ETHICAL AND PROFESSIONAL STANDARDS, QUANTITATIVE METHODS, AND ECONOMICS

CFA® PROGRAM CURRICULUM
2013 • Level II • Volume 1

CFA Institute

WILEY

John Wiley & Sons, Inc.

ISBN 978-1-937537-06-7 (paper)
ISBN 978-1-937537-27-2 (ebk)

10 9 8 7 6 5 4 3 2 1

Please visit our website at
www.WileyGlobalFinance.com.

Contents

Ethical and Professional Standards

O indicates an optional segment

◎ indicates an optional segment

Contents

◙ indicates an optional segment

[O] indicates an optional segment

Contents

Quantitative Methods

○ indicates an optional segment

◙ indicates an optional segment

Contents

◐ indicates an optional segment

◉ indicates an optional segment

How to Use the CFA Program Curriculum

Congratulations on passing Level I of the Chartered Financial Analyst (CFA®) Program. This exciting and rewarding program of study reflects your desire to become a serious investment professional. You are embarking on a program noted for its high ethical standards and the breadth of knowledge, skills, and abilities it develops. Your commitment to the CFA Program should be educationally and professionally rewarding.

The credential you seek is respected around the world as a mark of accomplishment and dedication. Each level of the program represents a distinct achievement in professional development. Successful completion of the program is rewarded with membership in a prestigious global community of investment professionals. CFA charterholders are dedicated to life-long learning and maintaining currency with the ever-changing dynamics of a challenging profession. The CFA Program represents the first step towards a career-long commitment to professional education.

The CFA examination measures your mastery of the core skills required to succeed as an investment professional. These core skills are the basis for the Candidate Body of Knowledge (CBOK™). The CBOK consists of four components:

- A broad topic outline that lists the major top-level topic areas (CBOK Topic Outline)

- Topic area weights that indicate the relative exam weightings of the top-level topic areas

- Learning outcome statements (LOS) that advise candidates about the specific knowledge, skills, and abilities they should acquire from readings covering a topic area (LOS are provided in candidate study sessions and at the beginning of each reading)

- The CFA Program curriculum, readings, and end-of-reading questions, which candidates receive upon exam registration

Therefore, the keys to your success on the CFA exam is studying and understanding the CBOK™. The following sections provide background on the CBOK, the organization of the curriculum, and tips for developing an effective study program.

CURRICULUM DEVELOPMENT PROCESS

The CFA Program is grounded in the practice of the investment profession. Using the Global Body of Investment Knowledge (GBIK) collaborative website, CFA Institute performs a continuous practice analysis with investment professionals around the world to determine the knowledge, skills, and abilities (competencies) that are relevant to the profession. Regional expert panels and targeted surveys are conducted annually to verify and reinforce the continuous feedback from the GBIK collaborative website. The practice analysis process ultimately defines the CBOK. The CBOK contains the competencies that are generally accepted and applied by investment professionals. These competencies are used in practice in a generalist context and are expected to be demonstrated by a recently qualified CFA charterholder.

A committee consisting of practicing charterholders, in conjunction with CFA Institute staff, designs the CFA Program curriculum in order to deliver the CBOK to candidates. The examinations, also written by practicing charterholders, are designed to allow you to demonstrate your mastery of the CBOK as set forth in the CFA Program curriculum. As you structure your personal study program, you should emphasize mastery of the CBOK and the practical application of that knowledge. For more information on the practice analysis, CBOK, and development of the CFA Program curriculum, please visit www.cfainstitute.org.

ORGANIZATION OF THE CURRICULUM

The Level II CFA Program curriculum is organized into 10 topic areas. Each topic area begins with a brief statement of the material and the depth of knowledge expected.

Each topic area is then divided into one or more study sessions. These study sessions—18 sessions in the Level II curriculum—should form the basic structure of your reading and preparation.

Each study session includes a statement of its structure and objective, and is further divided into specific reading assignments. An outline illustrating the organization of these 18 study sessions can be found at the front of each volume.

The reading assignments are the basis for all examination questions, and are selected or developed specifically to teach the knowledge, skills, and abilities reflected in the CBOK. These readings are drawn from CFA Institute-commissioned content, textbook chapters, professional journal articles, research analyst reports, and cases. All readings include problems and solutions to help you understand and master the topic areas.

Reading-specific Learning Outcome Statements (LOS) are listed at the beginning of each reading. These LOS indicate what you should be able to accomplish after studying the reading. The LOS, the reading, and the end-of-reading questions are dependent on each other, with the reading and questions providing context for understanding the scope of the LOS.

You should use the LOS to guide and focus your study, as each examination question is based on an assigned reading and one or more LOS. The readings provide context for the LOS and enable you to apply a principle or concept in a variety of scenarios. The candidate is responsible for the entirety of all of the required material in a study session, the assigned readings as well as the end-of-reading questions and problems.

We encourage you to review the material on LOS (http://www.cfainstitute.org/cfaprogram/courseofstudy/Pages/cfa_los.aspx), including the descriptions of LOS "command words," (www.cfainstitute.org/Documents/cfa_and_cipm_los_command_words.pdf).

FEATURES OF THE CURRICULUM

OPTIONAL
SEGMENT

- **Required vs. Optional Segments** - You should read all of an assigned reading. In some cases, however, we have reprinted an entire chapter or article and marked certain parts of the reading as "optional." The CFA examination is based only on the required segments, and the optional segments are included only when they might help you to better understand the required segments (by seeing the required material in its full context). When an optional segment begins, you will see text and a dashed vertical bar in the outside margin that will continue until the optional segment ends, accompanied by another icon. *Unless the material is specifically marked as optional, you should assume it is required.* You should rely on the required segments and the reading-specific LOS in preparing for the examination.

END OPTIONAL
SEGMENT

- **Problems/Solutions** - *All questions and problems in the readings as well as their solutions (which are provided directly following the problems) are part of the curriculum and are required material for the exam.* When appropriate, we have included problems within and after the readings to demonstrate practical application and reinforce your understanding of the concepts presented. The questions and problems are designed to help you learn these concepts and may serve as a basis for exam questions. Many of these questions are adapted from past CFA examinations.

- **Margins** - The wide margins in each volume provide space for your note-taking.

- **Six-Volume Structure** - For portability of the curriculum, the material is spread over six volumes.

- **Glossary and Index** - For your convenience, we have printed a comprehensive glossary and index in each volume. Throughout the curriculum, a **bolded blue** word in a reading denotes a term defined in the glossary.

- **Source Material** - The authorship, publisher, and copyright owners are given for each reading for your reference. We recommend that you use this CFA Institute curriculum rather than the original source materials because the curriculum may include only selected pages from outside readings, updated sections within the readings, and contains problems and solutions tailored to the CFA Program.

- **LOS Self-Check** - We have inserted checkboxes next to each LOS that you can use to track your progress in mastering the concepts in each reading.

DESIGNING YOUR PERSONAL STUDY PROGRAM

Create a Schedule - An orderly, systematic approach to examination preparation is critical. You should dedicate a consistent block of time every week to reading and studying. Complete all reading assignments and the associated problems and solutions in each study session. Review the LOS both before and after you study each reading to ensure that you have mastered the applicable content and can demonstrate the knowledge, skill, or ability described by the LOS and the assigned reading. Use the LOS self-check to track your progress and highlight areas of weakness for later review.

As you prepare for your exam, we will e-mail you important exam updates, testing policies, and study tips. Be sure to read these carefully. Curriculum errata are periodically updated and posted on the study session page at www.cfainstitute.org. You may also sign up for an RSS feed to alert you to the latest errata update.

Successful candidates report an average of over 300 hours preparing for each exam. Your preparation time will vary based on your prior education and experience. For each level of the curriculum, there are 18 study sessions, so a good plan is to devote 15–20 hours per week, for 18 weeks, to studying the material. Use the final four to six weeks before the exam to review what you've learned and practice with sample and mock exams. This recommendation, however, may underestimate the hours needed for appropriate examination preparation depending on your individual circumstances, relevant experience, and academic background. You will undoubtedly adjust your study time to conform to your own strengths and weaknesses, and your educational and professional background.

You will probably spend more time on some study sessions than on others, but on average you should plan on devoting 15-20 hours per study session. You should allow ample time for both in-depth study of all topic areas and additional concentration on those topic areas for which you feel least prepared.

Online Sample Examinations - CFA Institute online sample examinations are intended to assess your exam preparation as you progress toward the end of your study. After each question, you will receive immediate feedback noting the correct response and indicating the relevant assigned reading, so you will be able to identify areas of weakness for further study. The 120-minute sample examinations reflect the question formats, topics, and level of difficulty of the actual CFA examinations. Aggregate data indicate that the CFA examination pass rate was higher among candidates who took one or more online sample examinations than among candidates who did not take the online sample examinations. For more information on the online sample examinations, please visit www.cfainstitute.org.

Online Mock Examinations - In response to candidate requests, CFA Institute has developed mock examinations that mimic the actual CFA examinations not only in question format and level of difficulty, but also in length and topic weight. The three-hour online mock exams simulate the morning and afternoon sessions of the actual CFA exam, and are intended to be taken after you complete your study of the full curriculum, so you can test your understanding of the CBOK and your readiness for the exam. The mock exams are available in a printable PDF format with feedback provided at the end of the exam, rather than after each question as with the sample exams. CFA Institute recommends that you take these mock exams at the final stage of your preparation toward the actual CFA examination. For more information on the online mock examinations, please visit www.cfainstitute.org.

Preparatory Providers - After you enroll in the CFA Program, you may receive numerous solicitations for preparatory courses and review materials. When considering a prep course make sure the provider is in compliance with the CFA Institute Prep Provider Guidelines Program (www.cfainstitute.org/partners/examprep/Pages/cfa_prep_provider_guidelines.aspx). Just remember, there are no shortcuts to success on the CFA examinations; reading and studying the CFA curriculum is the key to success on the examination. The CFA examinations reference only the CFA Institute assigned curriculum—no preparatory course or review course materials are consulted or referenced.

SUMMARY

Every question on the CFA examination is based on the content contained in the required readings and on one or more LOS. Frequently, an examination question is based on a specific example highlighted within a reading or on a specific end-of-reading question and/or problem and its solution. To make effective use of the CFA Program curriculum, please remember these key points:

1. All pages printed in the curriculum are required reading for the examination except for occasional sections marked as optional. You may read optional pages as background, but you will not be tested on them.

2. All questions, problems, and their solutions - printed at the end of readings - are part of the curriculum and are required study material for the examination.

3. You should make appropriate use of the online sample/mock examinations and other resources available at www.cfainstitute.org.

4. You should schedule and commit sufficient study time to cover the 18 study sessions, review the materials, and take sample/mock examinations.

5. **Note:** Some of the concepts in the study sessions may be superseded by updated rulings and/or pronouncements issued after a reading was published. Candidates are expected to be familiar with the overall analytical framework contained in the assigned readings. Candidates are not responsible for changes that occur after the material was written.

FEEDBACK

At CFA Institute, we are committed to delivering a comprehensive and rigorous curriculum for the development of competent, ethically grounded investment professionals. We rely on candidate and member feedback as we work to incorporate content, design, and packaging improvements. You can be assured that we will continue to listen to your suggestions. Please send any comments or feedback to curriculum@cfainstitute.org. Ongoing improvements in the curriculum will help you prepare for success on the upcoming examinations, and for a lifetime of learning as a serious investment professional.

Ethical and Professional Standards

TOPIC LEVEL LEARNING OUTCOME

The candidate should be able to demonstrate a thorough knowledge of the CFA Institute Code of Ethics and Standards of Professional Conduct, identify violations of the Code and Standards, and recommend appropriate corrective measures.

Indices		Percentage change	
Index (today)			2011
Mumbai			
Singapore			
Sydney			
Shanghai B	2,971.0	1.1%	-4.7%
Hong Kong	464.0	0.9%	-10.5%
Toronto	316.8	0.7%	-6.9%
Stockholm	22,700.9	0.5%	-4.2%
Mexico City	13,524.8	0.1%	4.1%

1

Ethical and Professional Standards

The readings in this study session present a framework for ethical conduct in the investment profession by focusing on the CFA Institute Code of Ethics and Standards of Professional Conduct (the Code and Standards) as well as the CFA Institute Soft Dollar Standards and the CFA Institute Research Objectivity Standards.

The principles and guidance presented in the CFA Institute *Standards of Practice Handbook* (*Handbook*) form the basis for the CFA Institute self-regulatory program to maintain the highest professional standards among investment practitioners. A clear understanding of the CFA Institute Code of Ethics and Standards of Professional Conduct (both found in the *Handbook*) should allow the practitioner to identify and appropriately resolve ethical conflicts. The resulting recognition for integrity should benefit both the individual and the profession. "Guidance" in the *Handbook* addresses the practical application of the Code of Ethics and Standards of Professional Conduct. The guidance reviews the purpose and scope of each Standard, presents recommended procedures for compliance, and provides examples of the Standard in practice.

The CFA Institute Soft Dollar Standards and CFA Institute Research Objectivity Standards address contemporary issues for which CFA Institute has believed further, more specific guidance is warranted. Both documents are consistent with and complement the CFA Institute Code of Ethics and Standards of Professional Conduct.

Soft-dollar payment arrangements, involving the investment manager's use of client brokerage to obtain services related to the manager's investment decision-making process, have become extremely complex. As a consequence, ethically ambiguous situations can arise in which it is not immediately clear that the manager remains in compliance with the obligation, under the CFA Institute Code of Ethics, to place client interests ahead of personal or firm interests. The Soft Dollar Standards provide guidance on what services and products are appropriate for purchase with client brokerage, the appropriate disclosure of soft-dollar practices, and the necessary record keeping.

Investment research objectivity should be the logical consequence of ethical conduct, consistent with the CFA Institute Code of Ethics and Standards of Professional Conduct, in which client interests are placed first and conflicts of interest are fully disclosed. When temptation or pressure leads to biased or misleading research reports, the integrity of all financial professionals is tainted. The CFA Institute Research Objectivity Standards present specific policies and procedures designed to create a research environment where conflicts of interests and opportunities for ethical lapses are minimized and disclosed.

READING ASSIGNMENTS

Reading 1   ***Code of Ethics and Standards of Professional Conduct***
           Standards of Practice Handbook, Tenth Edition

Reading 2   ***Guidance for Standards I–VII***
           Standards of Practice Handbook, Tenth Edition

Reading 3   ***CFA Institute Soft Dollar Standards***
           CFA Institute Soft Dollar Standards

Reading 4   ***CFA Institute Research Objectivity Standards***

1

Code of Ethics and Standards of Professional Conduct

LEARNING OUTCOMES	
Mastery	**The candidate should be able to:**
☐	**a** describe the six components of the Code of Ethics and the seven Standards of Professional Conduct;
☐	**b** explain the ethical responsibilities required by the Code and Standards, including the multiple sub-sections of each Standard.

PREFACE

The *Standards of Practice Handbook* (*Handbook*) provides guidance to the people who grapple with real ethical dilemmas in the investment profession on a daily basis; the *Handbook* addresses the professional intersection where theory meets practice and where the concept of ethical behavior crosses from the abstract to the concrete. The *Handbook* is intended for a diverse and global audience: CFA Institute members navigating ambiguous ethical situations; supervisors and direct/indirect reports determining the nature of their responsibilities to each other, to existing and potential clients, and to the broader financial markets; and candidates preparing for the Chartered Financial Analyst (CFA) examinations.

Recent events in the global financial markets have tested the ethical mettle of financial market participants, including CFA Institute members. The standards taught in the CFA Program and by which CFA Institute members and candidates must abide represent timeless ethical principles and professional conduct for all market conditions. Through adherence to these standards, which continue to serve as the model for ethical behavior in the investment professional globally, each market participant does his or her part to improve the integrity and efficient operations of the financial markets.

The *Handbook* provides guidance in understanding the interconnectedness of the principles and provisions of the Code of Ethics and Standards of Professional Conduct (Code and Standards). Individually, the principles outline the high level of ethical conduct required from CFA Institute members and candidates. However, applying the principles individually may not capture the complexity of ethical requirements related to the investment industry. The Code and Standards should be viewed and interpreted as an interwoven tapestry of ethical requirements. Through members' and candidates' adherence to these principles as a whole, the integrity of and trust in the capital markets are improved.

Evolution of the CFA Institute Code of Ethics and Standards of Professional Conduct

Generally, changes to the Code and Standards over the years have been minor. CFA Institute has revised the language of the Code and Standards and occasionally added a new standard to address a prominent issue of the day. For instance, in 1992, CFA Institute added the standard addressing performance presentation to the existing list of standards.

Major changes came in 2005 with the ninth edition of the *Handbook*. CFA Institute adopted new standards, revised some existing standards, and reorganized the standards. The revisions were intended to clarify the requirements of the Code and Standards and effectively convey to its global membership what constitutes "best practice" in a number of areas relating to the investment profession.

The Code and Standards must be regularly reviewed and updated if they are to remain effective and continue to represent the highest ethical standards in the global investment industry. CFA Institute strongly believes that revisions of the Code and Standards are not undertaken for cosmetic change but to add value by addressing legitimate concerns and improving comprehension.

Changes to the Code and Standards have far-reaching implications for the CFA Institute membership, the CFA Program, and the investment industry as a whole. CFA Institute members and candidates are *required* to adhere to the Code and Standards. In addition, the Code and Standards are increasingly being adopted, in whole or in part, by firms and regulatory authorities. Their relevance goes well beyond CFA Institute members and candidates.

Standards of Practice Handbook

The periodic revisions to the Code and Standards have come in conjunction with updates of the *Standards of Practice Handbook*. The *Handbook* is the fundamental element of the ethics education effort of CFA Institute and the primary resource for guidance in interpreting and implementing the Code and Standards. The *Handbook* seeks to educate members and candidates on how to apply the Code and Standards to their professional lives and thereby benefit their clients, employers, and the investing public in general. The *Handbook* explains the purpose of the Code and Standards and how they apply in a variety of situations. The sections discuss and amplify each standard and suggest procedures to prevent violations.

Examples in the "Application of the Standard" sections are meant to illustrate how the standard applies to hypothetical but factual situations. The names contained in the examples are fictional and are not meant to refer to any actual person or entity. Unless otherwise stated, individuals in each example are CFA Institute members and holders of the CFA designation. Because factual circumstances vary so widely and often involve gray areas, the explanatory material and examples are not intended to be all inclusive. Many examples set forth in the application sections involve standards that have legal counterparts; *members are strongly urged to discuss with their supervisors and legal and compliance departments the content of the Code and Standards and the members' general obligations under the Code and Standards*.

CFA Institute recognizes that the presence of any set of ethical standards may create a false sense of security unless the documents are fully understood, enforced, and made a meaningful part of everyday professional activities. The *Handbook* is intended to provide a useful frame of reference that suggests ethical professional behavior in the investment decision-making process. This section cannot cover every contingency or circumstance, however, and it does not attempt to do so. The development and interpretation of the Code and Standards are evolving processes; the Code and Standards will be subject to continuing refinement.

Summary of Changes in the Tenth Edition

The comprehensive review of the Code and Standards in 2005 resulted in principle requirements that remain applicable today. The review carried out for the tenth edition focused on updates to the guidance and examples within the *Handbook*. In the tenth edition, the changes relate primarily to the growing diversity of the CFA Institute membership and CFA Program candidate base and aim to make specific guidance easier to understand.

Clarification of Standard III(A)

Standard III(A) Duties to Clients—Loyalty, Prudence, and Care was shortened to improve clarity. The third sentence was deleted to avoid possible misinterpretations of the members' or candidates' required duties to their clients. The principle contained in the deleted sentence already has been established in Standard I(A) regarding the responsibility to adhere to the most strict legal, regulatory, or CFA Institute requirements.

> Deletion:
> In relationships with clients, Members and Candidates must determine applicable fiduciary duty and must comply with such duty to persons and interests to whom it is owed.

Why Ethics Matters

A new section was added to the *Handbook* to broaden the discussion of the importance of ethics to the investment profession. The chapter addresses market integrity and sustainability, the role of CFA Institute, and the importance of ongoing awareness of and education about changes in the investment industry.

Text Revisions

As the investment industry and, as a result, CFA Institute membership have become more global, the use of English that can be easily understood and translated into different languages has become critical. Therefore, in some places, CFA Institute has eliminated, modified, or added language for clarity, even though it is not the intent to change the meaning of a particular provision.

Guidance Table

To keep the *Handbook* as a primary resource for members and candidates as they tackle ethical dilemmas, bulleted tables were added to help the reader locate the guidance within a standard that is most applicable to the situations that may occur in daily professional life. The Code and Standards must not be viewed as something solely to be learned to pass the CFA examinations; its principles are intended to play an active role in everyday decision making.

Example Highlight

In a continued effort to assist readers in locating examples of situations similar to issues they are facing, this update includes a brief descriptive heading for each example in the "Application of the Standard" sections. The heading notes the principle being addressed or the nature of the example.

Cross-Standard Examples

To further highlight the applicability of multiple standards to a single set of facts, some examples are used several times. The single or slightly modified facts are accompanied by comments directed to the standard in question. The other standards using the same example are noted at the end of the comments.

CFA Institute Professional Conduct Program

All CFA Institute members and candidates enrolled in the CFA Program are required to comply with the Code and Standards. The CFA Institute Board of Governors maintains oversight and responsibility for the Professional Conduct Program (PCP), which, in conjunction with the Disciplinary Review Committee (DRC), is responsible for enforcement of the Code and Standards. The CFA Institute Bylaws and Rules of Procedure for Proceedings Related to Professional Conduct (Rules of Procedure) form the basic structure for enforcing the Code and Standards. The Rules of Procedure are based on two primary principles: 1) fair process to the member and candidate and 2) confidentiality of proceedings.

Professional Conduct staff, under the direction of the CFA Institute Designated Officer, conducts professional conduct inquiries. Several circumstances can prompt an inquiry. First, members and candidates must self-disclose on the annual Professional Conduct Statement all matters that question their professional conduct, such as involvement in civil litigation or a criminal investigation or being the subject of a written complaint. Second, written complaints received by Professional Conduct staff can bring about an investigation. Third, CFA Institute staff may become aware of questionable conduct by a member or candidate through the media or another public source. Fourth, CFA examination proctors may submit a violation report for any candidate suspected to have compromised his or her professional conduct during the examination.

When an inquiry is initiated, the Professional Conduct staff conducts an investigation that may include requesting a written explanation from the member or candidate; interviewing the member or candidate, complaining parties, and third parties; and collecting documents and records in support of its investigation. The Designated Officer, upon reviewing the material obtained during the investigation, may conclude the inquiry with no disciplinary sanction, issue a cautionary letter, or continue proceedings to discipline the member or candidate. If the Designated Officer finds that a violation of the Code and Standards occurred, the Designated Officer proposes a disciplinary sanction, which may be rejected or accepted by the member or candidate.

If the member or candidate does not accept the proposed sanction, the matter is referred to a hearing panel composed of DRC members and CFA Institute member volunteers affiliated with the DRC. The hearing panel reviews materials and presentations from the Designated Officer and from the member or candidate. The hearing panel's task is to determine whether a violation of the Code and Standards occurred and, if so, what sanction should be imposed.

Sanctions imposed by CFA Institute may have significant consequences; they include public censure, suspension of membership and use of the CFA designation, and revocation of the CFA charter. Candidates enrolled in the CFA Program who have violated the Code and Standards may be suspended from further participation in the CFA Program.

Adoption of the Code and Standards

The Code and Standards apply to individual members of CFA Institute and candidates in the CFA Program. CFA Institute does encourage firms to adopt the Code and

Standards, however, as part of a firm's code of ethics. Those who claim compliance should fully understand the requirements of each of the principles of the Code and Standards.

Once a party—nonmember or firm—ensures its code of ethics meets the principles of the Code and Standards, that party should make the following statement whenever claiming compliance:

> *"[Insert name of party] claims compliance with the CFA Institute Code of Ethics and Standards of Professional Conduct. This claim has not been verified by CFA Institute."*

CFA Institute welcomes public acknowledgement, when appropriate, that firms are complying with the CFA Institute Code of Ethics and Standards of Professional Conduct and encourages firms to notify us of the adoption plans. For firms that would like to distribute the Code and Standards to clients and potential clients, attractive one-page copies of the Code and Standards, including translations, are available on the CFA Institute website (www.cfainstitute.org).

CFA Institute has also published the Asset Manager Code of Professional Conduct (AMC), which is designed, in part, to help asset managers comply with the regulations mandating codes of ethics for investment advisers. Whereas the Code and Standards are aimed at individual investment professionals who are members of CFA Institute or candidates in the CFA Program, the AMC was drafted specifically for firms. The AMC provides specific, practical guidelines for asset managers in six areas: loyalty to clients, the investment process, trading, compliance, performance evaluation, and disclosure. The AMC and the appropriate steps to acknowledge adoption or compliance can be found on the CFA Institute website (www.cfainstitute.org).

Acknowledgments

CFA Institute is a not-for-profit organization that is heavily dependent on the expertise and intellectual contributions of member volunteers. Members devote their time as they share a mutual interest in the organization's mission to promote and achieve ethical practice in the investment profession. CFA Institute owes much to the volunteers' abundant generosity and energy in extending ethical integrity.

The CFA Institute Standards of Practice Council (SPC), a group consisting of CFA charterholder volunteers from many different countries, is charged with maintaining and interpreting the Code and Standards and ensuring that they are effective. The SPC draws its membership from a broad spectrum of organizations in the securities field, including brokers, investment advisers, banks, and insurance companies. In most instances, the SPC members have important supervisory responsibilities within their firms.

The SPC continually evaluates the Code and Standards, as well as the guidance in the *Handbook*, to ensure that they are:

- representative of high standards of professional conduct;
- relevant to the changing nature of the investment profession;
- globally applicable;
- sufficiently comprehensive, practical, and specific;
- enforceable; and
- testable for the CFA Program.

The SPC has spent countless hours reviewing and discussing revisions to the Code and Standards and updates to the guidance that makes up the tenth edition of the *Handbook*. Following is a list of the current and former members of the SPC who generously donated their time and energy to this effort.

Christopher C. Loop, CFA, Chair	Toshihiko Saito, CFA, Prior Chair
Karin B. Bonding, CFA	Jinliang Li, CFA
Jean-Francois Bouilly, CFA	Lynn S. Mander, CFA
Terence E. Burns, CFA	James M. Meeth, CFA
Sharon Craggs, CFA	Brian O'Keefe, CFA
Mario Eichenberger, CFA	Guy G. Rutherfurd, Jr., CFA
James E. Hollis, CFA	Sunil B. Singhania, CFA
Samuel B. Jones, CFA	Peng Lian Wee, CFA
Ulrike Kaiser-Boeing, CFA	

The chair and members of the SPC would like to thank the CFA Institute staff who supported this revision for their efforts to keep the process smooth and well organized.

This tenth edition of the *Standards of Practice Handbook* is dedicated to the late Mildred Hermann, who served in a variety of capacities with the CFA Institute predecessor organizations, the Financial Analysts Federation (FAF) and the Association for Investment Management and Research (AIMR). With a work ethic that knew no limits, she possessed an unfailing sense of fairness and uncompromising integrity—attributes she expected in all investment professionals.

As FAF/AIMR staff representative to the predecessor committees to the Standards of Practice Council, Mildred was instrumental in the development of the first edition of the *Standards of Practice Handbook* and continued her direct involvement with the four subsequent editions published up to her retirement in 1991. She proved to be a passionate and skilled technician whose prodigious intellect, range of knowledge, and seasoned judgment fused seamlessly to create a deeply informed understanding of regulatory trends and their implications for FAF/AIMR members and the investment profession at large.

Mildred's tenure was marked by her special brand of leadership, vision, and commitment in promoting the highest standards of ethical conduct and professional practice. As Rossa O'Reilly, CFA, former chair of the Board of Governors, aptly observed at her retirement, "Very few professionals have contributed as much or worked as diligently toward furthering the goals of the profession of investment analysis and portfolio management as Mildred Hermann." For those of us fortunate enough to have worked with Mildred, she is fondly remembered as a unique talent, quick wit, valued colleague, model of human decency, and a humble, beloved friend.

WHY ETHICS MATTERS

The adherence of investment professionals to ethical practices benefits all market participants and increases investor confidence in global financial markets. Clients are reassured that the investment professionals they hire operate with the clients' best interests in mind, and investment professionals benefit from the more efficient and transparent operation of the market that integrity promotes. Ethical practices instill public trust in markets and support the development of markets. Sound ethics is fundamental to capital markets and the investment profession.

The first decade of the 21st century has been but one of many times of crisis for the investment industry. This period, unfortunately, has encompassed many instances of unethical behavior—by business executives and investment professionals. The newspapers and airwaves have brimmed with a succession of accounting frauds and manipulations, Ponzi schemes, insider trading, and other misdeeds. Each case has resulted in heavy financial losses and stained reputations. Equally important has been the terrible toll these actions have taken on investors' trust. Trust is hard earned and easily lost; corporations and individuals can safeguard themselves by committing to the highest standards of ethics and professional conduct.

Ethics is not merely a virtue to be demonstrated by CFA Institute members and candidates. Ethics must permeate all levels of our profession. Serving the best interests of the investing clients and employers lies at the heart of what collectively must be done to ensure a sense of trust and integrity in the financial markets. Although the drive to achieve such a lofty collective objective is critically important, the drive must ultimately start in the workplace. It is imperative that top management foster a strong culture of ethics not just among CFA charterholders and candidates but among all staff members who are involved directly or indirectly with client relations, the investment process, record keeping, and beyond. In such a culture, all participants can see clear evidence of how extremely important ethics is when woven into the fabric of an organization, or in other words, all participants in the process will know that ethics genuinely matters.

Ethics and CFA Institute

An important goal of CFA Institute is to ensure that the organization and its members develop, promote, and follow the highest ethical standards in the investment industry. The CFA Institute Code of Ethics (Code) and Standards of Professional Conduct (Standards) are the foundation supporting the organization's quest to advance the interests of the global investment community by establishing and maintaining the highest standards of professional excellence and integrity. The Code is a set of principles that define the professional conduct CFA Institute expects from its members and candidates in the CFA Program. The Code works in tandem with the Standards, which outline conduct that constitutes fair and ethical business practices.

For more than 40 years, CFA Institute members and candidates in the CFA Program have been required to abide by the organization's Code and Standards. Periodically, CFA Institute has revised and updated its Code and Standards to ensure that they remain relevant to the changing nature of the investment profession and representative of the "highest standard" of professional conduct. Recent events have highlighted unethical actions in the areas of governance, investment ratings, financial product packaging and distribution, and outright investment fraud. Finance is a sophisticated and interconnected global industry; new investment opportunities and new financial instruments to make the most of those opportunities are constantly developing. Although the investment world has become a far more complex place since the first publication of the *Handbook*, distinguishing right from wrong remains the paramount principle of the Code and Standards.

Ethics and Market Sustainability

The increasingly interconnected nature of global finance brings to the fore an added consideration that was, perhaps, less relevant in years past. This consideration is that of *market sustainability*. In addition to committing to the highest levels of ethical behavior, today's investment professional, when making decisions, should consider the long-term health of the market as a whole. As recent events have demonstrated, the sum of apparently isolated and unrelated decisions, however innocuous when considered on an individual basis, when aggregated, can precipitate a market crisis. In an interconnected global economy and marketplace, each participant should strive to be aware of how his or her actions or products may be distributed to, used in, or have an impact on other regions or countries.

The much-discussed credit crisis that buffeted global financial markets highlights these concerns. Relying on esoteric structures, certain banks developed financial instruments that extended credit to consumers and companies that otherwise would not have had access to those monies. Clients purchased these instruments in a quest for yield in a low-interest-rate environment. But some of the higher-risk borrowers could not afford their loans and were not able to refinance them. Defaults soared, and some of the instruments collapsed. Many of the institutions that had purchased the instruments or retained stakes in them had not completed sufficient diligence on the instruments' structures and suffered horrendous losses. Established institutions toppled into ruin, wrecking lives and reputations. Had members of the investment profession considered with greater foresight the question of market sustainability in tandem with the needs and expectations of their clients, the magnitude of the crisis might have been lessened.

CFA Institute encourages all members and candidates to consider in their investment decision-making process the promotion and protection of the global financial markets as an aspect of the broader context of the application of the Code and Standards. Those in positions of authority have a special responsibility to consider the broader context of market sustainability in their development and approval of corporate policies, particularly those involving risk management and product development. In addition, corporate compensation strategies should not encourage otherwise ethically sound individuals to engage in unethical or questionable conduct for financial gain. Ethics, sustainability, and properly functioning capital markets are components of the same concept of protecting the interests of all.

Ethics and Regulation

Regulation alone will never fully anticipate and eliminate the causes of financial crises. Some individuals will try to and may well be able to circumvent the regulatory rules. Only strong ethical principles, at the level of the individual and the level of the firm, will limit abuses. Knowing the rules or regulations to apply in a particular situation, although important, is not sufficient to ensure ethical decision making. Individuals must be able both to recognize areas that are prone to ethical pitfalls and to identify those circumstances and influences that can impair ethical judgment.

The Code and Standards, as well as other voluntary ethical standards of the CFA Institute (e.g., the Global Investment Performance Standards, Soft Dollar Standards, Trade Management Guidelines, Research Objectivity Standards, and the Asset Manager Code of Professional Conduct), offer a foundation to adopt and build on in promoting an ethical corporate culture. The adoption of these standards is not limited to investment professionals and their firms affiliated with CFA Institute. National regulators might consider the *Handbook*'s guidance in fostering ethical identities within organizations and national systems.

In the future, the nature and level of regulation will depend on how companies comply with the rules already in place. Greater adherence to the spirit of current rules may well require fewer regulatory changes. Conversely, continued short-sightedness and disregard for the outcomes of particularly adverse practices may necessitate more stringent regulation. In this respect, the investment industry can have a positive effect on evolving regulation and, in that way, on its own operational environment. Through continuing education, investment professionals can reinforce and evaluate their personal ethical conduct.

Ethics Education and Awareness

New challenges will continually arise for members and candidates in applying the Code and Standards because ethical dilemmas are not unambiguously right or wrong.

The dilemma exists because the choice between right and wrong is not always clear. Even well-intentioned investment professionals can find themselves in circumstances that may tempt them to cut corners. Situational influences can overpower the best of intentions.

To assist members and candidates in adhering to the principles of the Code and Standards, CFA Institute has made a significant commitment to provide members and candidates with the resources to extend and deepen their understanding of the principles' applications. The publications from CFA Institute offer a wealth of material. *CFA Magazine* contains a section on ethics in most issues. The magazine contains not only vignettes describing potentially questionable situations and guidance related to the Code and Standards but also frequent articles on broad topics relevant to current and developing ethical issues. The *Financial Analysts Journal* also publishes articles related to ethics and professional conduct. Archived issues of these publications are available on the CFA Institute website (www.cfainstitute.org).

CFA Institute includes presentations on ethics in many of its sponsored conferences. These presentations vary as widely as the articles do, from staff-led training courses to discussion of market events by outside professionals with a view toward ethical education. These presentations highlight current trends and how improved ethical decision making may lead to different or even preferred outcomes in the future.

These various resources are available to members and candidates and the investment community at large. Those unable to attend an actual conference will find podcasts, webcasts, or transcripts available on the CFA Institute website (www.cfainstitute.org). Conferences and the presentations offered in the *CFA Institute Conference Proceedings Quarterly* also provide continuing education credits for those members participating in the program.

The Research Foundation of CFA Institute, a not-for-profit organization established to promote the development and dissemination of relevant research for investment practitioners worldwide, has contributed to continued ethical education through the commission and publication in 2007 of *The Psychology of Ethics in the Finance and Investment Industry*. In this monograph, Thomas Oberlechner, professor of psychology at Webster University in Vienna, discusses the role psychology plays in individuals' ethical or unethical decision making. He concludes that understanding the dynamic nature of ethical decision making allows us to understand why unethical decisions can be made by anyone and, hence, how to manage our ethical conduct.

Markets function to an important extent on trust. Recent events have shown the fragility of this foundation and the devastating consequences that can ensue when this foundation is fundamentally questioned. Investment professionals should remain mindful of the long-term health of financial markets and incorporate this concern for the market's sustainability in their investment decision making. CFA Institute and the Standards of Practice Council hope this edition of the *Handbook* will assist and guide investment professionals in meeting the ethical demands of the highly interconnected global capital markets.

CFA INSTITUTE CODE OF ETHICS AND STANDARDS OF PROFESSIONAL CONDUCT

Preamble

The CFA Institute Code of Ethics and Standards of Professional Conduct are fundamental to the values of CFA Institute and essential to achieving its mission to lead the investment profession globally by setting high standards of education, integrity, and professional excellence. High ethical standards are critical to maintaining the public's trust in financial markets and in the investment profession. Since their creation in the 1960s, the Code and Standards have promoted the integrity of CFA Institute members and served as a model for measuring the ethics of investment professionals globally, regardless of job function, cultural differences, or local laws and regulations. All CFA Institute members (including holders of the Chartered Financial Analyst [CFA] designation) and CFA candidates must abide by the Code and Standards and are encouraged to notify their employer of this responsibility. Violations may result in disciplinary sanctions by CFA Institute. Sanctions can include revocation of membership, revocation of candidacy in the CFA Program, and revocation of the right to use the CFA designation.

The Code of Ethics

Members of CFA Institute (including CFA charterholders) and candidates for the CFA designation ("Members and Candidates") must:

- Act with integrity, competence, diligence, respect, and in an ethical manner with the public, clients, prospective clients, employers, employees, colleagues in the investment profession, and other participants in the global capital markets.

- Place the integrity of the investment profession and the interests of clients above their own personal interests.

- Use reasonable care and exercise independent professional judgment when conducting investment analysis, making investment recommendations, taking investment actions, and engaging in other professional activities.

- Practice and encourage others to practice in a professional and ethical manner that will reflect credit on themselves and the profession.

- Promote the integrity of and uphold the rules governing capital markets.

- Maintain and improve their professional competence and strive to maintain and improve the competence of other investment professionals.

Standards of Professional Conduct

I. PROFESSIONALISM

A. Knowledge of the Law. Members and Candidates must understand and comply with all applicable laws, rules, and regulations (including the CFA Institute Code of Ethics and Standards of Professional Conduct) of any government, regulatory organization, licensing agency, or professional association governing their professional activities. In the event of conflict, Members and Candidates must comply with the more strict law, rule, or regulation. Members and Candidates must not knowingly participate or assist in and must dissociate from any violation of such laws, rules, or regulations.

B. Independence and Objectivity. Members and Candidates must use reasonable care and judgment to achieve and maintain independence and objectivity in their professional activities. Members and Candidates must not offer, solicit, or accept any gift, benefit, compensation, or consideration that reasonably could be expected to compromise their own or another's independence and objectivity.

C. Misrepresentation. Members and Candidates must not knowingly make any misrepresentations relating to investment analysis, recommendations, actions, or other professional activities.

D. **Misconduct.** Members and Candidates must not engage in any professional conduct involving dishonesty, fraud, or deceit or commit any act that reflects adversely on their professional reputation, integrity, or competence.

II. INTEGRITY OF CAPITAL MARKETS

A. **Material Nonpublic Information.** Members and Candidates who possess material nonpublic information that could affect the value of an investment must not act or cause others to act on the information.

B. **Market Manipulation.** Members and Candidates must not engage in practices that distort prices or artificially inflate trading volume with the intent to mislead market participants.

III. DUTIES TO CLIENTS

A. **Loyalty, Prudence, and Care.** Members and Candidates have a duty of loyalty to their clients and must act with reasonable care and exercise prudent judgment. Members and Candidates must act for the benefit of their clients and place their clients' interests before their employer's or their own interests.

B. **Fair Dealing.** Members and Candidates must deal fairly and objectively with all clients when providing investment analysis, making investment recommendations, taking investment action, or engaging in other professional activities.

C. **Suitability.**

1. When Members and Candidates are in an advisory relationship with a client, they must:

   a. Make a reasonable inquiry into a client's or prospective client's investment experience, risk and return objectives, and financial constraints prior to making any investment recommendation or taking investment action and must reassess and update this information regularly.

   b. Determine that an investment is suitable to the client's financial situation and consistent with the client's written objectives, mandates, and constraints before making an investment recommendation or taking investment action.

   c. Judge the suitability of investments in the context of the client's total portfolio.

2. When Members and Candidates are responsible for managing a portfolio to a specific mandate, strategy, or style, they must make only investment recommendations or take only investment actions that are consistent with the stated objectives and constraints of the portfolio.

D. **Performance Presentation.** When communicating investment performance information, Members and Candidates must make reasonable efforts to ensure that it is fair, accurate, and complete.

E. **Preservation of Confidentiality.** Members and Candidates must keep information about current, former, and prospective clients confidential unless:

1. The information concerns illegal activities on the part of the client or prospective client,

2. Disclosure is required by law, or

3. The client or prospective client permits disclosure of the information.

IV. **DUTIES TO EMPLOYERS**

  A. **Loyalty.** In matters related to their employment, Members and Candidates must act for the benefit of their employer and not deprive their employer of the advantage of their skills and abilities, divulge confidential information, or otherwise cause harm to their employer.

  B. **Additional Compensation Arrangements.** Members and Candidates must not accept gifts, benefits, compensation, or consideration that competes with or might reasonably be expected to create a conflict of interest with their employer's interest unless they obtain written consent from all parties involved.

  C. **Responsibilities of Supervisors.** Members and Candidates must make reasonable efforts to detect and prevent violations of applicable laws, rules, regulations, and the Code and Standards by anyone subject to their supervision or authority.

V. **INVESTMENT ANALYSIS, RECOMMENDATIONS, AND ACTIONS**

  A. **Diligence and Reasonable Basis.** Members and Candidates must:

  1. Exercise diligence, independence, and thoroughness in analyzing investments, making investment recommendations, and taking investment actions.

  2. Have a reasonable and adequate basis, supported by appropriate research and investigation, for any investment analysis, recommendation, or action.

  B. **Communication with Clients and Prospective Clients.** Members and Candidates must:

  1. Disclose to clients and prospective clients the basic format and general principles of the investment processes they use to analyze investments, select securities, and construct portfolios and must promptly disclose any changes that might materially affect those processes.

  2. Use reasonable judgment in identifying which factors are important to their investment analyses, recommendations, or actions and include those factors in communications with clients and prospective clients.

  3. Distinguish between fact and opinion in the presentation of investment analysis and recommendations.

  C. **Record Retention.** Members and Candidates must develop and maintain appropriate records to support their investment analyses, recommendations, actions, and other investment-related communications with clients and prospective clients.

VI. **CONFLICTS OF INTEREST**

  A. **Disclosure of Conflicts.** Members and Candidates must make full and fair disclosure of all matters that could reasonably be expected to impair their independence and objectivity or interfere with respective duties to their clients, prospective clients, and employer. Members and Candidates must ensure that such disclosures are prominent, are delivered in plain language, and communicate the relevant information effectively.

  B. **Priority of Transactions.** Investment transactions for clients and employers must have priority over investment transactions in which a Member or Candidate is the beneficial owner.

  C. **Referral Fees.** Members and Candidates must disclose to their employer, clients, and prospective clients, as appropriate, any compensation, consideration, or benefit received from or paid to others for the recommendation of products or services.

VII. **RESPONSIBILITIES AS A CFA INSTITUTE MEMBER OR CFA CANDIDATE**

A. **Conduct as Members and Candidates in the CFA Program.** Members and Candidates must not engage in any conduct that compromises the reputation or integrity of CFA Institute or the CFA designation or the integrity, validity, or security of the CFA examinations.

B. **Reference to CFA Institute, the CFA Designation, and the CFA Program.** When referring to CFA Institute, CFA Institute membership, the CFA designation, or candidacy in the CFA Program, Members and Candidates must not misrepresent or exaggerate the meaning or implications of membership in CFA Institute, holding the CFA designation, or candidacy in the CFA program.

Mumbai		
Singapore		
Sydney		
Shanghai B	297.0	1.1%
Hong Kong	4644.0	0.9%
Toronto	316.8	0.7%
Stockholm	22,700.9	0.5%
Mexico City	13,524.8	0.1%

Guidance for Standards I–VII

STANDARD I—PROFESSIONALISM

A. Knowledge of the Law

Members and Candidates must understand and comply with all applicable laws, rules, and regulations (including the CFA Institute Code of Ethics and Standards of Professional Conduct) of any government, regulatory organization, licensing agency, or professional association governing their professional activities. In the event of conflict, Members and Candidates must comply with the more strict law, rule, or regulation. Members and Candidates must not knowingly participate or assist in and must dissociate from any violation of such laws, rules, or regulations

Guidance

Highlights:

- *Relationship between the Code and Standards and Applicable Law*
- *Participation in or Association with Violations by Others*
- *Investment Products and Applicable Laws*

Members and candidates must understand the applicable laws and regulations of all the countries in which they trade securities or provide investment advice or other investment services. On the basis of their understanding, members and candidates must comply with the laws and regulations that directly govern their work. When questions arise, members and candidates should know their firm's policies and procedures for accessing compliance guidance. This standard does not require members and candidates to become experts, however, in compliance. Additionally, investment professionals are not required to have detailed knowledge of or be experts on all the laws that could potentially govern the member's or candidate's activities.

During times of changing regulations, members and candidates must remain vigilant in maintaining their knowledge of the requirements for their professional activities. The financial and ethical missteps in the first decade of the 21st century created an environment for swift and wide-ranging regulatory changes. As new local, regional, and global requirements are updated, members, candidates, and their firms must adjust their procedures and practices to remain in compliance.

Relationship between the Code and Standards and Applicable Law

Some members or candidates may live, work, or provide investment services to clients living in a country that has no law or regulation governing a particular action or that has laws or regulations that differ from the requirements of the Code and Standards. When applicable law and the Code and Standards require different conduct, members and candidates must follow the more strict of the applicable law or the Code and Standards.

"Applicable law" is the law that governs the member's or candidate's conduct. Which law applies will depend on the particular facts and circumstances of each case. The "more strict" law or regulation is the law or regulation that imposes greater restrictions on the action of the member or candidate or calls for the member or candidate to exert a greater degree of action that protects the interests of investors. For example, applicable law or regulation may not require members and candidates to disclose referral fees received from or paid to others for the recommendation of investment products or services. Because the Code and Standards impose this obligation, however, members and candidates must disclose the existence of such fees.

Members and candidates must adhere to the following principles:

- Members and candidates must comply with applicable law or regulation related to their professional activities.

- Members and candidates must not engage in conduct that constitutes a violation of the Code and Standards, even though it may otherwise be legal.

- In the absence of any applicable law or regulation or when the Code and Standards impose a higher degree of responsibility than applicable laws and regulations, members and candidates must adhere to the Code and Standards. Applications of these principles are outlined in Exhibit 1.

CFA Institute members are obligated to abide by the CFA Institute Articles of Incorporation, Bylaws, Code of Ethics, Standards of Professional Conduct, Rules of Procedure, Membership Agreement, and other applicable rules promulgated by CFA Institute, all as amended from time to time. CFA candidates who are not members must also abide by these documents (except for the Membership Agreement) as well as rules and regulations related to the administration of the CFA examination, the Candidate Responsibility Statement, and the Candidate Pledge.

Participation in or Association with Violations by Others

Members and candidates are responsible for violations in which they *knowingly* participate or assist. Although members and candidates are presumed to have knowledge of all applicable laws, rules, and regulations, CFA Institute acknowledges that members may not recognize violations if they are not aware of all the facts giving rise to the violations. Standard I(A) applies when members and candidates know or should know that their conduct may contribute to a violation of applicable laws, rules, regulations, or the Code and Standards.

If a member or candidate has reasonable grounds to believe that imminent or ongoing client or employer activities are illegal or unethical, the member or candidate must dissociate, or separate, from the activity. In extreme cases, dissociation may require a member or candidate to leave his or her employment. Members and candidates may take the following intermediate steps to dissociate from ethical violations of others when direct discussions with the person or persons committing the violation are unsuccessful. The first step should be to attempt to stop the behavior by bringing it to the attention of the employer through a supervisor or the firm's compliance department. If this attempt is unsuccessful, then members and candidates have a responsibility to step away and dissociate from the activity. Dissociation practices will differ on the basis of the member's or candidate's role in the investment industry. It may include removing one's name from written reports or recommendations, asking for a different assignment, or refusing to accept a new client or continue to advise a current client. Inaction combined with continuing association with those involved in illegal or unethical conduct may be construed as participation or assistance in the illegal or unethical conduct.

CFA Institute strongly encourages members and candidates to report potential violations of the Code and Standards committed by fellow members and candidates. Although a failure to report is less likely to be construed as a violation than a failure to dissociate from unethical conduct, the impact of inactivity on the integrity of capital markets can be significant. Although the Code and Standards do not compel members and candidates to report violations to their governmental or regulatory organizations unless such disclosure is mandatory under applicable law, such disclosure may be prudent under certain circumstances. Members and candidates should consult their legal and compliance advisers for guidance.

Additionally, CFA Institute encourages members, nonmembers, clients, and the investing public to report violations of the Code and Standards by CFA Institute members or CFA candidates by submitting a complaint in writing to the CFA Institute Professional Conduct Program via e-mail (pcprogram@cfainstitute.org) or the CFA Institute website (www.cfainstitute.org).

Investment Products and Applicable Laws

Members and candidates involved in creating or maintaining investment services or investment products or packages of securities and/or derivatives should be mindful of where these products or packages will be sold as well as their places of origination. The applicable laws and regulations of the countries or regions of origination and expected sale should be understood by those responsible for the supervision of the services or creation and maintenance of the products or packages. Members or candidates should make reasonable efforts to review whether associated firms that are distributing products or services developed by their employing firm also abide by the laws and regulations of the countries and regions of distribution. Members and candidates should undertake the necessary due diligence when transacting cross-border business to understand the multiple applicable laws and regulations in order to protect the reputation of their firm and themselves.

Exhibit 1	Global Application of the Code and Standards

Members and candidates who practice in multiple jurisdictions may be subject to varied securities laws and regulations. If applicable law is stricter than the requirements of the Code and Standards, members and candidates must adhere to applicable law; otherwise, they must adhere to the Code and Standards. The following chart provides illustrations involving a member who may be subject to the securities laws and regulations of three different types of countries:

(continued)

Exhibit 1	Continued

NS: country with no securities laws or regulations

LS: country with *less* strict securities laws and regulations than the Code and Standards

MS: country with *more* strict securities laws and regulations than the Code and Standards

Applicable Law	Duties	Explanation
Member resides in NS country, does business in LS country; LS law applies.	Member must adhere to the Code and Standards.	Because applicable law is less strict than the Code and Standards, the member must adhere to the Code and Standards.
Member resides in NS country, does business in MS country; MS law applies.	Member must adhere to the law of MS country.	Because applicable law is stricter than the Code and Standards, member must adhere to the more strict applicable law.
Member resides in LS country, does business in NS country; LS law applies.	Member must adhere to the Code and Standards.	Because applicable law is less strict than the Code and Standards, member must adhere to the Code and Standards.
Member resides in LS country, does business in MS country; MS law applies.	Member must adhere to the law of MS country.	Because applicable law is stricter than the Code and Standards, member must adhere to the more strict applicable law.
Member resides in LS country, does business in NS country; LS law applies, but it states that law of locality where business is conducted governs.	Member must adhere to the Code and Standards.	Because applicable law states that the law of the locality where the business is conducted governs and there is no local law, the member must adhere to the Code and Standards.
Member resides in LS country, does business in MS country; LS law applies, but it states that law of locality where business is conducted governs.	Member must adhere to the law of MS country.	Because applicable law of the locality where the business is conducted governs and local law is stricter than the Code and Standards, member must adhere to the more strict applicable law.
Member resides in MS country, does business in LS country; MS law applies.	Member must adhere to the law of MS country.	Because applicable law is stricter than the Code and Standards, member must adhere to the more strict applicable law.

Exhibit 1	Continued	

Applicable Law	Duties	Explanation
Member resides in MS country, does business in LS country; MS law applies, but it states that law of locality where business is conducted governs.	Member must adhere to the Code and Standards.	Because applicable law states that the law of the locality where the business is conducted governs and local law is less strict than the Code and Standards, member must adhere to the Code and Standards.
Member resides in MS country, does business in LS country with a client who is a citizen of LS country; MS law applies, but it states that the law of the client's home country governs.	Member must adhere to the Code and Standards.	Because applicable law states that the law of the client's home country governs (which is less strict than the Code and Standards), member must adhere to the Code and Standards.
Member resides in MS country, does business in LS country with a client who is a citizen of MS country; MS law applies, but it states that the law of the client's home country governs.	Member must adhere to the law of MS country.	Because applicable law states that the law of the client's home country governs and the law of the client's home country is stricter than the Code and Standards, the member must adhere to the more strict applicable law.

Recommended Procedures for Compliance

Members and Candidates

Suggested methods by which members and candidates can acquire and maintain understanding of applicable laws, rules, and regulations include the following:

- *Stay informed*: Members and candidates should establish or encourage their employers to establish a procedure by which employees are regularly informed about changes in applicable laws, rules, regulations, and case law. In many instances, the employer's compliance department or legal counsel can provide such information in the form of memorandums distributed to employees in the organization. Also, participation in an internal or external continuing education program is a practical method of staying current.

- *Review procedures*: Members and candidates should review, or encourage their employers to review, the firm's written compliance procedures on a regular basis to ensure that the procedures reflect current law and provide adequate guidance to employees about what is permissible conduct under the law and/or the Code and Standards. Recommended compliance procedures for specific items of the Code and Standards are discussed in this *Handbook* in the "Guidance" sections associated with each standard.

- *Maintain current files*: Members and candidates should maintain or encourage their employers to maintain readily accessible current reference copies of applicable statutes, rules, regulations, and important cases.

Distribution Area Laws

Members and candidates should make reasonable efforts to understand the applicable laws—both country and regional—for the countries and regions where their investment products are developed and are most likely to be distributed to clients.

Legal Counsel

When in doubt about the appropriate action to undertake, it is recommended that a member or candidate seek the advice of compliance personnel or legal counsel concerning legal requirements. If a potential violation is being committed by a fellow employee, it may also be prudent for the member or candidate to seek the advice of the firm's compliance department or legal counsel.

Dissociation

When dissociating from an activity that violates the Code and Standards, members and candidates should document the violation and urge their firms to attempt to persuade the perpetrator(s) to cease such conduct. To dissociate from the conduct, a member or candidate may have to resign his or her employment.

Firms

The formality and complexity of compliance procedures for firms depend on the nature and size of the organization and the nature of its investment operations. Members and candidates should encourage their firms to consider the following policies and procedures to support the principles of Standard I(A):

- *Develop and/or adopt a code of ethics*: The ethical culture of an organization starts at the top. Members and candidates should encourage their supervisors or managers to adopt a code of ethics. Adhering to a code of ethics facilitates solutions when people face ethical dilemmas and can prevent the need for employees to resort to a "whistleblowing" solution publicly alleging concealed misconduct. CFA Institute has published the *Asset Manager Code of Professional Conduct*, which firms may adopt or use as the basis for their codes (visit www.cfapubs.org/loi/ccb).

- *Provide information on applicable laws*: Pertinent information that highlights applicable laws and regulations might be distributed to employees or made available in a central location. Information sources might include primary information developed by the relevant government, governmental agencies, regulatory organizations, licensing agencies, and professional associations (e.g., from their websites); law firm memorandums or newsletters; and association memorandums or publications (e.g., *CFA Magazine*).

- *Establish procedures for reporting violations*: Firms might provide written protocols for reporting suspected violations of laws, regulations, or company policies.

Application of the Standard

Example 1   (Notification of Known Violations): Michael Allen works for a brokerage firm and is responsible for an underwriting of securities. A company official gives Allen information indicating that the financial statements Allen filed with the regulator overstate the issuer's earnings. Allen seeks the advice of the brokerage firm's general counsel, who states that it would be difficult for the regulator to prove that Allen has been involved in any wrongdoing.

> *Comment*: Although it is recommended that members and candidates seek the advice of legal counsel, the reliance on such advice does not absolve

a member or candidate from the requirement to comply with the law or regulation. Allen should report this situation to his supervisor, seek an independent legal opinion, and determine whether the regulator should be notified of the error.

Example 2   (Dissociating from a Violation): Lawrence Brown's employer, an investment banking firm, is the principal underwriter for an issue of convertible debentures by the Courtney Company. Brown discovers that the Courtney Company has concealed severe third-quarter losses in its foreign operations. The preliminary prospectus has already been distributed.

> *Comment*: Knowing that the preliminary prospectus is misleading, Brown should report his findings to the appropriate supervisory persons in his firm. If the matter is not remedied and Brown's employer does not dissociate from the underwriting, Brown should sever all his connections with the underwriting. Brown should also seek legal advice to determine whether additional reporting or other action should be taken.

Example 3   (Dissociating from a Violation): Kamisha Washington's firm advertises its past performance record by showing the 10-year return of a composite of its client accounts. Washington discovers, however, that the composite omits the performance of accounts that have left the firm during the 10-year period, whereas the description of the composite indicates the inclusion of all firm accounts. This omission has led to an inflated performance figure. Washington is asked to use promotional material that includes the erroneous performance number when soliciting business for the firm.

> *Comment*: Misrepresenting performance is a violation of the Code and Standards. Although she did not calculate the performance herself, Washington would be assisting in violating Standard I(A) if she were to use the inflated performance number when soliciting clients. She must dissociate herself from the activity. If discussing the misleading number with the person responsible is not an option for correcting the problem, she can bring the situation to the attention of her supervisor or the compliance department at her firm. If her firm is unwilling to recalculate performance, she must refrain from using the misleading promotional material and should notify the firm of her reasons. If the firm insists that she use the material, she should consider whether her obligation to dissociate from the activity requires her to seek other employment.

Example 4   (Following the Highest Requirements): James Collins is an investment analyst for a major Wall Street brokerage firm. He works in a developing country with a rapidly modernizing economy and a growing capital market. Local securities laws are minimal—in form and content—and include no punitive prohibitions against insider trading.

> *Comment*: Collins must abide by the requirements of the Codes and Standards that might be more strict than the rules of the developing country. He should be aware of the risks that a small market and the absence of a fairly regulated flow of information to the market represent to his ability to obtain information and make timely judgments. He should include this factor in formulating his advice to clients. In handling material nonpublic information that accidentally comes into his possession, he must follow Standard II(A)–Material Nonpublic Information.

Example 5   (Following the Highest Requirements): Laura Jameson works for a multinational investment adviser based in the United States. Jameson lives and works as a registered investment adviser in the tiny, but wealthy, island nation of Karramba. Karramba's securities laws state that no investment adviser registered and working in that country can participate in initial public offerings (IPOs) for the adviser's personal account. Jameson, believing that as a U.S. citizen working for a U.S.-based company she should comply only with U.S. law, has ignored this Karrambian law. In addition, Jameson believes that, as a charterholder, as long as she adheres to the Code and Standards requirement that she disclose her participation in any IPO to her employer and clients when such ownership creates a conflict of interest, she is meeting the highest ethical requirements.

> *Comment*: Jameson is in violation of Standard I(A). As a registered investment adviser in Karramba, Jameson is prevented by Karrambian securities law from participating in IPOs regardless of the law of her home country. In addition, because the law of the country where she is working is stricter than the Code and Standards, she must follow the stricter requirements of the local law rather than the requirements of the Code and Standards.

Example 6   (Laws and Regulations Based on Religious Tenets): Amanda Janney is employed as a fixed-income portfolio manager for a large international firm. She is on a team within her firm that is responsible for creating and managing a fixed-income hedge fund to be sold throughout the firm's distribution centers to high-net-worth clients. Her firm receives expressions of interest from potential clients from the Middle East who are seeking investments that comply with Islamic law. The marketing and promotional materials for the fixed-income hedge fund do not specify whether or not the fund is a suitable investment for an investor seeking compliance with Islamic law. Because the fund is being distributed globally, Janney is concerned about the reputation of the fund and the firm and believes disclosure of whether or not the fund complies with Islamic law could help minimize potential mistakes with placing this investment.

> *Comment:* As the financial market continues to become globalized, members and candidates will need to be aware of the differences between cultural and religious laws and requirements as well as the different governmental laws and regulations. Janney and the firm could be proactive in their efforts to acknowledge areas where the new fund may not be suitable for clients.

Example 7   (Reporting Potential Unethical Actions): Krista Blume is a junior portfolio manager for high-net-worth portfolios at a large global investment manager. She observes a number of new portfolios and relationships coming from a country in Europe where the firm did not have previous business and is told that a broker in that country is responsible for this new business. At a meeting on allocation of research resources to third-party research firms, Blume notes that this broker has been added to the list and is allocated payments for research. However, she knows the portfolios do not invest in securities in the broker's country. And she has not seen any research come from this broker. Blume asks her supervisor about the name being on the list and is told that someone in marketing is receiving the research and that the name being on the list is OK. She believes that what is going on may be that the broker is being paid for new business through the inappropriate research payments and wishes to dissociate from the misconduct.

> *Comment:* Blume should follow the firm's policies and procedures for reporting potential unethical activity, which may include discussions with her supervisor or someone in a designated compliance department. She should communicate her concerns appropriately while advocating for disclosure between the new broker relationship and the research payments.

B. Independence and Objectivity

Members and Candidates must use reasonable care and judgment to achieve and maintain independence and objectivity in their professional activities. Members and Candidates must not offer, solicit, or accept any gift, benefit, compensation, or consideration that reasonably could be expected to compromise their own or another's independence and objectivity.

Guidance

Highlights:

- *Buy-Side Clients*
- *Fund Manager Relationships*
- *Investment Banking Relationships*
- *Public Companies*
- *Credit Rating Agency Opinions*
- *Issuer-Paid Research*
- *Travel Funding*

Standard I(B) states the responsibility of CFA Institute members and candidates in the CFA Program to maintain independence and objectivity so that their clients will have the benefit of their work and opinions unaffected by any potential conflict of interest or other circumstance adversely affecting their judgment. Every member and candidate should endeavor to avoid situations that could cause or be perceived to cause a loss of independence or objectivity in recommending investments or taking investment action.

External sources may try to influence the investment process by offering analysts and portfolio managers a variety of benefits. Corporations may seek expanded research coverage; issuers and underwriters may wish to promote new securities offerings; brokers may want to increase commission business; and independent rating agencies may be influenced by the company requesting the rating. Benefits may include gifts, invitations to lavish functions, tickets, favors, or job referrals. One type of benefit is the allocation of shares in oversubscribed IPOs to investment managers for their personal accounts. This practice affords managers the opportunity to make quick profits that may not be available to their clients. Such a practice is prohibited under Standard I(B). Modest gifts and entertainment are acceptable, but special care must be taken by members and candidates to resist subtle and not-so-subtle pressures to act in conflict with the interests of their clients. Best practice dictates that members and candidates reject any offer of gift or entertainment that could be expected to threaten their independence and objectivity.

Receiving a gift, benefit, or consideration from a *client* can be distinguished from gifts given by entities seeking to influence a member or candidate to the detriment of other clients. In a client relationship, the client has already entered some type of compensation arrangement with the member, candidate, or his or her firm. A gift from a client could be considered supplementary compensation. The potential for obtaining influence to the detriment of other clients, although present, is not as great as in situations where no compensation arrangement exists. When possible, prior to accepting "bonuses" or gifts from clients, members and candidates should disclose to their employers such benefits offered by clients. If notification is not possible prior to acceptance, members and candidates must disclose to their employers benefits previously accepted from clients. Disclosure allows the employer of a member or candidate to make an independent determination about the extent to which the gift may affect the member's or candidate's independence and objectivity.

Members and candidates may also come under pressure from their own firms to, for example, issue favorable research reports or recommendations for certain companies with potential or continuing business relationships with the firm. The situation may be aggravated if an executive of the company sits on the bank or investment firm's board and attempts to interfere in investment decision making. Members and candidates acting in a sales or marketing capacity must be especially mindful of their objectivity in promoting appropriate investments for their clients.

Left unmanaged, pressures that threaten independence place research analysts in a difficult position and may jeopardize their ability to act independently and objectively. One of the ways that research analysts have coped with these pressures in the past is to use subtle and ambiguous language in their recommendations or to temper the tone of their research reports. Such subtleties are lost on some investors, however, who reasonably expect research reports and recommendations to be straightforward and transparent, and to communicate clearly an analyst's views based on unbiased analysis and independent judgment.

Members and candidates are personally responsible for maintaining independence and objectivity when preparing research reports, making investment recommendations, and taking investment action on behalf of clients. Recommendations must convey the member's or candidate's true opinions, free of bias from internal or external pressures, and be stated in clear and unambiguous language.

Members and candidates also should be aware that some of their professional or social activities within CFA Institute or its member societies may subtly threaten their independence or objectivity. When seeking corporate financial support for conventions, seminars, or even weekly society luncheons, the members or candidates responsible for the activities should evaluate both the actual effect of such solicitations on their independence and whether their objectivity might be perceived to be compromised in the eyes of their clients.

Buy-Side Clients

One source of pressure on sell-side analysts is buy-side clients. Institutional clients are traditionally the primary users of sell-side research, either directly or with soft dollar brokerage. Portfolio managers may have significant positions in the security of a company under review. A rating downgrade may adversely affect the portfolio's performance, particularly in the short term, because the sensitivity of stock prices to ratings changes has increased in recent years. A downgrade may also affect the manager's compensation, which is usually tied to portfolio performance. Moreover, portfolio performance is subject to media and public scrutiny, which may affect the manager's professional reputation. Consequently, some portfolio managers implicitly or explicitly support sell-side ratings inflation.

Portfolio managers have a responsibility to respect and foster the intellectual honesty of sell-side research. Therefore, it is improper for portfolio managers to threaten or engage in retaliatory practices, such as reporting sell-side analysts to the covered company in order to instigate negative corporate reactions. Although most portfolio managers do not engage in such practices, the perception by the research analyst that a reprisal is possible may cause concern and make it difficult for the analyst to maintain independence and objectivity.

Fund Manager Relationships

Research analysts are not the only people who must be concerned with maintaining their independence. Members and candidates who are responsible for hiring and retaining outside managers should not accepts gifts, entertainment, or travel funding that may be perceived as impairing their decisions. The use of secondary fund managers has evolved into a common practice to manage specific asset allocations. Both the primary and secondary fund managers often arrange educational and marketing events to inform others about their business strategies or investment process. Members and candidates must review the merits of each offer individually in determining whether they may attend yet maintain their independence.

Investment Banking Relationships

Some sell-side firms may exert pressure on their analysts to issue favorable research reports on current or prospective investment banking clients. For many of these firms, income from investment banking has become increasingly important to overall firm profitability because brokerage income has declined as a result of price competition. Consequently, firms offering investment banking services work hard to develop and maintain relationships with investment banking clients and prospects. These companies are often covered by the firm's research analysts because companies often select their investment banks on the basis of the reputation of their research analysts, the quality of their work, and their standing in the industry.

In some countries, research analysts frequently work closely with their investment banking colleagues to help evaluate prospective investment banking clients. In other countries, because of past abuses in managing the obvious conflicts of interest, regulators have established clear rules prohibiting the interaction of these groups. Although collaboration between research analysts and investment banking colleagues may benefit the firm and enhance market efficiency (e.g., by allowing firms to assess risks more accurately and make better pricing assumptions), it requires firms to carefully balance the conflicts of interest inherent in the collaboration. Having analysts work with investment bankers is appropriate only when the conflicts are adequately and effectively managed and disclosed. Firm managers have a responsibility to provide an environment in which analysts are neither coerced nor enticed into issuing research that does not reflect their true opinions. Firms should require public disclosure of actual conflicts of interest to investors.

Members, candidates, and their firms must adopt and follow perceived best practices in maintaining independence and objectivity in the corporate culture and protecting analysts from undue pressure by their investment banking colleagues. The "firewalls" traditionally built between these two functions must be managed to minimize conflicts of interest; indeed, enhanced firewall policies may go as far as prohibiting all communications between these groups. A key element of an enhanced firewall is separate reporting structures for personnel on the research side and personnel on the investment banking side. For example, investment banking personnel should not have any authority to approve, disapprove, or make changes to research reports or recommendations. Another element should be a compensation arrangement that minimizes the pressures on research analysts and rewards objectivity and accuracy. Compensation arrangements should not link analyst remuneration directly to investment banking assignments in which the analyst may participate as a team member. Firms should also regularly review their policies and procedures to determine whether analysts are adequately safeguarded and to improve the transparency of disclosures relating to conflicts of interest. The highest level of transparency is achieved when disclosures are prominent and specific rather than marginalized and generic.

Public Companies

Analysts may be pressured to issue favorable reports and recommendations by the companies they follow. Not every stock is a "buy," and not every research report is favorable—for many reasons, including the cyclical nature of many business activities and market fluctuations. For instance, a "good company" does not always translate into a "good stock" rating if the current stock price is fully valued. In making an investment recommendation, the analyst is responsible for anticipating, interpreting, and assessing a company's prospects and stock price performance in a factual manner. Many company managers, however, believe that their company's stock is undervalued, and these managers may find it difficult to accept critical research reports or ratings downgrades. Company managers' compensation may also be dependent on stock performance.

Due diligence in financial research and analysis involves gathering information from a wide variety of sources, including public disclosure documents (such as proxy statements, annual reports, and other regulatory filings) and also company management and investor-relations personnel, suppliers, customers, competitors, and other relevant sources. Research analysts may justifiably fear that companies will limit their ability to conduct thorough research by denying analysts who have "negative" views direct access to company managers and/or barring them from conference calls and other communication venues. Retaliatory practices include companies bringing legal action against analysts personally and/or their firms to seek monetary damages for the economic effects of negative reports and recommendations. Although few companies engage in such behavior, the perception that a reprisal is possible is a reasonable concern for analysts. This concern may make it difficult for them to conduct the comprehensive research needed to make objective recommendations. For further information and guidance, members and candidates should refer to the CFA Institute publication *Best Practice Guidelines Governing Analyst/Corporate Issuer Relations* (www.cfainstitute.org).

Credit Rating Agency Opinions

Credit rating agencies provide a service by grading the fixed-income products offered by companies. Analysts face challenges related to incentives and compensation schemes that may be tied to the final rating and successful placement of the product. Members and candidates employed at rating agencies should ensure that procedures and processes at the agencies prevent undue influences from a sponsoring company during the analysis. Members and candidates should abide by their agencies' and the industry's standards of conduct regarding the analytical process and the distribution of their reports.

The work of credit rating agencies also raises concerns similar to those inherent in investment banking relationships. Analysts may face pressure to issue ratings at a specific level because of other services the agency offers companies, namely, advising on the development of structured products. The rating agencies need to develop the necessary firewalls and protections to allow the independent operations of their different business lines.

When using information provided by credit rating agencies, members and candidates should be mindful of the potential conflicts of interest. And because of the potential conflicts, members and candidates may need to independently validate the rating granted.

Issuer-Paid Research

In light of the recent reduction of sell-side research coverage, many companies, seeking to increase visibility both in the financial markets and with potential investors, have hired analysts to produce research reports analyzing their companies. These reports bridge the gap created by the lack of coverage and can be an effective method of communicating with investors.

Issuer-paid research conducted by independent analysts, however, is fraught with potential conflicts. Depending on how the research is written and distributed, investors may be misled into believing that the research is from an independent source when, in reality, it has been paid for by the subject company.

Members and candidates must adhere to strict standards of conduct that govern how the research is to be conducted and what disclosures must be made in the report. Analysts must engage in thorough, independent, and unbiased analysis and must fully disclose potential conflicts of interest, including the nature of their compensation. Otherwise, analysts risk misleading investors.

Investors need clear, credible, and thorough information about companies, and they need research based on independent thought. At a minimum, issuer-paid research should include a thorough analysis of the company's financial statements based on publicly disclosed information, benchmarking within a peer group, and industry analysis. Analysts must exercise diligence, independence, and thoroughness in conducting their research in an objective manner. Analysts must distinguish between fact and opinion in their reports. Conclusions must have a reasonable and adequate basis and must be supported by appropriate research.

Independent analysts must also strictly limit the type of compensation that they accept for conducting issuer-paid research. Otherwise, the content and conclusions of the reports could reasonably be expected to be determined or affected by compensation from the sponsoring companies. Compensation that might influence the research report could be direct, such as payment based on the conclusions of the report, or indirect, such as stock warrants or other equity instruments that could increase in value on the basis of positive coverage in the report. In such instances, the independent analyst has an incentive to avoid including negative information or making negative conclusions. Best practice is for independent analysts, prior to writing their report, to negotiate only a flat fee for their work that is not linked to their conclusions or recommendations.

Travel Funding

The benefits related to accepting paid travel extend beyond the cost savings to the member or candidate, such as the chance to talk exclusively with the executives of a company. The problem is that members and candidates may be influenced by these discussions when flying on a corporate or chartered jet. Best practice dictates that members and candidates always use commercial transportation rather than accept paid travel arrangements from an outside company. Should commercial transportation be unavailable, members and candidates may accept modestly arranged travel to participate in appropriate information-gathering events, such as a property tour.

Recommended Procedures for Compliance

Members and candidates should adhere to the following practices and should encourage their firms to establish procedures to avoid violations of Standard I(B):

- *Protect the integrity of opinions*: Members, candidates, and their firms should establish policies stating that every research report concerning the securities of a corporate client should reflect the unbiased opinion of the analyst. Firms should also design compensation systems that protect the integrity of the investment decision process by maintaining the independence and objectivity of analysts.

- *Create a restricted list*: If the firm is unwilling to permit dissemination of adverse opinions about a corporate client, members and candidates should encourage the firm to remove the controversial company from the research universe and put it on a restricted list so that the firm disseminates only factual information about the company.

- *Restrict special cost arrangements*: When attending meetings at an issuer's headquarters, members and candidates should pay for commercial transportation and hotel charges. No corporate issuer should reimburse members or candidates for air transportation. Members and candidates should encourage issuers to limit the use of corporate aircraft to situations in which commercial transportation is not available or in which efficient movement could not otherwise be arranged. Members and candidates should take particular care that when frequent meetings are held between an individual issuer and an individual member or candidate, the issuer should not always host the member or candidate.

▪ *Limit gifts*: Members and candidates must limit the acceptance of gratuities and/or gifts to token items. Standard I(B) does not preclude customary, ordinary business-related entertainment as long as its purpose is not to influence or reward members or candidates. Firms should consider a strict value limit for acceptable gifts that is based on the local or regional customs and should address whether the limit is per gift or an aggregate annual value.

▪ *Restrict investments*: Members and candidates should encourage their investment firms to develop formal polices related to employee purchases of equity or equity-related IPOs. Firms should require prior approval for employee participation in IPOs, with prompt disclosure of investment actions taken following the offering. Strict limits should be imposed on investment personnel acquiring securities in private placements.

▪ *Review procedures*: Members and candidates should encourage their firms to implement effective supervisory and review procedures to ensure that analysts and portfolio managers comply with policies relating to their personal investment activities.

▪ *Independence policy*: Members, candidates, and their firms should establish a formal written policy on the independence and objectivity of research and implement reporting structures and review procedures to ensure that research analysts do not report to and are not supervised or controlled by any department of the firm that could compromise the independence of the analyst. More detailed recommendations related to a firm's policies regarding research objectivity are set forth in the CFA Institute statement *Research Objectivity Standards* (www.cfainstitute.org).

▪ *Appointed officer*: Firms should appoint a senior officer with oversight responsibilities for compliance with the firm's code of ethics and all regulations concerning its business. Firms should provide every employee with the procedures and policies for reporting potentially unethical behavior, violations of regulations, or other activities that may harm the firm's reputation.

Application of the Standard

Example 1 (Travel Expenses): Steven Taylor, a mining analyst with Bronson Brokers, is invited by Precision Metals to join a group of his peers in a tour of mining facilities in several western U.S. states. The company arranges for chartered group flights from site to site and for accommodations in Spartan Motels, the only chain with accommodations near the mines, for three nights. Taylor allows Precision Metals to pick up his tab, as do the other analysts, with one exception—John Adams, an employee of a large trust company who insists on following his company's policy and paying for his hotel room himself.

> *Comment*: The policy of the company where Adams works complies closely with Standard I(B) by avoiding even the appearance of a conflict of interest, but Taylor and the other analysts were not necessarily violating Standard I(B). In general, when allowing companies to pay for travel and/or accommodations in these circumstances, members and candidates must use their

judgment. They must be on guard that such arrangements not impinge on a member's or candidate's independence and objectivity. In this example, the trip was strictly for business and Taylor was not accepting irrelevant or lavish hospitality. The itinerary required chartered flights, for which analysts were not expected to pay. The accommodations were modest. These arrangements are not unusual and did not violate Standard I(B) as long as Taylor's independence and objectivity were not compromised. In the final analysis, members and candidates should consider both whether they can remain objective and whether their integrity might be perceived by their clients to have been compromised.

Example 2   (Research Independence): Susan Dillon, an analyst in the corporate finance department of an investment services firm, is making a presentation to a potential new business client that includes the promise that her firm will provide full research coverage of the potential client.

> *Comment*: Dillon may agree to provide research coverage, but she must not commit her firm's research department to providing a favorable recommendation. The firm's recommendation (favorable, neutral, or unfavorable) must be based on an independent and objective investigation and analysis of the company and its securities.

Example 3   (Research Independence and Intrafirm Pressure): Walter Fritz is an equity analyst with Hilton Brokerage who covers the mining industry. He has concluded that the stock of Metals & Mining is overpriced at its current level, but he is concerned that a negative research report will hurt the good relationship between Metals & Mining and the investment banking division of his firm. In fact, a senior manager of Hilton Brokerage has just sent him a copy of a proposal his firm has made to Metals & Mining to underwrite a debt offering. Fritz needs to produce a report right away and is concerned about issuing a less-than-favorable rating.

> *Comment*: Fritz's analysis of Metals & Mining must be objective and based solely on consideration of company fundamentals. Any pressure from other divisions of his firm is inappropriate. This conflict could have been eliminated if, in anticipation of the offering, Hilton Brokerage had placed Metals & Mining on a restricted list for its sales force.

Example 4   (Research Independence and Issuer Relationship Pressure): As in Example 3, Walter Fritz has concluded that Metals & Mining stock is overvalued at its current level, but he is concerned that a negative research report might jeopardize a close rapport that he has nurtured over the years with Metals & Mining's CEO, chief finance officer, and investment relations officer. Fritz is concerned that a negative report might result also in management retaliation—for instance, cutting him off from participating in conference calls when a quarterly earnings release is made, denying him the ability to ask questions on such calls, and/or denying him access to top management for arranging group meetings between Hilton Brokerage clients with top Metals & Mining managers.

> *Comment:* As in Example 3, Fritz's analysis must be objective and based solely on consideration of company fundamentals. Any pressure from Metals & Mining is inappropriate. Fritz should reinforce the integrity of his conclusions by stressing that his investment recommendation is based on relative valuation, which may include qualitative issues with respect to Metals & Mining's management.

Example 5   (Research Independence and Sales Pressure): As support for the sales effort of her corporate bond department, Lindsey Warner offers credit guidance to purchasers of fixed-income securities. Her compensation is closely linked to the performance of the corporate bond department. Near the quarter's end, Warner's firm has a large inventory position in the bonds of Milton, Ltd., and has been unable to sell the bonds because of Milton's recent announcement of an operating problem. Salespeople have asked her to contact large clients to push the bonds.

> *Comment*: Unethical sales practices create significant potential violations of the Code and Standards. Warner's opinion of the Milton bonds must not be affected by internal pressure or compensation. In this case, Warner must refuse to push the Milton bonds unless she is able to justify that the market price has already adjusted for the operating problem.

Example 6   (Research Independence and Prior Coverage): Jill Jorund is a securities analyst following airline stocks and a rising star at her firm. Her boss has been carrying a "buy" recommendation on International Airlines and asks Jorund to take over coverage of that airline. He tells Jorund that under no circumstances should the prevailing buy recommendation be changed.

> *Comment*: Jorund must be independent and objective in her analysis of International Airlines. If she believes that her boss's instructions have compromised her, she has two options: Tell her boss that she cannot cover the company under these constraints or take over coverage of the company, reach her own independent conclusions, and if they conflict with her boss's opinion, share the conclusions with her boss or other supervisors in the firm so that they can make appropriate recommendations. Jorund must issue only recommendations that reflect her independent and objective opinion.

Example 7   (Gifts and Entertainment from Related Party): Edward Grant directs a large amount of his commission business to a New York-based brokerage house. In appreciation for all the business, the brokerage house gives Grant two tickets to the World Cup in South Africa, two nights at a nearby resort, several meals, and transportation via limousine to the game. Grant fails to disclose receiving this package to his supervisor.

> *Comment*: Grant has violated Standard I(B) because accepting these substantial gifts may impede his independence and objectivity. Every member and candidate should endeavor to avoid situations that might cause or be perceived to cause a loss of independence or objectivity in recommending investments or taking investment action. By accepting the trip, Grant has opened himself up to the accusation that he may give the broker favored treatment in return.

Example 8   (Gifts and Entertainment from Client): Theresa Green manages the portfolio of Ian Knowlden, a client of Tisbury Investments. Green achieves an annual return for Knowlden that is consistently better than that of the benchmark she and the client previously agreed to. As a reward, Knowlden offers Green two tickets to Wimbledon and the use of Knowlden's flat in London for a week. Green discloses this gift to her supervisor at Tisbury.

> *Comment*: Green is in compliance with Standard I(B) because she disclosed the gift from one of her clients in accordance with the firm's policies. Members and candidates may accept bonuses or gifts from clients as long as they disclose them to their employers, because gifts in a client relationship are deemed less likely to affect a member's or candidate's objectivity and independence than gifts in other situations. Disclosure is required, however, so that supervisors can monitor such situations to guard against

employees favoring a gift-giving client to the detriment of other fee-paying clients (such as by allocating a greater proportion of IPO stock to the gift-giving client's portfolio).

Best practices for monitoring include comparing the transaction costs of the Knowlden account with the costs of other accounts managed by Green and other similar accounts within Tisbury. The supervisor could also compare the performance returns with the returns of other clients with the same mandate. This comparison will assist in determining whether a pattern of favoritism by Green is disadvantaging other Tisbury clients or the possibility that this favoritism could affect her future behavior.

Example 9 (Travel Expenses from External Manager): Tom Wayne is the investment manager of the Franklin City Employees Pension Plan. He recently completed a successful search for a firm to manage the foreign equity allocation of the plan's diversified portfolio. He followed the plan's standard procedure of seeking presentations from a number of qualified firms and recommended that his board select Penguin Advisors because of its experience, well-defined investment strategy, and performance record. The firm claims compliance with the Global Investment Performance Standards (GIPS) and has been verified. Following the selection of Penguin, a reporter from the *Franklin City Record* calls to ask if there was any connection between this action and the fact that Penguin was one of the sponsors of an "investment fact-finding trip to Asia" that Wayne made earlier in the year. The trip was one of several conducted by the Pension Investment Academy, which had arranged the itinerary of meetings with economic, government, and corporate officials in major cities in several Asian countries. The Pension Investment Academy obtains support for the cost of these trips from a number of investment managers, including Penguin Advisors; the Academy then pays the travel expenses of the various pension plan managers on the trip and provides all meals and accommodations. The president of Penguin Advisors was also one of the travelers on the trip.

> *Comment*: Although Wayne can probably put to good use the knowledge he gained from the trip in selecting portfolio managers and in other areas of managing the pension plan, his recommendation of Penguin Advisors may be tainted by the possible conflict incurred when he participated in a trip partly paid for by Penguin Advisors and when he was in the daily company of the president of Penguin Advisors. To avoid violating Standard I(B), Wayne's basic expenses for travel and accommodations should have been paid by his employer or the pension plan; contact with the president of Penguin Advisors should have been limited to informational or educational events only; and the trip, the organizer, and the sponsor should have been made a matter of public record. Even if his actions were not in violation of Standard I(B), Wayne should have been sensitive to the public perception of the trip when reported in the newspaper and the extent to which the subjective elements of his decision might have been affected by the familiarity that the daily contact of such a trip would encourage. This advantage would probably not be shared by firms competing with Penguin Advisors.

Example 10 (Research Independence and Compensation Arrangements): Javier Herrero recently left his job as a research analyst for a large investment adviser. While looking for a new position, he was hired by an investor-relations firm to write a research report on one of its clients, a small educational software company. The investor-relations firm hopes to generate investor interest in the technology company. The firm will pay Herrero a flat fee plus a bonus if any new investors buy stock in the company as a result of Herrero's report.

Comment: If Herrero accepts this payment arrangement, he will be in violation of Standard I(B) because the compensation arrangement can reasonably be expected to compromise his independence and objectivity. Herrero will receive a bonus for attracting investors, which provides an incentive to draft a positive report regardless of the facts and to ignore or play down any negative information about the company. Herrero should accept only a flat fee that is not tied to the conclusions or recommendations of the report. Issuer-paid research that is objective and unbiased can be done under the right circumstances as long as the analyst takes steps to maintain his or her objectivity and includes in the report proper disclosures regarding potential conflicts of interest.

Example 11   (Recommendation Objectivity and Service Fees): Two years ago, Bob Wade, trust manager for Central Midas Bank, was approached by Western Funds about promoting its family of funds, with special interest in the service-fee class of funds. To entice Central to promote this class, Western Funds offered to pay the bank a service fee of 0.25 percent. Without disclosing the fee being offered to the bank, Wade asked one of the investment managers to review Western's funds to determine whether they were suitable for clients of Central Midas Bank. The manager completed the normal due diligence review and determined that the new funds were fairly valued in the market with fee structures on a par with competitors. Wade decided to accept Western's offer and instructed the team of portfolio managers to exclusively promote these funds and the service-fee class to clients seeking to invest new funds or transfer from their current investments.

Now, two years later, the funds managed by Western begin to underperform their peers. Wade is counting on the fees to reach his profitability targets and continues to push these funds as acceptable investments for Central's clients.

Comment: Wade is violating Standard I(B) because the fee arrangement has affected the objectivity of his recommendations. Wade is relying on the fee as a component of the department's profitability and is unwilling to offer other products that may affect the fees received.

See also Standard VI(A)–Disclosure of Conflicts.

Example 12   (Recommendation Objectivity): Bob Thompson has been doing research for the portfolio manager of the fixed-income department. His assignment is to do sensitivity analysis on securitized subprime mortgages. He has discussed with the manager possible scenarios to use to calculate expected returns. A key assumption in such calculations is housing price appreciation (HPA) because it drives "prepays" (prepayments of mortgages) and losses. Thompson is concerned with the significant appreciation experienced over the previous five years as a result of the increased availability of funds from subprime mortgages. Thompson insists that the analysis should include a scenario run with negative 10 percent for the first year, negative 5 percent for the second year, and then (to project a worst-case scenario) 0 percent for Years 3 through 5. The manager replies that these assumptions are too dire because there has never been a time in their available database when HPA was negative.

Thompson conducts his research to better understand the risks inherent in these securities and evaluates these securities in the worst-case scenario, an unlikely but possible environment. Based on the results of the enhanced scenarios, Thompson does not recommend the purchase of the securitization. Against the general market trends, the manager follows Thompson's recommendation and does not invest. The following year, the housing market collapses. In avoiding the subprime investments, the manager's portfolio outperforms its peer group that year.

Comment: Thompson's actions in running the worst-case scenario against the protests of the portfolio manager are in alignment with the principles of

Standard I(B). Thompson did not allow his research to be pressured by the general trends of the market or the manager's desire to limit the research to historical norms.

See also Standard V(A)—Diligence and Reasonable Basis.

C. Misrepresentation

Members and Candidates must not knowingly make any misrepresentations relating to investment analysis, recommendations, actions, or other professional activities.

Guidance

Highlights:

- *Impact on Investment Practice*
- *Plagiarism*
- *Work Completed for Employer*

Trust is the foundation of the investment profession. Investors must be able to rely on the statements and information provided to them by those with whom the investors have trusted their financial well-being. Investment professionals who make false or misleading statements not only harm investors but also reduce the level of investor confidence in the investment profession and threaten the integrity of capital markets as a whole.

A misrepresentation is any untrue statement or omission of a fact or any statement that is otherwise false or misleading. A member or candidate must not knowingly omit or misrepresent information or give a false impression of a firm, organization, or security in the member's or candidate's oral representations, advertising (whether in the press or through brochures), electronic communications, or written materials (whether publicly disseminated or not). In this context, "knowingly" means that the member or candidate either knows or should have known that the misrepresentation was being made or that omitted information could alter the investment decision-making process.

Written materials include, but are not limited to, research reports, underwriting documents, company financial reports, market letters, newspaper columns, and books. Electronic communications include, but are not limited to, internet communications, webpages, chat rooms, and e-mails. Members and candidates who use webpages should regularly monitor materials posted on the site to ensure that the site contains current information. Members and candidates should also ensure that all reasonable precautions have been taken to protect the site's integrity and security and that the site does not misrepresent any information and does provide full disclosure.

The omission of a fact or outcome has increased in importance because of the growing use of technical analysis. Many members and candidates rely on models to scan for new investment opportunities, to develop investment vehicles, and to produce investment recommendations and ratings. Although not every model can test for every factor or outcome, members and candidates should ensure that their analyses incorporate a broad range of assumptions—from very positive scenarios to extremely negative scenarios. The omission from the analysis of potentially negative outcomes or of levels of risk outside the norm may misrepresent the true economic value of the investment.

Impact on Investment Practice

Members and candidates must not misrepresent any aspect of their practice, including (but not limited to) their qualifications or credentials, the qualifications or services provided by their firm, their performance record and the record of their firm, and the characteristics of an investment. Any misrepresentation made by a member or candidate relating to the member's or candidate's professional activities is a breach of this standard.

Members and candidates should exercise care and diligence when incorporating third-party information. Misrepresentations resulting from the use of the credit ratings, research, testimonials, or marketing materials of these outside parties become the responsibility of the investment professional when it affects that professional's business practices.

Investing through outside managers continues to expand as an acceptable method of investing in areas outside a firm's core competencies. Members and candidates must disclose their intended use of external managers and must not represent those managers' investment practices as their own. Although the level of involvement of outside managers may change over time, appropriate disclosures by members and candidates are important to avoiding misrepresentations, especially if the primary activity is to invest directly with a single external manager. Standard V(B)—Communication with Clients and Prospective Clients discusses in further detail communicating the firm's investment practices.

Standard I(C) prohibits members and candidates from guaranteeing clients any specific return on volatile investments. Most investments contain some element of risk that makes their return inherently unpredictable. For these investments, guaranteeing either a particular rate of return or a guaranteed preservation of investment capital (e.g., "I can guarantee that you will earn 8 percent on equities this year" or "I can guarantee that you will not lose money on this investment") is misleading to investors. Standard I(C) does not prohibit members and candidates from providing clients with information on investment products that have guarantees built into the structure of the product itself or for which an institution has agreed to cover any losses.

Plagiarism

Standard I(C) also prohibits plagiarism in the preparation of material for distribution to employers, associates, clients, prospects, or the general public. Plagiarism is defined as copying or using in substantially the same form materials prepared by others without acknowledging the source of the material or identifying the author and publisher of such material. Members and candidates must not copy (or represent as their own) original ideas or material without permission and must acknowledge and identify the source of ideas or material that is not their own.

The investment profession uses a myriad of financial, economic, and statistical data in the investment decision-making process. Through various publications and presentations, the investment professional is constantly exposed to the work of others and to the temptation to use that work without proper acknowledgment.

Misrepresentation through plagiarism in investment management can take various forms. The simplest and most flagrant example is to take a research report or study done by another firm or person, change the names, and release the material as one's own original analysis. This action is a clear violation of Standard I(C). Other practices include 1) using excerpts from articles or reports prepared by others either verbatim or with only slight changes in wording without acknowledgment, 2) citing specific quotations as attributable to "leading analysts" and "investment experts" without naming the specific references, 3) presenting statistical estimates of forecasts prepared by others and identifying the sources but without including the qualifying statements or caveats that may have been used, 4) using charts and graphs without stating their sources, and 5) copying proprietary computerized spreadsheets or algorithms without seeking the cooperation or authorization of their creators.

In the case of distributing third-party, outsourced research, members and candidates may use and distribute these reports as long as they do not represent themselves as the authors of such a report. Indeed, the member or candidate may add value for the client by sifting through research and repackaging it for clients. In such cases, clients should be fully informed that they are paying for the ability of the member or candidate to find the best research from a wide variety of sources. Members and candidates must not misrepresent their abilities, the extent of their expertise, or the extent of their work in a way that would mislead their clients or prospective clients. Members and candidates should disclose whether the research being presented to clients comes from another source, from either within or outside the member's or candidate's firm. This allows clients to understand who has the expertise behind the report or if the work is being done by the analyst, other members of the firm, or an outside party.

Standard 1(C) also applies to plagiarism in oral communications, such as through group meetings; visits with associates, clients, and customers; use of audio/video media (which is rapidly increasing); and telecommunications, including electronic data transfer and the outright copying of electronic media.

One of the most egregious practices in violation of this standard is the preparation of research reports based on multiple sources of information without acknowledging the sources. Examples of information from such sources include ideas, statistical compilations, and forecasts combined to give the appearance of original work. Although there is no monopoly on ideas, members and candidates must give credit where it is clearly due. Analysts should not use undocumented forecasts, earnings projections, asset values, and so on. Sources must be revealed to bring the responsibility directly back to the author of the report or the firm involved.

Work Completed for Employer

The preceding paragraphs address actions that would constitute a violation of Standard I(C). In some situations, however, members or candidates may use research conducted or models developed by others within the same firm without committing a violation. The most common example relates to the situation in which one (or more) of the original analysts is no longer with the firm. Research and models developed while employed by a firm are the property of the firm. The firm retains the right to continue using the work completed after a member or candidate has left the organization. The firm may issue future reports without providing attribution to the prior analysts. A member or candidate cannot, however, reissue a previously released report solely under his or her name.

Recommended Procedures for Compliance

Factual Presentations

Members and candidates can prevent unintentional misrepresentations of the qualifications or services they or their firms provide if each member and candidate understands the limit of the firm's or individual's capabilities and the need to be accurate and complete in presentations. Firms can provide guidance for employees who make written or oral presentations to clients or potential clients by providing a written list of the firm's available services and a description of the firm's qualifications. This list should suggest ways of describing the firm's services, qualifications, and compensation that are both accurate and suitable for client or customer presentations. Firms can also help prevent misrepresentation by specifically designating which employees are authorized to speak on behalf of the firm. Whether or not the firm provides guidance, members and candidates should make certain that they understand the services the firm can perform and its qualifications.

Qualification Summary

In addition, to ensure accurate presentations to clients, each member and candidate should prepare a summary of his or her own qualifications and experience and a list of the services the member or candidate is capable of performing. Firms can assist member and candidate compliance by periodically reviewing employee correspondence and documents that contain representations of individual or firm qualifications.

Verify Outside Information

When providing information to clients from third parties, members and candidates share a responsibility for the accuracy of the marketing and distribution materials that pertain to the third party's capabilities, services, and products. Misrepresentation by third parties can damage the member's or candidate's reputation, the reputation of the firm, and the integrity of the capital markets. Members and candidates should encourage their employers to develop procedures for verifying information of third-party firms.

Maintain Webpages

Members and candidates who publish webpages should regularly monitor materials posted on the site to ensure that the site contains current information. Members and candidates should also ensure that all reasonable precautions have been taken to protect the site's integrity, confidentiality, and security and that the site does not misrepresent any information and provides full disclosure.

Plagiarism Policy

To avoid plagiarism in preparing research reports or conclusions of analysis, members and candidates should take the following steps:

- *Maintain copies*: Keep copies of all research reports, articles containing research ideas, material with new statistical methodologies, and other materials that were relied on in preparing the research report.

- *Attribute quotations*: Attribute to their sources any direct quotations, including projections, tables, statistics, model/product ideas, and new methodologies prepared by persons other than recognized financial and statistical reporting services or similar sources.

- *Attribute summaries*: Attribute to their sources any paraphrases or summaries of material prepared by others. For example, to support his analysis of Brown Company's competitive position, the author of a research report on Brown might summarize another analyst's report on Brown's chief competitor, but the author of the Brown report must acknowledge in his own report the reliance on the other analyst's report.

Application of the Standard

Example 1   (Representing the Firm's Abilities): Allison Rogers is a partner in the firm of Rogers and Black, a small firm offering investment advisory services. She assures a prospective client who has just inherited US$1 million that "we can perform all the financial and investment services you need." Rogers and Black is well equipped to provide investment advice but, in fact, cannot provide asset allocation assistance or a full array of financial and investment services.

Comment: Rogers has violated Standard I(C) by orally misrepresenting the services her firm can perform for the prospective client. She must limit herself to describing the range of investment advisory services Rogers and Black can provide and offer to help the client obtain elsewhere the financial and investment services that her firm cannot provide.

Example 2   (Disclosure of Issuer-Paid Research): Anthony McGuire is an issuer-paid analyst hired by publicly traded companies to electronically promote their stocks. McGuire creates a website that promotes his research efforts as a seemingly independent analyst. McGuire posts a profile and a strong buy recommendation for each company on the website indicating that the stock is expected to increase in value. He does not disclose the contractual relationships with the companies he covers on his website, in the research reports he issues, or in the statements he makes about the companies in internet chat rooms.

Comment: McGuire has violated Standard I(C) because the internet site is misleading to potential investors. Even if the recommendations are valid and supported with thorough research, his omissions regarding the true relationship between himself and the companies he covers constitute a misrepresentation. McGuire has also violated Standard VI(A)—Disclosure of Conflicts by not disclosing the existence of an arrangement with the companies through which he receives compensation in exchange for his services.

Example 3   (Correction of Unintentional Errors): Hijan Yao is responsible for the creation and distribution of the marketing materials for his firm, which claims compliance with the GIPS standards. Yao creates and distributes a presentation of performance by the firm's Asian equity composite that states the composite has ¥350 billion in assets. In fact, the composite has only ¥35 billion in assets, and the higher figure on the presentation is a result of a typographical error. Nevertheless, the erroneous material is distributed to a number of clients before Yao catches the mistake.

Comment: Once the error is discovered, Yao must take steps to cease distribution of the incorrect material and correct the error by informing those who have received the erroneous information. Because Yao did not knowingly make the misrepresentation, however, he did not violate Standard I(C). Since his firm claims compliance with the GIPS standards, it must also comply with the GIPS Guidance Statement on Error Correction in relation to the error.

Example 4   (Noncorrection of Known Errors): Syed Muhammad is the president of an investment management firm. The promotional material for the firm, created by the firm's marketing department, incorrectly claims that Muhammad has an advanced degree in finance from a prestigious business school in addition to the CFA designation. Although Muhammad attended the school for a short period of time, he did not receive a degree. Over the years, Muhammad and others in the firm have distributed this material to numerous prospective clients and consultants.

Comment: Even though Muhammad may not have been directly responsible for the misrepresentation of his credentials in the firm's promotional material, he used this material numerous times over an extended period and should have known of the misrepresentation. Thus, Muhammad has violated Standard I(C).

Example 5   (Plagiarism): Cindy Grant, a research analyst for a Canadian brokerage firm, has specialized in the Canadian mining industry for the past 10 years. She recently read an extensive research report on Jefferson Mining, Ltd., by Jeremy Barton, another analyst. Barton provided extensive statistics on the mineral reserves, production capacity, selling rates, and marketing factors affecting Jefferson's operations. He also noted that initial drilling results on a new ore body, which had not been made public, might show the existence of mineral zones that could increase the life of Jefferson's main mines, but Barton cited no specific data as to the initial drilling results. Grant called an officer of Jefferson, who gave her the initial drilling results over the telephone. The data indicated that the expected life of the main mines would be tripled. Grant added these statistics to Barton's report and circulated it as her own report within her firm.

> *Comment*: Grant plagiarized Barton's report by reproducing large parts of it in her own report without acknowledgment.

Example 6   (Misrepresentation of Information): When Ricki Marks sells mortgage-backed derivatives called "interest-only strips" (IOs) to public pension plan clients, she describes them as "guaranteed by the U.S. government." Purchasers of the IOs are entitled only to the interest stream generated by the mortgages, however, not the notional principal itself. One particular municipality's investment policies and local law require that securities purchased by its public pension plans be guaranteed by the U.S. government. Although the underlying mortgages are guaranteed, neither the investor's investment nor the interest stream on the IOs is guaranteed. When interest rates decline, causing an increase in prepayment of mortgages, interest payments to the IOs' investors decline, and these investors lose a portion of their investment.

> *Comment*: Marks violated Standard I(C) by misrepresenting the terms and character of the investment.

Example 7   (Potential Information Misrepresentation): Khalouck Abdrabbo manages the investments of several high-net-worth individuals in the United States who are approaching retirement. Abdrabbo advises these individuals that a portion of their investments be moved from equity to bank-sponsored certificates of deposit and money market accounts so that the principal will be "guaranteed" up to a certain amount. The interest is not guaranteed.

> *Comment*: Although there is risk that the institution offering the certificates of deposits and money market accounts could go bankrupt, in the United States, these accounts are insured by the U.S. government through the Federal Deposit Insurance Corporation. Therefore, using the term "guaranteed" in this context is not inappropriate as long as the amount is within the government-insured limit. Abdrabbo should explain these facts to the clients.

Example 8   (Plagiarism): Steve Swanson is a senior analyst in the investment research department of Ballard and Company. Apex Corporation has asked Ballard to assist in acquiring the majority ownership of stock in the Campbell Company, a financial consulting firm, and to prepare a report recommending that stockholders of Campbell agree to the acquisition. Another investment firm, Davis and Company, had already prepared a report for Apex analyzing both Apex and Campbell and recommending an exchange ratio. Apex has given the Davis report to Ballard officers, who have passed it on to Swanson. Swanson reviews the Davis report and other available material on Apex and Campbell companies. From his analysis, he concludes that the common stocks of Campbell and Apex represent good value at their current prices; he believes, however, that the Davis report does not consider all the factors a Campbell stockholder would need to know to make a decision. Swanson reports his conclusions to the partner in charge, who tells him to "use the Davis report, change a few words, sign your name, and get it out."

Comment: If Swanson does as requested, he will violate Standard I(C). He could refer to those portions of the Davis report that he agrees with if he identifies Davis as the source; he could then add his own analysis and conclusions to the report before signing and distributing it.

Example 9   (Plagiarism): Claude Browning, a quantitative analyst for Double Alpha, Inc., returns in great excitement from a seminar. In that seminar, Jack Jorrely, a well-publicized quantitative analyst at a national brokerage firm, discussed one of his new models in great detail, and Browning is intrigued by the new concepts. He proceeds to test the model, making some minor mechanical changes but retaining the concepts, until he produces some very positive results. Browning quickly announces to his supervisors at Double Alpha that he has discovered a new model and that clients and prospective clients should be informed of this positive finding as ongoing proof of Double Alpha's continuing innovation and ability to add value.

Comment: Although Browning tested Jorrely's model on his own and even slightly modified it, he must still acknowledge the original source of the idea. Browning can certainly take credit for the final, practical results; he can also support his conclusions with his own test. The credit for the innovative thinking, however, must be awarded to Jorrely.

Example 10   (Plagiarism): Fernando Zubia would like to include in his firm's marketing materials some "plain-language" descriptions of various concepts, such as the price-to-earnings (P/E) multiple and why standard deviation is used as a measure of risk. The descriptions come from other sources, but Zubia wishes to use them without reference to the original authors. Would this use of material be a violation of Standard I(C)?

Comment: Copying verbatim any material without acknowledgement, including plain-language descriptions of the P/E multiple and standard deviation, violates Standard I(C). Even though these concepts are general, best practice would be for Zubia to describe them in his own words or cite the sources from which the descriptions are quoted. Members and candidates would be violating Standard I(C) if they were either responsible for creating marketing materials without attribution or knowingly use plagiarized materials.

Example 11   (Plagiarism): Through a mainstream media outlet, Erika Schneider learns about a study that she would like to cite in her research. Should she cite both the mainstream intermediary source as well as the author of the study itself when using that information?

Comment: In all instances, a member or candidate must cite the actual source of the information. Best practice for Schneider would be to obtain the information directly from the author and review it before citing it in a report. In that case, Schneider would not need to report how she found out about the information. For example, suppose Schneider read in the *Financial Times* about a study issued by CFA Institute; best practice for Schneider would be to obtain a copy of the study from CFA Institute, review it, and then cite it in her report. If she does not use any interpretation of the report from the *Financial Times* and the newspaper does not add value to the report itself, the newspaper is merely a conduit to the original information and does not need to be cited. If she does not obtain the report and review the information, Schneider runs the risk of relying on second-hand information that may misstate facts. If, for example, the *Financial Times* erroneously reported some information from the original CFA Institute study and Schneider copied that erroneous information without acknowledging CFA Institute, she could be the object of complaints. Best practice would be either to obtain the complete study from its original author and cite only that author or to use the information provided by the intermediary and cite both sources.

Example 12   (Misrepresentation of Information): Paul Ostrowski runs a two-person investment management firm. Ostrowski's firm subscribes to a service from a large investment research firm that provides research reports that can be repackaged by smaller firms for those firms' clients. Ostrowski's firm distributes these reports to clients as its own work.

> *Comment*: Ostrowski can rely on third-party research that has a reasonable and adequate basis, but he cannot imply that he is the author of such research. If he does, Ostrowski is misrepresenting the extent of his work in a way that misleads the firm's clients or prospective clients.

Example 13   (Misrepresentation of Information): Tom Stafford is part of a team within Appleton Investment Management responsible for managing a pool of assets for Open Air Bank, which distributes structured securities to offshore clients. He becomes aware that Open Air is promoting the structured securities as a much less risky investment than the investment management policy followed by him and the team to manage the original pool of assets. Also, Open Air has procured an independent rating for the pool that significantly overstates the quality of the investments. Stafford communicates his concerns to his team leader and supervisor, who responds that Open Air owns the product and is responsible for all marketing and distribution. Stafford's supervisor goes on to say that the product is outside of the U.S. regulatory regime that Appleton follows and that all risks of the product are disclosed at the bottom of page 184 of the prospectus.

> *Comment:* As a member of the investment team, Stafford is qualified to recognize the degree of accuracy of the materials that characterize the portfolio, and he is correct to be worried about Appleton's responsibility for a misrepresentation of the risks. Thus, he should continue to pursue the issue of Open Air's inaccurate promotion of the portfolio according to the firm's policies and procedures.
>
> The Code and Standards stress protecting the reputation of the firm and the sustainability and integrity of the capital markets. Misrepresenting the quality and risks associated with the investment pool may lead to negative consequences for others well beyond the direct investors.

Example 14   (Avoiding a Misrepresentation): Trina Smith is a fixed-income portfolio manager at a pension fund. She has observed that the market for highly structured mortgages is the focus of salespeople she meets and that these products represent a significant number of trading opportunities. In discussions about this topic with her team, Smith learns that calculating yields on changing cash flows within the deal structure requires very specialized vendor software. After more research, they find out that each deal is unique and that deals can have more than a dozen layers and changing cash flow priorities. Smith comes to the conclusion that, because of the complexity of these securities, the team cannot effectively distinguish between potentially good and bad investment options. To avoid misrepresenting their understanding, the team decides that the highly structured mortgage segment of the securitized market should not become part of the core of the fund's portfolio; they will allow some of the less complex securities to be part of the core.

> *Comment:* Smith is in compliance with Standard 1(C) by not investing in securities that she and her team cannot effectively understand. Because she

is not able to describe the risk and return profile of the securities to the pension fund beneficiaries and trustees, she appropriately limits the fund's exposure to this sector.

D. Misconduct

Members and Candidates must not engage in any professional conduct involving dishonesty, fraud, or deceit or commit any act that reflects adversely on their professional reputation, integrity, or competence.

Guidance

Whereas Standard I(A) addresses the obligation of members and candidates to comply with applicable law that governs their professional activities, Standard I(D) addresses *all* conduct that reflects poorly on the professional integrity, good reputation, or competence of members and candidates. Any act that involves lying, cheating, stealing, or other dishonest conduct is a violation of this standard if the offense reflects adversely on a member's or candidate's professional activities. Although CFA Institute discourages any sort of unethical behavior by members and candidates, the Code and Standards are primarily aimed at conduct and actions related to a member's or candidate's professional life.

Conduct that damages trustworthiness or competence may include behavior that, although it is not illegal, nevertheless negatively affects a member's or candidate's ability to perform his or her responsibilities. For example, abusing alcohol during business hours might constitute a violation of this standard because it could have a detrimental effect on the member's or candidate's ability to fulfill his or her professional responsibilities. Personal bankruptcy may not reflect on the integrity or trustworthiness of the person declaring bankruptcy, but if the circumstances of the bankruptcy involve fraudulent or deceitful business conduct, the bankruptcy may be a violation of this standard.

In some cases, the absence of appropriate conduct or the lack of sufficient effort may be a violation of Standard I(D). The integrity of the investment profession is built on trust. A member or candidate—whether an investment banker, rating or research analyst, or portfolio manager—is expected to conduct the necessary due diligence to properly understand the nature and risks of an investment before making an investment recommendation. By not taking these steps and, instead, relying on someone else in the process to have performed them, members or candidates may violate the trust their clients have placed in them. This loss of trust may have a significant impact on the reputation of the member or candidate and the operations of the financial market as a whole.

Individuals may attempt to abuse the CFA Institute Professional Conduct Program by actively seeking CFA Institute enforcement of the Code and Standards, and Standard I(D) in particular, as a method of settling personal, political, or other disputes unrelated to professional ethics. CFA Institute is aware of this issue, and appropriate disciplinary policies, procedures, and enforcement mechanisms are in place to address misuse of the Code and Standards and the Professional Conduct Program in this way.

Recommended Procedures for Compliance   (I. Professionalism)

In addition to ensuring that their own behavior is consistent with Standard I(D), to prevent general misconduct, members and candidates should encourage their firms to adopt the following policies and procedures to support the principles of Standard I(D):

■ *Code of ethics*: Develop and/or adopt a code of ethics to which every employee must subscribe and make clear that any personal behavior that reflects poorly on the individual involved, the institution as a whole, or the investment industry will not be tolerated.

■ *List of violations*: Disseminate to all employees a list of potential violations and associated disciplinary sanctions, up to and including dismissal from the firm.

■ *Employee references*: Check references of potential employees to ensure that they are of good character and not ineligible to work in the investment industry because of past infractions of the law.

Application of the Standard

Example 1   (Professionalism and Competence): Simon Sasserman is a trust investment officer at a bank in a small affluent town. He enjoys lunching every day with friends at the country club, where his clients have observed him having numerous drinks. Back at work after lunch, he clearly is intoxicated while making investment decisions. His colleagues make a point of handling any business with Sasserman in the morning because they distrust his judgment after lunch.

> *Comment*: Sasserman's excessive drinking at lunch and subsequent intoxication at work constitute a violation of Standard I(D) because this conduct has raised questions about his professionalism and competence. His behavior reflects poorly on him, his employer, and the investment industry.

Example 2   (Fraud and Deceit): Howard Hoffman, a security analyst at ATZ Brothers, Inc., a large brokerage house, submits reimbursement forms over a two-year period to ATZ's self-funded health insurance program for more than two dozen bills, most of which have been altered to increase the amount due. An investigation by the firm's director of employee benefits uncovers the inappropriate conduct. ATZ subsequently terminates Hoffman's employment and notifies CFA Institute.

> *Comment*: Hoffman violated Standard I(D) because he engaged in intentional conduct involving fraud and deceit in the workplace that adversely reflected on his integrity.

Example 3   (Fraud and Deceit): Jody Brink, an analyst covering the automotive industry, volunteers much of her spare time to local charities. The board of one of the charitable institutions decides to buy five new vans to deliver hot lunches to low-income elderly people. Brink offers to donate her time to handle purchasing agreements. To pay a long-standing debt to a friend who operates an automobile dealership—and to compensate herself for her trouble—she agrees to a price 20 percent higher than normal and splits the surcharge with her friend. The director of the charity ultimately discovers the scheme and tells Brink that her services, donated or otherwise, are no longer required.

> *Comment*: Brink engaged in conduct involving dishonesty, fraud, and misrepresentation and has violated Standard I(D).

Example 4   (Personal Actions and Integrity): Carmen Garcia manages a mutual fund dedicated to socially responsible investing. She is also an environmental activist. As the result of her participation in nonviolent protests, Garcia has been arrested on numerous occasions for trespassing on the property of a large petrochemical plant that is accused of damaging the environment.

> *Comment*: Generally, Standard I(D) is not meant to cover legal transgressions resulting from acts of civil disobedience in support of personal beliefs

because such conduct does not reflect poorly on the member's or candidate's professional reputation, integrity, or competence.

Example 5 (Professional Misconduct): Meredith Rasmussen works on a buy-side trading desk of an investment management firm and concentrates on in-house trades for a hedge fund subsidiary managed by a team at the investment management firm. The hedge fund has been very successful and is marketed globally by the firm. From her experience as the trader for much of the activity of the fund, Rasmussen has become quite knowledgeable about the hedge fund's strategy, tactics, and performance. When a distinct break in the market occurs, however, and many of the securities involved in the hedge fund's strategy decline markedly in value, Rasmussen observes that the reported performance of the hedge fund does not reflect this decline. In her experience, the lack of effect is a very unlikely occurrence. She approaches the head of trading about her concern and is told that she should not ask any questions, that the fund is big and successful and is not her concern. She is fairly sure something is not right, so she contacts the compliance officer, who also tells her to stay away from the issue of the hedge fund's reporting.

> *Comment:* Rasmussen has clearly come upon an error in policies, procedures, and compliance practices within the firm's operations. According to the firm's procedures for reporting potentially unethical activity, she should pursue the issue by gathering some proof of her reason for doubt. Should all internal communications within the firm not satisfy her concerns, Rasmussen should consider reporting the potential unethical activity to the appropriate regulator.
>
> See also Standard IV(A) for guidance on whistleblowing and Standard IV(C) for the duties of a supervisor.

STANDARD II—INTEGRITY OF CAPITAL MARKETS

A. Material Nonpublic Information

Members and Candidates who possess material nonpublic information that could affect the value of an investment must not act or cause others to act on the information.

Guidance

Highlights:

- *What Is "Material" Information?*
- *What Constitutes "Nonpublic" Information?*
- *Mosaic Theory*
- *Investment Research Reports*

Trading or inducing others to trade on material nonpublic information erodes confidence in capital markets, institutions, and investment professionals by supporting the idea that those with inside information and special access can take unfair advantage of the general investing public. Although trading on inside information may lead to short-term profits, in the long run, individuals and the profession as a whole will suffer from such trading. It will cause investors to avoid capital markets because the markets are perceived to be "rigged" in favor of the knowledgeable insider. Standard II(A) promotes and maintains a high level of confidence in market integrity, which is one of the foundations of the investment profession.

The prohibition on using this information goes beyond the direct buying and selling of individual securities or bonds. Members and candidates must not use material nonpublic information to influence their investment actions related to derivatives (e.g., swaps or option contracts), mutual funds, or other alternative investments. *Any* trading based on material nonpublic information constitutes a violation of Standard II(A). The expansion of financial products and the increasing interconnectivity of financial markets globally have resulted in new potential opportunities for trading on material nonpublic information.

What Is "Material" Information?

Information is "material" if its disclosure would probably have an impact on the price of a security or if reasonable investors would want to know the information before making an investment decision. In other words, information is material if it would significantly alter the total mix of information currently available about a security in such a way that the price of the security would be affected.

The specificity of the information, the extent of its difference from public information, its nature, and its reliability are key factors in determining whether a particular piece of information fits the definition of material. For example, material information may include, but is not limited to, information on the following:

- earnings;
- mergers, acquisitions, tender offers, or joint ventures;
- changes in assets or asset quality;
- innovative products, processes, or discoveries;
- new licenses, patents, registered trademarks, or regulatory approval/rejection of a product;
- developments regarding customers or suppliers (e.g., the acquisition or loss of a contract);
- changes in management;
- change in auditor notification or the fact that the issuer may no longer rely on an auditor's report or qualified opinion;
- events regarding the issuer's securities (e.g., defaults on senior securities, calls of securities for redemption, repurchase plans, stock splits, changes in dividends, changes to the rights of security holders, public or private sales of additional securities, and changes in credit ratings);
- bankruptcies;
- significant legal disputes;
- government reports of economic trends (employment, housing starts, currency information, etc.);
- orders for large trades before they are executed.

In addition to the substance and specificity of the information, the source or relative reliability of the information also determines materiality. The less reliable a source, the less likely the information provided would be considered material. For example, factual information from a corporate insider regarding a significant new contract for a company is likely to be material, whereas an assumption based on speculation by a competitor about the same contract is likely to be less reliable and, therefore, not material.

Also, the more ambiguous the effect of the information on price, the less material that information is considered. If it is unclear whether the information will affect the price of a security and to what extent, the information may not be considered material. The passage of time may also render information that was once important immaterial.

What Constitutes "Nonpublic" Information?

Information is "nonpublic" until it has been disseminated or is available to the marketplace in general (as opposed to a select group of investors). Dissemination can be defined as "made known to." For example, a company report of profits that is posted on the internet and distributed widely through a press release or accompanied by a filing has been effectively disseminated to the marketplace. Members and candidates must have a reasonable expectation that people have received the information before it can be considered public. It is not necessary, however, to wait for the slowest method of delivery. Once the information is disseminated to the market, it is public information that is no longer covered by this standard.

Members and candidates must be particularly aware of information that is selectively disclosed by corporations to a small group of investors, analysts, or other market participants. Information that is made available to analysts remains nonpublic until it is made available to investors in general. Corporations that disclose information on a limited basis create the potential for insider-trading violations.

Issues of selective disclosure often arise when a corporate insider provides material information to analysts in a briefing or conference call before that information is released to the public. Analysts must be aware that a disclosure made to a room full of analysts does not necessarily make the disclosed information "public." Analysts should also be alert to the possibility that they are selectively receiving material nonpublic information when a company provides them with guidance or interpretation of such publicly available information as financial statements or regulatory filings.

Mosaic Theory

A financial analyst gathers and interprets large quantities of information from many sources. The analyst may use significant conclusions derived from the analysis of public and nonmaterial nonpublic information as the basis for investment recommendations and decisions even if those conclusions would have been material inside information had they been communicated directly to the analyst by a company. Under the "mosaic theory," financial analysts are free to act on this collection, or mosaic, of information without risking violation.

The practice of financial analysis depends on the free flow of information. For the fair and efficient operation of the capital markets, analysts and investors must have the greatest amount of information possible to facilitate making well-informed investment decisions about how and where to invest capital. Accurate, timely, and intelligible communication are essential if analysts and investors are to obtain the data needed to make informed decisions about how and where to invest capital. These disclosures must go beyond the information mandated by the reporting requirements of the securities laws and should include specific business information about items used to guide a company's future growth, such as new products, capital projects, and the competitive environment. Analysts seek and use such information to compare and contrast investment alternatives.

Much of the information used by analysts comes directly from companies. Analysts often receive such information through contacts with corporate insiders, especially investor-relations staff and financial officers. Information may be disseminated in the form of press releases, through oral presentations by company executives in analysts' meetings or conference calls, or during analysts' visits to company premises. In seeking to develop the most accurate and complete picture of a company, analysts should also reach beyond contacts with companies themselves and collect information from other sources, such as customers, contractors, suppliers, and the companies' competitors.

Analysts are in the business of formulating opinions and insights that are not obvious to the general investing public about the attractiveness of particular securities. In the course of their work, analysts actively seek out corporate information not generally known to the market for the express purpose of analyzing that information, forming an opinion on its significance, and informing their clients, who can be expected to trade on the basis of the recommendation. Analysts' initiatives to discover and analyze information and communicate their findings to their clients significantly enhance market efficiency, thus benefiting all investors (see *Dirks v. Securities and Exchange Commission*). Accordingly, violations of Standard II(A) will *not* result when a perceptive analyst reaches a conclusion about a corporate action or event through an analysis of public information and items of nonmaterial nonpublic information.

Investment professionals should note, however, that although analysts are free to use mosaic information in their research reports, they should save and document all their research [see Standard V(C)—Record Retention]. Evidence of the analyst's knowledge of public and nonmaterial nonpublic information about a corporation strengthens the assertion that the analyst reached his or her conclusions solely through appropriate methods rather than through the use of material nonpublic information.

Investment Research Reports

When a particularly well-known or respected analyst issues a report or makes changes to his or her recommendation, that information alone may have an effect on the market and thus may be considered material. Theoretically, under Standard II(A), such a report would have to be made public before it was distributed to clients. The analyst is not a company insider, however, and does not have access to inside information. Presumably, the analyst created the report from information available to the public (mosaic theory) and by using his or her expertise to interpret the information. The analyst's hard work, paid for by the client, generated the conclusions. Simply because the public in general would find the conclusions material does not require that the analyst make his or her work public. Investors who are not clients of the analyst can either do the work themselves or become clients of the analyst for access to the analyst's expertise.

Recommended Procedures for Compliance

Achieve Public Dissemination

If a member or candidate determines that information is material, the member or candidate should make reasonable efforts to achieve public dissemination of the information. This effort usually entails encouraging the issuer company to make the information public. If public dissemination is not possible, the member or candidate must communicate the information only to the designated supervisory and compliance personnel within the member's or candidate's firm and must not take investment action or alter current investment recommendations on the basis of the information. Moreover, members and candidates must not knowingly engage in any conduct that may induce company insiders to privately disclose material nonpublic information.

Adopt Compliance Procedures

Members and candidates should encourage their firms to adopt compliance procedures to prevent the misuse of material nonpublic information. Particularly important is improving compliance in such areas as the review of employee and proprietary trading, documentation of firm procedures, and the supervision of interdepartmental communications in multiservice firms. Compliance procedures should suit the particular characteristics of a firm, including its size and the nature of its business.

Adopt Disclosure Procedures

Members and candidates should encourage their firms to develop and follow disclosure policies designed to ensure that information is disseminated to the marketplace in an equitable manner. For example, analysts from small firms should receive the same information and attention from a company as analysts from large firms receive. Similarly, companies should not provide certain information to buy-side analysts but not to sell-side analysts, or vice versa. Furthermore, a company should not discriminate among analysts in the provision of information or "blackball" particular analysts who have given negative reports on the company in the past.

Issue Press Releases

Companies should consider issuing press releases prior to analyst meetings and conference calls and scripting those meetings and calls to decrease the chance that further information will be disclosed. If material nonpublic information is disclosed for the first time in an analyst meeting or call, the company should promptly issue a press release or otherwise make the information publicly available.

Firewall Elements

An information barrier commonly referred to as a "firewall" is the most widely used approach to preventing the communication of material nonpublic information within firms. It restricts the flow of confidential information to those who need to know the information to perform their jobs effectively. The minimum elements of such a system include, but are not limited to, the following:

- substantial control of relevant interdepartmental communications, preferably through a clearance area within the firm in either the compliance or legal department;
- review of employee trading through the maintenance of "watch," "restricted," and "rumor" lists;
- documentation of the procedures designed to limit the flow of information between departments and of the actions taken to enforce those procedures;
- heightened review or restriction of proprietary trading while a firm is in possession of material nonpublic information.

Appropriate Interdepartmental Communications

Although documentation requirements must, for practical reasons, take into account the differences between the activities of small firms and those of large, multiservice firms, firms of all sizes and types benefit by improving the documentation of their internal enforcement of firewall procedures. Therefore, even at small firms, procedures concerning interdepartmental communication, the review of trading activity, and the investigation of possible violations should be compiled and formalized.

Physical Separation of Departments

As a practical matter, to the extent possible, firms should consider the physical separation of departments and files to prevent the communication of sensitive information that should not be shared. For example, the investment banking and corporate finance areas of a brokerage firm should be separated from the sales and research departments, and a bank's commercial lending department should be segregated from its trust and research departments.

Prevention of Personnel Overlap

There should be no overlap of personnel between the investment banking and corporate finance areas of a brokerage firm and the sales and research departments or between a bank's commercial lending department and its trust and research departments. For a firewall to be effective in a multiservice firm, an employee can be allowed to be on only one side of the firewall at any time. Inside knowledge may not be limited to information about a specific offering or the current financial condition of a company. Analysts may be exposed to much information about the company, including new product developments or future budget projections that clearly constitute inside knowledge and thus preclude the analyst from returning to his or her research function. For example, an analyst who follows a particular company may provide limited assistance to the investment bankers under carefully controlled circumstances when the firm's investment banking department is involved in a deal with the company. That analyst must then be treated as though he or she were an investment banker; the analyst must remain on the investment banking side of the wall until any information he or she learns is publicly disclosed. In short, the analyst cannot use any information learned in the course of the project for research purposes and cannot share that information with colleagues in the research department.

A Reporting System

A primary objective of an effective firewall procedure is to establish a reporting system in which authorized people review and approve communications between departments. If an employee behind a firewall believes that he or she needs to share confidential information with someone on the other side of the wall, the employee should consult a designated compliance officer to determine whether sharing the information is necessary and how much information should be shared. If the sharing is necessary, the compliance officer should coordinate the process of "looking over the wall" so that the necessary information will be shared and the integrity of the procedure will be maintained.

A single supervisor or compliance officer should have the specific authority and responsibility of deciding whether or not information is material and whether it is sufficiently public to be used as the basis for investment decisions. Ideally, the supervisor or compliance officer responsible for communicating information to a firm's research or brokerage area would not be a member of that area.

Personal Trading Limitations

Firms should consider restrictions or prohibitions on personal trading by employees and should carefully monitor both proprietary trading and personal trading by employees. Firms should require employees to make periodic reports (to the extent that such reporting is not already required by securities laws) of their own transactions and transactions made for the benefit of family members. Securities should be placed on a restricted list when a firm has or may have material nonpublic information. The broad distribution of a restricted list often triggers the sort of trading the list was developed to avoid. Therefore, a watch list shown to only the few people responsible for compliance should be used to monitor transactions in specified securities. The use of a watch list in combination with a restricted list is an increasingly common means of ensuring effective control of personal trading.

Record Maintenance

Multiservice firms should maintain written records of the communications between various departments. Firms should place a high priority on training and should consider instituting comprehensive training programs, particularly for employees in sensitive areas.

Proprietary Trading Procedures

Procedures concerning the restriction or review of a firm's proprietary trading while it possesses material nonpublic information will necessarily depend on the types of proprietary trading in which a firm may engage. A prohibition on all types of proprietary activity when a firm comes into possession of material nonpublic information is *not* appropriate. For example, when a firm acts as a market maker, a prohibition on proprietary trading may be counterproductive to the goals of maintaining the confidentiality of information and market liquidity. This concern is particularly important in the relationships between small, regional broker/dealers and small issuers. In many situations, a firm will take a small issuer public with the understanding that the firm will continue to be a market maker in the stock. In such instances, a withdrawal by the firm from market-making acts would be a clear tip to outsiders. Firms that continue market-making activity while in the possession of material nonpublic information should, however, instruct their market makers to remain passive to the market—that is, to take only the contra side of unsolicited customer trades.

In risk-arbitrage trading, the case for a trading prohibition is more compelling than it is in the case of market making. The impetus for arbitrage trading is neither passive nor reactive, and the potential for illegal profits is greater than in market making. The most prudent course for firms is to suspend arbitrage activity when a security is placed on the watch list. Those firms that continue arbitrage activity face a high hurdle in proving the adequacy of their internal procedures for preventing trading on material nonpublic information and must demonstrate a stringent review and documentation of firm trades.

Communication to All Employees

Written compliance policies and guidelines should be circulated to all employees of a firm. Policies and guidelines should be used in conjunction with training programs aimed at enabling employees to recognize material nonpublic information. Such information is not always clearly identifiable. Employees must be given sufficient training to either make an informed decision or to realize they need to consult a supervisor or compliance officer before engaging in questionable transactions.

Application of the Standard

Example 1   (Acting on Nonpublic Information): Frank Barnes, the president and controlling shareholder of the SmartTown clothing chain, decides to accept a tender offer and sell the family business at a price almost double the market price of its shares. He describes this decision to his sister (SmartTown's treasurer), who conveys it to her daughter (who owns no stock in the family company at present), who tells her husband, Staple. Staple, however, tells his stockbroker, Alex Halsey, who immediately buys SmartTown stock for himself.

> *Comment*: The information regarding the pending sale is both material and nonpublic. Staple has violated Standard II(A) by communicating the inside information to his broker. Halsey also has violated the standard by buying the shares on the basis of material nonpublic information.

Example 2   (Acting on Nonpublic Information): Josephine Walsh is riding an elevator up to her office when she overhears the chief financial officer (CFO) for the Swan Furniture Company tell the president of Swan that he has just calculated the company's earnings for the past quarter and they have unexpectedly and significantly dropped. The CFO adds that this drop will not be released to the public until next week. Walsh immediately calls her broker and tells him to sell her Swan stock.

Comment: Walsh has sufficient information to determine that the information is both material and nonpublic. By trading on the inside information, she has violated Standard II(A).

Example 3 (Controlling Nonpublic Information): Samuel Peter, an analyst with Scotland and Pierce Incorporated, is assisting his firm with a secondary offering for Bright Ideas Lamp Company. Peter participates, via telephone conference call, in a meeting with Scotland and Pierce investment banking employees and Bright Ideas' CEO. Peter is advised that the company's earnings projections for the next year have significantly dropped. Throughout the telephone conference call, several Scotland and Pierce salespeople and portfolio managers walk in and out of Peter's office, where the telephone call is taking place. As a result, they are aware of the drop in projected earnings for Bright Ideas. Before the conference call is concluded, the salespeople trade the stock of the company on behalf of the firm's clients and other firm personnel trade the stock in a firm proprietary account and in employee personal accounts.

> *Comment*: Peter has violated Standard II(A) because he failed to prevent the transfer and misuse of material nonpublic information to others in his firm. Peter's firm should have adopted information barriers to prevent the communication of nonpublic information between departments of the firm. The salespeople and portfolio managers who traded on the information have also violated Standard II(A) by trading on inside information.

Example 4 (Acting on Nonpublic Information): Madison & Lambeau, a well-respected broker/dealer, submits a weekly column to *Securities Weekly* magazine. Once published, the column usually affects the value of the stocks discussed. Ron George, an employee of Madison & Lambeau, knows that *Securities Weekly* is published by Ziegler Publishing, for which his nephew is the night foreman. George's nephew faxes him an advance copy of the weekly column before it is printed. George regularly trades in the securities mentioned in the Madison & Lambeau column prior to its distribution, and to date, he has realized a personal profit of US$42,000 as well as significant profits for his clients.

> *Comment*: George has violated Standard II(A) by trading on material nonpublic information. The Madison & Lambeau article is considered nonpublic until the magazine is distributed through the normal channels.

Example 5 (Acting on Nonpublic Information): Greg Newman and his wife, Nancy Newman, volunteer at a local charitable organization that delivers meals to the elderly. One morning, Nancy Newman receives a telephone call from Betsy Sterling, another volunteer, who asks if the Newmans can fill in for her and her husband that afternoon. Betsy Sterling indicates that her husband is busy at work because his company has just fired its chief financial officer for misappropriation of funds. Nancy Newman agrees to perform the volunteer work for the Sterlings and advises her husband of the situation. Greg Newman knows that Betsy Sterling's husband is the CEO at O'Hara Brothers Incorporated, and he determines that this information is not public. Then, he sells his entire holding of 3,000 shares of O'Hara Brothers. Three days later, the firing is announced and O'Hara Brothers stock drops in value.

> *Comment*: Because the information is material and nonpublic, Greg Newman has violated Standard II(A) by trading on this information.

Example 6 (Selective Disclosure of Material Information): Elizabeth Levenson is based in Taipei and covers the Taiwanese market for her firm, which is based in Singapore. She is invited, together with the other 10 largest shareholders of a manufacturing company, to meet the finance director of that company. During the meeting, the finance director states that the company expects its workforce to strike next Friday, which will cripple productivity and distribution. Can Levenson use this information as a basis to change her rating on the company from "buy" to "sell"?

> *Comment*: Levenson must first determine whether the material information is public. According to Standard II(A), if the company has not made this information public (a small-group forum does not qualify as a method of public dissemination), she cannot use the information.

Example 7 (Determining Materiality): Leah Fechtman is trying to decide whether to hold or sell shares of an oil-and-gas exploration company that she owns in several of the funds she manages. Although the company has underperformed the index for some time already, the trends in the industry sector signal that companies of this type might become takeover targets. While she is considering her decision, her doctor, who casually follows the markets, mentions that she thinks that the company in question will soon be bought out by a large multinational conglomerate and that it would be a good idea to buy the stock right now. After talking to various investment professionals and checking their opinions on the company as well as checking industry trends, Fechtman decides the next day to accumulate more stock in the oil-and-gas exploration company.

> *Comment*: Although information on an expected takeover bid may be of the type that is generally material and nonpublic, in this case, the source of information is unreliable, so the information cannot be considered material. Therefore, Fechtman is not prohibited from trading the stock on the basis of this information.

Example 8 (Applying the Mosaic Theory): Jagdish Teja is a buy-side analyst covering the furniture industry. Looking for an attractive company to recommend as a buy, he analyzes several furniture makers by studying their financial reports and visiting their operations. He also talks to some designers and retailers to find out which furniture styles are trendy and popular. Although none of the companies that he analyzes are a clear buy, he discovers that one of them, Swan Furniture Company (SFC), may be in trouble financially. Swan's extravagant new designs have been introduced at substantial cost. Even though these designs initially attracted attention, in the long run, the public is buying more conservative furniture from other makers. Based on this information and on a profit-and-loss analysis, Teja believes that Swan's next quarter's earnings will drop substantially. He issues a sell recommendation for SFC. Immediately after receiving that recommendation, investment managers start reducing the SFC stock in their portfolios.

> *Comment*: Information on quarterly earnings data is material and nonpublic. Teja arrived at his conclusion about the earnings drop on the basis of public information and on pieces of nonmaterial nonpublic information (such as opinions of designers and retailers). Therefore, trading based on Teja's correct conclusion is not prohibited by Standard II(A).

Example 9 (Applying the Mosaic Theory): Roger Clement is a senior financial analyst who specializes in the European automobile sector at Rivoli Capital. Because he has been repeatedly nominated by many leading industry magazines and newsletters as "best analyst" for the automobile industry, he is widely regarded as an authority on the sector. After speaking with representatives of Turgot Chariots, a European auto manufacturer with sales primarily in South Korea, as well as interviews with salespeople, labor leaders, his firm's Korean currency analysts, and banking officials, Clement has analyzed Turgot Chariots and concluded that 1) its newly introduced model will probably not meet sales anticipation, 2) its corporate restructuring strategy may well face serious opposition from the unions, 3) the depreciation of the Korean won should lead to pressure on margins for the industry in general and Turgot's market segment in particular, and 4) banks could take a tougher-than-expected stance in the upcoming round of credit renegotiations with the company. For these reasons, he changes his conclusion about the company from "market outperform" to "market underperform."

> *Comment*: To reach a conclusion about the value of the company, Clement has pieced together a number of nonmaterial or public bits of information that affect Turgot Chariots. Therefore, under the mosaic theory, Clement has not violated Standard II(A) in drafting the report.

Example 10 (Analyst Recommendations as Material Nonpublic Information): The next day, Clement is preparing to be interviewed on a global financial news television program where he will discuss his changed recommendation on Turgot Chariots for the first time in public. While preparing for the program, he mentions to the show's producers and Mary Zito, the journalist who will be interviewing him, the information he will be discussing. Just prior to going on the air, Zito sells her holdings in Turgot Chariots.

> *Comment*: When Zito receives advance notice of Clement's change of opinion, she knows it will have a material impact on the stock price, even if she is not totally aware of Clement's underlying reasoning. She is not a client of Clement but obtains early access to the material nonpublic information prior to publication. Her trades are thus based on material nonpublic information and violate Standard II(A).

Example 11 (Acting on Nonpublic Information): Timothy Holt is a portfolio manager for the Toro Aggressive Growth Fund, a large mutual fund with an aggressive-growth mandate. Because of its mandate, the fund is heavily invested in small-cap companies with strong growth potential. Based on an unfavorable analysis of McCardell Industries by his research department, Holt decides to liquidate the fund's holdings in this company. Holt knows that this action will be widely viewed as negative by the market and that the company's stock is likely to plunge. He contacts several family members to tell them to liquidate any of their holdings before Toro's holdings are sold.

> *Comment*: When Holt tells his family to sell stock in advance of Toro's trade, he is violating Standard II(A) by causing others to trade on material nonpublic information.

Example 12 (Acting on Nonpublic Information): Holt executes his sell order of McCardell Industries with Toro's broker, Karim Ahmed. Ahmed immediately recognizes the likely effect this order will have on the stock price of McCardell and sells his own holdings in the company prior to placing the order.

> *Comment*: Ahmed has violated Standard II(A) by trading on material nonpublic information.

Example 13 (Acting on Nonpublic Information): Ashton Kellogg is a retired investment professional who manages his own portfolio. He owns shares in National Savings, a large local bank. A close friend and golfing buddy, John Mayfield, is a senior executive at National. National has seen its stock drop considerably, and the news and outlook are not good. In a conversation about the economy and the banking industry on the golf course, Mayfield drops the information that National will surprise the investment community in a few days when it announces excellent earnings for the quarter. Kellogg is pleasantly surprised by this information, and thinking that Mayfield, as a senior executive, knows the law and would not disclose inside information, he doubles his position in the bank. Subsequently, National announces that it had good operating earnings but had to set aside reserves for anticipated significant losses on its loan portfolio. The combined news causes the stock to go down 60 percent.

> *Comment*: Even though Kellogg believes that Mayfield would not break the law by disclosing insider information and money was lost on the purchase, Kellogg should not have purchased additional shares of National. It is the member's or candidate's responsibility to make sure, before executing investment actions, that comments about earnings are not material non-public information. Kellogg has violated Standard II(A).

B. Market Manipulation

Members and Candidates must not engage in practices that distort prices or artificially inflate trading volume with the intent to mislead market participants.

Guidance

Highlights:

- *Information-Based Manipulation*
- *Transaction-Based Manipulation*

Standard II(B) requires that members and candidates uphold market integrity by prohibiting market manipulation. Market manipulation includes practices that distort security prices or trading volume with the intent to deceive people or entities that rely on information in the market. Market manipulation damages the interests of all investors by disrupting the smooth functioning of financial markets and lowering investor confidence. Although market manipulation may be less likely to occur in mature financial markets than in emerging markets, cross-border investing increasingly exposes all global investors to the potential for such practices.

Market manipulation includes 1) the dissemination of false or misleading information and 2) transactions that deceive or would be likely to mislead market participants by distorting the price-setting mechanism of financial instruments. The development of new products and technologies increases the incentives, means, and opportunities for market manipulation.

Information-Based Manipulation

Information-based manipulation includes, but is not limited to, spreading false rumors to induce trading by others. For example, members and candidates must refrain from "pumping up" the price of an investment by issuing misleading positive information or overly optimistic projections of a security's worth only to later "dump" the investment (sell ownership in it) once the price of the stock, fueled by the misleading information's effect on other market participants, reaches an artificially high level.

Transaction-Based Manipulation

Transaction-based manipulation involves instances where the member or candidate knew or should have known that his or her actions could very well affect the pricing of a security. This includes, but is not limited to, the following:

- transactions that artificially affect prices or volume to give the impression of activity or price movement in a financial instrument, which represent a diversion from the expectations of a fair and efficient market; and

■ securing a controlling, dominant position in a financial instrument to exploit and manipulate the price of a related derivative and/or the underlying asset.

Standard II(B) is not intended to preclude transactions undertaken on legitimate trading strategies based on perceived market inefficiencies. The intent of the action is critical to determining whether it is a violation of this standard.

Application of the Standard

Example 1   (Independent Analysis and Company Promotion): The principal owner of Financial Information Services (FIS) entered into an agreement with two microcap companies to promote the companies' stock in exchange for stock and cash compensation. The principal owner caused FIS to disseminate e-mails, design and maintain several internet sites, and distribute an online investment newsletter—all of which recommended investment in the two companies. The systematic publication of purportedly independent analyses and recommendations containing inaccurate and highly promotional and speculative statements increased public investment in the companies and led to dramatically higher stock prices.

> *Comment*: The principal owner of FIS violated Standard II(B) by using inaccurate reporting and misleading information under the guise of independent analysis to artificially increase the stock price of the companies. Furthermore, the principal owner violated Standard V(A)—Diligence and Reasonable Basis by not having a reasonable and adequate basis for recommending the two companies and violated Standard VI(A)—Disclosure of Conflicts by not disclosing to investors the compensation agreements (which constituted a conflict of interest).

Example 2   (Personal Trading Practices and Price): An employee of a broker/dealer acquired a significant ownership interest in several publicly traded microcap stocks and held the stock in various brokerage accounts in which the broker/dealer had a controlling interest. The employee orchestrated the manipulation of the stock price by artificially increasing the bid price for the stock through transactions among the various accounts.

> *Comment*: The employee of the broker/dealer violated Standard II(B) by distorting the price of the stock through false trading and manipulative sales practices.

Example 3   (Creating Artificial Price Volatility): Matthew Murphy is an analyst at Divisadero Securities & Co., which has a significant number of hedge funds among its most important brokerage clients. Some of the hedge funds hold short positions on Wirewolf Semiconductor. Two trading days before the publication of the quarter-end report, Murphy alerts his sales force that he is about to issue a research report on Wirewolf that will include the following opinion:

■ quarterly revenues are likely to fall short of management's guidance,

■ earnings will be as much as 5 cents per share (or more than 10 percent) below consensus, and

■ Wirewolf's highly respected chief financial officer may be about to join another company.

Knowing that Wirewolf has already entered its declared quarter-end "quiet period" before reporting earnings (and thus would be reluctant to respond to rumors), Murphy times the release of his research report specifically to sensationalize the negative aspects of the message in order to create significant downward pressure on

Wirewolf's stock—to the distinct advantage of Divisadero's hedge fund clients. The report's conclusions are based on speculation, not on fact. The next day, the research report is broadcast to all of Divisadero's clients and to the usual newswire services.

Before Wirewolf's investor-relations department can assess the damage on the final trading day of the quarter and refute Murphy's report, its stock opens trading sharply lower, allowing Divisadero's clients to cover their short positions at substantial gains.

> *Comment*: Murphy violated Standard II(B) by aiming to create artificial price volatility designed to have a material impact on the price of an issuer's stock. Moreover, by lacking an adequate basis for the recommendation, Murphy also violated Standard V(A)—Diligence and Reasonable Basis.

Example 4 (Personal Trading and Volume): Rajesh Sekar manages two funds—an equity fund and a balanced fund—whose equity components are supposed to be managed in accordance with the same model. According to that model, the funds' holdings in stock of Digital Design Inc. (DD) are excessive. Reduction of the DD holdings would not be easy, however, because the stock has low liquidity in the stock market. Sekar decides to start trading larger portions of DD stock back and forth between his two funds to slowly increase the price; he believes market participants will see growing volume and increasing price and become interested in the stock. If other investors are willing to buy the DD stock because of such interest, then Sekar will be able to get rid of at least some of his overweight position without inducing price decreases. In this way, the whole transaction will be for the benefit of fund participants, even if additional brokers' commissions are incurred.

> *Comment*: Sekar's plan would be beneficial for his funds' participants but is based on artificial distortion of both trading volume and the price of the DD stock and thus constitutes a violation of Standard II(B).

Example 5 ("Pump-Priming" Strategy): Sergei Gonchar is chairman of the ACME Futures Exchange, which is launching a new bond futures contract. To convince investors, traders, arbitrageurs, hedgers, and so on, to use its contract, the exchange attempts to demonstrate that it has the best liquidity. To do so, it enters into agreements with members in which they commit to a substantial minimum trading volume on the new contract over a specific period in exchange for substantial reductions of their regular commissions.

> *Comment*: The formal liquidity of a market is determined by the obligations set on market makers, but the actual liquidity of a market is better estimated by the actual trading volume and bid–ask spreads. Attempts to mislead participants about the actual liquidity of the market constitute a violation of Standard II(B). In this example, investors have been intentionally misled to believe they chose the most liquid instrument for some specific purpose, but they could eventually see the actual liquidity of the contract significantly reduced after the term of the agreement expires. If the ACME Futures Exchange fully discloses its agreement with members to boost transactions over some initial launch period, it will not violate Standard II(B). ACME's intent is not to harm investors but, on the contrary, to give them a better service. For that purpose, it may engage in a liquidity-pumping strategy, but the strategy must be disclosed.

Example 6 (Creating Artificial Price Volatility): Emily Gordon, an analyst of household products companies, is employed by a research boutique, Picador & Co. Based on information that she has gathered during a trip through Latin America, she believes that Hygene, Inc., a major marketer of personal care products, has generated better-than-expected sales from its new product initiatives in South America.

After modestly boosting her projections for revenue and for gross profit margin in her worksheet models for Hygene, Gordon estimates that her earnings projection of US$2.00 per diluted share for the current year may be as much as 5 percent too low. She contacts the chief financial officer (CFO) of Hygene to try to gain confirmation of her findings from her trip and to get some feedback regarding her revised models. The CFO declines to comment and reiterates management's most recent guidance of US$1.95 to US$2.05 for the year.

Gordon decides to try to force a comment from the company by telling Picador & Co. clients who follow a momentum investment style that consensus earnings projections for Hygene are much too low; she explains that she is considering raising her published estimate by an ambitious US$0.15 to US$2.15 per share. She believes that when word of an unrealistically high earnings projection filters back to Hygene's investor-relations department, the company will feel compelled to update its earnings guidance. Meanwhile, Gordon hopes that she is at least correct with respect to the earnings direction and that she will help clients who act on her insights to profit from a quick gain by trading on her advice.

> *Comment*: By exaggerating her earnings projections in order to try to fuel a quick gain in Hygene's stock price, Gordon is in violation of Standard II(B). Furthermore, by virtue of previewing her intentions of revising upward her earnings projections to only a select group of clients, she is in violation of Standard III(B)—Fair Dealing. Instead of what she did, it would have been acceptable for Gordon to write a report that:
>
> ■ framed her earnings projection in a range of possible outcomes,
>
> ■ outlined clearly the assumptions used in her Hygene models that took into consideration the findings from her trip through Latin America; and
>
> ■ distributed the report to all Picador & Co. clients in an equitable manner.

Example 7   (Pump and Dump Strategy): In an effort to pump up the price of his holdings in Moosehead & Belfast Railroad Company, Steve Weinberg logs on to several investor chat rooms on the internet to start rumors that the company is about to expand its rail network in anticipation of receiving a large contract for shipping lumber.

> *Comment*: Weinberg has violated Standard II(B) by disseminating false information about Moosehead & Belfast with the intent to mislead market participants.

Example 8   (Manipulating Model Inputs): Bill Mandeville supervises a structured financing team for Superior Investment Bank. His responsibilities include packaging new structured investment products and managing Superior's relationship with relevant rating agencies. To achieve the best rating possible, Mandeville uses mostly positive scenarios as model inputs—scenarios that reflect minimal downside risk in the assets underlying the structured products. The resulting output statistics in the rating request and underwriting prospectus support the idea that the new structured products have minimal potential downside risk. Additionally, Mandeville's compensation from Superior is partially based on both the level of the rating assigned and the successful sale of new structured investment products but does not have a link to the long-term performance of the instruments.

Mandeville is extremely successful and leads Superior as the top originator of structured investment products for the next two years. In the third year, the economy experiences difficulties and the values of the assets underlying structured products significantly decline. The subsequent defaults lead to major turmoil in the capital markets, the demise of Superior Investment Bank, and Mandeville's loss of employment.

> *Comment:* Mandeville manipulates the inputs of a model to minimize associated risk to achieve higher ratings. His understanding of structured

products allows him to skillfully decide which inputs to include in support of the desired rating and price. This information manipulation for short-term gain, which is in violation of Standard II(B), ultimately causes significant damage to many parties and the capital markets as a whole. Mandeville should have realized that promoting a rating and price with inaccurate information could cause not only a loss of price confidence in the particular structured product but also a loss of investor trust in the system. Such loss of confidence affects the ability of the capital markets to operate efficiently.

STANDARD III—DUTIES TO CLIENTS

A. Loyalty, Prudence, and Care

Members and Candidates have a duty of loyalty to their clients and must act with reasonable care and exercise prudent judgment. Members and Candidates must act for the benefit of their clients and place their clients' interests before their employer's or their own interests.

Guidance

Highlights:

- *Identifying the Actual Investment Client*
- *Developing the Client's Portfolio*
- *Soft Commission Policies*
- *Proxy Voting Policies*

Standard III(A) clarifies that client interests are paramount. A member's or candidate's responsibility to a client includes a duty of loyalty and a duty to exercise reasonable care. Investment actions must be carried out for the sole benefit of the client and in a manner the member or candidate believes, given the known facts and circumstances, to be in the best interest of the client. Members and candidates must exercise the same level of prudence, judgment, and care that they would apply in the management and disposition of their own interests in similar circumstances.

Prudence requires caution and discretion. The exercise of prudence by investment professionals requires that they act with the care, skill, and diligence in the circumstances that a reasonable person acting in a like capacity and familiar with such matters would use. In the context of managing a client's portfolio, prudence requires following the investment parameters set forth by the client and balancing risk and return. Acting with care requires members and candidates to act in a prudent and judicious manner in avoiding harm to clients.

Standard III(A) sets minimum expectations for members and candidates when fulfilling their responsibilities to their clients. Regulatory and legal requirements for such duties can vary across the investment industry depending on a variety of factors, including job function of the investment professional, the existence of an adviser/client relationship, and the nature of the recommendations being offered. From the perspective of the end user of financial services, these different standards can be arcane and confusing, leaving investors unsure of what level of service to expect from investment professionals they employ. The single standard of conduct described in Standard III(A) benefits investors by establishing a benchmark for the duties of loyalty, prudence, and care and clarifies that all CFA Institute members and candidates, regardless of job title, local laws, or cultural differences, are required to comply with these fundamental responsibilities. Investors hiring members or candidates who must adhere to the duty of loyalty, prudence, and care set forth in this standard can be confident that these responsibilities are a requirement regardless of any legally imposed fiduciary duties.

Standard III(A), however, is not a substitute for a member's or candidate's legal or regulatory obligations. Members and candidates must also understand and adhere to any legally imposed fiduciary responsibility they assume with each client. Fiduciary duties are often imposed by law or regulation when an individual or institution is charged with the duty of acting for the benefit of another party, such as managing investment assets. The duty required in fiduciary relationships exceeds what is acceptable in many other business relationships because a fiduciary is in an enhanced position of trust.

As stated in Standard I(A), members and candidates must abide by the most strict requirements imposed on them by regulators or the Code and Standards, including any legally imposed fiduciary duty. Standard III(A) establishes a minimum benchmark for the duties of loyalty, prudence, and care that are required of all members and candidates regardless of whether a legal fiduciary duty applies.

Members and candidates must also be aware of whether they have "custody" or effective control of client assets. If so, a heightened level of responsibility arises. Members and candidates are considered to have custody if they have any direct or indirect access to client funds. Members and candidates must manage any pool of assets in their control in accordance with the terms of the governing documents (such as trust documents and investment management agreements), which are the primary determinant of the manager's powers and duties. Whenever their actions are contrary to provisions of those instruments or applicable law, members and candidates are at risk of violating Standard III(A).

Identifying the Actual Investment Client

The first step for members and candidates in fulfilling their duty of loyalty to clients is to determine the identity of the "client" to whom the duty of loyalty is owed. In the context of an investment manager managing the personal assets of an individual, the client is easily identified. When the manager is responsible for the portfolios of pension plans or trusts, however, the client is not the person or entity who hires the manager but, rather, the beneficiaries of the plan or trust. The duty of loyalty is owed to the ultimate beneficiaries.

In some situations, an actual client or group of beneficiaries may not exist. Members and candidates managing a fund to an index or an expected mandate owe the duty of loyalty, prudence, and care to invest in a manner consistent with the stated mandate. The decisions of a fund's manager, although benefitting all fund investors, do not have to be based on an individual investor's requirements and risk profile. Client loyalty and care for those investing in the fund are the responsibility of members and candidates who have an advisory relationship with those individuals.

Situations involving potential conflicts of interest with respect to responsibilities to clients may be extremely complex because they may involve a number of competing interests. The duty of loyalty, prudence, and care applies to a large number of persons in varying capacities, but the exact duties may differ in many respects in accord with the relationship with each client or each type of account in which the assets are managed. Members and candidates must not only put their obligations to clients first in all dealings but must also endeavor to avoid all real or potential conflicts of interest.

Members and candidates with positions whose responsibilities do not include direct investment management also have "clients" that must be considered. Just as there are various types of advisory relationships, members and candidates must look at their roles and responsibilities when making a determination of who their clients are. Sometimes the client is easily identifiable; such is the case in the relationship between a company executive and the firm's public shareholders. At other times, the client may be the investing public as a whole, in which case, the goals of independence and objectivity of research surpass the goal of loyalty to a single organization.

Developing the Client's Portfolio

The duty of loyalty, prudence, and care owed to the individual client is especially important because the professional investment manager typically possesses greater knowledge in the investment arena than the client does. This disparity places the individual client in a vulnerable position; the client must trust the manager. The manager in these situations should ensure that the client's objectives and expectations for the performance of the account are realistic and suitable to the client's circumstances and that the risks involved are appropriate. In most circumstances, recommended investment strategies should relate to the long-term objectives and circumstances of the client.

Particular care must be taken to detect whether the goals of the investment manager or the firm in placing business, selling products, and executing security transactions potentially conflict with the best interests and objectives of the client. When members and candidates cannot avoid potential conflicts between their firm and clients' interests, they must provide clear and factual disclosures of the circumstances to the clients.

Members and candidates must follow any guidelines set by their clients for the management of their assets. Some clients, such as charitable organizations and pension plans, have strict investment policies that limit investment options to certain types or classes of investment or prohibit investment in certain securities. Other organizations have aggressive policies that do not prohibit investments by type but, instead, set criteria on the basis of the portfolio's total risk and return.

Investment decisions must be judged in the context of the total portfolio rather than by individual investment within the portfolio. The member's or candidate's duty is satisfied with respect to a particular investment if the individual has thoroughly considered the investment's place in the overall portfolio, the risk of loss and opportunity for gains, tax implications, and the diversification, liquidity, cash flow, and overall return requirements of the assets or the portion of the assets for which the manager is responsible.

Soft Commission Policies

An investment manager often has discretion over the selection of brokers executing transactions. Conflicts arise when an investment manager uses client brokerage to purchase research services that benefit the investment manager, a practice commonly called "soft dollars" or "soft commissions." Whenever members or candidates use client brokerage to purchase goods or services that do not benefit the client, they should disclose to clients the methods or policies followed in addressing the potential conflict. A member or candidate who pays a higher commission than he or she would normally pay to purchase goods or services, without corresponding benefit to the client, violates the duty of loyalty to the client.

From time to time, a client will direct a manager to use the client's brokerage to purchase goods or services for the client, a practice that is commonly called "directed brokerage." Because brokerage commission is an asset of the client and is used to benefit that client, not the manager, such a practice does not violate any duty of loyalty. A member or candidate is obligated to seek "best price" and "best execution," however, and be assured by the client that the goods or services purchased from the brokerage will benefit the account beneficiaries. "Best execution" refers to a trading process that seeks to maximize the value of the client's portfolio within the client's stated investment objectives and constraints. In addition, the member or candidate should disclose to the client that the client may not be getting best execution from the directed brokerage.

Proxy Voting Policies

The duty of loyalty, prudence, and care may apply in a number of situations facing the investment professional other than issues related directly to investing assets.

Part of a member's or candidate's duty of loyalty includes voting proxies in an informed and responsible manner. Proxies have economic value to a client, and members and candidates must ensure that they properly safeguard and maximize this value. An investment manager who fails to vote, casts a vote without considering the impact of the question, or votes blindly with management on nonroutine governance issues (e.g., a change in company capitalization) may violate this standard. Voting of proxies is an integral part of the management of investments.

A cost–benefit analysis may show that voting all proxies may not benefit the client, so voting proxies may not be necessary in all instances. Members and candidates should disclose to clients their proxy voting policies.

Recommended Procedures for Compliance

Regular Account Information

Members and candidates with control of client assets should submit to each client, at least quarterly, an itemized statement showing the funds and securities in the custody or possession of the member or candidate plus all debits, credits, and transactions that occurred during the period; should disclose to the client where the assets are to be maintained, as well as where or when they are moved; and should separate the client's assets from any other party's assets, including the member's or candidate's own assets.

Client Approval

If a member or candidate is uncertain about the appropriate course of action with respect to a client, the member or candidate should ask what he or she would expect or demand if the member or candidate were the client. If in doubt, a member or candidate should disclose the questionable matter in writing to the client and obtain client approval.

Firm Policies

Members and candidates should address and encourage their firms to address the following topics when drafting the statements or manuals containing their policies and procedures regarding responsibilities to clients:

- *Follow all applicable rules and laws*: Members and candidates must follow all legal requirements and applicable provisions of the Code and Standards.

- *Establish the investment objectives of the client*: Make a reasonable inquiry into a client's investment experience, risk and return objectives, and financial constraints prior to making investment recommendations or taking investment actions.

- *Consider all the information when taking actions*: When taking investment actions, members and candidates must consider the appropriateness and suitability of the investment relative to 1) the client's needs and circumstances, 2) the investment's basic characteristics, and 3) the basic characteristics of the total portfolio.

- *Diversify*: Members and candidates should diversify investments to reduce the risk of loss, unless diversification is not consistent with plan guidelines or is contrary to the account objectives.

- *Carry out regular reviews*: Members and candidates should establish regular review schedules to ensure that the investments held in the account adhere to the terms of the governing documents.

- *Deal fairly with all clients with respect to investment actions*: Members and candidates must not favor some clients over others and should establish policies for allocating trades and disseminating investment recommendations.

- *Disclose conflicts of interest*: Members and candidates must disclose all actual and potential conflicts of interest so that clients can evaluate those conflicts.

- *Disclose compensation arrangements*: Members and candidates should make their clients aware of all forms of manager compensation.

- *Vote proxies*: In most cases, members and candidates should determine who is authorized to vote shares and vote proxies in the best interests of the clients and ultimate beneficiaries.

- *Maintain confidentiality*: Members and candidates must preserve the confidentiality of client information.

- *Seek best execution*: Unless directed by the client as ultimate beneficiary, members and candidates must seek best execution for their clients. (Best execution is defined in the preceding text.)

- *Place client interests first*: Members and candidates must serve the best interests of clients.

Application of the Standard

Example 1 (Identifying the Client—Plan Participants): First Country Bank serves as trustee for the Miller Company's pension plan. Miller is the target of a hostile takeover attempt by Newton, Inc. In attempting to ward off Newton, Miller's managers persuade Julian Wiley, an investment manager at First Country Bank, to purchase Miller common stock in the open market for the employee pension plan. Miller's officials indicate that such action would be favorably received and would probably result in other accounts being placed with the bank. Although Wiley believes the stock to be overvalued and would not ordinarily buy it, he purchases the stock to support Miller's managers, to maintain Miller's good favor toward the bank, and to realize additional new business. The heavy stock purchases cause Miller's market price to rise to such a level that Newton retracts its takeover bid.

> *Comment*: Standard III(A) requires that a member or candidate, in evaluating a takeover bid, act prudently and solely in the interests of plan participants and beneficiaries. To meet this requirement, a member or candidate must carefully evaluate the long-term prospects of the company against the short-term prospects presented by the takeover offer and by the ability to invest elsewhere. In this instance, Wiley, acting on behalf of his employer, which was the trustee for a pension plan, clearly violated Standard III(A). He used the pension plan to perpetuate existing management, perhaps to the detriment of plan participants and the company's shareholders, and to benefit himself. Wiley's responsibilities to the plan participants and beneficiaries should have taken precedence over any ties of his bank to corporate managers and over his self-interest. Wiley had a duty to examine the takeover offer on its own merits and to make an independent decision. The guiding principle is the appropriateness of the investment decision to the

pension plan, not whether the decision benefitted Wiley or the company that hired him.

Example 2   (Client Commission Practices): JNI, a successful investment counseling firm, serves as investment manager for the pension plans of several large regionally based companies. Its trading activities generate a significant amount of commission-related business. JNI uses the brokerage and research services of many firms, but most of its trading activity is handled through a large brokerage company, Thompson, Inc. The reason is that the executives of the two firms have a close friendship. Thompson's commission structure is high in comparison with charges for similar brokerage services from other firms. JNI considers Thompson's research services and execution capabilities average. In exchange for JNI directing its brokerage to Thompson, Thompson absorbs a number of JNI overhead expenses, including those for rent.

> *Comment*: JNI executives are breaching their responsibilities by using client brokerage for services that do not benefit JNI clients and by not obtaining best price and best execution for their clients. Because JNI executives are not upholding their duty of loyalty, they are violating Standard III(A).

Example 3   (Brokerage Arrangements): Charlotte Everett, a struggling independent investment adviser, serves as investment manager for the pension plans of several companies. One of her brokers, Scott Company, is close to consummating management agreements with prospective new clients whereby Everett would manage the new client accounts and trade the accounts exclusively through Scott. One of Everett's existing clients, Crayton Corporation, has directed Everett to place securities transactions for Crayton's account exclusively through Scott. But to induce Scott to exert efforts to send more new accounts to her, Everett also directs transactions to Scott from other clients without their knowledge.

> *Comment*: Everett has an obligation at all times to seek best price and best execution on all trades. Everett may direct new client trades exclusively through Scott Company as long as Everett receives best price and execution on the trades or receives a written statement from new clients that she is *not* to seek best price and execution and that they are aware of the consequence for their accounts. Everett may trade other accounts through Scott as a reward for directing clients to Everett only if the accounts receive best price and execution and the practice is disclosed to the accounts. Because Everett does not disclose the directed trading, Everett has violated Standard III(A).

Example 4   (Brokerage Arrangements): Emilie Rome is a trust officer for Paget Trust Company. Rome's supervisor is responsible for reviewing Rome's trust account transactions and her monthly reports of personal stock transactions. Rome has been using Nathan Gray, a broker, almost exclusively for trust account brokerage transactions. When Gray makes a market in stocks, he has been giving Rome a lower price for personal purchases and a higher price for sales than he gives to Rome's trust accounts and other investors.

> *Comment*: Rome is violating her duty of loyalty to the bank's trust accounts by using Gray for brokerage transactions simply because Gray trades Rome's personal account on favorable terms. Rome is placing her own interests before those of her clients.

Example 5   (Client Commission Practices): Lauren Parker, an analyst with Provo Advisors, covers South American equities for her firm. She likes to travel to the markets for which she is responsible and decides to go on a trip to Chile, Argentina, and

Brazil. The trip is sponsored by SouthAM, Inc., a research firm with a small broker/dealer affiliate that uses the clearing facilities of a larger New York brokerage house. SouthAM specializes in arranging South American trips for analysts during which they can meet with central bank officials, government ministers, local economists, and senior executives of corporations. SouthAM accepts commission dollars at a ratio of 2 to 1 against the hard dollar costs of the research fee for the trip. Parker is not sure that SouthAM's execution is competitive, but without informing her supervisor, she directs the trading desk at Provo to start giving commission business to SouthAM so she can take the trip. SouthAM has conveniently timed the briefing trip to coincide with the beginning of Carnival season, so Parker also decides to spend five days of vacation in Rio de Janeiro at the end of the trip. Parker uses commission dollars to pay for the five days of hotel expenses.

> *Comment*: Parker is violating Standard III(A) by not exercising her duty of loyalty to her clients. She should have determined whether the commissions charged by SouthAM are reasonable in relation to the benefit of the research provided by the trip. She also should have determined whether best execution and prices could be received from SouthAM. In addition, the five extra days are not part of the research effort because they do not assist in the investment decision making. Thus, the hotel expenses for the five days should not be paid for with client assets.

Example 6 (Excessive Trading): Vida Knauss manages the portfolios of a number of high-net-worth individuals. A major part of her investment management fee is based on trading commissions. Knauss engages in extensive trading for each of her clients to ensure that she attains the minimum commission level set by her firm. Although the securities purchased and sold for the clients are appropriate and fall within the acceptable asset classes for the clients, the amount of trading for each account exceeds what is necessary to accomplish the client's investment objectives.

> *Comment*: Knauss has violated Standard III(A) because she is using the assets of her clients to benefit her firm and herself.

Example 7 (Managing Family Accounts): Adam Dill recently joined New Investments Asset Managers. To assist Dill in building a book of clients, both his father and brother opened new fee-paying accounts. Dill followed all the firm's procedures in noting his relationships with these clients and in developing their investment policy statements.

After several years, the number of Dill's clients has grown, but he still manages the original accounts of his family members. An IPO is coming to market that is a suitable investment for many of his clients, including his brother. Dill does not receive the amount of stock he requested, so to avoid any appearance of a conflict of interest, he does not allocate any shares to his brother's account.

> *Comment:* Dill has violated Standard III(A) because he is not acting for the benefit of his brother's account as well as his other accounts. The brother's account is a regular fee-paying account comparable to the accounts of his other clients. By not allocating the shares proportionately across *all* accounts for which he thought the IPO was suitable, Dill is disadvantaging specific clients.
>
> Dill would have been correct in not allocating shares to his brother's account if that account was being managed outside the normal fee structure of the firm.

Example 8 (Identifying the Client): Donna Hensley has been hired by a law firm to testify as an expert witness. Although the testimony is intended to represent impartial advice, she is concerned that her work may have negative consequences for the law firm. If the law firm is Hensley's client, how does she ensure that her testimony will not violate the required duty of loyalty, prudence, and care to one's client?

> *Comment:* In this situation, the law firm represents Hensley's employer and the aspect of "who is the client" is not well defined. When acting as an expert witness, Hensley is bound by the standard of independence and objectivity in the same manner as an independent research analyst would be bound. Hensley must not let the law firm influence the testimony she is to provide in the legal proceedings.

Example 9   (Identifying the Client): Jon Miller is a mutual fund portfolio manager. The fund is focused on the global financial services sector. Wanda Spears is a private wealth manager in the same city as Miller and is a friend of Miller. At a local CFA Institute society meeting, Spears mentions to Miller that her new client is an investor in Miller's fund. She states that the two of them now share a responsibility to this client.

> *Comment:* Spears' statement is not totally correct. Because she provides the advisory services to her new client, she alone is bound by the duty of loyalty to this client. Miller's responsibility is to manage the fund according to the investment policy statement of the fund. His actions should not be influenced by the needs of any particular fund investor.

B. Fair Dealing

Members and Candidates must deal fairly and objectively with all clients when providing investment analysis, making investment recommendations, taking investment action, or engaging in other professional activities.

Guidance

Highlights:

■ *Investment Recommendations*

■ *Investment Action*

Standard III(B) requires members and candidates to treat all clients fairly when disseminating investment recommendations or making material changes to prior investment recommendations or when taking investment action with regard to general purchases, new issues, or secondary offerings. Only through the fair treatment of all parties can the investment management profession maintain the confidence of the investing public.

When an investment adviser has multiple clients, the potential exists for the adviser to favor one client over another. This favoritism may take various forms—from the quality and timing of services provided to the allocation of investment opportunities.

The term "fairly" implies that the member or candidate must take care not to discriminate against any clients when disseminating investment recommendations or taking investment action. Standard III(B) does not state "equally" because members and candidates could not possibly reach all clients at exactly the same time—whether by printed mail, telephone (including text messaging), computer (including internet updates and e-mail distribution), facsimile (fax), or wire. Each client has unique needs, investment criteria, and investment objectives, so not all investment opportunities are suitable for all clients. In addition, members and candidates may provide more personal, specialized, or in-depth service to clients who are willing to pay for premium services through higher management fees or higher levels of brokerage. Members and candidates may differentiate their services to clients, but different levels of service must not disadvantage or negatively affect clients. In addition, the different service levels should be disclosed to clients and prospective clients and should be available to everyone (i.e., different service levels should not be offered selectively).

Standard III(B) covers conduct in two broadly defined categories—investment recommendations and investment action.

Investment Recommendations

The first category of conduct involves members and candidates whose primary function is the preparation of investment recommendations to be disseminated either to the public or within a firm for the use of others in making investment decisions. This group includes members and candidates employed by investment counseling, advisory, or consulting firms as well as banks, brokerage firms, and insurance companies. The criterion is that the member's or candidate's primary responsibility is the preparation of recommendations to be acted on by others, including those in the member's or candidate's organization.

An investment recommendation is any opinion expressed by a member or candidate in regard to purchasing, selling, or holding a given security or other investment. The opinion may be disseminated to customers or clients through an initial detailed research report, through a brief update report, by addition to or deletion from a list of recommended securities, or simply by oral communication. A recommendation that is distributed to anyone outside the organization is considered a communication for general distribution under Standard III(B).

Standard III(B) addresses the manner in which investment recommendations or changes in prior recommendations are disseminated to clients. Each member or candidate is obligated to ensure that information is disseminated in such a manner that all clients have a fair opportunity to act on every recommendation. Communicating with all clients on a uniform basis presents practical problems for members and candidates because of differences in timing and methods of communication with various types of customers and clients. Members and candidates should encourage their firms to design an equitable system to prevent selective or discriminatory disclosure and should inform clients about what kind of communications they will receive.

The duty to clients imposed by Standard III(B) may be more critical when members or candidates change their recommendations than when they make initial recommendations. Material changes in a member's or candidate's prior investment recommendations because of subsequent research should be communicated to all current clients; particular care should be taken that the information reaches those clients who the member or candidate knows have acted on or been affected by the earlier advice. Clients who do not know that the member or candidate has changed a recommendation and who, therefore, place orders contrary to a current recommendation should be advised of the changed recommendation before the order is accepted.

Investment Action

The second category of conduct includes those members and candidates whose primary function is taking investment action (portfolio management) on the basis of recommendations prepared internally or received from external sources. Investment action, like investment recommendations, can affect market value. Consequently, Standard III(B) requires that members or candidates treat all clients fairly in light of their investment objectives and circumstances. For example, when making investments in new offerings or in secondary financings, members and candidates should distribute the issues to all customers for whom the investments are appropriate in a manner consistent with the policies of the firm for allocating blocks of stock. If the issue is oversubscribed, then the issue should be prorated to all subscribers. This action should be taken on a round-lot basis to avoid odd-lot distributions. In addition, if the issue is oversubscribed, members and candidates should forgo any sales to themselves or their immediate families in order to free up additional shares for clients. If the investment professional's family-member accounts are managed similarly to the accounts of other clients of the firm, however, the family-member accounts should not be excluded from buying such shares.

Members and candidates must make every effort to treat all individual and institutional clients in a fair and impartial manner. A member or candidate may have multiple relationships with an institution; for example, the member or candidate may be a corporate trustee, pension fund manager, manager of funds for individuals employed by the customer, loan originator, or creditor. A member or candidate must exercise care to treat all clients fairly.

Members and candidates should disclose to clients and prospective clients the documented allocation procedures they or their firms have in place and how the procedures would affect the client or prospect. The disclosure should be clear and complete so that the client can make an informed investment decision. Even when complete disclosure is made, however, members and candidates must put client interests ahead of their own. A member's or candidate's duty of fairness and loyalty to clients can never be overridden by client consent to patently unfair allocation procedures.

Treating clients fairly also means that members and candidates should not take advantage of their position in the industry to the detriment of clients. For instance, in the context of IPOs, members and candidates must make bona fide public distributions of "hot issue" securities (defined as securities of a public offering that are trading at a premium in the secondary market whenever such trading commences because of the great demand for the securities). Members and candidates are prohibited from withholding such securities for their own benefit and must not use such securities as a reward or incentive to gain benefit.

Recommended Procedures for Compliance

Develop Firm Policies

Although Standard III(B) refers to a member's or candidate's responsibility to deal fairly and objectively with clients, members and candidates should also encourage their firms to establish compliance procedures requiring all employees who disseminate investment recommendations or take investment actions to treat customers and clients fairly. At the very least, a member or candidate should recommend appropriate procedures to management if none are in place. And the member or candidate should make management aware of possible violations of fair-dealing practices within the firm when they come to the attention of the member or candidate.

The extent of the formality and complexity of such compliance procedures depends on the nature and size of the organization and the type of securities involved. An investment adviser who is a sole proprietor and handles only discretionary accounts might not disseminate recommendations to the public, but that adviser should have formal written procedures to ensure that all clients receive fair investment action.

Good business practice dictates that initial recommendations be made available to all customers who indicate an interest. Although a member or candidate need not communicate a recommendation to all customers, the selection process by which customers receive information should be based on suitability and known interest, not on any preferred or favored status. A common practice to assure fair dealing is to communicate recommendations simultaneously within the firm and to customers.

Members and candidates should consider the following points when establishing fair-dealing compliance procedures:

■ *Limit the number of people involved*: Members and candidates should make reasonable efforts to limit the number of people who are privy to the fact that a recommendation is going to be disseminated.

■ *Shorten the time frame between decision and dissemination*: Members and candidates should make reasonable efforts to limit the amount of time that elapses between the decision to make an investment recommendation and the time the actual recommendation is disseminated. If a detailed institutional recommendation is in preparation that might take two or three weeks to publish, a short summary report including the conclusion might be published in advance. In an organization where both a research committee and an investment policy committee must approve a recommendation, the meetings should be held on the same day if possible. The process of reviewing, printing, and mailing reports or faxing or distributing them by e-mail necessarily involves the passage of time, sometimes long periods of time. In large firms with extensive review processes, the time factor is usually not within the control of the analyst who prepares the report. Thus, many firms and their analysts communicate to customers and firm personnel the new or changed recommendations by an update or "flash" report. The communication technique might be fax, e-mail, wire, or short written report.

■ *Publish guidelines for pre-dissemination behavior*: Guidelines are needed that prohibit personnel who have prior knowledge of an investment recommendation from discussing or taking any action on the pending recommendation.

■ *Simultaneous dissemination*: Members and candidates should establish procedures for the timing of dissemination of investment recommendations so that all clients are treated fairly—that is, are informed at approximately the same time. For example, if a firm is going to announce a new recommendation, supervisory personnel should time the announcement to avoid placing any client or group of clients at unfair advantage relative to other clients. A communication to all branch offices should be sent at the time of the general announcement. (When appropriate, the firm should accompany the announcement of a new recommendation with a statement that trading restrictions for the firm's employees are now in effect.) The trading restrictions should stay in effect until the recommendation is widely distributed to all relevant clients. Once this distribution has occurred, the member or candidate may follow up separately with individual clients, but members and candidates should not give favored clients advance information when such advance notification may disadvantage other clients.

■ *Maintain a list of clients and their holdings*: Members and candidates should maintain a list of all clients and the securities or other investments each client holds in order to facilitate notification of customers or clients of a change in an investment recommendation. If a particular security or other investment is to be sold, such a list can be used to ensure that all holders are treated fairly in the liquidation of that particular investment.

■ *Develop and document trade allocation procedures*: When formulating procedures for allocating trades, members and candidates should develop a set of guiding principles that ensure:

  ● fairness to advisory clients, both in priority of execution of orders and in the allocation of the price obtained in execution of block orders or trades,

  ● timeliness and efficiency in the execution of orders; and

  ● accuracy of the member's or candidate's records as to trade orders and client account positions.

With these principles in mind, members and candidates should develop or encourage their firm to develop written allocation procedures, with particular attention to procedures for block trades and new issues. Procedures to consider are as follows:

- requiring orders and modifications or cancellations of orders to be documented and time stamped;

- processing and executing orders on a first-in, first-out basis with consideration of bundling orders for efficiency as appropriate for the asset class or the security;

- developing a policy to address such issues as calculating execution prices and "partial fills" when trades are grouped, or in a block, for efficiency;

- giving all client accounts participating in a block trade the same execution price and charging the same commission;

- when the full amount of the block order is not executed, allocating partially executed orders among the participating client accounts pro rata on the basis of order size while not going below an established minimum lot size for some securities (e.g., bonds);

- when allocating trades for new issues, obtaining advance indications of interest, allocating securities by client (rather than portfolio manager), and providing a method for calculating allocations.

Disclose Trade Allocation Procedures

Members and candidates should disclose to clients and prospective clients how they select accounts to participate in an order and how they determine the amount of securities each account will buy or sell. Trade allocation procedures must be fair and equitable, and disclosure of inequitable allocation methods does not relieve the member or candidate of this obligation.

Establish Systematic Account Review

Member and candidate supervisors should review each account on a regular basis to ensure that no client or customer is being given preferential treatment and that the investment actions taken for each account are suitable for each account's objectives. Because investments should be based on individual needs and circumstances, an investment manager may have good reasons for placing a given security or other investment in one account while selling it from another account and should fully document the reasons behind both sides of the transaction. Members and candidates should encourage firms to establish review procedures, however, to detect whether trading in one account is being used to benefit a favored client.

Disclose Levels of Service

Members and candidates should disclose to all clients whether the organization offers different levels of service to clients for the same fee or different fees. Different levels of service should not be offered to clients selectively.

Application of the Standard

Example 1   (Selective Disclosure): Bradley Ames, a well-known and respected analyst, follows the computer industry. In the course of his research, he finds that a small, relatively unknown company whose shares are traded over the counter has just signed significant contracts with some of the companies he follows. After a considerable amount of investigation, Ames decides to write a research report on the small company and recommend purchase of its shares. While the report is being reviewed by the company for factual accuracy, Ames schedules a luncheon with several of his best clients to discuss the company. At the luncheon, he mentions the purchase recommendation scheduled to be sent early the following week to all the firm's clients.

> *Comment*: Ames has violated Standard III(B) by disseminating the purchase recommendation to the clients with whom he has lunch a week before the recommendation is sent to all clients.

Example 2 (Fair Dealing between Funds): Spencer Rivers, president of XYZ Corporation, moves his company's growth-oriented pension fund to a particular bank primarily because of the excellent investment performance achieved by the bank's commingled fund for the prior five-year period. Later, Rivers compares the results of his pension fund with those of the bank's commingled fund. He is startled to learn that, even though the two accounts have the same investment objectives and similar portfolios, his company's pension fund has significantly underperformed the bank's commingled fund. Questioning this result at his next meeting with the pension fund's manager, Rivers is told that, as a matter of policy, when a new security is placed on the recommended list, Morgan Jackson, the pension fund manager, first purchases the security for the commingled account and then purchases it on a pro rata basis for all other pension fund accounts. Similarly, when a sale is recommended, the security is sold first from the commingled account and then sold on a pro rata basis from all other accounts. Rivers also learns that if the bank cannot get enough shares (especially of hot issues) to be meaningful to all the accounts, its policy is to place the new issues only in the commingled account.

Seeing that Rivers is neither satisfied nor pleased by the explanation, Jackson quickly adds that nondiscretionary pension accounts and personal trust accounts have a lower priority on purchase and sale recommendations than discretionary pension fund accounts. Furthermore, Jackson states, the company's pension fund had the opportunity to invest up to 5 percent in the commingled fund.

> *Comment*: The bank's policy does not treat all customers fairly, and Jackson has violated her duty to her clients by giving priority to the growth-oriented commingled fund over all other funds and to discretionary accounts over nondiscretionary accounts. Jackson must execute orders on a systematic basis that is fair to all clients. In addition, trade allocation procedures should be disclosed to all clients when they become clients. Of course, in this case, disclosure of the bank's policy would not change the fact that the policy is unfair.

Example 3 (Fair Dealing and IPO Distribution): Dominic Morris works for a small regional securities firm. His work consists of corporate finance activities and investing for institutional clients. Arena, Ltd., is planning to go public. The partners have secured rights to buy an arena football league franchise and are planning to use the funds from the issue to complete the purchase. Because arena football is the current rage, Morris believes he has a hot issue on his hands. He has quietly negotiated some options for himself for helping convince Arena to do the financing through his securities firm. When he seeks expressions of interest, the institutional buyers oversubscribe the issue. Morris, assuming that the institutions have the financial clout to drive the stock up, then fills all orders (including his own) and decreases the institutional blocks.

> *Comment*: Morris has violated Standard III(B) by not treating all customers fairly. He should not have taken any shares himself and should have prorated the shares offered among all clients. In addition, he should have disclosed to his firm and to his clients that he received options as part of the deal [see Standard VI(A)—Disclosure of Conflicts].

Example 4   (Fair Dealing and Transaction Allocation): Eleanor Preston, the chief investment officer of Porter Williams Investments (PWI), a medium-sized money management firm, has been trying to retain a client, Colby Company. Management at Colby, which accounts for almost half of PWI's revenues, recently told Preston that if the performance of its account did not improve, it would find a new money manager. Shortly after this threat, Preston purchases mortgage-backed securities (MBS) for several accounts, including Colby's. Preston is busy with a number of transactions that day, so she fails to allocate the trades immediately or write up the trade tickets. A few days later, when Preston is allocating trades, she notes that some of the MBS have significantly increased in price and some have dropped. Preston decides to allocate the profitable trades to Colby and spread the losing trades among several other PWI accounts.

> *Comment*: Preston has violated Standard III(B) by failing to deal fairly with her clients in taking these investment actions. Preston should have allocated the trades prior to executing the orders, or she should have had a systematic approach to allocating the trades, such as pro rata, as soon as practical after they were executed. Among other things, Preston must disclose to the client that the adviser may act as broker for, receive commissions from, and have a potential conflict of interest regarding both parties in agency cross-transactions. After the disclosure, she should obtain from the client consent authorizing such transactions in advance.

Example 5   (Selective Disclosure): Saunders Industrial Waste Management (SIWM) publicly indicates to analysts that it is comfortable with the somewhat disappointing earnings per share projection of US$1.16 for the quarter. Bernard Roberts, an analyst at Coffey Investments, is confident that SIWM management has understated the forecasted earnings so that the real announcement will cause an "upside surprise" and boost the price of SIWM stock. The "whisper number" (rumored) estimate based on extensive research and discussed among knowledgeable analysts is higher than US$1.16. Roberts repeats the US$1.16 figure in his research report to all Coffey clients but informally tells his large clients that he expects the earnings per share to be higher, making SIWM a good buy.

> *Comment*: By not sharing his opinion regarding the potential for a significant upside earnings surprise with all clients, Roberts is not treating all clients fairly and has violated Standard III(B).

Example 6   (Additional Services for Select Clients): Jenpin Weng uses e-mail to issue a new recommendation to all his clients. He then calls his three largest institutional clients to discuss the recommendation in detail.

> *Comment*: Weng has not violated Standard III(B) because he widely disseminated the recommendation and provided the information to all his clients prior to discussing it with a select few. Weng's largest clients received additional personal service because they presumably pay higher fees or because they have a large amount of assets under Weng's management. If Weng had discussed the report with a select group of clients prior to distributing it to all his clients, he would have violated Standard III(B).

Example 7   (Minimum Lot Allocations): Lynn Hampton is a well-respected private wealth manager in her community with a diversified client base. She determines that a new 10-year bond being offered by Healthy Pharmaceuticals is appropriate for five of her clients. Three clients request to purchase US$10,000 each, and the other two request US$50,000 each. The minimum lot size is established at US$5,000, and the issue is oversubscribed at the time of placement. Her firm's policy is that odd-lot allocations, especially those below the minimum, should be avoided because they may affect the liquidity of the security at the time of sale.

Hampton is informed she will receive only US$55,000 of the offering for all accounts. Hampton distributes the bond investments as follows: The three accounts that requested US$10,000 are allocated US$5,000 each, and the two accounts that requested US$50,000 are allocated US$20,000 each.

> *Comment:* Hampton has not violated Standard III(B), even though the distribution is not on a complete pro rata basis because of the required minimum lot size. With the total allocation being significantly below the amount requested, Hampton ensured that each client received at least the minimum lot size of the issue. This approach allowed the clients to efficiently sell the bond later if necessary.

C. Suitability

1. When Members and Candidates are in an advisory relationship with a client, they must:

    a. Make a reasonable inquiry into a client's or prospective client's investment experience, risk and return objectives, and financial constraints prior to making any investment recommendation or taking investment action and must reassess and update this information regularly.

    b. Determine that an investment is suitable to the client's financial situation and consistent with the client's written objectives, mandates, and constraints before making an investment recommendation or taking investment action.

    c. Judge the suitability of investments in the context of the client's total portfolio.

2. When Members and Candidates are responsible for managing a portfolio to a specific mandate, strategy, or style, they must make only investment recommendations or take only investment actions that are consistent with the stated objectives and constraints of the portfolio.

Guidance

Highlights:

- *Developing an Investment Policy*
- *Understanding the Client's Risk Profile*
- *Updating an Investment Policy*
- *The Need for Diversification*
- *Managing to an Index or Mandate*

Standard III(C) requires that members and candidates who are in an investment advisory relationship with clients consider carefully the needs, circumstances, and objectives of the clients when determining the appropriateness and suitability of a given investment or course of investment action. An appropriate suitability determination will not, however, prevent some investments or investment actions from losing value.

In judging the suitability of a potential investment, the member or candidate should review many aspects of the client's knowledge, experience related to investing, and financial situation. These aspects include, but are not limited to, the risk profile of the investment as compared with the constraints of the client, the impact of the investment on the diversity of the portfolio, and whether the client has the means or net worth to assume the associated risk. The investment professional's determination of suitability should reflect only the investment recommendations or actions that a prudent person would be willing to undertake. Not every investment opportunity will be suitable for every portfolio, regardless of the potential return being offered.

The responsibilities of members and candidates to gather information and make a suitability analysis prior to making a recommendation or taking investment action fall on those members and candidates who provide investment advice in the course of an advisory relationship with a client. Other members and candidates may be simply executing specific instructions for retail clients when buying or selling securities, such as shares in mutual funds. These members and candidates and some others, such as sell-side analysts, may not have the opportunity to judge the suitability of a particular investment for the ultimate client. In cases of unsolicited trade requests that a member or candidate knows are unsuitable for the client, the member or candidate should refrain from making the trade or should seek an affirmative statement from the client that suitability is not a consideration.

Developing an Investment Policy

When an advisory relationship exists, members and candidates must gather client information at the inception of the relationship. Such information includes the client's financial circumstances, personal data (such as age and occupation) that are relevant to investment decisions, attitudes toward risk, and objectives in investing. This information should be incorporated into a written investment policy statement (IPS) that addresses the client's risk tolerance, return requirements, and all investment constraints (including time horizon, liquidity needs, tax concerns, legal and regulatory factors, and unique circumstances). Without identifying such client factors, members and candidates cannot judge whether a particular investment or strategy is suitable for a particular client. The IPS also should identify and describe the roles and responsibilities of the parties to the advisory relationship and investment process, as well as schedules for review and evaluation of the IPS. After formulating long-term capital market expectations, members and candidates can assist in developing an appropriate strategic asset allocation and investment program for the client, whether these are presented in separate documents or incorporated in the IPS or in appendices to the IPS.

Understanding the Client's Risk Profile

One of the most important factors to be considered in matching appropriateness and suitability of an investment with a client's needs and circumstances is measuring that client's tolerance for risk. The investment professional must consider the possibilities of rapidly changing investment environments and their likely impact on a client's holdings, both individual securities and the collective portfolio. The risk of many investment strategies can and should be analyzed and quantified in advance.

The use of synthetic investment vehicles and derivative investment products has introduced particular issues of risk. Members and candidates should pay careful attention to the leverage inherent in many of these vehicles or products when considering them for use in a client's investment program. Such leverage and limited liquidity, depending on the degree to which they are hedged, bear directly on the issue of suitability for the client.

Updating an Investment Policy

Updating the IPS should be repeated at least annually and also prior to material changes to any specific investment recommendations or decisions on behalf of the client. The effort to determine the needs and circumstances of each client is not a one-time occurrence. Investment recommendations or decisions are usually part of an ongoing process that takes into account the diversity and changing nature of portfolio and client characteristics. The passage of time is bound to produce changes that are important with respect to investment objectives.

For an individual client, important changes might include the number of dependents, personal tax status, health, liquidity needs, risk tolerance, amount of wealth beyond that represented in the portfolio, and extent to which compensation and other income provide for current-income needs. With respect to an institutional client, such changes might relate to the magnitude of unfunded liabilities in a pension fund, the withdrawal privileges in an employee savings plan, or the distribution requirements of a charitable foundation. Without efforts to update information concerning client factors, one or more factors could change without the investment manager's knowledge.

Suitability review can be done effectively only if the client fully discloses his or her complete financial portfolio, including those portions not managed by the member or candidate. If clients withhold information about their financial portfolio, the suitability analysis conducted by members and candidates cannot be expected to be complete; it must be based on the information provided.

The Need for Diversification

The investment profession has long recognized that the combination of several different investments is likely to provide a more acceptable level of risk exposure than having all assets in a single investment. The unique characteristics (or risks) of an individual investment may become partially or entirely neutralized when it is combined with other individual investments within a portfolio. Some reasonable amount of diversification is thus the norm for many portfolios, especially those managed by individuals or institutions that have some degree of legal fiduciary responsibility.

An investment with high relative risk on its own may be a suitable investment in the context of the entire portfolio or when the client's stated objectives contemplate speculative or risky investments. The manager may be responsible for only a portion of the client's total portfolio, or the client may not have provided a full financial picture. Members and candidates can be responsible for assessing the suitability of an investment only on the basis of the information and criteria actually provided by the client.

Managing to an Index or Mandate

Some members and candidates do not manage money for individuals but are responsible for managing a fund to an index or an expected mandate. The responsibility of these members and candidates is to invest in a manner consistent with the stated mandate. For example, a member or candidate who serves as the fund manager for a large-cap income fund would not be following the fund mandate by investing heavily in small-cap or start-up companies whose stock is speculative in nature. Members and candidates who manage pooled assets to a specific mandate are not responsible for determining the suitability of the fund as an investment for investors who may be purchasing shares in the fund. The responsibility for determining the suitability of an investment for clients can only be conferred on members and candidates who have an advisory relationship with clients.

Recommended Procedures for Compliance

Investment Policy Statement

To fulfill the basic provisions of Standard III(C), a member or candidate should put the needs and circumstances of each client and the client's investment objectives into a written investment policy statement. In formulating an investment policy for the client, the member or candidate should take the following into consideration:

- client identification—1) type and nature of client, 2) the existence of separate beneficiaries, and 3) approximate portion of total client assets that the member or candidate is managing;

- investor objectives—1) return objectives (income, growth in principal, maintenance of purchasing power) and 2) risk tolerance (suitability, stability of values);

- investor constraints—1) liquidity needs, 2) expected cash flows (patterns of additions and/or withdrawals), 3) investable funds (assets and liabilities or other commitments), 4) time horizon, 5) tax considerations, 6) regulatory and legal circumstances, 7) investor preferences, prohibitions, circumstances, and unique needs, and 8) proxy voting responsibilities and guidance;

- performance measurement benchmarks.

Regular Updates

The investor's objectives and constraints should be maintained and reviewed periodically to reflect any changes in the client's circumstances. Members and candidates should regularly compare client constraints with capital market expectations to arrive at an appropriate asset allocation. Changes in either factor may result in a fundamental change in asset allocation. Annual review is reasonable unless business or other reasons, such as a major change in market conditions, dictate more frequent review. Members and candidates should document attempts to carry out such a review if circumstances prevent it.

Suitability Test Policies

With the increase in regulatory required suitability tests, members and candidates should encourage their firms to develop related policies and procedures. The procedures will differ according to the size of the firm and scope of the services offered to its clients.

The test procedures should require the investment professional to look beyond the potential return of the investment and include the following:

- an analysis on the impact on the portfolio's diversification;

- a comparison of the investment risks with the client's assessed risk tolerance; and

- the fit of the investment with the required investment strategy.

Application of the Standard

Example 1   (Investment Suitability—Risk Profile): Caleb Smith, an investment adviser, has two clients: Larry Robertson, 60 years old, and Gabriel Lanai, 40 years old. Both clients earn roughly the same salary, but Robertson has a much higher risk tolerance because he has a large asset base. Robertson is willing to invest part of his assets very aggressively; Lanai wants only to achieve a steady rate of return with low volatility to pay for his children's education. Smith recommends investing 20 percent of both portfolios in zero-yield, small-cap, high-technology equity issues.

> *Comment*: In Robertson's case, the investment may be appropriate because of his financial circumstances and aggressive investment position, but this investment is not suitable for Lanai. Smith is violating Standard III(C) by applying Robertson's investment strategy to Lanai because the two clients' financial circumstances and objectives differ.

Example 2   (Investment Suitability—Entire Portfolio): Jessica Walters, an investment adviser, suggests to Brian Crosby, a risk-averse client, that covered call options be used in his equity portfolio. The purpose would be to enhance Crosby's income and partially offset any untimely depreciation in the portfolio's value should the stock market or other circumstances affect his holdings unfavorably. Walters educates Crosby about all possible outcomes, including the risk of incurring an added tax liability if a stock rises in price and is called away and, conversely, the risk of his holdings losing protection on the downside if prices drop sharply.

> *Comment*: When determining suitability of an investment, the primary focus should be on the characteristics of the client's entire portfolio, not the characteristics of single securities on an issue-by-issue basis. The basic characteristics of the entire portfolio will largely determine whether investment recommendations are taking client factors into account. Therefore, the most important aspects of a particular investment are those that will affect the characteristics of the total portfolio. In this case, Walters properly considers the investment in the context of the entire portfolio and thoroughly explains the investment to the client.

Example 3   (IPS Updating): In a regular meeting with client Seth Jones, the portfolio managers at Blue Chip Investment Advisors are careful to allow some time to review his current needs and circumstances. In doing so, they learn that some significant changes have recently taken place in his life. A wealthy uncle left Jones an inheritance that increased his net worth fourfold, to US$1,000,000.

> *Comment*: The inheritance has significantly increased Jones's ability (and possibly his willingness) to assume risk and has diminished the average yield required to meet his current-income needs. Jones's financial circumstances have definitely changed, so Blue Chip managers must update Jones's investment policy statement to reflect how his investment objectives have changed. Accordingly, the Blue Chip portfolio managers should consider a somewhat higher equity ratio for his portfolio than was called for by the previous circumstances, and the managers' specific common stock recommendations might be heavily tilted toward low-yield, growth-oriented issues.

Example 4   (Following an Investment Mandate): Louis Perkowski manages a high-income mutual fund. He purchases zero-dividend stock in a financial services company because he believes the stock is undervalued and is in a potential growth industry, which makes it an attractive investment.

> *Comment*: A zero-dividend stock does not seem to fit the mandate of the fund that Perkowski is managing. Unless Perkowski's investment fits within the mandate or is within the realm of allowable investments the fund has made clear in its disclosures, Perkowski has violated Standard III(C).

Example 5   (IPS Requirements and Limitations): Max Gubler, chief investment officer of a property/casualty insurance subsidiary of a large financial conglomerate, wants to improve the diversification of the subsidiary's investment portfolio and increase its returns. The subsidiary's investment policy statement provides for highly liquid investments, such as large-cap equities and government, supranational, and corporate bonds with a minimum credit rating of AA and maturity of no more than five years. In a recent presentation, a venture capital group offered very attractive prospective returns on some of its private equity funds that provide seed capital to ventures. An exit strategy was already contemplated, but investors would have to observe a minimum three-year lock-up period and a subsequent laddered exit option for a maximum of one-third of their shares per year. Gubler does not want to miss this opportunity. After extensive analysis, with the intent to optimize the return on the equity assets within the subsidiary's current portfolio, he invests 4 percent in this seed fund, leaving the portfolio's total equity exposure still well below its upper limit.

Comment: Gubler is violating Standard III(A)—Loyalty, Prudence, and Care as well as Standard III(C). His new investment locks up part of the subsidiary's assets for at least three years and up to as many as five years and possibly beyond. The IPS requires investments in highly liquid investments and describes accepted asset classes; private equity investments with a lock-up period certainly do not qualify. Even without a lock-up period, an asset class with only an occasional, and thus implicitly illiquid, market may not be suitable for the portfolio. Although an IPS typically describes objectives and constraints in great detail, the manager must also make every effort to understand the client's business and circumstances. Doing so should enable the manager to recognize, understand, and discuss with the client other factors that may be or may become material in the investment management process.

Example 6   (Submanager and IPS Reviews): Paul Ostrowski's investment management business has grown significantly over the past couple of years, and some clients want to diversify internationally. Ostrowski decides to find a submanager to handle the expected international investments. Because this will be his first subadviser, Ostrowski uses the CFA Institute model "request for proposal" to design a questionnaire for his search. By his deadline, he receives seven completed questionnaires from a variety of domestic and international firms trying to gain his business. Ostrowski reviews all the applications in detail and decides to select the firm that charges the lowest fees because doing so will have the least impact on his firm's bottom line.

Comment: When selecting an external or subadviser, Ostrowski needs to ensure that the new manager's services are appropriate for his clients. This due diligence includes comparing the risk profile of the clients with the investment strategy of the manager. In basing the decision on the fee structure alone, Ostrowski may be violating Standard III(C).

When clients ask to diversify into international products, it is an appropriate time to review and update the clients' IPS. Ostrowski's review may determine that the risk of international investments modifies the risk profiles of the clients or does not represent an appropriate investment.

See also Standard V(A)—Diligence and Reasonable Basis for further discussion of the review process needed in selecting appropriate submanagers.

Example 7   (Investment Suitability—Risk Profile): Samantha Snead, a portfolio manager for Thomas Investment Counsel, Inc., specializes in managing public retirement funds and defined-benefit pension plan accounts, all of which have long-term investment objectives. A year ago, Snead's employer, in an attempt to motivate and retain key investment professionals, introduced a bonus compensation system that rewards portfolio managers on the basis of quarterly performance relative to their peers and to certain benchmark indices. In an attempt to improve the short-term performance of her accounts, Snead changes her investment strategy and purchases several high-beta stocks for client portfolios. These purchases are seemingly contrary to the clients' investment policy statements. Following their purchase, an officer of Griffin Corporation, one of Snead's pension fund clients, asks why Griffin Corporation's portfolio seems to be dominated by high-beta stocks of companies that often appear among the most actively traded issues. No change in objective or strategy has been recommended by Snead during the year.

Comment: Snead violated Standard III(C) by investing the clients' assets in high-beta stocks. These high-risk investments are contrary to the long-term risk profile established in the clients' IPS. Snead has changed the investment strategy of the clients in an attempt to reap short-term rewards offered by her firm's new compensation arrangement, not in response to changes in clients' investment policy statements.

See also Standard VI(A)—Disclosure of Conflicts.

Example 8   (Investment Suitability): Andre Shrub owns and operates Conduit, an investment advisory firm. Prior to opening Conduit, Shrub was an account manager with Elite Investment, a hedge fund managed by his good friend Adam Reed. To attract clients to a new Conduit fund, Shrub offers lower-than-normal management fees. He can do so because the fund consists of two top-performing funds managed by Reed. Given his personal friendship with Reed and the prior performance record of these two funds, Shrub believes this new fund is a winning combination for all parties. Clients quickly invest with Conduit to gain access to the Elite funds. No one is turned away because Conduit is seeking to expand its assets under management.

> *Comment:* Shrub has violated Standard III(C) because the risk profile of the new fund may not be suitable for every client. As an investment adviser, Shrub needs to establish an investment policy statement for each client and recommend only investments that match that client's risk and return profile in that client's IPS. Shrub is required to act as more than a simple sales agent for Elite.
>
> Although Shrub cannot disobey the direct request of a client to purchase a specific security, he should fully discuss the risks of a planned purchase and provide reasons why it might not be suitable for a client. This requirement may lead members and candidates to decline new customers if those customers' requested investment decisions are significantly out of line with their stated requirements.
>
> See also Standard V(A)—Diligence and Reasonable Basis.

D. Performance Presentation

When communicating investment performance information, Members and Candidates must make reasonable efforts to ensure that it is fair, accurate, and complete.

Guidance

Standard III(D) requires members and candidates to provide credible performance information to clients and prospective clients and to avoid misstating performance or misleading clients and prospective clients about the investment performance of members or candidates or their firms. This standard encourages full disclosure of investment performance data to clients and prospective clients.

Standard III(D) covers any practice that would lead to misrepresentation of a member's or candidate's performance record, whether the practice involves performance presentation or performance measurement. This standard prohibits misrepresentations of past performance or reasonably expected performance. A member or candidate must give a fair and complete presentation of performance information whenever communicating data with respect to the performance history of individual accounts, composites or groups of accounts, or composites of an analyst's or firm's performance results. Furthermore, members and candidates should not state or imply that clients will obtain or benefit from a rate of return that was generated in the past.

The requirements of this standard are not limited to members and candidates managing separate accounts. Whenever a member or candidate provides performance information for which the manager is claiming responsibility, such as for pooled funds, the history must be accurate. Research analysts promoting the success or accuracy of their recommendations must ensure that their claims are fair, accurate, and complete.

If the presentation is brief, the member or candidate must make available to clients and prospects, on request, the detailed information supporting that communication. Best practice dictates that brief presentations include a reference to the limited nature of the information provided.

Recommended Procedures for Compliance

Apply GIPS Standards. For members and candidates who are showing the performance history of the assets they manage, compliance with the GIPS standards is the best method to meet their obligations under Standard III(D). Members and candidates should encourage their firms to comply with the GIPS standards.

Compliance without Applying GIPS Standards

Members and candidates can also meet their obligations under Standard III(D) by:

■ considering the knowledge and sophistication of the audience to whom a performance presentation is addressed;

■ presenting the performance of the weighted composite of similar portfolios rather than using a single representative account;

■ including terminated accounts as part of performance history with a clear indication of when the accounts were terminated;

■ including disclosures that fully explain the performance results being reported (for example, stating, when appropriate, that results are simulated when model results are used, clearly indicating when the performance record is that of a prior entity, or disclosing whether the performance is gross of fees, net of fees, or after tax); and

■ maintaining the data and records used to calculate the performance being presented.

Application of the Standard

Example 1 (Performance Calculation and Length of Time): Kyle Taylor of Taylor Trust Company, noting the performance of Taylor's common trust fund for the past two years, states in a brochure sent to his potential clients, "You can expect steady 25 percent annual compound growth of the value of your investments over the year." Taylor Trust's common trust fund did increase at the rate of 25 percent per year for the past year, which mirrored the increase of the entire market. The fund has never averaged that growth for more than one year, however, and the average rate of growth of all of its trust accounts for five years is 5 percent per year.

> *Comment*: Taylor's brochure is in violation of Standard III(D). Taylor should have disclosed that the 25 percent growth occurred only in one year. Additionally, Taylor did not include client accounts other than those in the firm's common trust fund. A general claim of firm performance should take into account the performance of all categories of accounts. Finally, by stating that clients can expect a steady 25 percent annual compound growth rate, Taylor is also violating Standard I(C)—Misrepresentation, which prohibits assurances or guarantees regarding an investment.

Example 2 (Performance Calculation and Asset Weighting): Anna Judd, a senior partner of Alexander Capital Management, circulates a performance report for the capital appreciation accounts for the years 1988 through 2004. The firm claims compliance with the GIPS standards. Returns are not calculated in accordance with the requirements of the GIPS standards, however, because the composites are not asset weighted.

Comment: Judd is in violation of Standard III(D). When claiming compliance with GIPS standards, firms must meet all of the requirements, make mandatory disclosures, and meet any other requirements that apply to that firm's specific situation. Judd's violation is not from any misuse of the data but from a false claim of GIPS compliance.

Example 3   (Performance Presentation and Prior Fund/Employer): Aaron McCoy is vice president and managing partner of the equity investment group of Mastermind Financial Advisors, a new business. Mastermind recruited McCoy because he had a proven six-year track record with G&P Financial. In developing Mastermind's advertising and marketing campaign, McCoy prepares an advertisement that includes the equity investment performance he achieved at G&P Financial. The advertisement for Mastermind does not identify the equity performance as being earned while at G&P. The advertisement is distributed to existing clients and prospective clients of Mastermind.

Comment: McCoy has violated Standard III(D) by distributing an advertisement that contains material misrepresentations about the historical performance of Mastermind. Standard III(D) requires that members and candidates make every reasonable effort to ensure that performance information is a fair, accurate, and complete representation of an individual's or firm's performance. As a general matter, this standard does not prohibit showing past performance of funds managed at a prior firm as part of a performance track record as long as showing that record is accompanied by appropriate disclosures about where the performance took place and the person's specific role in achieving that performance. If McCoy chooses to use his past performance from G&P in Mastermind's advertising, he should make full disclosure of the source of the historical performance.

Example 4   (Performance Presentation and Simulated Results): Jed Davis has developed a mutual fund selection product based on historical information from the 1990–95 period. Davis tested his methodology by applying it retroactively to data from the 1996–2003 period, thus producing simulated performance results for those years. In January 2004, Davis's employer decided to offer the product and Davis began promoting it through trade journal advertisements and direct dissemination to clients. The advertisements included the performance results for the 1996–2003 period but did not indicate that the results were simulated.

Comment: Davis violated Standard III(D) by failing to clearly identify simulated performance results. Standard III(D) prohibits members and candidates from making any statements that misrepresent the performance achieved by them or their firms and requires members and candidates to make every reasonable effort to ensure that performance information presented to clients is fair, accurate, and complete. Use of simulated results should be accompanied by full disclosure as to the source of the performance data, including the fact that the results from 1995 through 2003 were the result of applying the model retroactively to that time period.

Example 5   (Performance Calculation and Selected Accounts Only): In a presentation prepared for prospective clients, William Kilmer shows the rates of return realized over a five-year period by a "composite" of his firm's discretionary accounts that have a "balanced" objective. This composite consisted of only a few of the accounts, however, that met the balanced criterion set by the firm, excluded accounts under a certain asset level without disclosing the fact of their exclusion, and included accounts that did not have the balanced mandate because those accounts would boost the investment results. In addition, to achieve better results, Kilmer manipulated the narrow range of accounts included in the composite by changing the accounts that made up the composite over time.

> *Comment*: Kilmer violated Standard III(D) by misrepresenting the facts in the promotional material sent to prospective clients, distorting his firm's performance record, and failing to include disclosures that would have clarified the presentation.

E. Preservation of Confidentiality

Members and Candidates must keep information about current, former, and prospective clients confidential unless:

1. The information concerns illegal activities on the part of the client;
2. Disclosure is required by law; or
3. The client or prospective client permits disclosure of the information.

Guidance

Highlights:

- *Status of Client*
- *Compliance with Laws*
- *Electronic Information and Security*
- *Professional Conduct Investigations by CFA Institute*

Standard III(E) requires that members and candidates preserve the confidentiality of information communicated to them by their clients, prospective clients, and former clients. This standard is applicable when 1) the member or candidate receives information because of his or her special ability to conduct a portion of the client's business or personal affairs and 2) the member or candidate receives information that arises from or is relevant to that portion of the client's business that is the subject of the special or confidential relationship. If disclosure of the information is required by law or the information concerns illegal activities by the client, however, the member or candidate may have an obligation to report the activities to the appropriate authorities.

Status of Client

This standard protects the confidentiality of client information even if the person or entity is no longer a client of the member or candidate. Therefore, members and candidates must continue to maintain the confidentiality of client records even after the client relationship has ended. If a client or former client expressly authorizes the member or candidate to disclose information, however, the member or candidate may follow the terms of the authorization and provide the information.

Compliance with Laws

As a general matter, members and candidates must comply with applicable law. If applicable law requires disclosure of client information in certain circumstances, members and candidates must comply with the law. Similarly, if applicable law requires members and candidates to maintain confidentiality, even if the information concerns illegal activities on the part of the client, members and candidates should not disclose such information. When in doubt, members and candidates should consult with their employer's compliance personnel or legal counsel before disclosing confidential information about clients.

Electronic Information and Security

Because of the ever increasing volume of electronically stored information, members and candidates need to be particularly aware of possible accidental disclosures. Many employers have strict policies about storing client information on personal laptops or portable drives. Standard III(E) does not require members or candidates to become experts in information security technology, but they should have a thorough understanding of the policies of their employers. The size and operations of the firm will lead to differing policies for ensuring the security of confidential information maintained within the firm.

Professional Conduct Investigations by CFA Institute

The requirements of Standard III(E) are not intended to prevent members and candidates from cooperating with an investigation by the CFA Institute Professional Conduct Program (PCP). When permissible under applicable law, members and candidates shall consider the PCP an extension of themselves when requested to provide information about a client in support of a PCP investigation into their own conduct. Members and candidates are encouraged to cooperate with investigations into the conduct of others. Any information turned over to the PCP is kept in the strictest confidence. Members and candidates will not be considered in violation of this standard by forwarding confidential information to the PCP.

Recommended Procedures for Compliance

The simplest, most conservative, and most effective way to comply with Standard III(E) is to avoid disclosing any information received from a client except to authorized fellow employees who are also working for the client. In some instances, however, a member or candidate may want to disclose information received from clients that is outside the scope of the confidential relationship and does not involve illegal activities. Before making such a disclosure, a member or candidate should ask the following:

- In what context was the information disclosed? If disclosed in a discussion of work being performed for the client, is the information relevant to the work?
- Is the information background material that, if disclosed, will enable the member or candidate to improve service to the client?

Members and candidates need to understand and follow their firm's electronic information storage procedures. If the firm does not have procedures in place, members and candidates should encourage the development of procedures that appropriately reflect the firm's size and business operations.

Application of the Standard

Example 1 (Possessing Confidential Information): Sarah Connor, a financial analyst employed by Johnson Investment Counselors, Inc., provides investment advice to the trustees of City Medical Center. The trustees have given her a number of internal reports concerning City Medical's needs for physical plant renovation and expansion. They have asked Connor to recommend investments that would generate capital appreciation in endowment funds to meet projected capital expenditures. Connor is approached by a local businessman, Thomas Kasey, who is considering a substantial contribution either to City Medical Center or to another local hospital. Kasey wants to find out the building plans of both institutions before making a decision, but he does not want to speak to the trustees.

> *Comment*: The trustees gave Connor the internal reports so she could advise them on how to manage their endowment funds. Because the information

in the reports is clearly both confidential and within the scope of the confidential relationship, Standard III(E) requires that Connor refuse to divulge information to Kasey.

Example 2   (Disclosing Confidential Information): Lynn Moody is an investment officer at the Lester Trust Company. She has an advisory customer who has talked to her about giving approximately US$50,000 to charity to reduce her income taxes. Moody is also treasurer of the Home for Indigent Widows (HIW), which is planning its annual giving campaign. HIW hopes to expand its list of prospects, particularly those capable of substantial gifts. Moody recommends that HIW's vice president for corporate gifts call on her customer and ask for a donation in the US$50,000 range.

> *Comment*: Even though the attempt to help the Home for Indigent Widows was well intended, Moody violated Standard III(E) by revealing confidential information about her client.

Example 3   (Disclosing Possible Illegal Activity): Government officials approach Casey Samuel, the portfolio manager for Garcia Company's pension plan, to examine pension fund records. They tell her that Garcia's corporate tax returns are being audited and the pension fund is being reviewed. Two days earlier, Samuel had learned in a regular investment review with Garcia officers that potentially excessive and improper charges were being made to the pension plan by Garcia. Samuel consults her employer's general counsel and is advised that Garcia has probably violated tax and fiduciary regulations and laws.

> *Comment*: Samuel should inform her supervisor of these activities, and her employer should take steps, with Garcia, to remedy the violations. If that approach is not successful, Samuel and her employer should seek advice of legal counsel to determine the appropriate steps to be taken. Samuel may well have a duty to disclose the evidence she has of the continuing legal violations and to resign as asset manager for Garcia.

Example 4   (Disclosing Possible Illegal Activity): David Bradford manages money for a family-owned real estate development corporation. He also manages the individual portfolios of several of the family members and officers of the corporation, including the chief financial officer (CFO). Based on the financial records of the corporation and some questionable practices of the CFO that Bradford has observed, Bradford believes that the CFO is embezzling money from the corporation and putting it into his personal investment account.

> *Comment*: Bradford should check with his firm's compliance department or appropriate legal counsel to determine whether applicable securities regulations require reporting the CFO's financial records.

STANDARD IV—DUTIES TO EMPLOYERS

A. Loyalty

In matters related to their employment, Members and Candidates must act for the benefit of their employer and not deprive their employer of the advantage of their skills and abilities, divulge confidential information, or otherwise cause harm to their employer.

Guidance

Highlights:

- *Employer Responsibilities*
- *Independent Practice*
- *Leaving an Employer*
- *Whistleblowing*
- *Nature of Employment*

Standard IV(A) requires members and candidates to protect the interests of their firm by refraining from any conduct that would injure the firm, deprive it of profit, or deprive it of the member's or candidate's skills and ability. Members and candidates must always place the interests of clients above the interests of their employer but should also consider the effects of their conduct on the sustainability and integrity of the employer firm. In matters related to their employment, members and candidates must not engage in conduct that harms the interests of their employer. Implicit in this standard is the obligation of members and candidates to comply with the policies and procedures established by their employers that govern the employer–employee relationship—to the extent that such policies and procedures do not conflict with applicable laws, rules, regulations, or the Code and Standards.

This standard is not meant to be a blanket requirement to place employer interests ahead of personal interests in all matters. The standard does not require members and candidates to subordinate important personal and family obligations to their work. Members and candidates should enter into a dialogue with their employer about balancing personal and employment obligations when personal matters may interfere with their work on a regular or significant basis.

Employer Responsibilities

The employer–employee relationship imposes duties and responsibilities on both parties. Employers must recognize the duties and responsibilities that they owe to their employees if they expect to have contented and productive employees.

Members and candidates are encouraged to provide their employers with a copy of the Code and Standards. These materials will inform the employer of the responsibilities of a CFA Institute member or candidate in the CFA Program. The Code and Standards also serve as a basis for questioning employer policies and practices that conflict with these responsibilities.

Employers are not obligated to adhere to the Code and Standards. In expecting to retain competent employees who are members and candidates, however, they should not develop conflicting policies and procedures. The employer is responsible for a positive working environment, which includes an ethical workplace. Senior management has the additional responsibility to devise compensation structures and incentive arrangements that do not encourage unethical behavior.

Independent Practice

Included in Standard IV(A) is the requirement that members and candidates abstain from independent competitive activity that could conflict with the interests of their employer. Although Standard IV(A) does not preclude members or candidates from entering into an independent business while still employed, members and candidates who plan to engage in independent practice for compensation must notify their employer and describe the types of services the members or candidates will render to prospective independent clients, the expected duration of the services, and the compensation for the services. Members and candidates should not render services until they receive consent from their employer to all of the terms of the arrangement.

"Practice" means any service that the employer currently makes available for remuneration. "Undertaking independent practice" means engaging in competitive business, as opposed to making preparations to begin such practice.

Leaving an Employer

When members and candidates are planning to leave their current employer, they must continue to act in the employer's best interest. They must not engage in any activities that would conflict with this duty until their resignation becomes effective. It is difficult to define specific guidelines for those members and candidates who are planning to compete with their employer as part of a new venture. The circumstances of each situation must be reviewed to distinguish permissible preparations from violations of duty. Activities that might constitute a violation, especially in combination, include the following:

■ misappropriation of trade secrets;

■ misuse of confidential information;

■ solicitation of employer's clients prior to cessation of employment;

■ self-dealing (appropriating for one's own property a business opportunity or information belonging to one's employer); and

■ misappropriation of clients or client lists.

A departing employee is generally free to make arrangements or preparations to go into a competitive business before terminating the relationship with his or her employer as long as such preparations do not breach the employee's duty of loyalty. Members and candidates who are contemplating seeking other employment must not contact existing clients or potential clients prior to leaving their employer for purposes of soliciting their business for the new employer. Once notice is provided to the employer of the intent to resign, the member or candidate must follow the employer's policies and procedures related to notifying clients of his or her planned departure. In addition, the member or candidate must not take records or files to a new employer without the written permission of the previous employer.

Once an employee has left the firm, the skills and experience that an employee obtained while employed are not "confidential" or "privileged" information. Similarly, simple knowledge of the names and existence of former clients is generally not confidential information unless deemed such by an agreement or by law. Standard IV(A) does not prohibit experience or knowledge gained at one employer from being used at another employer. Firm records, however, or work performed on behalf of the firm that is stored in paper copy or electronically for the member's or candidate's convenience while employed should be erased or returned to the employer unless the firm gives permission to keep those records after employment ends.

The standard does not prohibit former employees from contacting clients of their previous firm as long as the contact information does not come from the records of the former employer or violate an applicable "noncompete agreement." Members and candidates are free to use public information after departing to contact former clients without violating Standard IV(A) as long as there is no specific agreement not to do so.

Employers often require employees to sign noncompete agreements that preclude a departing employee from engaging in certain conduct. Members and candidates should take care to review the terms of any such agreement when leaving their employer to determine what, if any, conduct those agreements may prohibit.

Whistleblowing

A member's or candidate's personal interests, as well as the interests of his or her employer, are secondary to protecting the integrity of capital markets and the interests of clients. Therefore, circumstances may arise (e.g., when an employer is engaged in illegal or unethical activity) in which members and candidates must act contrary to their employer's interests in order to comply with their duties to the market and clients. In such instances, activities that would normally violate a member's or candidate's duty to his or her employer (such as contradicting employer instructions, violating certain policies and procedures, or preserving a record by copying employer records) may be justified. Such action would be permitted only if the intent is clearly aimed at protecting clients or the integrity of the market, not for personal gain.

Nature of Employment

A wide variety of business relationships exists within the investment industry. For instance, a member or candidate may be an employee or an independent contractor. Members and candidates must determine whether they are employees or independent contractors in order to determine the applicability of Standard IV(A). This issue will be decided largely by the degree of control exercised by the employing entity over the member or candidate. Factors determining control include whether the member's or candidate's hours, work location, and other parameters of the job are set; whether facilities are provided to the member or candidate; whether the member's or candidate's expenses are reimbursed; whether the member or candidate seeks work from other employers; and the number of clients or employers the member or candidate works for.

A member's or candidate's duties within an independent contractor relationship are governed by the oral or written agreement between the member and the client. Members and candidates should take care to define clearly the scope of their responsibilities and the expectations of each client within the context of each relationship. Once the member or candidate establishes a relationship with a client, the member or candidate has a duty to abide by the terms of the agreement.

Recommended Procedures for Compliance

Employers may establish codes of conduct and operating procedures for their employees to follow. Members and candidates should fully understand the policies to ensure that they are not in conflict with the Code and Standards. The following topics identify policies that members and candidates should encourage their firms to adopt if the policies are not currently in their procedures.

Competition Policy

Members and candidates must understand any restrictions placed by the employer on offering similar services outside the firm while employed by the firm. The policy may outline the procedures for requesting approval to undertake the outside service or may be a strict prohibition of such service. If a member's or candidate's employer elects to have its employees sign a noncompete agreement as part of the employment agreement, members and candidates should ensure that the details are clear and fully explained prior to signing the agreement.

Termination Policy

Members and candidates should clearly understand the termination policies of their employer. The policy should establish clear procedures regarding the resignation process, including addressing how the termination will be disclosed to clients and staff. The firm's policy may also outline the procedures for transferring responsibilities of ongoing research responsibilities and account management.

Incident-Reporting Procedures

Members and candidates should be aware of their firm's policies related to whistle-blowing and encourage their firms to adopt industry best practices in this area. Many firms are required by regulatory mandates to establish confidential and anonymous reporting procedures that allow employees to report potentially unethical and illegal activities in the firm.

Employee Classification

Members and candidates should understand their status within their employer firm. Firms are encouraged to adopt a standardized classification structure—e.g., part time, full time, outside contractor—for their employees and indicate how each of the firm's policies applies to each employee class.

Application of the Standard

Example 1   (Soliciting Former Clients): Samuel Magee manages pension accounts for Trust Assets, Inc., but has become frustrated with the working environment and has been offered a position with Fiduciary Management. Before resigning from Trust Assets, Magee asks four big accounts to leave that firm and open accounts with Fiduciary. Magee also persuades several prospective clients to sign agreements with Fiduciary Management. Magee had previously made presentations to these prospects on behalf of Trust Assets.

> *Comment*: Magee violated the employee–employer principle requiring him to act solely for his employer's benefit. Magee's duty is to Trust Assets as long as he is employed there. The solicitation of Trust Assets' current clients and prospective clients is unethical and violates Standard IV(A).

Example 2   (Former Employer's Documents and Files): James Hightower has been employed by Jason Investment Management Corporation for 15 years. He began as an analyst but assumed increasing responsibilities and is now a senior portfolio manager and a member of the firm's investment policy committee. Hightower has decided to leave Jason Investment and start his own investment management business. He has been careful not to tell any of Jason's clients that he is leaving; he does not want to be accused of breaching his duty to Jason by soliciting Jason's clients before his departure. Hightower is planning to copy and take with him the following documents and information he developed or worked on while at Jason: 1) the client list, with addresses, telephone numbers, and other pertinent client information; 2) client account statements; 3) sample marketing presentations to prospective clients containing Jason's performance record; 4) Jason's recommended list of securities; 5) computer models to determine asset allocations for accounts with various objectives; 6) computer models for stock selection; and 7) personal computer spreadsheets for Hightower's major corporate recommendations, which he developed when he was an analyst.

> *Comment*: Except with the consent of their employer, departing members and candidates may not take employer property, which includes books, records, reports, and other materials, because taking such materials may interfere with their employer's business opportunities. Taking any employer records, even those the member or candidate prepared, violates Standard IV(A). Employer records include items stored in hard copy or any other medium (e.g., home computers, portable storage devices, cell phones).

Example 3   (Addressing Rumors): Reuben Winston manages all-equity portfolios at Target Asset Management (TAM), a large, established investment counselor. Ten years previously, Philpott & Company, which manages a family of global bond mutual funds, acquired TAM in a diversification move. After the merger, the combined operations prospered in the fixed-income business but the equity management business at TAM languished. Lately, a few of the equity pension accounts that had been with TAM before the merger have terminated their relationships with TAM. One day, Winston finds on his voice mail a message from a concerned client, "Hey! I just heard that Philpott is close to announcing the sale of your firm's equity management business to Rugged Life. What is going on?" Not being aware of any such deal, Winston and his associates are stunned. Their internal inquiries are met with denials from Philpott management, but the rumors persist. Feeling left in the dark, Winston contemplates leading an employee buyout of TAM's equity management business.

> *Comment*: An employee-led buyout of TAM's equity asset management business would be consistent with Standard IV(A) because it would rest on the permission of the employer and, ultimately, the clients. In this case, however, in which employees suspect the senior managers or principals are not truthful or forthcoming, Winston should consult legal counsel to determine appropriate action.

Example 4 (Ownership of Completed Prior Work): Laura Clay, who is unemployed, wants part-time consulting work while seeking a full-time analyst position. During an interview at Bradley Associates, a large institutional asset manager, Clay is told that the firm has no immediate research openings but would be willing to pay her a flat fee to complete a study of the wireless communications industry within a given period of time. Clay would be allowed unlimited access to Bradley's research files and would be welcome to come to the offices and use whatever support facilities are available during normal working hours. Bradley's research director does not seek any exclusivity for Clay's output, and the two agree to the arrangement on a handshake. As Clay nears completion of the study, she is offered an analyst job in the research department of Winston & Company, a brokerage firm, and she is pondering submitting the draft of her wireless study for publication by Winston.

> *Comment*: Although she is under no written contractual obligation to Bradley, Clay has an obligation to let Bradley act on the output of her study before Winston & Company or Clay use the information to their advantage. That is, unless Bradley gives permission to Clay and waives its rights to her wireless report, Clay would be in violation of Standard IV(A) if she were to immediately recommend to Winston the same transactions recommended in the report to Bradley. Furthermore, Clay must not take from Bradley any research file material or other property that she may have used.

Example 5 (Ownership of Completed Prior Work): Emma Madeline, a recent college graduate and a candidate in the CFA Program, spends her summer as an unpaid intern at Murdoch and Lowell. The senior managers at Murdoch are attempting to bring the firm into compliance with the GIPS standards, and Madeline is assigned to assist in its efforts. Two months into her internship, Madeline applies for a job at McMillan & Company, which has plans to become GIPS compliant. Madeline accepts the job with McMillan. Before leaving Murdoch, she copies the firm's software that she helped develop because she believes this software will assist her in her new position.

> *Comment*: Even though Madeline does not receive monetary compensation for her services at Murdoch, she has used firm resources in creating the software and is considered an employee because she receives compensation and benefits in the form of work experience and knowledge. By copying the software, Madeline violated Standard IV(A) because she misappropriated Murdoch's property without permission.

Example 6 (Soliciting Former Clients): Dennis Elliot has hired Sam Chisolm, who previously worked for a competing firm. Chisolm left his former firm after 18 years of employment. When Chisolm begins working for Elliot, he wants to contact his former clients because he knows them well and is certain that many will follow him to his new employer. Is Chisolm in violation of Standard IV(A) if he contacts his former clients?

> *Comment*: Because client records are the property of the firm, contacting former clients for any reason through the use of client lists or other information taken from a former employer without permission would be a violation of Standard IV(A). In addition, the nature and extent of the contact with former clients may be governed by the terms of any noncompete agreement signed by the employee and the former employer that covers contact with former clients after employment.
>
> Simple knowledge of the names and existence of former clients is not confidential information, just as skills or experience that an employee obtains while employed are not "confidential" or "privileged" information. The Code and Standards do not impose a prohibition on the use of experience or knowledge gained at one employer from being used at another employer. The Code and Standards also do not prohibit former employees from contacting clients of their previous firm, in the absence of a noncompete agreement. Members and candidates are free to use public information about their former firm after departing to contact former clients without violating Standard IV(A).
>
> In the absence of a noncompete agreement, as long as Chisolm maintains his duty of loyalty to his employer before joining Elliot's firm, does not take steps to solicit clients until he has left his former firm, and does not make use of material from his former employer without its permission after he has left, he is not in violation of the Code and Standards.

Example 7   (Starting a New Firm): Geraldine Allen currently works at a registered investment company as an equity analyst. Without notice to her employer, she registers with government authorities to start an investment company that will compete with her employer, but she does not actively seek clients. Does registration of this competing company with the appropriate regulatory authorities constitute a violation of Standard IV(A)?

> *Comment*: Allen's preparation for the new business by registering with the regulatory authorities does not conflict with the work for her employer if the preparations have been done on Allen's own time outside the office and if Allen will not be soliciting clients for the business or otherwise operating the new company until she has left her current employer.

Example 8   (Competing with Current Employer): Several employees are planning to depart their current employer within a few weeks and have been careful to not engage in any activities that would conflict with their duty to their current employer. They have just learned that one of their employer's clients has undertaken a request for proposal (RFP) to review and possibly hire a new investment consultant. The RFP has been sent to the employer and all of its competitors. The group believes that the new entity to be formed would be qualified to respond to the RFP and be eligible for the business. The RFP submission period is likely to conclude before the employees' resignations are effective. Is it permissible for the group of departing employees to respond to the RFP for their anticipated new firm?

> *Comment*: A group of employees responding to an RFP that their employer is also responding to would lead to direct competition between the employees and the employer. Such conduct violates Standard IV(A) unless the group of employees receives permission from their employer as well as the entity sending out the RFP.

Example 9   (Externally Compensated Assignments): Alfonso Mota is a research analyst with Tyson Investments. He works part time as a mayor for his hometown, a position for which he receives compensation. Must Mota seek permission from Tyson to serve as mayor?

> *Comment*: If Mota's mayoral duties are so extensive and time-consuming that they might detract from his ability to fulfill his responsibilities at Tyson, he should discuss his outside activities with his employer and come to a mutual agreement regarding how to manage his personal commitments with his responsibilities to his employer.

Example 10   (Soliciting Former Clients): After leaving her employer, Shawna McQuillen establishes her own money management business. While with her former employer, she did not sign a noncompete agreement that would have prevented her from soliciting former clients. Upon her departure, she does not take any of her client lists or contact information and she clears her personal computer of any employer records, including client contact information. She obtains the phone numbers of her former clients through public records and contacts them to solicit their business.

> *Comment*: McQuillen is not in violation of Standard IV(A) because she has not used information or records from her former employer and is not prevented by an agreement with her former employer from soliciting her former clients.

Example 11   (Whistleblowing Actions): Meredith Rasmussen works on a buy-side trading desk and concentrates on in-house trades for a hedge fund subsidiary managed by a team at the investment management firm. The hedge fund has been very successful and is marketed globally by the firm. From her experience as the trader for much of the activity of the fund, Rasmussen has become quite knowledgeable about the hedge fund's strategy, tactics, and performance. When a distinct break in the market occurs, however, and many of the securities involved in the hedge fund's strategy decline markedly in value, Rasmussen observes that the reported performance of the hedge fund does not reflect this decline. In her experience, the lack of any effect is a very unlikely occurrence. She approaches the head of trading about her concern and is told that she should not ask any questions, that the fund is big and successful and is not her concern. She is fairly sure something is not right, so she contacts the compliance officer, who also tells her to stay away from the issue of this hedge fund's reporting.

> *Comment*: Rasmussen has clearly come upon an error in policies, procedures, and compliance practices in the firm's operations. Having been unsuccessful in finding a resolution with her supervisor and the compliance officer, Rasmussen should consult the firm's whistleblowing policy to determine the appropriate next step toward informing management of her concerns. The potentially unethical actions of the investment management division are appropriate grounds for further disclosure, so Rasmussen's whistleblowing would not represent a violation of Standard IV(A).
>
> See also Standard I(D)—Misconduct and Standard IV(C)—Responsibilities of Supervisors.

Example 12   (Soliciting Former Clients): Angel Crome has been a private banker for YBSafe Bank for the past eight years. She has been very successful and built a considerable client portfolio during that time but is extremely frustrated by the recent loss of reputation by her current employer and subsequent client insecurity. A locally renowned headhunter contacted Crome a few days ago and offered her an interesting job with a competing private bank. This bank offers a substantial signing bonus for advisers with their own client portfolios. Crome figures that she can solicit at least 70 percent of her clients to follow her and gladly enters into the new employment contract.

> *Comment*: Crome may contact former clients upon termination of her employment with YBSafe Bank, but she is prohibited from using client records built and kept with her in her capacity as an employee of YBSafe Bank. Client lists are proprietary information of her former employer and must not be used for her or her new employer's benefit. The use of written, electronic, or any other form of records, other than publicly available information, to contact her former clients at YBSafe Bank will be a violation of Standard IV(A).

Example 13   (Notification of Code and Standards): Krista Smith is a relatively new assistant trader for the fixed-income desk of a major investment bank. She is on a team responsible for structuring collateralized debt obligations (CDOs) made up of securities in the inventory of the trading desk. At a meeting of the team, senior executives explain the opportunity to eventually separate the CDO into various risk-rated tranches to be sold to the clients of the firm. After the senior executives leave the meeting, the head trader announces various responsibilities of each member of the team and then says, "This is a good time to unload some of the junk we have been stuck with for a while and disguise it with ratings and a thick, unreadable prospectus, so don't be shy in putting this CDO together. Just kidding." Smith is worried by this remark and asks some of her colleagues what the head trader meant. They all respond that he was just kidding but that there is some truth in the remark because the CDO is seen by management as an opportunity to improve the quality of the securities in the firm's inventory.

Concerned about the ethical environment of the workplace, Smith decides to talk to her supervisor about her concerns and provides the head trader with a copy of the Code and Standards. Smith discusses the principle of placing the client above the interest of the firm and the possibility that the development of the new CDO will not adhere to this responsibility. The head trader assures Smith that the appropriate analysis will be conducted when determining the appropriate securities for collateral. Furthermore, the ratings are assigned by an independent firm and the prospectus will include full and factual disclosures. Smith is reassured by the meeting, but she also reviews the company's procedures and requirements for reporting potential violations of company policy and securities laws.

> *Comment*: Smith's review of the company policies and procedures for reporting violations allows her to be prepared to report through the appropriate whistleblower process if she decides that the CDO development process involves unethical actions by others. Smith's actions comply with the Code and Standards principles of placing the clients' interests first and being loyal to her employer. In providing her supervisor with a copy of the Code and Standards, Smith is highlighting the high level of ethical conduct she is required to adhere to in her professional activities.

B. Additional Compensation Arrangements

Members and Candidates must not accept gifts, benefits, compensation, or consideration that competes with or might reasonably be expected to create a conflict of interest with their employer's interest unless they obtain written consent from all parties involved.

Guidance

Standard IV(B) requires members and candidates to obtain permission from their employer before accepting compensation or other benefits from third parties for the services rendered to the employer or for any services that might create a conflict with their employer's interest. Compensation and benefits include direct compensation by the client and any indirect compensation or other benefits received from third parties. "Written consent" includes any form of communication that can be documented (for example, communication via computer e-mail that can be retrieved and documented).

Members and candidates must obtain permission for additional compensation/ benefits because such arrangements may affect loyalties and objectivity and create potential conflicts of interest. Disclosure allows an employer to consider the outside arrangements when evaluating the actions and motivations of members and candidates. Moreover, the employer is entitled to have full knowledge of all compensation/ benefit arrangements so as to be able to assess the true cost of the services members or candidates are providing.

Recommended Procedures for Compliance

Members and candidates should make an immediate written report to their employer specifying any compensation they propose to receive for services in addition to the compensation or benefits received from their employer. The details of the report should be confirmed by the party offering the additional compensation, including performance incentives offered by clients. This written report should state the terms of any agreement under which a member or candidate will receive additional compensation; "terms" include the nature of the compensation, the approximate amount of compensation, and the duration of the agreement.

Application of the Standard

Example 1 (Notification of Client Bonus Compensation): Geoff Whitman, a portfolio analyst for Adams Trust Company, manages the account of Carol Cochran, a client. Whitman is paid a salary by his employer, and Cochran pays the trust company a standard fee based on the market value of assets in her portfolio. Cochran proposes to Whitman that "any year that my portfolio achieves at least a 15 percent return before taxes, you and your wife can fly to Monaco at my expense and use my condominium during the third week of January." Whitman does not inform his employer of the arrangement and vacations in Monaco the following January as Cochran's guest.

> *Comment*: Whitman violated Standard IV(B) by failing to inform his employer in writing of this supplemental, contingent compensation arrangement. The nature of the arrangement could have resulted in partiality to Cochran's account, which could have detracted from Whitman's performance with respect to other accounts he handles for Adams Trust. Whitman must obtain the consent of his employer to accept such a supplemental benefit.

Example 2 (Notification of Outside Compensation): Terry Jones sits on the board of directors of Exercise Unlimited, Inc. In return for his services on the board, Jones receives unlimited membership privileges for his family at all Exercise Unlimited facilities. Jones purchases Exercise Unlimited stock for the client accounts for which it is appropriate. Jones does not disclose this arrangement to his employer because he does not receive monetary compensation for his services to the board.

> *Comment*: Jones has violated Standard IV(B) by failing to disclose to his employer benefits received in exchange for his services on the board of directors. The nonmonetary compensation may create a conflict of interest in the same manner as being paid to serve as a director.

Example 3   (Prior Approval for Outside Compensation): Jonathan Hollis is an analyst of oil-and-gas companies for Specialty Investment Management. He is currently recommending the purchase of ABC Oil Company shares and has published a long, well-thought-out research report to substantiate his recommendation. Several weeks after publishing the report, Hollis received a call from the investor-relations office of ABC Oil saying that Thomas Andrews, CEO of the company, saw the report and really liked the analyst's grasp of the business and his company. The investor-relations officer invited Hollis to visit ABC Oil to discuss the industry further. ABC Oil offers to send a company plane to pick Hollis up and arrange for his accommodations while visiting. Hollis, after gaining the appropriate approvals, accepts the meeting with the CEO but declines the offered travel arrangements.

Several weeks later, Andrews and Hollis meet to discuss the oil business and Hollis's report. Following the meeting, Hollis joins Andrews and the investment relations officer for dinner at an upscale restaurant near ABC Oil's headquarters.

Upon returning to Specialty Investment Management, Hollis provides a full review of the meeting to the director of research, including a disclosure of the dinner attended.

> *Comment*: Hollis's actions did not violate Standard IV(B). Through gaining approval before accepting the meeting and declining the offered travel arrangements, Hollis sought to avoid any potential conflicts of interest between his company and ABC Oil. Because the location of the dinner was not available prior to arrival and Hollis notified his company of the dinner upon his return, accepting the dinner should not impair his objectivity. By disclosing the dinner, Hollis has enabled Specialty Investment Management to assess whether it has any impact on future reports and recommendations by Hollis related to ABC Oil.

C. Responsibilities of Supervisors

Members and Candidates must make reasonable efforts to detect and prevent violations of applicable laws, rules, regulations, and the Code and Standards by anyone subject to their supervision or authority.

Guidance

Highlights:

- *Detection Procedures*
- *Compliance Procedures*
- *Inadequate Procedures*
- *Enforcement of Non-Investment-Related Policies*

Standard IV(C) states that members and candidates must take steps to prevent persons acting under their supervision from violating laws, rules, regulations, firm policies, or the Code and Standards.

Any investment professional who has employees subject to her or his control or influence—whether or not the employees are CFA Institute members, CFA charterholders, or candidates in the CFA Program—exercises supervisory responsibility. Members and candidates acting as supervisors must also have in-depth knowledge of the Code and Standards so that they can apply this knowledge in discharging their supervisory responsibilities.

The conduct that constitutes reasonable supervision in a particular case depends on the number of employees supervised and the work performed by those employees.

Members and candidates who supervise large numbers of employees cannot personally evaluate the conduct of their employees on a continuing basis. Although these members and candidates may delegate supervisory duties, such delegation does not relieve them of their supervisory responsibility. Their responsibilities under Standard IV(C) include instructing those subordinates to whom supervision is delegated about methods to prevent and detect violations of laws, rules, regulations, firm policies, and the Code and Standards.

Detection Procedures

Members and candidates with supervisory responsibility must make reasonable efforts to detect violations of laws, rules, regulations, firm policies, and the Code and Standards. They exercise reasonable supervision by establishing and implementing written compliance procedures and ensuring that those procedures are followed through periodic review. If a member or candidate has adopted reasonable procedures and taken steps to institute an effective compliance program, then the member or candidate may not be in violation of Standard IV(C) if he or she does not detect violations that occur despite these efforts. The fact that violations do occur may indicate, however, that the compliance procedures are inadequate. In addition, in some cases, merely enacting such procedures may not be sufficient to fulfill the duty required by Standard IV(C). A member or candidate may be in violation of Standard IV(C) if he or she knows or should know that the procedures designed to detect and prevent violations are not being followed.

Compliance Procedures

Members and candidates with supervisory responsibility must understand what constitutes an adequate compliance system for their firms and make reasonable efforts to see that appropriate compliance procedures are established, documented, communicated to covered personnel, and followed. "Adequate" procedures are those designed to meet industry standards, regulatory requirements, the requirements of the Code and Standards, and the circumstances of the firm. Once compliance procedures are established, the supervisor must also make reasonable efforts to ensure that the procedures are monitored and enforced.

To be effective, compliance procedures must be in place prior to the occurrence of a violation of the law or the Code and Standards. Although compliance procedures cannot be designed to anticipate every potential violation, they should be designed to anticipate the activities most likely to result in misconduct. Each compliance program must be appropriate for the size and nature of the organization. The member or candidate should review model compliance procedures or other industry programs to ensure that the firm's procedures meet the minimum industry standards.

Once a supervisor learns that an employee has violated or may have violated the law or the Code and Standards, the supervisor must promptly initiate an investigation to ascertain the extent of the wrongdoing. Relying on an employee's statements about the extent of the violation or assurances that the wrongdoing will not recur is not enough. Reporting the misconduct up the chain of command and warning the employee to cease the activity are also not enough. Pending the outcome of the investigation, a supervisor should take steps to ensure that the violation will not be repeated, such as placing limits on the employee's activities or increasing the monitoring of the employee's activities.

Inadequate Procedures

A member or candidate with supervisory responsibility should bring an inadequate compliance system to the attention of the firm's senior managers and recommend corrective action. If the member or candidate clearly cannot discharge supervisory responsibilities because of the absence of a compliance system or because of an inadequate compliance system, the member or candidate should decline in writing to accept supervisory responsibility until the firm adopts reasonable procedures to allow adequate exercise of supervisory responsibility.

Enforcement of Non-Investment-Related Policies

A member or candidate with supervisory responsibility should enforce policies related to investment and non-investment-related activities equally. Firms regularly establish policies related to attendance and acceptable workplace actions, such as mandatory vacations for specific positions. The equal enforcement of all firm policies assists in creating a strong ethical work environment where all rules are demonstrated to be important.

Recommended Procedures for Compliance

Codes of Ethics or Compliance Procedures

Members and candidates are encouraged to recommend that their employers adopt a code of ethics. Adoption of a code of ethics is critical to establishing a strong ethical foundation for investment advisory firms and their employees. Codes of ethics formally emphasize and reinforce the client loyalty responsibilities of investment firm personnel, protect investing clients by deterring misconduct, and protect the firm's reputation for integrity.

There is a distinction, however, between codes of ethics and the specific policies and procedures needed to ensure compliance with the codes and with securities laws and regulations. Although both are important, codes of ethics should consist of fundamental, principle-based ethical and fiduciary concepts that are applicable to all of the firm's employees. In this way, firms can best convey to employees and clients the ethical ideals that investment advisers strive to achieve. These concepts need to be implemented, however, by detailed, firmwide compliance policies and procedures. Compliance procedures assist the firm's personnel in fulfilling the responsibilities enumerated in the code of ethics and make probable that the ideals expressed in the code of ethics will be adhered to in the day-to-day operation of the firm.

Stand-alone codes of ethics should be written in plain language and should address general fiduciary concepts. They should be unencumbered by numerous detailed procedures. Codes presented in this way are the most effective in stressing to employees that they are in positions of trust and must act with integrity at all times. Mingling compliance procedures in the firm's code of ethics goes against the goal of reinforcing the ethical obligations of employees.

Separating the code of ethics from compliance procedures will also reduce, if not eliminate, the legal terminology and "boilerplate" language that can make the underlying ethical principles incomprehensible to the average person. Above all, to ensure that a culture of ethics and integrity is created rather than merely a focus on following the rules, the principles in the code of ethics must be stated in a way that is accessible and understandable to everyone in the firm.

Members and candidates should encourage their employers to provide their codes of ethics to clients. In this case also, a simple, straightforward code of ethics will be best understood by clients. Unencumbered by the compliance procedures, the code of ethics will be effective in conveying that the firm is committed to conducting business in an ethical manner and in the best interests of the clients.

Adequate Compliance Procedures

A supervisor complies with Standard IV(C) by identifying situations in which legal violations or violations of the Code and Standards are likely to occur and by establishing and enforcing compliance procedures to prevent such violations. Adequate compliance procedures should:

- be contained in a clearly written and accessible manual that is tailored to the firm's operations;
- be drafted so that the procedures are easy to understand;
- designate a compliance officer whose authority and responsibility are clearly defined and who has the necessary resources and authority to implement the firm's compliance procedures;
- describe the hierarchy of supervision and assign duties among supervisors;
- implement a system of checks and balances;
- outline the scope of the procedures;
- outline procedures to document the monitoring and testing of compliance procedures;
- outline permissible conduct; and
- delineate procedures for reporting violations and sanctions.

Once a compliance program is in place, a supervisor should:

- disseminate the contents of the program to appropriate personnel;
- periodically update procedures to ensure that the measures are adequate under the law;
- continually educate personnel regarding the compliance procedures;
- issue periodic reminders of the procedures to appropriate personnel;
- incorporate a professional conduct evaluation as part of an employee's performance review;
- review the actions of employees to ensure compliance and identify violators; and
- take the necessary steps to enforce the procedures once a violation has occurred.

Once a violation is discovered, a supervisor should:

- respond promptly;
- conduct a thorough investigation of the activities to determine the scope of the wrongdoing; and
- increase supervision or place appropriate limitations on the wrongdoer pending the outcome of the investigation.

Application of the Standard

Example 1   (Supervising Research Activities): Jane Mattock, senior vice president and head of the research department of H&V, Inc., a regional brokerage firm, has decided to change her recommendation for Timber Products from buy to sell. In line with H&V's procedures, she orally advises certain other H&V executives of her proposed actions before the report is prepared for publication. As a result of Mattock's conversation with Dieter Frampton, one of the executives of H&V accountable to Mattock, Frampton immediately sells Timber's stock from his own account and from certain discretionary client accounts. In addition, other personnel inform certain institutional customers of the changed recommendation before it is printed and disseminated to all H&V customers who have received previous Timber reports.

> *Comment*: Mattock has violated Standard IV(C) by failing to reasonably and adequately supervise the actions of those accountable to her. She did

not prevent or establish reasonable procedures designed to prevent dissemination of or trading on the information by those who knew of her changed recommendation. She must ensure that her firm has procedures for reviewing or recording any trading in the stock of a corporation that has been the subject of an unpublished change in recommendation. Adequate procedures would have informed the subordinates of their duties and detected sales by Frampton and selected customers.

Example 2   (Supervising Research Activities): Deion Miller is the research director for Jamestown Investment Programs. The portfolio managers have become critical of Miller and his staff because the Jamestown portfolios do not include any stock that has been the subject of a merger or tender offer. Georgia Ginn, a member of Miller's staff, tells Miller that she has been studying a local company, Excelsior, Inc., and recommends its purchase. Ginn adds that the company has been widely rumored to be the subject of a merger study by a well-known conglomerate and discussions between them are under way. At Miller's request, Ginn prepares a memo recommending the stock. Miller passes along Ginn's memo to the portfolio managers prior to leaving for vacation, and he notes that he has not reviewed the memo. As a result of the memo, the portfolio managers buy Excelsior stock immediately. The day Miller returns to the office, he learns that Ginn's only sources for the report were her brother, who is an acquisitions analyst with Acme Industries, the "well-known conglomerate," and that the merger discussions were planned but not held.

> *Comment*: Miller violated Standard IV(C) by not exercising reasonable supervision when he disseminated the memo without checking to ensure that Ginn had a reasonable and adequate basis for her recommendations and that Ginn was not relying on material nonpublic information.

Example 3   (Supervising Trading Activities): David Edwards, a trainee trader at Wheeler & Company, a major national brokerage firm, assists a customer in paying for the securities of Highland, Inc., by using anticipated profits from the immediate sale of the same securities. Despite the fact that Highland is not on Wheeler's recommended list, a large volume of its stock is traded through Wheeler in this manner. Roberta Ann Mason is a Wheeler vice president responsible for supervising compliance with the securities laws in the trading department. Part of her compensation from Wheeler is based on commission revenues from the trading department. Although she notices the increased trading activity, she does nothing to investigate or halt it.

> *Comment*: Mason's failure to adequately review and investigate purchase orders in Highland stock executed by Edwards and her failure to supervise the trainee's activities violate Standard IV(C). Supervisors should be especially sensitive to actual or potential conflicts between their own self-interests and their supervisory responsibilities.

Example 4   (Supervising Trading Activities and Record Keeping): Samantha Tabbing is senior vice president and portfolio manager for Crozet, Inc., a registered investment advisory and registered broker/dealer firm. She reports to Charles Henry, the president of Crozet. Crozet serves as the investment adviser and principal underwriter for ABC and XYZ public mutual funds. The two funds' prospectuses allow Crozet to trade financial futures for the funds for the limited purpose of hedging against market risks. Henry, extremely impressed by Tabbing's performance in the past two years, directs Tabbing to act as portfolio manager for the funds. For the benefit of its employees, Crozet has also organized the Crozet Employee Profit-Sharing Plan (CEPSP), a defined-contribution retirement plan. Henry assigns Tabbing to manage 20 percent of the assets of CEPSP. Tabbing's investment objective for her portion of CEPSP's assets is aggressive growth. Unbeknownst to Henry, Tabbing frequently places S&P 500 Index purchase and sale orders for the funds and the CEPSP without providing the futures commission merchants (FCMs) who take the orders with any prior or simultaneous designation of the account for which the trade has been placed. Frequently, neither Tabbing nor anyone else at Crozet completes an internal trade ticket to record the time an order was placed or the specific account for which the order was intended. FCMs often designate a specific account only after the trade, when Tabbing provides such designation. Crozet has no written operating procedures or compliance manual concerning its futures trading, and its compliance department does not review such trading. After observing the market's movement, Tabbing assigns to CEPSP the S&P 500 positions with more-favorable execution prices and assigns positions with less-favorable execution prices to the funds.

> *Comment*: Henry violated Standard IV(C) by failing to adequately super-vise Tabbing with respect to her S&P 500 trading. Henry further violated Standard IV(C) by failing to establish record-keeping and reporting proce-dures to prevent or detect Tabbing's violations.

Example 5 (Accepting Responsibility): Meredith Rasmussen works on a buy-side trading desk and concentrates on in-house trades for a hedge fund subsidiary managed by a team at the investment management firm. The hedge fund has been very successful and is marketed globally by the firm. From her experience as the trader for much of the activity of the fund, Rasmussen has become quite knowledgeable about the hedge fund's strategy, tactics, and performance. When a distinct break in the market occurs and many of the securities involved in the hedge fund's strategy decline markedly in value, however, Rasmussen observes that the reported performance of the hedge fund does not at all reflect this decline. From her experience, this lack of an effect is a very unlikely occurrence. She approaches the head of trading about her concern and is told that she should not ask any questions, that the fund is too big and successful and is not her concern. She is fairly sure something is not right, so she contacts the compliance officer and is again told to stay away from the hedge fund reporting issue.

> *Comment:* Rasmussen has clearly come upon an error in policies, proce-dures, and compliance practices within the firm's operations. According to Standard IV(C), the supervisor and the compliance officer have the respon-sibility to review the concerns brought forth by Rasmussen. Supervisors have the responsibility of establishing and encouraging an ethical culture in the firm. The dismissal of Rasmussen's question violates Standard IV(C) and undermines the firm's ethical operations.
>
> See also Standard I(D)—Misconduct and, for guidance on whistleblow-ing, Standard IV(A)—Loyalty.

Example 6 (Inadequate Procedures): Brendan Witt, a former junior sell-side technol-ogy analyst, decided to return to school to earn an MBA. To keep his research skills and industry knowledge sharp, Witt accepted a position with On-line and Informed, an independent internet-based research company. The position requires the publication of a recommendation and report on a different company every month. Initially, Witt is a regular contributor of new research and a participant in the associated discussion boards that generally have positive comments on the technology sector. Over time, his ability to manage his educational requirements and his work requirements begin to conflict with one another. Knowing a recommendation is due the next day for On-line, Witt creates a report based on a few news articles and what the conventional wisdom of the markets has deemed the "hot" security of the day.

> *Comment*: Allowing the report submitted by Witt to be posted highlights a lack of compliance procedures by the research firm. Witt's supervisor needs to work with the management of On-line to develop an appropriate

review process to ensure that all contracted analysts comply with the requirements.

See also Standard V(A)—Diligence and Reasonable Basis, as it relates to Witt's responsibility for substantiating a recommendation.

Example 7   (Inadequate Supervision): Michael Papis is the chief investment officer of his state's retirement fund. The fund has always used outside advisers for the real estate allocation, and this information is clearly presented in all fund communications. Thomas Nagle, a recognized sell-side research analyst and Papis's business school classmate, recently left the investment bank he worked for to start his own asset management firm, Accessible Real Estate. Nagle is trying to build his assets under management and contacts Papis about gaining some of the retirement fund's allocation. In the previous few years, the performance of the retirement fund's real estate investments was in line with the fund's benchmark but was not extraordinary. Papis decides to help out his old friend and also to seek better returns by moving the real estate allocation to Accessible. The only notice of the change in adviser appears in the next annual report in the listing of associated advisers.

> *Comment*: Papis's actions highlight the need for supervision and review at all levels in an organization. His responsibilities may include the selection of external advisers, but the decision to change advisers appears arbitrary. Members and candidates should ensure that their firm has appropriate policies and procedures in place to detect inappropriate actions such as the action taken by Papis.
>
> See also Standard V(A)—Diligence and Reasonable Basis, Standard V(B)—Communication with Clients and Prospective Clients, and Standard VI(A)—Disclosure of Conflicts.

STANDARD V—INVESTMENT ANALYSIS, RECOMMENDATIONS, AND ACTIONS

A. Diligence and Reasonable Basis

Members and Candidates must:

1. Exercise diligence, independence, and thoroughness in analyzing investments, making investment recommendations, and taking investment actions.

2. Have a reasonable and adequate basis, supported by appropriate research and investigation, for any investment analysis, recommendation, or action.

Guidance

Highlights:

■ *Defining Diligence and Reasonable Basis*

■ *Using Secondary or Third-Party Research*

■ *Quantitatively Oriented Research*

■ *Selecting External Advisers and Subadvisers*

■ *Group Research and Decision Making*

The application of Standard V(A) depends on the investment philosophy the member, candidate, or firm is following, the role of the member or candidate in the investment decision-making process, and the support and resources provided by the member's or candidate's employer. These factors will dictate the nature of the diligence and thoroughness of the research and the level of investigation required by Standard V(A).

The requirements for issuing conclusions based on research will vary in relation to the member's or candidate's role in the investment decision-making process, but the member or candidate must make reasonable efforts to cover all pertinent issues when arriving at a recommendation. Members and candidates enhance transparency by providing or offering to provide supporting information to clients when recommending a purchase or sale or when changing a recommendation.

Defining Diligence and Reasonable Basis

Every investment decision is based on a set of facts known and understood at the time. Clients turn to members and candidates for advice and expect these advisers to have more information and knowledge than they do. This information and knowledge is the basis from which members and candidates apply their professional judgment in taking investment actions and making recommendations.

At a basic level, clients want assurance that members and candidates are putting forth the necessary effort to support the recommendations they are making. Communicating the level and thoroughness of the information reviewed before the member or candidate makes a judgment allows clients to understand the reasonableness of the recommended investment actions.

As with determining the suitability of an investment for the client, the necessary level of research and analysis will differ with the product, security, or service being offered. In providing an investment service, members and candidates typically use a variety of resources, including company reports, third-party research, and results from quantitative models. A reasonable basis is formed through a balance of these resources appropriate for the security or decision being analyzed.

The following list provides some, but definitely not all, examples of attributes to consider while forming the basis for a recommendation:

- company's operating and financial history;
- current stage of the industry's business cycle;
- mutual fund's fee structure and management history;
- output and potential limitations of quantitative models;
- quality of the assets included in a securitization; and
- appropriateness of selected peer-group comparisons.

Even though an investment recommendation may be well-informed, downside risk remains for any investment. Members and candidates can base their decision only on the information available at the time the decision is made. The steps taken in developing a diligent and reasonable recommendation should minimize unexpected downside events.

Using Secondary or Third-Party Research

If members and candidates rely on secondary or third-party research, they must make reasonable and diligent efforts to determine whether such research is sound. Secondary research is defined as research conducted by someone else in the member's or candidate's firm. Third-party research is research conducted by entities outside the member's or candidate's firm, such as a brokerage firm, bank, or research firm. If a member or candidate has reason to suspect that either secondary or third-party research or information comes from a source that lacks a sound basis, the member or candidate must not rely on that information. Criteria that a member or candidate can use in forming an opinion on whether research is sound include the following:

- assumptions used;
- rigor of the analysis performed;
- date/timeliness of the research; and
- evaluation of the objectivity and independence of the recommendations.

A member or candidate may rely on others in his or her firm to determine whether secondary or third-party research is sound and use the information in good faith unless the member or candidate has reason to question its validity or the processes and procedures used by those responsible for the research. For example, a portfolio manager may not have a choice of a data source because the firm's senior managers conducted due diligence to determine which vendor would provide services; the member or candidate can use the information in good faith assuming the due diligence process was deemed adequate.

A member or candidate should verify that the firm has a policy about the timely and consistent review of approved research providers to ensure that the quality of the research continues to meet the necessary standards. If such a policy is not in place at the firm, the member or candidate should encourage the development and adoption of a formal review practice.

Quantitatively Oriented Research

Standard V(A) applies to the rapidly expanding use of quantitatively oriented research models, such as computer-generated screening and ranking of equity securities and the creation or valuation of derivative instruments. Models are being used for more than the back testing of investment strategies, and the continued development of models is an important part of capital market developments.

The importance and limitations of financial models became clear as the credit crisis unfolded in 2007 and 2008. In many cases the financial models used to value collateralized debt securities and related derivative products were poorly understood. Members and candidates need to have an understanding of the parameters used in the model or quantitative research. Although they are not required to become experts in the technical aspects of the models, they must be able to explain to their clients the importance of the quantitative research and how the results were used in the decision-making process.

Members and candidates need to consider the time horizon of the data used as inputs in financial models. The information from many commercially available databases may not effectively incorporate both positive and negative market cycles. In the development of a recommendation, the member or candidate may need to test the models by using volatility and performance expectations that represent scenarios outside the observable databases. In reviewing the computer models or the resulting output, members and candidates need to pay particular attention to the assumptions used in the analysis and the rigor of the analysis to ensure that the model incorporates negative market events.

Selecting External Advisers and Subadvisers

Financial instruments and asset allocation techniques continue to develop and evolve. This progression has led to the use of specialized managers to invest in specific asset classes or diversification strategies that complement a firm's in-house expertise. Standard V(A) applies to the level of review necessary in selecting an external adviser or subadviser.

Members and candidates need to ensure that their firms have standardized criteria for reviewing external advisers. Such criteria would include, but would not be limited to, the following:

- reviewing the adviser's established code of ethics;
- understanding the adviser's compliance and internal control procedures;
- assessing the quality of the published return information; and
- reviewing the adviser's adherence to its stated strategy.

CFA Institute published codes, standards, and guides to best practice provide members and candidates with examples of acceptable practices for external advisers and advice in selecting a new adviser. The following guides are available at the CFA Institute website (www.cfainstitute.org): Asset Manager Code of Professional Conduct, Global Investment Performance Standards, and Model Request for Proposal (for equity, credit, or real estate managers).

Group Research and Decision Making

Commonly, members and candidates are part of a group or team that is collectively responsible for producing investment analysis or research. The conclusions or recommendations of the group report represent the consensus of the group and are not necessarily the views of the member or candidate, even though the name of the member or candidate is included on the report. In some instances, the member or candidate will not agree with the view of the group. If, however, the member or candidate believes that the consensus opinion has a reasonable and adequate basis and is independent and objective, the member or candidate need not decline to be identified with the report. If the member or candidate is confident in the process, the member or candidate does not need to dissociate from the report even if it does not reflect his or her opinion.

Recommended Procedures for Compliance

Members and candidates should encourage their firms to consider the following policies and procedures to support the principles of Standard V(A):

- Establish a policy requiring that research reports, credit ratings, and investment recommendations have a basis that can be substantiated as reasonable and adequate. An individual employee (a supervisory analyst) or a group of employees (a review committee) should be appointed to review and approve such items prior to external circulation to determine whether the criteria established in the policy have been met.

- Develop detailed, written guidance for analysts (research, investment, or credit), supervisory analysts, and review committees that establishes the due diligence procedures for judging whether a particular recommendation has a reasonable and adequate basis.

- Develop measurable criteria for assessing the quality of research, the reasonableness and adequacy of the basis for any recommendation or rating, and the accuracy of recommendations over time. In some cases, firms may consider implementing compensation arrangements that depend on these measurable criteria and that are applied consistently to all related analysts.

- Develop detailed, written guidance that establishes minimum levels of scenario testing of all computer-based models used in developing, rating, and evaluating financial instruments. The policy should contain criteria related to the breadth of the scenarios tested, the accuracy of the output over time, and the analysis of cash flow sensitivity to inputs.

- Develop measurable criteria for assessing outside providers, including the quality of information being provided, the reasonableness and adequacy of the provider's collection practices, and the accuracy of the information over time. The established policy should outline how often the provider's products are reviewed.

- Adopt a standardized set of criteria for evaluating the adequacy of external advisers. The policy should include how often and on what basis the allocation of funds to the adviser will be reviewed.

Application of the Standard

Example 1   (Sufficient Due Diligence): Helen Hawke manages the corporate finance department of Sarkozi Securities, Ltd. The firm is anticipating that the government will soon close a tax loophole that currently allows oil-and-gas exploration companies to pass on drilling expenses to holders of a certain class of shares. Because market demand for this tax-advantaged class of stock is currently high, Sarkozi convinces several companies to undertake new equity financings at once before the loophole closes. Time is of the essence, but Sarkozi lacks sufficient resources to conduct adequate research on all the prospective issuing companies. Hawke decides to estimate the IPO prices on the basis of the relative size of each company and to justify the pricing later when her staff has time.

> *Comment*: Sarkozi should have taken on only the work that it could adequately handle. By categorizing the issuers by general size, Hawke has bypassed researching all the other relevant aspects that should be considered when pricing new issues and thus has not performed sufficient due diligence. Such an omission can result in investors purchasing shares at prices that have no actual basis. Hawke has violated Standard V(A).

Example 2   (Sufficient Scenario Testing): Babu Dhaliwal works for Heinrich Brokerage in the corporate finance group. He has just persuaded Feggans Resources, Ltd., to allow his firm to do a secondary equity financing at Feggans Resources' current stock price. Because the stock has been trading at higher multiples than similar companies with equivalent production, Dhaliwal presses the Feggans Resources managers to project what would be the maximum production they could achieve in an optimal scenario. Based on these numbers, he is able to justify the price his firm will be asking for the secondary issue. During a sales pitch to the brokers, Dhaliwal then uses these numbers as the base-case production levels that Feggans Resources will achieve.

> *Comment*: When presenting information to the brokers, Dhaliwal should have given a range of production scenarios and the probability of Feggans Resources achieving each level. By giving the maximum production level as the likely level of production, he has misrepresented the chances of achieving that production level and seriously misled the brokers. Dhaliwal has violated Standard V(A).

Example 3   (Developing a Reasonable Basis): Brendan Witt, a former junior sell-side technology analyst, decided to return to school to earn an MBA. To keep his research skills and industry knowledge sharp, Witt accepted a position with On-line and Informed, an independent internet-based research company. The position requires the publication of a recommendation and report on a different company every month. Initially, Witt is a regular contributor of new research and a participant in the associated discussion boards that generally have positive comments on the technology sector. Over time, his ability to manage his educational requirements and his work requirements begin to conflict with one another. Knowing a recommendation is due the next day for On-line, Witt creates a report based on a few news articles and what the conventional wisdom of the markets has deemed the "hot" security of the day.

> *Comment*: Witt's knowledge of and exuberance for technology stocks, a few news articles, and the conventional wisdom of the markets do not constitute, without more information, a reasonable and adequate basis for a stock recommendation that is supported by appropriate research and investigation. Therefore, Witt has violated Standard V(A).
>
> See also Standard IV(C)—Responsibilities of Supervisors as it relates to the firm's inadequate procedures.

Example 4 (Timely Client Updates): Kristen Chandler is an investment consultant in the London office of Dalton Securities, a major global investment consultant firm. One of her U.K. pension funds has decided to appoint a specialist U.S. equity manager. Dalton's global manager of research relies on local consultants to cover managers within their regions and, after conducting thorough due diligence, puts their views and ratings in Dalton's manager database. Chandler accesses Dalton's global manager research database and conducts a screen of all U.S. equity managers on the basis of a match with the client's desired philosophy/style, performance, and tracking-error targets. She selects the five managers that meet these criteria and puts them in a briefing report that is delivered to the client 10 days later. Between the time of Chandler's database search and the delivery of the report to the client, Chandler is told that Dalton has updated the database with the information that one of the firms that Chandler has recommended for consideration lost its chief investment officer, the head of its U.S. equity research, and the majority of its portfolio managers on the U.S. equity product—all of whom have left to establish their own firm. Chandler does not revise her report with this updated information.

> *Comment*: Chandler has failed to satisfy the requirement of Standard V(A). Although Dalton updated the manager ratings to reflect the personnel turnover at one of the firms, Chandler did not update her report to reflect the new information.

Example 5 (Group Research Opinions): Evelyn Mastakis is a junior analyst who has been asked by her firm to write a research report predicting the expected interest rate for residential mortgages over the next six months. Mastakis submits her report to the fixed-income investment committee of her firm for review, as required by firm procedures. Although some committee members support Mastakis's conclusion, the majority of the committee disagrees with her conclusion, and the report is significantly changed to indicate that interest rates are likely to increase more than originally predicted by Mastakis. Should Mastakis ask that her name be taken off the report when it is disseminated?

> *Comment*: The results of research are not always clear, and different people may have different opinions based on the same factual evidence. In this case, the committee may have valid reasons for issuing a report that differs from the analyst's original research. The firm can issue a report that is different from the original report of an analyst as long as there is a reasonable or adequate basis for its conclusions.
>
> Generally, analysts must write research reports that reflect their own opinion and can ask the firm not to put their name on reports that ultimately differ from that opinion. When the work is a group effort, however, not all members of the team may agree with all aspects of the report. Ultimately, members and candidates can ask to have their names removed from the report, but if they are satisfied that the process has produced results or conclusions that have a reasonable or adequate basis, members

or candidates do not have to dissociate from the report even when they do not agree with its contents. If Mastakis is confident in the process, she does not need to dissociate from the report even if it does not reflect her opinion.

Example 6   (Reliance on Third-Party Research): Gary McDermott runs a two-person investment management firm. McDermott's firm subscribes to a service from a large investment research firm that provides research reports. McDermott's firm makes investment recommendations on the basis of these reports.

> *Comment*: Members and candidates can rely on third-party research but must make reasonable and diligent efforts to determine that such research is sound. If McDermott undertakes due diligence efforts on a regular basis to ensure that the research produced by the large firm is objective and reasonably based, McDermott can rely on that research when making investment recommendations to clients.

Example 7   (Due Diligence in Submanager Selection): Paul Ostrowski's business has grown significantly over the past couple of years, and some clients want to diversify internationally. Ostrowski decides to find a submanager to handle the expected international investments. Because this will be his first subadviser, Ostrowski uses the CFA Institute model "request for proposal" to design a questionnaire for his search. By his deadline, he receives seven completed questionnaires from a variety of domestic and international firms trying to gain his business. Ostrowski reviews all the applications in detail and decides to select the firm that charges the lowest fees because doing so will have the least impact on his firm's bottom line.

> *Comment:* The selection of an external adviser or subadviser should be based on a full and complete review of the advisers' services, performance history, and cost structure. In basing the decision on the fee structure alone, Ostrowski may be violating Standard V(A).
>
> See also Standard III(C)—Suitability as it relates to the ability of the selected adviser to meet the needs of the clients.

Example 8   (Sufficient Due Diligence): Michael Papis is the chief investment officer of his state's retirement fund. The fund has always used outside advisers for the real estate allocation, and this information is clearly presented in all fund communications. Thomas Nagle, a recognized sell-side research analyst and Papis's business school classmate, recently left the investment bank he worked for to start his own asset management firm, Accessible Real Estate. Nagle is trying to build his assets under management and contacts Papis about gaining some of the retirement fund's allocation. In the previous few years, the performance of the retirement fund's real estate investments was in line with the fund's benchmark but was not extraordinary. Papis decides to help out his old friend and also to seek better returns by moving the real estate allocation to Accessible. The only notice of the change in adviser appears in the next annual report in the listing of associated advisers.

> *Comment*: Papis violated Standard V(A) in this example. His responsibilities may include the selection of the external advisers, but the decision to change investers appears to have been arbitrary. If Papis was dissatisfied with the current real estate adviser, he should have conducted a proper solicitation to select the most appropriate adviser.
>
> See also Standard IV(C)—Responsibilities of Supervisors, Standard V(B)—Communication with Clients and Prospective Clients, and Standard VI(A)—Disclosure of Conflicts.

Example 9 (Sufficient Due Diligence): Andre Shrub owns and operates Conduit, an investment advisory firm. Prior to opening Conduit, Shrub was an account manager with Elite Investment, a hedge fund managed by his good friend Adam Reed. To attract clients to a new Conduit fund, Shrub offers lower-than-normal management fees. He can do so because the fund consists of two top-performing funds managed by Reed. Given his personal friendship with Reed and the prior performance record of these two funds, Shrub believes this new fund is a winning combination for all parties. Clients quickly invest with Conduit to gain access to the Elite funds. No one is turned away because Conduit is seeking to expand its assets under management.

> *Comment:* Shrub violated Standard V(A) by not conducting a thorough analysis of the funds managed by Reed before developing the new Conduit fund. Due diligence must be applied more deeply than review of a single security. It includes a review of outside managers and investment funds. Shrub's reliance on his personal relationship with Reed and his prior knowledge of Elite are insufficient justification for the investments. The funds may be appropriately considered, but a full review of their operating procedures, reporting practices, and transparency are some elements of the necessary due diligence.
> See also Standard III(C)—Suitability.

Example 10 (Sufficient Due Diligence): Bob Thompson has been doing research for the portfolio manager of the fixed-income department. His assignment is to do sensitivity analysis on securitized subprime mortgages. He has discussed with the manager possible scenarios to use to calculate expected returns. A key assumption in such calculations is housing price appreciation (HPA) because it drives "prepays" (prepayments of mortgages) and losses. Thompson is concerned with the significant appreciation experienced over the previous five years as a result of the increased availability of funds from subprime mortgages. Thompson insists that the analysis should include a scenario run with negative 10 percent for the first year, negative 5 percent for the second year, and then (to project a worst-case scenario) 0 percent for Years 3 through 5. The manager replies that these assumptions are too dire because there has never been a time in their available database when HPA was negative.

Thompson conducts his research to better understand the risks inherent in these securities and evaluates these securities in the worst-case scenario, an unlikely but possible environment. Based on the results of the enhanced scenarios, Thompson does not recommend the purchase of the securitization. Against the general market trends, the manager follows Thompson's recommendation and does not invest. The following year, the housing market collapses. In avoiding the subprime investments, the manager's portfolio outperforms its peer group that year.

> *Comment*: Thompson's actions in running the scenario test with inputs beyond the historical trends available in the firm's databases adheres to the principles of Standard V(A). His concerns over recent trends provide a sound basis for further analysis. Thompson understands the limitations of his model, when combined with the limited available historical information, to accurately predict the performance of the funds if market conditions change negatively.
> See also Standard I(B)—Independence and Objectivity.

Example 11 (Use of Quantitatively Oriented Models): Espacia Liakos works in sales for Hellenica Securities, a firm specializing in developing intricate derivative strategies to profit from particular views on market expectations. One of her clients is Eugenie Carapalis, who has become convinced that commodity prices will become more volatile over the coming months. Carapalis asks Liakos to quickly engineer a strategy that will benefit from this expectation. Liakos turns to Hellenica's modelling group to fulfil this request. Because of the tight deadline, the modelling group outsources parts of the work to several trusted third parties. Liakos implements the disparate components of the strategy as the firms complete them.

Within a month, Carapalis is proven correct: Volatility across a range of commodities increases sharply. But her derivatives position with Hellenica returns huge losses, and the losses increase daily. Liakos investigates and realizes that, although each of the various components of the strategy had been validated, they had never been evaluated as an integrated whole. In extreme conditions, portions of the model worked at cross-purposes with other portions, causing the overall strategy to fail dramatically.

> *Comment:* Liakos violated Standard V(A). Members and candidates must understand the statistical significance of the results of the models they recommend and must be able to explain them to clients. Liakos did not take adequate care to ensure a thorough review of the whole model; its components were evaluated only individually. Because Carapalis clearly intended to implement the strategy as a whole rather than as separate parts, Liakos should have tested how the components of the strategy interacted as well as how they performed individually.

Example 12   (Successful Due Diligence/Failed Investment): Alton Newbury is an investment adviser to high-net-worth clients. A client with an aggressive risk profile in his investment policy statement asks about investing in the Top Shelf hedge fund. This fund, based in Calgary, Alberta, Canada, has reported 20 percent returns for the first three years. The fund prospectus states that its strategy involves long and short positions in the energy sector and extensive leverage. Based on his analysis of the fund's track record, the principals involved in managing the fund, the fees charged, and the fund's risk profile, Newbury recommends the fund to the client and secures a position in it. The next week, the fund announces that it has suffered a loss of 60 percent of its value and is suspending operations and redemptions until after a regulatory review. Newbury's client calls him in a panic and asks for an explanation.

> *Comment:* Newbury's actions were consistent with Standard V(A). Analysis of an investment that results in a reasonable basis for recommendation does not guarantee that the investment will have no downside risk. Newbury should discuss the analysis process with the client while reminding him or her that past performance does not lead to guaranteed future gains and that losses in an aggressive investment portfolio should be expected.

B. Communication with Clients and Prospective Clients

Members and Candidates must:

1. Disclose to clients and prospective clients the basic format and general principles of the investment processes they use to analyze investments, select securities, and construct portfolios and must promptly disclose any changes that might materially affect those processes.

2. Use reasonable judgment in identifying which factors are important to their investment analyses, recommendations, or actions and include those factors in communications with clients and prospective clients.

3. Distinguish between fact and opinion in the presentation of investment analyses and recommendations.

Guidance

Highlights:

- *Informing Clients of the Investment Process*
- *Different Forms of Communication*
- *Identifying Limitations of Analysis*
- *Distinction between Facts and Opinions in Reports*

Standard V(B) addresses member and candidate conduct with respect to communicating with clients. Developing and maintaining clear, frequent, and thorough communication practices is critical to providing high-quality financial services to clients. When clients understand the information communicated to them, they also can understand exactly how members and candidates are acting on their behalf, which gives clients the opportunity to make well-informed decisions about their investments. Such understanding can be accomplished only through clear communication.

Standard V(B) states that members and candidates should communicate in a recommendation the factors that were instrumental in making the investment recommendation. A critical part of this requirement is to distinguish clearly between opinions and facts. In preparing a research report, the member or candidate must present the basic characteristics of the security(ies) being analyzed, which will allow the reader to evaluate the report and incorporate information the reader deems relevant to his or her investment decision-making process.

Similarly, in preparing a recommendation about, for example, an asset allocation strategy, alternative investment vehicle, or structured investment product, the member or candidate should include factors that are relevant to whatever asset classes are being discussed. In all cases, the upside potential and downside risk expressed in terms of expected total returns should be among the factors communicated. Follow-on communication of any changes in the risk characteristics of a security or asset strategy would also be advisable.

Informing Clients of the Investment Process

Members and candidates must adequately describe to clients and prospective clients the manner in which the member or candidate conducts the investment decision-making process. The member or candidate must keep clients and other interested parties informed on an ongoing basis about changes to the investment process. Only by thoroughly understanding the nature of the investment product or service can a client determine whether changes to that product or service could materially affect his or her investment objectives.

Understanding the basic characteristics of an investment is of great importance in judging the suitability of that investment on a stand-alone basis, but it is especially important in determining the impact each investment will have on the characteristics of a portfolio. Although the risk and return characteristics of a common stock might seem to be essentially the same for any investor when the stock is viewed in isolation, the effects of those characteristics greatly depend on the other investments held. For instance, if the particular stock will represent 90 percent of an individual's investments, the stock's importance in the portfolio is vastly different from what it would be to an investor with a highly diversified portfolio for whom the stock will represent only 2 percent of the holdings.

A firm's investment policy may include the use of outside advisers to manage various portions of the clients' assets under management. Members and candidates should inform the clients about the specialization or diversification expertise provided by the external adviser(s). This information allows clients to understand the full mix of products and strategies being applied that may affect their investment objectives.

Different Forms of Communication

For purposes of Standard V(B), communication is not confined to a written report of the type traditionally generated by an analyst researching a security, company, or industry. A presentation of information can be made via any means of communication, including in-person recommendation or description, telephone conversation, media broadcast, or transmission by computer (e.g., on the internet). Furthermore, the nature of these communications is highly diverse—from one word ("buy" or "sell") to in-depth reports of more than 100 pages.

A communication may contain a general recommendation about the market, asset allocations, or classes of investments (e.g., stocks, bonds, real estate) or may relate to a specific security. If recommendations are contained in capsule form (such as a recommended stock list), members and candidates should notify clients that additional information and analyses are available from the producer of the report.

Identifying Limitations of Analysis

Investment advice based on quantitative research and analysis must be supported by readily available reference material and should be applied in a manner consistent with previously applied methodology; if changes in methodology are made, they should be highlighted. Members and candidates should outline known limitations of the analysis and conclusions contained in their investment advice. In evaluating the basic characteristics of the investment being recommended, members and candidates should consider in the report the potential total returns and the principal risks inherent in the expected returns, which may include credit risk, financial risk (specifically, the use of leverage or financial derivatives), and overall market risk.

Once the process has been completed, the member or candidate who prepares the report must include those elements that are important to the analysis and conclusions of the report so that the reader can follow and challenge the report's reasoning. A report writer who has done adequate investigation may emphasize certain areas, touch briefly on others, and omit certain aspects deemed unimportant. For instance, a report may dwell on a quarterly earnings release or new-product introduction and omit other matters as long as the analyst clearly stipulates the limits to the scope of the report.

Distinction between Facts and Opinions in Reports

Standard V(B) requires that opinion be separated from fact. Violations often occur when reports fail to separate the past from the future by not indicating that earnings estimates, changes in the outlook for dividends, and/or future market price information are *opinions* subject to future circumstances. In the case of complex quantitative analyses, analysts must clearly separate fact from statistical conjecture and should identify the known limitations of an analysis. Analysts may violate Standard V(B) by failing to identify the limits of statistically developed projections, because this omission leaves readers unaware of the limits of the published projections.

Recommended Procedures for Compliance

Because the selection of relevant factors is an analytical skill, determination of whether a member or candidate has used reasonable judgment in excluding and including information in research reports depends heavily on case-by-case review rather than a specific checklist. To assist in the after-the-fact review of a report, the member or candidate must maintain records indicating the nature of the research and should, if asked, be able to supply additional information to the client (or any user of the report) covering factors not included in the report.

Application of the Standard

Example 1   (Sufficient Disclosure of Investment System): Sarah Williamson, director of marketing for Country Technicians, Inc., is convinced that she has found the perfect formula for increasing Country Technician's income and diversifying its product base. Williamson plans to build on Country Technician's reputation as a leading money manager by marketing an exclusive and expensive investment advice letter to high-net-worth individuals. One hitch in the plan is the complexity of Country Technician's investment system—a combination of technical trading rules (based on historical price and volume fluctuations) and portfolio construction rules designed to minimize risk. To simplify the newsletter, she decides to include only each week's top-five "buy" and "sell" recommendations and to leave out details of the valuation models and the portfolio structuring scheme.

> *Comment*: Williamson's plans for the newsletter violate Standard V(B). Williamson need not describe the investment system in detail in order to implement the advice effectively, but she must inform clients of Country Technician's basic process and logic. Without understanding the basis for a recommendation, clients cannot possibly understand its limitations or its inherent risks.

Example 2   (Providing Opinions as Facts): Richard Dox is a mining analyst for East Bank Securities. He has just finished his report on Boisy Bay Minerals. Included in his report is his own assessment of the geological extent of mineral reserves likely to be found on the company's land. Dox completed this calculation on the basis of the core samples from the company's latest drilling. According to Dox's calculations, the company has more than 500,000 ounces of gold on the property. Dox concludes his research report as follows: "Based on the fact that the company has 500,000 ounces of gold to be mined, I recommend a strong BUY."

> *Comment*: If Dox issues the report as written, he will violate Standard V(B). His calculation of the total gold reserves for the property is an opinion, not a fact. Opinion must be distinguished from fact in research reports.

Example 3   (Proper Description of a Security): Olivia Thomas, an analyst at Government Brokers, Inc., which is a brokerage firm specializing in government bond trading, has produced a report that describes an investment strategy designed to benefit from an expected decline in U.S. interest rates. The firm's derivative products group has designed a structured product that will allow the firm's clients to benefit from this strategy. Thomas's report describing the strategy indicates that high returns are possible if various scenarios for declining interest rates are assumed. Citing the proprietary nature of the structured product underlying the strategy, the report does not describe in detail how the firm is able to offer such returns or the related risks in the scenarios, nor does the report address the likely returns of the strategy if, contrary to expectations, interest rates rise.

> *Comment*: Thomas has violated Standard V(B) because her report fails to describe properly the basic characteristics of the actual and implied risks of the investment strategy, including how the structure was created and the degree to which leverage was embedded in the structure. The report should include a balanced discussion of how the strategy would perform in the case of rising as well as falling interest rates, preferably illustrating how the strategies might be expected to perform in the event of a reasonable variety of interest rate and credit-risk-spread scenarios. If liquidity issues are relevant with regard to the valuation of either the derivatives or the

underlying securities, provisions the firm has made to address those risks should also be disclosed.

Example 4   (Notification of Fund Mandate Change): May & Associates is an aggressive-growth manager that has represented itself since its inception as a specialist at investing in small-cap U.S. stocks. One of May's selection criteria is a maximum capitalization of US$250 million for any given company. After a string of successful years of superior performance relative to its peers, May has expanded its client base significantly, to the point at which assets under management now exceed $3 billion. For liquidity purposes, May's chief investment officer (CIO) decides to lift the maximum permissible market-cap ceiling to US$500 million and change the firm's sales and marketing literature accordingly to inform prospective clients and third-party consultants.

> *Comment*: Although May's CIO is correct about informing potentially interested parties as to the change in investment process, he must also notify May's existing clients. Among the latter group might be a number of clients who not only retained May as a small-cap manager but also retained midcap and large-cap specialists in a multiple-manager approach. Such clients could regard May's change of criteria as a style change that distorts their overall asset allocations.

Example 5   (Notification of Fund Mandate Change): Rather than lifting the ceiling for its universe from US$250 million to US$500 million, May & Associates extends its small-cap universe to include a number of non-U.S. companies.

> *Comment*: Standard V(B) requires that May's CIO advise May's clients of this change because the firm may have been retained by some clients specifically for its prowess at investing in U.S. small-cap stocks. Other changes that require client notification are introducing derivatives to emulate a certain market sector or relaxing various other constraints, such as portfolio beta. In all such cases, members and candidates must disclose changes to all interested parties.

Example 6   (Notification of Changes to the Investment Process): RJZ Capital Management is an active value-style equity manager that selects stocks by using a combination of four multifactor models. The firm has found favorable results when back testing the most recent 10 years of available market data in a new dividend discount model (DDM) designed by the firm. This model is based on projected inflation rates, earnings growth rates, and interest rates. The president of RJZ decides to replace its simple model that uses price to trailing 12-months earnings with the new DDM.

> *Comment*: Because the introduction of a new and different valuation model represents a material change in the investment process, RJZ's president must communicate the change to the firm's clients. RJZ is moving away from a model based on hard data toward a new model that is at least partly dependent on the firm's forecasting skills. Clients would likely view such a model as a significant change rather than a mere refinement of RJZ's process.

Example 7   (Notification of Changes to the Investment Process): RJZ Capital Management loses the chief architect of its multifactor valuation system. Without informing its clients, the president of RJZ decides to redirect the firm's talents and resources toward developing a product for passive equity management—a product that will emulate the performance of a major market index.

> *Comment*: By failing to disclose to clients a substantial change to its investment process, the president of RJZ has violated Standard V(B).

Example 8 (Notification of Changes to the Investment Process): At Fundamental Asset Management, Inc., the responsibility for selecting stocks for addition to the firm's "approved" list has just shifted from individual security analysts to a committee consisting of the research director and three senior portfolio managers. Eleanor Morales, a portfolio manager with Fundamental Asset Management, thinks this change is not important enough to communicate to her clients.

> *Comment*: Morales must disclose the process change to all her clients. Some of Fundamental's clients might be concerned about the morale and motivation among the firm's best research analysts after such a change. Moreover, clients might challenge the stock-picking track record of the portfolio managers and might even want to monitor the situation closely.

Example 9 (Sufficient Disclosure of Investment System): Amanda Chinn is the investment director for Diversified Asset Management, which manages the endowment of a charitable organization. Because of recent staff departures, Diversified has decided to limit its direct investment focus to large-cap securities and supplement the needs for small-cap and midcap management by hiring outside fund managers. In describing the planned strategy change to the charity, Chinn's update letter states, "As investment director, I will directly oversee the investment team managing the endowment's large-capitalization allocation. I will coordinate the selection and ongoing review of external managers responsible for allocations to other classes." The letter also describes the reasons for the change and the characteristics external managers must have to be considered.

> *Comment*: Standard V(B) requires the disclosure of the investment process used to construct the portfolio of the fund. Changing the investment process from managing all classes of investments within the firm to the use of external managers is one example of information that needs to be communicated to clients. Chinn and her firm have embraced the principles of Standard V(B) by providing their client with relevant information. The charity can now make a reasonable decision about whether Diversified Asset Management remains the appropriate manager for its fund.

Example 10 (Notification of Changes to the Investment Process): Michael Papis is the chief investment officer of his state's retirement fund. The fund has always used outside advisers for the real estate allocation, and this information is clearly presented in all fund communications. Thomas Nagle, a recognized sell-side research analyst and Papis's business school classmate, recently left the investment bank he worked for to start his own asset management firm, Accessible Real Estate. Nagle is trying to build his assets under management and contacts Papis about gaining some of the retirement fund's allocation. In the previous few years, the performance of the retirement fund's real estate investments was in line with the fund's benchmark but was not extraordinary. Papis decides to help out his old friend and also to seek better returns by moving the real estate allocation to Accessible. The only notice of the change in adviser appears in the next annual report in the listing of associated advisers.

> *Comment*: Papis has violated Standard V(B). He attempted to hide the nature of his decision to change external managers by making only a limited disclosure. The plan recipients and the fund's trustees need to be aware when changes are made to ensure that operational procedures are being followed.
>
> See also Standard IV(C)—Responsibilities of Supervisors, Standard V(A)—Diligence and Reasonable Basis, and Standard VI(A)—Disclosure of Conflicts.

C. Record Retention

Members and Candidates must develop and maintain appropriate records to support their investment analyses, recommendations, actions, and other investment-related communications with clients and prospective clients.

Guidance

Highlights:

- *Records Are Property of the Firm*
- *Local Requirements*

Members and candidates must retain records that substantiate the scope of their research and reasons for their actions or conclusions. Which records are required to support recommendations and/or investment actions depends on the role of the member or candidate in the investment decision-making process. Records may be maintained either in hard copy or electronic form.

Some examples of supporting documentation that assists the member or candidate in meeting the requirements for retention are as follows:

- personal notes from meetings with the covered company;
- press releases or presentations issued by the covered company;
- computer-based model outputs and analyses;
- computer-based model input parameters;
- risk analyses of securities' impacts on a portfolio;
- selection criteria for external advisers;
- notes from clients from meetings to review investment policy statements;
- outside research reports.

Records Are Property of the Firm

As a general matter, records created as part of a member's or candidate's professional activity on behalf of his or her employer are the property of the firm. When a member or candidate leaves a firm to seek other employment, the member or candidate cannot take the property of the firm, including originals or copies of supporting records of the member's or candidate's work, to the new employer without the express consent of the previous employer. The member or candidate cannot use historical recommendations or research reports created at the previous firm because the supporting documentation is unavailable. For future use, the member or candidate must re-create the supporting records at the new firm with information gathered through public sources or directly from the covered company and not from memory or sources obtained at the previous employer.

Local Requirements

Local regulators often impose requirements on members, candidates, and their firms related to record retention that must be followed. Fulfilling such regulatory requirements also may satisfy the requirements of Standard V(C), but members and candidates should explicitly determine whether it does. In the absence of regulatory guidance, CFA Institute recommends maintaining records for at least seven years.

Recommended Procedures for Compliance

The responsibility to maintain records that support investment action generally falls with the firm rather than individuals. Members and candidates must, however, archive research notes and other documents, either electronically or in hard copy, that support their current investment-related communications. Doing so will assist their firms in complying with requirements for preservation of internal or external records.

Application of the Standard

Example 1　(Record Retention and IPS Objectives and Recommendations): One of Nikolas Lindstrom's clients is upset by the negative investment returns in his equity portfolio. The investment policy statement for the client requires that the portfolio manager follow a benchmark-oriented approach. The benchmark for the client includes a 35 percent investment allocation in the technology sector. The client acknowledges that this allocation was appropriate, but over the past three years, technology stocks have suffered severe losses. The client complains to the investment manager that so much money was allocated to this sector.

> *Comment*: For Lindstrom, having appropriate records is important to show that over the past three years the percentage of technology stocks in the benchmark index was 35 percent as called for in the IPS. Lindstrom should also have the IPS for the client stating that the benchmark was appropriate for the client's investment objectives. He should also have records indicating that the investment has been explained appropriately to the client and that the IPS was updated on a regular basis. Taking these actions, Lindstrom would be in compliance with Standard V(C).

Example 2　(Record Retention and Research Process): Malcolm Young is a research analyst who writes numerous reports rating companies in the luxury retail industry. His reports are based on a variety of sources, including interviews with company managers, manufacturers, and economists; onsite company visits; customer surveys; and secondary research from analysts covering related industries.

> *Comment*: Young must carefully document and keep copies of all the information that goes into his reports, including the secondary or third-party research of other analysts. Failure to maintain such files would violate Standard V(C).

Example 3　(Records as Firm, Not Employee, Property): Martin Blank develops an analytical model while he is employed by Grosse Point Investment Management, LLP (GPIM). While at the firm, he systematically documents the assumptions that make up the model as well as his reasoning behind the assumptions. As a result of the success of his model, Blank is hired to be the head of the research department of one of GPIM's competitors. Blank takes copies of the records supporting his model to his new firm.

> *Comment*: The records created by Blank supporting the research model he developed at GPIM are the records of GPIM. Taking the documents with him to his new employer without GPIM's permission violates Standard V(C). To use the model in the future, Blank must re-create the records supporting his model at the new firm.

STANDARD VI—CONFLICTS OF INTEREST

A. Disclosure of Conflicts

Members and Candidates must make full and fair disclosure of all matters that could reasonably be expected to impair their independence and objectivity or interfere with respective duties to their clients, prospective clients, and employer. Members and Candidates must ensure that such disclosures are prominent, are delivered in plain language, and communicate the relevant information effectively.

Guidance

Highlights:

- *Disclosure of Conflicts to Employers*
- *Disclosure to Clients*
- *Cross-Departmental Conflicts*
- *Conflicts with Stock Ownership*
- *Conflicts as a Director*

Best practice is to avoid actual conflicts or the appearance of conflicts of interest when possible. Conflicts of interest often arise in the investment profession. Conflicts can occur between the interests of clients, the interests of employers, and the member's or candidate's own personal interests. Common sources for conflict are compensation structures, especially incentive and bonus structures that provide immediate returns for members and candidates with little or no consideration of long-term value creation.

Identifying and managing these conflicts is a critical part of working in the investment industry and can take many forms. When conflicts cannot be reasonably avoided, clear and complete disclosure of their existence is necessary.

Standard VI(A) protects investors and employers by requiring members and candidates to fully disclose to clients, potential clients, and employers all actual and potential conflicts of interest. Once a member or candidate has made full disclosure, the member's or candidate's employer, clients, and prospective clients will have the information needed to evaluate the objectivity of the investment advice or action taken on their behalf.

To be effective, disclosures must be prominent and must be made in plain language and in a manner designed to effectively communicate the information. Members and candidates have the responsibility of determining how often, in what manner, and in what particular circumstances the disclosure of conflicts must be made. Best practices dictate updating disclosures when the nature of a conflict of interest changes materially—for example, if the nature of a conflict of interest deepens through the introduction of bonuses based on each quarter's profits as opposed to the previous review based on annual profits. In making and updating disclosures of conflicts of interest, members and candidates should err on the side of caution to ensure that conflicts are effectively communicated.

Disclosure of Conflicts to Employers

Disclosure of conflicts to employers may be appropriate in many instances. When reporting conflicts of interest to employers, members and candidates should give their employers enough information to assess the impact of the conflict. By complying with employer guidelines, members and candidates allow their employers to avoid potentially embarrassing and costly ethical or regulatory violations.

Reportable situations include conflicts that would interfere with rendering unbiased investment advice and conflicts that would cause a member or candidate to act not in the employer's best interest. The same circumstances that generate conflicts to be reported to clients and prospective clients also would dictate reporting to employers. Ownership of stocks analyzed or recommended, participation on outside boards, and financial or other pressures that could influence a decision are to be promptly reported to the employer so that their impact can be assessed and a decision made on how to resolve the conflict.

The mere appearance of a conflict of interest may create problems for members, candidates, and their employers. Therefore, many of the conflicts previously mentioned could be explicitly prohibited by an employer. For example, many employers restrict personal trading, outside board membership, and related activities to prevent situations that might not normally be considered problematic from a conflict-of-interest point of view but that could give the appearance of a conflict of interest. Members and candidates must comply with these restrictions. Members and candidates must take reasonable steps to avoid conflicts and, if they occur inadvertently, must report them promptly so that the employer and the member or candidate can resolve them as quickly and effectively as possible.

Standard VI(A) also deals with a member's or candidate's conflicts of interest that might be detrimental to the employer's business. Any potential conflict situation that could prevent clear judgment about or full commitment to the execution of the member's or candidate's duties to the employer should be reported to the member's or candidate's employer and promptly resolved.

Disclosure to Clients

Members and candidates must maintain their objectivity when rendering investment advice or taking investment action. Investment advice or actions may be perceived to be tainted in numerous situations. Can a member or candidate remain objective if, on behalf of the firm, the member or candidate obtains or assists in obtaining fees for services? Can a member or candidate give objective advice if he or she owns stock in the company that is the subject of an investment recommendation or if the member or candidate has a close personal relationship with the company managers? Requiring members and candidates to disclose all matters that reasonably could be expected to impair the member's or candidate's objectivity allows clients and prospective clients to judge motives and possible biases for themselves.

Often in the investment industry, a conflict, or the perception of a conflict, cannot be avoided. The most obvious conflicts of interest, which should always be disclosed, are relationships between an issuer and the member, candidate, or their firm (such as a directorship or consultancy by a member; investment banking, underwriting, and financial relationships; broker/dealer market-making activities; and material beneficial ownership of stock). For the purposes of Standard VI(A), members and candidates beneficially own securities or other investments if they have a direct or indirect pecuniary interest in the securities; have the power to vote or direct the voting of the shares of the securities or investments; or have the power to dispose or direct the disposition of the security or investment.

A member or candidate must take reasonable steps to determine whether a conflict of interest exists and disclose to clients any known conflicts of the member's or candidate's firm. Disclosure of broker/dealer market-making activities alerts clients that a purchase or sale might be made from or to the firm's principal account and that the firm has a special interest in the price of the stock.

Additionally, disclosures should be made to clients of fee arrangements, subadvisory agreements, or other situations involving nonstandard fee structures. Equally important is the disclosure of arrangements in which the firm benefits directly from investment recommendations. An obvious conflict of interest is the rebate of a portion of the service fee some classes of mutual funds charge to investors. Members and candidates should ensure that their firms disclose such relationships so clients can fully understand the costs of their investments and the benefits received by their investment manager's employer.

Cross-Departmental Conflicts

Other circumstances can give rise to actual or potential conflicts of interest. For instance, a sell-side analyst working for a broker/dealer may be encouraged, not only by members of her or his own firm but by corporate issuers themselves, to write research reports about particular companies. The buy-side analyst is likely to be faced with similar conflicts as banks exercise their underwriting and security-dealing powers. The marketing division may ask an analyst to recommend the stock of a certain company in order to obtain business from that company.

The potential for conflicts of interest also exists with broker-sponsored limited partnerships formed to invest venture capital. Increasingly, members and candidates are expected not only to follow issues from these partnerships once they are offered to the public but also to promote the issues in the secondary market after public offerings. Members, candidates, and their firms should attempt to resolve situations presenting potential conflicts of interest or disclose them in accordance with the principles set forth in Standard VI(A).

Conflicts with Stock Ownership

The most prevalent conflict requiring disclosure under Standard VI(A) is a member's or candidate's ownership of stock in companies that he or she recommends to clients and/or that clients hold. Clearly, the easiest method for preventing a conflict is to prohibit members and candidates from owning any such securities, but this approach is overly burdensome and discriminates against members and candidates.

Therefore, sell-side members and candidates should disclose any materially beneficial ownership interest in a security or other investment that the member or candidate is recommending. Buy-side members and candidates should disclose their procedures for reporting requirements for personal transactions. Conflicts arising from personal investing are discussed more fully in the guidance for Standard VI(B).

Conflicts as a Director

Service as a director poses three basic conflicts of interest. First, a conflict may exist between the duties owed to clients and the duties owed to shareholders of the company. Second, investment personnel who serve as directors may receive the securities or options to purchase securities of the company as compensation for serving on the board, which could raise questions about trading actions that might increase the value of those securities. Third, board service creates the opportunity to receive material nonpublic information involving the company. Even though the information is confidential, the perception could be that information not available to the public is being communicated to a director's firm—whether a broker, investment adviser, or other type of organization. When members or candidates providing investment services also serve as directors, they should be isolated from those making investment decisions by the use of firewalls or similar restrictions.

Recommended Procedures for Compliance

Members or candidates should disclose special compensation arrangements with the employer that might conflict with client interests, such as bonuses based on short-term performance criteria, commissions, incentive fees, performance fees, and referral fees.

If the member's or candidate's firm does not permit such disclosure, the member or candidate should document the request and may consider dissociating from the activity.

Members' and candidates' firms are encouraged to include information on compensation packages in firms' promotional literature. If a member or candidate manages a portfolio for which the fee is based on capital gains or capital appreciation (a performance fee), this information should be disclosed to clients. If a member, candidate, or a member's or candidate's firm has outstanding agent options to buy stock as part of the compensation package for corporate financing activities, the amount and expiration date of these options should be disclosed as a footnote to any research report published by the member's or candidate's firm.

Application of the Standard

Example 1   (Conflict of Interest and Business Relationships): Hunter Weiss is a research analyst with Farmington Company, a broker and investment banking firm. Farmington's merger and acquisition department has represented Vimco, a conglomerate, in all of Vimco's acquisitions for 20 years. From time to time, Farmington officers sit on the boards of directors of various Vimco subsidiaries. Weiss is writing a research report on Vimco.

> *Comment*: Weiss must disclose in his research report Farmington's special relationship with Vimco. Broker/dealer management of and participation in public offerings must be disclosed in research reports. Because the position of underwriter to a company entails a special past and potential future relationship with a company that is the subject of investment advice, it threatens the independence and objectivity of the report writer and must be disclosed.

Example 2   (Conflict of Interest and Business Stock Ownership): The investment management firm of Dover & Roe sells a 25 percent interest in its partnership to a multinational bank holding company, First of New York. Immediately after the sale, Margaret Hobbs, president of Dover & Roe, changes her recommendation for First of New York's common stock from "sell" to "buy" and adds First of New York's commercial paper to Dover & Roe's approved list for purchase.

> *Comment*: Hobbs must disclose the new relationship with First of New York to all Dover & Roe clients. This relationship must also be disclosed to clients by the firm's portfolio managers when they make specific investment recommendations or take investment actions with respect to First of New York's securities.

Example 3   (Conflict of Interest and Personal Stock Ownership): Carl Fargmon, a research analyst who follows firms producing office equipment, has been recommending purchase of Kincaid Printing because of its innovative new line of copiers. After his initial report on the company, Fargmon's wife inherits from a distant relative US$3 million of Kincaid stock. He has been asked to write a follow-up report on Kincaid.

> *Comment*: Fargmon must disclose his wife's ownership of the Kincaid stock to his employer and in his follow-up report. Best practice would be to avoid the conflict by asking his employer to assign another analyst to draft the follow-up report.

Example 4   (Conflict of Interest and Personal Stock Ownership): Betty Roberts is speculating in penny stocks for her own account and purchases 100,000 shares of Drew Mining, Inc., for 30 cents a share. She intends to sell these shares at the sign of any substantial upward price movement of the stock. A week later, her employer asks her to write a report on penny stocks in the mining industry to be published in two weeks. Even without owning the Drew stock, Roberts would recommend it in her report as a "buy." A surge in the price of the stock to the US$2 range is likely to result once the report is issued.

> *Comment*: Although this holding may not be material, Roberts must disclose it in the report and to her employer before writing the report because the gain for her will be substantial if the market responds strongly to her recommendation. The fact that she has only recently purchased the stock adds to the appearance that she is not entirely objective.

Example 5　(Conflict of Interest and Compensation Arrangement): Samantha Snead, a portfolio manager for Thomas Investment Counsel, Inc., specializes in managing public retirement funds and defined-benefit pension plan accounts, all of which have long-term investment objectives. A year ago, Snead's employer, in an attempt to motivate and retain key investment professionals, introduced a bonus compensation system that rewards portfolio managers on the basis of quarterly performance relative to their peers and to certain benchmark indices. In an attempt to improve the short-term performance of her accounts, Snead changes her investment strategy and purchases several high-beta stocks for client portfolios. These purchases are seemingly contrary to the clients' investment policy statements. Following their purchase, an officer of Griffin Corporation, one of Snead's pension fund clients, asks why Griffin Corporation's portfolio seems to be dominated by high-beta stocks of companies that often appear among the most actively traded issues. No change in objective or strategy has been recommended by Snead during the year.

> *Comment*: Snead has violated Standard VI(A) by failing to inform her clients of the changes in her compensation arrangement with her employer, which created a conflict of interest between her compensation and her clients' IPS. Firms may pay employees on the basis of performance, but pressure by Thomas Investment Counsel to achieve short-term performance goals is in basic conflict with the objectives of Snead's accounts.
>
> See also Standard III(C)—Suitability.

Example 6　(Conflict of Interest and Options and Compensation Arrangements): Wayland Securities works with small companies doing IPOs and/or secondary offerings. Typically, these deals are in the US$10 million to US$50 million range, and as a result, the corporate finance fees are quite small. To compensate for the small fees, Wayland Securities usually takes "agents options"—that is, rights (exercisable within a two-year time frame) to acquire up to an additional 10 percent of the current offering. Following an IPO performed by Wayland for Falk Resources, Ltd., Darcy Hunter, the head of corporate finance at Wayland, is concerned about receiving value for her Falk Resources options. The options are one month from expiring, and the stock is not doing well. She contacts John Fitzpatrick in the research department of Wayland Securities, reminds him that he is eligible for 30 percent of these options, and indicates that now would be a good time to give some additional coverage to Falk Resources. Fitzpatrick agrees and immediately issues a favorable report.

> *Comment*: For Fitzpatrick to avoid being in violation of Standard VI(A), he must indicate in the report the volume and expiration date of agent options outstanding. Furthermore, because he is personally eligible for some of the options, Fitzpatrick must disclose the extent of this compensation. He also must be careful that he does not violate his duty of independence and objectivity under Standard I(B).

Example 7　(Conflict of Interest and Compensation Arrangements): Gary Carter is a representative with Bengal International, a registered broker/dealer. Carter is approached by a stock promoter for Badger Company, who offers to pay Carter additional compensation for sales of Badger Company's stock to Carter's clients. Carter accepts the stock promoter's offer but does not disclose the arrangements to his clients or to his employer. Carter sells shares of the stock to his clients.

> *Comment*: Carter has violated Standard VI(A) by failing to disclose to clients that he is receiving additional compensation for recommending and selling Badger stock. Because he did not disclose the arrangement with Badger to his clients, the clients were unable to evaluate whether Carter's recommendations to buy Badger were affected by this arrangement. Carter's conduct also violated Standard VI(A) by failing to disclose to his employer monetary compensation received in addition to the compensation and benefits conferred by his employer. Carter was required by Standard VI(A) to disclose the arrangement with Badger to his employer so that his employer could evaluate whether the arrangement affected Carter's objectivity and loyalty.

Example 8 (Conflict of Interest and Directorship): Carol Corky, a senior portfolio manager for Universal Management, recently became involved as a trustee with the Chelsea Foundation, a large not-for-profit foundation in her hometown. Universal is a small money manager (with assets under management of approximately US$100 million) that caters to individual investors. Chelsea has assets in excess of US$2 billion. Corky does not believe informing Universal of her involvement with Chelsea is necessary.

> *Comment*: By failing to inform Universal of her involvement with Chelsea, Corky violated Standard VI(A). Given the large size of the endowment at Chelsea, Corky's new role as a trustee can reasonably be expected to be time-consuming, to the possible detriment of Corky's portfolio responsibilities with Universal. Also, as a trustee, Corky may become involved in the investment decisions at Chelsea. Therefore, Standard VI(A) obligates Corky to discuss becoming a trustee at Chelsea with her compliance officer or supervisor at Universal before accepting the position, and she should have disclosed the degree to which she would be involved in investment decisions at Chelsea.

Example 9 (Conflict of Interest and Personal Trading): Bruce Smith covers East European equities for Marlborough Investments, an investment management firm with a strong presence in emerging markets. While on a business trip to Russia, Smith learns that investing in Russian equity directly is difficult but that equity-linked notes that replicate the performance of the underlying Russian equity can be purchased from a New York–based investment bank. Believing that his firm would not be interested in such a security, Smith purchases a note linked to a Russian telecommunications company for his own account without informing Marlborough. A month later, Smith decides that the firm should consider investing in Russian equities by way of the equity-linked notes. He prepares a write-up on the market that concludes with a recommendation to purchase several of the notes. One note he recommends is linked to the same Russian telecom company that Smith holds in his personal account.

> *Comment*: Smith has violated Standard VI(A) by failing to disclose his purchase and ownership of the note linked to the Russian telecom company. Smith is required by the standard to disclose the investment opportunity to his employer and look to his company's policies on personal trading to determine whether it was proper for him to purchase the note for his own account. By purchasing the note, Smith may or may not have impaired his ability to make an unbiased and objective assessment of the appropriateness of the derivative instrument for his firm, but Smith's failure to disclose the

purchase to his employer impaired his employer's ability to decide whether his ownership of the security is a conflict of interest that might affect Smith's future recommendations. Then, when he recommended the particular telecom notes to his firm, Smith compounded his problems by not disclosing that he owned the notes in his personal account—a clear conflict of interest.

Example 10   (Conflict of Interest and Requested Favors): Michael Papis is the chief investment officer of his state's retirement fund. The fund has always used outside advisers for the real estate allocation, and this information is clearly presented in all fund communications. Thomas Nagle, a recognized sell-side research analyst and Papis's business school classmate, recently left the investment bank he worked for to start his own asset management firm, Accessible Real Estate. Nagle is trying to build his assets under management and contacts Papis about gaining some of the retirement fund's allocation. In the previous few years, the performance of the retirement fund's real estate investments was in line with the fund's benchmark but was not extraordinary. Papis decides to help out his old friend and also to seek better returns by moving the real estate allocation to Accessible. The only notice of the change in adviser appears in the next annual report in the listing of associated advisers.

> *Comment*: Papis has violated Standard VI(A) by not disclosing to his employer his personal relationship with Nagle. Disclosure of his past history with Nagle would allow his firm to determine whether the conflict may have impaired Papis's independence in deciding to change managers.
>
> See also Standard IV(C)—Responsibilities of Supervisors, Standard V(A)—Diligence and Reasonable Basis, and Standard V(B)—Communication with Clients and Prospective Clients.

Example 11   (Conflict of Interest and Business Relationships): Bob Wade, trust manager for Central Midas Bank, was approached by Western Funds about promoting its family of funds, with special interest in the service-fee class. To entice Central to promote this class, Western Funds offered to pay the bank a service fee of 0.25 percent. Without disclosing the fee being offered to the bank, Wade asked one of the investment managers to review the Western Funds family of funds to determine whether they were suitable for clients of Central. The manager completed the normal due diligence review and determined that the funds were fairly valued in the market with fee structures on a par with their competitors. Wade decided to accept Western's offer and instructed the team of portfolio managers to exclusively promote these funds and the service-fee class to clients seeking to invest new funds or transfer from their current investments. So as to not influence the investment managers, Wade did not disclose the fee offer and allowed that income to flow directly to the bank.

> *Comment*: Wade is violating Standard VI(A) by not disclosing the portion of the service fee being paid to Central. Although the investment managers may not be influenced by the fee, neither they nor the client have the proper information about Wade's decision to exclusively market this fund family and class of investments. Central may come to rely on the new fee as a component of the firm's profitability and may be unwilling to offer other products in the future that could affect the fees received.
>
> See also Standard I(B)—Independence and Objectivity.

B. Priority of Transactions

Investment transactions for clients and employers must have priority over investment transactions in which a Member or Candidate is the beneficial owner.

Guidance

Highlights:

- *Avoiding Potential Conflicts*
- *Personal Trading Secondary to Trading for Clients*
- *Standards for Nonpublic Information*
- *Impact on All Accounts with Beneficial Ownership*

Standard VI(B) reinforces the responsibility of members and candidates to give the interests of their clients and employers priority over their personal financial interests. This standard is designed to prevent any potential conflict of interest or the appearance of a conflict of interest with respect to personal transactions. Client interests have priority. Client transactions must take precedence over transactions made on behalf of the member's or candidate's firm or personal transactions.

Avoiding Potential Conflicts

Conflicts between the client's interest and an investment professional's personal interest may occur. Although conflicts of interest exist, nothing is inherently unethical about individual managers, advisers, or mutual fund employees making money from personal investments as long as 1) the client is not disadvantaged by the trade, 2) the investment professional does not benefit personally from trades undertaken for clients, and 3) the investment professional complies with applicable regulatory requirements.

Some situations occur where a member or candidate may need to enter a personal transaction that runs counter to current recommendations or what the portfolio manager is doing for client portfolios. For example, a member or candidate may be required at some point to sell an asset to make a college tuition payment or a down payment on a home, to meet a margin call, or so on. The sale may be contrary to the long-term advice the member or candidate is currently providing to clients. In these situations, the same three criteria given in the preceding paragraph should be applied in the transaction so as to not violate Standard VI(B).

Personal Trading Secondary to Trading for Clients

Standard VI(B) states that transactions for clients and employers must have priority over transactions in securities or other investments of which a member or candidate is the beneficial owner. The objective of the standard is to prevent personal transactions from adversely affecting the interests of clients or employers. A member or candidate having the same investment positions or being co-invested with clients does not always create a conflict. Some clients in certain investment situations require members or candidates to have aligned interests. Personal investment positions or transactions of members or candidates or their firm should never, however, adversely affect client investments.

Standards for Nonpublic Information

Standard VI(B) covers the activities of members and candidates who have knowledge of pending transactions that may be made on behalf of their clients or employers, who have access to nonpublic information during the normal preparation of research recommendations, or who take investment actions. Members and candidates are prohibited from conveying nonpublic information to any person whose relationship to the member or candidate makes the member or candidate a beneficial owner of the person's securities. Members and candidates must not convey this information to any other person if the nonpublic information can be deemed material.

Impact on All Accounts with Beneficial Ownership

Members or candidates may undertake transactions in accounts for which they are a beneficial owner only after their clients and employers have had adequate opportunity to act on a recommendation. Personal transactions include those made for the member's or candidate's own account, for family (including spouse, children, and other immediate family members) accounts, and for accounts in which the member or candidate has a direct or indirect pecuniary interest, such as a trust or retirement account. Family accounts that are client accounts should be treated like any other firm account and should neither be given special treatment nor be disadvantaged because of the family relationship. If a member or candidate has a beneficial ownership in the account, however, the member or candidate may be subject to preclearance or reporting requirements of the employer or applicable law.

Recommended Procedures for Compliance

Policies and procedures designed to prevent potential conflicts of interest, and even the appearance of a conflict of interest, with respect to personal transactions are critical to establishing investor confidence in the securities industry. Therefore, members and candidates should urge their firms to establish such policies and procedures. Because investment firms vary greatly in assets under management, types of clients, number of employees, and so on, each firm should have policies regarding personal investing that are best suited to the firm. Members and candidates should then prominently disclose these policies to clients and prospective clients.

The specific provisions of each firm's standards will vary, but all firms should adopt certain basic procedures to address the conflict areas created by personal investing. These procedures include the following:

■ *Limited participation in equity IPOs*: Some eagerly awaited IPOs rise significantly in value shortly after the issue is brought to market. Because the new issue may be highly attractive and sought after, the opportunity to participate in the IPO may be limited. Therefore, purchases of IPOs by investment personnel create conflicts of interest in two principal ways. First, participation in an IPO may have the appearance of taking away an attractive investment opportunity from clients for personal gain—a clear breach of the duty of loyalty to clients. Second, personal purchases in IPOs may have the appearance that the investment opportunity is being bestowed as an incentive to make future investment decisions for the benefit of the party providing the opportunity. Members and candidates can avoid these conflicts or appearances of conflicts of interest by not participating in IPOs.

  Reliable and systematic review procedures should be established to ensure that conflicts relating to IPOs are identified and appropriately dealt with by supervisors. Members and candidates should preclear their participation in IPOs, even in situations without any conflict of interest between a member's or candidate's participation in an IPO and the client's interests. Members and candidates should not benefit from the position that their clients occupy in the marketplace—through preferred trading, the allocation of limited offerings, and/or oversubscription.

■ *Restrictions on private placements*: Strict limits should be placed on investment personnel acquiring securities in private placements, and appropriate supervisory and review procedures should be established to prevent noncompliance.

  Firms do not routinely use private placements for clients (e.g., venture capital deals) because of the high risk associated with them. Conflicts related to private placements are more significant to members and candidates who manage large pools of assets or act as plan sponsors because these managers may be offered special opportunities, such as private placements, as a reward or an enticement for continuing to do business with a particular broker.

Participation in private placements raises conflict-of-interest issues that are similar to issues surrounding IPOs. Investment personnel should not be involved in transactions, including (but not limited to) private placements that could be perceived as favors or gifts that seem designed to influence future judgment or to reward past business deals.

Whether the venture eventually proves to be good or bad, managers have an immediate conflict concerning private placement opportunities. If and when the investments go public, participants in private placements have an incentive to recommend the investments to clients regardless of the suitability of the investments for their clients. Doing so increases the value of the participants' personal portfolios.

- *Establish blackout/restricted periods*: Investment personnel involved in the investment decision-making process should establish blackout periods prior to trades for clients so that managers cannot take advantage of their knowledge of client activity by "front-running" client trades (trading for one's personal account before trading for client accounts).

  Individual firms must decide who within the firm should be required to comply with the trading restrictions. At a minimum, all individuals who are involved in the investment decision-making process should be subject to the same restricted period. Each firm must determine specific requirements related to blackout and restricted periods that are most relevant to the firm while ensuring that the procedures are governed by the guiding principles set forth in the Code and Standards. Size of firm and type of securities purchased are relevant factors. For example, in a large firm, a blackout requirement is, in effect, a total trading ban because the firm is continually trading in most securities. In a small firm, the blackout period is more likely to prevent the investment manager from front-running.

- *Reporting requirements*: Supervisors should establish reporting procedures for investment personnel, including disclosure of personal holdings/beneficial ownerships, confirmations of trades to the firm and the employee, and preclearance procedures. Once trading restrictions are in place, they must be enforced. The best method for monitoring and enforcing procedures to eliminate conflicts of interest in personal trading is through reporting requirements, including the following:

  - **Disclosure of holdings in which the employee has a beneficial interest**. Disclosure by investment personnel to the firm should be made upon commencement of the employment relationship and at least annually thereafter. To address privacy considerations, disclosure of personal holdings should be handled in a confidential manner by the firm.

  - **Providing duplicate confirmations of transactions**. Investment personnel should be required to direct their brokers to supply to firms duplicate copies or confirmations of all their personal securities transactions and copies of periodic statements for all securities accounts. The duplicate confirmation requirement has two purposes: 1) The requirement sends a message that there is independent verification, which reduces the likelihood of unethical behavior, and 2) it enables verification of the accounting of the flow of personal investments that cannot be determined from merely looking at holdings.

- **Preclearance procedures**. Investment personnel should examine all planned personal trades to identify possible conflicts prior to the execution of the trades. Preclearance procedures are designed to identify possible conflicts before a problem arises.

■ *Disclosure of policies*: Upon request, members and candidates should fully disclose to investors their firm's policies regarding personal investing. The information about employees' personal investment activities and policies will foster an atmosphere of full and complete disclosure and calm the public's legitimate concerns about the conflicts of interest posed by investment personnel's personal trading. The disclosure must provide helpful information to investors; it should not be simply boilerplate language such as "investment personnel are subject to policies and procedures regarding their personal trading."

Application of the Standard

Example 1   (Personal Trading): Research analyst Marlon Long does not recommend purchase of a common stock for his employer's account because he wants to purchase the stock personally and does not want to wait until the recommendation is approved and the stock purchased by his employer.

> *Comment*: Long has violated Standard VI(B) by taking advantage of his knowledge of the stock's value before allowing his employer to benefit from that information.

Example 2   (Trading for Family Member Account): Carol Baker, the portfolio manager of an aggressive-growth mutual fund, maintains an account in her husband's name at several brokerage firms with which the fund and a number of Baker's other individual clients do a substantial amount of business. Whenever a hot issue becomes available, she instructs the brokers to buy it for her husband's account. Because such issues normally are scarce, Baker often acquires shares in hot issues but her clients are not able to participate in them.

> *Comment*: To avoid violating Standard VI(B), Baker must acquire shares for her mutual fund first and acquire them for her husband's account only after doing so, even though she might miss out on participating in new issues via her husband's account. She also must disclose the trading for her husband's account to her employer because this activity creates a conflict between her personal interests and her employer's interests.

Example 3   (Family Accounts as Equals): Erin Toffler, a portfolio manager at Esposito Investments, manages the retirement account established with the firm by her parents. Whenever IPOs become available, she first allocates shares to all her other clients for whom the investment is appropriate; only then does she place any remaining portion in her parents' account, if the issue is appropriate for them. She has adopted this procedure so that no one can accuse her of favoring her parents.

> *Comment*: Toffler has violated Standard VI(B) by breaching her duty to her parents by treating them differently from her other accounts simply because of the family relationship. As fee-paying clients of Esposito Investments, Toffler's parents are entitled to the same treatment as any other client of the firm. If Toffler has beneficial ownership in the account, however, and Esposito Investments has preclearance and reporting requirements for personal transactions, she may have to preclear the trades and report the transactions to Esposito.

Example 4   (Personal Trading and Disclosure): Gary Michaels is an entry-level employee who holds a low-paying job serving both the research department and the investment management department of an active investment management firm. He purchases a sports car and begins to wear expensive clothes after only a year of employment with the firm. The director of the investment management department, who has responsibility for monitoring the personal stock transactions of all employees, investigates and discovers that Michaels has made substantial investment gains by purchasing stocks just before they were put on the firm's recommended "buy" list. Michaels was regularly given the firm's quarterly personal transaction form but declined to complete it.

> *Comment*: Michaels violated Standard VI(B) by placing personal transactions ahead of client transactions. In addition, his supervisor violated the Standard IV(C)—Responsibilities of Supervisors by permitting Michaels to continue to perform his assigned tasks without having signed the quarterly personal transaction form. Note also that if Michaels had communicated information about the firm's recommendations to a person who traded the security, that action would be a misappropriation of the information and a violation of Standard II(A)—Material Nonpublic Information.

Example 5   (Trading Prior to Report Dissemination): A brokerage's insurance analyst, Denise Wilson, makes a closed-circuit TV report to her firm's branches around the country. During the broadcast, she includes negative comments about a major company in the insurance industry. The following day, Wilson's report is printed and distributed to the sales force and public customers. The report recommends that both short-term traders and intermediate investors take profits by selling that insurance company's stock. Seven minutes after the broadcast, however, Ellen Riley, head of the firm's trading department, had closed out a long "call" position in the stock. Then, shortly thereafter, Riley established a sizable "put" position in the stock. When asked about her activities, Riley claimed she took the actions to facilitate anticipated sales by institutional clients.

> *Comment*: Riley did not give customers an opportunity to buy or sell in the options market before the firm itself did. By taking action before the report was disseminated, Riley's firm may have depressed the price of the calls and increased the price of the puts. The firm could have avoided a conflict of interest if it had waited to trade for its own account until its clients had an opportunity to receive and assimilate Wilson's recommendations. As it is, Riley's actions violated Standard VI(B).

C. Referral Fees

Members and Candidates must disclose to their employer, clients, and prospective clients, as appropriate, any compensation, consideration, or benefit received from or paid to others for the recommendation of products or services

Guidance

Standard VI(C) states the responsibility of members and candidates to inform their employer, clients, and prospective clients of any benefit received for referrals of customers and clients. Such disclosures allow clients or employers to evaluate 1) any partiality shown in any recommendation of services and 2) the full cost of the services. Members and candidates must disclose when they pay a fee or provide compensation to others who have referred prospective clients to the member or candidate.

Appropriate disclosure means that members and candidates must advise the client or prospective client, before entry into any formal agreement for services, of any benefit given or received for the recommendation of any services provided by the member or candidate. In addition, the member or candidate must disclose the nature of the consideration or benefit—for example, flat fee or percentage basis; one-time or continuing benefit; based on performance; benefit in the form of provision of research or other noncash benefit—together with the estimated dollar value. Consideration includes all fees, whether paid in cash, in soft dollars, or in kind.

Recommended Procedures for Compliance

Members and candidates should encourage their employers to develop procedures related to referral fees. The firm may completely restrict such fees. If the firm does not adopt a strict prohibition of such fees, the procedures should indicate the appropriate steps for requesting approval.

Employers should have investment professionals provide to the clients notification of approved referral fee programs and provide the employer regular (at least quarterly) updates on the amount and nature of compensation received.

Application of the Standard

Example 1   (Disclosure of Referral Arrangements and Outside Parties): Brady Securities, Inc., a broker/dealer, has established a referral arrangement with Lewis Brothers, Ltd., an investment counseling firm. In this arrangement, Brady Securities refers all prospective tax-exempt accounts, including pension, profit-sharing, and endowment accounts, to Lewis Brothers. In return, Lewis Brothers makes available to Brady Securities on a regular basis the security recommendations and reports of its research staff, which registered representatives of Brady Securities use in serving customers. In addition, Lewis Brothers conducts monthly economic and market reviews for Brady Securities personnel and directs all stock commission business generated by referral accounts to Brady Securities.

Willard White, a partner in Lewis Brothers, calculates that the incremental costs involved in functioning as the research department of Brady Securities are US$20,000 annually.

Referrals from Brady Securities last year resulted in fee income of US$200,000 for Lewis Brothers, and directing all stock trades through Brady Securities resulted in additional costs to Lewis Brothers' clients of US$10,000.

Diane Branch, the chief financial officer of Maxwell Inc., contacts White and says that she is seeking an investment manager for Maxwell's profit-sharing plan. She adds, "My friend Harold Hill at Brady Securities recommended your firm without qualification, and that's good enough for me. Do we have a deal?" White accepts the new account but does not disclose his firm's referral arrangement with Brady Securities.

> *Comment*: White has violated Standard VI(C) by failing to inform the prospective customer of the referral fee payable in services and commissions for an indefinite period to Brady Securities. Such disclosure could have caused Branch to reassess Hill's recommendation and make a more critical evaluation of Lewis Brothers' services.

Example 2   (Disclosure of Interdepartmental Referral Arrangements): James Handley works for the trust department of Central Trust Bank. He receives compensation for each referral he makes to Central Trust's brokerage department and personal financial management department that results in a sale. He refers several of his clients to the personal financial management department but does not disclose the arrangement within Central Trust to his clients.

Comment: Handley has violated Standard VI(C) by not disclosing the referral arrangement at Central Trust Bank to his clients. Standard VI(C) does not distinguish between referral payments paid by a third party for referring clients to the third party and internal payments paid within the firm to attract new business to a subsidiary. Members and candidates must disclose all such referral fees. Therefore, Handley is required to disclose, at the time of referral, any referral fee agreement in place among Central Trust Bank's departments. The disclosure should include the nature and the value of the benefit and should be made in writing.

Example 3   (Disclosure of Referral Arrangements and Informing Firm): Katherine Roberts is a portfolio manager at Katama Investments, an advisory firm specializing in managing assets for high-net-worth individuals. Katama's trading desk uses a variety of brokerage houses to execute trades on behalf of its clients. Roberts asks the trading desk to direct a large portion of its commissions to Naushon, Inc., a small broker/dealer run by one of Roberts' business school classmates. Katama's traders have found that Naushon is not very competitive on pricing, and although Naushon generates some research for its trading clients, Katama's other analysts have found most of Naushon's research to be not especially useful. Nevertheless, the traders do as Roberts asks, and in return for receiving a large portion of Katama's business, Naushon recommends the investment services of Roberts and Katama to its wealthiest clients. This arrangement is not disclosed to either Katama or the clients referred by Naushon.

Comment: Roberts is violating Standard VI(C) by failing to inform her employer of the referral arrangement.

Example 4   (Disclosure of Referral Arrangements and Employer Compensation): Yeshao Wen is a portfolio manager for a bank. He receives additional monetary compensation from his employer when he is successful in assisting in the sales process and generation of assets under management. The assets in question will be invested in proprietary products, such as affiliate company mutual funds.

Comment: Standard VI(C) is meant to address instances where the investment advice provided by a member or candidate appears to be objective and independent but in fact is influenced by an unseen referral arrangement. It is not meant to cover compensation by employers to employees for generating new business when it would be obvious to potential clients that the employees are "referring" potential clients to the services of their employers.

If Wen is selling the bank's investment management services in general, he does not need to disclose to potential clients that he will receive a bonus for finding new clients and acquiring new assets under management for the bank. Potential clients are probably aware that it would be financially beneficial both to the portfolio manager and the manager's firm for the portfolio manager to sell the services of the firm and attract new clients.

In this example, however, the assets will be managed in "proprietary product offerings" of the manager's company (for example, an in-house mutual fund) and Wen will receive additional compensation for selling firm products. Some sophisticated investors may realize that it would be financially beneficial to the portfolio manager and the manager's firm if the investor were to buy the product offerings of the firm. Best practice dictates, however, that members or candidates acting as portfolio managers disclose to clients that they are compensated for selling firm products to clients. Such disclosure will meet the purpose of Standard VI(C), which is to allow investors to determine whether there is any partiality on the part of the portfolio manager making investment advice.

Example 5   (Disclosure of Referral Arrangements and Outside Organizations): Alex Burl is a portfolio manager at Helpful Investments, a local investment advisory firm. Burl is on the advisory board of his child's school, which is looking for ways to raise money to purchase new playground equipment for the school. Burl discusses a plan with his supervisor in which he will donate to the school a portion of his service fee from new clients referred by the parents of students at the school. Upon getting the approval from Helpful, Burl presents the idea to the school's advisory board and directors. The school agrees to announce the program at the next parent event and asks Burl to provide the appropriate written materials to be distributed. A week following the distribution of the flyers, Burl receives the first school-related referral. In establishing the client's investment policy statement, Burl clearly discusses the school's referral and outlines the plans for distributing the donation back to the school.

> *Comment*: Burl has not violated Standard VI(C) because he secured the permission of his employer, Helpful Investments, and the school prior to beginning the program and because he discussed the arrangement with the client at the time the investment policy statement was designed.

Example 6   (Disclosure of Referral Arrangements and Outside Parties): The sponsor of a state employee pension is seeking to hire a firm to manage the pension plan's emerging market allocation. To assist in the review process, the sponsor has hired Thomas Arrow as a consultant to solicit proposals from various advisers. Arrow is contracted by the sponsor to represent its best interest in selecting the most appropriate new manager. The process runs smoothly, and Overseas Investments is selected as the new manager.

The following year, news breaks that Arrow is under investigation by the local regulator for accepting kickbacks from investment managers after they are awarded new pension allocations. Overseas Investments is included in the list of firms allegedly making these payments. Although the sponsor is happy with the performance of Overseas since it has been managing the pension plan's emerging market funds, the sponsor still decides to have an independent review of the proposals and the selection process to ensure that Overseas was the appropriate firm for its needs. This review confirms that, even though Arrow was being paid by both parties, the recommendation of Overseas appeared to be objective and appropriate.

> *Comment*: Arrow has violated Standard VI(C) because he did not disclose the fee being paid by Overseas. Withholding this information raises the question of a potential lack of objectivity in the recommendations Overseas is making; this aspect is in addition to questions about the legality of having firms pay to be considered for an allocation.
>
> Regulators and governmental agencies may adopt requirements concerning allowable consultant activities. Local regulations sometimes include having a consultant register with the regulatory agency's ethics board. Regulator policies may include a prohibition on acceptance of payments from investment managers receiving allocations and require regular reporting of contributions made to political organizations and candidates. Arrow would have to adhere to these requirements as well as the Code and Standards.

STANDARD VII—RESPONSIBILITIES AS A CFA INSTITUTE MEMBER OR CFA CANDIDATE

A. Conduct as Members and Candidates in the CFA Program

Members and Candidates must not engage in any conduct that compromises the reputation or integrity of CFA Institute or the CFA designation or the integrity, validity, or security of the CFA examinations.

Guidance

Highlights:

- *Confidential Program Information*
- *Additional CFA Program Restrictions*
- *Expressing an Opinion*

Standard VII(A) covers the conduct of CFA Institute members and candidates involved with the CFA Program and prohibits any conduct that undermines the public's confidence that the CFA charter represents a level of achievement based on merit and ethical conduct. The standard's function is to hold members and candidates to a high ethical criterion while they are participating in or involved with the CFA Program. Conduct covered includes but is not limited to

- cheating or assisting others on the CFA examination or any other CFA Institute examination;
- disregarding the rules and policies of the CFA Program related to exam administration;
- providing confidential program or exam information to candidates or the public;
- disregarding or attempting to circumvent security measures established by CFA Institute for the CFA exam;
- improperly using the CFA designation in any form of communication;
- improperly using an association with CFA Institute to further personal or professional goals;
- misrepresenting information on the Professional Conduct Statement or in the CFA Institute Continuing Education Program.

Confidential Program Information

CFA Institute is vigilant about protecting the integrity of the CFA Program content and examination process. The CFA Program prohibits candidates from disclosing confidential material gained during the exam process.

Examples of information that cannot be disclosed by candidates sitting for an exam include but are not limited to

- specific details of questions appearing on the exam, and
- broad topical areas and formulas tested or not tested on the exam.

All aspects of the exam, including questions, broad topical areas, and formulas, tested or not tested, are considered confidential until such time as CFA Institute elects to release them publicly. This confidentiality requirement allows CFA Institute to maintain the integrity and rigor of the exam for future candidates. Standard VII(A) does not prohibit candidates from discussing nonconfidential information or curriculum material with others or in study groups in preparation for the exam.

Candidates increasingly use online forums and new technology as part of their exam preparations. CFA Institute actively polices blogs, forums, and related social networking groups for information considered confidential. The organization works with both individual candidates and the sponsors of online or offline services to promptly remove any and all violations. As noted in the discussion of Standard I(A)—Knowledge of the Law, candidates, members, and the public are encouraged to report suspected violations to CFA Institute.

Additional CFA Program Restrictions

The CFA Program examination administration policies define additional allowed and disallowed actions concerning the exams. Violating any of the testing policies, such as the calculator policy, personal belongings policy, or the Candidate Pledge, constitutes a violation of Standard VII(A). Candidates will find all of these policies on the CFA Program portion of the CFA Institute website (www.cfainstitute.org). Exhibit 2 provides the Candidate Pledge, which highlights the respect candidates must have for the integrity, validity, and security of the CFA exam.

Members may participate as volunteers in various aspects of the CFA Program. Standard VII(A) prohibits members from disclosing and/or soliciting confidential material gained prior to or during the exam and grading processes with those outside the CFA exam development process.

Examples of information that cannot be shared by members involved in developing, administering, or grading the exams include but are not limited to

- questions appearing on the exam or under consideration,
- deliberation related to the exam process, and
- information related to the scoring of questions.

Expressing an Opinion

Standard VII(A) does *not* cover expressing opinions regarding the CFA Program or CFA Institute. Members and candidates are free to disagree and express their disagreement with CFA Institute on its policies, procedures, or any advocacy positions taken by the organization. When expressing a personal opinion, a candidate is prohibited from disclosing content-specific information, including any actual exam question and the information as to subject matter covered or not covered in the exam.

Exhibit 2	Sample of CFA Program Testing Policies
Candidate Pledge	As a candidate in the CFA Program, I am obligated to follow Standard VII(A) of the CFA Institute Standards of Professional Conduct, which states that members and candidates must not engage in any conduct that compromises the reputation or integrity of CFA Institute or the CFA designation or the integrity, validity, or security of the CFA exam.

Exhibit 2	Continued

- Prior to this exam, I have not given or received information regarding the content of this exam. During this exam, I will not give or receive any information regarding the content of this exam.

- After this exam, I will not **disclose any portion of this exam** and I will not remove **any exam materials** from the testing room in original or copied form. I understand that all exam materials, including my answers, are the property of CFA Institute and will not be returned to me in any form.

- I will follow **all** rules of the CFA Program as stated on the CFA Institute website and the back cover of the exam book. My violation of any rules of the CFA Program will result in CFA Institute voiding my exam results and may lead to suspension or termination of my candidacy in the CFA Program.

Application of the Standard

Example 1   (Sharing Exam Questions): Travis Nero serves as a proctor for the administration of the CFA examination in his city. In the course of his service, he reviews a copy of the Level II exam on the evening prior to the exam's administration and provides information concerning the exam questions to two candidates who use it to prepare for the exam.

> *Comment*: Nero and the two candidates have violated Standard VII(A). By giving information about the exam questions to two candidates, Nero provided an unfair advantage to the two candidates and undermined the integrity and validity of the Level II exam as an accurate measure of the knowledge, skills, and abilities necessary to earn the right to use the CFA designation. By accepting the information, the candidates also compromised the integrity and validity of the Level II exam and undermined the ethical framework that is a key part of the designation.

Example 2   (Bringing Written Material into Exam Room): Loren Sullivan is enrolled to take the Level II CFA examination. He has been having difficulty remembering a particular formula, so prior to entering the exam room, he writes the formula on the palm of his hand. During the afternoon section of the exam, a proctor notices Sullivan looking at the palm of his hand. She asks to see his hand and finds the formula to be readable.

> *Comment*: Because Sullivan wrote down information from the Candidate Body of Knowledge (CBOK) and took that written information into the exam room, his conduct compromised the validity of his exam performance and violated Standard VII(A). Sullivan's conduct was also in direct contradiction of the rules and regulations of the CFA Program, the Candidate Pledge, and the CFA Institute Code and Standards.

Example 3   (Writing after Exam Period End): At the conclusion of the morning section of the Level I CFA examination, the proctors announce that all candidates are to stop writing immediately. John Davis has not completed the exam, so he continues to randomly fill in ovals on his answer sheet. A proctor approaches Davis's desk and reminds him that he should stop writing immediately. Davis, however, continues to complete the answer sheet. After the proctor asks him to stop writing two additional times, Davis finally puts down his pencil.

> *Comment*: By continuing to complete his exam after time was called, Davis has violated Standard VII(A). By continuing to write, Davis took unfair advantage of other candidates, and his conduct compromised the validity of his exam performance. Additionally, by not heeding the proctor's repeated instructions, Davis violated the rules and regulations of the CFA Program.

Example 4   (Sharing Exam Content): After completing Level II of the CFA Exam, Annabelle Rossi writes in her blog about her experience. She posts the following: "Level II is complete! I think I did fairly well on the exam. It was really difficult, but fair. I think I did especially well on the derivatives questions. And there were tons of them! I think I counted 18! The ethics questions were really hard. I'm glad I spent so much time on the Code and Standards. I was surprised to see there were no questions at all about IPO allocations. I expected there to be a couple. Well, off to celebrate getting through it. See you tonight?"

> *Comment*: Rossi did not violate Standard VII(A) when she wrote about how difficult she found the exam or how well she thinks she may have done. By revealing portions of the CBOK covered on the exam and areas not covered, however, she did violate Standard VII(A) and the Candidate Pledge. Depending on the time frame in which the comments were posted, Rossi not only may have assisted future candidates but also may have provided an unfair advantage to candidates sitting for the same exam, thereby undermining the integrity and validity of the Level II exam.

Example 5   (Sharing Exam Content): Level I candidate Etienne Gagne has been a frequent visitor to an internet forum designed specifically for CFA Program candidates. The week after completing the Level I examination, Gagne and several others begin a discussion thread on the forum about the most challenging questions and attempt to determine the correct answers.

> *Comment*: Gagne has violated Standard VII(A) by providing and soliciting confidential exam information, which compromises the integrity of the exam process and violates the Candidate Pledge. In trying to determine correct answers to specific questions, the group's discussion included question-specific details considered to be confidential to the CFA Program. CFA Institute works with candidates and the sponsors of such online discussion boards and forums to remove information of this specific nature from these websites.

Example 6   (Sharing Exam Content): CFA4Sure is a company that produces test-preparation materials for CFA Program candidates. Many candidates register for and use the company's products. The day after the CFA examination, CFA4Sure sends an e-mail to all its customers asking them to share with the company the hardest questions from the exam so that CFA4Sure can better prepare its customers for the next exam administration. Marisol Pena e-mails a summary of the questions she found most difficult on the exam.

> *Comment*: Pena has violated Standard VII(A) by disclosing a portion of the exam questions. The information provided is considered confidential until publicly released by CFA Institute. CFA4Sure is likely to use such feedback to refine its review materials for future candidates. Pena's sharing of the specific questions undermines the integrity of the exam while potentially making the exam easier for future candidates.
>
> If the CFA4Sure employees who participated in the solicitation of confidential CFA Program information are CFA Institute members or candidates, they also have violated Standard VII(A).

Example 7   (Sharing Exam Questions): Ashlie Hocking is in London writing Level II of the CFA examination. After completing the exam, she immediately attempts to contact her friend in Sydney, Australia, to tip him off about specific questions on the exam.

> *Comment*: Hocking has violated Standard VII(A) by attempting to give her friend an unfair advantage, thereby compromising the integrity of the CFA exam process.

Example 8   (Discussion of Exam Grading Guidelines and Results): Prior to participating in grading CFA examinations, Wesley Whitcomb is required to sign a CFA Institute Grader Agreement. As part of the Grader Agreement, Whitcomb agrees not to reveal or discuss the exam materials with anyone except CFA Institute staff or other graders. Several weeks after the conclusion of the CFA exam grading, Whitcomb tells several colleagues who are candidates in the CFA Program which question he graded. He also discusses the guideline answer and adds that few candidates scored well on the question.

> *Comment*: Whitcomb violated Standard VII(A) by breaking the Grader Agreement and disclosing information related to a specific question on the exam, which compromised the integrity of the exam process.

Example 9   (Compromising CFA Institute Integrity as a Volunteer): Jose Ramirez is an investor-relations consultant for several small companies that are seeking greater exposure to investors. He is also the program chair for the CFA Institute society in the city where he works. Ramirez schedules only companies that are his clients to make presentations to the society and excludes other companies.

> *Comment*: Ramirez, by using his volunteer position at CFA Institute to benefit himself and his clients, compromises the reputation and integrity of CFA Institute and thus violates Standard VII(A).

Example 10   (Compromising CFA Institute Integrity as a Volunteer): Marguerite Warrenski is a member of the CFA Institute GIPS Executive Committee, which oversees the creation, implementation, and revision of the GIPS standards. As a member of the Executive Committee, she has advance knowledge of confidential information regarding the GIPS standards, including any new or revised standards the committee is considering. She tells her clients that her Executive Committee membership will allow her to better assist her clients in keeping up with changes to the Standards and facilitating their compliance with the changes.

> *Comment*: Warrenski is using her association with the GIPS Executive Committee to promote her firm's services to clients and potential clients. In defining her volunteer position at CFA Institute as a strategic business advantage over competing firms and implying to clients that she would use confidential information to further their interests, Warrenski is compromising the reputation and integrity of CFA Institute and thus violating Standard VII(A). She may factually state her involvement with the Executive Committee but cannot infer any special advantage to her clients from such participation.

B. Reference to CFA Institute, the CFA Designation, and the CFA Program

When referring to CFA Institute, CFA Institute membership, the CFA designation, or candidacy in the CFA Program, Members and Candidates must not misrepresent or exaggerate the meaning or implications of membership in CFA Institute, holding the CFA designation, or candidacy in the CFA Program.

Guidance

Highlights:

- *CFA Institute Membership*
- *Using the CFA Designation*
- *Referring to Candidacy in the CFA Program*
- *Proper Usage of the CFA Marks*

Standard VII(B) is intended to prevent promotional efforts that make promises or guarantees that are tied to the CFA designation. Individuals may refer to their CFA designation, CFA Institute membership, or candidacy in the CFA Program but must not exaggerate the meaning or implications of membership in CFA Institute, holding the CFA designation, or candidacy in the CFA Program.

Standard VII(B) is not intended to prohibit factual statements related to the positive benefit of earning the CFA designation. However, statements referring to CFA Institute, the CFA designation, or the CFA Program that overstate the competency of an individual or imply, either directly or indirectly, that superior performance can be expected from someone with the CFA designation are not allowed under the standard.

Statements that highlight or emphasize the commitment of CFA Institute members, CFA charterholders, and CFA candidates to ethical and professional conduct or mention the thoroughness and rigor of the CFA Program are appropriate. Members and candidates may make claims about the relative merits of CFA Institute, the CFA Program, or the Code and Standards as long as those statements are implicitly or explicitly stated as the opinion of the speaker. Statements that do not express opinions have to be supported by facts.

Standard VII(B) applies to any form of communication, including but not limited to communications made in electronic or written form (such as on firm letterhead, business cards, professional biographies, directory listings, printed advertising, firm brochures, or personal resumes) and oral statements made to the public, clients, or prospects.

CFA Institute Membership

The term "CFA Institute member" refers to "regular" and "affiliate" members of CFA Institute who have met the membership requirements as defined in the CFA Institute Bylaws. Once accepted as a CFA Institute member, the member must satisfy the following requirements to maintain his or her status:

- remit annually to CFA Institute a completed Professional Conduct Statement, which renews the commitment to abide by the requirements of the Code and Standards and the CFA Institute Professional Conduct Program, and
- pay applicable CFA Institute membership dues on an annual basis.

If a CFA Institute member fails to meet any of these requirements, the individual is no longer considered an active member. Until membership is reactivated, individuals must not present themselves to others as active members. They may state, however, that they were CFA Institute members in the past or refer to the years when their membership was active.

Using the CFA Designation

Those who have earned the right to use the Chartered Financial Analyst designation may use the trademarks or registered marks "Chartered Financial Analyst" or "CFA" and are encouraged to do so but only in a manner that does not misrepresent or exaggerate the meaning or implications of the designation. The use of the designation may be accompanied by an accurate explanation of the requirements that have been met to earn the right to use the designation.

"CFA charterholders" are those individuals who have earned the right to use the CFA designation granted by CFA Institute. These people have satisfied certain requirements, including completion of the CFA Program and required years of acceptable work experience. Once granted the right to use the designation, individuals must also satisfy the CFA Institute membership requirements (see above) to maintain their right to use the designation.

If a CFA charterholder fails to meet any of the membership requirements, he or she forfeits the right to use the CFA designation. Until membership is reactivated, individuals must not present themselves to others as CFA charterholders. They may state, however, that they were charterholders in the past.

Referring to Candidacy in the CFA Program

Candidates in the CFA Program may refer to their participation in the CFA Program, but the reference must clearly state that an individual is a candidate in the CFA Program and must not imply that the candidate has achieved any type of partial designation. A person is a candidate in the CFA Program if:

■ the person's application for registration in the CFA Program has been accepted by CFA Institute, as evidenced by issuance of a notice of acceptance, and the person is enrolled to sit for a specified examination; or

■ the registered person has sat for a specified examination but exam results have not yet been received.

If an individual is registered for the CFA Program but declines to sit for an exam or otherwise does not meet the definition of a candidate as described in the CFA Institute Bylaws, then that individual is no longer considered an active candidate. Once the person is enrolled to sit for a future examination, his or her CFA candidacy resumes.

CFA candidates must never state or imply that they have a partial designation as a result of passing one or more levels or cite an expected completion date of any level of the CFA Program. Final award of the charter is subject to meeting the CFA Program requirements and approval by the CFA Institute Board of Governors.

If a candidate passes each level of the exam in consecutive years and wants to state that he or she did so, that is not a violation of Standard VII(B) because it is a statement of fact. If the candidate then goes on to claim or imply superior ability by obtaining the designation in only three years, however, he or she is in violation of Standard VII(B).

Exhibit 3 provides examples of proper and improper references to the CFA designation.

Exhibit 3	Proper and Improper References to the CFA Designation
Proper References	**Improper References**
"Completion of the CFA Program has enhanced my portfolio management skills."	"CFA charterholders achieve better performance results."
"John Smith passed all three CFA examinations in three consecutive years."	"John Smith is among the elite, having passed all three CFA examinations in three consecutive attempts."
"The CFA designation is globally recognized and attests to a charterholder's success in a rigorous and comprehensive study program in the field of investment management and research analysis."	"As a CFA charterholder, I am the most qualified to manage client investments."
"The credibility that the CFA designation affords and the skills the CFA Program cultivates are key assets for my future career development."	"As a CFA charterholder, Jane White provides the best value in trade execution."

(continued)

Exhibit 3	*Continued*

Proper References	Improper References
"I enrolled in the CFA Program to obtain the highest set of credentials in the global investment management industry."	"Enrolling as a candidate in the CFA Program ensures one of becoming better at valuing debt securities."
"I passed Level I of the CFA exam."	"CFA, Level II"
"I am a 2010 Level III CFA candidate."	"CFA, Expected 2011"
"I passed all three levels of the CFA Program and will be eligible for the CFA charter upon completion of the required work experience."	
"As a CFA charterholder, I am committed to the highest ethical standards."	

Proper Usage of the CFA Marks

Upon obtaining the CFA charter from CFA Institute, charterholders are given the right to use the CFA marks, including Chartered Financial Analyst®, CFA®, and the CFA Logo (a certification mark):

These marks are registered by CFA Institute in countries around the world.

The Chartered Financial Analyst and CFA marks must always be used either after a charterholder's name or as adjectives (never as nouns) in written documents or oral conversations. For example, to refer to oneself as "a CFA" or "a Chartered Financial Analyst" is improper.

The CFA Logo certification mark is used by charterholders as a distinctive visual symbol of the CFA designation that can be easily recognized by employers, colleagues, and clients. As a certification mark, it must be used only to directly refer to an individual charterholder or group of charterholders.

Exhibit 4 provides examples of correct and incorrect use of the marks. CFA charterholders should refer to the complete guidelines published by CFA Institute for additional and up-to-date information and examples illustrating proper and improper use of the CFA Logo, Chartered Financial Analyst mark, and CFA mark. These guidelines and the CFA logo are available on the CFA Institute website at www.cfainstitute.org/.

Exhibit 4	Correct and Incorrect Use of the Chartered Financial Analyst and CFA Marks	
Correct	**Incorrect**	**Principle**
He is one of two CFA charterholders in the company.	He is one of two CFAs in the company.	The CFA and Chartered Financial Analyst designations must always be used as adjectives, never as nouns or common names.
He earned the right to use the Chartered Financial Analyst designation.	He is a Chartered Financial Analyst.	
Jane Smith, CFA	Jane Smith, C.F.A.	No periods.

Exhibit 4	Continued

Correct	Incorrect	Principle
	John Doe, cfa	Always capitalize the letters "CFA".
John Jones, CFA	John, a CFA-type portfolio manager. The focus is on Chartered Financial Analysis. CFA-equivalent program. Swiss-CFA	Do not alter the designation to create new words or phrases.
John Jones, Chartered Financial Analyst	Jones Chartered Financial Analysts, Inc.	The designation must not be used as part of the name of a firm.
Jane Smith, CFA John Doe, Chartered Financial Analyst	Jane Smith, **CFA** John Doe, **Chartered Financial Analyst**	The CFA designation should not be given more prominence (e.g., larger, bold) than the charterholder's name.
Level I candidate in the CFA Program.	Chartered Financial Analyst (CFA), September 2011.	Candidates in the CFA Program must not cite the expected date of exam completion and award of charter.
Passed Level I of the CFA examination in 2010.	CFA Level I. CFA degree expected in 2011.	No designation exists for someone who has passed Level I, Level II, or Level III of the exam. The CFA designation should not be referred to as a degree.
I have passed all three levels of the CFA Program and may be eligible for the CFA charter upon completion of the required work experience.	CFA (Passed Finalist)	A candidate who has passed Level III but has not yet received his or her charter cannot use the CFA or Chartered Financial Analyst designation.
CFA, 2009, CFA Institute, (optional: Charlottesville, Virginia, USA)	CFA, 2009, CFA Society of the UK	In citing the designation in a resume, a charterholder should use the date that he or she received the designation and should cite CFA Institute as the conferring body.

Recommended Procedures for Compliance

Misuse of a member's CFA designation or CFA candidacy or improper reference to it is common by those in a member's or candidate's firm who do not possess knowledge of the requirements of Standard VII(B). As an appropriate step to reduce this risk, members and candidates should disseminate written information about Standard VII(B) and the accompanying guidance to their firm's legal, compliance, public relations, and marketing departments (see www.cfainstitute.org/).

For materials that refer to employees' affiliation with CFA Institute, members and candidates should encourage their firms to create templates that are approved by a central authority (such as the compliance department) as being consistent with Standard VII(B). This practice promotes consistency and accuracy in the firm of references to CFA Institute membership, the CFA designation, and CFA candidacy.

Application of the Standard

Example 1   (Passing Exams in Consecutive Years): An advertisement for AZ Investment Advisors states that all the firm's principals are CFA charterholders and all passed the three examinations on their first attempt. The advertisement prominently links this fact to the notion that AZ's mutual funds have achieved superior performance.

> *Comment*: AZ may state that all principals passed the three examinations on the first try as long as this statement is true, but it must not be linked to performance or imply superior ability. Implying that 1) CFA charterholders achieve better investment results and 2) those who pass the exams on the first try may be more successful than those who do not violates Standard VII(B).

Example 2   (Right to Use CFA Designation): Five years after receiving his CFA charter, Louis Vasseur resigns his position as an investment analyst and spends the next two years traveling abroad. Because he is not actively engaged in the investment profession, he does not file a completed Professional Conduct Statement with CFA Institute and does not pay his CFA Institute membership dues. At the conclusion of his travels, Vasseur becomes a self-employed analyst accepting assignments as an independent contractor. Without reinstating his CFA Institute membership by filing his Professional Conduct Statement and paying his dues, he prints business cards that display "CFA" after his name.

> *Comment*: Vasseur has violated Standard VII(B) because his right to use the CFA designation was suspended when he failed to file his Professional Conduct Statement and stopped paying dues. Therefore, he no longer is able to state or imply that he is an active CFA charterholder. When Vasseur files his Professional Conduct Statement, resumes paying CFA Institute dues to activate his membership, and completes the CFA Institute reinstatement procedures he will be eligible to use the CFA designation.

Example 3   ("Retired" CFA Institute Membership Status): After a 25-year career, James Simpson retires from his firm. Because he is not actively engaged in the investment profession, he does not file a completed Professional Conduct Statement with CFA Institute and does not pay his CFA Institute membership dues. Simpson designs a plain business card (without a corporate logo) to hand out to friends with his new contact details, and he continues to put "CFA" after his name.

> *Comment*: Simpson has violated Standard VII(B). Because he failed to file his Professional Conduct Statement and ceased paying dues, his membership has been suspended and he must give up the right to use the CFA designation. CFA Institute has procedures, however, for reclassifying a member and charterholder as "retired" and reducing the annual dues. If he wants to obtain retired status, he needs to file the appropriate paperwork with CFA Institute. When Simpson receives his notification from CFA Institute that his membership has been reclassified as retired and he resumes paying reduced dues, his membership will be reactivated and his right to use the CFA designation will be reinstated.

Example 4   (CFA Logo—Individual Use Only): Asia Futures Ltd is a small quantitative investment advisory firm. The firm takes great pride in the fact that all its employees are CFA charterholders. To underscore this fact, the firm's senior partner is proposing to change the firm's letterhead to include the following:

Asia Futures Ltd.

> *Comment*: The CFA Logo is a certification mark intended to identify *individual* charterholders and must not be incorporated in a company name, confused with a company logo, or placed in such close proximity to a company name or logo as to give the reader the idea that the certification mark certifies the company. The only appropriate use of the CFA logo is on the business card or letterhead of each individual CFA charterholder.

Example 5   (Stating Facts about CFA Designation and Program): Rhonda Reese has been a CFA charterholder since 2000. In a conversation with a friend who is considering enrolling in the CFA Program, she states that she has learned a great deal from the CFA Program and that many firms require their employees to be CFA charterholders. She would recommend the CFA Program to anyone pursuing a career in investment management.

> *Comment*: Reese's comments comply with Standard VII(B). Her statements refer to facts: The CFA Program enhanced her knowledge, and many firms require the CFA designation for their investment professionals.

Example 6   (Order of Professional and Academic Designations): Tatiana Prittima has earned both her CFA designation and a PhD in finance. She would like to cite both her accomplishments on her business card but is unsure of the proper method for doing so.

> *Comment*: The order of designations cited on such items as resumes and business cards is a matter of personal preference. Prittima is free to cite the CFA designation either before or after citing her PhD.

PRACTICE PROBLEMS FOR READING 2

Unless otherwise stated in the question, all individuals in the following questions are CFA Institute members or candidates in the CFA Program and, therefore, are subject to the CFA Institute Code of Ethics and Standards of Professional Conduct.

1. Smith, a research analyst with a brokerage firm, decides to change his recommendation for the common stock of Green Company, Inc., from a "buy" to a "sell." He mails this change in investment advice to all the firm's clients on Wednesday. The day after the mailing, a client calls with a buy order for 500 shares of Green Company. In this circumstance, Smith should:

    A. accept the order.

    B. advise the customer of the change in recommendation before accepting the order.

    C. not accept the order because it is contrary to the firm's recommendation.

2. Which statement about a manager's use of client brokerage commissions violates the Code and Standards?

    A. A client may direct a manager to use that client's brokerage commissions to purchase goods and services for that client.

    B. Client brokerage commissions should be used to benefit the client and should be commensurate with the value of the brokerage and research services received.

    C. Client brokerage commissions may be directed to pay for the investment manager's operating expenses.

3. Jamison is a junior research analyst with Howard & Howard, a brokerage and investment banking firm. Howard & Howard's mergers and acquisitions department has represented the Britland Company in all of its acquisitions for the past 20 years. Two of Howard & Howard's senior officers are directors of various Britland subsidiaries. Jamison has been asked to write a research report on Britland. What is the best course of action for her to follow?

    A. Jamison may write the report but must refrain from expressing any opinions because of the special relationships between the two companies.

    B. Jamison should not write the report because the two Howard & Howard officers serve as directors for subsidiaries of Britland.

    C. Jamison may write the report if she discloses the special relationships with the company in the report.

4. Which of the following statements clearly *conflicts* with the recommended procedures for compliance presented in the CFA Institute *Standards of Practice Handbook*?

    A. Firms should disclose to clients the personal investing policies and procedures established for their employees.

    B. Prior approval must be obtained for the personal investment transactions of all employees.

    C. For confidentiality reasons, personal transactions and holdings should not be reported to employers unless mandated by regulatory organizations.

5. Bronson provides investment advice to the board of trustees of a private university endowment fund. The trustees have provided Bronson with the fund's financial information, including planned expenditures. Bronson receives a phone call on Friday afternoon from Murdock, a prominent alumnus, requesting that Bronson fax him comprehensive financial information about

the fund. According to Murdock, he has a potential contributor but needs the information that day to close the deal and cannot contact any of the trustees. Based on the CFA Institute Standards, Bronson should:

   A. send Murdock the information because disclosure would benefit the client.

   B. not send Murdock the information to preserve confidentiality.

   C. send Murdock the information, provided Bronson promptly notifies the trustees.

6. Miller heads the research department of a large brokerage firm. The firm has many analysts, some of whom are subject to the Code and Standards. If Miller delegates some supervisory duties, which statement best describes her responsibilities under the Code and Standards?

   A. Miller's supervisory responsibilities do not apply to those subordinates who are not subject to the Code and Standards.

   B. Miller no longer has supervisory responsibility for those duties delegated to her subordinates.

   C. Miller retains supervisory responsibility for all subordinates despite her delegation of some duties.

7. Willier is the research analyst responsible for following Company X. All the information he has accumulated and documented suggests that the outlook for the company's new products is poor, so the stock should be rated a weak "hold." During lunch, however, Willier overhears a financial analyst from another firm whom he respects offer opinions that conflict with Willier's forecasts and expectations. Upon returning to his office, Willier releases a strong "buy" recommendation to the public. Willier:

   A. violated the Standards by failing to distinguish between facts and opinions in his recommendation.

   B. violated the Standards because he did not have a reasonable and adequate basis for his recommendation.

   C. was in full compliance with the Standards.

8. An investment management firm has been hired by ETV Corporation to work on an additional public offering for the company. The firm's brokerage unit now has a "sell" recommendation on ETV, but the head of the investment banking department has asked the head of the brokerage unit to change the recommendation from "sell" to "buy." According to the Standards, the head of the brokerage unit would be permitted to:

   A. increase the recommendation by no more than one increment (in this case, to a "hold" recommendation).

   B. place the company on a restricted list and give only factual information about the company.

   C. assign a new analyst to decide if the stock deserves a higher rating.

9. Albert and Tye, who recently started their own investment advisory business, have registered to take the Level III CFA examination. Albert's business card reads, "Judy Albert, CFA Level II." Tye has not put anything about the CFA designation on his business card, but promotional material that he designed for the business describes the CFA requirements and indicates that Tye participates in the CFA Program and has completed Levels I and II. According to the Standards:

   A. Albert has violated the Standards but Tye has not.

   B. Tye has violated the Standards but Albert has not.

   C. both Albert and Tye have violated the Standards.

10. Scott works for a regional brokerage firm. He estimates that Walkton Industries will increase its dividend by US$1.50 a share during the next year. He realizes that this increase is contingent on pending legislation that would, if enacted, give Walkton a substantial tax break. The U.S. representative for Walkton's home district has told Scott that, although she is lobbying hard for the bill and prospects for its passage are favorable, concern of the U.S. Congress over the federal deficit could cause the tax bill to be voted down. Walkton Industries has not made any statements about a change in dividend policy. Scott writes in his research report, "We expect Walkton's stock price to rise by at least US$8.00 a share by the end of the year because the dividend will increase by US$1.50 a share. Investors buying the stock at the current time should expect to realize a total return of at least 15 percent on the stock." According to the Standards:

   A. Scott violated the Standards because he used material inside information.

   B. Scott violated the Standards because he failed to separate opinion from fact.

   C. Scott violated the Standards by basing his research on uncertain predictions of future government action.

11. Which *one* of the following actions will help to ensure the fair treatment of brokerage firm clients when a new investment recommendation is made?

   A. Informing all people in the firm in advance that a recommendation is to be disseminated.

   B. Distributing recommendations to institutional clients prior to individual accounts.

   C. Minimizing the time between the decision and the dissemination of a recommendation.

12. The mosaic theory holds that an analyst:

   A. violates the Code and Standards if the analyst fails to have knowledge of and comply with applicable laws.

   B. can use material public information and nonmaterial nonpublic information in the analyst's analysis.

   C. should use all available and relevant information in support of an investment recommendation.

13. Jurgen is a portfolio manager. One of her firm's clients has told Jurgen that he will compensate her beyond the compensation provided by her firm on the basis of the capital appreciation of his portfolio each year. Jurgen should:

   A. turn down the additional compensation because it will result in conflicts with the interests of other clients' accounts.

   B. turn down the additional compensation because it will create undue pressure on her to achieve strong short-term performance.

   C. obtain permission from her employer prior to accepting the compensation arrangement.

14. One of the discretionary accounts managed by Farnsworth is the Jones Corporation employee profit-sharing plan. Jones, the company president, recently asked Farnsworth to vote the shares in the profit-sharing plan in favor of the slate of directors nominated by Jones Corporation and against the directors sponsored by a dissident stockholder group. Farnsworth does not want to lose this account because he directs all the account's trades to a brokerage firm that provides Farnsworth with useful information about tax-free investments. Although this information is not of value in managing

the Jones Corporation account, it does help in managing several other accounts. The brokerage firm providing this information also offers the lowest commissions for trades and provides best execution. Farnsworth investigates the director issue, concludes that the management-nominated slate is better for the long-run performance of the company than the dissident group's slate, and votes accordingly. Farnsworth:

A. violated the Standards in voting the shares in the manner requested by Jones but not in directing trades to the brokerage firm.

B. did not violate the Standards in voting the shares in the manner requested by Jones or in directing trades to the brokerage firm.

C. violated the Standards in directing trades to the brokerage firm but not in voting the shares as requested by Jones.

15. Brown works for an investment counseling firm. Green, a new client of the firm, is meeting with Brown for the first time. Green used another counseling firm for financial advice for years, but she has switched her account to Brown's firm. After spending a few minutes getting acquainted, Brown explains to Green that she has discovered a highly undervalued stock that offers large potential gains. She recommends that Green purchase the stock. Brown has committed a violation of the Standards. What should she have done differently?

A. Brown should have determined Green's needs, objectives, and tolerance for risk before making a recommendation of any type of security.

B. Brown should have thoroughly explained the characteristics of the company to Green, including the characteristics of the industry in which the company operates.

C. Brown should have explained her qualifications, including her education, training, experience, and the meaning of the CFA designation.

16. Grey recommends the purchase of a mutual fund that invests solely in long-term U.S. Treasury bonds. He makes the following statements to his clients:

Statement 1 "The payment of the bonds is guaranteed by the U.S. government; therefore, the default risk of the bonds is virtually zero."

Statement 2 "If you invest in the mutual fund, you will earn a 10 percent rate of return each year for the next several years based on historical performance of the market."

Did Grey's statements violate the CFA Institute Code and Standards?

A. Neither statement violated the Code and Standards.

B. Only Statement 1 violated the Code and Standards.

C. Only Statement 2 violated the Code and Standards.

17. Anderb, a portfolio manager for XYZ Investment Management Company—a registered investment organization that advises investment firms and private accounts—was promoted to that position three years ago. Bates, her supervisor, is responsible for reviewing Anderb's portfolio account transactions and her required monthly reports of personal stock transactions. Anderb has been using Jonelli, a broker, almost exclusively for brokerage transactions for the portfolio account. For securities in which Jonelli's firm makes a market, Jonelli has been giving Anderb lower prices for personal purchases and higher prices for personal sales than Jonelli gives to Anderb's portfolio accounts and other investors. Anderb has been filing monthly reports with Bates only for those months in which she has no personal transactions, which is about every

fourth month. Which of the following is *most likely* to be a violation of the Code and Standards?

    A. Anderb failed to disclose to her employer her personal transactions.

    B. Anderb owned the same securities as those of her clients.

    C. Bates allowed Anderb to use Jonelli as her broker for personal trades.

18. Which of the following is a correct statement of a member's or candidate's duty under the Code and Standards?

    A. In the absence of specific applicable law or other regulatory requirements, the Code and Standards govern the member's or candidate's actions.

    B. A member or candidate is required to comply only with applicable local laws, rules, regulations, or customs, even though the Code and Standards may impose a higher degree of responsibility or a higher duty on the member or candidate.

    C. A member or candidate who trades securities in a securities market where no applicable local laws or stock exchange rules regulate the use of material nonpublic information may take investment action based on material nonpublic information.

19. Ward is scheduled to visit the corporate headquarters of Evans Industries. Ward expects to use the information he obtains there to complete his research report on Evans stock. Ward learns that Evans plans to pay all of Ward's expenses for the trip, including costs of meals, hotel room, and air transportation. Which of the following actions would be the *best* course for Ward to take under the Code and Standards?

    A. Accept the expense-paid trip and write an objective report.

    B. Pay for all travel expenses, including costs of meals and incidental items.

    C. Accept the expense-paid trip but disclose the value of the services accepted in the report.

20. Which of the following statements is *correct* under the Code and Standards?

    A. CFA Institute members and candidates are prohibited from undertaking independent practice in competition with their employer.

    B. Written consent from the employer is necessary to permit independent practice that could result in compensation or other benefits in competition with a member's or candidate's employer.

    C. Members and candidates are prohibited from making arrangements or preparations to go into a competitive business before terminating their relationship with their employer.

21. Smith is a financial analyst with XYZ Brokerage Firm. She is preparing a purchase recommendation on JNI Corporation. Which of the following situations is *most likely* to represent a conflict of interest for Smith that would have to be disclosed?

    A. Smith frequently purchases items produced by JNI.

    B. XYZ holds for its own account a substantial common stock position in JNI.

    C. Smith's brother-in-law is a supplier to JNI.

22. Michelieu tells a prospective client, "I may not have a long-term track record yet, but I'm sure that you'll be very pleased with my recommendations and service. In the three years that I've been in the business, my equity-oriented clients have averaged a total return of more than 26 percent a year." The statement is true, but Michelieu only has a few clients, and one of his clients took a large position in a penny stock (against Michelieu's advice) and realized

a huge gain. This large return caused the average of all of Michelieu's clients to exceed 26 percent a year. Without this one investment, the average gain would have been 8 percent a year. Has Michelieu violated the Standards?

A. No.

B. Yes, because the statement misrepresents Michelieu's track record.

C. Yes, because the Standards prohibit members from guaranteeing future results.

23. An investment banking department of a brokerage firm often receives material nonpublic information that could have considerable value if used in advising the firm's brokerage clients. In order to conform to the Code and Standards, which one of the following is the best policy for the brokerage firm?

A. Permanently prohibit both "buy" and "sell" recommendations of the stocks of clients of the investment banking department.

B. Establish physical and informational barriers within the firm to prevent the exchange of information between the investment banking and brokerage operations.

C. Monitor the exchange of information between the investment banking department and the brokerage operation.

24. Stewart has been hired by Goodner Industries, Inc., to manage its pension fund. Stewart's duty of loyalty, prudence, and care is owed to:

A. the management of Goodner.

B. the participants and beneficiaries of Goodner's pension plan.

C. the shareholders of Goodner.

25. Which of the following statements is a stated purpose of disclosure in Standard VI(C)—Referral Fees?

A. Disclosure will allow the client to request discounted service fees.

B. Disclosure will help the client evaluate any possible partiality shown in the recommendation of services.

C. Disclosure means advising a prospective client about the referral arrangement once a formal client relationship has been established.

26. Rose, a portfolio manager for a local investment advisory firm, is planning to sell a portion of his personal investment portfolio to cover the costs of his child's academic tuition. Rose wants to sell a portion of his holdings in Household Products, but his firm recently upgraded the stock to "strong buy." Which of the following describes Rose's options under the Code and Standards?

A. Based on his firm's "buy" recommendation, Rose cannot sell the shares because he would be improperly prospering from the inflated recommendation.

B. Rose is free to sell his personal holdings once his firm is properly informed of his intentions.

C. Rose can sell his personal holdings but only when a client of the firm places an order to buy shares of Household.

27. A former hedge fund manager, Jackman, has decided to launch a new private wealth management firm. From his prior experiences, he believes the new firm needs to achieve US$1 million in assets under management in the first year. Jackman offers a $10,000 incentive to any adviser who joins his firm with the minimum of $200,000 in committed investments. Jackman places notice of the opening on several industry web portals and career search sites. Which of the following is *correct* according to the Code and Standards?

A. A member or candidate is eligible for the new position and incentive if he or she can arrange for enough current clients to switch to the new firm and if the member or candidate discloses the incentive fee.

B. A member or candidate may not accept employment with the new firm because Jackman's incentive offer violates the Code and Standards.

C. A member or candidate is not eligible for the new position unless he or she is currently unemployed because soliciting the clients of the member's or candidate's current employer is prohibited.

28. Carter works for Invest Today, a local asset management firm. A broker that provides Carter with proprietary research through client brokerage arrangements is offering a new trading service. The broker is offering low-fee, execution-only trades to complement its traditional full-service, execution-and-research trades. To entice Carter and other asset managers to send additional business its way, the broker will apply the commissions paid on the new service toward satisfying the brokerage commitment of the prior full-service arrangements. Carter has always been satisfied with the execution provided on the full-service trades, and the new low-fee trades are comparable to the fees of other brokers currently used for the accounts that prohibit soft dollar arrangements.

A. Carter can trade for his accounts that prohibit soft dollar arrangements under the new low-fee trading scheme.

B. Carter cannot use the new trading scheme because the commissions are prohibited by the soft dollar restrictions of the accounts.

C. Carter should trade only through the new low-fee scheme and should increase his trading volume to meet his required commission commitment.

29. Rule has worked as a portfolio manager for a large investment management firm for the past 10 years. Rule earned his CFA charter last year and has decided to open his own investment management firm. After leaving his current employer, Rule creates some marketing material for his new firm. He states in the material, "In earning the CFA charter, a highly regarded credential in the investment management industry, I further enhanced the portfolio management skills learned during my professional career. While completing the examination process in three consecutive years, I consistently received the highest possible scores on the topics of Ethics, Alternative Investments, and Portfolio Management." Has Rule violated Standard VII(B)—Reference to CFA Institute, the CFA Designation, and the CFA Program in his marketing material?

A. Rule violated Standard VII(B) in stating that he completed the exams in three consecutive years.

B. Rule violated Standard VII(B) in stating that he received the highest scores in the topics of Ethics, Alternative Investments, and Portfolio Management.

C. Rule did not violate Standard VII(B).

30. Stafford is a portfolio manager for a specialized real estate mutual fund. Her firm clearly describes in the fund's prospectus its soft dollar policies. Stafford decides that entering the CFA Program will enhance her investment decision-making skill and decides to use the fund's soft dollar account to pay the registration and exam fees for the CFA Program. Which of the following statements is *most likely* correct?

A. Stafford did not violate the Code and Standards because the prospectus informed investors of the fund's soft dollar policies.

    B. Stafford violated the Code and Standards because improving her investment skills is not a reasonable use of the soft dollar account.

    C. Stafford violated the Code and Standards because the CFA Program does not meet the definition of research allowed to be purchased with brokerage commissions.

31. Long has been asked to be the keynote speaker at an upcoming investment conference. The event is being hosted by one of the third-party investment managers currently used by his pension fund. The manager offers to cover all conference and travel costs for Long and make the conference registrations free for three additional members of his investment management team. To ensure that the conference obtains the best speakers, the host firm has arranged for an exclusive golf outing for the day following the conference on a local championship-caliber course. Which of the following is *least likely* to violate Standard I(B)?

    A. Long may accept only the offer to have his conference-related expenses paid by the host firm.

    B. Long may accept the offer to have his conference-related expenses paid and may attend the exclusive golf outing at the expense of the hosting firm.

    C. Long may accept the entire package of incentives offered to speak at this conference.

32. Andrews, a private wealth manager, is conducting interviews for a new research analyst for his firm. One of the candidates is Wright, an analyst with a local investment bank. During the interview, while Wright is describing his analytical skills, he mentions a current merger in which his firm is acting as the adviser. Andrews has heard rumors of a possible merger between the two companies, but no releases have been made by the companies concerned. Which of the following actions by Andrews is *least likely* a violation of the Code and Standards?

    A. Waiting until the next day before trading on the information to allow time for it to become public.

    B. Notifying all investment managers in his firm of the new information so none of their clients are disadvantaged.

    C. Placing the securities mentioned as part of the merger on the firm's restricted trading list.

33. Pietro, president of Local Bank, has hired the bank's market maker, Vogt, to seek a merger partner. Local is currently not listed on a stock exchange and has not reported that it is seeking strategic alternatives. Vogt has discussed the possibility of a merger with several firms, but they have all decided to wait until after the next period's financial data are available. The potential buyers believe the results will be worse than the results of prior periods and will allow them to pay less for Local Bank.

Pietro wants to increase the likelihood of structuring a merger deal quickly. Which of the following actions would *most likely* be a violation of the Code and Standards?

    A. Pietro could instruct Local Bank to issue a press release announcing that it has retained Vogt to find a merger partner.

    B. Pietro could place a buy order for 2,000 shares (or four times the average weekly volume) through Vogt for his personal account.

    C. After confirming with Local's chief financial officer, Pietro could instruct Local to issue a press release reaffirming the firm's prior announced earnings guidance for the full fiscal year.

34. ABC Investment Management acquires a new, very large account with two concentrated positions. The firm's current policy is to add new accounts for the purpose of performance calculation after the first full month of management. Cupp is responsible for calculating the firm's performance returns. Before the end of the initial month, Cupp notices that one of the significant holdings of the new accounts is acquired by another company, causing the value of the investment to double. Because of this holding, Cupp decides to account for the new portfolio as of the date of transfer, thereby allowing ABC Investment to reap the positive impact of that month's portfolio return.

    A. Cupp did not violate the Code and Standards because the GIPS standards allow composites to be updated on the date of large external cash flows.

    B. Cupp did not violate the Code and Standards because companies are allowed to determine when to incorporate new accounts into their composite calculation.

    C. Cupp violated the Code and Standards because the inclusion of the new account produces an inaccurate calculation of the monthly results according to the firm's stated policies.

35. Cannan has been working from home on weekends and occasionally saves correspondence with clients and completed work on her home computer. Because of worsening market conditions, Cannan is one of several employees released by her firm. While Cannan is looking for a new job, she uses the files she saved at home to request letters of recommendation from former clients. She also provides to prospective clients some of the reports as examples of her abilities.

    A. Cannan is violating the Code and Standards because she did not receive permission from her former employer to keep or use the files after her employment ended.

    B. Cannan did not violate the Code and Standards because the files were created and saved on her own time and computer.

    C. Cannan violated the Code and Standards because she is prohibited from saving files on her home computer.

36. Quinn sat for the Level III CFA exam this past weekend. He updates his resume with the following statement:

    "In finishing the CFA Program, I improved my skills related to researching investments and managing portfolios. I will be eligible for the CFA charter upon completion of the required work experience."

    A. Quinn violated the Code and Standards by claiming he improved his skills through the CFA Program.

    B. Quinn violated the Code and Standards by incorrectly stating that he is eligible for the CFA charter.

    C. Quinn did not violate the Code and Standards with his resume update.

37. During a round of golf, Rodriguez, chief financial officer of Mega Retail, mentions to Hart, a local investment adviser and long-time personal friend, that Mega is having an exceptional sales quarter. Rodriguez expects the results to be almost 10 percent above the current estimates. The next day, Hart initiates the purchase of a large stake in the local exchange-traded retail fund for her personal account.

    A. Hart violated the Code and Standards by investing in the exchange-traded fund that included Mega Retail.

    B. Hart did not violate the Code and Standards because she did not invest directly in securities of Mega Retail.

    C. Rodriguez did not violate the Code and Standards because the comments made to Hart were not intended to solicit an investment in Mega Retail.

38. Park is very frustrated after taking her Level II exam. While she was studying for the exam, to supplement the curriculum provided, she ordered and used study material from a third-party provider. Park believes the additional material focused her attention on specific topic areas that were not tested while ignoring other areas. She posts the following statement on the provider's discussion board: "I am very dissatisfied with your firm's CFA Program Level II material. I found the exam extremely difficult and myself unprepared for specific questions after using your product. How could your service provide such limited instructional resources on the analysis of inventories and taxes when the exam had multiple questions about them? I will not recommend your products to other candidates."

    A. Park violated the Code and Standards by purchasing third-party review material.

    B. Park violated the Code and Standards by providing her opinion on the difficulty of the exam.

    C. Park violated the Code and Standards by providing specific information on topics tested on the exam.

39. Paper was recently terminated as one of a team of five managers of an equity fund. The fund had two value-focused managers and terminated one of them to reduce costs. In a letter sent to prospective employers, Paper presents, with written permission of the firm, the performance history of the fund to demonstrate his past success.

    A. Paper did not violate the Code and Standards.

    B. Paper violated the Code and Standards by claiming the performance of the entire fund as his own.

    C. Paper violated the Code and Standards by including the historical results of his prior employer.

40. Townsend was recently appointed to the board of directors of a youth golf program that is the local chapter of a national not-for-profit organization. The program is beginning a new fund-raising campaign to expand the number of annual scholarships it provides. Townsend believes many of her clients make annual donations to charity. The next week in her regular newsletter to all clients, she includes a small section discussing the fundraising campaign and her position on the organization's board.

    A. Townsend did not violate the Code and Standards.

    B. Townsend violated the Code and Standards by soliciting donations from her clients through the newsletter.

    C. Townsend violated the Code and Standards by not getting approval of the organization before soliciting her clients.

The following information relates to Questions 41–46[1]

Anne Boswin, CFA, is a senior fixed-income analyst at Greenfield Financial Corporation. Boswin develops financial models for predicting changes in bond prices. On the premise that bonds of firms targeted for leveraged buyouts (LBOs) often decline in value, Boswin develops a model to predict which firms are likely to be subject to LBOs.

---

1 This case was written by Sarah W. Peck, PhD.

Boswin works closely with another analyst, Robert Acertado, CFA. Acertado uses Boswin's model frequently to identify potential LBO targets for further research. Using the model and his extensive research skills, Acertado makes timely investment recommendations and develops a strong track record.

Based on this record, Acertado receives an employment offer from the asset management division of Smith & Garner Investments, Inc., a diversified financial services firm. With Boswin's consent, Acertado downloads the model before leaving Greenfield.

At Smith & Garner, Acertado presents the idea of predicting LBO targets as a way to identify bonds that might decline in value and thus be good sell recommendations. After Acertado walks his boss through the model, the supervisor comments, "I like your idea and your model, Robert. I can see that we made the right decision in hiring you."

Because Smith & Garner has both an Investment Banking (IB) and Asset Management (AM) division, Acertado's supervisor reminds him that he should not attempt to contact or engage in conversation with anyone from the Investment Banking division. The supervisor also directs him to eat in the East end of the company cafeteria. "The West end is reserved for the IB folks, and you may laugh at this, but we actually put up a wall between the two ends. If anyone were to accuse us of not having a firewall, we could actually point to it!" Robert's supervisor also tells him, "There should be absolutely no conversation about divisional business while in the hall and elevator that serves as a common access to the cafeteria for both divisions. We are very strict about this."

The following week, Acertado is riding alone in the elevator when it stops on an IB floor. As the doors begin to slide open, Acertado hears a voice whispering, "I am so pleased that we were able to put the financing together for Country Industries. I was concerned because the leverage will go to 80%—higher than our typical deal." As soon as the doors open enough to reveal that the elevator is occupied, all conversation stops.

Late that afternoon, Acertado uses the LBO model to measure the probability of Country Industries receiving an LBO offer. According to the model, the probability is 62%—slightly more than the 60% Acertado generally requires before conducting additional research. It is late in the afternoon and Acertado has little time to research the matter fully before the end of the trading day. He checks his inputs to the model. In the interest of time, Acertado immediately recommends selling Country Industries' senior bonds held in any long-only accounts. He also recommends establishing positions in derivatives contracts that will benefit from a decline in the value of Country Industries' bonds.

The next morning, after the firm has established the derivatives positions he recommended, Acertado calls Boswin. Knowing that his former associate will be preparing Greenfield's monthly newsletter, he tells her, "I ran Country Industries through your model and I think it is likely that they will receive an LBO offer." Acertado explains some of the inputs he used in the model. At the conclusion of the conversation Boswin responds, "You may be right. Country Industries sounds like a possible LBO candidate, and thus, a sell rating on their senior bonds would be in order. If I'm lucky, I can finish researching the issue in time to include the recommendation in the upcoming newsletter. Thanks. It was good talking with you, Robert."

After the conversation with Acertado, Boswin quickly runs Country Industries through the model. Based on her inputs, the model calculates that the probability of an LBO is 40 percent—not enough, in Boswin's opinion, to justify further research. She wonders if there is a discrepancy between her inputs and Acertado's. Pressed for time, Boswin resumes her work on the upcoming newsletter rather than investigating the matter.

Acertado soon begins searching the internet for information on companies that the model predicts have more than a 60% probability of an LBO offer. He scours blogs and company websites looking for signs of a potential offer. He uses evidence of rumored offers in developing sell recommendations on various corporations' bonds.

41. When downloading the model from Greenfield Financial Corporation, does Acertado violate any CFA Institute Standards of Practice and Professional Conduct?

    A. No.

    B. Yes, because he does not have written permission from Boswin.

    C. Yes, because he does not have permission from Greenfield Financial Corporation.

42. When using the model at Smith & Garner, Acertado is *least likely* to violate the Standard relating to:

    A. misrepresentation.

    B. loyalty to employer.

    C. material nonpublic information.

43. When making the recommendation regarding Country Industries, does Acertado violate any CFA Institute Standards?

    A. No.

    B. Yes, relating to diligence and reasonable basis.

    C. Yes, relating to material nonpublic information.

44. In his phone conversation with Boswin, Acertado *least likely* violates the CFA Institute Standard relating to:

    A. suitability.

    B. integrity of capital markets.

    C. preservation of confidentiality.

45. When analyzing the probability of an LBO of Country Industries, does Boswin violate any CFA Institute Standards?

    A. No.

    B. Yes, relating to independence and objectivity.

    C. Yes, relating to diligence and reasonable basis.

46. When searching blogs, does Acertado violate any CFA Institute Standards?

    A. No.

    B. Yes, because he misuses company resources.

    C. Yes, because he seeks inside information on the blogs.

The following information relates to Questions 47–52[2]

Erik Brecksen, CFA, a portfolio manager at Apfelbaum Kapital, is a strong advocate of the CFA program. He displays the CFA logo on both his letterhead and business cards and prefers to hire only CFA candidates or charterholders. Brecksen recently recruited Hans Grohl, a CFA candidate and recent MBA graduate from a top university with excellent quantitative analysis skills. After receiving Grohl's letter of acceptance, Brecksen instructs the personnel department to order business cards and letterhead for Grohl, telling them, "Use mine as a template. Just change the name, title, and other information as necessary." When Grohl arrives for his first day of work, he receives business cards and letterhead displaying his name, the firm name, and the CFA logo.

Apfelbaum Kapital stresses "top-down" fundamental analysis and uses a team approach to investment management. The firm's investment professionals, all of whom are CFA charterholders or candidates, attend weekly investment committee

---

2 This case was written by David S. Krause, PhD, and Dorothy C. Kelly, CFA.

meetings. At the meetings, analysts responsible for different industrial sectors present their research and recommendations. Following each presentation, the investment committee, consisting of senior portfolio managers, questions the analyst about the recommendation. If the majority of the committee agrees with the recommendation, the recommendation is approved and the stock is placed on a restricted list while the firm executes the necessary trades.

Apfelbaum considers its research proprietary. It is intended for the sole use of its investment professionals and is not distributed outside the firm. The names of all the investment personnel associated with the sector or investment class are listed on each research report regardless of their actual level of contribution to the report.

On Grohl's first day of work, Brecksen assigns him responsibility for a company that Brecksen covered previously. He provides Grohl with his past research including all of his files and reports. Brecksen instructs Grohl to report back when he has finished his research and is ready to submit his own research report on the company.

Grohl reads Brecksen's old reports before studying the financial statements of the company and its competitors. Taking advantage of his quantitative analysis skills, Grohl then conducts a detailed multi-factor analysis. Afterward, he produces a written buy recommendation using Brecksen's old research reports as a guide for format and submits a draft to Brecksen for review.

Brecksen reviews the work and indicates that he is not familiar with multi-factor analysis. He tells Grohl that he agrees with the buy recommendation, but instructs Grohl to omit the multi-factor analysis from the report. Grohl attempts to defend his research methodology, but is interrupted when Brecksen accepts a phone call. Grohl follows Brecksen's instructions and removes all mention of the multi-factor analysis from the final report. Brecksen presents the completed report at the weekly meeting with both his and Grohl's names listed on the document. After Brecksen's initial presentation, the committee turns to Grohl and asks about his research. Grohl takes the opportunity to mention the multi-factor analysis. Satisfied, the committee votes in favor of the recommendation and congratulates Grohl on his work.

Ottie Zardt, CFA, has worked as a real estate analyst for Apfelbaum for the past 18 months. A new independent rating service has determined that Zardt's recommendations have resulted in an excess return of 12% versus the industry's return of 2.7% for the past twelve months. After learning about the rating service, Zardt immediately updates the promotional material he is preparing for distribution at an upcoming industry conference. He includes a reference to the rating service and quotes its returns results and other information. Before distributing the material at the conference, he adds a footnote stating "Past performance is no guarantee of future success."

47. According to the CFA Institute Standards of Professional Conduct, may Brecksen and Grohl both use the letterhead and business cards provided by Apfelbaum Kapital?

   A. Yes.

   B. No, because candidates may not use the logo.

   C. No, because the logo may not be used on company letterhead.

48. When preparing the initial draft for Brecksen's review, does Grohl violate any CFA Standards?

   A. No.

   B. Yes, because he used Brecksen's research reports without permission.

   C. Yes, because he did not use reasonable judgment in identifying which factors were important to the analysis.

49. When instructing Grohl to eliminate the multi-factor analysis from the research report, does Brecksen violate any CFA Standards?

    A. No.

    B. Yes, relating to record retention.

    C. Yes, relating to diligence and reasonable basis.

50. When removing the multi-factor analysis from his research report, does Grohl violate any CFA Standards?

    A. No.

    B. Yes, because he no longer has a reasonable basis for his recommendation.

    C. Yes, because he is required to make full and fair disclosure of all relevant information.

51. When listing their names on the research report, do Brecksen and Grohl violate any CFA Standards?

    A. No.

    B. Yes, because Brecksen misrepresents his authorship.

    C. Yes, because Grohl should dissociate from the report.

52. When distributing the material at the industry conference, does Zardt violate any CFA Standards?

    A. No.

    B. Yes, because Zardt does not verify the accuracy of the information.

    C. Yes, because analysts cannot claim performance or promote the accuracy of their recommendations.

The following information relates to Questions 53–58[3]

Samuel Telline, CFA, is a portfolio manager at Aiklin Investments with discretionary authority over all of his accounts. One of his clients, Alan Caper, Chief Executive Officer (CEO) of Ellipse Manufacturing, invites Telline to lunch.

At the restaurant, the CEO reveals the reason for the lunch. "As you know Reinhold Partners has made an unsolicited cash offer for all outstanding shares of Ellipse Manufacturing. Reinhold has made it clear that I will not be CEO if they are successful. I can assure you that our shareholders will be better off in the long term if I'm in charge." Caper then shows Telline his projections for a new plan designed to boost both sales and operating margins.

"I know that your firm is the trustee for our firm's Employee Stock Ownership Plan (ESOP). I hope that the trustee will vote in the best interest of our shareholders—and that would be a vote against the takeover offer."

After looking through Caper's business plans, Telline says, "This plan looks good. I will recommend that the trustee vote against the offer."

Caper responds, "I remember my friend Karen Leighton telling me that the Leighton Family's Trust is managed by your firm. Perhaps the trustee could vote those shares against the acquisition as well. Karen Leighton is a close friend. I am sure that she would agree."

Telline responds, "The Family Trust is no longer managed by Aiklin." He adds, "I understand that the Trust is very conservatively managed. I doubt it that it would have holdings in Ellipse Manufacturing." Telline does not mention that although the Family Trust has changed investment managers, Karen Leighton remains an important client at Aiklin with significant personal holdings in Ellipse.

After lunch, Telline meets with Sydney Brown, CFA, trustee of the Ellipse ESOP. He shows her Caper's plan for improvements. "I think the plan is a good one and Caper is

3 This case was written by Sarah W. Peck, PhD.

one of the firm's most profitable accounts. We don't want to lose him." Brown agrees to analyze the plan. After thoroughly analyzing both the plan and the takeover offer, Brown concludes that the takeover offer is best for the shareholders in the ESOP and votes the plan's shares in favor of the takeover offer.

A few months later the acquisition of Ellipse by Reinhold Partners is completed. Caper again meets Telline for lunch. "I received a generous severance package and I'm counting on you to manage my money well for me. While we are on the subject, I would like to be more aggressive with my portfolio. With my severance package, I can take additional risk." Telline and Caper discuss his current financial situation, risk tolerance, and financial objectives throughout lunch. Telline agrees to adjust Caper's investment policy statement (IPS) to reflect his greater appetite for risk and his increased wealth.

Back at the office, Telline realizes that with the severance package, Caper is now his wealthiest client. He also realizes that Caper's increased appetite for risk gives him a risk profile similar to that of another client. He pulls a copy of the other client's investment policy statement (IPS) and reviews it quickly before realizing that the two clients have very different tax situations. Telline quickly revises Caper's IPS to reflect the changes in his financial situation. He uses the other client's IPS as a reference when revising the section relating to Caper's risk tolerance. He then files the revised IPS in Caper's file.

The following week, an Aiklin analyst issues a buy recommendation on a small technology company with a promising software product. Telline reads the report carefully and concludes it would be suitable under Caper's new IPS. Telline places an order for 10,000 shares in Caper's account and then calls Caper to discuss the stock in more detail. Telline does not purchase the stock for any other clients. Although the one client has the same risk profile as Caper, that client does not have cash available in his account and Telline determines that selling existing holdings does not make sense.

In a subsequent telephone conversation, Caper expresses his lingering anger over the takeover. "You didn't do enough to persuade Aiklin's clients to vote against the takeover. Maybe I should look for an investment manager who is more loyal." Telline tries to calm Caper but is unsuccessful. In an attempt to change the topic of conversation, Telline states, "The firm was just notified of our allocation of a long-awaited IPO. Your account should receive a significant allocation. I would hate to see you lose out by moving your account." Caper seems mollified and concludes the phone call, "I look forward to a long-term relationship with you and your firm."

Aiklin distributes a copy of its firm policies regarding IPO allocations to all clients annually. According to the policy, Aiklin allocates IPO shares to each investment manager and each manager has responsibility for allocating shares to accounts for which the IPO is suitable. The statement also discloses that Aiklin offers different levels of service for different fees.

After carefully reviewing the proposed IPO and his client accounts, Telline determines that the IPO is suitable for 11 clients including Caper. Because the deal is oversubscribed, he receives only half of the shares he expected. Telline directs 50% of his allocation to Caper's account and divides the remaining 50% between the other ten accounts, each with a value equal to half of Caper's account.

53. When discussing the Leighton Family Trust, does Telline violate any CFA Institute Standards of Professional Conduct?

   A. No.

   B. Yes, relating to duties to clients.

   C. Yes, relating to misrepresentation.

54. When deciding how to vote the ESOP shares, does Brown violate any CFA Institute Standards?

   A. No.

   B. Yes, relating to loyalty, prudence, and care.

   C. Yes, relating to diligence and reasonable basis.

55. The Standard *least likely* to provide guidance for Telline when working with the clients' investment policy statements would be the Standard relating to:

   A. suitability.

   B. fair dealing.

   C. loyalty, prudence, and care.

56. Does Telline violate any CFA Institute Standards when he places the buy order for shares in the technology company for Caper's account?

   A. No.

   B. Yes, relating to fair dealing.

   C. Yes, relating to diligence and reasonable basis.

57. Is Aiklin's policy with respect to IPO allocations consistent with required and recommended CFA Institute Standards?

   A. Yes.

   B. No, because the IPO policy disadvantages certain clients.

   C. No, because the different levels of service disadvantage certain clients.

58. Does Telline violate any CFA Institute Standards in his allocation of IPO shares to Caper's account?

   A. No.

   B. Yes, because the IPO is not suitable for Caper.

   C. Yes, because he does not treat all his clients fairly.

The following information relates to Questions 59–64[4]

Adam Craw, CFA, is chief executive officer (CEO) of Crawfood, a European private equity firm specializing in food retailers. The retail food industry has been consolidating during the past two years as private equity funds have closed numerous deals and taken many companies private.

   Crawfood recently hired Lillian Voser, a CFA Level II candidate, as a controller. On Voser's first day of work, the head of personnel informs her that by signing the employment contract, Voser agrees to comply with the company's code of ethics and compliance manual. She hands Voser copies of the code and compliance manual without further comment. Voser spends the next hour reading both documents. An excerpt from the compliance manual appears in Exhibit 1.

Exhibit 1	Crawfood Company Compliance Manual Excerpts

   1. Employees must not accept gifts, benefits, compensation, or consideration that competes with, or might reasonably be expected to create a conflict of interest with their employer's interest unless they obtain written consent from all parties involved.

(continued)

---

4 This case was written by Anne-Katrin Scherer, CFA.

Exhibit 1	Continued

2. Officers have responsibility for ensuring that their direct reports—that is, employees whom they directly supervise—adhere to applicable laws, rules, and regulations.

3. Employees in possession of material nonpublic information should make reasonable efforts to achieve public dissemination of the information if such actions would not breach a duty.

4. Employees shall not trade or cause others to trade in securities of food retailers that may be potential takeover targets of their employer.

When she enters her new office that afternoon, Voser finds a large gift basket sent by her sister. The card reads "Congratulations on your new position." The basket is filled with expensive high-quality food items from Greenhornfood—a local small, publicly-traded food retailer, which produces many delicatessen products under its own brand name.

During the next two weeks, Voser meets with all of Crawfood's upper management, including the CEO. In his office, Craw praises Voser's efforts to complete the CFA program. "The program is demanding, but it is worthwhile." Craw then explains his investment strategy for choosing Crawfood's acquisition targets. He points to a large map on the wall with multi-colored pins marking Crawfood's previous takeovers. The map shows acquisitions in all the major cities of Germany with one exception—the home of Crawfood headquarters. Craw remarks, "We are currently in talks for another purchase. Confidentiality prohibits me from discussing it any further, but you will hear more about it soon."

Introduced to Greenhornfood by her sister, Voser quickly becomes a loyal customer. She considers it the best food retailer in the vicinity and she frequently purchases its products.

The following week, the local newspaper features an article about Greenhornfood and its young founders. The article describes the company's loyal and growing customer base as well as its poor quarterly financial results. Voser notes that the stock has steadily declined during the past twelve months. She concludes that the company has an inexperienced management team, but its popular product line and loyal customer base make the company a potential acquisition target. Voser calls her sister and recommends that she purchase Greenhornfood shares because "it would be an attractive acquisition for a larger company." Based on Voser's recommendation, her sister buys €3,000 worth of shares.

During the following two weeks the stock price of Greenhornfood continues to decline. Voser's sister is uncertain of what she should do with her position. She seeks Voser's advice. Voser recommends that her sister wait another few days before making her decision and promises to analyze the situation in the meantime.

While walking by Craw's office the following day, Voser sees a document with Greenhornfood's distinctive logo and overhears the company's name through an open office door. That evening, Voser tells her sister, "with the price decline, the stock is even more attractive." She recommends that her sister increase her position. Based on her recommendation her sister buys an additional €3,000 worth of Greenhornfood shares.

One month later, Crawfood publicly announces the acquisition of Greenhornfood Company at a 20% premium to the previous day's closing price. Following the announcement, Voser's sister boasts about Voser's excellent recommendation and timing to her broker.

Regulatory authorities initiate an investigation into suspicious trading in Greenhornfood shares and options preceding the formal announcement of the acquisition. Craw receives a letter from regulatory authorities stating that he is the subject of a formal investigation into his professional conduct surrounding the acquisition. He learns from the compliance officer that Voser is also under investigation. The compliance officer provides no details and out of respect for Voser's privacy, Craw makes no inquiries.

The situation remains unchanged and the matter is still pending with regulatory authorities several months later when Craw receives his annual Professional Conduct Statement (PCS) from CFA Institute. He reviews the text asking "In the last two years, have you been . . . the subject of . . . any investigation . . . in which your professional conduct, in either a direct or supervisory capacity, was at issue?"

59. Are Excerpts 2 and 3 of Crawfood's compliance procedures consistent with the CFA Institute Standards of Professional Conduct?

    A. Yes.

    B. No, because Excerpt 2 applies only to officers and their direct reports.

    C. No, because Excerpt 3 does not require employees to achieve public dissemination.

60. According to the CFA Institute Standards, must Voser obtain permission from her supervisor before accepting the Greenhornfood gift basket?

    A. No.

    B. Yes, because the value of the basket is higher than €50.

    C. Yes, because consent is required by the company's compliance procedures.

61. When making her initial recommendation to purchase Greenhornfood company shares, Voser *most likely* violates the Standard relating to:

    A. loyalty to employer.

    B. integrity of capital markets.

    C. diligence and reasonable basis.

62. When recommending the purchase of additional Greenhornfood company shares, Voser *least likely* violates the Standard relating to:

    A. loyalty to employer.

    B. integrity of capital markets.

    C. diligence and reasonable basis.

63. Does Craw violate any CFA Institute Standards?

    A. No.

    B. Yes, because he passes material nonpublic information to Voser.

    C. Yes, because he does not make reasonable efforts to prevent violations of applicable law.

64. According to the CFA Standards, Craw must disclose to CFA Institute the investigation into:

    A. his conduct.

    B. Voser's conduct.

    C. neither his conduct nor Voser's conduct.

SOLUTIONS FOR READING 2

1. B is correct. This question involves Standard III(B)—Fair Dealing. Smith disseminated a change in the stock recommendation to his clients but then received a request contrary to that recommendation from a client who probably had not yet received the recommendation. Prior to executing the order, Smith should take additional steps to ensure that the customer has received the change of recommendation. Answer A is incorrect because the client placed the order prior to receiving the recommendation and, therefore, does not have the benefit of Smith's most recent recommendation. Answer C is also incorrect; simply because the client request is contrary to the firm's recommendation does not mean a member can override a direct request by a client. After Smith contacts the client to ensure that the client has received the changed recommendation, if the client still wants to place a buy order for the shares, Smith is obligated to comply with the client's directive.

2. C is correct. This question involves Standard III(A)—Loyalty, Prudence, and Care and the specific topic of soft dollars or soft commissions. Answer C is the correct choice because client brokerage commissions may not be directed to pay for the investment manager's operating expenses. Answer B describes how members and candidates should determine how to use brokerage commissions—that is, if the use is in the best interests of clients and is commensurate with the value of the services provided. Answer A describes a practice that is commonly referred to as "directed brokerage." Because brokerage is an asset of the client and is used to benefit the client, not the manager, such practice does not violate a duty of loyalty to the client. Members and candidates are obligated in all situations to disclose to clients their practices in the use of client brokerage commissions.

3. C is correct. This question involves Standard VI(A)—Disclosure of Conflicts. The question establishes a conflict of interest in which an analyst, Jamison, is asked to write a research report on a company that is a client of the analyst's employer. In addition, two directors of the company are senior officers of Jamison's employer. Both facts establish that there are conflicts of interest that must be disclosed by Jamison in her research report. Answer B is incorrect because an analyst is not prevented from writing a report simply because of the special relationship the analyst's employer has with the company as long as that relationship is disclosed. Answer A is incorrect because whether or not Jamison expresses any opinions in the report is irrelevant to her duty to disclose a conflict of interest. Not expressing opinions does not relieve the analyst of the responsibility to disclose the special relationships between the two companies.

4. C is correct. This question asks about compliance procedures relating to personal investments of members and candidates. The statement in answer C clearly conflicts with the recommended procedures in the *Standards of Practice Handbook*. Employers should compare personal transactions of employees with those of clients on a regular basis regardless of the existence of a requirement by any regulatory organization. Such comparisons ensure that employees' personal trades do not conflict with their duty to their clients, and the comparisons can be conducted in a confidential manner. The statement in answer A does not conflict with the procedures in the *Handbook*. Disclosure of such policies will give full information to clients regarding potential conflicts of interest on the part of those entrusted to manage their money. Answer B is incorrect because firms are encouraged to establish policies whereby employees clear their personal holdings and transactions with their employers.

5. B is correct. This question relates to Standard III(A)—Loyalty, Prudence, and Care and Standard III(E)—Preservation of Confidentiality. In this case, the member manages funds of a private endowment. Clients, who are, in this case, the trustees of the fund, must place some trust in members and candidates. Bronson cannot disclose confidential financial information to anyone without the permission of the fund, regardless of whether the disclosure may benefit the fund. Therefore, answer A is incorrect. Answer C is incorrect because Bronson must notify the fund and obtain the fund's permission before publicizing the information.

6. C is correct. Under Standard IV(C)—Responsibilities of Supervisors, members and candidates may delegate supervisory duties to subordinates but such delegation does not relieve members or candidates of their supervisory responsibilities. As a result, answer B is incorrect. Moreover, whether or not Miller's subordinates are subject to the Code and Standards is irrelevant to her supervisory responsibilities. Therefore, answer A is incorrect.

7. B is correct. This question relates to Standard V(A)—Diligence and Reasonable Basis. The opinion of another financial analyst is not an adequate basis for Willier's action in changing the recommendation. Answer C is thus incorrect. So is answer A because, although it is true that members and candidates must distinguish between facts and opinions in recommendations, the question does not illustrate a violation of that nature. If the opinion overheard by Willier had sparked him to conduct additional research and investigation that justified a change of opinion, then a changed recommendation would be appropriate.

8. B is correct. This question relates to Standard I(B)—Independence and Objectivity. When asked to change a recommendation on a company stock to gain business for the firm, the head of the brokerage unit must refuse in order to maintain his independence and objectivity in making recommendations. He must not yield to pressure by the firm's investment banking department. To avoid the appearance of a conflict of interest, the firm should discontinue issuing recommendations about the company. Answer A is incorrect; changing the recommendation in any manner that is contrary to the analyst's opinion violates the duty to maintain independence and objectivity. Answer C is incorrect because merely assigning a new analyst to decide whether the stock deserves a higher rating will not address the conflict of interest.

9. A is correct. Standard VII(B)—Reference to CFA Institute, the CFA Designation, and the CFA Program is the subject of this question. The reference on Albert's business card implies that there is a "CFA Level II" designation; Tye merely indicates in promotional material that he is participating in the CFA Program and has completed Levels I and II. Candidates may not imply that there is some sort of partial designation earned after passing a level of the CFA exam. Therefore, Albert has violated Standard VII(B). Candidates may communicate that they are participating in the CFA Program, however, and may state the levels that they have completed. Therefore, Tye has not violated Standard VII(B).

10. B is correct. This question relates to Standard V(B)—Communication with Clients and Prospective Clients. Scott has issued a research report stating that he expects the price of Walkton Industries stock to rise by US$8 a share "because the dividend will increase" by US$1.50 per share. He has made this statement knowing that the dividend will increase only if Congress enacts certain legislation, an uncertain prospect. By stating that the dividend will increase, Scott failed to separate fact from opinion.

    The information regarding passage of legislation is not material nonpublic information because it is conjecture, and the question does not state whether the U.S. Representative gave Scott her opinion on the passage of the legislation in confidence. She could have been offering this opinion to anyone who asked. Therefore, statement A is incorrect. It may be acceptable to base a recommendation, in part, on an expectation of future events, even though they may be uncertain. Therefore, answer C is incorrect.

11. C is correct. This question, which relates to Standard III(B)—Fair Dealing, tests the knowledge of the procedures that will assist members and candidates in treating clients fairly when making investment recommendations. The steps listed in C will all help ensure the fair treatment of clients. Answer A may have negative effects on the fair treatment of clients. The more people who know about a pending change, the greater the chance that someone will inform some clients before the information's release. The firm should establish policies that limit the number of people who are aware in advance that a recommendation is to be disseminated. Answer B, distributing recommendations to institutional clients before distributing them to individual accounts, discriminates among clients on the basis of size and class of assets and is a violation of Standard III(B).

12. B is correct. This question deals with Standard II(A)—Material Nonpublic Information. The mosaic theory states that an analyst may use material public information and nonmaterial nonpublic information in creating a larger picture than shown by any individual piece of information and the conclusions the analyst reaches become material only after the pieces are assembled. Answers A and C are accurate statements relating to the Code and Standards but do not describe the mosaic theory.

13. C is correct. This question involves Standard IV(B)—Additional Compensation Arrangements. The arrangement described in the question—whereby Jurgen would be compensated beyond the compensation provided by her firm, on the basis of an account's performance—is not a violation of the Standards as long as Jurgen discloses the arrangement in writing to her employer and obtains permission from her employer prior to entering into the arrangement. Answers A and B are incorrect; although the private compensation arrangement could conflict with the interests of other clients and lead to short-term performance pressures, members and candidates may enter into such agreements as long as they have disclosed the arrangements to their employer and obtained permission for the arrangement from their employer.

14. B is correct. This question relates to Standard III(A)—Loyalty, Prudence, and Care—specifically, a member's or candidate's responsibility for voting proxies and the use of client brokerage. According to the facts stated in the question, Farnsworth did not violate Standard III(A). Although the company president asked Farnsworth to vote the shares of the Jones Corporation profit-sharing plan a certain way, Farnsworth investigated the issue and concluded, independently, the best way to vote. Therefore, even though his decision coincided with the wishes of the company president, Farnsworth is not in violation of his responsibility to be loyal and to provide care to his clients. In this case, the participants and the beneficiaries of the profit-sharing plan are the clients, not the company's management. Had Farnsworth not investigated the issue or had he yielded to the president's wishes and voted for a slate of directors that he had determined was not in the best interest of the company, Farnsworth would have violated his responsibilities to the beneficiaries of the plan. In addition, because the brokerage firm provides the lowest commissions and best execution for securities transactions, Farnsworth has met his obligations to the client in using this brokerage firm. It does not matter that the brokerage firm also provides research information that is not useful for the

account generating the commission, because Farnsworth is not paying extra money of the client's for that information.

15. A is correct. In this question, Brown is providing investment recommendations before making inquiries about the client's financial situation, investment experience, or investment objectives. Brown is thus violating Standard III(C)—Suitability. Answers B and C provide examples of information members and candidates should discuss with their clients at the outset of the relationship, but these answers do not constitute a complete list of those factors. Answer A is the best answer.

16. C is correct. This question involves Standard I(C)—Misrepresentation. Statement 1 is a factual statement that discloses to clients and prospects accurate information about the terms of the investment instrument. Statement 2, which guarantees a specific rate of return for a mutual fund, is an opinion stated as a fact and, therefore, violates Standard I(C). If Statement 2 were rephrased to include a qualifying statement, such as "in my opinion, investors may earn. . .," it would not be in violation of the Standards.

17. A is correct. This question involves three of the Standards. Anderb, the portfolio manager, has been obtaining more favorable prices for her personal securities transactions than she gets for her clients, which is a breach of Standard III(A)—Loyalty, Prudence, and Care. In addition, she violated Standard I(D)—Misconduct by failing to adhere to company policy and by hiding her personal transactions from her firm. Anderb's supervisor, Bates, violated Standard IV(C)—Responsibilities of Supervisors; although the company had requirements for reporting personal trading, Bates failed to adequately enforce those requirements. Answer B does not represent a violation because Standard VI(B)—Priority of Transactions requires that personal trading in a security be conducted after the trading in that security of clients and the employer. The Code and Standards do not prohibit owning such investments, although firms may establish policies that limit the investment opportunities of members and candidates. Answer C does not represent a violation because the Code and Standards do not contain a prohibition against employees using the same broker they use for their personal accounts that they also use for their client accounts. This arrangement should be disclosed to the employer so that the employer may determine whether a conflict of interest exists.

18. A is correct. This question relates to Standard I(A)—Knowledge of the Law—specifically, global application of the Code and Standards. Members and candidates who practice in multiple jurisdictions may be subject to various securities laws and regulations. If applicable law is more strict than the requirements of the Code and Standards, members and candidates must adhere to applicable law; otherwise, members and candidates must adhere to the Code and Standards. Therefore, answer A is correct. Answer B is incorrect because members and candidates must adhere to the higher standard set by the Code and Standards if local applicable law is less strict. Answer C is incorrect because when no applicable law exists, members and candidates are required to adhere to the Code and Standards, and the Code and Standards prohibit the use of material nonpublic information.

19. B is correct. The best course of action under Standard I(B)—Independence and Objectivity is to avoid a conflict of interest whenever possible. Therefore, for Ward to pay for all his expenses is the correct answer. Answer C details a course of action in which the conflict would be disclosed, but the solution is not as appropriate as avoiding the conflict of interest. Answer A would not be

the best course because it would not remove the appearance of a conflict of interest; even though the report would not be affected by the reimbursement of expenses, it could appear to be.

20. B is correct. Under Standard IV(A)—Loyalty, members and candidates may undertake independent practice that may result in compensation or other benefit in competition with their employer as long as they obtain consent from their employer. Answer C is not consistent with the Standards because the Standards allow members and candidates to make arrangements or preparations to go into competitive business as long as those arrangements do not interfere with their duty to their current employer. Answer A is not consistent with the Standards because the Standards do not include a complete prohibition against undertaking independent practice.

21. B is correct. This question involves Standard VI(A)—Disclosure of Conflicts—specifically, the holdings of an analyst's employer in company stock. Answers A and C do not describe conflicts of interest that Smith would have to disclose. Answer A describes the use of a firm's products, which would not be a required disclosure. In answer C, the relationship between the analyst and the company through a relative is so tangential that it does not create a conflict of interest necessitating disclosure.

22. B is correct. This question relates to Standard I(C)—Misrepresentation. Although Michelieu's statement about the total return of his clients' accounts on average may be technically true, it is misleading because the majority of the gain resulted from one client's large position taken against Michelieu's advice. Therefore, this statement misrepresents the investment performance the member is responsible for. He has not taken steps to present a fair, accurate, and complete presentation of performance. Answer A is incorrect because Michelieu's statement is a misrepresentation of his performance history. Answer C is incorrect because Michelieu does not guarantee future results.

23. B is correct. The best policy to prevent violation of Standard II(A)—Material Nonpublic Information is the establishment of firewalls in a firm to prevent exchange of insider information. The physical and informational barrier of a firewall between the investment banking department and the brokerage operation prevents the investment banking department from providing information to analysts on the brokerage side who may be writing recommendations on a company stock. Prohibiting recommendations of the stock of companies that are clients of the investment banking department is an alternative, but answer A states that this prohibition would be permanent, which is not the best answer. Once an offering is complete and the material nonpublic information obtained by the investment banking department becomes public, resuming publishing recommendations on the stock is not a violation of the Code and Standards because the information of the investment banking department no longer gives the brokerage operation an advantage in writing the report. Answer C is incorrect because no exchange of information should be occurring between the investment banking department and the brokerage operation, so monitoring of such exchanges is not an effective compliance procedure for preventing the use of material nonpublic information.

24. B is correct. Under Standard III(A)—Loyalty, Prudence, and Care, members and candidates who manage a company's pension fund owe these duties to the participants and beneficiaries of the pension plan, not the management of the company or the company's shareholders.

25. B is correct. Answer B gives one of the two primary reasons listed in the *Handbook* for disclosing referral fees to clients under Standard VI(C)—Referral

Fees. (The other is to allow clients and employers to evaluate the full cost of the services.) Answer A is inconsistent because Standard VI(C) does not require members or candidates to discount their fees when they receive referral fees. Answer C is inconsistent with Standard VI(C) because disclosure of referral fees, to be effective, should be made to prospective clients before entering into a formal client relationship with them.

26. B is correct. Standard VI(B)—Priority of Transactions does not limit transactions of company employees that differ from current recommendations as long as the sale does not disadvantage current clients. Thus, answer A is incorrect. Answer C is incorrect because the Standard does not require the matching of personal and client trades.

27. C is correct. Standard IV(A)—Loyalty discusses activities permissible to members and candidates when they are leaving their current employer; soliciting clients is strictly prohibited. Thus, answer A is inconsistent with the Code and Standards even with the required disclosure. Answer B is incorrect because the offer does not directly violate the Code and Standards. There may be out-of-work members and candidates who can arrange the necessary commitments without violating the Code and Standards.

28. A is correct. The question relates to Standard III(A)—Loyalty, Prudence, and Care. Carter believes the broker offers effective execution at a fee that is comparable with those of other brokers, so he is free to use the broker for all accounts. Answer B is incorrect because the accounts that prohibit soft dollar arrangements do not want to fund the purchase of research by Carter. The new trading scheme does not incur additional commissions from clients, so it would not go against the prohibitions. Answer C is incorrect because Carter should not incur unnecessary or excessive "churning" of the portfolios (excessive trading) for the purpose of meeting the brokerage commitments of soft dollar arrangements.

29. B is correct. According to Standard VII(B)—Reference to CFA Institute, the CFA Designation, and the CFA Program, CFA Program candidates do not receive their actual scores on the exam. Topic and subtopic results are grouped into three broad categories, and the exam is graded only as "pass" or "fail." Although a candidate may have achieved a topical score of "above 70 percent," she or he cannot factually state that she or he received the highest possible score because that information is not reported. Thus, answer C is incorrect. Answer A is incorrect as long as the member or candidate actually completed the exams consecutively. Standard VII(B) does not prohibit the communication of factual information about completing the CFA Program in three consecutive years.

30. C is correct. According to Standard III(A)—Loyalty, Prudence, and Care, the CFA Program would be considered a personal or firm expense and should not be paid for with the fund's brokerage commissions. Soft dollar accounts should be used only to purchase research services that directly assist the investment manager in the investment decision-making process, not to assist the management of the firm or to further education. Thus, answer A is incorrect. Answer B is incorrect because the reasonableness of how the money is used is not an issue; the issue is that educational expense is not research.

31. A is correct. Standard I(B)—Independence and Objectivity emphasizes the need for members and candidates to maintain their independence and objectivity. Best practices dictate that firms adopt a strict policy not to accept compensation for travel arrangements. At times, however, accepting paid travel would not compromise one's independence and objectivity. Answers B

and C are incorrect because the added benefits—free conference admission for additional staff members and an exclusive golf retreat for the speaker—could be viewed as inducements related to the firm's working arrangements and not solely related to the speaking engagement. Should Long wish to bring other team members or participate in the golf outing, he or his firm should be responsible for the associated fees.

32. C is correct. The guidance to Standard II(A)—Material Nonpublic Information recommends adding securities to the firm's restricted list when the firm has or may have material nonpublic information. By adding these securities to this list, Andrews would uphold this standard. Because waiting until the next day will not ensure that news of the merger is made public, answer A is incorrect. Negotiations may take much longer between the two companies, and the merger may never happen. Andrews must wait until the information is disseminated to the market before he trades on that information. Answer B is incorrect because Andrews should not disclose the information to other managers; no trading is allowed on material nonpublic information.

33. B is correct. Through placing a personal purchase order that is significantly greater than the average volume, Pietro is violating Standard IIB—Market Manipulation. He is attempting to manipulate an increase in the share price and thus bring a buyer to the negotiating table. The news of a possible merger and confirmation of the firm's earnings guidance may also have positive effects on the price of Local Bank, but Pietro's action in instructing the release of the information does not represent a violation through market manipulation. Announcements of this nature are common and practical to keep investors informed. Thus, answers A and C are incorrect.

34. C is correct. Cupp violated Standard III(D)—Performance Presentations when he deviated from the firm's stated policies solely to capture the gain from the holding being acquired. Answer A is incorrect because the firm does not claim GIPS compliance and the GIPS standards require external cash flows to be treated in a consistent manner with the firm's documented policies. Answer B is incorrect because the firm does not state that it is updating its composite policies. If such a change were to occur, all cash flows for the month would have to be reviewed to ensure their consistent treatment under the new policy.

35. A is correct. According to Standard V(C)—Record Retention, Cannan needed the permission of her employer to maintain the files at home after her employment ended. Without that permission, she should have deleted the files. All files created as part of a member's or candidate's professional activity are the property of the firm, even those created outside normal work hours. Thus, answer B is incorrect. Answer C is incorrect because the Code and Standards do not prohibit using one's personal computer to complete work for one's employer.

36. B is correct. According to Standard VII(B)—Reference to CFA Institute, the CFA Designation, and the CFA Program, Quinn cannot claim to have finished the CFA Program or be eligible for the CFA charter until he officially learns that he has passed the Level III exam. Until the results for the most recent exam are released, those who sat for the exam should continue to refer to themselves as "candidates." Thus, answer C is incorrect. Answer A is incorrect because members and candidates may discuss areas of practice in which they believe the CFA Program improved their personal skills.

37. A is correct. Hart's decision to invest in the retail fund appears directly correlated with Rodriguez's statement about the successful quarter of Mega Retail and thus violates Standard II(A)—Material Nonpublic Information.

Rodriguez's information would be considered material because it would influence the share price of Mega Retail and probably influence the price of the entire exchange-traded retail fund. Thus, answer B is incorrect. Answer C is also incorrect because Rodriguez shared information that was both material and nonpublic. Company officers regularly have such knowledge about their firms, which is not a violation. The sharing of such information, however, even in a conversation between friends, does violate Standard II(A).

38. C is correct. Standard VII(A)—Conduct as Members and Candidates in the CFA Program prohibits providing information to candidates or the public that is considered confidential to the CFA Program. In revealing that questions related to the analysis of inventories and analysis of taxes were on the exam, Park has violated this standard. Answer B is incorrect because the guidance for the standard explicitly acknowledges that members and candidates are allowed to offer their opinions about the CFA Program. Answer A is incorrect because candidates are not prohibited from using outside resources.

39. B is correct. Paper has violated Standard III(D)—Performance Presentation by not disclosing that he was part of a team of managers that achieved the results shown. If he had also included the return of the portion he directly managed, he would not have violated the standard. Thus, answer A is incorrect. Answer C is incorrect because Paper received written permission from his prior employer to include the results.

40. A is correct. Townsend has not provided any information about her clients to the leaders or managers of the golf program; thus, she has not violated Standard III(E)—Preservation of Confidentiality. Providing contact information about her clients for a direct-mail solicitation would have been a violation. Answer B is incorrect because the notice in the newsletter does not violate Standard III(E). Answer C is incorrect because the golf program's fund-raising campaign had already begun, so discussing the opportunity to donate was appropriate.

41. C is correct. Boswin, as an employee, developed the model on behalf of Greenfield. Therefore, Greenfield, not Boswin, is the owner of the model. Acertado violates Standard IV(A) Duties to Employers: Loyalty when he downloads the model without proper written permission from Greenfield Financial. Acertado is misappropriating employer assets.

42. C is correct. Acertado is least likely to violate Standard II(A) regarding Material Nonpublic Information when using the model at Smith and Garner. Acertado likely violated Standard IV(A), Loyalty, when he used the model. The Standard prohibits members who leave an employer from taking records or files—such as the model—without the written permission of the employer. Acertado also likely violated Standard I(C)—Misrepresentation when he failed to correct his supervisor's impression that the investment idea and the model were Acertado's creation.

43. C is correct. Acertado violates Standard II(A)—Material Nonpublic Information. He has a reasonable belief that the conversation that he overhears is from a reliable source and would have a material impact on security prices. According to the CFA Standards, he must not act, nor cause others to act on the information. Acertado does not violate the Standard relating to Diligence and Reasonable Basis because he bases the recommendation on a reliable model and checks his inputs prior to making the recommendation.

44. A is correct. Acertado least likely violates Standard III(C), which relates to suitability during his phone conversation with Boswin. According to the Standard, members in an advisory relationship with a client must determine

an investment's suitability within the context of the client's portfolio. The Standard also requires that members make reasonable inquiries into a client or prospective client's investment experience; risk and return objectives; and financial constraints prior to making investment recommendations. Boswin is neither a client nor a prospective client, thus Acertado is not bound by the Standard of Suitability during their conversation. Acertado is, however, in jeopardy of violating other Standards—specifically those relating to Integrity of Capital Markets and Preservation of Confidentiality by revealing material nonpublic information about a Smith & Garner client. According to Standard II(A), Acertado, who is in possession of material nonpublic information, must not act, nor cause others to act on the information. According to Standard III(E), members must keep information about current, former, and prospective clients confidential.

45. A is correct. Boswin uses her usual process in researching Country Industries. She is not in possession of material nonpublic information and she maintains her objectivity. Her use of the model provides a reasonable basis for the decision not to pursue additional research or make an investment recommendation regarding Country Industries.

46. A is correct. Blogs and company websites are in the public domain and thus do not constitute inside information. Acertado's use of blog sites to supplement his current research process is acceptable.

47. B is correct. The CFA logo is a certification mark intended to identify individual charterholders and may not be incorporated into a company's name or logo. Standard VII(B) indicates that the use of the CFA logo is appropriate on the business card or letterhead of an individual CFA charterholder.

48. A is correct. Grohl exercised diligence, independence, and thoroughness in analyzing the company and its competitors. Brecksen provided his research reports for Grohl's use and using the reports as a guide was appropriate. Standard V(A) requires that members distinguish between fact and opinion in communicating investment recommendations to clients. The Standard does not apply to investment recommendations communicated to supervisors or internal investment committees.

49. A is correct. Brecksen does not consider the multi-factor analysis a critical component of the analysis or the resulting investment recommendation and thus, under Standards V(A) and (C), is not required to maintain a record of the analysis within the completed report.

    Apfelbaum uses traditional "top-down" fundamental analysis in the investment process. The report followed the traditional format of previous reports on the same company. It contained a complete fundamental analysis and recommendation—indicating diligence and reasonable basis. The report also contained a multi-factor analysis—which is a quantitative analysis tool. If quantitative analysis were the basis of the investment recommendation, it would constitute a change in the general investment principles used by the firm. According to Standard V(B)—Communications with Clients and Prospective Clients, Brecksen and Grohl would be required to promptly disclose those changes to clients and prospective clients.

50. A is correct. Removing the multi-factor analysis from the research report does not constitute a violation. Grohl diligently prepared the internal document according to the firm's traditional format with a complete fundamental analysis and recommendation—indicating diligence and a reasonable basis for his recommendation. It would be wise for Grohl to retain records of the multi-factor analysis but he need not retain the analysis in the research report

to comply with Standards V(A)—Diligence and Reasonable Basis or V(C)—
Record Retention.

51. A is correct. According to Standard V(A)—Diligence and Reasonable Basis, research report conclusions or recommendations may represent the consensus of a group and not necessarily the views of the individual members listed. If the member believes that the consensus opinion has a reasonable basis, then he need not dissociate from the report.

52. B is correct. Zardt violated the Standard relating to Performance Presentation because he did not verify the accuracy of the return information before its distribution. According to Standard III(D), analysts may promote the success or accuracy of their recommendations, but they must make reasonable efforts to ensure that the information is fair, accurate, and complete. In addition to providing attribution, Zardt should take steps to ensure the accuracy of the data prior to distributing the material.

53. B is correct. Telline has a duty to preserve the confidentiality of current, former, and prospective clients. Telline violates Standard III(E)—Preservation of Confidentiality when he reveals that the firm managed the assets of Leighton Family Trust.

54. A is correct. Brown conducts an independent and careful analysis of the plans' benefits for shareholders as well as the takeover offer. In doing so she puts the client's interests ahead of the firm's. Brown's actions are consistent with Standard III(A)—Loyalty, Prudence, and Care; Standard V(A)—Diligence and Reasonable Basis; and Standard III(B)—Fair Dealing.

55. B is correct. Telline is not likely to receive appropriate guidance on developing or revising investment policy statements from the Standard relating to Fair Dealing. Standard III(B) provides members with guidance on treating clients fairly when making investment recommendations, providing investment analysis, or taking investment action. Telline could obtain guidance from the Standards relating to Loyalty, Prudence, and Care and Suitability. Both Standard III(A) and (C) provide guidance for members in determining client objectives and the suitability of investments.

56. A is correct. Telline determines that the other client does not have the cash available in his account and selling existing holdings does not make sense. Moreover, Telline is careful to consider the investment's suitability for Caper's account. Telline's actions are consistent with CFA Institute Standards III(A)—Loyalty, Prudence, and Care and III(B)—Fair Dealing.

57. B is correct. The firm violates Standard III(B)—Fair Dealing. Under Aiklin's policy, some clients for whom an IPO is suitable may not receive their pro-rata share of the issue. CFA Standards recommend that firms allocate IPOs on a pro-rata basis to clients, not to portfolio managers.

58. C is correct. Telline violates Standard III(B)—Fair Dealing by over-allocating shares to Caper. Telline carefully reviews both the proposed IPO and his client accounts to determine suitability. He fails to allocate the IPO shares on a pro-rata basis to all clients for whom the investment is suitable.

59. B is correct. Excerpt 2 is inconsistent with CFA Standards because it addresses only officers and only their direct reports, that is, employees whom they directly supervise. Standard IV (C) states that "any investment professionals who have employees subject to their control or influence" exercise supervisory responsibility. According to *The Standards of Practice Handbook*, "members and candidates who supervise large numbers of employees cannot personally evaluate the conduct of their employees on a continuing basis. Although these members . . . may delegate supervisory duties, such delegation does not relieve them of their supervisory responsibility." Excerpt 3 is consistent with CFA Standards. It is based on a quote from the *Standards of Practice Handbook* stating that "if a member or candidate determines that information is material, the member . . . should make reasonable efforts to achieve public dissemination." Members are not required to achieve public dissemination and those bound by a duty of loyalty or a duty to preserve confidentiality would refrain from doing so because it would breach their duty.

60. A is correct. According to Standard I(B)—Independence and Objectivity, members must use reasonable care and judgment to achieve and maintain independence and objectivity in their professional activities. Although it was sent to Voser's office, the gift basket is a private gift from Voser's sister and not likely to affect Voser's professional activities. According to Excerpt 4 of the Crawfood compliance manual and Standard IV(B)—Additional Compensation Arrangements, employees must obtain permission from their employer before accepting gifts, compensation, or other benefits that compete with, or might create a conflict of interest with, the employer's interests. The gift basket does not create a conflict or compete with the employer's interests.

61. A is correct. Voser most likely violated the Standard relating to loyalty to employer, Standard IV(A). While Voser used public information to develop the recommendation to purchase Greenhornfood shares, the company compliance guide states that she should not trade or cause others to trade in securities of companies that may be potential takeover targets. Voser's recommendation caused her sister to trade in Greenhornfood, violating the company's compliance policies, and possibly harming her employer in its attempt to acquire Greenhornfood.

By advising others to invest in a food retailer that she considered an attractive acquisition target, Voser deprived her employer of the advantage of her skills and abilities and may have caused harm to her employer. Voser could have recommended Greenhornfood to Craw rather than her sister as an acquisition target. Although the sister's trade in Greenhornfood was small, a large trade might have moved the stock price and caused harm to Crawfood in terms of additional cost.

62. C is correct. Voser least likely violated the Standard relating to diligence and reasonable basis. Voser initially applied the mosaic theory and had a reasonable basis for the trade as required by Standard V(A). Eventually, she came into possession of material nonpublic information (corporate logo on a document, overheard conversation). According to Standard II(A), once in possession of material nonpublic information, she is prohibited from acting or causing others to act. Voser also violated her duty of loyalty to her employer, Standard IV(A), by encouraging others to trade in Greenhornfood and possibly harming Crawfood's attempts to acquire the smaller company at an attractive price.

63. C is correct. Craw did not adequately fulfill his responsibilities as a supervisor. While he may have delegated supervisory duties to Voser's immediate supervisor, such delegation does not relieve him of his supervisory responsibility. As stated in the *Standards of Practice Handbook*, members and candidates with supervisory responsibility also must understand what constitutes an adequate compliance system for their firms and make reasonable efforts to see that appropriate compliance procedures are established, documented, communicated to covered personnel, and followed. "Adequate" procedures are those designed to meet industry standards, regulatory requirements, the requirements of the Code and Standards, and the circumstances of the firm. Once compliance procedures are established, the supervisor must also make reasonable efforts to ensure that the procedures are monitored and enforced. According to Standard IV(C)—Responsibilities of Supervisors, adequate compliance procedures require that once a violation is discovered, Craw conduct a thorough investigation to determine the scope of wrongdoing.

64. A is correct. As stated on page ix of the *Standards of Practice Handbook*, "Members and candidates must self disclose on the annual Professional Conduct Statement all matters that question their professional conduct, such as involvement in civil litigation, a criminal investigation, or being the subject of a written complaint." Standard VII(A)—Conduct as Members and Candidates in the CFA Program prohibits conduct that compromises the reputation of the CFA designation including misrepresenting information on the Professional Conduct Statement. Members are encouraged but not required to report violations of others. At a minimum, Craw should remind Voser of her duty to report the investigation.

Index			
Japan (Nikkei)			
Seoul			
Tokyo (Comp.)			
Mumbai			
Singapore	18,355.7		−11.1%
Sydney			−4.5%
Shanghai B	2971.0	1.1%	−4.7%
Hong Kong	4644.0	0.9%	−10.5%
Toronto	316.8	0.7%	−6.9%
Stockholm	22,700.9	0.5%	−4.2%
Mexico City	13,524.8	0.1%	4.1%

3

CFA Institute Soft Dollar Standards

LEARNING OUTCOMES

Mastery	The candidate should be able to:
☐	**a** define soft-dollar arrangements, and state the general principles of the Soft Dollar Standards;
☐	**b** evaluate company soft-dollar practices and policies;
☐	**c** determine whether a product or service qualifies as "permissible research" that can be purchased with client brokerage.

INTRODUCTION

1

CFA Institute Soft Dollar Standards provide guidance to investment professionals worldwide through the articulation of high ethical standards for CFA Institute members dealing with "soft dollar" issues. CFA Institute Soft Dollar Standards are consistent with and complement the existing CFA Institute Standards of Professional Conduct that all CFA Institute members and candidates in the CFA Program are required to follow.

The purposes of the Standards are to define "soft dollars," identify what is "allowable" research, establish standards for soft dollar use, create model disclosure guidelines, and provide guidance for client-directed brokerage arrangements.

The Soft Dollar Standards are *voluntary* standards for members. If a CFA Institute member claims compliance with the Standards, then certain of these Standards are mandatory (i.e., they *must* be followed to claim compliance) and others are recommended (i.e., they *should* be followed). CFA Institute strongly encourages members to adopt the required and recommended Standards. If the Soft Dollar Standards are adopted, compliance will not supplant the responsibility to comply with applicable law.[1] CFA Institute members should comply at all times with the relevant laws of the countries in which they do business. In situations in which these Standards impose a higher degree of responsibility or disclosure than, but do not conflict with, local law, the member is held to the mandatory provisions of these Standards.

---

1 For example, in the United States, the Securities Exchange Act of 1934, Investment Company Act of 1940, and Investment Advisers Act of 1940 all address the use of client commissions in soft dollar arrangements. The U.S. Department of Labor also provides regulations regarding directed brokerage practices concerning ERISA-covered pension plans.

BACKGROUND

In 1975, the U.S. Congress created a "safe harbor" under Section 28(e) of the Securities and Exchange Act of 1934 to protect investment managers from claims that they had breached their fiduciary duties by using their client commissions to pay a higher commission to acquire investment research than they might have paid for "execution" services. According to Securities and Exchange Commission (SEC) Staff, the protection of Section 28(e) is available only for securities transactions conducted on an agency basis.[2] Since that time, the soft dollar area has undergone considerable expansion, both in terms of actual usage and the types of products and services for which safe harbor protection is claimed. The complexity of these practices, including technologically sophisticated research tools and the existence of "mixed-use" products, has resulted in a fair amount of legitimate confusion surrounding the appropriate use of soft dollars.

CFA Institute seeks to provide ethical standards for CFA Institute members and those in the industry that engage in soft dollar practices and also emphasizes the paramount duty of the investment manager, as a fiduciary, to place the interests of clients before those of the investment manager. In particular, the Soft Dollar Standards focus on six key areas:

- Definitions—to enable all parties dealing with soft dollar practices to have a common understanding of all of the different aspects of soft dollars.

- Research—to give clear guidance to investment managers on what products and services are appropriate for a manager to purchase with client brokerage.

- Mixed-Use Products—to clarify the manager's duty to clearly justify the use of client brokerage to pay a portion of a mixed-use product.

- Disclosure—to obligate investment managers to clearly disclose their soft dollar practices and give detailed information to each client when requested.

- Record Keeping—to ensure that the client can 1) receive assurances that what the investment manager is doing with the client's brokerage can be supported in an "audit," and 2) receive important information on request.

- Client-Directed Brokerage—to clarify the manager's role and fiduciary responsibilities with respect to clients.

OVERVIEW

CFA Institute Soft Dollar Standards focus on the member's obligations to its clients. Although the Standards primarily focus on the obligations of the member as investment manager, they may be applicable to other parties involved in soft dollar practices, including brokers, plan sponsors, and trustees. Each of these parties, however, has its own set of obligations that should be considered prior to participating in any soft dollar arrangement.

CFA Institute Soft Dollar Standards are ethical principles intended to ensure:

- full and fair disclosure of an investment manager's use of a client's brokerage[3];

---

2 According to the SEC staff, securities transactions conducted on a principal basis cannot claim Section 28(e) "safe harbor" protection. Both principal transactions and those agency transactions unable to qualify for "safe harbor" protection are not necessarily illegal but are evaluated based on the existence of full disclosure, informed client consent, and other fundamental fiduciary principles, including placing the client's interests first.

3 The term "Brokerage" is described in the definitions section of the Standards.

- consistent presentation of information so that the client, broker, and other applicable parties can clearly understand an investment manager's brokerage practices;

- uniform disclosure and record keeping to enable an investment manager's client to have a clear understanding of how the investment manager is using the client's brokerage; and

- high standards of ethical practices within the investment industry.

No finite set of standards can cover all potential situations or anticipated future developments concerning the types of investment research available to investment managers. However, meeting the objective of full and fair disclosure and ensuring that the "client comes first" obligates an investment manager to disclose fully and clearly to its client the investment manager's practice when addressing any potential conflict concerning the payment methods for investment research.

CFA Institute Soft Dollar Standards are based on the following set of fundamental principles that an investment manager should consider when attempting to comply:

- an investment manager is a fiduciary and, as such, must disclose all relevant aspects concerning any benefit the manager receives through a client's brokerage;

- proprietary research and third-party research are to be treated the same in evaluating soft dollar arrangements, because the research that an investment manager receives from each is paid for with client brokerage;

- research should be purchased with client brokerage only if the primary use of the research, whether a product or a service, directly assists the investment manager in its investment decision-making process and not in the management of the investment firm; and

- when in doubt, the research should be paid for with investment manager assets, not client brokerage.

COMPARISON WITH CURRENT PRACTICES

CFA Institute Soft Dollar Standards seek to clarify certain areas of brokerage practices that have been a source of confusion for CFA Institute members. By emphasizing the basic fiduciary responsibilities of CFA Institute members with respect to their client's assets, the Soft Dollar Standards are intended to illuminate the line between permissible and impermissible uses of client brokerage. In this respect, the Standards do not create "new law" but address well-established principles applicable to the investment manager–client relationship.

In other respects, a reiteration of the current "soft dollar" practices would fail to adequately address the issues raised by the complexity of current brokerage practices faced by CFA Institute members. The Soft Dollar Standards, therefore, depart from certain well-established practices in the soft dollar area and address practices beyond those that currently claim Section 28(e) safe harbor protection.

The Soft Dollar Standards are not to be read as in any way changing the scope of activities that the SEC determines to fall within the safe harbor. Instead they are separate, ethical standards applicable to a variety of practices implicated in Soft Dollar Arrangements. Thus, these Standards will impose higher standards of conduct in certain areas on CFA Institute members that voluntarily elect to comply with the Standards, as follows:

1. **Definition of Soft Dollar Arrangements**

   a. *Proprietary, in addition to third-party, research.*

      Traditionally, soft dollar arrangements are understood to address those products or services provided to the investment manager by someone other than the executing broker, products or services that are commonly known as "third-party" research. Such an approach is deficient in light of the range of products and services provided by both third-party research providers and "in-house" research departments of brokerage firms. Thus, any meaningful Standards must also recognize the importance of research provided by the executing broker, commonly known as "proprietary" or "in-house" research.

      For purposes of the Soft Dollar Standards, "soft dollar arrangements" include proprietary, as well as third-party, research arrangements and seek to treat both categories the same. Although these Standards do *not* suggest an "unbundling" of proprietary research, they do require the investment manager to provide certain basic information regarding the types of research obtained with client brokerage through proprietary research arrangements. Moreover, these Standards should not be read to require research obtained either through third-party or proprietary arrangements to be attributed on an account-by-account basis or otherwise to require a "tracing" of products or services.

   b. *Principal, in addition to agency, trades.*

      Traditionally, the term "soft dollars" refers to commissions generated by trades conducted on an agency basis.[4] However, such an approach fails to recognize that research may be obtained through the use of "spreads" or "discounts" generated by trades conducted on a principal basis. For the purposes of the Soft Dollar Standards, soft dollar arrangements include transactions conducted on an agency *or* principal basis.

2. **Definition of Research**

   Traditionally, "allowable" research in the soft dollar context is evaluated by whether it provides lawful and appropriate assistance to an investment manager in the investment decision-making process. This approach, however, leaves CFA Institute members with inadequate guidance. Consequently, the Soft Dollar Standards embrace a definition of research that requires the primary use of the soft dollar product or service to directly assist the investment manager in its investment decision-making process and not in the management of the investment firm.

   In many cases, this determination may not lend itself to absolute precision, but an investment manager must use its best judgment as a fiduciary to justify the use of client brokerage to pay for a product or service. The Standards suggest the use of a three-tiered analysis to aid CFA Institute members in determining whether a product or service is research. Such an approach is intended to provide needed guidance for CFA Institute members in determining when it is appropriate to use client brokerage to purchase a product or service.

3. **Enhanced Disclosure**

   Disclosure of a CFA Institute member's brokerage practices will provide the member's client with a means of evaluating the member's soft dollar practices and how client brokerage is used. Under the Soft Dollar Standards, the CFA Institute member must disclose to its clients certain information, the majority of which the member is already required under current law to disclose, or to

---

4 As noted above, the "safe harbor" provided by Section 28(e) of the Securities Exchange Act of 1934, as interpreted by the SEC staff, applies only to those transactions conducted on an agency, not principal, basis.

maintain, in order to meet federal disclosure requirements. Moreover, although the Soft Dollar Standards require the CFA Institute member to disclose the *availability* of additional information, this information does not actually have to be provided, unless it is specifically requested by the client.

4. **Compliance Statement**

Finally, the Soft Dollar Standards contemplate the use of a voluntary statement of compliance. Only a claim of compliance with these Standards requires an investment manager to comply with all of the mandatory provisions of these Standards and only as to the client brokerage that its compliance statement relates. Thus, an investment manager that claims compliance with the Soft Dollar Standards must provide the client with a statement that any brokerage arrangement with respect to *that* client's account comports with the mandatory provisions of these Standards. Such a compliance statement will help to ensure the continued integrity of the Standards and provide clients with additional assurance with respect to how their brokerage is used by their investment manager.

DEFINITIONS

For purposes of the CFA Institute Soft Dollar Standards, the following terms apply:

Agency Trade refers to a transaction involving the payment of a commission.

Best Execution refers to executing Client transactions so that the Client's total cost is the most favorable under the particular circumstances at that time.

Broker refers to any person or entity that provides securities execution services.

Brokerage refers to the amount on any trade retained by a Broker to be used directly or indirectly as payment for execution services and, when applicable, Research supplied to the Investment Manager or its Client in connection with Soft Dollar Arrangements or for benefits provided to the Client in Client-Directed Brokerage Arrangements. For these purposes, trades may be conducted on an agency *or* principal basis.

Brokerage Arrangement refers to an arrangement whereby a Broker provides services or products that are in addition to execution. Brokerage Arrangements include Investment Manager-Directed and Client-Directed Brokerage Arrangements.

Brokerage and Research Services refers to services and/or products provided by a Broker to an Investment Manager through a Brokerage Arrangement.

Client refers to the entity, including a natural person, investment fund, or separate account, designated to receive the benefits, including income, from the Brokerage generated through Securities Transactions. A Client may be represented by a trustee or other Fiduciary, who may or may not have Investment Discretion.

Client-Directed Brokerage Arrangement refers to an arrangement whereby a Client directs that trades for its account be executed through a specific Broker in exchange for which the Client receives a benefit in addition to execution services. Client-Directed Brokerage Arrangements include rebates, commission banking, and commission recapture programs through which the Broker provides the Client with cash or services or pays certain obligations of the Client. A Client may also direct the use of limited lists of brokers—not for the purpose of reducing Brokerage costs but to effect various other goals (e.g., increased diversity by using minority-owned brokers) or geographical concentration.

Commission refers to the amount paid to the Broker in addition to the price of the security and applicable regulatory fees on an Agency Trade.

Fiduciary refers to any entity, or a natural person, including a CFA Institute member, that has discretionary authority or responsibility for the management of a Client's assets or other relationships of special trust.

Investment Decision-Making Process refers to the quantitative and qualitative processes and related tools used by the Investment Manager in rendering investment advice to its Clients, including financial analysis, trading and risk analysis, securities selection, broker selection, asset allocation, and suitability analysis.

Investment Discretion refers to the sole or shared authority (whether or not exercised) to determine what securities or other assets to purchase or sell on behalf of a Client.

Investment Manager refers to any entity, or a natural person, including a CFA Institute member, that serves in the capacity of asset manager to a Client. The Investment Manager may have sole, shared, or no Investment Discretion over an account.

Investment Manager-Directed Brokerage Arrangement refers to Proprietary and Third-Party Research Arrangements.

Member refers to any individual who is required to comply with the CFA Institute Code of Ethics and Standards of Professional Conduct in accordance with the CFA Institute Bylaws.

Mixed-Use refers to services and/or products, provided to an Investment Manager by a Broker through a Brokerage Arrangement, that have the capacity to be used for both the Investment Decision-Making Process *and* management of the investment firm.

Principal Trade refers to a transaction involving a "discount" or a "spread."

Proprietary Research Arrangement refers to an arrangement whereby the Investment Manager directs a Broker to effect Securities Transactions for Client accounts in exchange for which the Investment Manager receives Research from, and/or access to, the "in-house" staffs of the brokerage firms.

Provided by a Broker refers to 1) in Proprietary Research Arrangements, Research developed by the Broker and 2) in Third-Party Research Arrangements, Research for which the obligation to pay is between the Broker and Third-Party Research Provider, not between the Investment Manager and Third-Party Research Provider.

Research refers to services and/or products provided by a Broker, the primary use of which must directly assist the Investment Manager in its Investment Decision-Making Process and not in the management of the investment firm.

Section 28(e) Safe Harbor refers to the "safe harbor" set forth in Section 28(e) of the U.S. Securities Exchange Act of 1934, which provides that an Investment Manager that has Investment Discretion over a Client account is not in breach of its fiduciary duty when paying more than the lowest Commission rate available if it determines in good faith that the rate paid is commensurate with the value of Brokerage and Research Services provided by the Broker.

Securities Transactions refers to any transactions involving a Broker, whether conducted on an agency basis or principal basis.

Soft Dollar Arrangement refers to an arrangement whereby the Investment Manager directs transactions to a Broker, in exchange for which the Broker provides Brokerage and Research Services to the Investment Manager. Soft Dollar Arrangements include Proprietary and Third-Party Research Arrangements but do *not* include Client-Directed Brokerage Arrangements. Soft Dollar Arrangements are sometimes referred to herein as Investment Manager-Directed Brokerage Arrangements, where applicable.

Third-Party Research Arrangement refers to an arrangement whereby the Investment Manager directs a Broker to effect Securities Transactions for Client accounts in exchange for which the Investment Manager receives Research provided by the Broker, which has been generated by an entity *other than* the executing Broker.

CFA INSTITUTE SOFT DOLLAR STANDARDS

I. General

Principles

A. These Soft Dollar Standards apply to all CFA Institute Members' Proprietary and Third-Party Research Arrangements, with or without Commissions, and recognize two fundamental principles:

1. Brokerage is the property of the Client.

2. The Investment Manager has an ongoing duty to ensure the quality of transactions effected on behalf of its Client, including:

   a. seeking to obtain Best Execution;

   b. minimizing transaction costs; and

   c. using Client Brokerage to benefit Clients.

Required

B. An Investment Manager in Soft Dollar Arrangements must always act for the benefit of its Clients and place Clients' interests before its own.

C. An Investment Manager may not allocate a Client's Brokerage based on the amount of Client referrals the Investment Manager receives from a Broker.

Clarification: With respect to mutual funds, the Investment Manager's Client is the fund. However, in this context, the fund's board, not the fund, establishes the policies with respect to the use of certain brokers.

II. Relationships with Clients

Required

A. The Investment Manager must disclose to the Client that it may engage in Soft Dollar Arrangements prior to engaging in such Arrangements involving that Client's account.

Recommended

B. The Investment Manager should assure that, over time, all Clients receive the benefits of Research purchased with Client Brokerage.

1. *Agency Trades.* While it is permissible for the Investment Manager to use a Client's Brokerage derived from Agency Trades to obtain Research that may not directly benefit that particular Client at that particular time, the Investment Manager should endeavor to ensure that, over a reasonable period of time, the Client receives the benefit of Research purchased with other Clients' Brokerage.

2. *Principal Trades.* The Investment Manager should determine if the particular Principal Trade is subject to certain fiduciary requirements (e.g., ERISA, Investment Company Act of 1940) which require that Client Brokerage derived from Principal Trades must benefit the Client account generating the Brokerage. If such requirements do not apply, it is permissible to use Client Brokerage derived from Principal Trades to benefit Client accounts other than the account generating the Brokerage if the Investment Manager discloses this practice and obtains prior consent from the Client.

Clarification: Certain fiduciary statutes require that brokerage derived from a Principal Trade must directly benefit the Client account generating the Trade. In such situations, even consent by the Client will not waive this legal requirement. Compliance with the Soft Dollar Standards should not be read to, in any way, absolve one's responsibilities to comply fully with the applicable law regarding Principal Trades.

III. Selection of Brokers

Principle

A. Selecting Brokers to execute Clients' Securities Transactions is a key component of the Investment Manager's ability to add value to its Client portfolios. The failure to obtain Best Execution may result in impaired performance for the Client.

Required

B. In selecting Brokers, the Investment Manager must consider the capabilities of the Broker to provide Best Execution.

Recommended

C. In evaluating the Broker's capability to provide Best Execution, the Investment Manager should consider the Broker's financial responsibility, the Broker's responsiveness to the Investment Manager, the Commission rate or spread involved, and the range of services offered by the Broker.

Clarification: These criteria are relevant components to the Broker's ability to obtain the most favorable total cost under the particular circumstances at that time.

IV. Evaluation of Research

Required

A. In determining whether to use Client Brokerage to pay for Research, the Investment Manager must use the following criteria:

1. Whether the Research under consideration meets the definition of Research contained in these Standards.

2. Whether the Research benefits the Investment Manager's Client(s).

3. Whether the Investment Manager is able to document the basis for the determinations.

4. Whether under certain fiduciary regulations (e.g., ERISA, the Investment Company Act of 1940) for Principal Trades, the Research directly benefits the Client account generating the trade. If the Principal Trades are not subject to such regulations, the Research may benefit Client accounts other than those generating the trade if the Investment Manager has made disclosure and obtained prior Client consent.

B. The inability to decide and document that the Research meets the above criteria requires that the Investment Manager *not* pay for such Research with Client Brokerage.

C. In determining the portion of Mixed-Use Research to be paid with Client Brokerage, the Investment Manager must:

1. Be able to make a reasonable, justifiable, and documentable allocation of the cost of the Research according to its expected usage.

2. Pay with Client Brokerage only the portion of the Research that is actually used by the Investment Manager in the Investment Decision-Making Process.

3. Reevaluate the Mixed-Use Research allocation at least annually.

V. Client-Directed Brokerage

Principle

A. Because Brokerage is an asset of the Client, not the Investment Manager, the practice of Client-Directed Brokerage does not violate any investment manager duty per se.

B. In a Client-Directed Brokerage Arrangement:

Required

1. The Investment Manager must not use Brokerage from another Client account to pay for a product or service purchased under the Client-Directed Brokerage Arrangement.

Recommended

2. The Investment Manager should disclose to the Client:

    a. the Investment Manager's duty to continue to seek to obtain Best Execution, and

    b. that arrangements that require the Investment Manager to commit a certain percentage of Brokerage may affect the Investment Manager's ability to i) seek to obtain Best Execution and ii) obtain adequate Research.

3. The Investment Manager should attempt to structure the Client-Directed Brokerage Arrangement in a manner that comports with Appendix 3A to the Soft Dollar Standards.

VI. Disclosure

In addition to disclosure required elsewhere in the Soft Dollar Standards:

Required

A. An Investment Manager must clearly disclose, with specificity and in "plain language," its policies with respect to all Soft Dollar Arrangements, including:

1. *To Clients and potential Clients.* An Investment Manager must disclose whether it may use the Research to benefit Clients other than those whose trades generated the Brokerage. This disclosure must address whether the trades generating the Brokerage involved transactions conducted on a principal basis.

2. *To Clients.* An Investment Manager must disclose i) the types of Research received through Proprietary or Third-Party Research Arrangements; ii) the extent of use; and iii) whether any affiliated Broker is involved.

Clarification: Description of the types and use of Research should be appropriate to the type of Research Arrangement involved. The disclosures required or recommended in the Soft Dollar Standards do not contemplate an "unbundling" of Proprietary Research Arrangements. Instead, the description of Research should, in the judgment of the Investment Manager, provide Clients with the ability to understand the type of Research involved *in the degree of detail* appropriate to the source of the Research.

B. To claim compliance with these Standards for any Client account, an Investment Manager must provide the Client with a statement that any Soft Dollar Arrangements with respect to the particular Client account comport with the CFA Institute Soft Dollar Standards. This statement must be provided at least annually.

Clarification: This statement is required only if the Investment Manager is claiming compliance with the Soft Dollar Standards. If applicable, the statement is to be provided to the individual Client to which the claim is being made.

C. An Investment Manager must prominently disclose in writing to its Client that additional information in accordance with the CFA Institute Soft Dollar Standards concerning the Investment Manager's Soft Dollar Arrangements is available on request. Such additional information should include the following on at least an annual basis.

Clarification: Although certain additional information is suggested, the Soft Dollar Standards are intended to preserve the ability of the Client and Investment Manager to determine what other information may be relevant in light of particular Client needs or types of accounts.

1. *On a firmwide basis.* A description of the products and services that were received from Brokers pursuant to a Soft Dollar Arrangement, regardless of whether the product or service derives from Proprietary or Third-Party Research Arrangements, detailed by Broker.

2. *For a specific Client account:*

    a. the total amount of Commissions generated for that Client through a Soft Dollar Arrangement, detailed by Broker; and

    b. the total amount of Brokerage directed by that Client through Directed Brokerage Arrangements.

Clarification: The disclosure required in this section is intended to provide the requesting Client with certain basic items of information: a description of what the entire firm obtained through Soft Dollar Arrangements, the identity of brokers providing those products and services, the total amount of Directed Brokerage attributable to the Client, and the total amount of Commissions generated for the requesting Client's account.

3. The aggregate percentage of the Investment Manager's Brokerage derived from Client-Directed Brokerage Arrangements and the amount of that Client's Directed Brokerage, as a percentage of that aggregate.

    a. The Investment Manager is not obligated to report amounts of Client-Directed Brokerage that constitute less than 10 percent of the Manager's aggregate amount of Client-Directed Brokerage.

Recommended

When requested by a Client:

D. The Investment Manager should provide a description of the product or service obtained through Brokerage generated from the Client's account.

E. The Investment Manager should provide the aggregate dollar amount of Brokerage paid from all accounts over which the Manager has Investment Discretion.

VII. Record Keeping

Required

The Investment Manager must maintain, when applicable, all records that:

A. are required by applicable law;

B. are necessary to supply Clients on a timely basis with the information required by Soft Dollar Standard VI;

C. document arrangements, oral or written, obligating the Investment Manager to generate a specific amount of Brokerage;

D. document arrangements with Clients pertaining to Soft Dollar or Client-Directed Brokerage Arrangements;

E. document any agreements with Brokers pertaining to Soft Dollar Arrangements;

F. document transactions with Brokers involving Soft Dollar Arrangements, including 1) a list of Proprietary or Third-Party Research providers and 2) a description of the service or product obtained from the provider;

G. document the bases of allocation in determining to use Client Brokerage to pay for any portion of a Mixed-Use service or product;

H. indicate how the services and products obtained through Soft Dollar Arrangements directly assist the Investment Manager in the Investment Decision-Making Process;

I. show compliance with the CFA Institute Soft Dollar Standards, including the identity of the Investment Manager personnel responsible for determining such compliance;

J. copies of all Client disclosures and authorizations.

APPENDIX A

Recommended Practices for Client-Directed Brokerage Arrangements

In Client-Directed Brokerage Arrangements:

A. When directed by a Fiduciary, the Investment Manager should receive written assurance from the Fiduciary that the Client-Directed Brokerage Arrangement will solely benefit the Client's account.

B. The Investment Manager should attempt to structure Client-Directed Brokerage Arrangements so that:

   1. they do not require the commitment of a certain portion of Brokerage to a single Broker, and

   2. Commissions are negotiated and seeking to obtain Best Execution is still relevant.

C. The Investment Manager should request from its Client in any Client-Directed Brokerage Arrangement written instructions that:

   1. restate the Investment Manager's continuing responsibility for seeking to obtain Best Execution,

   2. list the eligible Brokers,

   3. specify the approximate target percentage or dollar amount of transactions to be directed, and

   4. state procedures for monitoring the Arrangements.

D. The Investment Manager should regularly communicate with the Client for the purpose of jointly evaluating the Client-Directed Brokerage Arrangement, including:

   1. the potential for achieving Best Execution,

   2. the list of Brokers and their trading skills,

   3. the target percentage of transactions to be directed to the selected Brokers, and

   4. the Investment Manager's trading style and liquidity needs.

APPENDIX B

Permissible Research Guidance

Central to whether a product or service constitutes "Research" that can be paid for with Client Brokerage is whether the product or service provides lawful and appropriate assistance to the Investment Manager in carrying out its investment decision-making responsibilities. This determination pivots on whether the product or service aids the Investment Decision-Making Process instead of the general operation of the firm.

CFA Institute Soft Dollar Standards add guidance by requiring that the primary use of the Research must directly assist the Investment Manager in its Investment Decision-Making Process and not in the management of the investment firm.

Formulating what is allowable Research is not subject to hard and fast rules. Rather, the context in which something is used and the particulars of an Investment Manager's business form the framework for this determination. In evaluating a practice, the substance of *actual* usage will prevail over the *form* of some possible usage.

Three-Level Analysis

CFA Institute Soft Dollar Standards assist the Investment Manager in making this determination by setting forth a three-level analysis to assist the Investment Manager in determining whether a product or service is Research. In the vast majority of cases, if the criteria of all three levels are satisfied, the Investment Manager can then feel comfortable in using Client Brokerage to pay for the Research. When conducting the analysis, the Investment Manager must consider the ethical framework of the Soft Dollar Standards. In conjunction with the Soft Dollar Standards' Client disclosure requirements, an Investment Manager must be able to explain to its Client how the Research—and when applicable, its component parts—assists in the Investment Decision-Making Process. Stated another way, the Investment Manager should only obtain Research with Client Brokerage if the Manager would feel comfortable disclosing and explaining the decision in a face-to-face meeting with the Client.

Level I—Define the Product or Service   The first step is for the Investment Manager to define the product or service to be purchased with Client Brokerage. In most instances, the product or service is clearly defined (e.g., an industry report). However, many products and services consist of different components that are related only to the ability of the product or service to assist the Investment Manager in its Investment Decision-Making Process (e.g., a computer work station that runs Research software). For such multicomponent products or services, the Investment Manager, consistent with the Soft Dollar Standards' ethical framework, must narrowly construe the component parts that are necessary for the products or services to directly assist the Investment Manager in the Investment Decision-Making Process.

For example, the computer work station could be considered a closely related component of the product or service that constitutes the "Research." The electricity needed to run the computer, however, is not closely related and, if paid with Client Brokerage, would violate the ethical principles of the Soft Dollar Standards.

Level II—Determine Usage   The second step is for the Investment Manager to determine that the primary use of the product or service, as defined by the Investment Manager in the Level I analysis, will directly assist the Investment Manager in its Investment Decision-Making Process.

For example, an Investment Manager subscribes to the Bloomberg Service and uses this service only to enable all persons visiting the Investment Manager's offices to look up the price of securities and analyze market trends. Under the Level I analysis, the Investment Manager defines the service as the market data received from Bloomberg, plus the Bloomberg supplied terminal and the dedicated line necessary to receive the Bloomberg service in the Investment Manager's offices. However, under the Level II analysis, the Investment Manager does not use the Bloomberg service to directly assist it in its Investment Decision-Making Process. To the contrary, the Investment Manager subscribes to the Bloomberg Service as a benefit to the firm. The Bloomberg Service, therefore, cannot be paid for with Client Brokerage.

Level III—Mixed-Use Analysis   The third step occurs only after the Investment Manager determines that the product or service is Research by completing the Level I and Level II analysis above. The Investment Manager must then determine what portion of the Research is used by the Investment Manager to directly assist it in the Investment Decision-Making Process. If less than 100 percent of the Research is used for assistance in its Investment Decision-Making Process, the Investment Manager must consider the Research as Mixed-Use Research. With Mixed-Use Research, the Investment Manager can use Client Brokerage to pay for only that portion of the Research used by the Investment Manager in the Investment Decision-Making Process and not in the management of the investment firm.

For example, if the Bloomberg service discussed in the Level II analysis was actually used 50 percent of the time to determine market and industry trends as part of the Investment Manager's Investment Decision-Making Process, the Investment Manager could pay for 50 percent of the Bloomberg service with Client Brokerage.

Conclusion

The Investment Manager can establish that the product or service is Research that can be purchased with Client Brokerage only after the Investment Manager has taken two steps. First, the Investment Manager must have defined the product or service (Level I analysis). Second, the Investment Manager must have determined that the primary use of the product or service will directly assist the Investment Manager in the Investment Decision-Making Process rather than in the management of the investment firm (Level II analysis). The final step is for the Investment Manager to determine what portion of the Research will be used by the Investment Manager in the Investment Decision-Making Process and pay only for that portion with Client Brokerage (Level III analysis).

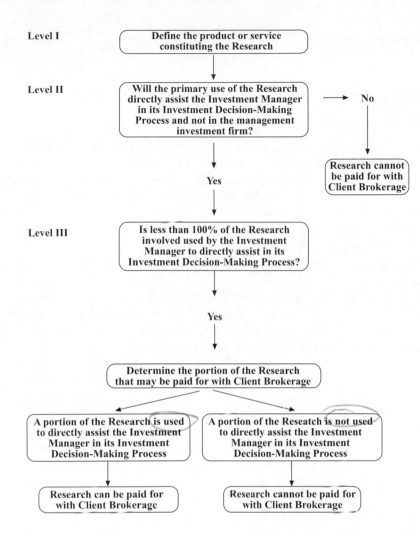

Level I
Define the product or service constituting the Research

Level II
Will the primary use of the Research directly assist the Investment Manager in its Investment Decision-Making Process and not in the management investment firm?

No

Yes

Research cannot be paid for with Client Brokerage

Level III
Is less than 100% of the Research involved used by the Investment Manager to directly assist in its Investment Decision-Making Process?

Yes

Determine the portion of the Research that may be paid for with Client Brokerage

A portion of the Research is used to directly assist the Investment Manager in its Investment Decision-Making Process

A portion of the Reseatch is not used to directly assist the Investment Manager in its Investment Decision-Making Process

Research can be paid for with Client Brokerage

Research cannot be paid for with Client Brokerage

APPENDIX C

Case Study under the CFA Institute Soft Dollar Standards

XYZ Firm is an Investment Manager that seeks to comply with the CFA Institute Soft Dollar Standards and claim such compliance. XYZ, a member of CFA Institute, manages a variety of accounts: separate accounts, including accounts of employee benefit plans subject to ERISA, accounts of non-ERISA institutional investors, and accounts of wealthy individuals; several collective investment vehicles, including a group trust for employee benefit plans subject to ERISA and/or governmental plans; a "hedge fund" for institutional and other "sophisticated" individual investors; and three SEC-registered investment companies, including an equity fund, a fixed-income fund, and a money market fund.

XYZ executes trades for its Client accounts with several broker–dealers who conduct trades for XYZ on both a principal and agency basis. Some of the broker–dealers have offered to provide XYZ with the following products and/or services for XYZ's own use, to be paid for with XYZ's Client Brokerage business: 1) desks and office equipment; 2) trading room television sets that receive the Financial News Network and other financial news services supplied by cable and satellite television services; 3) the Bloomberg Service, which includes a Bloomberg terminal; and 4) software that will assist XYZ in analyzing economic trends in industries followed by the Firm, as well as a widely available computer work station on which to install and operate the software. In addition, XYZ has received the following requests from Clients: 5) a pension fund Client subject to ERISA has requested that XYZ direct a portion of its Brokerage from its separate account to Broker ABC to obtain research information to be provided to the plan trustees; 6) a public pension plan has requested that XYZ direct a portion of its Brokerage to Broker ABC in return for cash credits to be paid to the Plan; 7) a non-ERISA institutional investor in XYZ's hedge fund has requested that XYZ direct a portion of the hedge fund's brokerage to Broker ABC to compensate Broker ABC for research services provided to the institutional investor; and, 8) the SEC-registered investment companies have requested that XYZ direct a portion of the equity fund's Brokerage to Broker ABC in return for credits to be used to reduce or eliminate all of the registered investment companies' custodian fees.

What steps or other actions must or should XYZ take to comply with the Soft Dollar Standards and/or other CFA Institute Standards of Professional Conduct?

Discussion

XYZ Firm is facing a set of decisions that typically confronts Investment Managers in connection with their use of Client Brokerage. XYZ should approach these decisions in a logical and systematic fashion to identify all relevant issues and ensure compliance with applicable law and CFA Institute Soft Dollar Standards. As an initial matter, XYZ should clearly isolate and identify the proposed transactions contemplated. Then, in order to determine compliance with applicable law and CFA Institute Soft Dollar Standards, XYZ should 1) consider fundamental principles that apply to the conduct of CFA Institute members, 2) identify applicable laws and regulations and analyze the proposed transactions in light of those laws and regulations, and 3) identify the CFA Institute Soft Dollar Standards and analyze the proposed transactions in light of those Standards. XYZ may pursue the proposed transactions only after satisfying itself that the transactions pass this systematic, multilevel analysis.

Isolate and Define the Proposed Transactions. One of the benefits of the CFA Institute Soft Dollar Standards is that they help Investment Managers to clearly define their practices as they relate to their Clients' Brokerage. By referring to the definitions contained in the Soft Dollar Standards, XYZ should determine that the broker–dealers' offer to provide the products and services in Transactions 1–4 described in the "Facts" section possibly constitutes a Soft Dollar Arrangement. Because XYZ is contemplating directing transactions to the broker–dealers to receive execution on trades and to receive products and services that will benefit XYZ directly, this offer may meet the CFA Institute Soft Dollar Standards definition of a Soft Dollar Arrangement. An additional measure of whether Transactions 1–4 qualify as Soft Dollar Arrangements under the CFA Institute Soft Dollar Standards is whether the products and services received by XYZ qualify as Research as defined in the Soft Dollar Standards. Transactions 5–8 may constitute Client-Directed Brokerage Arrangements, as defined in the CFA Institute Soft Dollar Standards, if XYZ determines that the *clients* are directing that their trades be routed through specific broker–dealers in order that the *clients* may receive benefits *in addition to* execution services.

Fundamental Principles. In considering the transactions that have been proposed, XYZ should adhere to a set of fundamental principles contained in three of the CFA Institute Standards that generally govern a member's conduct in this area. Standard I (Fundamental Responsibilities) of the CFA Institute Standards of Professional Conduct requires that a member be familiar and comply with all applicable laws governing their professional activities. XYZ is thus charged with a duty to know and apply the provisions of law that are implicated by the proposed transactions. Even if XYZ has adopted the CFA Institute Soft Dollar Standards, compliance with these Standards does not absolve XYZ of the responsibility to comply with applicable law. For situations in which the CFA Institute Standards impose a higher degree of responsibility or disclosure than, but do not conflict with, applicable law, XYZ must adhere to the provisions of the CFA Institute Standards *in addition to* any provisions of applicable law.

Moreover, Standard I of the CFA Institute Soft Dollar Standards contains fundamental principles that govern any of XYZ's activities involving Soft Dollar Arrangements. Standard I states that 1) Brokerage is the property of the Client and 2) XYZ has an ongoing duty to ensure the quality of transactions effected on behalf of its Clients, which includes:

- seeking to obtain Best Execution;
- minimizing transactions costs; and
- using Client Brokerage to benefit Clients.

These principles are reflected in the CFA Institute Soft Dollar Standards' requirement that XYZ, in considering a Soft Dollar Arrangement, must act for the benefit of its Clients and place its Clients' interests before its own.

Finally, Standard V of the CFA Institute Soft Dollar Standards, governing Client-Directed Brokerage Arrangements, requires that XYZ must not use Brokerage from another Client account to pay for a product or service purchased under the Client-Directed Brokerage Arrangement.

Applicable Laws and Regulations. Members are expected at all times to comply with the applicable laws of the countries in which they do business. For example, in the United States, the Securities Exchange Act of 1934, Investment Company Act of 1940, Investment Advisers Act of 1940, and Employment Retirement Income Security Act of 1974 would govern certain or possibly all of the transactions that XYZ is considering. Regardless of the country in which XYZ is doing business, as a threshold matter, it must analyze each transaction for compliance with applicable law. Only those transactions that comply with local laws are eligible for subsequent analysis under the CFA Institute Soft Dollar Standards.

Applicable Relevant Standards. Assuming each of the proposed transactions has "survived" the first two stages of analysis, they must still comply with provisions of the CFA Institute Soft Dollar Standards in order for XYZ to pursue them. Because XYZ has previously determined that each of the transactions qualifies as a possible Soft Dollar Arrangement (depending on whether the products or services qualify as Research under the CFA Institute Soft Dollar Standards) or a Client-Directed Brokerage Arrangement (depending on whether XYZ's Client is directing its trades to receive a benefit), XYZ must satisfy the following three broad requirements to claim compliance with the Soft Dollar Standards:

- Determine that each arrangement is permitted by the CFA Institute Soft Dollar Standards.
- Disclose the Investment Manager's Soft Dollar policies to its Clients.
- Maintain the specified records.

A. *Determinations of Eligibility.* Standard III of the CFA Institute Soft Dollar Standards requires that, as an initial matter in selecting any broker, XYZ must consider the capabilities of the broker to provide Best Execution. Once XYZ has satisfied itself that a particular broker will provide Best Execution, XYZ must next evaluate any additional research provided by the broker under the following four criteria specified in Soft Dollar Standard IV:

- The research under consideration must meet the definition of Research contained in the Soft Dollar Standards.
- The Research must benefit XYZ's clients.
- XYZ must be able to document the basis for its determination.
- Under certain fiduciary regulations (i.e., ERISA, the Investment Company Act of 1940), for trades conducted on a principal basis, the Research must directly benefit the Client account generating the trade. If not so limited by such regulations, the Research must directly benefit the Client account generating the trade, unless XYZ has made disclosure and obtained prior Client consent.

The meaning of the term "Research" is crucial to XYZ's evaluation under Soft Dollar Standard IV. "Research" is defined in the CFA Institute Soft Dollar Standards to mean services and/or products the primary use of which must directly assist the Investment Manager in its Investment Decision-Making Process and not in the management of the investment firm.

Transaction 1—Use of Client Brokerage to Pay for Desks and Office Equipment   Transaction 1 would not qualify for Research as defined in the Soft Dollar Standards because desks and office equipment would not satisfy the Soft Dollar Standards' definition of Research. Although XYZ should be able to determine that desks and office equipment do not qualify as Research based on the plain terms of the definition, the result becomes clear when XYZ applies the three-level analysis. Under that analysis, XYZ would first define the products or services that it desires to purchase with Client Brokerage. The desks are a discrete and simple product that can be clearly identified. Although office equipment is a somewhat general term, XYZ should also be able to clearly identify the office equipment being offered (e.g., photocopier, fax machine, etc.). XYZ next would analyze the primary use of these products to determine whether they will directly assist XYZ's Investment Decision-Making Process. At this point, XYZ clearly should understand that desks and most office equipment cannot be considered to aid directly in the Investment Decision-Making Process and hence do not qualify as Research under the CFA Institute Soft Dollar Standards. Because the Soft Dollar Standards only permit XYZ to receive Research as defined in the CFA Institute Soft Dollar Standards, XYZ could not engage in Transaction 1 and claim compliance with the CFA Institute Soft Dollar Standards.

Transaction 2—Use of Client Brokerage to Pay for Trading Room Television Sets   Transaction 2 involves a service that is more difficult than office equipment to analyze under the definition of Research contained in the Soft Dollar Standards. The service that XYZ desires to purchase is really a composite of products and services that may or may not qualify as Research under the definition provided in the Soft Dollar Standards. XYZ's first task is to define the service under the first level of analysis. Accordingly, XYZ should narrowly construe the component parts that are *necessary* for the service at issue in this example (i.e., financial news networks) to assist XYZ in its Investment Decision-Making Process. In this situation, XYZ could reasonably conclude that the component parts (i.e., television sets, individual financial news services, and cable or satellite providers) are necessary for the total service to assist XYZ in its Investment Decision-Making Process. Thus, the service is potentially eligible to be paid for with client brokerage, *provided* that the total service satisfies the next level of analysis.

Applying the next level of analysis would allow XYZ to conclude that the service may qualify as Research if the primary use of the service is to directly aid the Investment Manager in its Investment Decision-Making Process. Even if financial news services have a broader use than to provide data to Investment Managers for purposes of making investment decisions, it would be consistent with the Soft Dollar Standards for XYZ to conclude that such services meet the primary use analysis—if based on actual use.

Transaction 3—Use of Client Brokerage to Pay for the Bloomberg Service   Transaction 3 involves a similar analysis under the definition of Research contained in the CFA Institute Soft Dollar Standards. As with Transaction 2, XYZ's first step is to define the products or services that XYZ proposes to purchase with Client Brokerage. Again, XYZ should narrowly construe the component parts and could reasonably conclude that the Bloomberg terminal is a necessary component to receive the Bloomberg Service.

In applying the next level of analysis, XYZ may also reasonably conclude that the primary use of the Bloomberg Service, with its specific focus on real-time market news and analysis, does directly aid in the Investment Decision-Making Process. The service, therefore, may satisfy the first two levels of analyzing the definition of Research contained in the Soft Dollar Standards. However, if XYZ uses the Bloomberg Service and terminal to allow Clients to access financial information, the primary use of the service would not be to assist XYZ in its Investment Decision-Making Process, and the service would not qualify as Research under the CFA Institute Soft Dollar Standards. If XYZ uses the Bloomberg Service and terminal both in its own Investment Decision-Making Process and for Client purposes, at the third level of analysis, XYZ must make a good faith determination as to what portion of the service is actually used in the Investment Decision-Making Process. Only this portion may be paid for with Client Brokerage. XYZ must reevaluate this allocation on an annual basis.

Transaction 4—Use of Client Brokerage to Pay for Software and Computer Workstations   At this point, XYZ should be comfortable applying the three-level analysis required to define Research under the Soft Dollar Standards. Transaction 4 involves the same analysis that confronted XYZ in the first three transactions. In defining the product in Transaction 4 (i.e., the research software), XYZ might reasonably determine that each of the component parts (the software and workstation) is necessary for the product to assist in the Investment Decision-Making Process.

Furthermore, XYZ might reasonably conclude under the second level of analysis that the software (and its component parts) will directly aid XYZ's Investment Decision-Making Process. If the primary use of the software is to directly assist XYZ in its Investment Decision-Making Process (as indicated by Level II analysis), XYZ may purchase the software using Client Brokerage. However, as with Transaction 3, only that portion actually used by XYZ in its Investment Decision-Making Process (as determined by Level III analysis) may be paid for with Client Brokerage, and any mixed-use allocation must be reevaluated annually.

Client-Directed Transactions. The eligibility of Transactions 5–8 must be determined under the portions of the CFA Institute Soft Dollar Standards related to Client-Directed Brokerage Arrangements. Standard V of the CFA Institute Soft Dollar Standards requires that, in considering Transactions 5–8, XYZ must not use Brokerage from another Client account to pay for a product or service purchased under the Client-Directed Brokerage Arrangement. Standard V also recommends that XYZ attempt to structure the Client-Directed Brokerage Arrangement in accordance with certain recommended practices under the CFA Institute Soft Dollar Standards.

Transaction 5—Directing of Brokerage by ERISA Client to Benefit Plan Trustees   In considering Transaction 5, XYZ must be particularly cognizant of the definition of Client contained in the Soft Dollar Standards. The Standards define Client to refer to "the entity, including a natural person, investment fund, or separate account, designated to receive the benefits, including income, from the Brokerage generated through Securities Transactions."

Although this definition of Client also recognizes that a Client may be represented by a trustee or other Fiduciary, XYZ must be sensitive to the fundamental principle contained in Standard I of the CFA Institute Soft Dollar Standards that stresses that Brokerage is the property of the *Client*, not the trustee or Fiduciary representing the Client. XYZ should immediately question whether Transaction 5 qualifies as a Client-Directed Brokerage Arrangement because the additional benefit flows not to the Client but to the Client's trustees. Because Transaction 5 likely does not qualify as a proper Client-Directed Brokerage Arrangement, if XYZ were to pursue it, XYZ would be violating the fundamental principle that requires the use of Client Brokerage to benefit Clients. XYZ should, therefore, decline to pursue Transaction 5.

Transaction 6—Directing of Brokerage by Public Pension Plan to Obtain Cash Credits for the Plan   Transaction 6, however, would be a permissible Client-Directed Brokerage Arrangement under the Soft Dollar Standards because Client Brokerage would be used to generate cash credits that solely benefit the Client. XYZ should attempt to structure the arrangement in conformity with the recommended practices for Client-Directed Brokerage Arrangements that are contained in the Soft Dollar Standards, which would require XYZ to:

■ Disclose to the Client XYZ's duty to continue to seek to obtain Best Execution.

■ Disclose to the Client that committing a certain percentage of the Client's Brokerage to a particular broker–dealer may affect XYZ's ability to seek to obtain Best Execution and purchase adequate Research.

■ XYZ should receive written assurance from the plan trustees that the Client-Directed Brokerage Arrangement will solely benefit plan beneficiaries.

■ XYZ should attempt to structure the Client-Directed Brokerage Arrangement so that it does not require the commitment of a certain portion of Brokerage to a single broker and so that commissions are negotiated and seeking to obtain Best Execution is still relevant.

■ XYZ should request from the Client written instructions that 1) restate XYZ's continuing responsibility for seeking to obtain Best Execution, 2) list eligible brokers, 3) specify the target percentage of transactions to be directed, and 4) state procedures for monitoring the arrangement.

■ XYZ should regularly communicate with the Client for the purpose of jointly evaluating the Client-Directed Brokerage Arrangement, including 1) the potential for achieving Best Execution, 2) the list of brokers and their trading skills, 3) the target percentage of transactions to be directed to selected brokers, 4) XYZ's trading style and liquidity needs, and 5) other factors identified by the Client as relevant to the selection of brokers.

Transaction 7—Directing of Brokerage by Institutional Investor in Hedge Fund to Compensate Broker for Research Provided to Investor   Transaction 7 raises issues under Standard V of the CFA Institute Soft Dollar Standards because Standard V requires that XYZ not use Brokerage from another Client account to pay for a product or service purchased under the Client-Directed Brokerage Arrangement. In Transaction 7, XYZ's hedge fund is a commingled pool containing numerous investors. The CFA Institute Soft Dollar Standards define Client to refer to the beneficiaries of an *entity*, including, as in this case, *all* of the beneficiaries of an investment fund. However, the product or service purchased under this particular Client-Directed Brokerage Arrangement has benefited *only* the institutional investor in the hedge fund, not all of the Client's underlying investors and thus may be construed to violate the principles in Standard V of the CFA Institute Soft Dollar Standards. XYZ, therefore, should not pursue Transaction 7.

Transaction 8—Directing of a Portion of One Fund's Brokerage by Three Investment Companies to Benefit All Three Companies   Transaction 8 raises similar concerns as Transactions 5 and 7. XYZ is apparently directed by three distinct Clients (each of the three registered funds) to direct brokerage of one Client (i.e., the equity fund) to benefit all three Clients. XYZ should not pursue this arrangement because it would violate the principle in Standard V of the CFA Institute Soft Dollar Standards, which states that brokerage from another Client account should not be used to pay for a product or service purchased under a Client-Directed Brokerage Arrangement.

B.   *Disclosure.* In order to claim compliance with the CFA Institute Soft Dollar Standards, XYZ must also meet specific disclosure obligations relating to its Brokerage practices. In addition to XYZ's disclosure obligations described above in the discussion of the transactions, XYZ must clearly disclose the following information relating to its Soft Dollar and Client-Directed Brokerage Arrangements:

- XYZ must disclose to Clients and potential Clients whether XYZ may use the Research to benefit Clients other than those whose trades generated the Brokerage and whether the trades generating the Brokerage involved transactions conducted on a principal basis.

- XYZ must disclose to Clients 1) a description of the types of Research received through the arrangements, 2) the extent of its use, and 3) whether any broker affiliate of XYZ was involved.

- XYZ must provide each Client with a statement that any Soft Dollar or Client-Directed Brokerage Arrangements with respect to its account comport with the CFA Institute Soft Dollar Standards (this statement must be provided at least annually).

- XYZ must disclose in writing to its Clients that additional information in accordance with the CFA Institute Soft Dollar Standards concerning XYZ's Soft Dollar and Client-Directed Brokerage Arrangements is available on request. Such additional information should include 1) a firmwide description of the products and services that were received from each broker pursuant to a Soft Dollar Arrangement, including the identity of those Brokers; 2) for a specific Client account, the total amount of Commissions generated for the Client through Soft Dollar Arrangements, detailed by Broker and reporting the amount of Brokerage directed by the Client to specific brokers; and 3) the aggregate percentage of XYZ Brokerage derived from Client-Directed Brokerage Arrangements and the amount of the particular Client's Directed Brokerage as a percentage of the aggregate, subject to a 10 percent *de minimis* amount.

C. *Record Keeping*. In addition to the eligibility determinations and disclosure obligations, in order to claim compliance with the CFA Institute Soft Dollar Standards, XYZ must also maintain, when applicable, all records that:

- are required by applicable law;

- are necessary to supply Clients on a timely basis with the information required by Soft Dollar Standard VI;

- document arrangements, oral or written, obligating the Investment Manager to generate a specific amount of Brokerage;

- document arrangements with Clients pertaining to Soft Dollar or Client-Directed Brokerage Arrangements;

- document any agreements with Brokers pertaining to Soft Dollar Arrangements;

- document transactions with Brokers involving Soft Dollar Arrangements, including 1) a list of Proprietary or Third-Party Research providers and 2) a description of the service or product obtained from the provider;

- document the bases of allocation in determining to use Client Brokerage to pay for any portion of a Mixed-Use service or product;

- indicate how the services and products obtained through Soft Dollar Arrangements directly assist XYZ in the Investment Decision-Making Process;

- show compliance with the CFA Institute Soft Dollar Standards, including the identity of XYZ personnel responsible for determining such compliance;

- are copies of all Client disclosures and authorizations.

PRACTICE PROBLEMS FOR READING 3

The following information relates to Questions 1–6[1]

Portfolio manager Elsa Wirk, CFA, is a partner at LEV Capital Management, a long-only domestic equity manager. In addition to her portfolio management duties, Wirk is responsible for determining compliance with CFA Institute Soft Dollar Standards. In her morning mail, Wirk receives a notice that the local regulatory agency has issued a new rule about the use of client brokerage. According to the new rule, research to be paid with client brokerage "must include value-added analysis."

As part of her compliance duties, on a periodic basis Wirk evaluates the various brokers and research services used by LEV. Her assistant develops a worksheet of the brokerage firms' quoted commission rates for domestic stock trades. In addition, Wirk studies trading reports on each firm showing the average spread for all trades for each of the past 12 months and ranks the firms on an aggregate basis. Finally, Wirk evaluates research and other services available through soft dollars. Several firms offer proprietary and third-party research arrangements which LEV believes are valuable to the firm and its clients. Wirk polls staff members on the value of the services provided. After completing the research, Wirk develops a list of "preferred brokers" based on their commission structure, execution history, and research services. She instructs the firm's trading desk to direct trades to the preferred brokers whenever possible.

Babbit Financial is one of Wirk's preferred brokers. Babbit charges commissions of $0.05 per share and offers a variety of products and services including proprietary research. For firms that generate a minimum dollar amount of brokerage commissions, Babbit offers a subscription service that provides raw data feeds of historic price and economic information. Wirk is confident that the amount of brokerage directed to its preferred brokers will exceed the required minimum. LEV will be able to use the raw data feeds for research activities as well as valuing client portfolios.

Norton Investments, which recently launched a new hedge fund, is also a preferred broker. Norton charges commissions of $0.06 per share and provides third-party research including reports from Anderson Financial. Anderson produces excellent research in the area of derivatives and Wirk believes its reports will be useful to LEV in developing proprietary structured products.

Wirk is planning a meeting with a prospective client. The prospective client, a pension fund, requires that its advisers comply with CFA Institute Soft Dollar Standards. In preparation, Wirk sends the pension fund a packet containing the following information:

Soft Dollar Arrangements

LEV engages in soft dollar arrangements with brokers in which commission dollars generated by client trades pay for investment research and brokerage products and services. The commission paid to such brokers may be higher than the commission another broker would charge for the same transaction. The research purchased with brokerage benefits all clients and not only those whose trades generated the brokerage.

---

1 This case was written by Sarah W. Peck, PhD, and Dorothy C. Kelly, CFA.

LEV uses commissions on securities purchased or sold in client accounts to pay for the following services:

Research Provider	Broker	Description of Service
Alpha Financial	ABC	Stock market quotations and monitoring
Statbase	LMN	Statistical database
Mod-Allocator	ABC	Asset allocation modeling
Performance Analyst	PQR	Asset allocation backtesting

At the meeting, the pension fund trustees inform LEV that, by law, 20% of the fund's brokerage must be directed to three local minority-owned brokers. Wirk tells the pension fund board that, "We have a fiduciary duty to seek best execution for all client trades. The requirement to commit 20% of brokerage to specific firms may affect our ability to seek and obtain best execution. It may also adversely affect our ability to obtain adequate research for the fund."

The trustees respond that they "will continue to increase diversity by using minority-owned brokers and to support the regional economy by using local brokers." They also inform Wirk that they have entered into commission recapture programs with all three minority-owned firms. The commission recapture programs provide the pension fund with cash rebates that the pension fund uses to pay certain administrative expenses.

Wirk replies that to comply with the trustees' request, she will need written instructions identifying the eligible brokers, the approximate target percentage to be directed to each, and procedures for monitoring the arrangements. The pension fund soon signs a contract with LEV naming Wirk as portfolio manager.

The following month, Wirk directs the trading desk to purchase 10,000 shares of a mid-capitalization stock for the pension fund. The trading desk has three choices. Babbit would execute the trade on a principal basis rather than charge its normal commission. Norton would charge its normal commission of $0.06 to execute the trade. Framer, an agency broker that is not on Wirk's list of preferred brokers, specializes in the stock and would charge a commission of $0.05 per share. The head trader believes that Framer will execute the shares with minimal market impact.

1. Is directing brokerage to Wirk's preferred brokers consistent with both the required and recommended CFA Institute Soft Dollar Standards?

   A. Yes.

   B. Only if the preferred broker offers best execution.

   C. Only if the preferred broker offers research services of appropriate value.

2. According to the CFA Institute Soft Dollar Standards, is it permissible for Wirk to pay for some portion of Babbit's subscription service with client brokerage?

   A. Yes.

   B. No, because the service does not include value-added analysis.

   C. No, because the service requires a minimum dollar amount of transactions.

3. Is the purchase of Anderson reports with client brokerage consistent with both the required and recommended CFA Institute Soft Dollar Standards?

   A. Yes.

   B. No, because the reports are from a third-party.

   C. No, because the reports do not support the investment decision-making process.

4. Is the written information that Wirk provides to the potential client consistent with both the required and recommended CFA Institute Soft Dollar Standards?

    A. Yes.

    B. No, because it does not address whether trades generating brokerage involve transactions conducted on a principal basis.

    C. No, because it does not indicate that all soft dollar arrangements comply with the CFA Institute Soft Dollar Standards.

5. Are Wirk's oral statements about the pension fund's proposed directed brokerage arrangement consistent with both the required and recommended CFA Institute Soft Dollar Standards?

    A. Yes.

    B. No, because Wirk should disclose the information in writing.

    C. No, because Wirk was misrepresenting the facts—the arrangement will not affect Wirk's ability to obtain adequate research.

6. Are the written instructions that Wirk requests from the pension plan consistent with recommended practices of the CFA Institute Soft Dollar Standards?

    A. Yes.

    B. No, because Wirk should also request written instructions that relieve LEV of responsibility to seek best execution.

    C. No, because Wirk should also request written instructions that restate LEV's responsibility to seek best execution.

SOLUTIONS FOR READING 3

1. B is correct. According to the general principles of the CFA Institute Soft Dollar
    Standards, LEV has an ongoing duty to ensure the quality of transactions made
    on its behalf including seeking to obtain best execution.

2. B is correct. Compliance with the Soft Dollar Standards does not absolve Wirk
    of her responsibility to comply fully with applicable law. According to the local
    regulatory authority, permissible research must include value-added analysis.
    Raw data feeds of historical prices would not qualify as permissible research
    according to the regulatory agency's rules.

3. C is correct. According to the Standards, research paid by client brokerage
    must directly assist the investment manager in investment decision-making.
    Anderson's research on structured products will not assist LEV, a long-only
    domestic equity manager, in its current investment decision-making, but more
    likely will benefit new product development.

4. B is correct. The Standards require that an investment manager disclose its
    policies with respect to soft dollar arrangements to both clients and potential
    clients. The disclosure must address whether trades generating brokerage
    involve transactions conducted on a principal basis.

5. A is correct. In cases of client-directed brokerage, the Standards recommend
    that the manager disclose his duty to continue to seek to obtain best execution;
    the client-directed brokerage arrangement may affect the manager's ability to
    seek to obtain best execution.

6. C is correct. In a client-directed brokerage arrangement, the Standards
    recommend that investment managers request written instructions that restate
    the manager's continuing responsibility to seek to obtain best execution.

4

CFA Institute Research Objectivity Standards

(ROS)

GUIDING PRINCIPLES

1

CFA Institute has been concerned for some time that allegations of ethical misconduct and lack of objectivity and independence of research analysts weaken investor confidence in the financial markets and taint the reputations of all investment professionals. CFA Institute believes that the vast majority of investment professionals, particularly CFA Institute members who must attest annually to their adherence to the CFA Institute Code of Ethics and Standards of Professional Conduct, have professional integrity and should be able to conduct their professional activities free from pressure to bias their research and recommendations.

Therefore, the guiding principles that support the CFA Institute-ROS (Research Objectivity Standards) directly reflect the CFA Institute Code of Ethics:

- To act with integrity, competence, dignity, and in an ethical manner when dealing with the public, clients, prospects, employers, employees, and fellow CFA Institute members.

- To practice and encourage others to practice in a professional and ethical manner that will reflect credit on CFA Institute members and their profession.

- To strive to maintain and improve their competence and the competence of others in the profession.

- To use reasonable care and exercise independent judgment.

These principles, in concert with the CFA Institute mission "to advance the interests of the global investment community by establishing and maintaining the highest standards of professional excellence and integrity," provide the motivation and philosophical basis for undertaking this project to develop the CFA Institute-ROS.

(ROS)

2 COMPARISON WITH THE NEW YORK STOCK EXCHANGE AND NATIONAL ASSOCIATION OF SECURITIES DEALERS RULES

In the United States, the New York Stock Exchange (NYSE) and the National Association of Securities Dealers (NASD) recently issued new rules for their members relating to the issues of analyst independence and objectivity. CFA Institute commented on the adequacy of these rules when proposed by the NYSE, NASD, and the U.S. Securities and Exchange Commission. CFA Institute was generally supportive of these rules, which closely reflect the recommendations of the CFA Institute Task Force on Analyst Independence and the CFA Institute-ROS in their draft form.

Despite the implementation of the NYSE/NASD rules, CFA Institute still sees a definite need to go forward with the CFA Institute-ROS. As a global organization, CFA Institute believes that the ethical conflicts facing research analysts are worldwide and not just relevant to those working in the United States. The CFA Institute-ROS are designed so that there will be no conflict for firms between the NYSE/NASD rules and the CFA Institute-ROS.

3 OVERVIEW OF THE CFA INSTITUTE RESEARCH OBJECTIVITY STANDARDS

The CFA Institute-ROS are intended to be specific, measurable standards for managing and disclosing conflicts of interest that may impede a research analyst's ability to conduct independent research and make objective recommendations. Based on the ethical principles of placing the interests of investing clients before one's own, or the firm's, and of full and fair disclosure of conflicts of interest, the CFA Institute-ROS provide ethical standards and accompanying specific recommended practices to guide investment firms worldwide, and their respective employees, in achieving objectivity and independence of research reports.

Firms that adopt the CFA Institute-ROS demonstrate their commitment to manage conflicts of interest effectively and to provide full and fair disclosure of these conflicts to all investors who have access to their research. CFA Institute believes that firms that claim adoption will benefit from the competitive advantage that a commitment to, and reputation for, integrity yields.

A fundamental principle of ethical investment practice is that the best interests of the investing client must always take precedence over the interests of investment professionals and their employers. Every investment professional is personally responsible for ensuring that his or her independence and objectivity is maintained when preparing research reports, making investment recommendations, and taking investment action on behalf of clients. The CFA Institute Code of Ethics and Standards of Professional Conduct (CFA Institute Code and Standards), to which all CFA Institute members, Chartered Financial Analyst™ (CFA®) charterholders, and CFA candidates must adhere, already embody these principles. Therefore, the CFA Institute-ROS are designed to complement, not replace, the CFA Institute Code and Standards. CFA Institute believes that firms that comply with the CFA Institute-ROS will provide an appropriate working environment for their investment professionals—one that promotes ethical behavior and facilitates compliance with the CFA Institute Code and Standards.

Adoption of the CFA Institute-ROS cannot ensure the accuracy of research reports and recommendations. Future events are inherently uncertain. Regardless of the comprehensiveness and sophistication of the methodology used in the financial analysis, the actual event will often differ from the forecast on which investment recommendations are made. However, CFA Institute believes that firms that adopt the CFA Institute-ROS will instill confidence in investors and demonstrate that their research and recommendations have a reasonable and adequate basis, clearly differentiate between fact and opinion, and fully convey the opinion of the author(s).

Finally, CFA Institute recognizes that no finite set of guidelines or recommended practices will be exhaustive, nor will it address all future developments in the investment industry's structure and practices. Good ethics is always a work-in-progress. Therefore, CFA Institute encourages firms that adopt the CFA Institute-ROS to strive continuously to comply not only with the principles set forth in the Standards themselves, but also with the recommended procedures for compliance. In doing so, CFA Institute recommends that firms work to achieve the following objectives when designing policies and procedures to implement the CFA Institute-ROS:

A. To prepare research reports, make investment recommendations, and take investment actions; and develop policies, procedures, and disclosures that always place the interests of investing clients before their employees' or the firm's interests.

B. To facilitate full, fair, meaningful, and specific disclosures of potential and actual conflicts of interest of the firm or its employees to its current and prospective clients.

C. To promote the creation and maintenance of effective policies and procedures that would minimize and manage conflicts of interest that may jeopardize the independence and objectivity of research.

D. To support self-regulation through voluntary industry development of, and adherence to, specific, measurable, and demonstrable standards that promote and reward independent and objective research.

E. To provide a work environment for all investment professionals that supports, encourages, and rewards ethical behavior and supports CFA Institute members, CFA charterholders, and CFA candidates in their adherence to the CFA Institute Code and Standards.

DEFINITIONS

The following terms are used in the CFA Institute-ROS with the meanings specified:

Compliance and legal department: Department within a firm responsible for 1) implementing and enforcing a firm's policies and procedures and 2) ensuring that a firm and its employees are in compliance with applicable laws, rules, and regulations.

Corporate issuer: Company or corporation obtaining funding from public capital markets.

Covered employee: Firm employee who 1) conducts research, writes research reports, and/or makes investment recommendations; or assists in the research process; 2) takes investment action on behalf of clients or the firm, or who comes in contact with investment recommendations or decisions during the decision-making process; or 3) may benefit, personally or professionally, from influencing research reports or recommendations.

Immediate family: Individual(s) whose principal residence is the same as the principal residence of the subject person.

(CROS)

Investment advisory relationship: Asset management relationship that entails entire, shared, or partial investment discretion over client funds.

Investment banking: Corporate finance activities, such as acting as an underwriter in an offering for a subject company, acting as a financial adviser in a merger or acquisition, providing venture capital, lines of credit or other similar products, making a market in a security, or serving as a placement agent for corporate issuers.

Investment manager: Individual employed by an investment management firm (e.g., mutual fund, investment adviser, pension funds) to research securities and/or take investment action to purchase or sell securities for client accounts or for the firm's own account, whether or not such person has the title of "investment manager."

Personal investments and trading: Purchases and sales of a particular security including maintaining long-, short-, and other derivative positions in which an individual has a financial interest.

Public appearance: Participation in a seminar; open forum (including an interactive electronic forum); radio, television, or other media interview; or other public speaking activity in which a research analyst or investment manager makes a recommendation or offers an opinion.

Quiet period: Period during which covered employees are prohibited from issuing research reports or recommendations on, and publicly speaking about, a specific subject company.

Research analyst: Person who is primarily responsible for, contributes to, or is connected with, the preparation of the substance of a research report or the basis for a recommendation, whether or not any such person has the title of "research analyst."

Research report: Written or electronic communication that firms sell or distribute to clients or the general public, which presents information about a corporate issuer and may express an opinion or make a recommendation about the investment potential of the corporate issuer's equity securities, fixed income securities, or derivatives of such securities.

Restricted period: A period of time during which a firm prohibits its covered employees from trading specified securities.

Subject company: Corporate issuer whose securities are the subject of a research report or recommendation.

Supervisory analyst: Designated person responsible for reviewing research reports to assess and maintain the quality and integrity of research reports.

4 INVESTMENT BANKS, BROKER-DEALERS AND OTHER FIRMS THAT SELL RESEARCH

The following standards are applicable to firms, such as investment banks, broker-dealers, and independent research firms, that employ investment professionals to research issuers and make recommendations about these issuers' securities, and that sell these research reports and recommendations for either hard currency or soft commissions ("sell-side" firms).

Requirements

1.0 *Research Objectivity Policy*

Firms must have:

a. a formal written policy on the independence and objectivity of research (Policy) that must be:

    i. made available to clients and prospective clients (both investing and corporate); and

    ii. disseminated to all firm employees;

b. supervisory procedures that reasonably ensure that the firm and its covered employees comply with the provisions of the policy and all applicable laws and regulations; and

c. a senior officer of the firm who attests annually to clients and prospective clients to the firm's implementation of, and adherence to, the Policy.

2.0 *Public Appearances*

Firms that permit research analysts and other covered employees to present and discuss their research and recommendations in public appearances must require these employees to fully disclose personal and firm conflicts of interest to the host or interviewer and, whenever possible, to the audience.

3.0 *Reasonable and Adequate Basis*

Firms must require research reports and recommendations to have a basis that can be substantiated as reasonable and adequate. An individual employee (supervisory analyst who is someone other than the author) or a group of employees (review committee) must be appointed to review and approve all research reports and recommendations.

4.0 *Investment Banking*

Firms that engage in, or collaborate on, investment banking activities must:

a. establish and implement effective policies and procedures that:

    i. segregate research analysts from the investment banking department; and

    ii. ensure that investment banking objectives or employees do not have the ability to influence or affect research or recommendations;

b. implement reporting structures and review procedures that ensure that research analysts do not report to, and are not supervised or controlled by, investment banking or another department of the firm that could compromise the independence of the analyst; and

c. implement procedures that prevent investment banking or corporate finance departments from reviewing, modifying, approving, or rejecting research reports and recommendations on their own authority.

5.0 *Research Analyst Compensation*

Firms must establish and implement salary, bonus, and other compensation for research analysts that:

a. align compensation with the quality of the research and the accuracy of the recommendations over time; and

b. do not directly link compensation to investment banking or other corporate finance activities on which the analyst collaborated (either individually or in the aggregate).

6.0 *Relationships with Subject Companies*

Firms must implement policies and procedures that manage the working relationships that research analysts develop with the management of subject companies.
    Research analysts must be prohibited from:

a. sharing with, or communicating to, a subject company, prior to publication, any section of a research report that might communicate the research analyst's proposed recommendation, rating, or price target; and

b. directly or indirectly promising a subject company or other corporate issuer a favorable report or a specific price target, or from threatening to change reports, recommendations, or price targets.

7.0 *Personal Investments and Trading*

Firms must have policies and procedures that:

a. manage covered employees' "personal investments and trading activities" effectively;

b. ensure that covered employees do not share information about the subject company or security with any person who could have the ability to trade in advance of ("front run") or otherwise disadvantage investing clients;

c. ensure that covered employees and members of their immediate families do not have the ability to trade in advance of or otherwise disadvantage investing clients relative to themselves or the firm;

d. prohibit covered employees and members of their immediate families from trading in a manner that is contrary to, or inconsistent with, the employees' or the firm's most recent, published recommendations or ratings, except in circumstances of extreme financial hardship; and

e. prohibit covered employees and members of their immediate families from purchasing or receiving securities prior to an IPO for subject companies and other companies in the industry or industries assigned.

8.0 *Timeliness of Research Reports and Recommendations*

Firms must issue research reports on subject companies on a timely and regular basis.

9.0 *Compliance and Enforcement*

Firms must:

a. have effective enforcement of their policies and compliance procedures to ensure research objectivity;

b. implement appropriate disciplinary sanctions for covered employees, up to and including dismissal from the firm, for violations;

c. monitor and audit the effectiveness of compliance procedures; and

d. maintain records of the results of internal audits.

10.0 *Disclosure*

Firms must provide full and fair disclosure of all conflicts of interest to which the firm or its covered employees are subject.

11.0 *Rating System*

Firms must establish a rating system that:

a. is useful for investors and for investment decision-making; and

b. provides investors with information for assessing the suitability of the security to their own unique circumstances and constraints.

Recommended Procedures for Compliance

1.0 *Research Objectivity Policy*

An effective Research Objectivity Policy would clearly identify and describe the job title, function and department of covered employees. It should also identify whether covered employees are personally subject to a code of ethics and standards of professional conduct and provide the code and standards, if applicable. Covered employees should include those who conduct research, write research reports, and make recommendations, those who come in contact with research and recommendations, and those who may benefit from influencing research and recommendations.

Covered employees should be regularly trained on their responsibilities under the Policy and be required to attest annually in writing to their understanding of and adherence to it.

Full disclosure of the conflicts of interest that covered employees may face is a critical element of any Policy. These conflicts may include collaboration with investment banking or corporate finance; participation in marketing activities; necessary ongoing working relationships with corporate issuers; personal investments and trading; and firm investments and trading. The Policy should discuss each conflict that a firm's covered employees may face and how the firm's policies and procedures manage those conflicts effectively.

Since compensation is a major motivator of employee decision-making and actions, the Policy should clearly describe the factors on which compensation of research analysts is based.

Firms should also disclose in the Policy the conditions under which a research report can be purchased or acquired by clients, prospective clients, and investors in general.

It is recommended that firms post the Policy on their website for easy access by clients and prospective clients.

2.0 *Public Appearances*

A public appearance includes participation in a seminar; forum (including an interactive electronic forum); radio, television, or other media interview; or other public speaking activity in which a research analyst makes a recommendation or offers an opinion.

At a minimum, firms that permit covered employees to present and discuss research and recommendations in public or open forums (whether the audience consists of investment professionals, investing clients, or the general investing public) have a responsibility to ensure that the audience of such presentations has sufficient information to make informed judgments about the objectivity of the research and recommendations. Firms should also recognize that their employees have a responsibility to provide sufficient information to the audience to assess the suitability of the investment in light of their specific circumstances and constraints. Speakers should remind audience members to judge the suitability of the investment in light of their own unique situation.

Covered employees who make public appearances should be prepared to make full disclosure of all conflicts of interest, either their own or their firms', about which they could reasonably be expected to know. Firms should require research analysts who participate in public appearances to make the following disclosures to the interviewer or the audience as appropriate: 1) whether the research analyst knows (or has reason to know) whether the subject company is an investment banking or other corporate finance client of the firm; and 2) whether the research analyst has participated, or is participating, in marketing activities for the subject company.

Firms should provide the full research reports on the subject companies discussed to members of the audience at a reasonable price. At a minimum, the covered employee should disclose to the interviewer or audience whether a written research report is available to members of the audience who are not clients of the firm, the approximate cost, and how a viewer, listener, or reader might acquire the report.

Firms should make copies of the full research report available for purchase or review; for example via the firm's website.

3.0 *Reasonable and Adequate Basis*

Firms should develop detailed, written guidance for research analysts, supervisory analysts, and review committees that establish due diligence procedures for judging whether or not there is a reasonable and adequate basis for a particular recommendation.

When recommending a purchase, sale, or change in recommendation, firms should provide, or offer to provide, supporting information to investing clients. When making a recommendation, firms should disclose the current market price of the security in question.

4.0 *Investment Banking*

Collaboration between the research and investment banking activities of the firm creates severe conflicts of interest for research analysts. Firms need effective policies and procedures in place to safeguard the independence and objectivity of research analysts. Specifically, firms should prohibit research analysts from sharing with, or communicating to, members of the investment banking or corporate finance department, prior to publication, any section of the research report that might communicate the research analyst's proposed recommendation. The compliance or legal department should act as an intermediary for all communications between the research analyst and investment banking or corporate finance. Firms may permit investment banking or corporate finance personnel to review a research report only to verify factual information or to identify potential conflicts of interest. It is recommended that all written and oral communications between a research analyst and investment banking or corporate finance be documented and conducted with the compliance or legal department acting as an intermediary.

Firms should implement quiet periods for initial public offerings (IPOs) and secondary offerings of securities. Quiet periods should be of sufficient length to ensure that research reports and recommendations will not be based on inside information gained by the research analyst through investment banking sources. However, firms may issue an information-only research report concerning the effects of a significant event on a subject company if authorized by the compliance or legal departments. Quiet periods of 30 calendar days from issuance for IPOs and at least 10 calendar days from issuance for secondary offerings are recommended.

It is recommended that firms prohibit research analysts from participating in marketing activities, including "roadshows," for IPOs and secondary offerings in order to further the integrity of the ensuing quiet period. If firms permit research analysts to participate in such activities, the research analysts should disclose this participation in all interviews and public appearances.

5.0 *Research Analyst Compensation*

Firms should develop measurable criteria for assessing the quality of research including the reasonableness and adequacy of the basis for any recommendation and the accuracy of recommendations over time. Firms should implement compensation arrangements that depend on these measurable criteria and that are applied consistently to all research analysts. It is recommended that such criteria form a part of the Policy and be made available to clients and prospective clients.

Although direct linking of analyst's compensation with investment banking and corporate finance activities is prohibited, firms should disclose the extent to which research analyst compensation in general is dependent upon the firm's investment banking revenues.

6.0 *Relationships with Subject Companies*

In order to conduct quality research and develop a reasonable and adequate basis for a recommendation, research analysts, who rely on company financial reports and other documents for their research and as part of the basis for their recommendation, need the ability to communicate with subject-company management and participate fully in conference calls and other subject-company investor and analyst-relations activities. Maintaining appropriate working relationships with subject-company personnel is an important aspect of the research analyst's responsibilities.

Firms should establish and implement policies and procedures that govern these relationships, including policies regarding material gifts, company-sponsored and -paid trips, and communications with company management. Firms should have a clear, written definition of what constitutes "material."

Firms should implement procedures that ensure that only those sections of the report containing facts that could be reasonably checked or verified by the subject company are shared prior to publication.

It is recommended that the compliance or legal department receive a draft research report before sections are shared with the subject company, approve in advance all changes to a research report or recommendation that occur as a consequence of subject-company verification, and that the research analyst provide written justification for any changes that occur after verification by the subject company. It is also recommended that firms retain supporting documentation including the original report, the sections shared with the subject company, and any subsequent changes to the report or recommendation.

7.0 *Personal Investments and Trading*

Permitting research analysts and other covered employees to invest and trade in the securities of subject companies and industries may better align their personal interests with the interests of investing clients provided that precautions are taken to ensure that the interests of investing clients are always placed before the interests of the employee, members of their immediate families, and the firm.

Firms that permit covered employees and members of their immediate families to invest and trade in the securities, including derivative securities, of subject companies should require notification to, and approval by, the compliance or legal department in advance of all trades of securities in subject companies in the industry or industries assigned to that covered employee.

Firms should have specific policies and procedures that adequately prevent "front running" of investing client trades. These procedures should include restricted periods before and after issuing a research report. Restricted periods of at least 30 calendar days before and five calendar days after report issuance are recommended, with exceptions permitted on the announcement of significant news or events by the subject company if investing clients are given adequate notice and the ability to trade. However, restrictions on purchases or sales of securities need not apply to the securities of a diversified investment company or other investment fund over which the covered employees or members of their immediate families have no investment discretion or control.

When research analysts are permitted to invest and trade in the securities of the companies they cover, it is critical that firms prohibit them from trading contrary to the published recommendations of the firm on these companies. When research analysts trade contrary to their own investment recommendations, investing clients and prospective investing clients are rightly concerned about the quality and independence of the recommendation. Although there may be legitimate investment-management objectives for selling a security that the analyst recommends that investing clients purchase (e.g., the need to re-balance a diversified portfolio), investors are sent a mixed message that may cause concern and confusion.

There is one instance in which research analysts may be permitted to sell contrary to their recommendation. This is the case where the analyst would suffer "extreme financial hardship" if he or she could not liquidate these securities. To be clear and consistent about how this exception is applied, firms should have clear definitions of what constitutes extreme financial hardship and should also require a significant change in the employee's personal financial circumstances. Advance approval by the compliance or legal departments should be required. Appropriate documentation of the hardship conditions and the decision process should be retained.

Firms should require covered employees to provide to the firm or its compliance or legal department a complete list of all personal investments in which they or members of their immediate families have a financial interest. This list should be provided on a regular basis, but at least annually.

Firms should establish policies and procedures that prevent short-term trading of securities by covered employees. It is recommended that covered employees be required to hold securities for a minimum of 60 calendar days, except in the case of extreme financial hardship.

8.0 *Timeliness of Research Reports and Recommendations*

Firms have a fiduciary responsibility to investing clients to provide them with adequate and timely information on subject companies. To this end, firms should require research reports to be issued and recommendations or ratings to be confirmed or updated on a regular basis. It is recommended that reports and recommendations be issued at least quarterly, with additional updates recommended when there is an announcement of significant news or events by, or that might impact, the subject company.

Firms should not quietly and unobtrusively discontinue coverage of a subject company. When coverage of a subject company is being discontinued, firms should require the research analyst to issue a "final" research report that includes a recommendation. The final report should clearly explain the reason for discontinuing coverage.

9.0 *Compliance and Enforcement*

Firms should disseminate a list of activities that would be considered violations and resulting disciplinary sanctions to all covered employees. Firms should also disseminate a list of activities that would be considered violations and resulting disciplinary sanctions to all clients (both investing and corporate) and prospective clients. It is recommended that firms provide this information on their websites in conjunction with the publication of the research objectivity policy.

10.0 *Disclosure*

To be full and fair, disclosures should be comprehensive and complete, be presented prominently in the supporting documents or on the firm's website, be written in plain language that is easily understood by the average reader, and be designed to inform rather than obscure the nature of the conflicts of interest faced by the covered employee or the firm. It is recommended that such disclosure, or a page reference to the disclosure, be made on the front of the research report.

Firms that engage in investment banking or other corporate finance activities should disclose whether the subject company is currently an investment banking or other corporate finance client (corporate client) of the firm. It is recommended that firms disclose in the research report whether they have received compensation during the previous 12 months or expect to receive compensation in the next 3 months from a subject company that is a corporate client.

Firms should review all of their communications with investing clients to determine the most appropriate method of communicating conflicts of interest. Such communications would include advertisements, market letters, research reports, sales literature, electronic communications, and communications with the press and other media. In addition to disclosures in research reports, firms should determine the appropriate communications method(s) to inform investing clients of the following:

1. whether the firm makes a market in securities of a subject company;

2. whether the firm managed or co-managed a recent initial public or secondary offering of a subject company;

3. whether the research analyst or firm owns securities or any financial instrument that might reasonably be expected to benefit from the recommendation; or

4. whether the firm, an allied or affiliated firm, or the covered employee or a member of that employee's immediate family is a director, officer, or advisory board member of the subject company.

Firms should ensure that all conflicts of interest are disclosed in research reports. It is recommended that firms disclose the following in the research reports of all subject companies:

1. whether the subject company is a corporate client;

2. whether the firm or any of its affiliates holds one percent (1%) or more of any class of the outstanding common equity of the subject company as of five (5) business days prior to the issuance of the research report;

3. whether the firm makes a market in the securities of the subject company;

4. whether the firm permits the author(s) or members of their immediate families to invest or trade in the securities of the subject company;

5. whether the author(s) or members of their immediate families have a financial interest in any financial instrument that might reasonably be expected to benefit from the recommendation;

6. whether firm management, or the author(s) or members of their immediate families, are directors, officers, or advisory board members of the subject company; and

7. whether the author(s) of the report received a material gift from the subject company in the previous 12 months.

When the subject company is also a corporate client, it is recommended that firms also disclose the following in research reports and on their websites:

1. the nature of the corporate client relationship (e.g., initial public offering, merger and acquisition, etc.);

2. whether the firm received fees or revenues from the subject company in the previous 12 months or is expected to receive fees or revenues in the next 3 months;

3. whether the author(s) of the report assisted the firm in non-research activities and the specific nature of those activities (e.g., evaluated a subject company for acceptability as a corporate client, marketing activities); and

4. whether the compensation of the author(s) was dependent upon participation in investment banking or corporate finance activities.

Firms should provide appropriate statistical or other quantitative and qualitative presentations of information about their recommendations or ratings. In some jurisdictions, firms are required to provide distributions of their ratings by category and how these ratings have changed over time. Firms should provide information about prices of the securities of the subject company. It is recommended that price information be presented for a period of at least three years prior to the issuance of the research report. Firms should also provide information in connection with these price charts that identifies ratings and the dates of rating changes and provide information that identifies when and if the author(s) or research analysts changed the rating during that period.

Firms should disclose the valuation methods used to determine price targets and provide a description of the risk that may impede achieving those targets.

11.0 *Rating System*

One-dimensional rating systems do not provide sufficient information with which investors can make informed investment decisions. Therefore, firms should implement a rating system that incorporates the following: 1) recommendation or rating categories, 2) time horizon categories, and 3) risk categories.

Recommendation or rating categories may be absolute (e.g., buy, hold, sell) or relative (e.g., market outperform, neutral, or underperform). If the recommendation categories are relative, the firm should clearly identify the relevant benchmark, index, or objective.

Time horizon categories should clearly identify whether the time horizon measures the period over which the expected price target would be achieved or sustained.

Firms should require that communications of a firm's rating or recommendation, including discussions in public appearances, always include all three elements of the rating.

Firms should prohibit covered employees from communicating a rating or recommendation that is different from the current published rating or recommendation.

Firms should provide clients and prospective clients with a complete description of the firm's rating system on request. Firms should regularly inform clients and prospective clients of the availability of this description and how a client or prospective client can acquire this description.

PRACTICE PROBLEMS FOR READING 4

The following information relates to Questions 1–6

CVG is a regional investment firm that provides investment banking and brokerage services. The firm has a small investment research staff and has recently adopted the CFA Institute Research Objectivity Standards, including both the required and recommended policies and procedures.

Andrei Kepsh is a junior research analyst at CVG. The director of research has assigned Kepsh to initiate coverage on a local biotechnology company, GeoTech. CVG owns and makes a market in GeoTech shares. CVG recently participated in the selling group, but was not an underwriter, for GeoTech's initial public offering. Kepsh was not personally involved in the sale of the IPO. As part of his research, Kepsh meets with GeoTech's director of investor relations, Nils Olsen.

Two weeks later, on 2 May, Kepsh gives Olsen a copy of his completed GeoTech report containing a "buy" recommendation, and asks Olsen to correct any misstatements of fact before the report is released to CVG's clients. The next morning, Kepsh sends a copy of the GeoTech report to CVG's director of research. Kepsh also delivers the GeoTech report to CVG's investment banking department, and requests a review of his report for any conflicts of interest before it is released to CVG's clients on 5 May.

On 5 May, Kepsh has lunch with Gentura Hirai, one of the firm's senior analysts. Hirai explains the CFA Institute Research Objectivity Standards and CVG's policies and procedures regarding research reports and recommendations. Hirai states that CVG requires that reports be updated annually, or more frequently if there is substantive new information on the subject company. Also, because the research staff is small, CVG initiates coverage based on availability of the analytical staff and prioritizes companies to be covered on the basis of expected market attraction. Coverage is discontinued on the same basis, with a final report sent to clients if staff time permits.

After the appropriate waiting period, Kepsh purchases GeoTech shares for his personal account. On 11 May, Kepsh is one of the speakers at a biotechnology investment conference that is open to the public. By the time Kepsh presents his report on GeoTech, the conference is behind schedule. To save time, Kepsh summarizes his report and recommendation and does not make any disclosure statements. After the presentation, a conference participant requests a copy of his report. Kepsh responds that the report is available to the audience for a nominal fee.

On 25 May, Kepsh sells shares of GeoTech to pay for a wedding anniversary gift for his wife. In the future, Kepsh expects that, based on CVG's policy, he will receive large bonuses from increased investment banking fees and brokerage commissions attributable to his recommendations.

1. In giving his report to Olsen, does Kepsh comply with the CFA Institute Research Objectivity Standards?

    A. No.

    B. Yes, because he submitted a copy to the director of research.

    C. Yes, because he asked Olsen to correct any misstatements of facts.

2. Does Kepsh's interaction with the investment banking department comply with the CFA Institute Research Objectivity Standards?

    A. Yes.

    B. No, only because the investment banking department has been provided with the report containing the recommendation.

    C. No, both because the investment banking department has been provided with the report containing the recommendation, and because he does not direct the report through the compliance department.

3. Do CVG's policies regarding updating reports and discontinuing coverage, respectively, conform with the CFA Institute Research Objectivity Standards?

	Updating of Reports	Discontinuing Coverage
A.	No	No
B.	No	Yes
C.	Yes	No

4. To be in compliance with the CFA Institute Research Objectivity Standards, Kepsh must inform the conference audience about all of the following, *except*:

    A. CVG's ownership of GeoTech shares.

    B. CVG's making a market in GeoTech shares.

    C. CVG's participation in the selling group for the public offering of GeoTech.

5. Does Kepsh's response to the conference participant's question about the availability of the GeoTech report conform to the CFA Institute Research Objectivity Standards?

    A. Yes.

    B. No, because CVG should provide its research reports only to its clients.

    C. No, because CVG should provide research reports at no charge to all members of the audience.

6. Are Kepsh's sale of shares and CVG's bonus policy, respectively, in conformity with the CFA Institute Research Objectivity Standards?

	Sales of Shares	Bonus Policy
A.	No	No
B.	No	Yes
C.	Yes	No

SOLUTIONS FOR READING 4

1. A is correct. The Standards prohibit sharing the entire report and the recommendation with the subject company.

2. C is correct. The Standards recommend that any contact with the investment banking department regarding a research report be documented in writing, directed through the compliance department, and limited only to verification of facts, such as conflicts of interest.

3. A is correct. The Standards recommend that reports and recommendations be updated at least quarterly and that when coverage of a subject company is being discontinued, firms should issue a final research report and recommendation.

4. C is correct. The Standards require disclosure only if the firm managed or co-managed an offering of GeoTech securities.

5. A is correct. The Standards recommend that an analyst making a public appearance to discuss a report should disclose to the audience that the report is available at a reasonable price.

6. A is correct. The Standards prohibit Kepsh from trading in a manner that is contrary to the employee's or firm's most recent published recommendations. The Standards also prohibit direct linking of analyst compensation with investment banking activities.

Ethical and Professional Standards

Application

This study session uses case studies as an aid to understanding and internalizing the values and standards presented in the CFA Institute Code of Ethics and Standards of Professional Conduct.

The cases present realistic but fictional situations that closely approximate how individuals practicing in the investment industry encounter ethical issues in their day-to-day activities. The discussions following each case identify key violations of the Standards of Professional Conduct, recommend corrective actions, and when appropriate, present policy statements a firm could use in seeking to prevent the violations. The *Standards Reporter* readings present regulatory actions taken in response to actual occurrences and explain how the violations would be viewed from the perspective of the Code of Ethics and Standards of Professional Conduct.

Widespread recognition exists that certain situations create a relationship in which an elevated level of fidelity, due diligence, and prudence is required of the investment manager. Historically, the term "fiduciary" has been defined in country-specific laws and regulations, making generic definitions difficult. Nonetheless, the underlying principles of the prudent investor rule, presented in "Prudence in Perspective," capture much of what is expected of investment professionals entrusted with the prudent management of client assets.

READING ASSIGNMENTS

Reading 5   *The Glenarm Company*
                Ethics Cases

Reading 6   *Preston Partners*
                Ethics Cases

5

The Glenarm Company

by Glen A. Holden Jr., CFA

LEARNING OUTCOMES

Mastery	The candidate should be able to:
☐	**a** evaluate the practices and policies presented;
☐	**b** explain the appropriate action to take in response to conduct that violates the CFA Institute Code of Ethics and Standards of Professional Conduct.

CASE FACTS

Peter Sherman, CFA, recently joined the Glenarm Company after five years at Pearl Investment Management. He is very excited about the new job and believes he will make a big contribution to Glenarm. His first task is to identify attractive Latin American companies for Glenarm's emerging markets portfolio. Sherman, knowing many of these companies through his consulting contacts, approaches the task enthusiastically. He believes the Glenarm Company will clearly benefit from his knowledge about these companies and has no need to know about his consulting on the side.

Sherman's Background

Sherman had joined Pearl Investment Management, a small equity-oriented firm, as a junior research analyst. Pearl entered the international investing arena shortly after Sherman arrived, and Sherman performed well as he gained experience, particularly in researching emerging market securities. Sherman also spent some time handling client relations in the account administration department. More than a year ago, Sherman had earned his CFA designation.

Sherman's role at Pearl grew when several of his boss's foreign investment banking contacts hired Pearl to research companies and industries in Latin America in order to better position themselves vis-à-vis their local competitors.

When Pearl expanded its research department to accommodate these new projects, the company made Sherman its primary analyst for emerging markets. The firm encouraged Sherman to develop expertise in this area, and he capitalized on his position by serving as a consultant to several third-world companies to assist them in attracting U.S. and European investors, an arrangement that Sherman fully disclosed to Pearl. Pearl did not own stock in any of the companies that Sherman consulted with.

Shortly after Sherman's research responsibilities at Pearl expanded, he received a call from John Lawrence, an acquaintance in the local CFA Institute financial analysts society and a partner of the Glenarm Company, one of Pearl's competitors. Lawrence indicated that his company was looking for an individual with Sherman's background and asked him if he would be interested in becoming a portfolio manager at Glenarm.

Glenarm

The Glenarm Company is a small equity-oriented management firm. Glenarm was recently investigated, censured, and fined by the U.S. Securities and Exchange Commission for a number of violations related to its portfolio management practices. The latest censure was Glenarm's third in the past 13 years. The firm's partners are desperate to rehabilitate their reputation and stem the steady outflow of clients.

No one in the firm other than Lawrence is a member of CFA Institute or the local society, but the Glenarm partners have accepted Lawrence's reasoning that hiring a CFA charterholder as a portfolio manager will enhance the credentials of the firm, will demonstrate a commitment to professionalism in their practice, and is their best chance to expand their client base. Lawrence believes Sherman is an excellent prospect.

The Glenarm partners believe Sherman may be able to bring some business with him if he joins the firm. While at Pearl, Sherman developed client contacts through his duties with the research department and through handling client relations. He also has some knowledge of investment management clients by virtue of his interaction with the portfolio managers. To entice him, Glenarm offers Sherman a large portion of the first-year investment management fee for all the Pearl clients he is able to solicit and bring to Glenarm. Although he has reservations because of Glenarm's past problems with the SEC, Sherman decides that the opportunity is too good to pass up. Also, he can continue his consulting work. So, he agrees to join Glenarm as a portfolio manager.

The Transition

In preparation for his move to Glenarm but while he is still at Pearl, Sherman pays social calls on several local Pearl clients after business hours to inform them that he will be leaving Pearl and encourage them to switch their accounts to Glenarm. He also contacts a number of accounts that Pearl has been actively soliciting but that have not yet committed to hire Pearl as their investment manager. He also contacts prospects that Pearl has rejected in the past as too small or incompatible with the firm's business to determine if they are interested in hiring Glenarm. As a result of this activity, Sherman convinces several of Pearl's clients and prospects to hire Glenarm as their investment management company but to delay any action until he has joined Glenarm.

In his last week at Pearl, Sherman identifies material that he has worked on to take with him to his new job, including:

- sample marketing presentations he prepared;
- computer program models for stock selection and asset allocation that he developed;
- research material on several companies Sherman has been following;
- news articles he collected that contain potential research ideas; and
- a list of companies that Sherman suggested in the past deserved further research and possible investment and that were rejected by Pearl.

Several activities in the case are or could be in violation of the CFA Institute Code of Ethics and Standards of Professional Conduct (Code and Standards). Identify possible violations and state what actions are required by Sherman and/or Glenarm to correct the potential violations, and make a short policy statement a firm could use to prevent the violations.

CASE DISCUSSION

This case depicts violations or possible violations of the CFA Institute Code and Standards related to a member's duties toward the member's employer: the duty to disclose to one's employer additional compensation arrangements and the duty to disclose conflicts of interest to the employer.

Loyalty to One's Employer

Standard IV(A)—Duties to Employer: Loyalty, states that in matters related to their employment, members and candidates must act for the benefit of their employer and not deprive their employer of the advantage of their skills and abilities, divulge confidential information, or otherwise cause harm to their employer. Sherman's solicitation of clients and prospects and his plans to take Pearl property for the benefit of Glenarm are a breach of Standard IV(A).

Standard IV(A) does not preclude members from seeking alternative employment, but it does obligate a member to protect the interests of the employer by refraining from any conduct that could deprive an employer of profit or the benefits of the member's skills and abilities. An employee is free to make arrangements to leave any employer and go into competitive business—so long as the employee's preparations to leave do not breach the employee's duty of loyalty to the current employer.

In this instance, Sherman had an obligation to act in the best interests of Pearl while he was still an employee of Pearl. He had a duty not to engage in any activities that would be detrimental to Pearl's business until his resignation date became effective. The following activities by Sherman violated this duty of loyalty and, as a result, violated Standard IV(A).

Solicitation of clients and prospects. Sherman's solicitation of clients on behalf of Glenarm while he was still employed at Pearl is a clear violation of Standard IV(A). Attempting to lure clients from Pearl to another investment company undermined Pearl's business, and the fact that such activity was carried out "after hours" or in a social context is irrelevant; the damage to Pearl's business was the same. Even after leaving Pearl, Sherman must abide by any additional legal and contractual obligations between him and Pearl that would prevent solicitation of clients.

Soliciting potential clients of Pearl was also a violation of Standard IV(A). When engaging in such activity, Sherman was attempting to interfere with Pearl's business opportunities for his own benefit and the benefit of his future employer. Solicitation of clients and prospects cannot begin until Sherman has left Pearl and begun to work for Glenarm.

Sherman's contact of prospects that Pearl had not pursued because of their size or investment objectives does not constitute a violation of Standard IV(A) so long as the contacts were not in competition with Pearl in any way. Sherman could solicit business for his new employer on his own time when that activity did not interfere with his responsibilities at Pearl or take away a business opportunity from Pearl.

Misappropriation of employer property. Except with the consent of the employer, departing employees may not take property of the employer. Even material prepared by the departing employee is the property of the employer, and taking that property is a violation of the employee's duty to the employer. Employees must obtain permission to take with them any work or work product prepared in the course of the employee's employment or on behalf of the employer.

In this case, all the material mentioned as taken by Sherman was the property of Pearl. Sample marketing material prepared by Sherman, computer program models for stock selection and asset allocation that he developed, and research material and news articles that he collected are all Pearl's property because Sherman's efforts in creating or gathering these materials were undertaken in the context of his employment with and for the benefit of Pearl. Even the list of rejected research ideas was Pearl's property; those ideas were generated by Sherman for Pearl's consideration and use. The analyst that Pearl hires to replace Sherman might benefit by reviewing the list of ideas considered and rejected by the firm.

Actions Required

Sherman should have refrained from solicitation of any of Pearl's clients or prospects until he had left Pearl. Sherman should have obtained Pearl's permission to take copies of any work he prepared on behalf of Pearl in the course of his employment there. Without such permission, Sherman should not have taken any material that could have even remotely been considered Pearl's property.

Policy Statement for a Firm

"Employees shall not undertake any independent practice that could result in compensation or other benefit in competition with the firm unless they obtain written consent from the firm and the person or entity for whom they undertake independent practice. Departing employees shall not engage in any activities that would be in conflict with this policy, including soliciting firm clients or prospects, removing firm property, or misuse of confidential information."

Disclosure of Additional Compensation and Conflicts

Under Standard IV(B)—Duties to Employers: Disclosure of Additional Compensation Arrangements, CFA Institute members and candidates must not accept gifts, benefits, compensation, or consideration that competes with, or might reasonably be expected to create a conflict of interest with, their employer's interest unless they obtain written consent from all parties involved. Because such arrangements may affect an employee's loyalties and objectivity and may create conflicts of interest, employers must receive notice of these arrangements so that they can evaluate employees' actions and motivations.

In the case, Sherman disclosed his consulting arrangements to Pearl but not to Glenarm. Thus, he was violating Standard IV(B). Although Sherman's consulting activities might have uncovered investment opportunities for Glenarm clients, the arrangements had the potential to affect Sherman's ability to render objective advice and to divert Sherman's energies away from managing Glenarm clients' portfolios. Sherman should have given Glenarm written information on his independent practice so that the firm could make an informed determination about whether the outside activities impaired his ability to perform his responsibilities with the firm.

Sherman's consulting arrangements are also a violation of Standard VI(A)—Disclosure of Conflicts, and Standard I(B)—Independence and Objectivity. Under Standard VI(A), Sherman must make full and fair disclosure of all matters that could reasonably be expected to impair their independence and objectivity or interfere with respective duties to their employer, clients, and prospective clients. Members and candidates must ensure that such disclosures are prominent, are delivered in plain language, and communicate the relevant information effectively. Sherman could wind up receiving consulting fees from the same companies about which he is writing research reports for Glenarm's internal use. Thus, the consulting could compromise Sherman's independence and objectivity and would violate Standard I(B).

Actions Required

Sherman must disclose to Glenarm all outside compensation arrangements and describe in detail the activities that gave rise to this compensation. He must obtain written permission in advance of entering into these relationships.

Policy Statement for a Firm

"Employees shall disclose to the firm in writing all monetary compensation or other benefits that they receive for their services that are in addition to compensation or benefits conferred by the firm. Employees shall also disclose all matters that reasonably could be expected to interfere with their duty to this firm or ability to make unbiased and objective recommendations."

Mumbai			−11.7%
Singapore			−4.5%
Sydney	2971.0	1.1%	−4.7%
Shanghai B	4644.0	0.0%	−10.5%
Hong Kong	316.8	0.7%	−6.9%
Toronto	22,700.9	0.5%	−4.2%
Stockholm	13,524.8	0.1%	4.1%
Mexico City			

6

Preston Partners

by Jules A. Huot, CFA

LEARNING OUTCOMES

Mastery	The candidate should be able to:
☐	**a** evaluate the practices and policies presented;
☐	**b** explain the appropriate action to take in response to conduct that violates the CFA Institute Code of Ethics and Standards of Professional Conduct.

CASE FACTS

Sheldon Preston, CFA, the senior partner in Preston Partners, is sitting in his office and pondering the actions he should take in light of the activities of one of his portfolio managers, Gerald Smithson, CFA.

Preston Partners is a medium-sized investment management firm that specializes in managing large-capitalization portfolios of U.S. equities for pension funds and personal accounts. As president, Preston has made it a habit to review each day all the Preston Partner trades and the major price changes in the portfolios. Yesterday, he discovered some deeply disturbing information. Several weeks previously, when Preston was on a two-week vacation, Smithson had added to all his clients' portfolios the stock of Utah BioChemical Company, a client of Preston Partners, and of Norgood PLC, a large northern European manufacturer and distributor of drugs and laboratory equipment headquartered in the United Kingdom. Preston had known of a strong, long-standing relationship between Smithson and the president of Utah BioChemical. Indeed, among Smithson's clients were the personal portfolio of Arne Okapuu, president and CEO of Utah BioChemical, and the Utah BioChemical pension fund. Yesterday came the announcement that Utah BioChemical intended to merge with Norgood PLC, and with that news, the share prices of both companies increased more than 40 percent.

Preston Partners had adopted the CFA Institute Code of Ethics and Standards of Professional Conduct as part of the firm's own policy and procedures manual. Preston had written the manual himself but, because he had been pressed for time, had stuck to the key elements rather than addressing all policies in detail. He made sure that every employee received a copy of the manual when he or she joined the firm. Preston thought surely Smithson knew the local securities laws and the Code and Standards even if he hadn't read the manual. Extremely upset, Preston called Smithson into his office for an explanation.

While on vacation in Britain, Smithson narrated, he had seen Okapuu in a restaurant dining with someone he recognized as the chairman of Norgood. Their conversation appeared to be intense but very upbeat. Smithson did not attempt to greet Okapuu. Later, Smithson called on an old analyst friend in London, Andrew Jones, and asked him for some information on Norgood, the stock of which was trading as American Depositary Receipts (ADRs) on the New York Stock Exchange. Jones sent Smithson his firm's latest research report, which was recommending a "hold" on the Norgood stock.

Smithson was already somewhat familiar with the biochemical industry because his large accounts owned other stocks in the industry. Nevertheless, when he returned to the United States, he gathered together several trade journals for background, obtained copies of the two companies' annual reports, and carried out his own due diligence on Utah BioChemical and Norgood.

After thoroughly analyzing both companies' financial history, product lines, and market positions, Smithson concluded that each company's stock was selling at an attractive price based on his valuation. The earnings outlook for Norgood was quite positive, primarily because of the company's presence in the European Union and its strong supplier relationships. Norgood's stock price had shown little volatility but had risen consistently in the past, and the company currently had a strong balance sheet. Utah BioChemical, a leader in the biochemical industry, at one time had been a high-growth stock but had been in a slump in recent years. Based on his analysis of the new products in Utah's pipeline, however, and their market potential, Smithson projected strong sales and cash flow for Utah BioChemical in the future.

Through his research, Smithson also recognized that Utah BioChemical and Norgood were in complementary businesses. Reflecting on what he had seen on his trip to London, Smithson began to wonder if Okapuu was negotiating a merger with or takeover of Norgood. Convinced of the positive prospects for Utah BioChemical and Norgood, Smithson put in a block trade for 50,000 shares of each company. The purchase orders were executed during the next two weeks.

Smithson had not personally executed a block trade for some time; he usually left execution up to an assistant. Because this trade was so large, however, he decided to handle it himself. He glanced at the section on block trades in Preston Partners' policy and procedures manual, but the discussion was not clear on methods for allocating shares. So, he decided to allocate the shares by beginning with his largest client accounts and working down to the small accounts. Smithson's clients ranged from very conservative personal trust accounts to pension funds with aggressive objectives and guidelines.

At the time of Smithson's decision to make the share purchases, Utah BioChemical was trading at $10 a share and the Norgood ADRs were trading at $12 a share. During the next two weeks, the price for each company's shares rose several dollars, but no merger or takeover announcement was made—until yesterday.

> Several activities in this case are or could be violations of the CFA Institute Code and Standards. Identify possible violations, state what actions Preston and/or Smithson should take to correct the potential violations, and make a short policy statement a firm could use to prevent the violations.

CASE DISCUSSION

Gerald Smithson's story describes some perfectly legitimate actions but also some actions in clear violation of the CFA Institute Code and Standards. In researching and making the decision to purchase shares of Utah BioChemical and Norgood for his client accounts, Smithson complied with Standard V(A)—Diligence and Reasonable Basis. He observed a meeting between the heads of two public companies in related businesses, which sparked his interest in researching the companies further. He already had some knowledge of the biochemical industry through some clients' investments and through his relationship with Arne Okapuu, and he carried out his own due diligence on the companies. Smithson had a reasonable basis, supported by appropriate research and investigation, for his investment decision, and he exercised diligence and thoroughness in taking investment action.

Smithson neither possessed nor acted on insider information. He did not actually overhear a conversation; rather, after his research was complete, he "put two and two together" and speculated that the executives might have been discussing a merger or takeover. Viewing the two company leaders together was only one piece of his "mosaic" and was only a small factor in his investment decision-making process. If Smithson had based his decisions solely on his chance viewing of the dinner meeting, the investment decisions would have been inappropriate. Smithson failed to comply, however, with aspects of the Standards related to the suitability of the investments for his clients and the allocation of trades. In addition, Sheldon Preston failed to exercise his supervisory responsibilities.

Responsibilities to Clients and Interactions with Clients

Smithson purchased shares in Utah BioChemical Company and Norgood PLC for all of his client portfolios without first determining the suitability or appropriateness of the shares for each account. The case states that the investment objectives and guidelines for Smithson's accounts ranged from conservative, for his personal trust accounts, to aggressive, for his pension fund clients. Norgood, with its stable stock price, financial strength, and positive earnings outlook, appears to be a conservative stock that would fit within the guidelines of Smithson's more conservative accounts. It may or may not fit the more aggressive guidelines established for some of Smithson's pension fund clients.

Utah BioChemical, however, is probably too volatile to be included in a conservative account and thus may not have been appropriate or suitable for some of the firm's personal trust clients. Therefore, Smithson may have violated Standard III(C)—Suitability, in regard to the appropriateness and suitability of the investment actions he took. Under Standard III(C), an investment manager must consider the client's tolerance for risk, needs, circumstances, goals, and preferences, in matching a client with an investment.

Actions Required

The case does not make clear whether Smithson's clients have written investment objectives and guideline policy statements. If they do not, Preston should direct Smithson to prepare such written guidelines for all accounts. Smithson should review the guidelines for every account for which he bought shares of Utah BioChemical and Norgood and assess the characteristics of those investments in light of the objectives of the clients and their portfolios. In those accounts for which either investment is unsuitable and inappropriate, he should sell those shares, and Preston Partners should reimburse the accounts for any losses sustained by them.

Policy Statement for a Firm

"For each client of the firm, portfolio managers, in consultation with the client, shall prepare a written investment policy statement setting out the objectives, the constraints, and the asset-mix policy that meets the needs and circumstances of the client. Managers shall insert this analysis in each client's file. Portfolio managers shall review and confirm the investment policy statements at least annually and whenever the client's business or personal circumstances create a need to review them. In their client relationships, portfolio managers should be alert to any changes in the clients' circumstances that would require a policy review. When taking investment action, portfolio managers shall consider the appropriateness and suitability of an investment to the needs and circumstances of the client. Managers must satisfy themselves that the basic characteristics of the investment meet the written guidelines for the client's account."

Allocation of Trades

Standard III(B)—Fair Dealing, states that members shall deal fairly with clients when taking investment actions. In this case, the firm did not have detailed written guidelines for allocating block trades to client accounts. So, Smithson simply allocated trades to his largest accounts first, at more favorable prices, which discriminated against the smaller accounts. Certain small clients were disadvantaged financially because of Smithson's block-trade allocation method.

Standard III(B) arises out of the investment manager's duty of loyalty to clients embodied in the CFA Institute Code and Standards. Without loyalty, the client cannot trust or rely on the investment manager.

Whenever an investment manager has two or more clients, he or she faces the possibility of showing one client preference over the other. The Code and Standards require that the investment advisor treat each client fairly but do not specify the allocation method to be used. Moreover, treating all clients fairly does not mean that all clients must be treated equally. Equal treatment, given clients' different needs, objectives, and constraints, would be impossible.

Action Required

Because Preston Partners has only vague policies for portfolio managers on allocating block trades, Preston needs to formulate some detailed guidelines. The trade allocation procedures should be based on guiding principles that ensure 1) fairness to clients, both in priority of execution of orders and in the allocation of the price obtained in the execution of block trades, 2) timeliness and efficiency in the execution of trades, and 3) accuracy in the investment manager's records for trade orders and maintenance of client account positions. In advance of each trade, portfolio managers should be required to write down the account for which the trade is being made and the number of shares being traded.

Block trades are often executed throughout a day or week, which results in many small trades at different prices. To assure that all accounts receive the same average price for each segment of the trade, trades should be allocated to the appropriate accounts just prior to or immediately following each segment of the block trade on a pro rata basis. For example, if 5,000 shares of Norgood and 5,000 shares of Utah BioChemical traded on Day 1, Smithson would have immediately allocated each set of shares to each appropriate account according to the relative size of the account. Each account would thus pay the same average price. If 10,000 more shares traded later that day, or the next day, or so on, Smithson would follow the same procedure. Procedures for trade allocation should be disclosed to clients in writing at the outset of the client's relationship with the firm. Obtaining full disclosure and the client's consent does not, however, relieve the manager of the responsibility to deal fairly with clients under the Code and Standards.

Policy Statement for a Firm

"All client accounts participating in a block trade shall receive the same execution price and be charged the same commission, if any. All trade allocations to client accounts shall be made on a pro rata basis prior to or immediately following part or all of a block trade."

Responsibilities of Supervisors

Preston Partners did not have in place supervisory procedures that would have prevented Smithson's allocation approach. Preston's failure to adopt adequate procedures violated Standard IV(C)—Responsibilities of Supervisors. Preston Partners had adopted the Code and Standards; thus, anyone in the firm with supervisory responsibility should have been thoroughly familiar with the obligation of supervisors under the Code and Standards to make reasonable efforts to detect and prevent violations of applicable laws, rules, and regulations. Supervisors and managers should understand what constitutes an adequate compliance program and must establish proper compliance procedures, preferably designed to prevent rather than simply uncover violations.

The case notes that certain sections of the policy and procedures manual were unclear. Supervisors have a responsibility to ensure that compliance policies are clear and well developed. Supervisors and managers must document the procedures and disseminate them to staff. In addition to distributing the policy and procedures manual, they have a responsibility to ensure adequate training of each new employee concerning the key policies and procedures of the firm. Periodic refresher training sessions for all staff are also recommended.

Ultimately, supervisors must take the necessary steps to monitor the actions of all investment professionals and enforce the established policies and procedures.

Actions Required

Preston should assure that proper procedures are established that would have prevented the violation committed by Smithson. Preston should assume the responsibility or appoint someone within the firm to become the designated compliance officer whose responsibility is to assure that all policies, procedures, laws, and regulations are being followed by employees.

Policy Statement for a Firm

"Employees in a supervisory role are responsible for the actions of those under their supervision with regard to compliance with the firm's policies and procedures and any securities laws and regulations that govern employee activities."

Index		Pct. Percentage change
		Prev. day 2011
Seoul		5.7%
Johan. (Comp)		1.0% -1.1%
Mumbai		1.0%
Singapore	18,357.9	1.4% -4.5%
Sydney		1.1% -4.7%
Shanghai B	2,971.0	0.9%
Hong Kong	4,644.0	0.9% -10.5%
Toronto	316.8	0.7% -6.9%
Stockholm	22,700.9	0.5% -4.2%
Mexico City	13,524.8	0.1% 4.1%

Super Selection

by Paul F. Van Schyndel, CFA

LEARNING OUTCOMES

Mastery	The candidate should be able to:
☐	a evaluate the practices and policies presented;
☐	b explain the appropriate action to take in response to conduct that violates the CFA Institute Code of Ethics and Standards of Professional Conduct.

CASE FACTS

1

Patricia Cuff, chief financial officer and compliance officer for Super Selection Investment Advisors, has just finished reviewing the brokerage account statement for one of Super Selection's portfolio managers, Karen Trader. When a disgruntled board member of Atlantis Medical Devices (AMD) informed her of Trader's possible misconduct, Cuff decided to investigate Trader's relationship with AMD, a company whose stocks Trader recently bought for all her portfolios. As a result, Cuff obtained and is now reviewing Trader's brokerage statements, which were not previously submitted by Trader. Cuff is concerned about possible violations of the company's standards of professional conduct and her responsibilities as a compliance officer and member of CFA Institute to act on those violations.

Super Selection is a medium-size, rapidly growing money manager registered with the U.S. Securities and Exchange Commission to manage both separate accounts and mutual funds. Super Selection has subscribed to the CFA Institute Code of Ethics and Standards of Professional Conduct by incorporating the CFA Institute Code and Standards into the firm's compliance manual.

Trader has been a portfolio manager for Super Selection for almost five years. She loves the job because of the people she meets and the money she is able to earn. She has been particularly pleased to keep up her friendship with Josey James, a former college classmate and now the president of AMD, a rapidly growing local biotech company.

Over the past five years, James has provided Trader with information on attractive stocks in Trader's field—biotechnology—on which Trader capitalized for her Super Selection portfolios and her personal portfolio. Because she was able to act more quickly on her personal trades than her Super Selection trades, Trader has often purchased stocks of the companies recommended by James for her own account prior to purchasing them for her clients. As a result, the performance of her personal portfolio has been better than the performance of her other portfolios.

Three years ago, James asked Trader to serve as an outside director for AMD and, despite AMD's uncertain prospects at the time, Trader eagerly accepted the offer. Because AMD was in shaky financial condition until recently, the company compensated its directors with stock options rather than cash payments. For the past several years, directors received options exercisable into 200,000 shares in AMD stock. AMD's shares were not traded anywhere, however, so this compensation was essentially worthless, and Trader has not reported her relationship with AMD to Super Selection. This year, with AMD's sales setting records and earnings up, directors started receiving quarterly director fees of $5,000.

Several months ago, the AMD board voted to issue shares of stock to the public to raise needed cash. The market for initial public offerings (IPOs) was very hot, with valuations of biotech companies at record levels; so, AMD top managers believed the moment was opportune to go public. A public market for AMD shares was very appealing to many board members. Trader, for example, was eager to exercise her stock options so that she could cash in on their value. She had just begun construction of a new home, which was putting significant pressure on her cash flow. Trader voted, with the majority of the board, to go public as soon as possible—before the new-issue market soured.

Shortly before the public offering date, Trader received a frantic phone call from James asking for a favor. James indicated that the IPO market had reversed course in the preceding few days; valuations of biotech companies were falling rapidly. James was afraid that investor interest in AMD had slowed so much that the IPO would be threatened. James asked Trader to commit to purchasing a large amount of the AMD offering for her Super Selection accounts to provide enough support for the offering to proceed as planned.

Trader had previously decided that AMD was a questionable investment for her accounts. As an AMD director, however, she also wanted to see a successful IPO, so she offered to reevaluate that decision. In this reevaluation, AMD's stock price seemed high to Trader. Moreover, if she wanted to achieve the desired volume, AMD stock would then represent a higher percentage of Trader's Super Selection portfolios than most holdings. Nevertheless, Trader decided to purchase the shares as James suggested, and when the IPO was effective, she placed the order for the separate accounts and the mutual funds that she managed.

> Explain what violations of the CFA Institute Code and Standards have occurred and the steps that Trader should have taken to avoid the violations. What responsibility does Cuff, as compliance officer, have? What actions should Cuff take now?

CASE DISCUSSION

Several violations of the Code and Standards have occurred as a result of Karen Trader's involvement with an outside company.

Trader is neither a CFA charterholder nor a member of CFA Institute, but she is bound by the CFA Institute Code and Standards to the extent that they are incorporated in her firm's compliance policies. Patricia Cuff's responsibility to take action regarding violations of the Code and Standards arises from her duties as a CFA Institute member, as a compliance officer, and as a senior manager of Super Selection.

Responsibilities of Supervisors

Those with legal or compliance responsibilities, such as the designated compliance officer, do not become supervisors solely because they occupy such named positions. Generally, determining whether an individual has supervisory responsibilities depends on whether employees are subject to that individual's control or influence. In other words, does the individual have the authority, for example, to hire, fire, reward, and punish an employee. In this case, even though Trader does not report directly to Cuff, we assume Cuff supervises the actions of all employees of the firm (and has the power to hire, fire, reward, and punish them) in her dual responsibilities as CFO and compliance officer. Therefore, she must comply with the Standard IV(C)—Responsibilities of Supervisors.

As a supervisor, Cuff has a responsibility to take appropriate steps to prevent any violation by those she oversees of applicable statutes, regulations, or CFA Institute Standards. As compliance officer, she must also ensure that the firm's compliance policies are being followed and that violations of these policies are addressed.

Actions Required

As a supervisor, Cuff should take corrective action after discovering the violations by reporting them to senior management. Cuff and Super Selection's senior managers should then take affirmative steps to ensure that the appropriate action is taken to address the misconduct.

As compliance officer, Cuff should direct or monitor a thorough investigation of Trader's actions, recommend limitations on Trader's activities (such as monitoring all trading done in her client accounts, prohibiting her from personal trading, and imposing sanctions on her, including fines), implement procedures designed to prevent and detect future misconduct, and ensure that her recommendations are carried out.

The senior managers should also consult an attorney to determine whether Trader's actions should be reported to local legal or regulatory bodies. If senior management fails to act, Cuff may need to take additional steps, such as disclosing the incident to Super Selection's board of directors and to the appropriate regulatory authorities, and may need to resign from the firm.

Policy Statement for the Firm

"Employees in a supervisory role are responsible for the actions of the employees they supervise regarding compliance with the firm's policies and procedures and any securities laws and regulations that govern the employees' activities. When supervisors become aware of a violation of securities laws or firm policies, they must notify the compliance officer and senior management and/or ensure that appropriate steps are taken to address the violation."

Employees and the Employer/Supervisor

Trader has responsibilities under Standard VI(A)—Disclosure of Conflicts. Trader violated this standard by 1) failing to disclose the conflict of interest that she had as a result of her ownership of AMD stock options and 2) failing to disclose to her employer the compensation she received as a director of AMD. The stock options and the cash compensation both should have been disclosed.

Actions Required

To avoid the violation, Trader should have disclosed to her employer the compensation she was receiving as an AMD director, whether cash or any other benefit, and should have disclosed her ownership of the AMD stock options and her directorship. This disclosure would have provided her employer and clients the information necessary to evaluate the objectivity of her investment advice and actions.

Cuff, since discovering the violation, needs to ensure that proper disclosure is made to clients and a thorough review is made of Trader's client accounts and her personal accounts to determine whether any conflicts have occurred in addition to the IPO violation. If conflicts are discovered, Cuff has a responsibility to take appropriate action—e.g., limit behavior, impose sanctions, and so on.

Policy Statement for the Firm

"All personnel are required to inform their supervisors of any outside activities, such as board directorships, in which they are engaged or into which they propose to enter and receive approval for these activities prior to engaging in them. Employees shall disclose all conflicts of interest to clients and Super Selection prior to engaging in any activity that could be influenced by such conflicts."

Reasonable Basis

Trader had previously determined that AMD was not a suitable investment for her clients. Under pressure from James, Trader has reversed her stance on AMD and has thus violated Standard V(A)—Diligence and Reasonable Basis.

Actions Required

Trader should have diligently and thoroughly researched AMD again prior to making a decision on investing in this security for her clients' accounts. Once having concluded that AMD was not appropriate, she should not change her opinion, without adequate foundation. Trader must also inform clients of any conflicts she has as an AMD director and as an owner of AMD stock options.

Cuff should periodically—at least annually—review investment actions taken for clients by Super Selection employees to determine whether those actions were taken on a reasonable and adequate basis.

Policy Statement for the Firm

"Portfolio managers must consider all applicable relevant factors for each investment recommendation. Recommendations should be made in view of client objectives and the basic characteristics of the investment to be bought or sold."

Duties to Clients

By investing in and influencing the public offering of AMD in order to boost the price of this stock, Trader misused her professional position for personal benefits and breached her duty of loyalty to her clients by placing her interests before her clients' interests, thus violating Standard III(A)—Loyalty, Prudence and Care.

Although Trader, as a director of AMD, has a duty to that companies' shareholders, she cannot void her obligation to her clients at Super Selection and in the case situation, should have acted in client interests first.

Actions Required

Trader should have taken investment actions that were for the sole benefit of her clients. She should not have been swayed by her ownership of any company into taking an investment action for her clients that she might not have taken in the absence of that ownership. Cuff must thoroughly investigate Trader's activities to see whether other breaches of Standard III(A) have occurred. Following this type of breach and any others, Cuff must limit the activities of the wrongdoers, ensure the implementation of procedures to prevent and detect future occurrences, and follow up to make sure that her recommendations are carried out.

Policy Statement for the Firm

"Employees have a responsibility to identify those persons and interests to which they owe duties of loyalty, prudence, and care. Employees must comply with any fiduciary duties imposed on them by law or regulation."

Investment Recommendations and Actions

Trader violated Standard III(C.1)—Suitability, when she purchased AMD stock for her clients and did not take into consideration their needs and circumstances.

Actions Required

Trader should have considered clients' needs and circumstances prior to taking investment actions and should not have taken these actions to benefit herself or her friends. Cuff should establish a periodic review—to occur at least annually—to compare the suitability of investment actions taken for client accounts with their written investment policy statements.

Policy Statement for the Firm

"The objectives and constraints of each client's portfolio should be put into a written investment policy statement. In taking action or making investment recommendations for clients, employees should consider the needs and circumstances of the client and the basic characteristics of the investment and portfolio involved. No recommendation should be made unless it has been reasonably determined to be suitable for the client's financial situation, investment experience, and objectives."

Priority of Transactions

Trader violated Standard VI(B)—Priority of Transactions, by trading prior to her clients' trades and may have benefited from the impact of her clients' trades on the stock price.

Actions Required

In this instance, Trader circumvented Super Selection's procedures by not reporting trades and brokerage accounts. Nevertheless, Cuff should have made efforts to ensure that Super Selection's policies were being followed. Cuff should review her firm's policies and procedures to make sure they are adequate and determine whether any adjustments should be made to implement or improve them. If adjustments are necessary, she should carry them out. Cuff should also make sure that employees of Super Selection are periodically informed of the Code and Standards and its requirements so as to eliminate any uncertainty about which employees are covered and what responsibilities they have to comply with these standards. Cuff needs to investigate Trader's personal transactions thoroughly and recommend appropriate sanctions for Trader's behavior. Cuff must also ensure that her recommended sanctions are followed to completion.

Policy Statement for the Firm

"The interests of customers will always be given priority over the personal financial interests of the firm's personnel—particularly when securities are being traded or investment actions are being taken. All personal trades by employees of the firm will be pre-cleared in accordance with the firm's compliance policies. In addition, personal trades will be monitored for suspicious activity, such as conflicts of interest and trading on material nonpublic information. Any violator of these priority and pre-clearance policies will be subject to sanctions, including loss of employment."

8

Trade Allocation: Fair Dealing and Disclosure

LEARNING OUTCOMES

Mastery	The candidate should be able to:
☐	**a** evaluate trade allocation practices, and determine whether compliance exists with the CFA Institute Standards of Professional Conduct addressing fair dealing and client loyalty;
☐	**b** describe appropriate actions to take in response to trade allocation practices that do not adequately respect client interests.

The U.S. Securities and Exchange Commission (SEC) continues to focus its enforcement efforts on trade allocation issues. In the most recent enforcement action involving trade allocation practices, *In the Matter of McKenzie Walker Investment Management, Inc. and Richard McKenzie, Jr.*, the SEC censured and fined a registered investment advisor for failing to disclose its trade allocation practices. However, the SEC order in the *McKenzie Walker* matter makes clear that the firm's trade allocation practices themselves came under scrutiny.

The SEC found that McKenzie Walker did not prescribe any objective procedures or formulas for allocating trades among clients or maintain any internal control mechanism to ensure that portfolio managers allocated trades fairly. Instead, the firm allocated trades on an *ad hoc* basis according to clients' needs and objectives, the profitability of the trade, the type of client account, and in some instances, the client's relationship with the firm or its principal. Neither McKenzie Walker's compliance officer nor anyone else at the firm was required to review trade allocation practices to assess whether all accounts received an equitable allocation of trades consistent with their internal objectives.

According to the SEC, in allocating trades, McKenzie Walker significantly favored the firm's performance-based fee accounts over its asset-based fee accounts. The firm used profitable equity trades as well as hot initial public offerings (IPOs) to boost the performance of performance-based accounts in general and certain accounts in particular. The performance-based fee accounts received profitable equity trades (trades that resulted in a gain during the time interval between the execution of a trade and its allocation to an account at the end of the day) at approximately twice the rate of the asset-based fee accounts. The asset-based fee accounts received only 2 percent of the approximately $910,000 gross trading profits that McKenzie Walker earned for its clients by trading hot IPOs in the calendar year 1992. The asset-based accounts were also allocated all of the trading losses for poorly performing IPOs, which resulted in net losses for those accounts. In contrast, the performance-based fee accounts received 98 percent of the gross IPO trading profits and no trading losses. Among the performance-based fee accounts, the firm favored certain clients, including a former colleague and a former business partner of Richard McKenzie, Jr., and one of the firm's lawyers.

The SEC found that McKenzie Walker failed to disclose its practice of favoring its performance-based fee clients in the allocation of equity trades and hot IPOs. The SEC concluded that McKenzie Walker willfully violated Section 206(2) of the Investment Advisers Act of 1940 by "failing to disclose to its clients, current or prospective, that it engaged in a practice of generally favoring its performance-based fee clients in the allocation of equity trades and hot IPOs, and specifically favoring certain of its performance-based fee clients over such clients." The SEC censured the firm, ordered that the firm disgorge $224,683 plus $35,974 in prejudgment interest, and pay a $100,000 civil fine.

It is interesting to note that McKenzie Walker was not censured for the firm's trade allocation practices per se but, rather, for failing to disclose its trade allocation practices.

Under the CFA Institute Standards of Professional Conduct, however, in addition to fully disclosing their procedures, members must also adopt trade allocation procedures that treat clients in an equitable manner.

CFA Institute Standard III(B)—Fair Dealing states that members must deal fairly and objectively with all clients. To fulfill these duties, members must draft and adhere to allocation procedures that ensure that investment opportunities are allocated to all clients in an appropriate and fair manner. All clients for whom a new issue or secondary offering is suitable should have an opportunity to participate in the offering if they so choose. Members or their firms should adopt an objective formula or procedure for allocating investments to all customers for whom the investments are appropriate.

The CFA Institute *Standards of Practice Handbook* suggests steps to ensure that adequate trade allocation practices are followed. CFA Institute members and their firms are encouraged to:

■ obtain advance indications of client interest for new issues;

■ allocate new issues by client rather than by portfolio manager;

■ adopt a pro rata or similar objective method or formula for allocating trades;

■ treat clients fairly in terms of both trade execution order and price;

■ execute orders timely and efficiently;

■ keep accurate records of trades and client accounts; and

■ periodically review all accounts to ensure that all clients are being treated fairly.

Without adequate trade allocation procedures, members and their firms risk breaching the fiduciary duties owed to their investment management clients. CFA Institute Standard III(A)—Loyalty, Prudence, and Care, states that members have a duty of loyalty to their clients and must place clients' interests above their own. Members should strive to avoid all real or potential conflicts of interest. Allocating hot IPOs to selected clients in the hopes of receiving additional future business or increased fees creates an obvious conflict of interest and breaches members' duty to clients. Such practices are detrimental to the interests of those clients not given the opportunity to participate in the offering. The establishment of objective allocation procedures assists members in complying with their fiduciary duties.

Once trade allocation procedures are established, they must be disclosed. As the SEC stated in its order in the *McKenzie Walker* case, a reasonable investor would consider it important to know these allocation procedures. Disclosure must be sufficient to give the client or potential client full knowledge of the procedures and enable the client to make an informed decision regarding the handling of his or her account.

In summary, full and fair disclosure of a firm's allocation procedures is a minimum step toward meeting the goal of fair dealing. Disclosure of unfair allocation procedures does not, however, relieve CFA Institute members of their duties of fair dealing and fiduciary trust to all clients.

9

Changing Investment Objectives

LEARNING OUTCOMES

Mastery	The candidate should be able to:
☐	**a** evaluate the disclosure of investment objectives and basic policies and determine whether they comply with the CFA Institute Standards of Professional Conduct;
☐	**b** describe appropriate actions needed to ensure adequate disclosure of the investment process.

The U.S. Securities and Exchange Commission (SEC) sanctioned Mitchell Hutchins Asset Management (Mitchell Hutchins), a registered broker-dealer and investment adviser, for the failure to trade securities for an investment fund within the limits of the stated fund objectives.

Mitchell Hutchins commenced management of the PaineWebber Short-Term U.S. Government Income Fund (the Fund) in 1993, marketing it as a higher-yield and somewhat higher-risk alternative to money market funds and bank certificates of deposit. The prospectus disclosed that the Fund's investment objective was to achieve the highest level of income consistent with preservation of capital and low volatility of net asset value. The appendix to the prospectus also disclosed that the Fund had "no present intention" of investing in certain classes of interest only (IO) and principal only (PO) stripped mortgage-backed securities.

Contrary to the Fund's low-volatility investment objective and "no present intention" statement, the Fund's portfolio manager began investing in certain IO and PO securities in the fall of 1993. When interest rates increased sharply in February 1994, the Fund incurred significant losses, performing well below comparable funds.

The SEC found that the fund manager improperly deviated from the investment policy recited in its registration statement without shareholder approval. The SEC also found that Mitchell Hutchins violated the antifraud provisions of the federal securities laws by marketing the Fund as a low-volatility investment, when ultimately it was not.

By investing in securities outside the Fund's stated objectives, the portfolio manager's conduct violated Standard III(C.2)—Duties to Clients and Standard V(B.1)—Communication with Clients and Prospective Clients, of CFA Institute's Standards of Professional Conduct. Standard III(C.2) states that when members and candidates are responsible for managing a portfolio to a specific mandate, strategy, or style, they must only make investment recommendations or take investment actions that are consistent with the stated objectives and constraints of the portfolio. Standard V(B.1) states that members must disclose to clients the basic format and general principles of the investment processes by which securities are selected and portfolios are constructed and shall promptly disclose to clients and prospects any change that might materially affect those processes.

Standard III(C.2) protects investors by ensuring that when members manage a portfolio to a specific mandate or strategy, such as in the case of a mutual fund, that they adhere to the stated investment strategy. This allows investors to judge the suitability of the fund for themselves and protects them from style drift and exposure to investment strategies, asset classes, and risks other than those explicitly stated.

In much the same way, Standard V(B.1) protects investors by supplying them with enough information to have an adequate understanding of and to make informed decisions about an investment product or service that is being offered. Undisclosed changes by a manager in the investment strategy of a portfolio may be contrary to the investor's goals. Knowing the key elements of and principles behind the investment allows investors to choose investment products and services that are suitable and appropriate to their investment objectives.

CFA Institute members can take several steps to help ensure that they abide by the principles of Standard III(C.2) and V(B.1). First, when managing a separate portfolio, members should make a reasonable inquiry into a client's financial situation, investment experience, and investment objectives. This information should be updated at least annually. Second, members should disclose the basic format and general principles of the investment processes by which securities are selected and portfolios are constructed at the outset of the relationship, and on a regular basis thereafter. Third, members should implement regular internal checks for each account to ensure that portfolio characteristics meet the account's investment mandate, or the stated investment strategy in the case of pooled funds. Finally, if members wish to change the investment objectives or strategies of portfolios they manage, then members must notify clients and investors of the potential change. Members should fully disclose the impact that the change will have on the portfolio and secure documented authorization of the change in strategy from the client.

The SEC censured the firm, issued a cease-and-desist order, imposed a civil penalty of $500,000, and ordered the appointment of an independent consultant to review and make any appropriate recommendations concerning Mitchell Hutchins' policies and procedures.

10

Prudence in Perspective

by John Train and Thomas A. Melfe

LEARNING OUTCOMES

Mastery	The candidate should be able to:
☐	**a** explain the basic principles of the new Prudent Investor Rule;
☐	**b** explain the general fiduciary standards to which a trustee must adhere;
☐	**c** distinguish between the old Prudent Man Rule and the new Prudent Investor Rule;
☐	**d** explain key factors that a trustee should consider when investing and managing trust assets.

THE MEANING OF PRUDENCE

Prudence is a process, not a result. A trustee must act prudently in all he does for a trust and its beneficiaries.

Prudence is a flexible and unspecific standard of care, permitting wide discretion within general rules. It lacks the "safe harbor" features found in some other regulatory areas, such as federal securities and tax law, which tell you exactly what you should do.

CARE, SKILL, AND CAUTION

The principle of prudence consists of the three elements, care, skill, and caution.

Administrative prudence means exercising care, skill, and caution in safekeeping trust assets, disposing of trust income and principal, maintaining trust records and keeping beneficiaries informed, and treating beneficiaries impartially.

There is also *investment prudence*, which means exercising care, skill, and caution when dealing with any aspect of a trust's investments. For instance, before investing any funds, a trustee should establish investment objectives that suit the purposes of the trust and needs of the beneficiaries; act diligently in selecting investments; determine the risk tolerance of a trust and choose only investments that suit that risk level;

diversify the trust's holdings; focus on the portfolio's liquidity; determine whether to ask the advice of experts; and make certain that the investments themselves are advantageous to both the income and the remainder beneficiaries.

It helps greatly in understanding the new Prudent Investor Rule to see how it evolved from the old Prudent Man Rule, so we include a section to elucidate that background.

3   THE OLD PRUDENT MAN RULE: *HARVARD V. AMORY*

The new Prudent Investor Rule, the subject of this reading, derives from the old Prudent Man Rule. The Old Rule arose from a celebrated 1830 Massachusetts court decision, *Harvard College v. Amory*. Amory was a trustee of a $50,000 testamentary trust. The income went to the decedent's widow for life. At her death the remainder passed to Harvard and Massachusetts General Hospital in equal shares. The will gave Amory broad power to invest the trust fund, including in stocks according to "his best judgment and discretion." Amory invested the entire $50,000 fund in stocks that yielded 8 percent in dividends. Five years after the trust was established, the widow died. Amory filed his account with the court, showing a trust value of only $38,000. When he asked the court for his discharge, Harvard and Massachusetts General Hospital objected, demanding that he restore the $12,000 of lost capital. Judge Putnam, who heard the case, ruled in favor of Amory. The keystone of his decision was a phrase that has become graven in trust lore: "Do what you will, the capital is at hazard." He went on to pronounce a legal principle that became a universal standard for fiduciary conduct, known as the "Prudent Man Rule":

> All that can be required of a trustee to invest, is, that he shall conduct himself faithfully and exercise a sound discretion. He is to observe how men of prudence, discretion, and intelligence manage their own affairs, not in regard to speculation, but in regard to the permanent disposition of their funds, considering the probable income, as well as the probable safety of the capital to be invested.

Over the next century the philosophies of state legislatures and courts changed from favoring flexibility in trust investing to a desire for more certainty and conservatism. In the first half of the twentieth century, most states enacted lists of specific types of investments that trustees were permitted to make, and courts established a series of subrules on what was prudent and what was not. Thus the flexibility and discretion of *Harvard v. Amory* rule gave way to rules and restrictions.

The following are some examples of restrictions tacked on to the Old Rule by state courts and legislatures:

■ Certain types of investments were imprudent per se and thus not allowed for trusts.

■ Each investment in a trust portfolio, rather than the portfolio as a whole, had to satisfy the tests of prudence.

■ A trustee was required to perform duties personally, not delegate them to others.

■ Investment in mutual funds or index funds was an improper delegation of duty by the trustee.

The various restrictions grafted onto *Harvard v. Amory* by state legislatures and courts ultimately impaired its value by reducing its flexibility. They tended to backtrack toward earlier conservative and protective theories of trust investing, although not without struggles. Some institutions attempted to buck the restrictive trend by adopting model language echoing Judge Putnam's opinion.

In 1942 the American Bankers Association promulgated its Model Prudent Man Investment Statute, which both parroted and slightly modified Judge Putnam's words:

> In acquiring, investing, reinvesting, exchanging, retaining, selling, and managing property for the benefit of another, a fiduciary shall exercise the judgment and care under the circumstances then prevailing, which men of prudence, discretion, and intelligence exercise in the management of their own affairs, not in regard to speculation but in regard to the permanent disposition of their funds, considering the probable income as well as probable safety of their capital.

In 1959 the *Restatement of the Law, Trusts* (Second)—the Bible of American trust law principles—used different language with the same impact:

> In making investments of trust funds the trustee is under a duty to the beneficiary in the absence of provisions in the terms of the trust or of a statute otherwise providing, to make such investments and only such investments as a prudent man would make of his own property having in view the preservation of the estate and the amount and regularity of the income to be derived.

In 1972 the National Conference of Commissioners on Uniform State Laws issued a model Uniform Management of Institutional Funds (*not* private trusts) Act, which at this writing has been adopted by many states. This model legislation imposed a variation of the Prudent Man Rule on trustees and directors of not-for-profit institutions such as universities, hospitals, museums, and charitable foundations.

As recently as 1974, the National Conference of Commissioners on Uniform State Laws adopted the following wording for its Uniform Probate Code Prudent Man Rule:

> Except as otherwise provided by the terms of the trust, the trustee shall observe the standards in dealing with the trust assets that would be observed by a prudent man dealing with the property of another, and if the trustee has special skills or expertise, he is under duty to use those skills.

Also in 1974, Congress rejected many of these restrictive subrules when it enacted the Employee Retirement Income Security Act (ERISA), governing employee benefit trusts. ERISA incorporated its own prudent man rule, adopting many recommendations of the legal and investment communities. In its formulation, Congress sought to "avoid repeating the mistake of freezing its rules against future learning and developments." Its prudent man section states:

> The fiduciary shall discharge his duties with the care, skill, prudence, and diligence under the circumstances then prevailing that a prudent man acting in a like capacity and familiar with such matters would use in the conduct of an enterprise of a like character and with like aims; and by diversifying the investments of the plans so as to minimize the risk of large losses, unless under the circumstances it is clearly prudent not to do so.

Over time the states' additions and restrictions had resulted in so many prohibitions that trust investing departed from how the real-life prudent man was handling his own investments—the heart of the Old Rule! By the late 1950s, the *accretions* to the Rule *became* the Rule. In reaction to the restrictive court rulings and legislation, a counterreformation arose. The trust industry and the legal profession disagreed with the ultraconservatism of the modified Rule. Feminism influenced a name change to the "Prudent Person Rule." Lawyers countered its strictures by writing investment powers into wills and trust agreements that authorized the trustee to invest in his sole discretion, without regard to state law restrictions, even if the securities were non-income-producing, unseasoned, or speculative, essentially drafting out the constricting parts of a state's Prudent Man Rule. Some banks included in their specimen clauses for wills and trusts a provision that the trustee could invest in any securities that were eligible for the bank's own investment management accounts. Some drafters of wills and trusts allowed the trustee to invest in "alternative investments, such as venture capital, covered options, precious metals and natural resources."

Eventually, the entire trust community accepted the view that the old Prudent Man Rule placed trusts at a disadvantage by depriving them of newer investment variations. State legislatures began to join the movement, eliminating the legal lists that dictated what trusts could invest in, and replacing them with Prudent Man standards similar to *Harvard v. Amory*. In 1970 New York State adopted the following Prudent Man Rule:

> A fiduciary holding funds for investment may invest the same in such securities as would be acquired by prudent men of discretion and intelligence in such matters who are seeking a reasonable income and preservation of their capital, provided, however, that nothing in this subparagraph shall limit the effect of any will, agreement court order or other instrument creating or defining the investment powers of a fiduciary, or shall restrict the authority of a court of proper jurisdiction to instruct the fiduciary in the interpretation or administration of the express terms of any will, agreement or other instrument or in the administration of the property under the fiduciary's care.

Finally, in 1994 the National Conference of Commissioners of Uniform State Laws published its Uniform Prudent Investor Act, with the stated purpose of updating private trust investment law "in recognition of the alterations that have occurred in investment practice . . ." This Act draws upon the revised standards for prudent trust investment promulgated by the American Law Institute in its Third Restatement (1992), Section 227. It reads as follows:

> The trustee is under a duty to the beneficiaries to invest and manage the funds of the trust as a prudent investor would, in light of the purposes, terms, distribution requirements, and other circumstances of the trust.
>
> **a.** This standard requires the exercise of reasonable care, skill, and caution, and is to be applied to investments not in isolation but in the context of the trust portfolio and as a part of an overall investment strategy, which should incorporate risk and return objectives reasonably suitable to the trust.
>
> **b.** In making and implementing investment decisions, the trustee has a duty to diversify the investments of the trust unless, under the circumstances, it is prudent not to do so.
>
> **c.** In addition, the trustee must:
>
>> **1.** conform to fundamental fiduciary duties of loyalty and impartiality;
>>
>> **2.** act with prudence in deciding whether and how to delegate authority and in the selection and supervision of agents; and
>>
>> **3.** incur only costs that are reasonable in amount and appropriate to the investment responsibilities of the trusteeship.
>
> **d.** The trustee's duties under this Section are subject to the rule of § 228, dealing primarily with contrary investment provisions of a trust or statute.

The Old Rule, lumbered with so many restrictions over the years, was thus finally freed up.

THE NEW PRUDENT INVESTOR RULE = Third Restatement

The American Law Institute's 1992 *Restatement of the Law Third, Trusts* is not itself the law, but it is the definitive commentary on the law. Lawyers, professional trustees, and the courts often turn to it for guidance. It has greatly influenced the development of American trust law.

The sponsors of the Third Restatement concluded that the inflexibility imposed by the courts had placed unjustified liability upon trustees and inhibited the exercise of investment judgment. The American Law Institute's reporter says that the New Rule liberates expert trustees "to pursue challenging, rewarding, nontraditional strategies" and provides unsophisticated trustees with reasonably clear guidance to practical courses of investment.

So the essence of the New Rule is that no investments or techniques are imprudent per se—a radical departure, considering that the Old Rule held that investments that were speculative or non-income-producing were intrinsically imprudent.

The New Rule contains five basic principles:

1. Diversification is fundamental to risk minimization and is therefore ordinarily required of trustees.

2. Risk and return are so directly related that trustees have a duty to analyze and make conscious decisions concerning the levels of risk appropriate to the purposes of the trust.

3. Trustees have a duty to avoid fees, transaction costs, and other expenses that are not justified by the objectives of the investment program.

4. The fiduciary's duty of impartiality requires a conscious balancing of current income and growth.

5. Trustees may have a duty, as well as the authority, to delegate as prudent investors would.

The Third Restatement's new Prudent Investor Rule is intended for a trust only if it is consistent with the terms of a trust and with state law. Generally, the terms of the trust will control. Assuming that a state has adopted the New Rule, or permits a trust to adopt it, then the terms of the trust will dictate whether the New Rule applies to its investment activity.

The terms of a trust may expand or limit the provisions of the Third Restatement's New Rule. In general, a trustee can properly make investments as expressly or implicitly authorized by the terms of the trust. Thus a trust's terms will control a trustee's investment duties and authorities, even if different from the Rule, so long as they do not conflict with the law. But absent contrary provisions (or silence) in the terms of the trust, the Restatement's New Rule will govern, if a state has adopted it.

While the Restatement mainly addresses the administration of private trusts, it is also generally appropriate to charitable or public funds. The New Rule is also intended to guide executors and administrators of estates, guardians, conservators, and the like.

Even though the Restatement's New Rule does not directly apply to nonprivate trustees, it is the safest route for them to follow, since courts and regulators who supervise these other fiduciaries will probably turn to the Restatement for guidance, just as they looked to the previous Restatement in the days of the Old Rule.

Duty to Conform to General Fiduciary Standards

Of the standards to which a trustee must adhere, the most important are that he must exercise care, skill, and caution, and must manifest loyalty and impartiality. His compliance with these duties is judged as of the time an investment decision is made, and *not* with the benefit of hindsight or subsequent developments, nor on the outcome of his investment decisions. This is just as it was under Judge Putnam's rule.

Loyalty means that a trustee must be free of conflicts of interest in managing a trust's investments, and must act solely in the interests of the beneficiaries. Impartiality means that a trustee must recognize the divergent interests of different beneficiaries. He must resolve these differences "in a fair and reasonable manner," whatever that may mean.

Care includes obtaining relevant information on the circumstances and requirements of the trust and its beneficiaries, on the contents and resources of the trust estate, and about the available investment choices. The duty of care may also require a trustee to seek the advice of others.

Skill means that although a person of ordinary intelligence, without financial experience, may serve as a trustee, he should obtain the guidance of specialists in order to meet the skill criterion. Furthermore, unlike the Old Rule, which in general forbade investment delegation, the Restatement holds that a trustee may in some instances have a duty to delegate investment authority to others. In so delegating, "the trustee must exercise appropriate care and skill in selecting and supervising agents and in determining the degree and terms of the delegation." If, on the other hand, a trustee possesses more than ordinary skill, he must use it.

The New Rule requires caution when investing trust funds, with a view to both safety of capital and securing a reasonable return. Safety of capital includes preserving its real, as against nominal, value; that is, seeking to limit the erosion of the trust's purchasing power due to inflation.

In a major departure from the Old Rule, the New Rule defines reasonable return as total return: capital growth as well as income. Furthermore, under the New Rule, capital growth does not necessarily mean only preservation of the trust's purchasing power but may extend to growth in the real value of principal in appropriate cases.[1] The Restatement continues:

> In balancing the return objectives between flow of income and growth of principal, emphasis depends not only on the purposes and distribution requirements of the trust, but also on its other circumstances and specific terms, such as the beneficiaries' tax positions and whether the trustee has power to invade principal.

Caution and Risk Management

The Old Rule requires caution in making investments. This has been interpreted as a duty to avoid speculation and undue risk and follows from the "risk-averse" duty of caution.

That duty survives under the New Rule, but it is altered. After declaring that all investments, even U.S. Treasury obligations, and all investment strategies involve some risk, the Restatement asserts that the duty of caution does not call for the total avoidance of risk by trustees but rather for its "prudent management," taking account of inflation, volatility, illiquidity, and the like, in addition to potential loss.

This emphasis on active risk management in trusts is new. Its importance is shown by its specific inclusion in the Restatement's phrase "an overall investment strategy, which should incorporate risk and return objectives reasonably suitable to the trust." Risk management by a trustee is viewed by the Restatement as requiring that careful attention be given to each trust's particular "risk tolerance," defined as its tolerance for volatility,

---

1 We note that this is a remarkable line of reasoning. It is in reality quite enough to preserve buying power in real terms while providing a reasonable income that rises to offset inflation. Seeking much more than this—swinging for the fences—may achieve much less. Nevertheless, says the New Rule, it is permissible to try, if this endeavor is consistent with the situation of the trust. And these days many of the finest growth companies pay very low dividends, while rewarding their shareholders by reducing the number of shares outstanding through open-market purchases.

given the needs of the beneficiaries. Under the New Rule, the trustee has an affirmative duty to assess its risk tolerance and actively manage the risk element of its investments.

Diversification

The Restatement declares:

> In making and implementing investment decisions, the trustee has a duty to diversify the investments of the trust unless, under the circumstances, it is prudent not to do so.

This duty was included as a separate one in the preceding Second Restatement, but not as part of that edition's prudent investment standard. In the Third Restatement, the duty is elevated to the standard itself, to show "its centrality in fiduciary investing," and perhaps to encourage the states to adopt diversification as a requirement in their Prudent Investor statutes. Strange as it seems, trust portfolio diversification has not always been mandated by state law, even though it has for many years been almost universally followed in trust portfolios.

The Third Restatement also declares that "no objective, general legal standard can be set for a degree of risk that is or is not prudent," and it acknowledges that "the degree of risk permitted for a particular trust is ultimately a matter for interpretation and judgment. This requires that a trustee make reasonable efforts to ascertain the purposes of the trust and to understand the types of investments suitable to those purposes in light of all the relevant circumstances."

THE UNIFORM PRUDENT INVESTOR ACT = Model Act

5

The Third Restatement is dedicated exclusively to the *investment* and related duties of trustees. Based on its new Prudent Investor Rule, another institution, the National Conference of Commissioners on Uniform State Laws, whose charter is to promote uniformity among the fifty states in certain areas of the law, in 1994 promulgated the Uniform Prudent Investor Act, which we will call the Model Act.

Many states responded to the Model Act by revising their Prudent Man statutes to conform to the Act. Others adopted the entire Model Act with only slight modifications.

The Model Act is the wave of the future. All trustees of private trusts must understand its provisions, even trustees in states that have not yet adopted it. To that end we will describe its more important sections.

Like the Third Restatement from which it flows, the Model Act makes five fundamental changes in the old rules governing private trust investing:

1. The standard of prudence applies to the trust portfolio as a whole, rather than to each individual investment on its own.

2. The trade-off between investment risk and return is the fiduciary's central consideration.

3. All specific restrictions on the types of investments that a trustee may use are abrogated; a trustee may invest in anything that plays an appropriate role in achieving the risk/return objectives of the trust and that meets the requirements of prudent investing.

4. The traditional duty to diversify investments is integrated into the Prudent Investment Standard.

5. Delegation by a trustee is permissible, subject to certain safeguards.

For the text of the Model Act, see Appendix 10B.

SUMMARY OF THE MODEL ACT

The heart of the Model Act is its Section 2, setting forth a new standard of prudence to which the trustees it governs must adhere, unless the trust instrument provides otherwise. The Act's prudence standard provides that:

a. A trustee shall invest and manage trust assets as a prudent investor would, by considering the purpose, terms, distribution requirements, and other circumstances of the trust. In satisfying this standard, the trustee shall exercise reasonable care, skill, and caution.

b. A trustee's investment and management decisions respecting individual assets must be evaluated not in isolation but in the context of the trust portfolio as a whole and as a part of an overall investment strategy having risk and return objectives reasonably suited to the trust.

Risk/Reward

The Act incorporates a risk-reward ratio concept into the Model Act's new Prudence Standard. A Comment invokes "the main theme of modern investment practice, sensitivity to the risk/return curve." The Comment explains that risk varies with financial and other circumstances, and thus with a trust's purpose and the circumstances of the beneficiaries.

Strategy

A trustee must 1) develop an overall portfolio strategy designed to achieve expected present and future distributions to its beneficiaries and 2) do so with proper regard for risk and return. Unlike the Old Rule's focus on the prudence of individual investment holdings and avoiding risk, the new standard recognizes the relationship of the potential for reward to a trust from accepting risk and focuses on the trustee's duty to manage that risk over the portfolio as a whole, not taking each holding in isolation. This departure is a most noteworthy feature of the Model Act and New Rule.

The Act identifies *key factors* that a trustee should consider when investing and managing trust assets, notably:

■ general economic conditions

■ the possible effect of inflation or deflation

■ the expected tax consequences for the beneficiaries of investment decisions or strategies

■ the role that each investment or course of action plays within the overall trust portfolio

■ the expected total return from income and capital appreciation

■ the beneficiaries' other resources

■ needs for liquidity, regularity of income, and preservation or appreciation of capital

■ an asset's special relationship or special value, if any, to the purposes of the trust or to the beneficiaries

The Model Act further states a trustee need not satisfy all of these factors for each investment but only those "as are relevant to the trust or its beneficiaries."

The Model Act also includes three *investment policy* provisions:

1. A trustee shall make a reasonable effort to verify the facts relevant to the investment and management of trust assets.

2. A trustee may invest in any kind of property or type of investment consistent with the standards of the Act.

3. A trustee possessing special skills or expertise, or who is selected as trustee based upon the representation of having such skills, has a duty to use those special skills or expertise.

The first provision invokes a trustee's traditional duty to investigate before investing; that is, to analyze information likely to bear on an investment's value or safety. Examples offered are financial reports, auditor's reports, records of title, and the like—routine steps taken by investment analysts.

The second, in a major change for trustees of private trusts, declares the policy that no kind of property or investment is inherently imprudent. Under the Old Rule a variety of investments had been categorized by the courts as imprudent, such as venture capital, futures, options, lower-rated bonds, and stocks of new and untried enterprises. Conversely, the Model Act's Commentary also points out that long-term bonds, which were historically considered ideal for trusts, are now thought to incur a level of risk and volatility perhaps inappropriate for some trusts.

In underscoring its belief that no specific investments or techniques should be deemed imprudent per se, the Model Act's Commentary opines that trust beneficiaries are better protected by the Act's emphasis on close attention to risk/return objectives than by an attempt to predict categories of investment that are intrinsically imprudent. The Act espouses the view that the trustee's task is to invest at a risk level suitable to the purposes of the trust, whether that level is speculative or conservative.

The third provision reaffirms a policy of the old Prudent Man Rule. That policy distinguished between amateur and professional trustees, holding that the standard of prudence is "relational," meaning that the standard for professional trustees is higher than that for laymen.

Diversification

The Model Act and the Third Restatement both emphasize the importance of diversification to reduce risk in a trust portfolio. A trustee should diversify a trust's investments unless, owing to special circumstances, he reasonably determines that the purposes of the trust are better served by putting most of his eggs in a single basket. They even acknowledge that there is no automatic rule or method for identifying how much diversification is enough.

The duty to diversify might not apply if a trust held a block of low-basis stock, where the capital gains tax cost of selling it would outweigh the benefit of diversifying, or if by selling a stock the trust would lose control of a business.

Initial Review

The Act provides that the trustee of a new trust, or of an old trust to which new assets are being added, or a successor trustee, should conduct a review immediately and decide whether to retain or dispose of those assets. This provision applies to investments that were suitable when acquired but subsequently became unsuitable. The provision derives from the Restatement's admonition that a trustee must constantly monitor a trust's investments.

Loyalty

The Model Act includes a separate section on the duty of loyalty, which it calls "the most characteristic rule of trust law," namely to "invest and manage the trust assets solely in the interest of the beneficiaries."

Impartiality

Another traditional duty, also subject to a separate section in the Model Act, is the duty of a trustee to act impartially, taking into account any differing interests of the beneficiaries, whether successive, such as income beneficiaries and remaindermen, or simultaneous, as within a class of income beneficiaries.

This duty is the hardest for a trustee to fulfill to all the beneficiaries' satisfaction. It often forces him to adopt compromise investment strategies: to play it safe as between an income beneficiary wanting high income and prospective remaindermen wanting high growth. The supposed failure to meet this duty of impartiality often gives rise to remaindermens' claims when the trust terminates that the trustee violated the impartiality duty by giving the income beneficiaries too much income.

Some trusts avoid the problem by eliminating the duty of impartiality. For example, if the settlor's widow is the income beneficiary, and clearly the preferred beneficiary, and if the testator wants the trustee to pursue a high-income investment strategy, he can simply relieve the trustee of the duty to be impartial vis-à-vis the remaindermen. A fine solution is to distribute 4 percent a year, say, of the running three-year average total capital.

Costs

The Act provides that a trustee may only incur costs that are appropriate and reasonable. Trustees are thus obliged to make comparisons on transaction and agent costs such as brokerage commissions, and to calculate the cost-benefit ratio, considering the trust's size and ability to bear such costs. These costs include the trustee's own compensation. Although he has a duty to *control* costs, a trustee is not obliged to pay only the *lowest* costs.

The Model Act preserves the time-honored principle that compliance with the Prudent Investor Rule is to be determined in light of the circumstances at the time of the trustee's action, not by hindsight. A trustee is not an insurer or guarantor.

Delegation

A key feature of the Model Act breaks with the past and permits a trustee to delegate investment and management functions that he previously had to perform personally if a prudent investor with similar skills would reasonably delegate them under the circumstances. Still, a trustee must act prudently in the following:

- selecting the agent
- establishing the scope and terms of the delegation
- periodically reviewing the agent's actions

An agent who accepts delegation by a trustee is subject to the jurisdiction of the courts of the state in which the trust is resident.

The Model Act provides that a trustee who complies with its requirements for delegating investment and management functions to an agent will *not* be liable to the beneficiaries or to the trust for the agent's decisions or actions. Not every state is likely to accept this provision. New York's version of the Model Act, for instance, omits it.

The Model Act provides that it shall apply to trusts in existence upon, and created after, the date it is enacted by an adopting state. As to existing trusts, it applies only to investment decisions and actions made after its effective date.

APPENDIX A

The New Prudent Investor Rule

From the *Restatement of the Law Third, Trusts* (Prudent Investor Rule):

§ 227. General Standard of Prudent Investment

The trustee is under a duty to the beneficiaries to invest and manage the funds of the trust as a prudent investor would, in light of the purposes, terms, distributions requirements, and other circumstances of the trust.

a. This standard requires the exercise of reasonable care, skill, and caution, and is to be applied to investments not in isolation but in the context of the trust portfolio and as a part of an overall investment strategy, which should incorporate risk and return objectives reasonably suitable to the trust.

b. In making and implementing investment decisions, the trustee has a duty to diversify the investments of the trust unless, under the circumstances, it is prudent not to do so.

c. In addition, the trustee must:

    1. conform to fundamental fiduciary duties of loyalty (§ 170) and impartiality (§ 183);

    2. act with prudence in deciding whether and how to delegate authority and in the selection and supervision of agents (§ 171); and

    3. incur only costs that are reasonable in amount and appropriate to the investment responsibilities of the trusteeship (§ 188).

d. The trustee's duties under this Section are subject to the rule of § 228, dealing primarily with contrary investment provisions of a trust or statute.

APPENDIX B

Uniform Prudent Investor Act of 1994

Section

1. Prudent Investor Rule.
2. Standard of Care; Portfolio Strategy; Risk and Return Objectives.
3. Diversification.
4. Duties at Inception of Trusteeship.
5. Loyalty.
6. Impartiality.
7. Investment Costs.
8. Reviewing Compliance.
9. Delegation of Investment and Management Functions.

Section

10. Language Invoking Standard of [Act].
11. Application to Existing Trusts.
12. Uniformity of Application and Construction.
13. Short Title.
14. Severability.
15. Effective Date.
16. Repeals.

§ 1 Prudent Investor Rule.

a. Except as otherwise provided in subsection (b), a trustee who invests and manages trust assets owes a duty to the beneficiaries of the trust to comply with the prudent investor rule set forth in this [Act].

b. The prudent investor rule, a default rule, may be expanded, restricted, eliminated, or otherwise altered by the provisions of a trust. A trustee is not liable to a beneficiary to the extent that the trustee acted in reasonable reliance on the provisions of the trust.

§ 2 Standard of Care; Portfolio Strategy; Risk and Return Objectives.

a. A trustee shall invest and manage trust assets as a prudent investor would, but considering the purposes, terms, distribution requirements, and other circumstances of the trust. In satisfying this standard, the trustee shall exercise reasonable care, skill, and caution.

b. A trustee's investment and management decisions respecting individual assets must be evaluated not in isolation but in the context of the trust portfolio as a whole and as a part of an overall investment strategy having risk and return objectives reasonably suited to the trust.

Reprinted by permission of HBS Press. From *Investing and Managing Trusts under the New Prudent Investor Rule: A Guide for Trustees, Investment Advisors, and Lawyers,* by John Train and Thomas A. Melfe, pages 165–169. Copyright © 1999.

c.   Among circumstances that a trustee shall consider in investing and managing trust assets are such of the following as are relevant to the trust or its beneficiaries:

    1.   general economic conditions;

    2.   the possible effect of inflation or deflation;

    3.   the expected tax consequences of investment decisions or strategies;

    4.   the role that each investment or course of action plays within the overall trust portfolio, which may include financial assets, interests in closely held enterprises, tangible and intangible personal property, and real property;

    5.   the expected total return from income and the appreciation of capital;

    6.   other resources of the beneficiaries;

    7.   needs for liquidity, regularity of income, and preservation or appreciation of capital; and

    8.   an asset's special relationship or special value, if any, to the purposes of the trust or to one or more of the beneficiaries.

d.   A trustee shall make a reasonable effort to verify facts relevant to the investment and management of trust assets.

e.   A trustee may invest in any kind of property or type of investment consistent with the standards of this [Act].

f.   A trustee who has special skills or expertise, or is named trustee in reliance upon the trustee's representation that the trustee has special skills or expertise, has a duty to use those special skills or expertise.

§ 3   Diversification.

A trustee shall diversify the investments of the trust unless the trustee reasonably determines that, because of special circumstances, the purposes of the trust are better served without diversifying.

§ 4   Duties at Inception of Trusteeship.

Within a reasonable time after accepting a trusteeship or receiving trust assets, a trustee shall review the trust assets and make and implement decisions concerning the retention and disposition of assets, in order to bring the trust portfolio into compliance with the purposes, terms, distribution requirements, and other circumstances of the trust, and with the requirements of this [Act].

§ 5   Loyalty.

A trustee shall invest and manage the trust assets solely in the interest of the beneficiaries.

§ 6   Impartiality.

If a trust has two or more beneficiaries, the trustee shall act impartially in investing and managing the trust assets, taking into account any differing interests of the beneficiaries.

§ 7   Investment Costs.

In investing and managing trust assets, a trustee may only incur costs that are appropriate and reasonable in relation to the assets, the purposes of the trust, and the skills of the trustee.

§ 8   Reviewing Compliance.

Compliance with the prudent investor rule is determined in light of the facts and circumstances existing at the time of a trustee's decision or action and not by hindsight.

§ 9   Delegation of Investment and Management Functions.

a. A trustee may delegate investment and management functions that a prudent trustee of comparable skills could properly delegate under the circumstances. The trustee shall exercise reasonable care, skill, and caution in:

1. selecting an agent;

2. establishing the scope and terms of the delegation, consistent with the purposes and terms of the trust; and

3. periodically reviewing the agent's actions in order to monitor the agent's performance and compliance with the terms of the delegation.

b. In performing a delegated function, an agent owes a duty to the trust to exercise reasonable care to comply with the terms of the delegation.

c. A trustee who complies with the requirements of subsection (a) is not liable to the beneficiaries or to the trust for the decisions or actions of the agent to whom the function was delegated.

d. By accepting the delegation of a trust function from the trustee of a trust that is subject to the law of this State, an agent submits to the jurisdiction of the courts of this State.

§ 10   Language Invoking Standard of [Act].

The following terms or comparable language in the provisions of a trust, unless otherwise limited or modified, authorizes any investment or strategy permitted under this [Act]: "investments permissible by law for investment of trust funds," "legal investments," "authorized investments," "using the judgment and care under the circumstances then prevailing that persons of prudence, discretion, and intelligence exercise in the management of their own affairs, not in regard to speculation but in regard to the permanent disposition of their funds, considering the probable income as well as the probable safety of their capital," "prudent man rule," "prudent trustee rule," "prudent person rule," and "prudent investor rule."

§ 11   Application to Existing Trusts.

This [Act] applies to trusts existing on and created after its effective date. As applied to trusts existing on its effective date, this [Act] governs only decisions or actions occurring after that date.

§ 12   Uniformity of Application and Construction.

This [Act] shall be applied and construed to effectuate its general purpose to make uniform the law with respect to the subject of this [Act] among the States enacting it.

§ 13   Short Title.

This [Act] may be cited as the "[Name of Enacting State] Uniform Prudent Investor Act."

§ 14   Severability.

If any provision of this [Act] or its application to any person or circumstance is held invalid, the invalidity does not affect other provisions or applications of this [Act] which can be given effect without the invalid provision or application, and to this end the provisions of this [Act] are severable.

§ 15   Effective Date.

This [Act] takes effect _____.

§ 16   Repeals.

The following acts and parts of acts are repealed:

1.
2.
3.

PRACTICE PROBLEMS FOR READING 10

The following information relates to Questions 1–6

Praveen Shankar is employed as an analyst for Front Hall Investments (FHI), an asset management firm. Shankar is also a CFA candidate studying for the Level III exam.

Based on the past four monthly observations, Shankar observes that auto industry stock returns show a strong positive correlation with changes in hourly wages. As a result, his latest investment strategy report recommends that, in his opinion, adjustments to portfolio holdings of auto industry common stocks should be based on the national labor department's monthly release of hourly wage data.

The national labor department was scheduled to release hourly wage data on Thursday, 17 August. However, a clerical error causes the news of a dramatic increase in hourly wages to be released on the labor department's website on Tuesday, 15 August. Shankar assumes that he is the only analyst who notices the information on the website, and recommends that FHI's clients increase their holdings in auto industry common stocks. When the investment community subsequently learns of the wage data, the prices of auto industry common stocks rise significantly. During the following week, Shankar and FHI receive favorable publicity as a result of his timely recommendation.

Norah Pankow, CFA, Shankar's supervisor, is program director for the local CFA Society. Pankow selects only her own clients and brokers as seminar speakers for the society, and she tells Shankar, "Just as I had hoped, the seminars have been very positive for FHI's business." One of Pankow's other initiatives for the society is to create a publicly available web log (blog) on the internet. The blog's purpose is to give local society members a forum to discuss matters related to the CFA Program. To help generate discussion among the members, Shankar participates in the blog by listing several of the most recent, unpublished, Level II exam questions nearly word for word. He notes in his blog posting that the questions are from the exam that took place earlier.

At the end of August, Shankar sits in on a meeting between Pankow and Gerry Byrd, president of FHI. Pankow, who serves as a trustee for a pension plan, expresses concern that one of the pension plan's largest equity investments has underperformed. Pankow fears that, based on the results of this investment, her actions as a fiduciary will be criticized. Shankar states, "A trustee's compliance with the trustee's fiduciary duty is evaluated as of the date the investment decisions are made." Pankow responds, "I believe that a trustee's fiduciary compliance is based on whether the investment turned out to produce total returns that increased the wealth of the trust beneficiaries." Byrd responds, "I think that both of your views are valid and defensible, and at FHI we have supported either approach depending on the circumstances."

Impressed with Shankar's knowledge, Byrd requests that Shankar review FHI's compliance policy and compare it with the CFA Institute Code of Ethics and Standards of Professional Conduct. Key components of FHI's compliance policy are presented in Exhibit 1.

Exhibit 1	Front Hall Investments Key Components of Compliance Policy

1. Employees must not knowingly make any misrepresentation related to their investment analyses, recommendations, actions, and other professional activities.

2. Employees must not engage in any dishonest, fraudulent, or deceitful professional conduct, or commit any act that reflects adversely on their professional reputation, integrity, or competence.

Shankar offers to prepare a list of possible improvements to FHI's code if he sees that any are needed. As the conversation concludes, Byrd shows Shankar FHI's proposed new corporate letterhead, which Byrd says "will demonstrate our strong commitment to comply with CFA Institute Standards." Exhibit 2 shows the proposed letterhead.

Exhibit 2	Proposed Corporate Letterhead for Front Hall Investments

Front Hall Investments, committed to the highest standards of practice

One month later, Shankar advises Pankow that he will be leaving FHI for a new job. Prior to leaving FHI, at social events during nonworking hours, Shankar approaches two individuals to become clients of his new firm:

- Bill Homan oversees the investment of assets for a large nonprofit organization. Homan is not a client of FHI, but FHI employees had met with Homan several times over the last three months and were hoping he would hire FHI to manage the large-capitalization value portion of the nonprofit organization's equity portfolio.

- Lin Cheung had recently approached FHI concerning the overall management of an endowment fund. FHI had decided not to accept this fund as a client because of its small size and an investment objective that differed from the expertise and focus of FHI.

1. Does Shankar violate any CFA Institute Standards of Professional Conduct in recommending that clients increase their holdings of auto industry common stocks?

   A. No.

   B. Yes, because his recommendation did not have a reasonable basis.

   C. Yes, because his recommendation did not distinguish between fact and opinion.

2. Are Pankow and Shankar, respectively, in compliance with CFA Institute Standards with respect to:

	Pankow's selection of seminar leaders?	Shankar's blog posting?
A.	No	No
B.	No	Yes
C.	Yes	No

3. Are Shankar's statement and Pankow's response about fiduciary responsibility consistent with the New Prudent Investor Rule?

	Shankar's Statement	Pankow's Response
A.	No	No
B.	No	Yes
C.	Yes	No

4. Is the FHI compliance policy in Exhibit 1 consistent with CFA Institute Standards?

   A. Only component #1 is compliant with CFA Institute Standards.

   B. Only component #2 is compliant with CFA Institute Standards.

   C. Both components #1 and #2 are consistent with CFA Institute Standards.

5. Would FHI be in compliance with CFA Institute Standards if it used its proposed new letterhead?

    A. Yes.

    B. No, because not all of FHI's employees are CFA charterholders.

    C. No, because the CFA logo is not to be used by any firm on its corporate letterhead.

6. Did Shankar violate CFA Institute Standards in his discussions with Homan and/or Cheung?

    A. Yes, with Cheung only.

    B. Yes, with Homan only.

    C. Yes, with both Cheung and Homan.

The following information relates to Questions 7–11 and is based on "Guidance for Standards I–VII" and this reading

Jorge Aznar, the newly-hired compliance officer at Scott Bancorp (SB), is updating the firm's compliance manual. Aznar sets up a meeting with Anita Portillo, CFA, a portfolio manager at SB who specializes in individually-managed equity portfolios, to learn more about some of the daily processes of the firm's employees.

During the meeting, Aznar discusses the firm's policies related to proxy voting. With respect to portfolios managed for individuals, SB does not require that all proxies be voted in every instance and does not disclose its proxy-voting policies to clients. Portillo explains that SB recently conducted a cost-benefit analysis and found that the costs of evaluating all proxy-related issues outweigh the potential benefit to the clients.

Aznar turns the discussion to the firm's policies related to personal investing. SB requires investment personnel to disclose holdings in which the employee has a beneficial interest when he or she begins employment and on an annual basis thereafter. While employees are required to obtain preclearance for all personal trades and provide copies of periodic statements for all securities accounts, they are not required to direct their brokers to supply duplicate confirmations.

Portillo mentions to Aznar that she has substantially increased the bank's assets under management this year. This was the result of a relationship she established with a small advisory firm that specializes in structuring portfolios for individuals with conservative investment profiles. She states that in addition to these new individual accounts, JNR Manufacturing has hired her to manage a portion of its pension plan.

In reviewing Portillo's accounts, Aznar expresses concern over some high-risk alternative investments in some of the portfolios. He believes these high-risk assets are unsuitable for investors with conservative profiles and is concerned that Portillo may be violating her fiduciary duty by purchasing these assets. Portillo explains that she frequently includes small amounts of these types of investments in portfolios that do not have explicit prohibitions against them in an effort to boost the expected return and enhance diversification, and only does so after a thorough analysis of the investments and their place in each client's overall portfolio, including any tax implications, liquidity needs, and the overall return requirements for each account.

Aznar is unconvinced and worries about any legal implications that might arise with respect to these types of high-risk investments, particularly with regard to JNR Manufacturing's pension plan, for which SB is trustee. Portillo remarks, "According to the new Prudent Investor Rule, diversification is normally required of trustees unless it is clearly imprudent to do so. Moreover, unlike the old Prudent Man Rule, the new Prudent Investor Rule holds that no investments and/or techniques are necessarily considered imprudent." Portillo also explains that the new Prudent Investor Rule requires trustees to use care, skill, and caution. Portillo states, "While a trustee may not delegate investment authority, he may seek the guidance of specialists in order to meet the skill criterion."

The following day, Portillo receives a call from Wayne Seboro, president of JNR Manufacturing. Seboro informs Portillo that JNR is being targeted for a hostile takeover and attempts to persuade Portillo to support the company's resistance by voting the shares held in JNR's pension portfolio in opposition to the bid. Seboro indicates that Portillo's support would likely prompt JNR to commit a large amount of additional funds to the portfolio. While Portillo's initial analysis suggests the takeover would be beneficial to shareholders, she believes that the additional business could decrease overall costs to all clients of SB, including JNR Manufacturing's pension plan participants. After further consideration, Portillo decides to vote the shares in favor of the bid.

7. Is SB's proxy-voting policy consistent with the requirements and recommendations of the CFA Institute Standards with respect to voting and disclosure?

   A. Yes.

   B. No, it is not consistent with respect to voting only.

   C. No, it is not consistent with respect to disclosure only.

8. Are SB's policies related to personal investing consistent with the required and recommended procedures provided for by the CFA Institute Standards?

   A. Yes.

   B. No, they are not consistent with respect to the requirement to supply duplicate confirmations.

   C. No, they are not consistent with respect to the disclosure of holdings in which the employee has a beneficial interest.

9. Does Portillo's inclusion of high-risk alternative investments in the accounts she manages for individuals violate any CFA Institute Standards?

   A. No.

   B. Yes, with respect to suitability.

   C. Yes, with respect to diligence and reasonable basis.

10. Are Portillo's remarks consistent with the new Prudent Investor Rule with respect to diversification and investments?

   A. Yes.

   B. No, they are not consistent with respect to investments only.

   C. No, they are not consistent with respect to diversification only.

11. Are Portillo's statements regarding the skill criterion consistent with the new Prudent Investor Rule with respect to the delegation of investment authority and seeking the guidance of specialists?

   A. Yes.

   B. No, they are not consistent with respect to seeking the guidance of specialists only.

   C. No, they are not consistent with respect to the delegation of investment authority only.

SOLUTIONS FOR READING 10

1. B is correct. Shankar's analysis based on four observations does not constitute a reasonable basis for making an investment recommendation.

2. A is correct. Both have compliance issues. Improperly using one's position as a society leader to benefit oneself or one's clients is a violation. Posting exam questions, even after the exam is completed, compromises the integrity of the examination.

3. C is correct. The view expressed in Shankar's statement is consistent with the New Prudent Investor Rule which states that compliance is judged as of the time an investment decision is made, and *not* with the benefit of hindsight or subsequent developments, nor on the outcome of investment decisions. The view expressed in Pankow's response is inconsistent with the New Prudent Investor Rule.

4. C is correct. Both elements of the compliance policy are consistent with the CFA Institute Standard relating to Professionalism.

5. C is correct. Firms are not permitted to incorporate the CFA logo in their corporate names or letterheads.

6. B is correct. The Standard relating to Duties to Employers prohibits members who are contemplating other employment from soliciting either existing or potential clients prior to leaving the employer. Shankar is permitted to solicit Cheung on behalf of the new firm because Cheung is not a prospective FHI client. Homan, however, is clearly a prospective client.

7. C is correct. Members and candidates should disclose their proxy-voting policies to clients.

8. B is correct. Standard VI(B) provides recommended procedures for compliance that state that investment personnel should be required to direct their brokers to supply duplicate copies or confirmations to their firms of all their personal securities transactions.

9. A is correct. No violations took place. Guidance for Standard III(A) states, "Investment decisions may be judged in the context of the total portfolio rather than by individual investments within the portfolio." The member or candidate's duty is satisfied with respect to a particular investment if he or she has thoroughly considered the investment's place in the overall portfolio, the risk of loss and opportunity for gains, tax implications, and the diversification, liquidity, cash flow, and overall return requirements of the assets or the portion of the assets for which the manager is responsible.

10. A is correct. Under the New Prudent Investor Rule, both of these remarks are correct; diversification is one of the basic investment principles that determine prudent practice, and is normally required of trustees unless it is clearly imprudent to do so. Additionally, unlike the old Prudent Man Rule which held that investments that were speculative or non-income-producing were intrinsically imprudent, the New Prudent Investor Rule holds that no investments are imprudent per se.

11. C is correct. Unlike the old Prudent Man Rule, which in general forbade investment delegation, the Restatement holds that a trustee may in some instance have a duty to delegate investment authority to others.

Quantitative Methods

TOPIC LEVEL LEARNING OUTCOME

The candidate should be able to explain and demonstrate the use of regression and time series analyses in investment decision-making.

Market			
Mumbai			−11.1%
Singapore			−4.5%
Sydney	2971.0	1.1%	−4.7%
Shanghai B	4644.0	0.9%	−10.5%
Hong Kong	316.8	0.7%	−6.9%
Toronto	22,700.9	0.5%	−4.2%
Stockholm	13,524.8	0.1%	4.1%
Mexico City			

Quantitative Methods for Valuation

This study session begins with a discussion of linear correlation and then focuses on linear regression, one of the most widely used statistical techniques in financial modeling. In addition to a discussion of building and interpreting multiple regression models, the readings present information about testing the significance of the estimated parameters and verifying the whole regression model. It also is important to understand the assumptions behind the structure of regression models, to make corrections if the observed variables do not exhibit the assumed properties, and to avoid misspecification of the models.

Time-series analysis is used to describe the dynamic behavior of an economic or financial variable, to forecast its future values, and to detect relations between the time series of different variables. Indeed, regression models must be treated within a time-series context if the variables are measured over time. Regression reports for such models should include standard time-series tests to ensure that the results of the regression are interpreted correctly. Using time-series analysis to explain the past and predict the future of a data series is useful in analyzing company and industry data. Model assumptions and the consequences of model misspecification must be considered in any application. In addition, time-series properties, such as stationarity and mean reversion, have important consequences for security valuation.

READING ASSIGNMENTS

Reading 11 *Correlation and Regression*

Quantitative Methods for Investment Analysis, Second Edition, by Richard A. DeFusco, CFA, Dennis W. McLeavey, CFA, Jerald E. Pinto, CFA, and David E. Runkle, CFA

11

Correlation and Regression

by Richard A. DeFusco, CFA, Dennis W. McLeavey, CFA, Jerald E. Pinto, CFA, and David E. Runkle, CFA

LEARNING OUTCOMES

Mastery	The candidate should be able to:
☐	**a** calculate and interpret a sample covariance and a sample correlation coefficient, and interpret a scatter plot;
☐	**b** explain limitations to correlation analysis, including outliers and spurious correlation;
☐	**c** formulate a test of the hypothesis that the population correlation coefficient equals zero, and determine whether the hypothesis is rejected at a given level of significance;
☐	**d** distinguish between the dependent and independent variables in a linear regression;
☐	**e** explain the assumptions underlying linear regression, and interpret the regression coefficients;
☐	**f** calculate and interpret the standard error of estimate, the coefficient of determination, and a confidence interval for a regression coefficient;
☐	**g** formulate a null and alternative hypothesis about a population value of a regression coefficient, and determine the appropriate test statistic and whether the null hypothesis is rejected at a given level of significance;
☐	**h** calculate a predicted value for the dependent variable, given an estimated regression model and a value for the independent variable, and calculate and interpret a confidence interval for the predicted value of a dependent variable;
☐	**i** describe the use of analysis of variance (ANOVA) in regression analysis, interpret ANOVA results, and calculate and interpret an F-statistic;
☐	**j** explain limitations of regression analysis.

Quantitative Methods for Investment Analysis, Second Edition, by Richard A. DeFusco, CFA, Dennis W. McLeavey, CFA, Jerald E. Pinto, CFA, and David E. Runkle, CFA. Copyright © 2004 by CFA Institute.

INTRODUCTION

As a financial analyst, you will often need to examine the relationship between two or more financial variables. For example, you might want to know whether returns to different stock market indexes are related and, if so, in what way. Or you might hypothesize that the spread between a company's return on invested capital and its cost of capital helps to explain the company's value in the marketplace. Correlation and regression analysis are tools for examining these issues.

This reading is organized as follows. In Section 2, we present correlation analysis, a basic tool in measuring how two variables vary in relation to each other. Topics covered include the calculation, interpretation, uses, limitations, and statistical testing of correlations. Section 3 introduces basic concepts in regression analysis, a powerful technique for examining the ability of one or more variables (independent variables) to explain or predict another variable (the dependent variable).

CORRELATION ANALYSIS

We have many ways to examine how two sets of data are related. Two of the most useful methods are scatter plots and correlation analysis. We examine scatter plots first.

2.1 Scatter Plots

A **scatter plot** is a graph that shows the relationship between the observations for two data series in two dimensions. Suppose, for example, that we want to graph the relationship between long-term money growth and long-term inflation in six industrialized countries to see how strongly the two variables are related. Table 1 shows the average annual growth rate in the money supply and the average annual inflation rate from 1970 to 2001 for the six countries.

Table 1	Annual Money Supply Growth Rate and Inflation Rate by Country, 1970–2001	
Country	**Money Supply Growth Rate (%)**	**Inflation Rate (%)**
Australia	11.66	6.76
Canada	9.15	5.19
New Zealand	10.60	8.15
Switzerland	5.75	3.39
United Kingdom	12.58	7.58
United States	6.34	5.09
Average	9.35	6.03

Source: International Monetary Fund.

To translate the data in Table 1 into a scatter plot, we use the data for each country to mark a point on a graph. For each point, the *x*-axis coordinate is the country's annual average money supply growth from 1970–2001, and the *y*-axis coordinate is the country's annual average inflation rate from 1970–2001. Figure 1 shows a scatter plot of the data in Table 1.

| Figure 1 | Scatter Plot of Annual Money Supply Growth Rate and Inflation Rate by Country, 1970–2001 |

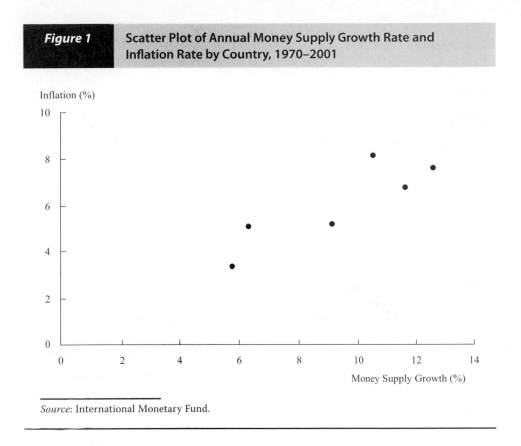

Source: International Monetary Fund.

Note that each observation in the scatter plot is represented as a point, and the points are not connected. The scatter plot does not show which observation comes from which country; it shows only the actual observations of both data series plotted as pairs. For example, the rightmost point shows the data for the United Kingdom. The data plotted in Figure 1 show a fairly strong linear relationship with a positive slope. Next we examine how to quantify this linear relationship.

2.2 Correlation Analysis

In contrast to a scatter plot, which graphically depicts the relationship between two data series, **correlation analysis** expresses this same relationship using a single number. The correlation coefficient is a measure of how closely related two data series are. In particular, the correlation coefficient measures the direction and extent of **linear association** between two variables. A correlation coefficient can have a maximum value of 1 and a minimum value of –1. A correlation coefficient greater than 0 indicates a positive linear association between the two variables: When one variable increases (or decreases), the other also tends to increase (or decrease). A correlation coefficient less than 0 indicates a negative linear association between the two variables: When one increases (or decreases), the other tends to decrease (or increase). A correlation coefficient of 0 indicates no linear relation between the two variables.[1] Figure 2 shows the scatter plot of two variables with a correlation of 1.

---

1 Later, we show that variables with a correlation of 0 can have a strong nonlinear relation.

| Figure 2 | Variables with a Correlation of 1 |

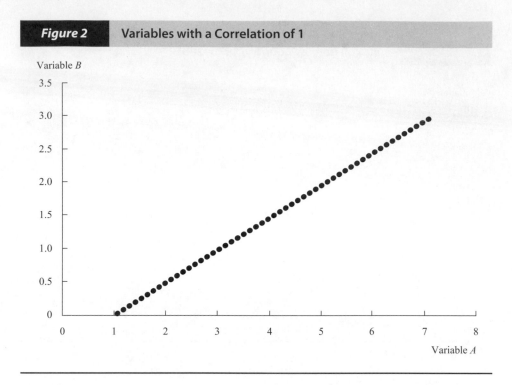

Note that all the points on the scatter plot in Figure 2 lie on a straight line with a positive slope. Whenever variable *A* increases by one unit, variable *B* increases by half a unit. Because all of the points in the graph lie on a straight line, an increase of one unit in *A* is associated with exactly the same half-unit increase in *B*, regardless of the level of *A*. Even if the slope of the line in the figure were different (but positive), the correlation between the two variables would be 1 as long as all the points lie on that straight line.

Figure 3 shows a scatter plot for two variables with a correlation coefficient of –1. Once again, the plotted observations fall on a straight line. In this graph, however, the line has a negative slope. As *A* increases by one unit, *B* decreases by half a unit, regardless of the initial value of *A*.

| Figure 3 | Variables with a Correlation of –1 |

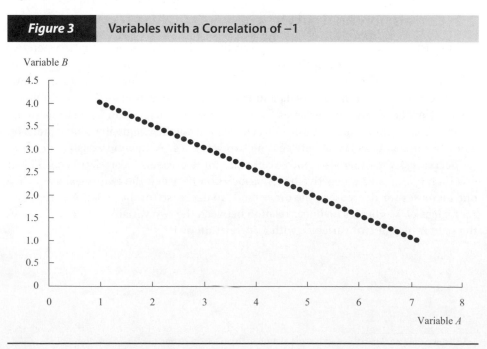

Figure 4 shows a scatter plot of two variables with a correlation of 0; they have no linear relation. This graph shows that the value of A tells us absolutely nothing about the value of B.

Figure 4	Variables with a Correlation of 0

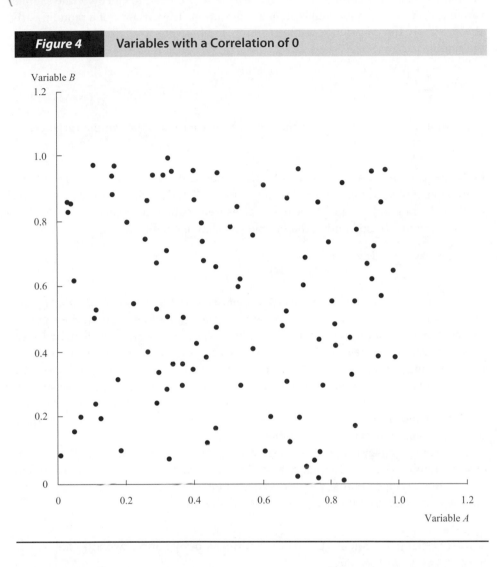

2.3 Calculating and Interpreting the Correlation Coefficient

To define and calculate the correlation coefficient, we need another measure of linear association: covariance. We have previously defined covariance as the expected value of the product of the deviations of two random variables from their respective population means. That was the definition of population covariance, which we would also use in a forward-looking sense. To study historical or sample correlations, we need to use sample covariance. The sample covariance of X and Y, for a sample of size n, is

$$\text{Cov}(X,Y) = \sum_{i=1}^{n}(X_i - \bar{X})(Y_i - \bar{Y})/(n-1) \tag{1}$$

The sample covariance is the average value of the product of the deviations of observations on two random variables from their sample means.[2] If the random variables are returns, the unit of covariance would be returns squared.

---

2 The use of $n-1$ in the denominator is a technical point; it ensures that the sample covariance is an unbiased estimate of population covariance.

The sample correlation coefficient is much easier to explain than the sample covariance. To understand the sample correlation coefficient, we need the expression for the sample standard deviation of a random variable X. We need to calculate the sample variance of X to obtain its sample standard deviation. The variance of a random variable is simply the covariance of the random variable with itself. The expression for the sample variance of X, s_X^2, is

$$s_X^2 = \sum_{i=1}^{n}(X_i - \bar{X})^2 \Big/ (n-1)$$

The sample standard deviation is the positive square root of the sample variance:

$$s_X = \sqrt{s_X^2}$$

Both the sample variance and the sample standard deviation are measures of the dispersion of observations about the sample mean. Standard deviation uses the same units as the random variable; variance is measured in the units squared.

The formula for computing the sample correlation coefficient is

$$r = \frac{\text{Cov}(X,Y)}{s_X s_Y} \tag{2}$$

The correlation coefficient is the covariance of two variables (X and Y) divided by the product of their sample standard deviations (s_x and s_y). Like covariance, the correlation coefficient is a measure of linear association. The correlation coefficient, however, has the advantage of being a simple number, with no unit of measurement attached. It has no units because it results from dividing the covariance by the product of the standard deviations. Because we will be using sample variance, standard deviation, and covariance in this reading, we will repeat the calculations for these statistics.

Table 2 shows how to compute the various components of the correlation equation (Equation 2) from the data in Table 1.[3] The individual observations on countries' annual average money supply growth from 1970–2001 are denoted X_i, and individual observations on countries' annual average inflation rate from 1970–2001 are denoted Y_i. The remaining columns show the calculations for the inputs to correlation: the sample covariance and the sample standard deviations.

Table 2	Sample Covariance and Sample Standard Deviations: Annual Money Supply Growth Rate and Inflation Rate by Country, 1970–2001				
Country	Money Supply Growth Rate X_i	Inflation Rate Y_i	Cross-Product $(X_i - \bar{X})(Y_i - \bar{Y})$	Squared Deviations $(X_i - \bar{X})^2$	Squared Deviations $(Y_i - \bar{Y})^2$
Australia	0.1166	0.0676	0.000169	0.000534	0.000053
Canada	0.0915	0.0519	0.000017	0.000004	0.000071
New Zealand	0.1060	0.0815	0.000265	0.000156	0.000449

3 We have not used full precision in the table's calculations. We used the average value of the money supply growth rate of 0.5608/6 = 0.0935, rounded to four decimal places, in the cross-product and squared deviation calculations, and similarly, we used the mean inflation rate as rounded to 0.0603 in those calculations. We computed standard deviation as the square root of variance rounded to six decimal places, as shown in the table. Had we used full precision in all calculations, some of the table's entries would be different and the computed value of correlation would be 0.8709 rather than 0.8702, not materially affecting our conclusions.

	Money Supply Growth Rate X_i	Inflation Rate Y_i	Cross-Product $(X_i - \bar{X})(Y_i - \bar{Y})$	Squared Deviations $(X_i - \bar{X})^2$	Squared Deviations $(Y_i - \bar{Y})^2$
Country					
Switzerland	0.0575	0.0339	0.000950	0.001296	0.000697
United Kingdom	0.1258	0.0758	0.000501	0.001043	0.000240
United States	0.0634	0.0509	0.000283	0.000906	0.000088
Sum	0.5608	0.3616	0.002185	0.003939	0.001598
Average	0.0935	0.0603			
Covariance			0.000437		
Variance				0.000788	0.000320
Standard deviation				0.028071	0.017889

Notes:
1. Divide the cross-product sum by $n - 1$ (with $n = 6$) to obtain the covariance of X and Y.
2. Divide the squared deviations sums by $n - 1$ (with $n = 6$) to obtain the variances of X and Y.
Source: International Monetary Fund.

Using the data shown in Table 2, we can compute the sample correlation coefficient for these two variables as follows:

$$r = \frac{\text{Cov}(X,Y)}{s_x s_y} = \frac{0.000437}{(0.028071)(0.017889)} = 0.8702$$

The correlation coefficient of approximately 0.87 indicates a strong linear association between long-term money supply growth and long-term inflation for the countries in the sample. The correlation coefficient captures this strong association numerically, whereas the scatter plot in Figure 1 shows the information graphically.

What assumptions are necessary to compute the correlation coefficient? Correlation coefficients can be computed validly if the means and variances of X and Y, as well as the covariance of X and Y, are finite and constant. Later, we will show that when these assumptions are not true, correlations between two different variables can depend greatly on the sample that is used.

2.4 Limitations of Correlation Analysis

Correlation measures the linear association between two variables, but it may not always be reliable. Two variables can have a strong **nonlinear relation** and still have a very low correlation. For example, the relation $B = (A - 4)^2$ is a nonlinear relation contrasted to the linear relation $B = 2A - 4$. The nonlinear relation between variables A and B is shown in Figure 5. Below a level of 4 for A, variable B decreases with increasing values of A. When A is 4 or greater, however, B increases whenever A increases. Even though these two variables are perfectly associated, the correlation between them is 0.[4]

4 The perfect association is the quadratic relationship $B = (A - 4)^2$.

| Figure 5 | Variables with a Strong Nonlinear Association |

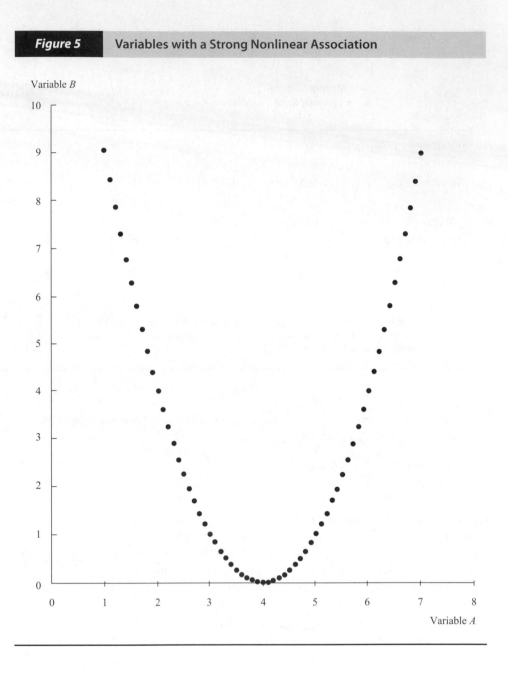

Correlation also may be an unreliable measure when outliers are present in one or both of the series. Outliers are small numbers of observations at either extreme (small or large) of a sample. Figure 6 shows a scatter plot of the monthly returns to the Standard & Poor's 500 Index and the monthly inflation rate in the United States during the 1990s (January 1990 through December 1999).

Figure 6	U.S. Inflation and Stock Returns in the 1990s

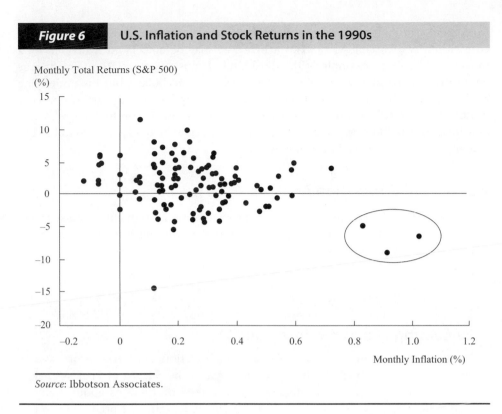

Source: Ibbotson Associates.

In the scatter plot in Figure 6, most of the data lie clustered together with little discernible relation between the two variables. In three cases, however (the three circled observations), inflation was greater than 0.8 percent in a particular month and stock returns were strongly negative. These observations are outliers. If we compute the correlation coefficient for the entire data sample, that correlation is –0.2997. If we eliminate the three outliers, however, the correlation is –0.1347.

The correlation in Figure 6 is quite sensitive to excluding only three observations. Does it make sense to exclude those observations? Are they noise or news? One possible partial explanation of Figure 6 is that during the 1990s, whenever inflation was very high during a month, market participants became concerned that the Federal Reserve would raise interest rates, which would cause the value of stocks to decline. This story offers one plausible explanation for how investors reacted to large inflation announcements. Consequently, the outliers may provide important information about market reactions during this period. Therefore, the correlation that includes the outliers may make more sense than the correlation that excludes them.

As a general rule, we must determine whether a computed sample correlation changes greatly by removing a few outliers. But we must also use judgment to determine whether those outliers contain information about the two variables' relationship (and should thus be included in the correlation analysis) or contain no information (and should thus be excluded).

Keep in mind that correlation does not imply causation. Even if two variables are highly correlated, one does not necessarily cause the other in the sense that certain values of one variable bring about the occurrence of certain values of the other. Furthermore, correlations can be spurious in the sense of misleadingly pointing towards associations between variables.

The term **spurious correlation** has been used to refer to 1) correlation between two variables that reflects chance relationships in a particular data set, 2) correlation induced by a calculation that mixes each of two variables with a third, and 3) correlation between two variables arising not from a direct relation between them but from their relation to a third variable. As an example of the second kind of spurious correlation, two variables that are uncorrelated may be correlated if divided by a third variable. As an example of the third kind of spurious correlation, height may be positively correlated with the extent of a person's vocabulary, but the underlying relationships are between age and height and between age and vocabulary. Investment professionals must be cautious in basing investment strategies on high correlations. Spurious correlation may suggest investment strategies that appear profitable but actually would not be so, if implemented.

2.5 Uses of Correlation Analysis

In this section, we give examples of correlation analysis for investment. Because investors' expectations about inflation are important in determining asset prices, inflation forecast accuracy will serve as our first example.

Example 1

Evaluating Economic Forecasts (1)

Investors closely watch economists' forecasts of inflation, but do these forecasts contain useful information? In the United States, the Survey of Professional Forecasters (SPF) gathers professional forecasters' predictions about many economic variables.[5] Since the early 1980s, SPF has gathered predictions on the U.S. inflation rate using the change in the U.S. consumer price index (CPI) for all urban consumers and all items to measure inflation. If these forecasts of inflation could perfectly predict actual inflation, the correlation between forecasts and inflation would be 1.

Figure 7 shows a scatter plot of the mean forecast of current-quarter percentage change in CPI from previous quarter and actual percentage change in CPI, on an annualized basis, from the first quarter of 1983 to the last quarter of 2002.[6] In this scatter plot, the forecast for each quarter is plotted on the x-axis and the actual change in the CPI is plotted on the y-axis.

---

5 The survey was originally developed by Victor Zarnowitz for the American Statistical Association and the National Bureau of Economic Research. Starting in 1990, the survey has been directed by Dean Croushore of the Federal Reserve Bank of Philadelphia.

6 In this scatter plot, the actual change in CPI is from the Federal Reserve's economic and financial database, available at the website of the Federal Reserve Bank of St. Louis.

Figure 7	Actual Change in CPI versus Predicted Change

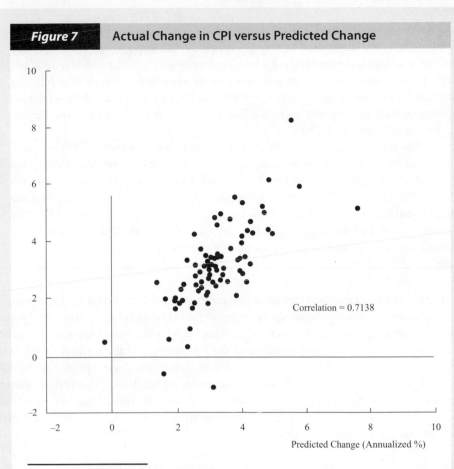

Correlation = 0.7138

Predicted Change (Annualized %)

Source: Federal Reserve Banks of Philadelphia and St. Louis.

As Figure 7 shows, a fairly strong linear association exists between the forecast and the actual inflation rate, suggesting that professional forecasts of inflation might be useful in investment decision-making. In fact, the correlation between the two series is 0.7138. Although there is no causal relation here, there is a direct relation because forecasters assimilate information to forecast inflation.

One important issue in evaluating a portfolio manager's performance is determining an appropriate benchmark for the manager. In recent years, style analysis has been an important component of benchmark selection.[7]

Example 2

Style Analysis Correlations

Suppose a portfolio manager uses small-cap stocks in an investment portfolio. By applying style analysis, we can try to determine whether the portfolio manager uses a small-cap growth style or a small-cap value style.

---

7 See, for example, Sharpe (1992) and Buetow, Johnson, and Runkle (2000).

In the United States, the Russell 2000 Growth Index and the Russell 2000 Value Index are often used as benchmarks for small-cap growth and small-cap value managers, respectively. Correlation analysis shows, however, that the returns to these two indexes are very closely associated with each other. For the 20 years ending in 2002 (January 1983 to December 2002), the correlation between the monthly returns to the Russell 2000 Growth Index and the Russell 2000 Value Index was 0.8526.

If the correlation between the returns to the two indexes were 1, there would be absolutely no difference in equity management style between small-cap value and small-cap growth. If we knew the return to one style, we could be certain about the return to the other style. Because the returns to the two indexes are highly correlated, we can say that very little difference exists between the two return series, and therefore, we may not be able to justify distinguishing between small-cap growth and small-cap value as different investment styles.

The previous examples in this reading have examined the correlation between two variables. Often, however, investment managers need to understand the correlations among many asset returns. For example, investors who have any exposure to movements in exchange rates must understand the correlations of the returns to different foreign currencies and other assets in order to determine their optimal portfolios and hedging strategies.[8] In the following example, we see how a correlation matrix shows correlation between pairs of variables when we have more than two variables. We also see one of the main challenges to investment managers: Investment return correlations can change substantially over time.

Example 3

Exchange Rate Return Correlations

The exchange rate return measures the periodic domestic currency return to holding foreign currency. Suppose a change in inflation rates in the United Kingdom and the United States results in the U.S. dollar price of a pound changing from $1.50 to $1.25. If this change occurred in one month, the return in that month to holding pounds would be (1.25 − 1.50)/1.50 = −16.67 percent, in terms of dollars.

Table 3 shows a correlation matrix of monthly returns in U.S. dollars to holding Canadian, Japanese, Swedish, or British currencies.[9] To interpret a correlation matrix, we first examine the top panel of this table.

The first column of numbers of that panel shows the correlations between USD returns to holding the Canadian dollar and USD returns to holding Canadian, Japanese, Swedish, and British currencies. Of course, any variable is perfectly correlated with itself, and so the correlation between USD returns to holding the Canadian dollar and USD returns to holding the Canadian dollar is 1. The second row of this column shows that the correlation between USD returns to holding the Canadian dollar and USD returns to holding the Japanese yen was 0.2593 from 1980 to 1989. The remaining correlations in the panel show how the USD returns to other combinations of currency holdings were correlated during this period.

---

8 See, for example, Clarke and Kritzman (1996).
9 Data for the 1980s run from January 1980 through December 1989. Data for the 1990s run from January 1990 through December 1999.

Table 3	Correlations of Monthly U.S. Dollar Returns to Selected Foreign Currency Returns			

1980–1989	Canada	Japan	Sweden	United Kingdom
Canada	1.000			
Japan	0.2593	1.0000		
Sweden	0.2834	0.6576	1.0000	
United Kingdom	0.3925	0.6068	0.6840	1.0000

1990–1999	Canada	Japan	Sweden	United Kingdom
Canada	1.0000			
Japan	−0.0734	1.0000		
Sweden	0.1640	0.2860	1.0000	
United Kingdom	0.0475	0.2906	0.6444	1.0000

Source: Ibbotson Associates.

Note that Table 3 omits many of the correlations. For example, Column 2 of the panel omits the correlation between USD returns to holding yen and USD returns to holding Canadian dollars. This correlation is omitted because it is identical to the correlation between USD returns to holding Canadian dollars and USD returns to holding yen shown in Row 2 of Column 1. Other omitted correlations would also have been duplicative. In fact, correlations are always symmetrical: The correlation between X and Y is always the same as the correlation between Y and X.

If you compare the two panels of this table, you will find that many of the currency return correlations changed dramatically between the 1980s and the 1990s. In the 1980s, for example, the correlation between the return to holding Japanese yen and the return to holding either Swedish kronor (0.6576) or British pounds (0.6068) was almost as high as the correlation between the return to holding kronor and the return to holding pounds (0.6840). In the 1990s, however, the correlation between yen returns and either krona or pound returns dropped by more than half (to 0.2860 and 0.2906, respectively), but the correlation between krona and pound returns hardly changed at all (0.6444). Some of the correlations between returns to the Canadian dollar and returns to other currencies dropped even more dramatically. In the 1980s, the correlation between Canadian dollar returns and Japanese yen returns was 0.2593. By the 1990s, that correlation actually became negative (−0.0734). The correlation between the Canadian dollar returns and British pound returns dropped from 0.3925 in the 1980s to 0.0475 in the 1990s.

Optimal asset allocation depends on expectations of future correlations. With less than perfect positive correlation between two assets' returns, there are potential risk-reduction benefits to holding both assets. Expectations of future correlation may be based on historical sample correlations, but the variability in historical sample correlations poses challenges. We discuss these issues in detail in the reading on portfolio concepts.

In the next example, we extend the discussion of the correlations of stock market indexes begun in Example 2 to indexes representing large-cap, small-cap, and broad-market returns. This type of analysis has serious diversification and asset allocation consequences because the strength of the correlations among the assets tells us how successfully the assets can be combined to diversify risk.

Example 4

Correlations among Stock Return Series

Table 4 shows the correlation matrix of monthly returns to three U.S. stock indexes during the period January 1971 to December 1999 and in three subperiods (the 1970s, 1980s, and 1990s).[10] The large-cap style is represented by the return to the S&P 500 Index, the small-cap style is represented by the return to the Dimensional Fund Advisors U.S. Small-Stock Index, and the broad-market returns are represented by the return to the Wilshire 5000 Index.

Table 4	Correlations of Monthly Returns to Various U.S. Stock Indexes		
1971–1999	**S&P 500**	**U.S. Small-Stock**	**Wilshire 5000**
S&P 500	1.0000		
U.S. Small-Stock	0.7615	1.0000	
Wilshire 5000	0.9894	0.8298	1.0000
1971–1979	**S&P 500**	**U.S. Small-Stock**	**Wilshire 5000**
S&P 500	1.0000		
U.S. Small-Stock	0.7753	1.0000	
Wilshire 5000	0.9906	0.8375	1.0000
1980–1989	**S&P 500**	**U.S. Small-Stock**	**Wilshire 5000**
S&P 500	1.0000		
U.S. Small-Stock	0.8440	1.0000	
Wilshire 5000	0.9914	0.8951	1.0000
1990–1999	**S&P 500**	**U.S. Small-Stock**	**Wilshire 5000**
S&P 500	1.0000		
U.S. Small-Stock	0.6843	1.0000	
Wilshire 5000	0.9858	0.7768	1.0000

Source: Ibbotson Associates.

The first column of numbers in the top panel of Table 4 shows nearly perfect positive correlation between returns to the S&P 500 and returns to the Wilshire 5000: The correlation between the two return series is 0.9894. This result should

---

10 The 1970s data have an initiation date of January 1971 because that is the starting date of the Wilshire 5000 total return series.

not be surprising, because both the S&P 500 and the Wilshire 5000 are value-weighted indexes, and large-cap stock returns receive most of the weight in both indexes. In fact, the companies that make up the S&P 500 have about 80 percent of the total market value of all companies included in the Wilshire 5000.

Small stocks also have a reasonably high correlation with large stocks. In the total sample, the correlation between the S&P 500 returns and the U.S. Small-Stock returns is 0.7615. The correlation between U.S. Small-Stock returns and returns to the Wilshire 5000 is slightly higher (0.8298). This result is also not too surprising because the Wilshire 5000 contains small-cap stocks and the S&P 500 does not. The second, third, and fourth panels of Table 4 show that correlations among the various stock market return series show some variation from decade to decade. For example, the correlation between returns to the S&P 500 and U.S. small-cap stocks dropped from 0.8440 in the 1980s to 0.6843 in the 1990s.[11]

For asset allocation purposes, correlations among asset classes are studied carefully with a view toward maintaining appropriate diversification based on forecasted correlations.

Example 5

Correlations of Debt and Equity Returns

Table 5 shows the correlation matrix for various U.S. debt returns and S&P 500 returns using monthly data from January 1926 to December 2002.

Table 5	Correlations among U.S. Stock and Debt Returns, 1926–2002				
All	S&P 500	U.S. Long-Term Corp.	U.S. Long-Term Govt.	U.S. 30-Day T-Bill	High-Yield Corp.
S&P 500	1.0000				
U.S. Long-Term Corp.	0.2143	1.0000			
U.S. Long-Term Govt.	0.1466	0.8480	1.0000		
U.S. 30-Day T-bill	−0.0174	0.0970	0.1119	1.0000	
High-Yield Corp.	0.6471	0.4274	0.3131	0.0174	1.0000

Source: Ibbotson Associates.

The first column of numbers, in particular, shows the correlations of S&P 500 returns with various debt returns. Note that S&P 500 returns are almost completely uncorrelated (−0.0174) with 30-day Treasury bill returns for this period. Long-term corporate debt returns are somewhat more correlated (0.2143) with S&P 500 returns. Returns on high-yield corporate bonds have the highest

[handwritten: 0 = uncorrelated]

---

11 The correlation coefficient for the 1990s was less than that for the 1980s at the 0.01 significance level. A test for this type of hypothesis on the correlation coefficient can be conducted using Fisher's z-transformation. See Daniel and Terrell (1995) for information on this method.

correlation (0.6471) with S&P 500 total returns. This high correlation is understandable; high-yield debt securities behave partially as equities because of their high default risk. If a company defaults, holders of high-yield debt typically lose most of their investment.

Long-term government bonds, however, have a low correlation (0.1466) with S&P 500 returns. We expect some correlation between these variables because interest rate increases reduce the present value of future cash flows for both bonds and stocks. The relatively low correlation between these two return series, however, shows that other factors affect the returns on stocks besides interest rates. Without these other factors, the correlation between bond and stock returns would be higher.

The second column of numbers in Table 5 shows that the correlation between long-term government bond and corporate bond returns is quite high (0.8480) for this time period. Although this correlation is the highest in the entire matrix, it is not 1. The correlation is less than 1 because the default premium for long-term corporate bonds changes, whereas U.S. government bonds do not incorporate a default premium. As a result, changes in required yields for government bonds have a correlation less than 1 with changes in required yields for corporate bonds, and return correlations between government bonds and corporate bonds are also below 1. Note also that the correlation of high-yield corporate bond returns with long-term government bond returns (0.3131), indicated in the third column of numbers, is less than half the correlation of high-yield corporate bond returns with S&P 500 returns. This relatively low correlation is another indicator that high-yield bond returns behave more similarly to equity returns than to debt returns.

Note finally that 30-day T-bill returns have a very low correlation with all other return series. In fact, the correlations between T-bill returns and other return series are lower than any of the other correlations in this table.

In the final example of this section, correlation is used in a financial statement setting to show that net income is an inadequate proxy for cash flow.

Example 6

Correlations among Net Income, Cash Flow from Operations, and Free Cash Flow to the Firm

Net income (NI), cash flow from operations (CFO), and free cash flow to the firm (FCFF) are three measures of company performance that analysts often use to value companies. Differences in these measures for given companies would not cause differences in the relative valuation if the measures were highly correlated.

CFO equals net income plus the net noncash charges that were subtracted to obtain net income, minus the company's investment in working capital during the same time period. FCFF equals CFO plus net-of-tax interest expense, minus the company's investment in fixed capital over the time period. FCFF may be interpreted as the cash flow available to the company's suppliers of capital (debtholders and shareholders) after all operating expenses have been paid and necessary investments in working and fixed capital have been made.[12]

---

12 For more on these three measures and their use in equity valuation, see Stowe, Robinson, Pinto, and McLeavey (2002). The statements in the footnoted paragraph explain the relationships among these measures according to U.S. GAAP. Stowe et al. also discuss the relationships among these measures according to international accounting standards.

Some analysts base their valuations only on NI, ignoring CFO and FCFF. If the correlations among NI, CFO, and FCFF were very high, then an analyst's decision to ignore CFO and FCFF would be easy to understand because NI would then appear to capture everything one needs to know about cash flow.

Table 6 shows the correlations among NI, CFO, and FCFF for a group of six publicly traded U.S. companies involved in retailing women's clothing for 2001. Before computing the correlations, we normalized all of the data by dividing each company's three performance measures by the company's revenue for the year.[13]

Table 6	Correlations among Performance Measures: U.S. Women's Clothing Stores, 2001		
	NI	CFO	FCFF
NI	1.0000		
CFO	0.6959	1.0000	
FCFF	0.4045	0.8217	1.0000

Source: Compustat.

Because CFO and FCFF include NI as a component (in the sense that CFO and FCFF can be obtained by adding and subtracting various quantities from NI), we might expect that the correlations between NI and CFO and between NI and FCFF would be positive. Table 6 supports that conclusion. These correlations with NI, however, are much smaller than the correlation between CFO and FCFF (0.8217). The lowest correlation in the table is between NI and FCFF (0.4045). This relatively low correlation shows that NI contained some but far from all the information in FCFF for these companies in 2001. Later in this reading, we will test whether the correlation between NI and FCFF is significantly different from zero.

2.6 Testing the Significance of the Correlation Coefficient

Significance tests allow us to assess whether apparent relationships between random variables are the result of chance. If we decide that the relationships do not result from chance, we will be inclined to use this information in predictions because a good prediction of one variable will help us predict the other variable. Using the data in Table 2, we calculated 0.8702 as the sample correlation between long-term money growth and long-term inflation in six industrialized countries between 1970 and 2001. That estimated correlation seems high, but is it significantly different from 0? Before we can answer this question, we must know some details about the distribution of the underlying variables themselves. For purposes of simplicity, let us assume that both of the variables are normally distributed.[14]

---

13 The results in this table are based on data for all women's clothing stores (U.S. Occupational Health and Safety Administration Standard Industrial Classification 5621) with a market capitalization of more than $250 million at the end of 2001. The market-cap criterion was used to eliminate microcap firms, whose performance-measure correlations may be different from those of higher-valued firms.

14 Actually, we must assume that the variables come from a bivariate normal distribution. If two variables, X and Y, come from a bivariate normal distribution, then for each value of X the distribution of Y is normal. See, for example, Ross (1997) or Greene (2003).

We propose two hypotheses: the null hypothesis, H_0, that the correlation in the population is 0 ($\rho = 0$); and the alternative hypothesis, H_a, that the correlation in the population is different from 0 ($\rho \neq 0$).

The alternative hypothesis is a test that the correlation is not equal to 0; therefore, a two-tailed test is appropriate. As long as the two variables are distributed normally, we can test to determine whether the null hypothesis should be rejected using the sample correlation, r. The formula for the t-test is

$$t = \frac{r\sqrt{n-2}}{\sqrt{1-r^2}}$$

(3)

This test statistic has a t-distribution with $n - 2$ degrees of freedom if the null hypothesis is true. One practical observation concerning Equation 3 is that the magnitude of r needed to reject the null hypothesis H_0: $\rho = 0$ decreases as sample size n increases, for two reasons. First, as n increases, the number of degrees of freedom increases and the absolute value of the critical value t_c decreases. Second, the absolute value of the numerator increases with larger n, resulting in larger-magnitude t-values. For example, with sample size $n = 12$, $r = 0.58$ results in a t-statistic of 2.252 that is just significant at the 0.05 level ($t_c = 2.228$). With a sample size $n = 32$, a smaller sample correlation $r = 0.35$ yields a t-statistic of 2.046 that is just significant at the 0.05 level ($t_c = 2.042$); the $r = 0.35$ would not be significant with a sample size of 12 even at the 0.10 significance level. Another way to make this point is that sampling from the same population, a false null hypothesis H_0: $\rho = 0$ is more likely to be rejected as we increase sample size, all else equal.

Example 7

Testing the Correlation between Money Supply Growth and Inflation

Earlier in this reading, we showed that the sample correlation between long-term money supply growth and long-term inflation in six industrialized countries was 0.8702 during the 1970–2001 period. Suppose we want to test the null hypothesis, H_0, that the true correlation in the population is 0 ($\rho = 0$) against the alternative hypothesis, H_a, that the correlation in the population is different from 0 ($\rho \neq 0$). Recalling that this sample has six observations, we can compute the statistic for testing the null hypothesis as follows:

$$t = \frac{0.8702\sqrt{6-2}}{\sqrt{1 - 0.8702^2}} = 3.532$$

The value of the test statistic is 3.532. As the table of critical values of the t-distribution for a two-tailed test shows, for a t-distribution with $n - 2 = 6 - 2 = 4$ degrees of freedom at the 0.05 level of significance, we can reject the null hypothesis (that the population correlation is equal to 0) if the value of the test statistic is greater than 2.776 or less than −2.776. The fact that we can reject the null hypothesis of no correlation based on only six observations is quite unusual; it further demonstrates the strong relation between long-term money supply growth and long-term inflation in these six countries.

Sig 0.05
So look for 0.025!

Example 8

Testing the Krona–Yen Return Correlation

The data in Table 3 showed that the sample correlation between the USD monthly returns to Swedish kronor and Japanese yen was 0.2860 for the period from January 1990 through December 1999. If we observe this sample correlation, can we reject a null hypothesis that the underlying or population correlation equals 0?

With 120 months from January 1990 through December 1999, we use the following statistic to test the null hypothesis, H_0, that the true correlation in the population is 0, against the alternative hypothesis, H_a, that the correlation in the population is different from 0:

$$t = \frac{0.2860\sqrt{120 - 2}}{\sqrt{1 - 0.2860^2}} = 3.242$$

At the 0.05 significance level, the critical level for this test statistic is 1.98 ($n = 120$, degrees of freedom = 118). When the test statistic is either larger than 1.98 or smaller than −1.98, we can reject the hypothesis that the correlation in the population is 0. The test statistic is 3.242, so we can reject the null hypothesis.

Note that the sample correlation coefficient in this case is significantly different from 0 at the 0.05 level, even though the coefficient is much smaller than that in the previous example. The correlation coefficient, though smaller, is still significant because the sample is much larger (120 observations instead of 6 observations).

The above example shows the importance of sample size in tests of the significance of the correlation coefficient. The following example also shows the importance of sample size and examines the relationship at the 0.01 level of significance as well as at the 0.05 level.

Example 9

The Correlation between Bond Returns and T-Bill Returns

Table 5 showed that the sample correlation between monthly returns to U.S. government bonds and monthly returns to 30-day T-bills was 0.1119 from January 1926 through December 2002. Suppose we want to test whether the correlation coefficient is statistically significantly different from zero. There are 924 months during the period January 1926 to December 2002. Therefore, to test the null hypothesis, H_0 (that the true correlation in the population is 0), against the alternative hypothesis, H_a (that the correlation in the population is different from 0), we use the following test statistic:

$$t = \frac{0.1119\sqrt{924 - 2}}{\sqrt{1 - 0.1119^2}} = 3.4193$$

At the 0.05 significance level, the critical value for the test statistic is approximately 1.96. At the 0.01 significance level, the critical value for the test statistic is approximately 2.58. The test statistic is 3.4193, so we can reject the null hypothesis of no correlation in the population at both the 0.05 and 0.01 levels. This example shows that, in large samples, even relatively small correlation coefficients can be significantly different from zero.

In the final example of this section, we explore another situation of small sample size.

Example 10

Testing the Correlation between Net Income and Free Cash Flow to the Firm

Earlier in this reading, we showed that the sample correlation between NI and FCFF for six women's clothing stores was 0.4045 in 2001. Suppose we want to test the null hypothesis, H_0, that the true correlation in the population is 0 ($\rho = 0$) against the alternative hypothesis, H_a, that the correlation in the population is different from 0 ($\rho \neq 0$). Recalling that this sample has six observations, we can compute the statistic for testing the null hypothesis as follows:

$$t = \frac{0.4045\sqrt{6-2}}{\sqrt{1-0.4045^2}} = 0.8846$$

With $n - 2 = 6 - 2 = 4$ degrees of freedom and a 0.05 significance level, we reject the null hypothesis that the population correlation equals 0 for values of the test statistic greater than 2.776 or less than −2.776. In this case, however, the t-statistic is 0.8846, so we cannot reject the null hypothesis. Therefore, for this sample of women's clothing stores, there is no **statistically significant** correlation between NI and FCFF, when each is normalized by dividing by sales for the company.[15]

The scatter plot creates a visual picture of the relationship between two variables, while the correlation coefficient quantifies the existence of any linear relationship. Large absolute values of the correlation coefficient indicate strong linear relationships. Positive coefficients indicate a positive relationship and negative coefficients indicate a negative relationship between two data sets. In Examples 8 and 9, we saw that relatively small sample correlation coefficients (0.2860 and 0.1119) can be statistically significant and thus might provide valuable information about the behavior of economic variables.

Next we will introduce linear regression, another tool useful in examining the relationship between two variables.

3   LINEAR REGRESSION

3.1 Linear Regression with One Independent Variable

As a financial analyst, you will often want to understand the relationship between financial or economic variables, or to predict the value of one variable using information about the value of another variable. For example, you may want to know the impact of changes in the 10-year Treasury bond yield on the earnings yield of the S&P 500

---

15 It is worth repeating that the smaller the sample, the greater the evidence in terms of the magnitude of the sample correlation needed to reject the null hypothesis of zero correlation. With a sample size of 6, the absolute value of the sample correlation would need to be greater than 0.81 (carrying two decimal places) for us to reject the null hypothesis. Viewed another way, the value of 0.4045 in the text would be significant if the sample size were 24, because $0.4045(24 - 2)^{1/2}/(1 - 0.4045^2)^{1/2} = 2.075$, which is greater than the critical t-value of 2.074 at the 0.05 significance level with 22 degrees of freedom.

(the earnings yield is the reciprocal of the price-to-earnings ratio). If the relationship between those two variables is linear, you can use linear regression to summarize it.

Linear regression allows us to use one variable to make predictions about another, test hypotheses about the relation between two variables, and quantify the strength of the relationship between the two variables. The remainder of this reading focuses on linear regression with a single independent variable. In the next reading, we will examine regression with more than one independent variable.

Regression analysis begins with the dependent variable (denoted Y), the variable that you are seeking to explain. The independent variable (denoted X) is the variable you are using to explain changes in the dependent variable. For example, you might try to explain small-stock returns (the dependent variable) based on returns to the S&P 500 (the independent variable). Or you might try to explain inflation (the dependent variable) as a function of growth in a country's money supply (the independent variable).

Linear regression assumes a linear relationship between the dependent and the independent variables. The following regression equation describes that relation:

$$Y_i = b_0 + b_1 X_i + \varepsilon_i, \ i = 1,\ldots,n \tag{4}$$

This equation states that the **dependent variable**, Y, is equal to the intercept, b_0, plus a slope coefficient, b_1, times the **independent variable**, X, plus an **error term**, ε. The error term represents the portion of the dependent variable that cannot be explained by the independent variable. We refer to the intercept b_0 and the slope coefficient b_1 as the **regression coefficients**.

Regression analysis uses two principal types of data: cross-sectional and time series. Cross-sectional data involve many observations on X and Y for the same time period. Those observations could come from different companies, asset classes, investment funds, people, countries, or other entities, depending on the regression model. For example, a cross-sectional model might use data from many companies to test whether predicted earnings-per-share growth explains differences in price-to-earnings ratios (P/Es) during a specific time period. The word "explain" is frequently used in describing regression relationships. One estimate of a company's P/E that does not depend on any other variable is the average P/E. If a regression of a P/E on an independent variable tends to give more accurate estimates of P/E than just assuming that the company's P/E equals the average P/E, we say that the independent variable helps *explain* P/Es because using that independent variable improves our estimates. Finally, note that if we use cross-sectional observations in a regression, we usually denote the observations as $i = 1, 2, \ldots, n$.

Time-series data use many observations from different time periods for the same company, asset class, investment fund, person, country, or other entity, depending on the regression model. For example, a time-series model might use monthly data from many years to test whether U.S. inflation rates determine U.S. short-term interest rates.[16] If we use time-series data in a regression, we usually denote the observations as $t = 1, 2, \ldots, T$.[17]

Exactly how does linear regression estimate b_0 and b_1? Linear regression, also known as linear least squares, computes a line that best fits the observations; it chooses values for the intercept, b_0, and slope, b_1, that minimize the sum of the squared vertical distances between the observations and the regression line. Linear regression chooses the **estimated** or fitted **parameters** $\hat{b}_0$ and $\hat{b}_1$ in Equation 4 to minimize[18]

---

16 A mix of time-series and cross-sectional data, also known as panel data, is now frequently used in financial analysis. The analysis of panel data is an advanced topic that Greene (2003) discusses in detail.
17 In this reading, we primarily use the notation $i = 1, 2, \ldots, n$ even for time series to prevent confusion that would be caused by switching back and forth between different notations.
18 Hats over the symbols for coefficients indicate estimated values.

$$\sum_{i=1}^{n} \left(Y_i - \hat{b}_0 - \hat{b}_1 X_i \right)^2 \tag{5}$$

In this equation, the term $\left(Y_i - \hat{b}_0 - \hat{b}_1 X_i \right)^2$ means (dependent variable – predicted value of dependent variable)^2. Using this method to estimate the values of $\hat{b}_0$ and $\hat{b}_1$, we can fit a line through the observations on X and Y that best explains the value that Y takes for any particular value of X.[19]

Note that we never observe the population parameter values b_0 and b_1 in a regression model. Instead, we observe only $\hat{b}_0$ and $\hat{b}_1$, which are estimates of the population parameter values. Thus predictions must be based on the parameters' estimated values, and testing is based on estimated values in relation to the hypothesized population values.

Figure 8 gives a visual example of how linear regression works. The figure shows the linear regression that results from estimating the regression relation between the annual rate of inflation (the dependent variable) and annual rate of money supply growth (the independent variable) for six industrialized countries from 1970 to 2001 ($n = 6$).[20] The equation to be estimated is Long-term rate of inflation = $b_0 + b_1$ (Long-term rate of money supply growth) + ε.

| Figure 8 | Fitted Regression Line Explaining the Inflation Rate Using Growth in the Money Supply by Country, 1970–2001 |

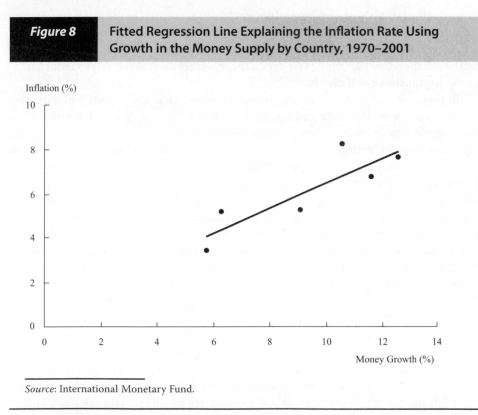

Source: International Monetary Fund.

The distance from each of the six data points to the fitted regression line is the regression residual, which is the difference between the actual value of the dependent variable and the predicted value of the dependent variable made by the regression equation. Linear regression chooses the estimated coefficients $\hat{b}_0$ and $\hat{b}_1$ in Equation 4 such that the sum of the squared vertical distances is minimized. The estimated regression equation is Long-term inflation = 0.0084 + 0.5545 (Long-term money supply growth).[21]

---

19 For a discussion of the precise statistical sense in which the estimates of b_0 and b_1 are optimal, see Greene (2003).

20 These data appear in Table 2.

21 We entered the monthly returns as decimals.

According to this regression equation, if the long-term money supply growth is 0 for any particular country, the long-term rate of inflation in that country will be 0.84 percent. For every 1-percentage-point increase in the long-term rate of money supply growth for a country, the long-term inflation rate is predicted to increase by 0.5545 percentage points. In a regression such as this one, which contains one independent variable, the slope coefficient equals $Cov(Y, X)/Var(X)$. We can solve for the slope coefficient using data from Table 2, excerpted here:

| Table 2 | (excerpted) | | | | |

	Money Supply Growth Rate X_i	Inflation Rate Y_i	Cross-Product $(X_i - \bar{X})(Y_i - \bar{Y})$	Squared Deviations $(X_i - \bar{X})^2$	Squared Deviations $(Y_i - \bar{Y})^2$
Sum	0.5608	0.3616	0.002185	0.003939	0.001598
Average	0.0935	0.0603			
Covariance			**0.000437**		
Variance				**0.000788**	0.000320
Standard deviation				0.028071	0.017889

$$Cov(Y, X) = 0.000437$$
$$Var(X) = 0.000788$$
$$Cov(Y, X)/Var(X) = 0.000437/0.000788$$
$$\hat{b}_1 = 0.5545$$

In a linear regression, the regression line fits through the point corresponding to the means of the dependent and the independent variables. As shown in Table 1 (excerpted below), from 1970 to 2001, the mean long-term growth rate of the money supply for these six countries was 9.35 percent, whereas the mean long-term inflation rate was 6.03 percent.

| Table 1 | (excerpted) | |

	Money Supply Growth Rate	Inflation Rate
Average	9.35%	6.03%

Because the point (9.35, 6.03) lies on the regression line $\hat{b}_0 = \bar{Y} - \hat{b}_1\bar{X}$, we can solve for the intercept using this point as follows:

$$\hat{b}_0 = 0.0603 - 0.5545(0.0935) = 0.0084$$

We are showing how to solve the linear regression equation step by step to make the source of the numbers clear. Typically, an analyst will use the data analysis function on a spreadsheet or a statistical package to perform linear regression analysis. Later, we will discuss how to use regression residuals to quantify the uncertainty in a regression model.

3.2 Assumptions of the Linear Regression Model

We have discussed how to interpret the coefficients in a linear regression model. Now we turn to the statistical assumptions underlying this model. Suppose that we have n observations on both the dependent variable, Y, and the independent variable, X, and we want to estimate Equation 4:

$$Y_i = b_0 + b_1 X_i + \varepsilon_i, i = 1,...,n$$

To be able to draw valid conclusions from a linear regression model with a single independent variable, we need to make the following six assumptions, known as the classic normal linear regression model assumptions:

1. The relationship between the dependent variable, Y, and the independent variable, X is linear in the parameters b_0 and b_1. This requirement means that b_0 and b_1 are raised to the first power only and that neither b_0 nor b_1 is multiplied or divided by another regression parameter (as in b_0/b_1, for example). The requirement does not exclude X from being raised to a power other than 1.

2. The independent variable, X, is not random.[22]

3. The expected value of the error term is 0: $E(\varepsilon) = 0$.

4. The variance of the error term is the same for all observations: $E\left(\varepsilon_i^2\right) = \sigma_\varepsilon^2$, $i = 1,...,\text{n}$.

5. The error term, ε, is uncorrelated across observations. Consequently, $E(\varepsilon_i \varepsilon_j) = 0$ for all i not equal to j.[23]

6. The error term, ε, is normally distributed.[24]

Now we can take a closer look at each of these assumptions.

Assumption 1 is critical for a valid linear regression. If the relationship between the independent and dependent variables is nonlinear in the parameters, then estimating that relation with a linear regression model will produce invalid results. For example, $Y_i = b_0 e^{b_1 X_i} + \varepsilon_i$ is nonlinear in b_1, so we could not apply the linear regression model to it.[25]

Even if the dependent variable is nonlinear, linear regression can be used as long as the regression is linear in the parameters. So, for example, linear regression can be used to estimate the equation $Y_i = b_0 + b_1 X_i^2 + \varepsilon_i$

Assumptions 2 and 3 ensure that linear regression produces the correct estimates of b_0 and b_1.

Assumptions 4, 5, and 6 let us use the linear regression model to determine the distribution of the estimated parameters $\hat{b}_0$ and $\hat{b}_1$ and thus test whether those coefficients have a particular value.

■ Assumption 4, that the variance of the error term is the same for all observations, is also known as the homoskedasticity assumption. The reading on regression analysis discusses how to test for and correct violations of this assumption.

---

22 Although we assume that the independent variable in the regression model is not random, that assumption is clearly often not true. For example, it is unrealistic to assume that the monthly returns to the S&P 500 are not random. If the independent variable is random, then is the regression model incorrect? Fortunately, no. Econometricians have shown that even if the independent variable is random, we can still rely on the results of regression models given the crucial assumption that the error term is uncorrelated with the independent variable. The mathematics underlying this reliability demonstration, however, are quite difficult. See, for example, Greene (2003) or Goldberger (1998).

23 $\text{Var}(\varepsilon_i) = E[\varepsilon_i - E(\varepsilon_i)]^2 = E(\varepsilon_i - 0)^2 = E(\varepsilon_i)^2$. $\text{Cov}(\varepsilon_i, \varepsilon_j) = E\{[\varepsilon_i - E(\varepsilon_i)][\varepsilon_j - E(\varepsilon_j)]\} = E[(\varepsilon_i - 0)(\varepsilon_j - 0)] = E(\varepsilon_i \varepsilon_j) = 0$.

24 If the regression errors are not normally distributed, we can still use regression analysis. Econometricians who dispense with the normality assumption use chi-square tests of hypotheses rather than F-tests. This difference usually does not affect whether the test will result in a particular null hypothesis being rejected.

25 For more information on nonlinearity in the parameters, see Gujarati (2003).

- Assumption 5, that the errors are uncorrelated across observations, is also necessary for correctly estimating the variances of the estimated parameters $\hat{b}_0$ and $\hat{b}_1$. The reading on multiple regression discusses violations of this assumption.

- Assumption 6, that the error term is normally distributed, allows us to easily test a particular hypothesis about a linear regression model.[26]

Example 11

Evaluating Economic Forecasts (2)

If economic forecasts were completely accurate, every prediction of change in an economic variable in a quarter would exactly match the actual change that occurs in that quarter. Even though forecasts can be inaccurate, we hope at least that they are unbiased—that is, that the expected value of the forecast error is zero. An unbiased forecast can be expressed as E(Actual change − Predicted change) = 0. In fact, most evaluations of forecast accuracy test whether forecasts are unbiased.[27]

Figure 9 repeats Figure 7 in showing a scatter plot of the mean forecast of current-quarter percentage change in CPI from the previous quarter and actual percentage change in CPI, on an annualized basis, from the first quarter of 1983 to the last quarter of 2002, but it adds the fitted regression line for the equation Actual percentage change = $b_0 + b_1$ (Predicted percentage change) + ε. If the forecasts are unbiased, the intercept, b_0, should be 0 and the slope, b_1, should be 1. We should also find E(Actual change − Predicted change) = 0. If forecasts are actually unbiased, as long as $b_0 = 0$ and $b_1 = 1$, the error term [Actual change − $b_0 - b_1$(Predicted change)] will have an expected value of 0, as required by Assumption 3 of the linear regression model. With unbiased forecasts, any other values of b_0 and b_1 would yield an error term with an expected value different from 0.

---

26 For large sample sizes, we may be able to drop the assumption of normality by appeal to the central limit theorem; see Greene (2003). Asymptotic theory shows that, in many cases, the test statistics produced by standard regression programs are valid even if the error term is not normally distributed. Non-normality of some financial time series can be quite severe. With severe non-normality, even with a relatively large number of observations, invoking asymptotic theory to justify using test statistics from linear regression models may be inappropriate.

27 See, for example, Keane and Rumble (1990).

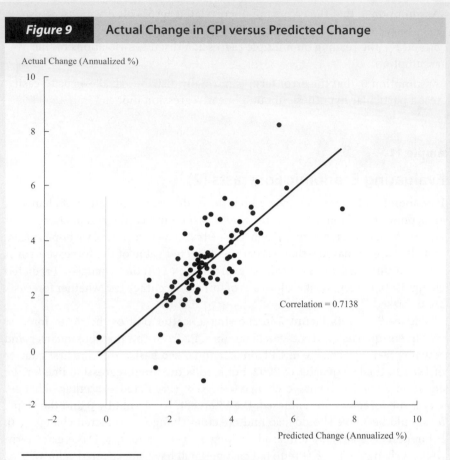

Figure 9   **Actual Change in CPI versus Predicted Change**

Actual Change (Annualized %)

Correlation = 0.7138

Predicted Change (Annualized %)

Source: Federal Reserve Banks of Philadelphia and St. Louis.

If $b_0 = 0$ and $b_1 = 1$, our best guess of actual change in CPI would be 0 if professional forecasters' predictions of change in CPI were 0. For every 1-percentage-point increase in the prediction of change by the professional forecasters, the regression model would predict a 1-percentage-point increase in actual change.

The fitted regression line in Figure 9 comes from the equation Actual change $= -0.0140 + 0.9637$(Predicted change). Note that the estimated values of both b_0 and b_1 are close to the values $b_0 = 0$ and $b_1 = 1$ that are consistent with unbiased forecasts. Later in this reading, we discuss how to test the hypotheses that $b_0 = 0$ and $b_1 = 1$.

3.3 The Standard Error of Estimate

The linear regression model sometimes describes the relationship between two variables quite well, but sometimes it does not. We must be able to distinguish between these two cases in order to use regression analysis effectively. Therefore, in this section and the next, we discuss statistics that measure how well a given linear regression model captures the relationship between the dependent and independent variables.

Figure 9, for example, shows a strong relation between predicted inflation and actual inflation. If we knew professional forecasters' predictions for inflation in a particular quarter, we would be reasonably certain that we could use this regression model to forecast actual inflation relatively accurately.

In other cases, however, the relation between the dependent and independent variables is not strong. Figure 10 adds a fitted regression line to the data on inflation and stock returns in the 1990s from Figure 6. In this figure, the actual observations are generally much farther from the fitted regression line than in Figure 9. Using the estimated regression equation to predict monthly stock returns assuming a particular level of inflation might result in an inaccurate forecast.

As noted, the regression relation in Figure 10 is less precise than that in Figure 9. The standard error of estimate (sometimes called the standard error of the regression) measures this uncertainty. This statistic is very much like the standard deviation for a single variable, except that it measures the standard deviation of $\hat{\varepsilon}_i$, the residual term in the regression.

The formula for the standard error of estimate (SEE) for a linear regression model with one independent variable is

$$\text{SEE} = \left(\frac{\sum_{i=1}^{n}\left(Y_i - \hat{b}_0 - \hat{b}_1 X_i\right)^2}{n-2} \right)^{1/2} = \left(\frac{\sum_{i=1}^{n}\left(\hat{\varepsilon}_i\right)^2}{n-2} \right)^{1/2} \qquad (6)$$

In the numerator of this equation, we are computing the difference between the dependent variable's actual value for each observation and its predicted value $\left(\hat{b}_0 + \hat{b}_1 X_i\right)$ for each observation. The difference between the actual and predicted values of the dependent variable is the regression residual, $\hat{\varepsilon}_i$.

Equation 6 looks very much like the formula for computing a standard deviation, except that $n-2$ appears in the denominator instead of $n-1$. We use $n-2$ because the sample includes n observations and the linear regression model estimates two parameters $\left(\hat{b}_0 \text{ and } \hat{b}_1\right)$; the difference between the number of observations and the number of parameters is $n-2$. This difference is also called the degrees of freedom; it is the denominator needed to ensure that the estimated standard error of estimate is unbiased.

| Figure 10 | Fitted Regression Line Explaining Stock Returns by Inflation during the 1990s |

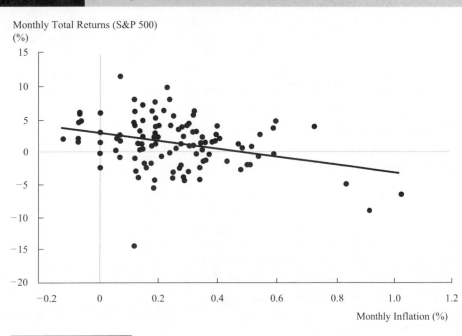

Source: Ibbotson Associates.

Example 12

Computing the Standard Error of Estimate

Recall that the estimated regression equation for the inflation and money supply growth data shown in Figure 8 was $Y_i = 0.0084 + 0.5545X_i$. Table 7 uses this estimated equation to compute the data needed for the standard error of estimate.

Table 7		Computing the Standard Error of Estimate			
Country	Money Supply Growth Rate X_i	Inflation Rate Y_i	Predicted Inflation Rate $\hat{Y}_i$	Regression Residual $Y_i - \hat{Y}_i$	Squared Residual $\left(Y_i - \hat{Y}_i\right)^2$
Australia	0.1166	0.0676	0.0731	−0.0055	0.000030
Canada	0.0915	0.0519	0.0591	−0.0072	0.000052
New Zealand	0.1060	0.0815	0.0672	0.0143	0.000204
Switzerland	0.0575	0.0339	0.0403	−0.0064	0.000041
United Kingdom	0.1258	0.0758	0.0782	−0.0024	0.000006
United States	0.0634	0.0509	0.0436	0.0073	0.000053
Sum					0.000386

Source: International Monetary Fund.

The first and second columns of numbers in Table 7 show the long-term money supply growth rates, X_i, and long-term inflations rates, Y_i, for the six countries. The third column of numbers shows the predicted value of the dependent variable from the fitted regression equation for each observation. For the United States, for example, the predicted value of long-term inflation is 0.0084 + 0.5545(0.0634) = 0.0436 or 4.36 percent. The next-to-last column contains the regression residual, which is the difference between the actual value of the dependent variable, Y_i, and the predicted value of the dependent variable, $\left(\hat{Y}_i = \hat{b}_0 + \hat{b}_1 X_i\right)$. So for the United States, the residual is equal to 0.0509 − 0.0436 = 0.0073 or 0.73 percent. The last column contains the squared regression residual. The sum of the squared residuals is 0.000386. Applying the formula for the standard error of estimate, we obtain

$$\left(\frac{0.000386}{6-2}\right)^{1/2} = 0.009823$$

Thus the standard error of estimate is about 0.98 percent.

Later, we will combine this estimate with estimates of the uncertainty about the parameters in this regression to determine confidence intervals for predicting inflation rates from money supply growth. We will see that smaller standard errors result in more accurate predictions.

3.4 The Coefficient of Determination

Although the standard error of estimate gives some indication of how certain we can be about a particular prediction of Y using the regression equation, it still does not tell us how well the independent variable explains variation in the dependent variable. The coefficient of determination does exactly this: It measures the fraction of the total variation in the dependent variable that is explained by the independent variable.

We can compute the coefficient of determination in two ways. The simpler method, which can be used in a linear regression with one independent variable, is to square the correlation coefficient between the dependent and independent variables. For example, recall that the correlation coefficient between the long-term rate of money growth and the long-term rate of inflation between 1970 and 2001 for six industrialized countries was 0.8702. Thus the coefficient of determination in the regression shown in Figure 8 is $(0.8702)^2 = 0.7572$. So in this regression, the long-term rate of money supply growth explains approximately 76 percent of the variation in the long-term rate of inflation across the countries between 1970 and 2001. (Relatedly, note that the square root of the coefficient of determination in a one-independent-variable linear regression, after attaching the sign of the estimated slope coefficient, gives the correlation coefficient between the dependent and independent variables.)

The problem with this method is that it cannot be used when we have more than one independent variable.[28] Therefore, we need an alternative method of computing the coefficient of determination for multiple independent variables. We now present the logic behind that alternative.

If we did not know the regression relationship, our best guess for the value of any particular observation of the dependent variable would simply be $\bar{Y}$, the mean of the dependent variable. One measure of accuracy in predicting Y_i based on $\bar{Y}$ is the

sample variance of Y_i, $\sum_{i=1}^{n} \dfrac{(Y_i - \bar{Y})^2}{n-1}$. An alternative to using $\bar{Y}$ to predict a particular

observation Y_i is using the regression relationship to make that prediction. In that case, our predicted value would be $\hat{Y}_i = \hat{b}_0 + \hat{b}_1 X_i$. If the regression relationship works well, the error in predicting Y_i using $\hat{Y}_i$ should be much smaller than the error

in predicting Y_i using $\bar{Y}$. If we call $\sum_{i=1}^{n}\left(Y_i - \bar{Y}\right)^2$ the total variation of Y and $\sum_{i=1}^{n}\left(Y_i - \hat{Y}_i\right)^2$

the unexplained variation from the regression, then we can measure the explained variation from the regression using the following equation:

Total variation = Unexplained variation + Explained variation   **(7)**

The coefficient of determination is the fraction of the total variation that is explained by the regression. This gives us the relationship

$$R^2 = \frac{\text{Explained variation}}{\text{Total variation}} = \frac{\text{Total variation} - \text{Unexplained variation}}{\text{Total variation}}$$
$$= 1 - \frac{\text{Unexplained variation}}{\text{Total variation}}$$ **(8)**

Note that total variation equals explained variation plus unexplained variation, as shown in Equation 7. Most regression programs report the coefficient of determination as R^2.[29]

---

28 We will discuss such models in the reading on multiple regression.
29 As we illustrate in the tables of regression output later in this reading, regression programs also report multiple R, which is the correlation between the actual values and the forecast values of Y. The coefficient of determination is the square of multiple R.

Example 13

Inflation Rate and Growth in the Money Supply

Using the data in Table 7, we can see that the unexplained variation from the regression, which is the sum of the squared residuals, equals 0.000386. Table 8 shows the computation of total variation in the dependent variable, the long-term rate of inflation.

Table 8	Computing Total Variation			
Country	Money Supply Growth Rate X_i	Inflation Rate Y_i	Deviation from Mean $Y_i - \overline{Y}$	Squared Deviation $(Y_i - \overline{Y})^2$
Australia	0.1166	0.0676	0.0073	0.000053
Canada	0.0915	0.0519	−0.0084	0.000071
New Zealand	0.1060	0.0815	0.0212	0.000449
Switzerland	0.0575	0.0339	−0.0264	0.000697
United Kingdom	0.1258	0.0758	0.0155	0.000240
United States	0.0634	0.0509	−0.0094	0.000088
	Average:	0.0603	Sum:	0.001598

Source: International Monetary Fund.

The average inflation rate for this period is 6.03 percent. The next-to-last column shows the amount each country's long-term inflation rate deviates from that average; the last column shows the square of that deviation. The sum of those squared deviations is the total variation in Y for the sample (0.001598), shown in Table 8.

The coefficient of determination for the regression is

$$\frac{\text{Total variation} - \text{Unexplained variation}}{\text{Total variation}} = \frac{0.001598 - 0.000386}{0.001598} = 0.7584$$

Note that this method gives the same result rounded to two decimal places, 0.76, that we obtained earlier (the difference at greater decimal places results from rounding). We will use this method again in the reading on multiple regression; when we have more than one independent variable, this method is the only way to compute the coefficient of determination.

3.5 Hypothesis Testing

In this section, we address testing hypotheses concerning the population values of the intercept or slope coefficient of a regression model. This topic is critical in practice. For example, we may want to check a stock's valuation using the capital asset pricing model; we hypothesize that the stock has a market-average beta or level of systematic risk. Or we may want to test the hypothesis that economists' forecasts of the inflation rate are unbiased (not overestimates or underestimates, on average). In each case, does the evidence support the hypothesis? Questions such as these can be addressed with hypothesis tests within a regression model. Such tests are often t-tests of the value of the intercept or slope coefficient(s). To understand the concepts involved in this test, it is useful to first review a simple, equivalent approach based on confidence intervals.

We can perform a hypothesis test using the confidence interval approach if we know three things: 1) the estimated parameter value, $\hat{b}_0$ or $\hat{b}_1$, 2) the hypothesized value of the parameter, b_0 or b_1, and 3) a confidence interval around the estimated parameter. A confidence interval is an interval of values that we believe includes the true parameter value, b_1, with a given degree of confidence. To compute a confidence interval, we must select the significance level for the test and know the standard error of the estimated coefficient.

Suppose we regress a stock's returns on a stock market index's returns and find that the slope coefficient ($\hat{b}_1$) is 1.5 with a standard error ($s_{\hat{b}_1}$) of 0.200. Assume we used 62 monthly observations in our regression analysis. The hypothesized value of the parameter (b_1) is 1.0, the market average slope coefficient. The estimated and the population slope coefficients are often called beta, because the population coefficient is often represented by the Greek symbol beta (β) rather than the b_1 we use in this reading. Our null hypothesis is that $b_1 = 1.0$ and $\hat{b}_1$ is the estimate for b_1. We will use a 95 percent confidence interval for our test, or we could say that the test has a significance level of 0.05.

Our confidence interval will span the range $\hat{b}_1 - t_c s_{\hat{b}_1}$ to $\hat{b}_1 + t_c s_{\hat{b}_1}$ or

$$\hat{b}_1 \pm t_c s_{\hat{b}_1} \tag{9}$$

where t_c is the critical t value.[30] The critical value for the test depends on the number of degrees of freedom for the t-distribution under the null hypothesis. The number of degrees of freedom equals the number of observations minus the number of parameters estimated. In a regression with one independent variable, there are two estimated parameters, the intercept term and the coefficient on the independent variable. For 62 observations and two parameters estimated in this example, we have 60 degrees of freedom (62 − 2). For 60 degrees of freedom, the table of critical values in the back of the book shows that the critical t-value at the 0.05 significance level is 2.00. Substituting the values from our example into Equation 9 gives us the interval

$$\hat{b}_1 \pm t_c s_{\hat{b}_1} = 1.5 \pm 2.00(0.200)$$
$$= 1.5 \pm 0.400$$
$$= 1.10 \text{ to } 1.90$$

Under the null hypothesis, the probability that the confidence interval includes b_1 is 95 percent. Because we are testing $b_1 = 1.0$ and because our confidence interval does not include 1.0, we can reject the null hypothesis. Therefore, we can be 95 percent confident that the stock's beta is different from 1.0.

In practice, the most common way to test a hypothesis using a regression model is with a t-test of significance. To test the hypothesis, we can compute the statistic

$$t = \frac{\hat{b}_1 - b_1}{s_{\hat{b}_1}} \tag{10}$$

This test statistic has a t-distribution with $n - 2$ degrees of freedom because two parameters were estimated in the regression. We compare the absolute value of the t-statistic to t_c. If the absolute value of t is greater than t_c, then we can reject the null hypothesis. Substituting the values from the above example into this relationship gives the t-statistic associated with the probability that the stock's beta equals 1.0 ($b_1 = 1.0$).

---

30 We use the t-distribution for this test because we are using a sample estimate of the standard error, s_b, rather than its true (population) value.

$$t = \frac{\hat{b}_1 - b_1}{s_{\hat{b}_1}}$$

$$= (1.5 - 1.0)/0.200$$

$$= 2.50$$

Because $t > t_c$, we reject the null hypothesis that $b_1 = 1.0$.

The t-statistic in the example above is 2.50, and at the 0.05 significance level, $t_c = 2.00$; thus we reject the null hypothesis because $t > t_c$. This statement is equivalent to saying that we are 95 percent confident that the interval for the slope coefficient does not contain the value 1.0. If we were performing this test at the 0.01 level, however, t_c would be 2.66 and we would not reject the hypothesis because t would not be greater than t_c at this significance level. A 99 percent confidence interval for the slope coefficient does contain the value 1.0.

The choice of significance level is always a matter of judgment. When we use higher levels of confidence, the t_c increases. This choice leads to wider confidence intervals and to a decreased likelihood of rejecting the null hypothesis. Analysts often choose the 0.05 level of significance, which indicates a 5 percent chance of rejecting the null hypothesis when, in fact, it is true (a Type I error). Of course, decreasing the level of significance from 0.05 to 0.01 decreases the probability of Type I error, but it increases the probability of Type II error—failing to reject the null hypothesis when, in fact, it is false.

Often, financial analysts do not simply report whether or not their tests reject a particular hypothesis about a regression parameter. Instead, they report the p-value or probability value for a particular hypothesis. The p-value is the smallest level of significance at which the null hypothesis can be rejected. It allows the reader to interpret the results rather than be told that a certain hypothesis has been rejected or accepted. In most regression software packages, the p-values printed for regression coefficients apply to a test of null hypothesis that the true parameter is equal to 0 against the alternative that the parameter is not equal to 0, given the estimated coefficient and the standard error for that coefficient. For example, if the p-value is 0.005, we can reject the hypothesis that the true parameter is equal to 0 at the 0.5 percent significance level (99.5 percent confidence).

The standard error of the estimated coefficient is an important input for a hypothesis test concerning the regression coefficient (and for a confidence interval for the estimated coefficient). Stronger regression results lead to smaller standard errors of an estimated parameter and result in tighter confidence intervals. If the standard error ($s_{\hat{b}_1}$) in the above example were 0.100 instead of 0.200, the confidence interval range would be half as large and the t-statistic twice as large. With a standard error this small, we would reject the null hypothesis even at the 0.01 significance level because we would have $t = (1.5 - 1)/0.1 = 5.00$ and $t_c = 2.66$.

With this background, we can turn to hypothesis tests using actual regression results. The next three examples illustrate hypothesis tests in a variety of typical investment contexts.

Example 14

Estimating Beta for General Motors Stock

You are an investor in General Motors stock and want an estimate of its beta. As in the text example, you hypothesize that GM has an average level of market risk and that its required return in excess of the risk-free rate is the same as the market's required excess return. One regression that summarizes these statements is

$$(R - R_F) = \alpha + \beta(R_M - R_F) + \varepsilon \qquad\qquad (11)$$

where R_F is the periodic risk-free rate of return (known at the beginning of the period), R_M is the periodic return on the market, R is the periodic return to the stock of the company, and β is the covariance of stock and market return divided by the variance of the market return, $\text{Cov}(R, R_M)/\sigma_M^2$. Estimating this equation with linear regression provides an estimate of β, $\hat{\beta}$, which tells us the size of the required return premium for the security, given expectations about market returns.[31]

Suppose we want to test the null hypothesis, H_0, that $\beta = 1$ for GM stock to see whether GM stock has the same required return premium as the market as a whole. We need data on returns to GM stock, a risk-free interest rate, and the returns to the market index. For this example, we use data from January 1998 through December 2002 ($n = 60$). The return to GM stock is R. The monthly return to 30-day Treasury bills is R_F. The return to the S&P 500 is R_M.[32] We are estimating two parameters, so the number of degrees of freedom is $n - 2 = 60 - 2 = 58$. Table 9 shows the results from the regression $(R - R_F) = \alpha + \beta(R_M - R_F) + \varepsilon$.

Table 9	Estimating Beta for GM Stock

Regression Statistics

Multiple R	0.5549
R-squared	0.3079
Standard error of estimate	0.0985
Observations	60

	Coefficients	Standard Error	t-Statistic
Alpha	0.0036	0.0127	0.2840
Beta	1.1958	0.2354	5.0795

Source: Ibbotson Associates and Bloomberg L.P.

We are testing the null hypothesis, H_0, that β for GM equals 1 ($\beta = 1$) against the alternative hypothesis that β does not equal 1 ($\beta \neq 1$). The estimated $\hat{\beta}$ from the regression is 1.1958. The estimated standard error for that coefficient in the regression, $s_{\hat{\beta}}$ is 0.2354. The regression equation has 58 degrees of freedom (60 − 2), so the critical value for the test statistic is approximately $t_c = 2.00$ at the 0.05 significance level. Therefore, the 95 percent confidence interval for the data for any particular hypothesized value of β is shown by the range

$$\hat{\beta} \pm t_c s_{\hat{\beta}}$$

$$1.1958 \pm 2.00(0.2354)$$

$$0.7250 \text{ to } 1.6666$$

---

31 Beta (β) is typically estimated using 60 months of historical data, but the data-sample length sometimes varies. Although monthly data is typically used, some financial analysts estimate β using daily data. For more information on methods of estimating β, see Reilly and Brown (2003). The expected excess return for GM stock above the risk-free rate $(R - R_F)$ is $\beta(R_M - R_F)$, given a particular excess return to the market above the risk-free rate $(R_M - R_F)$. This result holds because we regress $(R - R_F)$ against $(R_M - R_F)$. For example, if a stock's beta is 1.5, its expected excess return is 1.5 times that of the market portfolio.

32 Data on GM stock returns came from Bloomberg. Data on T-bill returns and S&P 500 returns came from Ibbotson Associates.

In this case, the hypothesized parameter value is $\beta = 1$, and the value 1 falls inside this confidence interval, so we cannot reject the hypothesis at the 0.05 significance level. This means that we cannot reject the hypothesis that GM stock has the same systematic risk as the market as a whole.

Another way of looking at this issue is to compute the t-statistic for the GM beta hypothesized parameter using Equation 10:

$$t = \frac{\hat{\beta} - \beta}{s_{\hat{\beta}}} = \frac{1.1958 - 1.0}{0.2354} = 0.8318$$

This t-statistic is less than the critical t-value of 2.00. Therefore, neither approach allows us to reject the null hypothesis. Note that the t-statistic associated with $\hat{\beta}$ in the regression results in Table 9 is 5.0795. Given the significance level we are using, we cannot reject the null hypothesis that $\beta = 1$, but we can reject the hypothesis that $\beta = 0$.[33]

Note also that the R^2 in this regression is only 0.3079. This result suggests that only about 31 percent of the total variation in the excess return to GM stock (the return to GM above the risk-free rate) can be explained by excess return to the market portfolio. The remaining 69 percent of GM stock's excess return variation is the nonsystematic component, which can be attributed to company-specific risk.

In the next example, we show a regression hypothesis test with a one-sided alternative.

Example 15

Explaining Company Value Based on Returns to Invested Capital

Some financial analysts have argued that one good way to measure a company's ability to create wealth is to compare the company's return on invested capital (ROIC) to its weighted-average cost of capital (WACC). If a company has an ROIC greater than its cost of capital, the company is creating wealth; if its ROIC is less than its cost of capital, it is destroying wealth.[34]

Enterprise value (EV) is a market-price-based measure of company value defined as the market value of equity and debt minus the value of cash and investments. Invested capital (IC) is an accounting measure of company value defined as the sum of the book values of equity and debt. Higher ratios of EV to IC should reflect greater success at wealth creation in general. Mauboussin (1996) argued that the spread between ROIC and WACC helps explains the ratio of EV to IC. Using data on companies in the food-processing industry, we can test the relationship between EV/IC and (ROIC–WACC) using the regression model given in Equation 12.

$$\text{EV}_i/\text{IC}_i = b_0 + b_1(\text{ROIC}_i - \text{WACC}_i) + \varepsilon_i \tag{12}$$

where the subscript i is an index to identify the company. Our null hypothesis is $H_0: b_1 \leq 0$, and we specify a significance level of 0.05. If we reject the null

---

hypothesis, we have evidence of a statistically significant relationship between EV/IC and (ROIC–WACC). We estimate Equation 12 using data from nine food-processing companies for 2001.[35] The results of this regression are displayed in Table 10 and Figure 11.

Table 10	Explaining Enterprise Value/Invested Capital by the ROIC–WACC Spread

Regression Statistics

Multiple R	0.9469
R-squared	0.8966
Standard error of estimate	0.7422
Observations	9

	Coefficients	Standard Error	t-Statistic
Intercept	1.3478	0.3511	3.8391
Spread	30.0169	3.8519	7.7928

Source: Nelson (2003).

Figure 11	Fitted Regression Line Explaining Enterprise Value/Invested Capital Using ROIC–WACC Spread for the Food Industry

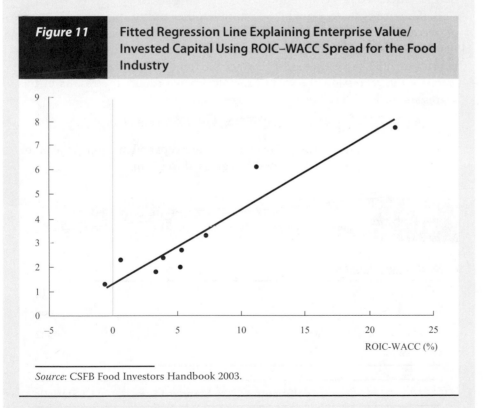

ROIC-WACC (%)

Source: CSFB Food Investors Handbook 2003.

We reject the null hypothesis based on the t-statistic of approximately 7.79 on estimated slope coefficient. There is a strong positive relationship between

---

35 Our data comes from Nelson (2003). Many sell-side analysts use this type of regression. It is one of the most frequently used cross-sectional regressions in published analyst reports.

the return spread (ROIC–WACC) and the ratio of EV to IC in our sample of companies. Figure 11 illustrates the strong positive relationship. The R^2 of 0.8966 indicates that the return spread explains about 90 percent of the variation in the ratio of EV to IC among the food-processing companies in the sample in 2001. The coefficient on the return spread of 30.0169 implies that the predicted increase in EV/IC is 0.01(30.0169) = 0.3002 or about 30 percent for a 1-percentage-point increase in the return spread, for our sample of companies.

In the final example of this section, we show that the null hypothesis can involve a slope coefficient of 1 just as well as a slope of 0.

Example 16

Testing whether Inflation Forecasts Are Unbiased

Example 11 introduced the concept of testing for bias in forecasts. That example showed that if a forecast is unbiased, its expected error is 0. We can examine whether a time-series of forecasts for a particular economic variable is unbiased by comparing the forecast at each date with the actual value of the economic variable announced after the forecast. If the forecasts are unbiased, then, by definition, the average realized forecast error should be close to 0. In that case, the value of b_0 (the intercept) should be 0 and the value of b_1 (the slope) should be 1, as discussed in Example 11.

Refer once again to Figure 9, which shows the current-quarter predictions of percentage change in CPI made by professional economic forecasters and the actual percentage change from the first quarter of 1983 through the fourth quarter of 2002 ($n = 80$). To test whether the forecasts are unbiased, we must estimate the regression shown in Example 11. We report the results of this regression in Table 11. The equation to be estimated is

$$\text{Actual percentage change in CPI}_t = b_0 + b_1(\text{Predicted change}_t) + \varepsilon_t$$

This regression estimates two parameters (the intercept and the slope); therefore, the regression has $n - 2 = 80 - 2 = 78$ degrees of freedom.

Table 11	Testing whether Forecasts of CPI Are Unbiased (Dependent Variable: CPI Change Expressed in Percent)

Regression Statistics

Multiple R	0.7138
R-squared	0.5095
Standard error of estimate	1.0322
Observations	80

	Coefficients	Standard Error	t-Statistic
Intercept	−0.0140	0.3657	−0.0384
Forecast (slope)	0.9637	0.1071	9.0008

Sources: Federal Reserve Banks of Philadelphia and St. Louis. ■

We can now test two null hypotheses about the parameters in this regression. Our first null hypothesis is that the intercept in this regression is 0 ($H_0: b_0 = 0$). The alternative hypothesis is that the intercept does not equal 0 ($H_a: b_0 \neq 0$). Our second null hypothesis is that the slope coefficient in this regression is 1 ($H_0: b_1 = 1$). The alternative hypothesis is that the slope coefficient does not equal 1 ($H_a: b_1 \neq 1$).

To test the hypotheses about b_0 and b_1, we must first decide on a critical value based on a particular significance level and then construct the confidence intervals for each parameter. If we choose the 0.05 significance level, with 78 degrees of freedom, the critical value, t_c, is approximately 1.99. The estimated value of the parameter $\hat{b}_0$ is −0.0140, and the estimated value of the standard error for $\hat{b}_0\left(s_{\hat{b}_0}\right)$ is 0.3657. Let B_0 stand for any particular hypothesized value. Therefore, under the null hypothesis that $b_0 = B_0$, a 95 percent confidence interval for b_0 is

$$\hat{b}_0 \pm t_c s_{\hat{b}_0}$$

$$-0.0140 \pm 1.99(0.3657)$$

$$-0.7417 \text{ to } 0.7137$$

In this case, B_0 is 0. The value of 0 falls within this confidence interval, so we cannot reject the first null hypothesis that $b_0 = 0$. We will explain how to interpret this result shortly.

Our second null hypothesis is based on the same sample as our first null hypothesis. Therefore, the critical value for testing that hypothesis is the same as the critical value for testing the first hypothesis ($t_c = 1.99$). The estimated value of the parameter $\hat{b}_1$ is 0.9637, and the estimated value of the standard error for $\hat{b}_1, s_{\hat{b}_1}$, is 0.1071. Therefore, the 95 percent confidence interval for any particular hypothesized value of b_1 can be constructed as follows:

$$\hat{b}_1 \pm t_c s_{\hat{b}_1}$$

$$0.9637 \pm 1.99(0.1071)$$

$$0.7506 \text{ to } 1.1768$$

In this case, our hypothesized value of b_1 is 1. The value 1 falls within this confidence interval, so we cannot reject the null hypothesis that $b_1 = 1$ at the 0.05 significance level. Because we did not reject either of the null hypotheses ($b_0 = 0$, $b_1 = 1$) about the parameters in this model, we cannot reject the hypothesis that the forecasts of CPI change were unbiased.[36]

As an analyst, you often will need forecasts of **economic growth** to help you make recommendations about asset allocation, expected returns, and other investment decisions. The hypothesis tests just conducted suggest that you cannot reject the hypothesis that the CPI predictions in the Survey of Professional Forecasters are unbiased. If you need an unbiased forecast of future percentage change in CPI for your asset-allocation decision, you might want to use these forecasts.

---

[36] Jointly testing the hypothesis $b_0 = 0$ and $b_1 = 1$ would require us to take into account the covariance of $\hat{b}_0$ and $\hat{b}_1$. For information on testing joint hypotheses of this type, see Greene (2003).

3.6 Analysis of Variance in a Regression with One Independent Variable

Analysis of variance (ANOVA) is a statistical procedure for dividing the total variability of a variable into components that can be attributed to different sources.[37] In regression analysis, we use ANOVA to determine the usefulness of the independent variable or variables in explaining variation in the dependent variable. An important statistical test conducted in analysis of variance is the F-test. The F-statistic tests whether all the slope coefficients in a linear regression are equal to 0. In a regression with one independent variable, this is a test of the null hypothesis H_0: $b_1 = 0$ against the alternative hypothesis H_a: $b_1 \neq 0$.

To correctly determine the test statistic for the null hypothesis that the slope coefficient equals 0, we need to know the following:

- the total number of observations (n);

- the total number of parameters to be estimated (in a one-independent-variable regression, this number is two: the intercept and the slope coefficient);

- the sum of squared errors or residuals, $\sum_{i=1}^{n} \left(Y_i - \hat{Y}_i\right)^2$, abbreviated SSE.

  This value is also known as the residual sum of squares; and

- the regression sum of squares, $\sum_{i=1}^{n} \left(\hat{Y}_i - \bar{Y}\right)^2$, abbreviated RSS. This value is the amount of total variation in Y that is explained in the regression equation. Total variation (TSS) is the sum of SSE and RSS.

The F-test for determining whether the slope coefficient equals 0 is based on an F-statistic, constructed using these four values. The F-statistic measures how well the regression equation explains the variation in the dependent variable. The F-statistic is the ratio of the average regression sum of squares to the average sum of the squared errors. The average regression sum of squares is computed by dividing the regression sum of squares by the number of slope parameters estimated (in this case, one). The average sum of squared errors is computed by dividing the sum of squared errors by the number of observations, n, minus the total number of parameters estimated (in this case, two: the intercept and the slope). These two divisors are the degrees of freedom for an F-test. If there are n observations, the F-test for the null hypothesis that the slope coefficient is equal to 0 is here denoted $F_{\text{# slope parameters}, n- \text{# parameters}} = F_{1, n-2}$, and the test has 1 and $n - 2$ degrees of freedom.

Suppose, for example, that the independent variable in a regression model explains none of the variation in the dependent variable. Then the predicted value for the regression model, $\hat{Y}_i$, is the average value of the dependent variable $\bar{Y}$. In this case, the regression sum of squares $\sum_{i=1}^{n}\left(\hat{Y}_i - \bar{Y}\right)^2$ is 0. Therefore, the F-statistic is 0. If the independent variable explains little of the variation in the dependent variable, the value of the F-statistic will be very small.

The formula for the F-statistic in a regression with one independent variable is

$$F = \frac{\text{RSS}/1}{\text{SSE}/(n-2)} = \frac{\text{Mean regression sum of squares}}{\text{Mean squared error}} \quad (13)$$

---

[37] In this reading, we focus on regression applications of ANOVA, the most common context in which financial analysts will encounter this tool. In this context, ANOVA is used to test whether all the regression slope coefficients are equal to 0. Analysts also use ANOVA to test a hypothesis that the means of two or more populations are equal. See Daniel and Terrell (1995) for details.

If the regression model does a good job of explaining variation in the dependent variable, then this ratio should be high. The explained regression sum of squares per estimated parameter will be high relative to the unexplained variation for each degree of freedom. Critical values for this F-statistic are given in Appendix D at the end of this volume.

Even though the F-statistic is commonly computed by regression software packages, analysts typically do not use ANOVA and F-tests in regressions with just one independent variable. Why not? In such regressions, the F-statistic is the square of the t-statistic for the slope coefficient. Therefore, the F-test duplicates the t-test for the significance of the slope coefficient. This relation is not true for regressions with two or more slope coefficients. Nevertheless, the one-slope coefficient case gives a foundation for understanding the multiple-slope coefficient cases.

Often, mutual fund performance is evaluated based on whether the fund has positive alpha—significantly positive excess risk-adjusted returns.[38] One commonly used method of risk adjustment is based on the capital asset pricing model. Consider the regression

$$(R_i - R_F) = \alpha_i + \beta_i(R_M - R_F) + \varepsilon_i \tag{14}$$

where R_F is the periodic risk-free rate of return (known at the beginning of the period), R_M is the periodic return on the market, R_i is the periodic return to Mutual Fund i, and β_i is the fund's beta. A fund has zero risk-adjusted excess return if $\alpha_i = 0$. If $\alpha_i = 0$, then $(R_i - R_F) = \beta_i(R_M - R_F) + \varepsilon_i$ and taking expectations, $E(R_i) = R_F + \beta_i(R_M - R_F)$, implying that β_i completely explains the fund's mean excess returns. If, for example, $\alpha_i > 0$, the fund is earning higher returns than expected given its beta.

In summary, to test whether a fund has a positive alpha, we must test the null hypothesis that the fund has no risk-adjusted excess returns (H_0: $\alpha = 0$) against the alternative hypothesis of nonzero risk-adjusted returns (H_a: $\alpha \neq 0$).

Example 17

Performance Evaluation: The Dreyfus Appreciation Fund

Table 12 presents results evaluating the excess return to the Dreyfus Appreciation Fund from January 1998 through December 2002. Note that the estimated beta in this regression, $\hat{\beta}_i$, is 0.7902. The Dreyfus Appreciation Fund was estimated to be about 0.8 times as risky as the market as a whole.

Table 12	Performance Evaluation of Dreyfus Appreciation Fund, January 1998 to December 2002

Regression Statistics

Multiple R	0.9280
R-squared	0.8611
Standard error of estimate	0.0174
Observations	60

ANOVA	Degrees of Freedom (df)	Sum of Squares (SS)	Mean Sum of Squares (MSS)	F
Regression	1	0.1093	0.1093	359.64

(continued)

---

38 Note that the Greek letter alpha, α, is traditionally used to represent the intercept in Equation 14 and should not be confused with another traditional usage of α to represent a significance level.

Table 12	Continued			
ANOVA	**Degrees of Freedom (df)**	**Sum of Squares (SS)**	**Mean Sum of Squares (MSS)**	**F**
Residual	58	0.0176	0.0003	
Total	59	0.1269		

	Coefficients	**Standard Error**	**t-Statistic**
Alpha	0.0009	0.0023	0.4036
Beta	0.7902	0.0417	18.9655

Source: Center for Research in Security Prices, University of Chicago.

Note also that the estimated alpha ($\hat{\alpha}$) in this regression is positive (0.0009). The value of the coefficient is only a little more than one-third the size of the standard error for that coefficient (0.0023), so the t-statistic for the coefficient is only 0.4036. Therefore, we cannot reject the null hypothesis ($\alpha = 0$) that the fund did not have a significant excess return beyond the return associated with the market risk of the fund. This result means that the returns to the fund were explained by the market risk of the fund and there was no additional statistical significance to the excess returns to the fund during this period.[39]

Because the t-statistic for the slope coefficient in this regression is 18.9655, the p-value for that coefficient is less than 0.0001 and is approximately zero. Therefore, the probability that the true value of this coefficient is actually 0 is microscopic.

How can we use an F-test to determine whether the slope coefficient in this regression is equal to 0? The ANOVA portion of Table 12 provides the data we need. In this case:

■ the total number of observations (n) is 60;
■ the total number of parameters to be estimated is 2 (intercept and slope);
■ the sum of squared errors or residuals, SSE, is 0.0176; and
■ the regression sum of squares, RSS, is 0.1093.

Therefore, the F-statistic to test whether the slope coefficient is equal to 0 is

$$\frac{0.1093/1}{0.0176/(60-2)} = 360.19$$

(The slight difference from the F-statistic in Table 12 is due to rounding.) The ANOVA output would show that the p-value for this F-statistic is less than 0.0001 and is exactly the same as the p-value for the t-statistic for the slope coefficient. Therefore, the F-test tells us nothing more than we already knew from the t-test. Note also that the F-statistic (359.64) is the square of the t-statistic (18.9655).

---

[39] This example introduces a well-known investment use of regression involving the capital asset pricing model. Researchers, however, recognize qualifications to the interpretation of alpha from a linear regression. The systematic risk of a managed portfolio is controlled by the portfolio manager. If, as a consequence, portfolio beta is correlated with the return on the market (as could result from market timing), inferences on alpha based on least-squares beta, as here, can be mistaken. This advanced subject is discussed in Dybvig and Ross (1985a) and (1985b).

3.7 Prediction Intervals

Financial analysts often want to use regression results to make predictions about a dependent variable. For example, we might ask, "How fast will the sales of XYZ Corporation grow this year if real GDP grows by 4 percent?" But we are not merely interested in making these forecasts; we also want to know how certain we should be about the forecasts' results. For example, if we predicted that sales for XYZ Corporation would grow by 6 percent this year, our prediction would mean more if we were 95 percent confident that sales growth would fall in the interval from 5 percent to 7 percent, rather than only 25 percent confident that this outcome would occur. Therefore, we need to understand how to compute confidence intervals around regression forecasts.

We must take into account two sources of uncertainty when using the regression model $Y_i = b_0 + b_1 X_i + \varepsilon_i, i = 1, \ldots, n$ and the estimated parameters, $\hat{b}_0$ and $\hat{b}_1$, to make a prediction. First, the error term itself contains uncertainty. The standard deviation of the error term, σ_ε, can be estimated from the standard error of estimate for the regression equation. A second source of uncertainty in making predictions about Y, however, comes from uncertainty in the estimated parameters $\hat{b}_0$ and $\hat{b}_1$.

If we knew the true values of the regression parameters, b_0 and b_1, then the variance of our prediction of Y, given any particular predicted (or assumed) value of X, would simply be s^2, the squared standard error of estimate. The variance would be s^2 because the prediction, $\hat{Y}$, would come from the equation $\hat{Y} = b_0 + \hat{b}_1 X$ and $\left(Y - \hat{Y}\right) = \varepsilon$.

Because we must estimate the regression parameters $\hat{b}_0$ and $\hat{b}_1$ however, our prediction of Y, $\hat{Y}$, given any particular predicted value of X, is actually $\hat{Y} = \hat{b}_0 + \hat{b}_1 X$. The estimated variance of the prediction error, s_f^2 of Y, given X, is

$$s_f^2 = s^2 \left[1 + \frac{1}{n} + \frac{\left(X - \bar{X}\right)^2}{(n-1)s_x^2} \right] \tag{15}$$

This estimated variance depends on:

- the squared standard error of estimate, s^2;
- the number of observations, n;
- the value of the independent variable, X, used to predict the dependent variable;
- the estimated mean, $\bar{X}$; and
- variance, s_x^2 of the independent variable.[40]

Once we have this estimate of the variance of the prediction error, determining a prediction interval around the prediction is very similar to estimating a confidence interval around an estimated parameter, as shown earlier in this reading. We need to take the following four steps to determine the prediction interval for the prediction:

1. Make the prediction.
2. Compute the variance of the prediction error using Equation 15.
3. Choose a significance level, α, for the forecast. For example, the 0.05 level, given the degrees of freedom in the regression, determines the critical value for the forecast interval, t_c.
4. Compute the $(1 - \alpha)$ percent prediction interval for the prediction, namely

$$\hat{Y} \pm t_c s_f.$$

---

40 For a derivation of this equation, see Pindyck and Rubinfeld (1998).

Example 18

Predicting the Ratio of Enterprise Value to Invested Capital

We continue with the example of explaining the ratio of enterprise value to invested capital among food-processing companies by the spread between the return to invested capital and the weighted-average cost of capital (ROIC–WACC). In Example 15, we estimated the regression given in Table 10.

Table 10	Explaining Enterprise Value/Invested Capital by the ROIC-WACC Spread (repeated)

Regression Statistics

Multiple R	0.9469
R-squared	0.8966
Standard error of estimate	0.7422
Observations	9

	Coefficients	Standard Error	t-Statistic
Intercept	1.3478	0.3511	3.8391
Spread	30.0169	3.8519	7.7928

Source: Nelson (2003).

You are interested in predicting the ratio of enterprise value to invested capital for a company if the return spread between ROIC and WACC is 10 percentage points. What is the 95 percent confidence interval for the ratio of enterprise value to invested capital for that company?

Using the data provided in Table 10, take the following steps:

1. Make the prediction: Expected EV/IC = 1.3478 + 30.0169(0.10) = 4.3495. This regression suggests that if the return spread between ROIC and WACC (X_i) is 10 percent, the EV/IC ratio will be 4.3495.

2. Compute the variance of the prediction error. To compute the variance of the forecast error, we must know:

   - the standard error of the estimate of the equation, $s = 0.7422$ (as shown in Table 10);

   - the mean return spread, $\bar{X} = 0.0647$ (this computation is not shown in the table); and

   - the variance of the mean return spread in the sample, $s_x^2 = 0.004641$ (this computation is not shown in the table).

Using these data, you can compute the variance of the forecast error (s_f^2) for predicting EV/IC for a company with a 10 percent spread between ROIC and WACC.

$$s_f^2 = 0.7422^2 \left[1 + \frac{1}{9} + \frac{(0.10 - 0.0647)^2}{(9-1)0.004641} \right]$$

$$= 0.630556$$

In this example, the variance of the forecast error is 0.630556, and the standard deviation of the forecast error is $s_f = (0.630556)^{1/2} = 0.7941$.

3. Determine the critical value of the t-statistic. Given a 95 percent confidence interval and $9 - 2 = 7$ degrees of freedom, the critical value of the t-statistic, t_c, is 2.365 using the tables in the back of this volume.

4. Compute the prediction interval. The 95 percent confidence interval for EV/IC extends from $4.3495 - 2.365(0.7941)$ to $4.3495 + 2.365(0.7941)$, or 2.4715 to 6.2275.

In summary, if the spread between the ROIC and the WACC is 10 percent, the 95 percent prediction interval for EV/IC will extend from 2.4715 to 6.2275. The small sample size is reflected in the relatively large prediction interval.

3.8 Limitations of Regression Analysis

Although this reading has shown many of the uses of regression models for financial analysis, regression models do have limitations. First, regression relations can change over time, just as correlations can. This fact is known as the issue of **parameter instability**, and its existence should not be surprising as the economic, tax, regulatory, political, and institutional contexts in which financial markets operate change. Whether considering cross-sectional or time-series regression, the analyst will probably face this issue. As one example, cross-sectional regression relationships between stock characteristics may differ between growth-led and value-led markets. As a second example, the time-series regression estimating the beta often yields significantly different estimated betas depending on the time period selected. In both cross-sectional and time-series contexts, the most common problem is sampling from more than one population, with the challenge of identifying when doing so is an issue.

A second limitation to the use of regression results specific to investment contexts is that public knowledge of regression relationships may negate their future usefulness. Suppose, for example, an analyst discovers that stocks with a certain characteristic have had historically very high returns. If other analysts discover and act upon this relationship, then the prices of stocks with that characteristic will be bid up. The knowledge of the relationship may result in the relation no longer holding in the future.

Finally, if the regression assumptions listed in Section 3.2 are violated, hypothesis tests and predictions based on linear regression will not be valid. Although there are tests for violations of regression assumptions, often uncertainty exists as to whether an assumption has been violated. This limitation will be discussed in detail in the reading on multiple regression.

SUMMARY

- A scatter plot shows graphically the relationship between two variables. If the points on the scatter plot cluster together in a straight line, the two variables have a strong linear relation.

- The sample correlation coefficient for two variables X and Y is $r = \dfrac{\text{Cov}(X,Y)}{s_x s_y}$.

- If two variables have a very strong linear relation, then the absolute value of their correlation will be close to 1. If two variables have a weak linear relation, then the absolute value of their correlation will be close to 0.

- The squared value of the correlation coefficient for two variables quantifies the percentage of the variance of one variable that is explained by the other. If the correlation coefficient is positive, the two variables are directly related; if the correlation coefficient is negative, the two variables are inversely related.

- If we have n observations for two variables, we can test whether the population correlation between the two variables is equal to 0 by using a t-test. This test statistic has a t-distribution with $n - 2$ degrees of freedom if the null hypothesis of 0 correlation is true.

- Even one outlier can greatly affect the correlation between two variables. Analysts should examine a scatter plot for the variables to determine whether outliers might affect a particular correlation.

- Correlations can be spurious in the sense of misleadingly pointing toward associations between variables.

- The dependent variable in a linear regression is the variable that the regression model tries to explain. The independent variables are the variables that a regression model uses to explain the dependent variable.

- If there is one independent variable in a linear regression and there are n observations on the dependent and independent variables, the regression model is $Y_i = b_0 + b_1 X_i + \varepsilon_i$, $i = 1, \ldots, n$, where Y_i is the dependent variable, X_i is the independent variable, and ε_i is the error term. In this model, the coefficient b_0 is the intercept. The intercept is the predicted value of the dependent variable when the independent variable has a value of zero. In this model, the coefficient b_1 is the slope of the regression line. If the value of the independent variable increases by one unit, then the model predicts that the value of the dependent variable will increase by b_1 units.

- The assumptions of the classic normal linear regression model are the following:
  - A linear relation exists between the dependent variable and the independent variable.
  - The independent variable is not random.
  - The expected value of the error term is 0.
  - The variance of the error term is the same for all observations (homoskedasticity).
  - The error term is uncorrelated across observations.
  - The error term is normally distributed.

- The estimated parameters in a linear regression model minimize the sum of the squared regression residuals.

- The standard error of estimate measures how well the regression model fits the data. If the SEE is small, the model fits well.

- The coefficient of determination measures the fraction of the total variation in the dependent variable that is explained by the independent variable. In a linear regression with one independent variable, the simplest way to compute the coefficient of determination is to square the correlation of the dependent and independent variables.

- To calculate a confidence interval for an estimated regression coefficient, we must know the standard error of the estimated coefficient and the critical value for the t-distribution at the chosen level of significance, t_c.

- To test whether the population value of a regression coefficient, b_1, is equal to a particular hypothesized value, B_1, we must know the estimated coefficient, $\hat{b}_1$, the standard error of the estimated coefficient, $s_{\hat{b}_1}$, and the critical value for the t-distribution at the chosen level of significance, t_c. The test statistic for this hypothesis is $\left(\hat{b}_1 - B_1\right)/s_{\hat{b}_1}$. If the absolute value of this statistic is greater than t_c, then we reject the null hypothesis that $b_1 = B_1$.

- In the regression model $Y_i = b_0 + b_1 X_i + \varepsilon_i$, if we know the estimated parameters, $\hat{b}_0$ and $\hat{b}_1$, for any value of the independent variable, X, then the predicted value of the dependent variable Y is $\hat{Y} = \hat{b}_0 + \hat{b}_1 X$.

- The prediction interval for a regression equation for a particular predicted value of the dependent variable is $\hat{Y} \pm t_c s_f$ where s_f is the square root of the estimated variance of the prediction error and t_c is the critical level for the t-statistic at the chosen significance level. This computation specifies a $(1 - \alpha)$ percent confidence interval. For example, if $\alpha = 0.05$, then this computation yields a 95 percent confidence interval.

PRACTICE PROBLEMS FOR READING 11

1. Variable X takes on the values shown in the following table for five observations. The table also shows the values for five other variables, Y_1 through Y_5. Which of the variables Y_1 through Y_5 have a zero correlation with variable X?

X	Y₁	Y₂	Y₃	Y₄	Y₅
1	7	2	4	4	1
2	7	4	2	1	2
3	7	2	0	0	3
4	7	4	2	1	4
5	7	2	4	4	5

2. Use the data sample below to answer the following questions.

$$\sum_{i=1}^{n} X_i = 220 \quad \sum_{i=1}^{n} \left(X_i - \bar{X}\right)^2 = 440 \quad \sum_{i=1}^{n} \left(X_i - \bar{X}\right)\left(Y_i - \bar{Y}\right) = -568$$

$$\sum_{i=1}^{n} Y_i = 385 \quad \sum_{i=1}^{n} \left(Y_i - \bar{Y}\right)^2 = 1120 \quad n = 11$$

A. Calculate the sample mean, variance, and standard deviation for X.

B. Calculate the sample mean, variance, and standard deviation for Y.

C. Calculate the sample covariance between X and Y.

D. Calculate the sample correlation between X and Y.

3. Statistics for three variables are given below. X is the monthly return for a large-stock index, Y is the monthly return for a small-stock index, and Z is the monthly return for a corporate bond index. There are 60 observations.

$$\bar{X} = 0.760 \quad \sum_{i=1}^{n} \left(X_i - \bar{X}\right)^2 = 769.081 \quad \sum_{i=1}^{n} \left(X_i - \bar{X}\right)\left(Y_i - \bar{Y}\right) = 720.535$$

$$\bar{Y} = 1.037 \quad \sum_{i=1}^{n} \left(Y_i - \bar{Y}\right)^2 = 1243.309 \quad \sum_{i=1}^{n} \left(X_i - \bar{X}\right)\left(Z_i - \bar{Z}\right) = 231.007$$

$$\bar{Z} = 0.686 \quad \sum_{i=1}^{n} \left(Z_i - \bar{Z}\right)^2 = 183.073 \quad \sum_{i=1}^{n} \left(Y_i - \bar{Y}\right)\left(Z_i - \bar{Z}\right) = 171.816$$

A. Calculate the sample variance and standard deviation for X, Y, and Z.

B. Calculate the sample covariance between X and Y, X and Z, and Y and Z.

C. Calculate the sample correlation between X and Y, X and Z, and Y and Z.

4. Home sales and interest rates should be negatively related. The following table gives the number of annual unit sales for Packard Homes and mortgage rates for four recent years. Calculate the sample correlation between sales and mortgage rates.

Year	Unit Sales	Interest Rate (%)
2000	50	8.0
2001	70	7.0
2002	80	6.0
2003	60	7.0

5. The following table shows the sample correlations between the monthly returns for four different mutual funds and the S&P 500. The correlations are based on 36 monthly observations. The funds are as follows:

Fund 1	Large-cap fund
Fund 2	Mid-cap fund
Fund 3	Large-cap value fund
Fund 4	Emerging markets fund
S&P 500	U.S. domestic stock index

	Fund 1	Fund 2	Fund 3	Fund 4	S&P 500
Fund 1	1				
Fund 2	0.9231	1			
Fund 3	0.4771	0.4156	1		
Fund 4	0.7111	0.7238	0.3102	1	
S&P 500	0.8277	0.8223	0.5791	0.7515	1

Test the null hypothesis that each of these correlations, individually, is equal to zero against the alternative hypothesis that it is not equal to zero. Use a 5 percent significance level.

6. Bouvier Co. is a Canadian company that sells forestry products to several Pacific Rim customers. Bouvier's sales are very sensitive to exchange rates. The following table shows recent annual sales (in millions of Canadian dollars) and the average exchange rate for the year (expressed as the units of foreign currency needed to buy one Canadian dollar).

Year i	Exchange Rate X_i	Sales Y_i
1	0.40	20
2	0.36	25
3	0.42	16
4	0.31	30
5	0.33	35
6	0.34	30

A. Calculate the sample mean and standard deviation for X (the exchange rate) and Y (sales).

B. Calculate the sample covariance between the exchange rate and sales.

C. Calculate the sample correlation between the exchange rate and sales.

D. Calculate the intercept and coefficient for an estimated linear regression with the exchange rate as the independent variable and sales as the dependent variable.

7. Julie Moon is an energy analyst examining electricity, oil, and natural gas consumption in different regions over different seasons. She ran a regression explaining the variation in energy consumption as a function of temperature. The total variation of the dependent variable was 140.58, the explained variation was 60.16, and the unexplained variation was 80.42. She had 60 monthly observations.

   A. Compute the coefficient of determination.

   B. What was the sample correlation between energy consumption and temperature?

   C. Compute the standard error of the estimate of Moon's regression model.

   D. Compute the sample standard deviation of monthly energy consumption.

8. You are examining the results of a regression estimation that attempts to explain the unit sales growth of a business you are researching. The analysis of variance output for the regression is given in the table below. The regression was based on five observations ($n = 5$).

   ANOVA

	df	SS	MSS	F	Significance F
Regression	1	88.0	88.0	36.667	0.00904
Residual	3	7.2	2.4		
Total	4	95.2			

   A. How many independent variables are in the regression to which the ANOVA refers?

   B. Define Total SS.

   C. Calculate the sample variance of the dependent variable using information in the above table.

   D. Define Regression SS and explain how its value of 88 is obtained in terms of other quantities reported in the above table.

   E. What hypothesis does the F-statistic test?

   F. Explain how the value of the F-statistic of 36.667 is obtained in terms of other quantities reported in the above table.

   G. Is the F-test significant at the 5 percent significance level?

9. The first table below contains the regression results for a regression with monthly returns on a large-cap mutual fund as the dependent variable and monthly returns on a market index as the independent variable. The analysis is performed using only 12 monthly returns (in percent). The second table provides summary statistics for the dependent and independent variables.

   A. What is the predicted return on the large-cap mutual fund for a market index return of 8.00 percent?

   B. Find a 95 percent prediction interval for the expected mutual fund return.

   Regression Statistics

Multiple R	0.776
R-squared	0.602
Standard error	4.243
Observations	12

	Coefficients	Standard Error	t-Statistic	p-Value
Intercept	−0.287	1.314	−0.219	0.831
Slope coefficient	0.802	0.206	3.890	0.003

Statistic	Market Index Return	Large-Cap Fund Return
Mean	2.30%	1.56%
Standard deviation	6.21%	6.41%
Variance	38.51	41.13
Count	12	12

10. Industry automobile sales should be related to consumer sentiment. The following table provides a regression analysis in which sales of automobiles and light trucks (in millions of vehicles) are estimated as a function of a consumer sentiment index.

Regression Statistics

Multiple R	0.80113
R-squared	0.64181
Standard error	0.81325
Observations	120

	Coefficients	Standard Error	t-Statistic	p-Value
Intercept	6.071	0.58432	10.389	0
Slope coefficient	0.09251	0.00636	14.541	0

For the independent variable and dependent variable, the means, standard deviations, and variances are as follows:

	Sentiment Index X	Automobile Sales (Millions of Units) Y
Mean	91.0983	14.4981
Standard deviation	11.7178	1.35312
Variance	137.3068	1.83094

A. Find the expected sales and a 95 percent prediction interval for sales if the sentiment index has a value of 90.

B. Find the expected sales and a 95 percent prediction interval for sales if the sentiment index has a value of 100.

11. Use the following information to create a regression model:

$$\sum_{i=1}^{n} X_i = 81 \quad \sum_{i=1}^{n}(X_i - \bar{X})^2 = 60 \quad \sum_{i=1}^{n}(X_i - \bar{X})(Y_i - \bar{Y}) = 84$$

$$\sum_{i=1}^{n} X_i^2 = 789$$

$$\sum_{i=1}^{n} Y_i = 144 \quad \sum_{i=1}^{n}(Y_i - \bar{Y})^2 = 144 \quad \sum_{i=1}^{n}\left(Y_i - \hat{b}_0 - \hat{b}_1 X_i\right)^2 = 26.4$$

$$n = 9$$

A. Calculate the sample mean, variance, and standard deviation for X and for Y.

B. Calculate the sample covariance and the correlation between X and Y.

C. Calculate $\hat{b}_0$ and $\hat{b}_1$ for a regression of the form $Y_i = \hat{b}_0 + \hat{b}_1 X_i$.

For the remaining three parts of this question, assume that the calculations shown above already incorporate the correct values for $\hat{b}_0$ and $\hat{b}_1$.

D. Find the total variation, explained variation, and unexplained variation.

E. Find the coefficient of determination.

F. Find the standard error of the estimate.

12. The bid–ask spread for stocks depends on the market liquidity for stocks. One measure of liquidity is a stock's trading volume. Below are the results of a regression analysis using the bid–ask spread at the end of 2002 for a sample of 1,819 NASDAQ-listed stocks as the dependent variable and the natural log of trading volume during December 2002 as the independent variable. Several items in the regression output have been intentionally omitted. Use the reported information to fill in the missing values.

Regression Statistics	
Multiple R	X2
R-squared	X1
Standard error	X3
Observations	1819

ANOVA	df	SS	MSS	F	Significance F
Regression	X5	14.246	X7	X9	0
Residual	X6	45.893	X8		
Total	X4	60.139			

	Coefficients	Standard Error	t-Statistic	p-Value	Lower 95%	Upper 95%
Intercept	0.55851	0.018707	29.85540	0	0.52182	0.59520
Slope coefficient	−0.04375	0.001842	X10	0	X11	X12

13. An economist collected the monthly returns for KDL's portfolio and a diversified stock index. The data collected are shown below:

Month	Portfolio Return (%)	Index Return (%)
1	1.11	−0.59
2	72.10	64.90
3	5.12	4.81
4	1.01	1.68
5	−1.72	−4.97
6	4.06	−2.06

The economist calculated the correlation between the two returns and found it to be 0.996. The regression results with the KDL return as the dependent variable and the index return as the independent variable are given as follows:

Regression Statistics

Multiple R	0.996
R-squared	0.992
Standard error	2.861
Observations	6

ANOVA	df	SS	MSS	F	Significance F
Regression	1	4101.62	4101.62	500.79	0
Residual	4	32.76	8.19		
Total	5	4134.38			

	Coefficients	Standard Error	t-Statistic	p-Value
Intercept	2.252	1.274	1.768	0.1518
Slope	1.069	0.0477	22.379	0

When reviewing the results, Andrea Fusilier suspected that they were unreliable. She found that the returns for Month 2 should have been 7.21 percent and 6.49 percent, instead of the large values shown in the first table. Correcting these values resulted in a revised correlation of 0.824 and the revised regression results shown as follows:

Regression Statistics

Multiple R	0.824
R-squared	0.678
Standard error	2.062
Observations	6

ANOVA	df	SS	MSS	F	Significance F
Regression	1	35.89	35.89	8.44	0.044
Residual	4	17.01	4.25		
Total	5	52.91			

	Coefficients	Standard Error	t-Statistic	p-Value
Intercept	2.242	0.863	2.597	0.060
Slope	0.623	0.214	2.905	0.044

Explain how the bad data affected the results.

14. Diet Partners charges its clients a small management fee plus a percentage of gains whenever portfolio returns are positive. Cleo Smith believes that strong incentives for portfolio managers produce superior returns for clients. In order to demonstrate this, Smith runs a regression with the Diet Partners' portfolio return (in percent) as the dependent variable and its management fee (in percent) as the independent variable. The estimated regression for a 60-month period is

$$\text{RETURN} = -3.021 + 7.062 \,(\text{FEE})$$
$$(-7.28) \quad (14.95)$$

The calculated t-values are given in parentheses below the intercept and slope coefficients. The coefficient of determination for the regression model is 0.794.

A. What is the predicted RETURN if FEE is 0 percent? If FEE is 1 percent?

B. Using a two-tailed test, is the relationship between RETURN and FEE significant at the 5 percent level?

C. Would Smith be justified in concluding that high fees are good for clients?

The following information relates to Questions 15–20

Kenneth McCoin, CFA, is a fairly tough interviewer. Last year, he handed each job applicant a sheet of paper with the information in the following table, and he then asked several questions about regression analysis. Some of McCoin's questions, along with a sample of the answers he received to each, are given below. McCoin told the applicants that the independent variable is the ratio of net income to sales for restaurants with a market cap of more than $100 million and the dependent variable is the ratio of cash flow from operations to sales for those restaurants. Which of the choices provided is the best answer to each of McCoin's questions?

Regression Statistics

Multiple R	0.8623
R-squared	0.7436
Standard error	0.0213
Observations	24

ANOVA	df	SS	MSS	F	Significance F
Regression	1	0.029	0.029000	63.81	0
Residual	22	0.010	0.000455		
Total	23	0.040			

	Coefficients	Standard Error	t-Statistic	p-Value
Intercept	0.077	0.007	11.328	0
Slope	0.826	0.103	7.988	0

15. What is the value of the coefficient of determination?

   A. 0.8261.

   B. 0.7436.

   C. 0.8623.

16. Suppose that you deleted several of the observations that had small residual values. If you re-estimated the regression equation using this reduced sample, what would likely happen to the standard error of the estimate and the R-squared?

	Standard Error of the Estimate	R-Squared
A.	Decrease	Decrease
B.	Decrease	Increase
C.	Increase	Decrease

17. What is the correlation between X and Y?

   A. −0.7436.

   B. 0.7436.

   C. 0.8623.

18. Where did the F-value in the ANOVA table come from?

   A. You look up the F-value in a table. The F depends on the numerator and denominator degrees of freedom.

   B. Divide the "Mean Square" for the regression by the "Mean Square" of the residuals.

   C. The F-value is equal to the reciprocal of the t-value for the slope coefficient.

19. If the ratio of net income to sales for a restaurant is 5 percent, what is the predicted ratio of cash flow from operations to sales?

   A. $0.007 + 0.103(5.0) = 0.524$.

   B. $0.077 − 0.826(5.0) = −4.054$.

   C. $0.077 + 0.826(5.0) = 4.207$.

20. Is the relationship between the ratio of cash flow to operations and the ratio of net income to sales significant at the 5 percent level?

   A. No, because the R-squared is greater than 0.05.

   B. No, because the p-values of the intercept and slope are less than 0.05.

   C. Yes, because the p-values for F and t for the slope coefficient are less than 0.05.

The following information relates to Questions 21–26

Howard Golub, CFA, is preparing to write a research report on Stellar Energy Corp. common stock. One of the world's largest companies, Stellar is in the business of refining and marketing oil. As part of his analysis, Golub wants to evaluate the sensitivity of the stock's returns to various economic factors. For example, a client recently asked Golub whether the price of Stellar Energy Corporation stock has tended to rise following increases in retail energy prices. Golub believes the association between the two variables to be negative, but he does not know the strength of the association.

Golub directs his assistant, Jill Batten, to study the relationships between Stellar monthly common stock returns versus the previous month's percent change in the U.S. Consumer Price Index for Energy (CPIENG), and Stellar monthly common stock returns versus the previous month's percent change in the U.S. Producer Price Index for Crude Energy Materials (PPICEM). Golub wants Batten to run both a correlation and a linear regression analysis. In response, Batten compiles the summary statistics shown in Exhibit 1 for the 248 months between January 1980 and August 2000. All of the data are in decimal form, where 0.01 indicates a 1 percent return. Batten also runs a regression analysis using Stellar monthly returns as the dependent variable and the monthly change in CPIENG as the independent variable. Exhibit 2 displays the results of this regression model.

Exhibit 1	Descriptive Statistics		
	Monthly Return Stellar Common Stock	Lagged Monthly Change	
		CPIENG	PPICEM
Mean	0.0123	0.0023	0.0042
Standard Deviation	0.0717	0.0160	0.0534
Covariance, Stellar vs. CPIENG	−0.00017		
Covariance, Stellar vs. PPICEM	−0.00048		
Covariance, CPIENG vs. PPICEM	0.00044		
Correlation, Stellar vs. CPIENG	−0.1452		

Exhibit 2	Regression Analysis with CPIENG

Regression Statistics

Multiple R	0.1452
R-squared	0.0211
Standard error of the estimate	0.0710
Observations	248

	Coefficients	Standard Error	t-Statistic
Intercept	0.0138	0.0046	3.0275
Slope coefficient	−0.6486	0.2818	−2.3014

21. Batten wants to determine whether the sample correlation between the Stellar and CPIENG variables (−0.1452) is statistically significant. The critical value for the test statistic at the 0.05 level of significance is approximately 1.96. Batten should conclude that the statistical relationship between Stellar and CPIENG is:

A. significant, because the calculated test statistic has a lower absolute value than the critical value for the test statistic.

B. significant, because the calculated test statistic has a higher absolute value than the critical value for the test statistic.

C. not significant, because the calculated test statistic has a higher absolute value than the critical value for the test statistic.

22. Did Batten's regression analyze cross-sectional or time-series data, and what was the expected value of the error term from that regression?

	Data Type	Expected Value of Error Term
A.	Time-series	0
B.	Time-series	ε_i
C.	Cross-sectional	0

23. Based on the regression, which used data in decimal form, if the CPIENG decreases by 1.0 percent, what is the expected return on Stellar common stock during the next period?

    A. 0.0073 (0.73 percent).

    B. 0.0138 (1.38 percent).

    C. 0.0203 (2.03 percent).

24. Based on Batten's regression model, the coefficient of determination indicates that:

    A. Stellar's returns explain 2.11 percent of the variability in CPIENG.

    B. Stellar's returns explain 14.52 percent of the variability in CPIENG.

    C. Changes in CPIENG explain 2.11 percent of the variability in Stellar's returns.

25. For Batten's regression model, the standard error of the estimate shows that the standard deviation of:

    A. the residuals from the regression is 0.0710.

    B. values estimated from the regression is 0.0710.

    C. Stellar's observed common stock returns is 0.0710.

26. For the analysis run by Batten, which of the following is an *incorrect* conclusion from the regression output?

    A. The estimated intercept coefficient from Batten's regression is statistically significant at the 0.05 level.

    B. In the month after the CPIENG declines, Stellar's common stock is expected to exhibit a positive return.

    C. Viewed in combination, the slope and intercept coefficients from Batten's regression are not statistically significant at the 0.05 level.

SOLUTIONS FOR READING 11

1. The three variables Y_2 through Y_4 have a zero correlation with X. (Y_1 has zero covariance with X; but because Y_1 has no variation, its correlation with X is undefined.) Notice that although Y_3 and Y_4 are clearly nonlinearly related to X (decreasing and then increasing as the value of X increases), their overall linear relationship with X is zero. Variable Y_5 has a correlation of 1.0 with X.

2. **A.** The sample mean, variance, and standard deviation of X are

$$\bar{X} = \sum_{i=1}^{n} X_i / n = 220/11 = 20$$

$$s_X^2 = \sum_{i=1}^{n} \left(X_i - \bar{X} \right)^2 / (n-1) = 440/10 = 44$$

$$s_X = \sqrt{s_X^2} = \sqrt{44} = 6.633$$

B. The sample mean, variance, and standard deviation of Y are

$$\bar{Y} = \sum_{i=1}^{n} Y_i / n = 385/11 = 35$$

$$s_Y^2 = \sum_{i=1}^{n} \left(Y_i - \bar{Y} \right)^2 / (n-1) = 1120/10 = 112$$

$$s_Y = \sqrt{s_Y^2} = \sqrt{112} = 10.583$$

C. The sample covariance between X and Y is

$$\text{Cov}(X,Y) = \sum_{i=1}^{n} \left[\left(X_i - \bar{X} \right)\left(Y_i - \bar{Y} \right) \right] / (n-1) = -568/10 = -56.8$$

D. The sample correlation between X and Y is

$$r = \frac{\text{Cov}(X, Y)}{s_x s_y} = \frac{-56.8}{6.633 \times 10.583} = -0.809$$

3. **A.** The sample variances and standard deviations are

$$s_X^2 = \sum_{i=1}^{n} \left(X_i - \bar{X} \right)^2 / (n-1) = 769.081/59 = 13.035$$

$$s_X = \sqrt{13.035} = 3.610$$

$$s_Y^2 = \sum_{i=1}^{n} \left(Y_i - \bar{Y} \right)^2 / (n-1) = 1243.309/59 = 21.073$$

$$s_Y = \sqrt{21.073} = 4.591$$

$$s_Z^2 = \sum_{i=1}^{n} \left(Z_i - \bar{Z} \right)^2 / (n-1) = 183.073/59 = 3.103$$

$$s_Z = \sqrt{3.103} = 1.762$$

B. The sample covariances are

$$\text{Cov}(X,Y) = \sum_{i=1}^{n}(X_i - \bar{X})(Y_i - \bar{Y})/(n-1) = 720.535/59 = 12.212$$

$$\text{Cov}(X,Z) = \sum_{i=1}^{n}(X_i - \bar{X})(Z_i - \bar{Z})/(n-1) = 231.007/59 = 3.915$$

$$\text{Cov}(Y,Z) = \sum_{i=1}^{n}(Y_i - \bar{Y})(Z_i - \bar{Z})/(n-1) = 171.816/59 = 2.912$$

C. The sample correlations are

$$r_{XY} = \frac{\text{Cov}(X, Y)}{s_X s_Y} = \frac{12.212}{(3.610)(4.591)} = 0.737$$

$$r_{XZ} = \frac{\text{Cov}(X, Z)}{s_X s_Z} = \frac{3.915}{(3.610)(1.762)} = 0.615$$

$$r_{YZ} = \frac{\text{Cov}(Y, Z)}{s_Y s_Z} = \frac{2.912}{(4.591)(1.762)} = 0.360$$

4. Sample mean sales are $(50 + 70 + 80 + 60)/4 = 260/4 = 65$.

Sample mean interest rate is $(8.0 + 7.0 + 6.0 + 7.0)/4 = 28.0/4 = 7.0$.

Sample variance of sales is $[(50 - 65)^2 + (70 - 65)^2 + (80 - 65)^2 + (60 - 65)^2]/3 = 500/3 = 166.7$.

Sample standard deviation of sales is the square root of the variance, or 12.91.

Sample variance of interest rates is $[(8 - 7)^2 + (7 - 7)^2 + (6 - 7)^2 + (7 - 7)^2]/3 = 2/3 = 0.666667$.

Sample standard deviation of interest rates is the square root of this result, or 0.8165.

Sample covariance between sales and interest rates is $[(50 - 65)(8 - 7) + (70 - 65)(7 - 7) + (80 - 65)(6 - 7) + (60 - 65)(7 - 7)]/3 = -30/3 = -10$.

Sample correlation is the covariance divided by the product of the standard deviations:

$$r = \frac{\text{Cov}(X, Y)}{s_x s_y} = \frac{-10}{(12.91)(0.8165)} = -0.9487$$

5. The critical t-value for $n - 2 = 34$ df, using a 5 percent significance level and a two-tailed test, is 2.032. First, take the smallest correlation in the table, the correlation between Fund 3 and Fund 4, and see if it is significantly different from zero. Its calculated t-value is

$$t = \frac{r\sqrt{n-2}}{\sqrt{1-r^2}} = \frac{0.3102\sqrt{36-2}}{\sqrt{1-0.3102^2}} = 1.903$$

This correlation is not significantly different from zero. If we take the next lowest correlation, between Fund 2 and Fund 3, this correlation of 0.4156 has a calculated t-value of 2.664. So this correlation is significantly different from zero at the 5 percent level of significance. All of the other correlations in the table (besides the 0.3102) are greater than 0.4156, so they too are significantly different from zero.

6. The following table provides several useful calculations:

Year i	Exchange Rate X_i	Sales Y_i	$(X_i - \overline{X})^2$	$(Y_i - \overline{Y})^2$	$(X_i - \overline{X})(Y_i - \overline{Y})$
1	0.4	20	0.0016	36	−0.24
2	0.36	25	0.0000	1	0.00
3	0.42	16	0.0036	100	−0.60
4	0.31	30	0.0025	16	−0.20
5	0.33	35	0.0009	81	−0.27
6	0.34	30	0.0004	16	−0.08
Sum	2.16	156	0.0090	250	−1.39

A. The sample mean and standard deviation of the exchange rate are

$$\overline{X} = \sum_{i=1}^{n} X_i / n = 2.16/6 = 0.36$$

and

$$s_X = \sqrt{\sum_{i=1}^{n} (X_i - \overline{X})^2 / (n-1)} = \sqrt{0.009/5} = 0.042426$$

The sample mean and standard deviation of sales are

$$\overline{Y} = \sum_{i=1}^{n} Y_i / n = 156/6 = 26$$

and

$$s_Y = \sqrt{\sum_{i=1}^{n} (Y_i - \overline{Y})^2 / (n-1)} = \sqrt{250/5} = 7.0711$$

B. The sample covariance between the exchange rate and sales is

$$\text{Cov}(X, Y) = \sum_{i=1}^{n} (X_i - \overline{X})(Y_i - \overline{Y})/(n-1) = -1.39/5 = -0.278$$

C. The sample correlation between the exchange rate and sales is

$$r = \frac{\text{Cov}(X, Y)}{s_x s_y} = \frac{-0.278}{(0.042426)(7.0711)} = -0.927$$

D. We want to estimate a regression equation of the form $Y_i = b_0 + b_1 X_i + \varepsilon_i$. Noting that division by $(n-1)$ in the numerator cancels with division by $(n-1)$ in the denominator in the expression for the slope coefficient, the estimates of the slope coefficient and the intercept are

$$\hat{b}_1 = \frac{\sum_{i=1}^{n} (Y_i - \overline{Y})(X_i - \overline{X})}{\sum_{i=1}^{n} (X_i - \overline{X})^2} = \frac{-1.39}{0.009} = -154.44$$

and

$$\hat{b}_1 = \overline{Y} - \hat{b}_1 \overline{X} = 26 - (-154.44)(0.36) = 26 + 55.6 = 81.6$$

So the regression equation is $Y_i = 81.6 - 154.44X_i$.

7. **A.** The coefficient of determination is

$$\frac{\text{Explained variation}}{\text{Total variation}} = \frac{60.16}{140.58} = 0.4279$$

B. For a linear regression with one independent variable, the absolute value of correlation between the independent variable and the dependent variable equals the square root of the coefficient of determination, so the correlation is $\sqrt{0.4279} = 0.6542$. (The correlation will have the same sign as the slope coefficient.)

C. The standard error of the estimate is

$$\left(\sum_{i=1}^{n} \frac{\left(Y_i - \hat{b}_0 - \hat{b}_1 X_i\right)^2}{n-2} \right)^{1/2} = \left(\frac{\text{Unexplained variation}}{n-2} \right)^{1/2}$$

$$= \sqrt{\frac{80.42}{60-2}} = 1.178$$

D. The sample variance of the dependent variable is

$$\sum_{i=1}^{n} \frac{\left(Y_i - \overline{Y}\right)^2}{n-1} = \frac{\text{Total variation}}{n-1} = \frac{140.58}{60-1} = 2.3827$$

The sample standard deviation is $\sqrt{2.3827} = 1.544$.

8. **A.** The degrees of freedom for the regression is the number of slope parameters in the regression, which is the same as the number of independent variables in the regression. Because regression df = 1, we conclude that there is one independent variable in the regression.

B. Total SS is the sum of the squared deviations of the dependent variable Y about its mean.

C. The sample variance of the dependent variable is the total SS divided by its degrees of freedom ($n - 1 = 5 - 1 = 4$ as given). Thus the sample variance of the dependent variable is 95.2/4 = 23.8.

D. The Regression SS is the part of total sum of squares explained by the regression. Regression SS equals the sum of the squared differences between predicted values of the Y and the sample mean of Y: $\sum_{i=1}^{n}\left(\hat{Y}_i - \overline{Y}\right)^2$.

In terms of other values in the table, Regression SS is equal to Total SS minus Residual SS: 95.2 – 7.2 = 88.

E. The F-statistic tests whether all the slope coefficients in a linear regression are equal to 0.

F. The calculated value of F in the table is equal to the Regression MSS divided by the Residual MSS: 88/2.4 = 36.667.

G. Yes. The significance of 0.00904 given in the table is the p-value of the test (the smallest level at which we can reject the null hypothesis). This value of 0.00904 is less than the specified significance level of 0.05, so we reject the null hypothesis. The regression equation has significant explanatory power.

9. **A.** For the large-cap fund, the predicted rate of return, $\hat{Y}$, is

$$\hat{Y} = \hat{b}_0 + \hat{b}_1 X = -0.287 + 0.802(8.00) = 6.129$$

B. The estimated variance of the prediction error, s_f^2, of Y, given X, is

$$s_f^2 = s^2 \left[1 + \frac{1}{n} + \frac{\left(X - \bar{X}\right)^2}{(n-1)s_x^2} \right]$$

$$= 4.243^2 \left[1 + \frac{1}{12} + \frac{(8.00 - 2.30)^2}{(12-1)(38.51)} \right] = 20.884$$

The standard deviation of the prediction error is the square root of this number: 4.57. For 10 degrees of freedom, the critical t-value is 2.228. A 95 percent prediction interval is $\hat{Y} \pm t_c s_f$, or $6.129 \pm 2.228(4.57)$, or 6.129 ± 10.182.

$$\text{Prob}\left(-4.053 < Y < 16.311\right) = 0.95$$

10. A. For a sentiment index of 90, predicted auto sales, $\hat{Y}$, are
$\hat{Y} = \hat{b}_0 + \hat{b}_1 X = 6.071 + 0.09251(90) = 14.397$ (about 14.4 million vehicles). The estimated variance of the prediction error, s_f^2, of Y, given X, is

$$s_f^2 = s^2 \left[1 + \frac{1}{n} + \frac{\left(X - \bar{X}\right)^2}{(n-1)s_x^2} \right]$$

$$= 0.81325^2 \left[1 + \frac{1}{120} + \frac{(90 - 91.0983)^2}{(120-1)(137.3068)} \right] = 0.66694$$

The standard deviation of the prediction error is the square root of this number: 0.8167. For 118 degrees of freedom and a 0.05 level of significance, the critical t-value is approximately 1.98. The 95 percent prediction interval for $X = 90$ is $\hat{Y} \pm t_c s_f$, or $14.397 \pm 1.98(0.8167)$, or 14.397 ± 1.617.

$$\text{Prob}\left(12.780 < Y < 16.014\right) = 0.95$$

B. For a sentiment index of 100, predicted auto sales, $\hat{Y}$, are

$$Y = \hat{b}_0 + \hat{b}_1 X = 6.071 + 0.09251(100) = 15.322$$

The estimated variance of the prediction error, s_f^2, of Y, given X, is

$$s_f^2 = s^2 \left[1 + \frac{1}{n} + \frac{\left(X - \bar{X}\right)^2}{(n-1)s_x^2} \right]$$

$$= 0.81325^2 \left[1 + \frac{1}{120} + \frac{(100 - 91.0983)^2}{(120-1)(137.3068)} \right] = 0.67009$$

The standard deviation of the prediction error is the square root of this number: 0.81859. For 118 degrees of freedom, the critical t-value is approximately 1.98. A 95 percent prediction interval would be $\hat{Y} \pm t_c s_f$, or $15.322 \pm 1.98(0.81859)$, or 15.322 ± 1.621.

$$\text{Prob}\left(13.701 < Y < 16.943\right) = 0.95$$

11. A. The sample size is $n = 9$.

For X, the sample mean is $\bar{X} = \sum_{i=1}^{n} X_i / n = 81/9 = 9$, the sample variance is

$s_X^2 = \sum_{i=1}^{n} \left(X_i - \bar{X}\right)^2 / (n-1) = 60/8 = 7.5$, and the sample standard deviation

is $s_X = \sqrt{7.5} = 2.7386$.

For Y, the sample mean is $\bar{Y} = \sum_{i=1}^{n} Y_i/n = 144/9 = 16$, the sample variance is

$$s_Y^2 = \sum_{i=1}^{n}(Y_i - \bar{Y})^2 \Big/ (n-1) = 144/8 = 18,$$ and the sample standard deviation

is $s_Y = \sqrt{18} = 4.2426$.

B. The sample covariance is

$$\text{Cov}(X, Y) = \sum_{i=1}^{n}(X_i - \bar{X})(Y_i - \bar{Y})/(n-1) = 84/8 = 10.5$$

The sample correlation between X and Y is

$$r = \frac{\text{Cov}(X, Y)}{s_x s_y}$$

$$= \frac{10.5}{(2.7386)(4.2426)} = 0.9037$$

C. The coefficients for the regression equation are

$$\hat{b}_1 = \frac{\sum_{i=1}^{n}(Y_i - \bar{Y})(X_i - \bar{X})}{\sum_{i=1}^{n}(X_i - \bar{X})^2} = \frac{84}{60} = 1.4,$$ and

$$\hat{b}_0 = \bar{Y} - \hat{b}_1\bar{X} = 16 - 1.4(9) = 3.4$$

So the regression equation is $\hat{Y}_i = 3.4 + 1.4X_i$.

D. The total variation is $\sum_{i=1}^{n}(Y_i - \bar{Y})^2 = 144$, and the unexplained variation is

$$\sum_{i=1}^{n}(Y_i - \hat{b}_0 - \hat{b}_1 X_i)^2 = 26.4.$$ So the explained variation is $144 - 26.4 = 117.6$.

E. The coefficient of variation, the R-squared, is

$$\frac{\text{Explained variation}}{\text{Total variation}} = \frac{117.6}{144} = 0.81667$$

F. The standard error of the estimate is

$$\text{SEE} = \left[\sum_{i=1}^{n} \frac{(Y_i - \hat{b}_0 - \hat{b}_1 X_i)^2}{n-2} \right]^{1/2}$$

$$= \left(\frac{26.4}{9-2} \right)^{1/2} = 1.942$$

12. The R-squared (**X1**) is Explained variation/Total variation = 14.246/60.139 = 0.2369. The Multiple R (**X2**) is the correlation between the two variables, which is the square root of the R-squared, or $\sqrt{0.2369} = 0.4867$. The standard error (**X3**) is the square root of unexplained variation divided by $(n-2)$, which is $\sqrt{45.893/(1,819 - 2)} = 0.1589$.

The Total df, **X4**, is the sample size minus 1, or $n - 1 = 1,819 - 1 = 1,818$. The Regression df (**X5**) is equal to the number of independent variables, which is

1. The Residual df (**X6**) is the difference between the Total df and Regression df, which is also $n - (k + 1)$ where n is the sample size (1,819) and k is the number of independent variables (1). X6 is $1,819 - (1 + 1) = 1,817$. MSS is the "mean square," which is the sum of squares divided by the degrees of freedom. For **X7**, the MSS regression is $14.246/1 = 14.246$. For **X8**, the MSS residual is $45.893/1,817 = 0.025258$. The F (**X9**) is testing the hypothesis that the regression coefficient equals zero, and it is equal to MSS regression/ MSS residual, or $14.246/0.025258 = 564.02$. This F has 1 df in the numerator and 1,817 df in the denominator. This value for F is extremely large, and the probability of an F this large is practically zero.

X10, the calculated t-value for the slope coefficient, is the coefficient divided by its standard error: $t = -0.04375/0.00184 = -23.75$. This is an extremely large negative t, with a probability of practically zero. (Notice that the square root of the F is equal to the t for a regression with one independent variable.) Finally, **X11** and **X12** are the upper and lower bounds for a 95 percent confidence interval for the slope coefficient. The critical t for a two-tailed test at the 5 percent significance level with 1,817 degrees of freedom is approximately 1.96. The lower bound, **X11**, is $\hat{b}_1 - t_c s_{\hat{b}_1} = -0.04375 - 1.96(0.001842) = -0.04736$. The upper bound, **X12**, is $\hat{b}_1 + t_c s_{\hat{b}_1} = -0.04375 + 1.96(0.001842) = -0.04014$.

13. The Month 2 data point is an outlier, lying far away from the other data values. Because this outlier was caused by a data entry error, correcting the outlier improves the validity and reliability of the regression. In this case, the true correlation is reduced from 0.996 to 0.824. The revised R-squared is substantially lower (0.678 versus 0.992). The significance of the regression is also lower, as can be seen in the decline of the F-value from 500.79 to 8.44 and the decline in the t-statistic of the slope coefficient from 22.379 to 2.905.

    The total sum of squares and regression sum of squares were greatly exaggerated in the incorrect analysis. With the correction, the slope coefficient changes from 1.069 to 0.623. This change is important. When the index moves up or down, the original model indicates that the portfolio return goes up or down by 1.069 times as much, while the revised model indicates that the portfolio return goes up or down by only 0.623 times as much. In this example, incorrect data entry caused the outlier. Had it been a valid observation, not caused by a data error, then the analyst would have had to decide whether the results were more reliable including or excluding the outlier.

14. **A.** If FEE = 0%, RETURN = $-3.021 + 7.062(0) = -3.021\%$.

     If FEE = 1%, RETURN = $-3.021 + 7.062(1) = 4.041\%$.

    B. The calculated t-value for the coefficient of FEE is 14.95. The critical t-value for 58 degrees of freedom, a two-tailed test, and a 5 percent significance level is 2.00. Because the calculated t exceeds the critical t, we may conclude that the coefficient of FEE is not equal to zero and that the relationship between RETURN and FEE is significant.

    C. Smith's analysis is inadequate to conclude that high fees are good. Clearly, high returns cause high fees (because of the compensation contract that Diet Partners has with its clients). The regression may be recognizing this relationship. Unfortunately, the reverse may not be true—that fees cause returns. As an analogy, assume that income taxes are a function of income. A regression of income as a function of income taxes would find a strong positive relationship. Does this mean that taxes cause income, or the reverse? Smith's experiment is too simplistic to address the issue of whether a particular compensation contract is good or bad for client returns.

15. B is correct. The coefficient of determination is the same as R-squared.

16. C is correct. Deleting observations with small residuals will degrade the strength of the regression, resulting in an *increase* in the standard error and a *decrease* in R-squared.

17. C is correct. For a regression with one independent variable, the correlation is the same as the Multiple R with the sign of the slope coefficient. Because the slope coefficient is positive, the correlation is 0.8623.

18. B is correct. This answer describes the calculation of the F-statistic.

19. C is correct. To make a prediction using the regression model, multiply the slope coefficient by the forecast of the independent variable and add the result to the intercept.

20. C is correct. The p-value reflects the strength of the relationship between the two variables. In this case the p value is less than 0.05, and thus the regression of the ratio of cash flow from operations to sales on the ratio of net income to sales is significant at the 5 percent level.

21. B is correct because the calculated test statistic is

$$t = \frac{r\sqrt{n-2}}{\sqrt{1-r^2}}$$

$$= \frac{-0.1452\sqrt{248-2}}{\sqrt{1-(-0.1452)^2}} = -2.3017$$

Because the absolute value of $t = -2.3017$ is greater than 1.96, the correlation coefficient is statistically significant. For a regression with one independent variable, the t-value (and significance) for the slope coefficient (which is -2.3014) should equal the t-value (and significance) of the correlation coefficient. The slight difference between these two t-values is caused by rounding error.

22. A is correct because the data are time series, and the expected value of the error term, $E(\varepsilon)$, is 0.

23. C is correct. From the regression equation, Expected return $= 0.0138 + -0.6486(-0.01) = 0.0138 + 0.006486 = 0.0203$, or 2.03 percent.

24. C is correct. R-squared is the coefficient of determination. In this case, it shows that 2.11 percent of the variability in Stellar's returns is explained by changes in CPIENG.

25. A is correct, because the standard error of the estimate is the standard deviation of the regression residuals.

26. C is the correct response, because it is a false statement. The slope and intercept are both statistically significant.

Indices		World Percentage change
Japan (Nikkei)		
Seoul		
Jakarta (Comp)		-11.1%
Mumbai		
Singapore		-4.5%
Sydney	29,110	-4.7%
Shanghai B	4,644.0	-10.5%
Hong Kong	316.8	-6.9%
Toronto	22,700.9	-4.2%
Stockholm	13,524.8	4.1%
Mexico City		

12

Multiple Regression and Issues in Regression Analysis

by Richard A. DeFusco, CFA, Dennis W. McLeavey, CFA, Jerald E. Pinto, CFA, and David E. Runkle, CFA

LEARNING OUTCOMES

Mastery	The candidate should be able to:
☐	**a** formulate a multiple regression equation to describe the relation between a dependent variable and several independent variables, determine the statistical significance of each independent variable, and interpret the estimated coefficients and their *p*-values;
☐	**b** formulate a null and an alternative hypothesis about the population value of a regression coefficient, calculate the value of the test statistic, determine whether to reject the null hypothesis at a given level of significance by using a one-tailed or two-tailed test, and interpret the results of the test;
☐	**c** calculate and interpret 1) a confidence interval for the population value of a regression coefficient and 2) a predicted value for the dependent variable, given an estimated regression model and assumed values for the independent variables;
☐	**d** explain the assumptions of a multiple regression model;
☐	**e** calculate and interpret the *F*-statistic, and describe how it is used in regression analysis;
☐	**f** distinguish between and interpret the R^2 and adjusted R^2 in multiple regression;
☐	**g** evaluate how well a regression model explains the dependent variable by analyzing the output of the regression equation and an ANOVA table;
☐	**h** formulate a multiple regression equation by using dummy variables to represent qualitative factors, and interpret the coefficients and regression results;
☐	**i** explain the types of heteroskedasticity and the effects of heteroskedasticity and serial correlation on statistical inference;
☐	**j** describe multicollinearity, and explain its causes and effects in regression analysis;
☐	**k** describe the effects of model misspecification on the results of a regression analysis, and explain how to avoid the common forms of misspecification;

Quantitative Methods for Investment Analysis, Second Edition, by Richard A. DeFusco, CFA, Dennis W. McLeavey, CFA, Jerald E. Pinto, CFA, and David E. Runkle, CFA. Copyright © 2004 by CFA Institute.

Mastery	The candidate should be able to:
☐	l describe models with qualitative dependent variables;
☐	m interpret the economic meaning of the results of multiple regression analysis, and evaluate a regression model and its results.

1 INTRODUCTION

As financial analysts, we often need to use more-sophisticated statistical methods than correlation analysis or regression involving a single independent variable. For example, a trading desk interested in the costs of trading NASDAQ stocks might want information on the determinants of the bid–ask spread on the NASDAQ. A mutual fund analyst might want to know whether returns to a technology mutual fund behaved more like the returns to a growth stock index or like the returns to a value stock index. An investor might be interested in the factors that determine whether analysts cover a stock. We can answer these questions using linear regression with more than one independent variable—multiple linear regression.

In Sections 2 and 3, we introduce and illustrate the basic concepts and models of multiple regression analysis. These models rest on assumptions that are sometimes violated in practice. In Section 4, we discuss three major violations of a regression assumption. We address practical concerns such as how to diagnose an assumption violation and what remedial steps to take when a model assumption has been violated. Section 5 outlines some guidelines for building good regression models and discusses ways that analysts sometimes go wrong in this endeavor. In a number of investment applications, we are interested in the probability that one of two outcomes occurs: For example, we may be interested in whether a stock has analyst coverage or not. Section 6 discusses a class of models, qualitative dependent variable models, that addresses such questions.

2 MULTIPLE LINEAR REGRESSION

As investment analysts, we often hypothesize that more than one variable explains the behavior of a variable in which we are interested. The variable we seek to explain is called the dependent variable. The variables that we believe explain the dependent variable are called the independent variables.[1] A tool that permits us to examine the relationship (if any) between the two types of variables is multiple linear regression. **Multiple linear regression** allows us to determine the effect of more than one independent variable on a particular dependent variable.

To give an example of how we might use this tool, suppose we want to know whether the bid–ask spread for stocks trading in a dealer market is affected by the number of market makers (dealers) for that stock and the market capitalization of the stock. We can address this question using the following **multiple linear regression model**:

$$Y_i = b_0 + b_1 X_{1i} + b_2 X_{2i} + \varepsilon_i$$

where

---

[1] Independent variables are also called explanatory variables or regressors.

Y_i = the natural logarithm of the bid–ask spread for stock i (the dependent variable)

X_{1i} = the natural logarithm of the number of market makers for stock i

X_{2i} = the natural logarithm of the market capitalization of company i

ε_i = the error term

Of course, linear regression models can use more than two independent variables to explain the dependent variable. A **multiple linear regression model** has the general form

$$Y_i = b_0 + b_1 X_{1i} + b_2 X_{2i} + \ldots + b_k X_{ki} + \varepsilon_i, i = 1,2,\ldots,n \qquad (1)$$

where

Y_i = the ith observation of the dependent variable Y

X_{ji} = the ith observation of the independent variable X_j, j = 1, 2, ..., k

b_0 = the intercept of the equation

$b_1, \ldots, b_k$ = the slope coefficients for each of the independent variables

ε_i = the error term

n = the number of observations

A slope coefficient, b_j, measures how much the dependent variable, Y, changes when the independent variable, X_j, changes by one unit, holding all other independent variables constant. For example, if $b_1 = 1$ and all of the other independent variables remain constant, then we predict that if X_1 increases by one unit, Y will also increase by one unit. If $b_1 = -1$ and all of the other independent variables are held constant, then we predict that if X_1 increases by one unit, Y will decrease by one unit. Multiple linear regression estimates $b_0, \ldots, b_k$. In this reading, we will refer to both the intercept, b_0, and the slope coefficients, $b_1, \ldots, b_k$, as **regression coefficients**. As we proceed with our discussion, keep in mind that a regression equation has k slope coefficients and $k + 1$ regression coefficients.

In practice, we use software to estimate a multiple regression model. Example 1 presents an application of multiple regression analysis in investment practice. In the course of discussing a hypothesis test, Example 1 presents typical regression output and its interpretation.

Example 1

Explaining the Bid–Ask Spread

As the manager of the trading desk at an investment management firm, you have noticed that the average bid–ask spreads of different NASDAQ-listed stocks can vary widely. When the ratio of a stock's bid–ask spread to its price is higher than for another stock, your firm's costs of trading in that stock tend to be higher. You have formulated the hypothesis that NASDAQ stocks' percentage bid–ask spreads are related to the number of market makers and the company's stock market capitalization. You have decided to investigate your hypothesis using multiple regression analysis.

You specify a regression model in which the dependent variable measures the percentage bid–ask spread and the independent variables measure the number of market makers and the company's stock market capitalization. The regression is estimated using data from December 2002 for 1,819 NASDAQ-listed stocks. Based on earlier published research exploring bid–ask spreads, you express the dependent and independent variables as natural logarithms, a so-called **log-log regression model**. A log-log regression model may be appropriate when one believes that proportional changes in the dependent variable bear a constant relationship to proportional changes in the independent variable(s), as we illustrate below. You formulate the multiple regression:

$$Y_i = b_0 + b_1 X_{1i} + b_2 X_{2i} + \varepsilon_i \tag{2}$$

where

> Y_i = the natural logarithm of (bid–ask spread/stock price) for stock i
>
> X_{1i} = the natural logarithm of the number of NASDAQ market makers for stock i
>
> X_{2i} = the natural logarithm of the market capitalization (measured in millions of dollars) of company i

In a log-log regression such as Equation 2, the slope coefficients are interpreted as elasticities, assumed to be constant. For example, b_2 = –0.75 means that for a 1 percent increase in the market capitalization, we expect bid–ask spread/stock price to decrease by 0.75 percent, holding all other independent variables constant.[2]

Reasoning that greater competition tends to lower costs, you suspect that the greater the number of market makers, the smaller the percentage bid–ask spread. Therefore, you formulate a first null hypothesis and alternative hypothesis:

$$H_0: b_1 \geq 0$$
$$H_a: b_1 < 0$$

The null hypothesis is the hypothesis that the "suspected" condition is not true. If the evidence supports rejecting the null hypothesis and accepting the alternative hypothesis, you have statistically confirmed your suspicion.[3]

You also believe that the stocks of companies with higher market capitalization may have more-liquid markets, tending to lower percentage bid–ask spreads. Therefore, you formulate a second null hypothesis and alternative hypothesis:

$$H_0: b_2 \geq 0$$
$$H_a: b_2 < 0$$

Table 1	Results from Regressing ln(Bid–Ask Spread/Price) on ln(Number of Market Makers) and ln(Market Cap)

	Coefficient	Standard Error	t-Statistic
Intercept	–0.7586	0.1369	–5.5416
ln(Number of NASDAQ market makers)	–0.2790	0.0673	–4.1427
ln(Company's market cap)	–0.6635	0.0246	–27.0087

ANOVA	df	SS	MSS	F	Significance F
Regression	2	2,681.6482	1,340.8241	1,088.8325	0.00
Residual	1,816	2,236.2820	1.2314		
Total	1,818	4,917.9302			

---

2 Note that $\Delta(\ln X) \approx \Delta X / X$, where Δ represents "change in" and $\Delta X / X$ is a proportional change in X. We discuss the model further in Example 11.

3 An alternative valid formulation is a two-sided test ($H_0: b_1 = 0$ versus $H_a: b_1 \neq 0$) which reflects the beliefs of the researcher less strongly. A two-sided test could also be conducted for the hypothesis on market capitalization that we discuss next.

Table 1	Continued				
ANOVA	**df**	**SS**	**MSS**	**F**	**Significance F**
Residual standard error			1.1097		
Multiple R-squared			0.5453		
Observations			1,819		

Source: FactSet, NASDAQ.

For both tests, we use a t-test, rather than a z-test, because we do not know the population variance of b_1 and b_2. Suppose that you choose a 0.01 significance level for both tests. Table 1 shows the results of estimating this linear regression using data from December 2002.

If the regression result is not significant, we follow the useful principle of not proceeding to interpret the individual regression coefficients. Thus the analyst might look first at the ANOVA section, which addresses the regression's overall significance.

- The ANOVA (analysis of variance) section reports quantities related to the overall explanatory power and significance of the regression. SS stands for sum of squares, and MSS stands for mean sum of squares (SS divided by df). The F-test reports the overall significance of the regression. For example, an entry of 0.01 for the significance of F means that the regression is significant at the 0.01 level. In Table 1, the regression is even more significant because the significance of F is 0 at two decimal places. Later in the reading, we will present more information on the F-test.

Having ascertained that the overall regression is highly significant, an analyst might turn to the first listed column in the first section of the regression output.

- The Coefficients column gives the estimates of the intercept, b_0, and the slope coefficients, b_1 and b_2. These estimates are all negative, but are they significantly negative? The Standard Error column gives the standard error (the standard deviation) of the estimated regression coefficients. The test statistic for hypotheses concerning the population value of a regression coefficient has the form (Estimated regression efficient − Hypothesized population value of the regression coefficient) / (Standard error of the regression coefficient). This is a t-test. Under the null hypothesis, the hypothesized population value of the regression coefficient is 0. Thus (Estimated regression coefficient)/(Standard error of the regression coefficient) is the t-statistic given in the third column. For example, the t-statistic for the intercept is $-0.7586/0.1369 = -5.5416$, ignoring the effects of rounding errors. To evaluate the significance of the t-statistic we need to determine a quantity called degrees of freedom (df).[4] The calculation is Degrees of freedom = Number of observations − (Number of independent variables + 1) = $n - (k + 1)$.

- The final section of Table 1 presents two measures of how well the estimated regression fits or explains the data. The first is the standard deviation of the regression residual, the residual standard error. This

---

4 To calculate the degrees of freedom lost in the regression, we add 1 to the number of independent variables to account for the intercept term.

standard deviation is called the standard error of estimate (SEE). The second measure quantifies the degree of linear association between the dependent variable and all of the independent variables jointly. This measure is known as multiple R^2 or simply R^2 (the square of the correlation between predicted and actual values of the dependent variable).[5] A value of 0 for R^2 indicates no linear association; a value of 1 indicates perfect linear association. The final item in Table 1 is the number of observations in the sample (1,819).

Having reviewed the meaning of typical regression output, we can return to complete the hypothesis tests.

The estimated regression supports the hypothesis that the greater the number of market makers, the smaller the percentage bid–ask spread: We reject H_0: $b_1 \geq 0$ in favor of H_a: $b_1 < 0$. The results also support the belief that the stocks of companies with higher market capitalization have lower percentage bid–ask spreads: We reject H_0: $b_2 \geq 0$ in favor of H_a: $b_2 < 0$. To see that the null hypothesis is rejected for both tests, we can use t-test tables. For both tests, df = 1,819 − 3 = 1,816. The tables do not give critical values for degrees of freedom that large. The critical value for a one-tailed test with df = 200 at the 0.01 significance level is 2.345; for a larger number of degrees of freedom, the critical value would be even smaller in magnitude. Therefore, in our one-sided tests, we reject the null hypothesis in favor of the alternative hypothesis if

$$t = \frac{\hat{b}_j - b_j}{s_{\hat{b}_j}} = \frac{\hat{b}_j - 0}{s_{\hat{b}_j}} < -2.345$$

where

$\hat{b}_j$ = the regression estimate of b_j, j = 1, 2

b_j = the hypothesized value[6] of the coefficient (0)

$s_{\hat{b}_j}$ = the estimated standard error of $\hat{b}_j$

The t-values of −4.1427 and −27.0087 for the estimates of b_1 and b_2, respectively, are both less than −2.345.

Before proceeding further, we should address the interpretation of a prediction stated in natural logarithm terms. We can convert a natural logarithm to the original units by taking the antilogarithm. To illustrate this conversion, suppose that a particular stock has five NASDAQ market makers and a market capitalization of $100 million. The natural logarithm of the number of NASDAQ market makers is equal to ln 5 = 1.6094, and the natural logarithm of the company's market cap (in millions) is equal to ln 100 = 4.6052. With these values, the regression model predicts that the natural log of the ratio of the bid–ask spread to the stock price will be −0.7586 + (−0.2790 × 1.6094) + (−0.6635 × 4.6052) = −4.2632. We take the antilogarithm of −4.2632 by raising e to that power: $e^{-4.2632}$ = 0.0141. The predicted bid–ask spread will be 1.41 percent of the stock price.[7] Later we state the assumptions of the multiple regression model; before using an estimated regression to make predictions in actual practice, we should assure ourselves that those assumptions are satisfied.

---

5 Multiple R^2 is also known as the multiple coefficient of determination, or simply the coefficient of determination.

6 To economize on notation in stating test statistics, in this context we use b_j to represent the hypothesized value of the parameter (elsewhere we use it to represent the unknown population parameter).

7 The operation illustrated (taking the antilogarithm) recovers the value of a variable in the original units as $e^{\ln X} = X$.

In Table 1, we presented output common to most regression software programs. Many software programs also report p-values for the regression coefficients.[8] For each regression coefficient, the p-value would be the smallest level of significance at which we can reject a null hypothesis that the population value of the coefficient is 0, in a two-sided test. The lower the p-value, the stronger the evidence against that null hypothesis. A p-value quickly allows us to determine if an independent variable is significant at a conventional significance level such as 0.05, or at any other standard we believe is appropriate.

Having estimated Equation 1, we can write

$$\hat{Y}_i = \hat{b}_0 + \hat{b}_1 X_{1i} + \hat{b}_2 X_{2i}$$
$$= -0.7586 - 0.2790 X_{1i} - 0.6635 X_{2i}$$

where $\hat{Y}_i$ stands for the predicted value of Y_i, and $\hat{b}_0$, $\hat{b}_1$, and $\hat{b}_2$, stand for the estimated values of b_0, b_1, and b_2, respectively. How should we interpret the estimated slope coefficients -0.2790 and -0.6635?

Interpreting the slope coefficients in a multiple linear regression model is different than doing so in the one-independent-variable regressions explored in the reading on correlation and regression. Suppose we have a one-independent-variable regression that we estimate as $\hat{Y}_i = 0.50 + 0.75 X_{1i}$. The interpretation of the slope estimate 0.75 is that for every 1 unit increase in X_1, we expect Y to increase by 0.75 units. If we were to add a second independent variable to the equation, we would generally find that the estimated coefficient on X_1 is *not* 0.75 unless the second independent variable were uncorrelated with X_1. The slope coefficients in a multiple regression are known as **partial regression coefficients** or **partial slope coefficients** and need to be interpreted with care.[9] Suppose the coefficient on X_1 in a regression with the second independent variable was 0.60. Can we say that for every 1-unit increase in X_1, we expect Y to increase by 0.60 units? Not without qualification. For every 1-unit increase in X_1, we still expect Y to increase by 0.75 units when X_2 is not held constant. We would interpret 0.60 as the expected increase in Y for a 1-unit increase X_1 *holding the second independent variable constant*.

To explain what the shorthand reference "holding the second independent constant" refers to, if we were to regress X_1 on X_2, the residuals from that regression would represent the part of X_1 that is uncorrelated with X_2. We could then regress Y on those residuals in a 1-independent-variable regression. We would find that the slope coefficient on the residuals would be 0.60; by construction, 0.60 would represent the expected effect on Y of a 1-unit increase in X_1 after removing the part of X_1 that is correlated with X_2. Consistent with this explanation, we can view 0.60 as the expected net effect on Y of a 1-unit increase in X_1, after accounting for any effects of the other independent variables on the expected value of Y. To reiterate, a partial regression coefficient measures the expected change in the dependent variable for a one-unit increase in an independent variable, holding all the other independent variables constant.

To apply this process to the regression in Table 1, we see that the estimated coefficient on the natural logarithm of market capitalization is -0.6635. Therefore, the model predicts that an increase of 1 in the natural logarithm of the company's market capitalization is associated with a -0.6635 change in the natural logarithm of the ratio of the bid–ask spread to the stock price, holding the natural logarithm of the number of market makers constant. We need to be careful not to expect that the natural

---

8 The entry 0.00 for the significance of F was a p-value for the F-test.
9 The terminology comes from the fact that they correspond to the partial derivatives of Y with respect to the independent variables. Note that in this usage, the term "regression coefficients" refers just to the slope coefficients.

logarithm of the ratio of the bid–ask spread to the stock price would differ by –0.6635 if we compared two stocks for which the natural logarithm of the company's market capitalization differed by 1, because in all likelihood the number of market makers for the two stocks would differ as well, which would affect the dependent variable. The value –0.6635 is the expected net effect of difference in log market capitalizations, net of the effect of the log number of market makers on the expected value of the dependent variable.

2.1 Assumptions of the Multiple Linear Regression Model

Before we can conduct correct statistical inference on a multiple linear regression model (a model with more than one independent variable estimated using ordinary least squares), we need to know the assumptions underlying that model.[10] Suppose we have n observations on the dependent variable, Y, and the independent variables, X_1, $X_2, \ldots, X_k$, and we want to estimate the equation $Y_i = b_0 + b_1 X_{1i} + b_2 X_{2i} + \ldots + b_k X_{ki} + \varepsilon_i$.

In order to make a valid inference from a multiple linear regression model, we need to make the following six assumptions, which as a group define the classical normal multiple linear regression model:

1. The relationship between the dependent variable, Y, and the independent variables, $X_1, X_2, \ldots, X_k$, is linear as described in Equation 1.

2. The independent variables $(X_1, X_2, \ldots, X_k)$ are not random.[11] Also, no exact linear relation exists between two or more of the independent variables.[12]

3. The expected value of the error term, conditioned on the independent variables, is 0: $E(\varepsilon \mid X_1, X_2, \ldots, X_k) = 0$.

4. The variance of the error term is the same for all observations:[13] $E\left(\varepsilon_i^2\right) = \sigma_\varepsilon^2$.

5. The error term is uncorrelated across observations: $E(\varepsilon_i \varepsilon_j) = 0, j \neq i$.

6. The error term is normally distributed.

Note that these assumptions are almost exactly the same as those for the single-variable linear regression model. Assumption 2 is modified such that no exact linear relation exists between two or more independent variables or combinations of independent variables. If this part of Assumption 2 is violated, then we cannot compute linear regression estimates.[14] Also, even if no exact linear relationship exists between two or more independent variables, or combinations of independent variables, linear regression may encounter problems if two or more of the independent variables or combinations thereof are highly correlated. Such a high correlation is known as multicollinearity, which we will discuss later in this reading. We will also discuss the consequences of supposing that Assumptions 4 and 5 are met if, in fact, they are violated.

---

10 Ordinary least squares (OLS) is an estimation method based on the criterion of minimizing the sum of the squared residuals of a regression.

11 As discussed in the reading on correlation and regression, even though we assume that independent variables in the regression model are not random, often that assumption is clearly not true. For example, the monthly returns to the S&P 500 are not random. If the independent variable is random, then is the regression model incorrect? Fortunately, no. Even if the independent variable is random but uncorrelated with the error term, we can still rely on the results of regression models. See, for example, Greene (2003) or Goldberger (1998).

12 No independent variable can be expressed as a linear combination of any set of the other independent variables. Technically, a constant equal to 1 is included as an independent variable associated with the intercept in this condition.

13 $\text{Var}(\varepsilon) = E(\varepsilon^2)$ and $\text{Cov}(\varepsilon_i \varepsilon_j) = E(\varepsilon_i \varepsilon_j)$ because $E(\varepsilon) = 0$.

14 When we encounter this kind of linear relationship (called perfect collinearity), we cannot compute the matrix inverse needed to compute the linear regression estimates. See Greene (2003) for a further description of this issue.

Although Equation 1 may seem to apply only to cross-sectional data because the notation for the observations is the same ($i = 1, . . ., n$), all of these results apply to time-series data as well. For example, if we analyze data from many time periods for one company, we would typically use the notation $Y_t, X_{1t}, X_{2t}, . . ., X_{kt}$, in which the first subscript denotes the variable and the second denotes the tth time period.

Example 2

Factors Explaining Pension Fund Performance

Ambachtsheer, Capelle, and Scheibelhut (1998) tested to see which factors affect the performance of pension funds. Specifically, they wanted to know whether the risk-adjusted net value added (RANVA) of 80 U.S. and Canadian pension funds depended on the size of the individual fund and the proportion of the fund's assets that were passively managed (indexed). Using data from 80 funds for four years (1993 to 1996), the authors regressed RANVA on the size of the pension fund and the fraction of pension fund assets that were passively managed.[15] They used the equation

$$RANVA_i = b_0 + b_1 Size_i + b_2 Passive_i + \varepsilon_i$$

where

$RANVA_i$ = the average RANVA (in percent) for fund i from 1993 to 1996
$Size_i$ = the $\log_{10}$ of average assets under management for fund i
$Passive_i$ = the fraction (decimal) of passively managed assets in fund i

Table 2 shows the results of their analysis.[16]

Table 2	Results from Regressing RANVA on Size and Passive Management		
	Coefficients	**Standard Error**	***t*-Statistic**
Intercept	−2.1	0.45	−4.7
Size	0.4	0.14	2.8
Passive management	0.8	0.42	1.9

Source: Ambachtsheer, Capelle, and Scheibelhut (1998).

Suppose we use the results in Table 2 to test the null hypothesis that a pension fund's size had no effect on its RANVA. Our null hypothesis is that the coefficient on the size variable equals 0 ($H_0: b_1 = 0$), and our alternative hypothesis is that the coefficient does not equal 0 ($H_a: b_1 \neq 0$). The *t*-statistic for testing that hypothesis is

---

15 As mentioned in an earlier footnote, technically a constant equal to 1 is included as an independent variable associated with the intercept term in a regression. Because all the regressions reported in this reading include an intercept term, we will not separately mention a constant as an independent variable in the remainder of this reading.

16 Size is the log base 10 of average assets. A log transformation is commonly used for independent variables that can take a wide range of values; company size and fund size are two such variables. One reason to use the log transformation is to improve the statistical properties of the residuals. If the authors had not taken the log of assets and instead used assets as the independent variable, the regression model probably would not have explained RANVA as well.

$$\frac{\hat{b}_1 - b_1}{s_{\hat{b}_1}} = \frac{0.4 - 0}{0.14} = 2.8$$

With 80 observations and three coefficients, the t-statistic has $80 - 3 = 77$ degrees of freedom. At the 0.05 significance level, the critical value for t is about 1.99. The computed t-statistic on the size coefficient is 2.8, which suggests strongly that we can reject the null hypothesis that size is unrelated to RANVA. The estimated coefficient of 0.4 implies that every 10-fold increase in fund size (an increase of 1 in $Size_i$) is associated with an expected 0.4 percentage point increase (40 basis points) in $RANVA_i$ *holding constant the fraction of passively managed assets*. Because $Size_i$ is the base 10 log of average assets, an increase of 1 in Size is the same as a 10-fold increase in fund assets.

Of course, no causal relation between size and RANVA is clear: Funds that are more successful may attract more assets. This regression equation is consistent with that result, as well as the result that larger funds perform better. On one hand, we could argue that larger funds are more successful. On the other hand, we could argue that more successful funds attract more assets and become larger.

Now suppose we want to test the null hypothesis that passive management is not related to RANVA; we want to test whether the coefficient on the fraction of assets under passive management equals 0 ($H_0: b_2 = 0$) against the alternative hypothesis that the coefficient on the fraction of assets under passive management does not equal 0 ($H_a: b_2 \neq 0$). The t-statistic to test this hypothesis is

$$\frac{\hat{b}_2 - b_2}{s_{\hat{b}_2}} = \frac{0.8 - 0}{0.42} = 1.9$$

The critical value of the t-test is 1.99 at the 0.05 significance level and about 1.66 at the 0.10 level. Therefore, at the 0.10 significance level, we can reject the null hypothesis that passive management has no effect on fund returns; however, we cannot do so at the 0.05 significance level. Although researchers typically use a significance level of 0.05 or smaller, these results and others like them are strong enough that many pension plan sponsors have increased the use of passive management for pension fund assets. We can interpret the coefficient on passive management of 0.8 as implying that an increase of 0.10 in the proportion of a fund's passively managed assets is associated with an expected 0.08 percentage point increase (8 basis points) in RANVA for the fund, holding Size constant.

Example 3

Explaining Returns to the Fidelity Select Technology Fund

Suppose you are considering an investment in the Fidelity Select Technology Fund (FSPTX), a U.S. mutual fund specializing in technology stocks. You want to know whether the fund behaves more like a large-cap growth fund or a large-cap value fund.[17] You decide to estimate the regression

$$Y_t = b_0 + b_1 X_{1t} + b_2 X_{2t} + \varepsilon_t$$

---

[17] This regression is related to return-based style analysis, one of the most frequent applications of regression analysis in the investment profession. For more information, see Sharpe (1988), who pioneered this field, and Buetow, Johnson, and Runkle (2000).

where

Y_t = the monthly return to the FSPTX
X_{1t} = the monthly return to the S&P 500/BARRA Growth Index
X_{2t} = the monthly return to the S&P 500/BARRA Value Index

The S&P 500/BARRA Growth and Value indexes represent predominantly large-cap growth and value stocks, respectively.

Table 3 shows the results of this linear regression using monthly data from January 1998 through December 2002. The estimated intercept in the regression is 0.0079. Thus, if both the return to the S&P 500/BARRA Growth Index and the return to the S&P 500/BARRA Value Index equal 0 in a specific month, the regression model predicts that the return to the FSPTX will be 0.79 percent. The coefficient on the large-cap growth index is 2.2308, and the coefficient on the large-cap value index return is –0.4143. Therefore, if in a given month the return to the S&P 500/BARRA Growth Index was 1 percent and the return to the S&P 500/BARRA Value Index was –2 percent, the model predicts that the return to the FSPTX would be 0.0079 + 2.2308(0.01) –0.4143(–0.02) = 3.85 percent.

Table 3   **Results from Regressing the FSPTX Returns on the S&P 500/BARRA Growth and Value Indexes**

	Coefficient	Standard Error	t-Statistic
Intercept	0.0079	0.0091	0.8635
S&P 500/BARRA Growth Index	2.2308	0.2299	9.7034
S&P 500/BARRA Value Index	–0.4143	0.2597	–1.5953

ANOVA	df	SS	MSS	F	Significance F
Regression	2	0.8649	0.4324	86.4483	5.48E-18
Residual	57	0.2851	0.0050		
Total	59	1.1500			
Residual standard error			0.0707		
Multiple R-squared			0.7521		
Observations			60		

Source: Ibbotson Associates.

We may want to know whether the coefficient on the returns to the S&P 500/BARRA Value Index is statistically significant. Our null hypothesis states that the coefficient equals 0 (H_0: b_2 = 0); our alternative hypothesis states that the coefficient does not equal 0 (H_a: $b_2 \neq 0$).

Our test of the null hypothesis uses a t-test constructed as follows:

$$t = \frac{\hat{b}_2 - b_2}{s_{\hat{b}_2}} = \frac{-0.4143 - 0}{0.2597} = -1.5953$$

where

$\hat{b}_2$ = the regression estimate of b_2
b_2 = the hypothesized value[18] of the coefficient (0)
$s_{\hat{b}_2}$ = the estimated standard error of $\hat{b}_2$

This regression has 60 observations and three coefficients (two independent variables and the intercept); therefore, the t-test has $60 - 3 = 57$ degrees of freedom. At the 0.05 significance level, the critical value for the test statistic is about 2.00. The absolute value of the test statistic is 1.5953. Because the test statistic's absolute value is less than the critical value ($1.5953 < 2.00$), we fail to reject the null hypothesis that $b_2 = 0$. (Note that the t-tests reported in Table 3, as well as the other regression tables, are tests of the null hypothesis that the population value of a regression coefficient equals 0.)

Similar analysis shows that at the 0.05 significance level, we cannot reject the null hypothesis that the intercept equals 0 ($H_0: b_0 = 0$) in favor of the alternative hypothesis that the intercept does not equal 0 ($H_a: b_0 \neq 0$). Table 3 shows that the t-statistic for testing that hypothesis is 0.8635, a result smaller in absolute value than the critical value of 2.00. However, at the 0.05 significance level we *can* reject the null hypothesis that the coefficient on the S&P 500/BARRA Growth Index equals 0 ($H_0: b_1 = 0$) in favor of the alternative hypothesis that the coefficient does not equal 0 ($H_a: b_1 \neq 0$). As Table 3 shows, the t-statistic for testing that hypothesis is 9.70, a result far above the critical value of 2.00. Thus multiple regression analysis suggests that returns to the FSPTX are very closely associated with the returns to the S&P 500/BARRA Growth Index, but they are not related to S&P 500/BARRA Value Index (the t-statistic of -1.60 is not statistically significant).

2.2 Predicting the Dependent Variable in a Multiple Regression Model

Financial analysts often want to predict the value of the dependent variable in a multiple regression based on assumed values of the independent variables. We have previously discussed how to make such a prediction in the case of only one independent variable. The process for making that prediction with multiple linear regression is very similar.

To predict the value of a dependent variable using a multiple linear regression model, we follow these three steps:

1. Obtain estimates $\hat{b}_0, \hat{b}_1, \hat{b}_2, \ldots, \hat{b}_k$ of the regression parameters $b_0, b_1, b_2, \ldots, b_k$.
2. Determine the assumed values of the independent variables, $\hat{X}_{1i}, \hat{X}_{2i}, \ldots, \hat{X}_{ki}$.
3. Compute the predicted value of the dependent variable, $\hat{Y}_i$, using the equation

$$\hat{Y}_i = \hat{b}_0 + \hat{b}_1 \hat{X}_{1i} + \hat{b}_2 \hat{X}_{2i} + \ldots + \hat{b}_k \hat{X}_{ki} \tag{3}$$

Two practical points concerning using an estimated regression to predict the dependent variable are in order. First, we should be confident that the assumptions of the regression model are met. Second, we should be cautious about predictions based on values of the independent variables that are outside the range of the data on which the model was estimated; such predictions are often unreliable.

---

18 To economize on notation in stating test statistics, in this context we use b_2 to represent the hypothesized value of the parameter (elsewhere we use it to represent the unknown population parameter).

Example 4

Predicting a Pension Fund's RANVA

In Example 2, we explained the RANVA for U.S. and Canadian pension funds based on the log base 10 of the assets under management for a fund ($Size_i$) and the fraction of assets in the fund that were passively managed ($Passive_i$).

$$RANVA_i = b_0 + b_1 Size_i + b_2 Passive_i + \varepsilon_i$$

Now we can use the results of the regression reported in Table 2 (excerpted here) to predict the performance (RANVA) for a pension fund.

Table 2	(excerpt)

	Coefficients
Intercept	−2.1
Size	0.4
Passive management	0.8

Suppose that a particular fund has assets under management of $10 million, and 25 percent of the assets are passively managed. The log base 10 of the assets under management equals $\log(10,000,000) = 7$. The fraction of assets in the fund that are passively managed is 0.25. Accordingly, the predicted RANVA for that fund, based on the regression, is $-2.1 + (0.4 \times 7) + (0.8 \times 0.25) = 0.9$ percent (90 basis points). The regression predicts that the RANVA will be 90 basis points for a pension fund with assets under management of $10 million, 25 percent of which are passively managed.

When predicting the dependent variable using a linear regression model, we encounter two types of uncertainty: uncertainty in the regression model itself, as reflected in the standard error of estimate, and uncertainty about the estimates of the regression model's parameters. In the reading on correlation and regression, we presented procedures for constructing a prediction interval for linear regression with one independent variable. For multiple regression, however, computing a prediction interval to properly incorporate both types of uncertainty requires matrix algebra, which is outside the scope of this reading.[19]

2.3 Testing whether All Population Regression Coefficients Equal Zero

Earlier, we illustrated how to conduct hypothesis tests on regression coefficients individually. But what about the significance of the regression as a whole? As a group, do the independent variables help explain the dependent variable? To address this question, we test the null hypothesis that all the slope coefficients in a regression are simultaneously equal to 0. In this section, we discuss **analysis of variance (ANOVA)**, which provides information about a regression's explanatory power and the inputs for an F-test of the above null hypothesis.

If none of the independent variables in a regression model helps explain the dependent variable, the slope coefficients should all equal 0. In a multiple regression,

---

19 For more information, see Greene (2003).

however, we cannot test the null hypothesis that *all* slope coefficients equal 0 based on *t*-tests that *each individual* slope coefficient equals 0, because the individual tests do not account for the effects of interactions among the independent variables. For example, a classic symptom of multicollinearity is that we can reject the hypothesis that all the slope coefficients equal 0 even though none of the *t*-statistics for the individual estimated slope coefficients is significant. Conversely, we can construct unusual examples in which the estimated slope coefficients are significantly different from 0 although jointly they are not.

To test the null hypothesis that all of the slope coefficients in the multiple regression model are jointly equal to 0 (H_0: $b_1 = b_2 = \ldots = b_k = 0$) against the alternative hypothesis that at least one slope coefficient is not equal to 0 we must use an *F*-test. The *F*-test is viewed as a test of the regression's overall significance.

To correctly calculate the test statistic for the null hypothesis, we need four inputs:

- total number of observations, n;
- total number of regression coefficients to be estimated, $k + 1$, where k is the number of slope coefficients;
- sum of squared errors or residuals, $\sum_{i=1}^{n}\left(Y_i - \hat{Y}_i\right)^2 = \sum_{i=1}^{n}\hat{\varepsilon}_i^2$, abbreviated SSE, also known as the residual sum of squares (unexplained variation);[20] and
- regression sum of squares, $\sum_{i=1}^{n}\left(\hat{Y}_i - \bar{Y}\right)^2$, abbreviated RSS.[21] This amount is the variation in Y from its mean that the regression equation explains (explained variation).

The *F*-test for determining whether the slope coefficients equal 0 is based on an *F*-statistic calculated using the four values listed above. The *F*-statistic measures how well the regression equation explains the variation in the dependent variable; it is the ratio of the mean regression sum of squares to the mean squared error.

We compute the mean regression sum of squares by dividing the regression sum of squares by the number of slope coefficients estimated, k. We compute the mean squared error by dividing the sum of squared errors by the number of observations, n, minus $(k + 1)$. The two divisors in these computations are the degrees of freedom for calculating an *F*-statistic. For n observations and k slope coefficients, the *F*-test for the null hypothesis that the slope coefficients are all equal to 0 is denoted $F_{k, n-(k+1)}$. The subscript indicates that the test should have k degrees of freedom in the numerator (numerator degrees of freedom) and $n - (k + 1)$ degrees of freedom in the denominator (denominator degrees of freedom).

The formula for the *F*-statistic is

$$F = \frac{\dfrac{RSS}{k}}{\dfrac{SSE}{\left[n-(k+1)\right]}} = \frac{\text{Mean regression sum of squares}}{\text{Mean squared error}} = \frac{MSR}{MSE} \qquad (4)$$

where MSR is the mean regression sum of squares and MSE is the mean squared error. In our regression output tables, MSR and MSE are the first and second quantities under the MSS (mean sum of squares) column in the ANOVA section of the output. If the regression model does a good job of explaining variation in the dependent variable, then the ratio MSR/MSE will be large.

---

20 In a table of regression output, this is the number under "SS" column in the row "Residual."
21 In a table of regression output, this is the number under the "SS" column in the row "Regression."

What does this F-test tell us when the independent variables in a regression model explain none of the variation in the dependent variable? In this case, each predicted value in the regression model, $\hat{Y}_i$, has the average value of the dependent variable, $\bar{Y}$, and the regression sum of squares, $\sum_{i=1}^{n}\left(\hat{Y}_i = \bar{Y}\right)^2$ is 0. Therefore, the F-statistic for testing the null hypothesis (that all the slope coefficients are equal to 0) has a value of 0 when the independent variables do not explain the dependent variable at all.

To specify the details of making the statistical decision when we have calculated F, we reject the null hypothesis at the α significance level if the calculated value of F is greater than the upper α critical value of the F distribution with the specified numerator and denominator degrees of freedom. Note that we use a one-tailed F-test.[22]

We can illustrate the test using Example 1, in which we investigated whether the natural log of the number of NASDAQ market makers and the natural log of the stock's market capitalization explained the natural log of the bid–ask spread divided by price. Assume that we set the significance level for this test to $\alpha = 0.05$ (i.e., a 5 percent probability that we will mistakenly reject the null hypothesis if it is true). Table 1 (excerpted here) presents the results of variance computations for this regression.

Table 1	(excerpt)				
ANOVA	**df**	**SS**	**MSS**	**F**	**Significance F**
Regression	2	2,681.6482	1,340.8241	1,088.8325	0.00
Residual	1,816	2,236.2820	1.2314		
Total	1,818	4,917.9302			

This model has two slope coefficients ($k = 2$), so there are two degrees of freedom in the numerator of this F-test. With 1,819 observations in the sample, the number of degrees of freedom in the denominator of the F-test is $n - (k + 1) = 1{,}819 - 3 = 1{,}816$. The sum of the squared errors is 2,236.2820. The regression sum of squares is 2,681.6482. Therefore, the F-test for the null hypothesis that the two slope coefficients in this model equal 0 is

$$\frac{2681.6482/2}{2236.2820/1{,}816} = 1{,}088.8325$$

This test statistic is distributed as an $F_{2,\,1{,}816}$ random variable under the null hypothesis that the slope coefficients are equal to 0. In the table for the 0.05 significance level, we look at the second column, which shows F-distributions with two degrees of freedom in the numerator. Near the bottom of the column, we find that the critical value of the F-test needed to reject the null hypothesis is between 3.00 and 3.07.[23] The actual value of the F-test statistic at 1,088.83 is much greater, so we reject the null hypothesis that coefficients of both independent variables equal 0. In fact, Table 1 under "Significance F," reports a p-value of 0. This p-value means that the smallest level of significance at which the null hypothesis can be rejected is practically 0. The large value for this F-statistic implies a minuscule probability of incorrectly rejecting the null hypothesis (a mistake known as a Type I error).

---

[22] We use a one-tailed test because MSR necessarily increases relative to MSE as the explanatory power of the regression increases.

[23] We see a range of values because the denominator has more than 120 degrees of freedom but less than an infinite number of degrees of freedom.

2.4 Adjusted R^2

In the reading on correlation and regression, we presented the coefficient of determination, R^2, as a measure of the goodness of fit of an estimated regression to the data. In a multiple linear regression, however, R^2 is less appropriate as a measure of whether a regression model fits the data well (goodness of fit). Recall that R^2 is defined as

$$\frac{\text{Total variation} - \text{Unexplained variation}}{\text{Total variation}}$$

The numerator equals the regression sum of squares, RSS. Thus R^2 states RSS as a fraction of the total sum of squares, $\sum_{i=1}^{n}(Y_i - \bar{Y})^2$. If we add regression variables to the model, the amount of unexplained variation will decrease, and RSS will increase, if the new independent variable explains any of the unexplained variation in the model. Such a reduction occurs when the new independent variable is even slightly correlated with the dependent variable and is not a linear combination of other independent variables in the regression.[24] Consequently, we can increase R^2 simply by including many additional independent variables that explain even a slight amount of the previously unexplained variation, even if the amount they explain is not statistically significant.

Some financial analysts use an alternative measure of goodness of fit called **adjusted R^2, or $\bar{R}^2$.** This measure of fit does not automatically increase when another variable is added to a regression; it is adjusted for degrees of freedom. Adjusted R^2 is typically part of the multiple regression output produced by statistical software packages.

The relation between R^2 and $\bar{R}^2$ is

$$\bar{R}^2 = 1 - \left(\frac{n-1}{n-k-1}\right)(1 - R^2)$$

where n is the number of observations and k is the number of independent variables (the number of slope coefficients). Note that if $k \geq 1$, then R^2 is strictly greater than adjusted R^2. When a new independent variable is added, $\bar{R}^2$ can decrease if adding that variable results in only a small increase in R^2. In fact, $\bar{R}^2$ can be negative, although R^2 is always nonnegative.[25] If we use $\bar{R}^2$ to compare regression models, it is important that the dependent variable be defined the same way in both models and that the sample sizes used to estimate the models are the same.[26] For example, it makes a difference for the value of $\bar{R}^2$ if the dependent variable is GDP (gross domestic product) or ln(GDP), even if the independent variables are identical. Furthermore, we should be aware that a high $\bar{R}^2$ does not necessarily indicate that the regression is well specified in the sense of including the correct set of variables.[27] One reason for caution is that a high $\bar{R}^2$ may reflect peculiarities of the dataset used to estimate the regression. To evaluate a regression model, we need to take many other factors into account, as we discuss in Section 5.1.

---

24 We say that variable y is a linear combination of variables x and z if $y = ax + bz$ for some constants a and b. A variable can also be a linear combination of more than two variables.

25 When $\bar{R}^2$ is negative, we can effectively consider its value to be 0.

26 See Gujarati (2003). The value of adjusted R^2 depends on sample size. These points hold if we are using R^2 to compare two regression models.

27 See Mayer (1975, 1980).

USING DUMMY VARIABLES IN REGRESSIONS

Often, financial analysts need to use qualitative variables as independent variables in a regression. One type of qualitative variable, called a **dummy variable**, takes on a value of 1 if a particular condition is true and 0 if that condition is false.[28] For example, suppose we want to test whether stock returns were different in January than during the remaining months of a particular year. We include one independent variable in the regression, X_{1t}, that has a value of 1 for each January and a value of 0 for every other month of the year. We estimate the regression model

$$Y_t = b_0 + b_1 X_{1t} + \varepsilon_t$$

In this equation, the coefficient b_0 is the average value of Y_t in months other than January, and b_1 is the difference between the average value of Y_t in January and the average value of Y_t in months other than January.

We need to exercise care in choosing the number of dummy variables in a regression. The rule is that if we want to distinguish among n categories, we need $n - 1$ dummy variables. For example, to distinguish between *during January* and *not during January* above ($n = 2$ categories), we used one dummy variable ($n - 1 = 2 - 1 = 1$). If we want to distinguish between each of the four quarters in a year, we would include dummy variables for three of the four quarters in a year. If we make the mistake of including dummy variables for four rather than three quarters, we have violated Assumption 2 of the multiple regression model and cannot estimate the regression. The next example illustrates the use of dummy variables in a regression with monthly data.

Example 5

Month-of-the-Year Effects on Small-Stock Returns

For many years, financial analysts have been concerned about seasonality in stock returns.[29] In particular, analysts have researched whether returns to small stocks differ during various months of the year. Suppose we want to test whether total returns to one small-stock index, the Russell 2000 Index, differ by month. Using data from January 1979 (the first available date for the Russell 2000 data) through the end of 2002, we can estimate a regression including an intercept and 11 dummy variables, one for each of the first 11 months of the year. The equation that we estimate is

$$\text{Returns}_t = b_0 + b_1 \text{Jan}_t + b_2 \text{Feb}_t + \ldots + b_{11} \text{Nov}_t + \varepsilon_t$$

where each monthly dummy variable has a value of 1 when the month occurs (e.g., $\text{Jan}_1 = \text{Jan}_{13} = 1$, as the first observation is a January) and a value of 0 for the other months. Table 4 shows the results of this regression.

The intercept, b_0, measures the average return for stocks in December because there is no dummy variable for December.[30] This equation estimates that the average return in December is 3.01 percent ($\hat{b}_0 = 0.0301$). Each of the estimated coefficients for the dummy variables shows the estimated difference between returns in that month and returns for December. So, for example, the estimated additional return in January is 0.03 percent higher than December ($\hat{b}_1 = 0.0003$). This gives a January return prediction of 3.04 percent (3.01 December + 0.03 additional).

---

28 Not all qualitative variables are simple dummy variables. For example, in a trinomial choice model (a model with three choices), a qualitative variable might have the value 0, 1, or 2.

29 For a discussion of this issue, see Siegel (1998).

30 When $\text{Jan}_t = \text{Feb}_t = \ldots = \text{Nov}_t = 0$, the return is not associated with January through November so the month is December and the regression equation simplifies to $\text{Returns}_t = b_0 + \varepsilon_t$. Because $E(\text{Returns}_t) = b_0 + E(\varepsilon_t) = b_0$, the intercept b_0 represents the mean return for December.

Table 4	Results from Regressing Russell 2000 Returns on Monthly Dummy Variables	

	Coefficient	Standard Error	t-Statistic
Intercept	0.0301	0.0116	2.5902
January	0.0003	0.0164	0.0176
February	−0.0111	0.0164	−0.6753
March	−0.0211	0.0164	−1.2846
April	−0.0141	0.0164	−0.8568
May	−0.0137	0.0164	−0.8320
June	−0.0200	0.0164	−1.2164
July	−0.0405	0.0164	−2.4686
August	−0.0230	0.0164	−1.4025
September	−0.0375	0.0164	−2.2864
October	−0.0393	0.0164	−2.3966
November	−0.0059	0.0164	−0.3565

ANOVA	df	SS	MSS	F	Significance F
Regression	11	0.0543	0.0049	1.5270	0.1213
Residual	276	0.8924	0.0032		
Total	287	0.9467			
Residual standard error		0.0569			
Multiple R-squared		0.0574			
Observations		288			

Source: Ibbotson Associates.

The low R^2 in this regression (0.0574), however, suggests that a month-of-the-year effect in small-stock returns may not be very important for explaining small-stock returns. We can use the F-test to analyze the null hypothesis that jointly, the monthly dummy variables all equal 0 (H_0: $b_1 = b_2 = \ldots = b_{11} = 0$). We are testing for significant monthly variation in small-stock returns. Table 4 shows the data needed to perform an analysis of variance. The number of degrees of freedom in the numerator of the F-test is 11; the number of degrees of freedom in the denominator is $[288 - (11 + 1)] = 276$. The regression sum of squares equals 0.0543, and the sum of squared errors equals 0.8924. Therefore, the F-statistic to determine whether all of the regression slope coefficients are jointly equal to 0 is

$$\frac{0.0543/11}{0.8924/276} = 1.53$$

Appendix D (the F-distribution table) at the end of this volume shows the critical values for this F-test. If we choose a significance level of 0.05 and look in Column 11 (because the numerator has 11 degrees of freedom), we see that the critical value is 1.87 when the denominator has 120 degrees of freedom. The denominator actually has 276 degrees of freedom, so the critical value of the

F-statistic is smaller than 1.87 (for df = 120) but larger than 1.79 (for an infinite number of degrees of freedom). The value of the test statistic is 1.53, so we clearly cannot reject the null hypothesis that all of the coefficients jointly are equal to 0.

The *p*-value of 0.1213 shown for the *F*-test in Table 4 means that the smallest level of significance at which we can reject the null hypothesis is roughly 0.12, or 12 percent—above the conventional level of 5 percent. Among the 11 monthly dummy variables, July, September, and October have a *t*-statistic with an absolute value greater than 2. Although the coefficients for these dummy variables are statistically significant, we have so many insignificant estimated coefficients that we cannot reject the null hypothesis that returns are equal across the months. This test suggests that the significance of a few coefficients in this regression model may be the result of random variation. We may thus want to avoid portfolio strategies calling for differing investment weights for small stocks in different months.

Example 6

Determinants of Spreads on New High-Yield Bonds

Fridson and Garman (1998) used data from 1995 and 1996 to examine variables that may explain the initial yield spread between a newly issued high-yield bond and a Treasury bond with similar maturity. They built a model of yield spreads using variables that affect the creditworthiness and interest-rate risk of the bond. Their model included the following factors:

- rating: Moody's senior-equivalent rating;
- zero-coupon status: Dummy variable (0 = no, 1 = yes);
- BB-B spread: Yield differential (Merrill Lynch Single-B Index minus Double-B Index, in basis points);
- seniority: Dummy variable (0 = senior, 1 = subordinated);
- callability: Dummy variable (0 = noncallable, 1 = callable);
- term: Maturity (years);
- first-time issuer: Dummy variable (0 = no, 1 = yes);
- underwriter type: Dummy variable (0 = investment bank, 1 = commercial bank);
- interest rate change.

Table 5 shows the authors' results.

Table 5	Multiple Regression Model of New High-Yield Issue Spread, 1995–96		
	Coefficient	**Standard Error**	***t*-Statistic**
Intercept	−213.67	63.03	−3.39
Rating	66.19	4.13	16.02
Zero-coupon status	136.54	32.82	4.16

(continued)

Table 5	Continued		
	Coefficient	**Standard Error**	***t*-Statistic**
BB-B spread	95.31	24.82	3.84
Seniority	41.46	11.95	3.47
Callability	51.65	15.42	3.35
Term	−8.51	2.71	−3.14
First-time issuer	25.23	10.97	2.30
Underwriter type	28.13	12.67	2.22
Interest rate change	40.44	19.08	2.12
R-squared	0.56		
Observations	428		

Source: Fridson and Garman (1998).

We can summarize Fridson and Garman's findings as follows:

■ Bond rating has the highest significance level of any coefficient in the regression. This result should not be surprising, because the rating captures rating agencies' estimates of the risk involved with the bond.

■ Zero-coupon status increases the yield spread because zero-coupon bonds have more interest rate risk than coupon bonds of a similar maturity.

■ The BB-B spread affects yields because it captures the market's evaluation of how much influence rating differentials have on credit risk.

■ Seniority affects yields because subordinated debt has a much lower recovery rate in the case of default.

■ Callability increases yields because it limits upside potential on the bond if yields decline.

■ Term actually reduces the yield spread. Perhaps term enters with a negative coefficient because the market is willing to buy long-term debt only from high-quality companies; lower-quality companies must issue shorter-term debt.

■ First-time issuers must pay a premium because the market does not know much about them.

■ Bonds underwritten by commercial banks have a premium over bonds underwritten by investment banks, most likely because the market believes that investment banks have a competitive edge in attracting high-quality corporate clients.

■ Interest-rate increases in Treasuries during the previous month cause yield spreads to widen, presumably because the market believes that increasing interest rates will worsen the economic prospects of companies issuing high-yield debt.

Note that all of the coefficients in this regression model are statistically significant at the 0.05 level. The smallest absolute value of a *t*-statistic in this table is 2.12.

VIOLATIONS OF REGRESSION ASSUMPTIONS

In Section 2.1, we presented the assumptions of the multiple linear regression model. Inference based on an estimated regression model rests on those assumptions being satisfied. In applying regression analysis to financial data, analysts need to be able to diagnose violations of regression assumptions, understand the consequences of violations, and know the remedial steps to take. In the following sections we discuss three regression violations: **heteroskedasticity**, serial correlation, and multicollinearity.

4.1 Heteroskedasticity

p. 336

So far, we have made an important assumption that the variance of error in a regression is constant across observations. In statistical terms, we assumed that the errors were homoskedastic. Errors in financial data, however, are often **heteroskedastic**: the variance of the errors differs across observations. In this section, we discuss how heteroskedasticity affects statistical analysis, how to test for heteroskedasticity, and how to correct for it.

We can see the difference between homoskedastic and heteroskedastic errors by comparing two graphs. Figure 1 shows the values of the dependent and independent variables and a fitted regression line for a model with homoskedastic errors. There is no systematic relationship between the value of the independent variable and the regression residuals (the vertical distance between a plotted point and the fitted regression line). Figure 2 shows the values of the dependent and independent variables and a fitted regression line for a model with heteroskedastic errors. Here, a systematic relationship is visually apparent: On average, the regression residuals grow much larger as the size of the independent variable increases.

4.1.1 *The Consequences of Heteroskedasticity*

What are the consequences when the assumption of constant error variance is violated? Although heteroskedasticity does not affect the consistency[31] of the regression parameter estimators, it can lead to mistakes in inference. When errors are heteroskedastic, the F-test for the overall significance of the regression is unreliable.[32] Furthermore, t-tests for the significance of individual regression coefficients are unreliable because heteroskedasticity introduces bias into estimators of the standard error of regression coefficients. If a regression shows significant heteroskedasticity, the standard errors and test statistics computed by regression programs will be incorrect unless they are adjusted for heteroskedasticity.

---

31 Informally, an estimator of a regression parameter is consistent if the probability that estimates of a regression parameter differ from the true value of the parameter decreases as the number of observations used in the regression increases. The regression parameter estimates from ordinary least squares are consistent regardless of whether the errors are heteroskedastic or homoskedastic. For a more advanced discussion, see Greene (2003).

32 This unreliability occurs because the mean squared error is a biased estimator of the true population variance given heteroskedasticity.

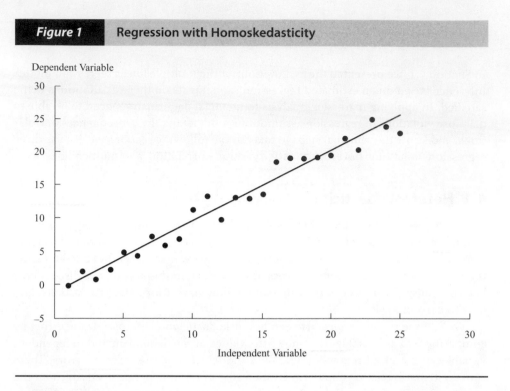

Figure 1   **Regression with Homoskedasticity**

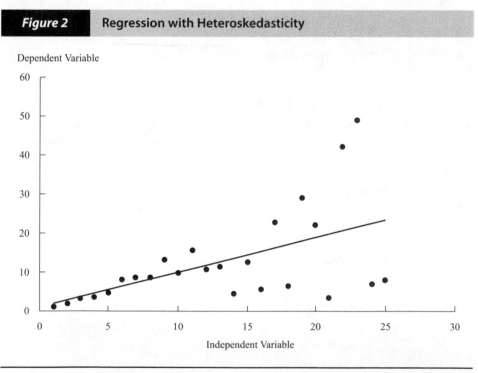

Figure 2   **Regression with Heteroskedasticity**

In regressions with financial data, the most likely result of heteroskedasticity is that the estimated standard errors will be underestimated and the t-statistics will be inflated. When we ignore heteroskedasticity, we tend to find significant relationships where none actually exist.[33] The consequences in practice may be serious if we are using regression analysis in the development of investment strategies. As Example 7 shows, the issue impinges even on our understanding of financial models.

---

33 Sometimes, however, failure to adjust for heteroskedasticity results in standard errors that are too large (and t-statistics that are too small).

Example 7

Heteroskedasticity and Tests of an Asset Pricing Model

MacKinlay and Richardson (1991) examined how heteroskedasticity affects tests of the capital asset pricing model (CAPM).[34] These authors argued that if the CAPM is correct, they should find no significant differences between the risk-adjusted returns for holding small stocks versus large stocks. To implement their test, MacKinlay and Richardson grouped all stocks on the New York and American exchanges by market-value decile with annual reassignment. They then tested for systematic differences in risk-adjusted returns across market-capitalization-based stock portfolios. They estimated the following regression:

$$r_{i,t} = \alpha_i + \beta_i r_{m,t} + \varepsilon_{i,t}$$

where

$r_{i,t}$ = excess return (return above the risk-free rate) to portfolio i in period t

$r_{m,t}$ = excess return to the market as a whole in period t

The CAPM formulation hypothesizes that excess returns on a portfolio are explained by excess returns on the market as a whole. That hypothesis implies that $\alpha_i = 0$ for every i; on average, no excess return accrues to any portfolio after taking into account its systematic (market) risk.

Using data from January 1926 to December 1988 and a market index based on equal-weighted returns, MacKinlay and Richardson failed to reject the CAPM at the 0.05 level when they assumed that the errors in the regression model are normally distributed and homoskedastic. They found, however, that they could reject the CAPM when they corrected their test statistics to account for heteroskedasticity. They rejected the hypothesis that there are no size-based, risk-adjusted excess returns in historical data.[35]

We have stated that effects of heteroskedasticity on statistical inference can be severe. To be more precise about this concept, we should distinguish between two broad kinds of heteroskedasticity: unconditional and conditional.

Unconditional heteroskedasticity occurs when heteroskedasticity of the error variance is not correlated with the independent variables in the multiple regression. Although this form of heteroskedasticity violates Assumption 4 of the linear regression model, it creates no major problems for statistical inference.

The type of heteroskedasticity that causes the most problems for statistical inference is **conditional heteroskedasticity**—heteroskedasticity in the error variance that is correlated with (conditional on) the values of the independent variables in the regression. Fortunately, many statistical software packages easily test and correct for conditional heteroskedasticity.

4.1.2 *Testing for Heteroskedasticity*

Because of conditional heteroskedasticity's consequences on inference, the analyst must be able to diagnose its presence. The Breusch–Pagan test is widely used in finance research because of its generality.[36]

---

34 For more on the CAPM, see Bodie, Kane, and Marcus (2001), for example.

35 MacKinlay and Richardson also show that when using value-weighted returns, one can reject the CAPM whether or not one assumes normally distributed returns and homoskedasticity.

36 Some other tests require more-specific assumptions about the functional form of the heteroskedasticity. For more information, see Greene (2003).

Breusch and Pagan (1979) suggested the following test for conditional heteroskedasticity: Regress the squared residuals from the estimated regression equation on the independent variables in the regression. If no conditional heteroskedasticity exists, the independent variables will not explain much of the variation in the squared residuals. If conditional heteroskedasticity is present in the original regression, however, the independent variables will explain a significant portion of the variation in the squared residuals. The independent variables can explain the variation because each observation's squared residual will be correlated with the independent variables if the independent variables affect the variance of the errors.

Breusch and Pagan showed that under the null hypothesis of no conditional heteroskedasticity, nR^2 (from the regression of the squared residuals on the independent variables from the original regression) will be a χ^2 random variable with the number of degrees of freedom equal to the number of independent variables in the regression.[37] Therefore, the null hypothesis states that the regression's squared error term is uncorrelated with the independent variables. The alternative hypothesis states that the squared error term is correlated with the independent variables. Example 8 illustrates the Breusch–Pagan test for conditional heteroskedasticity.

Example 8

Testing for Conditional Heteroskedasticity in the Relation between Interest Rates and Expected Inflation

Suppose an analyst wants to know how closely nominal interest rates are related to expected inflation to determine how to allocate assets in a fixed income portfolio. The analyst wants to test the Fisher effect, the hypothesis suggested by Irving Fisher that nominal interest rates increase by 1 percentage point for every 1 percentage point increase in expected inflation.[38] The Fisher effect assumes the following relation between nominal interest rates, real interest rates, and expected inflation:

$$i = r + \pi^e$$

where

i = the nominal interest rate

r = the real interest rate (assumed constant)

π^e = the expected rate of inflation

To test the Fisher effect using time-series data, we could specify the following regression model for the nominal interest rate:

$$i_t = b_0 + b_1 \pi_t^e + \varepsilon_t \tag{5}$$

Noting that the Fisher effect predicts that the coefficient on the inflation variable is 1, we can state the null and alternative hypotheses as

$H_0: b_1 = 1$

$H_a: b_1 \neq 1$

We might also specify a 0.05 significance level for the test. Before we estimate Equation 5, we must decide how to measure expected inflation (π_t^e) and the nominal interest rate (i_t).

---

37 The Breusch–Pagan test is distributed as a χ^2 random variable in large samples. The constant 1 technically associated with the intercept term in a regression is not counted here in computing the number of independent variables. For more on the Breusch–Pagan test, see Greene (2003).

38 For more on the Fisher effect, see, for example, Mankiw (2000).

The Survey of Professional Forecasters (SPF) has compiled data on the quarterly inflation expectations of professional forecasters.[39] We use those data as our measure of expected inflation. We use three-month Treasury bill returns as our measure of the (risk-free) nominal interest rate.[40] We use quarterly data from the fourth quarter of 1968 to the fourth quarter of 2002 to estimate Equation 5. Table 6 shows the regression results.

To make the statistical decision on whether the data support the Fisher effect, we calculate the following t-statistic, which we then compare to its critical value.

$$t = \frac{\hat{b}_1 - b_1}{s_{\hat{b}_1}} = \frac{0.8774 - 1}{0.0812} = -1.5099$$

With a t-statistic of -1.5099 and $137 - 2 = 135$ degrees of freedom, the critical t-value is about 1.98. If we have conducted a valid test, we cannot reject at the 0.05 significance level the hypothesis that the true coefficient in this regression is 1 and that the Fisher effect holds. The t-test assumes that the errors are homoskedastic. Before we accept the validity of the t-test, therefore, we should test whether the errors are conditionally heteroskedastic. If those errors prove to be conditionally heteroskedastic, then the test is invalid.

Table 6	Results from Regressing T-Bill Returns on Predicted Inflation		
	Coefficient	**Standard Error**	**t-Statistic**
Intercept	0.0304	0.0040	7.6887
Inflation prediction	0.8774	0.0812	10.8096
Residual standard error		0.0220	
Multiple R-squared		0.4640	
Observations		137	
Durbin–Watson statistic		0.4673	

Source: Federal Reserve Bank of Philadelphia, U.S. Department of Commerce.

We can perform the **Breusch–Pagan test** for conditional heteroskedasticity on the squared residuals from the Fisher effect regression. The test regresses the squared residuals on the predicted inflation rate. The R^2 in the squared residuals regression (not shown here) is 0.1651. The test statistic from this regression, nR^2, is $137 \times 0.1651 = 22.619$. Under the null hypothesis of no conditional heteroskedasticity, this test statistic is a χ^2 random variable with one degree of freedom (because there is only one independent variable).

We should be concerned about heteroskedasticity only for large values of the test statistic. Therefore, we should use a one-tailed test to determine whether we

---

[39] For this example, we use the annualized median SPF prediction of current-quarter growth in the GDP deflator (GNP deflator before 1992).

[40] Our data on Treasury bill returns are based on three-month T-bill yields in the secondary market. Because those yields are stated on a discount basis, we convert them to a compounded annual rate so they will be measured on the same basis as our data on inflation expectations. These returns are risk-free because they are known at the beginning of the quarter and there is no default risk.

can reject the null hypothesis. The critical value of the test statistic for a variable from a χ^2 distribution with one degree of freedom at the 0.05 significance level is 3.84. The test statistic from the Breusch–Pagan test is 22.619, so we can reject the hypothesis of no conditional heteroskedasticity at the 0.05 level. In fact, we can even reject the hypothesis of no conditional heteroskedasticity at the 0.01 significance level, because the critical value of the test statistic in the case is 6.63. As a result, we conclude that the error term in the Fisher effect regression is conditionally heteroskedastic. The standard errors computed in the original regression are not correct, because they do not account for heteroskedasticity. Therefore, we cannot accept the t-test as valid.

In Example 8, we concluded that a t-test that we might use to test the Fisher effect was not valid. Does that mean that we cannot use a regression model to investigate the Fisher effect? Fortunately, no. A methodology is available to adjust regression coefficients' standard error to correct for heteroskedasticity. Using an adjusted standard error for $\hat{b}_1$, we can reconduct the t-test. As we shall see in the next section, using this valid t-test we still do not reject the null hypothesis in Example 8.

4.1.3 *Correcting for Heteroskedasticity*

Financial analysts need to know how to correct for heteroskedasticity, because such a correction may reverse the conclusions about a particular hypothesis test—and thus affect a particular investment decision. In Example 7, for instance, MacKinlay and Richardson reversed their investment conclusions after correcting their model's significance tests for heteroskedasticity.

We can use two different methods to correct the effects of conditional heteroskedasticity in linear regression models. The first method, computing **robust standard errors**, corrects the standard errors of the linear regression model's estimated coefficients to account for the conditional heteroskedasticity. The second method, **generalized least squares**, modifies the original equation in an attempt to eliminate the heteroskedasticity. The new, modified regression equation is then estimated under the assumption that heteroskedasticity is no longer a problem.[41] The technical details behind these two methods of correcting for conditional heteroskedasticity are outside the scope of this volume.[42] Many statistical software packages can easily compute robust standard errors, however, and we recommend using them.[43]

Returning to the subject of Example 8 concerning the Fisher effect, recall that we concluded that the error variance was heteroskedastic. If we correct the regression coefficients' standard errors for conditional heteroskedasticity, we get the results shown in Table 7. In comparing the standard errors in Table 7 with those in Table 6, we see that the standard error for the intercept changes very little, but the standard error for the coefficient on predicted inflation (the slope coefficient) increases by about 25.5 percent (from 0.0812 to 0.1019). Note also that the regression coefficients are the same in both tables, because the results in Table 7 correct only the standard errors in Table 6.

---

41 Generalized least squares requires econometric expertise to implement correctly on financial data. See Greene (2003), Hansen (1982), and Keane and Runkle (1998).

42 For more details on both methods, see Greene (2003).

43 Robust standard errors are also known as **heteroskedasticity-consistent standard errors** or **White-corrected standard errors**.

Table 7	Results from Regressing T-Bill Returns on Predicted Inflation (Standard Errors Corrected for Conditional Heteroskedasticity)		
	Coefficients	**Standard Error**	**t-Statistic**
Intercept	0.0304	0.0038	8.0740
Inflation prediction	0.8774	0.1019	8.6083
Residual standard error		0.0220	
Multiple R-squared		0.4640	
Observations		137	

Source: Federal Reserve Bank of Philadelphia, U.S. Department of Commerce.

We can now conduct a valid t-test of the null hypothesis that the slope coefficient has a true value of 1, using the robust standard error for $\hat{b}_1$. We find that $t = (0.8774 - 1)/0.1019 = -1.2031$. In absolute value, this number is still much smaller than the critical value of 1.98 needed to reject the null hypothesis that the slope equals 1.[44] Thus, in this particular example, even though conditional heteroskedasticity was statistically significant, correcting for it had no effect on the result of the hypothesis test about the slope of the predicted inflation coefficient. In other cases, however, our statistical decision might change based on using robust standard errors in the t-test. Example 7 concerning tests of the CAPM is a case in point.

4.2 Serial Correlation

A more common—and potentially more serious—problem than violation of the homoskedasticity assumption is the violation of the assumption that regression errors are uncorrelated across observations. Trying to explain a particular financial relation over a number of periods is risky, because errors in financial regression models are often correlated through time.

When regression errors are correlated across observations, we say that they are **serially correlated** (or autocorrelated). Serial correlation most typically arises in time-series regressions. In this section, we discuss three aspects of serial correlation: its effect on statistical inference, tests for it, and methods to correct for it.

4.2.1 *The Consequences of Serial Correlation*

As with heteroskedasticity, the principal problem caused by serial correlation in a linear regression is an incorrect estimate of the regression coefficient standard errors computed by statistical software packages. As long as none of the independent variables is a lagged value of the dependent variable (a value of the dependent variable from a previous period), then the estimated parameters themselves will be consistent and need not be adjusted for the effects of serial correlation. If, however, one of the independent variables is a lagged value of the dependent variable—for example, if the T-bill return from the previous month was an independent variable in the Fisher effect regression—then serial correlation in the error term will cause all the parameter estimates from linear regression to be inconsistent and they will not be valid estimates of the true parameters.[45]

---

44 Remember, this is a two-tailed test.
45 We address this issue in the reading on time-series analysis.

In this reading, we assume that none of the independent variables is a lagged value of the dependent variable. When that is the case, the effect of serial correlation appears in the regression coefficient standard errors. We will examine it here for the positive serial correlation case, because that case is so common. **Positive serial correlation** is serial correlation in which a positive error for one observation increases the chance of a positive error for another observation. Positive serial correlation also means that a negative error for one observation increases the chance of a negative error for another observation.[46] In examining positive serial correlation, we make the common assumption that serial correlation takes the form of **first-order serial correlation**, or serial correlation between adjacent observations. In a time-series context, that assumption means the sign of the error term tends to persist from one period to the next.

Although positive serial correlation does not affect the consistency of the estimated regression coefficients, it does affect our ability to conduct valid statistical tests. First, the *F*-statistic to test for overall significance of the regression may be inflated because the mean squared error (MSE) will tend to underestimate the population error variance. Second, positive serial correlation typically causes the ordinary least squares (OLS) standard errors for the regression coefficients to underestimate the true standard errors. As a consequence, if positive serial correlation is present in the regression, standard linear regression analysis will typically lead us to compute artificially small standard errors for the regression coefficient. These small standard errors will cause the estimated *t*-statistics to be inflated, suggesting significance where perhaps there is none. The inflated *t*-statistics may, in turn, lead us to incorrectly reject null hypotheses about population values of the parameters of the regression model more often than we would if the standard errors were correctly estimated. This Type I error could lead to improper investment recommendations.[47]

4.2.2 *Testing for Serial Correlation*

We can choose from a variety of tests for serial correlation in a regression model,[48] but the most common is based on a statistic developed by Durbin and Watson (1951); in fact, many statistical software packages compute the Durbin–Watson statistic automatically. The equation for the Durbin–Watson test statistic is

$$DW = \frac{\sum_{t=2}^{T}\left(\hat{\varepsilon}_t - \hat{\varepsilon}_{t-1}\right)^2}{\sum_{t=1}^{T}\hat{\varepsilon}_t^2} \qquad (6)$$

where $\hat{\varepsilon}_t$ is the regression residual for period t. We can rewrite this equation as

$$\frac{\dfrac{1}{T-1}\sum_{t=2}^{T}\left(\hat{\varepsilon}_t^2 - 2\hat{\varepsilon}_t\hat{\varepsilon}_{t-1} + \hat{\varepsilon}_{t-1}^2\right)}{\dfrac{1}{T-1}\sum_{t=1}^{T}\hat{\varepsilon}_t^2}$$

$$\approx \frac{Var\left(\hat{\varepsilon}_t\right) - 2\,Cov\left(\hat{\varepsilon}_t,\hat{\varepsilon}_{t-1}\right) + Var\left(\hat{\varepsilon}_{t-1}\right)}{Var\left(\hat{\varepsilon}_t\right)}$$

---

46 In contrast, with **negative serial correlation**, a positive error for one observation increases the chance of a negative error for another observation, and a negative error for one observation increases the chance of a positive error for another.

47 OLS standard errors need not be underestimates of actual standard errors if negative serial correlation is present in the regression.

48 See Greene (2003) for a detailed discussion of tests of serial correlation.

If the variance of the error is constant through time, then we expect $\text{Var}\left(\hat{\varepsilon}_t\right) = \hat{\sigma}_\varepsilon^2$ for all t, where we use $\hat{\sigma}_\varepsilon^2$ to represent the estimate of the constant error variance. If, in addition, the errors are also not serially correlated, then we expect $\text{Cov}\left(\hat{\varepsilon}_t, \hat{\varepsilon}_{t-1}\right) = 0$. In that case, the Durbin–Watson statistic is approximately equal to

$$\frac{\hat{\sigma}_\varepsilon^2 - 0 + \hat{\sigma}_\varepsilon^2}{\hat{\sigma}_\varepsilon^2} = 2$$

This equation tells us that if the errors are homoskedastic and not serially correlated, then the Durbin–Watson statistic will be close to 2. Therefore, we can test the null hypothesis that the errors are not serially correlated by testing whether the Durbin–Watson statistic differs significantly from 2.

If the sample is very large, the Durbin–Watson statistic will be approximately equal to $2(1 - r)$, where r is the sample correlation between the regression residuals from one period and those from the previous period. This approximation is useful because it shows the value of the Durbin–Watson statistic for differing levels of serial correlation. The Durbin–Watson statistic can take on values ranging from 0 (in the case of serial correlation of + 1) to 4 (in the case of serial correlation of −1):

- If the regression has no serial correlation, then the regression residuals will be uncorrelated through time and the value of the Durbin–Watson statistic will be equal to $2(1 - 0) = 2$.

- If the regression residuals are positively serially correlated, then the Durbin–Watson statistic will be less than 2. For example, if the serial correlation of the errors is 1, then the value of the Durbin–Watson statistic will be 0.

- If the regression residuals are negatively serially correlated, then the Durbin–Watson statistic will be greater than 2. For example, if the serial correlation of the errors is −1, then the value of the Durbin–Watson statistic will be 4.

Returning to Example 8, which explored the Fisher effect, as shown in Table 6 the Durbin–Watson statistic for the OLS regression is 0.4673. This result means that the regression residuals are positively serially correlated:

$$DW = 0.4673$$
$$\approx 2(1 - r)$$
$$r \approx 1 - DW/2$$
$$= 1 - 0.4673/2$$
$$= 0.766$$

This outcome raises the concern that OLS standard errors may be incorrect because of positive serial correlation. Does the observed Durbin–Watson statistic (0.4673) provide enough evidence to warrant rejecting the null hypothesis of no positive serial correlation?

We should reject the null hypothesis of no serial correlation if the Durbin–Watson statistic is below a critical value, d^*. Unfortunately, Durbin and Watson also showed that, for a given sample, we cannot know the true critical value, d^*. Instead, we can determine only that d^* lies either between two values, d_u (an upper value) and d_l (a lower value), or outside those values. Figure 3 depicts the upper and lower values of d^* as they relate to the results of the Durbin–Watson statistic.

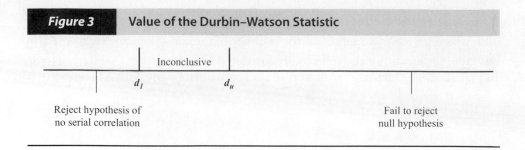

Figure 3   **Value of the Durbin–Watson Statistic**

From Figure 3, we learn the following:

■ When the Durbin–Watson (DW) statistic is less than d_l, we reject the null hypothesis of no positive serial correlation.

■ When the DW statistic falls between d_l and d_u, the test results are inconclusive.

■ When the DW statistic is greater than d_u, we fail to reject the null hypothesis of no positive serial correlation.[49]

Returning to Example 8, the Fisher effect regression has one independent variable and 137 observations. The Durbin–Watson statistic is 0.4673. We can reject the null hypothesis of no correlation in favor of the alternative hypothesis of positive serial correlation at the 0.05 level because the Durbin–Watson statistic is far below d_l for $k = 1$ and $n = 100$ (1.65). The level of d_l would be even higher for a sample of 137 observations. This finding of significant positive serial correlation suggests that the OLS standard errors in this regression probably significantly underestimate the true standard errors.

4.2.3 *Correcting for Serial Correlation*

We have two alternative remedial steps when a regression has significant serial correlation. First, we can adjust the coefficient standard errors for the linear regression parameter estimates to account for the serial correlation. Second, we can modify the regression equation itself to eliminate the serial correlation. We recommend using the first method for dealing with serial correlation; the second method may result in inconsistent parameter estimates unless implemented with extreme care.

The most prevalent method for adjusting standard errors was developed by Hansen (1982) and is a standard feature in many statistical software packages.[50] An additional advantage of Hansen's method is that it simultaneously corrects for conditional heteroskedasticity.[51]

Table 8 shows the results of correcting the standard errors from Table 6 for serial correlation and heteroskedasticity using Hansen's method. Note that the coefficients for both the intercept and the slope are exactly the same as in the original regression. The robust standard errors are now much larger, however—about twice the OLS standard errors. Because of the severe serial correlation in the regression error, OLS greatly underestimates the uncertainty about the estimated parameters in the regression.

Note also that the Durbin–Watson statistic has not changed from Table 6. The serial correlation has not been eliminated, but the standard error has been corrected to account for the serial correlation.

---

49 Of course, sometimes serial correlation in a regression model is negative rather than positive. For a null hypothesis of no serial correlation, the null hypothesis is rejected if $DW < d_l$ (indicating significant positive serial correlation) or if $DW > 4 - d_l$ (indicating significant negative serial correlation).

50 This correction is known by various names, including serial-correlation consistent standard errors, serial correlation and heteroskedasticity adjusted standard errors, robust standard errors, and Hansen–White standard errors. Analysts may also say that they use the Newey–West method for computing robust standard errors.

51 We do not always use Hansen's method to correct for serial correlation and heteroskedasticity because sometimes the errors of a regression are not serially correlated.

Table 8	Results from Regressing T-Bill Returns on Predicted Inflation (Standard Errors Corrected for Conditional Heteroskedasticity and Serial Correlation)		
	Coefficient	**Standard Error**	**t-Statistic**
Intercept	0.0304	0.0069	4.4106
Inflation prediction	0.8774	0.1729	5.0730
Residual standard error		0.0220	
Multiple R-squared		0.4640	
Observations		137	
Durbin–Watson statistic		0.4673	

Source: Federal Reserve Bank of Philadelphia, U.S. Department of Commerce.

Now suppose we want to test our original null hypothesis (the Fisher effect) that the coefficient on the predicted inflation term equals 1 ($H_0: b_1 = 1$) against the alternative that the coefficient on the inflation term is not equal to 1 ($H_a: b_1 \neq 1$). With the corrected standard errors, the value of the test statistic for this null hypothesis is

$$\frac{\hat{b}_1 - b_1}{s_{\hat{b}_1}} = \frac{0.8774 - 1}{0.1729} = -0.7091$$

The critical values for both the 0.05 and 0.01 significance level are much larger than 0.7091 (absolute value of the t-test statistic), so we cannot reject the null hypothesis.

In this particular case, our conclusion about the Fisher effect was not affected by serial correlation, but the standard error on the slope coefficient after taking into account serial correlation and conditional heteroskedasticity (0.1729) is more than double the OLS standard error (0.0812). Therefore, for some hypotheses, serial correlation and conditional heteroskedasticity could have had a big effect on whether we accepted or rejected those hypotheses.[52]

4.3 Multicollinearity

The second assumption of the multiple linear regression model is that no exact linear relationship exists between two or more of the independent variables. When one of the independent variables is an exact linear combination of other independent variables, it becomes mechanically impossible to estimate the regression. That case, known as perfect collinearity, is much less of a practical concern than multicollinearity.[53] **Multicollinearity** occurs when two or more independent variables (or combinations of independent variables) are highly (but not perfectly) correlated with each other. With multicollinearity we can estimate the regression, but the interpretation of the regression output becomes problematic. Multicollinearity is a serious practical concern because approximate linear relationships among financial variables are common.

---

52 Serial correlation can also affect forecast accuracy.
53 To give an example of perfect collinearity, suppose we tried to explain a company's credit ratings with a regression that included net sales, cost of goods sold, and gross profit as independent variables. Because Gross profit = Net sales − Cost of goods sold by definition, there is an exact linear relationship between these variables. This type of blunder is relatively obvious (and easy to avoid).

4.3.1 *The Consequences of Multicollinearity*

Although the presence of multicollinearity does not affect the consistency of the OLS estimates of the regression coefficients, the estimates become extremely imprecise and unreliable. Furthermore, it becomes practically impossible to distinguish the individual impacts of the independent variables on the dependent variable. These consequences are reflected in inflated OLS standard errors for the regression coefficients. With inflated standard errors, *t*-tests on the coefficients have little power (ability to reject the null hypothesis).

4.3.2 *Detecting Multicollinearity*

In contrast to the cases of heteroskedasticity and serial correlation, we shall not provide a formal statistical test for multicollinearity. In practice, multicollinearity is often a matter of degree rather than of absence or presence.[54]

The analyst should be aware that using the magnitude of pairwise correlations among the independent variables to assess multicollinearity, as has occasionally been suggested, is generally not adequate. Although very high pairwise correlations among independent variables can indicate multicollinearity, it is not necessary for such pairwise correlations to be high for there to be a problem of multicollinearity.[55] Stated another way, high pairwise correlations among the independent variables are not a necessary condition for multicollinearity, and low pairwise correlations do not mean that multicollinearity is not a problem. The only case in which correlation between independent variables may be a reasonable indicator of multicollinearity occurs in a regression with exactly two independent variables.

The classic symptom of multicollinearity is a high R^2 (and significant *F*-statistic) even though the *t*-statistics on the estimated slope coefficients are not significant. The insignificant *t*-statistics reflect inflated standard errors. Although the coefficients might be estimated with great imprecision, as reflected in low *t*-statistics, the independent variables *as a group* may do a good job of explaining the dependent variable, and a high R^2 would reflect this effectiveness. Example 9 illustrates this diagnostic.

Example 9

Multicollinearity in Explaining Returns to the Fidelity Select Technology Fund

In Example 3 we regressed returns to the Fidelity Select Technology Fund (FSPTX) on returns to the S&P 500/BARRA Growth Index and the S&P 500/BARRA Value Index. Table 9 shows the results of our regression, which uses data from January 1998 through December 2002. The *t*-statistic of 9.7034 on the growth index return is greater than 2.0, indicating that the coefficient on the growth index differs significantly from 0 at standard significance levels. On the other hand, the *t*-statistic on the value index return is −1.5953 and thus is not statistically significant. This result suggests that the returns to the FSPTX are linked to the returns to the growth index and not closely associated with the returns to the value index. The coefficient on the growth index, however, is 2.23. This result implies that returns on the FSPTX are more volatile than are returns on the growth index.

---

54 See Kmenta (1986).

55 Even if pairs of independent variables have low correlation, there may be linear combinations of the independent variables that are very highly correlated, creating a multicollinearity problem.

Table 9	Results from Regressing the FSPTX Returns on the S&P 500/BARRA Growth and Value Indexes

	Coefficient	Standard Error	t-Statistic
Intercept	0.0079	0.0091	0.8635
S&P 500/BARRA Growth Index	2.2308	0.2299	9.7034
S&P 500/BARRA Value Index	−0.4143	0.2597	−1.5953

ANOVA	df	SS	MSS	F	Significance F
Regression	2	0.8649	0.4324	86.4483	5.48E-18
Residual	57	0.2851	0.0050		
Total	59	1.1500			
Residual standard error	0.0707				
Multiple R-squared	0.7521				
Observations	60				

Source: Ibbotson Associates.

Note also that this regression explains a significant amount of the variation in the returns to the FSPTX. Specifically, the R^2 from this regression is 0.7521. Thus approximately 75 percent of the variation in the returns to the FSPTX is explained by returns to the S&P 500/BARRA growth and value indexes.

Now suppose we run another linear regression that adds returns to the S&P 500 itself to the returns to the S&P 500/BARRA Growth and Value indexes. The S&P 500 includes the component stocks of these two style indexes, so we are introducing a severe multicollinearity problem.

Table 10 shows the results of that regression. Note that the R^2 in this regression has changed almost imperceptibly from the R^2 in the previous regression (increasing from 0.7521 to 0.7539), but now the standard errors of the coefficients are much larger. Adding the return to the S&P 500 to the previous regression does not explain any more of the variance in the returns to the FSPTX than the previous regression did, but now none of the coefficients is statistically significant. This is the classic case of multicollinearity mentioned in the reading.

Table 10	Results from Regressing the FSPTX Returns on Returns to the S&P 500/BARRA Growth and Value Indexes and the S&P 500 Index

	Coefficient	Standard Error	t-Statistic
Intercept	0.0072	0.0092	0.7761
S&P 500/BARRA Growth Index	−1.1324	5.2443	−0.2159
S&P 500/BARRA Value Index	−3.4912	4.8004	−0.7273
S&P 500 Index	6.4436	10.0380	0.6419

(continued)

Table 10	Continued					
ANOVA		**df**	**SS**	**MSS**	**F**	**Significance *F***
Regression		3	0.8670	0.2890	57.1751	4.73E-17
Residual		56	0.2830	0.0051		
Total		59	1.1500			
Residual standard error				0.0711		
Multiple *R*-squared				0.7539		
Observations				60		

Source: Ibbotson Associates.

Multicollinearity may be a problem even when we do not observe the classic symptom of insignificant *t*-statistics but a highly significant *F*-test. Advanced textbooks provide further tools to help diagnose multicollinearity.[56]

4.3.3 *Correcting for Multicollinearity*

The most direct solution to multicollinearity is excluding one or more of the regression variables. In the example above, we can see that the S&P 500 total returns should not be included if both the S&P 500/BARRA Growth and Value Indexes are included, because the returns to the entire S&P 500 Index are a weighted average of the return to growth stocks and value stocks. In many cases, however, no easy solution is available to the problem of multicollinearity, and you will need to experiment with including or excluding different independent variables to determine the source of multicollinearity.

4.4 Heteroskedasticity, Serial Correlation, Multicollinearity: Summarizing the Issues

We have discussed some of the problems that heteroskedasticity, serial correlation, and multicollinearity may cause in interpreting regression results. These violations of regression assumptions, we have noted, all lead to problems in making valid inferences. The analyst should check that model assumptions are fulfilled before interpreting statistical tests.

Table 11	Problems in Linear Regression and Their Solutions		
Problem	**Effect**		**Solution**
Heteroskedasticity	Incorrect standard errors		Use robust standard errors (corrected for conditional heteroskedasticity)
Serial correlation	Incorrect standard errors (additional problems if a lagged value of the dependent variable is used as an independent variable)		Use robust standard errors (corrected for serial correlation)
Multicollinearity	High R^2 and low *t*-statistics		Remove one or more independent variables; often no solution based in theory

---

56 See Greene (2003).

Table 11 gives a summary of these problems, the effect they have on the linear regression results (an analyst can see these effects using regression software), and the solutions to these problems.

MODEL SPECIFICATION AND ERRORS IN SPECIFICATION

Until now, we have assumed that whatever regression model we estimate is correctly specified. **Model specification** refers to the set of variables included in the regression and the regression equation's functional form. In the following, we first give some broad guidelines for correctly specifying a regression. Then we turn to three types of model misspecification: misspecified functional form, regressors that are correlated with the error term, and additional time-series misspecification. Each of these types of misspecification invalidates statistical inference using OLS; most of these misspecifications will cause the estimated regression coefficients to be inconsistent.

5.1 Principles of Model Specification

In discussing the principles of model specification, we need to acknowledge that there are competing philosophies about how to approach model specification. Furthermore, our purpose for using regression analysis may affect the specification we choose. The following principles have fairly broad application, however.

- *The model should be grounded in cogent economic reasoning.* We should be able to supply the economic reasoning behind the choice of variables, and the reasoning should make sense. When this condition is fulfilled, we increase the chance that the model will have predictive value with new data. This approach contrasts to the variable-selection process known as **data mining**. With data mining, the investigator essentially develops a model that maximally exploits the characteristics of a specific dataset.

- *The functional form chosen for the variables in the regression should be appropriate given the nature of the variables.* As one illustration, consider studying mutual fund **market timing** based on fund and market returns alone. One might reason that for a successful timer, a plot of mutual fund returns against market returns would show curvature, because a successful timer would tend to increase (decrease) beta when market returns were high (low). The model specification should reflect the expected nonlinear relationship.[57] In other cases, we may transform the data such that a regression assumption is better satisfied.

- *The model should be parsimonious.* In this context, "parsimonious" means accomplishing a lot with a little. We should expect each variable included in a regression to play an essential role.

- *The model should be examined for violations of regression assumptions before being accepted.* We have already discussed detecting the presence of heteroskedasticity, serial correlation, and multicollinearity. As a result of such diagnostics, we may conclude that we need to revise the set of included variables and/or their functional form.

---

57 This example is based on Treynor and Mazuy (1966), an early regression study of mutual fund timing. To capture curvature, they included a term in the squared market excess return, which does not violate the assumption of the multiple linear regression model that relationship between the dependent and independent variables is linear *in the coefficients.*

■ *The model should be tested and be found useful out of sample before being accepted.* The term "out of sample" refers to observations outside the dataset on which the model was estimated. A plausible model may not perform well out of sample because economic relationships have changed since the sample period. That possibility is itself useful to know. A second explanation, however, may be that relationships have not changed but that the model explains only a specific dataset.

Having given some broad guidance on model specification, we turn to a discussion of specific model specification errors. Understanding these errors will help an analyst develop better models and be a more informed consumer of investment research.

5.2 Misspecified Functional Form

Whenever we estimate a regression, we must assume that the regression has the correct functional form. This assumption can fail in several ways:

■ One or more important variables could be omitted from regression.

■ One or more of the regression variables may need to be transformed (for example, by taking the natural logarithm of the variable) before estimating the regression.

■ The regression model pools data from different samples that should not be pooled.

First, consider the effects of omitting an important independent variable from a regression (omitted variable bias). If the true regression model was

$$Y_i = b_0 + b_1 X_{1i} + b_2 X_{2i} + \varepsilon_i \qquad (7)$$

but we estimate the model[58]

$$Y_i = a_0 + a_1 X_{1i} + \varepsilon_i$$

then our regression model would be misspecified. What is wrong with the model?

If the omitted variable (X_2) is correlated with the remaining variable (X_1), then the error term in the model will be correlated with (X_1), and the estimated values of the regression coefficients a_0 and a_1 would be biased and inconsistent. In addition, the estimates of the standard errors of those coefficients will also be inconsistent, so we can use neither the coefficients estimates nor the estimated standard errors to make statistical tests.

Example 10

Omitted Variable Bias and the Bid–Ask Spread

In this example, we extend our examination of the bid–ask spread to show the effect of omitting an important variable from a regression. In Example 1, we showed that the natural logarithm of the ratio [(Bid–ask spread)/Price] was significantly related to both the natural logarithm of the number of market makers and the natural logarithm of the market capitalization of the company. We repeat Table 1 from Example 1 below.

---

[58] We use a different regression coefficient notation when X_{2i} is omitted, because the intercept term and slope coefficient on X_{1i} will generally not be the same as when X_{2i} is included.

Table 1	Results from Regressing ln(Bid–Ask Spread/Price) on ln(Number of Market Makers) and ln(Market Cap) (repeated)

	Coefficients	Standard Error	t-Statistic
Intercept	−0.7586	0.1369	−5.5416
ln(Number of NASDAQ market makers)	−0.2790	0.0673	−4.1427
ln(Company's market cap)	−0.6635	0.0246	−27.0087

ANOVA	df	SS	MSS	F	Significance F
Regression	2	2,681.6482	1,340.8241	1,088.8325	0.00
Residual	1,816	2,236.2820	1.2314		
Total	1,818	4,917.9302			
Residual standard error			1.1097		
Multiple R-squared			0.5453		
Observations			1,819		

Source: FactSet, NASDAQ.

If we did not include the natural log of market capitalization as an independent variable in the regression, and we regressed the natural logarithm of the ratio [(Bid–ask spread)/Price] only on the natural logarithm of the number of market makers for the stock, the results would be as shown in Table 12.

Table 12	Results from Regressing ln(Bid–Ask Spread/Price) on ln(Number of Market Makers)

	Coefficients	Standard Error	t-Statistic
Intercept	−0.1229	0.1596	−0.7698
ln(Number of NASDAQ market makers)	−1.6629	0.0517	−32.1519

ANOVA	df	SS	MSS	F	Significance F
Regression	1	1,783.3549	1,783.3549	1,033.7464	0.00
Residual	1,817	3,134.5753	1.7251		
Total	1,818	4,917.9302			
Residual standard error			1.3134		
Multiple R-squared			0.3626		
Observations			1,819		

Source: FactSet, NASDAQ.

Note that the coefficient on ln(Number of NASDAQ market makers) fell from −0.2790 in the original (correctly specified) regression to −1.6629 in the misspecified regression. Also, the intercept rose from −0.7586 in the correctly specified regression to −0.1229 in the misspecified regression. These results illustrate that omitting an independent variable that should be in the regression can cause the remaining regression coefficients to be inconsistent.

A second common cause of misspecification in regression models is the use of the wrong form of the data in a regression, when a transformed version of the data is appropriate. For example, sometimes analysts fail to account for curvature or non-linearity in the relationship between the dependent variable and one or more of the independent variables, instead specifying a linear relation among variables. When we are specifying a regression model, we should consider whether economic theory suggests a nonlinear relation. We can often confirm the nonlinearity by plotting the data, as we will illustrate in Example 11 below. If the relationship between the variables becomes linear when one or more of the variables is represented as a proportional change in the variable, we may be able to correct the misspecification by taking the natural logarithm of the variable(s) we want to represent as a proportional change. Other times, analysts use unscaled data in regressions, when scaled data (such as dividing net income or cash flow by sales) are more appropriate. In Example 1, we scaled the bid–ask spread by stock price because what a given bid–ask spread means in terms of transactions costs for a given size investment depends on the price of the stock; if we had not scaled the bid–ask spread, the regression would have been misspecified.

Example 11

Nonlinearity and the Bid–Ask Spread

In Example 1, we showed that the natural logarithm of the ratio [(Bid–ask spread)/Price] was significantly related to both the natural logarithm of the number of market makers and the natural logarithm of the company's market capitalization. But why did we take the natural logarithm of each of the variables in the regression? We began a discussion of this question in Example 1, which we continue now.

What does theory suggest about the nature of the relationship between the ratio (Bid–ask spread)/Price, or the percentage bid–ask spread, and its determinants (the independent variables)? Stoll (1978) builds a theoretical model of the determinants of percentage bid–ask spread in a dealer market. In his model, the determinants enter multiplicatively in a particular fashion. In terms of the independent variables introduced in Example 1, the functional form assumed is

$$\left[(\text{Bid–ask spread})/\text{Price}\right]_i = c\left(\text{Number of market makers}\right)_i^{b_1}$$

$$\times\left(\text{Market capitalization}\right)_i^{b_2}$$

where c is a constant. The relationship of the percentage bid–ask spread with the number of market makers and market capitalization is not linear in the original variables.[59] If we take natural log of both sides of the above model, however, we have a log-log regression that is linear in the transformed variables:[60]

---

59 The form of the model is analogous to the Cobb–Douglas production function in economics.
60 We have added an error term to the model.

$$Y_i = b_0 + b_1 X_{1i} + b_2 X_{2i} + \varepsilon_i$$

where

Y_i = the natural logarithm of the ratio (Bid–ask spread) / Price for stock i

b_0 = a constant that equals $\ln(c)$

X_{1i} = the natural logarithm of the number of market makers for stock i

X_{2i} = the natural logarithm of the market capitalization of company i

ε_i = the error term

As mentioned in Example 1, a slope coefficient in the log-log model is interpreted as an elasticity, precisely, the partial elasticity of the dependent variable with respect to the independent variable ("partial" means holding the other independent variables constant).

We can plot the data to assess whether the variables are linearly related after the logarithmic transformation. For example Figure 4 shows a scatterplot of the natural logarithm of the number of market makers for a stock (on the X axis) and the natural logarithm of (Bid–ask spread)/Price (on the Y axis), as well as a regression line showing the linear relation between the two transformed variables. The relation between the two transformed variables is clearly linear.

Figure 4	Linear Regression When Two Variables Have a Linear Relation

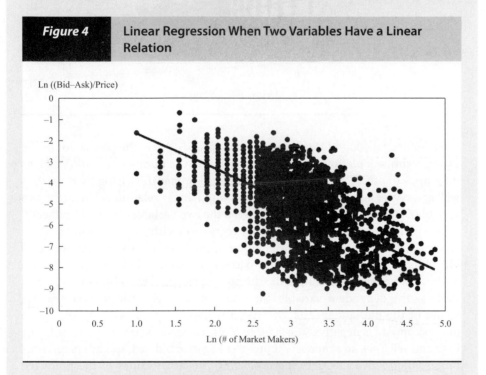

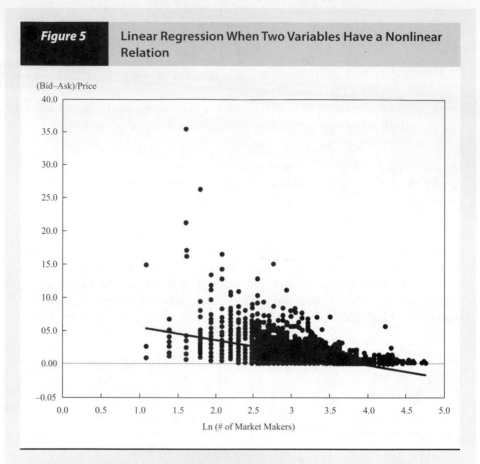

| Figure 5 | Linear Regression When Two Variables Have a Nonlinear Relation |

If we do not take log of the ratio (Bid–ask spread)/Price, the plot is not linear. Figure 5 shows a plot of the natural logarithm of the number of market makers for a stock (on the *X* axis) and the ratio (Bid–ask spread)/Price (on the *Y* axis), as well as a regression line that attempts to show a linear relation between the two variables. We see that the relation between the two variables is very nonlinear.[61] Consequently, we should not estimate a regression with (Bid–ask spread)/Price as the dependent variable. Consideration of the need to ensure that predicted bid–ask spreads are positive would also lead us to not use (Bid–ask spread)/Price as the dependent variable. If we use the nontransformed ratio (Bid–ask spread)/Price as the dependent variable, the estimated model could predict negative values of the bid–ask spread. This result would be nonsensical; in reality, no bid–ask spread is negative (it is hard to motivate traders to simultaneously buy high and sell low), so a model that predicts negative bid–ask spreads is certainly misspecified.[62] We illustrate the problem of negative values of the predicted bid–ask spreads now.

Table 13 shows the results of a regression with (Bid–ask spread)/Price as the dependent variable and the natural logarithm of the number of market makers and the natural logarithm of the company's market capitalization as the independent variables.

---

[61] The relation between (Bid–ask spread)/Price and ln(Market cap) is also nonlinear, while the relation between ln(Bid–ask spread)/Price and ln(Market cap) is linear. We omit these scatterplots to save space.
[62] In our data sample, the bid–ask spread for each of the 1,819 companies is positive.

| Table 13 | Results from Regressing Bid–Ask Spread/Price on ln(Number of Market Makers) and ln(Market Cap) | | |

	Coefficients	Standard Error	t-Statistic
Intercept	0.0658	0.0024	27.6430
ln(Number of NASDAQ market makers)	−0.0045	0.0012	−3.8714
ln(Company's market cap)	−0.0068	0.0004	−15.8679

ANOVA	df	SS	MSS	F	Significance F
Regression	2	0.3185	0.1592	427.8174	0.00
Residual	1816	0.6760	0.0004		
Total	1818	0.9944			
Residual standard error		0.0193			
Multiple R-squared		0.3203			
Observations	1,819				

Source: FactSet, NASDAQ.

Suppose that for a particular NASDAQ-listed stock, the number of market makers is 20 and the market capitalization is $5 billion. Therefore, the natural log of the number of market makers equals ln 20 = 2.9957 and the natural log of the stock's market capitalization (in millions) is ln 5,000 = 8.5172. In this case, the predicted ratio of bid–ask spread to price is $0.0658 + (2.9957 \times -0.0045) + (-0.0068 \times 8.5172) = -0.0056$. Therefore, the model predicts that the ratio of bid–ask spread to stock price is −0.0056 or −0.56 percent of the stock price. Thus the predicted bid–ask spread is negative, which does not make economic sense. This problem could be avoided by using log of (Bid–ask spread)/Price as the dependent variable.[63]

Often, analysts must decide whether to scale variables before they compare data across companies. For example, in financial statement analysis, analysts often compare companies using **common size statements**. In a common size income statement, all the line items in a company's income statement are divided by the company's revenues.[64] Common size statements make comparability across companies much easier. An analyst can use common size statements to quickly compare trends in gross margins (or other income statement variables) for a group of companies.

Issues of comparability also appear for analysts who want to use regression analysis to compare the performance of a group of companies. Example 12 illustrates this issue.

---

63 Whether the natural log of the percentage bid–ask spread, Y, is positive or negative, the percentage bid–ask spread found as eY is positive, because a positive number raised to any power is positive. The constant e is positive ($e \approx 2.7183$).

64 For more on common size statements, see White, Sondhi, and Fried (2003). Free cash flow and cash flow from operations are discussed in Stowe, Robinson, Pinto, and McLeavey (2002).

Example 12

Scaling and the Relation between Cash Flow from Operations and Free Cash Flow

Suppose an analyst wants to explain free cash flow to the firm as a function of cash flow from operations in 2001 for 11 family clothing stores in the United States with market capitalizations of more than $100 million as of the end of 2001.

To investigate this issue, the analyst might use free cash flow as the dependent variable and cash flow from operations as the independent variable in single-independent-variable linear regression. Table 14 shows the results of that regression. Note that the t-statistic for the slope coefficient for cash flow from operations is quite high (6.5288), the significance level for the F-statistic for the regression is very low (0.0001), and the R-squared is quite high. We might be tempted to believe that this regression is a success and that for a family clothing store, if cash flow from operations increased by $1.00, we could confidently predict that free cash flow to the firm would increase by $0.3579.

Table 14	Results from Regressing the Free Cash Flow on Cash Flow from Operations for Family Clothing Stores

	Coefficients	Standard Error	t-Statistic
Intercept	0.7295	27.7302	0.0263
Cash flow from operations	0.3579	0.0548	6.5288

ANOVA	df	SS	MSS	F	Significance F
Regression	1	245,093.7836	245,093.7836	42.6247	0.0001
Residual	9	51,750.3139	5,750.0349		
Total	10	296,844.0975			

Residual standard error	75.8290
Multiple R-squared	0.8257
Observations	11

Source: Compustat.

But is this specification correct? The regression does not account for size differences among the companies in the sample.

We can account for size differences by using common size cash flow results across companies. We scale the variables by dividing cash flow from operations and free cash flow to the firm by the company's sales before using regression analysis. We will use (Free cash flow to the firm/Sales) as the dependent variable and (Cash flow from operations/Sales) as the independent variable. Table 15 shows the results of this regression. Note that the t-statistic for the slope coefficient on (Cash flow from operations/Sales) is 1.6262, so it is not significant at the 0.05 level. Note also that the significance level of the F-statistic is 0.1383, so we cannot reject at the 0.05 level the hypothesis that the regression does not explain variation in (Free cash flow/Sales) among family clothing stores. Finally, note that the R-squared in this regression is much lower than that of the previous regression.

Table 15	Results from Regressing the Free Cash Flow/Sales on Cash Flow from Operations/Sales for Family Clothing Stores

	Coefficient	Standard Error	t-Statistic
Intercept	−0.0121	0.0221	−0.5497
Cash flow from operations/Sales	0.4749	0.2920	1.6262

ANOVA	df	SS	MSS	F	Significance F
Regression	1	0.0030	0.0030	2.6447	0.1383
Residual	9	0.0102	0.0011		
Total	10	0.0131			

Residual standard error	0.0336
Multiple R-squared	0.2271
Observations	11

Source: Compustat.

Which regression makes more sense? Usually, the scaled regression makes more sense. We want to know what happens to free cash flow (as a fraction of sales) if a change occurs in cash flow from operations (as a fraction of sales). Without scaling, the results of the regression can be based solely on scale differences across companies, rather than based on the companies' underlying economics.

A third common form of misspecification in regression models is pooling data from different samples that should not be pooled. This type of misspecification can best be illustrated graphically. Figure 6 shows two clusters of data on variables X and Y, with a fitted regression line. The data could represent the relationship between two financial variables at two stages of a company's growth, for example.

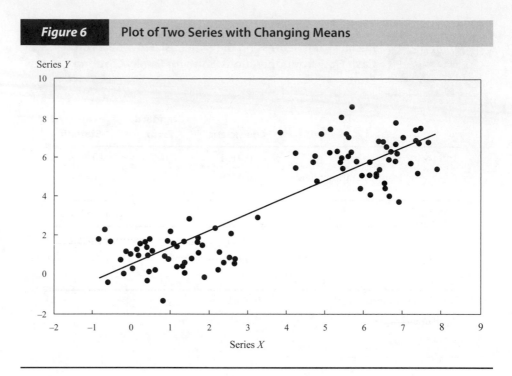

Figure 6   Plot of Two Series with Changing Means

In each cluster of data on X and Y, the correlation between the two variables is virtually 0. Because the means of both X and Y are different for the two clusters of data in the combined sample, X and Y are highly correlated. The correlation is spurious (misleading), however, because it reflects scale differences across companies.

5.3 Time-Series Misspecification (Independent Variables Correlated with Errors)

In the previous section, we discussed the misspecification that arises when a relevant independent variable is omitted from a regression. In this section, we discuss problems that arise from the kinds of variables included in the regression, particularly in a time-series context. In models that use time-series data to explain the relations among different variables, it is particularly easy to violate Regression Assumption 3, that the error term has mean 0, conditioned on the independent variables. If this assumption is violated, the estimated regression coefficients will be biased and inconsistent.

Three common problems that create this type of time-series misspecification are:

■ including lagged dependent variables as independent variables in regressions with serially correlated errors;

■ including a function of a dependent variable as an independent variable, sometimes as a result of the incorrect dating of variables; and

■ independent variables that are measured with error.

The next examples demonstrate these problems.

Suppose that an analyst has estimated a linear regression with significant serial correlation in the errors. That serial correlation could be corrected by the methods discussed previously in this reading. Nevertheless, suppose that the analyst includes as an additional independent variable the first lagged value of the dependent variable. For example, the analyst might use the regression equation

$$Y_t = b_0 + b_1 X_{1t} + b_2 Y_{t-1} + \varepsilon_t \tag{8}$$

Because we assume that the error term is serially correlated, by definition the error term is correlated with the dependent variable. Consequently, the lagged dependent variable, Y_{t-1}, will be correlated with the error term, violating the assumption that the independent variables are uncorrelated with the error term. As a result, the estimates of the regression coefficients will be biased and inconsistent.

Example 13

Fisher Effect with a Lagged Dependent Variable

In our discussion of serial correlation, we concluded from a test using the Durbin–Watson test that the error term in the Fisher effect equation (Equation 5) showed positive (first-order) serial correlation, using three-month T-bill returns as the dependent variable and inflation expectations of professional forecasters as the independent variable. Observations on the dependent and independent variables were quarterly. Table 16 modifies that regression by including the previous quarter's three-month T-bill returns as an additional independent variable.

Table 16	Results from Regressing T-Bill Returns on Predicted Inflation and Lagged T-Bill Returns		
	Coefficient	**Standard Error**	***t*-Statistic**
Intercept	0.0046	0.0040	1.5718
Inflation prediction	0.2753	0.0631	4.3610
Lagged T-bill return	0.7553	0.0495	15.2510
Residual standard error		0.0134	
Multiple R-squared		0.8041	
Observations		137	

Source: Federal Reserve Bank of Philadelphia, U.S. Department of Commerce.

At first glance, these regression results look very interesting—the coefficient on the lagged T-bill return appears to be highly significant. But on closer consideration, we must ignore these regression results, because the regression is fundamentally misspecified. As long as the error term is serially correlated, including lagged T-bill returns as an independent variable in the regression will cause all the coefficient estimates to be biased and inconsistent. Therefore, this regression is not usable for either testing a hypothesis or for forecasting.

A second common time-series misspecification in investment analysis is to forecast the past. What does that mean? If we forecast the future (say we predict at time t the value of variable Y in period $t + 1$), we must base our predictions on information we knew at time t. We could use a regression to make that forecast using the equation

$$Y_{t+1} = b_0 + b_1 X_{1t} + \varepsilon_{t+1} \tag{9}$$

In this equation, we predict the value of Y in time $t + 1$ using the value of X in time t. The error term, ε_{t+1}, is unknown at time t and thus should be uncorrelated with X_{1t}.

Unfortunately, analysts sometimes use regressions that try to forecast the value of a dependent variable at time $t + 1$ based on independent variable(s) that are functions of the value of the dependent variable at time $t + 1$. In such a model, the independent variable(s) would be correlated with the error term, so the equation would be misspecified. As an example, an analyst may try to explain the cross-sectional returns for a group of companies during a particular year using the market-to-book ratio and the market capitalization for those companies at the end of the year.[65] If the analyst believes that such a regression predicts whether companies with high market-to-book ratios or high market capitalizations will have high returns, the analyst is mistaken. For any given period, the higher the return during the period, the higher the market capitalization at the end of the period. It is also true that the higher the return during the period, the higher the market-to-book ratio at the end of the period. So in this case, if all the cross-sectional data come from period $t + 1$, a high value of the dependent variable (returns) actually causes a high value of the independent variables (market cap and market-to-book), rather than the other way around. In this type of misspecification, the regression model effectively includes the dependent variable on both the right-and left-hand sides of the regression equation.

The third common time-series misspecification arises when an independent variable is measured with error. Suppose a financial theory tells us that a particular variable X_t, such as expected inflation, should be included in the regression model. We do not observe X_t; instead, we observe actual inflation, $Z_t = X_t + u_t$, where u_t is an error term that is uncorrelated with X_t. Even in this best of circumstances, using Z_t in the regression instead of X_t will cause the regression coefficient estimates to be biased and inconsistent. Let's see why. If we want to estimate the regression

$$Y_t = b_0 + b_1 X_t + \varepsilon_t$$

but we observe Z_t not X_t, then we would estimate

$$Y_t = b_0 + b_1 Z_t + \left(-b_1 u_t + \varepsilon_t\right)$$

But because $Z_t = X_t + u_t$, Z_t is correlated with the error term $\left(-b_1 u_t + \varepsilon_t\right)$. Therefore, our estimated model violates the assumption that the error term is uncorrelated with the independent variable. Consequently, the estimated regression coefficients will be biased and inconsistent.

Example 14

The Fisher Effect with Measurement Error

Recall from Example 8 on the Fisher effect that we could not reject the hypothesis that three-month T-bill returns moved one-for-one with expected inflation.

Table 6	Results from Regressing T-Bill Returns on Predicted Inflation (repeated)		
	Coefficient	**Standard Error**	**t-Statistic**
Intercept	0.0304	0.0040	7.6887
Inflation prediction	0.8774	0.0812	10.8096
Residual standard error		0.0220	
Multiple R-squared		0.4640	
Observations		137	
Durbin–Watson statistic		0.4673	

Source: Federal Reserve Bank of Philadelphia, U.S. Department of Commerce.

---

[65] "Market-to-book ratio" is the ratio of price per share divided by book value per share.

What if we used actual inflation instead of expected inflation as the independent variable? Note first that

$$\pi = \pi^e + v$$

where

π = actual rate of inflation

π^e = expected rate of inflation

v = the difference between actual and expected inflation

Because actual inflation measures expected inflation with error, the estimators of the regression coefficients using T-bill yields as the independent variable and actual inflation as the independent variable will not be consistent.[66]

Table 17 shows the results of using actual inflation as the independent variable. The estimates in this table are quite different from those presented in the previous table. Note that the slope coefficient on actual inflation is much lower than the slope coefficient on predicted inflation in the previous regression. This result is an illustration of a general proposition: In a single-independent-variable regression, if we select a version of that independent variable that is measured with error, the estimated slope coefficient on that variable will be biased toward 0.[67]

Table 17	Results from Regressing T-Bill Returns on Actual Inflation		
	Coefficient	**Standard Error**	***t*-Statistic**
Intercept	0.0432	0.0034	12.7340
Actual inflation	0.5066	0.0556	9.1151
Residual standard error		0.0237	
Multiple R-squared		0.3810	
Observations		137	

Source: Federal Reserve Bank of Philadelphia, U.S. Department of Commerce.

5.4 Other Types of Time-Series Misspecification

By far the most frequent source of misspecification in linear regressions that use time series from two or more different variables is nonstationarity. Very roughly **nonstationarity** means that a variable's properties, such as mean and variance, are not constant through time. We will postpone our discussion about stationarity, but we can list some examples in which we need to use stationarity tests before we use regression statistical inference.[68]

■ Relations among time series with trends (for example, the relation between consumption and GDP).

---

66 A consistent estimator is one for which the probability of estimates close to the value of the population parameter increases as sample size increases.

67 This proposition does not generalize to regressions with more than one independent variable. Of course, we ignore serially-correlated errors in this example, but because the regression coefficients are inconsistent (due to measurement error), testing or correcting for serial correlation is not worthwhile.

68 We include both unit root tests and tests for cointegration in the term "stationarity tests."

- Relations among time series that may be **random walks** (time series for which the best predictor of next period's value is this period's value). Exchange rates are often random walks.

The time-series examples in this reading were carefully chosen such that nonstationarity was unlikely to be an issue for any of them. But nonstationarity can be a very severe problem for analyzing the relations among two or more time series in practice. Analysts must understand these issues before they apply linear regression to analyzing the relations among time series. Otherwise, they may rely on invalid statistical inference.

6 MODELS WITH QUALITATIVE DEPENDENT VARIABLES

Financial analysts often need to be able to explain the outcomes of a qualitative dependent variable. **Qualitative dependent variables** are dummy variables used as dependent variables instead of as independent variables.

For example, to predict whether or not a company will go bankrupt, we need to use a qualitative dependent variable (bankrupt or not) as the dependent variable and use data on the company's financial performance (e.g., return on equity, debt-to-equity ratio, or debt rating) as independent variables. Unfortunately, linear regression is not the best statistical method to use for estimating such a model. If we use the qualitative dependent variable bankrupt (1) or not bankrupt (0) as the dependent variable in a regression with financial variables as the independent variables, the predicted value of the dependent variable could be much greater than 1 or much lower than 0. Of course, these results would be invalid. The probability of bankruptcy (or of anything, for that matter) cannot be greater than 100 percent or less than 0 percent. Instead of a linear regression model, we should use probit, logit, or discriminant analysis for this kind of estimation.

Probit and **logit models** estimate the probability of a discrete outcome given the values of the independent variables used to explain that outcome. The **probit model**, which is based on the normal distribution, estimates the probability that $Y = 1$ (a condition is fulfilled) given the value of the independent variable X. The logit model is identical, except that it is based on the logistic distribution rather than the normal distribution.[69] Both models must be estimated using maximum likelihood methods.[70]

Another technique to handle qualitative dependent variables is **discriminant analysis**. In his Z-score and Zeta analysis, Altman (1968, 1977) reported on the results of discriminant analysis. Altman uses financial ratios to predict the qualitative dependent variable bankruptcy. Discriminant analysis yields a linear function, similar to a regression equation, which can then be used to create an overall score. Based on the score, an observation can be classified into the bankrupt or not bankrupt category.

Qualitative dependent variable models can be useful not only for portfolio management but also for business management. For example, we might want to predict whether a client is likely to continue investing in a company or to withdraw assets from the company. We might also want to explain how particular demographic characteristics might affect the probability that a potential investor will sign on as a new client, or evaluate the effectiveness of a particular direct-mail advertising campaign based on the demographic characteristics of the target audience. These issues can be analyzed with either probit or logit models.

---

69 The logistic distribution $e^{(b_0 + b_1 X)} / \left[1 + e^{(b_0 + b_1 X)}\right]$ is easier to compute than the cumulative normal distribution. Consequently, logit models gained popularity when computing power was expensive.
70 For more on probit and logit models, see Greene (2003).

Example 15

Explaining Analyst Coverage

Suppose we want to investigate what factors determine whether at least one analyst covers a company. We can employ a probit model to address the question. The sample consists of 2,047 observations on public companies in 1999. All data come from Disclosure, Inc. The analyst coverage data on Disclosure come from I/B/E/S.

The variables in the probit model are as follows:

ANALYSTS = the discrete dependent variable, which takes on a value of 1 if at least one analyst covers the company and a value of 0 if no analysts cover the company

LNVOLUME = the natural log of trading volume in the most recent week

LNMV = the natural log of market value

ESTABLISHED = a dummy independent variable that takes on a value of 1 if the company's financial data has been audited for at least five years

LNTA = the natural log of total assets (book value)

LNSALES = the natural log of net sales

In this attempt to explain analyst coverage, the market (volume and value) and the book (value and sales) variables might be expected to explain coverage through various dimensions of size and, hence, importance.[71] The audit history variable reflects a possible comfort level that analysts could be expected to have with audited statements. The model includes three variables (LNMV, LNTA, and LNSALES) that we may expect to be correlated. Based on analysis not shown here, our probit regression did not exhibit the classic symptom of multicollinearity. Table 18 shows the results of the probit estimation.

Table 18	Explaining Analyst Coverage Using a Probit Model		
	Coefficient	**Standard Error**	**t-Statistic**
Intercept	−7.9738	0.4362	−18.2815
LNVOLUME	0.1574	0.0158	9.9482
LNMV	0.4442	0.0369	12.0268
ESTABLISHED	0.3168	0.1045	3.0320
LNTA	0.0548	0.0296	1.8494
LNSALES	0.0507	0.0266	1.9059
Percent correctly predicted		73.67	

Source: Disclosure, Inc.

As Table 18 shows, three coefficients (besides the intercept) have t-statistics with an absolute value greater than 2.0. The coefficient on LNVOLUME has a t-statistic of 9.95. That value is far above the critical value at the 0.05 level for the t-statistic (1.96), so we can reject at the 0.05 level of significance the null hypothesis that the coefficient on LNVOLUME equals 0, in favor of the alternative hypothesis that the coefficient is not equal to 0. The second coefficient with an

---

71 For more information on tests of multicollinearity, see Greene (2003)

absolute value greater than 2 is LNMV, which has a *t*-statistic of 12.03. We can also reject at the 0.05 level of significance the null hypothesis that the coefficient on LNMV is equal to 0, in favor of the alternative hypothesis that the coefficient is not equal to 0. Finally, the coefficient on ESTABLISHED has a *t*-statistic of 3.03. We can reject at the 0.05 level of significance the null hypothesis that the coefficient on ESTABLISHED is equal to 0.

Neither of the two remaining independent variables is statistically significant at the 0.05 level in this probit analysis. Neither of the *t*-statistics on these two variables is larger in absolute value than 1.91, so neither one reaches the critical value of 1.96 needed to reject the null hypothesis (that the associated coefficient is significantly different from 0). This result shows that once we take into account a company's market value, trading volume, and the existence of a five-year audit history, the other factors—book value of assets and value of sales—have no power to explain whether at least one analyst will cover the company.

SUMMARY

In this reading, we have presented the multiple linear regression model and discussed violations of regression assumptions, model specification and misspecification, and models with qualitative variables.

- The general form of a multiple linear regression model is $Y_i = b_0 + b_1X_{1i} + b_2X_{2i} + \ldots + b_kX_{ki} + \varepsilon_i$

- We conduct hypothesis tests concerning the population values of regression coefficients using *t*-tests of the form

$$t = \frac{\hat{b}_j - b_j}{s_{\hat{b}_j}}$$

- The lower the *p*-value reported for a test, the more significant the result.

- The assumptions of classical normal multiple linear regression model are as follows:

  1. A linear relation exists between the dependent variable and the independent variables.

  2. The independent variables are not random. Also, no exact linear relation exists between two or more of the independent variables.

  3. The expected value of the error term, conditioned on the independent variables, is 0.

  4. The variance of the error term is the same for all observations.

  5. The error term is uncorrelated across observations.

  6. The error term is normally distributed.

- To make a prediction using a multiple linear regression model, we take the following three steps:

  1. Obtain estimates of the regression coefficients.

  2. Determine the assumed values of the independent variables.

  3. Compute the predicted value of the dependent variable.

- When predicting the dependent variable using a linear regression model, we encounter two types of uncertainty: uncertainty in the regression model itself, as reflected in the standard error of estimate, and uncertainty about the estimates of the regression coefficients.

- The *F*-test is reported in an ANOVA table. The *F*-statistic is used to test whether at least one of the slope coefficients on the independent variables is significantly different from 0.

$$ F = \frac{\text{RSS}/k}{\text{SSE}/[n - (k + 1)]} = \frac{\text{Mean regression sum of squares}}{\text{Mean squared error}} $$

  Under the null hypothesis that all the slope coefficients are jointly equal to 0, this test statistic has a distribution of $F_{k, n-(k+1)}$, where the regression has n observations and k independent variables. The *F*-test measures the overall significance of the regression.

- R^2 is nondecreasing in the number of independent variables, so it is less reliable as a measure of goodness of fit in a regression with more than one independent variable than in a one-independent-variable regression.

  Analysts often choose to use adjusted R^2 because it does not necessarily increase when one adds an independent variable.

- Dummy variables in a regression model can help analysts determine whether a particular qualitative independent variable explains the model's dependent variable. A dummy variable takes on the value of 0 or 1. If we need to distinguish among n categories, the regression should include $n - 1$ dummy variables. The intercept of the regression measures the average value of the dependent variable of the omitted category, and the coefficient on each dummy variable measures the average incremental effect of that dummy variable on the dependent variable.

- If a regression shows significant conditional heteroskedasticity, the standard errors and test statistics computed by regression programs will be incorrect unless they are adjusted for heteroskedasticity.

- One simple test for conditional heteroskedasticity is the Breusch–Pagan test. Breusch and Pagan showed that, under the null hypothesis of no conditional heteroskedasticity, nR^2 (from the regression of the squared residuals on the independent variables from the original regression) will be a χ^2 random variable with the number of degrees of freedom equal to the number of independent variables in the regression.

- The principal effect of serial correlation in a linear regression is that the standard errors and test statistics computed by regression programs will be incorrect unless adjusted for serial correlation. Positive serial correlation typically inflates the *t*-statistics of estimated regression coefficients as well as the *F*-statistic for the overall significance of the regression.

- The most commonly used test for serial correlation is based on the Durbin–Watson statistic. If the Durbin–Watson statistic differs sufficiently from 2, then the regression errors have significant serial correlation.

- Multicollinearity occurs when two or more independent variables (or combinations of independent variables) are highly (but not perfectly) correlated with each other. With multicollinearity, the regression coefficients may not be individually statistically significant even when the overall regression is significant as judged by the *F*-statistic.

- Model specification refers to the set of variables included in the regression and the regression equation's functional form. The following principles can guide model specification:

- The model should be grounded in cogent economic reasoning.
- The functional form chosen for the variables in the regression should be appropriate given the nature of the variables.
- The model should be parsimonious.
- The model should be examined for violations of regression assumptions before being accepted.
- The model should be tested and be found useful out of sample before being accepted.

■ If a regression is misspecified, then statistical inference using OLS is invalid and the estimated regression coefficients may be inconsistent.

■ Assuming that a model has the correct functional form, when in fact it does not, is one example of misspecification. There are several ways this assumption may be violated:

- One or more important variables could be omitted from the regression.
- One or more of the regression variables may need to be transformed before estimating the regression.
- The regression model pools data from different samples that should not be pooled.

■ Another type of misspecification occurs when independent variables are correlated with the error term. This is a violation of Regression Assumption 3, that the error term has a mean of 0, and causes the estimated regression coefficients to be biased and inconsistent. Three common problems that create this type of time-series misspecification are:

- including lagged dependent variables as independent variables in regressions with serially correlated errors;
- including a function of dependent variable as an independent variable, sometimes as a result of the incorrect dating of variables; and
- independent variables that are measured with error.

■ Probit and logit models estimate the probability of a discrete outcome (the value of a qualitative dependent variable, such as whether a company enters bankruptcy) given the values of the independent variables used to explain that outcome. The probit model, which is based on the normal distribution, estimates the probability that $Y = 1$ (a condition is fulfilled) given the values of the independent variables. The logit model is identical, except that it is based on the logistic distribution rather than the normal distribution.

PRACTICE PROBLEMS FOR READING 12

1. With many U.S. companies operating globally, the effect of the U.S. dollar's strength on a U.S. company's returns has become an important investment issue. You would like to determine whether changes in the U.S. dollar's value and overall U.S. equity market returns affect an asset's returns. You decide to use the S&P 500 Index to represent the U.S. equity market.

   A. Write a multiple regression equation to test whether changes in the value of the dollar and equity market returns affect an asset's returns. Use the notations below.

   R_{it} = return on the asset in period t
   R_{Mt} = return on the S&P 500 in period t
   ΔX_t = change in period t in the log of a trade-weighted index of the foreign exchange value of U.S. dollar against the currencies of a broad group of major U.S. trading partners.

   B. You estimate the regression for Archer Daniels Midland Company (NYSE: ADM). You regress its monthly returns for the period January 1990 to December 2002 on S&P 500 Index returns and changes in the log of the trade-weighted exchange value of the U.S. dollar. The table below shows the coefficient estimates and their standard errors.

   Coefficient Estimates from Regressing ADM's Returns: Monthly Data, January 1990–December 2002

	Coefficient	Standard Error
Intercept	0.0045	0.0062
R_{Mt}	0.5373	0.1332
ΔX_t	−0.5768	0.5121
n = 156		

   Source: FactSet, Federal Reserve Bank of Philadelphia.

   Determine whether S&P 500 returns affect ADM's returns. Then determine whether changes in the value of the U.S. dollar affect ADM's returns. Use a 0.05 significance level to make your decisions.

   C. Based on the estimated coefficient on R_{Mt}, is it correct to say that "for a 1 percentage point increase in the return on the S&P 500 in period t, we expect a 0.5373 percentage point increase in the return on ADM"?

2. One of the most important questions in financial economics is what factors determine the cross-sectional variation in an asset's returns. Some have argued that book-to-market ratio and size (market value of equity) play an important role.

   A. Write a multiple regression equation to test whether book-to-market ratio and size explain the cross-section of asset returns. Use the notations below.

Practice Problems and Solutions: 1–16 taken from *Quantitative Methods for Investment Analysis*, Second Edition, by Richard A. DeFusco, CFA, Dennis W. McLeavey, CFA, Jerald E. Pinto, CFA, and David E. Runkle, CFA. Copyright © 2004 by CFA Institute. All other problems and solutions copyright © CFA Institute.

$$(B/M)_i = \text{book-to-market ratio for asset } i$$

$$R_i = \text{return on asset } i \text{ in a particular month}$$

$$Size_i = \text{natural log of the market value of equity for asset } i$$

B. The table below shows the results of the linear regression for a cross-section of 66 companies. The size and book-to-market data for each company are for December 2001. The return data for each company are for January 2002.

	Results from Regressing Returns on the Book-to-Market Ratio and Size	
	Coefficient	**Standard Error**
Intercept	0.0825	0.1644
$(B/M)_i$	−0.0541	0.0588
$Size_i$	−0.0164	0.0350
$n = 66$		

Source: FactSet.

Determine whether the book-to-market ratio and size are each useful for explaining the cross-section of asset returns. Use a 0.05 significance level to make your decision.

3. There is substantial cross-sectional variation in the number of financial analysts who follow a company. Suppose you hypothesize that a company's size (market cap) and financial risk (debt-to-equity ratios) influence the number of financial analysts who follow a company. You formulate the following regression model:

$$(\text{Analyst following})_i = b_0 + b_1 Size_i + b_2 (D/E)_i + \varepsilon_i$$

where

$$(\text{Analyst following})_i = \text{the natural log of } (1 + n), \text{ where } n_i \text{ is the}$$
$$\text{number of analysts following company}_i$$
$$Size_i = \text{the natural log of the market capitalization of}$$
$$\text{company } i \text{ in millions of dollars}$$
$$(D/E)_i = \text{the debt-to-equity ratio for company}_i$$

In the definition of Analyst following, 1 is added to the number of analysts following a company because some companies are not followed by any analysts, and the natural log of 0 is indeterminate. The following table gives the coefficient estimates of the above regression model for a randomly selected sample of 500 companies. The data are for the year 2002.

	Coefficient	Standard Error	t-Statistic
Coefficient Estimates from Regressing Analyst Following on Size and Debt-to-Equity Ratio			
Intercept	−0.2845	0.1080	−2.6343
$Size_i$	0.3199	0.0152	21.0461
$(D/E)_i$	−0.1895	0.0620	−3.0565
$n = 500$			

Source: First Call/Thomson Financial, Compustat.

A. Consider two companies, both of which have a debt-to-equity ratio of 0.75. The first company has a market capitalization of $100 million, and the second company has a market capitalization of $1 billion. Based on the above estimates, how many more analysts will follow the second company than the first company?

B. Suppose the *p*-value reported for the estimated coefficient on $(D/E)_i$ is 0.00236. State the interpretation of 0.00236.

4. In early 2001, U.S. equity marketplaces started trading all listed shares in minimal increments (ticks) of $0.01 (decimalization). After decimalization, bid–ask spreads of stocks traded on the NASDAQ tended to decline. In response, spreads of NASDAQ stocks cross-listed on the Toronto Stock Exchange (TSE) tended to decline as well. Researchers Oppenheimer and Sabherwal (2003) hypothesized that the percentage decline in TSE spreads of cross-listed stocks was related to company size, the predecimalization ratio of spreads on NASDAQ to those on the TSE, and the percentage decline in NASDAQ spreads. The following table gives the regression coefficient estimates from estimating that relationship for a sample of 74 companies. Company size is measured by the natural logarithm of the book value of company's assets in thousands of Canadian dollars.

	Coefficient	t-Statistic
Coefficient Estimates from Regressing Percentage Decline in TSE Spreads on Company Size, Predecimalization Ratio of NASDAQ to TSE Spreads, and Percentage Decline in NASDAQ Spreads		
Intercept	−0.45	−1.86
$Size_i$	0.05	2.56
$(Ratio\ of\ spreads)_i$	−0.06	−3.77
$(Decline\ in\ NASDAQ\ spreads)_i$	0.29	2.42
$n = 74$		

Source: Oppenheimer and Sabherwal (2003).

The average company in the sample has a book value of assets of C$900 million and a predecimalization ratio of spreads equal to 1.3. Based on the above model, what is the predicted decline in spread on the TSE for a company with these average characteristics, given a 1 percent decline in NASDAQ spreads?

5. The "neglected-company effect" claims that companies that are followed by fewer analysts will earn higher returns on average than companies that are followed by many analysts. To test the neglected-company effect, you have collected data on 66 companies and the number of analysts providing earnings estimates for each company. You decide to also include size as an independent variable, measuring size as the log of the market value of the company's equity, to try to distinguish any small-company effect from a neglected-company effect. The small-company effect asserts that small-company stocks may earn average higher risk-adjusted returns than large-company stocks.

The table below shows the results from estimating the model $R_i = b_0 + b_1 \text{Size}_i + b_2(\text{Number of analysts})_i + \varepsilon_i$ for a cross-section of 66 companies. The size and number of analysts for each company are for December 2001. The return data are for January 2002.

Results from Regressing Returns on Size and Number of Analysts

	Coefficient	Standard Error	t-Statistic
Intercept	0.0388	0.1556	0.2495
Size_i	−0.0153	0.0348	−0.4388
$(\text{Number of analysts})_i$	0.0014	0.0015	0.8995

ANOVA	df	SS	MSS
Regression	2	0.0094	0.0047
Residual	63	0.6739	0.0107
Total	65	0.6833	
Residual standard error	0.1034		
R-squared	0.0138		
Observations	66		

Source: First Call/Thomson Financial, FactSet.

A. What test would you conduct to see whether the two independent variables are *jointly* statistically related to returns (H_0: $b_1 = b_2 = 0$)?

B. What information do you need to conduct the appropriate test?

C. Determine whether the two variables jointly are statistically related to returns at the 0.05 significance level.

D. Explain the meaning of adjusted R^2 and state whether adjusted R^2 for the regression would be smaller than, equal to, or larger than 0.0138.

6. Some developing nations are hesitant to open their equity markets to foreign investment because they fear that rapid inflows and outflows of foreign funds will increase volatility. In July 1993, India implemented substantial equity market reforms, one of which allowed foreign institutional investors into the Indian equity markets. You want to test whether the volatility of returns of stocks traded on the Bombay Stock Exchange (BSE) increased after July 1993, when foreign institutional investors were first allowed to invest in India. You have collected monthly return data for the BSE from February 1990 to December 1997. Your dependent variable is a measure of return volatility

of stocks traded on the BSE; your independent variable is a dummy variable
that is coded 1 if foreign investment was allowed during the month and 0
otherwise.

You believe that market return volatility actually *decreases* with the opening up
of equity markets. The table below shows the results from your regression.

	Results from Dummy Regression for Foreign Investment in India with a Volatility Measure as the Dependent Variable		
	Coefficient	**Standard Error**	***t*-Statistic**
Intercept	0.0133	0.0020	6.5351
Dummy	−0.0075	0.0027	−2.7604
$n = 95$			

Source: FactSet.

A. State null and alternative hypotheses for the slope coefficient of the
dummy variable that are consistent with testing your stated belief about
the effect of opening the equity markets on stock return volatility.

 **B.** Determine whether you can reject the null hypothesis at the 0.05
significance level (in a one-sided test of significance).

C. According to the estimated regression equation, what is the level of return
volatility before and after the market-opening event?

7. Both researchers and the popular press have discussed the question as to
which of the two leading U.S. political parties, Republicans or Democrats, is
better for the stock market.

A. Write a regression equation to test whether overall market returns, as
measured by the annual returns on the S&P 500 Index, tend to be higher
when the Republicans or the Democrats control the White House. Use the
notations below.

R_{Mt} = return on the S&P 500 in period t

$Party_i$ = the political party controlling the White House (1 for a
Republican president; 0 for a Democratic president) in period t

B. The table below shows the results of the linear regression from Part A
using annual data for the S&P 500 and a dummy variable for the party that
controlled the White House. The data are from 1926 to 2002.

	Results from Regressing S&P 500 Returns on a Dummy Variable for the Party That Controlled the White House, 1926–2002		
	Coefficient	**Standard Error**	***t*-Statistic**
Intercept	0.1494	0.0323	4.6270
$Party_t$	−0.0570	0.0466	−1.2242

(continued)

p.845 ?

	Continued				
ANOVA	df	SS	MSS	F	Significance F
Regression	1	0.0625	0.0625	1.4987	0.2247
Residual	75	3.1287	0.0417		
Total	76	3.1912			
Residual standard error		0.2042			
R-squared		0.0196			
Observations		77			

Source: FactSet.

Based on the coefficient and standard error estimates, verify to two decimal places the t-statistic for the coefficient on the dummy variable reported in the table.

C. Determine at the 0.05 significance level whether overall U.S. equity market returns tend to differ depending on the political party controlling the White House.

8. Problem 3 addressed the cross-sectional variation in the number of financial analysts who follow a company. In that problem, company size and debt-to-equity ratios were the independent variables. You receive a suggestion that membership in the S&P 500 Index should be added to the model as a third independent variable; the hypothesis is that there is greater demand for analyst coverage for stocks included in the S&P 500 because of the widespread use of the S&P 500 as a benchmark.

A. Write a multiple regression equation to test whether analyst following is systematically higher for companies included in the S&P 500 Index. Also include company size and debt-to-equity ratio in this equation. Use the notations below.

$$(\text{Analyst following})_i = \text{natural log of } (1 + \text{Number of analysts following company } i)$$
$$\text{Size}_i = \text{natural log of the market capitalization of company } i \text{ in millions of dollars}$$
$$(\text{D/E})_i = \text{debt-to-equity ratio for company } i$$
$$\text{S\&P}_i = \text{inclusion of company } i \text{ in the S\&P 500 Index (1 if included, 0 if not included)}$$

In the above specification for analyst following, 1 is added to the number of analysts following a company because some companies are not followed by any analyst, and the natural log of 0 is indeterminate.

B. State the appropriate null hypothesis and alternative hypothesis in a two-sided test of significance of the dummy variable.

C. The following table gives estimates of the coefficients of the above regression model for a randomly selected sample of 500 companies. The data are for the year 2002. Determine whether you can reject the null hypothesis at the 0.05 significance level (in a two-sided test of significance).

	Coefficient	Standard Error	*t*-Statistic
Coefficient Estimates from Regressing Analyst Following on Size, Debt-to-Equity Ratio, and S&P 500 Membership, 2002			
Intercept	−0.0075	0.1218	−0.0616
$Size_i$	0.2648	0.0191	13.8639
$(D/E)_i$	−0.1829	0.0608	−3.0082
$S\&P_i$	0.4218	0.0919	4.5898
$n = 500$			

Source: First Call/Thomson Financial, Compustat.

D. Consider a company with a debt-to-equity ratio of 2/3 and a market capitalization of $10 billion. According to the estimated regression equation, how many analysts would follow this company if it were not included in the S&P 500 Index, and how many would follow if it were included in the index?

E. In Problem 3, using the sample, we estimated the coefficient on the size variable as 0.3199, versus 0.2648 in the above regression. Discuss whether there is an inconsistency in these results.

9. You believe there is a relationship between book-to-market ratios and subsequent returns. The output from a cross-sectional regression and a graph of the actual and predicted relationship between the book-to-market ratio and return are shown below.

Results from Regressing Returns on the Book-to-Market Ratio

	Coefficient	Standard Error	*t*-Statistic
Intercept	12.0130	3.5464	3.3874
$\left(\dfrac{\text{Book value}}{\text{Market value}}\right)_i$	−9.2209	8.4454	−1.0918

ANOVA	df	SS	MSS	F	Significance F
Regression	1	154.9866	154.9866	1.1921	0.2831
Residual	32	4162.1895	130.0684		
Total	33	4317.1761			
Residual standard error		11.4048			
R-squared		0.0359			
Observations		34			

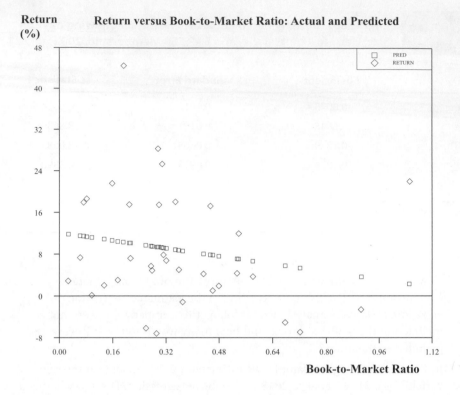

Return versus Book-to-Market Ratio: Actual and Predicted

A. You are concerned with model specification problems and regression assumption violations. Focusing on assumption violations, discuss symptoms of conditional heteroskedasticity based on the graph of the actual and predicted relationship.

B. Describe in detail how you could formally test for conditional heteroskedasticity in this regression.

C. Describe a recommended method for correcting for conditional heteroskedasticity.

P. 349

10. You are examining the effects of the January 2001 NYSE implementation of the trading of shares in minimal increments (ticks) of $0.01 (decimalization). In particular, you are analyzing a sample of 52 Canadian companies cross-listed on both the NYSE and the Toronto Stock Exchange (TSE). You find that the bid–ask spreads of these shares decline on both exchanges after the NYSE decimalization. You run a linear regression analyzing the decline in spreads on the TSE, and find that the decline on the TSE is related to company size, predecimalization ratio of NYSE to TSE spreads, and decline in the NYSE spreads. The relationships are statistically significant. You want to be sure, however, that the results are not influenced by conditional heteroskedasticity. Therefore, you regress the squared residuals of the regression model on the three independent variables. The R^2 for this regression is 14.1 percent. Perform a statistical test to determine if conditional heteroskedasticity is present.

11. You are analyzing if institutional investors such as mutual funds and pension funds prefer to hold shares of companies with less volatile returns. You have the percentage of shares held by institutional investors at the end of 1998 for a random sample of 750 companies. For these companies, you compute the standard deviation of daily returns during that year. Then you regress the institutional holdings on the standard deviation of returns. You find that the regression is significant at the 0.01 level and the F-statistic is 12.98. The R^2 for this regression is 1.7 percent. As expected, the regression coefficient of the standard deviation of returns is negative. Its t-statistic is -3.60, which is also significant at the 0.01 level. Before concluding that institutions prefer to hold shares of less volatile stocks, however, you want to be sure that the regression results are not influenced by conditional heteroskedasticity. Therefore, you regress the squared residuals of the regression model on the standard deviation of returns. The $R2$ for this regression is 0.6 percent.

A. Perform a statistical test to determine if conditional heteroskedasticity is present.

B. In view of your answer to Part A, what remedial action, if any, is appropriate?

12. In estimating a regression based on monthly observations from January 1987 to December 2002 inclusive, you find that the coefficient on the independent variable is positive and significant at the 0.05 level. You are concerned, however, that the t-statistic on the independent variable may be inflated because of serial correlation between the error terms. Therefore, you examine the Durbin–Watson statistic, which is 1.8953 for this regression.

A. Based on the value of the Durbin–Watson statistic, what can you say about the serial correlation between the regression residuals? Are they positively correlated, negatively correlated, or not correlated at all?

B. Compute the sample correlation between the regression residuals from one period and those from the previous period.

C. Perform a statistical test to determine if serial correlation is present. Assume that the critical values for 192 observations when there is a single independent variable are about 0.09 above the critical values for 100 observations.

13. The book-to-market ratio and the size of a company's equity are two factors that have been asserted to be useful in explaining the cross-sectional variation in subsequent returns. Based on this assertion, you want to estimate the following regression model:

$$R_i = b_0 + b_1\left(\frac{\text{Book}}{\text{Market}}\right)_i + b_2\text{Size}_i + \varepsilon_i$$

where

R_i = Return of Company i's shares (in the following period)

$\left(\frac{\text{Book}}{\text{Market}}\right)_i$ = Company i's book-to-market ratio

Size_i = Market value of Company i's equity

A colleague suggests that this regression specification may be erroneous, because he believes that the book-to-market ratio may be strongly related to (correlated with) company size.

A. To what problem is your colleague referring, and what are its consequences for regression analysis?

B. With respect to multicollinearity, critique the choice of variables in the regression model above.

Regression of Return on Book-to-Market and Size			
	Coefficient	**Standard Error**	**t-Statistic**
Intercept	14.1062	4.220	3.3427
$\left(\dfrac{\text{Book}}{\text{Market}}\right)_i$	–12.1413	9.0406	–1.3430
Size_i	–0.00005502	0.00005977	–0.92047
R-squared	0.06156		
Observations	34		

Correlation Matrix		
	Book-to-Market Ratio	**Size**
Book-to-Market Ratio	1.0000	
Size	–0.3509	1.0000

C. State the classic symptom of multicollinearity and comment on that basis whether multicollinearity appears to be present, given the additional fact that the F-test for the above regression is not significant.

14. You are analyzing the variables that explain the returns on the stock of the Boeing Company. Because overall market returns are likely to explain a part of the returns on Boeing, you decide to include the returns on a value-weighted index of all the companies listed on the NYSE, AMEX, and NASDAQ as an independent variable. Further, because Boeing is a large company, you also decide to include the returns on the S&P 500 Index, which is a value-weighted index of the larger market-capitalization companies. Finally, you decide to include the changes in the U.S. dollar's value. To conduct your test, you have collected the following data for the period 1990–2002.

R_t = monthly return on the stock of Boeing in month t

R_{ALLt} = monthly return on a value-weighted index of all the companies listed on the NYSE, AMEX, and NASDAQ in month t

R_{SPt} = monthly return on the S&P 500 Index in month t

ΔX_t = change in month t in the log of a trade-weighted index of the foreign exchange value of the U.S. dollar against the currencies of a broad group of major U.S. trading partners

The following table shows the output from regressing the monthly return on Boeing stock on the three independent variables.

Regression of Boeing Returns on Three Explanatory Variables: Monthly Data, January 1990–December 2002

	Coefficient	Standard Error	t-Statistic
Intercept	0.0026	0.0066	0.3939
R_{ALLt}	−0.1337	0.6219	−0.2150
R_{SPt}	0.8875	0.6357	1.3961
ΔX_t	0.2005	0.5399	0.3714

ANOVA	df	SS	MSS
Regression	3	0.1720	0.0573
Residual	152	0.8947	0.0059
Total	155	1.0667	

Residual standard error	0.0767
R-squared	0.1610
Observations	156

Source: FactSet, Federal Reserve Bank of Philadelphia.

From the t-statistics, we see that none of the explanatory variables is statistically significant at the 5 percent level or better. You wish to test, however, if the three variables *jointly* are statistically related to the returns on Boeing.

A. Your null hypothesis is that all three population slope coefficients equal 0—that the three variables *jointly* are statistically not related to the returns on Boeing. Conduct the appropriate test of that hypothesis.

B. Examining the regression results, state the regression assumption that may be violated in this example. Explain your answer.

C. State a possible way to remedy the violation of the regression assumption identified in Part B.

15. You are analyzing the cross-sectional variation in the number of financial analysts that follow a company (also the subject of Problems 3 and 8). You believe that there is less analyst following for companies with a greater debt-to-equity ratio and greater analyst following for companies included in the S&P 500 Index. Consistent with these beliefs, you estimate the following regression model.

$$(\text{Analyst following})_i = b_0 + b_1 (\text{D/E})_i + b_2 (\text{S\&P})_i + \varepsilon_i$$

where

$(\text{Analysts following})_i$ = natural log of $(1 + \text{Number of analysts following company } i)$

$(\text{D/E})_i$ = debt − to − equity ratio for company i

$\text{S\&P}_i$ = inclusion of company i in the S&P 500 Index $(1$ if included; 0 if not included$)$

In the preceding specification, 1 is added to the number of analysts following a company because some companies are not followed by any analysts, and the natural log of 0 is indeterminate. The following table gives the coefficient estimates of the above regression model for a randomly selected sample of 500 companies. The data are for the year 2002.

	Coefficient Estimates from Regressing Analyst Following on Debt-to-Equity Ratio and S&P 500 Membership, 2002		
	Coefficient	Standard Error	t-Statistic
Intercept	1.5367	0.0582	26.4038
$(D/E)_i$	−0.1043	0.0712	−1.4649
$S\&P_i$	1.2222	0.0841	14.5327
$n = 500$			

Source: First Call/Thomson Financial, Compustat.

You discuss your results with a colleague. She suggests that this regression specification may be erroneous, because analyst following is likely to be also related to the size of the company.

A. What is this problem called, and what are its consequences for regression analysis?

B. To investigate the issue raised by your colleague, you decide to collect data on company size also. You then estimate the model after including an additional variable, Size i, which is the natural log of the market capitalization of company i in millions of dollars. The following table gives the new coefficient estimates.

	Coefficient Estimates from Regressing Analyst Following on Size, Debt-to-Equity Ratio, and S&P 500 Membership, 2002		
	Coefficient	Standard Error	t-Statistic
Intercept	−0.0075	0.1218	−0.0616
$Size_i$	0.2648	0.0191	13.8639
$(D/E)_i$	−0.1829	0.0608	−3.0082
$S\&P_i$	0.4218	0.0919	4.5898
$n = 500$			

Source: First Call/Thomson Financial, Compustat.

What do you conclude about the existence of the problem mentioned by your colleague in the original regression model you had estimated?

16. You have noticed that hundreds of non-U.S. companies are listed not only on a stock exchange in their home market but also on one of the exchanges in the United States. You have also noticed that hundreds of non-U.S. companies are listed only in their home market and not in the United States. You are trying to predict whether or not a non-U.S. company will choose to list on a U.S. exchange. One of the factors that you think will affect whether or not a company lists in the United States is its size relative to the size of other companies in its home market.

    A. What kind of a dependent variable do you need to use in the model?

    B. What kind of a model should be used?

The following information relates to Questions 17–22

Gary Hansen is a securities analyst for a mutual fund specializing in small-capitalization growth stocks. The fund regularly invests in initial public offerings (IPOs). If the fund subscribes to an offer, it is allocated shares at the offer price. Hansen notes that IPOs frequently are underpriced, and the price rises when open market trading begins. The initial return for an IPO is calculated as the change in price on the first day of trading divided by the offer price. Hansen is developing a regression model to predict the initial return for IPOs. Based on past research, he selects the following independent variables to predict IPO initial returns:

Underwriter rank	=	1–10, where 10 is highest rank
Pre-offer price adjustment[a]	=	(Offer price – Initial filing price)/Initial filing price
Offer size ($ millions)	=	Shares sold × Offer price
Fraction retained[a]	=	Fraction of total company shares retained by insiders

[a]Expressed as a decimal

    Hansen collects a sample of 1,725 recent IPOs for his regression model. Regression results appear in Exhibit 1, and ANOVA results appear in Exhibit 2.

Exhibit 1	Hansen's Regression Results Dependent Variable: IPO Initial Return (Expressed in Decimal Form, i.e., 1% = 0.01)

Variable	Coefficient (b_j)	Standard Error	t-Statistic
Intercept	0.0477	0.0019	25.11
Underwriter rank	0.0150	0.0049	3.06
Pre-offer price adjustment	0.4350	0.0202	21.53
Offer size	−0.0009	0.0011	−0.82
Fraction retained	0.0500	0.0260	1.92

Exhibit 2	Selected ANOVA Results for Hansen's Regression

	Degrees of Freedom (df)	Sum of Squares (SS)
Regression	4	51.433
Residual	1,720	91.436
Total	1,724	142.869
	Multiple R-squared = 0.36	

    Hansen wants to use the regression results to predict the initial return for an upcoming IPO. The upcoming IPO has the following characteristics:

- underwriter rank = 6;
- pre-offer price adjustment = 0.04;
- offer size = $40 million;
- fraction retained = 0.70.

Because he notes that the pre-offer price adjustment appears to have an important effect on initial return, Hansen wants to construct a 95 percent confidence interval for the coefficient on this variable. He also believes that for each 1 percent increase in pre-offer price adjustment, the initial return will increase by less than 0.5 percent, holding other variables constant. Hansen wishes to test this hypothesis at the 0.05 level of significance.

Before applying his model, Hansen asks a colleague, Phil Chang, to review its specification and results. After examining the model, Chang concludes that the model suffers from two problems: 1) conditional heteroskedasticity, and 2) omitted variable bias. Chang makes the following statements:

Statement 1   "Conditional heteroskedasticity will result in consistent coefficient estimates, but both the t-statistics and F-statistic will be biased, resulting in false inferences."

Statement 2   "If an omitted variable is correlated with variables already included in the model, coefficient estimates will be biased and inconsistent and standard errors will also be inconsistent."

Selected values for the t-distribution and F-distribution appear in Exhibits 3 and 4, respectively.

Exhibit 3	Selected Values for the t-Distribution (df = ∞)
Area in Right Tail	***t*-Value**
0.050	1.645
0.025	1.960
0.010	2.326
0.005	2.576

Exhibit 4	Selected Values for the F-Distribution (α = 0.01) (df1/df2: Numerator/ Denominator Degrees of Freedom)

		df1	
		4	∞
	4	16.00	13.50
df2	∞	3.32	1.00

17. Based on Hansen's regression, the predicted initial return for the upcoming IPO is *closest* to:

    A. 0.0943.

    B. 0.1064.

    C. 0.1541.

18. The 95 percent confidence interval for the regression coefficient for the pre-offer price adjustment is *closest* to:

    A. 0.156 to 0.714.

    B. 0.395 to 0.475.

    C. 0.402 to 0.468.

19. The *most* appropriate null hypothesis and the *most* appropriate conclusion regarding Hansen's belief about the magnitude of the initial return relative to that of the pre-offer price adjustment (reflected by the coefficient b_j) are:

	Null Hypothesis	Conclusion about b_j (0.05 Level of Significance)
A.	$H_0: b_j = 0.5$	Reject H_0
B.	$H_0: b_j \geq 0.5$	Fail to reject H_0
C.	$H_0: b_j \geq 0.5$	Reject H_0

20. The *most* appropriate interpretation of the multiple R squared for Hansen's model is that:

   A. unexplained variation in the dependent variable is 36 percent of total variation.

   B. correlation between predicted and actual values of the dependent variable is 0.36.

   C. correlation between predicted and actual values of the dependent variable is 0.60.

21. Is Chang's Statement 1 correct?

   A. Yes.

   B. No, because the model's F-statistic will not be biased.

   C. No, because the model's t-statistics will not be biased.

22. Is Chang's Statement 2 correct?

   A. Yes.

   B. No, because the model's coefficient estimates will be unbiased.

   C. No, because the model's coefficient estimates will be consistent.

The following information relates to Questions 23–28

Adele Chiesa is a money manager for the Bianco Fund. She is interested in recent findings showing that certain business condition variables predict excess U.S. stock market returns (one-month market return minus one-month T-bill return). She is also familiar with evidence showing how U.S. stock market returns differ by the political party affiliation of the U.S. President. Chiesa estimates a multiple regression model to predict monthly excess stock market returns accounting for business conditions and the political party affiliation of the U.S. President:

Excess stock market return$_t$

$= a_0 + a_1 \text{Default spread}_{t-1} + a_2 \text{Term spread}_{t-1} + a_3 \text{Pres party dummy}_{t-1} + e_t$

Default spread is equal to the yield on Baa bonds minus the yield on Aaa bonds. Term spread is equal to the yield on a 10-year constant-maturity U.S. Treasury index minus the yield on a 1-year constant-maturity U.S. Treasury index. Pres party dummy is equal to 1 if the U.S. President is a member of the Democratic Party and 0 if a member of the Republican Party.

Chiesa collects 432 months of data (all data are in percent form, i.e., 0.01 = 1 percent). The regression is estimated with 431 observations because the independent variables are lagged one month. The regression output is in Exhibit 1. Exhibits 2 through 5 contain critical values for selected test statistics.

Exhibit 1	**Multiple Regression Output (the Dependent Variable Is the One-Month Market Return in Excess of the One-Month T-Bill Return)**		
	Coefficient	**t-Statistic**	**p-Value**
Intercept	−4.60	−4.36	<0.01
Default spread$_{t-1}$	3.04	4.52	<0.01
Term spread$_{t-1}$	0.84	3.41	<0.01
Pres party dummy$_{t-1}$	3.17	4.97	<0.01

Number of observations = 431

Test statistic from Breusch–Pagan (BP) test = 7.35

R^2 = 0.053

Adjusted R^2 = 0.046

Durbin–Watson (DW) = 1.65

Sum of squared errors (SSE) = 19,048

Regression sum of squares (SSR) = 1,071

An intern working for Chiesa has a number of questions about the results in Exhibit 1:

Question 1   How do you test to determine whether the overall regression model is significant?

Question 2   Does the estimated model conform to standard regression assumptions? For instance, is the error term serially correlated, or is there conditional heteroskedasticity?

Question 3   How do you interpret the coefficient for the Pres party dummy variable?

Question 4   Default spread appears to be quite important. Is there some way to assess the precision of its estimated coefficient? What is the economic interpretation of this variable?

After responding to her intern's questions, Chiesa concludes with the following statement: "Predictions from Exhibit 1 are subject to parameter estimate uncertainty, but not regression model uncertainty."

Exhibit 2	**Critical Values for the Durbin–Watson Statistic (α = 0.05)**	
	K = 3	
N	**d$_l$**	**d$_u$**
420	1.825	1.854
430	1.827	1.855
440	1.829	1.857

Exhibit 3	Table of the Student's t-Distribution (One-Tailed Probabilities for df = ∞)

P	t
0.10	1.282
0.05	1.645
0.025	1.960
0.01	2.326
0.005	2.576

Exhibit 4	Values of χ^2

	Probability in Right Tail			
df	0.975	0.95	0.05	0.025
1	0.0001	0.0039	3.841	5.024
2	0.0506	0.1026	5.991	7.378
3	0.2158	0.3518	7.815	9.348
4	0.4840	0.7110	9.488	11.14

Exhibit 5	Table of the F-Distribution (Critical Values for Right-Hand Tail Area Equal to 0.05) Numerator: df1 and Denominator: df2

	df1				
df2	1	2	3	4	427
1	161	200	216	225	254
2	18.51	19.00	19.16	19.25	19.49
3	10.13	9.55	9.28	9.12	8.53
4	7.71	6.94	6.59	6.39	5.64
427	3.86	3.02	2.63	2.39	1.17

23. Regarding the intern's Question 1, is the regression model as a whole significant at the 0.05 level?

    A. No, because the calculated F-statistic is less than the critical value for F.

    B. Yes, because the calculated F-statistic is greater than the critical value for F.

    C. Yes, because the calculated χ^2 statistic is greater than the critical value for χ^2.

24. Which of the following is Chiesa's *best* response to Question 2 regarding serial correlation in the error term? At a 0.05 level of significance, the test for serial correlation indicates that there is:

    A. no serial correlation in the error term.

    B. positive serial correlation in the error term.

    C. negative serial correlation in the error term.

25. Regarding Question 3, the Pres party dummy variable in the model indicates that the mean monthly value for the excess stock market return is:

   A. 1.43 percent larger during Democratic presidencies than Republican presidencies.

   B. 3.17 percent larger during Democratic presidencies than Republican presidencies.

   C. 3.17 percent larger during Republican presidencies than Democratic presidencies.

26. In response to Question 4, the 95 percent confidence interval for the regression coefficient for the default spread is *closest* to:

   A. 0.13 to 5.95.

   B. 1.72 to 4.36.

   C. 1.93 to 4.15.

27. With respect to the default spread, the estimated model indicates that when business conditions are:

   A. strong, expected excess returns will be higher.

   B. weak, expected excess returns will be lower.

   C. weak, expected excess returns will be higher.

28. Is Chiesa's concluding statement correct regarding parameter model uncertainty and regression model uncertainty?

   A. Yes.

   B. No, predictions are not subject to parameter estimate uncertainty.

   C. No, predictions are subject to regression model uncertainty and parameter model uncertainty.

SOLUTIONS FOR READING 12

1. A. $R_{it} = b_0 + b_1 R_{Mt} + b_2 \Delta X_t + \varepsilon_{it}$

  B. We can test whether the coefficient on the S&P 500 Index returns is statistically significant. Our null hypothesis is that the coefficient is equal to 0 ($H_0\!: b_1 = 0$); our alternative hypothesis is that the coefficient is not equal to 0 ($H_a\!: b_1 \neq 0$). We construct the t-test of the null hypothesis as follows:

$$\frac{\hat{b}_1 - b_1}{s_{\hat{b}_1}} = \frac{0.5373 - 0}{0.1332} = 4.0338$$

where

$\hat{b}_1$ = regression estimate of b_1

b_1 = the hypothesized value of the coefficient $(\text{here}, 0)$

$s_{\hat{b}_1}$ = the estimated standard error of $\hat{b}_1$

Because this regression has 156 observations and three regression coefficients, the t-test has $156 - 3 = 153$ degrees of freedom. At the 0.05 significance level, the critical value for the test statistic is between 1.98 and 1.97. The absolute value of the test statistic is 4.0338; therefore, we can reject the null hypothesis that $b_1 = 0$.

Similarly, we can test whether the coefficient on the change in the value of the U.S. dollar is statistically significant in this regression. Our null hypothesis is that the coefficient is equal to 0 ($H_0\!: b_2 = 0$); our alternative hypothesis is that the coefficient is not equal to 0 ($H_a\!: b_2 \neq 0$). We construct the t-test as follows:

$$\frac{\hat{b}_2 - b_2}{s_{\hat{b}_2}} = \frac{-0.5768 - 0}{0.5121} = -1.1263$$

As before, the t-test has 153 degrees of freedom, and the critical value for the test statistic is between 1.98 and 1.97 at the 0.05 significance level. The absolute value of the test statistic is 1.1263; therefore, we cannot reject the null hypothesis that $b_2 = 0$.

Based on the above t-tests, we conclude that S&P 500 Index returns do affect ADM's returns but that changes in the value of the U.S. dollar do not affect ADM's returns.

  C. The statement is not correct. To make it correct, we need to add the qualification "holding ΔX constant" to the end of the quoted statement.

2. A. $R_i = b_0 + b_1 (\text{B/M})_i + b_2 \text{Size}_i + \varepsilon_i$

  B. We can test whether the coefficients on the book-to-market ratio and size are individually statistically significant using t-tests. For the book-to-market ratio, our null hypothesis is that the coefficient is equal to 0 ($H_0\!:$ $b_1 = 0$); our alternative hypothesis is that the coefficient is not equal to 0 ($H_a\!: b_1 \neq 0$). We can test the null hypothesis using a t-test constructed as follows:

$$\frac{\hat{b}_1 - b_1}{s_{\hat{b}_1}} = \frac{-0.0541 - 0}{0.0588} = -0.9201$$

where

$\hat{b}_1$ = regression estimate of b_1

b_1 = the hypothesized value of the coefficient (here, 0)

$s_{\hat{b}_1}$ = the estimated standard error of $\hat{b}_1$

This regression has 66 observations and three coefficients, so the t-test has $66 - 3 = 63$ degrees of freedom. At the 0.05 significance level, the critical value for the test statistic is about 2.0. The absolute value of the test statistic is 0.9201; therefore, we cannot reject the null hypothesis that $b_1 = 0$. We can conclude that the book-to-market ratio is not useful in explaining the cross-sectional variation in returns for this sample.

We perform the same analysis to determine whether size (as measured by the log of the market value of equity) can help explain the cross-sectional variation in asset returns. Our null hypothesis is that the coefficient is equal to 0 (H_0: $b_2 = 0$); our alternative hypothesis is that the coefficient is not equal to 0 (H_a: $b_2 \neq 0$). We can test the null hypothesis using a t-test constructed as follows:

$$\frac{\hat{b}_2 - b_2}{s_{\hat{b}_2}} = \frac{-0.0164 - 0}{0.0350} = -0.4686$$

where

$\hat{b}_2$ = regression estimate of b_1

b_2 = the hypothesized value of the coefficient (here, 0)

$s_{\hat{b}_2}$ = the estimated standard error of $\hat{b}_2$

Again, because this regression has 66 observations and three coefficients, the t-test has $66 - 3 = 63$ degrees of freedom. At the 0.05 significance level, the critical value for the test statistic is about 2.0. The absolute value of the test statistic is 0.4686; therefore, we cannot reject the null hypothesis that $b_2 = 0$. We can conclude that asset size is not useful in explaining the cross-sectional variation of asset returns in this sample.

3. A. The estimated regression is (Analyst following)$_i$ = $-0.2845 + 0.3199$Size$_i -$ $0.1895(D/E)_i + \varepsilon_i$. Therefore, the prediction for the first company is

$$(\text{Analyst following})_i = -0.2845 + 0.3199(\ln 100) - 0.1895(0.75)$$
$$= -0.2845 + 1.4732 - 0.1421 = 1.0466$$

Recalling that (Analyst following)$_i$ is the natural log of $(1 + n_i)$, where n_i is the number of analysts following company i; it follows that $1 + n_1 = e^{1.0466} = 2.848$, approximately. Therefore, $n_1 = 2.848 - 1 = 1.848$, or about two analysts. Similarly, the prediction for the second company is as follows:

$$(\text{Analyst following})_i = -0.2845 + 0.3199(\ln 1{,}000) - 0.1895(0.75)$$
$$= -0.2845 + 2.2098 - 0.1421 = 1.7832$$
$$= 1.7832$$

Thus, $1 + n_2 = e^{1.7832} = 5.949$, approximately. Therefore, $n_2 = 5.949 - 1 = 4.949$, or about five analysts.

The model predicts that $5 - 2 = 3$ more analysts will follow the second company than the first company.

B. We would interpret the p-value of 0.00236 as the smallest level of significance at which we can reject a null hypothesis that the population value of the coefficient is 0, in a two-sided test. Clearly, in this regression the debt-to-equity ratio is a highly significant variable.

4. The estimated model is

Percentage decline in TSE spread of company i

$= -0.45 + 0.05 \, \text{Size}_i - 0.06(\text{Ratio of spreads})_i$

$+0.29(\text{Decline in NASDAQ spreads})_i$

Therefore, the prediction is

Percentage decline in TSE spread

$= -0.45 + 0.05(\ln 900{,}000) - 0.06(1.3) + 0.29(1)$

$= -0.45 + 0.69 - 0.08 + 0.29 = 0.45$

[handwritten: ← not –1 b/c defined in name "Decline" (?)]

The model predicts that for a company with average sample characteristics, the spread on the TSE declines by 0.45 percent for a 1 percent decline in NASDAQ spreads.

5. A. To test the null hypothesis that all the slope coefficients in the regression model are equal to 0 ($H_0: b_1 = b_2 = 0$) against the alternative hypothesis that at least one slope coefficient is not equal to 0, we must use an F-test.

B. To conduct the F-test, we need four inputs, all of which are found in the ANOVA section of the table in the statement of the problem:

i. total number of observations, n

ii. total number of regression coefficients to be estimated, $k + 1$

iii. sum of squared errors or residuals, $\sum_{i=1}^{n}(Y_i - \hat{Y}_i)^2$ abbreviated SSE, and

iv. regression sum of squares, $\sum_{i=1}^{n}(\hat{Y}_i - \bar{Y})^2$ abbreviated RSS

C. The F-test formula is

$$F = \frac{\text{RSS}/k}{\text{SSE}/[n - (k + 1)]} = \frac{0.0094/2}{0.6739/[66 - (2 + 1)]} = 0.4394$$

The F-statistic has degrees of freedom $F\{k, [n - (k + 1)]\} = F(2, 63)$. From the F-test table, for the 0.05 significance level, the critical value for $F(2, 63)$ is about 3.15, so we cannot reject the hypothesis that the slope coefficients are both 0. The two independent variables are jointly statistically unrelated to returns.

D. Adjusted R^2 is a measure of goodness of fit that takes into account the number of independent variables in the regression, in contrast to R^2. We can assert that adjusted R^2 is smaller than $R^2 = 0.0138$ without the need to perform any calculations. (However, adjusted R^2 can be shown to equal -0.0175 using an expression in the text on the relationship between adjusted R^2 and R^2.)

6. A. You believe that opening markets actually reduces return volatility; if that belief is correct, then the slope coefficient would be negative, $b_1 < 0$. The null hypothesis is that the belief is not true: $H_0: b_1 \geq 0$. The alternative hypothesis is that the belief is true: $H_a: b_1 < 0$.

B. The critical value for the t-statistic with $95 - 2 = 93$ degrees of freedom at the 0.05 significance level in a one-sided test is about 1.66. For the one-sided test stated in Part A, we reject the null hypothesis if the t-statistic on the slope coefficient is less than -1.66. As the t-statistic of $-2.7604 < -1.66$, we reject the null. Because the dummy variable takes on a value of 1 when foreign investment is allowed, we can conclude that the volatility was lower with foreign investment.

C. According to the estimated regression, average return volatility was 0.0133 (the estimated value of the intercept) before July 1993 and 0.0058 (= 0.0133 − 0.0075) after July 1993.

7. **A.** The appropriate regression model is $R_{Mt} = b_0 + b_1\,\text{Party}_t + \varepsilon_t$.

B. The t-statistic reported in the table for the dummy variable tests whether the coefficient on Party_t is significantly different from 0. It is computed as follows:

$$\frac{\hat{b}_1 - b_1}{s_{\hat{b}_1}} = \frac{-0.0570 - 0}{0.0466} = -1.22$$

where

$\hat{b}_1$ = regression estimate of b_1

b_1 = the hypothesized value of the coefficient $\left(\text{here}, 0\right)$

$s_{\hat{b}_1}$ = the estimated standard error of $\hat{b}_1$

To two decimal places, this value is the same as the t-statistic reported in the table for the dummy variable, as expected. The problem specified two decimal places because the reported regression output reflects rounding; for this reason, we often cannot exactly reproduce reported t-statistics.

C. Because the regression has 77 observations and two coefficients, the t-test has $77 - 2 = 75$ degrees of freedom. At the 0.05 significance level, the critical value for the two-tailed test statistic is about 1.99. The absolute value of the test statistic is 1.2242; therefore, we do not reject the null hypothesis that $b_1 = 0$. We can conclude that the political party in the White House does not, on average, affect the annual returns of the overall market as measured by the S&P 500.

8. **A.** The regression model is as follows:

$$\left(\text{Analyst following}\right)_i = b_0 + b_1\text{Size}_i + b_2\left(\text{D/E}\right)_i + b_3\text{S\&P}_i + \varepsilon_i$$

where $\left(\text{Analyst following}\right)_i$ is the natural log of $(1 +$ number of analysts following company $i)$; Size_i is the natural log of the market capitalization of company i in millions of dollars; $\left(\text{D/E}\right)_i$ is the debt-to-equity ratio for company i, and $\text{S\&P}_i$ is a dummy variable with a value of 1 if the company i belongs to the S&P 500 Index and 0 otherwise.

B. The appropriate null and alternative hypotheses are $H_0: b_3 = 0$ and $H_a: b_3 \neq 0$, respectively.

C. The t-statistic to test the null hypothesis can be computed as follows:

$$\frac{\hat{b}_3 - b_3}{s_{\hat{b}_3}} = \frac{0.4218 - 0}{0.0919} = 4.5898$$

This value is, of course, the same as the value reported in the table. The regression has 500 observations and 4 regression coefficients, so the t-test has $500 - 4 = 496$ degrees of freedom. At the 0.05 significance level, the critical value for the test statistic is between 1.96 and 1.97. Because the value of the test statistic is 4.5898 we can reject the null hypothesis that b_3 = 0. Thus a company's membership in the S&P 500 appears to significantly influence the number of analysts who cover that company.

D. The estimated model is

$$(\text{Analyst following})_i = -0.0075 + 0.2648\text{Size}_i - 0.1829(\text{D/E})_i$$
$$+ 0.4218\text{S\&P}_i + \varepsilon_i$$

Therefore the prediction for number of analysts following the indicated company that is not part of the S&P 500 Index is

$$(\text{Analyst following})_i = -0.0075 + 0.2648(\text{In } 10,000)$$
$$-0.1829(2/3) + 0.4218(0)$$
$$= -0.0075 + 2.4389 - 0.1219 + 0$$
$$= 2.3095$$

Recalling that $(\text{Analyst following})_i$ is the natural log of $(1 + n_i)$, where n_i is the number of analysts following company i; it ensues (coding the company under consideration as 1) that $1 + n_1 = e^{2.3095} = 10.069$, approximately. Therefore, the prediction is that $n_1 = 10.069 - 1 = 9.069$, or about nine analysts.

Similarly, the prediction for the company that is included in the S&P 500 Index is

$$(\text{Analyst following})_i = -0.0075 + 0.2648(\text{In } 10,000)$$
$$- 0.1829(2/3) + 0.4218(1)$$
$$= -0.0075 + 2.4389 - 0.1219 + 0.4218$$
$$= 2.7313$$

Coding the company that does belong to the S&P 500 as 2, $1 + n_2 = e^{2.7313} = 15.353$. Therefore, the prediction is that $n_2 = 15.353 - 1 = 14.353$, or about 14 analysts.

E. There is no inconsistency in the coefficient on the size variable differing between the two regressions. The regression coefficient on an independent variable in a multiple regression model measures the expected net effect on the expected value of the dependent variable for a one-unit increase in that independent variable, after accounting for any effects of the other independent variables on the expected value of the dependent variable. The earlier regression had one fewer independent variable; after the effect of S&P 500 membership on the expected value of the dependent variable is taken into account, it is to be expected that the effect of the size variable on the dependent variable will change. What the regressions appear to indicate is that the net effect of the size variable on the expected analyst following diminishes when S&P 500 membership is taken into account.

9. A. In a well-specified regression, the differences between the actual and predicted relationship should be random; the errors should not depend on the value of the independent variable. In this regression, the errors seem larger for smaller values of the book-to-market ratio. This finding indicates that we may have conditional heteroskedasticity in the errors, and consequently, the standard errors may be incorrect. We cannot proceed with hypothesis testing until we test for and, if necessary, correct for heteroskedasticity.

B. A test for heteroskedasticity is to regress the squared residuals from the estimated regression equation on the independent variables in the regression. As seen in Section 4.1.2, Breusch and Pagan showed that, under the null hypothesis of no conditional heteroskedasticity, $n \times R_2$ (from the regression of the squared residuals on the independent variables from the original regression) will be a χ^2 random variable, with the number of degrees of freedom equal to the number of independent variables in the regression.

C. One method to correct for heteroskedasticity is to use robust standard errors. This method uses the parameter estimates from the linear regression model but corrects the standard errors of the estimated parameters to account for the heteroskedasticity. Many statistical software packages can easily compute robust standard errors.

10. The test statistic is nR^2, where n is the number of observations and R^2 is the R^2 of the regression of squared residuals. So, the test statistic is $52 \times 0.141 = 7.332$. Under the null hypothesis of no conditional heteroskedasticity, this test statistic is a χ^2 random variable. There are three degrees of freedom, the number of independent variables in the regression. Appendix C, at the end of this volume, shows that for a one-tailed test, the test statistic critical value for a variable from a χ^2 distribution with 3 degrees of freedom at the 0.05 significance level is 7.815. The test statistic from the Breusch–Pagan test is 7.332. So, we cannot reject the hypothesis of no conditional heteroskedasticity at the 0.05 level. Therefore, we do not need to correct for conditional heteroskedasticity.

11. A. The test statistic is nR^2, where n is the number of observations and R^2 is the R^2 of the regression of squared residuals. So, the test statistic is $750 \times 0.006 = 4.5$. Under the null hypothesis of no conditional heteroskedasticity, this test statistic is a χ^2 random variable. Because the regression has only one independent variable, the number of degrees of freedom is equal to 1. Appendix C, at the end of this volume, shows that for a one-tailed test, the test statistic critical value for a variable from a χ^2 distribution with one degree of freedom at the 0.05 significance level is 3.841. The test statistic is 4.5. So, we can reject the hypothesis of no conditional heteroskedasticity at the 0.05 level. Therefore, we need to correct for conditional heteroskedasticity.

B. Two different methods can be used to correct for the effects of conditional heteroskedasticity in linear regression models. The first method involves computing robust standard errors. This method corrects the standard errors of the linear regression model's estimated parameters to account for the conditional heteroskedasticity. The second method is generalized least squares. This method modifies the original equation in an attempt to eliminate the heteroskedasticity. The new, modified regression equation is then estimated under the assumption that heteroskedasticity is no longer a problem.

Many statistical software packages can easily compute robust standard errors (the first method), and we recommend using them.

12. A. Because the value of the Durbin–Watson statistic is less than 2, we can say that the regression residuals are positively correlated. Because this statistic is fairly close to 2, however, we cannot say without a statistical test if the serial correlation is statistically significant.

B. From January 1987 through December 2002, there are 16 years, or $16 \times 12 = 192$ monthly returns. Thus the sample analyzed is quite large. Therefore, the Durbin–Watson statistic is approximately equal to $2(1 - r)$, where r is the sample correlation between the regression residuals from one period and those from the previous period.

$$DW = 1.8953 \approx 2(1 - r)$$

So, $r \approx 1 - DW/2 = 1 - 1.8953/2 = 0.0524$. Consistent with our answer to Part A, the correlation coefficient is positive.

C. Appendix E indicates that the critical values d_l and d_u for 100 observations when there is one independent variable are 1.65 and 1.69, respectively. Based on the information given in the problem, the critical values d_l and d_u for about 200 observations when there is one independent variable are about 1.74 and 1.78, respectively. Because the DW statistic of 1.8953 for our regression is above d_u, we fail to reject the null hypothesis of no positive serial correlation. Therefore, we conclude that there is no evidence of positive serial correlation for the error term.

13. A. This problem is known as multicollinearity. When some linear combinations of the independent variables in a regression model are highly correlated, the standard errors of the independent coefficient estimates become quite large, even though the regression equation may fit rather well.

B. The choice of independent variables presents multicollinearity concerns because market value of equity appears in both variables.

C. The classic symptom of multicollinearity is a high R^2 (and significant F-statistic) even though the t-statistics on the estimated slope coefficients are insignificant. Here a significant F-statistic does not accompany the insignificant t-statistics, so the classic symptom is not present.

14. A. To test the null hypothesis that all of the regression coefficients except for the intercept in the multiple regression model are equal to 0 (H_0: $b_1 = b_2 = b_3 = 0$) against the alternative hypothesis that at least one slope coefficient is not equal to 0, we must use an F-test.

$$F = \frac{RSS/k}{SSE/[n - (k + 1)]} = \frac{0.1720/3}{0.8947/[156 - (3 + 1)]} = 9.7403$$

The F-statistic has degrees of freedom $F\{k, [n - (k + 1)]\} = F(3, 152)$. From the F-test table, the critical value for $F(3, 120) = 2.68$ and $F(3, 152)$ will be less than $F(3, 120)$, so we can reject at the 0.05 significance level the null hypothesis that the slope coefficients are all 0. Changes in the three independent variables are jointly statistically related to returns.

[handwritten: F: $b_0 \neq b_1 \neq b_2 \neq 0$]

B. None of the t-statistics are significant, but the F-statistic is significant. This suggests the possibility of multicollinearity in the independent variables.

C. The apparent multicollinearity is very likely related to the inclusion of *both* the returns on the S&P 500 Index *and* the returns on a value-weighted index of all the companies listed on the NYSE, AMEX, and NASDAQ as independent variables. The value-weighting of the latter index, giving relatively high weights to larger companies such as those included in the S&P 500, may make one return series an approximate linear function of the other. By dropping one or the other of these two variables, we might expect to eliminate the multicollinearity.

15. A. Your colleague is indicating that you have omitted an important variable from the regression. This problem is called the omitted variable bias. If the omitted variable is correlated with an included variable, the estimated values of the regression coefficients would be biased and inconsistent.

Moreover, the estimates of standard errors of those coefficients would also be inconsistent. So, we cannot use either the coefficient estimates or the estimates of their standard errors to perform statistical tests.

B. A comparison of the new estimates with the original estimates clearly indicates that the original model suffered from the omitted variable bias due to the exclusion of company size from that model. As the t-statistics of the new model indicate, company size is statistically significant. Further, for the debt-to-equity ratio, the absolute value of the estimated coefficient substantially increases from 0.1043 to 0.1829, while its standard error declines. Consequently, it becomes significant in the new model, in contrast to the original model, in which it is not significant at the 5 percent level. The value of the estimated coefficient of the S&P 500 dummy substantially declines from 1.2222 to 0.4218. These changes imply that size should be included in the model.

16. **A.** You need to use a qualitative dependent variable. You could give a value of 1 to this dummy variable for a listing in the United States and a value of 0 for not listing in the United States.

B. Because you are using a qualitative dependent variable, linear regression is not the right technique to estimate the model. One possibility is to use either a probit or a logit model. Both models are identical, except that the logit model is based on logistic distribution while the probit model is based on normal distribution. Another possibility is to use discriminant analysis.

17. C is correct. The predicted initial return (IR) is:

$$IR = 0.0477 + (0.0150 \times 6) + (0.435 \times 0.04) - (0.0009 \times 40)$$
$$+ (0.05 \times 0.70) = 0.1541$$

18. B is correct. The 95% confidence interval is $0.435 \pm (0.0202 \times 1.96) = (0.395, 0.475)$.

19. C is correct. To test Hansen's belief about the direction and magnitude of the initial return, the test should be a one-tailed test. The alternative hypothesis is $H_1: b_j < 0.5$, and the null hypothesis is $H_0: b_j \geq 0.5$. The correct test statistic is: $t = (0.435 - 0.50)/0.0202 = -3.22$, and the critical value of the t-statistic for a one-tailed test at the 0.05 level is -1.645. The test statistic is significant, and the null hypothesis can be rejected at the 0.05 level of significance.

20. C is correct. The multiple R-squared for the regression is 0.36; thus, the model explains 36 percent of the variation in the dependent variable. The correlation between the predicted and actual values of the dependent variable is the square root of the R-squared or $\sqrt{0.36} = 0.60$

21. A is correct. Chang is correct because the presence of conditional heteroskedasticity results in consistent parameter estimates, but biased (up or down) standard errors, t-statistics, and F-statistics.

22. A is correct. Chang is correct because a correlated omitted variable will result in biased and inconsistent parameter estimates and inconsistent standard errors.

23. B is correct.

The F-test is used to determine if the regression model as a whole is significant.

$$F = \text{Mean square regression}(\text{MSR}) \div \text{Mean squared error}(\text{MSE})$$

$$\text{MSE} = \text{SSE}/\left[n - (k + 1)\right] = 19{,}048 \div 427 = 44.60$$

$$\text{MSR} = \text{SSR}/k = 1071 \div 3 = 357$$

$$F = 357 \div 44.60 = 8.004$$

The critical value for degrees of freedom of 3 and 427 with $\alpha = 0.05$ (one-tail) is $F = 2.63$ from Exhibit 5. The calculated F is greater than the critical value, and Chiesa should reject the null hypothesis that all regression coefficients are equal to zero.

24. B is correct. The Durbin–Watson test used to test for serial correlation in the error term, and its value reported in Exhibit 1 is 1.65. For no serial correlation, DW is approximately equal to 2. If DW $< d_l$ *the error terms are positively serially correlated.* Because the DW = 1.65 is less than $d_l = 1.827$ for $n = 431$ (see Exhibit 2), Chiesa should reject the null hypothesis of no serial correlation and conclude that there is evidence of positive serial correlation among the error terms.

25. B is correct. The coefficient for the Pres party dummy variable (3.17) represents the increment in the mean value of the dependent variable related to the Democratic Party holding the presidency. In this case, the excess stock market return is 3.17 percent greater in Democratic presidencies than in Republican presidencies.

26. B is correct. The confidence interval is computed as $a_1 \pm s(a_1) \times t(95\%, \infty)$. From Exhibit 1, $a_1 = 3.04$ and $t(a_1) = 4.52$, resulting in a standard error of $a_1 = s(a_1) = 3.04/4.52 = 0.673$. The critical value for t from Exhibit 3 is 1.96 for $p = 0.025$. The confidence interval for a_1 is $3.04 \pm 0.673 \times 1.96 = 3.04 \pm 1.31908$ or from 1.72092 to 4.35908.

27. C is correct. The default spread is typically larger when business conditions are poor, i.e., a greater probability of default by the borrower. The positive sign for default spread (see Exhibit 1) indicates that expected returns are positively related to default spreads, meaning that excess returns are greater when business conditions are poor.

28. C is correct. Predictions in a multiple regression model are subject to both parameter estimate uncertainty and regression model uncertainty.

Indices		World Percentage Change	2011
Japan (Nikkei)			
Seoul			
Johan. (Comp.)			-11.1%
Mumbai			-4.5%
Singapore	18,555.7		-4.7%
Sydney	2,971.0	1.1%	-4.7%
Shanghai B	4,644.0	0.8%	-10.5%
Hong Kong	316.8	0.7%	-6.9%
Toronto	22,700.9	0.5%	-4.2%
Stockholm	13,524.8	0.1%	4.1%
Mexico City			

13

Time-Series Analysis

by Richard A. DeFusco, CFA, Dennis W. McLeavey, CFA, Jerald E. Pinto, CFA, and David E. Runkle, CFA

LEARNING OUTCOMES

Mastery	The candidate should be able to:
☐	**a** calculate and evaluate the predicted trend value for a time series, modeled as either a linear trend or a log-linear trend, given the estimated trend coefficients;
☐	**b** describe factors that determine whether a linear or a log-linear trend should be used with a particular time series, and evaluate the limitations of trend models;
☐	**c** explain the requirement for a time series to be covariance stationary, and describe the significance of a series that is not stationary;
☐	**d** describe the structure of an autoregressive (AR) model of order p, and calculate one-and two-period ahead forecasts given the estimated coefficients;
☐	**e** explain how autocorrelations of the residuals can be used to test whether the autoregressive model fits the time series;
☐	**f** explain mean reversion, and calculate a mean-reverting level;
☐	**g** contrast in-sample and out-of-sample forecasts, and compare the forecasting accuracy of different time-series models based on the root mean squared error criterion;
☐	**h** explain the instability of coefficients of time-series models;
☐	**i** describe characteristics of random walk processes, and contrast them to covariance stationary processes;
☐	**j** describe implications of unit roots for time-series analysis, explain when unit roots are likely to occur and how to test for them, and demonstrate how a time series with a unit root can be transformed so it can be analyzed with an AR model;
☐	**k** describe the steps of the unit root test for nonstationarity, and explain the relation of the test to autoregressive time-series models;
☐	**l** explain how to test and correct for seasonality in a time-series model, and calculate and interpret a forecasted value using an AR model with a seasonal lag;

Quantitative Methods for Investment Analysis, Second Edition, by Richard A. DeFusco, CFA, Dennis W. McLeavey, CFA, Jerald E. Pinto, CFA, and David E. Runkle, CFA. Copyright © 2004 by CFA Institute.

Mastery	The candidate should be able to:
☐	**m** explain autoregressive conditional heteroskedasticity (ARCH), and describe how ARCH models can be applied to predict the variance of a time series;
☐	**n** explain how time-series variables should be analyzed for nonstationarity and/or cointegration before use in a linear regression;
☐	**o** determine the appropriate time-series model to analyze a given investment problem, and justify that choice.

1   INTRODUCTION TO TIME-SERIES ANALYSIS

As financial analysts, we often use time-series data to make investment decisions. A **time series** is a set of observations on a variable's outcomes in different time periods: the quarterly sales for a particular company during the past five years, for example, or the daily returns on a traded security. In this reading, we explore the two chief uses of time-series models: to explain the past and to predict the future of a time series. We also discuss how to estimate time-series models, and we examine how a model describing a particular time series can change over time. The following two examples illustrate the kinds of questions we might want to ask about time series.

Suppose it is the beginning of 2003 and we are managing a U.S.-based investment portfolio that includes Swiss stocks. Because the value of this portfolio would decrease if the Swiss franc depreciates with respect to the dollar, and vice-versa, holding all else constant, we are considering whether to hedge the portfolio's exposure to changes in the value of the franc. To help us in making this decision, we decide to model the time series of the franc/dollar exchange rate. Figure 1 shows monthly data on the franc/dollar exchange rate. (The data are monthly averages of daily exchange rates.) Has the exchange rate been more stable since 1987 than it was in previous years? Has the exchange rate shown a long-term trend? How can we best use past exchange rates to predict future exchange rates?

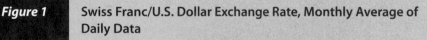

Figure 1	Swiss Franc/U.S. Dollar Exchange Rate, Monthly Average of Daily Data

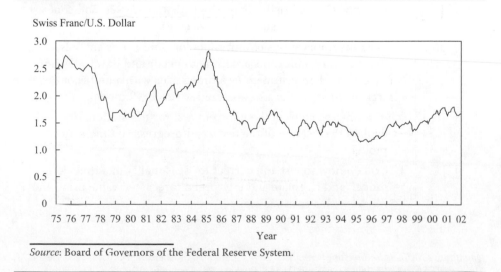

Source: Board of Governors of the Federal Reserve System.

As another example, suppose it is the beginning of 2001. We cover retail stores for a sell-side firm and want to predict retail sales for the coming year. Figure 2 shows monthly data on U.S. real retail sales. The data are inflation adjusted but not seasonally adjusted, hence the spikes around the holiday season at the turn of each year. Because the reported sales in the stores' financial statements are not seasonally adjusted, we model seasonally unadjusted retail sales. How can we model the trend in retail sales? How can we adjust for the extreme seasonality reflected in the peaks and troughs occurring at regular intervals? How can we best use past retail sales to predict future retail sales?

Figure 2	Monthly U.S. Real Retail Sales

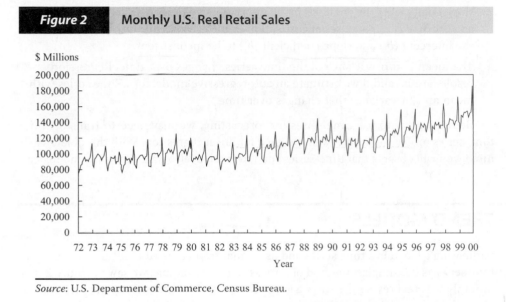

Source: U.S. Department of Commerce, Census Bureau.

Some fundamental questions arise in time-series analysis: How do we model trends? How do we predict the future value of a time series based on its past values? How do we model seasonality? How do we choose among time-series models? And how do we model changes in the variance of time series over time? We address each of these issues in this reading.

CHALLENGES OF WORKING WITH TIME SERIES

Throughout the reading, our objective will be to apply linear regression to a given time series. Unfortunately, in working with time series we often find that the assumptions of the linear regression model are not satisfied. To apply time-series analysis, we need to assure ourselves that the linear regression model assumptions are met. When those assumptions are not satisfied, in many cases we can transform the time series, or specify the regression model differently, so that the assumptions of the linear regression model are met.

We can illustrate assumption difficulties in the context of a common time-series model, an autoregressive model. Informally, an autoregressive model is one in which the independent variable is a lagged (that is, past) value of the dependent variable, such as the model $x_t = b_0 + b_1 x_{t-1} + \varepsilon_t$.[1] Specific problems that we often encounter in dealing with time series include the following:

---

[1] We could also write the equation as $y_t = b_0 + b_1 y_{t-1} + \varepsilon_t$.

- The residual errors are correlated instead of being uncorrelated. In the calculated regression, the difference between x_t and $b_0 + b_1 x_{t-1}$ is called the residual error. The linear regression assumes that this error term is not correlated across observations. The violation of that assumption is frequently more critical in terms of its consequences in the case of time-series models involving past values of the time series as independent variables than for other models (such as cross-sectional) in which the dependent and independent variables are distinct. As we discussed in the reading on multiple regression, in a regression in which the dependent and independent variables are distinct, serial correlation of the errors in this model does not affect the consistency of our estimates of intercept or slope coefficients. By contrast, in an autoregressive time-series regression such as $x_t = b_0 + b_1 x_{t-1} + \varepsilon_t$, serial correlation in the error term causes estimates of the intercept (b_0) and slope coefficient (b_1) to be inconsistent.

- The mean and/or variance of the time series changes over time. Regression results are invalid if we estimate an autoregressive model for a time series with mean and/or variance that changes over time.

Before we try to use time series for forecasting, we may need to transform the time-series model so that it is well specified for linear regression. With this objective in mind, you will observe that time-series analysis is relatively straightforward and logical.

3   TREND MODELS

Estimating a trend in a time series and using that trend to predict future values of the time series is the simplest method of forecasting. For example, we saw in Figure 2 that monthly U.S. real retail sales show a long-term pattern of upward movement—that is, a **trend**. In this section, we examine two types of trends—linear trends and log-linear trends—and discuss how to choose between them.

3.1 Linear Trend Models

The simplest type of trend is a **linear trend**, one in which the dependent variable changes at a constant rate with time. If a time series, y_t, has a linear trend, then we can model the series using the following regression equation:

$$y_t = b_0 + b_1 t + \varepsilon_t, \quad t = 1, 2, \ldots, T \tag{1}$$

where

y_t = the value of the time series at time t (value of the dependent variable)
b_0 = the y-intercept term
b_1 = the slope coefficient
t = time, the independent or explanatory variable
ε_t = a random-error term

In Equation 1, the trend line, $b_0 + b_1 t$, predicts the value of the time series at time t (where t takes on a value of 1 in the first period of the sample and increases by 1 in each subsequent period). Because the coefficient b_1 is the slope of the trend line, we refer to b_1 as the trend coefficient. We can estimate the two coefficients, b_0 and b_1, using ordinary least squares, denoting the estimated coefficients as $\hat{b}_0$ and $\hat{b}_1$.[2]

---

2 Recall that ordinary least squares is an estimation method based on the criterion of minimizing the sum of a regression's squared residuals.

Now we demonstrate how to use these estimates to predict the value of the time series in a particular period. Recall that t takes on a value of 1 in Period 1. Therefore, the predicted or fitted value of y_t in Period 1 is $\hat{y}_1 = \hat{b}_0 + \hat{b}_1(1)$. Similarly, in a subsequent period, say the sixth period, the fitted value is $\hat{y}_6 = \hat{b}_0 + \hat{b}_1(6)$. Now suppose that we want to predict the value of the time series for a period outside the sample, say period $T + 1$. The predicted value of y_t for period $T + 1$ is $\hat{y}_{T+1} = \hat{b}_0 + \hat{b}_1(T + 1)$. For example, if $\hat{b}_0$ is 5.1 and $\hat{b}_1$ is 2, then at $t = 5$ the predicted value of y_5 is 15.1 and at $t = 6$ the predicted value of y_6 is 17.1. Note that each consecutive observation in this time series increases by $\hat{b}_1 = 2$ irrespective of the level of the series in the previous period.

Example 1

The Trend in the U.S. Consumer Price Index

It is January 2001. As a fixed income analyst in the trust department of a bank, Lisette Miller is concerned about the future level of inflation and how it might affect portfolio value. Therefore, she wants to predict future inflation rates. For this purpose, she first needs to estimate the linear trend in inflation. To do so, she uses the monthly U.S. Consumer Price Index (CPI) inflation data, expressed as an annual percentage rate,[3] shown in Figure 3. The data include 192 months from January 1985 to December 2000, and the model to be estimated is $y_t = b_0 + b_1 t + \varepsilon_t, t = 1, 2, \ldots, 192$. Table 1 shows the results of estimating this equation. With 192 observations and two parameters, this model has 190 degrees of freedom. At the 0.05 significance level, the critical value for a t-statistic is 1.97. Both the intercept $\left(\hat{b}_0 = 4.1342\right)$ and the trend coefficient $\left(\hat{b}_1 = -0.0095\right)$ are statistically significant because the absolute values of t-statistics for both coefficients are well above the critical value. The estimated regression equation can be written as

$$y_t = 4.1342 - 0.0095t$$

Figure 3	**Monthly CPI Inflation, Not Seasonally Adjusted**

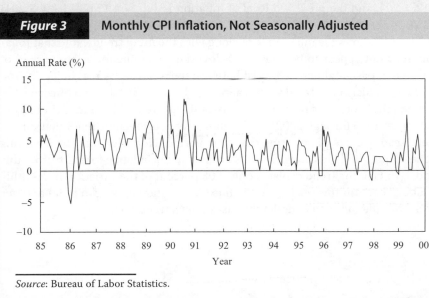

Source: Bureau of Labor Statistics.

---

3 In these data, 1 percent is represented as 1.0.

Table 1	Estimating a Linear Trend in Inflation Monthly Observations, January 1985–December 2000

Regression Statistics

R-squared	0.0408
Standard error	2.5544
Observations	192
Durbin–Watson	1.38

	Coefficient	Standard Error	t-Statistic
Intercept	4.1342	0.3701	11.1693
Trend	–0.0095	0.0033	–2.8445

Source: U.S. Bureau of Labor Statistics.

Because the trend line slope is estimated to be –0.0095, Miller concludes that the linear trend model's best estimate is that the annualized rate of inflation declined at a rate of about one one-hundredth of a percentage point per month during the sample time period.

In January 1985, the first month of the sample, the predicted value of inflation is $\hat{y}_1 = 4.1342 - 0.0095(1) = 4.1247$ percent. In December 2000, the 192nd or last month of the sample, the predicted value of inflation is $\hat{y}_{192} = 4.1342 - 0.0095(192) = 2.3177$ percent.[4] Note, though, that these predicted values are for in-sample periods. A comparison of these values with the actual values indicates how well Miller's model fits the data; however, a main purpose of the estimated model is to predict the level of inflation for out-of-sample periods. For example, for December 2001 (12 months after the end of the sample), $t = 192 + 12 = 204$, and the predicted level of inflation is $\hat{y}_{204} = 4.1342 - 0.0095(204) = 2.2041$ percent.

Figure 4 shows the inflation data along with the fitted trend. Note that inflation does not appear to be above or below the trend line for a long period of time. No persistent differences exist between the trend and actual inflation. The residuals (actual minus trend values) appear to be unpredictable and uncorrelated in time. Therefore, it is reasonable to use a linear trend line to model inflation rates from 1985 through 2000. Furthermore, we can conclude that inflation has been steadily decreasing during that time period. Note also that the R^2 in this model is quite low, indicating great uncertainty in the inflation forecasts from this model. In fact, the trend explains only 4.08 percent of the variation in monthly inflation. Later in this reading, we will examine whether we can build a better model of inflation than a model that uses only a trend line.

---

4 In reporting the final result (here, 2.3177), we use estimated regression coefficients without rounding; in stating the calculation, we use the regression coefficients with rounding, so carrying out the calculation with the rounded coefficients often results in slightly different answers.

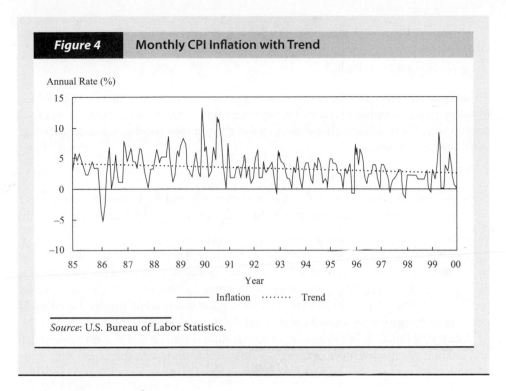

Figure 4 Monthly CPI Inflation with Trend

Source: U.S. Bureau of Labor Statistics.

3.2 Log-Linear Trend Models

Sometimes a linear trend does not correctly model the growth of a time series. In those cases, we often find that fitting a linear trend to a time series leads to persistent rather than uncorrelated errors. If the residuals from a linear trend model are persistent, we then need to employ an alternative model satisfying the conditions of linear regression. For financial time series, an important alternative to a linear trend is a log-linear trend. Log-linear trends work well in fitting time series that have exponential growth.

Exponential growth means constant growth at a particular rate. So, annual growth at a constant rate of 5 percent is exponential because the series continues to increase without an upper bound. How does exponential growth work? Suppose we describe a time series by the following equation:

$$y_t = e^{b_0 + b_1 t}, \ t = 1, 2, \ldots, T \tag{2}$$

Exponential growth is growth at a constant rate ($e^{b_1} - 1$) with continuous compounding. For instance, consider values of the time series in two consecutive periods. In Period 1, the time series has the value $y_1 = e^{b_0 + b_1(1)}$, and in Period 2, it has the value $y_2 = e^{b_0 + b_1(2)}$. The resulting ratio of the values of the time series in the first two periods is $y_2/y_1 = \left(e^{b_0 + b_1(2)}\right) / \left(e^{b_0 + b_1(1)}\right) = e^{b_1(1)}$. Generally, in any period t, the time series has the value $y_t = e^{b_0 + b_1(t)}$. In period $t + 1$, the time series has the value $y_{t+1} = e^{b_0 + b_1(t+1)}$. The ratio of the values in the periods ($t + 1$) and t is $y_{t+1}/y_t = e^{b_0 + b_1(t+1)} / e^{b_0 + b_1(t)} = e^{b_1(1)}$. Thus, the proportional rate of growth in the time series over two consecutive periods is always the same: $(y_{t+1} - y_t)/y_t = y_{t+1}/y_t - 1 = e^{b_1} - 1$.[5] Therefore, exponential growth is growth at a constant rate. Continuous compounding is a mathematical convenience that allows us to restate the equation in a form that is easy to estimate.

---

5 For example, if we use annual periods and $e^{b_1} = 1.04$ for a particular series, then that series grows by 1.04 − 1 = 0.04, or 4 percent a year.

If we take the natural log of both sides of Equation 2, the result is the following equation:

$$\ln y_t = b_0 + b_1 t, \qquad t = 1, 2, \dots, T$$

Therefore, if a time series grows at an exponential rate, we can model the natural log of that series using a linear trend.[6] Of course, no time series grows exactly at an exponential rate. Consequently, if we want to use a **log-linear model**, we must estimate the following equation:

$$\ln y_t = b_0 + b_1 t + \varepsilon_t, \qquad t = 1, 2, \dots, T \qquad\qquad (3)$$

Note that this equation is linear in the coefficients b_0 and b_1. In contrast to a linear trend model, in which the predicted trend value of y_t is $\hat{b}_0 + \hat{b}_1 t$, the predicted trend value of y_t in a log-linear trend model is $e^{\hat{b}_0 + \hat{b}_1 t}$ because $e^{\ln y t} = y_t$.

Examining Equation 3, we see that a log-linear model predicts that $\ln y_t$ will increase by b_1 from one time period to the next. The model predicts a constant growth rate in y_t of $e^{b_1} - 1$. For example, if $b_1 = 0.05$, then the predicted growth rate of y_t in each period is $e^{0.05} - 1 = 0.051271$ or 5.13 percent. In contrast, the linear trend model (Equation 1) predicts that y_t grows by a constant amount from one period to the next.

Example 2 illustrates the problem of nonrandom residuals in a linear trend model, and Example 3 shows a log-linear regression specification fit to the same data.

Example 2

A Linear Trend Regression for Quarterly Sales at Intel

In January 2000, technology analyst Ray Benedict wants to use Equation 1 to fit the data on quarterly sales for Intel Corporation shown in Figure 5. He uses 60 observations on Intel's sales from the first quarter of 1985 to the fourth quarter of 1999 to estimate the linear trend regression model $y_t = b_0 + b_1 t + \varepsilon_t, t = 1, 2, \dots, 60$. Table 2 shows the results of estimating this equation.

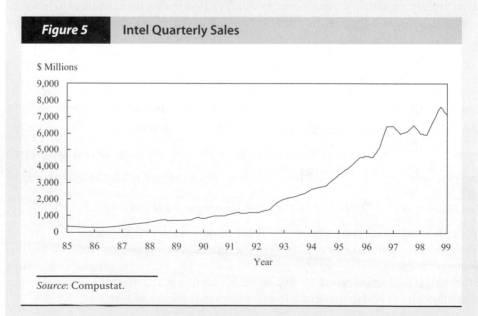

| Figure 5 | Intel Quarterly Sales |

Source: Compustat.

Table 2	Estimating a Linear Trend in Intel Sales

Regression Statistics

R-squared	0.8774
Standard error	871.6858
Observations	60
Durbin–Watson	0.13

	Coefficient	Standard Error	*t*-Statistic
Intercept	−1,318.7729	227.9585	−5.7852
Trend	132.4005	6.4994	20.3712

Source: Compustat.

At first glance, the results shown in Table 2 seem quite reasonable: Both the intercept and the trend coefficient are highly statistically significant. When Benedict plots the data on Intel's sales and the trend line, however, he sees a different picture. As Figure 6 shows, before 1989 the trend line is persistently below sales. Between 1989 and 1996, the trend line is persistently above sales, but after 1996, the trend line is once again persistently below sales.

Figure 6	Intel Quarterly Sales with Trend

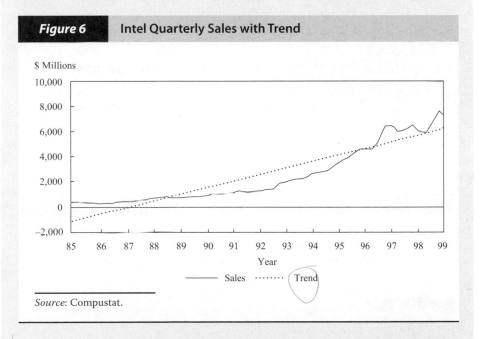

Source: Compustat.

Recall a key assumption underlying the regression model: that the regression errors are not correlated across observations. If a trend is persistently above or below the value of the time series, however, the residuals (the difference between the time series and the trend) are serially correlated. Figure 7 shows the residuals (the difference between sales and the trend) from estimating a linear trend model with the raw sales data. The figure shows that the residuals are persistent. Because of this persistent serial correlation in the errors of the trend model, using a linear trend to fit sales at Intel would be inappropriate, even though the

R^2 of the equation is high (0.88). The assumption of uncorrelated residual errors has been violated. Because the dependent and independent variables are not distinct, as in cross-sectional regressions, this assumption violation is serious and causes us to search for a better model.

Figure 7	Residual from Predicting Intel Sales with a Trend

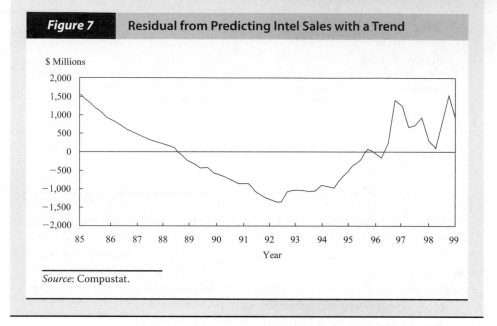

Source: Compustat.

Example 3

A Log-Linear Regression for Quarterly Sales at Intel

Having rejected a linear trend model in Example 2, technology analyst Benedict now tries a different model for the quarterly sales for Intel Corporation from the first quarter of 1985 to the fourth quarter of 1999. The curvature in the data plot shown in Figure 5 is a hint that an exponential curve may fit the data. Consequently, he estimates the following linear equation:

$$\ln y_t = b_0 + b_1 t + \varepsilon_t, \quad t = 1, 2, \ldots, 60$$

This equation seems to fit the sales data much better than did Equation 1. As Table 3 shows, the R^2 for this equation is 0.98 (the R^2 with Equation 1 was 0.88). An R^2 of 0.98 means that 98 percent of the variation in the natural log of Intel's sales is explained solely by a linear trend.

Table 3	Estimating a Linear Trend in Lognormal Intel Sales

Regression Statistics	
R-squared	0.9831
Standard error	0.1407
Observations	60
Durbin–Watson	0.30

Table 3	Continued		
	Coefficient	**Standard Error**	**t-Statistic**
Intercept	5.5529	0.0368	150.9809
Trend	0.0609	0.0010	58.0680

Source: Compustat.

Figure 8 shows how well a linear trend fits the natural log of Intel's sales. The natural logs of the sales data lie very close to the linear trend during the sample period, and log sales are not above or below the trend for long periods of time. Thus, a log-linear trend model seems much better suited for modeling Intel's sales than does a linear trend model.

How can Benedict use the results of estimating Equation 3 to predict Intel's sales in the future? Suppose Benedict wants to predict Intel's sales for the first quarter of 2000 ($t = 61$). The estimated value $\hat{b}_0$ is 5.5529, and the estimated value $\hat{b}_1$ is 0.0609. Therefore, the estimated model predicts that $\ln \hat{y}_{61} = 5.5529 + 0.0609(61) = 9.2673$ and that predicted sales are $\hat{y}_{61} = e^{\ln \hat{y}_{61}} = e^{9.2673} = \$10{,}585.63$ million.[7]

Figure 8	Natural Log of Intel Quarterly Sales

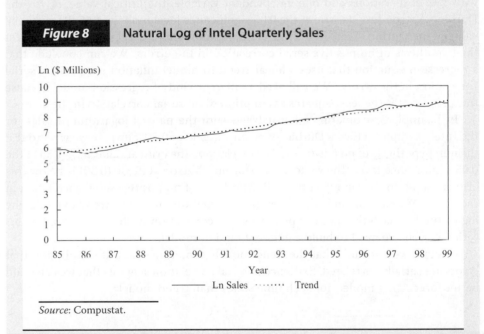

Ln ($ Millions)

Year

—— Ln Sales   ········ Trend

Source: Compustat.

How much different is this forecast from the prediction of the linear trend model? Table 2 showed that for the linear trend model, the estimated value of $\hat{b}_0$ is −1318.7729 and the estimated value of $\hat{b}_1$ is 132.4005. Thus, if we predict Intel's sales for the first quarter of 2000 ($t = 61$) using the linear trend model, the forecast is $\hat{y}_{61} = -1318.7729 + 132.4005(61) = \$6{,}757.66$ million. This forecast is far below the prediction made by the log-linear regression model. Later in this reading, we will examine whether we can build a better model of Intel's quarterly sales than a model that uses only a log-linear trend.

---

7 Note that $\hat{b}_1 = 0.0609$ implies that the exponential growth rate per quarter in Intel's sales will be 6.28 percent ($e^{0.0609} - 1 = 0.062793$).

3.3 Trend Models and Testing for Correlated Errors

Both the linear trend model and the log-linear trend model are single-variable regression models. If they are to be correctly specified, the regression-model assumptions must be satisfied. In particular, the regression error for one period must be uncorrelated with the regression error for all other periods.[8] In Example 2 in the previous section, we could infer an obvious violation of that assumption from a visual inspection of a plot of residuals (Figure 7). The log-linear trend model of Example 3 appeared to fit the data much better, but we still need to confirm that the uncorrelated errors assumption is satisfied. To address that question formally, we must carry out a Durbin–Watson test on the residuals.

In the reading on regression analysis, we showed how to test whether regression errors are serially correlated using the Durbin–Watson statistic. For example, if the trend models shown in Examples 1 and 3 really capture the time-series behavior of inflation and the log of Intel's sales, then the Durbin–Watson statistic for both of those models should not differ significantly from 2.0. Otherwise, the errors in the model are either positively or negatively serially correlated, and that correlation can be used to build a better forecasting model for those time series.

In Example 1, estimating a linear trend in the monthly CPI inflation yielded a Durbin–Watson statistic of 1.38. Is this result significantly different from 2.0? To find out, we need to test the null hypothesis of no positive serial correlation. For a sample with 192 observations and one independent variable, the critical value, d_l, for the Durbin–Watson test statistic at the 0.05 significance level is above 1.65. Because the value of the Durbin–Watson statistic (1.38) is below this critical value, we can reject the hypothesis of no positive serial correlation in the errors. We can conclude that a regression equation that uses a linear trend to model inflation has positive serial correlation in the errors.[9] We will need a different kind of regression model because this one violates the least-squares assumption of no serial correlation in the errors.

In Example 3, estimating a linear trend with the natural logarithm of sales for the Intel example yielded a Durbin–Watson statistic of 0.30. Suppose we wish to test the null hypothesis of no positive serial correlation. The critical value, d_l, is 1.55 at the 0.05 significance level. The value of the Durbin–Watson statistic (0.30) is below this critical value, so we can reject the null hypothesis of no positive serial correlation in the errors. We can conclude that a regression equation that uses a trend to model the log of Intel's quarterly sales has positive serial correlation in the errors. So, for this series as well, we need to build a different kind of model.

Overall, we conclude that the trend models sometimes have the limitation that errors are serially correlated. Existence of serial correlation suggests that we can build better forecasting models for such time series than trend models.

4   AUTOREGRESSIVE (AR) TIME-SERIES MODELS

A key feature of the log-linear model's depiction of time series and a key feature of time series in general is that current-period values are related to previous-period values. For example, Intel's sales for the current period are related to its sales in the

---

[8] Note that time-series observations, in contrast to cross-sectional observations, have a logical ordering: They must be processed in chronological order of the time periods involved. For example, we should not make a prediction of the inflation rate using a CPI series in which the order of the observations had been scrambled, because time patterns such as growth in the independent variables can negatively affect the statistical properties of the estimated regression coefficients.

[9] Significantly small values of the Durbin–Watson statistic indicate positive serial correlation; significantly large values point to negative serial correlation. Here the DW statistic of 1.38 indicates positive serial correlation. For more information, see the readings on regression analysis.

previous period. An **autoregressive model (AR)**, a time series regressed on its own past values, represents this relationship effectively. When we use this model, we can drop the normal notation of y as the dependent variable and x as the independent variable because we no longer have that distinction to make. Here we simply use x_t. For example, Equation 4 shows a first-order autoregression, AR(1), for the variable x_t:

$$x_t = b_0 + b_1 x_{t-1} + \varepsilon_t \tag{4}$$

Thus, in an AR(1) model, we use only the most recent past value of x_t to predict the current value of x_t. In general, a pth-order autoregression, AR(p), for the variable x_t is shown by

$$x_t = b_0 + b_1 x_{t-1} + b_2 x_{t-2} + \ldots + b_p x_{t-p} + \varepsilon_t \tag{5}$$

In this equation, p past values of x_t are used to predict the current value of x_t. In the next section we discuss a key assumption of time-series models that include lagged values of the dependent variable as independent variables.

4.1 Covariance-Stationary Series

Note that the independent variable (x_{t-1}) in Equation 4 is a random variable. This fact may seem like a mathematical subtlety, but it is not. If we use ordinary least squares to estimate Equation 4 when we have a randomly distributed independent variable that is a lagged value of the dependent variable, our statistical inference may be invalid. To conduct valid statistical inference, we must make a key assumption in time-series analysis: We must assume that the time series we are modeling is **covariance stationary**.[10]

What does it mean for a time series to be covariance stationary? The basic idea is that a time series is covariance stationary if its properties, such as mean and variance, do not change over time. A covariance stationary series must satisfy three principal requirements.[11] First, the expected value of the time series must be constant and finite in all periods: $E(y_t) = \mu$ and $|\mu| < \infty$, $t = 1, 2, \ldots, T$. Second, the variance of the time series must be constant and finite in all periods. Third, the covariance of the time series with itself for a fixed number of periods in the past or future must be constant and finite in all periods. The second and third requirements can be summarized as follows:[12]

$$\text{Cov}(y_t, y_{t-s}) = \lambda, \; |\lambda| < \infty, \; t = 1, 2, \ldots, T; \; s = 0, \; \pm 1, \; \pm 2, \ldots, \pm T$$

where λ signifies a constant. What happens if a time series is not covariance stationary but we model it using Equation 4? The estimation results will have no economic meaning. For a non-covariance-stationary time series, estimating the regression in Equation 4 will yield spurious results. In particular, the estimate of b_1 will be biased, and any hypothesis tests will be invalid.

How can we tell if a time series is covariance stationary? We can often answer this question by looking at a plot of the time series. If the plot shows roughly the same mean and variance through time without any significant seasonality, then we may want to assume that the time series is covariance stationary.

Some of the time series we looked at in Figures 1 to 4 appear to be covariance stationary. For example, the inflation data shown in Figure 3 appear to have roughly

---

10 "Weakly stationary" is a synonym for covariance stationary. Note that the terms "stationary" or "stationarity" are often used to mean "covariance stationary" or "covariance stationarity," respectively. You may also encounter the more restrictive concept of "strictly" stationary, which has little practical application. For details, see Diebold (2004).

11 In the first requirement, we will use the absolute value to rule out the case in which the mean is negative without limit (minus infinity).

12 When s in this equation equals 0, then this equation imposes the condition that the variance of the time series is finite. This is so because the covariance of a random variable with itself is its variance: $\text{Cov}(y_t, y_t) = \text{Var}(y_t)$.

the same mean and variance over the sample period. Many of the time series one encounters in business and investments, however, are not covariance stationary. For example, many time series appear to grow (or decline) steadily through time and so have a mean that is nonconstant, which implies that they are nonstationary. As an example, the time series of Intel's quarterly sales in Figure 5 clearly shows the mean increasing as time passes. Thus Intel's quarterly sales are not covariance stationary.[13] Macroeconomic time series such as those relating to income and consumption are often strongly trending as well. A time series with seasonality (regular patterns of movement with the year) also has a nonconstant mean, as do other types of time series that we discuss later.[14]

Figure 2 showed that monthly retail sales (not seasonally adjusted) are also not covariance stationary. Sales in December are always much higher than sales in other months (these are the regular large peaks), and sales in January are always much lower (these are the regular large drops after the December peaks). On average, sales also increase over time, so the mean of sales is not constant.

Later in the reading, we will show that we can often transform a nonstationary time series into a stationary time series. But whether a stationary time series is original or transformed, a caution applies: Stationarity in the past does not guarantee stationary in the future. There is always the possibility that a well-specified model will fail when the state of the world changes and yields a different underlying model that generates the time series.

4.2 Detecting Serially Correlated Errors in an Autoregressive Model

We can estimate an autoregressive model using ordinary least squares if the time series is covariance stationary and the errors are uncorrelated. Unfortunately, our previous test for serial correlation, the Durbin–Watson statistic, is invalid when the independent variables include past values of the dependent variable. Therefore, for most time-series models, we cannot use the Durbin–Watson statistic. Fortunately, we can use other tests to determine whether the errors in a time-series model are serially correlated. One such test reveals whether the autocorrelations of the error term are significantly different from 0. This test is a t-test involving a residual autocorrelation and the standard error of the residual autocorrelation. As background for the test, we next discuss autocorrelation in general before moving to residual autocorrelation.

The **autocorrelations** of a time series are the correlations of that series with its own past values. The order of the correlation is given by k where k represents the number of periods lagged. When $k = 1$, the autocorrelation shows the correlation of the variable in one period to its occurrence in the previous period. For example, the **kth order autocorrelation** (ρ_k) is

$$\rho_k = \frac{\text{Cov}(x_t, x_{t-k})}{\sigma_x^2} = \frac{E\left[(x_t - \mu)(x_{t-k} - \mu)\right]}{\sigma_x^2}$$

Note that we have the relationship $\text{Cov}(x_t, x_{t-k}) \leq \text{Var}(x_t)$ with equality holding when $k = 0$. This means that the absolute value of ρ_k is less than or equal to 1.

Of course, we can never directly observe the autocorrelations, ρ_k. Instead, we must estimate them. Thus we replace the expected value of x_t, μ, with its estimated value, $\bar{x}$, to compute the estimated autocorrelations. The kth order estimated autocorrelation of the time series x_t, which we denote $\hat{\rho}_k$, is

---

13 In general, any time series accurately described with a linear or log-linear trend model is not covariance stationary, although a transformation of the original series might be covariance stationary.
14 In particular, random walks are not covariance stationary.

$$\hat{\rho}_k = \frac{\sum\limits_{t=k+1}^{T} \left[(x_t - \bar{x})(x_{t-k} - \bar{x}) \right]}{\sum\limits_{t=1}^{T} (x_t - \bar{x})^2}$$

Analogous to the definition of autocorrelations for a time series, we can define the autocorrelations of the error term for a time-series model as[15]

$$\rho_{\varepsilon,k} = \frac{\mathrm{Cov}(\varepsilon_t, \varepsilon_{t-k})}{\sigma_\varepsilon^2}$$

$$= \frac{E\left[(\varepsilon_t - 0)(\varepsilon_{t-k} - 0)\right]}{\sigma_\varepsilon^2}$$

$$= \frac{E(\varepsilon_t, \varepsilon_{t-k})}{\sigma_\varepsilon^2}$$

where E stands for the expected value. We assume that the expected value of the error term in a time-series model is 0.[16]

We can determine whether we are using the correct time-series model by testing whether the autocorrelations of the error term (**error autocorrelations**) differ significantly from 0. If they do, the model is not specified correctly. We estimate the error autocorrelation using the sample autocorrelations of the residuals (**residual autocorrelations**) and their sample variance.

A test of the null hypothesis that an error autocorrelation at a specified lag equals 0 is based on the residual autocorrelation for that lag and the standard error of the residual correlation, which is equal to $1/\sqrt{T}$, where T is the number of observations in the time series.[17] Thus, if we have 100 observations in a time series, the standard error for each of the estimated autocorrelations is 0.1. We can compute the t-test of the null hypothesis that the error correlation at a particular lag equals 0, by dividing the residual autocorrelation at that lag by its standard error ($1/\sqrt{T}$).

How can we use information about the error autocorrelations to determine whether an autoregressive time-series model is correctly specified? We can use a simple three-step method. First, estimate a particular autoregressive model, say an AR(1) model. Second, compute the autocorrelations of the residuals from the model.[18] Third, test to see whether the residual autocorrelations differ significantly from 0. If significance tests show that the residual autocorrelations differ significantly from 0, the model is not correctly specified; we may need to modify it in ways that we will discuss shortly.[19] We now present an example to demonstrate how this three-step method works.

---

15 Whenever we refer to autocorrelation without qualification, we mean autocorrelation of the time series itself rather than autocorrelation of the error term or residuals.

16 This assumption is similar to the one made in the previous two readings about the expected value of the error term.

17 This calculation is derived in Diebold (2004).

18 We can compute these residual autocorrelations easily with most statistical software packages. In Microsoft Excel, for example, to compute the first-order residual autocorrelation, we compute the correlation of the residuals from observations 1 through $T - 1$ with the residuals from observations 2 through T.

19 Often, econometricians use additional tests for the significance of residual autocorrelations. For example, the Box–Pierce Q-statistic is frequently used to test the joint hypothesis that all autocorrelations of the residuals are equal to 0. For further discussion, see Diebold (2004).

Example 4

Predicting Gross Margins for Intel Corporation

Having investigated the time-series modeling of Intel Corporation's sales, analyst Ray Benedict decides to use a time-series model to predict Intel's gross margin [(Sales – Cost of goods sold)/Sales]. His observations on the dependent variable are 2Q:1985 through 4Q:1999. He does not know the best model for gross margin but believes that the current-period value will be related to the previous-period value. He decides to start out with a first-order autoregressive model, AR(1): Gross margin$_t = b_0 + b_1$(Gross margin$_{t-1}$) + ε_t. Table 4 shows the results of estimating this AR(1) model, along with the autocorrelations of the residuals from that model.

Table 4	Autoregression: AR(1) Model Gross Margin of Intel Quarterly Observations, April 1985–December 1999

Regression Statistics

R-squared	0.7784
Standard error	0.0402
Observations	59
Durbin–Watson	1.8446

	Coefficient	Standard Error	t-Statistic
Intercept	0.0834	0.0367	2.2705
Lag 1	0.8665	0.0612	14.1493

Autocorrelations of the Residual

Lag	Autocorrelation	Standard Error	t-Statistic
1	0.0677	0.1302	0.5197
2	−0.1929	0.1302	−1.4814
3	0.0541	0.1302	0.4152
4	−0.1498	0.1302	−1.1507

Source: Compustat.

The first thing to note about Table 4 is that both the intercept ($\hat{b}_0$=0.0834) and the coefficient on the first lag ($\hat{b}_1$= 0.8665) of the gross margin are highly significant in the regression equation.[20] The t-statistic for the intercept is about 2.3, whereas the t-statistic for the first lag of the gross margin is more than 14. With 59 observations and two parameters, this model has 57 degrees of freedom. At the 0.05 significance level, the critical value for a t-statistic is about 2.0. Therefore, Benedict must reject the null hypotheses that the intercept is equal to 0 ($b_0 = 0$) and the coefficient on the first lag is equal to 0 ($b_1 = 0$) in favor of the alternative hypothesis that the coefficients, individually, are not equal to 0.

---

20 The first lag of a time series is the value of the time series in the previous period.

But are these statistics valid? We will know when we test whether the residuals from this model are serially correlated.

At the bottom of Table 4, the first four autocorrelations of the residual are displayed along with the standard error and the t-statistic for each of those autocorrelations.[21] The sample has 59 observations, so the standard error for each of the autocorrelations is $1/\sqrt{59} = 0.1302$. Table 4 shows that none of the first four autocorrelations has a t-statistic larger than 1.50 in absolute value. Therefore, Benedict can conclude that none of these autocorrelations differs significantly from 0. Consequently, he can assume that the residuals are not serially correlated and that the model is correctly specified, and he can validly use ordinary least squares to estimate the parameters and the parameters' standard errors in the autoregressive model.[22]

Now that Benedict has concluded that this model is correctly specified, how can he use it to predict Intel's gross margin in the next period? The estimated equation is Gross margin$_t$ = 0.0834 + 0.8665(Gross margin$_{t-1}$) + ε_t. The expected value of the error term is 0 in any period. Therefore, this model predicts that gross margin in period $t + 1$ will be Gross margin$_{t+1}$ = 0.0834 + 0.8665(Gross margin$_t$). For example, if gross margin is 55 percent in this quarter (0.55), the model predicts that in the next quarter gross margin will increase to 0.0834 + 0.8665(0.55) = 0.5600 or 56.0 percent. On the other hand, if gross margin is currently 65 percent (0.65), the model predicts that in the next quarter, gross margin will fall to 0.0834 + 0.8665(0.65) = 0.6467 or 64.67 percent. As we show in the following section, the model predicts that gross margin will increase if it is below a certain level (62.50 percent) and decrease if it is above that level.

4.3 Mean Reversion

We say that a time series shows **mean reversion** if it tends to fall when its level is above its mean and rise when its level is below its mean. Much like the temperature in a room controlled by a thermostat, a mean-reverting time series tends to return to its long-term mean. How can we determine the value that the time series tends toward? If a time series is currently at its mean-reverting level, then the model predicts that the value of the time series will be the same in the next period. At its mean-reverting level, we have the relationship $x_{t+1} = x_t$. For an AR(1) model ($x_{t+1} = b_0 + b_1 x_t$), the equality $x_{t+1} = x_t$ implies the level $x_t = b_0 + b_1 x_t$, or that the mean-reverting level, x_t, is given by

$$x_t = \frac{b_0}{1 - b_1}$$

So the AR(1) model predicts that the time series will stay the same if its current value is $b_0/(1 - b_1)$, increase if its current value is below $b_0/(1 - b_1)$, and decrease if its current value is above $b_0/(1 - b_1)$.

In the case of gross margins for Intel, the mean-reverting level for the model shown in Table 4 is 0.0834/(1 − 0.8665) = 0.6250. If the current gross margin is above 0.6250, the model predicts that the gross margin will fall in the next period. If the current gross margin is below 0.6250, the model predicts that the gross margin will rise in the next period. As we will discuss later, all covariance-stationary time series have a finite mean-reverting level.

---

21 For seasonally unadjusted data, analysts often compute the same number of autocorrelations as there are observations in a year (for example, four for quarterly data). The number of autocorrelations computed also often depends on sample size, as discussed in Diebold (2004).

22 Statisticians have many other tests for serial correlation of the residuals in a time-series model. For details, see Diebold (2004).

4.4 Multiperiod Forecasts and the Chain Rule of Forecasting

Often, financial analysts want to make forecasts for more than one period. For example, we might want to use a quarterly sales model to predict sales for a company for each of the next four quarters. To use a time-series model to make forecasts for more than one period, we must examine how to make multiperiod forecasts using an AR(1) model. The one-period-ahead forecast of x_t from an AR(1) model is as follows:

$$\hat{x}_{t+1} = \hat{b}_0 + \hat{b}_1 x_t \tag{6}$$

If we want to forecast x_{t+2} using an AR(1) model, our forecast will be based on

$$\hat{x}_{t+2} = \hat{b}_0 + \hat{b}_1 x_{t+1} \tag{7}$$

Unfortunately, we do not know x_{t+1} in period t, so we cannot use Equation 7 directly to make a two-period-ahead forecast. We can, however, use our forecast of x_{t+1} and the AR(1) model to make a prediction of x_{t+2}. The **chain rule of forecasting** is a process in which the next period's value, predicted by the forecasting equation, is substituted into the equation to give a predicted value two periods ahead. Using the chain rule of forecasting, we can substitute the predicted value of x_{t+1} into Equation 7 to get $\hat{x}_{t+2} = \hat{b}_0 + \hat{b}_1 \hat{x}_{t+1}$. We already know $\hat{x}_{t+1}$ from our one-period-ahead forecast in Equation 6. Now we have a simple way of predicting x_{t+2}.

Multiperiod forecasts are more uncertain than single-period forecasts because each forecast period has uncertainty. For example, in forecasting x_{t+2}, we first have the uncertainty associated with forecasting x_{t+1} using x_t, and then we have the uncertainty associated with forecasting x_{t+2} using the forecast of x_{t+1}. In general, the more periods a forecast has, the more uncertain it is.[23]

Example 5

Multiperiod Prediction of Intel's Gross Margin

Suppose that at the beginning of 2000, we want to predict Intel's gross margin in two periods using the model shown in Table 4. Assume that Intel's gross margin in the current period is 65 percent. The one-period-ahead forecast of Intel's gross margin from this model is 0.6467 = 0.0834 + 0.8665(0.65). By substituting the one-period-ahead forecast, 0.6467, back into the regression equation, we can derive the following two-period-ahead forecast: 0.6438 = 0.0834 + 0.8665(0.6467). Therefore, if the current gross margin for Intel is 65 percent, the model predicts that Intel's gross margin in two quarters will be 64.38 percent.

Example 6

Modeling U.S. CPI Inflation

Analyst Lisette Miller has been directed to build a time-series model for monthly U.S. inflation. Inflation and expectations about inflation, of course, have a significant effect on bond returns. Beginning with January 1971, she selects as data the annualized monthly percentage change in the CPI. Which model should Miller use?

The process of model selection parallels that of Example 4 relating to Intel's gross margins. The first model Miller estimates is an AR(1) model, using the

---

23 If a forecasting model is well specified, the prediction errors from the model will not be serially correlated. If the prediction errors for each period are not serially correlated, then the variance of a multiperiod forecast will be higher than the variance of a single-period forecast.

previous month's inflation rate as the independent variable: $\text{Inflation}_t = b_0 + b_1$ $\text{Inflation}_{t-1} + \varepsilon_t$, $t = 1, 2, \ldots, 359$. To estimate this model, she uses monthly CPI inflation data from January 1971 to December 2000 ($t = 1$ denotes February 1971). Table 5 shows the results of estimating this model.

Table 5	Monthly CPI Inflation at an Annual Rate: AR(1) Model Monthly Observations, February 1971–December 2000

Regression Statistics

R-squared	0.3808
Standard error	3.4239
Observations	359
Durbin–Watson	2.3059

	Coefficient	Standard Error	t-Statistic
Intercept	1.9658	0.2803	7.0119
Lag 1	0.6175	0.0417	14.8185

Autocorrelations of the Residual

Lag	Autocorrelation	Standard Error	t-Statistic
1	−0.1538	0.0528	−2.9142
2	0.1097	0.0528	2.0782
3	0.0657	0.0528	1.2442
4	0.0920	0.0528	1.7434

Source: U.S. Bureau of Labor Statistics.

As Table 5 shows, both the intercept ($\hat{b}_0 = 1.9658$) and the coefficient on the first lagged value of inflation ($\hat{b}_1 = 0.6175$) are highly statistically significant, with large t-statistics. With 359 observations and two parameters, this model has 357 degrees of freedom. The critical value for a t-statistic at the 0.05 significance level is about 1.97. Therefore, Miller can reject the individual null hypotheses that the intercept is equal to 0 ($b_0 = 0$) and the coefficient on the first lag is equal to 0 ($b_1 = 0$) in favor of the alternative hypothesis that the coefficients, individually, are not equal to 0.

Are these statistics valid? Miller will know when she tests whether the residuals from this model are serially correlated. With 359 observations in this sample, the standard error for each of the estimated autocorrelations is $1/\sqrt{359}$ = 0.0528. The critical value for the t-statistic is 1.97. Because both the first and the second estimated autocorrelation have t-statistics larger than 1.97 in absolute value, Miller concludes that the autocorrelations are significantly different from 0. This model is thus misspecified because the residuals are serially correlated.

If the residuals in an autoregressive model are serially correlated, Miller can eliminate the correlation by estimating an autoregressive model with more lags of the dependent variable as explanatory variables. Table 6 shows the result of estimating a second time-series model, an AR(2) model using the same data as in the analysis shown in Table 5.[24] With 358 observations and three parameters, this model has 355 degrees of freedom. Because the degrees of freedom are almost the same as those for the estimates shown in Table 5, the critical value of the t-statistic at the 0.05 significance level also is almost the same (1.97). If she estimates the equation with two lags, Inflation$_t = b_0 + b_1$ Inflation$_{t-1} + b_2$ Inflation$_{t-2} + \varepsilon_t$, Miller finds that all three of the coefficients in the regression model (an intercept and the coefficients on two lags of the dependent variable) differ significantly from 0. The bottom portion of Table 6 shows that none of the first four autocorrelations of the residual has a t-statistic greater in absolute value than the critical value of 1.97. Therefore, Miller fails to reject the hypothesis that the individual autocorrelations of the residual equal 0. She concludes that this model is correctly specified because she finds no evidence of serial correlation in the residuals.

Table 6	Monthly CPI Inflation at an Annual Rate: AR(2) Model Monthly Observations, March 1971–December 2000

Regression Statistics

Multiple R	0.6479
R-squared	0.4197
Standard error	3.3228
Observations	358
Durbin–Watson	2.0582

	Coefficient	Standard Error	t-Statistic
Intercept	1.4609	0.2913	5.0147
Lag 1	0.4634	0.0514	9.0117
Lag 2	0.2515	0.0514	4.8924

Autocorrelations of the Residual

Lag	Autocorrelation	Standard Error	t-Statistic
1	−0.0320	0.0529	−0.6048
2	−0.0982	0.0529	−1.8574
3	−0.0114	0.0529	−0.2150
4	0.0320	0.0529	0.6053

Source: U.S. Bureau of Labor Statistics.

In the previous example, the analyst selected an AR(2) model because the residuals from the AR(1) model were serially correlated. Suppose that in a given month, inflation had been 4 percent at an annual rate in the previous month and 3 percent in the month before that. The AR(1) model shown in Table 5 predicted that

---

24 Note that Table 6 shows only 358 observations in the regression because the extra lag of inflation requires the estimation sample to start one month later than the regression in Table 5. (With two lags, inflation for January and February 1971 must be known in order to estimate the equation starting in March 1971.)

inflation in the next month would be 1.9658 + 0.6175(4) = 4.44 percent approximately, whereas the AR(2) model shown in Table 6 predicts that inflation in the next month will be 1.4609 + 0.4634(4) + 0.2515(3) = 4.07 percent approximately. If the analyst had used the incorrect AR(1) model, she would have predicted inflation to be 37 basis points higher (4.44 percent versus 4.07 percent) than using the AR(2) model. This incorrect forecast could have adversely affected the quality of her company's investment choices.

4.5 Comparing Forecast Model Performance

One way to compare the forecast performance of two models is to compare the variance of the forecast errors that the two models make. The model with the smaller forecast error variance will be the more accurate model, and it will also have the smaller standard error of the time-series regression. (This standard error usually is reported directly in the output for the time-series regression.)

In comparing forecast accuracy among models, we must distinguish between in-sample forecast errors and out-of-sample forecast errors. **In-sample forecast errors** are the residuals from a fitted time-series model. For example, when we estimated a linear trend with raw inflation data from January 1971 to December 2000, the in-sample forecast errors were the residuals from January 1971 to December 2000. If we use this model to predict inflation outside this period, the differences between actual and predicted inflation are **out-of-sample forecast errors**.

Example 7

In-Sample Forecast Comparisons of U.S. CPI Inflation

In Example 6, the analyst compared an AR(1) forecasting model of monthly U.S. inflation with an AR(2) model of monthly U.S. inflation and decided that the AR(2) model was preferable. Table 5 showed that the standard error from the AR(1) model of inflation is 3.4239, and Table 6 showed that the standard error from the AR(2) model is 3.3228. Therefore, the AR(2) model had a lower in-sample forecast error variance than the AR(1) model, which is consistent with our belief that the AR(2) model was preferable. Its standard error is 3.3228/3.4239 = 97.05 percent of the forecast error of the AR(1) model.

Often, we want to compare the forecasting accuracy of different models after the sample period for which they were estimated. We wish to compare the out-of-sample forecast accuracy of the models. Out-of-sample forecast accuracy is important because the future is always out of sample. Although professional forecasters distinguish between out-of-sample and in-sample forecasting performance, many articles that analysts read contain only in-sample forecast evaluations. Analysts should be aware that out-of-sample performance is critical for evaluating a forecasting model's real-world contribution.

Typically, we compare the out-of-sample forecasting performance of forecasting models by comparing their **root mean squared error (RMSE)**, which is the square root of the average squared error. The model with the smallest RMSE is judged most accurate. The following example illustrates the computation and use of RMSE in comparing forecasting models.

Example 8

Out-of-Sample Forecast Comparisons of U.S. CPI Inflation

Suppose we want to compare the forecasting accuracy of the AR(1) and AR(2) models of U.S. inflation estimated over 1971 to 2000, using data on U.S. inflation from January 2001 to December 2002.

Table 7	Out-of-Sample Forecast Error Comparisons: January 2001–December 2002 U.S. CPI Inflation (Annualized)						
Date	Infl(*t*)	Infl(*t*–1)	Infl(*t*–2)	AR(1) Error	Squared Error	AR(2) Error	Squared Error
2001							
January	7.8556	−0.6871	0.6918	6.3141	39.8681	6.5392	42.7611
February	4.9042	7.8556	−0.6871	−1.9122	3.6564	−0.0242	0.0006
March	2.7648	4.9042	7.8556	−2.2291	4.9689	−2.9440	8.6669
April	4.8729	2.7648	4.9042	1.1999	1.4399	0.8976	0.8058
May	5.5638	4.8729	2.7648	0.5892	0.3472	1.1497	1.3217
June	2.0448	5.5638	4.8729	−3.3564	11.2656	−3.2196	10.3660
July	−3.3192	2.0448	5.5638	−6.5475	42.8703	−7.1267	50.7892
August	0.0000	−3.3192	2.0448	0.0837	0.0070	−0.4369	0.1909
September	5.5446	0.0000	−3.3192	3.5788	12.8078	4.9183	24.1899
October	−3.9642	5.5446	0.0000	−9.3536	87.4891	−7.9944	63.9110
November	−2.0072	−3.9642	5.5446	−1.5252	2.3261	−3.0252	9.1519
December	−4.6336	−2.0072	−3.9642	−5.3600	28.7299	−4.1675	17.3685
2002							
January	2.7505	−4.6336	−2.0072	3.6459	13.2927	3.9416	15.5365
February	4.8476	2.7505	−4.6336	1.1834	1.4005	3.2772	10.7404
March	6.9619	4.8476	2.7505	2.0029	4.0118	2.5630	6.5692
April	6.9218	6.9619	4.8476	0.6573	0.4320	1.0158	1.0319
May	0.0000	6.9218	6.9619	−6.2397	38.9339	−6.4190	41.2034
June	0.6695	0.0000	6.9218	−1.2963	1.6804	−2.5319	6.4105
July	1.3423	0.6695	0.0000	−1.0369	1.0751	−0.4288	0.1839
August	4.0719	1.3423	0.6695	1.2773	1.6315	1.8207	3.3148
September	2.0105	4.0719	1.3423	−2.4694	6.0981	−1.6747	2.8047
October	2.0072	2.0105	4.0719	−1.2000	1.4400	−1.4092	1.9860
November	0.0000	2.0072	2.0105	−3.2051	10.2728	−2.8965	8.3900
December	−2.6157	0.0000	2.0072	−4.5814	20.9893	−4.5812	20.9876
				Average	14.0431	Average	14.5284
				RMSE	3.7474	RMSE	3.8116

Source: U.S. Bureau of Labor Statistics.

For each month from January 2001 to December 2002, the first column of numbers in Table 7 shows the actual annualized inflation rate during the month. The second and third columns show the rate of inflation in the previous two months. The fourth column shows the out-of-sample errors from the AR(1) model shown in Table 5. The fifth column shows the squared errors from the AR(1) model. The sixth column shows the out-of-sample errors from the AR(2) model shown in Table 6. The final column shows the squared errors from the AR(2) model. The bottom of the table displays the average squared error and the RMSE. According to these measures, the AR(1) model was slightly more accurate than the AR(2) model in its out-of-sample forecasts of inflation from January 2001 to December 2002. The RMSE from the AR(1) model was only 3.7474/3.8116 = 98.32 percent as large as the RMSE from the AR(2) model. Therefore, even though the AR(2) model was more accurate in-sample, the AR(1) model was slightly more accurate out of sample. Of course, this was a small sample to use in evaluating out-of-sample forecasting performance. Although we seem to have conflicting information about whether to choose an AR(1) or an AR(2) model here, we must also consider regression coefficient stability. We will continue the comparison between these two models in the following section.

4.6 Instability of Regression Coefficients

One of the important issues an analyst faces in modeling a time series is the sample period to use. The estimates of regression coefficients of the time-series model can change substantially across different sample periods used for estimating the model. Often, the regression coefficient estimates of a time-series model estimated using an earlier sample period can be quite different from those of a model estimated using a later sample period. Similarly, the estimates can be different between models estimated using relatively shorter and longer sample periods. Further, the choice of model for a particular time series can also depend on the sample period. For example, an AR(1) model may be appropriate for the sales of a company in one particular sample period, but an AR(2) model may be necessary for an earlier or later sample period (or for a longer or shorter sample period). Thus the choice of a sample period is an important decision in modeling a financial time series.

Unfortunately, there is usually no clear-cut basis in economic or financial theory for determining whether to use data from a longer or shorter sample period to estimate a time-series model. We can get some guidance, however, if we remember that our models are valid only for covariance-stationary time series. For example, we should not combine data from a period when exchange rates were fixed with data from a period when exchange rates were floating. The exchange rates in these two periods would not likely have the same variance because exchange rates are usually much more volatile under a floating-rate regime than when rates are fixed. Similarly, many U.S. analysts consider it inappropriate to model U.S. inflation or interest-rate behavior since the 1960s as a part of one sample period, because the Federal Reserve had distinct policy regimes during this period. The best way to determine appropriate samples for time-series estimation is to look at graphs of the data to see if the time series looks stationary before estimation begins. If we know that a government policy changed on a specific date, we might also test whether the time-series relation was the same before and after that date.

In the following example, we illustrate how the choice of a longer versus a shorter period can affect the decision of whether to use, for example, a first- or second-order time-series model. We then show how the choice of the time-series model (and the associated regression coefficients) affects our forecast. Finally, we discuss which sample period, and accordingly which model and corresponding forecast, is appropriate for the time series analyzed in the example.

Example 9

Instability in Time-Series Models of U.S. Inflation

In Example 6, analyst Lisette Miller concluded that U.S. CPI inflation should be modeled as an AR(2) time series. A colleague examined her results and questioned estimating one time-series model for inflation in the United States since 1971, given that Federal Reserve policy changed dramatically in the late 1970s and early 1980s. He argues that the inflation time series from 1971 to 2000 has two **regimes** or underlying models generating the time series: one running from 1971 through 1984, and another starting in 1985. Therefore, the colleague suggests that Miller estimate a new time-series model for U.S. inflation starting in 1985. Because of his suggestion, Miller first estimates an AR(1) model for inflation using data for a shorter sample period from 1985 to 2000. Table 8 shows her AR(1) estimates.

Table 8	Autoregression: AR(1) Model Monthly CPI Inflation at an Annual Rate, February 1985–December 2000

Regression Statistics	
R-squared	0.1540
Standard error	2.4641
Observations	191
Durbin–Watson	1.9182

	Coefficient	Standard Error	t-Statistic
Intercept	2.1371	0.2859	7.4747
Lag 1	0.3359	0.0690	4.8716

Autocorrelations of the Residual			
Lag	Autocorrelation	Standard Error	t-Statistic
1	0.0284	0.0724	0.3922
2	−0.0900	0.0724	−1.2426
3	−0.0141	0.0724	−0.1955
4	−0.0297	0.0724	−0.4103

Source: U.S. Bureau of Labor Statistics.

The bottom part of Table 8 shows that the first four autocorrelations of the residuals from the AR(1) model are quite small. None of these autocorrelations has a *t*-statistic larger than 1.97, the critical value for significance. Consequently, Miller cannot reject the null hypothesis that the residuals are serially uncorrelated. The AR(1) model is correctly specified for the sample period from 1985 to 2000, so there is no need to estimate the AR(2) model. This conclusion is very different from that reached in Example 6 using data from 1971 to 2000. In that example, Miller initially rejected the AR(1) model because its residuals exhibited serial correlation. When she used a larger sample, an AR(2) model initially appeared to fit the data much better than did an AR(1) model.

How deeply does our choice of sample period affect our forecast of future inflation? Suppose that in a given month, inflation was 4 percent at an annual rate, and the month before that it was 3 percent. The AR(1) model shown in Table 8 predicts that inflation in the next month will be 2.1371 + 0.3359(4) = approximately 3.48 percent. Therefore, the forecast of the next month's inflation using the 1985 to 2000 sample is 3.48 percent. Remember from the analysis following Example 6 that the AR(2) model for the 1971 to 2000 sample predicts inflation of 4.07 percent in the next month. Thus, using the correctly specified model for the shorter sample produces an inflation forecast almost 0.6 percentage points below the forecast made from the correctly specified model for the longer sample period. Such a difference might substantially affect a particular investment decision.

Which model is correct? Figure 9 suggests an answer. Monthly U.S. inflation was, on average, so much higher and so much more volatile during the mid-1970s to early 1980s than it was after 1984 that inflation is probably not a covariance-stationary time series from 1971 to 2000. Therefore, we can reasonably believe that the data have more than one regime and Miller should estimate a separate model for inflation from 1985 to 2000, as shown above. As the example shows, judgment and experience (such as knowledge of government policy changes) play a vital role in determining how to model a time series. Simply relying on autocorrelations of the residuals from a time-series model cannot tell us the correct sample period for our analysis.

Figure 9	Monthly CPI Inflation

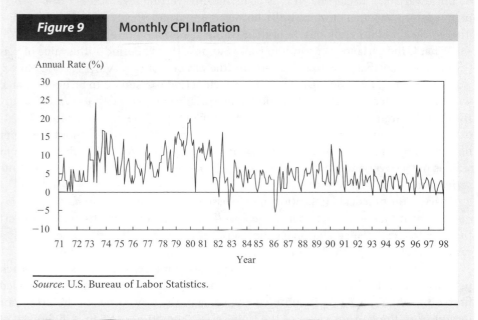

Source: U.S. Bureau of Labor Statistics.

RANDOM WALKS AND UNIT ROOTS

So far, we have examined those time series in which the time series has a tendency to revert to its mean level as the change in a variable from one period to the next follows a mean-reverting pattern. In contrast, there are many financial time series in which the changes follow a random pattern. We discuss these "random walks" in the following section.

5.1 Random Walks

A random walk is one of the most widely studied time-series models for financial data. A **random walk** is a time series in which the value of the series in one period is the value of the series in the previous period plus an unpredictable random error. A random walk can be described by the following equation:

$$x_t = x_{t-1} + \varepsilon_t, \; E(\varepsilon_t) = 0, \; E(\varepsilon_t^2) = \sigma^2, \; E(\varepsilon_t \varepsilon_s) = 0 \text{ if } t \neq s \qquad\qquad (8)$$

Equation 8 means that the time series x_t is in every period equal to its value in the previous period plus an error term, ε_t, that has constant variance and is uncorrelated with the error term in previous periods. Note two important points. First, this equation is a special case of an AR(1) model with $b_0 = 0$ and $b_1 = 1$.[25] Second, the expected value of ε_t is zero. Therefore, the best forecast of x_t that can be made in period $t - 1$ is x_{t-1}. In fact, in this model, x_{t-1} is the best forecast of x in every period after $t - 1$.

Random walks are quite common in financial time series. For example, many studies have tested and found that currency exchange rates follow a random walk. Consistent with the second point made above, some studies have found that sophisticated exchange rate forecasting models cannot outperform forecasts made using the random walk model, and that the best forecast of the future exchange rate is the current exchange rate.

Unfortunately, we cannot use the regression methods we have discussed so far to estimate an AR(1) model on a time series that is actually a random walk. To see why this is so, we must determine why a random walk has no finite mean-reverting level or finite variance. Recall that if x_t is at its mean-reverting level, then $x_t = b_0 + b_1 x_t$, or $x_t = b_0/(1 - b_1)$. In a random walk, however, $b_0 = 0$ and $b_1 = 1$, so $b_0/(1 - b_1) = 0/0$. Therefore, a random walk has an undefined mean-reverting level.

What is the variance of a random walk? Suppose that in Period 1, the value of x_1 is 0. Then we know that $x_2 = 0 + \varepsilon_2$. Therefore, the variance of $x_2 = \text{Var}(\varepsilon_2) = \sigma^2$. Now $x_3 = x_2 + \varepsilon_3 = \varepsilon_2 + \varepsilon_3$. Because the error term in each period is assumed to be uncorrelated with the error terms in all other periods, the variance of $x_3 = \text{Var}(\varepsilon_2) + \text{Var}(\varepsilon_3) = 2\sigma^2$. By a similar argument, we can show that for any period t, the variance of $x_t = (t - 1)\sigma^2$. But this means that as t grows large, the variance of x_t grows without an upper bound: It approaches infinity. This lack of upper bound, in turn, means that a random walk is not a covariance-stationary time series, because a covariance-stationary time series must have a finite variance.

What is the practical implication of these issues? *We cannot use standard regression analysis on a time series that is a random walk.* We can, however, attempt to convert the data to a covariance-stationary time series if we suspect that the time series is a random walk. In statistical terms, we can difference it.

We difference a time series by creating a new time series, say y_t, that in each period is equal to the difference between x_t and x_{t-1}. This transformation is called **first-differencing** because it subtracts the value of the time series in the first prior period from the current value of the time series. Sometimes the first difference of x_t is written as $\Delta x_t = x_t - x_{t-1}$. Note that the first difference of the random walk in Equation 8 yields

$$y_t = x_t - x_{t-1} = \varepsilon_t, \; E(\varepsilon_t) = 0, \; E(\varepsilon_t^2) = \sigma^2, \; E(\varepsilon_t \varepsilon_s) = 0 \text{ for } t \neq s$$

The expected value of ε_t is 0. Therefore, the best forecast of y_t that can be made in period $t - 1$ is 0. This implies that the best forecast is that there will be no change in the value of the current time series, x_{t-1}.

The first-differenced variable, y_t, is covariance stationary. How is this so? First, note that this model ($y_t = \varepsilon_t$) is an AR(1) model with $b_0 = 0$ and $b_1 = 0$. We can compute the mean-reverting level of the first-differenced model as $b_0/(1 - b_1) = 0/1 = 0$. Therefore, a first-differenced random walk has a mean-reverting level of 0. Note also that the variance of y_t in each period is $\text{Var}(\varepsilon_t) = \sigma^2$. Because the variance and the mean of y_t are constant and finite in each period, y_t is a covariance-stationary time series and

---

25 Equation 8 with a nonzero intercept added (as in Equation 9 given later) is sometimes referred to as a random walk with drift.

we can model it using linear regression.[26] Of course, modeling the first-differenced series with an AR(1) model does not help us predict the future, as $b_0 = 0$ and $b_1 = 0$. We simply conclude that the original time series is, in fact, a random walk.

Had we tried to estimate an AR(1) model for a time series that was a random walk, our statistical conclusions would have been incorrect because AR models cannot be used to estimate random walks or any time series that is not covariance stationary. The following example illustrates this issue with exchange rates.

Example 10

The Yen/U.S. Dollar Exchange Rate

Financial analysts often assume that exchange rates are random walks. Consider an AR(1) model for the Japanese yen/U.S. dollar exchange rate. Table 9 shows the results of estimating the model using month-end observations from January 1975 to December 2002.

Table 9	Yen/U.S. Dollar Exchange Rate: AR(1) Model Month-End Observations, January 1975–December 2002

Regression Statistics

R-squared	0.9914
Standard error	5.9006
Observations	336
Durbin–Watson	1.8492

	Coefficient	Standard Error	t-Statistic
Intercept	1.0223	0.9268	1.1092
Lag 1	0.9910	0.0050	196.4517

Autocorrelations of the Residual

Lag	Autocorrelation	Standard Error	t-Statistic
1	0.0706	0.0546	1.2930
2	0.0364	0.0546	0.6667
3	0.0864	0.0546	1.5824
4	0.0566	0.0546	1.0366

Source: U.S. Federal Reserve Board of Governors.

The results in Table 9 suggest that the yen/U.S. dollar exchange rate is a random walk because the estimated intercept does not appear to be significantly different from 0 and the estimated coefficient on the first lag of the exchange rate is very close to 1. Can we use the t-statistics in Table 9 to test whether the exchange rate is a random walk? Unfortunately, no, because the standard errors in an AR model are invalid if the model is estimated on a random walk

---

26 All the covariances are finite, for two reasons: The variance is finite, and the covariance of a time series with its own past value can be no greater than the variance of the series.

(remember, a random walk is not covariance stationary). If the exchange rate is, in fact, a random walk, we might come to an incorrect conclusion based on faulty statistical tests and then invest incorrectly. We can use a test presented in the next section to test whether the time-series is a random walk.

Suppose the exchange rate is a random walk, as we now suspect. If so, the first-differenced series, $y_t = x_t - x_{t-1}$, will be covariance stationary. We present the results from estimating $y_t = b_0 + b_1 y_{t-1} + \varepsilon_t$ in Table 10. If the exchange rate is a random walk, then $b_0 = 0$ and $b_1 = 0$ and the error term will not be serially correlated.

Table 10	First-Differenced Yen/U.S. Dollar Exchange Rate: AR(1) Model Month-End Observations, January 1975–December 2002

Regression Statistics

R-squared	0.0053
Standard error	5.9133
Observations	336
Durbin–Watson	1.9980

	Coefficient	Standard Error	t-Statistic
Intercept	−0.4963	0.3244	−1.5301
Lag 1	0.0726	0.0547	1.3282

Autocorrelations of the Residual			
Lag	Autocorrelation	Standard Error	t-Statistic
1	−0.0045	0.0546	−0.0824
2	0.0259	0.0546	0.4744
3	0.0807	0.0546	1.4780
4	0.0488	0.0546	0.8938

Source: U.S. Federal Reserve Board of Governors.

In Table 10, neither the intercept nor the coefficient on the first lag of the first-differenced exchange rate differs significantly from 0, and no residual auto-correlations differ significantly from 0.[27] These findings are consistent with the yen/U.S. dollar exchange rate being a random walk.

We have concluded that the differenced regression is the model to choose. Now we can see that we would have been seriously misled if we had based our model choice on an R^2 comparison. In Table 9, the R^2 is 0.9914, whereas in Table 10 the R^2 is 0.0053. How can this be, if we just concluded that the model in Table 10 is the one that we should use? In Table 9, the R^2 measures how well the exchange rate in one period predicts the exchange rate in the next period. If the exchange rate is a random walk, its current value will be an extremely good predictor of its value in the next period, and thus the R^2 will be extremely high.

---

27 See Greene (2003) for a test of the joint hypothesis that both regression coefficients are equal to 0.

At the same time, if the exchange rate is a random walk, then changes in the exchange rate should be completely unpredictable. Table 10 estimates whether changes in the exchange rate from one month to the next can be predicted by changes in the exchange rate over the previous month. If they cannot be predicted, the R^2 in Table 10 should be very low. In fact, it is low (0.0053). This comparison provides a good example of the general rule that we cannot necessarily choose which model is correct solely by comparing the R^2 from the two models.

The exchange rate is a random walk, and changes in a random walk are by definition unpredictable. Therefore, we cannot profit from an investment strategy that predicts changes in the exchange rate.

To this point, we have discussed only simple random walks; that is, random walks without drift. In a random walk without drift, the best predictor of the time series in the next period is its current value. A random walk with drift, however, should increase or decrease by a constant amount in each period. The equation describing a random walk with drift is a special case of the AR(1) model:

$$x_t = b_0 + b_1 x_{t-1} + \varepsilon_t$$
$$b_1 = 1, b_0 \neq 0, \text{ or} \tag{9}$$
$$x_t = b_0 + x_{t-1} + \varepsilon_t, E(\varepsilon_t) = 0$$

A random walk with drift has $b_0 \neq 0$ compared to a simple random walk, which has $b_0 = 0$.

We have already seen that $b_1 = 1$ implies an undefined mean-reversion level and thus nonstationarity. Consequently, we cannot use an AR model to analyze a time series that is a random walk with drift until we transform the time series by taking first differences. If we first-difference Equation 9, the result is $y_t = x_t - x_{t-1}, y_t = b_0 + \varepsilon_t, b_0 \neq 0$.

5.2 The Unit Root Test of Nonstationarity

In this section, we discuss how to use random walk concepts to determine whether a time series is covariance stationary. This approach focuses on the slope coefficient in the random-walk-with-drift case of an AR(1) model in contrast with the traditional autocorrelation approach which we discuss first.

The examination of the autocorrelations of a time series at various lags is a well-known prescription for inferring whether or not a time series is stationary. Typically, for a stationary time series, either autocorrelations at all lags are statistically indistinguishable from zero, or the autocorrelations drop off rapidly to zero as the number of lags becomes large. Conversely, the autocorrelations of a nonstationary time series do not exhibit those characteristics. However, this approach is less definite than a currently more popular test for nonstationarity known as the Dickey–Fuller test for a unit root.

We can explain what is known as the unit root problem in the context of an AR(1) model. If a time series comes from an AR(1) model, then to be covariance stationary the absolute value of the lag coefficient, b_1, must be less than 1.0. We could not rely on the statistical results of an AR(1) model if the absolute value of the lag coefficient were greater than or equal to 1.0 because the time series would not be covariance stationary. If the lag coefficient is equal to 1.0, the time series has a **unit root**: it is a random walk and is not covariance stationary.[28] By definition, all random walks, with or without a drift term, have unit roots.

---

28 When b_1 is greater than 1 in absolute value, we say that there is an explosive root. For details, see Diebold (2004).

How do we test for unit roots in a time series? If we believed that a time series, x_t, was a random walk with drift, it would be tempting to estimate the parameters of the AR(1) model $x_t = b_0 + b_1 x_{t-1} + \varepsilon_t$ using linear regression and conduct a t-test of the hypothesis that $b_1 = 1$. Unfortunately, if $b_1 = 1$, then x_t is not covariance stationary and the t-value of the estimated coefficient, $\hat{b}_1$, does not actually follow the t-distribution; consequently, a t-test would be invalid.

Dickey and Fuller (1979) developed a regression-based unit root test based on a transformed version of the AR(1) model $x_t = b_0 + b_1 x_{t-1} + \varepsilon_t$. Subtracting x_{t-1} from both sides of the AR(1) model produces

$$x_t - x_{t-1} = b_0 + (b_1 - 1)x_{t-1} + \varepsilon_t$$

or

$$x_t - x_{t-1} = b_0 + g_1 x_{t-1} + \varepsilon_t, \, E(\varepsilon_t) = 0 \tag{10}$$

where $g_1 = (b_1 - 1)$. If $b_1 = 1$, then $g_1 = 0$ and thus a test of $g_1 = 0$ is a test of $b_1 = 1$. If there is a unit root in the AR(1) model, then g_1 will be 0 in a regression where the dependent variable is the first difference of the time series and the independent variable is the first lag of the time series. The null hypothesis of the Dickey–Fuller test is $H_0: g_1 = 0$—that is, that the time series has a unit root and is nonstationary—and the alternative hypothesis is $H_a: g_1 < 0$, that the time series does not have a unit root and is stationary.

To conduct the test, one calculates a t-statistic in the conventional manner for $\hat{g}_1$ but instead of using conventional critical values for a t-test, one uses a revised set of values computed by Dickey and Fuller; the revised set of critical values are larger in absolute value than the conventional critical values. A number of software packages incorporate Dickey–Fuller tests.[29]

Example 11

Intel's Quarterly Sales (1)

Earlier, we concluded that we could not model the log of Intel's quarterly sales using only a time-trend line (as shown in Example 3). Recall that the Durbin–Watson statistic from the log-linear regression caused us to reject the hypothesis that the errors in the regression were serially uncorrelated. Suppose, instead, that the analyst decides to model the log of Intel's quarterly sales using an AR(1) model. He uses ln Sales$_t = b_0 + b_1$ ln Sales$_{t-1} + \varepsilon_t$.

Before he estimates this regression, the analyst should use the Dickey–Fuller test to determine whether there is a unit root in the log of Intel's quarterly sales. If he uses the sample of quarterly data on Intel's sales from the first quarter of 1985 through the fourth quarter of 1999, takes the natural log of each observation, and computes the Dickey–Fuller t-test statistic, the value of that statistic might cause him to fail to reject the null hypothesis that there is a unit root in the log of Intel's quarterly sales.

If a time series appears to have a unit root, how should we model it? One method that is often successful is to first-difference the time series (as discussed previously) and try to model the first-differenced series as an autoregressive time series. The following example demonstrates this method.

---

[29] Dickey and Fuller developed three separate tests of the hypothesis that $g_1 = 0$ assuming the following models: random walk, random walk with drift, or random walk with drift and trend. The critical values for the Dickey–Fuller tests for the three models are different. For more on this topic, see Greene (2003) or Hamilton (1994).

Example 12

Intel's Quarterly Sales (2)

Suppose you are convinced—from looking at the plot of the time series—that the log of Intel's quarterly sales is not covariance stationary (it has a unit root). So you create a new series, y_t, that is the first difference of the log of Intel's quarterly sales. Figure 10 shows that series.

If you compare Figure 10 to Figures 6 and 8, you will see that first-differencing the log of Intel's quarterly sales eliminates the strong upward trend that was present in both Intel's sales and the log of Intel's sales. Because the first-differenced series has no strong trend, you are better off assuming that the differenced series is covariance stationary rather than assuming that Intel's sales or the log of Intel's sales is a covariance-stationary time series.

Figure 10	Log Difference, Intel Quarterly Sales

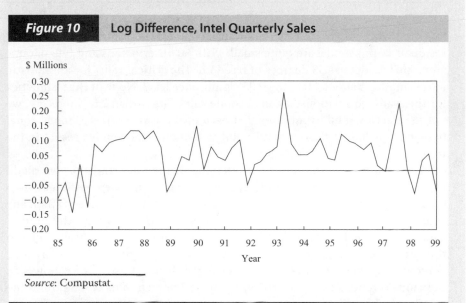

Source: Compustat.

Now suppose you decide to model the new series using an AR(1) model. You use $\ln(\text{Sales}_t) - \ln(\text{Sales}_{t-1}) = b_0 + b_1[\ln(\text{Sales}_{t-1}) - \ln(\text{Sales}_{t-2})] + \varepsilon_t$. Table 11 shows the results of that regression.

Table 11	Log Differenced Sales: AR(1) Model Intel Corporation Quarterly Observations, January 1985–December 1999

Regression Statistics

R-squared	0.0946
Standard error	0.0758
Observations	60
Durbin–Watson	1.9709

	Coefficient	Standard Error	t-Statistic
Intercept	0.0352	0.0114	3.0875
Lag 1	0.3064	0.1244	2.4620

(continued)

Table 11	Continued		
Autocorrelations of the Residual			
Lag	Autocorrelation	Standard Error	t-Statistic
1	−0.0140	0.1291	−0.1088
2	−0.0855	0.1291	−0.6624
3	−0.0582	0.1291	−0.4506
4	0.2125	0.1291	1.6463

Source: Compustat.

The lower part of Table 11 shows that the first four autocorrelations of residuals in this model are quite small. With 60 observations and two parameters, this model has 58 degrees of freedom. The critical value for a t-statistic in this model is about 2.0 at the 0.05 significance level. None of the t-statistics for these autocorrelations has an absolute value larger than 2.0. Therefore, we fail to reject the null hypotheses that each of these autocorrelations is equal to 0 and conclude instead that no significant autocorrelation is present in the residuals.

This result suggests that the model is well specified and that we could use the estimates. Both the intercept ($\hat{b}_0 = 0.0352$) and the coefficient ($\hat{b}_1 = 0.3064$) on the first lag of the new first-differenced series are statistically significant. How can we interpret the estimated coefficients in the model? The value of the intercept (0.0352) implies that if sales have not changed in the current quarter ($y_t = \ln \text{Sales}_t - \ln \text{Sales}_{t-1} = 0$), sales will grow by 3.52 percent next quarter.[30] If sales have changed during this quarter, however, the model predicts that sales will grow by 3.52 percent plus 0.3064 times the sales growth in this quarter.

Suppose we wanted to use this model soon after the end of the fourth quarter of 1999 to predict Intel's sales for the first quarter of 2000. Let us say that t is the fourth quarter of 1999, so $t - 1$ is the third quarter of 1999 and $t + 1$ is the first quarter of 2000. Then we would have to compute $\hat{y}_{t+1} = 0.0352 + 0.3064\, y_t$. To compute $\hat{y}_{t+1}$, we need to know $y_t = \ln \text{Sales}_t - \ln \text{Sales}_{t-1}$. In the third quarter of 1999, Intel's sales were $7,328 million, so $\ln (\text{Sales}_{t-1}) = \ln 7,328 = 8.8995$. In the fourth quarter of 1999, Intel's sales were $8,212 million, so $\ln (\text{Sales}_t) = \ln 8,212 = 9.0134$. Thus $y_t = 9.0134 - 8.8995 = 0.1139$. Therefore, $\hat{y}_{t+1} = 0.0352 + 0.3064(0.1139) = 0.0701$. If $\hat{y}_{t+1} = 0.0701$, then $0.0701 = \ln (\text{Sales}_{t+1}) - \ln (\text{Sales}_t) = \ln (\text{Sales}_{t+1}/\text{Sales}_t)$. If we exponentiate both sides of this equation, the result is

$$e^{0.0701} = \left(\text{Sales}_{t+1}/\text{Sales}_t\right)$$

$$\text{Sales}_{t+1} = \text{Sales}_t\, e^{0.0701}$$

$$= \$8,212 \text{ million} \times 1.0726$$

$$= \$8,808 \text{ million}$$

Thus, based on fourth quarter sales for 1999, this model would have predicted that Intel's sales in the first quarter of 2000 would be $8,808 million. This sales forecast might have affected our decision to buy Intel's stock at the time.

---

30 Note that 3.52 percent is the exponential growth rate, not [(Current quarter sales/Previous quarter sales) − 1]. The difference between these two methods of computing growth is usually small.

MOVING-AVERAGE TIME-SERIES MODELS

So far, many of the forecasting models we have used have been autoregressive models. Because most financial time series have the qualities of an autoregressive process, autoregressive time-series models are probably the most frequently used time-series models in financial forecasting. Some financial time series, however, seem to follow more closely another kind of time-series model called a moving-average model. For example, as we will see later, returns on the Standard & Poor's 500 Index can be better modeled as a moving-average process than as an autoregressive process.

In this section, we present the fundamentals of moving-average models so that you can ask the right questions when presented with them. We first discuss how to smooth past values with a moving average and then how to forecast a time series using a moving-average model. Even though both methods include the words "moving average" in the name, they are very different.

6.1 Smoothing Past Values with an n-Period Moving Average

Suppose you are analyzing the long-term trend in the past sales of a company. In order to focus on the trend, you may find it useful to remove short-term fluctuations or noise by smoothing out the time series of sales. One technique to smooth out period-to-period fluctuations in the value of a time series is an **n-period moving average**. An n-period moving average of the current and past $n - 1$ values of a time series, x_t, is calculated as

$$\frac{x_t + x_{t-1} + \ldots + x_{t-(n-1)}}{n} \tag{11}$$

The following example demonstrates how to compute a moving average of Intel's quarterly sales.

Example 13

Intel's Quarterly Sales (3)

Suppose we want to compute the four-quarter moving average of Intel's sales at the end of the fourth quarter of 1999. Intel's sales in the previous four quarters were 1Q:1999, $7,103 million; 2Q:1999, $6,746 million; 3Q:1999, $7,328 million; and 4Q:1999, $8,212 million. The four-quarter moving average of sales as of the first quarter of 2000 is thus (7,103 + 6,746 + 7,328 + 8,212)/4 = $7,347.25 million.

We often plot the moving average of a series with large fluctuations to help discern any patterns in the data. Figure 11 shows monthly real (inflation-adjusted) retail sales for the United States from January 1972 to December 2000, along with a 12-month moving average of the data.[31]

---

[31] A 12-month moving average is the average value of a time series over each of the last 12 months. Although the sample period starts in 1972, data from 1971 are used to compute the 12-month moving average for the months of 1972.

Figure 11   Monthly U.S. Real Retail Sales and 12-Month Moving Average of Retail Sales

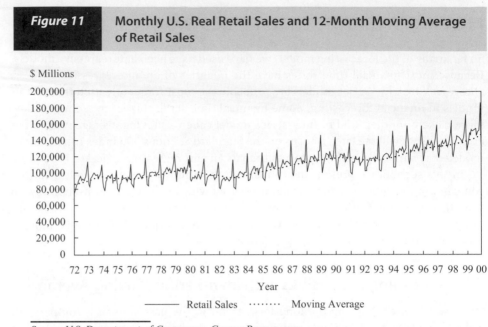

Source: U.S. Department of Commerce, Census Bureau.

As Figure 11 shows, each year has a very strong peak in retail sales (December) followed by a sharp drop in sales (January). Because of the extreme seasonality in the data, a 12-month moving average can help us focus on the long-term movements in retail sales instead of seasonal fluctuations. Note that the moving average does not have the sharp seasonal fluctuations of the original retail sales data. Rather, the moving average of retail sales grows steadily, for example, from 1985 through 1990, then declines until 1993, and grows steadily thereafter. We can see that trend more easily by looking at a 12-month moving average than by looking at the time series itself.

Figure 12 shows monthly crude oil prices in the United States along with a 12-month moving average of oil prices. Although these data do not have the same sharp regular seasonality displayed in the retail sales data in Figure 11, the moving average smoothes out the monthly fluctuations in oil prices to show the longer-term movements.

Figure 12   Monthly Oil Price and 12-Month Moving Average of Prices

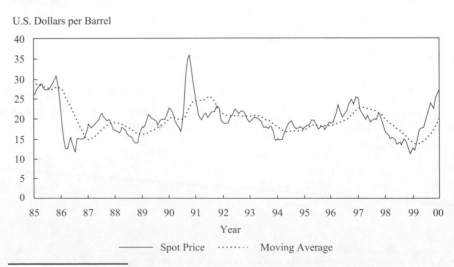

Source: Dow Jones Energy Service.

Figure 12 also shows one weakness with a moving average: It always lags large movements in the actual data. For example, when oil prices fell sharply in late 1985 and remained relatively low, the moving average fell only gradually. When oil prices rose quickly in 1999, the moving average also lagged. Consequently, a simple moving average of the recent past, though often useful in smoothing out a time series, may not be the best predictor of the future. A main reason for this is that a simple moving average gives equal weight to all the periods in the moving average. In order to forecast the future values of a time series, it is often better to use a more sophisticated moving-average time-series model. We discuss such models below.

6.2 Moving-Average Time-Series Models for Forecasting

Suppose that a time series, x_t, is consistent with the following model:

$$x_t = \varepsilon_t + \theta \varepsilon_{t-1}, \; E(\varepsilon_t) = 0, \; E(\varepsilon_t^2) = \sigma^2, \; E(\varepsilon_t \varepsilon_s) = 0 \text{ for } t \neq s \tag{12}$$

This equation is called a moving-average model of order 1, or simply an MA(1) model. Theta (θ) is the parameter of the MA(1) model.[32]

Equation 12 is a moving-average model because in each period, x_t is a moving average of ε_t and ε_{t-1}, two uncorrelated random variables that each have an expected value of zero. Unlike the simple moving-average model of Equation 11, this moving-average model places different weights on the two terms in the moving average (1 on ε_t, and θ on ε_{t-1}).

We can see if a time series fits an MA(1) model by looking at its autocorrelations to determine whether x_t is correlated only with its preceding and following values. First, we examine the variance of x_t in Equation 12 and its first two autocorrelations. Because the expected value of x_t is 0 in all periods and ε_t is uncorrelated with its own past values, the first autocorrelation is not equal to 0, but the second and higher autocorrelations are equal to 0. Further analysis shows that all autocorrelations except for the first will be equal to 0 in an MA(1) model. Thus for an MA(1) process, any value x_t is correlated with x_{t-1} and x_{t+1} but with no other time-series values; we could say that an MA(1) model has a memory of one period.

Of course, an MA(1) model is not the most complex moving-average model. A qth order moving-average model, denoted MA(q) and with varying weights on lagged terms, can be written as

$$x_t = \varepsilon_t + \theta_1 \varepsilon_{t-1} + \ldots \theta_q \varepsilon_{t-q}, \; E(\varepsilon_t) = 0, \; E(\varepsilon_t^2) = \sigma^2,$$

$$E(\varepsilon_t \varepsilon_s) = 0 \text{ for } t \neq s \tag{13}$$

How can we tell whether an MA(q) model fits a time series? We examine the autocorrelations. For an MA(q) model, the first q autocorrelations will be significantly different from 0, and all autocorrelations beyond that will be equal to 0; an MA(q) model has a memory of q periods. This result is critical for choosing the right value of q for an MA model. We discussed this result above for the specific case of $q = 1$ that all autocorrelations except for the first will be equal to 0 in an MA(1) model.

How can we distinguish an autoregressive time series from a moving-average time series? Once again, we do so by examining the autocorrelations of the time series itself. The autocorrelations of most autoregressive time series start large and decline gradually, whereas the autocorrelations of an MA(q) time series suddenly drop to 0 after the first q autocorrelations. We are unlikely to know in advance whether a time

---

32 Note that a moving-average time-series model is very different from a simple moving average, as discussed in Section 6.1. The simple moving average is based on observed values of a time series. In a moving-average time-series model, we never directly observe, ε_t or any other ε_{t-j}, but we can infer how a particular moving-average model will imply a particular pattern of serial correlation for a time series, as we discuss below.

series is autoregressive or moving average. Therefore, the autocorrelations give us our best clue about how to model the time series. Most time series, however, are best modeled with an autoregressive model.

Example 14

A Time-Series Model for Monthly Returns on the S&P 500

Are monthly returns on the S&P autocorrelated? If so, we may be able to devise an investment strategy to exploit the autocorrelation. What is an appropriate time-series model for S&P 500 monthly returns?

Table 12 shows the first six autocorrelations of returns to the S&P 500 using monthly data from January 1991 to December 2002. Note that all of the autocorrelations are quite small. Do they reach significance? With 144 observations, the critical value for a t-statistic in this model is about 1.98 at the 0.05 significance level. None of the autocorrelations has a t-statistic larger in absolute value than the critical value of 1.98. Consequently, we fail to reject the null hypothesis that those autocorrelations, individually, do not differ significantly from 0.

Table 12	Annualized Monthly Returns to the S&P 500 January 1991–December 2002

	Autocorrelations		
Lag	**Autocorrelation**	**Standard Error**	**t-Statistic**
1	−0.0090	0.0833	−0.1083
2	−0.0207	0.0833	−0.2481
3	0.0020	0.0833	0.0240
4	−0.0730	0.0833	−0.8756
5	0.1143	0.0833	1.3717
6	−0.0007	0.0833	−0.0082

Observations   144

Source: Ibbotson Associates.

If returns on the S&P 500 were an MA(q) time series, then the first q autocorrelations would differ significantly from 0. None of the autocorrelations is statistically significant, however, so returns to the S&P 500 appear to come from an MA(0) time series. An MA(0) time series in which we allow the mean to be nonzero takes the following form:[33]

$$x_t = \mu + \varepsilon_t, E(\varepsilon_t) = 0, E(\varepsilon_t^2) = \sigma^2, E(\varepsilon_t\varepsilon_s) = 0 \text{ for } t \neq s \tag{14}$$

which means that the time series is not predictable. This result should not be too surprising, as most research suggests that short-term returns to stock indexes are difficult to predict.

---

[33] On the basis of investment theory and evidence, we expect that the mean monthly return on the S&P 500 is positive ($\mu > 0$). We can also generalize Equation 13 for an MA(q) time series by adding a constant term, μ. Including a constant term in a moving-average model does not change the expressions for the variance and autocovariances of the time series. A number of early studies of weak-form market efficiency used Equation 14 as the model for stock returns. See Garbade (1982).

We can see from this example how examining the autocorrelations allowed us to choose between the AR and MA models. If returns to the S&P 500 had come from an AR(1) time series, the first autocorrelation would have differed significantly from 0 and the autocorrelations would have declined gradually. Not even the first autocorrelation is significantly different from 0, however. Therefore, we can be sure that returns to the S&P 500 do not come from an AR(1) model—or from any higher-order AR model, for that matter. This finding is consistent with our conclusion that the S&P 500 series is MA(0).

SEASONALITY IN TIME-SERIES MODELS

As we analyze the results of the time-series models in this reading, we encounter complications. One common complication is significant seasonality, a case in which the series shows regular patterns of movement within the year. At first glance, seasonality might appear to rule out using autoregressive time-series models. After all, autocorrelations will differ by season. This problem can often be solved, however, by using seasonal lags in an autoregressive model.

A seasonal lag is usually the value of the time series one year before the current period, included as an extra term in an autoregressive model. Suppose, for example, that we model a particular quarterly time series using an AR(1) model, $x_t = b_0 + b_1 x_{t-1} + \varepsilon_t$. If the time series had significant seasonality, this model would not be correctly specified. The seasonality would be easy to detect because the seasonal autocorrelation (in the case of quarterly data, the fourth autocorrelation) of the error term would differ significantly from 0. Suppose this quarterly model has significant seasonality. In this case, we might include a seasonal lag in the autoregressive model and estimate

$$x_t = b_0 + b_1 x_{t-1} + b_2 x_{t-4} + \varepsilon_t \tag{15}$$

to test whether including the seasonal lag would eliminate statistically significant autocorrelation in the error term.

In Examples 15 and 16, we illustrate how to test and adjust for seasonality in a time-series model. We also illustrate how to compute a forecast using an autoregressive model with a seasonal lag.

Example 15

Seasonality in Sales at Medtronic

We want to predict sales for Medtronic, Inc. Based on the previous results in this reading, we determine that the first difference of the log of sales is probably covariance stationary. Using quarterly data from the first quarter of 1985 to the last quarter of 2001, we estimate an AR(1) model using ordinary least squares on the first-differenced data. We estimate the following equation: (ln Sales$_t$ – ln Sales$_{t-1}$) = b_0 + b_1(ln Sales$_{t-1}$ – ln Sales$_{t-2}$) + ε_t. Table 13 shows the results of the regression.

Table 13	Log Differenced Sales: AR(1) Model Medtronic, Inc., Quarterly Observations, January 1985–December 2001

Regression Statistics

R-squared	0.1619
Standard error	0.0693
Observations	68
Durbin–Watson	2.0588

	Coefficient	Standard Error	t-Statistic
Intercept	0.0597	0.0091	6.5411
Lag 1	−0.4026	0.1128	−3.5704

Autocorrelations of the Residual

Lag	Autocorrelation	Standard Error	t-Statistic
1	−0.0299	0.1213	−0.2463
2	−0.1950	0.1213	−1.6077
3	−0.1138	0.1213	−0.9381
4	0.4072	0.1213	3.3581

Source: Compustat.

The first thing to note in Table 13 is the strong seasonal autocorrelation of the residuals. The bottom portion of the table shows that the fourth autocorrelation has a value of 0.4072 and a t-statistic of 3.36. With 68 observations and two parameters, this model has 66 degrees of freedom.[34] The critical value for a t-statistic is about 2.0 at the 0.05 significance level. Given this value of the t-statistic, we must reject the null hypothesis that the fourth autocorrelation is equal to 0 because the t-statistic is larger than the critical value of 2.0.

In this model, the fourth autocorrelation is the seasonal autocorrelation because this AR(1) model is estimated with quarterly data. Table 13 shows the strong and statistically significant seasonal autocorrelation that occurs when a time series with strong seasonality is modeled without taking the seasonality into account. Therefore, the AR(1) model is misspecified, and we should not use it for forecasting.

Suppose we decide to use an autoregressive model with a seasonal lag because of the seasonal autocorrelation. We are modeling quarterly data, so we estimate Equation 15: $(\ln \text{Sales}_t - \ln \text{Sales}_{t-1}) = b_0 + b_1 (\ln \text{Sales}_{t-1} - \ln \text{Sales}_{t-2}) + b_2(\ln \text{Sales}_{t-4} - \ln \text{Sales}_{t-5}) + \varepsilon_t$. The estimates of this equation appear in Table 14.

---

[34] Although the sample period begins in 1985, we use prior observations for the lags. Otherwise, the model would have fewer degrees of freedom because the sample size would be reduced with each increase in the number of lags.

Table 14	Log Differenced Sales: AR(1) Model with Seasonal Lag Medtronic, Inc., Quarterly Observations, January 1985– December 2001

Regression Statistics

R-squared	0.3219
Standard error	0.0580
Observations	68
Durbin–Watson	2.0208

	Coefficient	Standard Error	t-Statistic
Intercept	0.0403	0.0096	4.1855
Lag 1	−0.2955	0.1058	−2.7927
Lag 4	0.3896	0.0995	3.9159

Autocorrelations of the Residual

Lag	Autocorrelation	Standard Error	t-Statistic
1	−0.0108	0.1213	−0.0889
2	−0.0957	0.1213	−0.7889
3	0.0075	0.1213	0.0621
4	−0.0340	0.1213	−0.2801

Source: Compustat.

Note the autocorrelations of the residual shown at the bottom of Table 14. When we include a seasonal lag in the regression, none of the t-statistics on the first four autocorrelations remains significant.

Now that we know that the residuals of this model do not have significant serial correlation, we can assume that the model is correctly specified. How can we interpret the coefficients in this model? To predict the current quarter's sales growth at Medtronic, we need to know two things: sales growth in the previous quarter and sales growth four quarters ago. If sales remained constant in each of those two quarters, the model in Table 14 predicts that sales will grow by 0.0403 (4.03 percent) in the current quarter. If sales grew by 1 percent last quarter and by 2 percent four quarters ago, then the model predicts that sales growth this quarter will be 0.0403 − 0.2955(0.01) + 0.3896(0.02) = 0.0451 or 4.51 percent.[35] Notice also that the R^2 in the model with the seasonal lag (0.3219 in Table 14) was almost two times higher than the R^2 in the model without the seasonal lag (0.1619 in Table 13). Again, the seasonal lag model does a much better job of explaining the data.

---

35 Note that all of these growth rates are exponential growth rates.

Example 16

Retail Sales Growth

We want to predict the growth in U.S. monthly retail sales so that we can decide whether to recommend discount store stocks. We decide to use non-seasonally adjusted data on retail sales, adjusted for inflation. To begin with, we estimate an AR(1) model with observations on the annualized monthly growth in real retail sales from February 1972 to December 2000. We estimate the following equation: Sales growth$_t = b_0 + b_1$ Sales growth$_{t-1} + \varepsilon_t$. Table 15 shows the results from this model.

The autocorrelations of the residuals from this model, shown at the bottom of Table 15, indicate that seasonality is extremely significant in this model. With 347 observations and two parameters, this model has 345 degrees of freedom. At the 0.05 significance level, the critical value for a t-statistic is about 1.97. The 12th-lag autocorrelation (the seasonal autocorrelation, because we are using monthly data) has a value of 0.8739 and a t-statistic of 16.28. The t-statistic on this autocorrelation is larger than the critical value (1.97) implying that we can reject the null hypothesis that the 12th autocorrelation is 0. Note also that many of the other t-statistics for autocorrelations shown in the table differ significantly from 0. Consequently, the model shown in Table 15 is misspecified, so we cannot rely on it to forecast sales growth.

Suppose we add the seasonal lag of sales growth (the 12th lag) to the AR(1) model to estimate the equation Sales growth$_t = b_0 + b_1$(Sales growth$_{t-1}$) + b_2(Sales growth$_{t-12}$) + ε_t. Table 16 presents the results of estimating this equation. The estimated value of the seasonal autocorrelation (the 12th autocorrelation) has fallen to 0.0335. None of the first 12 autocorrelations has a t-statistic with an absolute value greater than the critical value of 1.97 at the 0.05 significance level. We can conclude that there is no significant serial correlation in the residuals from this model. Because we can reasonably believe that the model is correctly specified, we can use it to predict retail sales growth. Note that the R^2 in Table 16 is 0.8149, much larger than the R^2 in Table 15 (computed by the model without the seasonal lag).

Table 15	Monthly Real Retail Sales Growth: AR(1) Model February 1972–December 2000

Regression Statistics

R-squared	0.0659
Standard error	2.3520
Observations	347
Durbin–Watson	2.1008

	Coefficient	Standard Error	t-Statistic
Intercept	1.2170	0.1357	8.9666
Lag 1	−0.2577	0.0522	−4.9349

Autocorrelations of the Residual

Lag	Autocorrelation	Standard Error	t-Statistic
1	−0.0552	0.0537	−1.0288

Table 15	Continued		

Autocorrelations of the Residual

Lag	Autocorrelation	Standard Error	t-Statistic
2	−0.1536	0.0537	−2.8619
3	0.1774	0.0537	3.3044
4	−0.1020	0.0537	−1.8996
5	−0.1320	0.0537	−2.4582
6	−0.2676	0.0537	−4.9841
7	−0.1366	0.0537	−2.5455
8	−0.0923	0.0537	−1.7186
9	0.1655	0.0537	3.0832
10	−0.1732	0.0537	−3.2273
11	−0.0623	0.0537	−1.1597
12	0.8739	0.0537	16.2793

Source: U.S. Department of Commerce.

How can we interpret the coefficients in the model? To predict growth in retail sales in this month, we need to know last month's retail sales growth and retail sales growth 12 months ago. If retail sales remained constant both last month and 12 months ago, the model in Table 16 predicts that retail sales will grow at an annual rate of approximately 15 percent this month. If retail sales grew at an annual rate of 5 percent last month and at an annual rate of 10 percent 12 months ago, the model in Table 16 predicts that retail sales will grow in the current month at an annual rate of $0.1516 - 0.0490(0.05) + 0.8857(0.10)$ = 0.2377 or 23.8 percent.

Table 16	Monthly Real Retail Sales Growth: AR(1) Model with Seasonal Lag February 1972–December 2000

Regression Statistics

R-squared	0.8149
Standard error	1.0487
Observations	347
Durbin–Watson	2.4301

	Coefficient	Standard Error	t-Statistic
Intercept	0.1516	0.0669	2.2652
Lag 1	−0.0490	0.0239	−2.0484
Lag 12	0.8857	0.0237	37.3028

(continued)

Table 16	Continued		

Autocorrelations of the Residual

Lag	Autocorrelation	Standard Error	t-Statistic
1	−0.0699	0.0537	−1.3019
2	−0.0107	0.0537	−0.1985
3	0.0946	0.0537	1.7630
4	−0.0556	0.0537	−1.0355
5	−0.0319	0.0537	−0.5936
6	0.0289	0.0537	0.5386
7	−0.0933	0.0537	−1.7382
8	0.0062	0.0537	0.1150
9	−0.0111	0.0537	−0.2059
10	−0.0523	0.0537	−0.9742
11	0.0377	0.0537	0.7026
12	0.0335	0.0537	0.6231

Source: U.S. Department of Commerce.

8 AUTOREGRESSIVE MOVING-AVERAGE MODELS

So far, we have presented autoregressive and moving-average models as alternatives for modeling a time series. The time series we have considered in examples have usually been explained quite well with a simple autoregressive model (with or without seasonal lags).[36] Some statisticians, however, have advocated using a more general model, the autoregressive moving-average (ARMA) model. The advocates of ARMA models argue that these models may fit the data better and provide better forecasts than do plain autoregressive (AR) models. However, as we discuss later in this section, there are severe limitations to estimating and using these models. Because you may encounter ARMA models, we provide a brief overview below.

An ARMA model combines both autoregressive lags of the dependent variable and moving-average errors. The equation for such a model with p autoregressive terms and q moving-average terms, denoted ARMA(p, q), is

$$x_t = b_0 + b_1 x_{t-1} + \ldots + b_p x_{t-p} + \varepsilon_t + \theta_1 \varepsilon_{t-1} + \ldots + \theta_q \varepsilon_{t-q}$$

$$E(\varepsilon_t) = 0, \ E(\varepsilon_t^2) = \sigma^2, \ E(\varepsilon_t \varepsilon_s) = 0 \text{ for } t \neq s$$

(16)

where $b_1, b_2, \ldots, b_p$ are the autoregressive parameters and $\theta_1, \theta_2, \ldots, \theta_q$ are the moving-average parameters.

Estimating and using ARMA models has several limitations. First, the parameters in ARMA models can be very unstable. In particular, slight changes in the data sample or the initial guesses for the values of the ARMA parameters can result in very different final estimates of the ARMA parameters. Second, choosing the right ARMA model is more of an art than a science. The criteria for deciding on p and q for a particular

---

[36] For the returns on the S&P 500 (see Example 14), we chose a moving-average model over an autoregressive model.

time series are far from perfect. Moreover, even after a model is selected, that model may not forecast well.

To reiterate, ARMA models can be very unstable, depending on the data sample used and the particular ARMA model estimated. Therefore, you should be skeptical of claims that a particular ARMA model provides much better forecasts of a time series than any other ARMA model. In fact, in most cases, you can use an AR model to produce forecasts that are just as accurate as those from ARMA models without nearly as much complexity. Even some of the strongest advocates of ARMA models admit that these models should not be used with fewer than 80 observations, and they do not recommend using ARMA models for predicting quarterly sales or gross margins for a company using even 15 years of quarterly data.

AUTOREGRESSIVE CONDITIONAL HETEROSKEDASTICITY MODELS

9

Up to now, we have ignored any issues of heteroskedasticity in time-series models and have assumed homoskedasticity. **Heteroskedasticity** is the dependence of the error term variance on the independent variable; **homoskedasticity** is the independence of the error term variance from the independent variable. We have assumed that the error term's variance is constant and does not depend on the value of the time series itself or on the size of previous errors. At times, however, this assumption is violated and the variance of the error term is not constant. In such a situation, the standard errors of the regression coefficients in AR, MA, or ARMA models will be incorrect, and our hypothesis tests would be invalid. Consequently, we can make poor investment decisions based on those tests.

 ← error var constant

For example, suppose you are building an autoregressive model of a company's sales. If heteroskedasticity is present, then the standard errors of the regression coefficients of your model are incorrect. It is likely that due to heteroskedasticity, one or more of the lagged sales terms may appear statistically significant when in fact they are not. Therefore, if you use this model for your decision making, you may make some suboptimal decisions.

In work responsible in part for his shared Nobel Prize in Economics for 2003, Robert F. Engle in 1982 first suggested a way of testing whether the variance of the error in a particular time-series model in one period depends on the variance of the error in previous periods. He called this type of heteroskedasticity autoregressive conditional heteroskedasticity (ARCH).

As an example, consider the ARCH(1) model

$$\varepsilon_t \sim N\left(0, a_0 + a_1 \varepsilon_{t-1}^2\right) \tag{17}$$

where the distribution of ε_t, conditional on its value in the previous period, ε_{t-1}, is normal with mean 0 and variance $a_0 + a_1 \varepsilon_{t-1}^2$. If $a_1 = 0$, the variance of the error in every period is just a_0. The variance is constant over time and does not depend on past errors. Now suppose that $a_1 > 0$. Then the variance of the error in one period depends on how large the squared error was in the previous period. If a large error occurs in one period, the variance of the error in the next period will be even larger.

Engle shows that we can test whether a time series is ARCH(1) by regressing the squared residuals from a previously estimated time-series model (AR, MA, or ARMA) on a constant and one lag of the squared residuals. We can estimate the linear regression equation

$$\hat{\varepsilon}_t^2 = a_0 + a_1 \hat{\varepsilon}_{t-1}^2 + u_t \qquad\qquad (18)$$

where u_t is an error term. If the estimate of a_1 is statistically significantly different from zero, we conclude that the time series is ARCH(1). If a time-series model has ARCH(1) errors, then the variance of the errors in period $t + 1$ can be predicted in period t using the formula $\hat{\sigma}_{t+1}^2 = \hat{a}_0 + \hat{a}_1 \hat{\varepsilon}_t^2$.

Example 17

Testing for ARCH(1) in Monthly Inflation

Analyst Lisette Miller wants to test whether monthly data on CPI inflation contain autoregressive conditional heteroskedasticity. She could estimate Equation 18 using the residuals from the time-series model. As discussed in Example 8, if she modeled monthly CPI inflation from 1971 to 2000, she would conclude that an AR(1) model was the best autoregressive model to use to forecast inflation out of sample. Table 17 shows the results of testing whether the errors in that model are ARCH(1).

Because the t-statistic for the coefficient on the previous period's squared residuals is greater than 7.5, Miller easily rejects the null hypothesis that the variance of the error does not depend on the variance of previous errors. Consequently, the test statistics she computed in Table 5 are not valid, and she should not use them in deciding her investment strategy.

Table 17	Test for ARCH(1) in an AR(1) Model Residuals from Monthly CPI Inflation at an Annual Rate February 1971–December 2000

Regression Statistics

R-squared	0.1376
Standard error	26.3293
Observations	359
Durbin–Watson	1.9126

	Coefficient	Standard Error	t-Statistic
Intercept	7.2958	1.5050	4.8478
Lag 1	0.3687	0.0488	7.5483

Source: U.S. Bureau of Labor Statistics.

It is possible Miller's conclusion—that the AR(1) model for monthly inflation has ARCH in the errors—may have been due to the sample period employed (1971 to 2000). In Example 9, she used a shorter sample period of 1985 to 2000 and concluded that monthly CPI inflation follows an AR(1) process. (These results were shown in Table 8.) Table 17 shows that errors for a time-series model of inflation for the entire sample (1971 to 2000) have ARCH errors. Do the errors estimated with a shorter sample period (1985 to 2000) also display ARCH? For the shorter sample period, Miller estimated an AR(1) model using monthly inflation data.[37] Now she tests to see whether the errors display ARCH. Table 18 shows the results.

---

[37] The AR(1) results are reported in Example 9.

In this sample, the coefficient on the previous period's squared residual is quite small and has a t-statistic of only 1.4205. Consequently, Miller fails to reject the null hypothesis that the errors in this regression have no autoregressive conditional heteroskedasticity. This is additional evidence that the AR(1) model for 1985 to 2000 is a good fit. The error variance appears to be homoskedastic, and Miller can rely on the t-statistics. This result again confirms that a single AR process for the entire 1971–2000 period is misspecified (it does not describe the data well).

Table 18	Test for ARCH(1) in an AR(1) Model Monthly CPI Inflation at an Annual Rate February 1985–December 2000

Regression Statistics

R-squared	0.0106
Standard error	11.2593
Observations	191
Durbin–Watson	1.9969

	Coefficient	Standard Error	t-Statistic
Intercept	5.3939	0.9224	5.8479
Lag 1	0.1028	0.0724	1.4205

Source: U.S. Bureau of Labor Statistics.

Suppose a model contains ARCH(1) errors. What are the consequences of that fact? First, if ARCH exists, the standard errors for the regression parameters will not be correct. In case ARCH exists, we will need to use generalized least squares[38] or other methods that correct for heteroskedasticity to correctly estimate the standard error of the parameters in the time-series model. Second, if ARCH exists and we have it modeled, for example as ARCH(1), we can predict the variance of the errors. Suppose, for instance, that we want to predict the variance of the error in inflation using the estimated parameters from Table 17: $\hat{\sigma}_t^2 = 7.2958 + 0.3687\hat{\varepsilon}_{t-1}^2$. If the error in one period were 0 percent, the predicted variance of the error in the next period would be $7.2958 + 0.3687(0) = 7.2958$. If the error in one period were 1 percent, the predicted variance of the error in the next period would be $7.2958 + 0.3687(1^2) = 7.6645$.

Engle and other researchers have suggested many generalizations of the ARCH(1) model, including ARCH(p) and generalized autoregressive conditional heteroskedasticity (GARCH) models. In an ARCH(p) model, the variance of the error term in the current period depends linearly on the squared errors from the previous p periods: $\hat{\sigma}_t^2 = a_0 + a_1\varepsilon_{t-1}^2 + \ldots + a_p\varepsilon_{t-p}^2$ GARCH models are similar to ARMA models of the error variance in a time series. Just like ARMA models, GARCH models can be finicky and unstable: Their results can depend greatly on the sample period and the initial guesses of the parameters in the GARCH model. Financial analysts who use GARCH models should be well aware of how delicate these models can be, and they should examine whether GARCH estimates are robust to changes in the sample and the initial guesses about the parameters.[39]

---

38 See Greene (2003).

39 For more on ARCH, GARCH, and other models of time-series variance, see Hamilton (1994).

(cointegration)

10   REGRESSIONS WITH MORE THAN ONE TIME SERIES

Up to now, we have discussed time-series models only for one time series. Although in the readings on correlation and regression and on multiple regression we used linear regression to analyze the relationship among different time series, in those readings we completely ignored unit roots. A time series that contains a unit root is not covariance stationary. If any time series in a linear regression contains a unit root, ordinary least squares estimates of regression test statistics may be invalid.

To determine whether we can use linear regression to model more than one time series, let us start with a single independent variable; that is, there are two time series, one corresponding to the dependent variable and one corresponding to the independent variable. We will then extend our discussion to multiple independent variables.

We first use a unit root test, such as the Dickey–Fuller test, for each of the two time series to determine whether either of them has a unit root.[40] There are several possible scenarios related to the outcome of these tests. One possible scenario is that we find that neither of the time series has a unit root. Then we can safely use linear regression to test the relations between the two time series. Otherwise, we may have to use additional tests, as we discuss later in this section.

Example 18

Unit Roots and the Fisher Effect

In Example 8 in the reading on multiple regression, we examined the Fisher effect by estimating the regression relation between expected inflation and risk-free U.S. Treasury bill (T-bill) returns. We used a sample of 137 quarterly observations from the fourth quarter of 1968 until the fourth quarter of 2002 on the expected inflation and risk-free T-bill returns. We used linear regression to analyze the relationship between the two time series. The results of this regression would be valid if both the time series are covariance stationary; that is, neither of the two time series has a unit root. So, if we compute the Dickey–Fuller *t*-test statistic of the hypothesis of a unit root separately for each time series and find that we can reject the null hypothesis that the risk-free T-bill return series has a unit root and the null hypothesis that the expected inflation time series has a unit root, then we can use linear regression to analyze the relation between the two series. In that case, the results of our analysis of the Fisher effect would be valid.

A second possible scenario is that we reject the hypothesis of a unit root for the independent variable but fail to reject the hypothesis of a unit root for the dependent variable. In this case, the error term in the regression would not be covariance stationary. Therefore, one or more of the following linear regression assumptions would be violated: 1) that the expected value of the error term is 0, 2) that the variance of the error term is constant for all observations, and 3) that the error term is uncorrelated across observations. Consequently, the estimated regression coefficients and standard errors would be inconsistent. The regression coefficients might appear significant, but those results would be spurious.[41] Thus we should not use linear regression to analyze the relation between the two time series in this scenario.

A third possible scenario is the reverse of the second scenario: We reject the hypothesis of a unit root for the dependent variable but fail to reject the hypothesis of a unit root for the independent variable. In this case also, like the second scenario,

---

40 For theoretical details of unit root tests, see Greene (2003) or Hamilton (1994). Unit root tests are available in some econometric software packages, such as EViews.

41 The problem of spurious regression for nonstationary time series was first discussed by Granger and Newbold (1974).

the error term in the regression would not be covariance stationary, and we cannot use linear regression to analyze the relation between the two time series.

Example 19

Unit Roots and Predictability of Stock Market Returns by Price-to-Earnings Ratio

Johann de Vries is analyzing the performance of the South African stock market. He examines whether the percentage change in the Johannesburg Stock Exchange (JSE) All Share Index can be predicted by the price-to-earnings ratio (P/E) for the index. Using monthly data from January 1983 to December 2002, he runs a regression using $(P_t - P_{t-1})/P_{t-1}$ as the dependent variable and P_{t-1}/E_{t-2} as the independent variable, where P_t is the value of the JSE index at time t and E_t is the earnings on the index. De Vries finds that the regression coefficient is statistically significant and the value of the R-squared for the regression is quite high. What additional analysis should he perform before accepting the regression as valid?

De Vries needs to perform unit root tests for each of the two time series. If one of the two time series has a unit root, implying that it is not stationary, the results of the linear regression are not meaningful and cannot be used to conclude that stock market returns are predictable by P/E.[42]

The next possibility is that both time series have a unit root. In this case, we need to establish whether the two time series are **cointegrated** before we can rely on regression analysis.[43] Two time series are cointegrated if a long-term financial or economic relationship exists between them such that they do not diverge from each other without bound in the long run. For example, two time series are cointegrated if they share a common trend.

In the fourth scenario, both time series have a unit root but are not cointegrated. In this scenario, as in the second and third scenarios above, the error term in the linear regression will not be covariance stationary, some regression assumptions will be violated, the regression coefficients and standard errors will not be consistent, and we cannot use them for hypothesis tests. Consequently, linear regression of one variable on the other would be meaningless.

Finally, the fifth possible scenario is that both time series have a unit root, but they are cointegrated. In this case, the error term in the linear regression of one time series on the other will be covariance stationary. Accordingly, the regression coefficients and standard errors will be consistent, and we can use them for hypothesis tests. However, we should be very cautious in interpreting the results of a regression with cointegrated variables. The cointegrated regression estimates the long-term relation between the two series but may not be the best model of the short-term relation between the two series. Short-term models of cointegrated series (error correction models) are discussed in Engle and Granger (1987) and Hamilton (1994), but these are specialist topics.

Now let us look at how we can test for cointegration between two time series that each have a unit root as in the last two scenarios above.[44] Engle and Granger suggest this test: If y_t and x_t are both time series with a unit root, we should do the following:

---

42 Barr and Kantor (1999) contains evidence that the P/E time series is nonstationary.

43 Engle and Granger (1987) first discussed cointegration.

44 Consider a time series, x_t, that has a unit root. For many such financial and economic time series, the first difference of the series, $x_t - x_{t-1}$, is stationary. We say that such a series, whose first difference is stationary, has a *single* unit root. However, for some time series, even the first difference may not be stationary and further differencing may be needed to achieve stationarity. Such a time series is said to have *multiple* unit roots. In this section, we consider only the case in which each nonstationary series has a single unit root (which is quite common).

1. Estimate the regression $y_t = b_0 + b_1 x_t + \varepsilon_t$.

2. Test whether the error term from the regression in Step 1 has a unit root using a Dickey–Fuller test. Because the residuals are based on the estimated coefficients of the regression, we cannot use the standard critical values for the Dickey–Fuller test. Instead, we must use the critical values computed by Engle and Granger, which take into account the effect of uncertainty about the regression parameters on the distribution of the Dickey–Fuller test.

3. If the (Engle–Granger) Dickey–Fuller test fails to reject the null hypothesis that the error term has a unit root, then we conclude that the error term in the regression is not covariance stationary. Therefore, the two time series are not cointegrated. In this case any regression relation between the two series is spurious.

4. If the (Engle–Granger) Dickey–Fuller test rejects the null hypothesis that the error term has a unit root, then we conclude that the error term in the regression is covariance stationary. Therefore, the two time series are cointegrated. The parameters and standard errors from linear regression will be consistent and will let us test hypotheses about the long-term relation between the two series.

Example 20

Testing for Cointegration between Intel Sales and Nominal GDP

Suppose we want to test whether the natural log of Intel's sales and the natural log of GDP are cointegrated (that is, whether there is a long-term relation between GDP and Intel sales). We want to test this hypothesis using quarterly data from the first quarter of 1985 through the fourth quarter of 1999. Here are the steps:

1. Test whether the two series each have a unit root. If we cannot reject the null hypothesis of a unit root for both series, implying that both series are nonstationary, we must then test whether the two series are cointegrated.

2. Having established that each series has a unit root, we estimate the regression $\ln (\text{Intel Sales}_t) = b_0 + b_1 \ln \text{GDP}_t + \varepsilon_t$, then conduct the (Engle–Granger) Dickey–Fuller test of the hypothesis that there is a unit root in the error term of this regression using the residuals from the estimated regression. If we reject the null hypothesis of a unit root in the error term of the regression, we reject the null hypothesis of no cointegration. That is, the two series would be cointegrated. If the two series are cointegrated, we can use linear regression to estimate the long-term relation between the natural log of Intel Sales and the natural log of GDP.

We have so far discussed models with a single independent variable. We now extend the discussion to a model with two or more independent variables, so that there are three or more time series. The simplest possibility is that none of the time series in the model has a unit root. Then, we can safely use multiple regression to test the relation among the time series.

Example 21

Unit Roots and Returns to the Fidelity Select Technology Fund

In Example 3 in the reading on multiple regression, we used multiple linear regression to examine whether returns to either the S&P 500/BARRA Growth Index or the S&P 500/BARRA Value Index explain returns to the Fidelity Select Technology Fund using 60 monthly observations between January 1998 and December 2002. Of course, if any of the three time series has a unit root, then the results of our regression analysis may be invalid. Therefore, we could use a Dickey–Fuller test to determine whether any of these series has a unit root.

If we reject the hypothesis of unit roots for all three series, we can use linear regression to analyze the relation among the series. In that case the results of our analysis of the factors affecting returns to the Fidelity Select Technology Fund would be valid.

If at least one time series (the dependent variable or one of the independent variables) has a unit root while at least one time series (the dependent variable or one of the independent variables) does not, the error term in the regression cannot be covariance stationary. Consequently, we should not use multiple linear regression to analyze the relation among the time series in this scenario.

Another possibility is that each time series, including the dependent variable and each of the independent variables, has a unit root. If this is the case, we need to establish whether the time series are cointegrated. To test for cointegration, the procedure is similar to that for a model with a single independent variable. First, estimate the regression $y_t = b_0 + b_1 x_{1t} + b_2 x_{2t} + \ldots + b_k x_{kt} + \varepsilon_t$. Then conduct the (Engle–Granger) Dickey–Fuller test of the hypothesis that there is a unit root in the errors of this regression using the residuals from the estimated regression.

If we cannot reject the null hypothesis of a unit root in the error term of the regression, we cannot reject the null hypothesis of no cointegration. In this scenario, the error term in the multiple regression will not be covariance stationary, so we cannot use multiple regression to analyze the relationship among the time series.

If we can reject the null hypothesis of a unit root in the error term of the regression, we can reject the null hypothesis of no cointegration. However, modeling three or more time series that are cointegrated may be difficult. For example, an analyst may want to predict a retirement services company's sales based on the country's GDP and the total population over age 65. Although the company's sales, GDP, and the population over 65 may each have a unit root and be cointegrated, modeling the cointegration of the three series may be difficult, and doing so is beyond the scope of this volume. Analysts who have not mastered all these complex issues should avoid forecasting models with multiple time series that have unit roots: The regression coefficients may be inconsistent and may produce incorrect forecasts.

OTHER ISSUES IN TIME SERIES

Time-series analysis is an extensive topic and includes many highly complex issues. Our objective in this reading has been to present those issues in time series that are the most important for financial analysts and can also be handled with relative ease.

In this section, we briefly discuss some of the issues that we have not covered but could be useful for analysts.

In this reading, we have shown how to use time-series models to make forecasts. We have also introduced the RMSE as a criterion for comparing forecasting models. However, we have not discussed measuring the uncertainty associated with forecasts made using time-series models. The uncertainty of these forecasts can be very large, and should be taken into account when making investment decisions. Fortunately, the same techniques apply to evaluating the uncertainty of time-series forecasts as apply to evaluating the uncertainty about forecasts from linear regression models. To accurately evaluate forecast uncertainty, we need to consider both the uncertainty about the error term and the uncertainty about the estimated parameters in the time-series model. Evaluating this uncertainty is fairly complicated when using regressions with more than one independent variable.

In this reading, we used the U.S. CPI inflation series to illustrate some of the practical challenges analysts face in using time-series models. We used information on U.S. Federal Reserve policy to explore the consequences of splitting the inflation series in two. In financial time-series work, we may suspect that a time series has more than one regime but not have the information to attempt to sort the data into different regimes. If you face such a problem, you may want to investigate other methods, especially switching regression models, to identify multiple regimes using only the time series itself.

If you are interested in these and other advanced time-series topics, you can learn more in Diebold (2004) and Hamilton (1994).

SUGGESTED STEPS IN TIME-SERIES FORECASTING

The following is a step-by-step guide to building a model to predict a time series.

1. Understand the investment problem you have, and make an initial choice of model. One alternative is a regression model that predicts the future behavior of a variable based on hypothesized causal relationships with other variables. Another is a time-series model that attempts to predict the future behavior of a variable based on the past behavior of the same variable.

2. If you have decided to use a time-series model, compile the time series and plot it to see whether it looks covariance stationary. The plot might show important deviations from covariance stationarity, including the following:
    - a linear trend;
    - an exponential trend;
    - seasonality; or
    - a significant shift in the time series during the sample period (for example, a change in mean or variance).

3. If you find no significant seasonality or shift in the time series, then perhaps either a linear trend or an exponential trend will be sufficient to model the time series. In that case, take the following steps:
    - Determine whether a linear or exponential trend seems most reasonable (usually by plotting the series).
    - Estimate the trend.
    - Compute the residuals.
    - Use the Durbin–Watson statistic to determine whether the residuals have significant serial correlation. If you find no significant serial correlation in

the residuals, then the trend model is sufficient to capture the dynamics of the time series and you can use that model for forecasting.

4. If you find significant serial correlation in the residuals from the trend model, use a more complex model, such as an autoregressive model. First, however, reexamine whether the time series is covariance stationary. Following is a list of violations of stationarity, along with potential methods to adjust the time series to make it covariance stationary:

   - If the time series has a linear trend, first-difference the time series.
   - If the time series has an exponential trend, take the natural log of the time series and then first-difference it.
   - If the time series shifts significantly during the sample period, estimate different time-series models before and after the shift.
   - If the time series has significant seasonality, include seasonal lags (discussed in Step 7).

5. After you have successfully transformed a raw time series into a covariance-stationary time series, you can usually model the transformed series with a short autoregression.[45] To decide which autoregressive model to use, take the following steps:

   - Estimate an AR(1) model.
   - Test to see whether the residuals from this model have significant serial correlation.
   - If you find no significant serial correlation in the residuals, you can use the AR(1) model to forecast.

6. If you find significant serial correlation in the residuals, use an AR(2) model and test for significant serial correlation of the residuals of the AR(2) model.

   - If you find no significant serial correlation, use the AR(2) model.
   - If you find significant serial correlation of the residuals, keep increasing the order of the AR model until the residual serial correlation is no longer significant.

7. Your next move is to check for seasonality. You can use one of two approaches:

   - Graph the data and check for regular seasonal patterns.
   - Examine the data to see whether the seasonal autocorrelations of the residuals from an AR model are significant (for example, the fourth autocorrelation for quarterly data) and whether the autocorrelations before and after the seasonal autocorrelations are significant. To correct for seasonality, add seasonal lags to your AR model. For example, if you are using quarterly data, you might add the fourth lag of a time series as an additional variable in an AR(1) or an AR(2) model.

8. Next, test whether the residuals have autoregressive conditional heteroskedasticity. To test for ARCH(1), for example, do the following:

   - Regress the squared residual from your time-series model on a lagged value of the squared residual.
   - Test whether the coefficient on the squared lagged residual differs significantly from 0.

---

45 Most financial time series can be modeled using an autoregressive process. For a few time series, a moving-average model may fit better. To see if this is the case, examine the first five or six autocorrelations of the time series. If the autocorrelations suddenly drop to 0 after the first q autocorrelations, a moving-average model (of order q) is appropriate. If the autocorrelations start large and decline gradually, an autoregressive model is appropriate.

- If the coefficient on the squared lagged residual does not differ significantly from 0, the residuals do not display ARCH and you can rely on the standard errors from your time-series estimates.

- If the coefficient on the squared lagged residual does differ significantly from 0, use generalized least squares or other methods to correct for ARCH.

9. Finally, you may also want to perform tests of the model's out-of-sample forecasting performance to see how the model's out-of-sample performance compares to its in-sample performance.

Using these steps in sequence, you can be reasonably sure that your model is correctly specified.

SUMMARY

- The predicted trend value of a time series in period t is $\hat{b}_0 + \hat{b}_1 t$ in a linear trend model; the predicted trend value of a time series in a log-linear trend model is $e^{\hat{b}_0 + \hat{b}_0 t}$.

- Time series that tend to grow by a constant amount from period to period should be modeled by linear trend models, whereas time series that tend to grow at a constant rate should be modeled by log-linear trend models.

- Trend models often do not completely capture the behavior of a time series, as indicated by serial correlation of the error term. If the Durbin–Watson statistic from a trend model differs significantly from 2, indicating serial correlation, we need to build a different kind of model.

- An autoregressive model of order p, denoted AR(p), uses p lags of a time series to predict its current value: $x_t = b_0 + b_1 x_{t-1} + b_2 x_{t-2} + \ldots + b_p x_{t-p} + \varepsilon_t$.

- A time series is covariance stationary if the following three conditions are satisfied: First, the expected value of the time series must be constant and finite in all periods. Second, the variance of the time series must be constant and finite in all periods. Third, the covariance of the time series with itself for a fixed number of periods in the past or future must be constant and finite in all periods. Inspection of a nonstationary time-series plot may reveal an upward or downward trend (nonconstant mean) and/or nonconstant variance. The use of linear regression to estimate an autoregressive time-series model is not valid unless the time series is covariance stationary.

- For a specific autoregressive model to be a good fit to the data, the autocorrelations of the error term should be 0 at all lags.

- A time series is mean reverting if it tends to fall when its level is above its long-run mean and rise when its level is below its long-run mean. If a time series is covariance stationary, then it will be mean reverting.

- The one-period-ahead forecast of a variable x_t from an AR(1) model made in period t for period $t + 1$ is $\hat{x}_{t+1} = \hat{b}_0 + \hat{b}_1 x_t$. This forecast can be used to create the two-period ahead forecast from the model made in period t, $\hat{x}_{t+2} = \hat{b}_0 + \hat{b}_1 x_{t+1}$. Similar results hold for AR(p) models.

- In-sample forecasts are the in-sample predicted values from the estimated time-series model. Out-of-sample forecasts are the forecasts made from the estimated time-series model for a time period different from the one for which the model was estimated. Out-of-sample forecasts are usually more valuable in evaluating the forecasting performance of a time-series model than are in-sample forecasts. The root mean squared error (RMSE), defined as the square root of the average squared forecast error, is a criterion for comparing the forecast accuracy of different time-series models; a smaller RMSE implies greater forecast accuracy.

- Just as in regression models, the coefficients in time-series models are often unstable across different sample periods. In selecting a sample period for estimating a time-series model, we should seek to assure ourselves that the time series was stationary in the sample period.

- A random walk is a time series in which the value of the series in one period is the value of the series in the previous period plus an unpredictable random error. If the time series is a random walk, it is not covariance stationary. A random walk with drift is a random walk with a nonzero intercept term. All random walks have unit roots. If a time series has a unit root, then it will not be covariance stationary.

- If a time series has a unit root, we can sometimes transform the time series into one that is covariance stationary by first-differencing the time series; we may then be able to estimate an autoregressive model for the first-differenced series.

- An n-period moving average of the current and past $(n - 1)$ values of a time series, x_t, is calculated as $[x_t + x_{t-1} + \ldots + x_{t-(n-1)}]/n$.

- A moving-average model of order q, denoted MA(q), uses q lags of a random error term to predict its current value.

- The order q of a moving average model can be determined using the fact that if a time series is a moving-average time series of order q, its first q autocorrelations are nonzero while autocorrelations beyond the first q are zero.

- The autocorrelations of most autoregressive time series start large and decline gradually, whereas the autocorrelations of an MA(q) time series suddenly drop to 0 after the first q autocorrelations. This helps in distinguishing between autoregressive and moving-average time series.

- If the error term of a time-series model shows significant serial correlation at seasonal lags, the time series has significant seasonality. This seasonality can often be modeled by including a seasonal lag in the model, such as adding a term lagged four quarters to an AR(1) model on quarterly observations.

- The forecast made in time t for time $t + 1$ using a quarterly AR(1) model with a seasonal lag would be $x_{t+1} = \hat{b}_0 + \hat{b}_1 x_t + \hat{b}_2 x_{t-3}$.

- ARMA models have several limitations: the parameters in ARMA models can be very unstable; determining the AR and MA order of the model can be difficult; and even with their additional complexity, ARMA models may not forecast well.

- The variance of the error in a time-series model sometimes depends on the variance of previous errors, representing autoregressive conditional heteroskedasticity (ARCH). Analysts can test for first-order ARCH in a time-series model by regressing the squared residual on the squared residual from the previous period. If the coefficient on the squared residual is statistically significant, the time-series model has ARCH(1) errors.

- If a time-series model has ARCH(1) errors, then the variance of the errors in period $t + 1$ can be predicted in period t using the formula $\hat{\sigma}_{t+1}^2 = \hat{a}_0 + \hat{a}_1 \hat{\varepsilon}_t^2$.

- If linear regression is used to model the relationship between two time series, a test should be performed to determine whether either time series has a unit root:

  - If neither of the time series has a unit root, then we can safely use linear regression.

- If one of the two time series has a unit root, then we should not use linear regression.

- If both time series have a unit root and the time series are cointegrated, we may safely use linear regression; however, if they are not cointegrated, we should not use linear regression. The (Engle–Granger) Dickey–Fuller test can be used to determine if time series are cointegrated.

PRACTICE PROBLEMS FOR READING 13

Note: In the Problems and Solutions for this reading, we use the hat (^) to indicate an estimate if we are trying to differentiate between an estimated and an actual value. However, we suppress the hat when we are clearly showing regression output.

1. The civilian unemployment rate (UER) is an important component of many economic models. Table 1 gives regression statistics from estimating a linear trend model of the unemployment rate: $UER_t = b_0 + b_1 t + \varepsilon_t$.

Table 1	Estimating a Linear Trend in the Civilian Unemployment Rate Monthly Observations, January 1996–December 2000

Regression Statistics

R-squared	0.9314
Standard error	0.1405
Observations	60
Durbin–Watson	0.9099

	Coefficient	Standard Error	t-Statistic
Intercept	5.5098	0.0367	150.0363
Trend	−0.0294	0.0010	−28.0715

A. Using the regression output in the above table, what is the model's prediction of the unemployment rate for July 1996, midway through the first year of the sample period?

B. How should we interpret the Durbin–Watson (DW) statistic for this regression? What does the value of the DW statistic say about the validity of a *t*-test on the coefficient estimates?

2. Figure 1 compares the predicted civilian unemployment rate (PRED) with the actual civilian unemployment rate (UER) from January 1996 to December 2000. The predicted results come from estimating the linear time trend model $UER_t = b_0 + b_1 t + \varepsilon_t$.

What can we conclude about the appropriateness of this model?

Practice Problems and Solutions: *Quantitative Methods for Investment Analysis*, Second Edition, by Richard A. DeFusco, CFA, Dennis W. McLeavey, CFA, Jerald E. Pinto, CFA, and David E. Runkle, CFA. Copyright © 2004 by CFA Institute.

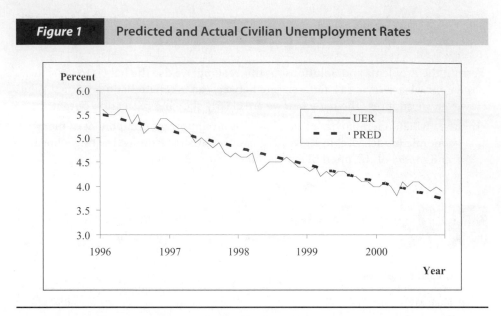

Figure 1   Predicted and Actual Civilian Unemployment Rates

3. You have been assigned to analyze automobile manufacturers and as a first step in your analysis, you decide to model monthly sales of lightweight vehicles to determine sales growth in that part of the industry. Figure 2 gives lightweight vehicle monthly sales (annualized) from January 1992 to December 2000.

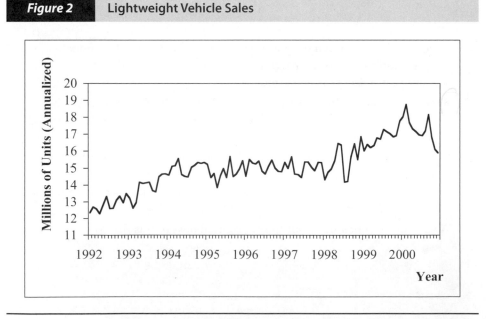

Figure 2   Lightweight Vehicle Sales

Monthly sales in the lightweight vehicle sector, Sales$_t$, have been increasing over time, but you suspect that the growth rate of monthly sales is relatively constant. Write the simplest time-series model for Sales$_t$ that is consistent with your perception.

4. Figure 3 shows a plot of the first differences in the civilian unemployment rate (UER) between January 1996 and December 2000, $\Delta UER_t = UER_t - UER_{t-1}$.

Figure 3	Change in Civilian Unemployment Rate

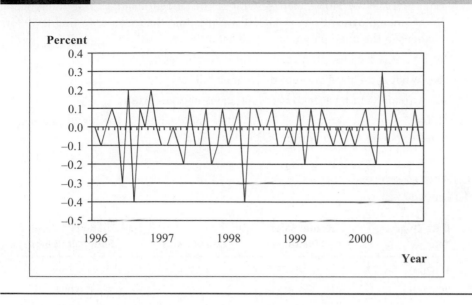

A. Has differencing the data made the new series, ΔUER_t, covariance stationary? Explain your answer.

B. Given the graph of the change in the unemployment rate shown in the figure, describe the steps we should take to determine the appropriate autoregressive time-series model specification for the series ΔUER_t.

5. Table 2 gives the regression output of an AR(1) model on first differences in the unemployment rate. Describe how to interpret the DW statistic for this regression.

Table 2	Estimating an AR(1) Model of Changes in the Civilian Unemployment Rate Monthly Observations, March 1996–December 2000

Regression Statistics

R-squared	0.2184
Standard error	0.1202
Observations	58
Durbin–Watson	2.1852

	Coefficient	Standard Error	t-Statistic
Intercept	−0.0405	0.0161	−2.5110
ΔUER_{t-1}	−0.4674	0.1181	−3.9562

6. Assume that changes in the civilian unemployment rate are covariance stationary and that an AR(1) model is a good description for the time series of changes in the unemployment rate. Specifically, we have $\Delta UER_t = -0.0405 - 0.4674\Delta UER_{t-1}$ (using the coefficient estimates given in the previous problem). Given this equation, what is the mean-reverting level to which changes in the unemployment rate converge?

7. Suppose the following model describes changes in the civilian unemployment rate: $\Delta UER_t = -0.0405 - 0.4674\Delta UER_{t-1}$. The current change (first difference) in the unemployment rate is 0.0300. Assume that the mean-reverting level for changes in the unemployment rate is −0.0276.

   A. What is the best prediction of the next change?

   B. What is the prediction of the change following the next change?

   C. Explain your answer to Part B in terms of equilibrium.

8. Table 3 gives the actual sales, log of sales, and changes in the log of sales of Cisco Systems for the period 1Q:2001 to 4Q:2001.

Table 3

Date Quarter: Year	Actual Sales ($ Millions)	Log of Sales	Changes in Log of Sales $\Delta \ln (\text{Sales}_t)$
1Q:2001	6,519	8.7825	0.1308
2Q:2001	6,748	8.8170	0.0345
3Q:2001	4,728	8.4613	−0.3557
4Q:2001	4,298	8.3659	−0.0954
1Q:2002			
2Q:2002			

Forecast the first- and second-quarter sales of Cisco Systems for 2002 using the regression $\Delta \ln (\text{Sales}_t) = 0.0661 + 0.4698\Delta \ln (\text{Sales}_{t-1})$.

9. Table 4 gives the actual change in the log of sales of Cisco Systems from 1Q:2001 to 4Q:2001, along with the forecasts from the regression model $\Delta \ln (\text{Sales}_t) = 0.0661 + 0.4698\Delta \ln (\text{Sales}_{t-1})$ estimated using data from 3Q:1991 to 4Q:2000. (Note that the observations after the fourth quarter of 2000 are out of sample.)

Table 4

Date	Actual Values of Changes in the Log of Sales $\Delta \ln (\text{Sales}_t)$	Forecast Values of Changes in the Log of Sales $\Delta \ln (\text{Sales}_t)$
1Q:2001	0.1308	0.1357
2Q:2001	0.0345	0.1299
3Q:2001	−0.3557	0.1271
4Q:2001	−0.0954	0.1259

   A. Calculate the RMSE for the out-of-sample forecast errors.

   B. Compare the forecasting performance of the model given with that of another model having an out-of-sample RMSE of 20 percent.

10. A. The AR(1) model for the civilian unemployment rate, $\Delta UER_t = -0.0405 - 0.4674\Delta UER_{t-1}$, was developed with five years of data. What would be the drawback to using the AR(1) model to predict changes in the civilian

unemployment rate 12 months or more ahead, as compared with one
month ahead?

B. For purposes of estimating a predictive equation, what would be the
drawback to using 30 years of civilian unemployment data rather than only
five years?

11. Figure 4 shows monthly observations on the natural log of lightweight vehicle
sales, ln (Sales$_t$), for the period January 1992 to December 2000.

Figure 4	Lightweight Vehicle Sales

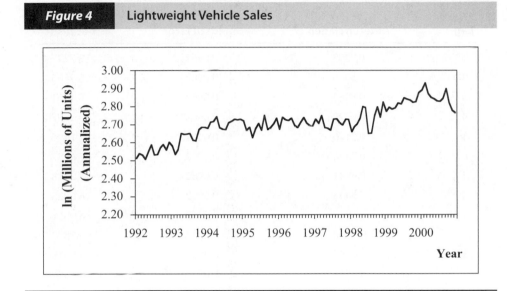

A. Using the figure, comment on whether the specification ln (Sales$_t$) = b_0 +
b_1[ln (Sales$_{t-1}$)] + ε_t is appropriate.

B. State an appropriate transformation of the time series.

12. Figure 5 shows a plot of first differences in the log of monthly lightweight
vehicle sales over the same period as in Problem 11. Has differencing the data
made the resulting series, Δln (Sales$_t$) = ln (Sales$_t$) − ln (Sales$_{t-1}$), covariance
stationary?

Figure 5	Change in Natural Log of Lightweight Vehicle Sales

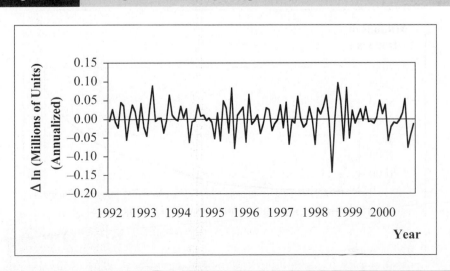

13. Using monthly data from January 1992 to December 2000, we estimate the following equation for lightweight vehicle sales: $\Delta \ln(\text{Sales}_t) = 2.7108 + 0.3987\Delta \ln(\text{Sales}_{t-1}) + \varepsilon_t$. Table 5 gives sample autocorrelations of the errors from this model.

Table 5	Different Order Autocorrelations of Differences in the Logs of Vehicle Sales		
Lag	**Autocorrelation**	**Standard Error**	**t-Statistic**
1	0.9358	0.0962	9.7247
2	0.8565	0.0962	8.9005
3	0.8083	0.0962	8.4001
4	0.7723	0.0962	8.0257
5	0.7476	0.0962	7.7696
6	0.7326	0.0962	7.6137
7	0.6941	0.0962	7.2138
8	0.6353	0.0962	6.6025
9	0.5867	0.0962	6.0968
10	0.5378	0.0962	5.5892
11	0.4745	0.0962	4.9315
12	0.4217	0.0962	4.3827

A. Use the information in the table to assess the appropriateness of the specification given by the equation.

B. If the residuals from the AR(1) model above violate a regression assumption, how would you modify the AR(1) specification?

14. Figure 6 shows the quarterly sales of Cisco Systems from 1Q:1991 to 4Q:2000.

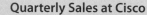

Figure 6	Quarterly Sales at Cisco

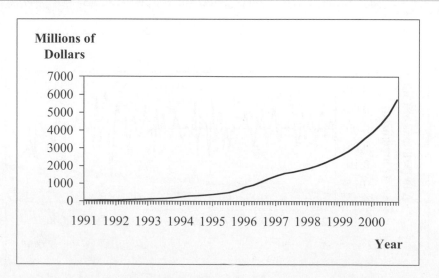

Table 6 gives the regression statistics from estimating the model $\Delta \ln(\text{Sales}_t) = b_0 + b_1 \Delta \ln(\text{Sales}_{t-1}) + \varepsilon_t$.

Table 6	Change in the Natural Log of Sales for Cisco Systems Quarterly Observations, 3Q:1991–4Q:2000

Regression Statistics

R-squared	0.2899
Standard error	0.0408
Observations	38
Durbin–Watson	1.5707

	Coefficient	Standard Error	*t*-Statistic
Intercept	0.0661	0.0175	3.7840
$\Delta \ln(\text{Sales}_{t-1})$	0.4698	0.1225	3.8339

A. Describe the salient features of the quarterly sales series.

B. Describe the procedures we should use to determine whether the AR(1) specification is correct.

C. Assuming the model is correctly specified, what is the long-run change in the log of sales toward which the series will tend to converge?

15. Figure 7 shows the quarterly sales of Avon Products from 1Q:1992 to 2Q:2002. Describe the salient features of the data shown.

Figure 7	Quarterly Sales at Avon

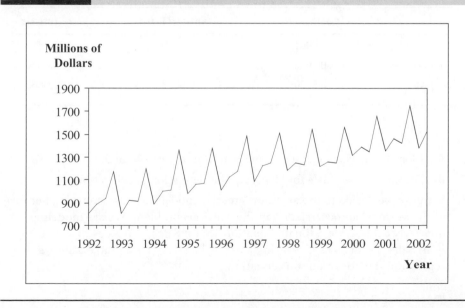

16. Table 7 below shows the autocorrelations of the residuals from an AR(1) model fit to the changes in the gross profit margin (GPM) of The Home Depot, Inc.

Table 7	Autocorrelations of the Residuals from Estimating the Regression $\Delta GPM_t = 0.0006 - 0.3330_1 \Delta GPM_{t-1} + \varepsilon_t$ 1Q:1992–4Q:2001 (40 Observations)

Lag	Autocorrelation
1	−0.1106
2	−0.5981
3	−0.1525
4	0.8496
5	−0.1099

Table 8 shows the output from a regression on changes in the GPM for Home Depot, where we have changed the specification of the AR regression.

Table 8	Change in Gross Profit Margin for Home Depot 1Q:1992–4Q:2001

Regression Statistics

R-squared	0.9155
Standard error	0.0057
Observations	40
Durbin–Watson	2.6464

	Coefficient	Standard Error	t-Statistic
Intercept	−0.0001	0.0009	−0.0610
ΔGPM_{t-1}	−0.0608	0.0687	−0.8850
ΔGPM_{t-4}	0.8720	0.0678	12.8683

    A. Identify the change that was made to the regression model.

    B. Discuss the rationale for changing the regression specification.

17. Suppose we decide to use an autoregressive model with a seasonal lag because of the seasonal autocorrelation in the previous problem. We are modeling quarterly data, so we estimate Equation 15: $(\ln Sales_t - \ln Sales_{t-1}) = b_0 + b_1(\ln Sales_{t-1} - \ln Sales_{t-2}) + b_2(\ln Sales_{t-4} - \ln Sales_{t-5}) + \varepsilon_t$. Table 9 shows the regression statistics from this equation.

Table 9	Log Differenced Sales: AR(1) Model with Seasonal Lag Johnson & Johnson Quarterly Observations, January 1985– December 2001

Regression Statistics

R-squared	0.4220
Standard error	0.0318
Observations	68
Durbin–Watson	1.8784

	Coefficient	Standard Error	t-Statistic
Intercept	0.0121	0.0053	2.3055
Lag 1	−0.0839	0.0958	−0.8757
Lag 4	0.6292	0.0958	6.5693

Autocorrelations of the Residual

Lag	Autocorrelation	Standard Error	t-Statistic
1	0.0572	0.1213	0.4720
2	−0.0700	0.1213	−0.5771
3	0.0065	0.1213	−0.0532
4	−0.0368	0.1213	−0.3033

A. Using the information in Table 9, determine if the model is correctly specified.

B. If sales grew by 1 percent last quarter and by 2 percent four quarters ago, use the model to predict the sales growth for this quarter.

18. Describe how to test for autoregressive conditional heteroskedasticity (ARCH) in the residuals from the AR(1) regression on first differences in the civilian unemployment rate, $\Delta UER_t = b_0 + b_1 \Delta UER_{t-1} + \varepsilon_t$.

19. Suppose we want to predict the annualized return of the five-year T-bill using the annualized return of the three-month T-bill with monthly observations from January 1993 to December 2002. Our analysis produces the data shown in Table 10.

Table 10	Regression with 3-Month T-Bill as the Independent Variable and 5-Year Treasury Bill as the Dependent Variable Monthly Observations, January 1993 to December 2002

Regression Statistics

R-squared	0.5829
Standard error	0.6598
Observations	120
Durbin–Watson	0.1130

	Coefficient	Standard Error	*t*-Statistic
Intercept	3.0530	0.2060	14.8181
Three-month	0.5722	0.0446	12.8408

Can we rely on the regression model in Table 10 to produce meaningful predictions? Specify what problem might be a concern with this regression.

SOLUTIONS FOR READING 13

1. **A.** The estimated forecasting equation is $UER_t = 5.5098 - 0.0294(t)$. The data begin in January 1996, and July 1996 is period 7. Thus the linear trend model predicts the unemployment rate to be $UER_7 = 5.5098 - 0.0294(7) = 5.3040$ or approximately 5.3 percent.

    B. The DW statistic is designed to detect positive serial correlation of the errors of a regression equation. Under the null hypothesis of no positive serial correlation, the DW statistics is 2.0. Positive serial correlation will lead to a DW statistic that is less than 2.0. From the table in Problem 1, we see that the DW statistic is 0.9099. To see whether this result is significantly less than 2.0, refer to the Durbin–Watson table in Appendix E at the end of this volume, in the column marked $k = 1$ (one independent variable) and the row corresponding to 60 observations. We see that $d_l = 1.55$. Because our DW statistic is clearly less than d_l, we reject the null hypothesis of no serial correlation at the 0.05 significance level.

    The presence of serial correlation in the error term violates one of the regression assumptions. The standard errors of the estimated coefficients will be biased downward, so we cannot conduct hypothesis testing on the coefficients.

2. The difference between UER and its forecast value, PRED, is the forecast error. In an appropriately specified regression model, the forecast errors are randomly distributed around the regression line and have a constant variance. We can see that the errors from this model specification are persistent. The errors tend first to be above the regression line and then, starting in 1997, they tend to be below the regression line until 2000 when they again are persistently above the regression line. This persistence suggests that the errors are positively serially correlated. Therefore, we conclude that the model is not appropriate for making estimates.

3. A log-linear model captures growth at a constant rate. The log-linear model $\ln(Sales_t) = b_0 + b_1 t + \varepsilon_t$ would be the simplest model consistent with a constant growth rate for monthly sales. Note that we would need to confirm that the regression assumptions are satisfied before accepting the model as valid.

4. **A.** The plot of the series ΔUER_t seems to fluctuate around a constant mean; its volatility appears to be constant throughout the period. Our initial judgment is that the differenced series is covariance stationary.

    B. The change in the unemployment rate seems covariance stationary, so we should first estimate an AR(1) model and test to see whether the residuals from this model have significant serial correlation. If the residuals do not display significant serial correlation, we should use the AR(1) model. If the residuals do display significant serial correlation, we should try an AR(2) model and test for serial correlation of the residuals of the AR(2) model. We should continue this procedure until the errors from the final AR(p) model are serially uncorrelated.

5. The DW statistic cannot be appropriately used for a regression that has a lagged value of the dependent variable as one of the explanatory variables. To test for serial correlation, we need to examine the autocorrelations.

6. When a covariance-stationary series is at its mean-reverting level, the series will tend not to change until it receives a shock (ε_t). So, if the series ΔUER_t is at the mean-reverting level, $\Delta UER_t = \Delta UER_{t-1}$. This implies that $\Delta UER_t = -0.0405 - 0.4674\Delta UER_t$, so that $(1 + 0.4674)\Delta UER_t = -0.0405$ and $\Delta UER_t = -0.0405/$

(1 + 0.4674) = −0.0276. The mean-reverting level is −0.0276. In an AR(1) model, the general expression for the mean-reverting level is $b_0/(1 - b_1)$.

7. **A.** The predicted change in the unemployment rate for next period is −5.45 percent, found by substituting 0.0300 into the forecasting model: −0.0405 − 0.4674(0.03) = −0.0545.

   B. If we substitute our one-period-ahead forecast of −0.0545 into the model (using the chain rule of forecasting), we get a two-period ahead forecast of −0.0150 or −1.5 percent.

   C. The answer to Part B is quite close to the mean-reverting level of −0.0276. A stationary time series may need many periods to return to its equilibrium, mean-reverting level.

8. The forecast of sales is $4,391 million for the first quarter of 2002 and $4,738 million for the second quarter of 2002, as the following table shows.

Date	Sales ($ Millions)	Log of Sales	Actual Values of Changes in the Log of Sales Δln (Sales$_t$)	Forecast Values of Changes in the Log of Sales Δln (Sales$_t$)
1Q:2001	6,519	8.7825	0.1308	
2Q:2001	6,748	8.8170	0.0345	
3Q:2001	4,728	8.4613	−0.3557	
4Q:2001	4,298	8.3659	−0.0954	
1Q:2002	4,391	8.3872		0.0213
2Q:2002	4,738	8.4633		0.0761

We find the forecasted change in the log of sales for the first quarter of 2002 by inputting the value for the change in the log of sales from the previous quarter into the equation Δln (Sales$_t$) = 0.0661 + 0.4698Δln (Sales$_{t-1}$). Specifically, Δln (Sales$_t$) = 0.0661 + 0.4698(−0.0954) = 0.0213, which means that we forecast the log of sales in the first quarter of 2002 to be 8.3659 + 0.0213 = 8.3872.

Next, we forecast the change in the log of sales for the second quarter of 2002 as Δln (Sales$_t$) = 0.0661 + 0.4698(0.0213) = 0.0761. Note that we have to use our first-quarter 2002 estimated value of the change in the log of sales as our input for Δln (Sales$_{t-1}$) because we are forecasting past the period for which we have actual data.

With a forecasted change of 0.0761, we forecast the log of sales in the second quarter of 2002 to be 8.3872 + 0.0761 = 8.4633.

We have forecasted the log of sales in the first and second quarters of 2002 to be 8.3872 and 8.4633, respectively. Finally, we take the antilog of our estimates of the log of sales in the first and second quarters of 2002 to get our estimates of the level of sales: $e^{8.3872}$ = 4,391 and $e^{8.4633}$ = 4,738, respectively, for sales of $4,391 million and $4,738 million.

9. **A.** The RMSE of the out-of-sample forecast errors is approximately 27 percent. Out-of-sample error refers to the difference between the realized value and the forecasted value of Δln (Sales$_t$) for dates beyond the estimation period. In this case, the out-of-sample period is 1Q:2001 to 4Q:2001. These are the four quarters for which we have data that we did not use to obtain the estimated model Δln (Sales$_t$) = 0.0661 + 0.4698Δln (Sales$_{t-1}$).

   The steps to calculate RMSE are as follows:

i. Take the difference between the actual and the forecast value. This is the error.

ii. Square the error.

iii. Sum the squared errors.

iv. Divide by the number of forecasts.

v. Take the square root of the average.

We show the calculations for RMSE in the table below.

Actual Values of Changes in the Log of Sales $\Delta\ln(\text{Sales}_t)$	Forecast Values of Changes in the Log of Sales $\Delta\ln(\text{Sales}_t)$	Error (Column 1 – Column 2)	Squared Error (Column 3 Squared)
0.1308	0.1357	−0.0049	0.0000
0.0345	0.1299	−0.0954	0.0091
−0.3557	0.1271	−0.4828	0.2331
−0.0954	0.1259	−0.2213	0.0490
		Sum	0.2912
		Mean	0.0728
		RMSE	0.2698

B. The lower the RMSE, the more accurate the forecasts of a model in forecasting. Therefore, the model with the RMSE of 20 percent has greater accuracy in forecasting than the model in Part A, which has an RMSE of 27 percent.

10. A. Predictions too far ahead can be nonsensical. For example, the AR(1) model we have been examining, $\Delta\text{UER}_t = -0.0405 - 0.4674\Delta\text{UER}_{t-1}$, taken at face value, predicts declining civilian unemployment into the indefinite future. Because the civilian unemployment rate will probably not go below 3 percent frictional unemployment and cannot go below 0 percent unemployment, this model's long-range forecasts are implausible. The model is designed for short-term forecasting, as are many time-series models.

B. Using more years of data for estimation may lead to nonstationarity even in the series of first differences in the civilian unemployment rate. As we go further back in time, we increase the risk that the underlying civilian unemployment rate series has more than one regime (or true model). If the series has more than one regime, fitting one model to the entire period would not be correct. Note that when we have good reason to believe that a time series is stationary, a longer series of data is generally desirable.

11. A. The graph of $\ln(\text{Sales}_t)$ appears to trend upward over time. A series that trends upward or downward over time often has a unit root and is thus not covariance stationary. Therefore, using an AR(1) regression on the undifferenced series is probably not correct. In practice, we need to examine regression statistics to confirm visual impressions such as this.

B. The most common way to transform a time series with a unit root into a covariance-stationary time series is to difference the data—that is, to create a new series $\Delta\ln(\text{Sales}_t) = \ln(\text{Sales}_t) - \ln(\text{Sales}_{t-1})$.

12. The plot of the series $\Delta\ln(\text{Sales}_t)$ appears to fluctuate around a constant mean; its volatility seems constant throughout the period. Differencing the data appears to have made the time series covariance stationary.

13. **A.** In a correctly specified regression, the residuals must be serially uncorrelated. We have 108 observations, so the standard error of the autocorrelation is $1/\sqrt{T}$, or in this case $1/\sqrt{108} = 0.0962$. The t-statistic for each lag is significant at the 0.01 level. We would have to modify the model specification before continuing with the analysis.

B. Because the residuals from the AR(1) specification display significant serial correlation, we should estimate an AR(2) model and test for serial correlation of the residuals of the AR(2) model. If the residuals from the AR(2) model are serially uncorrelated, we should then test for seasonality and ARCH behavior. If any serial correlation remains in the residuals, we should estimate an AR(3) process and test the residuals from that specification for serial correlation. We should continue this procedure until the errors from the final AR(p) model are serially uncorrelated. When serial correlation is eliminated, we should test for seasonality and ARCH behavior.

14. **A.** The series has a steady upward trend of growth, suggesting an exponential growth rate. This finding suggests transforming the series by taking the natural log and differencing the data.

B. First, we should determine whether the residuals from the AR(1) specification are serially uncorrelated. If the residuals are serially correlated, then we should try an AR(2) specification and then test the residuals from the AR(2) model for serial correlation. We should continue in this fashion until the residuals are serially uncorrelated, then look for seasonality in the residuals. If seasonality is present, we should add a seasonal lag. If no seasonality is present, we should test for ARCH. If ARCH is not present, we can conclude that the model is correctly specified.

C. If the model $\Delta\ln(\text{Sales}_t) = b_0 + b_1[\Delta\ln(\text{Sales}_{t-1})] + \varepsilon_t$ is correctly specified, then the series $\Delta\ln(\text{Sales}_t)$ is covariance stationary. So, this series tends to its mean-reverting level, which is $b_0/(1 - b_1)$ or $0.0661/(1 - 0.4698) = 0.1247$.

15. The quarterly sales of Avon show an upward trend and a clear seasonal pattern, as indicated by the repeated regular cycle.

16. **A.** A second explanatory variable, the change in the gross profit margin lagged four quarters, ΔGPM_{t-4}, was added.

B. The model was augmented to account for seasonality in the time series (with quarterly data, significant autocorrelation at the fourth lag indicates seasonality). The standard error of the autocorrelation coefficient equals 1 divided by the square root of the number of observations: $1/\sqrt{40}$ or 0.1581. The autocorrelation at the fourth lag (0.8496) is significant: $t = 0.8496/0.1581 = 5.37$. This indicates seasonality, and accordingly we added ΔGPM_{t-4}. Note that in the augmented regression, the coefficient on ΔGPM_{t-4} is highly significant. (Although the autocorrelation at second lag is also significant, the fourth lag is more important because of the rationale of seasonality. Once the fourth lag is introduced as an independent variable, we might expect that the second lag in the residuals would not be significant.)

17. **A.** In order to determine whether this model is correctly specified, we need to test for serial correlation among the residuals. We want to test whether we can reject the null hypothesis that the value of each autocorrelation is 0 against the alternative hypothesis that each is not equal to 0. At the 0.05 significance level, with 68 observations and three parameters, this model has 65 degrees of freedom. The critical value of the t-statistic needed to reject the null hypothesis is thus about 2.0. The absolute value of the t-statistic for each autocorrelation is below 0.60 (less than 2.0), so we cannot reject the null hypothesis that each autocorrelation is not significantly different from 0. We have determined that the model is correctly specified.

B. If sales grew by 1 percent last quarter and by 2 percent four quarters ago, then the model predicts that sales growth this quarter will be $0.0121 - 0.0839 \ln(1.01) + 0.6292 \ln(1.02) = e^{0.02372} - 1 = 2.40\%$.

18. We should estimate the regression $\Delta UER_t = b_0 + b_1 \Delta UER_{t-1} + \varepsilon_t$ and save the residuals from the regression. Then we should create a new variable, $\hat{\varepsilon}_t^2$, by squaring the residuals. Finally, we should estimate $\hat{\varepsilon}_t^2 = a_0 + a_1 \hat{\varepsilon}_{t-1}^2 + u_t$ and test to see whether a_1 is statistically different from 0.

19. To determine whether we can use linear regression to model more than one time series, we should first determine whether any of the time series has a unit root. If none of the time series has a unit root, then we can safely use linear regression to test the relations between the two time series. Note that if one of the two variables has a unit root, then our analysis would not provide valid results; if both of the variables have unit roots, then we would need to evaluate whether the variables are cointegrated.

Singapore	18.		-11.1%
Sydney			-4.5%
Shanghai B	2471.0		-4.7%
Hong Kong	4644.0	0.5%	-10.5%
Toronto	316.8	0.7%	-6.9%
Stockholm	22,700.9	0.5%	-4.2%
Mexico City	13,524.8	0.1%	4.1%

Economics

TOPIC LEVEL LEARNING OUTCOME

The candidate should be able to explain and demonstrate the use of economic concepts and methods in the determination and forecasting of currency exchange rates, the analysis of economic growth, the analysis of business and financial market regulation, and the evaluation of investment markets.

Index		Week Percentage change	
(prev. close)		prev. close	2011
Johan. (Comp.)		1.7%	
Mumbai			-11.7%
Singapore			-4.5%
Sydney	2971.0	1.1%	-4.7%
Shanghai B	4644.0	0.9%	-10.5%
Hong Kong	316.8	0.7%	-6.9%
Toronto	22,700.9	0.5%	-4.2%
Stockholm	13,524.8	0.1%	4.1%
Mexico City			

Economics for Valuation

This study session builds on the principles of economics from Level I and links them to the valuation process. The readings explain how the economic environment affects a firm's performance.

The first reading describes theories of exchange rate determination and how these can be used to forecast exchange rates. Most large firms do not exclusively trade within their own borders, but transact business with companies or individuals outside their own country. Foreign exchange fluctuations have an impact on profitability and valuation of a company.

The second reading describes factors affecting economic growth and how economic growth affects investment decisions and stock market appreciation. The final reading in the study session describes regulation, its purposes, and its potential effects on a firm's operating environment. Regulation has potential effects at both the macro level on the economy and the micro level on companies and individuals.

READING ASSIGNMENTS

Reading 14 *Currency Exchange Rates: Determination and Forecasting*
by Michael R. Rosenberg and William A. Barker, CFA

Reading 15 *Economic Growth and the Investment Decision*
by Paul Kutasovic, CFA

Reading 16 *Economics of Regulation*
by Chester S. Spatt

Index			
Singapore			−11.9%
Sydney			−4.5%
Shanghai B	2719.0	1.1%	−4.7%
Hong Kong	4644.0	0.9%	−10.5%
Toronto	316.8	0.7%	−6.9%
Stockholm	22,700.9	0.5%	−4.2%
Mexico City	13,524.8	0.1%	4.1%

READING

14

Currency Exchange Rates: Determination and Forecasting

by Michael R. Rosenberg and William A. Barker, CFA

LEARNING OUTCOMES

Mastery	The candidate should be able to:
☐	**a** calculate and interpret the bid–ask spread on a spot or forward foreign currency quotation and describe the factors that affect the bid–offer spread;
☐	**b** identify a triangular arbitrage opportunity, and calculate its profit, given the bid–offer quotations for three currencies;
☐	**c** distinguish between spot and forward rates and calculate the forward premium/discount for a given currency;
☐	**d** calculate the mark-to-market value of a forward contract;
☐	**e** explain international parity relations—covered and uncovered interest rate parity, purchasing power parity, and the international Fisher effect;
☐	**f** describe relations among the international parity conditions;
☐	**g** evaluate the use of the current spot rate, the forward rate, purchasing power parity, and uncovered interest parity to forecast future spot exchange rates;
☐	**h** explain approaches to assessing the long-run fair value of an exchange rate;
☐	**i** describe the carry trade and its relation to uncovered interest rate parity and calculate the profit from such a strategy;
☐	**j** explain how flows in the balance of payment accounts affect currency exchange rates;
☐	**k** describe the Mundell–Fleming model, the monetary approach, and the asset market (portfolio balance) approach to exchange rate determination;
☐	**l** forecast the direction of the expected change in an exchange rate based on balance of payment, Mundell–Fleming, monetary, and asset market approaches to exchange rate determination;
☐	**m** explain the potential impacts of monetary and fiscal policies on exchange rates;
☐	**n** describe the objectives and effectiveness of central bank intervention and capital controls;
☐	**o** describe warning signs of a currency crisis;
☐	**p** describe the use of technical analysis in forecasting exchange rates.

INTRODUCTION

Niels Bohr, the famous Danish physicist, once joked that "prediction is very difficult, especially about the future." No words could better express the difficulties associated with exchange rate forecasting. As anyone involved in the business of currency forecasting can attest, it can be a humbling experience. Alan Greenspan, former U.S. Federal Reserve chairman, famously noted that "having endeavored to forecast exchange rates for more than half a century, I have understandably developed significant humility about my ability in this area." Bill Gross, co-chief investment officer at PIMCO, once commented that "if you think writing about the fortunes of the stock market is tricky, try getting your arms around currencies."

The purpose of this reading is to provide readers with tools that will better enable them to get their "arms around currencies." Economists have developed a wide range of theories to explain how exchange rates are determined. This reading will discuss the main theories in detail—starting with the basic international parity building blocks, moving on to long-run equilibrium models, and then digging deeper into the important medium-term cyclical drivers such as monetary policy, fiscal policy, current account balances, and capital flow trends.

In addition, the reading reviews the empirical evidence to assess how well our theoretical models stack up in practice. In short, the empirical evidence shows that "real world" exchange rates have large and persistent deviations from their theoretical long-run equilibrium values. Indeed, most studies conclude that for short- and medium-term horizons, up to perhaps a few years, a random walk characterizes exchange rate movements better than most fundamentals-based exchange rate models. Most studies find that models that work well in one period fail in others. Most studies also find that models that work for one set of exchange rates fail to work for others.

One of the key reasons why fundamentals-based models perform so poorly in the short run is that changes in fundamental economic variables such as relative money supplies, interest rates, inflation rates, economic growth rates, and current account balances simply do not exhibit anywhere near the variability that exchange rates exhibit on a monthly or quarterly basis. As a result, researchers are often unable to unearth any significant contemporaneous relationship between changes in macroeconomic variables and changes in exchange rates over short- and medium-term horizons. Exchange rates may move in the direction suggested by economic fundamentals in the long run, but the often chaotic behavior of exchange rates over short- and medium-term periods is capable of generating so much noise that it tends to obscure any discernible relationship between macroeconomic time series and short- and medium-term exchange rate movements.

Given the shortcomings of most fundamentals-based models, currency strategists and market participants often have felt compelled to turn to non-fundamentals-based forecasting tools to get a better handle on shorter-run exchange rate trends. Such forecasting tools include technically based trend-following trading rules and order flow, sentiment, and positioning indicators. Unfortunately, recent studies show that the predictive value of these forecasting tools is either mixed or nonexistent.

On a more positive note, there is evidence that certain systematic foreign exchange investment strategies have rewarded currency managers with relatively high excess returns over fairly long periods of time (that is, in excess of the risk-free rate of return). One such strategy that has attracted a lot of interest among international investors is the so-called foreign exchange (FX) carry trade. FX carry trades entail going long a basket of high-yielding currencies and simultaneously going short a basket of low-yielding currencies. Although the empirical evidence suggests that the excess returns on this strategy have been fairly attractive, investors need to be mindful that carry trades are prone to crash when market conditions become volatile. Hence, investors need to overlay simple carry trade strategies with well-thought-out risk management systems to help protect against downside risks.

This reading will discuss in detail various approaches that economists and market strategists have devised on how to best position oneself in the currency markets. The reader should develop a general understanding of the fundamental and technical forces that affect exchange rates over short-, medium- and long-run horizons. At the same time, the reader should develop an appreciation of the issues that one is likely to face in devising a successful and profitable exchange rate forecasting/trading strategy.

The reading proceeds as follows:

- Section 2 reviews the basic concepts of the foreign exchange market covered in the CFA Level I curriculum readings and expands this previous coverage to incorporate more material on bid–offer spreads.

- In Section 3, we begin to examine determinants of exchange rates, starting with longer-term interrelationships among exchange rates, interest rates, and inflation rates embodied in the international parity conditions. Despite their empirical shortcomings, these parity conditions form the key building blocks for many long-run exchange rate models. We then examine alternative approaches for determining long-term "fair value" for a currency, and we use this expanded approach to derive an explanatory framework that shows how medium-term factors can cause observed exchange rates to fluctuate around a path to long-term equilibrium.

- Section 4 examines the FX carry trade, a profitable trading strategy that exploits exchange rate deviations from uncovered interest rate parity (one of the international parity conditions).

- Section 5 examines the relationship between a country's exchange rate and its balance of payments using the analytical framework developed earlier in Section 3.

- In Section 6, we examine how monetary and fiscal policies can *indirectly* influence exchange rates by influencing the various factors described in our exchange rate model from Section 3.

- Section 7 examines *direct* public sector actions in foreign exchange markets, either through capital controls or by foreign exchange market intervention (buying and selling currencies for policy purposes).

- Section 8 examines historical episodes of currency crises and some leading indicators that may signal increased likelihood of a crisis.

- Having examined the longer- and medium-term influences on exchange rates, in Section 9 we examine some of the tools for predicting exchange rate movements over shorter time horizons: technical analysis; order flow, sentiment, and positioning measures; and indicators derived from options and futures markets.

A final section summarizes the key points of the reading.

FOREIGN EXCHANGE MARKET CONCEPTS

We begin with a brief review of some of the basic conventions of the FX market that were covered in the CFA Level I curriculum.

An exchange rate is the price of the *base* currency expressed in terms of the *price* currency. For example, a USD/EUR rate of 1.3650 means the euro, the base currency, costs 1.3650 U.S. dollars (an appendix defines the three-letter currency codes used in this reading). The exact notation used to represent exchange rates can vary widely between sources, and occasionally the same exchange rate notation will be used by different sources to mean completely different things. *The reader should be aware that the notation used here may not be the same as that encountered elsewhere.* To avoid confusion, this reading will identify exchange rates using the convention of "P/B" referring to the price of the base currency "B" expressed in terms of the price currency "P."[1]

The spot exchange rate is usually for settlement on the second business day after the trade date, referred to as T+2 settlement.[2] In foreign exchange markets—as in other financial markets—market participants confront a two-sided price in the form of a bid price and an offer price (also called an ask price) quoted by potential counterparties. The bid price is the price, defined in terms of the price currency, at which the counterparty providing a two-sided price quote is willing to buy one unit of the base currency. Similarly, the offer price is the price, in terms of the price currency, at which that counterparty is willing to sell one unit of the base currency. For example, given a price request from a client, a dealer might quote a two-sided price on the spot USD/EUR exchange rate of 1.3648/1.3652. This means that the dealer is willing to pay USD 1.3648 to buy one euro and that the dealer will sell one euro for USD 1.3652.

There are two points to bear in mind about bid–offer quotes:

1. *The offer price is always higher than the bid price.* The bid–offer spread—the difference between the offer price and the bid price—is the compensation that counterparties seek for providing foreign exchange to other market participants.

2. *The counterparty in the transaction who inquires for a two-sided price quote will have the option (but not the obligation) to deal at either the bid (to sell the base currency) or offer (to buy the base currency) price quoted to them by the dealer.* The inquirer can pass on the price quote, but if the inquirer deals, the jargon in the market is that this counterparty has either "*hit the bid*" or "*paid the offer.*" To determine whether the bid or offer side of the market should be used in terms of describing a foreign exchange transaction, one should (a) determine which currency is the base currency in the currency quote and (b) determine whether the base currency is being sold (hit the bid) or bought (pay the offer).

We will distinguish here between the bid–offer pricing a *client receives from a dealer* and the pricing a *dealer receives from the interbank market.* Dealers buy and sell foreign exchange among themselves in what is called the interbank market.[3] This global network for exchanging currencies among professional market participants allows dealers to adjust their inventories and risk positions, distribute foreign currencies to end users who need them, and transfer foreign exchange rate risk to market participants who are willing to bear it. The interbank market is typically for dealing

---

1 Notation is generally not standardized in global foreign exchange markets, and there are several common ways of expressing the same currency pair (e.g., JPY/USD, USD:JPY, $/¥). What is common in FX markets, however, is the concept of a "base" and "price" currency when setting exchange rate prices. Later in the reading, we will sometimes switch to discussing a "domestic" and a "foreign" currency quoted as foreign/domestic (*f/d*). This will be *only an illustrative device* for more easily explaining various theoretical concepts. The candidate should be aware that describing currency pairs in terms of "foreign" and "domestic" currencies is not done in professional FX markets. This is because what is the "foreign" and what is the "domestic" currency depend on where one is located, which can lead to confusion. For instance, what is "foreign" and what is "domestic" for a Middle Eastern investor trading CHF against GBP with the New York branch of a European bank, with the trade ultimately booked at the bank's headquarters in Paris?

2 The exception among the major currencies is CAD/USD, for which standard spot settlement is T+1.

3 Although we refer to this as the interbank market, many non-bank entities now can access this market. These non-bank entities include institutional asset managers, hedge funds, and other large, sophisticated market participants. Detailed discussion of this topic is beyond the scope of this reading.

sizes of at least 1 million units of the base currency. Of course, the dealing amount can be larger than 1 million units; indeed, interbank market trades generally are measured in terms of multiples of a million units of the base currency.

The bid–offer spread a dealer provides to most clients typically is slightly wider than the bid–offer spread observed in the interbank market. For example, if the quote in the interbank USD/EUR spot market is 1.3649/1.3651 (two "pips" wide), the dealer might quote a client a bid–offer of 1.3648/1.3652 (four pips wide) for a spot USD/EUR transaction. When the dealer buys (sells) the base currency from (to) a client, the dealer typically wants to turn around and sell (buy) the base currency in the interbank market. This offsetting transaction allows the dealer to both get out of the risk exposure assumed by providing a two-sided price to the client and also make a profit. Continuing our example, suppose the dealer's client hits the dealer's bid and sells EUR to the dealer for USD 1.3648. The dealer is now long EUR (and short USD) and wants to cover this position in the interbank market. To do this, the dealer sells the EUR in the interbank market by hitting the interbank bid. As a result, the dealer *bought* EUR from the client at USD 1.3648 and then *sold* the EUR in the interbank for USD 1.3649. This gives the dealer a profit of USD 0.0001 (one pip) for every EUR transacted. This one pip translates into a profit of USD 100 per EUR million bought from the client. If, instead of hitting his bid, the client paid the offer (1.3652), then the dealer could pay the offer in the interbank market (1.3651), earning a profit of one pip.

The size of the bid–offer spread, in pips, quoted to dealers' clients in the FX market can vary widely across exchange rates and is not constant over time, even for a single exchange rate. The size of this bid/offer spread depends primarily on three factors: the bid–offer spread in the interbank foreign exchange market for the two currencies involved, the size of the transaction, and the relationship between the dealer and the client. We examine each factor in turn.

The size of the bid–offer spread quoted in the interbank market depends on the liquidity in this market, which in turn depends on several factors, including the following:

1. *The currency pair involved.* Market participation is greater for some currency pairs than others. Liquidity in the major currency pairs—for example, USD/EUR, JPY/USD, or USD/GBP—can be considerable. These markets are almost always deep with bids and offers from market participants around the world. In other currency pairs, particularly some of the more obscure currency cross rates (for example, MXN/CHF), market participation is much thinner and consequently the bid–offer spread in the interbank market will be wider.

2. *The time of day.* The interbank FX markets are most liquid when the major FX trading centers are open. Business hours in London and New York—the two largest FX trading centers—overlap from approximately 8:00 a.m. to 11:00 a.m. New York time. The interbank FX market for most currency pairs is typically most liquid during these hours. After London closes, liquidity is thinner through the New York afternoon. The Asian session starts when dealers in Tokyo, Singapore, and Hong Kong open for business, typically by 7:00 p.m. New York time. For most currency pairs, however, the Asian session is not as liquid as the London and New York sessions. Although FX markets are open 24 hours a day on business days, between the time New York closes and the time Asia opens, liquidity in interbank markets can be very thin, because Sydney, Australia tends to be the only active trading center during these hours. For reference, the chart below shows a 24-hour period from midnight (00:00) to midnight (24:00) London time, corresponding Standard Times in Tokyo and New York, and the *approximate* hours of the most liquid trading periods in each market.

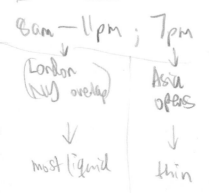

Standard Time and Approximate FX Trading Hours in Major Markets: Midnight to Midnight London Time							
Tokyo	09:00	13:00	17:00	21:00	01:00 Day+1	05:00 Day+1	09:00 Day+1
London	00:00	04:00	08:00	12:00	16:00	20:00	24:00
New York	19:00 Day−1	23:00 Day−1	03:00	07:00	11:00	15:00	19:00

3. *Market volatility.* As in any financial market, when major market participants have greater uncertainty about the factors influencing market pricing, they will attempt to reduce their risk exposures and/or charge a higher price for taking on risk. In the FX market, this response implies wider bid–offer spreads in both the interbank and broader markets. Geopolitical events (e.g., war, civil strife), market crashes, and major data releases (e.g., U.S. nonfarm payrolls) are among the factors that influence spreads and liquidity.

The size of the transaction can also affect the bid–offer spread shown by a dealer to clients. Typically, the larger the transaction, the further away from the current spot exchange rate the dealing price will be. Hence, a client who asks a dealer for a two-sided spot CAD/USD price on, for example, USD 50 million will be shown a wider bid–offer spread than a client who asks for a price on USD 1 million. The wider spread reflects the greater difficulty the dealer faces in "laying off" the foreign exchange risk of the position in the interbank FX market.[4]

The relationship between the dealer and the client can also affect the size of the bid–offer spread shown to clients. For many clients, the spot foreign exchange business is only one business service among many that a dealer provides to the client. For example, the dealer firm might also transact in bond and/or equity securities with the same client. In a competitive business environment, in order to win the client's business for these other services, the dealer might provide a tighter (i.e., smaller) bid–offer spot exchange rate quote. The dealer might also give tighter bid–offer quotes in order to win repeat FX business. A client's credit risk can also be a factor. A client with a poor credit profile may be quoted a wider bid–offer spread than one with good credit. Given the short settlement cycle for spot FX transactions (typically two business days), however, credit risk is not the most important factor in determining the client's bid–offer spread on spot exchange rates.

2.1 Arbitrage Constraints on Spot Exchange Rate Quotes

The bid–offer quotes a dealer shows in the interbank FX market must respect two arbitrage constraints; otherwise the dealer creates riskless arbitrage opportunities for other interbank market participants.[5]

---

4 Smaller dealing sizes can also affect the bid–offer quote shown to clients. "Retail" quotes are typically for dealing sizes less than 1 million units of the base currency and can range all the way down to foreign exchange transactions conducted by individuals (for example, going to a local bank in order to purchase foreign currency for an overseas holiday). Depending on the dealing venue, the bid–offer spreads for these retail transactions can be very large compared with the interbank market. Whereas the bid–offer spread in the interbank market for most liquid currency pairs can be a pip or two, going to the teller window at a local bank branch or using a credit card to conduct FX transactions can result in a retail bid–offer spread of several hundreds of pips.

5 We will confine our attention to the interbank FX market because arbitrage presumes the ability to deal simultaneously with different market participants and in different markets, to be able to access "wholesale" bid–offer quotes, and to have the market sophistication to spot arbitrage opportunities. These criteria are typically limited to interbank market participants—that is, the professional FX market.

First, the bid shown by a dealer in the interbank market cannot be higher than the current interbank offer, and the offer shown by a dealer cannot be lower than the current interbank bid. If the bid–offer quotes shown by a dealer are inconsistent with the interbank market quotes, other market participants will buy from the cheaper source and sell to the more expensive source. This arbitrage will eventually bring the two prices back into line. For example, suppose that the current spot USD/EUR price in the interbank market is 1.3649/1.3651. If a dealer showed a misaligned price quote of 1.3652/1.3654, then other market participants would pay the offer in the interbank market, *buying* EUR at a price of USD 1.3651, and then *sell* the EUR to the dealer by hitting the dealer's bid at USD 1.3652—thereby making a riskless profit of one pip on the trade. This arbitrage would continue as long as the dealer's bid–offer quote violates the arbitrage constraint.

Second, the cross-rate bids (offers) posted by a dealer must be lower (higher) than the implied cross-rate offers (bids) available in the interbank market. Recall that given exchange rate quotes for the currency pairs A/B and C/B, we can back out the implied cross rate of A/C, and that this implied cross-rate A/C must be consistent with the A/B and C/B rates. This again reflects the basic principle of arbitrage: If identical financial products are priced differently, then market participants will buy the cheaper one and sell the more expensive one until the price difference is eliminated. In the context of FX cross rates, there are two ways to trade currency A against currency C: (1) using the cross rate A/C or (2) using the A/B and C/B rates. Because, in the end, both methods involve selling (buying) currency C in order to buy (sell) currency A, the exchange rate using these two approaches must be consistent.

To illustrate this **triangular arbitrage** among three currencies, suppose that the interbank market bid–offer in USD/EUR is 1.3649/1.3651 and that the bid–offer in JPY/USD is 76.64/76.66. We need to use these two interbank bid–offer quotes to calculate the market-implied bid–offer quote on the JPY/EUR cross rate.

Let us begin by considering the transactions required to *sell* JPY and *buy* EUR, going through the JPY/USD and USD/EUR currency pairs. We can view this intuitively as follows:

Sell JPY Buy EUR	=	Sell JPY Buy USD	then	Sell USD Buy EUR

Note that the "Buy USD" and "Sell USD" in the expressions on the right-hand side of the equal sign will cancel out to give the JPY/EUR cross rate. In equation form, we can represent this relationship as follows:

$$\left(\frac{JPY}{EUR}\right) = \left(\frac{JPY}{USD}\right)\left(\frac{USD}{EUR}\right)$$

Now, let's take account of the bid–offer rates in order to do the JPY/EUR calculation.

i. The left-hand side of the above equal sign is "Sell JPY, Buy EUR." In the JPY/EUR price quote, the EUR is the base currency and buying it means paying the offer; i.e., we will be calculating the *offer* rate in JPY/EUR.

ii. The first term on the right-hand side of the equal sign is "Sell JPY, Buy USD." Because the USD is the base currency in the JPY/USD quote, buying it means paying the *offer*.

iii. The second term on the right-hand side of the equal sign is "Sell USD, Buy EUR." Because the EUR is the base currency in the USD/EUR price quote, buying it means paying the *offer*.

Combining all of this together conceptually and putting in the relevant offer rates leads to:

$$\left(\frac{JPY}{EUR}\right)_{offer} = \left(\frac{JPY}{USD}\right)_{offer}\left(\frac{USD}{EUR}\right)_{offer} = 76.66 \times 1.3651 = 104.65$$

Perhaps not surprisingly, calculating the implied JPY/EUR *bid* rate uses the same process as above (now using "Buy the JPY, Sell the EUR" for the left-hand side of the equation). This leads to:

$$\left(\frac{JPY}{EUR}\right)_{bid} = \left(\frac{JPY}{USD}\right)_{bid}\left(\frac{USD}{EUR}\right)_{bid} = 76.64 \times 1.3649 = 104.61$$

As one would expect, the implied cross-rate bid is less than the offer: 104.61/104.65.

This simple formula seems relatively straightforward: To get the implied *bid* cross-rate, simply multiply the *bid* rates for the other two currencies. One must be cautious about the quoting conventions used for the currencies, however, because this simple formula is *not always the case*. Depending on quoting conventions, it may be necessary to *invert* one of the quotes in order to complete the calculation.

This is best illustrated with an example. Consider the case of calculating the implied GBP/EUR cross rate given USD/GBP and USD/EUR quotes. In this case, simple multiplication will not work, and we have to invert the USD/GBP quote:

$$\frac{GBP}{EUR} \neq \left(\frac{USD}{GBP}\right)\left(\frac{USD}{EUR}\right)$$

Instead, we have

$$\frac{GBP}{EUR} = \left(\frac{GBP}{USD}\right)\left(\frac{USD}{EUR}\right) = \left(\frac{USD}{GBP}\right)^{-1}\left(\frac{USD}{EUR}\right)$$

The implied *bid* rate from this expression is the rate at which the customer can "buy the GBP, sell the EUR," because the EUR is the base currency in the GBP/EUR quote. Conceptually, calculating the implied *bid* rate for GBP/EUR proceeds by

Buy GBP Sell EUR	=	Buy GBP Sell USD	then	Buy USD Sell EUR

As we saw above, however, we need to *invert* USD/GBP in order to get GBP/USD, the first expression to the right of the equal sign. Let's assume that the bid–offer in USD/GBP is 1.5644/1.5646. Inverting this expression gives the bid–offer in GBP/USD as equal to 0.63914/0.63922. Note that the bid must always be smaller than the offer. Hence, to get the GBP/USD *bid*, we are using the inverse of the USD/GBP *offer*. Similarly, the GBP/USD *offer* is calculated by inverting the USD/GBP *bid*. (Note that we extended the calculated GBP/USD quotes to five decimal places to avoid truncation errors in subsequent calculations.)

As before, let's use 1.3649/1.3651 as the bid–offer in USD/EUR. We then combine all this together conceptually and mathematically to calculate the GBP/EUR *bid* rate:

$$\left(\frac{GBP}{EUR}\right)_{bid} = \left(\frac{GBP}{USD}\right)_{bid}\left(\frac{USD}{EUR}\right)_{bid} = 0.63914 \times 1.3649 = 0.8724$$

Similarly, for the implied GBP/EUR *offer* rate:

$$\left(\frac{GBP}{EUR}\right)_{offer} = \left(\frac{GBP}{USD}\right)_{offer}\left(\frac{USD}{EUR}\right)_{offer} = 0.63922 \times 1.3651 = 0.8726$$

Note that the implied *bid* rate is less than the implied *offer* rate, as it must be to prevent arbitrage.

We conclude this section on arbitrage constraints with some simple observations:

■ The arbitrage constraint on implied cross rates is similar to that for spot rates (posted bid rates cannot be higher than the market's offer; posted offer rates cannot be lower than the market's bid). The only difference is that this second arbitrage constraint is applied *across* currency pairs instead of involving a *single* currency pair.

- In reality, violations of these arbitrage constraints almost never occur. Both human traders and automatic trading algorithms are constantly on alert for any pricing inefficiencies and will arbitrage them away almost instantly.

- Market participants never have to calculate cross rates *manually* because electronic dealing machines (which are essentially just specialized computers) will automatically calculate cross bid–offer rates given any two underlying bid–offer rates.

Example 1

Bid–Offer Rates

The following are spot rate quotes in the interbank market:

USD/EUR	1.4559/1.4561
JPY/USD	81.87/81.89
CAD/USD	0.9544/0.9546
SEK/USD	6.8739/6.8741

1. What is the bid–offer on the SEK/EUR cross rate implied by the interbank market?

   A. 0.2118/0.2119

   B. 4.7209/4.7214

   C. 10.0077/10.0094

2. What is the bid–offer on the JPY/CAD cross rate implied by the interbank market?

   A. 78.13/78.17

   B. 85.781/85.785

   C. 85.76/85.80

3. If a dealer quoted a bid–offer rate of 85.73/85.75 in JPY/CAD, then a triangular arbitrage would involve buying:

   A. CAD in the interbank market and selling it to the dealer, for a profit of JPY 0.01 per CAD.

   B. JPY from the dealer and selling it in the interbank market, for a profit of CAD 0.01 per JPY.

   C. CAD from the dealer and selling it in the interbank market, for a profit of JPY 0.01 per CAD.

4. If a dealer quoted a bid–offer of 85.74/85.81 in JPY/CAD, then you could:

   A. not make any arbitrage profits.

   B. make arbitrage profits buying JPY from the dealer and selling it in the interbank market.

   C. make arbitrage profits buying CAD from the dealer and selling it in the interbank market.

5. A market participant is considering the following transactions:

   Transaction 1: Buy CAD 100 million against the USD at 15:30 London time.

   Transaction 2: Sell CAD 100 million against the KRW at 21:30 London time.

   Transaction 3: Sell CAD 10 million against the USD at 15:30 London time.

Given the proposed transactions, what is the *most likely* ranking of the bid–ask spreads, from tightest to widest, under normal market conditions?

A. Transaction 1, 2, 3

B. Transaction 2, 1, 3

C. Transaction 3, 1, 2

Solution to 1:

C is correct. Using the intuitive equation-based approach,

$$\frac{SEK}{EUR} = \frac{SEK}{USD} \times \frac{USD}{EUR}$$

Hence, to calculate the SEK/EUR bid (offer) rate, we multiply the SEK/USD and USD/EUR bid (offer) rates to get:

Bid:	10.0077 = 6.8739 × 1.4559
Offer:	10.0094 = 6.8741 × 1.4561

Solution to 2:

C is correct. Using the intuitive equation-based approach,

$$\frac{JPY}{CAD} = \frac{JPY}{USD} \times \left(\frac{CAD}{USD}\right)^{-1} = \frac{JPY}{\cancel{USD}} \times \frac{\cancel{USD}}{CAD}$$

This equation shows that we have to invert the CAD/USD quotes to get the USD/CAD bid–offer rates of 1.04756/1.04778. That is, given the CAD/USD quotes of 0.9544/0.9546, take the inverse of each and interchange bid and offer, such that the USD/CAD quotes are (1/0.9546)/(1/0.9544) or 1.04756/1.04778. Multiplying the JPY/USD and USD/CAD bid–offer rates then leads to:

Bid:	85.76 = 81.87 × 1.04756
Offer:	85.80 = 81.89 × 1.04778

Solution to 3:

C is correct. The interbank-implied cross rate for JPY/CAD is 85.76/85.80 (the answer to Question 2). Hence, the dealer is posting an offer rate to sell the CAD (the base currency in the quote) too cheaply, at a rate below the interbank bid rate (85.75 versus 85.76, respectively). Hence triangular arbitrage would involve buying CAD from the dealer (paying the dealer's offer) and selling CAD in the interbank market (hitting the interbank bid) for a profit of JPY 0.01 (85.76 – 85.75) per CAD transacted.

Solution to 4:

→ you cannot arbitrage

A is correct. The arbitrage relationship is not violated. The dealer's bid (offer) is not above (below) the interbank market's offer (bid). The implied interbank cross rate for JPY/CAD is 85.76/85.80 (the solution to Question 2).

Solution to 5:

C is correct. The CAD/USD currency pair is most liquid when New York and London are both in their most liquid trading periods at the same time (approximately 8:00 a.m. to 11:00 a.m. New York time, or about 13:00 to 16:00 London time). Transaction 3 is for a smaller amount than Transaction 1. Transaction 2 is for a less liquid currency pair (KRW/CAD is traded less than CAD/USD) and occurs outside of normal dealing hours in all three major centers (London, North America, and Asia); the transaction is also for a large amount.

2.2 Forward Markets

Outright forward contracts (often referred to simply as forwards) are agreements to exchange one currency for another on a future date at an exchange rate agreed on today. In contrast to spot rates, forward contracts are any exchange rate transactions that occur with settlement longer than the usual T+2 settlement for spot delivery.

Forward exchange rates must satisfy an arbitrage relationship that equates the investment return on two alternative but equivalent investments. To simplify the explanation of this arbitrage relationship, and to focus on the intuition behind forward rate calculations, we will ignore the bid–offer spread on exchange rates and money market instruments. In addition, we will alter our exchange rate notation somewhat from price/base currency (P/B) to "foreign/domestic currency (f/d)." We will also assume that the domestic currency for an investor is the base currency in the standard exchange rate quotation. Using this (f/d) notation will make it easier to illustrate the choice an investor faces between domestic and foreign investments, as well as the arbitrage relationships that equate the returns on these investments when their risk characteristics are equal.

Consider an investor with one unit of domestic currency to invest for one year. The investor faces two alternatives:

A. One alternative is to invest cash for one year at the domestic risk-free rate (i_d). At the end of the year, the investment would be worth $(1+i_d)$.

B. The other alternative is to convert the domestic currency to foreign currency at the spot rate of $S_{f/d}$ and invest for one year at the foreign risk-free rate (i_f). At the end of the period, the investor would have $S_{f/d}(1+i_f)$ units of foreign currency. These funds then must be converted back to the investor's domestic currency. If the exchange rate to be used for this end-of-year conversion is set at the start of the period using a one-year forward contract, then the investor will have eliminated the foreign exchange risk associated with converting at an unknown future spot rate. Letting $F_{f/d}$ denote the forward rate, the investor would obtain $(1/F_{f/d})$ units of the domestic currency for each unit of foreign currency sold forward. Hence, in domestic currency, at the end of the year the investment would be worth $S_{f/d}(1+i_f)(1/F_{f/d})$.

Because each of the two investments above (A and B) is risk free, they must have the same return. Otherwise investors could earn a riskless arbitrage profit by selling (going short) one investment and investing in the other. In particular, investors could borrow in one currency, lend in the other, and use the spot and forward exchange markets to eliminate currency risk. Equating the returns on these two alternative investments—that is, putting investments A and B on opposite sides of the equal sign—leads to the following relationship:

$$(1 + i_d) = S_{f/d}(1 + i_f)\left(\frac{1}{F_{f/d}}\right)$$

To help see the intuition behind forward rate calculations, note that the right-hand side of the expression (for investment B) also shows the chronological order of this investment: Convert from domestic to foreign currency at the spot rate $(S_{f/d})$; invest this foreign currency amount at the foreign risk-free interest rate $(1 + i_f)$; and then at maturity, convert the foreign currency investment proceeds back into the domestic currency using the forward rate $(1/F_{f/d})$.

For simplicity, we assumed a one-year horizon in the preceding example. However, the argument holds for any investment horizon. The risk-free assets used in this arbitrage relationship are typically bank deposits quoted using the London Interbank

Offered Rate (LIBOR) for the currencies involved. The day count convention for almost all LIBOR deposits is Actual/360.[6] Incorporating this day count convention into our arbitrage formula leads to

$$\left(1 + i_d\left[\frac{Actual}{360}\right]\right) = S_{f/d}\left(1 + i_f\left[\frac{Actual}{360}\right]\right)\left(\frac{1}{F_{f/d}}\right)$$

This equation can be rearranged to isolate the forward rate:

$$F_{f/d} = S_{f/d}\left(\frac{1 + i_f\left[\frac{Actual}{360}\right]}{1 + i_d\left[\frac{Actual}{360}\right]}\right) \qquad (1)$$

This equation is known as **covered interest rate parity.** Our previous work shows that covered interest rate parity is based on an arbitrage relationship among risk-free interest rates and spot and forward exchange rates. Because of this arbitrage relationship between alternative investments, Equation 1 can also be described as saying that the covered (i.e., currency-hedged) interest rate differential between the two markets is zero.

The covered interest rate parity equation can also be rearranged to give an expression for the forward premium or discount:

$$F_{f/d} - S_{f/d} = S_{f/d}\left(\frac{\left[\frac{Actual}{360}\right]}{1 + i_d\left[\frac{Actual}{360}\right]}\right)(i_f - i_d).$$

The domestic currency will trade at a forward premium ($F_{f/d} > S_{f/d}$) if, and only if, the foreign risk-free interest rate exceeds the domestic risk-free interest rate ($i_f > i_d$). The premium or discount is proportional to the spot exchange rate ($S_{f/d}$), proportional to the interest rate differential ($i_f - i_d$) between the markets, and approximately proportional to the time to maturity (Actual/360).

Finally, although for simplicity's sake we have developed the **covered interest rate parity** equation (Equation 1) in terms of foreign and domestic currencies (using the notation f/d), this equation can equivalently be expressed in our more standard exchange rate quoting convention of price and base currencies (P/B):

$$F_{P/B} = S_{P/B}\left(\frac{1 + i_P\left[\frac{Actual}{360}\right]}{1 + i_B\left[\frac{Actual}{360}\right]}\right)$$

When dealing in professional FX markets, it is perhaps more useful to think of the covered interest rate parity equation and the calculation of forward rates in this P/B notation rather than foreign/domestic (f/d) notation. This is because domestic and foreign are relative concepts that depend on where one is located, and because of the potential for confusion, these terms are not used for currency quotes in professional FX markets.

---

6 This means that interest is calculated as if there are 360 days in a year. However, the actual number of days the funds are on deposit is used to calculate the interest payable. The main exception to the Actual/360 day count convention is the GBP, for which the convention is Actual/365. For the purposes of this reading, we will use Actual/360 consistently in order to avoid complication. In practice, however, one should confirm and apply the correct day count convention for each rate. Applying incorrect day counts could give the illusion of an arbitrage opportunity where none actually exists.

Example 2

Calculating the Forward Premium (Discount)

The following table shows the mid-market (i.e., average of the bid and offer) for the current CAD/AUD spot exchange rate as well as for AUD and CAD 270-day LIBOR (annualized):

Spot (CAD/AUD)	1.0145
270-day LIBOR (AUD)	4.87%
270-day LIBOR (CAD)	1.41%

The forward premium (discount) for a 270-day forward contract for CAD/AUD would be *closest* to:

A. −0.0346.

B. −0.0254.

C. +0.0261.

Solution:

B is correct. The equation to calculate the forward premium (discount) is:

$$F_{P/B} - S_{P/B} = S_{P/B} \left(\frac{\left[\dfrac{Actual}{360}\right]}{1 + i_B\left[\dfrac{Actual}{360}\right]} \right)(i_P - i_B)$$

Because AUD is the base currency in the CAD/AUD quote, putting in the information from the table leads to:

$$F_{P/B} - S_{P/B} = 1.0145 \left(\frac{\left[\dfrac{270}{360}\right]}{1 + 0.0487\left[\dfrac{270}{360}\right]} \right)(0.0141 - 0.0487) = -0.0254$$

In professional FX markets, forward exchange rates are typically quoted in terms of points. The points on a forward rate quote are simply the difference between the forward exchange rate quote and the spot exchange rate quote; that is, the forward premium or discount, with the points scaled so that they can be related to the last decimal place in the spot quote. Forward points are adjustments to the spot price of the base currency, using our standard price/base currency notation.

This means that forward rate quotes in professional FX markets are typically shown as the bid–offer on the spot rate and the number of forward points at each maturity.[7] For illustration purposes, let's assume that the bid–offer for the spot and forward points for the USD/EUR exchange rate are as shown in Exhibit 1:

Exhibit 1	Sample Spot and Forward Quotes (Bid–Offer)

Maturity	Spot Rate or Forward Points
Spot (USD/EUR)	1.3549/1.3651
One month	−5.6/−5.1
Three months	−15.9/−15.3
Six months	−37.0/−36.3
Twelve months	−94.3/−91.8

---

7 "Maturity" is defined in terms of the time between spot settlement—usually T+2—and the settlement of the forward contract.

One should note several aspects of this exhibit. First, as always, the offer in the bid–offer quote is larger than the bid. In this example, the forward points are negative (i.e., the forward rate for the EUR is at a discount to the spot rate), but the bid is a smaller number (−5.6, versus −5.1 at the one-month maturity). Second, the absolute number of forward points is an increasing function of the term of the forward contract. Third, because this is an OTC market, a client is not restricted to dealing *only* at the dates/maturities shown. Dealers typically quote standard forward dates, but forward deals can be for any forward date the client requires. The forward points for these non-standard (referred to as "broken") forward dates will typically be interpolated on the basis of the points shown for the standard settlement dates. Fourth, to convert any of these quoted forward points into a forward rate, one would divide the number of points by 10,000 (to scale down to the fourth decimal place, the last decimal place in the USD/EUR spot quote) and then add the result to the spot exchange rate quote.[8] However, one must be careful about which side of the market (bid or offer) is being quoted. For example, suppose a market participant was *selling* the EUR forward against the USD. Given the USD/EUR quoting convention, the EUR is the base currency. This means the market participant must use the *bid* rates (i.e., the market participant will hit the bid) given the USD/EUR quoting convention. Using the data in Exhibit 1, the three-month forward *bid* rate in this case would be based on the bid for both the spot and the forward points, and hence would be:

$$1.3549 + \left(\frac{-15.9}{10,000} \right) = 1.35331$$

This means that the market participant would be selling EUR three months forward at a price of USD 1.35331 per EUR. Fifth, the quoted points are already scaled to each maturity—they are not annualized—so there is no need to adjust them.

The situation is slightly different when calculating forward exchange rates for an FX swap. An FX swap transaction consists of simultaneous spot and forward transactions, where the base currency is being bought (sold) spot and sold (bought) forward. FX swaps are used for a variety of purposes, such as swap financing as well as rolling either hedges or speculative positions forward in time as the underlying forward contract matures. Because swaps involve simultaneous and offsetting transactions—one is a buy, the other a sell, in terms of the base currency—a common spot rate is applied to both the spot leg of the transaction and to the calculation of the forward rate. Because the client is not being charged a bid–offer spread on the spot rate, it is standard practice to use the mid-market spot exchange rate for the swap transaction. The forward points will still be based on either the bid or offer, however, depending on whether the market participant is buying or selling the base currency forward. This method of quoting swap pricing is applied whenever a dealer's client transacts simultaneous spot and forward deals in the same base currency.

We now turn to considering what determines the bid–offer spread for forward swap points quoted by dealers to clients. When we discussed *spot* bid–offer rates, we indicated that the bid–offer spread depends on three factors: the interbank market liquidity of the underlying currency pair, the size of the transaction, and the relationship between the client and the dealer. These same factors also apply to bid–offer spreads for forward points. For forward bid–offer spreads, we can also add a fourth factor: the term of the forward contract. Generally, the longer the term of the forward contract, the wider the bid–offer. This relationship holds because, as the term of the contract increases,

- liquidity in the forward market tends to decline;
- the exposure to counterparty credit risk increases; and

---

[8] Because the JPY/USD exchange rate is quoted to only two decimal places, forward points for the dollar–yen currency pair are divided by 100.

■   the interest rate risk of the contract increases (forward rates are based on interest rate differentials, and a longer duration equates to higher price sensitivity to movements in interest rates).

Finally, we consider the mark-to-market of forward contracts. As with other financial instruments, the mark-to-market value of forward contracts reflects the profit (or loss) that would be realized from closing out the position at current market prices. To close out a forward position, it must be offset with an equal and opposite forward position using the spot exchange rate and forward points available in the market when the offsetting position is created. When a forward contract is initiated, the forward rate is such that no cash changes hands (i.e., the mark-to-market value of the contract at initiation is zero). From that moment onward, however, the mark-to-market value of the forward contract will change as the spot exchange rate changes and as interest rates change in either of the two currencies.

Let's look at an example. Suppose that a market participant bought GBP 10 million for delivery against the AUD in six months at an "all-in" forward rate of 1.6100 AUD/GBP. (The all-in forward rate is simply the sum of the spot rate and the forward points, appropriately scaled to size.) Three months later, the market participant wants to close out this forward contract. This would require selling GBP 10 million three months forward using the AUD/GBP spot exchange rate and forward points in effect at that time.[9] Assume the bid–offer for spot and forward points three months prior to the settlement date are as follows:

Spot rate (AUD/GBP)	1.6210/1.6215
Three-month points	130/140

To sell GBP (the base currency in the AUD/GBP quote), we will be calculating the *bid* side of the market. Hence, the appropriate all-in three-month forward rate to use is:

$$1.6210 + 130/10,000 = 1.6340$$

This means that the market participant originally bought GBP 10 million at an AUD/GBP rate of 1.6100 and subsequently sold them at a rate of 1.6340. These GBP amounts will net to zero at settlement date (GBP 10 million both bought and sold), but the AUD amounts will not, because the forward rate has changed. The AUD cash flow at settlement date will equal

$$(1.6340 - 1.6100) \times 10,000,000 = +AUD\ 240,000$$

This is a cash *inflow* because the market participant was long the GBP with the original forward position and the GBP subsequently appreciated (the AUD/GBP rate increased).

This cash flow will be paid at settlement day, which is still three months away. To calculate the mark-to-market on the dealer's position, this cash flow must be discounted to the present. The present value of this amount is found by discounting the settlement day cash flow by the three-month discount rate. Because this amount is in AUD, we use the three-month AUD discount rate. Let's use LIBOR and suppose that three-month AUD LIBOR is 4.80 percent (annualized). The present value of this future AUD cash flow is then:

$$\frac{AUD\ 240,000}{1 + 0.048 \left[\dfrac{90}{360} \right]} = AUD\ 237,154$$

---

9 Note that the offsetting forward contract is defined in terms of the original position taken: The original position in this example was long GBP 10 million, so the offsetting contract is short GBP 10 million. There is an ambiguity here, however: To be *long* GBP 10 million at 1.6100 AUD/GBP is equivalent to being *short* AUD 16,100,000 (10,000,000 × 1.6100) at the same forward rate. To avoid this ambiguity, for the purposes of this reading we will state what the relevant forward position is for mark-to-market purposes. The net gain or loss from the transaction will be reflected in the alternate currency.

This is the mark-to-market value of the original long GBP 10 million six-month forward when it is closed out three months prior to settlement.

To summarize, the process for marking to market a forward position is relatively straightforward:

1. Create an equal and offsetting forward position to the original forward position. (In the example above, the market participant was long GBP 10 million forward, so the offsetting forward contract would be to sell GBP 10 million.)

2. Determine the appropriate all-in forward rate for this new, offsetting forward position. If the base currency of the exchange rate quote is being sold (bought), then use the bid (offer) side of the market.

3. Calculate the cash flow at settlement day. This amount will be based on the original contract size times the difference between the original forward rate and that calculated in step 2. If the currency the market participant was originally long (short) subsequently appreciated (depreciated), then there will be a cash *inflow*. Otherwise there will be is a cash *outflow*. (In the above example, the market participant was long the GBP, which subsequently appreciated, leading to a cash inflow at settlement day.)

4. Calculate the present value of this cash flow at the future settlement date. The currency of the cash flow and the discount rate must match. (In the example above, the cash flow at the settlement date was in AUD, so an AUD LIBOR was used to calculate the present value.)

Example 3

Forward Rates and the Mark-to-Market of Forward Positions

Six months ago, a dealer sold CHF 1 million forward against the GBP for a 180-day term at an all-in rate of 1.4850 (CHF/GBP). Today, the dealer wants to roll this position forward for another six months (i.e., the dealer will use an FX swap to roll the position forward). The following are the current spot rate and forward points being quoted for the CHF/GBP currency pair:

Spot rate (CHF/GBP)	1.4939/1.4941
One month	−8.3/−7.9
Two month	−17.4/−16.8
Three month	−25.4/−24.6
Four month	−35.4/−34.2
Five month	−45.9/−44.1
Six month	−56.5/−54.0

1. The current all-in bid rate for delivery of GBP against the CHF in three months is *closest* to:

   A. 1.49136.

   B. 1.49150.

   C. 1.49164.

2. The cash flow that the dealer will realize on the settlement date is *closest* to an:

   A. inflow of GBP 4,057.

   B. inflow of GBP 8,100.

   C. outflow of GBP 5,422.

3. The all-in rate that the dealer will use today to sell the CHF six months forward against the GBP is *closest* to:

    A. 1.48825.

    B. 1.48835.

    C. 1.48860.

Some time ago, Laurier Bay Capital, an investment fund based in Los Angeles, hedged a long exposure to the New Zealand dollar by selling NZD 10 million forward against the USD; the all-in forward price was 0.7900 (USD/NZD). Three months prior to the settlement date, Laurier Bay wants to mark this forward position to market. The bid–offer for the USD/NZD spot rate, the three-month forward points, and the three-month LIBORs (annualized) are as follows:

Spot rate (USD/NZD)	0.7825/0.7830
Three-month points	−12.1/−10.0
Three-month LIBOR (NZD)	3.31%
Three-month LIBOR (USD)	0.31%

4. The mark-to-market for Laurier Bay's forward position is *closest* to:

    A. −USD 87,100.

    B. +USD 77,437.

    C. +USD 79,938.

Now suppose that instead of having a long exposure to the NZD, Laurier Bay Capital had a long forward exposure to the USD, which it hedged by selling USD 10 million forward against the NZD at an all-in forward rate of 0.7900 (USD/NZD). Three months prior to settlement date, it wants to close out this short USD forward position.

5. Using the above table, the mark-to-market for Laurier Bay's short USD forward position is *closest* to:

    A. −NZD 141,117.

    B. −NZD 139,959.

    C. −NZD 87,100.

Solution to 1:

A is correct. The current all-in three month bid rate for GBP (the base currency) is equal to $1.4939 + (−25.4/10,000) = 1.49136$.

Solution to 2:

A is correct because 180 days ago, the dealer sold 1 million CHF against the GBP for 1.4850. Today, the dealer will have to buy CHF 1 million to settle the maturing forward contract, so the CHF amounts will net to zero on settlement day. Because these CHF amounts net to zero, the cash flow on settlement day is measured in GBP. The GBP amount is calculated as follows: 180 days ago, the dealer sold CHF 1 million against the GBP at a rate of 1.4850, which is equivalent to buying GBP 673,400.67 (1,000,000/1.4850). That is, based on the forward contract, the dealer will receive GBP 673,400.67 on settlement day. Today, the dealer is buying CHF 1 million at a spot rate of 1.4940 (the mid-market spot rate, because this is an FX swap). This transaction is equivalent to selling GBP 669,344.04 (1,000,000/1.4940). That is, based on the spot transaction, the dealer will pay out GBP 669,344.04 on settlement day. Combining these two legs of the swap transaction, we have:

$$\frac{1,000,000}{1.4850} - \frac{1,000,000}{1.4940} = \text{GBP } 4,056.63$$

This is a cash inflow for the dealer because the dealer went short the CHF (long the GBP) and the CHF depreciated against the GBP (equivalently, the GBP appreciated against the CHF) over the life of the forward contract.

Solution to 3:

buy base currency

C is correct. The dealer will sell CHF against the GBP, which is equivalent to buying GBP (the base currency) against the CHF. Hence the *offer* side of the market will be used for forward points, and because this is a FX swap, the mid-market on the spot quote will be used. Hence the all-in forward price will be 1.4940 + (−54.0/10,000) = 1.48860.

Solution to 4:

C is correct. Laurier Bay sold NZD 10 million forward to the settlement date at an all-in forward rate of 0.7900 (USD/NZD). To mark this position to market, it would need an offsetting forward transaction involving buying NZD 10 million three months forward to the settlement date. The NZD amounts on settlement date net to zero. For the offsetting forward contract, because the NZD is the base currency in the USD/NZD quote, buying NZD forward means paying the offer for both the spot rate and forward points. This leads to an all-in three-month forward rate of 0.7830 − 0.0010 = 0.7820. On settlement day, Laurier Bay will receive USD 7,900,000 (NZD 10,000,000 × 0.7900 USD/NZD) from the original forward contract and pay out USD 7,820,000 (NZD 10,000,000 × 0.7820 USD/NZD) based on the offsetting forward contract. This gives a net cash flow on settlement day of 10,000,000 × (0.7900 − 0.7820) = +USD 80,000.

This is a cash inflow because Laurier Bay sold the NZD forward and the NZD depreciated against the USD. This USD cash inflow will occur in three months. To calculate the mark-to-market value of the original forward position, we need to calculate the present value of this USD cash inflow using the three-month USD discount rate (we use USD LIBOR for this purpose):

$$\frac{USD\ 80,000}{1 + 0.0031\left[\dfrac{90}{360}\right]} = +USD\ 79,938$$

Solution to 5:

B is correct. This is because Laurier Bay initially sold USD 10 million forward, and it will have to buy USD 10 million forward to the same settlement date (i.e., in three months' time) in order to close out the initial position. Buying USD using the USD/NZD currency pair is the same as selling the NZD. Because the NZD is the base currency in the USD/NZD quote, selling the NZD means calculating the *bid* rate:

$$0.7825 + (−12.1/10,000) = 0.78129$$

At settlement, the USD amounts will net to zero (10 million USD both bought and sold). The NZD amounts will not net to zero, however, because the all-in forward rate changed between the time Laurier Bay initiated the original position and when it closed out this position. At initiation, Laurier Bay contracted to sell USD 10,000,000 and receive NZD 12,658,228 (i.e., 10,000,000/0.7900) on the settlement date. To close out the original forward contract, Laurier Bay entered into an offsetting forward contract to receive USD 10,000,000 and pay out NZD 12,799,345 (i.e., 10,000,000/0.78129) at settlement. The difference between the NZD amounts that Laurier Bay will receive and pay out on the settlement date equals

$$NZD\ 12,658,228 − NZD\ 12,799,345 = −NZD\ 141,117$$

This is a cash *outflow* for Laurier Bay because the fund was *short* the USD in the original forward position and the USD subsequently *appreciated* (i.e., the NZD subsequently depreciated, because the all-in forward rate in USD/NZD dropped from 0.7900 to 0.78129). This NZD cash outflow occurs in three months' time, and we must calculate its present value using the three-month NZD LIBOR:

$$\frac{-NZD\ 141,117}{1 + 0.0331\left(\dfrac{90}{360}\right)} = -NZD\ 139,959$$

A LONG-TERM FRAMEWORK FOR EXCHANGE RATES

3

Having reviewed the basic tools of the FX market, we now turn our focus to how they are used in practice. At the heart of the trading decision in FX (and other) markets lies a view on future market prices and conditions. This outlook guides the market participant's decisions with respect to risk exposures, as well as whether currency hedges should be implemented and, if so, how they should be managed. Even the decision to be fully hedged, or to have no market exposure at all, implies an opinion that future market conditions are so uncertain that no sufficiently profitable active trading opportunities are available.

In this and the following sections, we lay out a framework for developing a view about future exchange rate movements, which should serve as a guide for how FX positions should be managed. We begin by examining international parity conditions, which describe the inter-relationships that jointly determine *long-run* movements in exchange rates, interest rates, and inflation. These parity conditions are the basic building blocks for describing long-term equilibrium levels for exchange rates. In subsequent sections, we expand beyond this simple view of how exchange rates are determined in a long-term, ideal world by bringing in a broader view of real-world factors that must be considered in forming an intelligent market opinion, especially over medium- and short-term horizons.

Always keep in mind that exchange rate movements reflect complex interactions among multiple forces. In trying to untangle this complex web of interactions, we must clearly delineate the following concepts:

1. **Long run versus short run:** Many of the factors that determine exchange rate movements exert subtle but persistent influences over long periods of time. Although a poor guide for short-term prediction, longer-term equilibrium values nevertheless act as an anchor for exchange rate movements. Exhibit 2 shows a stylized representation of movements in spot exchange rates within a convergence path centered on a long-run equilibrium exchange rate. The forces that affect long-run convergence to fair value are discussed more in the sections on international parity conditions and long-run equilibrium models. Subsequent sections discuss factors that help determine the medium- and short-term deviations within this convergence channel.

2. **Real versus nominal values:** Observable exchange rates (and interest rates) represent the prices of tradable financial products, but they are not inflation adjusted. In contrast, people save and invest to facilitate future purchases of *real* (inflation-adjusted) goods and services. Therefore, movements in real variables exert considerable influence over nominal variables, including nominal spot exchange rates. Hence, in some of the subsequent material, the focus will be on real variables in order to better conceptualize exchange rate determinants.

Nonetheless, only *nominal* exchange rates are tradable or used in mark-to-market calculations. Hence, it is necessary to be able to map expected movements in real rates back into expected future movements in nominal exchange (and interest) rates. Being able to form an opinion about future nominal exchange rate movements is the ultimate goal of the material covered in this and all subsequent sections of this reading.

3. **Expected versus unexpected changes:** In reasonably efficient markets, prices will adjust to reflect market participants' expectations of future developments. When a key factor, say inflation, is trending gradually in a particular direction, market pricing will eventually come to reflect expectations that this trend will continue. In contrast, large, unexpected movements in a variable (for example, a central bank intervening in the foreign exchange market) can lead to immediate, discrete price adjustments. This concept of expected versus unexpected changes is closely related to what might broadly be referred to as risk. For example, a moderate but steady rate of inflation will not have the same effect on market participants as an inflation rate that is very unpredictable. The latter clearly describes a riskier financial environment. Market pricing will reflect risk premia—that is, the compensation that traders and investors demand for being exposed to unpredictable outcomes. Whereas expectations of long-run equilibrium values tend to evolve slowly, risk premia—which are closely related to confidence and reputation—can change quickly in response to unexpected developments.

Exhibit 2	A Stylized Model of the Long-Term Trend in a Currency's Value

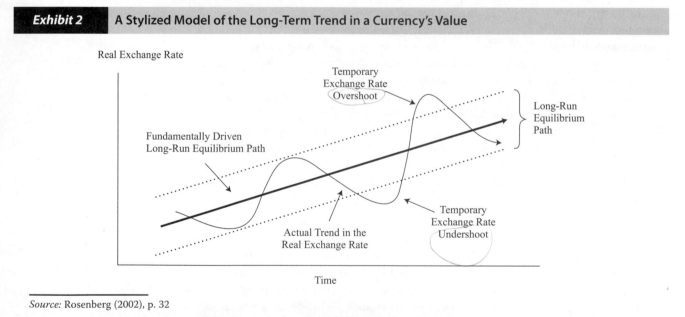

Source: Rosenberg (2002), p. 32

4. **Relative movements:** An exchange rate represents the relative price of one currency in terms of another. Hence, for exchange rate determination, the levels or variability of key factors in any particular country are typically much less important than the *differences* in these factors across countries. For example, knowing that inflation is increasing in Country A may not give much insight into the direction of the A/B exchange rate without also knowing what is happening with the inflation rate in Country B.

As a final word of caution—and this cannot be emphasized enough: *There is no simple formula, model, or approach that will allow market participants to precisely forecast exchange rates* (or any other financial prices) or to be able to make all trading decisions profitable. We live in an imperfect world where exchange rates and other financial prices can be highly erratic and hard to explain even after the fact, let alone predict in advance. Nonetheless, to operate in financial markets requires acceptance of these imperfections. It also requires that market participants have a market view to guide their decisions, even if this view requires significant revision as new information becomes available. The following sections provide a framework for formulating a view on FX markets, a guide for thinking through the complex forces driving exchange rates. As with all theory, however, it does not eliminate the need for insightful analysis of actual economic and market conditions.

3.1 International Parity Conditions

International parity conditions form the building blocks of most models of exchange rate determination. The key international parity conditions are as follows:

1. covered interest rate parity;

2. uncovered interest rate parity;

3. forward exchange rates as unbiased predictors of future spot exchange rates;

4. purchasing power parity;

5. the Fisher effect;

6. the international Fisher effect; and

7. real interest rate parity.

Parity conditions show how expected inflation differentials, interest rate differentials, forward exchange rates, current spot exchange rates, and expected future spot exchange rates would be linked in an ideal world. These conditions typically make simplifying assumptions, such as perfect information that is available to all market participants, risk neutrality, and freely adjustable market prices. If these international parity conditions held at all times, moving capital from one market to another would offer no profitable trading opportunities for international investors.

Most empirical studies find, however, that the key international parity conditions rarely hold in either the short or medium term. The exception is covered interest rate parity, which is the only one of the parity conditions that is enforced by an executable arbitrage relationship. There are often significant and persistent departures from purchasing power parity, uncovered interest rate parity, and real interest rate parity. In addition, forward exchange rates have typically been found to be poor predictors of future spot exchange rates.

The failure of international parity conditions raises an interesting question: Why bother to study them at all if they do not work? There are essentially two reasons. First, although the conditions are frequently violated, each reflects economic forces that should not be ignored altogether. Second, and perhaps even more importantly, from a trader/investor/analyst's perspective, international parity conditions truly become interesting only when they fail to hold, because it is only then that currency positions offer profitable opportunities. As mentioned earlier, the parity relationships are one of the most basic frameworks from which a more broadly based, long-term view of future market conditions can be constructed. Such a market outlook is a prerequisite for a market participant to manage longer-term risk exposures.

3.1.1 *Covered Interest Rate Parity*

We have already discussed covered interest rate parity in our examination of forward exchange rates. This parity condition describes a riskless arbitrage relationship in which *an investment in a foreign money market instrument that is completely hedged against exchange rate risk should yield exactly the same return as an otherwise identical domestic money market investment.* Given the spot exchange rate and the domestic and foreign yields, the forward exchange rate must equal the rate that gives these two alternative investment strategies—invest either in a domestic money market instrument or in a fully currency-hedged foreign money market instrument—exactly the same holding period return.[10] If one strategy gave a higher holding period return than the other, then an investor could short-sell the lower-yielding approach and invest the proceeds in the higher-yielding approach, earning riskless profits in the process. In real world financial markets, such a disparity would be quickly arbitraged away by alert market participants.

For covered interest rate parity to hold exactly, it must be assumed that there are zero transaction costs and that the underlying domestic and foreign money market instruments being compared are identical in terms of liquidity, maturity, and default risk. In most cases where capital is permitted to flow freely, spot and forward exchange markets are liquid, and financial market conditions are relatively stress-free, covered interest rate differentials are generally found to be close to zero; that is, Equation 1 in Section 2.2 holds.

3.1.2 *Uncovered Interest Rate Parity*

According to the **uncovered interest rate parity** condition, the *expected* return on an uncovered (i.e., unhedged) foreign currency investment should equal the return on a comparable domestic currency investment. The return on a risk-free domestic money market instrument is known with certainty for a domestic investor: It is the money market instrument's yield. However, an unhedged investment in a foreign currency money market instrument exposes a domestic investor to the risk of spot exchange rate movements between the time the investment is made and when it matures. Uncovered interest rate parity states that *the change in spot rate over the investment horizon should, on average, equal the differential in interest rates between the two countries. That is, the expected appreciation/depreciation of the exchange rate just offsets the yield differential, implying that the current forward exchange rate is an unbiased (i.e., correct on average) predictor of the future spot rate.*

An example will help illustrate how uncovered interest rate parity works. To explain the intuition behind this concept more easily, let's switch, as we did with the examples for covered interest parity, from the standard price/base currency notation (P/B) to foreign/domestic currency notation (*f/d*) in order to emphasize the choice between foreign and domestic investments. As before, we also will assume that for the investor, the base and domestic currencies are the same.

For our example, assume that this investor has a choice between owning a one-year domestic money market instrument and a one-year foreign-currency-denominated money market investment. We assume that this investor will not hedge the FX risk in the forward exchange market. Under the assumption of uncovered interest rate parity, the investor must compare the *known* return on the domestic investment with the *expected* all-in return on the unhedged foreign-currency-denominated investment (i.e., including the foreign yield as well as movements in the exchange rate, in $S_{f/d}$ terms). The ultimate investment choice between these two investments (domestic and foreign) will depend on which market offers the higher expected return on an unhedged basis.

To be concrete, let's assume that the return on the one-year foreign money market instrument is 10 percent, while the return on the one-year domestic money market instrument is 5 percent. From the investor's perspective, the expected return on the one-year domestic investment in domestic currency terms is known with complete

---

10 Note that the spot exchange rate, the forward exchange rate, and the two interest rates are actually determined simultaneously in the market. One should not think of one of them, say the forward exchange rate, being determined by the others.

certainty (i.e., 5 percent). This is not the case for the uncovered investment in the foreign currency money market instrument. In domestic currency terms, the investment return on an uncovered (or unhedged) foreign-currency-denominated investment is approximately equal to[11]

$$\left(1 + i_f\right)\left(1 - \%\Delta S_{f/d}\right) - 1 \cong i_f - \%\Delta S_{f/d}$$

The percentage change in $S_{f/d}$ enters with a minus sign because an *increase* in $S_{f/d}$ means the foreign currency *declines* in value, reducing the all-in return from the domestic currency perspective of our investor. An increase in $S_{f/d}$ means the base currency, the domestic currency in this case, is appreciating, and that the price (foreign) currency is depreciating.

This all-in return depends on *future* movements in the $S_{f/d}$ rate, which cannot be known until the end of the period. Consider three cases:

1. The $S_{f/d}$ rate is expected to remain unchanged.

2. The domestic currency is expected to appreciate by 10 percent.

3. The domestic currency is expected to appreciate by 5 percent.

In the first case, the investor would prefer the foreign-currency-denominated money market investment because it offers a 10 percent (= 10% – 0%) expected return, while the comparable domestic investment offers only 5 percent. In the second case, the investor would prefer the domestic investment because the expected return on the foreign-currency-denominated investment is 0 percent (= 10% – 10%). In the third case, uncovered interest rate parity holds because both investments offer a 5 percent (= 10% – 5%) expected return. In this case, the investor is assumed to be indifferent between the alternatives.

Note that in the third case, in which uncovered interest rate parity holds, although the *expected* return over the one-year investment horizon is the same, the *distribution* of possible total return outcomes is quite different. For our investor, the return on the domestic money market instrument is known with certainty. In contrast, the distribution of the all-in return on the foreign money market instrument embodies uncertainty with respect to the *future* $S_{f/d}$ rate. Hence, when we say that the investor would be indifferent between owning domestic and foreign investments because they both offer the same *expected* return (5 percent), we are assuming that the investor is *risk neutral*. Thus, uncovered interest rate parity assumes that there are enough risk-neutral investors to force equality of expected returns.

In terms of our example's foreign/domestic (*f/d*) notation, uncovered interest rate parity asserts

$$i_f - \%\Delta S_{f/d}^e = i_d$$

where $\%\Delta S_{f/d}^e$ is the expected change in the foreign currency price of the domestic currency over the investment horizon. This equation can be rearranged to restate the uncovered interest rate parity condition in terms of the expected change in the exchange rate:[12]

$$\%\Delta S_{f/d}^e = i_f - i_d \qquad (2)$$

---

11 The symbol $\cong$ indicates approximate equality. The approximation holds because the product ($i \times \%\Delta S$) is small compared to the interest rate (i) and the percentage change in the exchange rate (%ΔS). For simplicity of exposition, we will use the $\cong$ symbol when we introduce an approximation but will subsequently treat the relationship as an equality (=) unless the distinction is important for the issue being discussed.

12 The mathematically inclined reader may note that this equation cannot hold simultaneously for $S_{f/d}$ and $S_{d/f} (= 1/S_{f/d})$ because their percentage changes are not of exactly equal magnitude. This reflects our earlier approximation. Using the exact return on the unhedged foreign instrument would alleviate this issue at the expense of a less intuitive equation.

According to this equation, the expected change in the spot exchange rate over the investment horizon should be reflected in the interest rate differential. Using our example, if the yield spread between the foreign and domestic investments is 5 percent ($i_f - i_d = 5\%$), then this spread implicitly reflects the expectation that the domestic currency will strengthen versus the foreign currency by 5 percent ($\%\Delta S^e_{f/d} = 5\%$).

Note that with uncovered interest rate parity, the country with the *higher* interest rate or money market yield is expected to see the value of its currency *depreciate*. It is this depreciation of the currency that offsets the higher yield so that the (expected) all-in return on the two investment choices is the same. Hence, if the uncovered interest rate parity condition held consistently in the real world, it would rule out the possibility of earning excess returns from going long a high-yield currency and going short a low-yield currency. If uncovered interest rate parity held, the depreciation of the high-yield currency would exactly offset the yield advantage that the high-yield currency offers. Taking this to its logical conclusion, if uncovered interest rate parity held at all times, investors would have no incentive to shift capital from one currency to another because expected returns on otherwise identical money market investments would be equal across markets and risk-neutral investors would be indifferent among them.

Most studies find that uncovered interest rate parity fails to hold over short- and medium-term periods, although there is evidence that it works better over very long-term horizons. Over short- and medium-term periods, interest rate differentials have generally been found to be a poor predictor of future exchange rate changes. Indeed, most studies find that high-yield currencies fail to weaken in line with the path predicted by uncovered interest rate parity. That is, the rate of depreciation of the high-yield currency has been found to be less than the implied uncovered interest rate parity path. In many cases, high-yield currencies have been found to *strengthen*, not weaken, conflicting even more strongly with the implication of uncovered interest rate parity.

Such findings have significant implications for foreign exchange investment strategies. If high-yield currencies fail to depreciate in line with the path predicted by the uncovered interest rate parity condition, then high-yield currencies should exhibit a tendency to outperform low-yield currencies over time. If so, investors could adopt strategies that overweight high-yield currencies at the expense of low-yield currencies and generate attractive returns in the process. Such approaches are known as FX carry trade strategies. We will discuss them in greater depth in Section 4.

3.1.3 *Spot and Forward Rates as Predictors of Future Spot Rates*

The covered interest rate parity condition describes the relationship among the spot exchange rate, the forward exchange rate, and interest rates. Let's keep using the foreign/domestic exchange rate notation (f/d) to simplify the explanation. As we illustrated in Section 2, the arbitrage condition that underlies covered interest rate parity can be rearranged to give an expression for the forward premium or discount:

$$F_{f/d} - S_{f/d} = S_{f/d} \left(\frac{\left[\dfrac{Actual}{360} \right]}{1 + i_d \left[\dfrac{Actual}{360} \right]} \right) \left(i_f - i_d \right)$$

The domestic currency will trade at a forward premium ($F_{f/d} > S_{f/d}$) if, and only if, the foreign risk-free interest rate exceeds the domestic risk-free interest rate ($i_f > i_d$). For the sake of simplicity, assume that the investment horizon is one year, leading to:

$$F_{f/d} - S_{f/d} = S_{f/d} \left(\frac{i_f - i_d}{1 + i_d} \right) \cong S_{f/d} (i_f - i_d)$$

This equation can be re-expressed to show the forward discount or premium as a percentage of the spot rate:

$$\frac{F_{f/d} - S_{f/d}}{S_{f/d}} \cong i_f - i_d$$

As we showed previously, if uncovered interest parity holds—that is, investors are risk neutral—then the expected change in the spot rate is equal to the interest rate differential:

$$\%\Delta S^e_{f/d} = i_f - i_d$$

We can link these two equations by assuming that uncovered interest rate parity holds. If this is the case, then the forward premium (discount) on a currency, expressed in percentage terms, equals the expected percentage appreciation (depreciation) of the domestic currency:

$$\frac{F_{f/d} - S_{f/d}}{S_{f/d}} = \%\Delta S^e_{f/d} = i_f - i_d$$

It follows that the forward exchange rate equals the expected future spot exchange rate:

$$F_{f/d} = S^e_{f/d}$$

Thus, in theory, *the forward exchange rate will be an unbiased forecast of the future spot exchange rate if both covered and uncovered interest rate parity hold.*

In our previous example, foreign interest rates were assumed to be 5 percent higher (10% − 5%) than domestic interest rates. *Uncovered* interest parity would imply that the domestic currency was expected to appreciate by 5 percent against the foreign currency (i.e., $\%\Delta S^e_{f/d} = 5\%$). *Covered* interest rate parity would imply that the domestic currency must trade at a 5 percent forward premium (i.e., $\left(F_{f/d} - S_{f/d}\right)/S_{f/d} = 5\%$). The latter must hold because it is enforced by arbitrage. *So, asking whether the forward exchange rate is an unbiased predictor of the spot exchange rate is the same as asking whether uncovered interest rate parity holds.*

How might uncovered interest rate parity, and with it equality of the forward exchange rate and the expected future spot exchange rate, be enforced? It is not enforced by arbitrage, because there is no combination of trades that will lock in a certain profit. If the forward rate is above (below) speculators' expectation of the future spot rate, however, then risk-neutral speculators will buy the domestic currency in the spot (forward) market and simultaneously sell it in the forward (spot) market. If their expectations are correct, they will make a profit, on average. These transactions will push the forward premium into alignment with the consensus expectation of the future spot rate.

Note, however, that spot exchange rates are volatile and determined by a complex web of influences—interest rate differentials are only one among many factors. In other words, speculators can also lose. Moreover, speculators are rarely, if ever, truly risk neutral, and without an arbitrage relationship to enforce it, uncovered interest rate parity is often violated. *In general, this means that forward exchange rates are poor predictors of future spot exchange rates.*

Current spot exchange rates are not very good predictors of future spot exchange rates, either. Superficially, it might seem that spot rates could be used as a predictor, because movements in spot rates are so volatile that they often approximate a random walk:

$$S_{t+1} - S_t = \Delta S_{t+1} \cong \varepsilon_{t+1}$$

If the distribution for the error term has a mean of zero, then $E_t[\varepsilon_{t+1}] = 0$. This would imply that the expectation for the future spot exchange rate would be the current spot exchange rate $\left(E_t[S_{t+1}] = S_t\right)$. In practice, however, current spot rates are poor predictors of future spot rates because of the high volatility in exchange rate movements: Future spot exchange rates rarely equal current spot exchange rates and are often not even close. Also, without using *any* current information at all to attempt to predict future spot rates (such as current interest rate differentials), the random walk prediction can be slightly biased, on average.

Example 4

Covered and Uncovered Interest Parity; Predictors of Future Spot Rates

An Australian-based fixed income asset manager is deciding whether to allocate money between Australia and Japan. Note that the base currency in the exchange rate quote (AUD) is the domestic currency for the asset manager.

JPY/AUD spot rate (mid-market)	79.25
One-year forward points (mid-market)	−301.9
One-year Australian deposit rate	5.00%
One-year Japanese deposit rate	1.00%

1. Based on uncovered interest rate parity, over the next year, the expected change in the JPY/AUD rate is *closest* to a(n):

   A. decrease of 10 percent.

   B. decrease of 4 percent.

   C. increase of 4 percent.

2. The *best* explanation of why this prediction may not be very accurate is that:

   A. covered interest parity does hold in this case.

   B. the forward points indicate that a riskless arbitrage opportunity exists.

   C. there is no arbitrage condition that forces uncovered interest rate parity to hold.

3. Using the forward points to forecast the future JPY/AUD spot rate one year ahead assumes that:

   A. investors are risk neutral.

   B. spot rates follow a random walk.

   C. it is not necessary for uncovered interest rate parity to hold.

4. Forecasting that the JPY/AUD spot rate one year from now will equal 79.25 assumes that:

   A. investors are risk neutral.

   B. spot rates follow a random walk.

   C. it is necessary for uncovered interest rate parity to hold.

5. If the asset manager completely hedged the currency risk associated with a one-year Japanese deposit using a forward rate contract, the one-year all-in holding return, in AUD, would be *closest* to:

   A. 0 percent.

   B. 1 percent.

   C. 5 percent.

The fixed income manager collects the following information, and uses it along with the international parity conditions in order to estimate investment returns and future exchange rate movements.

Today's One-Year LIBOR		Currency Pair	Spot Rate Today
JPY	0.10%	JPY/USD	81.30
USD	0.10%	USD/GBP	1.5950
GBP	3.00%	JPY/GBP	129.67

6. If covered interest parity holds, the all-in, one-year investment return to a Japanese investor whose currency exposure to the GBP is fully hedged is *closest* to:

   A. 0.10 percent.

   B. 0.17 percent.

   C. 3.00 percent.

7. If uncovered interest parity holds, today's expected value for the JPY/GBP currency pair one year from now would be *closest* to:

   A. 126.02.

   B. 129.67.

   C. 130.05.

8. If uncovered interest parity holds, between today and one year from now the expected movement in the JPY/USD currency pair is *closest* to:

   A. −1.60 percent.

   B. +0.00 percent.

   C. +1.63 percent.

Solution to 1:

B is correct. The expected depreciation of the Australian dollar (decline in the JPY/AUD rate) is equal to the interest rate differential between Australia and Japan (5% − 1%).

Solution to 2:

C is correct. There is no arbitrage condition that forces uncovered interest rate parity to hold. In contrast, arbitrage virtually always ensures that covered interest rate parity holds. This is the case for our table, where the −302 point discount is calculated from the covered interest rate parity equation.

Solution to 3:

A is correct. Using forward rates (i.e., adding the forward points to the spot rate) to forecast future spot rates assumes that uncovered interest rate parity holds. In turn, uncovered interest rate parity assumes that investors are risk neutral. If these conditions hold, then movements in the spot exchange rate, although they *approximate* a random walk, will not actually be a random walk because current interest spreads will determine expected exchange rate movements.

Solution to 4:

B is correct. Assuming that the current spot exchange rate is the best predictor of future spot rates assumes that exchange rate movements follow a random walk. If uncovered interest rate parity holds, the current exchange rate will not be the best predictor unless the interest rate differential happens to be zero. Risk neutrality is needed to enforce uncovered interest rate parity, but it will not make the current spot exchange rate the best predictor of future spot rates.

Solution to 5:

C is correct. A fully hedged JPY investment would provide the same return as the AUD investment: 5 percent. This is covered interest rate parity, an arbitrage condition.

Solution to 6:

A is correct. If covered interest rate parity holds (and it very likely does, because this is a pure arbitrage relationship), then the all-in investment return to a Japanese investor in a one-year, fully hedged GBP LIBOR position would be identical to a one-year JPY LIBOR position: 0.10 percent. No calculations are necessary.

Solution to 7:

A is correct. If uncovered interest rate parity holds, then the expected spot rate one year forward is equal to the one-year forward exchange rate. This forward rate is calculated in the usual manner, given the spot exchange rates and LIBORs:

$$S^e = F = 129.67\left(\frac{1.001}{1.03}\right) = 126.02$$

Solution to 8:

B is correct. Given uncovered interest rate parity, the expected change in a spot exchange rate is equal to the interest rate differential. At the one-year term, there is no difference between USD and JPY LIBOR.

3.1.4 *Purchasing Power Parity*

So far, we have looked at the interrelationships between exchange rates and interest rate differentials. Now we turn to examining the relationship between exchange rates and inflation differentials. The basis for this relationship is known as purchasing power parity (PPP).

Various versions of PPP exist. The foundation for all of the versions is the law of one price. According to the **law of one price**, identical goods should trade at the same price across countries when valued in terms of a common currency. To simplify the explanation, as we did with our examples for covered and uncovered interest rate parity, let's continue to use the foreign/domestic currency quote convention (*f/d*) and the case where the base currency in the P/B notation is the domestic currency for the investor in the *f/d* notation.

The law of one price asserts that the foreign price of good $x(P_f^x)$ should equal the exchange rate-adjusted price of the identical good in the domestic country (P_d^x):

$$P_f^x = S_{f/d} \times P_d^x$$

For example, for a EUR-based consumer, if the price of good x in the euro area is €100 and the nominal exchange rate stands at 1.40 USD/EUR, then the price of good x in the United States should equal $140.

The **absolute version of PPP** simply extends the law of one price to the broad range of goods and services that are consumed in different countries. Using our example above but now expanded to include all goods and services, not just good x, the broad price level of the foreign country (P_f) should equal the currency-adjusted broad price level in the domestic country (P_d):

$$P_f = S_{f/d} \times P_d$$

This equation implicitly assumes that all domestic and foreign goods are tradable and that the domestic and foreign price indices include the same bundle of goods and services with the same exact weights in each country. Rearranging this equation and solving for the nominal exchange rate ($S_{f/d}$), the absolute version of PPP states that the nominal exchange rate will be determined by the ratio of the foreign and domestic broad price indices:

$$S_{f/d} = P_f / P_d$$

The absolute version of PPP asserts that the equilibrium exchange rate between two countries is determined entirely by the ratio of their national price levels. However, it is highly unlikely that one will find that this relationship actually holds in the real world. The absolute version of PPP assumes that goods arbitrage will equate the prices of all goods and service across countries, but if transaction costs are significant and/or not all goods and services are tradable, then goods arbitrage will be incomplete. Hence, sizable and persistent departures from absolute PPP are likely.

However, if it is assumed that transaction costs and other trade impediments are constant over time, it might be possible to show that *changes* in exchange rates and *changes* in national price levels are related, even if the relationship between exchange rate *levels* and national price *levels* does not hold. According to the **relative version of PPP**, the percentage change in the spot exchange rate $\left(\%\Delta S_{f/d}\right)$ will be completely determined by the difference between the foreign and domestic inflation rates $(\pi_f - \pi_d)$:[13]

$$\%\Delta S_{f/d} \cong \pi_f - \pi_d \qquad (3)$$

Intuitively, the relative version of PPP implies that the exchange rate changes to offset changes in competiveness arising from inflation differentials. For example, if the foreign inflation rate is assumed to be 10 percent while the domestic inflation rate is assumed to be 5 percent, then the $S_{f/d}$ exchange rate must rise by 5 percent ($\%\Delta S_{f/d} = 10\% - 5\% = 5\%$) in order to maintain the relative competitiveness of the two regions. (Stated in an equivalent manner, the currency of the high-inflation country should depreciate relative to the currency of the low-inflation country. Recall that an increase in $S_{f/d}$ means the domestic currency is appreciating and the foreign currency is depreciating.) If the $S_{f/d}$ exchange rate remained unchanged, the relatively higher foreign inflation rate would erode the competitiveness of foreign companies relative to domestic companies.

The *ex ante* **version of PPP** follows directly from the relative version of PPP. Whereas the relative version of PPP focuses on *actual* changes in exchange rates being driven by *actual* differences in national inflation rates in a given time period, the *ex ante* version of PPP focuses on *expected* changes in the spot exchange rate being entirely driven by *expected* differences in national inflation rates. *Ex ante* PPP tells us that countries that are expected to run *persistently* high inflation rates should expect to see their currencies depreciate over time, while countries that are expected to run relatively low inflation rates on a sustainable basis should expect to see their currencies appreciate over time. *Ex ante* PPP can be expressed as

---

[13] We will occasionally need to convert from a relationship expressed in levels of the relevant variables into a relationship among rates of change. If X = (Y × Z), then

(1+%ΔX) = (1+%ΔY)(1+ %ΔZ) and %ΔX ≈ %ΔY + %ΔZ because (%ΔY × %ΔZ) is "small."

Similarly, it can be shown that if X = (Y/Z), then

(1+%ΔX) = (1+%ΔY)/(1+ %ΔZ) and %ΔX ≈ %ΔY − %ΔZ

Applying this to the equation for absolute PPP gives Equation 3.

ex ante's

$$\%\Delta S^{\varepsilon}_{f/d} = \pi^{\varepsilon}_f - \pi^{\varepsilon}_d \qquad\qquad (4)$$

where it is understood that the use of expectations (the "*e*" superscript) indicates that we are now focused on *future* periods. That is, $\%\Delta S^{e}_{f/d}$ represents the expected percentage change in the spot exchange rate, while π^{e}_d and π^{e}_f represent the domestic and foreign inflation rates expected to prevail over the same period.

The idea that inflation differentials across countries will cause nominal exchange rates to adjust in order to re-equilibrate real purchasing power is closely related to the concept of real exchange rates. As was covered in Level I of the CFA curriculum, the **real exchange rate** of a currency captures the real purchasing power of that currency, defined in terms of the amount of *real* goods and services that it can purchase internationally. To derive the real exchange rate, the nominal exchange rate is adjusted for the inflation rate differential between the two countries involved in that currency pair.

An equivalent way of viewing the real exchange rate is that it represents the relative price levels in the domestic and foreign countries expressed in the same currency. Mathematically, we can represent the domestic price level in terms of the foreign currency as:

Domestic price level in foreign currency = $S_{f/d} \times P_d$

As before, the foreign price level expressed in terms of the foreign currency is P_f. The ratio between the domestic and foreign price levels is the real exchange rate $q_{f/d}$:

$$q_{f/d} = \left(\frac{S_{f/d}P_d}{P_f}\right) = S_{f/d}\left(\frac{P_d}{P_f}\right) \qquad\qquad (5)$$

For example, let's examine the case of a domestic consumer wanting to buy foreign goods. This means that the real exchange rate ($q_{f/d}$) will be an increasing function of the nominal spot exchange rate ($S_{f/d}$) and the domestic price level and a decreasing function of the foreign price level. This is written as:

$$q_{f/d} = S_{f/d} \times \left(\frac{CPI_d}{CPI_f}\right)$$

Note that for the domestic consumer, an increasing real exchange rate ($q_{f/d}$) means that it is becoming less expensive, in real terms, to shop in the foreign country: The amount of real goods and services that a domestic consumer can purchase is increasing. Just as an increase in $S_{f/d}$ is an appreciation of the domestic currency in nominal terms, an increase in the real exchange rate $q_{f/d}$ is an appreciation of the domestic currency in real, or inflation-adjusted, terms. (Recall that the domestic currency in our example is the base currency in the standard P/B notation.)

Real exchange rates exhibit a very important empirical property. Studies find that in the *long run*, real exchange rates between countries tend to stabilize around their average values—that is, they mean revert. Stated another way, nominal exchange rates gradually gravitate toward their PPP-based values. This means that, *although over shorter horizons nominal exchange rate movements may appear haphazard, over longer time horizons nominal exchange rates will tend to gravitate toward their long-run PPP equilibrium values.*

Exhibit 3 illustrates the success or lack thereof of the relative version of PPP at different time horizons: 1 year, 6 years, 12 years, and 24 years. Each chart plots the inflation differential (vertical axis) against the percentage change in the exchange rate (horizontal axis). If PPP holds, the points should fall along the upward-sloping diagonal line. As indicated in the chart, there is no clear relationship between changes in exchange rates and inflation differentials over a one-year time horizon. If the horizon is lengthened to six years and beyond, however, a strong positive relationship becomes apparent. Hence, *PPP appears to be a valid framework to assess long-run fair value in the*

FX markets, even though the path to PPP equilibrium is excruciatingly slow. Estimates place the half-life of PPP deviations at around three to five years. That is, on average it takes roughly three to five years to narrow a given PPP deviation by roughly 50 percent.

Exhibit 3	Impact of Relative Inflation Rates on Exchange Rates over Different Time Horizons

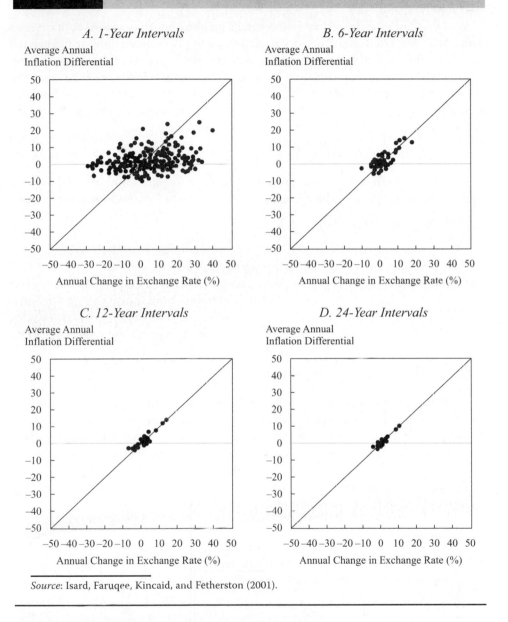

Source: Isard, Faruqee, Kincaid, and Fetherston (2001).

3.1.5 *The Fisher Effect and Real Interest Rate Parity*

So far, we have examined the relationship between exchange rates and interest rate differentials between countries, and between exchange rates and inflation differentials. Now we will begin to bring these concepts together by examining how exchange rates, interest rates, and inflation rates interact.

According to what economists call the Fisher effect, one can break down the nominal interest rate (i) in a given country into two parts: (1) the real interest rate in that particular country (r) and (2) the expected inflation rate (π^{ε}) in that country:

$$i = r + \pi^{\varepsilon}$$

To relate this concept to exchange rates—the relative price of a currency between *two* countries—we can write the Fisher equation for both the domestic country and a foreign country. If the Fisher effect holds, the nominal interest rates in both countries will equal the sum of their respective real interest rates and expected inflation rates:

$$i_d = r_d + \pi_d^\varepsilon;$$

$$i_f = r_f + \pi_f^\varepsilon$$

Because nominal interest rate differentials play an important role in both covered and uncovered interest rate parity calculations, let's take a closer look at the macro-economic forces that drive the trend in nominal yield spreads. Subtracting the top equation from the bottom equation shows that the nominal yield spread between the foreign and domestic countries $(i_f - i_d)$ equals the sum of two parts: (1) the foreign–domestic real yield spread $(r_f - r_d)$ and (2) the foreign–domestic expected inflation differential $(\pi_f^\varepsilon - \pi_d^\varepsilon)$:

$$i_f - i_d = \left(r_f - r_d\right) + (\pi_f^\varepsilon - \pi_d^\varepsilon)$$

We can rearrange this equation to solve for the foreign–domestic *real* interest rate differential instead of the domestic–foreign *nominal* interest rate differential:

$$\left(r_f - r_d\right) = (i_f - i_d) - (\pi_f^\varepsilon - \pi_d^\varepsilon)$$

To tie this material to our previous work on exchange rates, let's continue with our previous, simplifying convention of quoting the currencies using foreign/domestic notation (*f/d*). Now, if uncovered interest rate parity holds, then the nominal interest rate spread $(i_f - i_d)$ equals the expected change in the exchange rate (%$\Delta S^e_{f/d}$). Similarly, if *ex ante* PPP holds, the difference in expected inflation rates $(\pi_f^\varepsilon - \pi_d^\varepsilon)$ also equals the expected change in the exchange rate. Assuming that both uncovered interest rate parity and *ex ante* PPP hold leads to:

$$\left(r_f - r_d\right) = \%\Delta S^\varepsilon_{f/d} - \%\Delta S^\varepsilon_{f/d} = 0$$

According to this equation, if both uncovered interest rate parity and *ex ante* PPP hold, then the real yield spread between the domestic and foreign countries $(r_f - r_d)$ will be zero. If that is the case, then the level of real interest rates in the domestic country will be identical to the level of real interest rates in the foreign country. The proposition that real interest rates will converge to the same level across different markets is known as the **real interest rate parity** condition. This concept can be interpreted as an application of the law of one price to securities internationally:

$$(r_f - r_d) = 0$$

If real interest rates are equal across markets, such that $r_f - r_d = 0$, then it also follows that the foreign–domestic nominal yield spread will be solely determined by the foreign–domestic expected inflation differential.

$$i_f - i_d = \pi_f^\varepsilon - \pi_d^\varepsilon$$

This is known as the **international Fisher effect**.[14]

As noted above, the various parity relationships may seem of little empirical significance when examined over short time horizons. However, studies show that over longer time periods there is a discernible interaction between nominal interest rates, exchange rates, and inflation rates across countries, such that the international parity conditions described here serve as an anchor for longer-term exchange rate movements.

---

[14] The reader should be aware that some authors refer to uncovered interest rate parity as the international Fisher effect. We reserve this term for the relationship between nominal interest rate differentials and expected inflation differentials because the original (domestic) Fisher effect is a relationship between interest rates and expected inflation.

Example 5

PPP, Real Exchange Rates, and the International Fisher Effect

An Australian-based fixed income asset manager is deciding whether to allocate money between Australia and Japan. (As before, the AUD is the domestic currency.) Australia's one-year deposit rates are 5 percent, considerably higher than Japan's at 1 percent, but the Australian dollar is estimated to be roughly 10 percent overvalued relative to Japanese yen based on purchasing power parity. Before making her asset allocation, the asset manager considers the implications of interest rate differentials and PPP imbalances.

1. All else equal, which of the following events would restore the Australian dollar to its PPP value?

   A. The Japanese inflation rate increases by 4 percent.

   B. The Australian inflation rate decreases by 10 percent.

   C. The JPY/AUD exchange rate declines by 10 percent.

2. If both the Australian and Japanese CPI price levels increased by 5 percent, all else equal, then the change in the real exchange rate $q_{JPY/AUD}$ would be *closest* to:

   A. 0 percent.

   B. 5 percent.

   C. 10 percent.

3. If real interest rates in Japan and Australia were equal, then under the international Fisher effect, the inflation rate differential between Japan and Australia would be *closest* to:

   A. 0 percent.

   B. 4 percent.

   C. 10 percent.

4. According to the theory and empirical evidence regarding purchasing power parity, which of the following would *not* be true if PPP holds in the long run?

   A. An exchange rate's equilibrium path should be determined by the long-term trend in domestic relative to foreign price levels.

   B. Deviations from PPP might occur over short- and medium-term periods, but fundamental forces should eventually work to push exchange rates toward their long-term PPP path.

   C. High-inflation countries should tend to see their currencies appreciate over time.

5. Which of the following would *best* explain the failure of the absolute version of PPP to hold?

   A. Inflation rates vary across countries.

   B. Real interest rates are converging across countries.

   C. Trade barriers exist, and different product mixes are consumed across countries.

Solution to 1:

C is correct. If the Australian dollar is overvalued by 10 percent on a PPP basis, with all else held equal, a depreciation of the JPY/AUD rate by 10 percent would move the Australian dollar back to equilibrium.

Solution to 2:

A is correct. Based on our equation for the real exchange rate, these 5 percent changes would appear in both the numerator and denominator and cancel each other out.

Solution to 3:

B is correct. If the real interest rates were equal, then the difference in nominal yields would be explained by the difference in inflation rates (5% − 1%).

Solution to 4:

C is correct. According to PPP, high-inflation countries should see their currencies depreciate (at least, over the longer term) in order to re-equilibrate real purchasing power between countries.

Solution to 5:

C is correct. The absolute version of PPP assumes that all goods and services are identical, consumed in equal proportions across different countries, and freely tradable internationally.

3.1.6 *International Parity Conditions: Tying All the Pieces Together*

We now summarize the key international parity conditions and describe how they are all linked. We begin with the right-hand side of Exhibit 4. Starting in the lower right-hand corner, we note the following:

1. According to the theory of covered interest rate parity, arbitrage ensures that nominal interest rate spreads must equal the percentage forward premium (or discount).

2. According to the hypothesis of uncovered interest rate parity, the expected percentage appreciation (or depreciation) of the spot exchange rate should, on average, be reflected in the nominal interest rate spread.

3. If both covered and uncovered interest rate parity hold—that is, the nominal yield spread equals both the forward premium (or discount) and the expected percentage change in the spot exchange rate—then the forward exchange rate will be an unbiased predictor of the future spot exchange rate.

This brings us to the upper right-hand corner of Exhibit 4. Turning now to the left-hand side of the exhibit and beginning in the upper left-hand corner, we note the following:

4. According to the *ex ante* PPP approach to exchange rate determination, the expected change in the spot exchange rate should equal the expected difference in domestic and foreign inflation rates.

5. Assuming the Fisher effect holds in each market—that is, the nominal interest rate in each market equals the real interest rate plus the expected inflation rate—and also assuming that real interest rates across all markets are broadly the same (real interest rate parity), then the nominal yield spread between domestic and foreign markets will equal the domestic/foreign expected inflation differential, which is the international Fisher effect.

6. If *ex ante* PPP and Fisher effects hold, then expected inflation differentials should equal both the expected change in the exchange rate and the nominal interest rate differential. This implies that the expected change in the exchange rate equals the nominal interest rate differential, which is uncovered interest rate parity.

Uncovered interest rate parity, at the center of the exhibit, brings us back to the right-hand loop (Number 2 above) and, because covered interest rate parity is enforced by arbitrage (Number 1 above), implies that the forward exchange rate is an unbiased predictor of the future spot exchange rate (Number 3 above).

Exhibit 4 shows that if all the key international parity conditions held at all times, then the expected percentage change in the *spot* exchange rate would equal

- the forward premium or discount (expressed in percentage terms);
- the nominal yield spread between countries; and
- the difference in expected national inflation rates.

In other words, *if all these parity conditions held, it would be impossible for a global investor to earn consistent profits on currency movements*. If forward exchange rates accurately predicted the future path of spot exchange rates, there would be no way to make money in forward exchange speculation. If high-yield currencies fell in value versus low-yield currencies exactly in line with the path implied by nominal interest rate spreads, all markets would offer the same currency-adjusted total returns over time. Investors would have no incentive to shift funds from one market to another based solely on currency considerations.

Exhibit 4	How Spot Exchange Rates, Forward Exchange Rates, and Interest Rates Are Linked Internationally

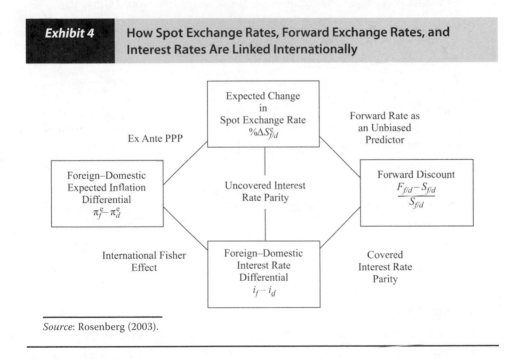

Source: Rosenberg (2003).

Example 6

The Relationships among the International Parity Conditions

1. Which of the following is a no-arbitrage condition?
   A. real interest rate parity
   B. covered interest rate parity
   C. uncovered interest rate parity

2. Forward rates are unbiased predictors of future spot rates if two parity conditions hold. Which of the following is *not* one of these conditions?

   A. real interest rate parity

   B. covered interest rate parity

   C. uncovered interest rate parity

3. The international Fisher effect requires all but which of the following to hold?

   A. *ex ante* PPP

   B. absolute PPP

   C. real interest rate parity

4. The forward premium/discount is determined by nominal interest rate differentials because of:

   A. the Fisher effect.

   B. covered interest parity.

   C. real interest rate parity.

5. If all of the key international parity conditions held at all times, then the expected percentage change in the spot exchange rate would equal all *except* which of the following?

   A. the real yield spread

   B. the nominal yield spread

   C. the expected inflation spread

Solution to 1:

B is correct. Covered interest rate parity is enforced by equating the investment return on two riskless investments (domestic and currency-hedged foreign).

Solution to 2:

A is correct. Both covered and uncovered interest rate parity must hold for the forward rate to be an unbiased predictor of the future spot rate. Real interest rate parity is not required.

Solution to 3:

B is correct. The international Fisher effect is based on real interest rate parity and *ex ante* PPP (not absolute PPP).

Solution to 4:

B is correct. The forward/premium is determined by covered interest rate arbitrage.

Solution to 5:

A is correct. If all the international parity conditions held, the real yield spread would equal zero regardless of expected changes in the spot exchange rate.

3.2 Assessing an Exchange Rate's Equilibrium Level

As noted earlier, there is evidence that PPP may be an appropriate framework with which to assess fair value in the FX markets over sufficiently long horizons. Nonetheless, the significant and persistent departures of observed exchange rates from such estimates of long-run equilibrium underscore the serious shortcomings of PPP as a real-time gauge of value. Hence, there have been many attempts to extend, supplement, or replace the parity-based framework for assessing a currency's short- or long-run equilibrium value.

Consider the dilemma facing FX forecasters and portfolio managers. Exchange rates tend to exhibit substantial noise over short time periods. From a strategic standpoint, an investor needs to be able to filter out such noise to get a better handle on the direction exchange rates are likely to take over the medium to long term. Knowing what constitutes a currency's real long-run equilibrium value would help investors better manage longer-term currency risk exposures.

From a policymaker's standpoint, knowing what constitutes a currency's real long-run equilibrium value would enable him or her to better quantify the degree of exchange rate misalignment that may exist at any point in time. If there is an interest in maintaining a level playing field among countries that engage in international trade, then it is incumbent upon global officials to closely monitor whether some countries might be attempting to gain an unfair competitive advantage by keeping their currencies significantly undervalued relative to the currencies of their trading partners.

In recent decades, exchange rate policies have often been at the center of debates among G–20 policymakers. In the 1980s and 1990s, the value of the Japanese yen was a major point of contention in United States/Japan trade negotiations. In the 2000s, the value of the Chinese yuan dominated United States/China trade talks. In response to the needs of its member countries, and in connection with its mandate to ensure the stability of the international monetary system, the International Monetary Fund (IMF) has been deeply involved in assessing the long-run value of exchange rates.

One of the IMF's core mandates is exchange rate surveillance. The IMF Consultative Group on Exchange Rate Issues (CGER) has used a three-pronged approach to derive long-run equilibrium exchange rate assessments for both developed and emerging market currencies:

1. The **macroeconomic balance approach** estimates how much exchange rates need to adjust in order to close the gap between the medium-term expectation for a country's current account imbalance and that country's normal (or sustainable) current account imbalance.

2. The **external sustainability approach** differs from the macroeconomic balance approach by focusing on stocks of outstanding assets or debt rather than on current account flows. The external sustainability approach calculates how much exchange rates would need to adjust to ensure that a country's net foreign-asset/GDP ratio or net foreign-liability/GDP ratio stabilizes at some benchmark level.

3. A **reduced-form econometric model** seeks to estimate the equilibrium path that a currency should take on the basis of the trends in several key macroeconomic variables, such as a country's net foreign asset position, its terms of trade, and its relative productivity.

The IMF finds that these three approaches are complementary in that they often generate similar assessments of fair value for most countries, although in some cases significant differences do arise.

The CGER estimates of long-run fair value help guide policymakers in determining how far exchange rates may be deviating from their long-run equilibrium levels. Interestingly, the IMF finds that the CGER estimates do have predictive value regarding future changes in *real* exchange rates. These methodologies frequently predict the *direction* of the change in the real exchange rates but unfortunately often miss in terms of *magnitude*. The IMF finds that its estimates of long-run fair value tend to over-predict both the future appreciation of undervalued currencies and the future depreciation of overvalued currencies. That is, currencies that are estimated to be significantly misaligned by the IMF tend to remain significantly misaligned in the future, although the magnitude of the misalignment tends to shrink over time.

These three IMF approaches can be viewed as an attempt to expand beyond the international parity conditions in order to explain some of the *mechanisms* that help bring exchange rates back toward their long-term equilibrium values. Exchange rates reflect the sum of all forces influencing trade and capital flows. Loosely speaking, the current account reflects the flows in the real economy while the capital account reflects financial flows. Because the balance of payments accounts must always balance, the current account must be matched by an equal and opposite balance in the capital account. This balance is achieved primarily by movements in exchange rates, which bring all the actions of the wide diversity of currency market participants into alignment. The IMF's three approaches largely represent different perspectives on this single equilibrating mechanism. Put somewhat simplistically, the macroeconomic balance approach focuses on the flows needed to achieve long-term equilibrium in the current account. (A country running a persistent current account deficit will eventually need to see its currency depreciate in order to restore its trade competitiveness.) In turn, the external sustainability approach focuses on the stock of net external debt that leads to long-term equilibrium in the capital account. As a hybrid approach, the reduced-form econometric model combines elements of both the current and capital accounts in a single, statistical equation.

In the following section, we derive a model of exchange rates that encapsulates both the long-run equilibrium value of a currency as well as some of the forces that drive exchange rate movements around this equilibrium level.

Example 7

Long-Run Equilibrium Exchange Rates

Various methods exist to calculate long-run equilibrium values for exchange rates, and the competing approaches do not always agree on what exchange rate level constitutes long-run equilibrium. The box diagram below focuses on two popular approaches to assess long-run fair value—PPP and the macroeconomic balance approach. Currencies that are out of line with fair value are likely to be characterized by one of the four cells (I, II, III, or IV) in the following box diagram.

Assessing Long-Run Fair Value in the FX Markets
Combinations of PPP Misalignment and Current Account Imbalance

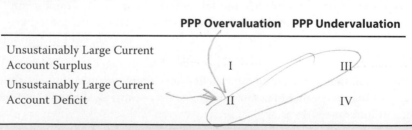

	PPP Overvaluation	PPP Undervaluation
Unsustainably Large Current Account Surplus	I	III
Unsustainably Large Current Account Deficit	II	IV

1. If a currency is described by Cell II, which of the following would *best* help bring the exchange rate closer to long-run fair value?

    A. Pursue policies to encourage currency depreciation.

    B. Pursue policies to encourage currency appreciation.

    C. The recommended course of action is unclear due to different recommended courses of action coming from PPP and current account balance considerations.

2. If a currency is described by Cell III, which of the following would *best* help bring the exchange rate closer to long-run fair value?

   A. Pursue policies to encourage currency depreciation.

   B. Pursue policies to encourage currency appreciation.

   C. The recommended course of action is unclear due to different recommended courses of action coming from PPP and current account balance considerations.

3. If a currency is described by Cell IV, which of the following would *best* help bring the exchange rate closer to long-run fair value?

   A. Pursue policies to encourage currency depreciation.

   B. Pursue policies to encourage currency appreciation.

   C. The recommended course of action is unclear due to different recommended courses of action coming from PPP and current account balance considerations.

Solution to 1:

A is correct. The currency is overvalued on a PPP basis (it should depreciate), and to obtain a sustainable current account, the domestic currency must depreciate against foreign currencies.

Solution to 2:

B is correct. The currency is undervalued on a PPP basis (it should appreciate), and to obtain a sustainable current account, the domestic currency must appreciate against foreign currencies.

Solution to 3:

C is correct. The currency is undervalued on a PPP basis, but to correct the current account deficit, it should depreciate.

3.3 Tying It Together: A Model That Includes Long-Term Equilibrium

Given the range of competing methodologies and the judgments that must be made in implementing them, it should not come as a surprise that there is often significant disagreement among both economists and market participants as to the appropriate fair value level for an exchange rate.

However, the attempt to define the long-run equilibrium value of a currency is not without merit. Most economists believe that there is an equilibrium level or a path to that equilibrium value that a currency will gravitate toward in the long run. Although medium-term cyclical deviations from the long-run equilibrium path can be both sizable and persistent, over the long run, fundamental forces should eventually drive the currency back toward its long-run equilibrium path. Evidence for both developed and emerging market economies suggests that misalignments tend to build up gradually over time. As these misalignments build, they are likely to generate serious economic imbalances that will eventually lead to correction of the underlying exchange rate misalignment.

At this stage, it is useful to develop a simple mathematical model of long-run exchange rate determination that will be helpful in subsequent discussions. The model incorporates the notion of long-run convergence of the real exchange rate to fair value and also demonstrates the role of real interest rate differentials. As before, to simplify the explanation and link it to our previous work, let's continue to use the foreign/domestic currency notation (*f/d*).

The model combines two assumptions. First, uncovered interest rate parity holds in the long run, implying that over a sufficiently long horizon,

$$\%\Delta S^{\varepsilon}_{f/d} = i_f - i_d \tag{6}$$

From the definition of the real exchange rate, we also know that

$$\%\Delta S^{\varepsilon}_{f/d} = \%\Delta q^{\varepsilon}_{f/d} - \left(\pi^{\varepsilon}_d - \pi^{\varepsilon}_f\right) \tag{7}$$

By subtracting Equation 6 from Equation 7, we can show that the expected change in the real exchange rate ($\% \Delta q^{\varepsilon}$) must equal the real interest rate differential ($r_f - r_d$):

$$\%\Delta q^{\varepsilon}_{f/d} = \left(i_f - \pi^{\varepsilon}_f\right) - (i_d - \pi^{\varepsilon}_d) \tag{8}$$

$$\%\Delta q^{\varepsilon}_{f/d} = (r_f - r_d) \tag{9}$$

The second assumption is that the real exchange rate is expected to converge to its long-run equilibrium value, $\overline{q}_{f/d}$. The long-run equilibrium may reflect PPP, one of the methods employed by the IMF, or some combination of estimates. Formally, we assume[15]

$$\%\Delta q^{\varepsilon}_{f/d} = \overline{q}_{f/d} - q_{f/d} \tag{10}$$

Combining Equations 9 and 10 gives

$$q_{f/d} = \overline{q}_{f/d} + \left(r_d - r_f\right) \tag{11}$$

The model can be extended to incorporate a risk premium (φ) that investors require in order to hold each country's securities. Among other factors, the required risk premium likely reflects the perceived sustainability of the country's external balances. Incorporating relative risk premia into the model yields:

$$q_{f/d} = \overline{q}_{f/d} + \left[\left(r_d - r_f\right) - \left(\varphi_d - \varphi_f\right)\right] \tag{12}$$

According to Equation 12, the level of the real exchange rate can be expressed as a function of three key variables: (1) the level of the real long-run equilibrium exchange rate, (2) the real interest rate differential, and (3) relative risk premia. With all else equal, a currency's real value would be expected to rise over time in response to (1) an upward revision in that currency's real long-term equilibrium value, (2) a rise in domestic relative to foreign real interest rates, and/or (3) a decline in domestic relative to foreign risk premia.

4   THE CARRY TRADE

According to uncovered interest rate parity, high-yield currencies are expected to depreciate in value, while low-yield currencies are expected to appreciate in value. If uncovered interest rate parity held at all times, investors would not be able to profit from a strategy that undertook long positions in baskets of high-yield currencies and short positions in baskets of low-yield currencies. The change in spot rates over the

---

15 The very careful reader will note that the two sides of equation (10) involve different units—the left-hand side is a percentage, while the right-hand side is in foreign currency units. Dividing the right hand side of Equation 10 by $q_{f/d}$ would make the units consistent. With this change, Equation 11 would become $q_{f/d} = \overline{q}_{f/d} + q_{f/d}(r_d - r_f)$. For simplicity, we will work with the slightly simpler versions of these equations given in the text.

tenor of the forward contracts would cancel out the interest rate differentials locked in at the inception of the position.

Uncovered interest rate parity is one of the most widely tested propositions in the field of international finance. Literally hundreds, if not thousands, of academic studies have tested whether uncovered interest rate parity has held for both developed and emerging market (EM) countries. Overwhelmingly, the evidence suggests that uncovered interest rate parity does *not* hold, at least over short- and medium-run time periods. These studies have generally found that *high-yield currencies, on average, have not depreciated, and low-yield currencies have not appreciated, to the levels predicted by interest rate differentials.*

These findings underscore the potential profitability of a trading strategy known as the **FX carry trade**, which involves taking on long positions in high-yield currencies and short positions in low-yield currencies. The latter are often referred to as "funding currencies." Historical evidence shows that such carry trade strategies often generate attractive excess returns over extended periods. One argument for the persistence of the carry trade is that the yields in higher interest rate countries are a risk premium for a more unstable economy, while low-yield currencies represent less risky markets. Although, history has demonstrated that carry trades generally earn positive excess returns in most market conditions, elevated levels of volatility and/or perceived risk in the financial markets can turn these excess returns into substantial losses very quickly. That is, small increases in asset market and/or FX volatility are unlikely to materially affect the positive excess returns earned on carry strategies. But during turbulent periods when asset price volatility and/or FX volatility rise sharply, the realized returns on long high-yield currency positions will tend to decline dramatically, while the realized returns on low-yield currencies will tend to rise just as dramatically.

To understand why, we need to recognize the nature of the risk and reward on the carry trade. The reward is the gradual accrual of the interest rate differential—essentially a flow of income that is unrelated to exchange rate volatility. The risk arises from the potential for adverse exchange rate movements—capital losses can occur virtually instantaneously. During periods of low turbulence, investors may feel relatively confident that exchange rate movements will not jeopardize the gradual accrual of the interest rate differential. In periods of high volatility, however, the risk of an adverse exchange rate movement rises sharply relative to the gradual flow of income, and investors may rush to unwind the carry trade. In the process, they sell the high-yielding currency basket and buy the low-yielding one, shifting realized returns sharply in favor of the low-yielding basket. The upshot is that *during periods of low volatility, carry trades tend to generate positive excess returns, but they are prone to significant crash risk in turbulent times.*

The tendency for carry trades to experience periodic crashes reveals itself in the distribution of carry trade returns. Academic studies find that the distribution of returns for G–10 and EM carry trades do not conform to a normal distribution. Rather, the distributions tend to be more peaked and to have fatter tails that are negatively skewed. The more peaked distribution around the mean implies that carry trades have typically generated a larger number of trades with small gains/ losses than would occur with the normal distribution. The negative skew and fat tails indicate that carry trades have tended to have more frequent and larger losses than would have been experienced had the distribution of returns been normal. That is, even though carry trades have generated positive excess returns on average in the past, the presence of a large, negative skew means that such strategies have been exposed to crash risk.

The primary reason for these crash risks relates to the fact that the carry trade is by nature a *leveraged* position: Investors borrow in the funding currency and invest the funds in a high-yielding currency. Like all leverage, this magnifies the impact of losses and gains relative to the investors' equity base. Moreover, because low-volatility regimes have tended to be the norm and often last for extended periods, investors can become complacent, allowing carry trade positions to grow to increasingly large levels in a search for yield. This crowded positioning tends to unwind rapidly when a shock to the market occurs, as many traders try to exit their position almost simultaneously before the leverage effects wipe out their equity. Another factor that accelerates the selling is that traders often leave stop-loss orders with their brokers that are triggered when price declines reach a certain level. These combined effects can lead to cascades of selling in which position liquidation begets further position liquidation. Finally, during periods of market turmoil, there is generally a flight to safety into those assets and currencies that seem to offer the most protection during times of uncertainty. This has typically favored low interest rate currencies (i.e., popular funding currencies) such as the Japanese yen and the Swiss franc, which are typically viewed as havens in times of market stress.

Recent research has focused on how one could best manage the downside crash risks associated with carry trades. One particular approach advocated by a number of investment banks and academics is to use a volatility filter to determine whether carry trade positions should be left open or closed. Under this approach, if the average level of FX volatility (and/or some other measure of market turbulence such as equity market volatility) were to trade below a specified threshold in the options market, then a signal would be generated to open carry trade positions. Likewise, if FX volatility or equity market volatility were to rise above a higher threshold, then a signal would be generated that those positions should be closed or reversed.

Another approach recommended by some observers is to combine valuation and carry into a single integrated strategy. Under this approach, purchasing power parity benchmarks can be used to determine whether carry trade positions should be opened or closed. That is, a valuation overlay would recommend that high yielders be overweighted and low yielders be underweighted when exchange rates lie inside prescribed PPP bands. If, instead, one or more of the high yielders were to become overvalued relative to their prescribed PPP threshold bands, the likelihood of a correction would increase and a valuation overlay would recommend closing or reversing the high-yield position. The opposite case would apply for low yielders.

These and other risk management tools are not foolproof, however, and investors need to be mindful of the considerable negative tail risks associated with carry trades.

From the perspective of policymakers, there is a clear concern that carry trade activities might be playing a major role in generating exchange rate misalignments around the world. As such activities have become a more important part of the FX landscape, there is a risk that a global search for yield could drive high-yield currencies deep into overvalued territory, which could have serious negative consequences for economic activity in high-yield markets. In such an environment, one runs the risk that the monetary authorities in high-yield markets might feel compelled to stem the inflow of capital into their market—for example, by introducing capital controls—to help prevent an unwarranted or undesired appreciation of their currencies.

Another policy-related danger of carry trade activities is that if a global search for yield encourages international investors to take on highly leveraged positions in carry trades, and if speculative positions begin to lean too heavily in one direction, a forced unwinding of highly leveraged carry trade positions could precipitate a serious currency or financial crisis. The carry trade unwind of 2008 illustrates the impact that these trades could have on exchange rates. During that period, high-yield developed market currencies such as the Australian dollar and the New Zealand dollar—as well as many high-yielding emerging market currencies—lost considerable ground, even though none of those high-yielding markets were at the epicenter of the 2007–2009 global financial crisis.

Example 8

Carry Trade Strategies

A currency fund manager is considering allocating a portion of her FX portfolio to carry trade strategies. The fund's investment committee asks the manager a number of questions about why she has chosen to become involved in FX carry trades and how she will manage the risk of potentially large downside moves associated with the unwinding of carry trades. Which of the following would be her *best* responses to the investment committee's questions?

1. Carry trades can be profitable when:
   A. covered interest rate parity does not hold.
   B. uncovered interest rate parity does not hold.
   C. the international Fisher effect does not hold.

2. Over time, the return distribution of the fund's FX carry trades is *most* likely to resemble a:
   A. normal distribution with fat tails.
   B. distribution with fat tails and a negative skew.
   C. distribution with thin tails and a positive skew.

3. The volatility of the fund's returns relative to its equity base is *best* explained by:
   A. leverage.
   B. low deposit rates in the funding currency.
   C. the yield spread between the high- and low-yielding currencies.

4. Which of these risk management strategies is *most* likely to reduce some of the negative tail risk associated with FX carry trades?
   A. Use forward contracts to sell the funding currency.
   B. Exit the carry trade position when implied FX volatility drops below a certain threshold.
   C. Exit the carry trade when the funding currency drops below its PPP level.

   A Tokyo-based asset manager enters into a carry trade position based on borrowing in yen and investing in one-year Australian LIBOR.

Today's One-Year LIBOR		Currency Pair	Spot Rate Today	Spot Rate One Year Later
JPY	0.10%	JPY/USD	81.30	80.00
AUD	4.50%	USD/AUD	1.0750	1.0803

5. After one year, the all-in return to this trade, measured in JPY terms, would be *closest* to:
   A. +1.84 percent.
   B. +3.23 percent.
   C. +5.02 percent.

Solution to 1:

B is correct. The carry trade is based on the supposition that uncovered interest rate parity does not hold.

Solution to 2:

B is correct. The "crash risk" of carry trades implies a fat-tailed distribution skewed towards a higher probability of large losses (compared with a normal distribution).

Solution to 3:

A is correct. Carry trades are leveraged trades (borrow in the funding currency, invest in the high-yield currency), and leverage increases the volatility in the investor's return on equity.

Solution to 4:

C is correct. One would want to exit the carry trade position when the likelihood of depreciation (appreciation) of the high-yield (low-yield) currency is building. When the funding currency is undervalued on a PPP basis, the likelihood that it might appreciate is increasing.

Solution to 5:

B is correct. To calculate the all-in return to a Japanese investor in a one-year AUD LIBOR deposit, we must first calculate the current and one year later JPY/AUD cross rates. Because one USD buys JPY 81.30 today, and one AUD buys USD 1.0750 today, today's JPY/AUD cross rate is the product of these two numbers: $81.30 \times 1.0750 = 87.40$ (rounding to two decimal places). Similarly, one year later the observed cross rate is $80.00 \times 1.0803 = 86.42$ (rounded to two decimal places). Accordingly, measured in yen, the investment return for the unhedged Australian LIBOR deposit is *closest* to:

$$\frac{1}{87.40}(1 + 4.50\%)86.42 = (1.0333)$$

Against this 3.33 percent *gross* return, however, the manager must charge the borrowing costs to fund the carry trade investment (one-year yen LIBOR was 0.10 percent). Hence, the *net* return on the carry trade is closest to 3.33% − 0.10% = 3.23%.

5　THE IMPACT OF BALANCE OF PAYMENTS FLOWS

The current account balance of a country represents the sum of all recorded transactions in traded goods, services, income, and net transfer payments in a country's overall balance of payments. Countries that run persistent current account deficits often see their currencies depreciate over time. Similarly, countries that run persistent current account surpluses often see their currencies appreciate over time.

Because the balance of payments accounts must always balance, the current account must be matched by an equal and opposite balance in the capital account.[16] Loosely speaking, the current account reflects the flows in the real economy, while the capital account reflects financial flows. Although this equality must always hold, it is not inconsequential. Decisions with respect to trade flows (the current account) and investment/financing flows (the capital account) are typically made by different entities with different perspectives and motivations. Their decisions are brought into

---

16 The official balance of payments accounts make a distinction between the "capital account" and the "financial account" based on the nature of the assets involved. For simplicity, we use the term "capital account" here to reflect all investment/financing flows.

alignment by changes in market prices and/or quantities. One of the key prices, perhaps *the* key price, in this process is the exchange rate.

It turns out that *investment/financing decisions are usually the dominant factor in determining exchange rate movements, at least in the short to intermediate term.* There are four main reasons for this. First, prices of real goods and services tend to adjust much more slowly than exchange rates and other asset prices. Second, production of real goods and services takes time, and demand decisions are subject to substantial inertia. In contrast, liquid financial markets allow virtually instantaneous redirection of financial flows. Third, whereas current spending/production decisions reflect only purchases/sales of current production, investment/financing decisions reflect not only the financing of current expenditures but also reallocation of existing portfolios. Fourth, *expected* exchange rate movements can induce very large short-term capital flows. This tends to make the *actual* exchange rate very sensitive to the currency views held by owners/managers of liquid assets.

In this section, we first examine the impact of current account imbalances on exchange rates. Then we take a closer look at capital flows.

5.1 Current Account Imbalances and the Determination of Exchange Rates

Current account trends influence the path of exchange rates over time through several mechanisms:

- The flow supply/demand channel
- The portfolio balance channel
- The debt sustainability channel

We briefly discuss each of these below.

5.1.1 *The Flow Supply/Demand Channel*

The flow supply/demand channel is based on a fairly simple model that focuses on the fact that purchases and sales of internationally traded goods and services require the exchange of domestic and foreign currencies in order to arrange payment for those goods and services. For example, if a country sold more goods and services than it purchased (i.e., the country was running a current account surplus), then the demand for its currency should rise, and vice versa. Such shifts in currency demand would tend to exert upward pressure on the value of the surplus nation's currency and downward pressure on the value of the deficit nation's currency.

Hence, we would expect to find that countries with persistent current account surpluses would see their currencies appreciate over time, and vice versa. The question remains whether such trends can go on indefinitely. At some point, domestic currency strength should contribute to deterioration in the trade competitiveness of the surplus nation while domestic currency weakness should contribute to an improvement in the trade competitiveness of the deficit nation. Thus, the exchange rate responses to these surpluses and deficits should eventually help eliminate—in the medium to long run—the source of the initial imbalances.[17]

The amount by which exchange rates must adjust to restore current accounts to balanced positions depends on a number of factors:

- The initial gap between imports and exports,
- The response of import and export prices to changes in the exchange rate, and

---

[17] Currency depreciation (appreciation) will improve (worsen) the current account if the generalized Marshall–Lerner condition is satisfied. This condition was developed and discussed in the CFA Level 1 curriculum.

- The response of import and export demand to the change in import and export prices.

Regarding the first factor, when the initial gap between imports and exports is relatively wide for a deficit nation, export growth would need to far outstrip import growth in percentage terms in order to narrow the current account deficit. Unless export demand is far more price elastic than import demand, a large initial deficit may require a substantial depreciation of the currency to bring about a meaningful correction of the trade imbalance.

Normally, a depreciation of the deficit country's currency should result in an increase in import prices in domestic currency terms and a decrease in the deficit country's export prices in foreign currency terms. However, empirical studies often find limited pass-through effects of exchange rate changes into traded goods prices. For example, many studies find that for every 1 percent decline in a currency's value, import prices rise by only 0.5 percent, and in some cases by even less because foreign producers tend to lower their profit margins in an effort to preserve market share. In light of the limited pass-through of exchange rate changes into traded goods prices, the exchange rate adjustment required to narrow a trade imbalance may be far larger than would otherwise be the case.

Even if traded goods prices ultimately adjust one-for-one with the change in exchange rates, the response of import and export demand to those price changes might not be sufficient to correct a sizable current account imbalance. In fact, many empirical studies find that the response of import and export demand to changes in traded goods prices is often quite sluggish. As a result, relatively long lags, lasting several years, can occur between (1) the onset of exchange rate changes, (2) the ultimate adjustment in traded goods prices, and (3) the eventual impact of those price changes on import demand, export demand, and the underlying current account imbalance.

5.1.2 *The Portfolio Balance Channel*

The second mechanism through which current account trends influence exchange rates is the so-called portfolio balance channel. Current account imbalances shift financial wealth from deficit nations to surplus nations. Over time, this may lead to shifts in global asset preferences, which in turn could exert a marked impact on the path of exchange rates. For example, nations running large current account surpluses versus the United States might find that their holdings of U.S. dollar–denominated assets exceed the amount they desire to hold in a portfolio context. Attempts to reduce their dollar holdings to desired levels could then have a profound, negative impact on the dollar's value.

5.1.3 *The Debt Sustainability Channel*

The third mechanism through which current account surpluses can affect exchange rates is the so-called debt sustainability channel. According to this channel, there should be some upper limit on the ability of countries to run persistently wide current account deficits. If a country runs a large and persistent current account deficit over time, eventually it will experience an unending rise in debt owed to foreign investors. If such investors believe that the deficit country's external debt is rising to unsustainable levels, they are likely to reason that a major depreciation of the deficit country's currency will be required at some point to ensure that the current account deficit narrows significantly and that the external debt stabilizes at a level deemed sustainable.

The existence of persistent current account imbalances will tend to alter the market's notion of what exchange rate level represents the true, real long-run equilibrium value. For deficit nations, ever-rising net external debt levels as a percent of GDP should give rise to steady (but not necessarily smooth) downward revisions in market expectations of the currency's real long-run equilibrium value. For surplus countries, ever-rising net external asset levels as a percentage of GDP should give rise to steady upward revisions of the currency's real long-run equilibrium value. Hence, one would expect currency values to move broadly in line with trends in debt and/ or asset accumulation.

Note that the debt sustainability channel is essentially the perspective underlying the IMF's external sustainability approach to determining the long-run equilibrium exchange rate.

Example 9

Persistent Current Account Deficits: The U.S. Current Account and the USD

The historical record indicates that the trend in the U.S. current account has been an important determinant of the long-term swings in the U.S. dollar's value but also that there can be rather long lags between the onset of a deterioration in the current account balance and an eventual decline in the dollar's value. For example, the U.S. current account balance deteriorated sharply in the first half of the 1980s, yet the dollar soared over that period. The reason for the dollar's strength over that period was that high U.S. real interest rates attracted large inflows of capital from abroad, which pushed the dollar higher despite the large U.S. external imbalance. Eventually, however, concerns on the part of market participants and policymakers regarding the sustainability of the ever-widening U.S. current account deficit triggered a major dollar decline in the second half of the 1980s.

History repeated itself in the second half of the 1990s, with the U.S. current account deficit once again deteriorating, yet the dollar soared over the same period. This time, the dollar's strength was driven by strong foreign direct investment and equity-related flows into the United States. Beginning in 2001, however, the ever-widening U.S. current account deficit, coupled with a decline in U.S. interest rates, made it more difficult for the United States to attract the foreign private capital needed to finance its current account deficit. The dollar eventually succumbed to the weight of ever-larger trade and current account deficits and began a multi-year slide starting in 2002–2003. Interestingly, the U.S. dollar has undergone three major downward cycles since the beginning of floating exchange rates: 1977–1978, 1985–1987, and 2002–2008. In each of those downward cycles, the dollar's slide was driven in large part by concerns over outsized U.S. current account deficits that were coupled with relatively low nominal and/or real short-term interest rates in the United States, which made it difficult to attract sufficient foreign capital to the United States to finance those deficits.

Example 10

Exchange Rate Adjustment in Surplus Nations—Japan and China

Japan and, more recently, China represent examples of countries with large current account surpluses and the pressure that those surpluses can bring to bear on their currencies. In the case of Japan, the rising trend in its current account surplus has tended to exert persistent upward pressure on the yen's value versus the dollar over time. Part of this upward pressure simply reflected the increase in demand for yen to make payment for Japan's merchandise exports. But some of the upward pressure on the yen might also have stemmed from rising commercial tensions between the United States and Japan.

> Protectionist sentiment in the United States rose steadily in line with the rising bilateral trade deficit that the United States ran with Japan in the post-war period. U.S. policymakers contended that the yen was undervalued and needed to rise. With the rising Japan–U.S. bilateral trade imbalance contributing to more heated protectionist rhetoric, Japan felt compelled to tolerate steady, upward pressure on the yen to placate U.S. demands for further exchange rate adjustments. As a result, the yen's value versus the dollar has tended to move in sync with the trend in Japan's current account surplus.
>
> In recent years, U.S. protectionist rhetoric has shifted to China. Given China's growing current account surplus, the Chinese currency has become a major point of contention between U.S. and Chinese authorities. The exchange rate regime between the Chinese yuan and the U.S. dollar can be characterized as a "crawling peg" in which the rate is allowed to fluctuate within a narrow band (currently ±0.5 percent) around a fixing level determined by the Chinese government. This fixing rate varies from day to day. In recent years, China has engineered a gradual appreciation of its currency. Nonetheless, the Chinese authorities have intervened aggressively to moderate the rate of appreciation, accumulating massive foreign exchange reserves in the process, and many economists argue that significant upward adjustment in the Chinese yuan's value is still needed to narrow China's large current account surplus.

5.2 Capital Flows and the Determination of Exchange Rates

Greater financial integration of the world's capital markets and the increased freedom of capital to flow across national borders have increased the importance of global financial flows in determining exchange rates, interest rates, and broad asset price trends. One can cite a litany of examples in which global financial flows either caused or contributed to overshooting exchange rates, interest rates, or asset price bubbles. Among them are the following:

- As described in Example 10 above, the dramatic rise in the U.S. dollar in the first half of the 1980s and again in the second half of the 1990s was powered by a significant rise in global demand for U.S. financial assets. The 1980s episode was powered by a major widening in yield spreads favoring the United States, while the 1990s rise was powered in part by a significant rise in global demand for U.S. equities during the New Economy/tech boom.

- Yen assets underperformed U.S. dollar assets over much of the 1995–2007 period, a 12-year span of ultra-low Japanese short-term interest rates that gave rise to what became known as the "yen carry trade" as both Japanese and global fund managers borrowed in yen and invested the proceeds in higher-yielding assets in other markets. Such actions helped push the value of the yen significantly lower on a trend basis. Periodically, however, such positions became overextended and vulnerable to sudden reversals. In the fall of 1998, a major unwinding of the yen carry trade led to the collapse of several major hedge funds.

- Australian and New Zealand dollar-denominated assets have both significantly outperformed U.S. dollar-denominated assets over the last two decades, driven in large measure by capital inflows attracted by the persistently higher short-term interest rates in those markets relative to the rest of the industrial world.

- In numerous cases, global capital flows have helped fuel boom-like conditions in emerging market economies for a while, and then suddenly, often without adequate warning, those flows stopped and then reversed—with the reversal often causing a major economic downturn, a possible sovereign default, a serious banking crisis, or a significant currency depreciation. A recent IMF study of 109 episodes of major capital inflow surges over the 1987–2007 period found that, in more than one-third of the cases, the inflows stopped abruptly.

Excessive surges in capital inflows to emerging markets have often planted the seeds of an economic or currency crisis by contributing to (1) an unwarranted real appreciation of the emerging market currency; (2) a huge buildup in external indebtedness by emerging market governments, businesses, or banks; (3) a financial asset or property market bubble; (4) a consumption binge that contributed to explosive growth in domestic credit and/or the current account deficit; or (5) an overinvestment in risky projects and questionable activities.

Because episodes of capital flow surges to emerging markets have often ended badly, emerging market policymakers have made a concerted effort in recent years to either resist such inflows through the use of capital controls or to prevent capital inflows from pushing currency values to overvalued levels by intervening more heavily in the foreign exchange market. In the following analysis, we will discuss the empirical evidence on the success, or lack thereof, of policymakers counteracting the negative consequences of capital flow surges.

5.2.1 *Real Interest Rate Differentials, Capital Flows and the Exchange Rate*

In Section 3.3, we developed a model in which real exchange rate movements around the long-run equilibrium are driven primarily by the response of capital flows to interest rate differentials, risk premia, and expectations with respect to exchange rate movements themselves. For ease of reference, we repeat Equation 12 here:

$$q_{f/d} = \overline{q}_{f/d} + \left[\left(r_d - r_f\right) - \left(\varphi_d - \varphi_f\right)\right]$$

Recall that $q_{f/d}$ is the real exchange rate, r_d and r_f are real interest rates, φ_d and φ_f are risk premia, and a bar over a variable indicates its long-run equilibrium value. Based on the above model, movements in real interest rate and risk premia differentials between countries can cause movements in the real exchange rate $q_{f/d}$ around its long-run equilibrium value $\overline{q}_{f/d}$.

This simple model can explain a wide range of phenomena such as (1) long-run cyclical trends in the U.S. dollar value, (2) the persistent excess returns that carry trade strategies have tended to offer, and (3) the impact of temporary bouts of risk aversion on exchange rates.

The trend in real interest rate differentials played a pivotal role in driving the U.S. dollar's value during several major exchange rate cycles. As shown in Exhibit 5, the decline of the dollar in the late 1970s, the dramatic rise in its value in the first half of the 1980s, and its subsequent decline in the second half of the 1980s can be explained, to a large extent, by changes in U.S.–foreign real yield spreads. (In exhibits 5 and 6, DEM/USD indicates the number of German Deutschemarks per U.S. dollar.) The dollar's surge in the 1990s can also be explained, in part, by trends in real yield spreads. Exhibit 6 shows that the dollar's decline in the first half of the 1990s coincided with a significant narrowing in U.S.–foreign real yield spreads, while the dollar's subsequent rise in the second half of the 1990s coincided with a significant widening in U.S.–foreign real yield spreads. To be sure, other forms of capital movements were at work during these dollar cycles—notably foreign direct investment and equity-related portfolio flows, particularly in the second half of the 1990s—but Exhibits 5 and 6 suggest that relative interest rate trends played a major role in each of the dollar's major upward and downward moves.

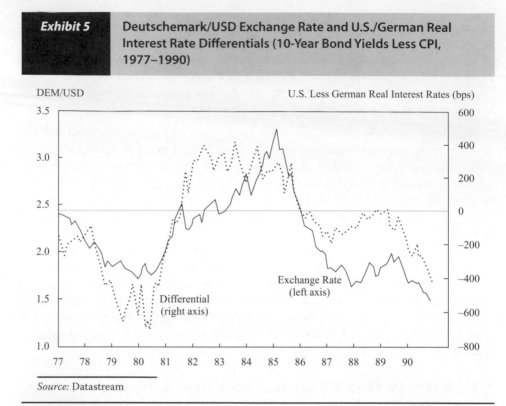

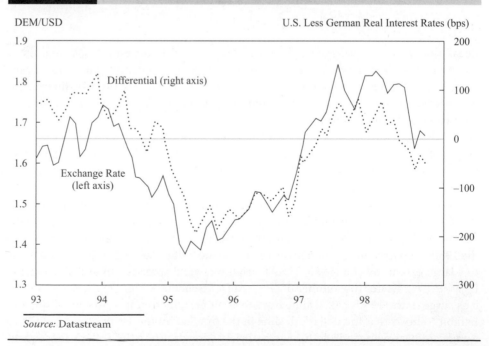

Interest rate differentials can play a major role in driving the relative total return performance of competing markets, even if interest rate spreads have little impact on the trend in exchange rates. Consider the case of the Turkish lira versus the U.S. dollar. The lira attracted a lot of interest on the part of global fund managers over the 2002–2010 period, in large part because of its attractive yield levels. Turkish–U.S. short-term yield spreads averaged over 1,000 basis points during much of this period.

As capital flowed into Turkey, the Turkish authorities intervened in the foreign exchange market in an attempt to keep the value of the lira broadly stable. As a result, international investors were not able to reap much in terms of currency gains over this period. Nevertheless, international investors were able to capture the high yields that Turkey offered, and over time, the cumulative effect was a significant outperformance of Turkish over U.S. assets during much of the 2002–2010 period. Indeed, a long Turkish lira/short U.S. dollar carry trade position generated significant long-run excess returns, mostly from the accumulated yield spread, while the return from the movement in the spot exchange rate was fairly small.

5.2.2 *Interest Rate Differentials, Carry Trades, and Exchange Rates*

Carry trades have generated significant positive excess returns for substantial periods in cases involving G–10 currencies as well as emerging market currencies. Sometimes those persistently positive excess returns show up in movements in the spot exchange rate, and sometimes the persistent returns show up in the contribution that cumulative yield spreads offer. Quite often, a combination of both factors jointly works to drive persistent positive excess returns. Equation 12 above provides a useful framework to understand how each of those factors has come into play in driving international capital flows toward markets offering higher yields.

To understand why a high-yield country might attract significant inflows of capital that could exert considerable upward pressure on the high-yield currency's value for persistent periods of time, it is useful to rewrite the equations above letting H and L denote the high-yield and low-yield currencies, respectively, with the high-yield currency as the base currency in the exchange rate:

$$q_{L/H} = \bar{q}_{L/H} + (r_H - r_L) - (\varphi_H - \varphi_L) \tag{13}$$

As a further step, we can break the real interest rate spread into its two constituent parts—the nominal interest rate spread and the expected inflation differential between the high-yield and low-yield countries:

$$q_{L/H} = \bar{q}_{L/H} + (i_H - i_L) - \left(\pi_H^\varepsilon - \pi_L^\varepsilon\right) - (\varphi_H - \varphi_L) \tag{14}$$

According to Equation 14, a high-yield currency's real value will tend to rise in the long run when the long-run equilibrium value of the high-yield currency ($\bar{q}_{L/H}$) is trending higher. Typically, however, oscillations around this long-run equilibrium trend can persist for relatively long periods of time (refer back to Exhibit 2 for an illustrative diagram of this process). These cyclical movements around the long-run equilibrium trend are often associated with movements in the differentials in Equation 14. That is, the real exchange rate $q_{L/H}$ will tend to rise, relative to its long-run equilibrium value $\bar{q}_{L/H}$, when (a) the nominal yield spread between the high- and low-yield market rises, (b) inflation expectations in the high-yield market decline relative to the low-yield market, and/or (c) the risk premium demanded by investors to hold the assets of the high-yield market declines relative to the low-yield market. It is important to recognize that movements in all of these various differentials can be gradual but persistent and thereby lead to persistent movements in the exchange rate.

Consider the case of a high-yield, inflation-prone emerging market country that wants to promote price stability and long-term sustainable growth. To achieve price stability, policymakers in the high-yield economy will initiate a tightening in monetary policy by gradually raising the level of domestic interest rates relative to yield levels in the rest of the world. Assuming that the tightening in domestic monetary policy is sustained, inflation expectations in the high-yield economy should gradually decline relative to the trend in inflation expectations in the rest of the world. The combination of sustained wide nominal yield spreads and a steady narrowing in relative inflation expectations should exert upward pressure on the real yield spread and thus on the high yield currency's value.

To achieve their long-run objectives of price stability and sustainable economic growth, policymakers in high-yield markets may not rely solely on a tight monetary policy. To reinforce initiatives on the monetary policy front, government authorities might also pursue policies that promote lower government deficits, liberalize financial markets, remove capital flow restrictions, attract foreign direct investment, promote privatization, and/or encourage better business practices. By encouraging an economic environment that promotes price stability, long-run growth, and a stronger and more stable financial system, such policies should also encourage investors to gradually demand a lower risk premium to hold the high-yield currency's assets.

All of these various government measures should gradually work to boost the long-run competitiveness of the high-yield country and, in the process, should lead market participants to gradually revise upward their assessment of the long-run equilibrium value of that country's currency ($\overline{q}_{L/H}$). And, as Equation 14 and Exhibit 2 indicate, an upward shift in the long-run trend for the high-yield country's equilibrium exchange rate should also cause the high-yield currency's real value ($q_{L/H}$) to move gradually higher as well. That is, over time, both changes in the trend for the long-run equilibrium exchange rate and the market forces driving oscillations around that long-run trend can work in concert to cause appreciation of the high-yield country's exchange rate.

What is noteworthy about Equation 14 is that only the interest rate spread is directly observable on the right-hand side of the equation. The trend in the long-run equilibrium exchange rate, relative inflation expectations, and relative risk premia might be working just as hard as interest rate spreads in affecting the high-yield currency's value, but because those variables are not directly observable, nominal yield spreads are often given most, if not all, of the credit for driving changes in exchange rates and thus for the profitability of FX carry trades.

These equations also help explain why FX carry trades are often able to generate positive excess returns even as nominal yield spreads stabilize or begin to narrow. As long as the combined impact of fiscal, economic, and monetary policy changes contributes to continued upward pressure on a high-yield currency's long-run equilibrium value, or lowers inflationary expectations in the high-yield market, or lowers a high yielder's risk premium, the net effect of these unobservable factors could lead to upward pressure on the high-yield currency's value and thereby offset the drag on the exchange rate coming from an observable decline in the yield spread. The important point to remember is that the profitability of FX carry trades sometimes depends on more than just the level and trend in the nominal yield spread.

The model also sheds light on why FX carry trades have tended to be profitable over long periods. The historical evidence suggests that the impact of nominal interest rate spreads on the exchange rate tends to be gradual. Monetary policymakers tend to adjust their official lending rates slowly over time—in part because of the uncertainty that policymakers face and in part because the authorities do not want to disrupt the financial markets. Because the monetary authorities in both the high-yield and low-yield countries are adjusting domestic policy rates gradually over time, a high-yield country should see its short-term interest rates rise slowly relative to interest rates in the low-yield country. These slowly evolving policy rates will therefore give rise to persistence of the positive interest rate carry enjoyed by the high-yield market and in the process encourage persistence of the positive excess returns earned by FX carry trades.

Similarly, the upward trend in the equilibrium exchange rate and the downward trends in inflation expectations and risk premia in the higher-yield market will also tend to proceed gradually. It often takes several years to determine whether structural economic changes will take root and boost the long-run competitiveness of the higher-yield country. In addition, although inflation will be favorably affected by tight monetary policies, fiscal discipline, and structural reforms, it may take several years to bring inflation expectations down to reasonably low and stable levels. Hence, all of the fundamental criteria that drive exchange rate trends over time, described in

Equation 14, are likely to proceed gradually. Because these fundamental drivers tend to reinforce each other over time, one should expect to observe trends in real exchange rate movements and persistence in carry trade returns.

5.2.3 *Equity Market Trends and Exchange Rates*

Although exchange rates and equity markets sometimes exhibit positive correlation, the relationship between equity market performance and exchange rates is not stable. For instance, between 1990 and 1995, the U.S. dollar fell and the Japanese yen soared while the U.S. equity market was strong and Japanese stocks were weak. In contrast, between 1995 and early 2000, the correlation between local equity market performances and the local currency's value turned strongly positive. The U.S. dollar soared in tandem with a rising U.S. equity market, while the yen weakened in tandem with a trend decline in the Japanese equity market. *Such instability in correlation between exchange rates and equity markets makes it difficult to form judgments on possible future currency moves based solely on expected equity market performances.*

The long-run correlation between the U.S. equity market and the dollar is very close to zero, but over short- to medium-term periods, rolling correlations tend to swing from being highly positive to being highly negative, depending on market conditions. In recent years, there has been a decidedly negative correlation, with the dollar declining when the U.S. equity market was rising and vice versa. Market observers attribute this recent behavior in the dollar to the U.S. dollar's role as a safe haven asset. When investors' appetite for risk is high—that is, the market is in "risk-on" mode—investor demand for risky assets such as equities tends to rise, which drives up their prices. At the same time, investor demand for safe haven assets such as the dollar tends to decline, which drives their values lower. The opposite has occurred when the market has been in "risk-off" mode.

Example 11

Capital Flows and Exchange Rates

Monique Kwan, a currency strategist at a major foreign exchange dealer, is responsible for formulating trading strategies for the currencies of both developed market (DM) and emerging market (EM) countries. She examines two specific countries—one DM and one EM—and notes that the DM country has what is considered a low-yield safe haven currency while the EM currency has a high-yield currency whose value is more exposed to fluctuations in the global economic growth rate. Kwan is trying to form an opinion about movements in the *real* exchange rate for the EM currency (i.e., for $q_{L/H}$).

1. All else equal, the real exchange rate for the EM currency ($q_{L/H}$) will *most likely* depreciate if the:

    A. long-run equilibrium value of the high-yield currency is revised upward.

    B. nominal yield spread between the EM and DM countries rises over time.

    C. expected inflation differential between the EM and DM countries is revised upward.

2. An increase in safe haven demand would *most likely*:

    A. increase the risk premium demanded by international investors to hold assets denominated in the EM currency.

    B. raise the excess return earned on carry trade strategies.

    C. exert upward pressure on the real value of the EM currency.

Kwan notes that the DM country is running a persistent current account deficit with the EM country. To isolate the influence of this chronic imbalance on exchange rates, she focuses only on the bilateral relationship between the EM and DM countries and makes the simplifying assumption that the external accounts of these two countries are otherwise balanced (i.e., there are no other current account deficits).

3. Over time, and all else equal, the persistent current account deficit with the EM country would *most likely* lead to:

   A. a large build-up of the EM country's assets held by the DM country.

   B. an increase in the trade competitiveness of the EM country.

   C. an upward revision in the long-run equilibrium real exchange rate $\bar{q}_{L/H}$.

Kwan notes that because of the high yield on the EM country's bonds, international investors have recently been reallocating their portfolios more heavily toward this country's assets. As a result of these capital inflows, the EM country has been experiencing boom-like conditions. She refers to the model in Equation 14 to estimate the effect of these capital flows on the real exchange for the EM currency.

4. Given the current boom-like conditions in the EM economy, in the *near term* these capital inflows are *most likely* to lead to:

   A. a decrease in π_H^e.

   B. an increase in ϕ_H.

   C. an increase in $q_{L/H}$.

5. If these capital inflows led to an unwanted appreciation in the real value of its currency, the EM country's government would *most likely*:

   A. impose capital controls.

   B. decrease taxes on consumption and investment.

   C. buy its currency in the foreign exchange market.

6. If government actions were ineffective and the EM country's bubble eventually burst, this would *most likely* be reflected in an increase in:

   A. ϕ_H.

   B. $q_{L/H}$.

   C. $\bar{q}_{L/H}$.

Finally, Kwan turns to examining the link between the value of the DM country's currency and movements in the DM country's main stock market index. One of her research associates tells her that, in general, the correlation between equity market returns and changes in exchange rates has been found to be highly positive over time.

7. The statement made by the research associate is:

   A. correct.

   B. incorrect, because the correlation is highly negative over time.

   C. incorrect, because the correlation is not stable and tends to converge toward zero in the long run.

Solution to 1:

C is correct. All else equal, if the expected inflation differential increases, the real interest rate differential decreases, which should lead to depreciation of the real exchange rate ($q_{L/H}$). See Equation 13 or 14.

Solution to 2:

A is correct. During times of intense risk aversion, investors will crowd into the safe haven currency. This tendency implies an increased risk premium demanded by investors to hold the EM currency.

Solution to 3:

C is correct. Over time, the DM country will see its level of external debt rise as a result of the chronic current account imbalance. Eventually, this trend should lead to a downward revision of the DM currency's real long-run equilibrium level (via the debt sustainability channel). This is equivalent to an *increase* in the EM currency's real long-run exchange rate. Because the EM (high-yielding) currency is the base currency in the $q_{L/H}$ notation, this means an increase in $\overline{q}_{L/H}$. A is incorrect because the DM country's current account deficit is likely to lead to a build-up in DM country assets held by the EM country. B is incorrect because at some point, the currency strength should contribute to deterioration in the trade competitiveness of the country with the trade surplus (the EM country).

Solution to 4:

C is correct. Given the current investor enthusiasm for the EM country's assets and the boom-like conditions in the country, it is most likely that in the near term, the real exchange rate $q_{L/H}$ is increasing. At the same time, expected inflation in the EM country π_H^e is also likely increasing and—given the enthusiasm for EM assets—that the risk premia ϕ_H is decreasing.

Solution to 5:

A is correct. To reduce unwanted appreciation of its exchange rate, the EM country would be most likely to impose capital controls to counteract the surging capital inflows. Because these inflows are often associated with overinvestment and consumption, the EM government would not be likely to encourage these activities through lower taxes. Nor would the EM country be likely to encourage further exchange rate appreciation by intervening in the market to *buy* its own currency.

Solution to 6:

A is correct. Episodes of surging capital flows into EM countries have often ended badly (a rapid reversal of these inflows as the bubble bursts). This is most likely to be reflected in an increase in the risk premium, ϕ_H. It is much less likely that a bursting bubble would be reflected in an increase in either the real exchange rate $q_{L/H}$ or its long-term equilibrium value $\overline{q}_{L/H}$.

Solution to 7:

C is correct. Correlations between equity returns and exchange rates are unstable in the short term and tend toward zero in the long run.

MONETARY AND FISCAL POLICIES

6

As the foregoing discussion indicates, monetary and fiscal policies can have a significant impact on exchange rate movements. We now examine the channels through which these impacts are transmitted.

6.1 The Mundell–Fleming Model

Developed in the early 1960s, the Mundell–Fleming model remains the textbook standard for the study of monetary and fiscal policy in open economies.[18] As such, it has substantial influence on the way economists and policymakers interpret economic and financial events.

The Mundell–Fleming model describes how changes in monetary and fiscal policy affect the level of interest rates and economic activity within a country, which in turn leads to changes in the direction and magnitude of trade and capital flows and ultimately to changes in the exchange rate. As was typical of macroeconomic models in the 1960s, the model focuses only on aggregate demand. Thus, the implicit assumption is that there is sufficient slack in the economy to allow changes in output without significant price level or inflation rate adjustments. The implications of the model must be interpreted in this context.

Standard macroeconomic arguments imply that expansionary monetary and fiscal policies increase aggregate demand and output. Expansionary monetary policy affects growth, in part, by reducing interest rates and thereby increasing investment and consumption spending. Expansionary fiscal policy increases spending, either directly or via lower taxes, and thus output in the short to medium run. At the same time, expansionary fiscal policy typically exerts upward pressure on interest rates as larger budget deficits need to be financed. Based on our exchange rate model and the interest rate movements that are induced, we should expect expansionary monetary policy to lead to capital outflows and thus downward pressure on the exchange rate, while expansionary fiscal policy should lead to capital inflows and upward pressure on the exchange rate. This is indeed the key mechanism embodied in the Mundell–Fleming model.

Although we are primarily interested in the issue of exchange rate determination and therefore the case of flexible exchange rates, it is useful to consider the implications of fixed exchange rates as well. Hence, we consider four cases involving both fixed and flexible exchange rates:

■ Expansionary Monetary Policy

● *With Flexible Exchange Rates:* Downward pressure on domestic interest rates will induce capital to flow to higher-yielding markets, putting downward pressure on the domestic currency. The more responsive capital flows are to interest rate differentials, the larger the depreciation of the currency. Depreciation of the currency will (eventually) increase net exports, reinforcing the aggregate demand impact of the expansionary monetary policy.

● *With Fixed Exchange Rates:* To prevent the exchange rate from depreciating, the monetary authority will have to buy its own currency in exchange for other currencies in the FX market. Doing so will tighten domestic credit conditions and offset the intended expansionary monetary policy. In the extreme case, expansionary monetary policy will be completely ineffective if the central bank is forced to fully offset the initial expansion of the money supply and allow the interest rate to rise back to its initial level. We also note that the monetary authority's ability to maintain the fixed exchange rate will be limited by its stock of foreign exchange reserves.

■ Expansionary Fiscal Policy

● *With Flexible Exchange Rates:* An expansionary fiscal policy will tend to exert upward pressure on domestic interest rates, which will in turn induce an inflow of capital from lower-yielding markets, putting upward pressure on the domestic currency. If capital flows are highly sensitive to

---

18 Mundell (1962, 1963) and Fleming (1962).

interest rate differentials, then the domestic currency will tend to appreciate substantially. On the other hand, if capital flows are very insensitive to interest rate differentials, then the currency will tend to depreciate rather than appreciate as the policy-induced increase in aggregate demand worsens the trade balance.

● *With Fixed Exchange Rates:* To prevent the domestic currency from appreciating, the monetary authority will have to sell its own currency in the FX market. This expansion of the domestic money supply will reinforce the aggregate demand impact of the expansionary fiscal policy.

Despite its simplicity, the Mundell–Fleming framework provides powerful insights. First, if domestic policymakers try to (1) pursue independent monetary policies, (2) permit capital to flow freely across national borders, and (3) commit to defend fixed exchange rates, they will eventually find that the three objectives cannot be satisfied at the same time. Second, the degree of capital mobility is critical to the effectiveness of monetary and fiscal policy in an open economy. In particular, policymakers may need to impose capital controls in order to both stabilize the exchange rate and make monetary policy a viable policy instrument for domestic objectives (e.g., employment and/or price stability). This may explain why a number of emerging market economies have taken steps in recent years to impose greater control over capital flows so they can maintain their monetary policy independence, on the one hand, and manage their exchange rates on the other.

The specific mix of monetary and fiscal policies that a country pursues can have a profound impact on its exchange rate. Consider first the case of high capital mobility. A restrictive (expansionary) domestic monetary policy under floating exchange rates will give rise to an appreciation (depreciation) of the domestic currency, with a greater change in the currency when capital flows are highly mobile. On the fiscal front, an expansionary (restrictive) fiscal policy will give rise to an appreciation (depreciation) of the domestic currency under conditions of high capital mobility. In Exhibit 7, we show that the combination of an expansionary fiscal policy and a restrictive monetary policy is extremely bullish for a currency when capital mobility is high; likewise, the combination of a restrictive fiscal and an expansionary monetary policy is bearish for a currency. The effect on the currency of fiscal and monetary policies that are both expansionary or both restrictive is ambiguous under conditions of high capital mobility.

Exhibit 7	Monetary–Fiscal Policy Mix and the Determination of Exchange Rates under Conditions of High Capital Mobility

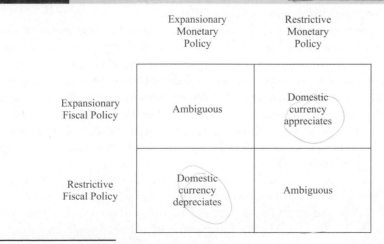

	Expansionary Monetary Policy	Restrictive Monetary Policy
Expansionary Fiscal Policy	Ambiguous	Domestic currency appreciates
Restrictive Fiscal Policy	Domestic currency depreciates	Ambiguous

Source: Rosenberg (1996), p. 132.

When capital mobility is low, the impact of monetary and fiscal policy changes on domestic interest rates will not induce major changes in capital flows. In such cases, monetary and fiscal policy effects on exchange rates will operate primarily through trade flows rather than capital flows. Hence, a uniformly restrictive fiscal/monetary policy mix will be bullish for a currency because this policy mix will tend to lead to an improvement in the trade balance. A uniformly expansionary fiscal/monetary policy mix will be bearish for a currency because the trade balance under such conditions would deteriorate. Combinations of expansionary fiscal and restrictive monetary policies or restrictive fiscal and expansionary monetary policies will have an ambiguous impact on aggregate demand and the trade balance, and hence on the exchange rate, under conditions of low capital mobility. Exhibit 8 summarizes these results.

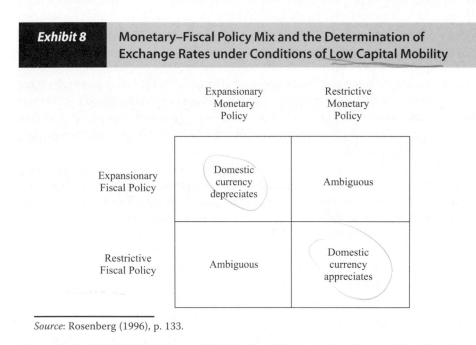

Exhibit 8	Monetary–Fiscal Policy Mix and the Determination of Exchange Rates under Conditions of Low Capital Mobility

	Expansionary Monetary Policy	Restrictive Monetary Policy
Expansionary Fiscal Policy	Domestic currency depreciates	Ambiguous
Restrictive Fiscal Policy	Ambiguous	Domestic currency appreciates

Source: Rosenberg (1996), p. 133.

Exhibit 7 is more relevant for the G–10 countries because capital mobility tends to be high in developed economies. Exhibit 8 is more relevant for emerging market economies that restrict the movement of capital.

A classic episode in which a dramatic shift in the policy mix caused dramatic changes in exchange rates was the case of Germany in 1990–1992. During that period, the German government pursued a highly expansionary fiscal policy to help facilitate German unification. At the same time, the Bundesbank pursued an extraordinarily tight monetary policy to combat the inflationary pressures associated with unification. The combined expansive fiscal/tight monetary policy mix drove interest rates sharply higher in Germany, and those higher interest rates were then transmitted to the rest of Europe via the pegged exchange rate regime known as the European Exchange Rate Mechanism (ERM). Higher interest rates led to a marked slowdown in European growth and to a marked rise in European unemployment. Recognizing that this deterioration in the European economic climate was unsustainable, currency speculators waged an attack on the ERM regime and eventually forced several members to abandon their ERM pegs. European central banks could no longer keep interest rates high enough to defend the ERM pegs and at the same time encourage a rebound in their domestic economies.

6.2 Monetary Models of Exchange Rate Determination

In the Mundell–Fleming model, monetary policy is transmitted to the exchange rate through its impact on interest rates and output. Changes in the price level and/ or the inflation rate play no role. Monetary models of exchange rate determination generally take the opposite perspective: Output is fixed and monetary policy affects exchange rates first and foremost through the price level and the rate of inflation. In this section, we briefly describe two variations of the monetary approach to exchange rate determination.

6.2.1 *The Monetary Approach with Flexible Prices*

The monetary approach is an extension of the classical quantity theory of money to an open economy. According to the quantity theory, money supply changes are the primary determinant of price level changes. In its most extreme version, the quantity theory asserts that an X percent rise in the domestic money supply will produce an X percent rise in the domestic price level. Assuming purchasing power parity holds —that is, that changes in exchange rates reflect changes in relative inflation rates—a money supply–induced increase (decrease) in domestic prices relative to foreign prices should lead to a proportional decline (increase) in the domestic currency's value.

In terms of the model we developed in Section 3.3, the monetary approach focuses on the long-run equilibrium path of the nominal exchange rate. Because it assumes that PPP holds at all times, the real exchange rate is assumed to be constant and equal to its long-run equilibrium value, $\bar{q}_{f/d}$. A discrete change in the money supply will cause a proportionate change in both the equilibrium and actual nominal exchange rates. A change in the future growth rate of the money supply would change the trajectory of both the equilibrium and actual exchange rates but, in the pure monetary approach model, would not have an immediate impact on the current exchange rate.

6.2.2 *The Dornbusch Overshooting Model*

One of the major shortcomings of the pure monetary approach is the assumption that purchasing power parity holds at all times—that is, in both the short and long run. Because purchasing power parity rarely holds in either the short or medium run, the monetary model may not provide a realistic explanation of the impact of monetary forces on the exchange rate.

To rectify that problem, Dornbusch (1976) constructed a modified monetary model of the exchange rate that assumes output prices exhibit limited flexibility in the short run but are fully flexible in the long run. The long-run flexibility of the price level ensures that any increase in the domestic money supply will give rise to a proportional increase in domestic prices and thus contribute to a depreciation of the domestic currency in the long run, which is consistent with the pure monetary model. If the domestic price level is assumed to be inflexible in the short run, however, the model implies that the exchange rate is likely to overshoot its long-run PPP path in the short run. With inflexible domestic prices in the short run, any increase in the nominal money supply results in an identical increase in the real money supply over the relevant short-term period, which in turn induces a decline in the domestic interest rate. Assuming capital is highly mobile, the decline in domestic interest rates will precipitate a capital outflow, which will cause the exchange rate to overshoot its new long-run equilibrium level to the downside on a short-run basis. Hence, in the short run, the domestic currency depreciates in both real and nominal terms. In the long run, once domestic prices rise and domestic interest rates rise in tandem, the exchange rate will recover from its overshoot level and move into line with the path predicted by the conventional monetary approach described in Section 6.2.1. The nominal exchange rate converges back to the path dictated by PPP as the domestic price level gradually adjusts and the real exchange rate returns to the equilibrium level.

6.3 The Taylor Rule and the Determination of Exchange Rates

The Mundell–Fleming and monetary models of exchange rates assume that a central bank targets, and can directly control, a country's money supply or its growth rate. Today, however, many major central banks tend to conduct policy via interest rate targets, not money supply targets. Although this practice does not invalidate the insights we have gleaned from the previous models, it is useful to consider the implications of combining a well-known interest rate targeting framework—the Taylor rule—with a basic exchange rate model.

Many central banks are charged with the responsibility of maintaining price stability and/or achieving maximum sustainable employment.[19] The key questions for individual central banks are, (1) what level of the policy rate will meet both of these policy objectives? and (2) How much should the policy rate rise or fall if inflation exceeds or falls short of the central bank's explicit or implicit inflation target or if the level of employment exceeds or falls short of the economy's maximum sustainable employment level?

John Taylor developed a simple mathematical rule prescribing the appropriate policy rate as a function of a central bank's neutral rate, its inflation and output targets, and observed deviations from those targets.[20] The Taylor rule is given by:

$$i = r_n + \pi + \alpha(\pi - \pi^*) + \beta(y - y^*) \tag{15}$$

where

i = the Taylor rule prescribed central bank policy rate
r_n = the neutral real policy rate
π = the current inflation rate
π^* = the central bank's target inflation rate
y = the log of the current level of output[21]
y^* = the log of the economy's potential/sustainable level of output

The neutral real rate, r_n, is expected to be consistent with growth at the economy's long-run potential growth rate with stable inflation at the target rate, π^*. The neutral nominal policy rate is equal to the neutral real rate plus the target rate of inflation, π^*.[22] According to the rule, the central bank should deviate from this neutral setting only if the actual rate of inflation deviates from the targeted inflation rate (π^*) and/ or the actual level of output (y) deviates from the economy's potential level of output (y^*). The magnitude of the policy rate adjustment to changes in the inflation gap ($\pi - \pi^*$) and the output gap ($y - y^*$) would be dictated by the policy response coefficients, alpha (α) and beta (β). As long as alpha and beta are both positive—Taylor proposed that alpha and beta each equal 0.5—the Taylor rule prescribes that the policy rate should rise in real terms relative to its neutral setting in response to positive inflation and output gaps (and fall in response to negative inflation and output gaps).

The Taylor rule has done a reasonably good job of explaining the trend in the U.S. federal funds rate over the Greenspan–Bernanke era, and it has done a fairly good job of explaining the trend in policy rates in other countries as well. In the United States, the actual federal funds rate has tended to move broadly in line with the recommendations of the original formulation of the Taylor rule.

---

19 For example, the U.S. Federal Reserve has a dual mandate. On the other hand, the Bank of Canada and the European Central Bank are explicitly charged only with price stability.
20 Taylor (1993).
21 Current and potential output are expressed as logarithms so that the difference, ($y - y^*$), measures the percentage deviation from potential output.
22 Inspection of Equation 15 shows that with this definition of the neutral nominal rate, policy will be neutral with respect to both the real and nominal interest rates only if both inflation and output are at their target levels. Various combinations of inflation and output gaps, e.g., stagflation, could imply that either the real policy rate or the nominal policy rate is at its neutral level, but not both.

Although the Taylor rule is used largely for explaining and predicting the future path of policy rates, recent research suggests that it may also provide valuable insights in determining exchange rates. To see how the Taylor rule can be used to explain the trend in exchange rates, let's first recast Equation 15 in real terms. This is shown in Equation 16 below:

$$r = (i - \pi) = r_n + \alpha(\pi - \pi^*) + \beta(y - y^*) \tag{16}$$

Now let's assume that the central banks in two countries—say the United States and the euro area—pursue monetary policy strategies that are broadly in line with the real policy rate recommendations of the Taylor rule, described in Equation 16. The yield spread between U.S. and euro area real policy rates will be determined by (1) the spread between U.S. and euro area neutral real rates, (2) the spread between the actual or expected U.S.–euro area inflation gaps, (3) the spread between the actual or expected U.S.–euro areas output gaps, and (4) the relative size of the respective policy response coefficients (α and β) that the Federal Reserve and European Central Bank normally follow.

Using the Taylor rule to substitute for the real interest rate differential in our real exchange rate model (Equation 12), letting the euro be the base currency, and for simplicity assuming the same policy response parameters in each market, we can write:

$$q_{USD/EUR} = \bar{q}_{USD/EUR} + \left(r_n^{EU} - r_n^{US} \right) + \alpha\left(\left(\pi_{EU} - \pi_{EU}^* \right) - \left(\pi_{US} - \pi_{US}^* \right) \right) +$$
$$\beta\left(\left(y_{EU} - y_{EU}^* \right) - \left(y_{US} - y_{US}^* \right) \right) - \left(\varphi_{EU} - \varphi_{US} \right). \tag{17}$$

Equation 17 indicates that each of the following should strengthen the euro versus the dollar in real terms:

- an increase in the market's estimate of the euro's long-run equilibrium value,
- an increase in the ECB's estimate of the policy-neutral real interest rate relative to the Fed's estimate of the policy-neutral real rate,
- an increase in the inflation gap in the euro area relative to the inflation gap in the United States,
- an increase in the output gap in the euro area relative to the output gap in the United States, and
- a decrease in the risk premium demanded for holding euro-denominated assets relative to the risk premium on dollar-denominated assets.

It is noteworthy that a rise in euro area inflation relative to the ECB's target implies appreciation of the euro, whereas a PPP framework would suggest that higher euro area inflation should be euro-negative. But in the Taylor rule framework, higher euro area inflation would compel the ECB to raise real interest rates, which would push the real interest rate differential in favor of the euro area. That, in turn, would be euro-positive. Thus bad news on euro area inflation turns out to be euro-positive, not euro-negative, as a pure monetary/purchasing power model would suggest.

6.4 Monetary Policy and Exchange Rates—The Historical Evidence

Historically, changes in monetary policy have had a profound impact on exchange rates. In the case of the U.S. dollar, the pursuit of a relatively easy monetary policy by the Federal Reserve drove U.S. real interest rates into negative territory in the late 1970s, which drove the U.S.–German real interest rate differential downward at that time. As shown earlier (Exhibit 5), this result contributed to a major decline in the dollar's value. The subsequent tightening of monetary policy by the Fed in the first half of the 1980s drove U.S. real interest rates up relative to real rates in Germany, which played a key role in driving the dollar higher during that period.

Japan's ultra-low interest rate policy in the second half of the 1990s and into the first decade of the 2000s helped contribute to a long period of subpar performance of yen assets versus U.S. dollar assets. From the spring of 1995 until mid-2007, a 12-year period, yen money market investments dramatically underperformed U.S. dollar money market investments in U.S. dollar terms. It is widely felt that Japan's ultra-low interest rate policy encouraged both Japanese and international investors to take on carry trades over much of this period, in which foreign exchange market participants borrowed heavily in yen and then invested those proceeds in higher-yielding currencies such as the Australian and New Zealand dollars.

Finally, history is replete with examples in which excessively expansionary monetary policies by central banks in emerging markets have planted the seeds of speculative attacks on their currencies. In the early 1980s, exchange rate crises in Argentina, Brazil, Chile, and Mexico were all preceded by sharp accelerations in domestic credit expansions. Emerging market policymakers appear to have learned the lessons of those past crises and policy mistakes. These policymakers have since moved toward more-flexible exchange rate regimes, embraced anti-inflation or inflation-targeting policies, and built huge arsenals of foreign exchange reserves, which are now well above historical norms, as a form of insurance that could be used to defend their currencies should the need ever arise.

Example 12

Monetary Policy and Exchange Rates

Monique Kwan, the currency strategist at a major foreign exchange dealer, is preparing a report on the outlook for several currencies that she follows. She begins by considering the outlook for the currency of a developed market (DM) country. This DM country has high capital mobility across its borders and a flexible exchange rate. It also has low levels of public and private debt.

Given these conditions, Kwan tries to assess the impact of each of the following policy changes using the Mundell–Fleming model and the Taylor Rule.

1. For the DM currency, increasing the degree of monetary easing will *most likely*:

   A. cause the currency to appreciate.

   B. cause the currency to depreciate.

   C. have an ambiguous effect on the currency.

2. The pursuit of an expansionary domestic fiscal policy by the DM country will *most likely*:

   A. cause the domestic currency's value to appreciate.

   B. cause the domestic currency's value to depreciate.

   C. have an ambiguous effect on the domestic currency's value.

Monique Kwan's assistant prepares the following information on the DM country:

Current policy rate (nominal)	2.00%
Neutral real policy rate	2.50%
Current inflation rate	1.00%
Target inflation rate	2.00%
Current output gap	0.50%

3. Assuming that the DM central bank is following the Taylor Rule and that the inflation and output gaps are equally weighted ($\alpha = \beta = 0.5$), the central bank will *most likely*:

   A. leave the policy rate unchanged.

   B. increase the policy rate by 1.00 percent.

   C. increase the policy rate by 1.25 percent.

After a period of adjustment, the current policy rate and the inflation rate are both at target levels and there is no output gap (i.e., equilibrium conditions prevail, according to the Taylor rule).

4. Given these initial equilibrium conditions, the central bank's policy response to:

   A. expansionary fiscal policy would result in lower policy rates.

   B. an increase in growth would lead to depreciation of the DM country's currency.

   C. an increase in inflation would lead to appreciation of the DM country's currency.

5. Given these initial equilibrium conditions, the central bank's policy response to a subsequent increase in the output gap would *most likely* lead to:

   A. tighter fiscal policy.

   B. an increase in the target policy rate.

   C. a depreciation of the DM country's currency.

Next, Kwan turns her attention to an emerging market that has low levels of public and private debt. Currently, the EM country has a fixed exchange rate but no controls over international capital mobility. However, the country is considering replacing its fixed exchange rate policy with a policy based on capital controls. These proposed controls are meant to reduce international capital mobility by limiting short-term investment flows ("hot money") in and out of its domestic capital markets.

Kwan uses the Mundell–Fleming model to assess the likely impact of various policy changes by the EM country.

6. To maintain the exchange rate peg while increasing the degree of monetary easing, the EM country will *most likely* have to:

   A. tighten fiscal policy.

   B. decrease interest rates.

   C. buy its own currency in the FX market.

7. After replacing its currency peg with capital controls, would its exchange rate be unaffected by a tightening in monetary policy?

   A. Yes.

   B. No, the domestic currency would appreciate.

   C. No, the domestic currency would depreciate.

8. After replacing its currency peg with capital controls, the simultaneous pursuit of a tight monetary policy and a highly expansionary fiscal policy by the EM country will *most likely*:

   A. cause the currency to appreciate.

   B. cause the currency to depreciate.

   C. have an ambiguous effect on the currency.

Solution to 1:

B is correct. A decrease in the policy rate would most likely cause capital to re-allocate to higher-yielding investments. This would lead to currency depreciation.

Solution to 2:

A is correct because an expansionary fiscal policy will lead to higher levels of government debt and interest rates, which will attract international capital flows. (In the long run, however, an excessive build-up in debt may eventually cause depreciation pressures on the currency. This is discussed in Section 6.5.)

Solution to 3:

C is correct. Under the Taylor rule, the prescribed central bank policy rate is equal to:

$$i = 2.50\% + 1.00\% + ½(1.00\% - 2.00\%) + ½(0.50\%) = 3.25\%$$

This requires a 1.25 percent increase from the current 2.00 percent policy rate.

Solution to 4:

C is correct. Above-target inflation will lead to monetary tightening, which should lead to currency appreciation. A is incorrect because an expansionary fiscal policy is likely to both lead to economic growth moving above potential and also add to inflationary pressures. Both effects should lead to an increase in the central bank's policy rate. B is incorrect because an increase in economic growth above potential, all else equal, will lead to an increase in the policy rate determined by the Taylor rule. A higher policy rate will likely lead to currency appreciation.

Solution to 5:

B is correct. An increase in the output gap $(y - y^*)$ means the economy is growing above potential. Under the Taylor rule, the central bank will tighten monetary policy. A is incorrect because the central bank does not control fiscal policy, only monetary policy. C is incorrect because an increase in the output gap will lead to a tightening of monetary policy, which, all else equal, should lead to currency appreciation, not depreciation.

Solution to 6:

C is correct. The looser monetary policy will lead to exchange rate depreciation. To counter this effect and maintain the currency peg, the central bank will have to intervene in the FX market, buying its own currency. A is incorrect because tighter fiscal policy is associated with lower interest rates and is therefore likely to increase rather than mitigate the downward pressure on the domestic currency. Similarly, B is incorrect because a move to lower interest rates would exacerbate the downward pressure on the currency and hence the pressure on the peg.

Solution to 7:

B is correct. In general, capital controls will not completely eliminate capital flows but will limit their magnitude and responsiveness to investment incentives such as interest rate differentials. At a minimum, flows directly related to financing international trade will typically be allowed. The exchange rate will still respond to monetary policy. With limited capital mobility, however, monetary policy's main influence is likely to come through the impact on aggregate demand and the trade balance. A tighter domestic monetary policy will most likely lead to higher interest rates and less domestic demand, including less demand for imported goods. With fewer imports, and exports held constant, there will be modest upward pressure on the currency.

Solution to 8:

C is correct because (1) capital mobility is low so the induced increase in interest rates is likely to exert only weak upward pressure on the currency, (2) the combined impact on aggregate demand is ambiguous, and (3) if aggregate demand increases, the downward pressure on the currency due to a worsening trade balance may or may not fully offset the upward pressure exerted by capital flows.

6.5 Fiscal Policy and the Determination of Exchange Rates

Virtually all of the exchange rate models that economists have devised agree that the pursuit of relatively easy domestic monetary policies will tend to exert downward pressure on a domestic currency's value, while the pursuit of relatively tight domestic monetary policies will tend to exert upward pressure on a domestic currency's value. In this section, we shift our focus to examine what role fiscal policy changes have in determining exchange rates.

Despite common agreement on the role of monetary policy in determining exchange rates, *fiscal policy's impact on exchange rates is ambiguous* because fiscal impulses are transmitted to exchange rates through a variety of channels, some of which transmit positive influences on a currency's value while others transmit negative influences. Whether a given change in fiscal policy will result in an increase or a decrease in a currency's value will depend on whether the positive channels dominate the negative ones or vice versa.

The Mundell–Fleming Model is essentially a short-run model of exchange rate determination. It makes no allowance for the long-term effects of budgetary imbalances that typically arise from sustained fiscal policy actions. The portfolio balance approach to exchange rate determination remedies this.

In the **portfolio balance approach**, global investors are assumed to hold a diversified portfolio of domestic and foreign assets, including bonds. Their desired allocation is assumed to vary in response to changes in expected return and risk considerations. In this framework, a steady increase in the supply of domestic bonds outstanding, generated by a continued widening of the government budget deficit, will be willingly held only if asset holders are compensated in the form of a higher expected return. Such a return could come from (1) higher interest rates and/or higher risk premium, (2) immediate *depreciation of the currency to a level sufficient to generate anticipation of gains from subsequent currency appreciation*, or (3) some combination of the two. The second mechanism, currency adjustments required to achieve or maintain global asset market equilibrium, is the crux of the portfolio balance approach.

One of the major insights one should draw from the portfolio balance model is that *in the long run, governments that run large budget deficits on a sustained basis could eventually see their currencies decline in value.*

The Mundell–Fleming and portfolio balance models can be combined into a single integrated framework in which expansionary fiscal policy under conditions of high capital mobility may be positive for a currency in the short run but negative in the long run. Exhibit 9 illustrates this concept. A domestic currency may rise in value when the stimulative fiscal policy is first put into place. As deficits mount over time and the government's debt obligations rise, however, the market will begin to wonder how that debt will be financed. If the volume of debt rises to levels that are believed to be unsustainable, the market may believe that pressure will eventually have to be brought to bear on the central bank to monetize the debt—that is, for the central bank to buy the government's debt with newly created money. Such a scenario would clearly lead to a rapid reversal of the initial currency appreciation.

Alternatively, the market may believe that the government's fiscal stance will eventually have to shift toward significant restraint to restore longer-run sustainable balance to its fiscal position. A reversal of the fiscal stance that initially drove the currency higher would set forces in motion for a reversal of the initial currency appreciation.

Exhibit 9   The Short- and Long-Run Response of Exchange Rates to Changes in Fiscal Policy

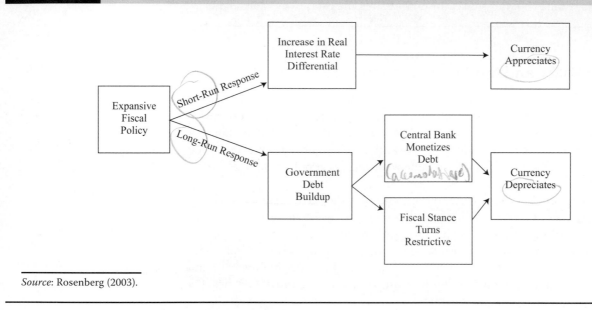

Source: Rosenberg (2003).

Example 13

Fiscal Policy and Exchange Rates

Monique Kwan is continuing her analysis of the foreign exchange rate outlook for selected countries. She examines a DM country that has a high degree of capital mobility and a floating-rate currency regime. Kwan notices that although the current outstanding stock of government debt is low, as a percentage of GDP, it is rising sharply as a result of expansionary fiscal policy. Moreover, projections for the government debt-to-GDP ratio point to further increases well into the future.

Kwan uses the Mundell–Fleming and portfolio balance models to form an opinion about both the short-run and long-run implications for the DM country's exchange rate.

1. Over the short run, Kwan is *most likely* to expect:

    A. appreciation of the DM's currency.

    B. an increase in the DM's asset prices.

    C. a decrease in the DM's risk premium.

2. Over the medium term, as the DM country's government debt becomes harder to finance, Kwan would be *most likely* to expect that:

    A. fiscal policy will turn more accommodative.

    B. the mark-to-market value of the debt will increase.

    C. monetary policy will become more accommodative.

3. Assuming that the DM country's government debt becomes harder to finance and there is no change in monetary policy, Kwan is *most likely* to expect that over the longer term, there will be a fiscal policy response that would lead to:

A. currency appreciation as yields rise.

B. currency depreciation as yields decline.

C. an ambiguous impact on the currency, depending on which effect prevails.

Solution to 1:

A is correct. The DM country currently has a low debt load (as a percentage of GDP), and in the short run, its expansionary fiscal policy will lead to higher interest rates and higher real rates relative to other countries. This path should lead to currency appreciation. The higher domestic interest rates will (all else equal) depress local asset prices (so B is incorrect), and the rising debt load is likely to increase rather than decrease the risk premium (so C is incorrect).

Solution to 2:

C is correct. This is because as government debt becomes harder to finance, the government will be tempted to monetize the debt through an accommodative monetary policy. A is incorrect because an inability to finance the debt will make it hard for fiscal policy to become more accommodative. B is incorrect because as investors demand a higher risk premium (a higher return) for holding the DM country's debt, the mark-to-market value of the debt will decline (i.e., bond prices will decline and bond yields will increase).

Solution to 3:

B is correct. As the DM country's debt ratios deteriorate, foreign investors will demand a higher rate of return to compensate them for the increased risks. Assuming that the central bank will not accommodate (monetize) the rising government debt, the most likely fiscal response is an eventual move towards fiscal consolidation—reducing the public deficit and debt levels that were causing the debt metrics to deteriorate. This policy adjustment would involve issuing fewer government bonds. All else equal, bond yields would decrease, leading to a weaker domestic currency.

A is not the most likely answer because currency appreciation is not likely to accompany rising yields when the government is having difficulty financing its deficit. There would be a rising risk premium (a deteriorating investor appetite) for holding DM assets and hence a currency appreciation would be unlikely despite high DM yields. To avoid paying these high yields on its debt, the DM government would eventually have to take measures to reduce its deficit spending. This approach would eventually help reduce investor risk aversion and DM yields. C is incorrect because given the deterioration in the DM's debt metrics, a depreciation of its exchange rate is likely to be an important part of the restoration of financial market equilibrium.

EXCHANGE RATE MANAGEMENT: INTERVENTION AND CONTROLS

Capital flow surges can be both a blessing and a curse. Capital inflows can be a blessing if they enable growing economies to bridge the gap between domestic investment and domestic savings. They can be a curse, however, if they fuel boom-like conditions, asset price bubbles, and an overshooting of the currency into overvalued territory. Problems arise when inflows of short-term capital eventually reverse, because the resulting outflow of capital can trigger a major economic downturn, a significant decline in asset prices, and a major depreciation of the currency.

Capital flow surges planted the seeds of three major currency crises in the 1990s—the ERM crisis in the fall of 1992, the Mexican peso crisis in late 1994, and the Asian currency and financial crisis in 1997–1998. Each crisis episode was preceded by a surge in capital inflows that led to a buildup of huge, highly leveraged speculative positions by local as well as international investors in currencies that eventually came under heavy speculative attack. In the run-up to the ERM crisis, investors—believing that European yield convergence would occur as European monetary union approached—took on highly leveraged long positions in the higher-yielding European currencies financed by short positions in the lower-yielding European currencies. Likewise, in the run-up to the Mexican peso crisis, investors and banks were highly leveraged and made extensive use of derivative products in taking on speculative long Mexican peso/short U.S. dollar positions. And in the run-up to the Asian financial crisis, Asian companies and banks were highly leveraged as they took on a huge volume of short-term dollar- and yen-denominated debt to fund local activities. In each case, the sudden unwinding of those leveraged long speculative positions triggered the attacks on the currencies.

Surges in capital inflows often are driven by a combination of "pull" and "push" factors, with both factors capable of generating bubble-like conditions. Pull factors represent a favorable set of developments that encourage overseas capital to flow toward a particular country. These factors include the following:

■ better economic management by policymakers;
■ expected declines in inflation and inflation volatility;
■ more-flexible exchange rate regimes;
■ improved current account balances;
■ declines in public and private sector debt burdens;
■ a significant buildup in FX reserves, which can be used as a buffer against future speculative attacks;
■ privatization of state-owned entities;
■ liberalization of financial markets;
■ lifting of foreign exchange regulations and controls;
■ strong and sustained economic growth, which works to enhance the expected long-run return on real and financial assets;
■ improved fiscal positions; and
■ sovereign ratings upgrades.

Push factors represent a favorable set of factors that emanate not from the recipient country per se but rather from the primary sources of internationally mobile capital, notably the investor base in industrial countries. The pursuit of low interest rate policies in industrial countries has often encouraged investors in those markets to move funds offshore to earn higher returns than can be earned domestically. Japan's ultra-low interest rates encouraged investors to move funds into higher-yielding markets in Australia, New Zealand, and Asia. The pursuit of a low interest rate policy by the Federal Reserve encouraged U.S. investors to allocate more of their funds to emerging markets in the mid and late 2000s. Another important push factor is the long-run trend in asset allocation by industrial country investors. For example, U.S. fund managers have traditionally had underweight exposures to emerging market assets, but with the weight of emerging market equities in broad global equity market indices on the rise, U.S. investor allocation to EM equities is likely to rise in lockstep. Because the

EM share of world GDP is now around 40 percent, up from 17 percent in the 1960s, the share of funds allocated to emerging markets is likely to increase on a trend basis. Notably, just a one percentage point annual increase in industrial country investor allocations to emerging market assets could add roughly $350 billion to $500 billion to the annual flow of net private capital to emerging markets. That amount would be a sizable chunk, considering that net private capital flows to emerging markets in 2010 was roughly $900 billion.

As indicated in Exhibit 10, net private capital inflows to emerging markets rose steadily between 2002 and 2007, posting nearly a six-fold increase over the period. Both push and pull factors contributed to that surge in capital flows. Net private capital flows to emerging markets tumbled in 2008 and 2009 as heightened risk aversion during the global financial crisis prompted investors to unwind some of their EM exposures in favor of U.S. assets. Since 2009, capital flows to emerging markets have once again started to rise. Emerging market investments appear to be gaining favor again in part because most EM economies appear to have weathered the global financial crisis better than most industrial economies, while the pursuit of ultra-low interest rate policies in the United States, euro area, and Japan has encouraged global investors to invest in higher-yielding EM assets.

Exhibit 10	Net Private Capital Flows to Emerging Markets

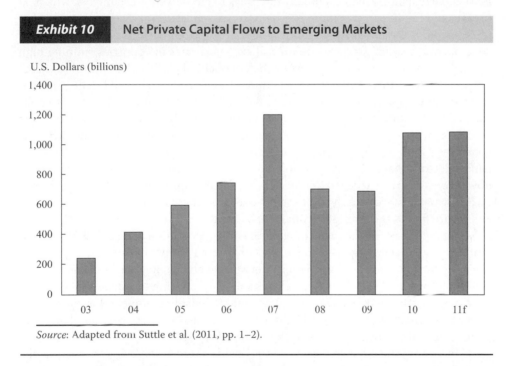

U.S. Dollars (billions)

Source: Adapted from Suttle et al. (2011, pp. 1–2).

The key question facing EM policymakers is how best to respond to the latest wave of capital inflows. As discussed earlier, some of the major crisis episodes of the 1990s were instigated, in part, by excessive surges in capital inflows that eventually were reversed. This time around, policymakers are intent on insuring that history does not repeat itself. Hence, policymakers appear to be making a concerted effort to either (a) resist or deflect such inflows through the use of capital controls or (b) prevent capital inflows from pushing EM currency values to overvalued levels by intervening more heavily in the foreign exchange market.

The International Monetary Fund offers the following guidelines to policymakers who face an unwanted surge in capital inflows: Assuming that the EM currency is undervalued, the appropriate policy response would be to allow the currency to appreciate. The danger, of course, is that the appreciation ends up being excessive, leading eventually to overvaluation and a loss of competitiveness. If the exchange rate is already fairly valued or overvalued, then the appropriate policy step would be to intervene. If there is no inflation threat, the authorities could engage in **unsterilized intervention**, which would expand the monetary base and encourage short-term interest rates to move lower. Lower interest rates, in turn, might help discourage future capital inflows. If, however, inflation is a concern, then this intervention would need to be sterilized. In a **sterilized intervention** operation, EM authorities would sell domestic securities to the private sector to mop up any excess liquidity created by its FX intervention activities. The end result would be that the monetary base and the level of short-term interest rates would not be altered by the intervention operation. If there are limits on the capacity of EM countries to engage in sterilized intervention operations, then a tightening in fiscal policy might be needed to help slow domestic demand and help alleviate some of the upward pressure on the EM currency.

If all of the above failed to stop the capital flow–induced upward pressure on the EM currency, then capital controls might have to be considered as a final line of resistance in preventing capital flows from pushing currency values and asset prices to undesirable levels. At one time, capital controls were frowned on as a policy tool for curbing undesired surges in capital inflows. It was generally felt that such controls tended to generate distortions in global trade and finance and that, in all likelihood, market participants would eventually find ways to circumvent the controls, which, in turn, would require an ever more pervasive set of regulations and controls to combat the evasion of the initial set of controls. It has also been felt that the use of capital controls to resist upward pressure on real exchange rates in countries running high current account surpluses might exacerbate global imbalances. Furthermore, many observers feared that capital controls imposed by one country could deflect capital flows to other countries, which could complicate monetary and exchange rate policies in those economies. Despite such concerns, the IMF believes that the benefits associated with capital controls may exceed the associated costs. Hence, the IMF now considers capital controls a legitimate part of EM policymakers' toolkit. Given the painful lessons that EM policymakers have learned from previous episodes of capital flow surges, it is now believed that under certain circumstances, capital controls may be needed to prevent exchange rates from overshooting, asset bubbles from forming, and future financial conditions from deteriorating.

Although a case can be made for central bank intervention and capital controls to limit the potential damage associated with unfettered inflows of overseas capital, the key issue for policymakers is whether intervention and capital controls will actually work in terms of (1) preventing currencies from appreciating too strongly, (2) reducing the aggregate volume of capital inflows, and (3) enabling monetary authorities to pursue independent monetary policies without having to worry whether changes in policy rates might attract too much capital from overseas.

Evidence on the effectiveness of central bank intervention suggests that, in the case of industrial countries, the volume of intervention is often quite small relative to the average daily turnover of G–10 currencies in the foreign exchange market. Hence, most studies conclude that the effect of intervention in developed market economies is either statistically insignificant or quantitatively unimportant. For most developed market countries, the ratio of official FX reserves held by the respective central banks to the average daily turnover of foreign exchange trading in that currency is negligible. With insufficient resources in most industrial countries' reserve arsenal, there simply is not enough firepower available to significantly affect the supply of and demand for foreign exchange.[23]

---

23 If a central bank is intervening in an effort to weaken, rather than strengthen, its own currency, it could (at least in principle) create and sell an unlimited amount of its currency and accumulate a correspondingly large quantity of FX reserves. As discussed above, however, persistent intervention in the FX market undermines the efficacy of monetary policy for domestic purposes.

The evidence on the effectiveness of central bank intervention in emerging market currencies is more mixed. Intervention appears to contribute to lower EM exchange rate volatility, but no statistically significant relationship has emerged between the level of EM exchange rates and intervention. Some studies find, however, that EM policymakers might have greater success than their industrial country counterparts in terms of their ability to influence the level and path of their exchange rates, because the ratio of EM central bank FX reserve holdings to average daily FX turnover in their domestic currencies is actually quite sizable. With considerably greater firepower in their reserve arsenals, emerging market central banks appear to be in a stronger position than their developed market counterparts to influence the level and path of their exchange rates. What's more, with emerging market central banks' FX reserve holdings expanding at a near record clip in the past decade, the effectiveness of sterilized intervention may be stronger now than in the past.

The evidence on the effectiveness of capital controls in terms of resisting or deflecting capital inflows is mixed. In a recent survey of empirical studies on the effectiveness of capital controls in emerging markets by Magud, Reinhart, and Rogoff (2011), the authors optimistically concluded that capital controls on inflows (1) make monetary policy more independent, (2) can alter the composition of capital flows, and (3) can reduce real exchange rate pressures in certain instances (although the evidence on this point is more controversial). The study also found, however, that "capital controls on inflows seem not to reduce the volume of net flows." To a large extent, *the relative success or lack thereof of controls on capital inflows hinges on the magnitude and persistence of the inflows that policymakers are seeking to resist. The more persistent those flows are, and the larger their magnitude, the less likely it is that capital controls will be effective* in stemming upward pressure on the real exchange rate.

Example 14

Exchange Rate Management: Intervention and Controls

Monique Kwan now turns her attention to an EM country that is experiencing a surge of capital inflows. This country recently improved its fiscal position through the privatization of state-owned assets and has seen its sovereign credit rating upgraded (both pull factors). Although the country's current policies allow a high degree of capital mobility, it is becoming concerned about the potential future impact of these capital inflows.

1. The EM country is *more likely* to engage in sterilized intervention if its:

    A. inflation rate is high.

    B. currency is undervalued.

    C. currency appreciation is caused by push factors rather than pull factors.

2. If the EM country used capital controls instead, this approach would:

    A. lead to a less independent monetary policy.

    B. be more likely to succeed when capital flows are less persistent.

    C. require that the ratio of foreign exchange reserves to FX market turnover be high.

Solution to 1:

A is correct. A country would likely choose sterilized intervention if it had a high inflation rate, because unsterilized intervention would add to the monetary base and possibly increase inflationary pressures. B is incorrect because an undervalued currency is likely to lessen the probability of intervention, sterilized or unsterilized, in response to capital inflows. C is incorrect because both push and pull factors can lead to bubble conditions, excessive exchange rate appreciation, and the unwanted build-up of excessive speculative positions.

Solution to 2:

B is correct. Although the empirical evidence is mixed, to a large extent the relative success of capital controls depends on the magnitude and persistence of the capital inflows that the policymakers are trying to resist (the less persistent, the higher the effectiveness). A successful capital control policy tends to increase, not decrease, monetary policy independence. As a regulatory measure, capital controls do not depend directly on the level of foreign exchange reserves. (This is in contrast to FX intervention, for which the likelihood of success would be enhanced by having relatively large foreign reserves.)

8   CURRENCY CRISES

History is replete with examples of currencies that have come under heavy selling pressure within short windows of time. These episodes often occurred suddenly, with many (if not most) investors surprised by the timing of the crisis.

If market participants correctly anticipated the onset of a currency crisis, one would expect to see a substantial widening in interest rate differentials to reflect the higher likelihood of a major currency depreciation as the impending crisis drew nearer. In addition, one would expect to see expectations of impending currency weakness built into the consensus forecasts of exchange rates by international economists. Finally, because many currency crisis episodes have coincided with banking and other forms of financial crises, one would expect that credit agency risk assessments would be signaling an impending crisis.

Unfortunately, a careful reading of the history of currency and financial crisis episodes suggests that this has not been the case. For example, interest rate differentials failed to widen measurably in anticipation of the ERM crisis of 1992–1993, the Mexican peso crisis of 1994–1995, or the Asian financial crisis of 1997–1998. More recently, risk premia embedded in many spread products in the U.S. financial markets failed to widen in advance of the 2007–2009 financial crisis. Particularly noteworthy is the fact that neither the consensus forecasts of private and government economists nor the risk assessments by credit rating agencies provided adequate warning of the impending financial shocks and the ensuing economic downturns.

If anything, the evidence seems more consistent with the view that market participants are taken by surprise when a crisis occurs. Indeed, more often than not, investors and borrowers tend to be leaning the wrong way in terms of their portfolio positioning at the time of an attack. Once a wave of selling begins, investors and borrowers must immediately reposition their portfolios to avoid excessive capital losses. Such repositioning often works to intensify selling pressure on the currency. It is this massive liquidation of vulnerable positions, often reinforced by speculative selling, that is largely responsible for the seemingly excessive exchange rate movements that typically occur during a currency crises.

Because most crisis episodes have not been adequately anticipated, economists at the IMF and at leading investment banks and think tanks have spent a great deal of time in recent years developing early warning systems to help policymakers and investors better position themselves the next time an impending crisis draws nearer. One of the problems in developing an early warning system is that views on the underlying causes of currency crises differ greatly. One school of thought contends that currency crises tend to be precipitated by deteriorating economic fundamentals, while a second school contends that currency crises can occur out of the blue, with no evidence of deteriorating fundamentals preceding them.

According to the first school of thought, evidence of a secular deterioration in economic fundamentals often precedes most crisis episodes. If currency crises tend to be preceded by weak economic fundamentals, and the trend in those economic fundamentals deteriorates steadily and predictably, then it should be possible to construct an early warning system to anticipate when a currency might be vulnerable.

The second school of thought argues that although evidence of deteriorating economic fundamentals might explain a relatively large number of currency collapses, there might be cases in which economies with relatively sound fundamentals could see their currencies come under attack because of (1) a sudden adverse shift in market sentiment totally unrelated to economic fundamentals or (2) contagion or spillover effects arising from crisis developments in other markets. If that is the case, then it might not be possible to construct a reliable early warning system to predict future currency crises.

Recognizing that no single model can correctly anticipate the onset of all crisis episodes, an early warning system might nevertheless be useful in assisting (1) fund managers in structuring their global investment portfolios and (2) policymakers in taking the necessary steps to avoid the impending crisis in the first place.

An ideal early warning system would need to incorporate a number of important features. First, it should have a strong record not only in terms of predicting actual crises but also in terms of avoiding the frequent issuance of false signals. Second, it should include macroeconomic indicators whose data are available on a timely basis. If data arrives with a long lag, one runs the risk that a crisis could be under way before the early warning system starts flashing red. Indeed, an ideal early warning system would be one that starts flashing red well in advance of an actual currency crisis allowing market participants sufficient time to adjust or hedge their portfolios before the crisis hits. Third, because currency crises tend to be triggered in countries with a number of economic problems, not just one, an ideal early warning system should be broad based, incorporating a wide range of symptoms that crisis-prone currencies might exhibit.

The IMF conducted a study analyzing the behavior of 10 key macroeconomic variables around the time of currency crises in 50 countries over the 1975–1997 period. Although the behavior of these variables often differed from one crisis to another, a number of stylized facts emerged from the study:

- In the period leading up to a crisis, the real exchange rate is substantially higher than its mean level during tranquil periods.
- Somewhat surprisingly, the trade balance displays no significant difference between its behavior in pre-crisis periods and in tranquil periods.
- Foreign exchange reserves tend to decline precipitously as the crisis approaches.
- On average, there is some deterioration in the terms of trade in the months leading up to a crisis.
- Inflation tends to be significantly higher in pre-crisis periods compared with tranquil periods.
- The ratio of M2, a measure of money supply, to bank reserves tends to rise in the 24-month period leading up to a crisis and then plummets sharply in the months immediately following a crisis.
- Broad money growth in nominal and real terms tends to rise sharply in the two years leading up to a currency crisis, peaking around 18 months before a crisis hits.
- Nominal private credit growth also tends to rise sharply in the period leading up to a crisis.

- Currency crises are often preceded by a boom–bust cycle in financial asset (equity) prices.

- Real economic activity displays no distinctive pattern ahead of a crisis but falls sharply in the aftermath.

Given the stylized behavior of these key economic variables prior to the onset of many major currency crises, model builders at the IMF and at leading investment banks have made numerous attempts to construct *composite* early warning systems that incorporate a number of key economic variables into a single index of crisis vulnerability. Although no single index can capture all of the economic and financial developments leading up to each and every crisis, such indices may nevertheless prove useful in assessing potential negative tail risks that might be lurking around the corner.

Example 15

Currency Crises

Monique Kwan now turns her attention to the likelihood of crises in various emerging market currencies. She discusses this matter with a research associate, who tells her that the historical record of currency crises shows that most of these episodes were not very well anticipated by investors (in terms of their positioning), by the bond markets (in terms of yield spreads between countries), or by major credit rating agencies and economists (in terms of the sovereign credit ratings or forecasts, respectively).

1. The research associate is *most likely*:
   A. correct.
   B. incorrect, because most credit rating agencies and economists typically changed their forecasts prior to a crisis.
   C. incorrect, because investor positioning and international yield differentials typically shift prior to a crisis.

Kwan delves further into the historical record of currency crises. She concludes that even countries with relatively sound economic fundamentals can fall victim to these crisis episodes and that these attacks can occur when sentiment shifts for reasons unrelated to economic fundamentals.

2. Kwan's conclusion is *most likely*:
   A. correct.
   B. incorrect, because there are few historical crises involving currencies of countries with sound economic fundamentals.
   C. incorrect, because there are few historical episodes in which a sudden adverse shift in market sentiment occurs that is unrelated to economic fundamentals.

To better advise the firm's clients on the likelihood of currency crises, Kwan tries to formulate an early warning system for these episodes. She recognizes that a typical currency crisis tends to be triggered by a number of economic problems, not just one.

3. Kwan's early warning system is *least likely* to indicate an impending crisis when there is:
   A. an expansionary monetary policy.
   B. an overly appreciated real exchange rate.
   C. rising foreign exchange reserves at the central bank.

4. Kwan's early warning system would *most likely* be better if it:

   A. had a strong record of predicting actual crises, even if it generates a lot of false signals.

   B. included a wide variety of economic indicators, including those for which data are available only with a significant lag.

   C. started flashing well in advance of an actual currency crisis to give market participants time to adjust or hedge their portfolio before the crisis hits.

Solution to 1:

A is correct. Currency crises often catch most market participants and analysts by surprise.

Solution to 2:

A is correct. Even countries with sound economic fundamentals can be subject to a currency crisis, including instances when market sentiment shifts for non-economic reasons.

Solution to 3:

C is correct. A high level of foreign exchange reserves held by a country typically decreases the likelihood of a currency crisis.

Solution to 4:

C is correct. Early warnings are a positive factor in judging the effectiveness of the system, whereas false signals and the use of lagged data would be considered negative factors.

SHORTER-TERM FORECASTING TOOLS

Correctly predicting the direction and magnitude of exchange rate movements on a more or less consistent basis is not an easy task. Economists have developed a range of theories to explain how exchange rates are determined, but the overwhelming body of evidence from hundreds of empirical studies indicates that fundamentals-based models, although useful in explaining the longer-term trends in exchange rates, have not had much success in explaining short- and medium-term trends. Indeed, a random walk characterizes exchange rate movements better than most conventional fundamentals-based exchange rate models in the short run.

Frustrated with the performance of such models, fund managers have turned to other types of forecasting tools to help them forecast the direction of exchange rates. Because the performance of fund managers is often evaluated over relatively short time spans, investor attention tends to focus on short-run forecasting tools such as technical analysis and order flow, sentiment, and positioning indicators for a better reading on the short-run pressures driving exchange rates. Although technical analysis has been widely used in the FX arena for decades, investor interest in order flow, sentiment, and positioning has been more recent. This newly found interest stems in part from the fact that data on order flow and positioning have only recently become more readily available.

9.1 Technical Analysis

Followers of technical analysis believe that the market tips its hand ahead of time as to the likely future direction of exchange rates. That is, if the upside and downside moves in exchange rates exhibit a tendency to recur in a systematic manner, then the study of past price action can allow investors to draw conclusions regarding the likely direction and magnitude of future price movements.

Technical trading rules come in many different forms. Some are designed to identify market trends or market reversals, while others are designed to identify

1. overbought or oversold conditions,

2. relative strength, and

3. support and resistance levels.

A recent survey found that approximately 90 percent of FX traders used some technical analysis input to help position themselves on an intraday, daily, or weekly basis.

The question, of course, is whether technical analysis represents a reliable approach to taking positions in the FX market. Numerous academic studies of the FX market conducted in the 1970s, 1980s, and early 1990s overwhelmingly concluded that a variety of trend-following trading rules—such as moving average crossover trading rules and filter rules—would have generated significant profits had such models been actively followed over those periods. But updated studies for the 1995–2010 period indicate that trend-following trading rules have not fared as well as they did in earlier periods. Indeed, those updated studies now find that whatever profitability previously existed for technical trading rules has vanished during the past 15 years.

The principal reason why trend-following trading rules have become less profitable since the mid-1990s is that persistent and pronounced exchange rate swings are not occurring as often as they did in the past. Most of the profits over the 1973–1995 period came from participating in a few correctly predicted and very large exchange rate moves. Because such large swings have become less frequent, the positive excess returns that could be earned by adhering to the dictates of trend-following rules have largely been eliminated.

A 2008 study by Pukthuanthong-Le and Thomas documents the decline in returns that trend-following trading rules offer. According to their findings, "the era of easy profits from simple trend-following strategies in major currencies is over." Exhibit 11 presents their findings for six key currencies versus the U.S. dollar, with returns broken down into six sub-periods: 1975–1979, 1980–1984, 1985–1989, 1990–1994, 1995–1999, and 2000–2006. As the exhibit shows, average annual excess returns were highly positive in the 1970s and 1980s but began to drop off in the 1990s and declined more substantially in the early 2000s.

Exhibit 11	Liquid Currencies' Mean Profit Performance Using Trend Trading Moving Average Rules, 1975–2006					
Currency	1975–79	1980–84	1985–89	1990–94	1995–99	2000–06
Japanese Yen	11.10	4.81	11.47	5.82	10.04	−2.29
German Mark/Euro	6.81	6.58	9.77	0.79	10.37	2.20
British Pound	11.03	7.80	3.31	1.21	−5.90	−0.17
Swiss Franc	6.70	6.31	7.98	2.55	−0.51	−0.22
Canadian Dollar	3.52	0.89	1.58	1.22	−0.96	0.11
Australian Dollar	–	–	−0.78	−0.09	−1.02	−1.44
Portfolio	7.83	5.28	5.66	1.92	2.00	−0.30

Source: Pukthuanthong-Le and Thomas, 2008.

Pukthuanthong-Le and Thomas do, however, offer a glimmer of hope for technically based traders. The authors suggest that "trending might be a feature confined to currencies in the early years of a floating rate regime." They find that significant positive excess returns could have been earned from 2002 to 2006 if FX traders applied moving average trading rules to selected emerging market currencies, such as the Brazilian real, Mexican peso, South African rand, and Russian ruble, although the peso market might have matured and may no longer be as profitable.

One reason for the success of technical-based trading in the emerging market currencies might be that the EM currency market is presently less crowded, similar to the G–10 market 30 years ago. A less crowded market implies that profitable trading opportunities might not have been completely arbitraged away.

Another reason for the success of technically based trading in emerging market currencies is that many such currencies have experienced significant real appreciation during the 2000s. Although it might not have been possible to observe and quantify all of the favorable structural and policy-related factors taking place in Asia, Latin America, and Eastern Europe/Middle East/Africa in real time, the net positive impact of these changes on currency values could have been indirectly captured by simple trend-following trading rules.

Interestingly, a case can be made for monitoring technical price action in the G–10 currencies as well, even though such activities are unlikely to add incremental return to a currency portfolio. A number of studies find that technical analysis may be useful for controlling risk, even if technically based strategies fail to boost average returns. A novel experiment conducted by Riccardo Curcio and Charles Goodhart (1992) of the London School of Economics involved separating their students into two groups to see which group could generate the best FX trading performance. One group formulated currency trading strategies with the assistance of a technically based forecasting service, while the other group did not. The results of the experiment indicated that the total return earned by both groups was roughly the same. That is, the use of a technical model input did not contribute to above-average total return performance. Interestingly, however, the standard deviation of returns was considerably smaller for the group using the technical model input than was the case for the group that received no assistance at all.

Curcio and Goodhart noted that without the assistance of technical analysis, students tended to follow extreme contrarian strategies that magnified the volatility of their total returns. The group of students that closely followed the dictates of a technically based trading system was able to avoid taking extreme contrarian positions. Hence, Curcio and Goodhart concluded that technically based trading systems might be useful for controlling risk, even if those strategies failed to enhance portfolio returns.

Curcio and Goodhart's findings have applicability for FX fund managers who implement carry trade strategies. Although carry trade strategies have been found to generate attractive returns over long periods, the distribution of those returns suggest that carry trades are prone to significant downside tail risk from time to time during carry trade unwinds. Therefore, a trend-following trading system overlaid on a carry trade strategy could warn investors to step aside when such unwinds are occurring.

9.2 Order Flow, Sentiment, and Positioning

If price trends are of limited use in predicting future exchange rate movements, what about other market indicators? Most studies find a positive, *contemporaneous* correlation between the trend in order flow, sentiment, and positioning indicators on the one hand and the trend in exchange rates on the other. The evidence is more mixed on whether these indicators have any value in terms of *predicting* the future direction of exchange rates on a short- to medium-term basis.

9.2.1 *FX Dealer Order Flow*

In recent years, market participants have become increasingly interested in FX dealer customer flow data. One of the characteristics that distinguishes the FX market from the world equity market is that the FX market has considerably less transparency. Equity market disclosure requirements mandate that all trades be posted instantly. Thus, volume and price data are instantly available to all parties. Not so in the FX market—no such disclosure requirements exist, which means that order flow information is not immediately available to all parties. Thus, a large FX dealer's order book could be of value to investors if the order flow data were shown to have predictive value on a short- to medium-term basis.

Most studies find a strong, positive, *contemporaneous* correlation between cumulative customer order flow and exchange rates over short periods of time (i.e., on an intraday or daily basis). Some studies find that a strong positive relationship holds even over several weeks. The evidence is more mixed on whether *lagged* order flow has predictive value for exchange rates. Because most investors are unlikely to have access to FX dealer flow data, the instant that customer trades are initiated, from an investor's perspective the important question is whether lagged order flow data can help in predicting the short-term path that exchange rates will take. The evidence to date is based on very limited data sets from only a few dealers and covering only short periods. Thus, the evidence is too fragmented to draw any firm conclusion on this question.

9.2.2 *Extracting Information from the Currency Options Market*

FX traders often use currency risk reversals to glean information on whether the FX market might be attaching a higher probability to a large currency appreciation than to a large currency depreciation, or vice versa. A **risk reversal** is a currency option position that consists of the purchase of an out-of-the-money (25 delta) call and the simultaneous sale of an out-of-the-money (25 delta) put, both on the base currency in the P/B exchange rate quote and both with the same expiration date.[24] Risk reversals are quoted in terms of the implied volatility spread between the 25 delta call and 25 delta put.[25] For example, if the price of the call implies an exchange rate volatility 2 percent larger than the implied volatility built into the put price, the risk reversal would be quoted at +2.0 percent. If the implied volatility on the put were 2 percent greater than the implied volatility on the call, the risk reversal would be quoted at −2 percent.

A risk reversal quoted at +2 percent (i.e., higher volatility in the call option price) would indicate that the market was attaching a higher probability to a large appreciation of the base currency than to a large depreciation. This would indicate that the market was willing to pay more to insure against the risk that the base currency will rise sharply than it was willing to pay to insure against the risk that the base currency will fall sharply.

The key issue for traders and investors is whether the level or trend in currency risk reversals can be used to correctly anticipate future exchange rate movements. The evidence indicates that there exists a high, contemporaneous correlation between the trend in risk reversals and the trend in exchange rates, but no statistically significant relationship exists between lagged risk reversal data and future exchange rate movements. Therefore, *risk reversals are capable of confirming an exchange rate's trend but cannot predict it.*

---

24 The delta of an option reflects the sensitivity of its price to the price of the underlying instrument. For standard put and call options, delta ranges (in absolute value) between zero (deep out-of-the-money options) and 1 (prices of deep in the money options change one-for-one with the underlying price) with at-the-money options having a delta of 0.5. In market jargon, delta is often multiplied by 100, so that a delta of 0.25 is referred to as "25 delta."

25 The values of standard put and call options increase as the volatility of the underlying asset price increases. Given an option pricing model such as the Black–Scholes model, the price of an option can be quoted in terms of the volatility implied by the market price.

9.2.3 *Information in the Size and Trend in Net Speculative Positions*

FX market participants closely monitor weekly changes in net positions of speculative accounts in the FX futures market to (1) glean whether speculative flows are moving in or out of particular currencies, which would indicate whether speculative flows were exerting significant upward or downward pressure on those currencies; or (2) assess whether such positions might be overbought or oversold. If speculative positions were overstretched, it might raise the probability that an unforeseen event or shock could prompt an unwinding of those overstretched positions and, in the process, cause a major reversal in the prevailing exchange rate trend.

The Commodity Futures Trading Commission's (CFTC's) weekly "Commitment of Traders" report contains data on long and short positions held by commercial and non-commercial (speculative) accounts in currency futures contracts that trade on the Chicago Mercantile Exchange. Analysts and market participants often focus on the level and trend in CFTC data on net positions of speculators to assess whether trends in investor positioning offer any insight into the likely direction that exchange rates might take in the future. Recent studies by the Federal Reserve Bank of New York and the Bank of England[26] do indeed find a strong, positive *contemporaneous* relationship between exchange rate movements and changes in net positions of speculative accounts. That is, a buildup of long speculative positions in a particular currency tends to be associated with an appreciation of that currency, and vice versa. These two studies, however, find that *changes in net speculative positions do not lead (i.e., predict) changes in exchange rates.* Nor do extreme overbought or oversold positions correctly anticipate major currency reversals. As we found in the case of FX options, the market simply does not tip its hand ahead of time as to what direction it intends to take.

Example 16

Technical Analysis and Flow, Sentiment, and Positioning Indicators

Monique Kwan turns her attention to forming short-term currency forecasts based on technical analysis as well as flow, sentiment, and positioning indicators. Her research associate tells her that both net speculative positioning indicators and options market indicators have done a good job of predicting exchange rate trends and market reversals over time.

1. The research associate is *most likely* incorrect:

    A. only with regard to options market indicators.

    B. only with regard to speculative positioning indicators.

    C. with regard to both speculative positioning and options market indicators.

    After investigating further, Kwan concludes that technical trading rules can be useful to investors for controlling downside risk, even if such trading rules fail to boost long-run total returns. She bases her conclusion on two findings. First, following the dictates of a technical-based trading system may help investors avoid taking extreme contrarian positions. Second, a trend-following trading system overlaid on a carry trade strategy could keep investors from leaning too heavily the wrong way when carry trade unwinds are occurring.

---

26 Klitgard and Weir (2004) and Mogford and Pain (2006).

2. Kwan is *most likely* correct:

    A. in both of her findings.

    B. only in regard to her first finding.

    C. only in regard to her second finding.

Kwan examines the order flow for the JPY/USD currency pair passing though the foreign exchange dealer she works for. She finds that net purchases of yen (against the dollar) have significantly exceeded net sales. Based on this finding, she draws two conclusions: first, that there are contemporaneous downward pressures on the JPY/USD spot rate; and second, that the JPY/USD spot rate will trend lower over the next few weeks.

3. Based on historical evidence, Kwan is *most likely* correct:

    A. in both of her conclusions.

    B. only in regard to her first conclusion.

    C. only in regard to her second conclusion.

Solution to 1:

C is correct. Studies find that although both speculative positioning indicators and options market–based indicators may have a *contemporaneous* correlation with exchange rate movements, they have weak predictive power.

Solution to 2:

A is correct. If properly deployed, technical trading rules can help manage both the risk of excessive positions as well as the crash risks of carry trades.

Solution to 3:

B is correct. The order flow shows net buying of the yen against the dollar, which means *contemporaneous* downward pressure on the JPY/USD currency pair. However, most studies find only weak predictive power from such order flow data.

SUMMARY

Exchange rates are one of the most difficult financial market prices to understand and therefore to forecast. There simply is no simple, robust framework—something akin to discounted cash flows in the valuation of equities and fixed income instruments—on which investors can rely in assessing the appropriate level and likely movements of exchange rates. Nonetheless, on-going globalization makes it increasingly important for investors to make informed judgments about exchange rates.

In this reading, we have described the various theories and modeling approaches that economists and foreign exchange strategists have devised to help explain and (hopefully) profit from exchange rate movements. On a theoretical level, we have described how changes in monetary policy, fiscal policy, current account trends, and capital flows affect exchange rate trends, as well as what role central bank intervention and capital controls can play in counteracting potentially undesirable exchange rate movements. The reading discusses the empirical evidence regarding the ability of our theoretical models to explain and predict exchange rate movements. The reader should have developed an understanding of the fundamental and technical forces that affect exchange rates over short-, medium- and long-run periods, as well as an appreciation of the difficulties one is likely to face in devising a successful and profitable exchange rate forecasting/trading strategy.

This reading makes the following points, among others:

- Spot exchange rates apply to trades for the next settlement date (usually T+2) for a given currency pair. Forward exchange rates apply to trades to be settled at any longer maturity.

- Market makers quote bid and offer prices (in terms of the *price currency*) at which they will buy or sell the *base currency*.

  - The offer price is always higher than the bid price.

  - The counterparty that asks for a two-sided price quote has the option (but not the obligation) to deal at either the bid or offer price quoted to them.

  - The bid–offer spread depends on (1) the currency pair involved, (2) the time of day, (3) market volatility, (4) the transaction size, and (5) the relationship between the dealer and client. Spreads are tightest in highly liquid currency pairs (e.g., USD/EUR), when the key market centers (e.g., London) are open, and when market volatility is relatively low.

- Absence of arbitrage requires the following:

  - The bid (offer) shown by a dealer in the interbank market cannot be higher (lower) than the current interbank offer (bid) price.

  - The cross rate bids (offers) posted by a dealer must be lower (higher) than the implied cross rate offers (bids) available in the interbank market. If not, then a triangular arbitrage opportunity arises.

- Forward exchange rates are quoted in terms of points to be added to the spot exchange rate. If the points are positive (negative), the base currency is trading at a forward premium (discount). The points are proportional to the interest rate differential and approximately proportional to the time to maturity.

- Forecasting the direction of exchange rate movements can be a daunting task. Most studies find that models that work well in one period or for one set of exchange rates fail to work well for others.

- International parity conditions show us how expected inflation, interest rate differentials, forward exchange rates, and expected future spot exchange rates are linked in an ideal world. According to theory, relative expected inflation rates should determine relative nominal interest rates; relative interest rates, in turn, should determine forward exchange rates; and forward exchange rates should correctly anticipate the path of the future spot exchange rate.

- International parity conditions tell us that countries with high (low) expected inflation rates should see their currencies depreciate (appreciate) over time, that high yield currencies should see their currencies depreciate relative to low yield currencies over time, and that forward exchange rates should function as unbiased predictors of future spot exchange rates.

- With the exception of covered interest rate parity, which is enforced by arbitrage, the key international parity conditions rarely hold in either the short or medium term. However, the parity conditions tend to hold over relatively long horizons.

- According to the theory of covered interest rate parity, an investment in a foreign-currency-denominated money market investment that is completely hedged against exchange rate risk in the forward market should yield exactly the same return as an otherwise identical domestic money market investment.

■ According to the theory of uncovered interest rate parity, the expected change in a domestic currency's value should be fully reflected in domestic–foreign interest rate spreads. If the uncovered interest rate parity condition always held, it would rule out the possibility of earning excess returns from going long a high-yield currency and short a low-yield currency.

■ According to the *ex ante* purchasing power parity condition, expected changes in exchange rates should equal the difference in expected national inflation rates.

■ Most studies find that high-yield currencies do not depreciate and low-yield currencies do not strengthen as much as yield spreads would suggest over short- to medium-term periods. Many investors exploit this anomaly by engaging in so-called carry trades that overweight high-yield currencies at the expense of low-yield currencies. Historically, such carry trades have generated attractive excess returns in benign market conditions but tend to perform poorly (i.e., are subject to crash risk) when market conditions are highly volatile.

■ If both *ex ante* purchasing power parity and uncovered interest rate parity held, real interest rates across all markets would be the same. This is real interest rate parity. Combining real interest rate parity with the fact that each country's nominal interest rate equals its real interest rate plus its expected inflation rate, we have the international Fisher effect: The nominal interest rate differential between two currencies equals the difference between the expected inflation rates.

■ If both covered and uncovered interest rate parity held, the market would set the forward exchange rate equal to the spot exchange rate that is expected to prevail in the future. That is, the forward exchange rate would serve as an unbiased predictor of the future spot exchange rate.

■ The purchasing power parity (PPP) approach to assessing long-run fair value probably has the widest following among international economists.

■ The macroeconomic balance approach to assessing long-run fair value in the foreign exchange market estimates how much exchange rates will need to adjust to bring a country's current account balance to a sustainable level.

■ The external debt sustainability approach to assessing long-run fair value in the foreign exchange market estimates what exchange rate level will ensure that a country's net external asset or liability position stabilizes at a viable level.

■ A useful model of longer-term exchange rate determination can be obtained by combining convergence to a long-run equilibrium real exchange rate with uncovered interest rate parity:

$$q_{f/d} = \bar{q}_{f/d} + \left[\left(r_d - r_f \right) - \left(\varphi_d - \varphi_f \right) \right]$$

■ For the most part, countries that run persistent current account deficits will see their currencies weaken over time. Similarly, countries that run persistent current account surpluses will tend to see their currencies appreciate over time.

■ The relationship between current account imbalances and changes in exchange rates is not contemporaneous. Indeed, large current account imbalances can persist for long periods of time before they trigger an adjustment in exchange rates.

■ A significant adjustment in exchange rates is often required to facilitate correction of a large current account gap. Many studies find long lags, perhaps lasting several years, between (1) the onset of the exchange rate change, (2) the adjustment in traded goods prices in response to the change in the exchange rate, and (3) the eventual effect of the change in traded goods prices on import and export demand.

■ Greater financial integration of the world's capital markets and the increased freedom of capital to flow across national borders have increased the importance of global capital flows in determining exchange rates.

■ Countries that run relatively tight monetary policies, introduce structural economic reforms, and lower outsized budget deficits will often see their currencies strengthen over time as capital flows respond positively to relatively high nominal interest rates, lower inflation expectations, a lower risk premium, and an upward revision in the market's assessment of what exchange rate level constitutes long-run fair value.

■ Monetary policy affects the exchange rate through a variety of channels. In the Mundell–Fleming model, it does so primarily through the interest rate sensitivity of capital flows, strengthening the currency when monetary policy is tightened and weakening it when monetary policy is eased. The more sensitive capital flows are to the change in interest rates, the greater the exchange rate's responsiveness to the change in monetary policy.

■ In the monetary model of exchange rate determination, monetary policy is deemed to have a direct impact on the actual and expected path of inflation, which, via purchasing power parity, translates into a corresponding impact on the exchange rate.

■ Although monetary policy impulses may be transmitted to exchange rates through a variety of channels, the end result is broadly the same—countries that pursue overly easy monetary policies will see their currencies depreciate over time. If a central bank wishes to slow or reverse a decline in the value of its currency, a move toward a tighter monetary policy would be helpful, if not required.

■ Fiscal policy has an ambiguous impact on the exchange rate. In the Mundell–Fleming model, an expansionary fiscal policy typically results in a rise in domestic interest rates and an increase in economic activity. The rise in domestic interest rates should induce a capital inflow, which is positive for the domestic currency, but the consequent rise in economic activity should contribute to a deterioration of the trade balance, which is negative for the domestic currency. The more mobile capital flows are, the greater the likelihood that the induced inflow of capital will dominate the deterioration in trade.

■ Under conditions of high capital mobility, countries that simultaneously pursue expansionary fiscal policies and relatively tight monetary policies should see their currencies strengthen over time.

■ The portfolio balance model of exchange rate determination asserts that a steady increase in the stock of government debt outstanding, perhaps generated by a steady widening of the government budget deficit over time, will be willingly held by investors only if they are compensated in the form of a higher expected return. The higher expected return could come from (1) higher interest rates and/or higher risk premium, (2) depreciation of the currency to a level sufficient to generate anticipation of gains from subsequent currency appreciation, or (3) some combination of the two.

■ Surges in capital inflows can be a curse if they fuel boom-like conditions, asset price bubbles, and an overshoot of exchange rates into overvalued territory. One of the major issues confronting policymakers in emerging market countries is how best to respond to excessive surges in capital flows.

■ The International Monetary Fund now considers capital controls to be a legitimate part of a policymaker's toolkit. Given the painful lessons from previous episodes of surging capital flows, the IMF feels that under certain circumstances, capital controls may be needed to prevent exchange rates from overshooting, asset price bubbles from forming, and future financial conditions from deteriorating.

■ The evidence indicates that intervention by industrial countries has had an insignificant impact on the course of exchange rates. The evidence is more mixed for emerging markets. Emerging market policymakers might have greater success in managing their exchange rates given their large arsenal of foreign exchange reserve holdings, which appear sizable relative to the limited turnover of FX transactions in many emerging markets.

■ Although each currency crisis episode is distinct in some respects, an IMF study of 50 episodes found the following stylized facts:

 ● Leading up to a crisis, the real exchange rate is substantially higher than its mean level during tranquil periods.

 ● The trade balance does not signal impending currency crisis.

 ● Foreign exchange reserves tend to decline precipitously as the crisis approaches.

 ● On average, the terms of trade deteriorate somewhat leading up to a crisis.

 ● Inflation tends to be significantly higher in pre-crisis periods.

 ● The ratio of M2 (a measure of money supply) to bank reserves tends to rise in the 24-month period leading up to a crisis, then plummets sharply in the months immediately following a crisis.

 ● Broad money growth in nominal and real terms tends to rise sharply in the two years leading up to a currency crisis, peaking around 18 months before a crisis hits.

 ● Nominal private credit growth tends to rise sharply in the period leading up to a crisis.

 ● Currency crises are often preceded by a boom–bust cycle in financial asset (equity) prices.

 ● Real economic activity does not display any distinctive pattern ahead of a crisis but falls sharply in the aftermath of a crisis.

■ Technical analysis is a popular trading tool for many, if not most, FX market participants. Numerous academic studies conducted in the 1970s, 1980s, and early 1990s concluded that a variety of trend-following trading rules would have generated significant profits had such models been actively followed during that period. However, updated studies for the post-1995 period indicate that trend-following trading rules have not fared as well since.

■ Although technical analysis may now be less useful as a strategic tool to enhance return, a number of studies show that technical analysis may be a useful tool in managing the downside risk associated with FX portfolios.

■ Most studies find that there exists a strong positive, *contemporaneous* relationship between cumulative order flow and exchange rates over short periods of time. However, the evidence is more mixed regarding whether order flow has *predictive* value for exchange rates.

■ Empirical studies find that neither the data on currency risk reversals nor data on the size and trend in reported net speculative positions on the futures market are useful for currency forecasting purposes.

REFERENCES

Curcio, Riccardo, and Charles A.E. Goodhart. 1992. "Chartism: A Controlled Experiment." *Journal of International Securities Markets*, vol. 7: 173–186.

Dornbusch, Rudiger. 1976. "Expectations and Exchange Rate Dynamics." *Journal of Political Economy*, vol. 84: 1161–1176.

Fleming, J. Marcus. 1962. "Domestic Financial Policies under Fixed and Floating Exchange Rates." *IMF Staff Papers*, vol. 9: 319–379.

International Monetary Fund. 1998. *IMF World Economic Outlook*, May 1998, Washington D.C.

International Monetary Fund. 2007. "Exchange Rates and the Adjustment of External Imbalances." *IMF World Economic Outlook*, April 2007, Ch. 3, pp. 81–120.

Isard, Peter, Hamid Faruqee, G. Russell Kincaid, and Martin Fetherston. 2001. "Methodology for Current Account and Exchange Rate Assessments." IMF Occasional Paper #209.

Klitgard, Thomas, and Laura Weir. 2004. "Exchange Rate Changes and Net Positions of Speculators in the Futures Market." *Economic Policy Review*. Federal Reserve Bank of New York, May 2004.

Magud, Nichols E., Carmen M. Reinhart, and Kenneth S. Rogoff. 2011. "Capital Controls: Myth and Reality—A Portfolio Balance Approach." Peterson Institute for International Economics, Working Paper No. 11-7.

Mogford, Caroline, and Darren Pain. 2006. "The Information Content of Aggregate Data on Financial Futures Positions."

Bank of England, *Quarterly Bulletin*, Spring 2006.

Mundell, Robert A. 1962. "The Appropriate Use of Monetary and Fiscal Policy for Internal and External Stability." *IMF Staff Papers*, vol. 9: 70–79.

Mundell, Robert A. 1963. "Capital Mobility and Stabilization Policy under Fixed and Flexible Exchange Rates." *Canadian Journal of Economics and Political Science*, vol. 29: 475–485.

Pukthuanthong-Le, Kuntara, and Lee R. Thomas. 2008. "Weak-Form Efficiency in Currency Markets." *Financial Analysts Journal*, vol. 64, no. 3 : 31–52.

Rosenberg, Michael R. 1996. *Currency Forecasting: A Guide to Fundamental and Technical Models of Exchange Rate Determination*. Chicago: Irwin Professional Publishing.

Rosenberg, Michael R. 2002. *Deutsche Bank Guide to Exchange Rate Determination*. Chicago: Irwin Professional Publishing.

Rosenberg, Michael R. 2003. *Exchange Rate Determination: Models and Strategies for Exchange Rate Forecasting*. New York: McGraw-Hill.

Suttle, Philip, Robin Koepke, Kristina Morkunaite, and Emre Tiftik. 2011. "Capital Flows to Emerging Market Economies." *IIF Research Note*, September 25. Institute of International Finance.

Taylor, John B. 1993. "Discretion versus Policy Rules in Practice." *Carnegie-Rochester Conference Series on Public Policy*, Vol. 39: 195–214.

APPENDIX

Currency Codes Used in This Reading

USD	U.S. dollar
EUR	euro
GBP	U.K. pound
JPY	Japanese yen
MXN	Mexican peso
CHF	Swiss franc
CAD	Canadian dollar
SEK	Swedish krona
AUD	Australian dollar
KRW	Korean won
NZD	New Zealand dollar

PRACTICE PROBLEMS FOR READING 14

The following information relates to Questions 1 – 6[1]

Ed Smith is a new trainee in the foreign exchange (FX) services department of a major global bank. Smith's focus is to assist senior FX trader, Feliz Mehmet, CFA. Mehmet mentions that an Indian corporate client exporting to the U.K. wants to estimate the potential hedging cost for a sale closing in one year. Smith is to determine the premium/discount for an annual (360 day) forward contract using the exchange rate data presented in Exhibit 1.

Exhibit 1	Select Currency Data for GBP and INR
Spot (INR/GBP)	79.5093
Annual (360-day) LIBOR (GBP)	5.43%
Annual (360-day) LIBOR (INR)	7.52%

Mehmet is also looking at two possible trades to determine their profit potential. The first trade involves a possible triangular arbitrage trade using the Swiss, U.S. and Brazilian currencies, to be executed based on a dealer's bid/offer rate quote of 0.5161/0.5163 in CHF/BRL and the interbank spot rate quotes presented in Exhibit 2.

p. 489

Exhibit 2	Interbank Market Quotes
Currency Pair	**Bid / Offer**
CHF/USD	0.9099 / 0.9101
BRL/USD	1.7790 / 1.7792

Mehmet is also considering a carry trade involving the USD and the Euro. He anticipates it will generate a higher return than buying a one-year domestic note at the current market quote due to low U.S. interest rates and his predictions of exchange rates in one year. To help Mehmet assess the carry trade, Mehmet provides Smith with selected current market data and his one year forecasts in Exhibit 3.

Exhibit 3	Spot Rates and Interest Rates for Proposed Carry Trade			
Today's one-year LIBOR		Currency pair (Price/Base)	Spot rate today	Projected spot rate in one year
USD	0.80%	CAD/USD	1.0055	1.0006
CAD	1.71%	EUR/CAD	0.7218	0.7279
EUR	2.20%			

p. 525

---

1 This item set was developed by Greg Gocek, CFA (Downers Grove, IL, USA).

Finally, Mehmet asks Smith to assist with a trade involving a U.S. multinational customer operating in Europe and Japan. The customer is a very cost conscious industrial company with a AA credit rating and strives to execute its currency trades at the most favorable bid/offer spread. Because its Japanese subsidiary is about to close on a major European acquisition in three business days, the client wants to lock in a trade involving the Japanese yen and the Euro as early as possible the next morning, preferably by 8:05 AM New York time.

At lunch, Smith and other FX trainees discuss how best to analyze currency market volatility from ongoing financial crises. The group agrees that a theoretical explanation of exchange rate movements, such as the framework of the international parity conditions, should be applicable across all trading environments. They note such analysis should enable traders to anticipate future spot exchange rates. But they disagree on which parity condition best predicts exchange rates, voicing several different assessments. Smith concludes the discussion on parity conditions by stating to the trainees:

> "I believe that in the current environment both covered and uncovered interest rate parity conditions are in effect."

The conversation next shifts to exchange rate assessment tools, specifically the techniques of the IMF Consultative Group on Exchange Rate Issues (CGER). CGER uses a three-part approach including the Macroeconomic Balance Approach, the External Sustainability Approach, and a Reduced Form Econometric Model. Smith asks Trainee #1 to describe the three approaches. In response, Trainee #1 makes the following statements to the other trainees and Smith:

Statement 1   Macroeconomic Balance focuses on the stocks of outstanding assets and liabilities

Statement 2   Reduced Form has a weakness in underestimating future appreciation of undervalued currencies.

Statement 3   External Sustainability centers on adjustments leading to long-term equilibrium in the capital account.

1. Based upon Exhibit 1, the forward premium (discount) for a 360-day INR/GBP forward contract is *closest* to:

    A. −1.546.

    B. 1.546

    C. 1.576

2. Based on Exhibit 2, the *most* appropriate recommendation regarding the triangular arbitrage trade is to:

    A. decline the trade, no arbitrage profits are possible.

    B. execute the trade, buy BRL in the interbank market and sell it to the dealer.

    C. execute the trade, buy BRL from the dealer and sell it in the interbank market.

3. Based on Exhibit 3, the potential all-in USD return on the carry trade is *closest* to:

    A. 1.04%.

    B. 1.40%.

    C. 1.84%.

4. The factor *least likely* to lead to a narrow bid/offer spread for the industrial company's needed currency trade is the:

    A. timing of its trade.

B. company's credit rating.

C. pair of currencies involved.

5. If Smith's statement on parity conditions is correct, future spot exchange rates are *most likely* to be forecast by:

A. current spot rates.

B. forward exchange rates.

C. inflation rate differentials.

6. Which of the following statements given by Trainee #1 in describing the approaches used by CGER is *most* accurate?

A. Statement 1

B. Statement 2

C. Statement 3

The following information relates to Questions 7 – 13[2]

Connor Wagener, a student at the University of Canterbury in New Zealand, has been asked to prepare a presentation on foreign exchange rates for his International Business course. Wagener has a basic understanding of exchange rates, but would like a practitioner's perspective, and he has arranged an interview with currency trader Hannah McFadden. During the interview, Wagener asks McFadden:

> "Could you explain what drives exchange rates? I'm curious as to why our New Zealand dollar was affected by the European debt crisis in 2011 and what other factors impact it."

In response, McFadden begins with a general discussion of exchange rates. She notes that international parity conditions illustrate how exchange rates are linked to expected inflation, interest rate differences, and forward exchange rates as well as current and expected future spot rates. McFadden states:

Statement 1   "Fortunately, the international parity condition most relevant for FX carry trades does not always hold."

McFadden continues her discussion:

> "FX carry traders go long (i.e. buy) high-yield currencies and fund their position by shorting, that is borrowing in, low-yield currencies. Unfortunately, crashes in currency values can occur which create financial crises as traders unwind their positions. For example, in 2008, the New Zealand dollar was negatively impacted when highly leveraged carry trades were unwound. In addition to investors, consumers and business owners can also affect currency exchange rates through their impact on their country's balance of payments. For example, if New Zealand consumers purchase more goods from China than New Zealand businesses sell to China, New Zealand will run a trade account deficit with China." McFadden further explains:

Statement 2   "A trade surplus will tend to cause the currency of the country in surplus to appreciate while a deficit will cause currency depreciation. Exchange rate changes will result in immediate adjustments in the prices of traded goods as well as in the demand for imports and exports. These changes will immediately correct the trade imbalance."

---

2 This item set was developed by Sue Ryan, CFA (East Hartland, Connecticut, USA).

McFadden next addresses the influence of monetary and fiscal policy on exchange rates:

> "Countries also exert significant influence on exchange rates through both the initial mix of their fiscal and monetary policies, and also by subsequent adjustments to those policies. Various models have been developed to identify how these policies affect exchange rates. The Mundell-Fleming model addresses how changes in both fiscal and monetary policies affect interest rates and ultimately exchange rates in the short-term." McFadden describes monetary models by stating:

> Statement 3   "Monetary models of exchange rate determination focus on the effects of inflation, price level changes, and risk premium adjustments."

McFadden continues her discussion:

> "So far, we've touched on balance of payments and monetary policy. The portfolio-balance model addresses the impacts of sustained fiscal policy on exchange rates. I must take a client call, but will return shortly. In the meantime, here is some relevant literature on the models I mentioned along with a couple of questions for you to consider:

> Question 1   Assume an emerging market (EM) country has restrictive monetary and fiscal policies under low capital mobility conditions. Are these policies likely to lead to currency appreciation, currency depreciation, or to have no impact?

> Question 2   Assume a developed market (DM) country has an expansive fiscal policy under high capital mobility conditions. Why is its currency most likely to depreciate in the long-run under an integrated Mundell-Fleming and portfolio-balance approach?"

Upon her return, Wagener and McFadden review the questions. McFadden notes that capital flows can have a significant impact on exchange rates and have contributed to currency crises in both EM and DM countries. She explains that central banks, like the Reserve Bank of New Zealand, use FX market intervention as a tool to manage exchange rates. McFadden states:

> Statement 4   "Some studies have found that EM central banks tend to be more effective in using exchange rate invention than DM central banks, primarily because of one important factor."

McFadden continues her discussion:

> Statement 5   "I mentioned that capital inflows could cause a currency crisis, leaving fund managers with significant losses. In the period leading up to a currency crisis, I would predict that an affected country's:

> Prediction 1 foreign exchange reserves will increase.

> Prediction 2 broad money growth in nominal and real terms will increase.

> Prediction 3 real exchange rate will be substantially higher than its mean level during tranquil periods.

After the interview, McFadden agrees to meet the following week to discuss more recent events on the New Zealand dollar.

7. The international parity condition McFadden is referring to in Statement 1 is:

    A. purchasing power parity.

    B. covered interest rate parity.

    C. uncovered interest rate parity.

8. In Statement 2, McFadden is *most likely* failing to consider the:

   A. initial gap between the country's imports and exports.

   B. price elasticity of export demand versus import demand.

   C. lag in the response of import and export demand to price changes.

9. The *least* appropriate factor used to describe the type of models mentioned in Statement 3 is:

   A. inflation.

   B. price level changes.

   C. risk premium adjustments.

10. The best response to Question 1 is that the policies will:

    A. have no impact.

    B. lead to currency appreciation.

    C. lead to currency depreciation.

11. The most likely response to Question 2 is a(n):

    A. increase in the price level.

    B. decrease in risk premiums.

    C. increase in government debt.

12. The factor that McFadden is *most likely* referring to in Statement 4 is:

    A. FX reserve levels.

    B. domestic demand.

    C. the level of capital flows.

13. Which of McFadden's predictions in Statement 5 is *least correct*?

    A. Prediction 1

    B. Prediction 2

    C. Prediction 3

SOLUTIONS FOR READING 14

1. C is correct. The equation to calculate the forward premium (discount) is:

$$F_{f/d} - S_{f/d} = S_{f/d} \left(\frac{\left[\dfrac{Actual}{360} \right]}{1 + i_d \left[\dfrac{Actual}{360} \right]} \right) (i_f - i_d)$$

$S_{f/d}$ is the spot rate with GBP the base currency or d, and INR the foreign currency or f. $S_{f/d}$ per Exhibit 1 is 79.5093, i_f is equal to 7.52% and i_d is equal to 5.43%.

With GBP as the base currency (i.e. the "domestic" currency) in the INR/GBP quote, substituting in the relevant base currency values from Exhibit 1 yields the following:

$$F_{f/d} - S_{f/d} = 79.5093 \left(\frac{\left[\dfrac{360}{360} \right]}{1 + 0.0573 \left[\dfrac{360}{360} \right]} \right) (0.0752 - 0.0543)$$

$$F_{f/d} - S_{f/d} = 79.5093 \left(\frac{1}{1.0543} \right) (0.0752 - 0.0543)$$

$$F_{f/d} - S_{f/d} = 1.576$$

2. B is correct. The dealer is posting an offer rate to buy BRL at a price that is too high. This overpricing is determined by calculating the interbank implied cross rate for the CHF/BRL using the intuitive equation-based approach:

   CHF/BRL = CHF/USD × (BRL/USD)⁻¹, or

   CHF/BRL = CHF/USD × USD/BRL

   Inverting the BRL/USD given quotes in Exhibit 2 determines the USD/BRL bid/offer rates of 0.56205/0.56211 (The bid of 0.56205 is the inverse of the BRL/USD offer, calculated as 1/1.7792; the offer of 0.56211 is the inverse of the BRL/USD bid, calculated as 1/1.7790). Multiplying the CHF/USD and USD/BRL bid/offer rates then leads to the interbank implied CHF/BRL cross rate of:

   Bid: 0.9099 × 0.56205 = 0.5114

   Offer: 0.9101 × 0.56211 = 0.5116

   Since the dealer is willing to buy BRL at 0.5161 but BRL can be purchased from the interbank market at 0.5116, so there is an arbitrage opportunity to buy BRL in the interbank market and sell them to the dealer for a profit of 0.0045 CHF (0.5161 − 0.5116) per BRL transacted.

3. A is correct. The carry trade involves borrowing in a lower yielding currency to invest in a higher yielding one and netting any profit after allowing for borrowing costs and exchange rate movements. The relevant trade is to borrow USD and lend in Euros. To calculate the all-in USD return from a one-year EUR LIBOR deposit, first determine the current and one-year later USD/EUR exchange rates. Because one USD buys CAD 1.0055 today, and one CAD buys EUR 0.7218 today, today's EUR/USD rate is the product of these two numbers: 1.0055 × 0.7218 = 0.7258. The projected rate one year later is: 1.0006 × 0.7279 = 0.7283. Accordingly, measured in dollars, the investment return for the unhedged EUR LIBOR deposit is equal to:

[handwritten margin note: ← p. 525 has reciprocal of first term, not third !]

$$(1.0055 \times 0.7218) \times (1 + 0.022) \times \left[1 / (1.0006 \times 0.7279) \right]$$
$$= 0.7258 \times (1.022)(1 / 0.7283) = 1.0184 - 1 = 1.84\%$$

[handwritten note: 1.022 × (0.7258 / 0.7283)]

However, the borrowing costs must be charged against this <u>gross</u> return to fund the carry trade investment (one-year USD LIBOR was 0.80%). The <u>net</u> return on the carry trade is thereby closest to: 1.84% − 0.80% = 1.04%.

4. B is correct. While credit ratings can affect spreads, the trade involves spot settlement, i.e. two business days after the trade date, so the spread quoted to this highly rated (AA) firm is not likely to be much tighter than the spread that would be quoted to a somewhat lower rated (but still high quality) firm. The relationship between the bank and client, the size of the trade, the time of day the trade is initiated, the currencies involved and the level of market volatility are likely to be more significant factors in determining the spread for this trade.

5. B is correct. By rearranging the terms of the equation defining covered interest rate parity, and assuming that uncovered interest rate parity is in effect, the forward exchange rate is equal to the expected future spot exchange rate, $F_{f/d} = S^e_{f/d}$, with the expected percentage change in the spot rate equal to the interest rate differential. Thus, the forward exchange rate is an unbiased forecast of the future spot exchange rate.

6. C is correct. The External Sustainability Approach deals with stocks (i.e. levels of) outstanding assets or debt and the financial flows associated with the capital account. The comment correctly states the External Sustainability Approach focuses on adjustments resulting in long-term equilibrium in the capital account.

7. C is correct. The carry trade strategy is dependent upon the fact that uncovered interest rate parity does not hold in the short or medium term. If uncovered interest rate parity held, it would mean that investors would receive identical returns from either an unhedged foreign currency investment or a domestic currency investment because the appreciation/depreciation of the exchange rate would offset the yield differential. However, during periods of low volatility, evidence shows that high yield currencies do not depreciate enough and low yield currencies do not appreciate enough to offset the yield differential.

8. C is correct. McFadden states that exchange rates will *immediately* correct the trade imbalance. She is describing the Flow Supply/Demand Channel, which assumes that trade imbalances will be corrected as the deficit country's currency depreciates, causing its exports to become more competitive and its imports to become more expensive. Studies indicate that there can be long lags between exchange rate changes, changes in the prices of traded goods and changes in the trade balance. In the short-run, exchange rates tend to be more responsive to investment and financing decisions.

9. C is correct. Risk premiums are more closely associated with the portfolio-balance approach. The portfolio balance approach addresses the impact of a country's net foreign asset/liability position. Under the portfolio balance approach, investors are assumed to hold a diversified portfolio of assets including foreign and domestic bonds. Investors will hold a country's bonds as long as they are compensated appropriately. Compensation may come in the form of higher interest rates and/or higher risk premium.

10. B is correct. The currency is likely to appreciate. The emerging market country has both a restrictive monetary policy and restrictive fiscal policy under conditions of low capital mobility. Low capital mobility indicates that interest

rate changes induced by monetary and fiscal policy will not cause large changes in capital flows. Implementation of restrictive policies should result in an improvement in the trade balance, which will result in currency appreciation.

11. C is correct. Expansionary fiscal policies result in currency depreciation in the long run. Under a portfolio-balance approach, the assumption is that investors hold a mix of domestic and foreign assets including bonds. Fiscal stimulus policies result in budget deficits which are often financed by debt. As the debt level rises, investors become concerned as to how the on-going deficit will be financed. The country's central bank may need to create more money in order to purchase the debt which would cause the currency to depreciate. Or, the government could adopt a more restrictive fiscal policy, which would also depreciate the currency.

12. A is correct. EM countries are better able to influence their exchange rates because their reserve levels as a ratio to average daily FX turnover are generally much greater than those of DM countries. This means that EM central banks are in a better position to affect currency supply and demand than DM countries where the ratio is negligible. EM policymakers use their foreign exchange reserves as a kind of insurance to defend their currencies, as needed.

15

Economic Growth and the Investment Decision

by Paul Kutasovic, CFA

LEARNING OUTCOMES

Mastery	The candidate should be able to:
☐	**a** describe and compare factors favoring and limiting economic growth in developed and developing economies;
☐	**b** describe the relation between the long-run rate of stock market appreciation and the sustainable growth rate of the economy;
☐	**c** explain the importance of potential GDP and its growth rate in the investment decisions of equity and fixed income investors;
☐	**d** distinguish between capital deepening investment and technological process and explain the impact of each on economic growth and labor productivity;
☐	**e** forecast potential GDP based on growth accounting relations;
☐	**f** explain the impact of natural resources on economic growth and evaluate the argument that limited availability of natural resources constrains economic growth;
☐	**g** explain the effects of demographics, immigration, and labor force participation on the rate and sustainability of economic growth;
☐	**h** explain how investment in physical capital, human capital, and technological development affects economic growth;
☐	**i** compare classical growth theory, neoclassical growth theory, and endogenous growth theory;
☐	**j** explain and evaluate convergence hypotheses;
☐	**k** explain the economic rationale for governments to provide incentives to private investment in technology and knowledge;
☐	**l** describe the expected impact of removing trade barriers on capital investment and profits, employment and wages, and growth in the economies involved.

1 INTRODUCTION

Forecasts of long-run economic growth are important for global investors. Equity prices reflect expectations of the future stream of earnings, which depend on expectations of future economic activity. This means that in the long term, the same factors that drive economic growth will be reflected in equity values. Similarly, the expected long-run growth rate of real income is a key determinant of the average real interest rate level in the economy, and therefore the level of real returns in general. In the shorter term, the relationship between actual and potential growth (i.e., the degree of slack in the economy) is a key driver of fixed income returns. Therefore, in order to develop global portfolio strategies and investment return expectations, investors must be able to identify and forecast the factors that drive long-term sustainable growth trends. Based on a country's long-term economic outlook, investors can then evaluate the long-term investment potential and risk of investing in the securities of companies located or operating in that country.

In contrast to the short-run fluctuations of the business cycle, the study of economic growth focuses on the long-run trend in aggregate output as measured by potential GDP. Over long periods of time, the actual growth rate of GDP should equal the rate of increase in potential GDP because, by definition, output in excess of potential GDP requires employing labor and capital beyond their optimum levels. Thus, the growth rate of potential GDP acts as an upper limit to growth and determines the economy's sustainable rate of growth. Increasing the growth rate of potential GDP is the key to raising the level of income, the level of profits, and the living standard of the population. Even small differences in the growth rate translate into large differences in the level of income over time.

What drives long-run growth? What distinguishes the "winners" from the "losers" in the long-run growth arena? Will poor countries catch up with rich countries over time? Can policies have a permanent effect on the sustainable growth rate? If so, how? If not, why not? These and other key questions are addressed in detail in this reading.

The reading is organized as follows: Section 2 examines the long-term growth record, focusing on the extent of growth variation across countries and across decades. Section 3 discusses the importance of economic growth to global investors and examines the relationship between investment returns and economic growth. Section 4 examines the factors that determine long-run economic growth. Section 5 presents the classical, neoclassical, and endogenous growth models. It also discusses whether poorer countries are converging to the higher income levels of the richer countries. Finally, Section 6 looks at the impact of international trade on economic growth. A summary and practice problems complete the reading.

2 GROWTH IN THE GLOBAL ECONOMY: DEVELOPED VS. DEVELOPING COUNTRIES

The first step in our study of long-term growth is to compare the economic performance of countries. GDP and per capita GDP are the best indicators economists have for measuring a country's standard of living and its level of economic development. Economic growth is calculated as the annual percentage change in real GDP or in real per capita GDP. Growth in real GDP measures how rapidly the total economy is expanding. Real per capita GDP reflects the average standard of living in each country—essentially the average level of material well-being. Growth in real GDP per capita (i.e., real GDP growing faster than the population) implies a rising standard of living.

Exhibit 1 presents data on the level of per capita GDP and the growth rate of GDP for various countries. Because each country reports its data in its own currency, each country's data must be converted into a common currency, usually the U.S. dollar. One can convert the GDP data into dollars using either current market exchange rates or the exchange rates implied by **purchasing power parity (PPP)**. Purchasing power parity is the idea that exchange rates move to equalize the purchasing power of different currencies. At the exchange rates implied by PPP, the cost of a typical basket of goods and services is the same across all countries. In other words, exchange rates should be at a level where you can buy the same goods and services with the equivalent amount of any country's currency.

| Exhibit 1 | Divergent Real GDP Growth among Countries |

	Average Annual Real GDP Growth (percent)				Real GDP Per Capita in Dollars[a]			
	1971–1980	1981–1990	1991–2000	2001–2010	1950	1970	1990	2010
Advanced Economies	3.2	3.1	2.8	1.6				
Canada	4.0	2.8	2.4	1.8	$12,053	$19,919	$31,1969	$41,288
United States	3.1	2.9	3.4	1.6	14,559	22,806	35,328	46,697
France	2.9	2.4	1.7	1.2	8,266	18,186	28,127	34,358
Germany	2.7	2.3	2.3	0.9	na	na	28,624	37,367
Ireland	4.7	3.9	7.1	2.6	5,496	9,869	18,812	36,433
Italy	3.4	2.2	1.7	0.3	5,954	16,522	27,734	31,069
Spain	3.0	3.0	2.9	2.1	3,964	11,444	21,830	30,504
United Kingdom	1.6	2.7	2.8	1.5	11,602	18,002	27,469	37,378
Hong Kong	9.2	6.5	3.9	4.1	3,128	8,031	24,734	43,324
Japan	4.3	4.0	1.3	0.8	3,048	15,413	29,813	34,828
Singapore	10.5	7.3	7.3	5.6	4,299	8,600	27,550	56,224
South Korea	7.4	9.1	7.2	4.2	1,185	3,009	12,083	30,079
Taiwan	10.9	7.9	6.5	3.8	1,425	3,948	15,465	36,413
Australia	3.2	3.3	3.4	3.0	13,219	21,444	30,628	45,951
New Zealand	1.6	2.5	2.9	2.3	13,795	18,255	22,331	31,223
Developing Countries	4.3	4.2	5.4	6.3				
Developing Asia	6.2	6.9	7.4	8.5				
China	10.4	9.1	10.4	10.5	402	698	1,677	8,569
India	3.9	5.9	5.6	7.5	658	922	1,390	3,575
Indonesia	8.4	5.4	4.0	5.2	804	1,182	2,517	4,740
Pakistan	4.5	6.0	3.9	4.8	666	985	1,645	2,600
Philippines	6.6	1.7	3.0	4.7	1,296	2,136	2,660	3,672
Vietnam	4.7	5.9	7.6	7.3	689	770	1,073	3,369
Middle East	2.9	3.0	4.0	4.9				
Egypt	5.9	5.9	4.4	4.9	1,132	1,560	3,137	5,306
Turkey	4.1	5.2	3.6	4.0	2,327	4,413	7,741	11,769
Saudi Arabia	11.0	1.7	2.7	3.3	5,060	17,292	20,399	22,951

(continued)

Exhibit 1	Continued

	Average Annual Real GDP Growth (percent)				Real GDP Per Capita in Dollars[a]			
	1971–1980	1981–1990	1991–2000	2001–2010	1950	1970	1990	2010
Latin America	6.5	1.6	3.3	3.4				
Argentina	2.9	−1.2	4.2	4.6	6,164	9,026	7,952	13,468
Brazil	8.8	1.5	2.5	3.6	2,365	4,324	6,959	9,589
Mexico	6.6	1.8	3.5	1.8	4,180	7,634	10,754	13,710
Peru	7.6	−0.8	4.0	5.7	3,464	5,786	4,516	8,671
Venezuela	1.6	1.9	2.1	3.5	8,104	11,590	9,028	10,560
Africa	3.5	2.5	2.4	5.7				
Botswana	17.1	10.9	6.4	4.2	449	774	3,731	5,311
Ethiopia	3.0	1.9	2.9	8.4	314	479	462	749
Kenya	7.4	4.3	1.7	4.1	791	1,113	1,359	1,376
Nigeria	7.4	2.0	1.9	8.7	814	1,183	1,203	2,037
South Africa	4.1	1.5	1.8	3.5	4,361	6,959	6,595	8,716

[a] The measure of GDP per capita is in constant U.S. dollar market prices for 2010 and adjusted for cross-country differences in the relative prices of goods and services using purchasing power parity (PPP).
Sources: International Monetary Fund, World Economic Outlook database for growth rates, and Conference Board, Total Economy Database (September 2011).

In general, the simple method of taking a country's GDP measured in its own currency and then multiplying by the current exchange rate to express it in another currency is not appropriate. Using market exchange rates has two problems. First, market exchange rates are very volatile. Changes in the exchange rate could result in large swings in measured GDP even if there is little or no growth in the country's economy. Second, market exchange rates are determined by financial flows and flows in tradable goods and services. This ignores the fact that much of global consumption is for non-tradable goods and services. Prices of non-traded goods and services differ by country. In particular, non-traded goods are generally less expensive in developing countries than in developed countries. For example, because labor is cheaper in Mexico City than in London, the prices of labor-intensive products, such as haircuts or taxi rides, are lower in Mexico City than in London. Failing to account for differences in the prices of non-traded goods and services across countries tends to understate the standard of living of consumers in developing countries. To compare standards of living across time or across countries, we need to use a common set of prices among a wide range of goods and services. Thus, cross-country comparisons of GDP should be based on purchasing power parity rather than current market exchange rates.

The countries in Exhibit 1 are divided into two categories, developed (or advanced) countries and developing countries. Developed countries are those with high per capita GDP.[1] These include the United States, Canada, Australia, Japan, and major economies in Europe. Growth in the large, developed economies generally slowed over the last few decades, with U.S. growth exceeding that of Europe and Japan. Also included in this group are such markets as Taiwan, South Korea, Singapore, Ireland, and Spain, which were poor in the 1950s but now have relatively high per capita real GDPs because of high rates of growth over the past 50 years.

---

1 There are no universally agreed upon criteria for classifying countries as advanced or developing. The International Monetary Fund (IMF) classifies 34 countries as advanced and 150 as developing. It says that "this classification is not based on strict criteria, economic or otherwise, and has evolved over time" (IMF 2011).

The second group of countries is the developing countries of Africa, Asia, and Latin America. Per capita GDP in these countries is lower than in the advanced countries, but GDP is generally growing at a faster rate than in the developed countries. Although the growth rates of the developing countries exceed those of the advanced countries, there is significant variation in economic performance among the developing countries. China and India are growing at a rapid rate. Between 1991 and 2010, the Chinese and Indian economies expanded at annual rates of 10.5 percent and 6.6 percent, respectively, compared with U.S. growth of 2.5 percent per year over this period. Meanwhile, growth in Latin America, Africa, and the Middle East has lagged behind Asia.

What explains the diverse experiences among the developing countries and between the developed and developing ones? Singapore, for example, had less than half the per capita GDP of the United States in 1970 but now has per capita GDP that exceeds that of the United States. South Korea and Taiwan have gone from among the poorest economies in the world to among the richest in one generation. In contrast, such countries as Ethiopia and Kenya have remained poor, with little growth in per capita GDP. The literature on economic growth focuses primarily on the role of capital and labor resources and the use of technology as sources of growth. In addition to these purely economic drivers, developed and developing countries differ with respect to the presence or absence of appropriate institutions that support growth. These institutions enable developing countries to raise their standards of living and eventually move into the ranks of the developed countries. We now examine some of the key institutions and requirements for growth.

2.1 Savings and Investment

One of the major problems for some of the developing countries is a low level of capital per worker. Countries accumulate capital through private and public sector (e.g., infrastructure) investment. But increasing the investment rate may be difficult in developing countries because low levels of disposable income can make it difficult to generate significant saving. The low saving rate contributes to a vicious cycle of poverty: Low savings lead to low levels of investment, which leads to slow GDP growth, which implies persistently low income and savings. Therefore, it is very difficult to design policies to increase domestic saving and investment rates in developing countries. The good news is that the savings of domestic residents are not the only source of investment funds. A developing country can break out of the cycle of low savings by attracting foreign investment.

2.2 Financial Markets and Intermediaries

In addition to the saving rate, growth depends on how efficiently saving is allocated within the economy. A role of the financial sector in any economy is to channel funds from savers to investment projects. Financial markets and intermediaries, such as banks, can promote growth in at least three ways. First, by screening those who seek funding and monitoring those who obtain funding, the financial sector channels financial capital (savings) to projects that are likely to generate the highest risk-adjusted returns. Second, the financial sector may encourage savings and assumption of risk by creating attractive investment instruments that facilitate risk transfer and diversification and enhance liquidity. Finally, the existence of well-developed financial markets and intermediaries can mitigate the credit constraints that companies might otherwise face in financing capital investments. For example, banks can aggregate small amounts of savings into a larger pool enabling them to finance larger projects that can exploit economies of scale. Evidence suggests that countries with better-functioning financial markets and intermediaries grow at a faster rate.[2] However, not all financial sector developments promote economic growth. Financial sector intermediation that results in declining credit standards and/or increasing leverage will increase risk and not necessarily increase long-run growth.

2.3 Political Stability, Rule of Law, and Property Rights

Stable and effective government, a well-developed legal and regulatory system, and respect for property rights are key ingredients for economic growth. Property rights are the legal arrangements that govern the protection of private property, including intellectual property. Clearly established property rights create the incentive for domestic households and companies to invest and save. A legal system—substantive and procedural laws[3]—is needed to establish and protect these rights. In developed countries these rights and arrangements are well established, but they may be lacking or ineffective in developing countries.

In addition, economic uncertainty increases when wars, military coups, corruption, and other sources of political instability are widespread. These factors raise investment risk, discourage foreign investment, and weaken growth. In many developing countries, especially those in Africa, the first priority in trying to enhance growth is to enact a legal system that establishes, protects, and enforces property rights.

2.4 Education and Health Care Systems

Inadequate education at all levels is a major impediment to growth for many developing countries. Many workers are illiterate, and few workers have the skills needed to use the latest technology. At the same time, many developing countries also suffer from a "brain drain," where the most highly educated individuals leave the developing country for the advanced countries. Basic education raises the skill level of the workforce and thus contributes to the country's potential for growth. In addition, because physical capital and human capital are often complementary, education can raise growth by increasing the productivity of existing physical capital. Thus, improving education, through both formal schooling and on-the-job training, is an important component of a sustainable growth strategy for a developing country. China and India are investing large amounts in education and have successfully graduated large numbers of students majoring in engineering and technology-related areas of study. This effort is significantly improving the quality of their workforces.

Empirical studies show that the allocation of education spending among different types and levels (primary, secondary, and post-secondary) of education is a key determinant of growth, especially in comparing growth in the developed countries with growth in the developing ones. The impact of education spending depends on whether the country is on the leading edge of technology and fostering innovation or simply relying on imitation as a source of growth. Typically, developed countries, such as the United States, Japan and western European nations, are on the leading edge of technology and need to invest in post-secondary education to encourage innovation and growth. For these countries, incremental spending on primary and secondary education will have a smaller impact on growth. In contrast, the developing countries, which largely apply technology developed elsewhere, should emphasize primary and secondary education. Such spending will improve growth by improving the countries' ability to absorb new technologies and to organize existing tasks more efficiently.

---

2 Levine (2005).
3 Substantive law focuses on the rights and responsibilities of entities and relationships among entities, and procedural law focuses on the protection and enforcement of the substantive laws.

Poor health is another obstacle to growth in the developing countries. Life expectancy rates are substantially lower in many developing countries. In Africa, tropical diseases are rampant and AIDS has had a devastating impact. As is evident in Exhibit 1, the growth rate of GDP in Botswana, a huge success story in the 1970s and 1980s, has slowed dramatically over the last two decades due, at least in part, to the AIDS epidemic.

2.5 Tax and Regulatory Systems

Tax and regulatory policies have an important impact on growth and productivity, especially at the company level. Analysis suggests that limited regulations encourage entrepreneurial activity and the entry of new companies. There is also a strong positive correlation between the entry of new companies and average productivity levels. Studies by the Organisation for Economic Co-Operation and Development (OECD) indicate that low administrative start-up cost is a key factor encouraging entrepreneurship.[4]

2.6 Free Trade and Unrestricted Capital Flows

Opening an economy to capital and trade flows has a major impact on economic growth. In an open economy, world savings can finance domestic investment. As a potential source of funds, foreign investment can break the vicious cycle of low income, low domestic savings, and low investment. Foreign investment can occur in two ways:

- Foreign companies can invest directly in a domestic economy (so-called foreign direct investment, or FDI) by building or buying property, plant, and equipment.

- Foreign companies and individuals can invest indirectly in a domestic economy by purchasing securities (equity and fixed income) issued by domestic companies.

Both of these forms of foreign investment will potentially increase the developing economy's physical capital stock, leading to higher productivity, employment and wages, and perhaps even increased domestic savings. This suggests that developing countries would benefit from policies that encourage investment from abroad, such as eliminating high tariffs on foreign imports (especially capital goods) and removing restrictions on foreign direct and indirect investments.

Brazil and India are examples of developing countries that have benefited from foreign investment. Foreign companies directly invested $48.5 billion in Brazil in 2010, an important source of investment spending for the Brazilian economy (see Exhibit 19 in Section 6). Foreign direct investment also provides developing countries with access to advanced technology developed and used in the advanced countries. In 1999, India enacted new regulations that liberalized direct and indirect foreign investments in Indian companies. Foreign institutional and venture capital investors were given greater flexibility to invest directly in Indian entities as well as in the Indian capital markets. These changes also made it easier for foreign companies to invest in plant and equipment. These developments contributed to the acceleration in India's economic growth over the last decade (see Exhibit 1).

Capital flows are just one way that the international economy affects economic growth. The other is through trade in goods and services. In general, free trade benefits an economy by providing its residents with more goods at lower costs. Domestic companies face increased competition, which limits their price discretion, but they also obtain access to larger markets. The evidence of the benefits of open markets is discussed later in the reading.

---

4 OECD (2003).

2.7 Summary of Factors Limiting Growth in Developing Countries

Developing countries differ significantly from developed countries in terms of their institutional structure and their legal and political environments. Lack of appropriate institutions and poor legal and political environments restrain growth in the developing economies and partially explain why these countries are poor and experience slow growth. Factors limiting growth include the following:

- Low rates of saving and investment
- Poorly developed financial markets
- Weak, or even corrupt, legal systems and failure to enforce laws
- Lack of property rights and political instability
- Poor public education and health services
- Tax and regulatory polices discouraging entrepreneurship
- Restrictions on international trade and flows of capital

Although these factors are not necessarily absent in developed countries, they tend to be more prevalent in developing countries. Policies that correct these issues, or mitigate their impact, enhance the potential for growth. In addition to these institutional restraints, as we will see in Section 4, growth in developing countries may be limited by a lack of physical, human, and public capital, as well as little or no innovation.

Example 1

Why Growth Rates Matter[a]

In 1950, Argentina and Venezuela were relatively wealthy countries with per capita levels of GDP of $6,164 and $8,104, respectively. Per capita GDPs in these Latin American countries were well above those of Japan, South Korea, and Singapore, which had per capita GDPs of $3,048, $1,185, and $4,299, respectively. By 2010, however, a dramatic change occurred in the relative GDPs per capita of these countries.

	Real GDP Per Capita in Dollars				
	Venezuela	**Argentina**	**Singapore**	**Japan**	**South Korea**
1950	$8,104	$6,164	$4,299	$3,048	$1,185
2010	$10,560	$13,468	$56,224	$34,828	$30,079

1. Calculate the annual growth rate in per capita GDP for each of the five countries over the period 1950–2010.

2. Explain the implication of the growth rates for these countries.

3. Suppose that GDP per capita in Argentina had grown at the same rate as in Japan from 1950 to 2010. How much larger would real per capita GDP have been in Argentina in 2010?

4. Venezuela plans to stimulate growth in its economy by substantially increasing spending on infrastructure, education, and health care. Nevertheless, foreign investment is discouraged, and reforms like

strengthening the legal system and encouraging private ownership have been largely ignored. Explain whether the measures described above could lead to faster economic growth.

Solution to 1:

The annual growth rates for the five countries are calculated as follows:

Argentina	$[(\$13,468/\$6,164)^{1/60}] - 1 = 1.31\%$
Venezuela	$[(\$10,560/\$8,104)^{1/60}] - 1 = 0.44\%$
Japan	$[(\$34,828/\$3,048)^{1/60}] - 1 = 4.14\%$
Singapore	$[(\$56,224/\$4,299)^{1/60}] - 1 = 4.38\%$
South Korea	$[(\$30,079/\$1,185)^{1/60}] - 1 = 5.54\%$

Solution to 2:

Differences in GDP growth rates sustained over a number of decades will significantly alter the relative incomes of countries. Nations that experience sustained periods of high growth will eventually become high-income countries and move up the income ladder. In contrast, countries with slow growth will experience relative declines in living standards. This is well illustrated in this example by a historic comparison of growth in Argentina and Venezuela with Japan, Singapore, and South Korea. In 1950, Argentina and Venezuela were relatively wealthy countries with per capita levels of GDP well above that of Japan, South Korea, and Singapore. Over the next 60 years, however, the rate of growth in per capita GDP was significantly slower in Venezuela and Argentina in comparison to the three Asian countries. This resulted in a dramatic change in the relative incomes of these countries. The per capita GDP of the three Asian countries rose sharply as each joined the ranks of developed countries. In contrast, Argentina and Venezuela stagnated and moved from the ranks of developed countries to developing country status. By 2010, per capita income in Singapore was more than five times higher than in Venezuela.

Over the long run, the rate of economic growth is an extremely important variable. Even small differences in growth rates matter because of the power of compounding. Thus, policy actions that affect the long-term growth rate even by a small amount will have a major economic impact.

Solution to 3:

Assuming Argentina had grown at the same rate as Japan since 1950, its GDP per capita in 2010 would have been $(\$6,164)(1 + 0.0414)^{60} = (\$6,164)(11.404) = \$70,294$, versus $13,468 from Exhibit 1.

If Argentina had grown at the same rate as Japan, it would have had by far the highest standard of living in the world in 2010. The question is why the growth rates in Argentina and Venezuela diverged so much from the three Asian countries.

Solution to 4:

The preconditions for economic growth are well-functioning financial markets, clearly defined property rights and rule of law, open international trade and flows of capital, an educated and healthy population, and tax and regulatory policies that encourage entrepreneurship. Investment in infrastructure would increase Venezuela's stock of physical capital, which would raise labor productivity and growth. Better education and health care would increase human capital and also increase productivity and growth. These measures would raise the growth prospects for Venezuela. However, what is missing is a legal system that could better enforce property rights, openness to international trade and foreign investment, and well-functioning capital markets. Without changes in these preconditions, a significant improvement in growth is unlikely to occur. The preconditions are summarized below:

Preconditions for Growth:	Impact of Planned Policy Action in Venezuela:
Saving and investment	Improve growth potential
Developed financial markets	No impact
Legal systems	No impact
Property rights and political stability	No impact
Education and health	Improve growth potential
Tax and regulatory polices discouraging entrepreneurship	No impact
Restrictions on international trade and flows of capital	No impact

[a] It should be noted that the global economy is evolving rapidly and past trends may or may not be sustained. Nonetheless, in order to provide concrete answers that do not require the reader to bring in additional information, our exercise solutions must assume past patterns are indicative of the future.

3   WHY POTENTIAL GROWTH MATTERS TO INVESTORS

The valuations of both equity and fixed income securities are closely related to the growth rate of economic activity. Anticipated growth in aggregate earnings is a fundamental driver of the equity market. Growth in an economy's productive capacity, measured by **potential GDP**, places a limit on how fast the economy can grow. The idea is that potential GDP is the maximum amount of output an economy can sustainably produce without inducing an increase in the inflation rate. A key question for equity investors, therefore, is whether earnings growth is also bounded or limited by the growth rate of potential GDP.

For earnings growth to exceed GDP growth, the ratio of corporate profits to GDP must trend upward over time. It should be clear that the share of profits in GDP cannot rise forever. At some point, stagnant labor income would make workers unwilling to work and would also undermine demand, making further profit growth unsustainable. Thus, in the long run, real earnings growth cannot exceed the growth rate of potential GDP.[5] Exhibit 2 illustrates the long-run stability of after-tax profits as a share of GDP using U.S. data derived from the National Income and Product Accounts (NIPA). The chart shows that since 1947, after-tax profits have ranged between 3.1 percent and 10.1 percent of GDP and have averaged around 6 percent of GDP. Note that there is neither an upward trend in the ratio of after-tax profits to GDP nor a move to a permanent increase in the ratio. The share of profits in 1947, at 8.5 percent, was essentially equal

---

5 Earnings growth for the overall national economy can differ from the growth of earnings per share in a country's equity market composites. This is due to the presence of new businesses that are not yet included in the equity indices and are typically growing at a faster rate than the mature companies that make up the composites. Thus, the earnings growth rate of companies making up the composites should be lower than the earnings growth rate for the overall economy.

to the 9.4 percent share at the end of the period in 2010. Because there is no trend in the ratio, the same factors that limit economic growth also set the upper limit or bound on the long-run growth of aggregate earnings.

Exhibit 2	U.S. After-Tax Corporate Profits as a Percentage of GDP

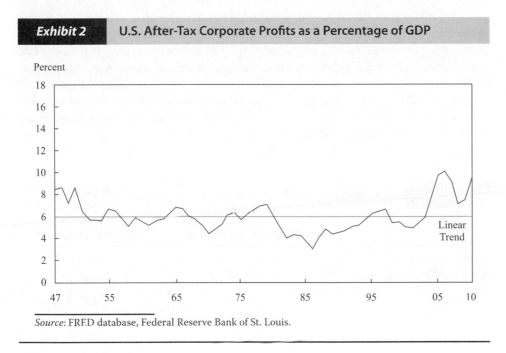

Source: FRED database, Federal Reserve Bank of St. Louis.

To examine the relationship between economic growth and stock prices, it is useful to express the aggregate value of the stock market as the product of key ratios. Letting P represent the aggregate value (price) of equities and E represent aggregate earnings, we can write:

$$P = GDP\left(\frac{E}{GDP}\right)\left(\frac{P}{E}\right)$$

This equation represents the aggregate value of equities as the product of GDP, corporate earnings as a share of GDP, and the price-to-earnings ratio for the market. Note that GDP may be interpreted as either real or nominal with a corresponding real or nominal interpretation of the other variables.

This equation can be expressed in terms of logarithmic rates of change over a time horizon T:

$$(1/T)\,\%\Delta P = (1/T)\%\Delta GDP + (1/T)\%\Delta(E/GDP) + (1/T)\%\Delta(P/E)$$

Thus, the percentage change in stock market value equals the percentage change in GDP plus the percentage change in the share of earnings (profit) in GDP plus the percentage change in the price-to-earnings multiple.[6] Over short to immediate horizons, all three of these factors contribute to appreciation or depreciation of the stock market. In the long run, however, the growth rate of GDP must dominate. As noted above, the ratio of earnings to GDP cannot rise forever. It cannot decline forever either because unprofitable businesses will disappear. Hence, the second term in the equation above must be approximately zero over long horizons (T). Similarly, the price-to-earnings ratio cannot grow or contract forever because investors will not pay

---

6 For simplicity, we have not explicitly incorporated issuance or repurchasing of shares. To do so, we would simply need to distinguish between aggregate stock market value and price per share. However, this would not alter our conclusions. Similarly, we could incorporate the dividend payout ratio into our argument, but again, this would not alter our conclusions.

an arbitrarily large price for a unit of earnings, nor will they give away earnings for nothing. Hence, the third term must also be approximately zero over long horizons. The conclusion is that the drivers of potential GDP are ultimately the drivers of stock market price performance.

Exhibit 3 shows the close relationship between economic growth and equity market appreciation over long horizons. Over the period 1946–2007, the S&P 500 Index returned 10.82 percent per year, of which 7.15 percent per year came from price appreciation. The price appreciation was almost exactly equal to the 6.95 percent growth rate of U.S. nominal GDP (real GDP growth plus inflation). Changes in the earnings-to-GDP and price-to-earnings ratios contributed only a combined 0.20 percent per year. As shown in the last column of the exhibit, these two ratios contributed much more to the volatility of the market than to its return.[7]

Exhibit 3	Decomposition of S&P 500 Returns: Log Returns, 1946–2007	
	Annual Return/Growth Rate	**Standard Deviation**
S&P 500 return	10.82%	15.31%
Real GDP growth	3.01	2.97
Inflation	3.94	3.29
EPS/GDP	−0.12	17.62
P/E	0.32	23.80
Dividend yield	3.67	1.49
Total	10.82	

Source: Stewart, Piros, and Heisler (2011).

Estimates of potential GDP and its growth rate are widely available. For example, both the OECD and the International Monetary Fund (IMF) provide such estimates as a basis for their intermediate-term and long-term forecasts of economic growth by country. In addition, central banks regularly make projections of potential GDP. The methods used to estimate potential GDP are examined later in the reading. The data in Exhibit 1 illustrate that simply extrapolating past GDP growth into the future may produce an incorrect forecast. A country's GDP growth rate can and does change over time. GDP growth can either slow down, as was the case for Japan (compare 1971–1990 with 1991–2010), or speed up, as was the case for Brazil over the last decade. Factors or policies that cause potential growth to increase or decrease by even a small amount will have a large impact on living standards and the future level of economic activity. The effect is analogous to the rate of return on a portfolio, where small differences in return compounded over many years result in a substantially higher or lower value for the portfolio. Being able to recognize these changes is critical for the global investor.

Estimates of an economy's growth potential are also relevant for global fixed income investors. One of the uses of potential GDP is to gauge inflationary pressures in the economy. Actual GDP growth above (below) the potential growth rate puts upward

---

7 It should be noted that the 1946–2007 time period was chosen because both endpoints correspond to fairly normal economic and market conditions. Selecting endpoints that correspond to crisis or bubble conditions would distort the role played by the various components of return.

(downward) pressure on inflation, which puts corresponding pressure on nominal interest rates and bond prices.[8]

The growth rate of potential GDP is also an important determinant of the level of real interest rates, and therefore real asset returns in general, in the economy. The real interest rate is essentially the real return that consumers/savers demand in exchange for postponing consumption. Faster growth in potential GDP means that consumers expect their real income to rise more rapidly. This implies that an extra unit of future income/consumption is less valuable than it would be if income were expected to grow more slowly. Hence, all else equal, the real interest rate will have to be higher in order to induce the savings needed to fund required capital accumulation. Thus, higher rates of potential GDP growth translate into higher real interest rates and higher expected real asset returns in general.

Potential GDP and its growth rate enter into fixed income analysis in other ways as well. Among them are the following:

1. A higher rate of potential GDP growth improves the general credit quality of fixed income securities because most such securities are ultimately backed by a flow of income even if the lender has a claim on specific underlying assets.

2. Central banks frequently explain their monetary policy decisions by referring to the level of "resource utilization" and the degree of "slack in the economy." In other words, monetary policy decisions are affected by the difference between an economy's estimated potential output and its actual operating level (referred to as the output gap) and by growth of actual GDP relative to the sustainable growth rate. Thus, fixed income investors need to closely monitor the output gap and growth rates of actual and potential GDP to assess the likelihood of a change in central bank policy.

3. Credit rating agencies use the growth rate of potential GDP as an input in evaluating the credit risk of sovereign debt or government-issued debt. All else equal, slower estimated potential GDP growth raises the perceived risk of these bonds.

4. Government budget deficits typically increase during recessions and decrease during expansions. In examining fiscal policy, actual fiscal positions are often judged relative to structural or cyclically adjusted deficits—the budgetary balance that would exist if the economy were operating at potential GDP.

Example 2

Impact on Equity and Fixed Income Investors

Your firm subscribes to asset class risk and return estimates generated by a large pension consultant. The equity market return estimates are based primarily on long-term average index returns. Following a multi-year period of very high equity returns driven by unusually high earnings growth and expanding P/E multiples, capital's share of total income as well as valuation multiples are near all-time highs. Based on the latest data, the vendor projects that your domestic equity market will return 13.5 percent per year—11 percent annual appreciation and 2.5 percent dividend yield—forever.

Your firm also subscribes to a macroeconomic forecasting service that provides, in addition to shorter-term projections, estimates of the long-term growth rate of potential GDP and the long-term inflation rate. This service forecasts

---

[8] Note that this is an argument about cyclical variations in growth and inflation around the economy's long-term potential growth rate. It does not imply that there is a long-run trade-off between growth and inflation.

3.25 percent real growth in the future and 3.75 percent inflation, down from 4.0 percent and 5.0 percent, respectively, over the last 75 years.

1. Why might you have greater confidence in the macroeconomic service's forecasts than in the pension consultant's equity market return forecast?

2. Assuming the macroeconomic forecasts are accurate, what implicit assumptions underlie the pension consultant's forecast of 11 percent equity market appreciation?

3. Assuming the macroeconomic forecasts are accurate, what would be a more reasonable forecast for long-term equity returns?

4. In addition to its long-term potential GDP forecast, the macroeconomic forecasting service estimates sluggish 1.5 percent GDP growth for the next year. Based on this short-term GDP forecast, the bond analyst at your firm recommends that the firm increase its fixed income investments. What assumptions underlie the bond analyst's forecast?

Solution to 1:

High volatility makes equity returns very hard to predict based on their own history. As illustrated in Exhibit 3, the high volatility of equity returns is due to the underlying volatility of earnings as a share of GDP and valuation ratios. Long-term real GDP growth rates tend to be far less volatile, especially for developed economies, such as the United States or the euro area, because long-term potential growth is governed by fundamental economic forces that tend to evolve slowly over time. Similarly, for countries with prudent monetary policies, inflation rates are much less volatile than stock prices. Thus, one could reasonably place much higher confidence in forecasts of long-term real and nominal (real growth plus inflation) GDP growth than in equity market return forecasts based on historical equity returns.

Solution to 2:

We can decompose the equity market appreciation rate into components due to (a) nominal GDP growth, (b) expansion/contraction of the share of profits in GDP, and (c) expansion/contraction of the P/E. The macroeconomic forecast indicates that nominal GDP will grow at 7 percent (3.25% real + 3.75% inflation). So the pension consultant's forecast of 11 percent equity market appreciation implies a 4 percent per year combined contribution from expansion in the P/E multiple and/or the profit share of GDP—*forever*.

Solution to 3:

Neither the P/E nor the profit share of GDP can grow at a non-negligible rate forever. A much more reasonable forecast of long-term equity market appreciation would be the projected 7 percent growth rate of nominal GDP.

Solution to 4:

With forecasted actual GDP growth well below the growth in potential GDP, the bond analyst assumes a growing output gap or slack in the economy. This slack may place downward pressure on inflation and reduce inflationary expectations. To close this gap, the central bank may need to lower short-term interest rates and ease policy. In such an environment, bond prices should rise.

DETERMINANTS OF ECONOMIC GROWTH

What are the forces driving long-run economic growth? The following sections discuss labor, physical and human capital, technology, and other factors, such as natural resources and public infrastructure, as inputs to economic growth and production functions and how changes in such inputs affect growth. Section 4.1 begins the discussion by presenting one of the simplest useful models of the production function.

4.1 Production Function

A production function is a model of the quantitative link between the inputs (factors of production), technology, and output. A two-factor aggregate production function with labor and capital as the inputs can be represented as:

$$Y = AF(K, L) \tag{1}$$

where Y denotes the level of aggregate output in the economy, L is the quantity of labor or number of workers or hours worked in the economy, and K is an estimate of the capital services provided by the stock of equipment and structures used to produce goods and services. The function $F(\ )$ embodies the fact that capital and labor can be used in various combinations to produce output.

In the production function above, A is a multiplicative scale factor referred to as **total factor productivity (TFP)**. Note that an increase in TFP implies a proportionate increase in output for any combination of inputs. Hence, TFP reflects the general level of productivity or technology in the economy. The state of technology embodies the cumulative effects of scientific advances, applied research and development, improvements in management methods, and ways of organizing production that raise the productive capacity of factories and offices.

It is worth noting that both the function $F(\ )$ and the scale factor A reflect technology. An innovation that makes it possible to produce the same output with the same amount of capital but fewer workers would be reflected in a change in the function $F(\ )$ because the relative productivity of labor and capital has been altered. In contrast, an increase in TFP does not affect the relative productivity of the inputs. As is standard in the analysis of economic growth, *unless stated otherwise, the level of "technology" should be interpreted as referring to TFP.*

In order to obtain concrete results, it is useful to use a specific functional form for the production function. The **Cobb–Douglas production function**, given by

$$F(K,L) = K^{\alpha} L^{1-\alpha} \tag{2}$$

is widely used because it is easy to analyze and does a good job of fitting the historic data relating inputs and output. The parameter α determines the shares of output (factor shares) paid by companies to capital and labor and is assumed to have a value between 0 and 1. The reason for this follows from basic microeconomics. In a competitive economy, factors of production are paid their marginal product. Profit maximization requires that the marginal product of capital equal the **rental price of capital** and the marginal product of labor equal the (real) wage rate. In the case of capital, the marginal product of capital (MPK) for the Cobb–Douglas production function is[9]

$$MPK = \alpha A K^{\alpha-1} L^{1-\alpha} = \alpha Y / K$$

---

9 The marginal product of capital is simply the derivative of output with respect to capital. This can be approximated as $\Delta Y / \Delta K \approx [A(K + \Delta K)^{\alpha} L^{1-\alpha} - A K^{\alpha} L^{1-\alpha}]/\Delta K \approx [A\alpha K^{\alpha-1}\Delta K L^{1-\alpha}]/\Delta K = A\alpha K^{\alpha-1} L^{1-\alpha} = \alpha Y / K$. The approximation becomes exact for very small increments, ΔK.

Setting the MPK equal to the rental price (r) of capital,

$$\alpha\, Y/K = r$$

If we solve this equation for α, we find that it equals the ratio of capital income, rK to output or GDP, Y. Thus, *α is the share of GDP paid out to the suppliers of capital*. A similar calculation shows that $1 - \alpha$ is the share of income paid to labor. This result is important because it is easy to estimate α for an economy by simply looking at capital's share of income in the national income accounts.

The Cobb–Douglas production function exhibits two important properties that explain the relationship between the inputs and the output. First, the Cobb–Douglas production function exhibits **constant returns to scale**. This means that if all the inputs into the production process are increased by the same percentage, then output rises by that percentage. Under the assumption of constant returns to scale, we can modify the production function (Equation 1) and examine the determinants of the quantity of output per worker. Multiplying the production function by $1/L$ gives

$$Y/L = AF(K/L, L/L) = AF(K/L, 1)$$

Defining $y = Y/L$ as the output per worker or (average) **labor productivity** and $k = K/L$ as the capital-to-labor ratio, the above expression becomes

$$y = AF(k,1)$$

Specifying the Cobb–Douglas production function in output per worker terms, where again lower case letters denote variables measured on a per capita basis, we get

$$y = Y/L = A(K/L)^{\alpha}(L/L)^{1-\alpha} = Ak^{\alpha} \qquad \text{(3)}$$

This equation tells us that the amount of goods a worker can produce (labor productivity) depends on the amount of capital available for each worker (capital-to-labor ratio), technology or TFP, and the share of capital in GDP (α). It is important to note that there are two different measures of productivity or efficiency in this equation. Labor productivity measures the output produced by a unit of labor and is measured by dividing the output (GDP) by the labor input used to produce that output ($y = Y/L$). TFP is a scale factor that multiplies the impact of the capital and labor inputs. Changes in TFP are estimated using a growth accounting method discussed in the next section.

A second important property of the model is the relation between an individual input and the level of output produced. The Cobb–Douglas production function exhibits **diminishing marginal productivity** with respect to each individual input. Marginal productivity is the extra output produced from a one-unit increase in an input keeping the other inputs unchanged. It applies to any input as long as the other inputs are held constant. For example, if we have a factory of a fixed size and we add more workers to the factory, the marginal productivity of labor measures how much additional output each additional worker will produce. Diminishing marginal productivity means that at some point the extra output obtained from each additional unit of the input will decline. To continue our example, if we hire more workers at the existing factory (fixed capital input in this case) each additional worker adds less to output than the previously hired worker does and average labor productivity (y) falls.

The significance of diminishing marginal returns in the Cobb–Douglas production function depends on the value of α. *A value of α close to zero means diminishing marginal returns to capital are very significant and the extra output made possible by additional capital declines quickly as capital increases.* In contrast, a value of α close to one means that the next unit of capital increases output almost as much as the previous unit of capital. In this case, diminishing marginal returns still occur but the impact is relatively small. Note that the exponents on the K and L variables in the Cobb–Douglas production function sum to one, indicating constant returns to scale—that is, there are no diminishing marginal returns if both inputs are increased proportionately.

4.2 Capital Deepening vs. Technological Progress

The property of diminishing marginal returns plays an important role in assessing the contribution of capital and technology to economic growth. Exhibit 4 shows the relationship between per capita output and the capital-to-labor ratio. It shows that adding more and more capital to a fixed number of workers increases per capita output but at a decreasing rate. Looking at Equation 3 and Exhibit 4, we can think of growth in per capita output coming from two sources: capital deepening and an improvement in technology, often referred to as technological progress.

Exhibit 4	Per Capita Production Function Capital Deepening vs. Technological (TFP) Progress

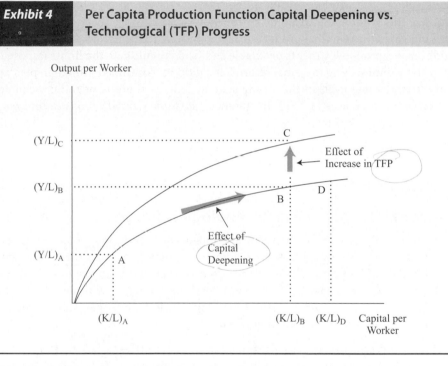

Capital deepening, an increase in the capital-to-labor ratio, is reflected in the exhibit by a move along the production function from point A to B. The increase in the capital-to-labor ratio reflects rising investment in the economy. The ratio will increase as long as the growth rate of capital (net investment) exceeds the growth rate of labor. However, once the capital-to-labor ratio becomes very high, as at point B, further additions to capital have relatively little impact on per capita output (e.g., moving to point D). This occurs because the marginal product of capital declines as more capital is added to the labor input.

At the point where the marginal product of capital equals its marginal cost, profit maximizing producers will stop adding capital (i.e., stop increasing the capital-to-labor ratio).[10] As we will discuss in Section 5, this point is very significant in the neoclassical model of growth because per capita growth in the economy will come to a halt.

---

10 To avoid confusion later, we must note that once technological progress (TFP growth) is introduced, the capital-to-labor ratio will have to keep increasing just to keep the marginal productivity of capital equal to its marginal cost. But the point remains: Once that equality is attained, companies will not increase the capital-to-labor ratio faster than is necessary to maintain that equality.

Once the economy reaches this steady state, capital deepening cannot be a source of sustained growth in the economy. Only when the economy is operating below the steady state and when the marginal product of capital exceeds its marginal cost can capital deepening raise per capita growth.

The neoclassical model's stark implication that more rapid capital accumulation—that is, higher rates of investment—cannot result in a permanently higher rate of per capita growth is somewhat disappointing. As we will see in our discussion of endogenous growth, capital accumulation can result in a permanently higher growth rate if the investment results not just in *more* capital (i.e., pure capital deepening) but also in new, innovative products and processes. That is, if the additional capital embodies new, more efficient methods of production or previously unavailable products, then more rapid capital accumulation can result in a permanently higher growth rate of per capita output.

In contrast to moves along a given production function, an improvement in TFP causes a proportional upward shift in the entire production function. As a result, the economy can produce higher output per worker for a given level of capital per worker. This is shown in Exhibit 4 by the move from B to C. Technological progress also increases the marginal product of capital relative to its marginal cost. This makes additional capital investments profitable and tends to mitigate the limits imposed on growth by diminishing marginal returns. In addition, continued growth in per capita output is possible even in the steady state as long as there is ongoing technological progress (increases in TFP). In summary, *sustained growth in per capita output requires progress in TFP.*

Example 3

Capital Deepening Vs. Technological Progress

One of main differences between developed and developing countries is the amount of capital available for each worker. Country A is an advanced economy with $100,000 of capital available for each worker and thus a high capital-to-labor ratio. In contrast, Country B is a developing country with only $5,000 of capital available for each worker. What impact will the following developments have on the growth rate of potential GDP?

1. An increase in business investment in both countries

2. An increase in the amount of spending on university research in both countries

3. An elimination of restrictions in Country B on the inflow of foreign investment

Solution to 1:

An increase in business investment will raise the capital-to-labor ratio in both countries. It results in capital deepening and a movement along the per worker production function. However, the impact on growth will be significantly different for the two countries. Country B will experience an increase in output per worker and thus in the growth rate of potential GDP. This is because Country B operates at a low level of capital per worker, at a point like A in Exhibit 4. Diminishing returns to capital are small, so any addition to capital has a major impact on growth. Country A operates at a point like B in Exhibit 4, so additions to capital have little impact on growth because of diminishing returns.

Solution to 2:

An increase in spending on university research will increase TFP and cause an upward shift in the production function in both countries. This can be seen in the move from point B to point C in Exhibit 4. The shift in the production function will raise growth in both countries and offset the negative impact of diminishing returns. This result shows that developing countries have the potential to grow through both capital deepening and technological progress, whereas improvement in potential GDP growth in developed countries is largely driven by technological progress.

Solution to 3:

The elimination of restrictions will result in higher foreign investment, which has the same impact as an increase in domestic business investment. This is again a movement along the production function such as from point A to B in Exhibit 4. With diminishing returns insignificant at low levels of capital to labor, the higher level of foreign investment will boost growth of potential GDP in Country B.

4.3 Growth Accounting

Since the publication of Solow's seminal work in 1957,[11] growth accounting has been used to analyze the performance of economies. The growth accounting equation is essentially the production function written in the form of growth rates. It starts with the Cobb–Douglas production function and decomposes the percentage change in output into components attributable to capital, labor, and technology:

$$\Delta Y / Y = \Delta A / A + \alpha \Delta K / K + (1 - \alpha)\Delta L / L \tag{4}$$

The **growth accounting equation** states that the growth rate of output equals the rate of technological change plus α times the growth rate of capital plus $(1 - \alpha)$ times the growth rate of labor. Because a 1 percent increase in capital leads to an $\alpha\%$ increase in output, α is the elasticity of output with respect to capital. Similarly, $(1 - \alpha)$ is the elasticity of output with respect to labor. Thus, in the Cobb–Douglas production function, the exponents α and $(1 - \alpha)$ play dual roles as both output elasticities and the shares of income paid to each factor. Note that the impact of any unspecified inputs (e.g., natural resources) is subsumed into the TFP component.

Data on output, capital, labor, and the elasticities of capital and labor are available for most developed countries. The rate of technological change is not directly measured and must therefore be estimated. The elasticities of capital and labor in the growth accounting equation are the relative shares of capital (α) and labor ($1 - \alpha$) in national income and are estimated from the GDP accounts. For the United States, the relative shares of labor and capital are approximately 0.7 and 0.3, respectively. This means that an increase in the growth rate of labor will have a significantly larger impact—roughly double—on potential GDP growth than will an equivalent increase in the growth rate of capital, holding all else equal. For example, because capital's share in GDP in the U.S. economy is 0.3, a 1 percent increase in the amount of capital available for each worker increases output by only 0.3 percent. An equivalent increase in the labor input would boost growth by 0.7 percent.

The growth accounting equation has a number of uses in studying an economy. First, Solow used the equation to estimate the contribution of technological progress to economic growth. Solow estimated the growth in TFP as a residual in the above

---

11 See Solow (1957).

equation by plugging in $\Delta Y/Y$, $\Delta K/K$, $\Delta L/L$, and α and solving for $\Delta A/A$. This residual measures the amount of output that cannot be explained by growth in capital or labor and can thus be regarded as progress in TFP.

Second, the growth accounting equation is used to empirically measure the sources of growth in an economy. In such studies, the growth accounting equation is used to quantify the contribution of each factor to long-term growth in an economy and answer such questions as the following: How important are labor and demographic factors to growth? What is the contribution of capital, and how important is capital deepening as a source of growth? What is the impact of TFP? The growth accounting equation can be expanded by considering different forms of capital and labor inputs, such as human capital and knowledge capital, and by considering the quality of the inputs as well.

Finally, the growth accounting equation is used to measure potential output. Potential GDP is estimated using Equation 4 with trend estimates of labor and capital and α estimated as one minus the labor share of GDP. The difficult task is estimating the growth rate of TFP, which, by definition, is a residual in the growth accounting equation.[12] The standard methodology treats TFP as exogenous and estimates its growth rate using various time-series models.

An alternative method of measuring potential GDP is the **labor productivity growth accounting equation**. It is very similar to the Solow approach but is simpler and models potential GDP as a function of the labor input and the productivity of the labor input. It avoids the need to estimate the capital input and the difficulty associated with computing total factor productivity. The disadvantage is that it incorporates both capital deepening and TFP progress in the productivity term in a way that can be difficult to analyze and to predict over long periods of time. Under this approach, the equation for estimating potential GDP is

$$
\begin{aligned}
\text{Growth rate in potential GDP} \;=\; & \text{Long-term growth rate of labor force} \\
& + \; \text{Long-term growth rate in labor productivity}
\end{aligned}
\tag{5}
$$

Thus, potential GDP growth is a combination of the long-term growth rate of the labor force and the long-term growth rate of labor productivity. If the labor force is growing at 1 percent per year and productivity per worker is rising at 2 percent per year, then potential GDP is rising at 3 percent per year.

4.4 Extending the Production Function

As a simplification, the production function in Equation 1 focused on only the labor and capital inputs. A more complete specification of the production function expands the list of inputs to include the following:

- Raw materials: natural resources such as oil, lumber, and available land (N)

- Quantity of labor: the number of workers in the country (L)

- Human capital: education and skill level of these workers (H)

- Information, computer, and telecommunications (ICT) capital: computer hardware, software, and communication equipment (K_{IT})

- Non-ICT capital: transport equipment, metal products and plant machinery other than computer hardware and communications equipment, and non-residential buildings and other structures (K_{NT})

---

12 TFP is computed as the growth in output less the growth in the factor inputs. These would include labor and capital in the traditional Solow two-factor production model. If the production function is expanded by including more inputs, the weighted growth rates of these inputs would also be subtracted from the growth in output.

- Public capital: infrastructure owned and provided by the government (K_p)
- Technological knowledge: the production methods used to convert inputs into final products, reflected by total factor productivity (A)

The expanded production function is expressed mathematically as:

$$Y = AF(N, L, H, K_{IT}, K_{NT}, K_P)$$

The impact of each of these inputs on economic growth is addressed in the following sections.

4.5 Natural Resources

Raw materials, including everything from available land to oil to water, are an essential input to growth. There are two categories of natural resources:

1. **Renewable resources** are those that are replenished, such as a forest. For example, if a tree is cut, a seedling can be planted and a new forest harvested in the future.

2. **Non-renewable resources** are finite resources that are depleted once they are consumed. Oil and coal are examples.

Although it seems intuitive that countries with more natural resources will be wealthier, the relation between resource endowment and growth is not so straight-forward. Natural resources do account for some of the differences in growth among countries. Today, Middle Eastern countries and such countries as Brazil and Australia have relatively high per capita incomes because of their resource base. Countries in the Middle East have large pools of oil. Brazil has an abundance of land suitable for large-scale agricultural production, allowing it to be a major exporter of coffee, soybeans, and beef.

Even though *access* to natural resources (e.g., via trade) is important, *ownership and production of natural resources is not necessary for a country to achieve a high level of income*. Countries in East Asia, such as Japan and South Korea, have experienced rapid economic growth but have few natural resources. In contrast, both Venezuela and Saudi Arabia have large oil reserves and are major producers of oil, yet both countries have experienced subpar growth in comparison to the natural-resource-poor countries of Singapore, Japan, and South Korea. As was examined in Example 1, economic growth in Venezuela over the last 60 years was well below that of Singapore, Japan, and South Korea.

For some countries, the presence of natural resources may even restrain growth, resulting in a "resource curse." Venezuela and Nigeria are two examples of countries blessed with resources yet with sluggish economic growth. There are two main reasons why this may occur. First, countries rich in natural resources may fail to develop the economic institutions necessary for growth. Second, countries rich in resources may suffer the **Dutch disease**, where currency appreciation driven by strong export demand for resources makes other segments of the economy, in particular manufac-turing, globally uncompetitive.[13] In this situation, the manufacturing sector contracts and the country does not participate in the TFP progress that occurs in countries with more vigorous manufacturing sectors.

In contrast, there is a long-standing concern that non-renewable natural resources will eventually limit growth. The idea is that a combination of rapid economic growth and a fixed stock of resources will cause resource depletion as the available pool of resources is used up. These concerns are probably overstated. Technological progress

---

13 Following the discovery of large natural gas fields in the Netherlands, the Dutch guilder appreciated and the manufacturing sector contracted.

(TFP from all sources) enables the economy to use fewer resources per unit of output and to develop substitutes. The growing scarcity of specific resources will increase their price and encourage a shift toward more plentiful substitutes. Finally, the share of national income going to land and resources has been declining for most countries, especially as the composition of output in the global economy shifts toward the use of more services.

Example 4

Impact of Natural Resources

The table below shows the share of world proved oil reserves as of 1990 for each of the 34 countries shown in Exhibit 1, along with the growth rate of real per capita GDP from 1990 to 2010. The simple correlation between the share of oil reserves and subsequent growth is not statistically different from zero.

	Percent of World Proved Oil Reserves: 1990	Real Per Capita GDP Growth (%) 1990–2010		Percent of World Proved Oil Reserves: 1990	Real Per Capita GDP Growth (%) 1990–2010
Saudi Arabia	25.75	3.00	Germany	0.04	1.60
Venezuela	5.85	2.80	France	0.02	1.45
Mexico	5.64	2.65	New Zealand	0.01	2.60
United States	2.62	2.50	Pakistan	0.01	4.35
China	2.40	10.45	Japan	0.01	1.05
Nigeria	1.60	5.25	Spain	0.00	2.50
Indonesia	0.82	4.60	Philippines	0.00	3.85
India	0.75	6.55	Taiwan	0.00	5.14
Canada	0.61	2.10	Botswana	0.00	5.29
Egypt	0.45	4.65	Ethiopia	0.00	5.61
United Kingdom	0.43	2.15	Hong Kong	0.00	4.00
Brazil	0.28	3.05	Ireland	0.00	4.83
Argentina	0.23	4.40	Kenya	0.00	2.89
Australia	0.17	3.20	Singapore	0.00	6.45
Italy	0.07	1.00	South Africa	0.00	2.65
Turkey	0.05	3.80	South Korea	0.00	5.69%
Peru	0.04	4.85	Vietnam	0.00	7.45%

Sources: U.S. Energy Information Administration (www.eia.gov) and Exhibit 1.

What might account for the fact that real per capita GDP growth appears to be unrelated to oil reserves, perhaps the single most economically important natural resource (aside from water)?

> **Solution:**
>
> Energy is a vital input for any economy. Thus, *access* to energy resources is critical. *Ownership* of raw energy resources, however, is not. Countries that are not self-sufficient in oil or other resources acquire what they need through trade. It should be noted that countries that lack oil may possess other types of energy resources, such as natural gas, coal, hydropower, or geothermal energy. In addition, countries can grow by emphasizing less energy intensive products, especially services, and adopting more energy efficient production methods. In sum, natural resources are important but not necessary for growth.

4.6 Labor Supply

As noted above, economic growth is affected by increases in inputs, mainly labor and capital. Growth in the number of people available for work (quantity of workforce) is an important source of economic growth and partially accounts for the superior growth performance of the United States among the advanced economies—in particular, relative to Europe and Japan. Most developing countries, such as China, India, and Mexico, have a large potential labor supply. We can measure the potential size of the labor input as the total number of hours available for work. This, in turn, equals the labor force times the average hours worked per worker. The **labor force** is defined as the working age population (ages 16 to 64) that is either employed or available for work but not working (i.e., unemployed). Thus, growth in the labor input depends on four factors: population growth, labor force participation, net migration, and average hours worked.

4.6.1 *Population Growth*

Long-term projections of the labor supply are largely determined by the growth of the working age population. Population growth is determined by fertility rates and mortality rates. Population growth rates are significantly lower in the developed countries than in the developing countries. As a result, there is an ongoing decline in the developed countries' share of the world's population. Note that although population growth may increase the growth rate of the overall economy, it has no impact on the rate of increase in *per capita* GDP.

The age mix of the population is also important. The percentage of the population over the age of 65 and the percentage below the age of 16 are key considerations. Some of the developed countries, especially European countries, Japan, and South Korea, are facing a growing demographic burden as the portion of non-working elders (over 65) grows as a share of the population. In contrast, growth in many developing countries will receive a demographic boost as the fraction of the population below the age of 16 begins to decline. Interestingly, China is similar to the advanced economies, with a growing proportion of the population over age 65.

Exhibit 5	Population Data for Selected Countries (millions)			
	2000	**2005**	**2010**	**Annual Growth (%)** **2000–2010**
France	59.1	61.2	63.0	0.64
Germany	82.2	82.3	81.6	−0.07

(continued)

Exhibit 5	Continued			
	2000	**2005**	**2010**	**Annual Growth (%) 2000–2010**
Ireland	3.8	4.0	4.5	1.71
Spain	40.3	43.4	46.1	1.35
United Kingdom	58.9	59.4	61.3	0.40
Russia	146.7	142.8	142.9	−0.26
Japan	126.9	127.8	127.6	0.06
United States	282.2	295.6	309.1	0.91
Mexico	98.4	103.9	108.4	0.97
China	1,267.4	1307.6	1341.4	0.57
India	1,024.3	1,110.0	1,190.5	1.52

Source: OECD Stat Extracts.

4.6.2 *Labor Force Participation*

In the short run, the growth rate of the labor force may differ from population growth because of changes in the participation rate. The **labor force participation rate** is defined as the percentage of the working age population in the labor force. It has trended upward in most countries over the last few decades because of rising participation rates among women. In contrast to population, an increase in the participation rate may raise the growth of per capita GDP. In many southern European countries, such as Greece and Italy, the participation rate among women is well below the rates in the United States and northern European countries (see Exhibit 6). Thus, rising participation rates among women in these countries could increase growth in the labor force and in potential GDP. This has been the case for Spain, where the female labor force participation rate rose from 52.0 percent in 2000 to 66.1 percent in 2010. It should be noted, however, that rising or falling labor force participation is likely to represent a transition to a new higher or lower level of participation rather than a truly permanent rate of change. Thus, although trends in participation may contribute to or detract from potential growth for substantial periods, one should be cautious in extrapolating such trends indefinitely.

Exhibit 6	Labor Force Data for Selected Countries (2010)			
	Percent of Population under Age 15	**Percent of Population over Age 65**	**Participation Rate: Male (%)**	**Participation Rate: Female (%)**
France	18.3	16.7	72.6	67.3
Germany	13.1	21.0	82.3	71.5
Greece	14.3	18.6	76.5	55.0
Ireland	21.5	11.4	79.5	63.4
Italy	14.1	20.0	73.5	51.5
Spain	15.0	17.0	80.4	66.1
Sweden	16.6	18.3	84.5	77.8
U.K.	17.7	15.9	82.8	70.5

Exhibit 6	Continued			

	Percent of Population under Age 15	Percent of Population over Age 65	Participation Rate: Male (%)	Participation Rate: Female (%)
Japan	13.3	22.7	93.8	68.5
U.S.	20.1	13.1	79.2	69.8
Mexico	28.1	5.9	83.2	48.3
Turkey	26.4	7.0	73.9	28.8

Source: OECD Stat Extracts.

Example 5

Impact of the Age Distribution on Growth: Mexico vs. Germany

Exhibits 5 and 6 provide population data for selected countries. The data show that the rate of population growth and the age composition vary significantly among countries. Thus, demographic factors can be expected to have a significant impact on relative growth rates across countries. This is very clear in the cases of Mexico and Germany. There was essentially zero growth in the population of Germany from 2000 to 2010, while the population of Mexico increased by 0.97 percent annually. The age composition of the two countries is also very different. How will the age distribution impact growth over the next decade?

Solution:

What is important for growth is the number of workers available to enter the workforce. Over the next decade, Mexico will receive a demographic benefit because of the high percentage of young people entering the workforce. This is because 28.1 percent of the population in 2010 was below the age of 15. In contrast, only 13.1 percent of the German population was below the age of 15. In addition, Germany is facing a demographic challenge given the high and growing share of its population over the age of 65. In Mexico, only 5.9 percent of the population is above the age of 65, compared with 21 percent in Germany. In sum, the lack of population growth and a rapidly aging population in Germany will limit its potential rate of growth. Germany must rely on high labor productivity growth, increase its workforce participation rate, or encourage immigration if it is to increase its near-term potential rate of growth. Meanwhile, potential GDP growth in Mexico should receive a boost from its favorable population trends.

4.6.3 Net Migration

Another factor increasing economic and population growth, especially among the developed countries, is immigration. Heightened immigration is a possible solution to the slowing labor force growth being experienced by many developed countries with low birthrates within the native population. The growth rate of the labor force in Ireland, Spain, the United Kingdom, and the United States has increased over the last decade because of immigration. As Exhibit 5 shows, the population growth rates for Ireland and Spain for the period 2000–2010, at 1.71 percent and 1.35 percent, respectively, were well above the population growth rates in other European countries. As shown in Exhibit 7, this is due to the impact of immigration. The open-border policies of both countries led to a significant population of immigrants that contributed to a large increase in labor input for both countries. As a consequence, both countries experienced GDP growth above the European average during this period (see Exhibit 1).

Exhibit 7	Ireland and Spain: Net Migration				
	2000–2007	**2008**	**2009**	**2010**	**Total 2000–2010**
Ireland	357,085	38,502	−7,800	−12,200	375,587
Spain	4,222,813	460,221	181,073	111,249	4,975,356

Source: OECD Stat Extracts.

Example 6

Potential Growth in Spain: Labor Input

The Investment Policy Committee of Global Invest Inc. reviewed a report on the growth prospects for Spain and noted that, with total hours worked growing at a 1.2 percent annual rate between 2000 and 2010, labor input had been a major source of growth for the economy. As of 2011, some members expected the growth rate of labor to slow considerably given projection from the OECD and IMF that immigration into Spain will fall to essentially zero over the next few years. A research assistant at the firm gathered demographic data on Spain from Exhibits 5–7 and other sources. The data are presented in the following table:

	2000	**2010**	**Annual Growth (2000–2010)**
Population (millions)	40.3	46.1	1.35%
Immigration since 2000 (millions)		4.975	
Percent of population under 15		15.0	
Percent of population over 65		17.0	
Male participation rate		80.4%	
Female participation rate		66.1%	
Unemployment rate		20.1%	

Using this information for Spain and Exhibits 5 and 6 for relevant comparison data, determine the following:

1. Whether a change in the trend growth rate of the labor input is likely over the next few years.

2. How the high unemployment rate of 20.1 percent is likely to affect the growth rate of the labor force.

Solution to 1:

The growth in the labor input depends on a number of factors, including the population growth rate, the labor force participation rate, and the percentage of the population below the age of 15. The labor force in Spain expanded sharply between 2000 and 2010 mainly because of a large 5.8 million person increase in the population, going from 40.3 million in 2000 to 46.1 million in

2010. Looking ahead, growth in the labor force is set to slow substantially for a number of reasons:

- The population increase between 2000 and 2010 is very misleading and not likely to be repeated in the future. Between 2000 and 2010, immigration raised the population of Spain by nearly 5 million people. Without the immigrants, the population of Spain between 2000 and 2010 would have grown by only about 825,000 or at an annual rate of 0.2 percent. With immigration, the population growth rate was 1.35 percent. The pace of immigration that occurred between 2000 and 2010 is not sustainable and is likely to slow. This will result in slower growth in the population and the labor force.

- In the short run, the growth rate of the labor force may differ from population growth because of changes in the participation rate. Looking at the data, the male participation rate in Spain, at 80.4 percent, is very high and, as shown in Exhibit 6, is above the male participation rates in France, Greece, and Italy and slightly below that of Germany. The female participation rate is low in comparison to northern European countries, such as Sweden. But it is higher than in Greece and Italy, which are probably a better comparison. Thus, little increase is likely in the male or female participation rates.

- Only 15 percent of the Spanish population is below the age of 15. The comparable figure from Exhibit 6 for the United Kingdom is 17.7 percent, for France 18.3 percent, for the United States 20.1 percent, and for Mexico 28.1 percent. Thus, Spain does not appear poised for a notable surge in young adults entering the labor force.

In summary, growth in the labor input in Spain should slow over the next few years and the growth rate of potential GDP should do the same.

Solution to 2:

Reducing the unemployment rate would mitigate some of the negative demographic factors because a reduction in the number of unemployed workers would boost utilization of the existing labor supply. This would represent a transition to a higher level of employment rather than a permanent increase in the potential growth rate. Nonetheless, it could boost potential growth for a substantial period.

4.6.4 *Average Hours Worked*

The contribution of labor to overall output is also affected by changes in the average hours worked per worker. Average hours worked is highly sensitive to the business cycle. However, the long-term trend in average hours worked has been toward a shorter workweek in the advanced countries. This development is the result of legislation, collective bargaining agreements, the growth of part-time and temporary work, and the impact of both the "wealth effect" and high tax rates on labor income, which cause workers in high-income countries to value leisure time relatively more highly than labor income.

Exhibit 8 provides data on average hours worked per year per person in the labor force for selected years since 1995. For most countries, the average number of hours worked per year has been declining. There is also a significant difference in hours worked across countries. In 2010, average hours worked per year in South Korea, at 2,193 hours, were 54.5 percent more than the 1,419 average hours worked per year in

Germany. The increase in female labor force participation rates may be contributing to the shorter average workweek because female workers disproportionately take on part-time, rather than full-time, jobs.

Exhibit 8	Average Hours Worked per Year per Person in Selected Countries			
	1995	**2000**	**2005**	**2010**
France	1,651	1,591	1,559	1,594
Germany	1,534	1,473	1,435	1,419
Greece	2,123	2,121	2,081	2,109
Ireland	1,875	1,719	1,654	1,664
Italy	1,859	1,861	1,819	1,778
Spain	1,733	1,731	1,688	1,663
Sweden	1,609	1,574	1,607	1,624
U.K.	1,743	1,711	1,676	1,647
Japan	1,884	1,821	1,775	1,733
South Korea	2,658	2,520	2,364	2,193
Canada	1,761	1,768	1,738	1,702
U.S.	1,840	1,832	1,795	1,778
Mexico	1,857	1,888	1,909	1,866
Turkey	1,876	1,937	1,918	1,877

Source: OECD Stat Extracts.

4.7 Labor Quality: Human Capital

In addition to the quantity of labor, the quality of the labor force is an important source of growth for an economy. **Human capital** is the accumulated knowledge and skills that workers acquire from education, training, or life experience. In general, better-educated and more skilled workers will be more productive and more adaptable to changes in technology or other shifts in market demand and supply.

An economy's human capital is increased through investment in education and on-the-job training. Like physical capital, investment in education is costly, but studies show that there is a significant return on that investment. That is, people with more education earn higher wages. In addition, education may also have a spillover or externality impact. Increasing the educational level of one person raises not only the output of that person but also the output of those around that person. The spillover effect operates through the link between education and advances in technology. Education not only improves the quality of the labor force, and thus the stock of human capital, but also encourages growth through innovation. Importantly, increased education, obtained both formally and via on-the-job training, could result in a permanent increase in the growth rate of an economy if the more educated workforce results in more innovations and a faster rate of technological progress. Investment in the health of the population is also a major contributor to human capital, especially in the developing countries.

4.8 Capital: ICT and Non-ICT

The physical capital stock increases from year to year as long as net investment (gross investment less the depreciation of the capital) is positive. Thus, countries with a higher rate of investment should have a growing physical capital stock and a higher rate of GDP growth.[14] Exhibit 9 shows the level of gross non-residential investment as a share of GDP. The exhibit shows significant variation across countries, with the investment share in the United States being low in comparison to other developed countries.

| Exhibit 9 | Business Investment as a Percentage of GDP |

	ICT Percent of GDP				Investment Percent of GDP			
	1990	**2000**	**2008**		**1990**	**2000**	**2008**	**2010**
Developed Countries								
France	2.6	3.7	3.2		21.5	19.5	21.1	19.1
Germany	3.1	3.6	2.7		22.8	21.5	19.4	17.3
Ireland	1.1	2.3	1.2		20.8	23.9	21.7	11.0
Italy	2.4	2.8	2.1		22.0	20.3	21.1	20.2
Spain	3.4	3.6	3.7		25.3	26.2	28.8	23.0
U.K.	3.3	5.1	4.2		20.5	17.1	16.6	15.0
Australia	3.6	5.5	4.6		23.6	22.0	29.4	27.6
Japan	4.9	3.7	3.1		32.5	25.4	23.2	20.2
South Korea	2.4	5.1	4.8		35.7	30.6	31.2	29.1
Singapore	3.2	5.4	4.9		35.2	33.1	30.2	23.8
Canada	2.8	3.9	3.6		21.3	19.2	22.6	22.2
U.S.	4.1	6.6	5.1		17.4	19.9	18.1	15.8
Developing Countries								
Brazil	NA	NA	NA		14.0	18.3	20.7	19.3
China	NA	NA	NA		24.9	35.1	44.0	48.2
India	NA	NA	NA		21.8	24.3	34.9	36.8
Mexico	NA	NA	NA		17.9	25.5	26.9	25.0
South Africa	NA	NA	NA		19.1	15.1	22.5	19.3

Source: OECD StatLink.

The correlation between economic growth and investment is high. Countries that devote a large share of GDP to investment, such as China, India, and South Korea, have high growth rates. The fastest-growing countries in Europe over the last decade, Ireland and Spain, have the highest investment-to-GDP ratios. Countries that devote a smaller share of GDP to investment, such as Brazil and Mexico, have slower growth rates. The data show why the Chinese economy has expanded at such a rapid rate: annual GDP growth rate in excess of 10 percent over the last two decades. Investment spending in China on new factories, equipment, and infrastructure as a percentage of GDP is the highest in the world. In recent years, China devoted over 40 percent of its GDP to investment spending.

As we discussed in Section 4.2, long-term sustainable growth cannot rely on pure capital deepening. How can we reconcile this notion with the strong correlation between investment spending and economic growth across countries? First, although diminishing marginal productivity will eventually limit the impact of capital deepening,

---

14 The impact on growth of *per capita* GDP will be somewhat smaller if the population is growing because a proportion of net investment simply provides the capital needed to maintain the capital-to-labor ratio.

investment-driven growth may last for a considerable period of time, especially in countries that start with relatively low levels of capital per worker.

A second, and closely related, explanation is that the impact of investment spending on available capital depends on the existing physical capital stock. As with the share of GDP devoted to investment, the stock of capital available per worker varies significantly across countries. In 2000, the average U.S. worker had $148,091 worth of capital, compared with $42,991 in Mexico and $6,270 in India.[15] The wide difference in physical capital per worker suggests that the positive impact of changes in the physical capital stock on growth is very significant in developing countries. Mexican workers have relatively little access to machinery or equipment, so adding even a little can make a big percentage difference. In developed countries, such as the United States, Japan, Germany, France, and the United Kingdom, the physical capital stock is so large that positive net investment in any given year has only a small percentage effect on the accumulated capital stock. For the developed countries, a sustained high level of investment over many years is required to have a meaningful relative impact on the physical capital stock even though the absolute size of the increase in any given year is still larger than in the developing countries.

Third, because physical capital is not really homogeneous, the composition of investment spending and the stock of physical capital matters for growth and productivity. Insights obtained from the endogenous theory of growth (discussed in Section 5) and from studies attempting to obtain a more accurate measure of TFP show that the composition of the physical capital stock is very important. These studies suggest that capital spending could be separated into two categories. The first is spending on information, computers, and telecommunications equipment (ICT investment). Capital spending on these goods is a measure of the impact of the information technology sector on economic growth. One of the key drivers of growth in the developed countries over the last decade has been the IT sector. Growth in the IT sector has been driven by technological innovation that has caused the price of key technologies, such as semiconductors, to fall dramatically. The steep decline in the price of high-technology capital goods has encouraged investment in IT at the expense of other assets.

The IT sector has grown very rapidly and has made a significant contribution to increasing the rate of economic and productivity growth. The greater use of IT equipment in various industries has resulted in **network externalities**. Computers allow people to interconnect through the internet and by e-mail, enabling them to work more productively. *The more people in the network, the greater the potential productivity gains.* The effects of the network externalities are largely captured in TFP rather than observed as a distinct, direct effect. The share of ICT investment in GDP is shown in Exhibit 9. The data show that in most countries, the IT sector is still relatively small and that between 2000 and 2008, IT spending declined as a share of GDP as the global recession disproportionately affected high-technology spending.

The other category of investment, non-ICT capital spending, includes non-residential construction, transport equipment, and machinery. High levels of capital spending for this category should eventually result in capital deepening and thus have less impact on potential GDP growth. In contrast, a growing share of ICT investments in the economy, through their externality impacts, may actually boost the growth rate of potential GDP.[16]

---

15 Heston, Summers, and Aten (2009).

16 It is worthwhile to note that there have been important "transformational technologies" at various stages of history. One need only think about the impact of the steam engine, the internal combustion engine, powered flight, atomic energy, vaccination, and so on, to realize that revolutionary advances are not unique to information, computers, and telecommunications. All of these are, to some extent, "general purpose technologies" (GPT) that affect production and/or innovation in many sectors of the economy. ICT capital clearly embodies this GPT characteristic. Nanotechnology could well become the next "super GPT," at which point investing in ICT may begin to look like mere capital deepening.

4.9 Technology

The most important factor affecting growth of per capita GDP is technology, especially in developed countries. Technology allows an economy to overcome some of the limits imposed by diminishing marginal returns and results in an upward shift in the production function, as we noted in Exhibit 4. Technological progress makes it possible to produce more and/or higher-quality goods and services with the same resources or inputs. It also results in the creation of new goods and services. Technological progress can also be one of the factors improving how efficiently businesses are organized and managed.

Technological change can be embodied in human capital (knowledge, organization, information, and experience base) and/or in new machinery, equipment, and software. Therefore, high rates of investment are important, especially investment in ICT goods. Countries can also innovate through expenditures, both public and private, on research and development (R&D). Expenditures on R&D and the number of patents issued, although not directly measuring innovation, provide some useful insight into innovative performance. Exhibit 10 shows R&D spending as a share of GDP for various countries. The developed countries spend the highest percentage of GDP on R&D because they must rely on innovation and the development of new products and production methods for growth.[17] In contrast, developing countries spend less on R&D because these countries can acquire new technology through imitation or copying the technology developed elsewhere. The embodiment of technology in capital goods can enable relatively poor countries to narrow the gap relative to the technology leaders.

Exhibit 10	Research and Development as a Percentage of GDP in Selected Countries		
	1990	**2000**	**2009**
France	2.3	2.2	2.2
Germany	2.6	2.5	2.8
Ireland	0.8	1.2	1.8
Italy	1.2	1.0	1.3
Spain	0.8	1.0	1.4
U.K.	2.1	1.8	1.9
Australia	1.3	1.5	2.2
Japan	3.0	3.0	3.4
South Korea	1.7	2.3	3.1
Singapore	1.1	1.9	2.9
Canada	1.5	1.9	2.0
U.S.	2.6	2.7	2.9
China	NA	1.0	1.7
India	NA	0.8	0.8
Mexico	NA	0.3	0.4

Source: OECD Stat Extracts.

---

17 The relationship between economic growth and R&D spending is not clear cut. Although technological innovation resulting from high R&D spending raises output and productivity in the long run, it may result in a cyclical slowing of growth as companies and workers are displaced by the new technologies. This is the Schumpeterian concept of creative destruction, which captures the double-edged nature of technological innovation.

The state of technology, as reflected by total factor productivity, embodies the cumulative effects of scientific advances, applied research and development, improvements in management methods, and ways of organizing production that raise the productive capacity of factories and offices. Because it is measured as a residual, TFP estimates are very sensitive to the measurements of the labor and capital inputs. Recent empirical work at the Conference Board and the OECD accounts for changes in the composition and quality of both the labor and capital inputs. The resulting measure of TFP should capture the technological and organizational improvements that increase output for a given level of inputs. Exhibit 11 provides data for the periods 1995–2005 and 2005–2009 on the growth rate in labor productivity and total factor productivity.[18] Labor productivity growth depends on both capital deepening and technological progress. The contribution of capital deepening can be measured as the difference between the growth rates of labor productivity and total factor productivity. For example, from 2005 to 2009, Ireland's labor productivity grew by 0.8 percent per year, of which 2.9 percent [0.8% − (−2.1%)] came from capital deepening, which offset the −2.1 percent decline in TFP. The larger the difference between the productivity growth measures, the more important capital deepening is as a source of economic growth. As we discussed previously, however, growth in per capita income cannot be sustained perpetually by capital deepening.

Exhibit 11	Labor and Total Factor Productivity					
	Growth in Hours Worked[a] (%)	Growth in Labor Prod. (%)	Growth in TFP (%)	Growth Due to Capital Deepening (%)	Growth in GDP (%)	Productivity Level 2010; GDP per Hour Worked ($)
Germany						53.6
1995–2005	−0.3	1.6	0.9	0.7	1.3	
2005–2009	0.2	0.2	0.1	0.1	0.4	
Ireland						50.3
1995–2005	3.2	4.1	1.7	2.4	7.3	
2005–2009	−0.8	0.8	−2.1	2.9	0.0	
United States						60.3
1995–2005	0.9	2.4	0.9	1.5	3.3	
2005–2009	−0.8	1.5	−0.5	2.0	0.7	
Japan						40.7
1995–2005	−1.0	2.1	0.4	1.7	1.1	
2005–2009	−1.3	0.8	−0.6	1.4	−0.5	
South Korea						27.9
1995–2005	0.0	4.3	2.4	1.9	4.3	
2005–2009	−0.5	2.8	2.0	0.8	2.3	
China						8.6
1995–2005	1.1	6.7	1.5	5.2	7.8	
2005–2008	1.2	10.3	4.2	6.1	11.5	
India						5.3
1995–2005	2.1	4.2	1.9	2.3	6.3	
2005–2008	2.2	6.0	2.4	3.6	8.2	

[18] Data for the developing countries are from 1995–2005 and 2005–2008. TFP data are not yet available for 2009 for these countries.

Exhibit 11	Continued					
	Growth in Hours Worked[a] (%)	Growth in Labor Prod. (%)	Growth in TFP (%)	Growth Due to Capital Deepening (%)	Growth in GDP (%)	Productivity Level 2010; GDP per Hour Worked ($)
Brazil						10.4
1995–2005	2.1	0.3	−0.3	0.6	2.4	
2005–2008	2.0	2.9	−0.5	3.4	4.9	
Mexico						16.8
1995–2005	2.2	1.4	0.4	1.0	3.6	
2005–2008	1.8	0.8	−0.1	0.9	2.6	

[a] Total hours worked is the preferred measure of labor quantity. However, this measure is not available for most developing countries (including China, India, Brazil, and Mexico). For these countries, total employment is used assuming that the change in total hours worked equals the change in employment. In this case, labor productivity is measured as output per worker, but for the developed countries labor productivity is output per hour.

Source: Conference Board Total Economy Database.

Exhibit 11 also provides data on the *level* of labor productivity or the amount of GDP produced per hour of work. The level of productivity depends on the accumulated stock of human and physical capital and is much higher among the developed countries. For example, China has a population of over 1.3 billion people, compared with slightly over 300 million people in the United States. Although the United States has significantly fewer workers than China because of its smaller population, its economy as measured by real GDP is much larger. This is because U.S. workers have historically been much more productive than Chinese workers. As shown in Exhibit 11, the United States has had the highest level of productivity in the world, producing over $60 of GDP per hour worked. In comparison, Chinese workers produce only $8.6 worth of GDP per hour worked. Thus, U.S. workers are seven times more productive than Chinese workers. In contrast to the *level* of productivity, the *growth rate* of productivity will typically be higher in the developing countries, where human and physical capital are scarce but growing rapidly and the impact of diminishing marginal returns is relatively small.

An understanding of productivity trends is critical for global investors. A permanent increase in the rate of labor productivity growth will increase the sustainable rate of economic growth and raise the upper boundary for earnings growth and the potential return on equities. In contrast, a low growth rate of labor productivity, if it persists over a number of years, suggests poor prospects for equity prices. A slowdown in productivity growth lowers both the long-run potential growth rate of the economy and the upper limit for earnings growth. Such a development would be associated with slow growth in profits and correspondingly low equity returns.

Example 7

Why the Sluggish Growth in the Japanese Economy?

As shown in Exhibit 1, annual growth in real GDP in Japan averaged 0.8 percent for 2000–2010 and a weak 1.3 percent in the prior decade. This growth is in sharp contrast to the 4.2 percent annual growth rate experienced from 1971 to 1990. The sluggish growth in Japan over the last decade should not be surprising.

The economy of Japan is growing at its potential rate of growth which is limited by the following:

1. The labor input is not growing. Population growth has been essentially zero since 2000 (Exhibit 5), and average hours worked per year per person is declining (Exhibit 8).

2. There has been a lack of technological innovation. The lack of growth in the labor input could be offset through higher productivity derived from innovation and more efficient use of available inputs. However, this is not occurring in Japan. Total factor productivity (Exhibit 11) increased at a sluggish 0.4 percent annual rate from 1995 to 2005 and declined between 2005 and 2009.

3. Diminishing returns to capital are very significant. Despite the negative growth in TFP, labor productivity growth remained relatively high. This means that all the growth in labor productivity in Japan was due to capital deepening (Exhibit 11). The problem for Japan, as discussed in Section 4.2, is that once the capital-to-labor ratio becomes high, further additions to capital have little impact on per capita output. Thus, the growth in labor productivity should slow.

Use the data for 2005–2009 and the labor productivity growth accounting equation to estimate the growth rate in potential GDP for Japan.

Solution:

To estimate the growth rate in potential GDP, we use Equation 5, given by

Growth rate of potential GDP = Long-term growth rate of labor force + Long-term growth rate in labor productivity

To use this equation, we need to project the growth rate in the labor input and labor productivity.

The hours worked data in Exhibit 11 are a potential source to use to estimate the growth rate of the labor input. Exhibit 11 shows the labor input for Japan declining by 1.3 percent per year between 2005 and 2009. The problem here is that the decline in hours worked is overstated because of the negative impact of the global recession on hours worked. As an alternative, the labor input should grow at the same rate as the population plus the net change in immigration. The population data in Exhibit 5 show essentially zero population growth in Japan for the period 2000–2010. This trend is likely to continue. Thus, a reasonable estimate for potential GDP growth in Japan is around 0.8 percent. We get this estimate by assuming no growth in the labor input and a 0.8 percent annual increase in labor productivity (using data from Exhibit 11 for 2005–2009).

4.10 Public Infrastructure

The final expansion of the definition of the capital input is public infrastructure investment. Roads, bridges, municipal water, dams, and, in some countries, electric grids are all examples of public capital. They have few substitutes and are largely complements to the production of private sector goods and services. Ashauer (1990) found that infrastructure investment is an important source of productivity growth and should be included as an input in the production function. As with R&D spending, the full impact of government infrastructure investment may extend well beyond the direct benefits of the projects because improvements in the economy's infrastructure generally boost the productivity of private investments.

4.11 Summary

Long-term sustainable growth is determined by the rate of expansion of real potential GDP. Expansion of the supply of factors of production (inputs) and improvements in technology are the sources of growth. The factors of production include human capital, ICT and non-ICT capital, public capital, labor, and natural resources. Data for the sources of growth are available from the OECD and the Conference Board. Exhibit 12 provides data from the Conference Board on the sources of output growth for various countries. These estimates are based on the growth accounting formula.[19]

Exhibit 12	Sources of Output Growth					
	Contribution from:					
	Labor Quantity (%)	Labor Quality (%)	Non-ICT Capital (%)	ICT Capital (%)	TFP (%)	Growth in GDP (%)
Germany						
1995–2005	−0.2	0.1	0.3	0.2	0.9	1.3
2005–2009	−0.6	0.1	0.5	0.3	0.1	0.4
Ireland						
1995–2005	2.0	0.3	2.6	0.7	1.7	7.3
2005–2009	−0.2	0.1	1.8	0.4	−2.1	0.0
United States						
1995–2005	0.6	0.3	0.7	0.8	0.9	3.3
2005–2009	0.1	0.1	0.5	0.5	−0.5	0.7
Japan						
1995–2005	−0.6	0.4	0.6	0.3	0.4	1.1
2005–2009	−0.6	0.1	0.4	0.2	−0.6	−0.5
South Korea						
1995–2005	−0.5	0.8	1.1	0.5	2.4	4.3
2005–2009	−0.7	0.0	0.8	0.2	2.0	2.3
China						
1995–2005	0.5	0.2	4.5	1.1	1.5	7.8
2005–2008	0.3	0.2	5.5	1.3	4.2	11.5
India						
1995–2005	1.0	0.2	2.7	0.5	1.9	6.3
2005–2008	1.1	0.1	3.7	0.9	2.4	8.2
Brazil						
1995–2005	0.8	0.1	1.1	0.7	−0.3	2.4
2005–2008	0.8	0.2	1.9	2.5	−0.5	4.9

(continued)

---

19 A standard growth accounting model (expanded version of Equation 4) is used to compute the contribution of each input to aggregate output (GDP) growth. The inputs include both the quantity and quality of labor and ICT and non-ICT capital. Each input is weighted by its share in national income, and TFP captures all sources of growth that are left unexplained by the labor and capital inputs.

Exhibit 12	Continued

	Contribution from:					
	Labor Quantity (%)	Labor Quality (%)	Non-ICT Capital (%)	ICT Capital (%)	TFP (%)	Growth in GDP (%)
Mexico						
1995–2005	1.2	0.2	1.4	0.4	0.4	3.6
2005–2008	1.1	0.1	1.3	0.2	–0.1	2.6

Source: Conference Board Total Economy Database.

Example 8

The Irish Economy

As shown in Exhibit 1, economic growth in Ireland since 1970 has been significantly higher than that experienced in the major European economies of Germany, France, and the United Kingdom. In 1970, the per capita GDP of Ireland, at $9,869, was 45.2 percent below the per capita income of the United Kingdom. In 2010, per capita GDP in Ireland, at $36,433, was only 2.5 percent below the United Kingdom's $37,371 per capita GDP. Like most of the global economy, Ireland fell into a deep recession in 2009, with GDP contracting by over 7 percent. To understand the factors driving the Irish economy and the prospects for future equity returns, use the data in Exhibits 11 and 12 and the population data below to address the following questions:

1. Using the growth accounting framework data, evaluate the sources of growth for the Irish economy from 1995 to 2009.

2. What is likely to happen to the potential rate of growth for Ireland? What are the prospects for equity returns?

	2000	2010	Annual Growth Rate
Population (millions)	3.8	4.5	1.71%
Net immigration total (2000–2010)		375,587	
Net immigration total (2009–2010)		–20,000	
Population less immigrants (millions)	3.8	4.1	0.8%

Solution to 1:

The sources of growth for an economy include labor quantity, labor quality, non-ICT capital, ICT capital, and TFP. The growth accounting data in Exhibit 12 indicate that economic growth in Ireland from 1995 to 2009 is explained by the following factors:

Input	Contribution: 1995–2005	Contribution: 2005–2009
Labor	**2.3%**	**–0.1%**
Labor quantity	2.0%	–0.2%
Labor quality	0.3%	0.1%

Input	Contribution: 1995–2005	Contribution: 2005–2009
Capital/Investment	3.3%	2.2%
Non-ICT capital	2.6%	1.8%
ICT capital	0.7%	0.4%
TFP	1.7%	−2.1%
Total: GDP growth	7.3%	0.0%

In sum, the main driver of growth for the Irish economy since 1995 has been capital spending. It accounted for over 45 percent of growth in 1995–2005 and has been the only factor contributing to growth in the Irish economy since 2005, offsetting the negative contribution from labor and TFP. Another way to look at growth in Ireland for the period 2005–2009 is that all the growth is through capital deepening. As shown in Exhibit 11, capital deepening added 2.9 percent to growth and by offsetting the decline in TFP caused an increase in labor productivity of 0.8 percent.

Solution to 2:

Looking forward, prospects for the economy are not as favorable as in the past. To estimate the growth rate in potential GDP, we use Equation 5, given by

$$\text{Growth rate of potential GDP} = \text{Long-term growth rate of labor force} \\ + \text{Long-term growth rate in labor productivity}$$

To use this equation, we need to project the growth rate in the labor input and labor productivity. The total hours worked data in Exhibit 11 are one potential source to use to estimate the growth rate of the labor input. Exhibit 11 shows the labor input declining by 0.8 percent between 2005 and 2009. The problem here is that the decline in hours worked is overstated because of the negative impact of the recession on hours worked. As an alternative, the labor input should grow at the same rate as the population plus the net change due to immigration. The population data for Ireland (given above) show that over half of the population growth between 2000 and 2010 was due to immigration. Since 2009, however, outward migration has replaced inward migration, reducing the growth rate in the labor input. Thus, if the 2000–2010 influx of immigrants is reversed over the next decade, a reasonable, perhaps somewhat conservative, estimate for labor force growth is zero. We also assume:

1. There is no increase in labor productivity coming from capital deepening as investment slows (resulting in essentially no growth in net investment and the physical capital stock).

2. TFP growth reverts to its average growth rate of 1.7 percent in the 1995–2005 time period (see Exhibit 11).

3. Labor productivity grows at the same rate as TFP.

Thus, growth in potential GDP is 0.0% + 1.7% = 1.7%.

In summary, despite the projected rebound in TFP growth, overall potential growth in Ireland is likely to decline as labor input growth and capital deepening no longer contribute to overall growth. As discussed in Section 3 of the reading, slower growth in potential GDP will limit potential earnings growth and equity price appreciation.

Example 9

Investment Outlook for China and India

The Investment Policy Committee at Global Invest Inc. is interested in increasing the firm's exposure to either India or China because of their rapid rates of economic growth. Economic growth in China has been close to 10 percent over the last few years, and India has grown over 7 percent. You are asked by the committee to do the following:

1. Determine the sources of growth for the two economies and review the data on productivity and investment using information from Exhibits 5, 9, 10, 11, and 12. Which of the two countries looks more attractive based on the sources of growth?

2. Estimate the long-term sustainable earnings growth rate using data from 1995 to 2008.

3. Make an investment recommendation.

Solution to 1:

The sources of economic growth include size of labor force, quality of labor force (human capital), ICT and non-ICT capital, natural resources, and technology. Looking at the sources of growth in Exhibit 12, we get the following:

Input	Percent Contribution: 1995–2005	Percent Contribution: 2005–2008
India		
Labor quantity	1.0	1.1
Labor quality	0.2	0.1
Non-ICT capital	2.7	3.7
ICT capital	0.5	0.9
TFP	1.9	2.4
Total: GDP growth	6.3	8.2
China		
Labor quantity	0.5	0.3
Labor quality	0.2	0.2
Non-ICT capital	4.5	5.5
ICT capital	1.1	1.3
TFP	1.5	4.2
Total: GDP growth	7.8	11.5

■ The contribution of the labor quantity input is more important to growth in India than in China. Labor quantity contributed 1 percent to India's GDP growth over 1995–2005 and 1.1 percent over 2005–2008. The equivalent numbers for China are 0.5 percent and 0.3 percent, respectively. Looking ahead, labor is likely to be a major factor adding to India's growth. The population of India (Exhibit 5) is growing at a faster rate than that of China. The annual growth rate in population from 2001 to 2010 was 1.52 percent in India versus 0.97 percent in China. Also, hours worked in India (Exhibit 11) are growing at a faster rate than in China. Therefore, the workforce and labor quantity input should grow faster in India. The edge here goes to India.

- The contribution to GDP made by the quality of the labor force is essentially identical in the two countries (0.2 percent in China versus 0.2 percent in India between 1995 and 2005 and 0.2 percent in China and 0.1 percent in India between 2005 and 2008). This factor is a tie.

- The contribution of non-ICT capital investment is significantly higher in China (4.5 percent in China versus 2.7 percent in India between 1995 and 2005 and 5.5 percent in China and 3.7 percent in India between 2005 and 2008). The edge goes to China.

- The contribution of ICT capital investment is significantly higher in China (1.1 percent in China versus 0.5 percent in India between 1995 and 2005 and 1.3 percent in China and 0.9 percent in India between 2005 and 2008). The edge goes to China.

- Both countries spend a high percentage of GDP on capital investment (Exhibit 9). In 2010, investment spending as a percentage of GDP was 48.2 percent in China and 36.8 percent in India. The Chinese share is higher, and this provides China with an edge unless diminishing marginal returns to capital deepening become an issue. However, this is not likely for a while given the low level of capital per worker in China. China and India still have a long way to go to converge with the developed economies. The advantage goes to China.

- The contribution of technological progress is measured by TFP. Comparing the two countries, TPF growth was higher in India over the period 1995–2005 (1.9 percent in India versus 1.5 percent in China). For the period 2005–2009, however, TFP growth was significantly higher in China (4.2 percent versus 2.4 percent). In addition, expenditures on R&D for 2009 (Exhibit 10) as a percentage of GDP were higher in China (1.7 percent in China and 0.8 percent in India). The edge here goes to China.

- Finally, growth in overall labor productivity (Exhibit 11) is considerably higher in China than India (10.3 percent in China versus 6.0 percent in India between 2005 and 2008). This is due to a greater increase in the capital-to-labor ratio in China (because of the high rate of investment, the physical capital stock is growing faster than the labor input) and due to faster technological progress in China. The edge here goes to China.

In sum, based on the sources of growth, China appears to be better positioned for growth in the future.

Solution to 2:

Estimates of potential GDP using the inputs from Exhibit 11 for China and India are

Growth rate in potential GDP = Long-term growth rate of labor force (equals growth in hours worked in Exhibit 11) + Long-term growth rate in labor productivity.

China (using 1995–2008)[a]

Growth in potential = 1.1% + 7.5% = 8.6%

India (using 1995–2008)

Growth in potential = 2.1% + 4.6% = 6.7%

Solution to 3:

Growth prospects in both countries are very attractive. However, China's growth potential is higher because of its greater level of capital spending and the greater contribution of technological progress toward growth. Long-term earnings growth is closely tied to the growth rate in potential GDP. Therefore, based on the previous calculations, earnings in China would be projected to grow at an annual rate of 8.6 percent, compared with 6.7 percent in India. Over the next decade, ignoring current valuation, the Chinese equity market would be projected to outperform the Indian market as its higher rate of sustainable growth translates into a higher rate of appreciation in equity values.[b]

---

[a] Calculated as geometric mean growth rates using data for the 1995–2005 and 2005–2008 subperiods.

[b] It bears repeating that the global economy is evolving rapidly and past trends may or may not be sustained. This is especially true of China and India. To provide concrete answers that do not require the reader to bring in additional information, our exercise solutions must assume past patterns are indicative of the future.

5   THEORIES OF GROWTH

The factors that drive long-term economic growth and determine the rate of sustainable growth in an economy are the subject of much debate among economists. The academic growth literature includes three main paradigms with respect to per capita growth in an economy—the classical, neoclassical, and endogenous growth models. Per capita economic growth under the classical model is only temporary because an exploding population with limited resources brings growth to an end. In the neoclassical model, long-run per capita growth depends solely on exogenous technological progress. The final model of growth attempts to explain technology within the model itself—thus the term endogenous growth.

5.1 Classical Model

Classical growth theory was developed by Thomas Malthus in his 1798 publication *Essay on the Principle of Population.* Commonly referred to as the Malthusian theory, it is focused on the impact of a growing population in a world with limited resources. The concerns of resource depletion and overpopulation are central themes within the Malthusian perspective on growth. The production function in the classical model is relatively simple and consists of a labor input with land as a fixed factor. The key assumption underlying the classical model is that population growth accelerates when the level of per capita income rises above the subsistence income, which is the minimum income needed to maintain life. This means that technological progress and land expansion, which increase labor productivity, translate into higher population growth. But because the labor input faces diminishing marginal returns, the additional output produced by the growing workforce eventually declines to zero. Ultimately, the population grows so much that labor productivity falls and per capita income returns back to the subsistence level.

The classical model predicts that in the long run, the adoption of new technology results in a larger but not richer population. Thus, the standard of living is constant over time even with technological progress, and there is no growth in per capita output. As a result of this gloomy forecast, economics was labeled the "dismal science."

The prediction from the Malthusian model failed for two reasons:

1. The link between per capita income and population broke down. In fact, as the growth of per capita income increased, population growth slowed rather than accelerating as predicted by the classical growth model.

2. Growth in per capita income has been possible because technological progress has been rapid enough to more than offset the impact of diminishing marginal returns.

Because the classical model's pessimistic prediction never materialized, economists changed the focus of the analysis away from labor to capital and to the neoclassical model.

5.2 Neoclassical Model

Robert Solow devised the mainstream neoclassical theory of growth in the 1950s.[20] The heart of this theory is the Cobb–Douglas production function discussed in Section 4.1. As before, the potential output of the economy is given by

$$Y = AF(K,L) = AK^{\alpha}L^{1-\alpha}$$

where K is the stock of capital, L is the labor input, and A is total factor productivity.[21] In the neoclassical model, both capital and labor are variable inputs each subject to diminishing marginal productivity.

The objective of the neoclassical growth model is to determine the long-run growth rate of output per capita and relate it to (a) the savings/investment rate, (b) the rate of technological change, and (c) population growth.

5.2.1 *Balanced or Steady State Rate of Growth*

As with most economic models, the neoclassical growth model attempts to find the equilibrium position toward which the economy will move. In the case of the Solow model, this equilibrium is the balanced or **steady state rate of growth** that occurs when the output-to-capital ratio is constant. Growth is balanced in the sense that capital per worker and output per worker grow at the same rate.

We begin the analysis by using the per capita version of the Cobb–Douglas production function given earlier in Equation 3:

$$y = Y/L = Ak^{\alpha}$$

where $k = K/L$. Using their definitions, the rates of change of capital per worker and output per worker are given by[22]

$$\Delta k/k = \Delta K/K - \Delta L/L$$

and

$$\Delta y/y = \Delta Y/Y - \Delta L/L$$

From the production function, the growth rate of output per worker is also equal to

$$\Delta y \, / \, y = \Delta A \, / \, A + \alpha \Delta k \, / \, k \qquad\qquad \textbf{(6)}$$

---

20 Solow (1957).

21 Our exposition of the neoclassical model with technological progress reflected in total factor productivity corresponds to what is known as "Hicks neutral" technical change. The neoclassical model is usually presented with "Harrod neutral" or "labor augmenting" technical change. In that formulation, the production function is given by $Y = F(K, BL)$, where B represents technological change and (BL) is interpreted as the "effective" labor supply. In general, this is not equivalent to our formulation using TFP. However, they are equivalent if, as we assume here, the function $F()$ has the Cobb–Douglas form. To see this, note that $[K^{\alpha}(BL)^{1-\alpha}] = [B^{1-\alpha}(K^{\alpha}L^{1-\alpha})] = [A(K^{\alpha}L^{1-\alpha})]$, where $A \equiv B^{1-\alpha}$ is total factor productivity.

22 Strictly speaking, these and other rate of change equations are exact only for changes over arbitrarily short periods ("continuous time").

The physical capital stock in an economy will increase because of gross investment (I) and decline because of depreciation. In a closed economy, investment must be funded by domestic saving. Letting s be the fraction of income (Y) that is saved, gross investment is given by $I = sY$. Assuming the physical capital stock depreciates at a constant rate, δ, the change in the physical capital stock is given by

$$\Delta K = sY - \delta K$$

Subtracting labor supply growth, $\Delta L / L \equiv n$, and rearranging gives

$$\Delta k/k = sY/K - \delta - n \tag{7}$$

In the steady state, the growth rate of capital per worker is equal to the growth rate of output per worker. Thus,

$$\Delta k/k = \Delta y/y = \Delta A/A + \alpha\Delta k/k$$

from which we get

$$\Delta y/y = \Delta k/k = (\Delta A/A)/(1 - \alpha)$$

Letting θ denote the growth rate of TFP (i.e., $\Delta A/A$), we see that the equilibrium sustainable growth rate of output per capita (= Growth rate of capital per worker) is a constant that depends only on the growth rate of TFP (θ) and the elasticity of output with respect to capital (α). Adding back the growth rate of labor (n) gives the sustainable growth rate of output.

$$\text{Growth rate of output per capita} = \frac{\theta}{1 - \alpha} \tag{8}$$

$$\text{Growth rate of output} = \frac{\theta}{1 - \alpha} + n$$

This is the key result of the neoclassical model. Note that $[\theta/(1 - \alpha)]$ is the steady state growth rate of labor productivity, so Equation 8 is consistent with the labor productivity growth accounting equation discussed in Section 4.3.

Substituting $[\theta/(1 - \alpha)]$ into the left-hand side of Equation 7 and rearranging gives the equilibrium output-to-capital ratio, denoted by the constant Ψ.

$$\frac{Y}{K} = \left(\frac{1}{s}\right)\left[\left(\frac{\theta}{1-\alpha}\right) + \delta + n\right] \equiv \Psi \tag{9}$$

In the steady state, the output-to-capital ratio is constant and the capital-to-labor ratio (k) and output per worker (y) grow at the same rate, given by $[\theta/(1 - \alpha)]$. On the steady state growth path, the marginal product of capital is also constant and, given the Cobb–Douglas production function, is equal to $\alpha(Y/K)$. The marginal product of capital is also equal to the real interest rate in the economy. Note that even though the capital-to-labor ratio (k) is rising at rate $[\theta/(1 - \alpha)]$ in the steady state, the increase in the capital-to-labor ratio (k) has no impact on the marginal product of capital, which is not changing. *Capital deepening is occurring, but it has no effect on the growth rate of the economy or on the marginal product of capital once the steady state is reached.*

Example 10

Steady State Rate of Growth for China, Japan, and Ireland

Earlier examples generated estimates of potential growth for China (11.5 percent), Japan (0.8 percent), and Ireland (1.7 percent). Given the data below,

1. Calculate the steady state growth rates from the neoclassical model for China, Japan, and Ireland.

2. Compare the steady state growth rates to the growth rates in potential GDP estimated in Examples 7–9 and explain the results.

	Labor Cost in Total Factor Cost (%)	TFP Growth (%)	Labor Force Growth (%)
China	46.5	2.5	1.2
Japan	57.3	0.2	0.0
Ireland	56.7	0.8	0.0

Sources: Conference Board Total Economy Database; labor cost and TFP growth are based on 1995–2009 data for Japan and Ireland and 1995–2008 data for China. Labor force growth estimates are from earlier examples.

Solution to 1:

Using Equation 8, the steady state growth rate in the neoclassical model is given by

$$\Delta Y / Y = (\theta)/(1 - \alpha) + n = \text{Growth rate of TFP scaled by labor factor share} + \text{Growth rate in the labor force}$$

Using the above equation and data, steady state growth rates for the three countries are estimated as follows:

China: The labor share of output $(1 - \alpha)$ is given by the average of the labor cost as a percentage of total factor cost, which is equal to 0.465 for China. The growth rate in the labor force is 1.2 percent, and the growth rate of TFP is 2.5 percent.

Steady state growth rate = 2.5%/0.465 + 1.2% = 6.58%

Japan: The labor share of output $(1 - \alpha)$ for Japan is 0.573. The growth rate in the labor force is 0.0 percent, and TFP growth is 0.2 percent.

Steady state growth rate = 0.2%/0.573 + 0.0% = 0.35%

Ireland: The labor share of output $(1 - \alpha)$ is 0.567 percent for Ireland. The growth rate in the labor force is 0.0 percent, and TFP growth is 0.8 percent.

Steady state growth rate = 0.8%/0.567 + 0.0% = 1.41%

Solution to 2:

The growth rate in potential GDP for China (8.6 percent, estimated in Example 9) is significantly above the estimated 6.58 percent steady state growth rate. The reason for this is that the economy of China is still in the process of converging to the higher income levels of the United States and the major economies in Europe. The physical capital stock is below the steady state, and capital deepening is a significant factor increasing productivity growth (see Exhibit 11) and the growth in potential GDP.

This is not the case for Japan and Ireland. Both countries are operating at essentially the steady state. The estimated growth rate in potential GDP for Japan (0.8 percent, from Example 7) is only slightly above its 0.35 percent steady state growth rate. Likewise, the estimated growth rate in potential GDP for Ireland (1.7 percent, from Example 8) is effectively equal to its estimated steady state growth rate of 1.4 percent. Operating close to the steady state means that capital investment in these countries, which results in an increasing capital-to-labor ratio, has no significant effect on the growth rate of the economy. Only changes in the growth rates of TFP and labor and in the labor share of output have an impact on potential GDP growth.

An intuitive way to understand the steady state equilibrium given in Equation 9 is to transform it into a savings/investment equation:

$$sy = \left[\left(\frac{\theta}{1-\alpha}\right) + \delta + n\right]k$$

Steady state equilibrium occurs at the output-to-capital ratio where the savings and actual gross investment per worker generated in the economy (sy) are just sufficient to (1) provide capital for new workers entering the workforce at rate n, (2) replace plant and equipment wearing out at rate δ, and (3) deepen the physical capital stock at the rate $[\theta/(1-\alpha)]$ required to keep the marginal product of capital equal to the rental price of capital.

Exhibit 13 shows the steady state equilibrium graphically. The straight line in the exhibit indicates the amount of investment required to keep the physical capital stock growing at the required rate. Because the horizontal axis is capital per worker, the slope of the line is given by $[\delta + n + \theta/(1-\alpha)]$. The curved line shows the amount of actual investment per worker and is determined by the product of the saving rate and the production function. It is curved because of diminishing marginal returns to the capital input in the production function. The intersection of the required investment and actual investment lines determines the steady state. Note that *this exhibit is a snapshot at a point in time.* Over time, the capital-to-labor ratio rises at rate $[\theta/(1-\alpha)]$ as the actual saving/investment curve $[sf(k)]$ shifts upward because of TFP growth, and *the equilibrium moves upward and to the right along the straight line.*

Exhibit 13	Steady State in the Neoclassical Model

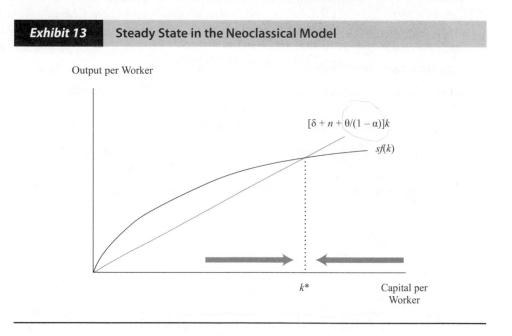

The impact of the various parameters in the model on the steady state can also be seen in the exhibit. At any point in time when the economy is on its steady state growth path, the exogenous factors—labor supply and TFP—are fixed. We would like to know what affect each of the parameters in the model has on the steady state capital-to-labor ratio and therefore on output per worker. For example, if there are two economies that differ only with respect to one parameter, what does that imply about their per capita incomes? All else the same, we can say the following regarding the impact of the parameters:

▪ Saving rate (s): An increase in the saving rate implies a higher capital-to-labor ratio (k) and higher output per worker (y) because a higher saving rate generates more saving/investment at every level of output. In Exhibit 14, the saving/investment curve [$sf(k)$] shifts upward from an initial steady state equilibrium at point A to a new equilibrium at point B. At the new equilibrium point, it intersects the required investment line [$\delta + n + \theta/(1 - \alpha)$] at higher capital-to-labor and output per worker ratios. Note that although the higher saving rate increases both k and y, it has no impact on the steady state growth rates of output per capita or output (Equation 8).

Exhibit 14　　　**Impact on the Steady State: Increase in the Saving Rate**

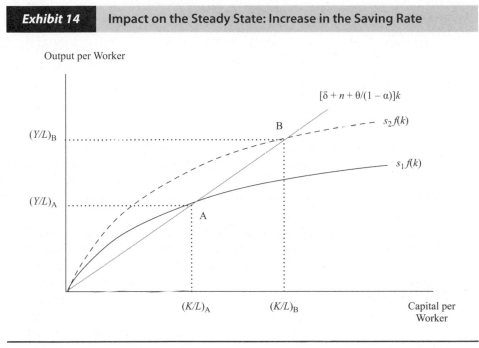

- <u>Labor force growth (n):</u> An increase in the labor force growth rate reduces the equilibrium capital-to-labor ratio because a corresponding increase in the steady state growth rate of capital is required. Given the gross saving/investment rate, this can only be achieved at a lower capital-to-labor ratio. Output per worker is correspondingly lower as well. In Exhibit 15, the higher population growth rate increases the slope of the required investment line. This shifts the steady state equilibrium from point A to point B, where it intersects the supply of saving/investment curve at lower capital-to-labor and output per worker ratios.

- <u>Depreciation rate (δ):</u> An increase in the depreciation rate reduces the equilibrium capital-to-labor and output per worker ratios because a given rate of gross saving generates less net capital accumulation. Graphically, it increases the slope of the required investment line and affects the steady state equilibrium in the same way as labor force growth (Exhibit 15).

- <u>Growth in TFP (θ):</u> An increase in the growth rate of TFP reduces the steady state capital-to-labor ratio and output per worker for given levels of labor input and TFP. This result must be interpreted with care. Raising the growth rate of TFP means that output per worker will grow faster in the future (Equation 8), but at a given point in time, a given supply of labor, and a given *level* of TFP, output per worker is lower than it would be with a slower TFP growth rate. In effect, the economy is on a steeper trajectory off a lower base of output per worker. Graphically, it is identical to Exhibit 15 in that faster TFP growth steepens the required investment line (increases the slope), which intersects with the available saving/investment curve at lower capital-to-labor and investment per worker ratios.

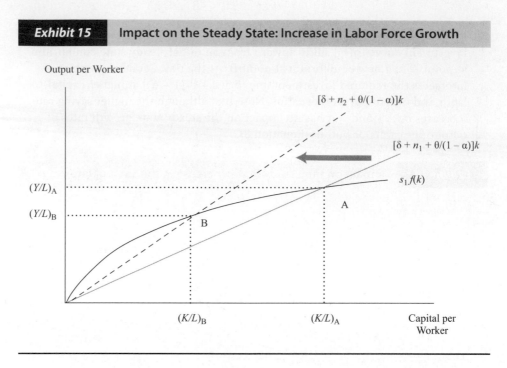

Exhibit 15   Impact on the Steady State: Increase in Labor Force Growth

In sum, such factors as the saving rate, the growth rate of the labor force, and the depreciation rate change the *level* of output per worker but do not permanently change the *growth rate* of output per worker. A permanent increase in the growth rate in output per worker can only occur if there is a change in the growth rate of TFP.

So far we have focused on the steady state growth path. What happens if the economy has not yet reached the steady state? During the transition to the steady state growth path, the economy can experience either faster or slower growth relative to the steady state. Using Equations 6, 7, and 9, we can write the growth rates of output per capita and the capital-to-labor ratio as, respectively,

$$\frac{\Delta y}{y} = \left(\frac{\theta}{1-\alpha}\right) + \alpha s\left(\frac{Y}{K} - \psi\right) = \left(\frac{\theta}{1-\alpha}\right) + \alpha s(y/k - \psi) \qquad \textbf{(10)}$$

and

$$\frac{\Delta k}{k} = \left(\frac{\theta}{1-\alpha}\right) + s\left(\frac{Y}{K} - \psi\right) = \left(\frac{\theta}{1-\alpha}\right) + s(y/k - \psi), \qquad \textbf{(11)}$$

where the second equality in each line follows from the definitions of y and k, which imply $(Y/K) = y/k$. These relationships are shown in Exhibit 16.

Exhibit 16	Dynamics in the Neoclassical Model

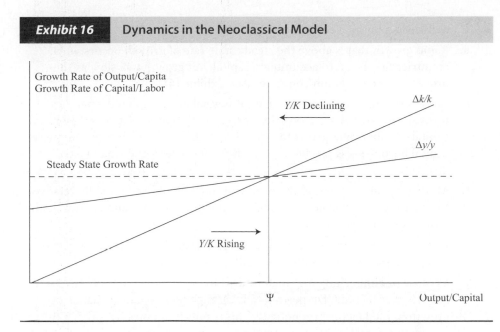

If the output-to-capital ratio is above its equilibrium level (ψ), the second term in Equations 10 and 11 is positive and the growth rates of output per capita and the capital-to-labor ratio are above the steady state rate [$\theta/(1 - \alpha)$]. This corresponds to a situation in which actual saving/investment exceeds required investment and above-trend growth in per capita output is driven by an above-trend rate of capital deepening. This situation usually reflects a relatively low capital-to-labor ratio but could, at least in principle, arise from high TFP. Because $\alpha < 1$, capital is growing faster than output and the output-to-capital ratio is falling. Over time, the growth rates of both output per capita and the capital-to-labor ratio decline to the steady state rate.

Of course, the converse is true if the output-to-capital ratio is below its steady state level. Actual investment is insufficient to sustain the trend rate of growth in the capital-to-labor ratio, and both output per capita and the capital-to-labor ratio grow more slowly. This situation usually corresponds to a relatively high and unsustainable capital-to-labor ratio, but could reflect relatively low TFP and hence relatively low output. Over time, output grows faster than capital, the output-to-capital ratio rises, and growth converges to the trend rate.

5.2.2 Implications of the Neoclassical Model

There are four major groups of conclusions from the neoclassical model:

1. Capital Accumulation

   a. Capital accumulation affects the level of output but not the growth rate in the long run.

   b. Regardless of its initial capital-to-labor ratio or initial level of productivity, a growing economy will move to a point of steady state growth.

   c. In a steady state, the growth rate of output equals the rate of labor force growth plus the rate of growth in TFP scaled by labor's share of income [$n + \theta/(1 - \alpha)$].[23] The growth rate of output does not depend on the accumulation of capital or the rate of business investment.

---

23 Readers who are familiar with the "labor-augmenting" technical change formulation of the neoclassical model should note that in that formulation, the rate of labor-augmenting technical change is also the growth rate of labor productivity. In our formulation, the growth rate of labor productivity is [$\theta/(1 - \alpha)$]. So both formulations imply that long-run growth equals the growth rate of the labor supply (n) plus a constant growth rate of labor productivity.

2. Capital Deepening vs. Technology

   a. Rapid growth that is above the steady state rate of growth occurs when countries first begin to accumulate capital; but growth will slow as the process of accumulation continues (see Exhibit 16).

   b. Long-term sustainable growth cannot rely solely on capital deepening investment—that is, on increasing the stock of capital relative to labor. If the capital-to-labor ratio grows too rapidly (i.e., faster than labor productivity), capital becomes less productive, resulting in slower rather than faster growth.

   c. More generally, increasing the supply of some input(s) too rapidly relative to other inputs will lead to diminishing marginal returns and cannot be the basis for sustainable growth.

   d. In the absence of improvements in TFP, the growth of labor productivity and per capita output would eventually slow.

   e. Because of diminishing marginal returns to capital, the only way to sustain growth in potential GDP per capita is through technological change or growth in total factor productivity. This results in an upward shift in the production function—the economy produces more goods and services for any given mix of labor and capital inputs.

3. Convergence

   a. Given the relative scarcity and hence high marginal productivity of capital and potentially higher saving rates in developing countries, the growth rates of developing countries should exceed those of developed countries.

   b. As a result, there should be a convergence of per capita incomes between developed and developing countries over time.

4. Effect of Savings on Growth

   a. The initial impact of a higher saving rate is to temporarily raise the rate of growth in the economy.[24] In response to the higher saving rate, growth exceeds the steady state growth rate during a transition period. However, the economy returns to the balanced growth path after the transition period.

   b. During the transition period, the economy moves to a higher level of per capita output and productivity.

   c. Once an economy achieves steady state growth, the growth rate does not depend on the percentage of income saved or invested. Higher savings cannot permanently raise the growth rate of output.

   d. However, countries with higher saving rates will have a higher level of per capita output, a higher capital-to-labor ratio, and a higher level of labor productivity.

Example 11

Comparative Statics and Transitional Growth in the Neoclassical Model

Beginning in steady state equilibrium, an economy's saving rate suddenly increases from 20 percent of income to 30 percent of income. Other key parameters describing the economy are as follows:

---

24 Mathematically, this can be seen as follows: Equation 9 indicates that an increase in the saving rate (s) reduces the steady state output-to-capital ratio (ψ). This makes the last term in Equations 10 and 11 positive, raising the growth rates of output per capita (y) and the capital-to-labor ratio (k) above the steady state rate.

Growth rate of TFP (θ)	= 0.02
Income share of capital (α)	= 0.35
Depreciation rate (δ)	= 0.10
Labor force growth rate (n)	= 0.01

The following table shows the output-to-capital ratio that will prevail in this economy at various points in time after the increase in the saving rate.

Years after Saving Rate Increase	Output-to-Capital Ratio
5	0.5947
10	0.5415
25	0.4857
50	0.4708
100	0.4693
New steady state	??

By rearranging the Cobb–Douglas production function (Equation 3), the proportional impact of the saving rate change on the capital-to-labor ratio can be expressed in terms of the proportional impact on the output-to-capital ratio. The proportional impact on per capita income can then be determined from the production function (Equation 3). Labeling the paths with and without the change in saving rate as "new" and "old" respectively, at each date we have:[a]

$$\frac{k_{new}}{k_{old}} = \left[\frac{\left(Y/K \right)_{new}}{\left(Y/K \right)_{old}} \right]^{\frac{1}{\alpha-1}}$$

and

$$\frac{y_{new}}{y_{old}} = \left(\frac{k_{new}}{k_{old}} \right)^{\alpha}$$

1. Using Equations 8 and 9, calculate the steady state growth rate of per capita income and the steady state output-to-capital ratio both before and after the change in the saving rate. What happens to the capital-to-labor ratio and output per capita?

2. Use the output-to-capital ratios given in the table above along with Equation 10 and your answers to Question 1 to determine the growth rate of per capita income that will prevail immediately following the change in the saving rate and at each of the indicated times after the change. Explain the pattern of growth rates.

3. Using the output-to-capital ratios given in the table above, calculate the proportional impact of the increased saving rate on the capital-to-labor ratio and on per capita income over time. With respect to these variables, how will the new steady state compare with the old steady state?

Solution to 1:

From Equation 8, the steady state growth rate of per capita income, both before and after the increase in the saving rate, is $\Delta y / y = \theta / (1 - \alpha) = 0.02 / (1 - 0.35) = 0.0308$, or 3.08 percent. From Equation 9, the steady state output-to-capital ratio is

$$\frac{Y}{K} = \left(\frac{1}{s}\right)\left[\left(\frac{\theta}{1-\alpha}\right) + \delta + n\right] \equiv \Psi$$

Using the parameter values given above, $[\theta/(1-\alpha) + \delta + n] = (0.0308 + 0.10 + 0.01) = 0.1408$, so the steady state output-to-capital ratio is $(0.1408/0.2) = 0.7040$ with the initial 20 percent saving rate and $(0.1408/0.30) = 0.4693$ with the new 30 percent saving rate. As shown in exhibit 14, both the capital-to-labor ratio and output per worker are at higher *levels* in the new steady state. But once the new steady state is achieved, they do not grow any faster than they did in the steady state with the lower saving rate.

Solution to 2

According to Equation 10, the growth rate of per capita income is given by

$$\frac{\Delta y}{y} = \left(\frac{\theta}{1-\alpha}\right) + \alpha s(y/k - \psi)$$

Immediately following the increase in the saving rate, the relevant value of ψ becomes the new steady state output-to-capital ratio (0.4693). The actual output-to-capital ratio does not change immediately, so y/k is initially still 0.7040. Plugging these values into the growth equation above gives the growth rate of per capita income:

$$\Delta y/y = 0.0308 + (0.35)(0.30)(0.7040 - 0.4693) = 0.0554, \text{ or } 5.54 \text{ percent}$$

Similar calculations using the output-to-capital ratios in the table above give the following:

Years after Saving Rate Increase	Output-to-Capital Ratio	Growth Rate of Per Capita Income (%)
0	0.7040	5.54
5	0.5947	4.39
10	0.5415	3.84
25	0.4857	3.25
50	0.4708	3.09
100	0.4693	3.08
New steady state	0.4693	3.08

The growth rate "jumps" from the steady state rate of 3.08 percent to 5.54 percent when the saving rate increases because the increase in saving/investment results in more rapid capital accumulation. Over time, the growth rate slows because the marginal productivity of capital declines as the capital-to-labor ratio increases. In addition, as the capital-to-labor ratio increases and the output-to-capital ratio declines, a greater portion of savings is required to maintain the capital-to-labor ratio, leaving a smaller portion for continued capital deepening. Roughly two-thirds of the growth acceleration has dissipated after 10 years.

Solution to 3:

Using the output-to-capital ratio that will prevail five years after the saving rate increase, the proportional impact on the capital-to-labor ratio and on per capita income will be

$$\frac{k_{new}}{k_{old}} = \left[\frac{(Y/K)_{new}}{(Y/K)_{old}}\right]^{\frac{1}{\alpha-1}} = \left[\frac{0.5947}{0.7040}\right]^{\frac{-1}{0.65}} = 1.2964$$

and

$$\frac{y_{new}}{y_{old}} = \left(\frac{k_{new}}{k_{old}}\right)^{\alpha} = 1.2964^{0.35} = 1.0951$$

Thus, after five years, the capital-to-labor ratio will be 29.64 percent higher than it would have been without the increase in the saving rate and per capita income will be 9.51 percent higher. Similar calculations for the other time periods give the following:

Years after Saving Rate Increase	Proportionate Increase (%) in:	
	Capital-to-Labor Ratio	**Per Capita Income**
0	0.00	0.00
5	29.64	9.51
10	49.74	15.18
25	77.01	22.12
50	85.71	24.19
100	86.68	24.42
New steady state	86.68	24.42

In the new steady state, the capital-to-labor ratio will be 86.68 percent higher at every point in time than it would have been in the old steady state. Per capita income will be 24.42 percent higher at every point in time. Both variables will be growing at the same rate (3.08 percent) as they would have been in the old steady state.

[a] Note that the output-to-capital ratio would have been constant on the original steady state path. Because of the impact of total factor productivity, the capital-to-labor ratio and output per capita are not constant even in steady state. In comparing "paths" for these variables, we isolate the impact of the saving rate change by canceling out the effect of TFP growth. Mathematically, we cancel out A in Equation 3 to get the equations shown here.

5.2.3 *Extension of the Neoclassical Model*

Solow (1957) used the growth accounting equation to determine the contributions of each factor to economic growth in the United States for the period 1909–1949. He reached the surprising conclusion that over 80 percent of the per capita growth in the United States was due to TFP. Denison (1985) authored another study examining U.S. growth for the period 1929–1982 using the Solow framework. His findings were similar to Solow's, with TFP explaining nearly 70 percent of U.S. growth. The problem with these findings is that the neoclassical model provides no explicit explanation of the economic determinants of technological progress or how TFP changes over time. Because technology is determined outside the model (i.e., exogenously), critics argue that the neoclassical model ignores the very factor driving growth in the economy. Technology is simply the residual or the part of growth that cannot be explained by other inputs, such as capital and labor. This lack of an explanation for technology led to growing dissatisfaction with the neoclassical model.

The other source of criticism of the neoclassical model is the prediction that the steady state rate of economic growth is unrelated to the rate of saving and investment. Long-run growth of output in the Solow model depends only on the rates of growth of the labor force and technology. Higher rates of investment and savings have only a transitory impact on growth. Thus, an increase in investment as a share of GDP from 10 percent to 15 percent of GDP will have a positive impact on the near-term growth rate but will not have a permanent impact on the ultimately sustainable percentage growth rate. This conclusion makes many economists uncomfortable. Mankiw (1995) provided evidence rebutting this hypothesis and showed that saving rates and growth rates are positively correlated across countries. Finally, the neoclassical model predicts that in an economy where the stock of capital is rising faster than labor productivity, the return to investment should decline with time. For the advanced countries, the evidence does not support this argument because returns have not fallen over time.

Critiques of the neoclassical model led to two lines of subsequent research on economic growth. The first approach, which was originated by Jorgenson (1966, 2000), is termed the augmented Solow approach. It remains in the neoclassical tradition in that diminishing marginal returns are critical and there is no explanation for the determinants of technological progress. Instead, this approach attempts to reduce empirically the portion of growth attributed to the unexplained residual labeled technological progress (TFP). The idea is to develop better measures of the inputs used in the production function and broaden the definition of investment by including human capital, research and development, and public infrastructure. In addition, the composition of capital spending is important. Higher levels of capital spending on high-technology goods will boost productivity more than spending on machine tools or structures.

By adding inputs like human capital to the production function, the augmented Solow model enables us to more accurately measure the contribution of technological progress to growth. However, the economy still moves toward a steady state growth path because even broadly defined capital is assumed to eventually encounter diminishing marginal returns. In essence, this line of research uses the growth accounting methodology and increases the number of inputs in the production function in order to provide a more accurate measure of technological progress. The second approach is the endogenous growth theory, which we examine in the next section.

5.3 Endogenous Growth Theory

The alternative to the neoclassical model is a series of models known as endogenous growth theory. These models focus on explaining technological progress rather than treating it as exogenous. In these models, self-sustaining growth emerges as a natural consequence of the model and the economy does not necessarily converge to a steady state rate of growth. Unlike the neoclassical model, there are *no diminishing marginal returns to capital for the economy as a whole* in the endogenous growth models. So increasing the saving rate permanently increases the rate of economic growth. These models also allow for the possibility of increasing returns to scale.

Romer (1986) provided a model of technological progress and a rationale for why capital does not experience diminishing marginal returns. He argued that capital accumulation is the main factor accounting for long-run growth, once the definition of capital is broadened to include such items as human or knowledge capital and research and development (R&D). R&D is defined as investment in new knowledge that improves the production process. In endogenous growth theory, knowledge or human capital and R&D spending are factors of production, like capital and labor, and have to be paid for through savings.

Companies spend on R&D for the same reason they invest in new equipment and build new factories: to make a profit. R&D spending is successful if it leads to the development of a new product or method of production that is successful in the marketplace. However, there is a fundamental difference between spending on new equipment and factories and on R&D. The final product of R&D spending is ideas. These ideas can potentially be copied and used by other companies in the economy. Thus, R&D expenditures have potentially large positive externalities or spillover effects. This means that spending by one company has a positive impact on other companies and increases the overall pool of knowledge available to all companies. Spending by companies on R&D and knowledge capital generates benefits to the economy as a whole that exceed the private benefit to the individual company making the R&D investment. Individual companies cannot fully capture all the benefits associated with creating new ideas and methods of production. Some of the benefits are external to the company, and so are the social returns associated with the investment in R&D and human capital.

This distinction between the private and social returns or benefits to capital is important because it solves an important microeconomic issue. The elimination of the assumption of diminishing marginal returns to capital implies constant returns to capital and increasing returns to all factors taken together. If individual companies could capture these scale economies, then all industries would eventually be dominated by a single company—a monopoly. There is simply no empirical evidence to support this implication. Separating private returns from social returns solves the problem. If companies face constant returns to scale for all private factors, there is no longer an inherent advantage for a company being large. But the externality or social benefit results in increasing returns to scale across the entire economy as companies benefit from the private spending of the other companies.

The role of R&D spending and the positive externalities associated with this spending have important implications for economic growth. In the endogenous growth model, the economy does not reach a steady growth rate equal to the growth of labor plus an exogenous rate of labor productivity growth. Instead, saving and investment decisions can generate self-sustaining growth at a permanently higher rate. This situation is in sharp contrast to the neoclassical model, in which only a transitory increase in growth above the steady state is possible. The reason for this difference is that because of the externalities on R&D, diminishing marginal returns to capital do not set in. The production function in the endogenous growth model is a straight line given by

$$y_e = f(k_e) = ck_e \tag{12}$$

where output per worker (y_e) is proportional to the stock of capital per worker (k_e), c is the (constant) marginal product of capital in the aggregate economy, and the subscript e denotes the endogenous growth model. In contrast, the neoclassical production function is a curved line that eventually flattens out (see Exhibit 4).

To understand the significance of introducing constant returns to aggregate capital accumulation, note that in this model the output-to-capital ratio is fixed ($= c$) and therefore output per worker (y_e) always grows at the same rate as capital per worker (k_e). Thus, faster or slower capital accumulation translates one for one into faster or slower growth in output per capita. Substituting Equation 12 into Equation 7 gives an equation for the growth rate of output per capita in the endogenous growth model:

$$\Delta y_e/y_e = \Delta k_e/k_e = sc - \delta - n$$

Because all the terms on the right-hand side of this equation are constant, this is both the long-run and short-run growth rate in this model. Examination of the equation shows that *a higher saving rate (s) implies a permanently higher growth rate*. This is the key result of the endogenous growth model.

The positive externalities associated with spending on R&D and knowledge capital suggest that spending by private companies on these inputs may be too low from an overall societal point of view. This is an example of a market failure where private companies under-invest in the production of these goods. In this case, there may be a role for government intervention to correct for the market failure by direct government spending on R&D and/or providing tax breaks and subsidies for private production of knowledge capital. Higher levels of spending on knowledge capital could translate into faster economic growth even in the long run. Finally, according to the endogenous growth theory, there is *no reason why the incomes of developed and developing countries should converge.* Because of constant or even increasing returns associated with investment in knowledge capital, the developed countries can continue to grow as fast as, or faster than, the developing countries. As a result, there is no reason to expect convergence of income over time. We now turn to the convergence debate in more detail.

Example 12

Neoclassical vs. Endogenous Growth Models

Consider again an economy with per capita income growing at a constant 3.08 percent rate and with a 20 percent saving rate, an output-to-capital ratio (c in the endogenous growth model, Equation 12) of 0.7040, a depreciation rate (δ) of 10 percent, and a 1 percent labor force growth (n).

1. Use the endogenous growth model to calculate the new steady state growth rate of per capita income if the saving rate increases to 23.5 percent.

2. How much higher will per capita income be in 10 years because of the higher saving rate? How does this compare with the impact calculated in Example 11 using the neoclassical model? What accounts for the difference?

3. In an effort to boost growth, the government is considering two proposals. One would subsidize all private companies that increase their investment spending. The second would subsidize only investments in R&D and/ or implementation of new technologies with potential for network externalities. Interpret these proposals in terms of the neoclassical and endogenous growth models and assess their likely impact on growth. (Focus only on "supply-side" considerations here.)

Solution to 1:

In the endogenous growth model the new growth rate of per capital income is

$$\Delta y_e / y_e = sc - \delta - n = (0.235)(0.7040) - 0.10 - 0.01 = 0.0554, \text{ or } 5.54 \text{ percent}$$

This is the same as the growth rate immediately following the increase in the saving rate (to 30 percent in that case) in the earlier example using the neoclassical model (Example 11). Unlike in the neoclassical model, in the endogenous growth model this higher growth rate will be sustained.

Solution to 2:

According to the endogenous growth model, per capita income will grow 2.46 percent (= 5.54% − 3.08%) faster with the higher saving rate. After 10 years, the cumulative impact of the faster growth rate will be

$$\exp(0.0246 \times 10) = \exp(0.246) = 1.2789$$

So, per capita income will be almost 28 percent higher than it would have been at the lower saving rate. This increase is substantially larger than the 15.18 percent cumulative increase after 10 years found in Example 11 assuming a much larger increase in the saving rate (to 30 percent instead of 23.5 percent) in the neoclassical model. The difference arises because the endogenous growth model assumes that capital accumulation is not subject to diminishing returns. Therefore, the growth rate is permanently, rather than temporarily, higher.

Solution to 3:

Subsidizing all private investment would tend to have a significant, pure capital deepening component. That is, companies would be encouraged to buy more, but not necessarily better, plant and equipment. The neoclassical model indicates that this is likely to result in a temporary surge in growth, but even if the higher rate of investment/saving is sustained, growth will again decline over time. On the positive side, this proposal is very likely to succeed, at least for a while, because it does not require investment in unproven technologies or ill-defined network effects. The impact of the other proposal is more uncertain but potentially much more powerful. If the investments in R&D and/or new technologies lead to new knowledge, greater efficiency, new products and methods, and/or network externalities, then the endogenous growth model suggests that growth is likely to be permanently enhanced.

5.4 Convergence Debate

As is evident in Exhibit 1, a wide gap separates the living standards in the developed and developing nations of the world. The question is, Will this difference persist forever or will the per capita income levels of the developing countries converge to those of the developed countries? Convergence means that countries with low per capita incomes should grow at a faster rate than countries with high per capita incomes. Thus, over time the per capita income of developing countries should converge toward that of the developed countries. Whether convergence occurs has major implications for the future growth prospects of developed versus developing countries. It also has important investment implications.

Neoclassical growth theory predicts two types of convergence: absolute convergence and conditional convergence. **Absolute convergence** means that developing countries, regardless of their particular characteristics, will eventually catch up with the developed countries and match them in per capita output. The neoclassical model assumes that all countries have access to the same technology. As a result, per capita income in all countries should eventually grow at the same rate. Thus, the model implies convergence of per capita *growth rates* among all countries. It does not, however, imply that the *level* of per capita income will be the same in all countries regardless of underlying characteristics; that is, it does not imply absolute convergence.

Conditional convergence means that convergence is conditional on the countries having the same saving rate, population growth rate, and production function. If these conditions hold, the neoclassical model implies convergence to the same *level* of per capita output as well as the same steady state growth rate. In terms of Exhibit 13, these economies would have the same k^* and thus the same steady state. If they start with different capital-to-labor ratios, their growth rates will differ in the transition to the steady state. The economy with a lower capital-to-labor ratio will experience more rapid growth of productivity and per capita income, but the differential will diminish until they finally converge. Countries with different saving rates or population growth rates and thus different steady state values for k^* will have different steady state *levels* of per capita income, but their growth rates of per capita output will still converge.

The data (see Exhibit 18) indicate that some of the poorer countries are diverging rather than converging to the income levels of the developed countries. Thus, in addition to the first two convergence concepts, we have the notion of **club convergence**, where only rich and middle-income countries that are members of the club are converging to the income level of the richest countries in the world. This means that the countries with the lowest per capita income in the club grow at the fastest rate. In contrast, countries outside the club continue to fall behind. Poor countries can join the club if they make appropriate institutional changes, such as those summarized in Section 2.7. Finally, countries may fall into a **non-convergence trap** if they do not implement necessary institutional reforms. For example, failure to reform labor markets has undermined growth in some European countries that have experienced weak growth in employment and high rates of unemployment over the last two decades. Certain institutional arrangements that initially enhance growth may later generate non-convergence traps if maintained too long. Import substitution policies enabled the Latin American countries to grow rapidly in the 1950s and 1960s but caused them to stagnate in the 1970s and 1980s.

If convergence, and especially club convergence, does occur, investing in countries with lower per capita incomes that are members of the club should, over long periods of time, provide a higher rate of return than investing in higher-income countries. Convergence means that the rate of growth of potential GDP should be higher in developing countries that have made the institutional changes that are a precondition for growth and that enable these countries to become members of the convergence club. With higher long-term growth in these economies, corporate profits should also grow at a faster rate. Given the faster rate of growth in earnings, stock prices may also rise at a faster rate. Of course, risk is also likely to be higher in these markets. Nonetheless, it is reasonable to conclude that long-term investors should allocate a risk-tolerance-appropriate portion of their assets to those developing economies that have become members of the convergence club.

Convergence between the developed and developing countries can occur in two ways. First, convergence takes place through capital accumulation and capital deepening. Exhibit 17 illustrates the difference between developed and developing countries using the per capita neoclassical production function. The developed countries operate at point B, so increases in capital have almost no impact on productivity. In contrast, developing countries operate at point A, where increases in capital significantly boost labor productivity.

Exhibit 17	Per Capita Production Function Developed vs. Developing Countries

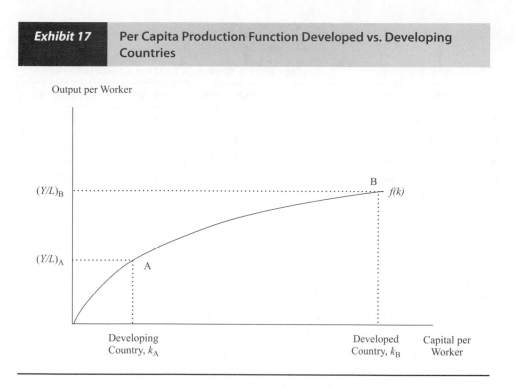

A second source of convergence is that developing countries can imitate or adopt technology already widely utilized in the advanced countries. Developing countries can learn from advanced countries as scientific and management practices spread with globalization. By importing technology from the advanced countries, the developing countries can achieve faster economic growth and converge to the income of the advanced countries. Japan had a successful imitation strategy in the 1950s and 1960s, as does China now. Technology transfers will narrow the income gap between developed and developing countries only if the poor countries invest the resources to master the technology and apply it to their economies. This spending is similar to R&D spending and allows the country to join the convergence club. The steady state rate of growth for members of the convergence club will be determined by the global rate of technological progress. Without such spending, the country will be left out and will continue to fall behind the developed countries.

In contrast to the neoclassical model, the endogenous growth model makes no prediction that convergence should occur. This model allows for countries that start with high per capita income and more capital to grow faster and stay ahead of the developing countries. If the externalities associated with knowledge and human capital are large, the higher-income country can maintain its lead through high rates of investment in these capital inputs.

If the convergence hypothesis is correct, there should be an inverse relation between the initial level of per capita real GDP and the growth rate in per capita GDP. Exhibit 18 shows the countries in Exhibit 1 in descending order of per capita income in 1950. If incomes are converging across countries, the poor countries in 1950 should have a higher growth rate between 1950 and 2010 than the rich countries.

| Exhibit 18 | Real Per Capita GDP by Country |

	Real GDP Per Capita in Dollars				Average Annual Growth in Real Per Capita GDP (%)			
	1950	1970	1990	2010	1950–1970	1970–1990	1990–2010	1950–2010
United States	14,559	22,806	35,328	46,697	2.27	2.21	1.40	1.96
New Zealand	13,795	18,255	22,331	31,223	1.41	1.01	1.69	1.37
Australia	13,219	21,444	30,628	45,951	2.45	1.80	2.05	2.10
Canada	12,053	19,919	31,196	41,288	2.54	2.27	1.41	2.07
United Kingdom	11,602	18,002	27,469	37,378	2.22	2.14	1.55	1.97
France	8,266	18,186	28,127	34,358	4.02	2.20	1.01	2.40
Venezuela	8,104	11,590	9,028	10,560	1.81	−1.24	0.79	0.44
Argentina	6,164	9,026	7,952	13,468	1.93	−0.63	2.67	1.31
Italy	5,954	16,522	27,734	31,069	5.24	2.62	0.57	2.79
Ireland	5,496	9,869	18,812	36,433	2.97	3.28	3.36	3.20
Saudi Arabia	5,060	17,292	20,399	22,951	6.34	0.83	0.59	2.55
South Africa	4,361	6,959	6,595	8,716	2.36	−0.27	1.40	1.16
Singapore	4,299	8,600	27,550	56,224	3.53	5.99	3.63	4.38
Mexico	4,180	7,634	10,754	13,710	3.06	1.73	1.22	2.00
Spain	3,964	11,444	21,830	30,504	5.44	3.28	1.69	3.46
Peru	3,464	5,786	4,516	8,671	2.60	−1.23	3.32	1.54
Hong Kong	3,128	8,031	24,734	43,324	4.83	5.79	2.84	4.48
Japan	3,048	15,413	29,813	34,828	8.44	3.35	0.78	4.14
Brazil	2,365	4,324	6,959	9,589	3.06	2.41	1.62	2.36
Turkey	2,327	4,413	7,741	11,769	3.25	2.85	2.12	2.74
Taiwan	1,425	3,948	15,465	36,413	5.23	7.07	4.37	5.55
Philippines	1,296	2,136	2,660	3,672	2.53	1.10	1.63	1.75
South Korea	1,185	3,009	12,083	30,079	4.77	7.20	4.67	5.54
Egypt	1,132	1,560	3,137	5,306	1.62	3.55	2.66	2.61
Nigeria	814	1,183	1,203	2,037	1.89	0.08	2.67	1.54
Indonesia	804	1,182	2,517	4,740	1.95	3.85	3.22	3.00
Kenya	791	1,113	1,359	1,376	1.72	1.00	0.06	0.93
Vietnam	689	770	1,073	3,369	0.56	1.67	5.89	2.68
Pakistan	666	985	1,645	2,600	1.98	2.60	2.32	2.29
India	658	922	1,390	3,575	1.70	2.07	4.84	2.86
Botswana	449	774	3,731	5,311	2.76	8.18	1.78	4.20
China	402	698	1,677	8,569	2.80	4.48	8.50	5.23
Ethiopia	314	479	462	749	2.13	−0.18	2.45	1.46

The results for the convergence hypothesis are mixed. The countries with the highest per capita income in 1950 were the United States, New Zealand, Australia, and Canada. The markets with the fastest growth rate over the period 1950–2010 were Taiwan, South Korea, and China, each growing at a rate above 5 percent. This result strongly supports convergence because the per capita incomes of all three countries in 1950 were well below that of the United States. In addition, the results for Japan, Singapore, and Spain showed a convergence to the level of income in the advanced economies. In total, 23 of the 32 countries grew faster than the United States over the period. However, Ethiopia, Kenya, Nigeria, the Philippines, Peru, South Africa, Argentina, Venezuela, and New Zealand fell further behind the United States. Interestingly, since 1990 convergence has been relatively strong overall, with 24 countries (75 percent) growing faster than the United States—including Ethiopia, Nigeria, the Philippines, Peru, South Africa, Argentina, and New Zealand—but has not continued among the most advanced economies as France, Japan, and Italy lagged the United States, Canada, and Australia.

The evidence seems to suggest that poorer countries may converge if they develop the appropriate legal, political, and economic institutions as discussed in Section 2.7. In addition, trade policy is an important factor, which we address in the next section.

GROWTH IN AN OPEN ECONOMY

6

The Solow model discussed in Section 5.2 assumed a closed economy in which domestic investment equals domestic savings and there is no international trade or capital flows. Opening up the economy to trade and financial flows can significantly affect the rate of growth in an economy for the following reasons:

1. A country can borrow or lend funds in global markets, and domestic investment can be funded by global savings. Thus, investment is not constrained by domestic savings.

2. Countries can shift resources into industries in which they have a comparative advantage and away from industries in which they are relatively inefficient, thereby increasing overall productivity.

3. Companies have access to a larger, global market for their products, allowing them to better exploit any economies of scale and increasing the potential reward for successful innovation.

4. Countries can import technology, thus increasing the rate of technological progress.

5. Global trade increases competition in the domestic market, forcing companies to produce better products, improve productivity, and keep costs low.

According to the neoclassical model, convergence should occur more quickly if economies are open and there is free trade and international borrowing and lending. Opening up the economy should increase the rate at which countries' capital-to-labor ratios converge. The dynamic adjustment process can be described as follows:

1. Developing countries have less capital per worker, and as a result, the marginal product of capital is higher. Thus, the rate of return on investments should be higher in countries with low capital-to-labor ratios and lower in countries with high capital-to-labor ratios.

2. Global savers, seeking higher returns on investments, will invest in the capital-poor countries. In an open economy, capital should flow from countries with high capital-to-labor ratios to those that are capital poor.

3. Because of the capital inflows, the physical capital stock in the developing countries should grow more rapidly than in rich countries even if the saving rate is low in the poorer countries. Faster capital growth will result in higher productivity growth, causing per capita incomes to converge.

4. Because capital flows must be matched by offsetting trade flows, capital-poor countries will tend to run a trade deficit as they borrow globally to finance domestic investment. In contrast, the developed countries will tend to run trade surpluses as they export capital.

5. During the transition to the new steady state, the inflows of capital will temporarily raise the rate of growth in the capital-poor country above the steady state rate of growth. At the same time, growth in the capital-exporting countries will be below the steady state.

6. Over time, the physical capital stock will rise in the capital-poor country, reducing the return on investments. As a result, the rate of investment and size of the country's trade deficit will decline. Growth will slow and approach the steady state rate of growth. If investment falls below the level of domestic savings, the country will eventually shift from a trade deficit to a trade surplus and become an exporter of capital.

7. In the Solow model, after the reallocation of world savings, there is no permanent increase in the rate of growth in an economy. Both the developed and developing countries grow at the steady state rate of growth.

In contrast to the neoclassical model, endogenous growth models predict that a more open trade policy will permanently raise the rate of economic growth. In these models, international trade increases global output through the following:

1. A selection effect, where increased competition from foreign companies forces less efficient domestic companies to exit and more efficient ones to innovate and raises the efficiency of the overall national economy.

2. A scale effect that allows producers to more fully exploit economies of scale by selling to a larger market.

3. A backwardness effect arising from less advanced countries or sectors of an economy catching up with the more advanced countries or sectors through knowledge spillovers.

Open trade also affects the innovation process by encouraging higher levels of spending on R&D and on human capital as companies invest to take advantage of access to larger markets and the greater flow of ideas and knowledge among countries. The rate of return to new investment increases, as does the rate of economic growth. In general, most countries gain from open trade, with the scale effect benefiting smaller countries and the backwardness effect benefiting the poorer, less developed countries. But trade can also retard growth in some cases, especially in small countries that lag behind the technology leaders. Opening these countries to trade may discourage domestic innovation because companies will recognize that, even if they innovate, they may lose out to more efficient foreign companies.

Example 13

The Entry of China and India into the Global Economy

China and India effectively entered the global economy in the 1980s as they shifted toward more market-oriented policies and opened up to global trade. Their impact on global growth was significant. In 2010, China and India accounted for 13.6 percent and 5.5 percent of world GDP, respectively, whereas the two countries combined for only 4.2 percent of global output in 1980. The entry of these two countries significantly increased the global supply of skilled and unskilled labor receiving low wages. As a result of the surge in available labor, global potential

GDP increased sharply. Economic theory suggests that the supply-side increase in the global capacity to produce goods and services would increase global output and put downward pressure on prices.

The neoclassical model of growth can provide us with some further insights into the impact of China and India entering the global economy. China and India are low-wage and capital-poor countries. In contrast, the United States, Japan, and Europe are high-wage and capital–rich countries. One would expect that the rate of return on capital would be higher in China and India and that capital would flow from the developed countries to China and India. Hence, both China and India would be expected to run trade deficits. This has been the case for India but, contrary to the prediction of the model, China has run trade surpluses. These surpluses stem from China's very high domestic saving rate—even higher than its high investment rate—as well as currency intervention that channels domestic saving into accumulation of foreign exchange reserves.

Nonetheless, China has experienced large foreign direct investment (see Exhibit 19) inflows, which have reinforced its already high private investment rate. As China and India accumulate capital, their capital-to-labor ratios, real wage levels, and per capita income should converge toward those of the advanced economies. Depending on global aggregate demand conditions, wages might even have to fall in the developed countries in the process of shifting wealth and income to the developing economies. Because of the surge in the global supply of labor, the overall share of labor in global income should decline relative to capital. In addition, global productivity should rise as China and India account for a rising share of global output. In sum, over the long run, the growing share of global GDP going to China and India will benefit the global economy as more efficient utilization of resources allows global potential GDP to grow more rapidly for an extended period.

Although both the neoclassical and endogenous models of growth show the benefits of open markets, over the last 50 years developing countries have pursued two contrasting strategies for economic development:

- *Inward-oriented policies* attempt to develop domestic industries by restricting imports. Instead of importing goods and services, these policies encourage the production of domestic substitutes, despite the fact that it may be more costly to do so. These policies are also called import substitution policies.

- *Outward-oriented policies* attempt to integrate domestic industries with those of the global economy through trade and make exports a key driver of growth.

Many African and Latin American countries pursued inward-oriented policies from the 1950s to the 1980s that resulted in poor GDP growth and inefficient industries producing low-quality goods. In contrast, many East Asian countries, such as Hong Kong, Singapore, and South Korea, pursued outward-oriented polices during this same time period, which resulted in high rates of GDP growth and convergence with developed countries. These countries also benefited from the positive effects of foreign direct investment, which suggests that more open and trade-oriented economies will grow at a faster rate. The evidence strongly supports this case.

In Example 1, we compared the economic performance of Argentina and Venezuela with that of Japan, South Korea, and Singapore. In 1950, the per capita GDP of the two Latin American countries was well above that of the three East Asian countries. By 2010, however, the per capita GDPs of the three Asian countries was well above those of Argentina and Venezuela. The difference in the growth rates between Argentina and Venezuela and the three Asian countries is explained largely by the openness of their economies. Argentina and Venezuela were relatively closed economies, whereas the Asian countries relied on foreign investment and open markets to fuel growth. China is now using the same approach and has achieved significant success. China's real per capita GDP (see Exhibit 1) increased from $698 in 1970 to $8,569 in 2010 following policy changes that opened the economy to global trade.

The good news is that many African and Latin American countries have removed trade barriers and are now pursuing more outward-oriented policies. These countries have seen better growth in recent years. Brazil is a good example. Exports of goods and services increased from $64.6 billion in 2000 to $249.9 billion in 2010, an increase of over 286 percent. As shown in Exhibit 19, exports as a share of GDP rose from 5.2 percent to 10.7 percent over this period.

Exhibit 19	Exports and Foreign Direct Investment of Selected Countries			
	1980	1990	2000	2010
Brazil				
Exports as percent of GDP	5.1	4.5	5.2	10.7
Inflows of foreign direct investment ($ billions)	NA	NA	$32.8	$48.5
China				
Exports as percent of GDP	5.9	7.5	9.3	17.2
Inflows of foreign direct investment ($ billions)	NA	NA	$38.4	$185.0
India				
Exports as percent of GDP	2.7	3.5	3.8	7.2
Inflows of foreign direct investment ($ billions)	NA	NA	$3.6	$24.6
Ireland				
Exports as percent of GDP	32.1	59.6	88.3	128.5
Inflows of foreign direct investment ($ billions)	NA	NA	$25.8	$26.3
Mexico				
Exports as percent of GDP	12.8	16.2	15.7	19.1
Inflows of foreign direct investment ($ billions)	NA	NA	$18.0	$19.6
South Africa				
Exports as percent of GDP	NA	11.6	10.7	16.1
Inflows of foreign direct investment ($ billions)	NA	NA	$0.9	$1.56
South Korea				
Exports as percent of GDP	NA	26.3	25.1	35.0
Inflows of foreign direct investment ($ billions)	NA	NA	$9.3	−$0.2
United States				
Exports as percent of GDP	8.8	9.1	10.9	12.7
Inflows of foreign direct investment ($ billions)	NA	NA	$159.2	$351.3

Source: OECD StatLink.

Example 14

Why Some Countries Converge and Others Do Not

As evident from the high rates of growth between 1950 and 2010 shown in Exhibit 18, China and South Korea are converging toward the income levels of the advanced countries but still have a long way to go, especially in the case of China. In contrast, the economies of Mexico and South Africa have not converged. Using the data in Exhibits 9 and 19, give some reasons why this has occurred.

Solution:

Two reasons largely account for the difference. First, growth in the Chinese and South Korean economies has been driven by high rates of business investment. As shown in Exhibit 9, investment as a share of GDP in 2010 was 48.2 percent in China, almost double the rate of 25.0 percent in Mexico and more than double the rate of 19.3 percent in South Africa. Although investment as a share of GDP in South Korea is lower than in China, it is well above that of Mexico and South Africa.

Second, both China and South Korea have pursued an aggressive export-driven, outward-oriented policy focusing on manufactured goods. In 2010, exports were 35 percent of GDP for South Korea and 17.2 percent of GDP for China (Exhibit 19). In addition, foreign direct investment is a major factor underlying growth in China.

The comparable export numbers for Mexico and South Africa are 19.1 percent and 16.1 percent of GDP, respectively. Despite the North American Free Trade Agreement (NAFTA), Mexico's exports as a share of GDP rose only modestly from 1990 to 2010. In contrast, exports as a share of GDP for China have nearly doubled since 2000. In addition, Mexico and South Africa attracted only a combined $21.2 billion in foreign direct investment in 2010, significantly less than that of Ireland—a smaller but much wealthier and very open country—and the $185 billion inflow of foreign investment into China. The upshot is that Mexico and South Africa have been more inward-oriented economies. These trends are changing, however, as many African and Latin American countries are increasingly relying on growing exports and foreign investment to increase GDP growth.

Example 15

Investment Prospects in Spain: Estimating the Sustainable Growth Rate

You are a financial analyst at Global Invest Inc., an investment management firm that runs a number of global mutual funds with a significant exposure to Spain. The Madrid General Index, which reached a crisis-induced low of 716 in March 2009, remains far below its November 2007 peak of 1725. The members of the investment policy committee at the firm believe the equity market in Spain is attractive and is currently being depressed by temporary problems in the banking and real estate markets of Spain, which they feel are overstated. They believe that higher profits will ultimately drive the market higher but are concerned about the long-term prospects and the sustainable rate of growth for Spain. One of the research assistants at the firm gathers the data shown in Exhibit 20 from the OECD and the Conference Board.

Exhibit 20	Growth Data for Spain						
	GDP in Billions of USD Adjusted for PPP	Gross Capital Spending as Percentage of GDP	Consumption of Fixed Capital (percent of GDP)	Labor Cost as Percentage of Total Factor Cost	Total Hours Worked (millions)	Output per Hour Worked in 2009 USD Adjusted for PPP	Growth in Total Factor Productivity (%)
2000	1,156.4	26.3	13.6	64.40	28,402	40.7	−0.87
2001	1,198.6	26.4	13.7	63.66	29,232	41.0	−0.78
2002	1,231.0	26.6	14.1	62.97	29,836	41.3	−0.57
2003	1,269.1	27.4	14.4	62.69	30,495	41.6	−0.21
2004	1,310.6	28.3	14.9	61.71	31,274	41.9	−0.58
2005	1,357.9	29.5	15.3	60.87	32,132	42.3	−0.65
2006	1,412.5	31.0	15.6	60.66	33,146	42.6	−0.28
2007	1,462.9	30.9	15.7	60.04	33,757	43.3	−0.07
2008	1,475.6	29.1	16.2	60.23	33,830	43.6	−1.63
2009	1,420.6	24.4	16.9	59.47	31,705	44.8	−1.61

Sources: OECD Stat Extracts and the Conference Board Total Economy Database.

From the Conference Board website, the physical capital stock for Spain was estimated at $2,177.2 billion (adjusted for purchasing power parity) in 1999. The research analyst calculated the physical capital stock (K) for Spain for the years 2000–2009 using the following equation:

$$K_t = K_{t-1} + I - D$$

where I is gross investment or gross capital spending and D is the depreciation or the consumption of fixed capital. So for 2000 and 2001, the physical capital stock is calculated as:

$$K_{2000} = \$2,177.2 + \$1,156.4 (0.263 - 0.136) = \$2,324.1 \text{ billion}$$

$$K_{2001} = \$2,324.1 + \$1,198.6 (0.264 - 0.137) = \$2,476.3 \text{ billion}$$

The physical capital stock for the remaining years is calculated in the same way and given by Exhibit 21.

Exhibit 21	Estimated Physical Capital Stock (USD billions)
2000	$2,324.1
2001	2,476.3
2002	2,630.2
2003	2,795.1
2004	2,970.8
2005	3,163.6
2006	3,381.1
2007	3,603.5
2008	3,793.8
2009	3,900.4

You are requested by the investment policy committee to use the above data to address the following:

1. Calculate the potential growth rate of the Spanish economy using the production function or growth accounting method (Equation 4), and determine the amount of growth attributed to each source.
2. Calculate the potential growth rate of the Spanish economy using the labor productivity method (Equation 5).
3. How significant are capital deepening and technology in explaining growth for Spain?
4. What is the steady state growth rate for Spain according to the neoclassical model?
5. Assess the implications of the growth analysis for future economic growth and equity prices in Spain.

Solution to 1:

The production function or growth accounting method estimates the growth in GDP using Equation 4:

Growth in potential GDP $= \alpha \Delta K/K + (1 - \alpha)\Delta L/L + \Delta A/A$

The annual growth rate in capital is calculated from Exhibit 21 as[a]

$(3,900.4/2,324.1)^{1/9} - 1 = 5.92\%$

The labor input is measured by the growth rate in total hours worked in the economy (Exhibit 20) and given by

$(31,705/28,402)^{1/9} - 1 = 1.23\%$

The growth rate in total factor productivity (Exhibit 20) is calculated by using a geometric average of the growth rates for 2000–2009 and is equal to –0.73 percent. Finally, the labor share of output is given by the average of the labor cost as a percentage of total factor cost, which is 61.7 percent for 2000–2009 (Exhibit 20). Thus, the share of capital (α) is $1 - 0.617 = 38.3\%$.

Using these numbers, the growth in potential GDP is

Growth in potential GDP $= \alpha \Delta K/K + (1 - \alpha)\Delta L/L + \Delta A/A$

$= (0.383)0.0592 + (0.617)0.0123 + (-0.0073) = 2.30\%$

Sources of growth for Spain over the period 2000–2009 were:

Capital	$(0.383) \times (0.0592) = 2.27\%$
Labor	$(0.617) \times (0.0123) = 0.76\%$
TFP	$= -0.73\%$

Solution to 2:

The labor productivity method estimates the growth in GDP using Equation 5:

Growth rate in potential GDP $=$ Long-term growth rate of labor force $+$
Long-term growth rate in labor productivity

As before, we use the growth in total hours worked to measure the growth in the labor force. The growth in labor productivity per hour worked is

$(44.8 / 40.7)^{1/9} - 1 = 1.07\%$

Growth in potential GDP $= 1.23\% + 1.07\% = 2.3\%$

Note that the estimate of potential GDP growth using the labor productivity approach is the same as that obtained from the growth accounting method. In general, the two methods are likely to give somewhat different estimates because they rely on different data inputs. The growth accounting method requires measurements of the physical capital stock and TFP. As discussed in Section 4.3, TFP is estimated using various time-series or econometric models of the component of growth that is not accounted for by the explicit factors of production. As a result, the estimate of TFP reflects the average (or "smoothed") behavior of the growth accounting residual. The labor productivity approach is simpler, and it avoids the need to estimate the capital input and TFP. In contrast to the estimated value of TFP, labor productivity is measured as a pure residual; that is, it is the part of

GDP growth that is not explained by the labor input (and only the labor input). The cost of the simplification is that the labor productivity approach does not allow a detailed analysis of the drivers of productivity growth.

Solution to 3:

Capital deepening occurs in an economy when there is an increase in the capital-to-labor ratio. The labor input for Spain is measured in terms of total hours worked in the economy. Thus, the capital-to-labor ratio for Spain is calculated by dividing the physical capital stock in Exhibit 21 by total hours worked in Exhibit 20. The results, shown in Exhibit 22, indicate that capital deepening was very significant in Spain: The amount of capital per hour worked increased from $81.83 in 2000 to $123.02 in 2009. In terms of the growth rate, the capital-to-labor ratio increased at an annual rate of 4.6 percent.

The contribution of TFP is measured by the growth in total factor productivity. In contrast to capital deepening, TFP made a negative contribution to growth; the average rate of growth for TFP from 2000 to 2009 was −0.73 percent. However, TFP is estimated using various statistical techniques, and given the uncertainty around these estimates, it should be viewed with some caution.

Exhibit 22	Estimated Capital-to-Labor Ratio ($ millions/hour worked)
2000	$81.83
2001	84.71
2002	88.16
2003	91.66
2004	94.99
2005	98.46
2006	102.01
2007	106.75
2008	112.14
2009	123.02

Solution to 4:

The steady state growth rate in the neoclassical model is estimated by (see Equation 8):

$$\Delta Y / Y = (\theta) / (1 - \alpha) + n = \text{Growth rate of TFP scaled by labor factor share}$$
$$+ \text{Growth rate in the labor force}$$

Steady state growth rate $= -0.73\% / (1 - 0.383) + 1.23\% = 0.05\%$

As expected, the growth rate in potential GDP (calculated as in the solutions to 1 and 2) is above the steady state growth rate. The reason for this is that the economy of Spain is still in the process of converging to the higher income levels of the United States and the major economies in Europe. The physical capital stock is below the steady state, and capital deepening is a significant factor increasing productivity growth and the growth in potential GDP. Steady state growth may be somewhat underestimated in our analysis given that TFP growth is likely to revert to the 1 percent annual rate of increase exhibited in other major developed economies. This is likely to be offset by a lower growth rate in the labor input (see Example 6).

Solution to 5:

The results suggest that potential GDP growth in Spain is approximately 2.3 percent. As we saw in Exhibit 1, the growth rate of actual GDP since early 2000 has been 2.1 percent per year, close to the previous estimate of potential but well above the steady state. The problem is that all the growth in potential GDP is due to the increase in the labor and capital inputs, with capital deepening being very significant as the capital-to-labor ratio is increasing at a 4.6 percent annual rate. The neoclassical model would suggest that the impact of capital deepening will decline over time and the economy will move toward a steady state rate of growth. Thus, growth based on capital deepening should not be sustainable over time. The other major question raised is whether the labor input can continue to grow at an annual rate of 1.2 percent. We examined this question in Example 6. In sum, potential GDP growth is likely to fall over time given Spain's reliance on capital deepening and the strong possibility that growth in the labor input is likely to slow. However, the reversion of TFP growth to levels more typical of other European economies should mitigate the decline. Even if TFP does rebound, slower growth in potential GDP in Spain will likely restrain future stock price increases.

---

[a] Using the 1999 capital stock as a base instead of the 2000 capital stock would give almost the same growth rate: $(3,900.4/2,177.2)^{1/10} - 1 = 6.00\%$.

SUMMARY

This reading focuses on the factors that determine the long-term growth trend in the economy. As part of the development of global portfolio equity and fixed-income strategies, investors must be able to determine both the near-term and the sustainable rates of growth within a country. Doing so requires identifying and forecasting the factors that determine the level of GDP and that determine long-term sustainable trends in economic growth.

- The sustainable rate of economic growth is measured by the rate of increase in the economy's productive capacity or potential GDP.

- Growth in real GDP measures how rapidly the total economy is expanding. Per capita GDP, defined as real GDP divided by population, measures the standard of living in each country.

- The growth rate of real GDP and the level of per capita real GDP vary widely among countries. As a result, investment opportunities differ by country.

- Equity markets respond to anticipated growth in earnings. Higher sustainable economic growth should lead to higher earnings growth and equity market valuation ratios, all other things being equal.

- The best estimate for the long-term growth in earnings for a given country is the estimate of the growth rate in potential GDP.

- In the long run, the growth rate of earnings cannot exceed the growth in potential GDP. Labor productivity is critical because it affects the level of the upper limit. A permanent increase in productivity growth will raise the upper limit on earnings growth and should translate into faster long-run earnings growth and a corresponding increase in stock price appreciation.

- For global fixed-income investors, a critical macroeconomic variable is the rate of inflation. One of the best indicators of short- to intermediate-term inflation trends is the difference between the growth rate of actual and potential GDP.

- Capital deepening, an increase in the capital-to-labor ratio, occurs when the growth rate of capital (net investment) exceeds the growth rate of labor. In a graph of output per capita versus the capital-to-labor ratio, it is reflected by a move along the curve (i.e., the production function).

- An increase in total factor productivity (TFP) causes a proportional upward shift in the entire production function.

- One method of measuring sustainable growth uses the production function and the growth accounting framework developed by Solow. It arrives at the growth rate of potential GDP by estimating the growth rates of the economy's capital and labor inputs plus an estimate of total factor productivity.

- An alternative method measures potential growth as the long-term growth rate of the labor force plus the long-term growth rate of labor productivity.

- The forces driving economic growth include the quantity and quality of labor and the supply of non-ICT and ICT capital, public capital, raw materials, and technological knowledge.

- The labor supply is determined by population growth, the labor force participation rate, and net immigration. The physical capital stock in a country increases with net investment. The correlation between long-run economic growth and the rate of investment is high.

- Technological advances are discoveries that make it possible to produce more or higher quality goods and services with the same resources or inputs. Technology is a major factor determining TFP. TFP is the main factor affecting long-term, sustainable economic growth rates in developed countries and also includes the cumulative effects of scientific advances, applied research and development, improvements in management methods, and ways of organizing production that raise the productive capacity of factories and offices.

- Total factor productivity, estimated using a growth accounting equation, is the residual component of growth once the weighted contributions of all explicit factors (e.g., labor and capital) are accounted for.

- Labor productivity is defined as output per worker or per hour worked. Growth in labor productivity depends on capital deepening and technological progress.

- The academic growth literature is divided into three theories—the classical view, the neoclassical model, and the new endogenous growth view.

- In the classical model, growth in per capita income is only temporary because an exploding population with limited resources brings per capita income growth to an end.

- In the neoclassical model, a sustained increase in investment increases the economy's growth rate only in the short run. Capital is subject to diminishing marginal returns, so long-run growth depends solely on population growth, progress in TFP, and labor's share of income.

- The neoclassical model assumes that the production function exhibits diminishing marginal productivity with respect to any individual input.

- The point at which capital per worker and output per worker are growing at equal, sustainable rates is called the steady state or balanced growth path for the economy. In the steady state, total output grows at the rate of labor force growth plus the rate of growth of TFP divided by the elasticity of output with respect to labor input.

- The following parameters affect the steady state values for the capital-to-labor ratio and output per worker: saving rate, labor force growth, growth in TFP, depreciation rate, and elasticity of output with respect to capital.

- The main criticism of the neoclassical model is that it provides no quantifiable prediction of the rate or form of TFP change. TFP progress is regarded as exogenous to the model.

- Endogenous growth theory explains technological progress within the model rather than treating it as exogenous. As a result, self-sustaining growth emerges as a natural consequence of the model and the economy does not converge to a steady state rate of growth that is independent of saving/investment decisions.

- Unlike the neoclassical model, where increasing capital will result in diminishing marginal returns, the endogenous growth model allows for the possibility of constant or even increasing returns to capital in the aggregate economy.

- In the endogenous growth model, expenditures made on R&D and for human capital may have large positive externalities or spillover effects. Private spending by companies on knowledge capital generates benefits to the economy as a whole that exceed the private benefit to the company.

- The convergence hypothesis predicts that the rates of growth of productivity and GDP should be higher in the developing countries. Those higher growth rates imply that the per capita GDP gap between developing and developed economies should narrow over time. The evidence on convergence is mixed.

- Countries fail to converge because of low rates of investment and savings, lack of property rights, political instability, poor education and health, restrictions on trade, and tax and regulatory policies that discourage work and investing.

- Opening an economy to financial and trade flows has a major impact on economic growth. The evidence suggests that more open and trade-oriented economies will grow at a faster rate.

REFERENCES

Ashauer, David. 1990. "Why Is Infrastructure Important?" In *Is There a Shortfall in Public Capital Investment?* Edited by Alicia Munnell. Federal Reserve Bank of Boston Conference Series No. 34.

Denison, Edward. 1985. *Trends in American Growth.* Washington, DC: Brookings Institution.

Heston, Alan, Robert Summers, and Bettina Aten. 2009. Penn World Table Version 6.3. Center for International Comparisons of Production, Income and Prices at the University of Pennsylvania (August).

IMF. 2011. "Statistical Appendix." In *World Economic Outlook* (September). Washington, DC: International Monetary Fund.

Jorgenson, Dale. 1966. "Technology in Growth Theory." Technology and Growth, Federal Reserve Bank of Boston Conference Series.

Jorgenson, Dale. 2000. "Raising the Speed limit: U.S. Economic Growth in the Information Age." *Brooking Papers on Economic Activity.*

Levine, R. 2005. "Finance and Growth: Theory and Evidence." In *Handbook of Economic Growth.* Edited by Philippe Aghion and Steven Durlauf. Amsterdam: Elsevier, B.V.

Mankiw, Gregory. 1995. "The Growth of Nations." *Brookings Papers on Economic Activity.*

OECD. 2003. *The Sources of Economic Growth in the OECD Countries.* Paris: Organisation for Economic Co-Operation and Development.

Romer, Paul. 1986. "Increasing Returns and Long-Run Growth." *Journal of Political Economy,* vol. 94, no. 5 (October): 1002–1037.

Solow, Robert. 1957. "Technical Change and the Aggregate Production Function." *Review of Economics and Statistics,* vol. 39, no. 3 (August): 312–320.

Stewart, Scott, Christopher Piros, and Jeffrey Heisler. 2011. *Running Money: Professional Portfolio Management.* McGraw-Hill/Irwin.

PRACTICE PROBLEMS FOR READING 15

The following information refers to Questions 1–6[1]

Hans Schmidt, CFA, is a portfolio manager with a boutique investment firm that specializes in sovereign credit analysis. Schmidt's supervisor asks him to develop estimates for GDP growth for three countries. Information on the three countries is provided in Exhibit 1.

Exhibit 1	Select Economic Data for Countries A, B, C	
Country	Economy	Capital Per Worker
A	Developed	High
B	Developed	High
C	Developing	Low

After gathering additional data on the three countries, Schmidt shares his findings with colleague, Sean O'Leary. After reviewing the data, O'Leary notes the following observations:

Observation 1   The stock market of Country A has appreciated considerably over the past several years. Also, the ratio of corporate profits to GDP for Country A has been trending upward over the past several years, and is now well above its historical average.

Observation 2   The government of Country C is working hard to bridge the gap between its standard of living and that of developed countries. Currently, the rate of potential GDP growth in Country C is high.

Schmidt knows that a large part of the analysis of sovereign credit is to develop a thorough understanding of what the potential GDP growth rate is for a particular country and the region in which the country is located. Schmidt is also doing research on Country D for a client of the firm. Selected economic facts on Country D are provided in Exhibit 2.

Exhibit 2	Select Economic Facts for Country D

- Slow GDP Growth
- Abundant Natural Resources
- Developed Economic Institutions

Prior to wrapping up his research, Schmidt schedules a final meeting with O'Leary to see if he can provide any other pertinent information. O'Leary makes the following statements to Schmidt:

1 This item set was developed by Karen Ashby, CFA (LaGrange, KY, USA).

Statement 1   Many countries that have the same population growth rate, savings rate and production function will have growth rates that converge over time.

Statement 2   Convergence between countries can occur more quickly if economies are open and there is free trade and international borrowing and lending; however, there is no permanent increase in the rate of growth in an economy from a more open trade policy.

1. Based upon Exhibit 1, the factor that would *most likely* have the greatest positive impact on the per capita GDP growth of Country A is:

   A. free trade.

   B. technology.

   C. saving and investment.

2. Based upon Observation 1, in the long run the ratio of profits to GDP in Country A is *most likely* to:

   A. remain near its current level.

   B. increase from its current level.

   C. decrease from its current level.

3. Based upon Observation 2, Country C is *most likely* to have:

   A. relatively low real asset returns.

   B. a relatively low real interest rate.

   C. a relatively high real interest rate.

4. Based upon Exhibit 2, the *least likely* reason for the current pace of GDP growth in Country D is:

   A. a persistently strong currency.

   B. strong manufacturing exports.

   C. strong natural resource exports.

5. The type of convergence described by O'Leary in Statement 1 is *best* described as:

   A. club convergence.

   B. absolute convergence.

   C. conditional convergence.

6. Which of the following growth models is *most* consistent with O'Leary's Statement 2?

   A. Classical

   B. Endogenous

   C. Neoclassical

The following information relates to Questions 7–15[2]

Victor Klymchuk, the chief economist at ECONO Consulting (EC), is reviewing the long-term GDP growth of three countries over the recent decade. Klymchuk is interested in forecasting the long term change in stock market value for each country. Exhibit 1 presents current country characteristics and historical information on selected economic variables for the three countries.

2 This item set was developed by Lou Lemos, CFA (Louisville, KY, USA)

| Exhibit 1 | Select Country Factors and Historical Economic Data |

		2000–2010			
	Country Factors	Growth in Hours Worked (%)	Growth in Labor Productivity (%)	Growth in TFP (%)	Growth in GDP (%)
Country A	■ High level of savings and investment				
	■ Highly educated workforce				
	■ Low tariffs on foreign imports				
	■ Limited natural resources	0.9	2.4	0.6	3.3
Country B	■ Developed financial markets				
	■ Moderate levels of disposable income				
	■ Significant foreign direct and indirect investments				
	■ Significant natural resources	-0.3	1.6	0.8	1.3
Country C	■ Politically unstable				
	■ Limited property rights				
	■ Poor public education and health				
	■ Significant natural resources	1.8	0.8	−0.3	2.6

Klymchuk instructs an associate economist at EC to assist him in forecasting the change in stock market value for each country. Klymchuk reminds the associate:

Statement 1   "Over short time horizons, percentage changes in GDP, the ratio of earnings to GDP, and the price-to-earnings ratio are important factors for describing the relationship between economic growth and stock prices. However, I am interested in a long-term stock market forecast."

A client is considering investing in the sovereign debt of Country A and Country B and asks Klymchuk his opinion of each country's credit risk. Klymchuk tells the client:

Statement 2   "Over the next 10 years, I forecast higher potential GDP growth for Country A and lower potential GDP growth for Country B. The capital per worker is similar and very high for both countries, but per capita output is greater for Country A."

The client tells Klymchuk that Country A will offer 50 year bonds and that he believes the bonds could be a good long-term investment given the higher potential GDP growth. Klymchuk responds to the client by saying:

Statement 3   "After the next 10 years, I think the sustainable rate of economic growth for Country A will be affected by a growing share of its population over the age of 65, a declining percentage under age 16, and minimal immigration."

The client is surprised to learn that Country C, a wealthy oil rich country with significant reserves, is experiencing sluggish economic growth and asks Klymchuk for an explanation. Klymchuk responds by stating:

Statement 4   "While countries with access to natural resources are often wealthier, the relationship between resource abundance and economic growth is not clear. My analysis shows that the presence of a dominant natural resource (oil) in Country C is constraining growth. Interestingly, Country A has few natural resources, but is experiencing a strong rate of increase in per capita GDP growth."

Klymchuk knows that growth in per capita income cannot be sustained by pure capital deepening. He asks the associate economist to determine how important capital deepening is as a source of economic growth for each country. Klymchuk instructs the associate to use the data provided in Exhibit 1.

Klymchuk and his associate debate the concept of convergence. The associate economist believes that developing countries, irrespective of their particular characteristics, will eventually equal developed countries in per capita output. Klymchuk responds as follows:

Statement 5   "Poor countries will only converge to the income levels of the richest countries if they make appropriate institutional changes."

7. Based upon the country factors provided in Exhibit 1, the country *most likely* to be considered a developing country is:
    A. Country A.
    B. Country B.
    C. Country C.

8. Based upon Exhibit 1, capital deepening as a source of growth was *most* important for:
    A. Country A.
    B. Country B.
    C. Country C.

9. Based upon Statement 1, over the requested forecast horizon, the factor that will *most likely* drive stock market performance is the percentage change in:
    A. GDP.
    B. the earnings to GDP ratio.
    C. the price-to-earnings ratio.

10. Based solely on the predictions in Statement 2, over the next decade Country B's sovereign credit risk will *most likely*:
    A. increase.
    B. decrease.
    C. not change.

11. Based upon Statement 2, the difference in per capita output between Country A and Country B is *most likely* due to differences in:

    A. capital deepening.

    B. capital per worker.

    C. total factor productivity.

12. Based upon Statement 3, after the next 10 years the growth rate of potential GDP for Country A will *most likely* be:

    A. lower.

    B. higher.

    C. unchanged.

13. Based upon Statement 4 and Exhibit 1, the sluggish economic growth in Country C is *least likely* to be explained by:

    A. limited labor force growth.

    B. export driven currency appreciation.

    C. poorly developed economic institutions.

14. Based upon Statement 4, the higher rate of per capita income growth in Country A is *least likely* explained by the:

    A. rate of investment.

    B. growth of its population.

    C. application of information technology.

15. The type of convergence described by Klymchuk in Statement 5 is *best* described as:

    A. club convergence.

    B. absolute convergence.

    C. conditional convergence.

The following information relates to Questions 16–21[3]

At a recent international finance and economics conference in Bamako, Mali, Jose Amaral of Brazil, and Lucinda Mantri of India, are discussing how to spur their countries' economic growth. Amaral believes that growth can be bolstered by removing institutional impediments, and suggests several possibilities for Brazil: launching a rural literacy program, clarifying property rights laws, and implementing a new dividend tax on foreign investors.

Mantri responds that, for India, capital deepening will be more effective, and has proposed the following ideas: building a group of auto and textile factories in the southern states, developing a north-south and east-west highway network, and sponsoring a patent initiative.

In response, Amaral says to Mantri:

> "Based on endogenous growth theory, one of those proposals is more likely to raise total factor productivity than result in pure capital deepening."

While Mantri recognizes that India lacks the significant natural resources of Brazil, she states that India can overcome this challenge by bolstering long-term growth through three channels:

---

3 This item set was developed by E. Shepard Farrar, CFA (Washington, DC, USA).

Channel 1: Deepening the capital base

Channel 2: Making investments in technology

Channel 3: Maintaining a low Rupee exchange rate

Each country's basic economic statistics were presented at the conference. Selected data for Brazil and India are presented in Exhibit 1. Adama Kanté, a fund manager based in Mali, is planning to increase the fund's allocation to international equities, and after some preliminary analysis, has determined the new allocation will be to Brazilian or Indian equities. After reviewing the data in Exhibit 1, Kanté decides that the allocation will be to Indian equities.

Exhibit 1	Economic Statistics, Brazil and India	
Economic Statistic	**Brazil**	**India**
GDP/capita, 2010	$9,589	$3,575
GDP/capita Growth, 1990-2010	1.62%	4.84%
GDP Growth, 2005-2008	4.9%	8.2%
- Growth due to Labor Productivity Component	2.9%	6.0%
- Growth due to Capital Deepening Component	3.4%	3.6%

Kanté is concerned about the low standard of living in Mali and its large informal sector. To improve per capita GDP, Kanté is considering five specific strategies:

Strategy 1: Lower the country's tax rate.

Strategy 2: Introduce policies that encourage the return of highly-educated Malian emigrants.

Strategy 3: Build day care centers to permit greater participation of women in the workforce.

Strategy 4: Impose high tariffs on imports to protect the country's nascent industries.

Strategy 5: Use economic development bank loans to improve the country's transport and manufacturing infrastructure.

16. Which of Amaral's initiatives is *least likely* to achieve his stated growth objective?

   A. Dividend tax

   B. Rural literacy

   C. Property rights

17. Which proposal for India is Amaral *most likely* referring to in his response to Mantri?

   A. Patent initiative

   B. Highway network

   C. Auto and textile factories

18. The channel that is *least likely* to help India overcome its challenge of lacking significant natural resources is:

    A. Channel 1.

    B. Channel 2.

    C. Channel 3.

19. Based upon Exhibit 1, which Indian economic statistic *least likely* supports Kanté's international equity allocation preference?

    A. GDP per capita

    B. Growth due to labor productivity

    C. Growth due to capital deepening

20. The strategy that is *least likely* to improve per capita GDP in Mali is:

    A. Strategy 1.

    B. Strategy 2.

    C. Strategy 3.

21. Which of the following strategies being considered by Kanté is *most likely* to undermine or delay convergence with developed economies?

    A. Strategy 2

    B. Strategy 4

    C. Strategy 5

SOLUTIONS FOR READING 15

1. B is correct. Country A is a developed country with a high level of capital per worker. Technological progress and/or more intensive use of existing technology can help developed countries increase productivity and thereby increase per capita GDP. Most developed countries have reasonably low trade barriers; thus, somewhat freer trade is likely to have only an incremental, and probably transitory, impact on per capita GDP growth. Also, since the country already has a high capital-to-labor ratio, increased saving/investment is unlikely to increase the growth rate substantially unless it embodies improved technology.

2. C is correct. The ratio of profits to GDP for Country A has been trending upward over the past several years, and is now well above its historical average. The ratio of profits to GDP cannot rise forever. At some point stagnant labor income would make workers unwilling to work without an increase in wages and would also undermine demand, making further expansion of profit margins unsustainable. Thus, it is likely that the ratio of profits to GDP will decline in the long run toward its historical average.

3. C is correct. A high growth rate of potential GDP would cause real incomes to rise more rapidly and also translate into higher real interest rates and higher expected/required real asset returns. The real interest rate is essentially the real return that consumers/savers demand in exchange for postponing consumption. Faster growth in potential GDP means that consumers expect their real income to rise more rapidly. This implies that an extra unit of future income/consumption is less valuable than it would be if income were expected to grow more slowly. All else the same, the real interest rate will have to be relatively high in order to induce the savings required to fund required/desired capital accumulation.

4. B is correct. Country D is a country with abundant resources and has developed the economic institutions necessary for growth, yet the country is experiencing slow economic growth. It is likely that Country D is experiencing the Dutch Disease, where currency appreciation driven by strong export demand for natural resources makes other segments of the economy, in particular manufacturing, globally uncompetitive. Strong manufacturing exports would indicate that Country D is globally competitive and likely to have adopted leading edge technology. Thus, it is unlikely that the slow growth reflects inability to maintain productivity growth. Similarly, strong exports would suggest adequate demand for its products. Thus, strong exports are unlikely to be the cause of slow growth.

5. C is correct. Conditional convergence means that convergence is conditional on the countries having the same savings rate, population growth rate, and production function. If these conditions hold, the neoclassical model implies convergence to the same *level* of per capita output as well as the same steady state growth rate.

6. C is correct. According to the neoclassical model, convergence should occur more quickly if economies are open and there is free trade and international borrowing and lending. Opening up the economy should increase the rate at which the capital-to-labor ratio converges among countries. However, in the neoclassical Solow model, after the reallocation of world savings, there is no permanent increase in the rate of growth in an economy. Both the developed and developing countries eventually grow at the same steady-state rate.

7. C is correct. Country C is the most likely to be a developing economy. Political instability, limited property rights and poor public education and health are all factors that limit economic growth, and thereby contribute to a relatively low standard of living.

8. A is correct. The associate economist can measure the effect of pure capital deepening by measuring the difference of the growth rates of labor productivity and total factor productivity (TFP). The larger the difference, the more important capital deepening is as a source of economic growth. From 2000-2010, Country A's labor productivity grew by 2.4% per year, of which 0.6% came from TFP growth and 1.8% from capital deepening (2.4% − 0.6% = 1.8%).

9. A is correct. In the long-run, the growth rate of GDP is the most important driver of stock market performance. Therefore, the associate economist should focus on the drivers of long run potential GDP growth. The ratio of earnings to GDP cannot increase indefinitely since that would imply that profit would eventually absorb all of GDP. This ratio cannot shrink forever either since unprofitable companies will go out of business. Thus, the annualized growth rate of the earnings to GDP ratio must be approximately zero over long time horizons and this ratio should not be a dominant factor in forecasting long term stock market performance. Similarly, the price-to-earnings ratio cannot grow or contract at a finite rate forever because investors will not pay an excessive price for each dollar of earnings, nor will they give away earnings for free. Therefore the rate of change in the price-to-earnings ratio must be approximately zero over long time horizons and should not be a dominant factor in the forecast of long term stock market performance.

10. A is correct. Credit rating agencies consider the growth rate of potential GDP when evaluating the credit risk of sovereign debt. The chief economist's expectation for lower potential GDP growth for Country B over the next decade increases the perceived credit risk of its sovereign bonds.

11. C is correct. The higher per capita output for Country A is most likely due to differences in the cumulative impact of technological progress embodied in total factor productivity. Technological progress raises the productive capacity of a country. Technological progress causes an upward shift in the entire production function, resulting in higher output per worker for a given level of capital per worker.

12. A is correct. Demographic factors can positively or negatively contribute to a country's sustainable rate of economic growth. After the next 10 years, Country A is expected to experience a growing share of the population over the age of 65 and a declining percentage of the population under the age of 16. All else the same this implies slower growth of the labor force and hence slower growth of potential GDP. Immigration could offset these demographic challenges. However, Statement 3 indicates that Country A is expected to experience minimal immigration.

13. A is correct. Country C is an example of a country endowed with an abundant natural resource yet experiencing slow economic growth. While labor force growth is an important source of economic growth, it is the least likely explanation of the sluggish economic growth in Country C. As shown in Exhibit 1, growth in total hours worked has accounted for most of Country C's growth. Furthermore, export driven currency appreciation and poorly developed economic institutions are both likely causes of sluggish growth in countries with abundant natural resources.

14. B is correct. Population growth can increase the growth rate of the overall economy, but does not impact the rate of increase in *per capita* GDP.

Therefore, population growth does not explain Country A's higher rate of per capita income growth. An increase in labor force participation could, however, raise the growth of per capita GDP.

15. A is correct. Klymchuk is referring to the concept of club convergence. The basic premise is that lower income members of the club are converging to the income levels of the richest countries. This implies that the countries with the lowest per capita income in the club grow at the fastest rate. Countries outside the club, however, continue to fall behind.

16. A is correct. Amaral's initiative to implement a new dividend tax is likely to impede inflows of equity capital by making equity investment in Brazil less attractive for foreign investors. Capital flows, or lack thereof, have a major impact on economic growth because, in an open economy, world savings can finance domestic investment. As a potential source of funds, foreign investment breaks the vicious cycle of low income, low domestic savings, and low investment.

17. A is correct. Mantri's proposal to sponsor a patent initiative, which is likely to result in technology investment and improvement, is likely to cause a proportional upward shift in the entire production function, allowing the economy to produce higher output per worker for a given level of capital per worker. Technological progress also increases the marginal product of capital relative to its marginal cost.

18. C is correct. Maintaining a low currency exchange rate is a policy aimed at maintaining demand for the country's exports. It would have little direct impact on the potential growth rate of aggregate supply. It might boost long term capacity growth indirectly, however, by encouraging adoption of leading edge technology. Nonetheless, it would not be expected to be as powerful as capital deepening and/or investment in technology.

19. A is correct. Kante's decision to invest in equities in India is supported by the country's strong economic growth. For global investors, economic growth is important since equity composite valuations depend to a great extent on both the level of economic output (GDP per capita and GDP overall) and on the rate of economic growth. Relative to Brazil, the growth rate in per capita GDP has been much higher, and furthermore, the growth rate in GDP has also been much higher than that of Brazil. In contrast to the growth rate, the relatively low *level* of GDP per capita in India is less likely to indicate attractive equity investment opportunities. Low per capita GDP suggests that India may lack sufficient industrial and financial infrastructure to support some types of industries. It also indicates that domestic purchasing power is relatively limited, decreasing the potential for higher-margin, domestically-oriented businesses.

20. A is correct. With Mali's low standard of living, i.e. GDP per capita, and large informal workforce, the tax rate is unlikely to be an impediment to growth, so lowering the tax rate is not likely to be a major contributor to growth.

21. B is correct. The strategy for Mali to impose high tariffs (trade restrictions) on imports is likely to undermine rather than enhance growth and therefore is not supportive of convergence with developed economies. Freer trade (fewer trade restrictions) tends to enhance growth by, for example, inducing a shift of resources into industries in which the country has a comparative thereby increasing overall productivity; forcing less efficient domestic companies to exit and more efficient ones to innovate; allowing domestic producers to more fully exploit economies of scale by selling to a larger market; and enabling less advanced sectors of an economy to catch up with more advanced countries or sectors through knowledge spillovers.

16

Economics of Regulation

by Chester S. Spatt

INTRODUCTION

Regulation is an extremely important topic because regulation not only has potential effects at the macro level on the economy, but also has potential effects at the micro level on companies and individuals. Regulation may develop either proactively in anticipation of consequences of changes in the environment or reactively in response to some occurrence(s). For example, changes that resulted from technological advances in the marketplace because of new means of communications and applications of computers have led to a variety of regulation, proactive and reactive. Regulation has also developed in response to financial crises and undesirable behaviors or actions that have occurred in the past.[1] Regulations are necessary because market solutions are not adequate for all situations.

A significant challenge on the financial regulation front is how to deal with systemic risk (the risk of failure of the financial system) and the consequences of risk taking by financial institutions. On other fronts, such issues as labor regulation, environmental regulation, and electronic privacy are receiving increased attention. Changes in regulatory structure and regulatory uncertainty can have substantial effects on business

---

[1] In some cases, these behaviors or actions were criminal and violated existing laws. One goal of regulators is to try to detect these activities earlier.

decisions. One of the significant challenges facing professionals in the finance industry is to anticipate and understand the consequences of potential changes in the regulatory environment and to specific regulations.

Section 2 of this reading provides an overview of regulation, including classifications of regulations and regulators, roles of regulations, and regulatory tools. Section 3 describes regulation of commerce and areas of focus in commercial regulation. Section 4 describes regulation of financial markets, including securities regulation and regulation of financial institutions. Section 5 describes the assessment of costs and benefits of regulation. Section 6 describes and illustrates an analysis of regulation. Section 7 summarizes the key points of the reading, and practice problems conclude the reading.

2 OVERVIEW OF REGULATION

Regulatory frameworks, among other effects, influence how businesses operate. A regulatory framework develops a set of rules or standards of conduct. Regulations may impose restrictions on and/or mandate how businesses interact with others, including other businesses, consumers, workers, and society in general. The regulations may also impose constraints on and/or mandate how businesses operate internally. It is important for an analyst to understand how regulation may affect the business environment, as well as individual industries or businesses. There is a separate discussion of regulation of financial markets, although that is part of the broad business environment. This section includes an overview of regulation, such as the classification of regulations and regulators, roles of regulations, and regulatory tools.

2.1 Classification of Regulations and Regulators

Regulations are sometimes enacted by legislative bodies (often these regulations are laws), but more typically arise from the determination of regulatory bodies. Regulatory bodies may be either governmental agencies or independent regulators (other regulators granted authority by a government or governmental agency). Regulatory bodies have legal authority to enact and enforce regulation within the parameters of the mandate given to them. In many instances, a legislative body enacts a statute at a broad level, leaving it to regulatory bodies to fill in implementation details.[2] Courts play a role in regulation as well—helping to interpret regulations and laws, defining permitted and not permitted regulatory practices, and in some instances, imposing sanctions for regulatory violations. Regulations can be classified as reflecting laws enacted by legislative bodies (**statutes**), rules issued by government agencies or other regulators (**administrative regulations or administrative law**), and interpretations of courts (**judicial law**).

Although government agencies make many regulatory determinations, **independent regulators** make some regulations. The authority of independent regulators comes from their recognition by a government body or agency but they are not government agencies per se. One distinction between government agencies and independent regulators is that the latter typically do not rely on government funding.

---

2 This description by the U.S. Securities and Exchange Commission (SEC) is illustrative of how the process works: "Rulemaking is the process by which federal agencies implement legislation passed by Congress and signed into law by the President. Major pieces of legislation, such as the Securities Act of 1933, the Securities Exchange Act of 1934, the Investment Company Act of 1940, and the Sarbanes-Oxley Act, provide the framework for the SEC's oversight of the securities markets. These statutes are drafted broadly, establishing basic principles and objectives. To ensure that the intent of Congress is carried out in specific circumstances—and as the securities markets evolve technologically, expand in size, and offer new products and services—the SEC engages in rulemaking." www.sec.gov/about/whatwedo.shtml

Some argue that an advantage of independent regulators is that they are to some extent immune from political influence and pressure. Some independent regulators are **self-regulating organizations**, private, non-governmental organizations that both represent and regulate their members. While these organizations may be independent of the government and to an extent immune from political pressure, they may be subject to pressure from their members. Self-regulating organizations given recognition and authority, including enforcement power, by a government body or agency, are independent regulators. However, not all self-regulating organizations are independent regulators. Some self-regulating organizations receive authority from their members, who agree to comply with the organization's rules and standards and its enforcement of these. This authority does not have the force of law; self-regulating organizations are not regulators unless they are given recognition and authority, including enforcement power, by a government body or agency.

In addition, regulatory authorities may reference the work of outside bodies in their regulations. Examples of these outside bodies are accounting standard–setting bodies, such as the IASB and FASB, and credit reporting agencies. Regulatory authorities retain the legal authority to enforce any regulation that references the work of these bodies. In the case of accounting standard–setting bodies—which are typically private sector, non-profit, self-regulated organizations—the requirement to prepare financial reports in accordance with specified accounting standards is the responsibility of regulatory authorities. The standard-setting bodies may set the standards, but the regulatory authorities recognize and enforce the standards. Ratings by credit-rating agencies—that are typically private sector, profit-oriented entities—were often referenced in regulations related to acceptable holding by certain entities. Issues with conflicts of interest, however, have resulted in efforts to reduce references to credit-rating agencies in regulations.[3]

The relatively simple classification of regulators (legislative bodies, government agencies, independent regulators, courts) and regulations (statutes, administrative regulations, and judicial law) is useful, but does not reflect the complexities and nuances that exist with respect to regulators and regulation. In some cases, the classification of a regulator is clear, and in other cases, the classification is ambiguous.

For example, the U.S. Securities and Exchange Commission (SEC), the government agency that regulates the securities markets in the United States, allocates some regulatory responsibilities to specified self-regulatory organizations (SROs). In this context, an SRO is a self-regulating organization and an independent regulator recognized and granted authority by a government agency or body. These SROs are funded independently rather than from the government. The Financial Industry Regulatory Authority (FINRA), one such SRO, describes itself as "the largest independent regulator for all securities firms doing business in the United States. FINRA's mission is to protect America's investors by making sure the securities industry operates fairly and honestly."[4] FINRA has the authority to enforce industry rules and federal securities laws. In this case, it is clear that FINRA is an independent regulator and an SRO. The U.S. Congress established the Public Company Accounting Oversight Board (PCAOB), a non-profit corporation, to oversee the audits of public companies. Previously, the audit profession was self-regulated. The PCAOB is funded primarily through the assessment of annual fees on public companies, brokers, and dealers. The SEC oversees the PCAOB. The PCAOB is an independent regulator rather than a government agency, but it is not an SRO.

---

3 Credit-rating agencies often are compensated by the entity requesting the rating; this practice has resulted in questions about the independence and reliability of such ratings. Perhaps the most significant source of conflict of interest is that the issuer selects the ratings that will be purchased and published (ratings shopping).

4 www.finra.org/AboutFINRA/

The role of SROs varies among countries. In some countries, such as in the United States, SROs have specific regulatory authority, and in other countries, self-regulating organizations are rarely or never recognized as independent regulators. For example: "One of the many significant recent legislative amendments that was introduced in Australia with the Financial Services Reform Act 2001 was the removal of the official regulatory standing of self-regulatory organizations (SROs). SROs, whether they are exchanges, industry associations, or some other form of peer group, have traditionally set standards of behaviour or codes of conduct for market participants."[5] According to Carson (2011), the role of self-regulation in Europe, with the exception of the United Kingdom, was limited because of civil law systems and resulting reliance on government supervision. In the United Kingdom and other countries with common-law systems, reliance on self-regulation has been more extensive. The roles of SROs in regulation range from non-existent to having some regulatory authority. Regulators are concerned with the corporate governance of SROs and the management of their conflicts of interest. The extent of the concern is a factor in deciding the regulatory role, if any, of the SRO in question.

In Singapore, "Statutory boards are entities separate from the government, with specific legislation governing their operations. Most, if not all, statutory boards impose charges on some or all of their services. Statutory boards that do not generate sufficient revenue to meet their expenses would receive grants from the government to finance their operations. These grants are funded from the government's annual budget." [6] The statutory boards are described as separate from the government, yet they are subject to specific legislation governing their operations and they may receive government funding. It is ambiguous whether Singapore's statutory boards are government agencies or independent regulators. The Singapore Economic Development Board (EDB), one such statutory board, describes itself as "the lead government agency for planning and executing strategies to enhance Singapore's position as a global business centre."[7] Another statutory board, the Accounting and Corporate Regulatory Authority (ACRA), describes itself as "the national regulator of business entities and public accountants in Singapore."[8] Although the EDB clearly identifies itself as a government agency, it is less clear whether the ACRA, given the description of a statutory board and the description of itself, should be classified as a government agency or an independent regulator.

Classifying regulatory bodies that exist in unions, such as the Union of South American Nations (UNASUR) and the European Union (EU), can present challenges. For example, the European Commission (EC), which has a mission to promote the general interest of the EU, can issue regulations, directives, and decisions. These are jointly referred to as EU law. Regulations have binding legal force throughout every EU member state on a par with national laws.[9] Directives identify desired results and require national authorities to put laws in place to achieve these.[10] Decisions are binding laws addressed to specific parties and are the result of specific cases.[11] Regulations appear to have the characteristics of administrative regulations. Directives appear to have the characteristics of statutes; these are at a broad level and another body needs to fill in the implementation details. Decisions appear more similar to judicial law. Thus, it is hard to classify the European Commission based on the type of regulation

5 www.asic.gov.au/asic/pdflib.nsf/lookupbyfilename/integration-financial-regulatory-authorities. pdf/$file/integration-financial-regulatory-authorities.pdf.

6 www.ifaq.gov.sg.

7 www.edb.gov.sg/edb/sg/en_uk/index/about_edb/what_we_do.html.

8 www.acra.gov.sg/About_ACRA/About_Us.htm.

9 http://ec.europa.eu/eu_law/introduction/what_regulation_en.htm.

10 http://ec.europa.eu/eu_law/introduction/what_directive_en.htm. Christensen, Hail, and Leuz (2011) use differences in the timing of the implementation of EU directives tightening the regulation of market abuse and transparency across countries to assess the impact of tighter securities regulation.

11 http://ec.europa.eu/eu_law/introduction/what_decision_en.htm.

issued. In choosing whether to issue a directive or regulation, the EC appears to take into account the desired outcome. For example, the European Market Infrastructure Regulation (EMIR) takes the form of a regulation rather than a directive. This choice reflects the EC's desire to build a harmonized regulatory framework across the EU. Regardless of how a regulatory body is classified, it is important to identify the regulators and regulations that might affect the entities or industry being analyzed.

Regulations address a broad range of issues and can be classified by their objectives. These include safety (for example, food, products), privacy (for example, financial information), protection (for example, intellectual property), environmental (for example, pollution), labor or employment (for example, workers' rights, employment practices), commerce or trade (for example, consumers' rights and protection, investors' protection, antitrust), and financial system (for example, prudential supervision of institutions, capital requirements, insider trading). It is difficult, if not impossible, to think of an area of life unaffected by regulation.

Although much of the focus of this reading is on the rules themselves and their development, impact, and implementation, regulatory enforcement and sanctions also play an important role. This division between development and enforcement of regulation also represents a possible way to classify laws or regulation. **Substantive law** focuses on the rights and responsibilities of entities and relationships among entities, and **procedural law** focuses on the protection and enforcement of the substantive laws. Regulators typically have responsibility for both substantive and procedural aspects of their regulations. In developing regulations, the regulator must implicitly consider the roles of regulation.

2.2 Economic Rationale for Regulation

Regulations are necessary because market solutions are not adequate for all situations. Conceptually, this need can be understood best using ideas from economic theory. One of the basic principles in economics is the "fundamental theorem of welfare economics." Assuming constant returns to scale, no frictions[12] and no externalities,[13] competitive market (equilibrium) allocations[14] are efficient or *Pareto optimal*. There is no way to redistribute resources and make some agents better off without making others worse off.[15] Furthermore, any efficient allocation of resources can be sustained as a market equilibrium for an appropriate set of prices. Hence, absent frictions and externalities, the market solution will be economically efficient so that there would be no benefit to regulatory intervention.

The case for regulatory intervention rests on the presence of **informational frictions** and **externalities**. Informational frictions result in a variety of issues, which regulators attempt to address. These issues include "adverse selection" (private information in the hands of some, but not all, market participants, which affects the consumption of goods or services), and "moral hazard" (incentive conflicts that arise from the delegation of decision making to agents or from contracts that will affect the behavior of one party to the detriment of the other party to the contract). Asymmetrical information, in general, may allow one entity to have an inherent advantage over another entity with

---

12 Examples of frictions are costs for or restraints on trading and asymmetrical information.
13 Externalities are spillover effects of production and consumption activities onto others who did not consent to participate in the activity. A positive externality provides a spillover benefit and a negative externality generates a spillover cost. For example, if one person does home improvements, neighbors may benefit from increases in their home values even though they have expended no resources to improve their properties. Similarly, if one home in a neighborhood is not maintained, neighbors may bear such costs as losses in property values or expenses incurred to keep pests off their property.
14 Market (equilibrium) allocations are ones in which (1) agents maximize utility given relative prices and (2) markets clear.
15 If resources can be redistributed such that any one agent can be made better off without making any other agent worse off, then the original allocation would not have been *Pareto optimal*.

which interaction occurs, and the resulting regulation focuses on establishing rights and responsibilities of entities and adjusting relationships among entities.

Many aspects of regulation reflect the provision of public goods, an externality issue. Although the consumption of a private good by a consumer would deny access to the same units by other consumers, many individuals can consume a public good simultaneously, and indeed, it can be difficult to exclude others from the public good. Many regulations represent an attempt to respond to a public goods or externality problem. In effect, because there are shared benefits from consuming the public good, markets would not produce the optimal amount of these goods. Classic examples of public goods include national defense and standard setting.

Some public goods are considered local public goods because those living in particular areas largely reap the benefits. This type of good is relevant to regulation in a global economy because those with jurisdiction undertake many regulatory decisions over particular geographic areas. Indeed, there can be strong spillover effects associated with such goods and even their regulation. Policymakers (regulators and legislators, for example) in various jurisdictions have become sensitive to the spillover effects of their actions.

2.2.1 *Regulatory Interdependencies*

An interesting facet of regulation is how regulated entities view the regulation. The answer is often context specific—while there are obviously many examples in which regulated companies fight against new proposed regulations, it is far from universal. Regulated company efforts to fight particular regulations tend to attract more public attention than when the companies are sympathetic to the contemplated regulations. Even more fundamentally, academics have argued that regulation often arises to enhance the interests of the regulated (see Stigler 1971), often called the "**regulatory capture**" theory. For example, regulatory actions and determinations can restrict potential competition and coordinate the choices of rivals. In the interaction between regulated entities and their regulators, the regulated entities may possess considerable expertise and knowledge and some of the individual regulators may even have had their intellectual roots in the industry or aspire to be in the industry in which the regulated entities operate. The interactions between regulated entities and their regulators may reinforce the perception (or reality) of regulatory capture.

Regulatory differences across jurisdictions can lead to shifts in location and behavior of entities because of **regulatory competition** and **regulatory arbitrage**. Regulators may compete to provide a regulatory environment designed to attract certain entities (regulatory competition). Entities may engage in regulatory arbitrage; for example, they may identify and use some aspect of regulations that allows them to exploit differences in economic substance and regulatory interpretation or in foreign and domestic regulatory regimes to their (the entities') benefit.

Interdependence in the actions of regulators with different objectives is important in the international arena. Many regulatory issues are relatively common ones around the globe. The commonality reflects both similarities in the challenges confronting different countries as well as the diffusion of the underlying problems around the globe. While issues such as systemic risk, moral hazard, global warming, and nuclear power regulation all reflect significant global concerns, regulators in different jurisdictions can have different perspectives or face different trade-offs when addressing specific issues. These different perspectives can lead to differences in regulatory treatments. Although such differences are often well justified, "regulatory competition" can undercut the effectiveness of enhanced regulation in particular countries and impose constraints on regulation. Sometimes regulatory cooperation and coordination is called for in an increasingly interconnected global economy.

An example in the aftermath of the global financial crisis, which was first identified as such in 2008 (hereafter, referred to as the 2008 global financial crisis although it lasted beyond 2008), concerned the push toward centralized clearing rather than bilateral settlement of derivatives transactions. Many European and Asian regulators were slower to respond than U.S. regulators. In the United States, the Dodd–Frank Act called for derivatives reforms to be fully resolved by July 2011, whereas the G–20 called for action by member nations by the end of 2012. A number of U.S.-based entities expressed fear that the U.S. markets would be greatly disadvantaged because of the extent of differences in the ultimate regulatory regimes.

In another example, consider issues related to global warming and pollution. How should governments manage and coordinate efforts and adjustments around the globe? The relevant externality is not simply within countries, but across countries. One of the challenging aspects of this issue is that countries are in very different situations. What are the institutional and governance mechanisms that would be appropriate to address this issue on a global basis? Although an economist's solution to the problem of pollution externalities might be to tax it in order to allocate the pollution to the parties that can absorb the cost, that leaves many questions open. How should one allocate "permits" to pollute among countries? Should countries have "the right" to pollute related to their past pollution? If not, how would one accommodate differences in living standards? How should one address the equity issues associated with low wealth and developing countries having a potential comparative advantage in absorbing pollution?[16]

The point of this overall discussion of interdependencies across jurisdictions is not to suggest global governance or a global regulator, but to recognize the reality and implications of diverse trade-offs and preferences among regional, national, and local regulators. To a degree, the presence of diverse and arguably competing jurisdictions influences the stances of national and regional regulators. Evidence exists that governments recognize the necessity for global regulatory cooperation and coordination. For example, the Basel Accords establish and promote internationally consistent capital requirements and risk management practices for larger international banks. The Basel Committee on Banking Supervision, among other functions, has evolved into a standard setter for bank supervision. The International Organization of Securities Commissions (IOSCO) is a self-regulating organization, but not a regulatory authority. Its members regulate a significant portion of the world's capital markets. This organization has established objectives and principles to guide securities and capital market regulation and its members agree to adhere to these.[17]

At the country level, the objectives of diverse government regulators can differ and potentially lead to regulations that seem inconsistent. Bank supervisors (whether as a function of the central bank, another entity, or combination of entities) focus on **prudential supervision**—regulation and monitoring of the safety and soundness of financial institutions in order to promote financial stability, reduce system-wide risks, and protect customers of financial institutions. The objectives of securities commissions, per IOSCO, are protecting investors; ensuring that markets are fair, efficient, and transparent; and reducing systemic risk. In some situations, these goals are quite

---

16 A memo that Larry Summers wrote in 1991, while chief economist of the World Bank, suggested that poor countries should bear much of the pollution (with compensation) and resulted in a political firestorm.
17 The member agencies currently assembled in the IOSCO have resolved, through its permanent structures
• to cooperate in developing, implementing, and promoting adherence to internationally recognised and consistent standards of regulation, oversight, and enforcement in order to protect investors, maintain fair, efficient and transparent markets, and seek to address systemic risks;
• to enhance investor protection and promote investor confidence in the integrity of securities markets, through strengthened information exchange and cooperation in enforcement against misconduct and in supervision of markets and market intermediaries; and
• to exchange information at both global and regional levels on their respective experiences in order to assist the development of markets, strengthen market infrastructure, and implement appropriate regulation. www.iosco.org/about/

different in their implications. The bank supervisor may be reluctant or even unwilling to release the results of the bank's tests of financial institutions in order to promote financial stability and avoid systemic risk because of a loss of confidence. The securities commission is more likely to advocate for the release of information that might be relevant to investors (see Spatt 2009).

A general conclusion is that regulation by different regulators, even with seemingly similar objectives, can lead to very different regulatory outcomes. The causes of this variation include different orientations of the regulators and objectives that are broadly stated and/or ill defined.

2.3 Regulatory Tools

Given a range of regulatory tools and measures, it is important to recognize that regulatory and governmental policies should be predictable as well as effective in achieving objectives. It is very difficult for any entity to function with confidence and success in an environment where the rules are unclear or in a state of flux (in other words, where there is considerable regulatory uncertainty). Regulatory choices or government policies that will be consistent over time are desirable. The most effective way to ensure time consistency is to focus on regulatory choices that the government will have an incentive to carry out over time. If these choices occur, the regulatory environment is likely to be stable despite the fact that, in many countries, governmental decision makers (with diverse political preferences) change on a regular basis. It is helpful to utilize regulatory tools that are consistent with maintaining a stable regulatory environment. Regulatory tools and government interventions in markets include the use of price mechanisms, such as taxes and subsidies; regulatory mandates and restrictions on behaviors, including establishing rights and responsibilities; provision of public goods; and public financing of private projects.

The issue of how to address pollution is a classic example in regulation. By taxing polluters (or subsidizing those who do not by using a suitable baseline), one can create a system in which marginal incentives are equated across economic agents. The advantage of such an arrangement is that, theoretically, the rights to pollute are redistributed in an "efficient" manner relative to a fixed allocation. In particular, the structure of the regulation allows market incentives to redistribute the pollution rights to those for whom they are the most valuable at the margin. There are important issues, however, about how to initially establish and distribute the amount of acceptable total pollution. In some situations, historical usage (amount of pollution produced) is used to allocate these. One problem is that marginal incentives may be altered in anticipation of this allocation. In other situations, the allocation is the outcome of a political process, which can lead to considerable lobbying. At the heart of this example is the use of a price mechanism to create the appropriate marginal incentives and an efficient allocation of resources. The "Coase Theorem" states that if an externality can be traded and there are no transaction costs, then the allocation of property rights will be efficient and the resource allocation will not depend on the initial assignment of property rights.

Governments can intervene in markets in ways other than through the price mechanism. These include restricting some activities (for example, insider trading, short selling), mandating some activities (for example, capital requirements for banks, registration with a securities commission for certain activities), providing public goods (for example, national defense, transportation infrastructure), and financing private projects (for example, loans to individuals or companies for specified activities that the government deems desirable to encourage). The extent of government provision of public goods and government financing of private projects depends on a number of factors including the political philosophy of the country and/or government in power, the structure of the government, and the country's gross domestic product. The problem of **systemic risk** (the risk of failure of the financial system) as a result of the failure of a major financial institution has emerged as an issue in many countries around the world in the aftermath of the 2008 global financial crisis. Systemic risk and **financial contagion** (a situation in which financial shocks spread from their place of origin to other locales; in essence, a faltering economy infects other, healthier economies) are examples of negative externalities. In the EU, the European Systemic Risk Board (ESRB), formed in December 2010, is an independent EU body tasked with macro-prudential oversight of the EU financial system. The Dodd–Frank Act enacted by the U.S. legislative body, among other objectives, attempts to mitigate systemic risk. U.S. regulatory bodies (rather than the legislature) are largely responsible for implementing the provisions of the Dodd–Frank Act. At the same time, policymakers may not have sufficiently clarified how to evaluate differences in systemic risk imposed by different financial institutions or even defined systemic risk except in broad terms.

It is difficult to assess the extent to which the new approaches created by legislation, such as the Dodd–Frank Act, and other regulatory changes, such as the creation of the ESRB, will reduce systemic risk. There are a number of reasons for this difficulty. The amount of underlying empirical data about systemic crises is very limited. By definition, these events are outliers on some metrics, and so, the types and sources of future crises are likely to be rather different. Regulations designed with a prior crisis in mind may not head off a future crisis (or even contain the seeds of one). It can be difficult to assess the potential effectiveness of regulatory actions before an event and even after the fact. The mere fact that a crisis does not occur is not necessarily evidence that the regulation was the reason that a crisis did not occur. It is also plausible that some regulatory responses have the unintended consequence of mitigating one source of risk while increasing another source of risk. All of these issues make effective regulation challenging to design.

Generally, more than one regulatory approach is feasible and worthy of consideration in a specific situation. Two examples that illustrate a range of possible regulatory responses are (a) conflict of interest policies and (b) trading restrictions on insiders. To illustrate the first situation, consider a hypothetical situation in which a potential employee of a regulator has some degree of financial exposure to a regulated company. Such exposure could come about in many ways (for example, spousal employment, a marketable position in an investment portfolio, an illiquid position resulting from past employment) and at a variety of financial levels. What types of regulatory restrictions might arise? Among the potential regulatory responses are the following: The individual is barred from employment at the agency. The individual is barred from working on specific (or all) projects involving the company in question. The individual sells the position; the sale can be voluntary or mandated. The individual is required to disclose the nature of his potential conflict to higher-level decision makers to whom he will be providing recommendations. Broadly, the alternative remedies include a bar on involvement, resolution of the conflict, or disclosure of it.

Turning to the case of corporate insiders, there are both potential regulatory and corporate restrictions. Examples of regulatory responses are a ban from trading on nonpublic information and a requirement that insiders disclose trades. The company may impose a blackout period during which insiders are banned from trading on the company's stock (these periods often precede earning announcements and continue shortly afterward). The appropriate remedy is dependent on the underlying "facts and circumstances," and arguably the appropriate standards would reflect the specific context. As stated previously, there often are alternative ways to tackle a particular regulatory issue. When evaluating potential regulatory responses to an issue and the effects of the potential regulation, it is important to consider a range of feasible responses.

An important aspect of effective regulation is the potential ability to impose sanctions on violators of the regulations; in other words, it is important to be able to enforce the regulations. IOSCO clearly identifies this aspect as one of the agreed

IOSCO's

upon principles of securities regulation, "The Regulator should have comprehensive enforcement powers."[18] Enforcement of securities regulations and regulations on businesses may include sanctions on the violating corporation (business or company), the individual violator(s), or both. Corporate sanctions may be appropriate when the company caused harm to others. The sanctions often involve monetary fines/fees/settlement, and in the case of individuals, the sanctions may involve prison terms. However, in some situations, such as cases of accounting fraud, stockholders may actually be the victims. In such instances, when the stockholders were harmed by the wrongdoing, the case for sanctions, such as fines, against the company is far from compelling. The sanctions may simply redistribute funds from current stockholders to the stockholders who were the specific victims, and the company incurs real resource costs.

For various reasons, it can be difficult to prosecute or achieve settlements with individual violators. First, it often is difficult to detect violations and to identify exactly which individuals were at fault. Furthermore, the individuals possess very strong incentives to fight in order to protect their reputation and livelihood. Indeed, individuals are often able to fight using corporate resources because of indemnification provisions in their employment contract. The intent of these provisions may be to protect a risk-averse executive against inadvertent liability and potentially align their interests with the stockholders' interests, but they may result in protecting an executive to the detriment of the stockholders. The incentive to fight individual sanctions may be especially strong not only because of financial costs, but also other costs, such as reputational costs.

Example 1

Overview of Regulation

Lee Ming, an analyst, is researching the use of self-regulation in securities markets by reading "Self-Regulation in Securities Markets" by John Carson (2011). The main factors identified as contributing to a trend of decreased reliance on self-regulation in securities markets are the following:

- Privatization of securities exchanges
- Intense competition
- Uncertainty regarding the effectiveness of self-regulation
- Internationalization
- Strengthening of government regulators
- Trend toward consolidation of financial regulators
- "Cooperative regulation"
- Pressure to increase efficiency and lower costs

Reasons there still is reliance on self-regulation include the following:

- Increases overall level of regulatory resources
- Uses knowledge and expertise of industry professionals
- Enables the regulator to focus on other priorities while relying on an SRO for front line supervision of its members and regulated markets

---

[18] International Organization of Securities Commissions, "Objectives and Principles of Securities Regulation," (June 2010).

In addition, Ming made note of the following statements, among others, in Carson's paper:

Statement 1   "In much of the world, the value of self-regulation is being debated anew. Forces, such as commercialization of exchanges, development of stronger statutory regulatory authorities, consolidation of financial services industry regulatory bodies, and globalization of capital markets, are affecting the scope and effectiveness of self-regulation." p.2

Statement 2   "IOSCO states that use of an SRO may be appropriate where an SRO exists that has the capacity to carry out the purpose of regulation and to enforce compliance with rules by its members, and where the SRO is subject to adequate oversight by the regulator." p.7

Statement 3   "France employs a similar approach, because regulations may provide that firms have a duty to implement standards set by associations such as the *Association française des marchés financiers* (AMAFI)." (Note that this organization was previously known as The French Association of Investment Firms.) p.8

Statement 4   "Even in countries where formal SROs [with regulatory powers] do not exist, as in Europe, a trend is observed toward increased use of securities industry bodies to support the regulatory system by providing guidance, codes of conduct, continuing education and so on." p. 12

Statement 5   "In many countries, the cost of government 'bailouts' and the need for significant government intervention in the financial system have raised demands for regulatory reform. Potential reforms may take several forms, ranging from (1) adoption of stronger laws and regulations to (2) changes in the structure of regulatory systems (including consolidating financial regulators), (3) improved governance and accountability of financial regulators, and (4) stronger supervision of compliance with laws and rules by financial institutions." p.53

1. In Statement 1, commercialization of exchanges *most likely* led to debates on and decline in reliance on self-regulation because of concerns about:

    A. regulatory capture.

    B. regulatory arbitrage.

    C. regulatory competition.

2. Given an objective of fair and efficient markets, the *most* important criterion from Statement 2 when using an SRO for regulatory purposes is:

    A. capacity of the SRO.

    B. adequate oversight by the regulator.

    C. ability of the SRO to enforce compliance.

3. Considering Statements 3 and 4, the Association française des marchés financiers is *most likely*:

    A. an independent regulator.

    B. a self-regulating organization.

    C. both an independent regulator and a self-regulating organization.

4. In response to the information in Statement 5, governments are *least likely* to increase reliance on:

    A. government agencies.

    B. independent regulators.

    C. self-regulating organizations.

5. Globalization of capital markets is *most likely* to result in increased concerns about:

    A. contagion.

    B. regulatory competition.

    C. Both contagion and regulatory competition.

6. The regulatory tools *least likely* to be used by self-regulating organizations are:

    A. price mechanisms.

    B. restrictions on behaviors.

    C. provision of public goods.

Solutions:

1. A is correct. Regulatory capture has always been a concern when SROs are used, but commercialization of exchanges has led to increased concern about conflicts of interest and regulatory capture.

2. B is correct. Adequate oversight by the regulator is a critical aspect in ensuring that the SRO fulfills its roles in a manner consistent with a fair and efficient market.

3. B is correct. The Association française des marchés financiers is a self-regulating organization that issues standards and guidance that are referenced by a regulator, but it is not a regulator, independent or otherwise; it is also not a formal SRO with regulatory powers. It is a standard-setting body but it has no regulatory authority; regulatory authorities recognize and enforce the standards. This role is similar to the role of many accounting standards boards.

4. C is correct. Governments are least likely to increase reliance on self-regulating organizations. There appears to be a desire for increased government intervention, stronger laws, and improved governance and accountability. The use of SROs is not consistent with these.

5. C is correct. Globalization is likely to result in increased concerns about contagion and regulatory competition. It is easier for a financial shock to spread. Governments may use their regulatory environment as a basis to attract entities from around the world.

6. A is correct. SROs are least likely to use price mechanisms. They typically regulate behaviors and often provide public goods in the form of standards.

REGULATION OF COMMERCE

Given the amount of regulation in existence, it is useful to have a framework within which to consider regulation. IOSCO developed a framework of matters to be addressed in the domestic laws of a jurisdiction to facilitate effective securities legislation. This framework is shown in Exhibit 1.

The framework is a useful, but by no means exhaustive, list of areas of regulation relevant to an analyst. For example, labor, consumer protection, and environmental laws, which are not included in the list, may significantly affect a business or industry. These laws often address issues of safety and health. Awareness of the basic types of laws that affect economies, financial systems, industries, and businesses is useful to an analyst. This knowledge will help the analyst to identify areas of concern and to consider proactively potential effects of regulations, existing and anticipated.

Exhibit 1	IOSCO's Legal Framework

Effective securities regulation depends on an appropriate legal framework. The matters to be addressed in the domestic laws of a jurisdiction include:

1. **Company Law**

    1.1 company formation

    1.2 duties of directors and officers

    1.3 regulation of takeover bids and other transactions intended to effect a change in control

    1.4 laws governing the issue and offer for sale of securities

    1.5 disclosure of information to security holders to enable informed voting decisions

    1.6 disclosure of material shareholdings

2. **Commercial Code/Contract Law**

    2.1 private right of contract

    2.2 facilitation of securities lending and hypothecation

    2.3 property rights, including rights attaching to securities, and the rules governing the transfer of those rights

3. **Taxation Laws**

    3.1 clarity and consistency, including, but not limited to, the treatment of investments and investment products

4. **Bankruptcy and Insolvency Laws**

    4.1 rights of security holders on winding up

    4.2 rights of clients on insolvency of intermediary

    4.3 netting

5. **Competition Law**

    5.1 prevention of anti-competitive practices

    5.2 prevention of unfair barriers to entry

    5.3 prevention of abuse of a market dominant position

6. **Banking Law**

7. **Dispute Resolution System**

    7.1 a fair and efficient judicial system (including the alternative of arbitration or other alternative dispute resolution mechanisms)

    7.2 enforceability of court orders and arbitration awards, including foreign orders and awards

Source: Annexure 3 in "Objectives and Principles of Securities Regulation" (May 2003): www.iosco.org/library/pubdocs/pdf/IOSCOPD154.pdf

As discussed previously, externalities (such as pollution) and public goods problems are critical to the operation of our national and global economies. Similarly, it is difficult to structure private markets for many of the kinds of infrastructure decisions that are central to the operation of society and the economy. The role of government regulation is critical to setting out an underlying framework and facilitating business decisions that involve a considerable degree of coordination.

The relevant decisions arise at a number of levels. Arguably, many of these would be within the domain of national governments, but some of the relevant externalities are global. While common examples involve environmental issues, such as pollution, global warming externalities across countries, and externalities associated with nuclear waste storage, there are other relevant externalities in a global economy. It is important to have international mechanisms to facilitate the coordination and acceptance of responsibilities across national governments (typically, national governments are best able to coordinate decisions within their respective countries). Some of these externalities have long-term consequences (costs) and implications. In fact, arguably some of these long-run consequences may be ones that are difficult to fully quantify and assess.

The role of governments is crucial for promoting commerce locally, nationally, regionally, and globally. Trade agreements are important to global commerce. Government is in a position to facilitate basic features of the business environment, such as establishing the legal framework for contracting and setting standards. Regulation is central to fundamental aspects of our labor markets, such as workers' and employers' rights and responsibilities and workplace safety. Immigration issues are handled through regulation. Fundamental safety regulations with respect to drugs (including the reliance on testing), food products, medical devices, and pollution are significant.

Several issues have emerged as particularly relevant in the context of globalization and the internet. One issue is the recognition and protection of intellectual property. Government policies regulate intellectual property, prescribing standards and processes that define and govern patents, trademarks, and copyrights. Although the legal standards are country specific, most countries recognize the importance of protecting intellectual property. At the same time, lack of enforcement and protection of intellectual property has emerged as an issue in some of the trading disputes around the globe. Setting technical standards is another issue given the focus on technology and electronic tools and resources. Even something as mundane as establishing domain names and the related standard setting requires some appropriate delegation of authority.

Privacy issues also have arisen in the context of the internet. Privacy is particularly important with respect to medical, financial, academic, and employment records. Entities, including businesses and governments, must be protective of the confidential data in their possession and maintain appropriate security procedures. The internet raises a broad set of issues involving privacy because of the depth of information potentially available about a person's situation (financial and personal), activities, interactions, and purchases. How internet software navigates these privacy concerns will influence both the perceptions and actions of regulators as well as the acceptance of software innovations and business models in the marketplace.

An appropriate legal environment is crucial for the successful operation of commerce. Clearly defined rules governing contracts, their interpretation, and each party's legal rights under a contract are necessary. A framework for financial liability and dealing with bankruptcy is necessary for suitable private incentives to enter into economic contracts, particularly those that require long-term commitments. Such activities as construction projects, energy exploration and extraction projects, and even such mundane activities as relocation decisions involve significant long-term, dynamic commitments. Pre-commitment by society to a well-defined set of rules and standards is crucial to facilitating the willingness of market participants to engage in long-term commitments.

For example, consider the situation in which a company needs to incur significant costs to start a project. These costs are unrecoverable if the project does not progress forward; in other words, these are sunk costs. Without a strong legal framework, the party expending the sunk costs would be reluctant to incur these because of the potential of a "hold out" problem in which the other side exploits the sunk costs to force renegotiation of the deal. Such contractual difficulties would destabilize the operation of businesses and weaken the economy.

One important role of a national government is to support and protect domestic business interests. A crucial issue in international economic negotiations is protecting businesses against unfair competition. An example of unfair competition is the ability of a company or companies from country X to sell goods at significantly lower prices than its competitors from other countries because of subsidies from government X. Protection of domestic businesses can take the form of tariff and/or non-tariff barriers. These protective mechanisms are sometimes challenged in the international context as giving domestic companies an unfair competitive edge. Analogously, international disputes about whether a country is manipulating or fixing its currency price often center on issues related to competitiveness.

Economics emphasizes the principle of comparative advantage and the value of free trade. Comparative advantage suggests that all countries should allocate their efforts to those goods or services for which development efforts are most productive at the margin. In some cases, protecting and/or encouraging domestic production, through mechanisms such as subsidies, can impose excess costs on certain sectors or the broader society. Any potential benefit associated with the subsidy should be compared with the potential distortion created by the government subsidy and the efficiency of the transformation between products. Basic economic principles focus on avoiding the distortion associated with the relative pricing of products because of the underlying transformation process. Similarly, restricting foreign ownership or imposing capital flow restrictions can provide some protection to a domestic economy but these come at a cost.

Interestingly, while in a global context, an implicit regulatory goal of government may be to restrict competition from other countries. In a domestic context, a regulatory goal is to promote competition (this goal can alternatively be viewed as monitoring and preventing activities that restrict or distort competition). There are several dimensions to this goal. Regulatory approval is typically required for mergers and acquisition of major companies. Regulators can effectively block a merger or acquisition, or suggest remedies to resolve a perceived issue (for example, divestiture of particular segments of the businesses to resolve an antitrust issue). When there are competing bids, the actions of the regulator can effectively decide the outcome based on their assessment of the effects of each bid. Considering the expected response of regulators on competition or antitrust grounds is a central aspect to the evaluation of mergers and acquisitions. An important question to consider, as is done by the regulators, is whether the merger will lead to the monopolization of particular markets and, if so, are there ways (such as by divestiture of specific geographic, product, or other segments) to avoid the particular problem.

Competition and antitrust laws also typically prohibit abusive and anticompetitive behavior, such as collusion on prices by companies that dominate a market. Some of the types of behavior that are problematic (beyond mergers that create monopoly power) include exclusive dealings and refusals to deal, pricing discrimination, and engaging in predatory pricing. In response to antitrust issues, regulators may not only impose monetary sanctions but may require companies to alter their business (for example, divest portions, change operating/marketing practices).

The definition of software products and the bundling of them has been an increasing concern with respect to competition. For example, in the late 1990s, Microsoft was subject to a significant challenge by the United States concerning bundling its web browser with the Windows operating system—the crucial issue was whether the bundling reflected innovation or an attempt to monopolize the browser market. Challenges to rivals under competition laws also represent a business strategy. An example of such a challenge is Microsoft's challenge in Europe that Google is unfairly impeding competition in the search engine market.

A significant issue that companies need to face in addressing antitrust (or lack of competition) issues is that in many cases they need to satisfy simultaneously a range of regulators. For example, a company may have to satisfy both the U.S. Department of Justice and the European Union, if the company plans to use a common product and market strategy across jurisdictions. Despite language and cultural differences, it often will be advantageous to follow a unified strategy around the globe because of business imperatives and likely overlapping views among regulators of competition. Many of the cases that are significant for the U.S. market are taking place in Europe or elsewhere.

4   REGULATION OF FINANCIAL MARKETS

The regulation of securities markets and financial institutions is especially important because of the consequences to society of failures in the financial system. These consequences range from micro- to macro-level. Potential consequences include financial losses to specific parties, an overall loss of confidence, and disruption of commerce. These consequences were evident in the 2008 global financial crisis. Securities regulation focuses on such goals as protecting investors, creating confidence in markets (a challenging subject), and enhancing capital formation. Although it is difficult to define tangibly what types of regulatory changes would enhance confidence in the financial system, increasing confidence is at least occasionally cited as one of the motives for securities regulation. Many of the rules oriented toward equitable access to information (which, in turn, encourages capital formation) and protecting small investors, implicitly serve the role of promoting confidence in the markets.

Regulators of financial institutions focus on such issues as protecting consumers and investors, ensuring safety and soundness of financial institutions, promoting smooth operation of the payments system, and maintaining access to credit. Other macroeconomic concerns of financial regulators include price stability, levels of employment/unemployment, and economic growth.

A key focus of regulators is maintaining the integrity of the markets and acting as a referee for its fairness. This role is distinct compared with financial stability regulation, which is more directly focused on specific outcomes. In addition to securities registration requirements, to facilitate and support the marketplace and the confidence of investors, disclosure requirements are important. Disclosures allow investors to use available information to assess the consequences for investing in and valuing financial instruments and to allow markets to operate. Securities market disclosures occur at various levels, in various forms, and with varied and sometimes unexpected consequences. For example, Sarbanes–Oxley, which required *timeliness* in disclosure of insider transactions,[19] largely resolved the problem of options backdating in the United States—although the architects of that legislation were not aware of the backdating issue.

The disclosure framework is wide-ranging and has high potential importance. The disclosure framework includes financial reporting requirements and accounting standards, prospectus disclosure requirements in conjunction with both securities offerings and annual reports, disclosure requirements in the context of proxy proposals and contests, mutual fund disclosure rules, and price transparency disclosure rules.

19 Disclosure of insider transactions has been a long-standing requirement in the securities markets in the United States.

Disclosure requirements tend to be oriented toward the protection of and provision of information to investors (whether used by investors directly or by service providers).

Many of the regulations governing securities markets are oriented toward mitigating agency problems that arise through delegation to intermediaries. For many financial transactions, parties need to act through others (agents), leading to the potential for agency conflicts. Among the range of examples of regulations addressing potential agency conflicts are those related to mutual fund fees and governance, the governance of listed companies, rules for proxy voting in companies, best execution requirements on broker/dealers, and treatment of "soft dollar" expenses by investment advisers in the trading process.

Securities regulators historically have tended to focus more directly on protecting retail investors (individual investors with modest resources and arguably less investment expertise). This tendency has resulted in a lesser focus on financial regulation of hedge funds, private equity, and venture capital funds because of the type of investors (institutional and affluent individual investors) that invest in these funds. For these larger investors, regulators have taken more of a "buyer beware" orientation. For larger investors, it is more difficult to define suitability standards. One approach is to require a more modest range of disclosure requirements related to offering memorandum for a variety of different types of transactions as well as basic antifraud rules. These modest regulations coupled with access requirements that are at least arguably related to the sophistication of investors have typically been the extent of regulation of hedge funds, private equity, and venture capital funds. The majority of securities regulations focus on protecting small investors.

Issues related to prudential supervision of financial institutions and financial stability were introduced earlier. Prudential supervision is regulation and monitoring of the safety and soundness of financial institutions in order to promote financial stability, reduce system-wide risks, and protect customers of financial institutions. This supervision is critical because of the cost that failure of a financial institution can impose on the economy and society. The failure of a bank can result in loss of savings and access to credit. The failure of an insurance company can result in unanticipated losses to those insured. If government-sponsored entities provide protection against these losses or the government chooses to cover all or a portion of these losses, the losses can be spread across a greater sector of society than those directly affected. Additionally, the resulting loss of confidence in the financial system can have far-reaching consequences. The types of regulations include those that focus on diversifying assets, managing and monitoring risk taking, and ensuring adequate capitalization. Monitoring and supervision are important aspects of the regulations. In addition, regulators may set up funds to provide insurance against losses and mandate premiums or fees be paid into these funds. The benefits of regulation generally do not come without associated costs. For example, regulations that result in the provision of insurance on certain activities may create a moral hazard situation and result in greater risk-taking incentives.

COST–BENEFIT ANALYSIS OF REGULATION 5

In assessing regulation and regulatory outcomes, it is important to assess the overall benefits and costs of regulatory proposals, to develop techniques to enhance the measurement of these, and to examine how economic principles guide regulators.[20]

---

20 This theme, and especially the importance of measurement and suitable statistical methods in policy formulation, are examined in more detail in Spatt (2011).

The general benefits of regulation as discussed in earlier sections may be clear but the measurement of the full impact of the regulation (both benefits and costs) can be challenging. In conducting cost–benefit analysis of regulation, it often is easier to assess the costs of regulation.

Regulatory burden refers to the costs of regulation for the regulated entity; this cost is sometimes viewed as the private costs of regulation or government burden. **Net regulatory burden** is the private costs of regulation less the private benefits of regulation. Understanding the regulatory process will help an analyst recognize the types of challenges that regulators and policymakers face and formulate expectations of regulatory outcomes. Costs and benefits of regulation are important to consider, but often difficult to assess. Many regulators focus narrowly on the implementation costs of regulation (for example, how many compliance attorneys at what cost will need to be hired), but in many instances the most significant costs are the indirect ones that relate to the way in which economic decisions and behavior are altered and market allocations changed.

Regulators view some of the costs associated with regulations as "unintended," but it is important to distinguish between two types of such costs. There may be implementation costs that were unanticipated (for example, it turns out more compliance lawyers need to be hired than originally thought) and indirect costs because of unintended consequences. It is important for regulators to recognize that their evaluation of potential rules should reflect the "unintended consequences" as well as the consequences that were the direct object of the rule making. Furthermore, regulatory filings, in response to proposed regulations, identify at least some of the "unintended consequences" prior to the implementation of the regulation. It is difficult to argue that such consequences were unanticipated and unintended if they were identified prior to the implementation of the regulation. Unintended consequences are reflective of underlying policy risk and may result in high, unanticipated costs.

Regulatory costs and benefits are especially difficult to assess on a prospective basis compared with a retrospective basis. An after-the-fact analysis allows a comparison of the item(s) of interest before and after the regulation occurs. This comparison allows for a more informed assessment of a regulation because the actual costs and benefits may be identifiable. Even a trial or pilot analysis may be appropriate and helpful in some instances (perhaps too complex to achieve in other instances) to more fully understand the import in advance of a proposed regulation. A potentially feasible and relevant approach in the context of an environment with frequent trading is to use natural experiments and trial phase-ins to generate data suitable for careful cost–benefit analysis.[21] This approach facilitates the assessment of statistical evidence to evaluate the effects prior to the full-blown implementation of the proposed regulation. Such approaches are more feasible for a trading rule in a market with high trading frequency that will generate considerable data and run little risk of disrupting the real economy.

Some regulators undertake relatively little retrospective analysis and assessment of the impact of previously enacted regulations. There has been some call for "sunset provisions" by which a regulation being implemented would be automatically removed after a number of years, unless the regulator took further action.[22] The use of sunset provisions would require regulators to undertake a new cost–benefit analysis to continue the regulation. An area of concern is whether regulators devote sufficient attention to assessing the consequences of their past actions. Greater focus on the economic impact of prior decisions would help enhance accountability. A post-implementation review, as is the case with any decision-making process, is a logical step.

---

21 Among the contexts in which such techniques have been utilized by U.S. securities regulators have been rules involving short sales, post-trade price reporting, and the tick size increment for trading.
22 See, for example, Romano (2005).

Within the United States, administrative law requires that federal regulatory agencies conduct a cost–benefit analysis to assess the consequences of their actions. Court rulings have struck down regulatory actions because inadequate economic and cost–benefit analyses were performed. For example, the U.S. Circuit Court of Appeals overturned the 2004 SEC rule requiring that mutual funds have independent chairs and at least 75 percent independent directors on such grounds.[23] More recently as reported in the *Economist*, "An appeals court rejected the Securities and Exchange Commission's proxy-access rules…. The judges ruled that the regulator had carried out insufficient cost–benefit analysis."[24] In the aftermath of the adoption of the Dodd–Frank Act in the United States, a number of legislators have expressed concern about the quality of the cost–benefit analyses of the financial regulatory agencies responsible for implementing the Act. This concern reveals an interesting perspective for assessing regulations.

Ideally, regulatory judgments should reflect economic principles and full consideration of the economic costs and benefits rather than the preferences of the current decision makers. Although the potential failure of the fundamental theorem of welfare economics suggests the potential relevance of regulation, it is important to use economic principles to identify and assess alternative remedies and specific actions.

ANALYSIS OF REGULATION

The effect of regulations can range from macro effects on an economy to micro effects on a business. These ultimately have implications for security analysis and valuation. Because regulations are constantly evolving, it is important to monitor issues of concern to regulators and ongoing developments to assess the implications of potential regulation. Using a framework, such as that shown in Exhibit 1, can help an analyst identify and focus on particular areas that potentially have significant effects on the industry or entity being analyzed.

When a regulatory environment shifts, lobbying by the potentially affected industry or business may occur; the affected industries and companies are anxious to convey their perspective on the impact of proposed regulations. Potential new regulation may be perceived as either costly or beneficial to the affected entities. Some regulations may work against particular market sectors or industries, while others may work in their favor. If a regulator is captive to those that they regulate, regulation is more likely to benefit those regulated. For example, regulation can create demand for particular products and can act as a barrier to entry against rivals. Regulation can change relative demands among products.

One interesting example is the effect of the SEC's Regulation National Market System (NMS) regarding competition among equity trading platforms in the United States. Regulation NMS, an example of a proactive regulation, was intended to take advantage of technological advances to achieve the objectives of efficient, competitive, fair, and orderly markets. Since the 2005 adoption of Regulation NMS, the market share of the trading floor of the New York Stock Exchange (NYSE) has fallen by about two thirds. Prior to Regulation NMS, NYSE "specialists" or market makers could take up to thirty seconds to react to orders sent by other platforms. The other platforms were checking whether the NYSE would execute at a more favorable price than the original platform quoted. This process provided considerable opportunity for an NYSE specialist to observe subsequent pricing, and to exploit the implicit optionality in the

---

23 See *Chamber of Commerce v. SEC*, 412 F.3d 133 (D.C. Cir. 2005) and 443 F.3d 890 (D.C. Cir. 2006).
24 *Economist*, 30 July 2011, p. 7. See also, *Business Roundtable and Chamber of Commerce v. SEC*, No. 10-1305 (D.C. Cir. 22 July 2011).

process. This process also made it hard for the rival platform to compete. Consequently, the NYSE could position itself to attract and concentrate much of the market liquidity, and so it emerged along the lines of a "natural monopoly." After Regulation NMS, which the NYSE had endorsed, the advantage to the NYSE diminished.[25] Because of the change in regulation, many new trading platforms developed and trading execution fragmented. Clearly, the structure of regulation plays a crucial role with respect to the viability of different order tactics and even the viability of the business models underlying different trading platforms.

The history of the money market mutual fund industry is another interesting example of how regulation can affect business models. Money market mutual funds in the United States first arose in response to Regulation Q in the early 1970s, which imposed a ceiling on the interest rates paid by banks for various types of bank deposits. When market interest rates rose above the ceiling, there was considerable migration from bank deposits toward marketed fixed-income instruments, such as Treasury bills and notes. Money market mutual funds developed in response to the binding Regulation Q rate ceilings. During the 2008 global financial crisis, the collapse of a major U.S. money market mutual fund (Reserve Fund), led to a run until the government launched a short-term insurance program to protect money market mutual fund balances. Government policy (motivated by an attempt to stabilize the financial system) helped to protect this product. However, in response to resulting pressures from banks and the new advantage that the money market fund industry obtained, the Federal Deposit Insurance Corporation then raised its insurance limit to $250,000 from $100,000. As this example illustrates, regulatory constraints have played a major role in the organization of short-term deposits in the United States. Changes in the effective regulatory structure have led to dramatic changes in the competitive landscape.

Another interesting class of issues occurs with respect to the allocation of the pricing of joint products. For example, it can be difficult to separate fully the underlying economics associated with the production, transmission, and distribution of energy products. Government regulation can affect the structure of the industry. For example, suppose there is a natural monopoly with respect to the distribution stage. How much should the provider of those services be able to obtain from the consumer or other companies providing upstream services, such as an energy product or access to a communication network? While for some products there is increased and vigorous competition, these issues are still very important with respect to the returns available from building various infrastructure. Although the market can sort out the allocation of profits and pricing across stages when there is vigorous competition at each stage, these issues are difficult in the face of a natural monopoly. Of course, monopoly power is at the root of one of the most important traditional uses of regulation—to set pricing and returns at utility providers. In many areas, a government regulator sets public utility prices because a utility provider has a monopolistic position.

At a global level, there has been an extensive debate about "network neutrality." Advocates of the principle of network neutrality argue that there should not be any restriction on access to networks (such as telephone and the internet) and assert that operators would otherwise attempt to restrict competition and create market power. Conversely, some ability to discriminate on the part of service providers may be desirable for developing and supporting the underlying infrastructure. The issues involving network neutrality are not fully resolved and likely to be ones of continuing conflict. Alternative government policies may lead to very different incentives and structures in the industry.

It also is interesting to reflect on industries or sectors that receive subsidies from government policy compared with those that pay taxes. This reflection provides a

---

25 See the discussion of the impact of Regulation NMS in Angel, Harris, and Spatt (2011).

means for understanding the extent to which government policy leads some sectors of the economy to be smaller and some sectors to be larger. For example, the policies of many governments have led the cigarette industry to shrink. Cigarette products often are heavily taxed, thereby reducing the size of the sector. Governments justify the heavy taxation based on externalities that are created by cigarette smoking (these include second-hand smoke and elevated health care costs for society). In contrast, many governments provide government-sponsored health care programs or heavily subsidized health care, which may increase the size of the health care sector. Because of government programs, the ultimate user pays directly only a small portion, if any, of the health care costs attributable to the user. Because the cost is not visible to or paid directly by the user, these health care policies may have the effect of encouraging the allocation of additional resources to the health care sector. While there may be justifications for policies that heavily tax or subsidize a sector, the link between government policies and the allocation of resources to a sector can be significant and should be considered. Once again, the importance and relevance of cost–benefit analysis is apparent.

6.1 Effects of Regulations

Some regulation is very specific and focused on a particular sector, whereas other regulation is wide ranging and may affect a number of sectors to varying degrees. Examples of regulations that focus on a particular sector are those focused on the financial sector. Financial institutions, including banks, are subject to extensive regulation from a variety of regulatory bodies. This regulation affects a variety of items, including a bank's financial and operating structures and risk management. A major regulatory challenge confronting banking supervisors is how much "capital" should be required for banks and other financial institutions. This issue is key for bank regulators globally —including central bankers and the Basel Committee on Banking Supervision. Increasing capital requirements may improve liquidity and stability of financial institutions and reduce reliance on indirect governmental guarantees and support.[26] Such proposals, however, have been controversial with the leadership of financial institutions, who view equity capital as substantially more costly than debt financing (this subject is discussed further later in this subsection). They argue that such regulation may reduce access to credit and hinder economic growth.

One of the lessons from the 2008 global financial crisis was that globally, many major financial institutions, including financial services firms, had excessive leverage. This leverage reflected the similarity in the exposures of many financial institutions, a factor in the spreading of losses from institution to institution in the financial system (contagion). Some of these institutions ultimately collapsed or received some sort of a bailout from a government. The similarity in exposures makes it doubtful that the financial difficulties simply reflected externalities rather than similar and apparently mistaken judgments.

An apparent conclusion of policymakers in the United States after the collapse of Lehman Brothers was that the imposition of losses on creditors would lead to a loss of confidence and systemic failure. Consequently, many participants in the financial system anticipate that bondholders of major companies are likely to be protected in the future, leading to limits on the extent that credit spreads can serve as a disciplinary mechanism and amplifying the willingness of companies to assume greater risks. The extent of this moral hazard may have been amplified because of what market participants inferred from government responses during the 2008 global financial crisis, which has manifested itself in terms of a funding advantage to banks that have greater systemic risk. To the degree that these institutions are largely debt-financed

---

26 Capital requirements are discussed in detail by Admati, DeMarzo, Hellwig, and Pfleiderer (2010).

rather than equity-financed, the cost of the company's risk bearing is understated (because it is subsidized by government) and the company's shareholders may not adequately internalize the company's risk-taking.

The responses of governments to, in effect, subsidize certain investors in financial institutions and the expected effects on moral hazard and on taxpayers are not unique to the United States. The Irish government guaranteed the liabilities of Irish banks at significant cost to Irish taxpayers. In 2008, Dexia, a Franco-Belgian financial services group, received a bailout from the French and Belgian governments. As reported on 4 October 2011 in the *Wall Street Journal*, "The French and Belgian governments, both part-owners of Dexia thanks to the previous bailout, committed Tuesday to safeguarding the bank's depositors and creditors. Even if this support calms markets short-term, the maneuver poses the danger of transferring more risk from the private sector to the public one."[27] It is very challenging to assess the costs and benefits of these decisions to the various stakeholders, including taxpayers.

In countries in which interest on debt, but not dividends on equity, is tax-deductible, taxpayers effectively subsidize the use of corporate debt as a source of capital. Requirements that financial institutions meet specified capital standards are essentially requirements that they have a significant portion of equity capital so that they bear most of the marginal funding cost. It is important to recognize what high capital standards are not—they are not a requirement that companies set aside as a "buffer" and hold (e.g., idle) amounts of capital as a reserve. High capital standards are an attempt to ensure that investors in the financial institutions are bearing the costs of the risk that the financial institutions choose to assume.

Under the Modigliani–Miller capital structure theory, in the absence of taxes and given certain other assumptions, equity and debt are substitutes for financing the company and capital structure is irrelevant to the value of the company.[28] To the extent that a company can reduce its overall funding cost by reducing its equity investment and increasing leverage, it reflects a government subsidy in the form of the tax advantage of debt. The addition of implicit or assumed guarantees, that the government will not allow the institution to fail, encourages increased leverage because this guarantee is in effect a government subsidy that will reduce overall funding costs. Some CEOs of financial institutions have not been sympathetic to high equity capital standards—this disagreement may reflect compensation arrangements focused on return on equity (ROE) rather than return on assets (ROA) and benefits of leverage due to the tax advantage of debt.

The bank supervision process is another aspect of regulation with important implications for the riskiness of a bank's contingent claims. Traditionally, supervision has had limited transparency; ratings and recommendations of bank supervisors have not been shared publicly. The stress tests undertaken in 2009 in the United States were cited as a major advance with respect to the bank supervision model (for example, see Bernanke 2009). In those tests, the financial institutions were subject to common shocks and stresses, which was an important innovation with respect to the supervisory model. Another key aspect of the implementation of the 2009 stress tests was the public disclosure of the funding needs of the financial institutions. Similar stress tests were and are being conducted in various parts of the world, including Europe. Issues about the disclosure of results—how much and what to disclose—and the adequacy of the tests are among the issues that regulators have had to address. Decisions about the appropriate amount of disclosure have varied among regulators.

Another cost–benefit consideration is the regulatory impact on funding costs in the capital market when a regulator essentially "infuses capital or writes checks." Although it is not common for a regulator to "write checks" (most do not have resources for

---

27 *Wall Street Journal*, "Dexia Looks for Bailout, Part Deux," (5 October 2011).
28 This is discussed in greater detail in Aggarwal, Drake, Kobor, and Noronha (2010).

such purposes), such a situation can arise with discount window borrowing from a central bank.[29] Discount window borrowers are likely to advocate that discount window transactions be kept confidential; they hope to avoid the adverse stigma associated with acknowledging their need to obtain "lender of last resort" financing.[30] Often, a central bank also supports this position of confidentiality; the central bank justifies this based on its objectives, such as maintaining confidence and stability in the financial system. Others may advocate for the release of this information because of the potential relevance to stakeholders, including customers and investors.

Judicial law may be required to resolve the issue of information availability in different parts of the world. In the United States, Bloomberg LP brought a Freedom of Information Act lawsuit to require disclosure of the discount window borrowers during the 2008 global financial crisis. The Federal Reserve fought the lawsuit unsuccessfully. Even with a lack of public disclosure about discount window borrowing, there is at least some empirical evidence suggesting that the marketplace penalizes financial institutions that borrow at the window (see Armantier, Ghysels, Sarkar, and Shrader 2011). It is plausible that, even in the absence of disclosure, participants in the financial markets are able to deduce that such borrowing has or is likely to occur; discount window borrowing is not the only information about an institution's financial condition available to market participants.

A final example of a regulatory issue with significant ramifications for funding costs concerns the extent to which regulators outsource the determination of regulatory treatment to rating agencies. Regulators may reference and rely on third-party ratings for regulatory purposes, such as capital requirements for financial institutions and suitability standards for particular investors or products. Ratings have an important impact on the pricing of bonds and the structuring of portfolios—for example, what bonds can be held in various types of accounts and funds (such as money market mutual funds). Those seeking ratings may engage in regulatory arbitrage (entities identify and use some aspect of regulations that allows them to exploit differences in economic substance and regulatory interpretation to their benefit) by shopping for a higher rating. The default rate of highly rated mortgage market financial instruments played an important role in the 2008 global financial crisis.

The collateralized mortgage-backed securities (MBS) structure is based on the securitization model of buying a pool of assets (mortgages, in this case) and assigning the income and principal returns into individual security tranches. It was subsequently found that in many cases, a pool of mortgages was transformed via securitization from individual mortgages with a lower average rating to a securitized pool of mortgages with a higher rating. The credit-rating agencies assigned the ratings to MBS and the ratings led to false comfort by investors about the quality of their holdings. Many observers believed that the "mistakes" of credit rating agencies and the process and standards implicitly sanctioned by regulators led to the development of a relatively common view. Considerable revaluation and systemic risk ensued when the degree of risk and quality of the underlying mortgage pools did not match the higher rating assigned by the rating agencies.

Because credit ratings were identified as a key source of systemic risk in the United States, the Dodd–Frank Act barred references to ratings in regulation. Globally, other regulators are reconsidering the roles and/or types of rating agencies; in the EU, some have advocated the creation of an EU-sponsored independent credit-rating agency. At

---

29 Although rare, other examples exist of regulators having resources to assist those they regulate. An example is the Trouble Asset Recovery Program (TARP) that was approved in the United States in late 2008. TARP in essence provided a "checkbook" to the Secretary of the Treasury. In the United States, access to resources potentially explains the power of the Fed compared with that of the SEC or Commodities and Futures Trading Commission (CFTC) during a financial crisis.

30 A recent study documents that borrowers are willing to pay a premium to access other Federal Reserve liquidity facilities rather than the discount window. See Armantier, Ghysels, Sarkar, and Shrader (2011).

the same time, regulators have struggled with how to replace ratings for regulatory purposes. For example, the use of credit default swap prices or yield spreads would be forward looking, but the underlying markets may lack sufficient liquidity and/or could be subject to manipulation. Even the price of the bonds could be manipulated. Although it is generally not referred to as "manipulation," the large scale purchases of European sovereign debt by the European Central Bank (ECB) can be viewed as distorting market pricing.[31] Transferring authority to organizations other than credit-rating agencies may not result in fundamental changes. It is difficult to identify an alternative approach that would eliminate the potential for systemic risk.

For some purposes, it may be helpful to have asset managers take responsibility for the classification and rating of the assets that they purchase (for example, develop suitability standards for the relevant account), but it is unclear how this approach could work with respect to capital standards. The discussion of the complexity of setting up a suitable system of capital regulation and the viability of risk-based models suggest that alternatives to the use of ratings by credit-rating agencies still may lead to systemic risk.

Despite the challenges with the credit-rating agency model, several aspects are worth emphasizing. While the discussion highlights some of the consequences in outsourcing the determination of regulatory treatment to rating agencies, to a degree there are similar challenges with many of the proposed alternatives. Reliance on intermediaries with a stake in the economic outcomes of the entity being assessed may align incentives of the assessor with those relying on the assessment. This approach, however, is not without potential conflict of interest issues. A possible benefit of the rating agency approach is that the rating agencies have the potential to provide objective guidance for financial instruments in regulatory contexts. The potential economies of scale in information production also suggest that there may be significant private incentives to outsource a portion of the information production that asset managers require. Even if regulators eliminate reference to ratings by credit-rating agencies, there may still be a viable role and business model for credit-rating agencies.

Environmental, property rights, and labor regulations are other examples of areas in which regulation plays an important role with a significant impact on society. Regulation in any of these areas may still focus on a particular industry. When analyzing an industry or business, it is important to consider the type of regulation that the industry is sensitive and susceptible to. For example, oil, gas, and mining companies, as well as certain types of manufacturers may be more sensitive to changes in the regulatory atmosphere with respect to environmental issues. Labor-intensive industries may be affected to a greater extent than a capital-intensive industry by regulatory changes with respect to labor conditions and rights. Pharmaceutical and technology companies may be sensitive to regulations with respect to intellectual property rights. Having a framework within which to consider regulation is very useful.

SUMMARY

Knowledge of regulation is important because regulation has potentially far-reaching and significant effects. These effects can range from macro-level effects on the economy to micro-level effects on individual entities and securities.

---

31 For example, C. Spatt and P. Wallison, "A Regulatory Blueprint for Mismanaging the Sovereign Debt Crisis," Shadow Financial Regulatory Committee Statement No. 320 (2011), points to this distortion. That discussion also highlights a range of other ways in which sovereign debtors have been unhappy with various market institutions (such as credit default swaps, short selling, and credit-rating agencies) and have attempted to diminish how sovereign debt would be disciplined by markets.

Regulation originates from a variety of sources and in a variety of areas. A framework that includes types of regulators and regulation as well as areas of regulation that may affect the entity of interest (including the economy as an entity) is useful. The framework will help in assessing possible effects of new regulation. It can also help in assessing the effects of regulation on various entities.

More than one regulator may develop regulations in response to a particular issue. Each of the relevant regulators may have different objectives and choose to address the issue using different regulatory tools.

In developing regulations, the regulator should consider costs and benefits. In the analysis, the net regulatory burden (private costs less private benefits of regulation) may also be relevant. Costs and benefits, regardless of the perspective, may be difficult to assess. A critical aspect of regulatory analysis, however, is assessing the costs and benefits of regulation.

Some key points of the reading are summarized below:

- Legislative bodies, regulatory bodies, and courts typically enact regulation.

- Regulatory bodies include government agencies and independent regulators granted authority by a government or governmental agency. Some independent regulators may be self-regulating organizations.

- Typically, legislative bodies enact broad laws or statutes; regulatory bodies issue administrative regulations, often implementing statutes; and courts interpret statutes and administrative regulations and these interpretations may result in judicial law.

- Regulators have responsibility for both substantive and procedural laws. The former focuses on rights and responsibilities of entities and relationships among entities. The latter focuses on the protection and enforcement of the former.

- The existence of informational frictions and externalities creates a need for regulation. Regulation is expected to have societal benefits and should be assessed using cost–benefit analysis.

- Regulation that arises to enhance the interests of regulated entities reflects regulatory capture.

- Regulatory competition is competition among different regulatory bodies to use regulation in order to attract certain entities.

- Regulatory arbitrage is the use of regulation by an entity to exploit differences in economic substance and regulatory interpretation or in regulatory regimes to the entity's benefit.

- Interdependence in the actions and potentially conflicting objectives of regulators is an important consideration for regulators, those regulated, and those assessing the effects of regulation.

- There are many regulatory tools available to regulators, including price mechanisms (such as taxes and subsidies), regulatory mandates and restrictions on behaviors, provision of public goods, and public financing of private projects.

- The choice of regulatory tool should be consistent with maintaining a stable regulatory environment. Stable does not mean unchanging, but rather refers to desirable attributes of regulation, including predictability, effectiveness in achieving objectives, time consistency, and enforceability.

- The breadth of regulation of commerce necessitates the use of a framework that identifies potential areas of regulation. This framework can be referenced to identity specific areas of regulation, existing and anticipated, that may affect the entity of interest.

- The regulation of securities markets and financial institutions is extensive and complex because of the consequences of failures in the financial system. These consequences include financial losses, loss of confidence, and disruption of commerce.

- The focus of regulators in financial markets includes prudential supervision, financial stability, market integrity, and economic growth among others.

- Regulators—in assessing regulation and regulatory outcomes—should conduct ongoing cost–benefit analyses, develop techniques to enhance the measurement of these, and use economic principles to guide them.

- Net regulatory burden to the entity of interest is an important consideration for an analyst.

REFERENCES

Admati, Anat, Peter DeMarzo, Martin Hellwig, and Paul Pfleiderer. 2010. "Fallacies, Irrelevant Facts and Myths in the Discussion of Capital Regulation: Why Bank Equity is Not Expensive." Working Paper No. 86, Rock Center for Corporate Governance at Stanford University.

Aggarwal, Raj, Pamela Drake, Adam Kobor, and Gregory Noronha. 2011. "Capital Structure." Charlottesville, VA: CFA Institute.

Angel, James, Lawrence Harris, and Chester Spatt. 2011. "Equity Trading in the 21st Century." *Quarterly Journal of Finance*, vol. 1: 1–53.

Armantier, Olivier, Eric Ghysels, Asani Sarkar, and Jeffrey Shrader. 2011. "Stigma in Financial Markets: Evidence from Liquidity Auctions and Discount Window Borrowing during the Crisis." Federal Reserve Bank of New York Staff Reports, No. 483.

Bernanke, Ben S. 2009. "The Supervisory Capital Assessment Program." Atlanta Federal Reserve Bank Financial Markets Conference speech (11 May).

Carson, John W. 2011. "Self-Regulation in Securities Markets." Working Paper No. 5542, World Bank Financial Sector Policy Group (http://ssrn.com/abstract=1747445).

Christensen, Hans, Luzi Hail, and Christian Leuz. 2011. "Capital-Market Effects of Securities Regulation: The Role of Prior Regulation, Implementation and Enforcement." NBER Working Paper 16737 (October).

Romano, Roberta. 2005. "The Sarbanes–Oxley Act and the Making of Quack Corporate Governance." *Yale Law Journal*, vol. 114, no. 7 (May): 1521–1611.

Spatt, Chester. 2009. "Regulatory Conflict: Market Integrity vs. Financial Stability." *University of Pittsburgh Law Review*, vol. 71, no. 3 (Winter): 625–639.

Spatt, Chester. 2011. "Measurement and Policy Formulation." Invited Lecture to the Society for Financial Econometrics meeting at the University of Chicago (June).

Stigler, George J. 1971. "The Economic Theory of Regulation." *Bell Journal of Economics*, vol. 2, no. 1 (Spring): 3–21.

PRACTICE PROBLEMS FOR READING 16

The following information relates to Questions 1 – 6[1]

Tiu Asset Management (TAM) recently hired Jonna Yun. Yun is a member of TAM's Global Equity portfolio team and is assigned the task of analyzing the effects of regulation on the U.S. financial services sector. In her first report to the team, Yun makes the following statements:

Statement 1   The Dodd-Frank Wall Street Reform and Consumer Protection Act (Dodd-Frank Act), enacted on July 21, 2010 by the U.S. Congress, will have a significant effect on U.S. banks and other financial services firms.

Statement 2   The U.S. Securities and Exchange Commission (SEC) allocates certain regulatory responsibilities to the Financial Industry Regulatory Authority (FINRA), with the goal of ensuring that the securities industry operates fairly and honestly.

Statement 3   The Dodd-Frank Act called for derivatives reforms, including shifting from bilateral to centralized derivatives settlement, by July 2011. The G-20 called for action by its members on derivatives reform by year-end 2012. The accelerated timeline of the Dodd-Frank Act concerned some U.S. firms.

Statement 4   Regulators use various tools to intervene in the financial services sector.

Statement 5   Regulations may bring benefits to the U.S. economy, but they may also have unanticipated costly effects.

Statement 6   Regulation Q imposed a ceiling on interest rates paid by banks for certain bank deposits.

1. The *most* appropriate classification of the Dodd-Frank Act, referred to in Statement 1, is a(n):
   A. statute.
   B. judicial law.
   C. administrative law.

2. The Financial Industry Regulatory Authority, referred to in Statement 2, is *best* classified as a:
   A. legislative body.
   B. government agency.
   C. self-regulatory organization.

3. What is the *most likely* basis for the concerns noted in Statement 3?
   A. Externalities
   B. Regulatory arbitrage
   C. Informational friction

4. The tools *least likely* to be used by regulators to intervene in financial markets are:
   A. blackout periods.
   B. capital requirements.
   C. insider trading restrictions.

---

[1] This item set was developed by E. Shepard Farrar, CFA (Washington, DC, USA).
Copyright © CFA Institute.

5. Which of the following is *most likely* an unanticipated effect of regulation?

   A. Hiring compliance lawyers

   B. Setting legal standards for contracts

   C. Establishing employers' rights and responsibilities

6. After Regulation Q was imposed, the demand for money market funds *most likely*:

   A. increased.

   B. decreased.

   C. remained unchanged.

SOLUTIONS FOR READING 16

1. A is correct. The Dodd-Frank Act, enacted by the U.S. Congress and signed into law, is an example of a statute (a law enacted by a legislative body).

2. C is correct. FINRA, the Financial Industry Regulatory Authority, is a self-regulatory organization (SRO) and an independent regulator. The reading states that it describes itself as "the largest independent regulator for all securities firms doing business in the United States. Our chief role is to protect investors by maintaining the fairness of the U.S. capital markets." FINRA oversees over 4,000 brokerage firms, 160,000 branch offices and 629,000 registered securities representatives. FINRA has, as noted by the reading, "a degree of official sanction but is not a government agency per se." FINRA is referred to specifically in the reading as an SRO.

3. B is correct. U.S. firms are likely to be concerned due to the earlier timing of the application of new (more stringent) regulations in the U.S. than in other G-20 countries. With more stringent regulations, some business may flow to less-stringent regulatory environments or jurisdictions.

4. A is correct. Blackout periods are established by *companies* in response to concerns about insider trading. Thus, blackout periods are not a tool used by government to intervene in the financial services sector. Capital requirements are utilized by government regulators to reduce systemic risk and financial contagion. Insider trading restrictions are used by regulators concerned about insiders using their greater knowledge to the disadvantage of others; insider trading restrictions respond to informational frictions.

5. A is correct. The hiring of more lawyers to deal with compliance is an example of an 'unintended' implementation cost. Establishing legal standards for contracts and employers' rights and responsibilities are objectives (intended consequences) of some regulation.

6. A is correct. Regulation Q set a ceiling on the interest rates paid by banks for various types of deposits, which resulted in investors' shifting funds to money market funds.

Glossary

Abandonment option The ability to terminate a project at some future time if the financial results are disappointing.

Abnormal earnings See *Residual income*.

Abnormal return The return on an asset in excess of the asset's required rate of return; the risk-adjusted return.

Absolute convergence The idea that developing countries, regardless of their particular characteristics, will eventually catch up with the developed countries and match them in per capita output.

Absolute valuation model A model that specifies an asset's intrinsic value.

Absolute version of PPP The extension of the law of one price to the broad range of goods and services that are consumed in different countries.

Accounting estimates Estimates of items such as the useful lives of assets, warranty costs, and the amount of uncollectible receivables.

Accrual basis Method of accounting in which the effect of transactions on financial condition and income are recorded when they occur, not when they are settled in cash.

Acquirer The company in a merger or acquisition that is acquiring the target.

Acquiring company The company in a merger or acquisition that is acquiring the target.

Acquisition The purchase of some portion of one company by another; the purchase may be for assets, a definable segment of another entity, or the purchase of an entire company.

Active factor risk The contribution to active risk squared resulting from the portfolio's different-than-benchmark exposures relative to factors specified in the risk model.

Active portfolio In the context of the Treynor-Black model, the portfolio formed by mixing analyzed stocks of perceived nonzero alpha values. This portfolio is ultimately mixed with the passive market index portfolio.

Active return The return on a portfolio minus the return on the portfolio's benchmark.

Active risk The standard deviation of active returns.

Active risk squared The variance of active returns; active risk raised to the second power.

Active specific risk or asset selection risk The contribution to active risk squared resulting from the portfolio's active weights on individual assets as those weights interact with assets' residual risk.

Add-on interest A procedure for determining the interest on a bond or loan in which the interest is added onto the face value of a contract.

Adjusted beta Historical beta adjusted to reflect the tendency of beta to be mean reverting.

Adjusted funds from operations Funds from operations (FFO) adjusted to remove any non-cash rent reported under straight-line rent accounting and to subtract maintenance-type capital expenditures and leasing costs, including leasing agents' commissions and tenants' improvement allowances.

Adjusted present value (APV)As an approach to valuing a company, the sum of the value of the company, assuming no use of debt, and the net present value of any effects of debt on company value.

Adjusted R^2 A measure of goodness-of-fit of a regression that is adjusted for degrees of freedom and hence does not automatically increase when another independent variable is added to a regression.

Administrative regulations or administrative law Rules issued by government agencies or other regulators.

Agency costs Costs associated with the conflict of interest present when a company is managed by non-owners. Agency costs result from the inherent conflicts of interest between managers and equity owners.

Agency costs of equity The smaller the stake that managers have in the company, the less is their share in bearing the cost of excessive perquisite consumption or not giving their best efforts in running the company.

Agency issues (also agency problems, or principal-agent problems) Conflicts of interest that arise when the agent in an agency relationship has goals and incentives that differ from the principal to whom the agent owes a fiduciary duty.

Agency problem A conflict of interest that arises when the agent in an agency relationship has goals and incentives that differ from the principal to whom the agent owes a fiduciary duty.

Alpha The return on an asset in excess of the asset's required rate of return; the risk-adjusted return.

American Depositary Receipt A negotiable certificate issued by a depositary bank that represents ownership in a non-U.S. company's deposited equity (i.e., equity held in custody by the depositary bank in the company's home market).

American option An option that can be exercised at any time until its expiration date.

Amortizing and accreting swaps A swap in which the notional principal changes according to a formula related to changes in the underlying.

Analysis of variance (ANOVA) The analysis of the total variability of a dataset (such as observations on the dependent variable in a regression) into components representing different sources of variation; with reference to regression, ANOVA provides the inputs for an F-test of the significance of the regression as a whole.

Arbitrage 1) The simultaneous purchase of an undervalued asset or portfolio and sale of an overvalued but equivalent asset or portfolio, in order to obtain a riskless profit on the price differential. Taking advantage of a market inefficiency in a risk-free manner. 2) The condition in a financial market in which equivalent assets or combinations of assets sell for two different prices, creating an opportunity to profit at no risk with no commitment of money. In a well-functioning financial market, few arbitrage opportunities are possible. 3) A risk-free operation that earns an expected positive net profit but requires no net investment of money.

Arbitrage opportunity   An opportunity to conduct an arbitrage; an opportunity to earn an expected positive net profit without risk and with no net investment of money.

Arbitrage portfolio   The portfolio that exploits an arbitrage opportunity.

Arrears swap   A type of interest rate swap in which the floating payment is set at the end of the period and the interest is paid at that same time.

Asset beta   The unlevered beta; reflects the business risk of the assets; the asset's systematic risk.

Asset purchase   An acquisition in which the acquirer purchases the target company's assets and payment is made directly to the target company.

Asset-based approach   Approach that values a private company based on the values of the underlying assets of the entity less the value of any related liabilities.

Asset-based valuation   An approach to valuing natural resource companies that estimates company value on the basis of the market value of the natural resources the company controls.

Asymmetric information   The differential of information between corporate insiders and outsiders regarding the company's performance and prospects. Managers typically have more information about the company's performance and prospects than owners and creditors.

At-the-money   An option in which the underlying value equals the exercise price.

Autocorrelation   The correlation of a time series with its own past values.

Autoregressive model (AR)   A time series regressed on its own past values, in which the independent variable is a lagged value of the dependent variable.

Available-for-sale investments   Debt and equity securities not classified as either held-to-maturity or held-for-trading securities. The investor is willing to sell but not actively planning to sell. In general, available-for-sale securities are reported at fair value on the balance sheet.

Backward integration   A merger involving the purchase of a target ahead of the acquirer in the value or production chain; for example, to acquire a supplier.

Backwardation   A condition in the futures markets in which the benefits of holding an asset exceed the costs, leaving the futures price less than the spot price.

Balance-sheet-based accruals ratio   The difference between net operating assets at the end and the beginning of the period compared to the average net operating assets over the period.

Balance-sheet-based aggregate accruals   The difference between net operating assets at the end and the beginning of the period.

Basic earnings per share   (EPS) Net earnings available to common shareholders (i.e., net income minus preferred dividends) divided by the weighted average number of common shares outstanding during the period.

Basis swap   1) An interest rate swap involving two floating rates. 2) A swap in which both parties pay a floating rate.

Bear hug   A tactic used by acquirers to circumvent target management's objections to a proposed merger by submitting the proposal directly to the target company's board of directors.

Benchmark   A comparison portfolio; a point of reference or comparison.

Benchmark value of the multiple   In using the method of comparables, the value of a price multiple for the comparison asset; when we have comparison assets (a group), the mean or median value of the multiple for the group of assets.

Bill-and-hold basis   Sales on a bill-and-hold basis involve selling products but not delivering those products until a later date.

Binomial model   A model for pricing options in which the underlying price can move to only one of two possible new prices.

Binomial tree   The graphical representation of a model of asset price dynamics in which, at each period, the asset moves up with probability p or down with probability $(1 - p)$.

Blockage factor   An illiquidity discount that occurs when an investor sells a large amount of stock relative to its trading volume (assuming it is not large enough to constitute a controlling ownership).

Bond indenture   A legal contract specifying the terms of a bond issue.

Bond option   An option in which the underlying is a bond; primarily traded in over-the-counter markets.

Bond yield plus risk premium method   An estimate of the cost of common equity that is produced by summing the before-tax cost of debt and a risk premium that captures the additional yield on a company's stock relative to its bonds. The additional yield is often estimated using historical spreads between bond yields and stock yields.

Bond-equivalent yield   The yield to maturity on a basis that ignores compounding.

Bonding costs   Costs borne by management to assure owners that they are working in the owners' best interest (e.g., implicit cost of non-compete agreements).

Book value   Shareholders' equity (total assets minus total liabilities) minus the value of preferred stock; common shareholders' equity.

Book value of equity   Shareholders' equity (total assets minus total liabilities) minus the value of preferred stock; common shareholders' equity.

Book value per share   The amount of book value (also called carrying value) of common equity per share of common stock, calculated by dividing the book value of shareholders' equity by the number of shares of common stock outstanding.

Bottom-up forecasting approach   A forecasting approach that involves aggregating the individual company forecasts of analysts into industry forecasts, and finally into macroeconomic forecasts.

Bottom-up investing   An approach to investing that focuses on the individual characteristics of securities rather than on macroeconomic or overall market forecasts.

Breakup value   The value derived using a sum-of-the-parts valuation.

Breusch–Pagan test   A test for conditional heteroskedasticity in the error term of a regression.

Broker   1) An agent who executes orders to buy or sell securities on behalf of a client in exchange for a commission. 2) *See* Futures commission merchants.

Brokerage   The business of acting as agents for buyers or sellers, usually in return for commissions.

Buy-side analysts   Analysts who work for investment management firms, trusts, and bank trust departments, and similar institutions.

Call   An option that gives the holder the right to buy an underlying asset from another party at a fixed price over a specific period of time.

Cannibalization   Cannibalization occurs when an investment takes customers and sales away from another part of the company.

Cap 1) A contract on an interest rate, whereby at periodic payment dates, the writer of the cap pays the difference between the market interest rate and a specified cap rate if, and only if, this difference is positive. This is equivalent to a stream of call options on the interest rate. 2) A combination of interest rate call options designed to hedge a borrower against rate increases on a floating-rate loan.

Cap rate See capitalization rate.

Capital allocation line (CAL) A graph line that describes the combinations of expected return and standard deviation of return available to an investor from combining the optimal portfolio of risky assets with the risk-free asset.

Capital asset pricing model (CAPM) An equation describing the expected return on any asset (or portfolio) as a linear function of its beta relative to the market portfolio.

Capital charge The company's total cost of capital in money terms.

Capital deepening An increase in the capital-to-labor ratio.

Capital market line (CML) The line with an intercept point equal to the risk-free rate that is tangent to the efficient frontier of risky assets; represents the efficient frontier when a risk-free asset is available for investment.

Capital rationing A capital rationing environment assumes that the company has a fixed amount of funds to invest.

Capital structure The mix of debt and equity that a company uses to finance its business; a company's specific mixture of long-term financing.

Capitalization of earnings method In the context of private company valuation, valuation model based on an assumption of a constant growth rate of free cash flow to the firm or a constant growth rate of free cash flow to equity.

Capitalization rate The divisor in the expression for the value of perpetuity. In the context of real estate, the divisor in the direct capitalization method of estimating value. The cap rate equals net operating income divided by value.

Capitalized cash flow method (capitalized cash flow model) In the context of private company valuation, valuation model based on an assumption of a constant growth rate of free cash flow to the firm or a constant growth rate of free cash flow to equity.

Capitalized cash flow model (method) In the context of private company valuation, valuation model based on an assumption of a constant growth rate of free cash flow to the firm or a constant growth rate of free cash flow to equity.

Capitalized income method In the context of private company valuation, valuation model based on an assumption of a constant growth rate of free cash flow to the firm or a constant growth rate of free cash flow to equity.

Caplet Each component call option in a cap.

Capped swap A swap in which the floating payments have an upper limit.

Carried interest A share of any profits that is paid to the general partner (manager) of an investment partnership, such as a private equity or hedge fund, as a form of compensation designed to be an incentive to the manager to maximize performance of the investment fund.

Carrying costs The costs of holding an asset, generally a function of the physical characteristics of the underlying asset.

Cash available for distribution Funds from operations (FFO) adjusted to remove any non-cash rent reported under straight-line rent accounting and to subtract maintenance-type capital expenditures and leasing costs, including leasing agents' commissions and tenants' improvement allowances.

Cash basis Accounting method in which the only relevant transactions for the financial statements are those that involve cash.

Cash offering A merger or acquisition that is to be paid for with cash; the cash for the merger might come from the acquiring company's existing assets or from a debt issue.

Cash settlement A procedure used in certain derivative transactions that specifies that the long and short parties engage in the equivalent cash value of a delivery transaction.

Cash-flow-statement-based accruals ratio The difference between reported net income on an accrual basis and the cash flows from operating and investing activities compared to the average net operating assets over the period.

Cash-flow-statement-based aggregate accruals The difference between reported net income on an accrual basis and the cash flows from operating and investing activities.

Cash-generating unit The smallest identifiable group of assets that generates cash inflows that are largely independent of the cash inflows of other assets or groups of assets.

Catalyst An event or piece of information that causes the marketplace to re-evaluate the prospects of a company.

Chain rule of forecasting A forecasting process in which the next period's value as predicted by the forecasting equation is substituted into the right-hand side of the equation to give a predicted value two periods ahead.

Cheapest-to-deliver A bond in which the amount received for delivering the bond is largest compared with the amount paid in the market for the bond.

Clean surplus accounting Accounting that satisfies the condition that all changes in the book value of equity other than transactions with owners are reflected in income. The bottom-line income reflects all changes in shareholders' equity arising from other than owner transactions. In the absence of owner transactions, the change in shareholders' equity should equal net income. No adjustments such as translation adjustments bypass the income statement and go directly to shareholders equity.

Clean surplus relation The relationship between earnings, dividends, and book value in which ending book value is equal to the beginning book value plus earnings less dividends, apart from ownership transactions.

Clientele effect The preference some investors have for shares that exhibit certain characteristics.

Club convergence The idea that only rich and middle-income countries sharing a set of favorable attributes (i.e., are members of the "club") will converge to the income level of the richest countries.

Cobb–Douglas production function A function of the form $Y = K^\alpha L^{1-\alpha}$ relating output (Y) to labor (L) and capital (K) inputs.

Cointegrated Describes two time series that have a long-term financial or economic relationship such that they do not diverge from each other without bound in the long run.

Commercial real estate properties Income-producing real estate properties, properties purchased with the intent to let, lease, or rent (in other words, produce income).

Common size statements Financial statements in which all elements (accounts) are stated as a percentage of a key figure such as revenue for an income statement or total assets for a balance sheet.

Company fundamental factors   Factors related to the company's internal performance, such as factors relating to earnings growth, earnings variability, earnings momentum, and financial leverage.

Company share-related factors   Valuation measures and other factors related to share price or the trading characteristics of the shares, such as earnings yield, dividend yield, and book-to-market value.

Comparables   (comps, guideline assets, guideline companies) Assets used as benchmarks when applying the method of comparables to value an asset.

Compiled financial statements   Financial statements that are not accompanied by an auditor's opinion letter.

Comprehensive income   All changes in equity other than contributions by, and distributions to, owners; income under clean surplus accounting; includes all changes in equity during a period except those resulting from investments by owners and distributions to owners; comprehensive income equals net income plus other comprehensive income.

Comps   Assets used as benchmarks when applying the method of comparables to value an asset.

Conditional convergence   The idea that convergence of per capita income is conditional on the countries having the same savings rate, population growth rate, and production function.

Conditional heteroskedasticity   Heteroskedasticity in the error variance that is correlated with the values of the independent variable(s) in the regression.

Conglomerate discount   The discount possibly applied by the market to the stock of a company operating in multiple, unrelated businesses.

Conglomerate merger   A merger involving companies that are in unrelated businesses.

Consolidation   The combining of the results of operations of subsidiaries with the parent company to present financial statements as if they were a single economic unit. The assets, liabilities, revenues and expenses of the subsidiaries are combined with those of the parent company, eliminating intercompany transactions.

Constant dividend payout ratio policy   A policy in which a constant percentage of net income is paid out in dividends.

Constant maturity swap   (or **CMT swap**) A swap in which the floating rate is the rate on a security known as a constant maturity treasury or CMT security.

Constant maturity treasury (CMT)   A hypothetical U.S. Treasury note with a constant maturity. A CMT exists for various years in the range of 2 to 10.

Constant returns to scale   The condition that if all inputs into the production process are increased by a given percentage, then output rises by that same percentage.

Contango   A situation in a futures market where the current futures price is greater than the current spot price for the underlying asset.

Contingent consideration   Potential future payments to the seller that are contingent on the achievement of certain agreed on occurrences.

Continuing earnings   Earnings excluding nonrecurring components.

Continuing residual income   Residual income after the forecast horizon.

Continuing value   The analyst's estimate of a stock's value at a particular point in the future.

Continuous time   Time thought of as advancing in extremely small increments.

Control premium   An increment or premium to value associated with a controlling ownership interest in a company.

Convenience yield   The nonmonetary return offered by an asset when the asset is in short supply, often associated with assets with seasonal production processes.

Conventional cash flow   A conventional cash flow pattern is one with an initial outflow followed by a series of inflows.

Conversion factor   An adjustment used to facilitate delivery on bond futures contracts in which any of a number of bonds with different characteristics are eligible for delivery.

Core earnings   Earnings excluding nonrecurring components.

Corporate governance   The system of principles, policies, procedures, and clearly defined responsibilities and accountabilities used by stakeholders to overcome the conflicts of interest inherent in the corporate form.

Corporate raider   A person or organization seeking to profit by acquiring a company and reselling it, or seeking to profit from the takeover attempt itself (e.g., greenmail).

Corporation   A legal entity with rights similar to those of a person. The chief officers, executives, or top managers act as agents for the firm and are legally entitled to authorize corporate activities and to enter into contracts on behalf of the business.

Cost approach   Approach that values a private company based on the values of the underlying assets of the entity less the value of any related liabilities. In the context of real estate, this approach estimates the value of a property based on what it would cost to buy the land and construct a new property on the site that has the same utility or functionality as the property being appraised.

Cost of carry   The cost associated with holding some asset, including financing, storage, and insurance costs. Any yield received on the asset is treated as a negative carrying cost.

Cost of debt   The cost of debt financing to a company, such as when it issues a bond or takes out a bank loan.

Cost of equity   The required rate of return on common stock.

Cost-of-carry model   A model for pricing futures contracts in which the futures price is determined by adding the cost of carry to the spot price.

Covariance stationary   Describes a time series when its expected value and variance are constant and finite in all periods and when its covariance with itself for a fixed number of periods in the past or future is constant and finite in all periods.

Covered interest arbitrage   A transaction executed in the foreign exchange market in which a currency is purchased (sold) and a forward contract is sold (purchased) to lock in the exchange rate for future delivery of the currency. This transaction should earn the risk-free rate of the investor's home country.

Covered interest rate parity   Relationship among the spot exchange rate, forward exchange rate, and the interest rates in two currencies that ensures that the return on a hedged (i.e., covered) foreign risk-free investment is the same as the return on a domestic risk-free investment.

Currency option   An option that allows the holder to buy (if a call) or sell (if a put) an underlying currency at a fixed exercise rate, expressed as an exchange rate.

Current credit risk   The risk associated with the possibility that a payment currently due will not be made.

Current exchange rate   For accounting purposes, the spot exchange rate on the balance sheet date.

Current rate method   Approach to translating foreign currency financial statements for consolidation in which all assets and liabilities are translated at the current exchange rate. The current rate method is the prevalent method of translation.

Cyclical businesses Businesses with high sensitivity to business- or industry-cycle influences.

DOWNREIT A variation of the UPREIT structure under which the REIT owns more than one partnership and may own properties at both the REIT level and the partnership level.

Daily settlement See *Marking to market*.

Data mining The practice of determining a model by extensive searching through a dataset for statistically significant patterns.

Day trader A trader holding a position open somewhat longer than a scalper but closing all positions at the end of the day.

"Dead-hand" provision A poison pill provision that allows for the redemption or cancellation of a poison pill provision only by a vote of continuing directors (generally directors who were on the target company's board prior to the takeover attempt).

Debt covenants Agreements between the company as borrower and its creditors.

Debt ratings An objective measure of the quality and safety of a company's debt based upon an analysis of the company's ability to pay the promised cash flows, as well as an analysis of any indentures.

Decision rule With respect to hypothesis testing, the rule according to which the null hypothesis will be rejected or not rejected; involves the comparison of the test statistic to rejection point(s).

Deep-in-the-money Options that are far in-the-money.

Deep-out-of-the-money Options that are far out-of-the-money.

Deferred revenue A liability account for money that has been collected for goods or services that have not yet been delivered; payment received in advance of providing a good or service.

Definition of value A specification of how "value" is to be understood in the context of a specific valuation.

Definitive merger agreement A contract signed by both parties to a merger that clarifies the details of the transaction, including the terms, warranties, conditions, termination details, and the rights of all parties.

Delivery A process used in a deliverable forward contract in which the long pays the agreed-upon price to the short, which in turn delivers the underlying asset to the long.

Delivery option The feature of a futures contract giving the short the right to make decisions about what, when, and where to deliver.

Delta The relationship between the option price and the underlying price, which reflects the sensitivity of the price of the option to changes in the price of the underlying.

Depreciated replacement cost In the context of real estate, the replacement cost of a building adjusted different types of depreciation.

Derivative A financial instrument whose value depends on the value of some underlying asset or factor (e.g., a stock price, an interest rate, or exchange rate).

Descriptive statistics The study of how data can be summarized effectively.

Diff swaps A swap in which the payments are based on the difference between interest rates in two countries but payments are made in only a single currency.

Diluted earnings per share (diluted EPS) Net income, minus preferred dividends, divided by the number of common shares outstanding considering all dilutive securities (e.g., convertible debt and options); the EPS that would result if all dilutive securities were converted into common shares.

Dilution A reduction in proportional ownership interest as a result of the issuance of new shares.

Diminishing marginal productivity When each additional unit of an input, keeping the other inputs unchanged, increases output by a smaller increment.

Direct capitalization method In the context of real estate, this method estimates the value of an income-producing property based on the level and quality of its net operating income.

Direct financing leases A type of finance lease, from a lessor perspective, where the present value of the lease payments (lease receivable) equals the carrying value of the leased asset. The revenues earned by the lessor are financing in nature.

Dirty surplus accounting Accounting in which some income items are reported as part of stockholders' equity rather than as gains and losses on the income statement; certain items of comprehensive income bypass the income statement and appear as direct adjustments to shareholders' equity.

Dirty-surplus items Items that affect comprehensive income but which bypass the income statement.

Discount To reduce the value of a future payment in allowance for how far away it is in time; to calculate the present value of some future amount. Also, the amount by which an instrument is priced below its face value.

Discount for lack of control An amount or percentage deducted from the pro rata share of 100 percent of the value of an equity interest in a business to reflect the absence of some or all of the powers of control.

Discount for lack of marketability An amount of percentage deducted from the value of an ownership interest to reflect the relative absence of marketability.

Discount interest A procedure for determining the interest on a loan or bond in which the interest is deducted from the face value in advance.

Discount rate Any rate used in finding the present value of a future cash flow.

Discounted abnormal earnings model A model of stock valuation that views intrinsic value of stock as the sum of book value per share plus the present value of the stock's expected future residual income per share.

Discounted cash flow (DCF) analysis In the context of merger analysis, it is an estimate of a target company's value found by discounting the company's expected future free cash flows to the present.

Discounted cash flow method Income approach that values an asset based on estimates of future cash flows discounted to present value by using a discount rate reflective of the risks associated with the cash flows. In the context of real estate, this method estimates the value of an income-producing property based by discounting future projected cash flows.

Discounted cash flow model A model of intrinsic value that views the value of an asset as the present value of the asset's expected future cash flows.

Discrete time Time thought of as advancing in distinct finite increments.

Discriminant analysis A multivariate classification technique used to discriminate between groups, such as companies that either will or will not become bankrupt during some time frame.

Diversified REITs REITs that own and operate in more than one type of property; they are more common in Europe and Asia than in the United States.

Divestiture The sale, liquidation, or spin-off of a division or subsidiary.

Dividend coverage ratio The ratio of net income to dividends.

Dividend discount model (also DDM) A present value model of stock value that views the intrinsic value of a stock as present value of the stock's expected future dividends.

Dividend displacement of earnings The concept that dividends paid now displace earnings in all future periods.

Dividend imputation tax system A taxation system which effectively assures that corporate profits distributed as dividends are taxed just once, at the shareholder's tax rate.

Dividend payout ratio The ratio of cash dividends paid to earnings for a period.

Dividend policy The strategy a company follows with regard to the amount and timing of dividend payments.

Dividend rate The most recent quarterly dividend multiplied by four.

Double taxation system Corporate earnings are taxed twice when paid out as dividends. First, corporate earnings are taxed regardless of whether they will be distributed as dividends or retained at the G-13 corporate level, and second, dividends are taxed again at the individual shareholder level.

Downstream A transaction between two affiliates, an investor company and an associate company such that the investor company records a profit on its income statement. An example is a sale of inventory by the investor company to the associate.

Due diligence Investigation and analysis in support of a recommendation; the failure to exercise due diligence may sometimes result in liability according to various securities laws.

Dummy variable A type of qualitative variable that takes on a value of 1 if a particular condition is true and 0 if that condition is false.

Duration A measure of an option-free bond's average maturity. Specifically, the weighted average maturity of all future cash flows paid by a security, in which the weights are the present value of these cash flows as a fraction of the bond's price. A measure of a bond's price sensitivity to interest rate movements.

Dutch disease A situation in which currency appreciation driven by strong export demand for resources makes other segments of the economy (particularly manufacturing) globally uncompetitive.

Dynamic hedging A strategy in which a position is hedged by making frequent adjustments to the quantity of the instrument used for hedging in relation to the instrument being hedged.

Earnings expectations management Attempts by management to encourage analysts to forecast a slightly lower number for expected earnings than the analysts would otherwise forecast.

Earnings game Management's focus on reporting earnings that meet consensus estimates.

Earnings management activity Deliberate activity aimed at influencing reporting earnings numbers, often with the goal of placing management in a favorable light; the opportunistic use of accruals to manage earnings.

Earnings surprise The difference between reported earnings per share and expected earnings per share.

Earnings yield Earnings per share divided by price; the reciprocal of the P/E ratio.

Economic obsolescence In the context of real estate, a reduction in value due to current economic conditions.

Economic profit See *Residual income.*

Economic sectors Large industry groupings.

Economic value added (EVA°) A commercial implementation of the residual income concept; the computation of EVA° is the net operating profit after taxes minus the cost of capital, where these inputs are adjusted for a number of items.

Economies of scale In reference to mergers, it is the savings achieved through the consolidation of operations and elimination of duplicate resources.

Edwards–Bell–Ohlson model A model of stock valuation that views intrinsic value of stock as the sum of book value per share plus the present value of the stock's expected future residual income per share.

Efficient frontier The portion of the minimum-variance frontier beginning with the global minimum-variance portfolio and continuing above it; the graph of the set of portfolios offering the maximum expected return for their level of variance of return.

Efficient portfolio A portfolio offering the highest expected return for a given level of risk as measured by variance or standard deviation of return.

Enterprise value (EV) Total company value (the market value of debt, common equity, and preferred equity) minus the value of cash and investments.

Enterprise value multiple A valuation multiple that relates the total market value of all sources of a company's capital (net of cash) to a measure of fundamental value for the entire company (such as a pre-interest earnings measure).

Entry price The price paid to buy an asset.

Equilibrium The condition in which supply equals demand.

Equity REIT A REIT that owns, operates, and/or selectively develops income-producing real estate.

Equity carve-out A form of restructuring that involves the creation of a new legal entity and the sale of equity in it to outsiders.

Equity charge The estimated cost of equity capital in money terms.

Equity forward A contract calling for the purchase of an individual stock, a stock portfolio, or a stock index at a later date at an agreed-upon price.

Equity options Options on individual stocks; also known as stock options.

Error autocorrelation The autocorrelation of the error term.

Eurodollar A dollar deposited outside the United States.

European option An option that can only be exercised on its expiration date.

Ex ante version of PPP Hypothesis that expected changes in the spot exchange rate are equal to expected differences in national inflation rates. An extension of relative purchasing power parity to expected future changes in the exchange rate.

Ex-dividend Trading ex-dividend refers to shares that no longer carry the right to the next dividend payment.

Ex-dividend date The first date that a share trades without (i.e., "ex") the dividend.

Ex-dividend price The price at which a share first trades without (i.e., "ex") the right to receive an upcoming dividend.

Excess earnings method Income approach that estimates the value of all intangible assets of the business by capitalizing future earnings in excess of the estimated return requirements associated with working capital and fixed assets.

Exchange for physicals (EFP) A permissible delivery procedure used by futures market participants, in which the long and short arrange a delivery procedure other than the normal procedures stipulated by the futures exchange.

Exchange ratio The number of shares that target stockholders are to receive in exchange for each of their shares in the target company.

Exercise (also **exercising the option**) The process of using an option to buy or sell the underlying.

Exercise price (also **strike price**, **striking price**, or **strike**) The fixed price at which an option holder can buy or sell the underlying.

Exercise rate (also **strike rate**) The fixed rate at which the holder of an interest rate option can buy or sell the underlying.

Exercise value (also **intrinsic value**) The value of an asset given a hypothetically complete understanding of the asset's investment characteristics; the value obtained if an option is exercised based on current conditions.

Exercising the option (also **exercise**) The process of using an option to buy or sell the underlying.

Exit price The price received to sell an asset or transfer a liability.

Expanded CAPM An adaptation of the CAPM that adds to the CAPM a premium for small size and company-specific risk.

Expected holding-period return The expected total return on an asset over a stated holding period; for stocks, the sum of the expected dividend yield and the expected price appreciation over the holding period.

Expenses Outflows of economic resources or increases in liabilities that result in decreases in equity (other than decreases because of distributions to owners); reductions in net assets associated with the creation of revenues.

Expiration date The date on which a derivative contract expires.

Exposure to foreign exchange risk The risk of a change in value of an asset or liability denominated in a foreign currency due to a change in exchange rates.

External growth Company growth in output or sales that is achieved by buying the necessary resources externally (i.e., achieved through mergers and acquisitions).

External sustainability approach An approach to assessing the equilibrium exchange rate that focuses on exchange rate adjustments required to ensure that a country's net foreign-asset/GDP ratio or net foreign-liability/GDP ratio stabilizes at a sustainable level.

Externalities Spillover effects of production and consumption activities onto others who did not consent to participate in the activity.

Externality The effect of an investment on other things besides the investment itself.

FX carry trade An investment strategy that involves taking on long positions in high-yield currencies and short positions in low-yield currencies.

Factor A common or underlying element with which several variables are correlated.

Factor betas An asset's sensitivity to a particular factor; a measure of the response of return to each unit of increase in a factor, holding all other factors constant.

Factor loadings See *factor betas*.

Factor price The expected return in excess of the risk-free rate for a portfolio with a sensitivity of 1 to one factor and a sensitivity of 0 to all other factors.

Factor risk premium (or factor price) The expected return in excess of the risk-free rate for a portfolio with a sensitivity of 1 to one factor and a sensitivity of 0 to all other factors.

Factor risk premium See *factor price*.

Factor sensitivity See *factor betas*.

Fair market value The market price of an asset or liability that trades regularly.

Fair value The amount at which an asset (or liability) could be bought (or incurred) or sold (or settled) in a current transaction between willing parties, that is, other than in a forced or liquidation sale; the price that would be received to sell an asset or paid to transfer a liability in an orderly transaction between market participants at the measurement date.

Fiduciary call A combination of a European call and a risk-free bond that matures on the option expiration day and has a face value equal to the exercise price of the call.

Finance lease (capital lease) Essentially, the purchase of some asset by the buyer (lessee) that is directly financed by the seller (lessor).

Financial contagion A situation where financial shocks spread from their place of origin to other locales; in essence, a faltering economy infects other, healthier economies.

Financial distress Heightened uncertainty regarding a company's ability to meet its various obligations because of lower or negative earnings.

Financial futures Futures contracts in which the underlying is a stock, bond, or currency.

Financial reporting quality The accuracy with which a company's reported financials reflect its operating performance and their usefulness for forecasting future cash flows.

Financial risk The risk that environmental, social, or governance risk factors will result in significant costs or other losses to a company and its shareholders; the risk arising from a company's obligation to meet required payments under its financing agreements.

Financial transaction A purchase involving a buyer having essentially no material synergies with the target (e.g., the purchase of a private company by a company in an unrelated industry or by a private equity firm would typically be a financial transaction).

First-differencing A transformation that subtracts the value of the time series in period $t - 1$ from its value in period t.

First-in, first-out (FIFO) The first in, first out, method of accounting for inventory, which matches sales against the costs of items of inventory in the order in which they were placed in inventory.

First-order serial correlation Correlation between adjacent observations in a time series.

Fixed-rate perpetual preferred stock Nonconvertible, non-callable preferred stock with a specified dividend rate that has a claim on earnings senior to the claim of common stock, and no maturity date.

Flip-in pill A poison pill takeover defense that dilutes an acquirer's ownership in a target by giving other existing target company shareholders the right to buy additional target company shares at a discount.

Flip-over pill A poison pill takeover defense that gives target company shareholders the right to purchase shares of the acquirer at a significant discount to the market price, which has the effect of causing dilution to all existing acquiring company shareholders.

Floor A combination of interest rate put options designed to hedge a lender against lower rates on a floating-rate loan.

Floor traders   Market makers that buy and sell by quoting a bid and an ask price. They are the primary providers of liquidity to the market.

Floored swap   A swap in which the floating payments have a lower limit.

Floorlet   Each component put option in a floor.

Flotation cost   Fees charged to companies by investment bankers and other costs associated with raising new capital.

Foreign currency transactions   Transactions that are denominated in a currency other than a company's functional currency.

Forward P/E   A P/E calculated on the basis of a forecast of EPS; a stock's current price divided by next year's expected earnings.

Forward contract   An agreement between two parties in which one party, the buyer, agrees to buy from the other party, the seller, an underlying asset at a later date for a price established at the start of the contract.

Forward dividend yield   A dividend yield based on the anticipated dividend during the next 12 months.

Forward integration   A merger involving the purchase of a target that is farther along the value or production chain; for example, to acquire a distributor.

Forward price or forward rate   The fixed price or rate at which the transaction scheduled to occur at the expiration of a forward contract will take place. This price is agreed on at the initiation date of the contract.

Forward rate agreement (FRA)   A forward contract calling for one party to make a fixed interest payment and the other to make an interest payment at a rate to be determined at the contract expiration.

Forward swap   A forward contract to enter into a swap.

Franking credit   A tax credit received by shareholders for the taxes that a corporation paid on its distributed earnings.

Free cash flow   The actual cash that would be available to the company's investors after making all investments necessary to maintain the company as an ongoing enterprise (also referred to as free cash flow to the firm); the internally generated funds that can be distributed to the company's investors (e.g., shareholders and bondholders) without impairing the value of the company.

Free cash flow hypothesis   The hypothesis that higher debt levels discipline managers by forcing them to make fixed debt service payments and by reducing the company's free cash flow.

Free cash flow method   Income approach that values an asset based on estimates of future cash flows discounted to present value by using a discount rate reflective of the risks associated with the cash flows.

Free cash flow to equity   The cash flow available to a company's common shareholders after all operating expenses, interest, and principal payments have been made, and necessary investments in working and fixed capital have been made.

Free cash flow to equity model   A model of stock valuation that views a stock's intrinsic value as the present value of expected future free cash flows to equity.

Free cash flow to the firm   The cash flow available to the company's suppliers of capital after all operating expenses (including taxes) have been paid and necessary investments in working and fixed capital have been made.

Free cash flow to the firm model   A model of stock valuation that views the value of a firm as the present value of expected future free cash flows to the firm.

Friendly transaction   A potential business combination that is endorsed by the managers of both companies.

Functional currency   The currency of the primary economic environment in which an entity operates.

Functional obsolescence   In the context of real estate, a reduction in value due to a design that differs from that of a new building constructed for the intended use of the property.

Fundamental beta   A beta that is based at least in part on fundamental data for a company.

Fundamental factor models   A multifactor model in which the factors are attributes of stocks or companies that are important in explaining cross-sectional differences in stock prices.

Fundamentals   Economic characteristics of a business such as profitability, financial strength, and risk.

Funds available for distribution   Funds from operations (FFO) adjusted to remove any non-cash rent reported under straight-line rent accounting and to subtract maintenance-type capital expenditures and leasing costs, including leasing agents' commissions and tenants' improvement allowances.

Funds from operations   Accounting net earnings excluding (1) depreciation charges on real estate, (2) deferred tax charges, and (3) gains or losses from sales of property and debt restructuring.

Futures commission merchants (FCMs)   Individuals or companies that execute futures transactions for other parties off the exchange.

Futures contract   A variation of a forward contract that has essentially the same basic definition but with some additional features, such as a clearinghouse guarantee against credit losses, a daily settlement of gains and losses, and an organized electronic or floor trading facility.

Gamma   A numerical measure of how sensitive an option's delta is to a change in the underlying.

Generalized least squares   A regression estimation technique that addresses heteroskedasticity of the error term.

Going-concern assumption   The assumption that the business will maintain its business activities into the foreseeable future.

Going-concern value   A business's value under a going-concern assumption.

Goodwill   An intangible asset that represents the excess of the purchase price of an acquired company over the value of the net assets acquired.

Gross domestic product   A money measure of the goods and services produced within a country's borders over a stated time period.

Gross lease   A lease under which the tenant pays a gross rent to the landlord who is responsible for all operating costs, utilities, maintenance expenses, and real estate taxes relating to the property.

Growth accounting equation   The production function written in the form of growth rates. For the basic Cobb–Douglas production function, it states that the growth rate of output equals the rate of technological change plus α times the growth rate of capital plus $(1-\alpha)$ times the growth rate of labor.

Growth option   (expansion option) The ability to make additional investments in a project at some future time if the financial results are strong.

Guideline assets   Assets used as benchmarks when applying the method of comparables to value an asset.

Guideline companies   Assets used as benchmarks when applying the method of comparables to value an asset.

Guideline public companies   Public-company comparables for the company being valued.

Guideline public company method   A variation of the market approach; establishes a value estimate based on the observed multiples from trading activity in the shares of public companies viewed as reasonably comparable to the subject private company.

Guideline transactions method   A variation of the market approach; establishes a value estimate based on pricing multiples derived from the acquisition of control of entire public or private companies that were acquired.

Harmonic mean   A type of weighted mean computed by averaging the reciprocals of the observations, then taking the reciprocal of that average.

Health care REITs   REITs that invest in skilled nursing facilities (nursing homes), assisted living and independent residential facilities for retired persons, hospitals, medical office buildings, or rehabilitation centers.

Hedge ratio   The relationship of the quantity of an asset being hedged to the quantity of the derivative used for hedging.

Hedging   A general strategy usually thought of as reducing, if not eliminating, risk.

Held for trading investments   Debt or equity securities acquired with the intent to sell them in the near term.

Held-to-maturity investments   Debt (fixed-income) securities that a company intends to hold to maturity; these are presented at their original cost, updated for any amortization of discounts or premiums.

Herfindahl–Hirschman Index (HHI)   A measure of market concentration that is calculated by summing the squared market shares for competing companies in an industry; high HHI readings or mergers that would result in large HHI increases are more likely to result in regulatory challenges.

Heteroskedastic   With reference to the error term of regression, having a variance that differs across observations.

Heteroskedasticity   The property of having a nonconstant variance; refers to an error term with the property that its variance differs across observations.

Heteroskedasticity-consistent standard errors   Standard errors of the estimated parameters of a regression that correct for the presence of heteroskedasticity in the regression's error term.

Historical exchange rates   For accounting purposes, the exchange rates that existed when the assets and liabilities were initially recorded.

Holding period return   The return that an investor earns during a specified holding period; a synonym for total return.

Homoskedasticity   The property of having a constant variance; refers to an error term that is constant across observations.

Horizontal merger   A merger involving companies in the same line of business, usually as competitors.

Hostile transaction   An attempt to acquire a company against the wishes of the target's managers.

Hotel REITs   REITs that own hotel properties but, similar to health care REITs, in many countries they must refrain from operating their properties themselves to maintain their tax-advantaged REIT status.

Human capital   The accumulated knowledge and skill that workers acquire from education, training, or life experience.

Hybrid REITs   REITs that own and operate income-producing real estate and invest in mortgages as well; REITs that have positions in both real estate assets and real estate debt.

Illiquidity discount   See *Liquidity discount.*

Impairment   Diminishment in value as a result of carrying (book) value exceeding fair value and/or recoverable value.

Impairment of capital rule   A legal restriction that dividends cannot exceed retained earnings.

Implied repo rate   The rate of return from a cash-and-carry transaction implied by the futures price relative to the spot price.

Implied volatility   The volatility that option traders use to price an option, implied by the price of the option and a particular option-pricing model.

In-process research and development   Research and development costs relating to projects that are not yet completed, such as have been incurred by a company that is being acquired.

In-sample forecast errors   The residuals from a fitted time-series model within the sample period used to fit the model.

In-the-money   Options that, if exercised, would result in the value received being worth more than the payment required to exercise.

Income approach   Valuation approach that values an asset as the present discounted value of the income expected from it. In the context of real estate, this approach estimates the value of a property based on an expected rate of return; the estimated value is the present value of the expected future income from the property, including proceeds from resale at the end of a typical investment holding period.

Incremental cash flow   The cash flow that is realized because of a decision; the changes or increments to cash flows resulting from a decision or action.

Indenture   A written contract between a lender and borrower that specifies the terms of the loan, such as interest rate, interest payment schedule, maturity, etc.

Independent projects   Independent projects are projects whose cash flows are independent of each other.

Independent regulators   Regulators recognized and granted authority by a government body or agency. They are not government agencies per se and typically do not rely on government funding.

Index amortizing swap   An interest rate swap in which the notional principal is indexed to the level of interest rates and declines with the level of interest rates according to a predefined schedule. This type of swap is frequently used to hedge securities that are prepaid as interest rates decline, such as mortgage-backed securities.

Indexing   An investment strategy in which an investor constructs a portfolio to mirror the performance of a specified index.

Industrial REITs   REITs that hold portfolios of single-tenant or multi-tenant industrial properties that are used as warehouses, distribution centers, light manufacturing facilities, and small office or "flex" space.

Industry structure   An industry's underlying economic and technical characteristics.

Information ratio   (also IR) Mean active return divided by active risk; or alpha divided by the standard deviation of diversifiable risk.

Informational frictions   Forces that restrict availability, quality, and/or flow of information and its use.

Initial margin requirement   The margin requirement on the first day of a transaction as well as on any day in which additional margin funds must be deposited.

Initial public offering   (also IPO) The initial issuance of common stock registered for public trading by a formerly private corporation.

Instability in the minimum-variance frontier   The characteristic of minimum-variance frontiers that they are sensitive to small changes in inputs.

Interest rate call   An option in which the holder has the right to make a known interest payment and receive an unknown interest payment.

Interest rate cap   A series of call options on an interest rate, with each option expiring at the date on which the floating loan rate will be reset, and with each option having the same exercise rate. A cap in general can have an underlying other than an interest rate.

Interest rate collar   A combination of a long cap and a short floor, or a short cap and a long floor. A collar in general can have an underlying other than an interest rate.

Interest rate floor   (also **floor**) A series of put options on an interest rate, with each option expiring at the date on which the floating loan rate will be reset, and with each option having the same exercise rate. A floor in general can have an underlying other than the interest rate.

Interest rate option   An option in which the underlying is an interest rate.

Interest rate parity   A formula that expresses the equivalence or parity of spot and forward rates, after adjusting for differences in the interest rates.

Interest rate put   An option in which the holder has the right to make an unknown interest payment and receive a known interest payment.

Internal rate of return   (IRR) Rate of return that discounts future cash flows from an investment to the exact amount of the investment; the discount rate that makes the present value of an investment's costs (outflows) equal to the present value of the investment's benefits (inflows).

International Fisher effect   Proposition that nominal interest rate differentials across currencies are determined by expected inflation differentials.

Intrinsic value   The value of an asset given a hypothetically complete understanding of the asset's investment characteristics; the value obtained if an option is exercised based on current conditions.

Inverse price ratio   The reciprocal of a price multiple, e.g., in the case of a P/E ratio, the "earnings yield" E/P (where P is share price and E is earnings per share).

Investment objectives   Desired investment outcomes; includes risk objectives and return objectives.

Investment strategy   An approach to investment analysis and security selection.

Investment value   The value to a specific buyer, taking account of potential synergies based on the investor's requirements and expectations.

Judicial law   Interpretations of courts.

Justified (fundamental) P/E   The price-to-earnings ratio that is fair, warranted, or justified on the basis of forecasted fundamentals.

Justified price multiple   The estimated fair value of the price multiple, usually based on forecasted fundamentals or comparables.

***k*th order autocorrelation**   The correlation between observations in a time series separated by *k* periods.

Labor force   Everyone of working age (ages 16 to 64) that either is employed or is available for work but not working.

Labor force participation rate   The percentage of the working age population that is in the labor force.

Labor productivity   The quantity of real GDP produced by an hour of labor. More generally, output per unit of labor input.

Labor productivity growth accounting equation   States that potential GDP growth equals the growth rate of the labor input plus the growth rate of labor productivity.

Lack of marketability discount   An extra return to investors to compensate for lack of a public market or lack of marketability.

Last-in, first-out (LIFO)   The last in, first out, method of accounting for inventory, which matches sales against the costs of items of inventory in the reverse order the items were placed in inventory (i.e., inventory produced or acquired last are assumed to be sold first).

Law of one price   Hypothesis that (1) identical goods should trade at the same price across countries when valued in terms of a common currency, or (2) two equivalent financial instruments or combinations of financial instruments can sell for only one price. The latter form is equivalent to the principle that no arbitrage opportunities are possible.

Leading P/E   A P/E calculated on the basis of a forecast of EPS; a stock's current price divided by next year's expected earnings.

Leading dividend yield   Forecasted dividends per share over the next year divided by current stock price.

Legal risk   The risk that failures by company managers to effectively manage a company's environmental, social, and governance risk exposures will lead to lawsuits and other judicial remedies, resulting in potentially catastrophic losses for the company; the risk that the legal system will not enforce a contract in case of dispute or fraud.

Legislative and regulatory risk   The risk that governmental laws and regulations directly or indirectly affecting a company's operations will change with potentially severe adverse effects on the company's continued profitability and even its long-term sustainability.

Lessee   The party obtaining the use of an asset through a lease.

Lessor   The owner of an asset that grants the right to use the asset to another party.

Leveraged buyout   (also LBO) A transaction whereby the target company management team converts the target to a privately held company by using heavy borrowing to finance the purchase of the target company's outstanding shares.

Leveraged recapitalization   A post-offer takeover defense mechanism that involves the assumption of a large amount of debt that is then used to finance share repurchases; the effect is to dramatically change the company's capital structure while attempting to deliver a value to target shareholders in excess of a hostile bid.

Limit down   A limit move in the futures market in which the price at which a transaction would be made is at or below the lower limit.

Limit move   A condition in the futures markets in which the price at which a transaction would be made is at or beyond the price limits.

Limit up   A limit move in the futures market in which the price at which a transaction would be made is at or above the upper limit.

Linear trend   A trend in which the dependent variable changes at a constant rate with time.

Liquidation To sell the assets of a company, division, or subsidiary piecemeal, typically because of bankruptcy; the form of bankruptcy that allows for the orderly satisfaction of creditors' claims after which the company ceases to exist.

Liquidation value The value of a company if the company were dissolved and its assets sold individually.

Liquidity discount A reduction or discount to value that reflects the lack of depth of trading or liquidity in that asset's market.

Liquidity risk The risk that a financial instrument cannot be purchased or sold without a significant concession in price due to the size of the market.

Local currency The currency of the country where a company is located.

Locals Market makers that buy and sell by quoting a bid and an ask price. They are the primary providers of liquidity to the market.

Locational obsolescence In the context of real estate, a reduction in value due to decreased desirability of the location of the building.

Locked limit A condition in the futures markets in which a transaction cannot take place because the price would be beyond the limits.

Log-linear model With reference to time-series models, a model in which the growth rate of the time series as a function of time is constant.

Log-log regression model A regression that expresses the dependent and independent variables as natural logarithms.

Logit model A qualitative-dependent-variable multiple regression model based on the logistic probability distribution.

London Interbank Offer Rate (LIBOR) The Eurodollar rate at which London banks lend dollars to other London banks; considered to be the best representative rate on a dollar borrowed by a private, high-quality borrower.

Long The buyer of a derivative contract. Also refers to the position of owning a derivative.

Long-term equity anticipatory securities (also **LEAPS**) Options originally created with expirations of several years.

Look-ahead bias A bias caused by using information that was not available on the test date.

Lower bound The lowest possible value of an option.

Macroeconomic balance approach An approach to assessing the equilibrium exchange rate that focuses on exchange rate adjustments needed to close the gap between the medium-term expectation for a country's current account balance and that country's normal (or sustainable) current account balance.

Macroeconomic factor A factor related to the economy, such as the inflation rate, industrial production, or economic sector membership.

Macroeconomic factor model A multifactor model in which the factors are surprises in macroeconomic variables that significantly explain equity returns.

Maintenance margin requirement The margin requirement on any day other than the first day of a transaction.

Managerialism theories Theories that posit that corporate executives are motivated to engage in mergers to maximize the size of their company rather than shareholder value.

Margin The amount of money that a trader deposits in a margin account. The term is derived from the stock market practice in which an investor borrows a portion of the money required to purchase a certain amount of stock. In futures markets, there is no borrowing so the margin is more of a down payment or performance bond.

Marginal investor An investor in a given share who is very likely to be part of the next trade in the share and who is therefore important in setting price.

Mark-to-market The revaluation of a financial asset or liability to its current market value or fair value.

Market approach Valuation approach that values an asset based on pricing multiples from sales of assets viewed as similar to the subject asset.

Market efficiency A finance perspective on capital markets that deals with the relationship of price to intrinsic value. The **traditional efficient markets formulation** asserts that an asset's price is the best available estimate of its intrinsic value. The **rational efficient markets formulation** asserts that investors should expect to be rewarded for the costs of information gathering and analysis by higher gross returns.

Market price of risk The slope of the capital market line, indicating the market risk premium for each unit of market risk.

Market risk premium The expected excess return on the market over the risk-free rate.

Market timing Asset allocation in which the investment in the market is increased if one forecasts that the market will outperform T-bills.

Market value The estimated amount for which a property should exchange on the date of valuation between a willing buyer and a willing seller in an arm's-length transaction after proper marketing wherein the parties had each acted knowledgeably, prudently, and without compulsion.

Market value of invested capital The market value of debt and equity.

Marking to market A procedure used primarily in futures markets in which the parties to a contract settle the amount owed daily. Also known as the *daily settlement*.

Markowitz decision rule A decision rule for choosing between two investments based on their means and variances.

Mature growth rate The earnings growth rate in a company's mature phase; an earnings growth rate that can be sustained long term.

Mean reversion The tendency of a time series to fall when its level is above its mean and rise when its level is below its mean; a mean-reverting time series tends to return to its long-term mean.

Mean–variance analysis An approach to portfolio analysis using expected means, variances, and covariances of asset returns.

Merger The absorption of one company by another; two companies become one entity and one or both of the pre-merger companies ceases to exist as a separate entity.

Method based on forecasted fundamentals An approach to using price multiples that relates a price multiple to forecasts of fundamentals through a discounted cash flow model.

Method of comparables An approach to valuation that involves using a price multiple to evaluate whether an asset is relatively fairly valued, relatively undervalued, or relatively overvalued when compared to a benchmark value of the multiple.

Minimum-variance frontier The graph of the set of portfolios that have minimum variance for their level of expected return.

Minimum-variance portfolio The portfolio with the minimum variance for each given level of expected return.

Minority Interest The proportion of the ownership of a subsidiary not held by the parent (controlling) company.

Mispricing   Any departure of the market price of an asset from the asset's estimated intrinsic value.

Mixed factor models   Factor models that combine features of more than one type of factor model.

Mixed offering   A merger or acquisition that is to be paid for with cash, securities, or some combination of the two.

Model specification   With reference to regression, the set of variables included in the regression and the regression equation's functional form.

Modified duration   A measure of a bond's price sensitivity to interest rate movements. Equal to the Macaulay duration of a bond divided by one plus its yield to maturity.

Molodovsky effect   The observation that P/Es tend to be high on depressed EPS at the bottom of a business cycle, and tend to be low on unusually high EPS at the top of a business cycle.

Momentum indicators   Valuation indicators that relate either price or a fundamental (such as earnings) to the time series of their own past values (or in some cases to their expected value).

Monetary assets and liabilities   Assets and liabilities with value equal to the amount of currency contracted for, a fixed amount of currency. Examples are cash, accounts receivable, mortgages receivable, accounts payable, bonds payable, and mortgages payable. Inventory is not a monetary asset. Most liabilities are monetary.

Monetary/nonmonetary method   Approach to translating foreign currency financial statements for consolidation in which monetary assets and liabilities are translated at the current exchange rate. Nonmonetary assets and liabilities are translated at historical exchange rates (the exchange rates that existed when the assets and liabilities were acquired).

Moneyness   The relationship between the price of the underlying and an option's exercise price.

Monitoring costs   Costs borne by owners to monitor the management of the company (e.g., board of director expenses).

Mortgage REITs   REITs that invest the bulk of their assets in interest-bearing mortgages, mortgage securities, or short-term loans secured by real estate.

Mortgage-backed securities   Asset-backed securitized debt obligations that represent rights to receive cash flows from portfolios of mortgage loans.

Mortgages   Loans with real estate serving as collateral for the loans.

Multi-family/residential REITs   REITs that invest in and manage rental apartments for lease to individual tenants, typically using one-year leases.

Multicollinearity   A regression assumption violation that occurs when two or more independent variables (or combinations of independent variables) are highly but not perfectly correlated with each other.

Multiple linear regression   Linear regression involving two or more independent variables.

Multiple linear regression model   A linear regression model with two or more independent variables.

Mutually exclusive projects   Mutually exclusive projects compete directly with each other. For example, if Projects A and B are mutually exclusive, you can choose A or B, but you cannot choose both.

NTM P/E   Next twelve months P/E: current market price divided by an estimated next twelve months EPS.

Negative serial correlation   Serial correlation in which a positive error for one observation increases the chance of a negative error for another observation, and vice versa.

Net asset balance sheet exposure   When assets translated at the current exchange rate are greater in amount than liabilities translated at the current exchange rate. Assets exposed to translation gains or losses exceed the exposed liabilities.

Net asset value   The difference between assets and liabilities, all taken at current market values instead of accounting book values.

Net asset value per share   Net asset value divided by the number of shares outstanding.

Net lease   A lease under which the tenant pays a net rent to the landlord as well as an additional amount based on the tenant's pro rata share of the operating costs, utilities, maintenance expenses, and real estate taxes relating to the property.

Net liability balance sheet exposure   When liabilities translated at the current exchange rate are greater than assets translated at the current exchange rate. Liabilities exposed to translation gains or losses exceed the exposed assets.

Net operating assets   The difference between operating assets (total assets less cash) and operating liabilities (total liabilities less total debt).

Net operating income   Gross rental revenue minus operating costs, but before deducting depreciation, corporate overhead, and interest expense. In the context of real estate, a measure of the income from the property after deducting operating expenses for such items as property taxes, insurance, maintenance, utilities, repairs, and insurance but before deducting any costs associated with financing and before deducting federal income taxes. It is similar to earnings before interest, taxes, depreciation, and amortization (EBITDA) in a financial reporting context.

Net operating profit less adjusted taxes (NOPLAT)   A company's operating profit with adjustments to normalize the effects of capital structure.

Net present value (NPV)   The present value of an investment's cash inflows (benefits) minus the present value of its cash outflows (costs).

Net realisable value   Estimated selling price in the ordinary course of business less the estimated costs necessary to make the sale.

Net regulatory burden   The private costs of regulation less the private benefits of regulation.

Net rent   A rent that consists of a stipulated rent to the landlord and a further amount based on their share of common area costs for utilities, maintenance, and property taxes.

Netting   When parties agree to exchange only the net amount owed from one party to the other.

Network externalities   The impact that users of a good, a service, or a technology have on other users of that product; it can be positive (e.g., a critical mass of users makes a product more useful) or negative (e.g., congestion makes the product less useful).

No-growth company   A company without positive expected net present value projects.

No-growth value per share   The value per share of a no-growth company, equal to the expected level amount of earnings divided by the stock's required rate of return.

Node   Each value on a binomial tree from which successive moves or outcomes branch.

Non-cash rent   An amount equal to the difference between the average contractual rent over a lease term (the straight-line rent) and the cash rent actually paid during a period. This figure is one of the deductions made from FFO to calculate AFFO.

Non-convergence trap A situation in which a country remains relative poor, or even falls further behind, because it fails to implement necessary institutional reforms and/or adopt leading technologies.

Non-renewable resources Finite resources that are depleted once they are consumed; oil and coal are examples.

Nonconventional cash flow In a nonconventional cash flow pattern, the initial outflow is not followed by inflows only, but the cash flows can flip from positive (inflows) to negative (outflows) again (or even change signs several times).

Nondeliverable forwards (NDFs) Cash-settled forward contracts, used predominately with respect to foreign exchange forwards.

Nonearning assets Cash and investments (specifically cash, cash equivalents, and short-term investments).

Nonmonetary assets and liabilities Assets and liabilities that are not monetary assets and liabilities. Nonmonetary assets include inventory, fixed assets, and intangibles, and nonmonetary liabilities include deferred revenue.

Nonstationarity With reference to a random variable, the property of having characteristics such as mean and variance that are not constant through time.

Normal EPS The earnings per share that a business could achieve currently under mid-cyclical conditions.

Normal backwardation The condition in futures markets in which futures prices are lower than expected spot prices.

Normal contango The condition in futures markets in which futures prices are higher than expected spot prices.

Normalized EPS The earnings per share that a business could achieve currently under mid-cyclical conditions.

Normalized P/E P/Es based on normalized EPS data.

Normalized earnings Earnings adjusted for nonrecurring, noneconomic, or other unusual items to eliminate anomalies and/or facilitate comparisons.

n-Period moving average The average of the current and immediately prior $n - 1$ values of a time series.

Off-market FRA A contract in which the initial value is intentionally set at a value other than zero and therefore requires a cash payment at the start from one party to the other.

Office REITs REITs that invest in and manage multi-tenanted office properties in central business districts of cities and suburban markets.

Offsetting A transaction in exchange-listed derivative markets in which a party re-enters the market to close out a position.

Operating lease An agreement allowing the lessee to use some asset for a period of time; essentially a rental.

Operating risk The risk attributed to the operating cost structure, in particular the use of fixed costs in operations; the risk arising from the mix of fixed and variable costs; the risk that a company's operations may be severely affected by environmental, social, and governance risk factors.

Operational risk The risk of loss from failures in a company's systems and procedures, or from external events.

Opportunity cost The value that investors forgo by choosing a particular course of action; the value of something in its best alternative use.

Opportunity set The set of assets available for investment.

Optimal capital structure The capital structure at which the value of the company is maximized.

Optimizer A specialized computer program or a spreadsheet that solves for the portfolio weights that will result in the lowest risk for a specified level of expected return.

Option A financial instrument that gives one party the right, but not the obligation, to buy or sell an underlying asset from or to another party at a fixed price over a specific period of time. Also referred to as contingent claims.

Option premium The amount of money a buyer pays and seller receives to engage in an option transaction.

Option price The amount of money a buyer pays and seller receives to engage in an option transaction.

Orderly liquidation value The estimated gross amount of money that could be realized from the liquidation sale of an asset or assets, given a reasonable amount of time to find a purchaser or purchasers.

Organic growth Company growth in output or sales that is achieved by making investments internally (i.e., excludes growth achieved through mergers and acquisitions).

Orthogonal Uncorrelated; at a right angle.

Other comprehensive income Changes to equity that bypass (are not reported in) the income statement; the difference between comprehensive income and net income.

Out-of-sample forecast errors The differences between actual and predicted value of time series outside the sample period used to fit the model.

Out-of-the-money Options that, if exercised, would require the payment of more money than the value received and therefore would not be currently exercised.

Overnight index swap (OIS) A swap in which the floating rate is the cumulative value of a single unit of currency invested at an overnight rate during the settlement period.

PEG The P/E-to-growth ratio, calculated as the stock's P/E divided by the expected earnings growth rate.

Pairs trading An approach to trading that uses pairs of closely related stocks, buying the relatively undervalued stock and selling short the relatively overvalued stock.

Partial regression coefficients or **partial slope coefficients** The slope coefficients in a multiple regression.

Partial slope coefficients or **partial regression coefficients** The slope coefficients in a multiple regression.

Partnership A business owned and operated by more than one individual.

Passive portfolio A market index portfolio.

Payer swaption A swaption that allows the holder to enter into a swap as the fixed-rate payer and floating-rate receiver.

Payoff The value of an option at expiration.

Payout policy The principles by which a company distributes cash to common shareholders by means of cash dividends and/or share repurchases.

Pecking order theory The theory that managers take into account how their actions might be interpreted by outsiders and thus order their preferences for various forms of corporate financing. Forms of financing that are least visible to outsiders (e.g., internally generated funds) are most preferable to managers and those that are most visible (e.g., equity) are least preferable.

Perfect capital markets Markets in which, by assumption, there are no taxes, transactions costs, or bankruptcy costs, and in which all investors have equal ("symmetric") information.

Performance appraisal The evaluation of risk-adjusted performance; the evaluation of investment skill.

Periodic inventory system An inventory accounting system in which inventory values and costs of sales are determined at the end of the accounting period.

Perpetual inventory system An inventory accounting system in which inventory values and costs of sales are continuously updated to reflect purchases and sales.

Perpetuity   A perpetual annuity, or a set of never-ending level sequential cash flows, with the first cash flow occurring one period from now.

Persistent earnings   Earnings excluding nonrecurring components.

Pet projects   Projects in which influential managers want the corporation to invest. Often, unfortunately, pet projects are selected without undergoing normal capital budgeting analysis.

Physical deterioration   In the context of real estate, a reduction in value due to wear and tear.

Plain vanilla swap   An interest rate swap in which one party pays a fixed rate and the other pays a floating rate, with both sets of payments in the same currency.

Poison pill   A pre-offer takeover defense mechanism that makes it prohibitively costly for an acquirer to take control of a target without the prior approval of the target's board of directors.

Poison puts   A pre-offer takeover defense mechanism that gives target company bondholders the right to sell their bonds back to the target at a pre-specified redemption price, typically at or above par value; this defense increases the need for cash and raises the cost of the acquisition.

Pooling of interests accounting method   A method of accounting in which combined companies were portrayed as if they had always operated as a single economic entity. Called pooling of interests under U.S. GAAP and uniting of interests under IFRS. (No longer allowed under U.S. GAAP or IFRS).

Portfolio balance approach   A theory of exchange rate determination that emphasizes the portfolio investment decisions of global investors and the requirement that global investors willingly hold all outstanding securities denominated in each currency at prevailing prices and exchange rates.

Portfolio performance attribution   The analysis of portfolio performance in terms of the contributions from various sources of risk.

Portfolio possibilities curve   A graphical representation of the expected return and risk of all portfolios that can be formed using two assets.

Position trader   A trader who typically holds positions open overnight.

Positive serial correlation   Serial correlation in which a positive error for one observation increases the chance of a positive error for another observation, and a negative error for one observation increases the chance of a negative error for another observation.

Potential GDP   The maximum amount of output an economy can sustainably produce without inducing an increase in the inflation rate. The output level that corresponds to full employment with consistent wage and price expectations.

Potential credit risk   The risk associated with the possibility that a payment due at a later date will not be made.

Premise of value   The status of a company in the sense of whether it is assumed to be a going concern or not.

Premium   The amount of money a buyer pays and seller receives to engage in an option transaction.

Present value model   A model of intrinsic value that views the value of an asset as the present value of the asset's expected future cash flows.

Present value of growth opportunities   (or **value of growth**) The difference between the actual value per share and the nogrowth value per share.

Presentation currency   The currency in which financial statement amounts are presented.

Price limits   Limits imposed by a futures exchange on the price change that can occur from one day to the next.

Price momentum   A valuation indicator based on past price movement.

Price multiples   The ratio of a stock's market price to some measure of value per share.

Price-setting option   The operational flexibility to adjust prices when demand varies from forecast. For example, when demand exceeds capacity, the company could benefit from the excess demand by increasing prices.

Priced risk   Risk for which investors demand compensation for bearing (e.g., equity risk, company-specific factors, macroeconomic factors).

Principal-agent problem   A conflict of interest that arises when the agent in an agency relationship has goals and incentives that differ from the principal to whom the agent owes a fiduciary duty.

Prior transaction method   A variation of the market approach; considers actual transactions in the stock of the subject private company.

Private market value   The value derived using a sum-of-the-parts valuation.

Probit model   A qualitative-dependent-variable multiple regression model based on the normal distribution.

Procedural law   The body of law that focuses on the protection and enforcement of the substantive laws.

Production-flexibility   The operational flexibility to alter production when demand varies from forecast. For example, if demand is strong, a company may profit from employees working overtime or from adding additional shifts.

Project sequencing   To defer the decision to invest in a future project until the outcome of some or all of a current project is known. Projects are sequenced through time, so that investing in a project creates the option to invest in future projects.

Prospective P/E   A P/E calculated on the basis of a forecast of EPS; a stock's current price divided by next year's expected earnings.

Protective put   An option strategy in which a long position in an asset is combined with a long position in a put.

Proxy fight   An attempt to take control of a company through a shareholder vote.

Proxy statement   A public document that provides the material facts concerning matters on which shareholders will vote.

Prudential supervision   Regulation and monitoring of the safety and soundness of financial institutions to promote financial stability, reduce system-wide risks, and protect customers of financial institutions.

Purchased in-process research and development costs   Costs of research and development in progress at an acquired company; often, part of the purchase price of an acquired company is allocated to such costs.

Purchasing power gain   A gain in value caused by changes in price levels. Monetary liabilities experience purchasing power gains during periods of inflation.

Purchasing power loss   A loss in value caused by changes in price levels. Monetary assets experience purchasing power losses during periods of inflation.

Purchasing power parity (PPP)   The idea that exchange rates move to equalize the purchasing power of different currencies.

Pure factor portfolio   A portfolio with sensitivity of 1 to the factor in question and a sensitivity of 0 to all other factors.

Put   An option that gives the holder the right to sell an underlying asset to another party at a fixed price over a specific period of time.

Put–call parity   An equation expressing the equivalence (parity) of a portfolio of a call and a bond with a portfolio of a put and the underlying, which leads to the relationship between put and call prices.

Put–call–forward parity   The relationship among puts, calls, and forward contracts.

Qualifying special purpose entity   Under U.S. GAAP, a special purpose entity structured to avoid consolidation that must meet qualification criteria.

Qualitative dependent variables   Dummy variables used as dependent variables rather than as independent variables.

Quality of earnings analysis   The investigation of issues relating to the accuracy of reported accounting results as reflections of economic performance; quality of earnings analysis is broadly understood to include not only earnings management, but also balance sheet management.

Random walk   A time series in which the value of the series in one period is the value of the series in the previous period plus an unpredictable random error.

Rational efficient markets formulation   See *Market efficiency.*

Real estate investment trusts   Tax-advantaged entities (companies or trusts) that typically own, operate, and—to a limited extent—develop income-producing real estate property.

Real estate operating companies   Regular taxable real estate ownership companies that operate in the real estate industry in countries that do not have a tax-advantaged REIT regime in place or are engaged in real estate activities of a kind and to an extent that do not fit within their country's REIT framework.

Real exchange rate   The relative purchasing power of two currencies, defined in terms of the *real* goods and services that each can buy at prevailing national price levels and nominal exchange rates. Measured as the ratio of national price levels expressed in a common currency.

Real interest rate parity   The proposition that real interest rates will converge to the same level across different markets.

Real options   Options that relate to investment decisions such as the option to time the start of a project, the option to adjust its scale, or the option to abandon a project that has begun.

Receiver swaption   A swaption that allows the holder to enter into a swap as the fixed-rate receiver and floating-rate payer.

Regime   With reference to a time series, the underlying model generating the times series.

Regression coefficients   The intercept and slope coefficient(s) of a regression.

Regulatory arbitrage   Entities identify and use some aspect of regulations that allows them to exploit differences in economic substance and regulatory interpretation or in foreign and domestic regulatory regimes to their (the entities) advantage.

Regulatory burden   The costs of regulation for the regulated entity.

Regulatory capture   Theory that regulation often arises to enhance the interests of the regulated.

Regulatory competition   Regulators may compete to provide a regulatory environment designed to attract certain entities.

Relative valuation models   A model that specifies an asset's value relative to the value of another asset.

Relative version of PPP   Hypothesis that changes in (nominal) exchange rates over time are equal to national inflation rate differentials.

Relative-strength indicators   Valuation indicators that compare a stock's performance during a period either to its own past performance or to the performance of some group of stocks.

Renewable resources   Resources that can be replenished, such as a forest.

Rental price of capital   The cost per unit of time to rent a unit of capital.

Replacement cost   In the context of real estate, the value of a building assuming it was built today using current construction costs and standards.

Replacement value   The market value of a swap.

Reporting unit   An operating segment or one level below an operating segment (referred to as a component).

Reputational risk   The risk that a company will suffer an extended diminution in market value relative to other companies in the same industry due to a demonstrated lack of concern for environmental, social, and governance risk factors.

Required rate of return   The minimum rate of return required by an investor to invest in an asset, given the asset's riskiness.

Residential properties   Properties that provide housing for individuals or families. Single-family properties may be owner-occupied or rental properties, whereas multi-family properties are rental properties even if the owner or manager occupies one of the units.

Residual autocorrelations   The sample autocorrelations of the residuals.

Residual dividend policy   A policy in which dividends are paid from any internally generated funds remaining after such funds are used to finance positive NPV projects.

Residual income   (or economic profit or abnormal earnings) Earnings for a given time period, minus a deduction for common shareholders' opportunity cost in generating the earnings.

Residual income method   Income approach that estimates the value of all intangible assets of the business by capitalizing future earnings in excess of the estimated return requirements associated with working capital and fixed assets.

Residual income model   (RIM) (also discounted abnormal earnings model or Edwards-Bell-Ohlson model) A model of stock valuation that views intrinsic value of stock as the sum of book value per share plus the present value of the stock's expected future residual income per share.

Residual loss   Agency costs that are incurred despite adequate monitoring and bonding of management.

Retail REITs   REITs that invest in such retail properties as regional shopping malls or community/neighborhood shopping centers.

Return on invested capital   (ROIC) The after-tax net operating profits as a percent of total assets or capital.

Revenue   The amount charged for the delivery of goods or services in the ordinary activities of a business over a stated period; the inflows of economic resources to a company over a stated period.

Reviewed financial statements   A type of non-audited financial statements; typically provide an opinion letter with representations and assurances by the reviewing accountant that are less than those in audited financial statements.

Rho   The sensitivity of the option price to the risk-free rate.

Risk reversal   An option position that consists of the purchase of an out-of-the-money call and the simultaneous sale of an out-of-the-money put with the same "delta," on the same underlying currency or security, and with the same expiration date.

Risk-neutral probabilities   Weights that are used to compute a binomial option price. They are the probabilities that would apply if a risk-neutral investor valued an option.

Risk-neutral valuation   The process by which options and other derivatives are priced by treating investors as though they were risk neutral.

Robust standard errors   Standard errors of the estimated parameters of a regression that correct for the presence of heteroskedasticity in the regression's error term.

Root mean squared error (RMSE)   The square root of the average squared forecast error; used to compare the out-of-sample forecasting performance of forecasting models.

Sales comparison approach   In the context of real estate, this approach estimates value based on what similar or comparable properties (comparables) transacted for in the current market.

Sales-type leases   A type of finance lease, from a lessor perspective, where the present value of the lease payments (lease receivable) exceeds the carrying value of the leased asset. The revenues earned by the lessor are operating (the profit on the sale) and financing (interest) in nature.

Sampling distribution   The distribution of all distinct possible values that a statistic can assume when computed from samples of the same size randomly drawn from the same population.

Scaled earnings surprise   Unexpected earnings divided by the standard deviation of analysts' earnings forecasts.

Scalper   A trader who offers to buy or sell futures contracts, holding the position for only a brief period of time. Scalpers attempt to profit by buying at the bid price and selling at the higher ask price.

Screening   The application of a set of criteria to reduce a set of potential investments to a smaller set having certain desired characteristics.

Seats   Memberships in a derivatives exchange.

Sector neutralizing   Measure of financial reporting quality by subtracting the mean or median ratio for a given sector group from a given company's ratio.

Securities offering   A merger or acquisition in which target shareholders are to receive shares of the acquirer's common stock as compensation.

Security market line (SML)   The graph of the capital asset pricing model.

Self-regulating organizations   Private, non-governmental organizations that both represent and regulate their members. Some self-regulating organizations are also independent regulators.

Sell-side analysts   Analysts who work at brokerages.

Sensitivity analysis   Analysis that shows the range of possible outcomes as specific assumptions are changed.

Serially correlated   With reference to regression errors, errors that are correlated across observations.

Settlement date   (or **payment date**) The date on which the parties to a swap make payments.

Settlement period   The time between settlement dates.

Settlement price   The official price, designated by the clearinghouse, from which daily gains and losses will be determined and marked to market.

Shareholders' equity   Total assets minus total liabilities.

Shark repellents   A pre-offer takeover defense mechanism involving the corporate charter (e.g., staggered boards of directors and supermajority provisions).

Sharpe's measure   Reward-to-volatility ratio; ratio of portfolio excess return to standard deviation.

Shopping center   REITs that invest in such retail properties as regional shopping malls or community/neighborhood shopping centers.

Short   The seller of a derivative contract. Also refers to the position of being short a derivative.

Sole proprietorship   A business owned and operated by a single person.

Special purpose vehicle   (also special purpose entity or variable interest entity) A non-operating entity created to carry out a specified purpose, such as leasing assets or securitizing receivables; can be a corporation, partnership, trust, limited liability, or partnership formed to facilitate a specific type of business activity.

Speculative value   (also **time value**) The difference between the market price of the option and its intrinsic value, determined by the uncertainty of the underlying over the remaining life of the option.

Spin-off   A form of restructuring in which shareholders of a parent company receive a proportional number of shares in a new, separate entity; shareholders end up owning stock in two different companies where there used to be one.

Split-off   A form of restructuring in which shareholders of the parent company are given shares in a newly created entity in exchange for their shares of the parent company.

Split-rate tax system   In reference to corporate taxes, a split-rate system taxes earnings to be distributed as dividends at a different rate than earnings to be retained. Corporate profits distributed as dividends are taxed at a lower rate than those retained in the business.

Stabilized NOI   In the context of real estate, the expected NOI when a renovation is complete.

Stable dividend policy   A policy in which regular dividends are paid that reflect long-run expected earnings. In contrast to a constant dividend payout ratio policy, a stable dividend policy does not reflect short-term volatility in earnings.

Standard deviation   The positive square root of the variance; a measure of dispersion in the same units as the original data.

Standard of value   A specification of how "value" is to be understood in the context of a specific valuation.

Standardized beta   With reference to fundamental factor models, the value of the attribute for an asset minus the average value of the attribute across all stocks, divided by the standard deviation of the attribute across all stocks.

Standardized unexpected earnings   (SUE) Unexpected earnings per share divided by the standard deviation of unexpected earnings per share over a specified prior time period.

Static trade-off theory of capital structure   A theory pertaining to a company's optimal capital structure; the optimal level of debt is found at the point where additional debt would cause the costs of financial distress to increase by a greater amount than the benefit of the additional tax shield.

Statistical factor models   A multifactor model in which statistical methods are applied to a set of historical returns to determine portfolios that best explain either historical return covariances or variances.

Statistical inference Making forecasts, estimates, or judgments about a larger group from a smaller group actually observed; using a sample statistic to infer the value of an unknown population parameter.

Statutes Laws enacted by legislative bodies.

Statutory merger A merger in which one company ceases to exist as an identifiable entity and all its assets and liabilities become part of a purchasing company.

Steady state rate of growth The constant growth rate of output (or output per capita) which can or will be sustained indefinitely once it is reached. Key ratios, such as the capital–output ratio, are constant on the steady-state growth path.

Sterilized intervention A policy measure in which a monetary authority buys or sells its own currency to mitigate undesired exchange rate movements and simultaneously offsets the impact on the money supply with transactions in other financial instruments (usually money market instruments).

Stock purchase An acquisition in which the acquirer gives the target company's shareholders some combination of cash and securities in exchange for shares of the target company's stock.

Storage REITs REITs that own and operate self-storage properties, sometimes referred to as mini-warehouse facilities.

Storage costs The costs of holding an asset, generally a function of the physical characteristics of the underlying asset.

Straight-line rent The average annual rent under a multi-year lease agreement that contains contractual increases in rent during the life of the lease. For example if the rent is $100,000 in Year 1, $105,000 in Year 2, and $110,000 in Year 3, the average rent to be recognized each year as revenue under straight-line rent accounting is ($100,000 + $105,000 + $110,000)/3 = $105,000.

Straight-line rent adjustment *See* Non-cash rent.

Strategic transaction A purchase involving a buyer that would benefit from certain synergies associated with owning the target firm.

Strike See *exercise price*.

Strike price See *exercise price*.

Strike rate (also **exercise rate**) The fixed rate at which the holder of an interest rate option can buy or sell the underlying.

Striking price See *exercise price*.

Subsidiary merger A merger in which the company being purchased becomes a subsidiary of the purchaser.

Substantive law The body of law that focuses on the rights and responsibilities of entities and relationships among entities.

Sum-of-the-parts valuation A valuation that sums the estimated values of each of a company's businesses as if each business were an independent going concern.

Sunk cost A cost that has already been incurred.

Supernormal growth Above average or abnormally high growth rate in earnings per share.

Surprise The actual value of a variable minus its predicted (or expected) value.

Survivorship bias Bias that may result when failed or defunct companies are excluded from membership in a group.

Sustainable growth rate The rate of dividend (and earnings) growth that can be sustained over time for a given level of return on equity, keeping the capital structure constant and without issuing additional common stock.

Swap spread The difference between the fixed rate on an interest rate swap and the rate on a Treasury note with equivalent maturity; it reflects the general level of credit risk in the market.

Swaption An option to enter into a swap.

Synthetic call The combination of puts, the underlying, and risk-free bonds that replicates a call option.

Synthetic forward contract The combination of the underlying, puts, calls, and risk-free bonds that replicates a forward contract.

Synthetic lease A lease that is structured to provide a company with the tax benefits of ownership while not requiring the asset to be reflected on the company's financial statements.

Synthetic put The combination of calls, the underlying, and risk-free bonds that replicates a put option.

Systematic factors Factors that affect the average returns of a large number of different assets.

Systemic risk The risk of failure of the financial system.

Takeover A merger; the term may be applied to any transaction, but is often used in reference to hostile transactions.

Takeover premium The amount by which the takeover price for each share of stock must exceed the current stock price in order to entice shareholders to relinquish control of the company to an acquirer.

Tangible book value per share Common shareholders' equity minus intangible assets from the balance sheet, divided by the number of shares outstanding.

Target The company in a merger or acquisition that is being acquired.

Target capital structure A company's chosen proportions of debt and equity.

Target company The company in a merger or acquisition that is being acquired.

Target payout ratio A strategic corporate goal representing the long-term proportion of earnings that the company intends to distribute to shareholders as dividends.

Technical indicators Momentum indicators based on price.

Temporal method A variation of the monetary/nonmonetary translation method that requires not only monetary assets and liabilities, but also nonmonetary assets and liabilities that are measured at their current value on the balance sheet date to be translated at the current exchange rate. Assets and liabilities are translated at rates consistent with the timing of their measurement value. This method is typically used when the functional currency is other than the local currency.

Tender offer A public offer whereby the acquirer invites target shareholders to submit ("tender") their shares in return for the proposed payment.

Terminal price multiples The price multiple for a stock assumed to hold at a stated future time.

Terminal share price The share price at a particular point in the future.

Terminal value of the stock (or continuing value of the stock) The analyst's estimate of a stock's value at a particular point in the future.

Termination date The date of the final payment on a swap; also, the swap's expiration date.

Theta The rate at which an option's time value decays.

Time series A set of observations on a variable's outcomes in different time periods.

Time to expiration The time remaining in the life of a derivative, typically expressed in years.

Time value (also **speculative value**) The difference between the market price of the option and its intrinsic value, determined by the uncertainty of the underlying over the remaining life of the option.

Time value decay   The loss in the value of an option resulting from movement of the option price towards its payoff value as the expiration day approaches.

Tobin's *q*   The ratio of the market value of debt and equity to the replacement cost of total assets.

Top-down forecasting approach   A forecasting approach that involves moving from international and national macroeconomic forecasts to industry forecasts and then to individual company and asset forecasts.

Top-down investing   An approach to investing that typically begins with macroeconomic forecasts.

Total factor productivity (TFP)   A multiplicative scale factor that reflects the general level of productivity or technology in the economy. Changes in total factor productivity generate proportional changes in output for any input combination.

Total invested capital   The sum of market value of common equity, book value of preferred equity, and face value of debt.

Total return swap   A swap in which one party agrees to pay the total return on a security. Often used as a credit derivative, in which the underlying is a bond.

Tracking error   **(tracking risk)** The standard deviation of the differences between a portfolio's returns and its benchmark's returns; a synonym of active risk.

Tracking portfolio   A portfolio having factor sensitivities that are matched to those of a benchmark or other portfolio.

Tracking risk   **(tracking error)** The standard deviation of the differences between a portfolio's returns and its benchmark's returns; a synonym of active risk.

Trailing P/E   (or current P/E) A stock's current market price divided by the most recent four quarters of earnings per share.

Trailing dividend yield   Current market price divided by the most recent quarterly per-share dividend multiplied by four.

Transaction exposure   The risk of a change in value between the transaction date and the settlement date of an asset or liability denominated in a foreign currency.

Trend   A long-term pattern of movement in a particular direction.

Triangular arbitrage   An arbitrage transaction involving three currencies which attempts to exploit inconsistencies among pair wise exchange rates.

UPREITs   An umbrella partnership REIT under which the REIT owns an operating partnership and serves as the general partner of the operating partnership. All or most of the properties are held in the operating partnership.

Unconditional heteroskedasticity   Heteroskedasticity of the error term that is not correlated with the values of the independent variable(s) in the regression.

Uncovered interest rate parity   The proposition that the expected return on an uncovered (i.e., unhedged) foreign currency (risk-free) investment should equal the return on a comparable domestic currency investment.

Underlying   An asset that trades in a market in which buyers and sellers meet, decide on a price, and the seller then delivers the asset to the buyer and receives payment. The underlying is the asset or other derivative on which a particular derivative is based. The market for the underlying is also referred to as the spot market.

Underlying earnings   Earnings excluding nonrecurring components.

Unearned revenue   A liability account for money that has been collected for goods or services that have not yet been delivered; payment received in advance of providing a good or service.

Unexpected earnings   The difference between reported earnings per share and expected earnings per share.

Unit root   A time series that is not covariance stationary is said to have a unit root.

Uniting of interests method   A method of accounting in which combined companies were portrayed as if they had always operated as a single economic entity. Called pooling of interests under U.S. GAAP and uniting of interests under IFRS. (No longer allowed under U.S. GAAP or IFRS).

Unlimited funds   An unlimited funds environment assumes that the company can raise the funds it wants for all profitable projects simply by paying the required rate of return.

Unsterilized intervention   A policy measure in which a monetary authority buys or sells its own currency to mitigate undesired exchange rate movements and does not offset the impact on the money supply with transactions in other financial instruments.

Upstream   A transaction between two affiliates, an investor company and an associate company such that the associate company records a profit on its income statement. An example is a sale of inventory by the associate to the investor company.

Valuation   The process of determining the value of an asset or service on the basis of variables perceived to be related to future investment returns, or on the basis of comparisons with closely similar assets.

Value at risk (VAR)   A money measure of the minimum value of losses expected during a specified time period at a given level of probability.

Value of growth   The difference between the actual value per share and the nogrowth value per share.

Variance   The expected value (the probability-weighted average) of squared deviations from a random variable's expected value.

Variation margin   Additional margin that must be deposited in an amount sufficient to bring the balance up to the initial margin requirement.

Vega   The relationship between option price and volatility.

Venture capital investors   Private equity investors in development-stage companies.

Vertical merger   A merger involving companies at different positions of the same production chain; for example, a supplier or a distributor.

Visibility   The extent to which a company's operations are predictable with substantial confidence.

Weighted average cost   An inventory accounting method that averages the total cost of available inventory items over the total units available for sale.

Weighted average cost of capital   (WACC)A weighted average of the after-tax required rates of return on a company's common stock, preferred stock, and long-term debt, where the weights are the fraction of each source of financing in the company's target capital structure.

Weighted harmonic mean   See *Harmonic mean.*

White knight   A third party that is sought out by the target company's board to purchase the target in lieu of a hostile bidder.

White squire   A third party that is sought out by the target company's board to purchase a substantial minority stake in the target—enough to block a hostile takeover without selling the entire company.

White-corrected standard errors   A synonym for robust standard errors.

Winner's curse   The tendency for the winner in certain competitive bidding situations to overpay, whether because of overestimation of intrinsic value, emotion, or information asymmetries.

Write-down   A reduction in the value of an asset as stated in the balance sheet.

Zero-cost collar   A transaction in which a position in the underlying is protected by buying a put and selling a call with the premium from the sale of the call offsetting the premium from the purchase of the put. It can also be used to protect a floating-rate borrower against interest rate increases with the premium on a long cap offsetting the premium on a short floor.

Index

8

Third Restatement of the Law. *see* Prudent Investor Rule

three-level analysis of permissible research, 187–189

three-step method for testing error autocorrelations, 423–425

time frame
  of decision and dissemination, 71
  and performance calculation, 82

time horizons
  and effect of uncovered interest rate parity, 506
  inflation and exchange rates for, 513
  for ratings systems, 212

Timeliness of Research Reports and Recommendations (CFA Institute ROS 8.0), 206, 210

time of day, size of bid–offer spread and, 487–488

time series
  autocorrelations of, 422–423
  defined, 410
  forecasts of, 443–445
  model misspecification of, 372–376
  ordering of, 420n.8
  regression analysis of, 285, 337

time-series analysis, 409–477
  about, 410–411
  autoregressive models, 420–433
    comparing forecast model performance, 429–431
    with conditional heteroskedasticity, 451–453
    covariance-stationary series, 421–422
    instability of regression coefficients, 431–433
    mean reversion, 425
    moving-average, 450–451
    multiperiod forecasts and chain rule of forecasting, 426–429
    serially correlated errors in, 422–425
  challenges with, 411–412
  forecasting with
    moving-average models, 443–445
    multiperiod forecasts and chain rule of forecasting, 426–429
    steps, 458–460
    uncertainty in, 458
  moving-average models, 441–445
    autoregressive, 450–451
    forecasting time series with, 443–445
    smoothing past values with, 441–443
  with multiple regimes, 458
  practice problems, 463–472
  random walks, 433–437
  regressions with multiple time series, 454–457
  seasonality in, 445–450
  solutions to problems, 473–477
  trend models, 412–420
    linear, 412–415
    log-linear, 415–419
    and testing for correlated errors, 420
  uncertainty in forecasts from, 458
  unit root test of nonstationarity, 437–440

Tokyo, Japan, 487, 488

total factor productivity (TFP), 591
  and capital deepening, 593–595

in growth accounting equation, 595–596

and steady state of growth equilibrium, 621

and technology, 608–609

and U.S. economic growth, 627

total variation, in ANOVA, 302

trade, free, 583, 671

trade allocation procedures, 72, 237–238

trade balance, 528, 636

trades
  agency, 178, 181
  carry, 522–526
    and capital flows, 533–535
    defined, 523
    example, 525–526
    returns on, 484–485
    risks and rewards on, 523–524
    with U.S. dollar and Turkish lira, 532–533
    yen, 530, 544
  principal, 178, 180, 181

trading
  excessive, 67
  insider, 665
  personal, 58, 59
    and conflict of interest, 123–124
    disclosure of, 128, 129
    limitations on, 52
    priority of transactions for, 125
  proprietary trading procedures, 53
  in Research Objectivity Standards, 206, 209–210
  risk-arbitrage, 53
  supervising trading activities, 100–101

trading volume, 59

transaction-based manipulation, 57–58

transaction size, bid–offer spread and, 488

transformation, of regression variables
  first-differencing, 434–437
  and model specification, 364, 366–369

transformational technologies, 606n.16

transitional growth, in neoclassical model, 624–627

travel expenses, 32–33, 35

travel funding, 31

trend-following trading rules, in FX market, 558–559

trend models
  linear, 412–415
  log-linear, 415–419
  and testing for correlated errors, 420
  time-series analysis, 412–420

trends, 412

triangular arbitrage, among currencies, 489–491

trinomial choice models, 345n.28

trustees, directing brokerage for benefit of, 194

trusteeship. *see* Duties at Inception of Trusteeship (Model Act § 4)

t-tests
  of autocorrelation, 422–423
  Dickey–Fuller test, 438
  for Fisher effect, 354, 355
  formula for, 282
  and *F*-test, 303, 304
  hypothesis testing with, 295

and multicollinearity, 360

in multiple linear regression, 333, 342

Turkey
  average hours worked, 604
  labor force participation rate, 601
  natural resources, 598
  real GDP per capita, 579, 634

Turkish lira, 532–533

12-month moving average, 441n.31

Type I errors, 343, 356

U

UER. *see* civilian unemployment rate

UNASUR. *see* Union of South American Nations

unbundling, of proprietary research, 178, 183

uncertainty
  in forecasts from time-series analysis, 458
  and predicting dependent variable with regression analysis, 341

unconditional heteroskedasticity, 351

uncovered interest rate parity
  and carry trades, 522–523
  in emerging and developed markets, 523
  in exchange rate determination, 504–506
  and international parity conditions, 516, 517
  and long-term equilibrium interest rates, 522
  in prediction of spot rates, 507–510

unethical actions, reporting, 26

unexpected changes, in exchange rates, 502

unfair competition, regulation against, 671

Uniformity of Application and Construction (Model Act § 12), 254

Uniform Management of Institutional Funds Act, 243

Uniform Probate Code Prudent Man Rule, 243

Uniform Prudent Investor Act (Model Act), 247–250
  adoption of, 247
  application to existing trusts (§ 11), 254
  delegation of investment and management functions (§ 9), 250, 254
  diversification (§ 3), 249, 253
  duties at inception of trusteeship (§ 4), 249, 253
  effective date (§ 15), 255
  impartiality (§ 6), 250, 253
  improvements to Prudent Man Rule in, 248–250
  investment costs (§ 7), 250, 253
  language invoking standard of [act] (§ 10), 254
  loyalty (§ 5), 249, 253
  Prudent Investor Rule (§ 1), 252
  repeals (§ 16), 255
  reviewing compliance (§ 8), 253
  severability (§ 14), 254
  short title (§ 13), 254